PRINCIPAL POLITICAL DIVISIONS OF THE WORLD

Identification of Numbers

EUROPE	ASIA	AUSTRALASIA
1. Denmark	1. Lebanon	1. British Malaya
2. Netherlands	2. Palestine	2. Sarawak
3. Belgium	3. Transjordan	3. Brunei
4. Switzerland	4. Yemen	4. British North Borneo
5. Austria	5. Pakistan	5. Timor
6. Czechoslovakia	6. Nepal	6. Northeast New Guinea
7. Hungary	7. Bhutan	7. Territory of Papua
8. Albania		8. Bismarck Archipelago
9. Bulgaria		
10. Greece		

World Political Geography

ASSOCIATE AUTHORS

Samuel F. Bemis, *Yale University*
Herman Beukema, *United States Military Academy*
Sax Bradford, *United States Department of State*
Albert S. Carlson, *Dartmouth College*
Alden Cutshall, *University of Illinois*
Gordon G. Darkenwald, *Hunter College of the City of New York*
Sigismond deR. Diettrich, *University of Florida*
Sidney E. Ekblaw, *University of Kansas City*
Franklin C. Erickson, *Boston University*
Weldon B. Gibson, *Stanford University*
Arthur R. Hall, *United States Department of State*
George W. Hoffman, *The University of Texas*
George D. Hubbard, *Emeritus, Oberlin College*
Ben F. Lemert, *Duke University*
George A. Lipsky, *University of California*
Michael Mansfield, *United States House of Representatives*
Shannon McCune, *Colgate University*
J. Warren Nystrom, *University of Pittsburgh*
Clarence B. Odell, *Encyclopaedia Britannica, Inc.*
George T. Renner, *Teachers College, Columbia University*
John K. Rose, *Library of Congress*
Joseph S. Roucek, *University of Bridgeport*
Joseph R. Schwendeman, *University of Kentucky*
Ruth S. Sutherland, *United States Department of the Army*
George Tatham, *University of Toronto*
Griffith Taylor, *University of Toronto*
L. W. Trueblood, *United States Department of the Army*
Richard L. Tuthill, *University of Kentucky*
Joseph E. Van Riper, *Syracuse University*
William Van Royen, *University of Maryland*
Carleton F. Waite, *New Mexico State Teachers College*
C. Langdon White, *Stanford University*

POLITICAL GEOGRAPHY

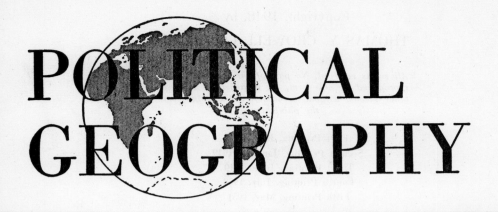

G. ETZEL PEARCY
Geographic Attaché,
U.S. Department of State

RUSSELL H. FIFIELD
Associate Professor of Political Science
University of Michigan

and

ASSOCIATES

Cartography by
ROBERT J. VOSKUIL

THOMAS Y. CROWELL COMPANY, New York

Preface

WHATEVER the future in a rapidly changing world, certain basic facts remain, and with them men must cope. Geographic location, physical environment, population, economic resources, cultural heritage, political aptitude, and other related factors have all exerted significant influences on the past accomplishments of men and nations and inevitably will continue to bear on their future hopes. The purpose of this book is to lay the groundwork for an understanding of how these forces have operated in centuries gone by and their probable effects in the years ahead. For those who have this background, world political developments will have added meaning as they unfold.

If the study of political geography is to offer an adequate grasp of the full range of national enterprise and international relations, it must be world wide in scope. For too long studies in the field have focused largely on the first-rate powers and their direct interrelations; seldom have such studies provided a comprehensive analysis of the lesser powers in whose regions the divergent interests of the great powers have already or may in the future come into conflict. This book, however, surveys the entire world and evaluates each of its segments, not only separately, but also in its relation to the rest of the world.

Of the thirty-nine chapters, more than three-fourths deal with the political regions into which the world is divided. Within these regions an effort has been made at least to mention and briefly qualify every place that interests or is likely to interest the statesmen of the world. In some cases these regions cut across international boundaries, and in others they ignore lines of empire. As a whole, however, they form a mosaic into which all the political entities of the world, large or small, fit logically. The remaining chapters deal with aspects of political geography that lend themselves to an over-all view rather than to regional treatment, such as the nature and scope of the field, oceanography, and population and boundary problems. Thus, this book, based primarily upon the *political area*, is truly global in its viewpoint and approach.

In the discussion of the functioning of each political area as a world unit, the content falls within four major fields of interest. First, *geography* accounts for the area itself and its inventory of physical and cultural possessions, including its relation to other areas. Second, *history* gives an insight into the accomplishments of the area. Rather than history in the usual sense, the survey highlights in large measure those events that have contributed most significantly to political progression or recession. Third, *international relations* provides the liaison between the area under consideration and other areas, and explains its external policies and practices. Fourth, *political science* analyzes the machinery, often intangible, that underlies the workings of the area in matters of state, both in developing an internal program and in dealing with other areas. Because of the inevitable overlapping of forces among these four fields, however, and the differences in conditions among the various areas, no attempt has been made to force into an identical pattern the organization of material dealing with each of the several areas.

Both in the text and in the accompanying tables areal measurement and population values for many areas and combinations of areas receive considerable attention.   Despite every effort to correlate these data, different area and population values do occasionally appear for the same political or geographic region.   The explanation for these discrepancies, which are apparent rather than actual, depends upon (1) whether the population figure is derived from a definite census or from a recent estimate; (2) whether the amount of territory includes or omits dependencies; and (3) whether exact figures or round numbers are given.

In this book the choice of place names follows no orthodox rule.   Either Anglicization of all names or the use of all names in accordance with the language of the region in which they appear would have resulted in the use of some little-known names to designate well-known places.   The plan adopted was extremely simple; namely, to use in each case that name which most commonly appears in English-language atlases, maps, and texts.   The editors believe that the ensuing ease of recognizing and looking up names will more than justify the seeming inconsistencies.

The maps, charts, and graphs constitute a distinctive feature.   With only a few exceptions all 139 of them were planned and drawn specifically for this book.   Although not designed to give the thorough coverage of an atlas, they do provide an orientation for the principal regions and topics, spotlight matters of geopolitical interest for each area, and delineate pertinent data involving areal distribution and statistical measurement that are difficult to grasp when presented only in textual form.

Thirty-four authors have contributed to the preparation of this volume.   This multiple authorship has marked advantages for a book of this type.   First, many of the authors are specialists on the subject of their writing.   Second, all of them have had the opportunity to devote their entire attention to a limited field.   The task of the editors has been to eliminate the expression of any personal prejudices and to achieve a unity in the overall pattern.   This they have attempted to perform without stifling the organization and creative ability of the individual authors while, at the same time, maintaining a logical sequence from chapter to chapter and facilitating a consistent method of study throughout.   The further responsibility of the political editor has been the planning of the political coverage of the book, the synchronization of the political with the geographical data, and a careful check to ensure the accurate portrayal of the international politics of the contemporary world.

The editors wish to express their gratitude to the coauthors.   Not only their scholarly contributions but their suggestions and criticisms have been invaluable in this joint effort to produce a book presenting a world picture of politics and geography in action.

G. ETZEL PEARCY
RUSSELL H. FIFIELD

July 16, 1948

Acknowledgments

THE editors wish to extend their thanks to a number of people for their help in making this book possible. Many constructive comments and criticisms relative to content and organization were given by Clarence F. Jones of Northwestern University, George T. Renner of Teachers College, Columbia University, and Otis P. Starkey of Indiana University. In addition, various parts of the manuscript were read and invaluable suggestions offered by Wallace W. Atwood, Sr. and George Hubbard Blakeslee, both formerly of Clark University, Isaiah Bowman of Johns Hopkins University, Mary E. Bradshaw of Berea College, J. Norman Carls, formerly of the Bureau of the Census, Katharine Elizabeth Crane of the Library of Congress, George B. Cressey of Syracuse University, George Kish of the University of Michigan, Walter M. Kollmorgen of the University of Kansas, Gustave Nuermberger, E. Taylor Parks, Ernest R. Perkins, and Bernadotte E. Schmitt, all four of the Department of State, and Samuel Van Valkenburg of Clark University.

For long hours of tireless effort the editors also wish to thank Gordon G. Darkenwald for a preliminary reading of the entire manuscript; George T. Renner for his writing of the introductions that appear at the beginning of each of the seven major parts of this book; and Vera Rigdon for editorial assistance on many of the chapters. Members of the Trans World Airline personnel in Washington, New York, and Kansas City are thanked collectively for their cooperation and assistance in providing maps and material to go into this book.

In numerous instances individual coauthors have asked that the editors express their appreciation and indebtedness to those who rendered valuable assistance in the writing of specific chapters. Sax Bradford extends thanks to Germano Jardim of the *Instituto Brasileiro de Geografia e Estatistica;* Weldon B. Gibson to the late Dr. Eliot G. Mears of Stanford University; Arthur R. Hall to S. W. Boggs of the Department of State, and Stephen B Jones of Yale University; George W. Hoffman to E. A. Speiser of the University of Pennsylvania, and Harry N. Howard of the Department of State; George A. Lipsky to Captain Wallace C. Magathan, Jr., formerly of the U. S. Military Academy, now with the American occupation forces in Germany, and Colonel Herman Beukema of the U. S. Military Academy; Shannon McCune to Guy-Harold Smith of Ohio State University; Clarence B. Odell to S. W. Boggs of the Department of State, and Frank W. Notestein and Irene B. Taeuber, both of the Office of Population Research, Princeton University; Joseph R. Schwendeman to Thomas Clark and Amry Vandenbosch, both of the University of Kentucky, and William Clayton Bower of the University of Chicago; Lester W. Trueblood to C. H. Chapman, formerly of the Burma Methodist Mission, and George F. Deasy of the United States War Department; Richard L. Tuthill to George T. Renner of Teachers College, Columbia University; and C. Langdon White to Dr. Fred Carlson, Ohio State University, Dr. Ronald Hilton, Stanford University, Dr. George McBride, U. S. Technical Advisor, Ecuador-Peru Boundary Demarcation Commission, Lima, Peru, and Quito, Ecuador, Dr. Victor M. Davila, San Marcos University, Lima, Peru and Dr. Albert A. Giesecke, U. S. Embassy, Lima, Peru.

For cartographical assistance Robert J. Voskuil expresses his appreciation to Mr. Anthony J. Sucher, Jr., Mr. and Mrs. Henry Frieswyk and Norman Greenawalt, all of the Department of State, and Bruce C. Ogilvie of the University of Georgia.

Contents

[The maps, charts, and diagrams for each chapter are enclosed in brackets]

PART ONE

The Nature and Scope of Political Geography

1. POLITICAL GEOGRAPHY AND ITS POINT OF VIEW   *George T. Renner*   3

The Utility of Political Geography, 3.   Some Definitions, 5.   Factors of Powerhood, 7.
Classifications of States, 8.   Characteristics of Power Areas, 10.

2. THE SUBSTANCE AND SCOPE OF POLITICAL GEOGRAPHY   *George T. Renner*   12

Geopolitical Schools of Thought, 12.   The Political Region or Area, 15.   The Study
of Political Geography, 20.

3. THE HISTORY AND DEVELOPMENT OF POLITICAL GEOGRAPHY   *G. Etzel Pearcy*   22

Modern Developments, 22.   The Rise of German Geopolitik, 23.   Founders of Geopolitics, 24.   Recent American Geopolitics, 32.   Conclusion, 33.

[The Geographical Pivot of History (Mackinder's Heartland), 26.   Relative Sizes
of the Europes of Napoleon and Hitler, 28.]

PART TWO

The World Powers

4. GEOGRAPHIC FOUNDATIONS OF CONTINENTAL UNITED STATES

Gordon G. Darkenwald   37

Territorial Expansion, 37.   Boundary Problems, 38.   World Location, 39.   Physical
Factors, 40.   Economic Factors, 42.   Population, 50.

[Territorial Acquisitions (1783–1853), 37.   Major Land Forms, 41.   Major Precipitation Zones, 41.   Virgin Forests (1620), 42.   Virgin Forests (1940), 43.   Land
Area by Major Economic Uses (1929), 45.   Industrial Production, 47.   Commercial Airlines, 50.   Population Density, 51.]

5. THE UNITED STATES AS A WORLD POWER   *Samuel Flagg Bemis*   53

Historical Background: Nineteenth Century, 53.   The New Frame of World Politics:
Twentieth Century, 54.   The American Colonial Empire, 56.   American Foreign Pol-
icy in the Far East, 57.   The "Washington
Period," 1922–37, 59.   The United States and World War II, 61.   The Atomic Age, 62.

[Panama Canal, 57.   War Declarations against Axis Powers by Latin American
Republics, 62.   The United States as a World Power, 63.]

ix

6. THE SOVIET UNION: A LAND-MASS POWER   *Richard L. Tuthill*   65

Historical Development, 66. Continentality of Russia, 67. Internal Political Structure, 68. Internal Economic Structure, 71. Geopolitical Problems, 79.

⎡ Major Political Divisions, 69. Parallel Chart of Government of U. S. S. R. and ⎤
⎢ Communist Party, 70. Major Industrial Regions and Railroads, 75. Major ⎥
⎣ Cities, 76. ⎦

7. THE SOVIET UNION IN WORLD POLITICS   *George A. Lipsky*   83

Russian Policy in the Pre-Soviet Past, 83. Soviet Foreign Policy, 1917–41, 87. The Soviet Union in World War II, 88. The Soviet Position in the Postwar World, 89. Soviet Regional Foreign Policy, 89. The Future, 95.

⎡ The Growth of the Russian State, 85. Soviet Russia and Its Peripheral Spheres ⎤
⎣ of Interest, 91. ⎦

8. GREAT BRITAIN AND THE DEPENDENT EMPIRE   *George Tatham*   96

The Commonwealth-Empire as a Whole, 96. *Great Britain:* Geographic Background, 99. Historical Survey of Great Britain, 101. Future Outlook, 109. *Eire and Northern Ireland:* Geographic Background, 110. Historical Survey, 111.

⎡ British Commonwealth-Empire, 97. Structure of the British Isles, 99. Land Use ⎤
⎢ of the British Isles, 100. Industrial Britain, 101. Population Density of the Brit- ⎥
⎣ ish Isles, 105. ⎦

9. THE BRITISH COMMONWEALTH OF NATIONS   *Griffith Taylor*   114

World Position of the Dominions, 114. *Canada:* Environment, 116. Internal Development, 117. Canada and the Outside World, 120. *Newfoundland,* 121. *Australasia:* The Environment of Australia, 122. Australian Internal Developments, 125. Australia and the Outside World, 126. The Australian Dependent Areas, 127. New Zealand, 127. *Union of South Africa:* Environment, 128. Cultural Development, 129. South Africa and the Outside World, 130.

⎡ Main Structures (Shields, Downfolds, Mountains) of the World, 115. Canada: ⎤
⎢ Major Economic Activities, 117. Canada: Settled Zones and Cultural Groups, ⎥
⎢ 118. Australia: Environment, Population Density, 123. South Africa: Po- ⎥
⎣ litical, Environment, 128. ⎦

PART THREE

Europe

10. THE GERMAN REICH: EUROPEAN PIVOTAL AREA   *Sigismond deR. Diettrich*   133

The Historical Factor, 133. The Location Factor, 135. The Site Factors, 139. The Human Factor, 146. Economic Factors, 148. Conclusion, 150.

⎡ Comparative Location, 136. German Reich (1937), 138. Germany (1871–1937), ⎤
⎣ 139. Postwar Occupation Zones, 140. ⎦

11. THE LOW COUNTRIES BETWEEN THE GREAT POWERS   *William Van Royen*   151

Physical Aspects, 151. Political Boundaries, 156. Divergence in Development of the Netherlands and Belgium, 157. The Changing Role of Geographic Location, 159. Present Economy of the Low Countries, 161. The Low Countries in the European and the World Economy, 164. Conclusions, 165. *Luxembourg,* 166.

⎡ Geographic Regions of the Low Countries, 153. Cities and Provinces of the Low ⎤
⎣ Countries, 155. ⎦

Contents

12. FRANCE AND ITS GEOGRAPHICAL SETTING   *George D. Hubbard*   167

The History and People of France, 167.   Physical Aspects, 170.   Political and Social
Aspects, 174.   Boundaries, 176.   Commerce, 177.   Cities, 178.   The French Colonial
Empire, 179.   Postwar France, 179.

[Regions of France, 169.   Cities and Rivers of France, 170.]

13. SWITZERLAND: A SUCCESSFUL NEUTRAL   *Franklin C. Erickson*   181

Geographical Structure, 181.   Historical Development, 182.   Human Factors, 186.   Economic Development, 187.   Political Factors, 189.   *Liechtenstein*, 190.

[Railroads and Airlines, 183.   Cantons, 184.   Languages, 186.   Distribution of
Religions, 187.]

14. ITALY IN THE MEDITERRANEAN   *Joseph R. Schwendeman*   191

The Italian People, 192.   Space Relationships, 193.   Physical Factors, 198.   National
Economy, 201.   Colonies, 205.   International Policy, 206.

[Italy and the Mediterranean, 191.   Cities and Railroads, Physical Features, 195.
The Istria Area, 196.   Franco-Italian Border (1947), 196.   The Mediterranean
Waist, 198.]

15. SPAIN AND PORTUGAL: POWERS OF THE PAST   *Sidney E. Ekblaw*   207

Location, 207.   Historical Development, 208.   The Environment, 210.   Peoples of
Spain and Portugal, 214.   Economic Factors, 217.   External Factors, 220.

[Gibraltar, 209.   Major Physical Features, 212.   Cities and Major Railways, 219.]

16. THE FIVE FENNO SCANDIC COUNTRIES   *Albert S. Carlson*   222

General Considerations, 222.   *Denmark:*   Physical Characteristics, 225.   Economy,
225.   World Relations, 226.   *Finland:*   Physical Features, 228.   Economy, 228.   International Politics, 229.   *Norway:*   Physical Geography, 230.   Economy, 231.   Implications of Location, 232.   *Sweden:*   Natural Regions, 233.   Industrial Development, 234.   Cultural and Political Aspects, 235.   *Iceland*, 235.   *Greenland*, 236.

[Comparative Location of Fenno Scandia and Alaska, 223.   The Fenno Scandic
Countries, 224.]

17. POLAND: A PERPETUAL PROBLEM   *George D. Hubbard*   237

Historical Evolution, 238.   Physical Aspects, 240.   Human Aspects, 244.   Economic
Aspects, 246.   Problems of the Future, 247.

[Poland (18th Century, 1919–39, 1939, 1945), 238.   Poland, prior to World
War II, 241.]

18. THE LESSER COUNTRIES OF CENTRAL EUROPE   *Joseph S. Roucek*   249

Influence of the Danube River, 249.   The Birth and Rebirth of the "Lesser Countries," 251.   *Czechoslovakia:*   Physical Aspects, 252.   Economic Evaluation, 253.   Geopolitical Implications, 254.   *Austria:*   The Republic, 256.   Cultural Aspects, 256.
The Rebirth of Austria, 257.   *Hungary:*   Geographic Aspects, 257.   Political Aspects,
258.

[Political, 249.   Major Physical Features of Southeastern Europe, 250.   Former
Austro-Hungarian Empire, 251.   Postwar Territorial Changes in Central Europe,
259.]

19. THE BALKAN STATES: PENINSULAR RIVALS   *Joseph S. Roucek*   260

Geographic Factors, 260.   Cultural and Political Factors, 261.   *Rumania:*   Geographic Background, 264.   National Economy, 264.   Historical Background, 265.
Political Problems, 266.   *Yugoslavia:*   Geographic Factors, 267.   National Economy,
268.   Historical Background, 268.   Territorial Problems, 269.   *Bulgaria:*   Geographic

Factors, 271. National Economy, 271. Historical Background, 272. The Bulgars and the Postwar Era, 272. *Greece:* Geographic Factors, 273. National Economy, 273. Historical Background, 274. Postwar Status, 275. *Albania:* Geographic Factors, 276. Historical Background, 276.

Political, 260. Major Railroads of Southeastern Europe, 261. Politico-Geographic Regions of Southeastern Europe, 263. Territorial Changes in Rumania and Bulgaria by Peace Treaties (1947), 266.

PART FOUR

Asia

20. TURKEY AND THE STRAITS   *G. Etzel Pearcy*   281

The Turkish National State: Historical Evolution, 282. Physical Landscape, 287. People, 288. National Economy, 289. *The Straits:* Importance of Location, 291. Political Issues, 292. Role of the Straits in the Atomic Age, 295.

Modern Turkey, 282. Growth and Maximum Extent of the Ottoman Empire, 283. Disintegration of the Ottoman Empire, 285. The Straits, 291.

21. THE ARAB WORLD   *George W. Hoffman*   296

Analysis of Environmental Elements, 297. Economic and Strategic Elements, 302. Historical and Social Elements, 304. Problems of the Present and the Future, 307.

Surface Features of the Eastern Mediterranean, 296. The Arab World, 297. Suez Canal and Environs, 301. Oil Concessions, 303. Partition of Palestine, 309.

22. THE MIDDLE EAST STATES OF IRAN AND AFGHANISTAN   *Ben F. Lemert*   313

Iran: Physical Features, 314. Human Aspects, 316. National Economy, 317. Political Aspects, 319. *Afghanistan:* Physical Features, 321. Cultural Aspects, 322. National Economy, 322. Political Aspects, 323.

Areal Comparison with the United States, 314. Iran: Political, 315. Afghanistan: Political, 321.

23. THE COMPLEXITY OF INDIA AND BURMA   *Lester W. Trueblood*   325

India: Physical Framework, 326. Historical Background, 328. The Economic Strength of India, 329. The People, 331. Political Framework under the British, 333. Pakistan and the Union of India, 334. *Ceylon, Bhutan, and Nepal,* 336. *Burma:* Physical Factors, 337. Historical Sketch, 338. Economic Aspects, 338. The People, 339. The Political Framework, 340.

India before Self-Government, 326. Political Units of India and Burma, 335. Early Stage in Partition of India, 336. The Burma Area, 337.

24. THE FOUNDATIONS OF MODERN CHINA   *Michael Mansfield*   341

Political Framework of China, 341. Historical Background, 343. Physical Features, 345. Economic Pattern, 347. The Human Element, 352. Politico-Geographic Aspects of Greater China, 355. Problems Facing the Chinese Republic, 356.

Greater China, 341. Provinces, 342. Major Transportation Routes, 349. Air Routes, 351. Hong Kong, 353. Gateway to Manchuria, 355.

25. KOREA, INDO-CHINA, AND SIAM: HISTORIC ASIATIC BUFFERS   *Shannon McCune*   358

Korea: Physical Factors, 359. Economic Pattern, 361. The People and Culture of Korea, 361. Historical Development of Korea, 362. Modern Korea, 363. *Indo-*

China: Physical Factors, 364. Human and Economic Factors in Indo-China, 365. Political Factors in Indo-China, 367. *Siam:* Physical Regions and Human Occupance, 370. Political Factors in Siam, 371. *Conclusion,* 372.

[Peripheral Location to China, 358. Korea: Physical, 360. Siam and Indo-China: Physical, 365.]

26. THE JAPANESE ISLES   *G. Etzel Pearcy and Carleton F. Waite*   373

Physical Factors, 373. Historical Factors, 375. Human Factors, 378. Economic Factors, 380. Aggressive Expansion, 383. Problems of Postwar Japan, 387.

[The Japanese Islands, 373. Principal Railroads, Industrial Centers, 381. Expansion of Japan to Empire, 385.]

PART FIVE

Africa and Australasia

27. AFRICA: A STUDY IN COLONIALISM   *George T. Renner*   393

Physical Characteristics, 393. Native Races, 395. Historical Backgrounds, 395. The Opening of Africa, 397. Independent African States, 406.

[Physical, 393. Climatic Controls, 394. Climates, 395. Native Races, 396. Roman Empire in Africa, 397. Germany and Italy in Africa, Portugal in Africa, 399. The British Sea Empire in Africa, 401. The French Land Empire in Africa, Spain and Belgium in Africa, 403. Africa about 1875, 406.]

28. A STRATEGIC APPRAISAL OF AFRICA   *George T. Renner*   408

Africa in Early Times, 408. Africa in the World-Ocean Age, 409. Africa in the Amphibian and Air Age, 410. Africa in the Atomic Power Age, 414.

[Africa's Location with Respect to the "World Island," 409. Africa in the Second World War, 412. Strategic Value of Africa in a Third World War, 414.]

29. THE MALAY ARCHIPELAGO AND OCEANIA   *Joseph E. Van Riper*   416

The Malay Archipelago: The Locational Factor, 417. Physical Setting and Human Settlement, 419. The People, 422. Economic Structure, 423. Major Political Trends, 427. *Oceania,* 428.

[Malay Archipelago: Locational Map, 416. Netherlands East Indies: Major Physical Features, 421. Malay Archipelago: Commercial Production, 423. Singapore, 424.]

30. THE PHILIPPINE ISLANDS   *Alden Cutshall*   430

Physical Setting, 431. People and Culture, 432. Government and Politics, 435. Economy, 435. Internal Problems, 436. Foreign Relations, 438.

[The Philippine Islands, 433.]

PART SIX

Latin America

31. THE CARIBBEAN: AN AMERICAN MEDITERRANEAN   *J. Warren Nystrom*   443

Space Factors, 444. Physical Characteristics, 446. Regional Economy, 449. People, 451. Historical Background, 453. The Caribbean and the United States, 454.

[The Caribbean Region (Showing Major Colonial Possessions), 445. West Indies, 446.]

32. THE UNITED STATES OF BRAZIL   *Sax Bradford*   458

Historical Background, 459. Human Factors, 462. Transportation: Man vs. Space, 463. Regions of Brazil, 464. Brazil in the Postwar World, 469.

⎡ Brazil in South America, 458. States, Territories, and Cities, 459. Regions and ⎤
⎣ Resources, 465. ⎦

33. THE STATES OF THE RIO DE LA PLATA   *Ruth S. Sutherland*   471

Argentina: Physical Characteristics, 471. Regions and Resources, 472. National Economy, 476. Historical Background, 478. Argentina and the United States, 481. *Paraguay:* Economy, 482. The People, 483. History and Foreign Relations, 483. *Uruguay:* History, 484. Population, 484. National Economy, 484.

⎡ States of the Rio de la Plata, 472. Argentina: Provinces and Regions, 473. ⎤
⎣ Apex of South America, 475. ⎦

34. PACIFIC SOUTH AMERICA   *C. Langdon White*   485

Physical Setting, 486. The People, 488. Cities, 491. Historical Highlights, 492. Economic Developments, 494. Political Relations, 497. Boundary Disputes, 499. Social Problems, 500. Pacific Islands, 500. Conclusion, 501.

⎡ Pacific Countries of South America, 487.   Physiographic Diagram of South Amer- ⎤
⎣ ica, 489. Inca Empire, 493. ⎦

PART SEVEN

Some Special Aspects of Political Geography

35. POLITICAL GEOGRAPHY OF THE OCEANS   *Weldon B. Gibson*   505

The Science of Oceanography, 505. History and the Sea, 506. World Ocean and Man's Environment, 509. The Polar Mediterranean, 513. Law of the High Seas, 515.

⎡ Currents of the Seven Seas, 510. Principal Ocean Trade Routes of the World, ⎤
⎣ 511. States of the Arctic Mediterranean, 513. ⎦

36. BOUNDARIES IN INTERNATIONAL RELATIONS   *Arthur R. Hall*   517

Development of Frontiers and Boundaries, 517. Types of Boundaries, 519. Boundary-Making, 521. Boundary Functions, 524. Solving Boundary Problems, 527.

⎡ Boundary Fluctuations in a Frontier Area, 518. Boundary Delimitation and ⎤
⎣ Demarcation, 525. ⎦

37. POPULATION FACTORS IN INTERNATIONAL AFFAIRS   *Clarence B. Odell*   528

National Greatness in Terms of Man Power, 529. Distribution and Density of the World's Population, 529. Trends of the World's Population Growth, 532. Political Significance of the Composition of the World's Population, 535. Population Policies and Controls, 537.

⎡ World: Population Estimates by Continental Areas (1650–2000), 533. Age and ⎤
⎣ Sex Composition of Population (1940), 539. ⎦

38. GRAND STRATEGY OF WORLD WAR II   *Herman Beukema*   541

Meaning and Application of Grand Strategy, 541. The Strategic Situation in August 1939, 542. War Plans in 1939, 544. Strategic Operations through 1942, 545. The Allied Offensives: European Theater, 548. The Allied Offenses: Pacific Theater, 550. The Strategy of Peace Enforcement, 552.

⎡ High Tide of Axis Success (Mid-1942), 547. The Siege of *Festung Europa*, 550. ⎤
⎣ Allied Offensive in the Pacific, 551. ⎦

39. GEOGRAPHY IN FUTURE WORLD POLITICS · *John K. Rose* · 554

The Population Variable, 555. The Land Variable, 556. The Energy Variable, 558. Other Resource Variables, 559. The Time Variable, 562. The Variable Economic Pattern, 565. Finale, 566.

Regions Unsuitable for Crop Growth, 557. Energy Reserves and Their Utilization in 1937 (Major Countries Only), 560. United States: Commercial Reserves of Certain Minerals in 1944, 561. World Air Route Pattern, 564–565.

APPENDICES · 567

Area and Population of the Countries of the World, 567. States of the Postwar World, 569. Territorial Changes and New States since World War II, 571. Area and Population of the World's "Empires," 573.

BIBLIOGRAPHY · 575

QUESTIONS AND TOPICS FOR FURTHER STUDY · 605

BIOGRAPHICAL NOTES · 629

INDEX · 637

PART ONE

The Nature and Scope of Political Geography

THE study of political geography is concerned with the association of the earth and the state, and the relationships between the two. The dynamic elements in political geography are people, ideas, and group motivations; the static elements are the earth factors of space, location, and material resources.

The potential riches and power of a state are primarily set by the natural resources within the space occupied by that state. The actual wealth and power of the state in question are the result of human ability and effort operating within the limits set by the environment. In all, there are more than eighty sovereign states in the world and these are equipped with space or land area in very unequal amounts. For example, in prewar Germany some 67,000,000 people lived on 181,000 square miles, whereas only about 11,500,000 Canadians inhabited a national area of 3,462,000 square miles. The Soviet Union possesses an area of more than 8,000,000 square miles, Monaco an area of but 0.6 square miles. That great republic, the United States of America, comprises almost 3,000,000 square miles; the little republic of Andorra includes only 191 square miles. Obviously, there is great discrepancy in the amount of terrestrial space allotted to the individual nations. Space per se, however, is of relatively minor importance; its chief significance consists in the amount of natural resources contained in any specific unit of space. In the quantity and quality of their natural resources the nations vary strikingly. Thus, little Belgium is richly equipped, large Mongolia or Pakistan is poorly endowed.

Even more striking than the contrasts in space and resources generally are the contrasts in social and economic development wrought by man. For example, the Dutch have shown a positive genius in developing a poor area; the Irish much less so. The Chinese have been highly successful in developing a numerous human society within a large, fairly well endowed area; the Brazilians have been less successful. The Americans have developed a highly mechanized civilization; the Bantus or Indonesians have not. The inhabitants of mountainous Switzerland have developed a vigorous pacifist society; the inhabitants of mountainous Afghanistan have developed a vigorous militaristic society; the inhabitants of mountainous Tibet have developed a feeble hermit society. The Hindus have been indifferent to world affairs; the Germans have disrupted the world with a series of great wars; the Scandinavians have been equally active in promoting peace. Whatever the reason for these differences, it is probable that human differences are involved. Indeed, human groups seem to vary as much in their culture, mass motivations, and attitude toward their neighbors as political regions differ in their areas and resources.

Only a few nations are strong enough to play the game of power politics. In the nineteenth century there were a larger number of states strong enough to be called Great Powers. With war becoming more and more a matter of industrial capacity, however, the number of states which could qualify as major nations slowly diminished. By 1914 there were eight Great Powers. During World War I these states were engaged in a colossal death struggle, from which but five Great Powers emerged. By 1939 two defeated nations had revived, rearmed, and assumed their positions as Great Powers. The seven Great Powers of that day, together with their smaller allies and victims, plunged into World War II. At the end of six years of exhaustive and highly mechanized warfare there were left but three Great Powers—the United States, the U. S. S. R., and the British Commonwealth and Empire.

Of these three Soviet Russia has immense advantages in geographic situation and location, a great and growing industry, and a population as numerous as that of Great Britain and the United States combined. Her resources are enormous: some geographers estimate that the U. S. S. R. has the greatest array of natural resources and is potentially the most nearly self-sufficing of all nations.

The study of the areas and resources of political units, together with the people who live in them, makes up the essence of political geography. This subject is closely related to the field designated as political science. These two social sciences are alike in that both of them study the state. The latter, however, is concerned with the *polity* and the *sovereignty* of the state, whereas the former is concerned with the *power* and *space relations* of the state.

Political geography has been defined in numerous ways. In general, these may be grouped into three broad schools of thought —the landscape school, the ecological school, and the organismic school. These are based upon somewhat different premises and involve the use of unlike methodologies, but yield not entirely dissimilar results.

In the United States, political geography was comparatively neglected until relatively recent times. In Germany it was developed much earlier. Before World War II the subject received an enormously enhanced amount of attention, but in a somewhat perverted direction, in the Reich. The organismic concept of the state, previously developed by

German scholars, was an idea which, when coupled with the pathology of the German national mass mind during the 1920's and 1930's, was readily adaptable to the Nazi demands for *Lebensraum*. The *Institut für Geopolitik* at the University of Munich thus extensively served both the Nazi party and the German General Staff, but there was no direct liaison between the latter and the *Institut*. When the geographically uninformed American people learned that certain facts and hypotheses of political geography, under the appellation of *Geopolitik*, were utilized in Nazi diplomacy and war, there was nothing in their previous experiences to explain such a situation. Many Americans, therefore, hastily condemned geopolitics as necessarily immoral. Some, indeed, included all geography in their castigations. A more geographically informed people would not have made such an error—especially when their own government was even then using geopolitical principles in shaping the pattern of victory.

Since the power and the space relations of states are primary considerations in political geography, most of the chapters of this book bear directly upon these two topics. At the outset, therefore, it may be stated categorically that most of the space relations conform to the geographical principles governing space relationships in general. As to political power, that must in the first analysis rest upon the basic principles of economic and military geography. At the same time the exercise of political power should conform to three principles:

I. National security lies in active participation in world affairs rather than in a retreat into a national or continental defense shell.

II. International justice must rest upon the triumph of the human spirit over force, that is, upon valuing the individual above the nation or any institution, either secular or sectarian.

III. World peace must be based upon international exercise of power to enforce justice, that is, the human community must continue its growth from tribal to local to provincial to national to global dimensions.

CHAPTER 1 | Political Geography and Its Point of View

DURING the recent war against the Axis, Americans generally became aware for the first time of the existence of political geography. Hardly had the flames died down at Pearl Harbor before a professor of geography was invited to head the operations-planning seminar of the United States Army General Staff; great numbers of American geographers were set to work plotting bombing objectives, studying invasion beaches, analyzing the concentrations of enemy industries, railroads, and populations, and doing many other sorts of government war research; and other geographers were engaged in such diverse tasks as secret intelligence work, aerial-photographic mosaic construction, instructional duties, cartography and map study. One eminent geographer was appointed to membership in a steering committee of three, set up by the President for the purpose of formulating national wartime policy. Eventually, many army officer-candidates were required to study political geography as a preparation for military leadership. All of these pieces of evidence indicated strongly that geography had many valuable applications to the business of war and defense.

The Utility of Political Geography

Wartime impacts. Oddly enough, the American people were not to learn of political geography from reading the ideas or observing the wartime achievements of their own geographers. Instead, they were to hear about it as something being cultivated by their German enemies. Moreover, they learned of it under the name of geopolitics (or Geopolitik to use the German spelling of the word).

Many Americans, because they had previously never heard of geopolitics, nor of anything even remotely resembling it, deduced that this whole field of knowledge was of very recent origin. Moreover, because they observed that some of the German political geographers ranted about Nordic "race superiority" and the "Aryan super-man" (as also did German anthropologists, historians, and others) they concluded that geopolitics was therefore intellectually fictitious. Furthermore, they observed that the Nazis were making use of geopolitics in formulating war strategy, that the leading German geopolitician was once a Major General of the Reich, and that many of the Nazi geopoliticians were bent upon world domination. They, therefore, inferred that political geography was a German National Socialist invention for conquering the world. Actually, none of these inferences was true.

Geography is one of mankind's oldest fields of learning, and whereas that subdivision of the subject known as political geography (and called by some people, geopolitics *) is relatively young, it is, nevertheless, quite old. In this connection, it may be pointed out that political geography was fathered by Immanuel Kant, who died in 1804, and developed by Friedrich Ratzel, who died a century later. Subsequently, political geography achieved considerable prestige in the educational system of Germany. Its seeds were transferred

* Geopolitics may be regarded as a shortened designation for political geography, just as geonomics is an abbreviated term for economic geography.

3

to Britain, France, the United States, and elsewhere. In the United States, it developed sturdily but it received little educational recognition, and achieved almost no prestige. One is, therefore, treated to the amazing spectacle of the American people learning about political geography from their enemies, unaware that there were, at the outbreak of World War II, more capable geographers in the United States than in Nazi Germany. The American people were generally unaware, too, that geopolitical principles were being used by the United States itself, almost from the outset of World War II, in fashioning the pattern of military victory. Thus, geopolitics was neither of recent origin nor fictitious in character, nor yet was it a German Nazi invention for conquering the world.

Popular reactions. After the partition of Czechoslovakia in 1939, the American people had their first large-scale introduction to the ideas and applications of German Nazi geopolitics. For more than six years prior to this, however, they had been seeing small bits of it in that program of tub thumping, sabre rattling, and lie mongering known as the "war of nerves." With the advent and progress of World War II (especially the early stages wherein the Axis won all the battles and diplomatic moves) they saw and heard more and more about it. When they encountered Geopolitik as a limited instrument of German statecraft, as a vehicle for Nazi propaganda, and in some respects as a blueprint for Axis strategy, the American people generally had no foundation of geographical education for evaluating and adjudging it. Accordingly, most of them were thoroughly confused and not a little disturbed. A great deal of ill-informed discussion took place. There was a fairly general tendency to label all geopolitics as an immoral science. Almost as common was the attempt to classify geopolitics as something quite different from political geography.

In the midst of all this confusion, the British-Canadian geographer, Griffith Taylor, appraised the situation discerningly and remarked that the writings of the modern German geographers, and by inference their interpretation by some American writers, "seem to imply that Geopolitics necessarily includes discussions of world domination and of racial superiority. To the present writer these are arbitrary and unnecessary extensions of the term Geopolitics. The latter may be defined as the study of the outstanding features of the situation and resources of a country with a view to determining its status in World Politics." *

Thus defined and clarified by Taylor, geopolitics might well be inferred to be synonymous with political geography, and consequently one may also infer that the dissimilarity between the two resulted, not from any difference between the subjects, but from differences between German geographers living under a national psychosis and non-German geographers in a democratic regime. Practically all geographers and most political scientists and historians did know that political geography and geopolitics had the same roots, and therefore they did not try to pose any basic dichotomy between the two terms. Nevertheless, this does not mean that political geography as set forth by the Nazis was not filled with a great deal of both humbug and malice, because it did contain much of both. It does, however, imply that geopolitics as a field of knowledge cannot be classified on the basis of how many spurious qualities were present in German Geopolitik in, say, the year 1938.

Moreover, to label geopolitics as an immoral science, was to box with a straw man. Science is neither moral nor immoral, it is amoral. It is only the ends to which science is used that may be moral or immoral. The Nazi leaders used German Geopolitik for low and mean purposes, but such use no more reflects upon either geopolitics or political geography than do the repulsive race doctrines held by the Nazis reflect upon the science of anthropology, or do the dark experiments performed upon the bodies of living Nazi victims discredit the acts of surgery and medicine. On the contrary geopolitics (even the Nazi Geopolitik) possessed many basic elements of strategic validity. Were this not true, it would be inconceivable how a second-rate country such as Germany could have come so near to conquering the entire world. American geopolitics, however,

* Griffith Taylor, "Canada's Role in Geopolitics," *Compass of the World*, Hans W. Weigert and Vilhjalmur Stefansson, editors (The Macmillan Company, 1944), 273.

proved even more valid than did German Geopolitik.

Professional indifference. All the activity in Nazi Germany prior to its territorial expansion failed to impress political geographers in the United States. As late as 1935 Hartshorne wrote, "Nowhere in English can I find an adequate summary, to say nothing of a discussion, of the notable developments of the past twenty years in political geography on the Continent, particularly by the Germans." *

Even after the war began and American geographers were perforce compelled to take note of such developments, the general consensus of opinion was that German Geopolitik was so fraudulent as not to qualify as bona fide geopolitics. Moreover, they regarded it as so patently dishonest as not even to merit serious refutation.

Applications. The evidence presented in the previous paragraphs indicates that geopolitics has a very great wartime utility. This held as true for Germany, which employed geopolitical distortions in order to obfuscate and intimidate its enemies, as it did for the United States, which operated on the premise that geopolitical truth was a most effective psychological weapon.

It would seem to be a fact, however, that geopolitics has an even greater utility in peacetime. It affords a way for a nation to appraise its own national strength and to estimate the strength of its enemies or possible enemies. It provides a system for projecting graphically one's probable military moves, and the probable military moves of one's enemy in the event of a war. Moreover, it also yields a system for graphically plotting the moves and counter moves in diplomatic relations. As such, it provides the basis for winning and maintaining peace.

Some Definitions

The social science of geography has been defined in numerous ways, each definition expressing a slightly different shade of meaning. Despite this, a fairly large number of American geographers would concur in defining it, at least tentatively, as *the study of human so-*ciety as viewed against its earth background. Expressed a little more dynamically, geography might be defined as *the strategy of men, space, and resources.* Political geography, or geopolitics, may be considered the political phase of such a study (in contrast to the subsciences of economic geography and social geography, which treat of its economic and cultural phases). Regardless of basic definitions, however, it is a truism that the principal *regional* aspect of political geography is the study of countries or national states, just as the regional aspects of economic and social geographies can be described as the study of economic regions and culture provinces respectively.

The state. The land surface of the earth is composed of several hundred major and many thousand minor political units or civil divisions. Political units are merely divisions of the earth's surface which possess enough *polity* * to make them recognizable as separate civic entities. Whether or not such units are to be considered as states depends upon the extent to which they possess sovereignty and independence. The exercise of sovereignty and independence is not, however, absolute. Consequently, it is seldom possible to determine the precise number of states in the world at any given time. At the moment of writing, there would seem to be approximately eighty-one states in existence. There are periods of time during which the pattern of states changes but little or not at all. There are others, notably during and immediately following major wars, wherein the pattern changes drastically. Old states may disappear: new ones may be born. Still others may be dismembered or rearranged into new combinations.

THE SIZE OF STATES. Careful scrutiny of the world's eighty-one states reveals that six of them are very small, even diminutive, in size:

Country	Square miles	
Luxembourg	998	
Andorra	191	
Liechtenstein	65	
San Marino	38	
Monaco	370	acres
Vatican State	108.7	acres

* Richard Hartshorne, "Recent Developments in Political Geography," *American Political Science Review*, 29 (October, 1935), 786.

* By *polity* is meant a politically organized community.

At the opposite extreme are the eight *
gigantic states of the earth:

Country	Square miles
Soviet Union	8,477,000
China	3,877,000
Canada	3,462,000
Brazil	3,286,000
United States	2,977,000
Australia	2,975,000
India (Hindustan)	1,200,000
Argentina	1,080,000

The remaining sovereign national units
vary in size from Mexico, with 760,000 square
miles, on down to Albania, with approximately 10,000 square miles, and Lebanon,
with some 3600. Nineteen are small (3000 to
39,999 square miles), eighteen are medium
(40,000 to 99,999 square miles), and thirty are
large (100,000 to 999,999 square miles). Arranged tabularly, these are as follows:

Category of size	Number
Diminutive states	6
Small states	19
Medium states	18
Large states	30
Gigantic states	8

Although classifications of size are useful
in helping to describe political units, they are
not indices of national power. A glance at
a table of national areas will show that India
is a gigantic or colossal state, France is a
large state, and Britain is of intermediate
size. Despite these comparative magnitudes,
Britain wields several times as much power
as does France, and enjoys an almost incomparably greater prestige than India.

DISTRIBUTION OF STATES. The nations of
the world are distributed over the continents
very unevenly. The following chart emphasizes this point:

Continent	Number of states
Europe	31
Asia	20
North America	12
South America	10
Africa	4
Australasia	4
Antarctica	0
Total	81

* If the Union of South Africa succeeds in annexing
Southwest Africa, and if Egypt obtains clear title to
the Anglo-Egyptian Sudan, these two nations will be
added to the list of gigantic states.

That distribution is not a function of area is
shown by the following figures:

Continent	Area in sq. mi.
Asia	16,494,000
Africa	11,530,000
North America	9,364,000
South America	7,097,000
Antarctica	5,363,000
Australasia	4,240,000
Europe	3,781,000

Nor does it, except in the case of Antarctica,
seem to be a function of population, as suggested by the following figures:

Continent	Population
Asia	1,157,000,000
Europe	524,000,000
North America	198,000,000
Africa	163,000,000
South America	97,000,000
Australasia	88,000,000
Antarctica	0

From a comparison of these several data it is
fairly obvious that neither population nor
land area is the yeast that causes national
states to arise. An examination of the figures
showing distribution of states by continents
reveals that whatever that yeast may be, it is
strongly present in Europe, Asia, North
America, and South America whereas it is but
weakly present in Africa and Australasia.
The first four continents contain seventy-
three states; the latter two contain but eight
states. This contrast suggests the factor,
which for the moment we may term nationalism, that lies at the root of the matter.
From this study we can conclude that the
assumption of power by the national state is
a vital factor in political geography and international politics.

Three centers of power. A close look at
not only the clustering of states in certain
areas, but at the actual relative strengths of
these states as well, indicates that there are,
geopolitically speaking, three regional centers of power in the world. The first of these
lies at the western end of Eurasia, and
stretches across western Europe, central Europe, eastern and southeastern Europe. The
second center, which lies at the opposite end
of Eurasia, centers in China, Korea, and
Japan but extends northward into Manchuria and Maritime Siberia and reaches
southward into southern and southeastern

Asia. The third center, which lies in eastern North America, includes most of the eastern part of the United States and southeastern Canada.

Although these three areas contain nearly three fourths of the world's population, they include only about one eighth of its land surface. The average density of population over the earth is about forty persons per square mile; in the power centers it averages about 230 per square mile. From this difference, one can infer that these power areas are much more productive than are terrestrial regions generally. Indeed, when examined geographically they are seen to possess:

(a) an abundance of fertile and arable land, under a climate that yields sufficient warmth and water for plant growth, the combination insuring a plentiful food supply;

(b) additional natural resources for manufactural industries;

(c) a location reasonably favorable to the flow of trade and the spread of ideas and other stimuli to human development.

In nearly every part of the world men have erected governments for the purposes of providing defense and group welfare and of promoting group ideas and interests. It is only in the world's three power areas, however, that governments have achieved great economic, diplomatic, and military strength.

The three power areas of the world are well mineralized regions, made up principally of accessible lowlands centered in the middle latitudes. They are also regions of large and dense populations, which are reservoirs of above-average human energy, skill, and education. Thus, the world's power centers are the result of the geographical interaction of select human stocks and superior natural environments. As a consequence, every powerful nation on earth lies in one or another of these three areas. Not all nations located in the areas in question, however, are possessed of power or even of national vigor.

Factors of Powerhood *

Natural advantages and resources. Although states are human in substance and man-made in origin, they are physical in foundation and structure. No real state ever possessed national strength nor even enjoyed well-being unless its natural environment afforded numerous and large physical advantages.* Chief among these are a geographic location which provides good access and yet allows for that security needed for social development, adequate area or space, an energizing climate, and abundant mineral, power, water, soil, and biotic resources.

A numerous, energetic population. Numerically, the populations of some states far exceed those of others. The extremes are represented on the one hand by China with 450,000,000 and India with 300,000,000 inhabitants, and on the other hand by Andorra with 5,200 and Vatican State with 1,100 inhabitants. For every different stage of development in the arts there is an optimum density of population. Some states exceed this optimum, others fall short of it—circumstances which vitally affect standards of living and industrial strength. More important than mere numbers, however, is the quality of a population. Owing to the results of overpopulation, poor dietary habits, and low public health standards, many countries contain large percentages of ill, undernourished, and inefficient people. Moreover, because of poverty or poor institutional practices, they may also include large numbers of uneducated and untrained persons. No state can be powerful unless it contains a relatively large proportion of intelligent, healthy, educated, and skilful people.

A common language and historical background. A common historical background and a stirring and heroic tradition are the cements that bind a population together. Even more effective as a unifier is a common language. Language is not only a medium of communication, but a vehicle whereby the culture of the historical past is brought to each individual in the present. Diversity in language and tradition, therefore, affords a serious national problem. Where such diversity exists, a state is strong only to the extent that it sets up such common bonds as will neutralize it.

Freedom of religion, education, and press. Attempts to regiment education, press, and

---

* Much of the material in this section dealing with the "Factors of Powerhood" was supplied by Dr. Richard L. Tuthill of the University of Kentucky.

* Each of these is treated in some detail in Chapter 2.

human minds in the interest of producing cultural unity are, paradoxically, the greatest disruptor of states. Mental and moral tyrannies are merely attempts by the herd mind to suppress those who are either intelligent enough or enterprising enough to have individual opinions. Such dissenting opinions and beliefs are not always right, but they are the visible evidences of the unquenchable freemasonry of the human mind and spirit. As such, they are the most valuable resource possessed by any nation. The extent to which they are conserved is a measure of the moral strength of a state.

An advanced technology. More than ever before, national strength today is a matter of technology. Scientific knowledge is more or less international and available to everyone. Knowledge of how peacetime factories and wartime weapons are built is, therefore, widespread; the ability to build them is not. Most of the constructions and gadgets of modern civilization are made by machines, not hands. Moreover, those same machines are themselves made not by hands, but by other machines, called machine tools. The creation of tools to make machine tools to make machines to manufacture industrial goods and weapons of war is called technology. This technology has been, and still is to a considerable extent, the monopoly of certain nations. Possession of technology helps to determine national power.

Capital goods and credit. Many nations are rich in machine tools and other capital goods; others are woefully lacking in them. Nations similarly vary in their possession of international credit and the ability to command both capital goods and consumer goods through trade. War invariably causes the expansion of capital equipment in certain countries and its destruction in others. Thus, the moment of industrial strength among nations shifts from time to time.

Balanced economic development. A balanced pattern of economic development, in which agricultural, extractive, manufactural, transportational, and commercial industries complement and supplement one another, is a goal of all major states. A British four-year plan, a Russian *Piatiletka,* a Nazi German autarky, a Polish three-year plan, a Japanese Co-Prosperity Sphere, or an American New Deal program all represent attempts to move in the direction of balanced economic patterns. Not only are some rational and others irrational, but their completion is often hindered by national armament programs and trade wars. In the long run, it seems probable that the development of industrial patterns is guided principally by basic economic considerations.

Internal political stability. During normal times a state is able to command loyalty, or at least passive acceptance, from its citizenry. During a period of war, economic depression, or other disaster a government may fall, or be rendered weak or impotent through dissension, or it may grow strong by reason of the support of its citizenry. The ability of a state to survive tests of internal support is one of the measures of powerhood.

Friendly relationships with other countries. The pattern of external relationships varies greatly from one state to another, the extent depending to a rather considerable degree upon the relative strength of each. In any instance the strength or weakness of a state is determined by all the elements previously listed. Fear, suspicion, covetousness, or aggressiveness on the part of a state sometimes make genuine cooperation with other states impossible; but despite the presence of one or more of these deterrents, seemingly friendly diplomatic and commercial relationships are often maintained. From such superficial dealings, however, there is usually a slow accumulation of international poison that has, in the past, invariably led to war.

Classifications of States

Major and minor powers. No state possesses all the elements of national powerhood in full measure. There is, therefore, no such thing as the ideal state. Even the strongest members of the world's family of nations contain one or more large (and perhaps fatal) weaknesses. The effects of this lack are evidenced in the constant rise or decline of nations on the power scale.

In the year 1914, just prior to World War I, the list of Major and Minor Powers looked about as follows:

Major powers	*Minor powers*
France	Spain
Great Britain	Netherlands
Germany	China

Major powers	Minor powers
Russia	Serbia
Austria-Hungary	Sweden
United States	Rumania
Italy	Turkey
Japan	

As a result of the war, however, Germany was defeated and disarmed; Austria-Hungary was dismembered; Turkey was trimmed down in size; Russia collapsed, and was overrun; France was bled white; Italy, the United Kingdom, and the United States were saddled with heavy debt; and Japan was stimulated to expand.

Soon after the war (1920), therefore, the list of powers appeared to be approximately as follows:

Major powers	Minor powers
Great Britain	Rumania
France	Poland
United States	Spain
Japan	Yugoslavia
Italy	China
	Sweden

The next two decades saw southern Ireland separate from the United Kingdom; Turkey reorganize; Soviet Russia climb to power; Spain crumple in revolution; Germany rearm; and nearly all countries stagger under the impact of an economic depression. By 1939, just before World War II, the alignment of powers was approximately as follows:

Major powers	Minor powers
Germany	Rumania
Great Britain	Poland
United States	Turkey
France	China
Soviet Union	Yugoslavia
Japan	Sweden
Italy	Argentina
	Brazil

The war against the Axis brought disastrous defeat to Germany, Japan, and Italy; collapse to France and several of the small powers; and near exhaustion to Britain. Brazil, aided by the United States, eclipsed its Latin American neighbors; and China surprised the world by resisting Japan for more than a decade.

It is interesting to note that only three great units emerged from World War II possessing any real military and political power. These were the United States, the Soviet Union, and the British Commonwealth and Empire.* However, when the United Nations organization was set up, China and France were arbitrarily, and not altogether justifiably, elevated to the rank of Major Powers; whether this move will ultimately be justified remains to be seen. Meanwhile, the three Axis nations were taken into custody. Italy has now been restored to the family of nations and should probably be rated as a Minor Power. At the moment, neither Germany nor Japan possesses any military strength, but both possess an enormous nuisance value in world politics. For that reason both may be regarded at present as potential Minor Powers, although it is conceivable that Germany at least may eventually rejoin the ranks of Major Powers. For the time being, therefore, the power alignment among nations is approximately as follows:

"Big Five" powers	Minor powers
United States	Brazil
Soviet Union	Argentina
Great Britain	Turkey
France	Sweden
China	Yugoslavia
	Poland
	Italy

Weak imperial states. In addition to some of the Major Powers, there are a number of states which possess colonies and other types of dependencies, despite the fact that they are too weak to hold them against attack. This group includes the Netherlands, Portugal, Spain, Norway, Denmark, and Belgium.

Weak metropolitan states. The vast majority of the world's nations consists of weak metropolitan states. These are merely home areas without dependencies. They are of two general types which combined number about fifty-seven. First, there are nations, such as Japan and Germany, which have been stripped of their colonies; and, second, there are those, such as Liberia, Switzerland, Bhutan, or El Salvador, which have never possessed, and conceivably may not want, colonies.

Feudal relict states. Lastly, there are the six diminutive states of Europe. They are

* Many critical observers believe that at the close of the war, Britain was on the verge of collapse and that she was sustained only by help from her dominions and the United States.

not real nations, but they have been vested with most of the political attributes of nations. Examined historically, they are seen in some cases to be mere tiny feudal relics.

Types of states summarized. The various types of states, when arranged in tabular fashion, show the following frequencies:

Major powers	5
Minor powers	7
Weak imperial states	6
Weak metropolitan states	57
Feudal relict states	6
Total	81

Characteristics of Power Areas

The European area. Southern Europe has one of the most benignant climates on earth—favorable to both man and his agriculture. Into this area penetrates a warm and relatively protected arm of the ocean, the Mediterranean Sea, the whole affording a nursery for early civilization. From this nursery area, civilization eventually spread via the mountain passes of Central Europe to the northern and eastern parts of the continent. During this expansion European men were subjected to three forces. First, because Europe is merely a peninsula on the great land mass of Asia, they were subjected to waves of invaders from the continent. Second, because the ocean reaches far into both northern and southern Europe, they were eventually tempted under favorable conditions to venture abroad. Third, because Europe is both physically fragmented and varied as to resources, they became culturally and industrially differentiated more than in any other part of the world.

Europeans were early stimulated into precocious cultural, political, and industrial development. Earlier than any other people they began to expand overseas. The first to expand were the Portuguese, the Spanish, and the Dutch. These were closely followed by the British and French. Russian land expansion extended across northern Asia to the Pacific in the seventeenth century. Finally came the German, Belgian, and Italian overseas movements. The European colonial daughter nations, such as the United States, Australia, New Zealand, Argentina, Chile, and South Africa, have in turn started

their own secondary waves of expansion.*

Today Europe is the most active of the geographical power areas. This small continent contains three of the Major Powers and a large number of Minor Powers; it contains about forty per cent of all the world's states; it contains all of the six diminutive states in its entirety. Any one of these four traits is enough to mark the European continent as unusual. Combined, they reveal it to be geopolitically pathological to a high degree. As a result of this condition Europe has long been the diplomatic and military storm center of the world. During the past century and a half, three world wars have originated on that troubled little continent and several additional smaller wars have been fought there.

The Eastern North American area. Eastern North America is richly equipped with coal, iron, and petroleum. It is penetrated by the St. Lawrence–Great Lakes system, and by the Ohio-Mississippi waterway. It is backed by the most productive agricultural domain on earth, the Mississippi Basin, and rendered accessible by the greatest network of railways, highways, and airways yet constructed by man.

Most of this great power area is comprised in one political jurisdiction, that of the United States, although Canada holds a small fringe along the north. Thus, this area is to all intents and purposes united, in contrast to the minutely divided European area. This unity has enabled the region to avoid conflict and competitive waste. Although its population is smaller than in the other power areas, it has developed organization, mechanization, and large-scale systems of production to such a point as to achieve world economic and political leadership.

The Oriental area. The eastern and southeastern Asiatic area consists of a series of large fertile river valleys and deltas separated by intervening uplands. Not only is it less well endowed with fuels, minerals, and forests than the other two power areas, but also, it is seriously overpopulated and politically disorganized. Much of the area is occupied by China, one of the "Big Five" nations. Despite the essential greatness of the

* The Asiatic Japanese also undertook a typical colonial program.

Chinese people and their civilization, China is presently torn by internal political strife. Augmenting this element of weakness, Japanese neighbors have despoiled the country; the Russians have reached across Asia and have thrust themselves into the realm; and the western Europeans and Americans have come by way of the ocean and have also intervened in Chinese affairs.

World struggle for power. These three great power areas are not set off from the rest of the world; instead, they grade into the nonpower areas almost imperceptibly, inviting expansion by strong states at the expense of the weak. Moreover, the great power areas are not isolated from one another, but lie open to intercontinental struggles for regional and global hegemony. Furthermore, the division of space and strength even between states within a power area is not fixed but, instead, is constantly in flux. Only the strongest states, however, can even hope to play important parts in modern global war and that struggle known as power politics. It is in response to the need for understanding the state and its role in war, peace, and power politics that the science of political geography was originated and developed.

CHAPTER 2 | The Substance and Scope of Political Geography

ALTHOUGH political geography has undergone more than a half century of sturdy growth, it has not yet been defined in terms acceptable to all political geographers. Instead, thinking in this field has proceeded in such diverse directions that several distinctly different patterns of thinking have developed. Three of the most significant of these schools of thought are:

(a) the Political Landscape School
(b) the Political Ecology School
(c) the Organismic School

Geopolitical Schools of Thought

The Political Landscape School. According to followers of one school of thought, political geography is a study of the political landscape. It devotes itself primarily to the observation, analysis, and recording of all political items in the total cultural landscape, and their integration into spatial patterns. In general, it concerns itself with the following items:

The Political Landscape

1. The area
   a. Location, size, form
   b. Core areas and nuclei
   c. Political subdivisions
      (1) Local
      (2) Subprovincial
      (3) Provincial
2. The internal pattern
   a. Differences
      (1) Race
      (2) Language
      (3) Religion
      (4) Party and political sentiments
      (5) Other

b. Distributions
   (1) Suffrage
   (2) Parliamentary representation
   (3) Other
3. Terminal elements
   a. Boundaries and their configuration
      (1) Irregularities
         (a) Protuberances
         (b) Embayments
      (2) Inliers and outliers
      (3) Disputed areas
   b. Frontier zones
      (1) Defensive positions
      (2) Militarized and demilitarized zones
      (3) Customs barriers
   c. Boundary and terminal structure
4. The external pattern
   a. International grouping
   b. Colonial patterns
   c. Other arrangements

This is a limited interpretation of political geography in that it restricts the subject to a study of the visible evidences of man's political organization and activity.* In actual practice, however, the work of the political geographers who lean toward this school of thinking tends to be considerably broader than this outline would suggest. Whittlesey, for instance, declares that ". . . the essence of political geography" is the "differentiation of political phenomena from place to place over the earth," and the "kernel of political geography is the political area." ** Hartshorne specifically states, "Political geography is the science of political areas, or more specif-

---

* The regional aspect of political geography under this definition tends to shape up into the concept of the German *Landschaft.*

** D. S. Whittlesey, *The Earth and the State* (Henry Holt and Company, 1944), iii, 585.

ically, the study of the state as a characteristic of areas in relation to the other characteristics of areas." *

The Political Ecology School. Under the ecological definition of geography the attention of the geographer is focused upon human society rather than upon the area itself. The political geographer of this school aims, therefore, not at the description and interpretation of a political area but at the description and interpretation of the ways in which men have accommodated their political behavior and structures to the character of their area. In other words, this school of thought defines political geography as the study of a social group's "politico-geographic adjustments to the natural environment of its area." ** In general, this political phase of human ecology concerns itself primarily with the following elements.†

Political Ecology

1. The human group
    a. Origins and growth
    b. Present ethnic traits
    c. The area occupied
        (1) Location
        (2) Space
        (3) Resource equipment
        (4) Areal growth
            (a) Lines of expansion
            (b) Historical stages of expansion
2. The economy by which the group maintains itself
    a. Patterns of resource use
        (1) Industries and related resources
        (2) Surpluses and deficits
        (3) Conservation practices
        (4) Trade in resources
    b. Social attitudes and social control
    c. The nationality structure
        (1) Minorities
        (2) Other differentiations
3. Adjustments for controlling the area
    a. National governmental arrangements
        (1) Monarchy
        (2) Federal republic
        (3) Confederacy
    b. Provincial governmental arrangements
        (1) Tribal state

    (2) Feudal state
    (3) Province, shire, canton, department, or American State
    (4) Soviet republic
    c. Local governmental arrangements
        (1) Tribal village
        (2) Feudal unit
        (3) City state
        (4) Others
            (a) Municipality
            (b) Soviet or commune
            (c) Township, county, borough, district
4. Adjustments in boundary delimitation
    a. Relationship to environmental factors
    b. Disputed points
5. External adjustments
    a. International governmental arrangements
        (1) Commonwealth of nations
        (2) Alliance or entente
        (3) League of nations
    b. Extra-national arrangements
        (1) Colonies
        (2) Mandates (trusteeships) and protectorates
        (3) Extraterritoriality
        (4) Buffer states and neutral zones
    c. Projected activities
        (1) Peace plans
        (2) Trade programs
        (3) War strategies
        (4) Others

Although the underlying motif in this school of thought is that of seeking to understand the state through a search for ecological relationships, its proponents often go considerably beyond these bounds. At the hands of many of them, political geography tends to become a national economy school of thought.* Under this organizing concept, political geographers essay to study the whole resource equipment, organization, and functional relations of a nation within the area which it occupies: how it produces, feeds itself, and extends and protects itself; what are its national objectives and ideals; and what problems grow out of this total economy. Bowman, who uses variants of this approach, says of his book, *The New World:* "The method of my book was to deal realistically with the political problems of the postwar world. . . . It sought to analyze real situations rather than justify any one of several

---

* R. Hartshorne, "Recent Developments in Political Geography," *American Political Science Review,* 29 (October, 1935), 804.

** C. L. White, and G. T. Renner, *Geography: An Introduction to Human Ecology* (D. Appleton–Century Co., 1936), 20.

† *Ibid.,* 20; 26–27.

* This tendency of the ecological approach to expand into a *national economy school* parallels the tendency of the political landscape approach to expand into a *science* of areas.

conflicting nationalistic policies." * Van Valkenburg likewise points in the direction of the national economy school of thinking when he defines political geography as the "geography of states" providing a "geographical interpretation of international relations." **

In short, the ecological approach to political geography involves the *power* aspect of the state. It includes a study of those human adjustments to environment that implicate the whole political behavior of society. It culminates in a picture of how a nation functions and what problems face it. In this sense political geography may be said to deal with a particular group of geographic problems, namely, those problems that arise out of society's contacts with its environment and that require the attention and action of organized government.

The Organismic School. A third major group of political geographers holds an organismic concept of the state. It regards the state as a geopolitical organism; that is, it considers the state as a living entity consisting of more than the sum total of all its citizens. In 1896 Ratzel set forth the idea that the state was an organic creature possessing a basic biotic need to expand. A few years later Kjellén elaborated this concept by saying that the state is a living organism whose body consists of territorial space; that the boundaries are the end organs of the state; that the producing regions are its limbs; that roads, railways, and waterways are its circulatory system; and that the administrative capital is its brain, heart, and lungs. After a further interval of time, Karl Haushofer wrote editorially ". . . political geography . . . is the doctrine of political organisms of space and their structure."

This idea of political units as organisms implies that each of the latter must have its own *Lebensraum,* or living space, and that the need for such space changes as the culture and vigor of a state wax or wane. It also implies that the behavior of a state, both inside and beyond its own *Raum,* is a major concern of political geography; that is, political geography is a basis upon which both programs of diplomacy and strategies of war should be formulated. As yet no one has delimited precisely the content of political geography under this defining concept, but the following tentative outline suggests the general direction of study.

The Geopolitical Organism

1. Physical properties of the area
   a. Location—accessibility and strategic quality
   b. Size—depth and defensibility
   c. Shape—vulnerability
   d. Surface character—penetrability
      (1) Landforms
      (2) Water features
      (3) Coastal features
      (4) Land-water arrangements
   e. Natural resources
      (1) Inventory
         (a) Soil, minerals, waters, fuels, biota
         (b) Surpluses and deficits
2. The people
   a. Races and ethnic groups
   b. Population—numbers, distribution, density
   c. The culture
      (1) Basic cultural elements
      (2) Skills, education, technology
      (3) Institutional organization
   d. The economy
      (1) Industries
      (2) Transport and trade
      (3) Production and productivity
      (4) Standard-of-living levels
      (5) Wants and demands
   e. Government
      (1) Polity
      (2) Civic attitudes
      (3) Political behavior
3. The anatomy of the political area
   a. The capital
   b. The core area
   c. The domain
      (1) The regions
      (2) The corridors of movement
   d. Boundaries
   e. The buffer zone
      (1) Buffer states
      (2) Spheres of influence
   f. Colonies and dependencies
   g. The *Raum* or "extended domain"
      (1) Land realm
      (2) Sea realm
      (3) The air sphere
4. The integrated population-area organism
   a. The record of growth and expansion
      (1) Historical stages
      (2) Avenues of expansion
   b. Vital trends in the population

* I. Bowman, "Geography vs Geopolitics," *The Geographical Review,* 32 (October, 1942), 653.
** S. Van Valkenburg, *Elements of Political Geography* (Prentice-Hall, 1939), vii.

    (1) Numbers
    (2) Health and quality
  c. The national plan
    (1) Population reduction for raising living standards
    (2) Population control for maintenance of living standards
    (3) Increasing population to be cared for by:
      (a) Industrialization and commercialization
      (b) Overseas colonization
      (c) Frontier overflow and peaceful pentration
      (d) Conquest and plunder
  d. The national strategy
    (1) Trade program in the extended domain
    (2) Military strategies
      (a) Defense
      (b) Offense
    (3) Diplomatic policies
      (a) Unilateral
      (b) Collective

Because Germany is a densely populated country hemmed in closely by a ring of continental neighbors, German political geographers of the organismic school have tended to concentrate their attention upon the question of *Lebensraum*. On the other hand, the political geographers of the spatially unrestricted Anglo-Saxon nations have put most of their attention upon the role of political geography in providing a basis for both interpreting international relations and guiding national behavior.

Thus, the organismic concept is a broad approach to the study of the state. It examines the economic life, the ethnic and social make-up, the government, constitutional law, and the history of an area in terms of the basic geography in which they are embedded. It is truly the political strategy of men, space, and resources. It culminates not in a mere study of the observable political landscape nor in a restricted study of the geopolitical problems emerging from the national economy. Instead, since it takes the view that the state is a biotic whole which is tied up with the location and resource-equipment of its area, it undertakes to evolve a space strategy for national policy, even a military grand strategy for expansion or defense.

As a general rule, German political geographers have tended to belong to either the political landscape or the organismic schools, with the latter predominating during the Nazi period. French geographers have leaned toward the landscape school, whereas American geographers have tended to divide between the landscape (science of area) school and the ecology (national economy) school.

How many Americans belong to the organismic (geopolitical organism) school is impossible to say. The German Nazis succeeded in attaching an objectionable odor to this philosophy of political geography, and hence British and American geographers have been reluctant to indentify themselves with it. Others of them have simply not been interested in espousing any specific academic pattern of thinking. This avoidance of any commitment apparently was also true of the British geopolitician, Sir Halford J. Mackinder, who enunciated his significant theory of the World Heartland merely to enhance the security of the British Empire and not to advance any school of thought.

Geopolitical thinking. The cleavage of political geographers into different schools of thought is, in the last analysis, a minor matter—of interest primarily to the philosopher. What is of real importance is the fact that any study of political geography, regardless of what approach is employed, reveals a great many significant data and ideas that are not generally known and appreciated. The study of this field also yields a set of directives for public policy and solutions to international problems that are quite different from those that political leaders are accustomed to following and that the public has been led to believe are correct. Most important of all, the study of political geography develops the ability to follow a method of highly valid geographical reasoning which is sorely needed as a guide to the conduct of foreign policy by the United States.

As a first step toward an understanding of geographical reasoning, a few selected geopolitical elements and concepts are presented in the pages that follow.

The Political Region or Area

Definition. A political region or area may be regarded as any piece of the earth's surface possessing governmental unity. In the main, this means a national state or some subdivision thereof. Occasionally, it refers to some combination of national states.

Physical properties of an area: SIZE. Perhaps the most obvious property of an area is its size or areal magnitude. Other things being equal, the larger a state is, the greater is the probability of its containing a numerous population and a rich and assorted array of natural resources, and therefore the greater is its likelihood of being politically strong and economically wealthy.

In the preceding chapter the great variability in the size of states is pointed out. If the world's largest and smallest states be compared, it becomes readily apparent that power today tends to accompany large or gigantic size rather than small or diminutive size. In ancient times, small or even diminutive areas, such as Athens, Sparta, Troy, Phoenicia, Carthage, Latium, or Judaea, possessed a positive advantage over large regions.* The populations of all the former early became integrated into dynamic wholes that moved quickly toward economic, social, and political power. This tendency existed because the means for exploring and developing a large area were lacking until relatively modern times. The United States with its colossal size became a great power primarily because its period of settlement largely coincided with the evolution of the river steamboat and the railroad. On the other hand, Soviet Russia, whose transportation pattern evolved late, is even now in the process of breaking down internal isolation and building a strong state. And China, Brazil, and India have yet to accomplish such a result.

The size of a state has a vital bearing upon that state's destiny in time of war. For instance, during the recent war, Belgium and the Netherlands were quickly overrun, despite determined resistance, because of their lack of areal depth. In contrast, both the Soviet Union and China were able to absorb into their enormous expanses great military invasions and yet live to expel the invaders.

FORM. The form or regional shape of a state is the result of two conditions: the configuration of its boundaries and the relation of the outer portions of its area to the central part. Form varies from *compact* through *protuberant, perforated,* and *attenuated,* to *fragmented.* Rumania, Poland, and France

* White and Renner, *op. cit.,* chapter XXVIII.

exemplify the compact state; Peru, Siam, and Mexico, the protuberant state. India and Pakistan, whose surfaces are interrupted by "native" states, may be termed perforated political units. Chile and Norway are classical examples of attenuated or elongated form; Japan and Denmark typify fragmented form.

Each of the types of areal form creates its own characteristic set of environmental conditions and problems. In general, compactness increases unity and decreases sectionalism and social cleavage in a state. In time of war the compact state is easier to defend; in peacetime it enjoys superior transportation and communication.

LOCATION. The most significant physical property of an area is its locus, or location. Location may be expressed in three ways: as mathematical location, as natural (physical) location, or as relative location.*

Mathematical location. Mathematical location, or, as it is sometimes termed, *position,* expresses the occurrence of an area on the globe. That is, it expresses it geomathematically in terms of the hemispheres, the climatic zones, latitude and longitude, the time belts, and land subdivision systems. Significantly, in the recent war against the Axis (1939–45) the "Big Five" of the United Nations and the three leading Axis Nations lay in the middle latitudes and in the northern or land hemisphere.

Natural location. Natural location, or *situation,* expresses the occurrence of an area physically, that is, in terms of land and water bodies (continents and oceans). Areas located in or adjacent to the ocean are regarded as maritime; those removed from the ocean, as continental. Littoral, peninsular, insular, and pelagic are varying degrees of maritime situation. In the same way, intermontane, piedmont, mesopotamian, and midland express various phases of continentality.

At the outbreak of World War II all of the Great Powers except the Soviet Union were maritime in varying degrees and enjoyed access to important ocean trade routes. The Soviet Union, which had very inadequate sea connections, was the epitome of continental situation. Japan lay in the Pa-

* C. L. White, and G. T. Renner, *Human Geography* (Appleton-Century-Crofts, 1948), chapters 35, 36, and 37.

cific, which carried about ten per cent of the world's commerce. All other Powers touched the Atlantic, which carried eighty per cent of the world commerce. Fortunately, the United States touched both the Atlantic and Pacific oceans.

Relative location. The occurrence of any political area with reference to other political areas is called *relative location.* This factor is sometimes paramount in the political life of a state. The location of Germany in the western doorway to the landlocked Russian state and the location of Japan at the eastern door go much farther in explaining the foreign policy of the Soviet Union today than does any economic or social ideology: twice since 1914 has Germany invaded the Russian area and killed millions of the Russian people; often since 1900 has Japan threatened the Asiatic interests of Russia.

Britain, lying adjacent to the Afro-Eurasian land mass, has in the past often remained aloof from, but has always been vitally interested in, the latter's political affairs. The United States, being peripherally located with respect to this great "World Island," has traditionally been isolationist in its sentiments. It has occasionally emerged from its isolationism to make desperate last-minute attempts to discharge its obligations toward world order.

At any given time in the earth's history there are some areas and even a few points which are highly strategic in their location. Gateways to continents, islands at the foci of sea lanes, "bottlenecks" between oceans, places suitable for use as the jumping-off points of transoceanic airways, great mountain passes, and other loci often possess immense geopolitical significance. They must, therefore, receive especial treatment in political geography. Since relative location is always dependent upon the development of the arts, however, technological changes require that all parts of the earth be constantly reassessed as to locational value.

SURFACE FEATURES. In any political area, surface features are important characteristics. The most important of these are the climatic features. The surface of the earth may be divided into four great climatic zones—tropical, subtropical (warm temperate), cyclonic (cool temperate), and polar. Each zone is further divided into two to four cli-

matic types—yielding a total of twelve to fifteen major types in the world. Some of these are stimulating to man, some are not; some are favorable for agriculture, some for pastoralism, some for forest industries. Arranged in a world pattern, they form a significant measuring stick for an evaluation of the basic potentialities of any area, either singly or comparatively.

In much the same way, land relief features may be classified into four major and some twenty minor types. Water features may be divided into three major and a dozen minor types. Coast-zone features may be classified into four major and ten minor categories. All of them may then be used as criteria for measuring the potentialities of regions or political areas. Among other things these surface characteristics determine penetrability during wartime and accessibility, usability, and areal cohesion during peacetime.

NATURAL RESOURCES. In one sense the physical characteristics of an area—climate, landforms, minerals, space, location, and others—are natural resources, all of them interrelated in the natural landscape. In the restricted sense, however, this term is applied only to those natural substances directly involved in the production of economic goods. Among these, minerals, fuels, water and water-power, soil, forest, grassland, wild game, and fisheries are the most important. As such things have been very capriciously distributed by the hand of Nature, there are great inequalities among political areas in their natural-resource equipment. Nevertheless, any state must depend upon the natural resources lying within its borders, or accessible to it through trade, to supply the physical bases of its industry and industrial production.

Although no nation is wholly self-sufficient in natural resources, some nations approach such a condition far more closely than others. For any state to enjoy internal well-being and power and prestige in external affairs, a fairly adequate resource equipment is a requisite. It is upon these fundamentals of wealth that the maintenance of a national economy in the present complicated civilization rests.

Social characteristics of an area. An area receives its physical properties from the hand of Nature and these are, and can be, but little modified by the hand of man. Such physical properties are relatively permanent traits of any political unit. Alongside these there are, in addition to the human inhabitants, many man-made structures and contrivances. Every area, therefore, except the few unpopulated parts of the world, exhibits an array of social characteristics in addition to its physical properties.

POPULATION. The number, density, and distribution of human inhabitants are significant aspects of any region. Total population is important as a source of man power but does not in itself create national strength. Indeed, it may even be a source of weakness.

The distribution of population often has an important bearing upon the cohesiveness and unity of the social group. Even more significant is the density of population. Australia with a population density of 2 per square mile, the United States with 45, and Java with 805, face entirely different sets of problems in their national economies. Vital trends in population are significant in making industrial and political forecasts. The generally stationary populations of western Europe, the overlarge and even growing human groups of the Orient, and the rapidly growing numbers in the Soviet Union pose quite different problems for the political geographer.

ECONOMIC PATTERNS. The real sinews of political strength lie in industrial development. Agricultural crops, pastoral products, wood and wood products, the output from fisheries, mines, and quarries, industrial fuels, and manufactured goods are indices of power. Inventories of industrial equipment, such as power plants, factories, mills, railroads, piers, bridges, highways, banks, stores, and warehouses, also help determine the political power potential of a state.

INSTITUTIONAL EQUIPMENT. The strength of a state rests in large measure upon its utilization of natural resources. The effectiveness of that utilization rests, in turn, upon the social, economic, and political organization of a state. This, finally, rests upon the ideologies motivating the people, and the institutions available for maintaining the organization of society. For instance, the German states before 1871 had the same natural resources as had the German Reich, but the altered institutions of the latter gave it an enormously enhanced economic and political

status. Czarist Russia and Soviet Russia afford an analogous contrast. Shinto Japan and a reconstructed quasi-democratic future Japan may eventually show a similar change.

NATIONALITY. A nation may be defined as a group of people held together by a common bond of social and political consciousness, and by common loyalty to certain ideologies and institutions. The national state is the expression of nationality, but it does not always coincide with the nation. For example, Bohemia under the Habsburg emperors ceased to be a state, but the Czechs remained a nation, and re-emerged as an independent political unit in 1918. Poland supplies an analogous example. On the other hand, Austria-Hungary was long a powerful state, but there was never such a thing as an Austro-Hungarian nationality. Today Soviet Russia is one of the world's most powerful states but is a union of sixteen major and nearly two hundred minor nationalities.

In order to appraise the strength of any state, the unifying factors should be studied and weighed carefully. These include the factors of race and ethnic character, language, religion, historical tradition, and social psychology. Where any of them show distinct variations, strong cleavages may appear within a population. Of these factors, language is perhaps the most potent. Where a common language is spoken, national unification is usually attainable, even where diverse racial and cultural groups are involved.

The anatomy of a political area. Structurally, a political area (that is, the state or any of its subdivisions) may consist of some seven anatomical parts or elements. These are: (a) the capital, (b) the core area, (c) the domain, (d) the boundaries, (e) buffer zones, (f) colonies and dependencies, (g) the *Raum,* or extended realm.

THE CAPITAL. The administrative center of a state is known as the capital. Because it is the focus of many political and cultural activities, a central location is most effective. In some instances, it is thus ideally placed, as for example, Madrid in Spain, Rome in Italy, Brussels in Belgium or Budapest in Hungary.

More often than not, the capital is marginal or adjacent or it may even be peripheral to the heart of a state. In the case of the United States the capital city, Washington, is distinctly peripheral to the country as a whole. Originally it was built on the bank of the Potomac in order to be midway between the northern and southern states. The westward expansion of the American people, however, has left the capital stranded on the extreme eastern periphery. Something similar has occurred in Brazil, Russia, and numerous other countries.

Often the fortunes of war and power politics will alter drastically the extent of a state and thereby change the locus of the capital. Warsaw, the Polish capital, originally lay in the center of Poland. Through conquest the area of Poland was extended eastward, expansion that left Warsaw relatively near the western margin. Later these eastern areas were lost to Russia, but German lands on the west were awarded to Poland by way of compensation. These changes have left Warsaw east of the heart area of the country less than one hundred miles from Soviet soil.

Sometimes the capital city is deliberately changed because of a shift in national policy. Czar Peter moved the Russian capital from Moscow to St. Petersburg (now Leningrad) in order to "Europeanize" his country. Then the Communist revolutionaries moved it back to Moscow in order to "redeem and nationalize" their country. In analogous manner, the capital of Japan was changed from Kyoto to Tokyo when the Japanese ceased to be a provincial people centering about the Inland Sea and began to aspire to the role of a Great Power facing into the Pacific Ocean. Capitals are often displaced from a true geometric center for many other reasons. Some capitals lie in the ancient cultural heart of a country which has subsequently spilled over its original confines, as in the case of Paris. Others have been located deliberately in such manner as to lie midway between two discordant ethnic minorities, as has been Ottawa, the capital of Canada.

THE CORE AREA. The core area of a state is usually the nucleus or cradle region in which the nation was germinated and nurtured. Much of the economic vitality, especially in an industrial state, frequently centers in the old political nucleus, or core area. Modern France originated in the Île de France district in the Paris Basin. Russia sprang from the little Muscovite duchy in the upper valley of the Oka River. England sprang from a group of little Saxon kingdoms in the London Basin or Thames drainage area.

In some instances nations have grown by the simple process of overflowing their cores and colonizing adjacent areas or conquering and assimilating neighboring peoples. Some countries possess more than one core. Canada, for instance, has a French core in the Lower St. Lawrence Valley and an English core in the Ontario Peninsula. Czechoslovakia is a triple-core state: a Czech core lies in the Bohemian Basin, a Moravian core in the Morava Gateway, and a Slovak core in the piedmont and foothills of the Tatra Mountains.

The United States originally possessed three cores: southern New England, the Hudson-Delaware-Chesapeake Lowland, and the Cape Fear-to-Altamaha section of the Atlantic Coastal Plain. All of these have been outgrown and supplanted by a new agricultural and industrial heart area in the upper Mississippi Basin—that is, the so-called Middle West. In similar fashion England during the Industrial Revolution shifted its economic nucleus from the agricultural Thames Valley to the coal-bearing Midland area.

The Danube River flows through the core areas of three states—that of Austria in the Upper Danube Valley, of Hungary in the Basin of the Middle Danube, and of Rumania on the Plains of the Lower Danube. Many of the political troubles of Europe stem from the unhappy fact that no one of these cores has been able to generate a state strong enough to absorb the entire Danube Valley.

THE DOMAIN. In all except diminutive and small states the core areas are surrounded by a more or less extensive domain. This latter is almost invariably less characteristically national than is the core. Moreover, it is usually differentiated into markedly dissimilar geographic regions, subregions, and districts, each of which makes an unique contribution to the national economy.

BOUNDARIES. The boundaries of a state are usually even more revealing than is the location of the capital. Often both the origin and the power of a state are implicit in the character, location, and form of the boundaries. Some national states, such as Bolivia, Afghanistan, and Austria, have only land boundaries; others, as for instance, Japan, Australia, and Cuba, have only sea boundaries. Some, as the United States, Italy, and Siam, have both land and sea boundaries.

In a few instances land boundaries are intricately crenulated, as found in the case of Belgium and Pakistan. In others, they are simple and regular, as in the case of Mexico, the United States, and Guatemala. In still others there are awkward extensions, troublesome embayments, or bewildering enclaves, inliers, and outliers. In not a few instances the boundary of one state seems to have been drawn deliberately in such a way as to exclude another state from frontage on the ocean or on a lake, a river, or land corridor.

BUFFER ZONES. Boundaries are always potential danger lines in relation to national states. In order to protect vital areas, and even to insulate the outlying regions of their domains, strong states have often attempted to surround, or partially surround, themselves with buffer zones. In some instances these are strips of demilitarized territory; in others, they are areas that have been annexed outright (as, for instance, Alsace-Lorraine, which has alternated between German and French annexation).

The Great Powers have frequently resorted to the creation, by mutual consent, of weak, nominally independent states in places where international friction is unusually severe. The classical example of this is Belgium on Britain's flank, between France and Germany. Another example is afforded by the action of the Great Powers at the Versailles Conference in creating a line of new countries across eastern Europe from Sweden to Turkey. This was a buffer zone (*Cordon Sanitaire*), whose purpose was to exclude communism from European affairs. After World War II Soviet Russia turned the tables and converted this area into a pro-Russian wall of buffer states (The Iron Curtain) as a protection against capitalist pressure.

COLONIES AND DEPENDENCIES. A colony or dependency is a piece of territory lying outside the metropolitan area of the state which controls it and often populated by "backward" people. From one fourth to one fifth of the land surface of the globe might be classed as colonial territory in one degree or another.

Only a few countries, some of them surprisingly small and weak, possess colonies. The holding of colonies and dependent areas enormously complicates world politics and reduces the chances of world peace.

THE EXTENDED AREA, OR "RAUM." All states at one time or another in their history manifest an urge toward expansion of one sort or another. In some instances this may result in military conquest; in others, colonization, trade penetration, or cultural expansion. In still others it may take the form of organization for defense and military security over a wide area. In any event the strong and growing state manifests a tendency to extend its influence over a hemisphere, a continent, or a major drainage basin, or around a partially enclosed sea or group of seas. Such realms have been termed "extended areas," "power provinces," or *"Raums."* They rest upon such concepts as America's *Monroe Doctrine,* Japan's *Greater East Asia Co-Prosperity Sphere,* Fascist Italy's *Mare Nostrum,* Nazi Germany's *Lebensraum,* Britain's *Freedom of the Seas* (freedom for all who conformed to Anglo-Saxon mores), and Soviet Russia's *Security Zone.*

The Study of Political Geography

Principal learning outcome. Regardless of the definition applied to political geography (that is, whether organismic, ecological, or landscape-descriptive) any serious study of the subject results in viewing the state and the earth in association. To view the state and the earth in association, however, is invariably to reveal a great number of relationships between the two. To perceive and examine these interrelationships of earth and state is usually to lay bare the geopolitical problems of the area under examination. Indeed, the most desirable outcome of the study of political geography is to be able to recognize and understand the geopolitical problems of the various countries of the world. These have previously been defined as "those problems which are environmental in origin but political in settlement." On the basis of this definition there are in general three groups of geopolitical problems for every national state: (a) internal, (b) external, (c) international.

Three groups of geopolitical problems: PROBLEMS OF AN INTERNAL OR DOMESTIC NATURE. Internal problems include all questions which arise out of society's contact with the natural environment, but which can be settled by a national government or a subdivision thereof. Some examples are land reclamation, flood control, population resettlement, title to oil lands, ownership and operation of coal mines, treatment of cultural or ethnic minorities,* and others.

PROBLEMS OF AN EXTERNAL NATURE. External problems include those questions which arise from or are associated with environmental causes within a state, but whose influence extends beyond its borders. Some examples are colonial problems, resource division (for example, fisheries, water resources, waterways, migratory fowl), trade programs, tariffs, and others.

PROBLEMS OF AN INTERNATIONAL NATURE. International problems include those problems arising out of, or associated with, environmental causes or geographical situations which require for solution the action of several or even all of the world's states. Some examples are collective security and world

* Treatment of minorities, if they consist of nationals or co-linguals of an adjacent nation, frequently becomes an external problem.

peace, Zionism and the Palestine question, and the occupation and demilitarization of Germany.

Major considerations. The study of political geography ordinarily involves five major considerations. In other words, when one undertakes the study of the geopolitics of a country or of any other specific political area, he usually finds that it is necessary to base that study upon the following five questions in the order listed:

(a) What people are involved?
(b) What natural resources, sites, and areas are involved?
(c) What tensions and stresses exist?
(d) What problems are created by these tensions and stresses
(e) What are their probable outcomes and solutions?

Interesting and profitable though it may be to speculate upon these problems, seldom can the answers be stated categorically. The geopolitician can discern *answers*, but *the answer* can be written only by the hand of history.

CHAPTER 3 | The History and Development of Political Geography

THE roots of political geography reach back into ancient history, the development of the subject being related to the growth of philosophy, history, political science, and mathematics. The Greek scholar, Herodotus (484 B.C.–425 B.C.), who is well known for his early historical writings, also showed an interest in geographical problems. It was Hecataeus, however, who has been awarded the title, "father of ancient geography"—this extended by reason of his general treatise on the earth. Plato (427 B.C.–347 B.C.)was intrigued by the relationship of the state to its area. In his *Republic* he raised certain considerations which still are of interest to political geographers today. Julius Caesar (100 B.C.–44 B.C.) used political geography as an adjunct to the writing of history in his *Gallic Wars*. Strabo, Pliny the Elder, Ptolemy, and later geographers continued the slow development of this embryonic subject. In all instances, however, the evolution of political geography was an unnoticed part of the development of geography in general.

Modern Developments

Origins. Immanuel Kant (1724–1804), in a memorable series of lectures delivered at the University of Königsberg, philosophically defined the field of geography and delineated its parts, one of which he termed political geography. As a consequence of his talks Kant has been regarded as not only the founder of modern geography but also the father of political geography. His geographical ideas produced few results except in central Europe, noticeably among the Germans. Friedrich List, Heinrich von Treitschke, Alexander von Humboldt, Karl Ritter, and Friedrich Ratzel were the most noteworthy of his German disciples.

Among these, Ratzel (1844–1904) must be regarded as the real founder of that science of political geography which Kant had fathered. In 1897 Ratzel's *Politische Geographie* was published—the first systematic treatment of political geography. As a professor of geography, his influence was considerable. For one thing, he was the teacher of the American, Ellen Churchill Semple, who later carried his philosophy of geography back to the United States. His teachings were cultivated vigorously in Germany and were carried to many other countries.

Expansion. In Germany political geography gradually became a political instrument of the state. In Great Britain it was generally ignored save for such small portions of it as seemed useful in governing the Empire. In France it was cultivated to a limited degree for an analogous reason and as a device for understanding the intentions of Germany. In the United States, as a result of the greatest economic development ever witnessed in the world's history, economic geography was much cultivated by American geographers, but political and social geography were accorded scant attention. World War I drew some attention to political geography, but not until World War II did the subject really achieve prestige in the United States. Among the men who have been outstanding in promoting the growth of political geography are Halford Mackinder and James Fairgrieve of Great Britain, J. Brunhes and C. Vallaux of France, Ewald Banse and Alfred Hettner of Germany, and Isaiah Bowman, Derwent Whittlesey, and others of the United States, and Rudolf Kjellén of Sweden.

Contrasts. Perhaps the most important event in the development of the political phase of geography was the publication of Bowman's *The New World: Problems in Political Geography* in 1921. A less important but equally significant occurrence was the founding of the *Zeitschrift für Geopolitik* under Karl Haushofer three years later. These two events highlight the contrast in the development of political geography in the United States and Germany.

In the United States, where man has always possessed "an abundance of resources distributed over a superabundance of area," most political geographers have been preoccupied with the study of the space relations of the state. Indeed, many American political geographers have defined political geography as the "science of areas." By the same token, they have rarely paid much attention to the power of the state.

In Germany, however, where more than sixty million people were concentrated within an area equal to the two American states of Oregon and Idaho, space and natural resources were more completely utilized than in most parts of the Western World. Moreover, since Germany was closely ringed about by a cordon of armed neighbor states and had few natural boundaries to separate her from her neighbors—indeed, a large number of German-speaking people lived outside those boundaries—German political geographers recognized the state's vital interest in matters relative to both space relations and power. As time went on, however, they became more and more preoccupied with a study of power. Eventually this study of national power became a morbid obsession with them.

The Rise of German Geopolitik

Incentives. At the end of World War I Germany received a crushing defeat and was compelled to sign a treaty far from its liking. Soon thereafter German political and military geographers began to ask themselves what were the reasons for Germany's defeat. Their quest for the answer to that query led to an added emphasis upon geographic study and teaching. The prestige of political and military geography had not, however, been enhanced by the defeat of the German army and the confiscation of the German navy. There was needed, therefore, a new name for the old subject.* Fortunately, this was already at hand in the word *Geopolitik*, which Kjellén in Sweden had coined a few years earlier.

It should be noted in connection with their geographical studies, however, that the stigma of national defeat and the psychoses of war-guilt denial and of Versailles-peace-treaty repudiation had left the German geographers in no normal state of mind. They were not really searching for the politico-geographic reasons for Germany's defeat; they were seeking a blueprint for German vindication and revival, and a strategy for eventual national victory.

Perversion. The preceding German geographers had done much to develop political geography (especially the organismic concept of the subject); but political geography is a sane, cautious and, above all else, an honest science. Its study did offer Germany the basis for partial vindication, a blueprint for a modest and sound postwar revival, and a strategy useful for either military defense or a limited expansion. These values, however, did not offer what most Germans of that day sought. Even the scientists had fallen victim to the psychosis of "all or nothing." They wanted total vindication, total escape from war guilt, and total revival of wealth and power. To achieve these ends, they were willing to convert political geography into *total geographical nonsense* if need be, and eventually to risk total war. Therefore, adoption of the new term *Geopolitik* fooled the German public into believing that here was something new, dynamic, and portentous of success; it enabled the German geographers themselves to escape the moral censorship of their science, and to sidestep their own scientific consciences.

After the death of Kjellén in 1922, Karl Haushofer became the leading protagonist of Geopolitik, and in 1923 he came into contact with some of the leaders of the Nazi movement. In and after 1924 he helped edit the

---

* At about this same time in the United States an American geographer suggested to his professional peers that they might use the term *geonomics* instead of economic geography, in order to make the American people more receptive to the idea of studying the subject on an adult level.

Zeitschrift für Geopolitik. This soon became the very vocal house organ for the *Institut für Geopolitik,* which Haushofer headed at the University of Munich.

Work of the Institut. The *Institut* eventually attracted to itself many able geographers and workers in cognate fields. It also included in its ranks inferior workers and "crackpots" of several varieties. These workers developed a considerable amount of "geopolitical" theory and began the collection of a vast array of data to be filed in the *Strategic Index* of the *Institut.* "The basic, incontestable truth is that Haushofer, directly in some instances, indirectly in others, coordinated, integrated, and rationalized the whole field of comparative geography for the uses of the Führer." * As time went by, the *Institut* became more and more an instrument for statecraft and a tool of the state—for which purposes it received a government subsidy in funds and patronage. "Geography, particularly war geography, became a national preoccupation which influenced and molded public opinion in postwar Germany from elementary school to university seminar, from street corner and bookstore to factory, club, beer-hall, and dinner table." **

Definitions. The Geopolitiker of Munich started with an organismic concept of the state and the practiced techniques of cartography and geographic research. Added to these were their *Weltanschauung,* or world perspective, and a motivation springing from the national pathology that characterized Germany between the two world wars. They defined their subject as "The science of the earth relationship to political developments." † Karl Haushofer asserted that the word *Politik* is not preceded by the prefix *geo* by accident. The prefix relates politics to the earth (ge = earth in Greek). The Geopolitiker of Munich also attempted to apply the principles and methods of geopolitics to "branch" sciences, such as psychology, medicine, and jurisprudence. The category of *Geo-Wissenschafte* was broadened to include

Geo-Psychologie, Geo-Medizin, and Geo-Jurisprudenz.

Geopolitical concepts in Germany centered around a number of subjects. The ideas of the organic state, living space (*Lebensraum*), and the organic frontier received considerable attention in German literature. The political power of the state was analyzed by the Munich Geopolitiker. A very important idea behind the political power of the state was its location with reference to a specific concept of the distribution of land masses and ocean spaces. The expression of the power of the state in wartime involved the study of *Wehr-Geopolitik,* or war geopolitics, for the *aim of power was war.* The German geopoliticians used not only the studies of Alfred T. Mahan on sea power but also the works of General Karl von Clausewitz on land power. Haushofer made use of the definition of war given by Clausewitz, namely, "war is a continuation of policy with other means." No writer on air power assumed the stature of either Mahan or Clausewitz in the thought and writing of the Men of Munich.

Founders of Geopolitics

Numerous men are associated with the field of geopolitics, but five stand out as leaders in its development and in writings that widely disseminated the subject in its various interpretations and implications. Two of these men were German, one was Swedish, one English, and one American. All five were born in the nineteenth century and all lived into the twentieth century—two surviving the end of World War II.

Friedrich Ratzel (1844–1904). A professor of geography at the Polytechnic Institute of Munich and later at the University of Leipzig, Ratzel developed political geography to a point where Geopolitik could easily appear, but he remained aloof from the problems of German foreign policy. He was a teacher of Ellen C. Semple, an outstanding geographer of the United States, and was also a friend of Max Haushofer, the father of Karl Haushofer. The latter used to accompany the older men on their walks along the Isar River. He accepted many more of Ratzel's ideas about the state than Ellen Semple did.

Ratzel taught that the state, a union of the people and the land, was a spatial organism

* Edmund A. Walsh, "Geopolitics and International Morals," *Compass of the World,* Hans W. Weigert and Vilhjalmur Stefansson, editors (Macmillan Company, 1944), 22.

** *Ibid.,* 24.

† Karl Haushofer, Erich Obst, Hermann Lautensach, and Otto Maull, *Bausteine zur Geopolitik* (Berlin, 1928), 27.

that grew in accordance with the processes of any other living organism. In 1896 he even published an article on "The Laws of the Territorial Growth of States." He began his *Politische Geographie,* first published in 1897, with a chapter on "The State as an Organism Fixed in the Soil." On one occasion Ratzel asserted that a state decayed as the result of a declining conception of space. He believed that space was a political force of great importance. In harmony with his general views, Ratzel's concept of the frontier is logical. According to him, the frontier was only a changing zone of assimilation. Frontiers were dynamic, reflecting the expansive force of aggressive countries. Boundary questions often led to war because a boundary might be an obstacle to the growth of the state. The idea of *Lebensraum,* or living space, is logically associated with the theory of the organic state and the dynamic boundary. Both Karl Haushofer and Adolf Hitler received many of their ideas regarding *Lebensraum* from Ratzel. However, Professor Ratzel was only a link in the chain of thought relative to *Lebensraum.*

Rudolf Kjellén (1864–1922). A pro-German Swede of World War I and a professor of government at the University of Göteborg, Kjellén expanded the ideas of Ratzel and applied them to world politics. The Swedish professor taught in his *Staten som lifsform,* first published in Stockholm in 1916, that the state, deep-rooted in historic and actual realities, had grown organically and had an appearance of the same basic type as an individual man or a living being. He believed that the most important attribute of the state was power. Power was more important in the existence of the state than law because law could be maintained only by power. He was the first to use the now familiar term *Geopolitik.*

In studying the state, Kjellén advocated an analysis based on the following: *Geopolitik,* or geography and the state; *Demopolitik,* or population and the state; *Oekopolitik,* or economic resources and the state; *Sociopolitik,* or social structure of the state; and *Kratopolitik,* or government of the state. It is significant to note that he placed the study of geography and the state first and the study of the government of the state last. Kjellén believed that the power of the maritime empires would pass to the compact land empires, which in turn would eventually control the seas. Kjellén foresaw the emergence of a few giant states in the world, with Germany as the great power in Europe, Africa, and western Asia. The thinking of the Men of Munich was greatly influenced by the studies of Kjellén. Dr. Haushofer and a group of followers enlarged, re-edited, and published some of Kjellén's works.

Alfred Thayer Mahan (1840–1914). The German geopoliticians derived many ideas from the publications of Alfred Thayer Mahan, a distinguished naval historian and a great exponent of sea power.* A graduate of the United States Naval Academy in 1859, he saw forty-one years of active service and was promoted to the rank of rear-admiral upon retiring in 1906. He was a lecturer on naval history and strategy at the Naval War College at Newport, becoming its president in 1886. In 1902–03 he was president of the American Historical Association. President Theodore Roosevelt, a genuine admirer, once stated: "There is no question you stand head and shoulders above the rest of us." Emperor William II of Germany had Mahan's *The Influence of Sea Power upon History* placed in the libraries of German naval ships.

The general thesis supported by Mahan cannot be found in any one of his numerous publications, but his ideas were expressed in a number of books and articles extending through almost a generation. He maintained that the prime prerequisite of world power was control of the seas. In his interpretation of history and his theory of sea power he believed that the oceanic powers would keep the supremacy of the seas that Great Britain had acquired during the Napoleonic conflict. Great Britain, having an excellent insular base at home and easily defended bases abroad, held a position of great strength that made her naval supremacy possible. Only the United States had a geographical position that rivaled that of Great Britain. The United States, having no powerful potential enemies on its borders, possessed the advantages of insularity and had secure access to the

* His great trilogy consisted of *The Influence of Sea Power upon History, 1660–1783,* published in 1890; *The Influence of Sea Power upon the French Revolution and Empire, 1793–1812,* published in 1892; and *The Life of Nelson,* published in 1897.

great resources of a continent. Mahan, walking in the vanguard of events, not only advocated American control of the Hawaiians and of the Caribbean but also favored the construction of an Isthmian Canal between the Atlantic and Pacific oceans. He believed that the United States might succeed Great Britain as the leading oceanic power.

This distinguished American naval officer thought that no state could be a great land and sea power at the same time. The problems involved in the defense of a land boundary against a strong continental rival would probably prevent any country from successfully competing for the supremacy of the sea. All of the continental states had to be on guard against their neighbors at the border. None of them, with the possible exception of France, possessed a geographical position well suited as a base for sea power. Mahan never seriously feared that a land-sea power in Eurasia could seize the control of the oceans from the Anglo-Saxons.

The ideas of this American naval historian can be appreciated only by a consideration of sea power at the time of the writing and publishing of his trilogy. In those days the navy of Queen Victoria (1837–1901) ruled the oceans of the world. The geographical basis of British sea power arose from the fact that Great Britain controlled the narrow waterways through which all seaborne commerce between the leading trade centers of the world was obliged to pass. Dover Strait between England and France, Gibraltar Strait and the Suez Canal at the western and eastern ends of the Mediterranean respectively, and Malacca Strait between Sumatra and Malaya were all under British domination. In fact, Great Britain in 1901 controlled all the ocean gateways to Europe, Asia, and Africa, and all the navigable passages among the Atlantic, Indian, and Pacific oceans.

Sir Halford Mackinder (1861–1947). Extremely influential in the development of German geopolitics was Sir Halford Mackinder—through no intention of his own. Dr. Edward Mead Earle of Princeton University has expressed the belief that the studies of Sir Halford Mackinder are at the present time more significant for an understanding of the dynamic forces of today than are Mahan's writings. Mackinder had been a professor of geography at the University of London, a

member of Parliament, a director of the London School of Economics, and vice-president of the Royal Geographical Society. Haushofer referred to him as "the most brilliant English geopolitican" and acknowledged a deep debt of gratitude to him as a geographer.

The contribution of Mackinder lies in his political perspective on the geographic distribution of the land masses and the bodies of water on earth. He has interpreted history as essentially a struggle between land and sea power. His first important statement on the subject came in a lecture on "The Geographical Pivot of History," delivered to the Royal Geographical Society in 1904. In 1919, as a warning to the statesmen of the Paris Peace Conference, he published *Democratic Ideals and Reality*. The Anglo-Saxon world paid little attention to the book, but Haushofer saw many implications in the volume.

In his thinking and writing Mackinder visualized the continents of Europe, Asia, and Africa as a World-Island, forming one land mass (see the map directly below). He noted

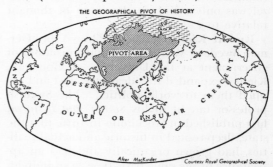

THE GEOGRAPHICAL PIVOT OF HISTORY

After MacKinder   Courtesy Royal Geographical Society

that nine twelfths of the world was water and only three twelfths land. Of the land, the World-Island had two twelfths, and the other land masses—principally North America, South America, and Australia—one twelfth. Also the World-Island had fourteen sixteenths of the population, and the other land areas two sixteenths.

The key to the World-Island was the pivot area, or the Heartland. At first Mackinder defined the Heartland as a vast area in Eurasia that was characterized by Arctic and interior drainage. This area stretched from the Volga River to eastern Siberia and from the Himalayas to the Arctic Sea. As delineated, it included most of the Iranian Upland in the southwest and much of the Mongolian Upland in the southeast. The pivot area was not vulnerable to sea power from the surrounding water, or world ocean. From a political viewpoint in 1904 the Heartland was entirely Russian in eastern Europe and largely Russian in Asia, although western China, part of Mongolia, Afghanistan, Baluchistan, and Iran were included except for a narrow coastal strip in the case of the latter two. Later, Mackinder extended the Heartland concept westward to include much or all of the Russian area in Europe. At present the Heartland is commonly understood to include all of the Soviet Union except the Far Eastern territories. Mackinder specifically excluded Lenaland in 1943.

Around Mackinder's Heartland in the area known as the "Inner or Marginal Crescent" was an arc of Coastland defined as an area of drainage into navigable seas (see the map on page 26). The Coastland included all of continental Europe except the Heartland portion of Russia. According to this concept the monsoon areas of Asia—India, southeast Asia, and most of China—were also included in the Coastland. The Outer or Offshore Islands were the British and Japanese homelands. The outlying islands in the Outer or Insular Crescent were largely made up by the Americas and Australia. Africa south of the Sahara Desert was considered a southern but secondary Heartland, connected by the bridge of Arabia to the northern or main Heartland. Mackinder wrote his thesis in three main points in late 1918:

Who rules East Europe commands the Heartland:
Who rules the Heartland commands the World-Island:
Who rules the World-Island commands the World.*

Mackinder believed firmly in the primary importance of the Heartland in Eurasia. He also recognized the strategic location of Germany in the peninsula of Europe with reference to the Heartland. The north, central, and west areas of the Heartland were a vast plain or great lowland broken only by the Ural Mountains. This vast lowland merged into the plains of northern Germany. Although in the past Europe had been frequently invaded from the steppes of Asia, why could not the direction of invasion be re-

versed? In 1904 Mackinder asserted in his address on "The Geographical Pivot of History" before the Royal Geographical Society:

The oversetting of the balance of power in favour of the pivot state, resulting in its expansion over the marginal lands of Euro-Asia, would permit of the use of vast continental resources for fleetbuilding, and the empire of the world would then be in sight. This might happen if Germany were to ally herself with Russia.

During World War II Mackinder stated in an article that his Heartland idea was "more valid and useful today than it was either twenty or forty years ago." In the same article he also stated,

All things considered, the conclusion is unavoidable that if the Soviet Union emerges from this war as conqueror of Germany, she must rank as the greatest land Power on the globe. Moreover, she will be the Power in the strategically strongest defensive position. The Heartland is the greatest natural fortress on earth. For the first time in history it is manned by a garrison sufficient both in number and quality.*

Karl Haushofer (1869–1946). Karl Haushofer first won attention as a German geopolitician in 1908, when he was sent on a mission to Japan as a military observer for the German General Staff. Although he had received a commission in the First Bavarian Artillery Regiment at the age of nineteen, this period was one of the most formative of his life. He not only studied the institutions of Japan but also became an expert on the Pacific and the Far East; and he learned to speak six foreign languages including Chinese, Japanese, Korean, and Russian. On his trip to Japan he traveled by way of the Mediterranean, the Red Sea, and the Indian Ocean. On his return he traveled across Russia from Vladivostok to the Reich.**

Haushofer received his doctorate *summa cum laude* from the University of Munich. By the end of World War I he had been promoted to the rank of a major general in the army of the Kaiser, but, while leading troops through the remains of the German border provinces after defeat, he determined on a

* Halford J. Mackinder, *Democratic Ideals and Reality* (Henry Holt and Company, 1942), 150.

* Halford J. Mackinder, "The Round World and the Winning of the Peace," *Foreign Affairs* (July, 1943), 601.
** Culmination of Haushofer's mission to Japan was the publication in 1913 of his *Dai Nihon: Greater Japan's Military Power, World Role, and Future.*

career of educating the new Germany. In the period that followed he laid aside his uniform to teach political geography and military history at the University of Munich.

In 1924, with Otto Maull and Erich Obst,

In theme the strength and weaknesses of a certain area (*Raum*) were compared with the location (*Lage*) of the region and the nature of the boundaries (*Grenzen*). Since the end of World War II some of the geographers at

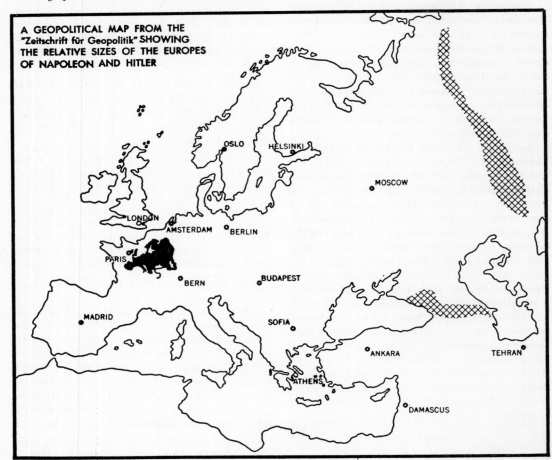

A GEOPOLITICAL MAP FROM THE "Zeitschrift für Geopolitik" SHOWING THE RELATIVE SIZES OF THE EUROPES OF NAPOLEON AND HITLER

he founded at Munich the *Zeitschrift für Geopolitik,* a monthly magazine intended chiefly for the lay reader and devoted to a discussion of geopolitical matters. Somewhat later, Dr. Albrecht Haushofer, the elder son of the professor-general, began to write regularly for the *Zeitschrift.* The issues contained "factual" articles and "dynamic" maps concerning all parts of the world (see the map on this page). Albrecht Haushofer specialized in the Atlantic region; his father wrote about the Indo-Pacific area.

The top organization of geopolitical research was the Institute of Geopolitics (*Institut für Geopolitik*) at Munich under the direction of Karl and Albrecht Haushofer.

the University of Munich have stated that Haushofer was not a scientific geographer but a gifted amateur with a flair for publicity.

Haushofer himself has published more on geopolitics than any other person. His articles in the *Zeitschrift,* his own books, and his publications in collaboration with others reveal the industry of the professor. The geographic area in which he was most interested was the Indo-Pacific realm. His *Die Geopolitik des Pazifischen Ozeans: Studien über die Wechselbeziehungen zwischen Geographie und Geschichte* (*Geopolitics of the Pacific Ocean: Studies on the Relationship between Geography and History*), first published in 1924, is his most important book. Of considerable consequence in Haushofer's writings is the fact that he called the attention of many Germans to the political significance in the theories and teachings of Ratzel, Kjellén, Mahan, and Mackinder.

The personal relation between Hitler and Haushofer was very limited. Haushofer was a university professor; Hitler had never been to college. Haushofer was a major general in the army of the Kaiser; Hitler was a corporal in World War I. Haushofer had traveled widely in the Pacific and Far East; Hitler had seen only a part of Europe. After World War I both worked in the Bavarian city of Munich, one in politics, the other in geopolitics. The link between the two men was Rudolf Hess, aide-de-camp to Haushofer during the war. While Hitler was in the Landsberg jail, following the Beer Hall Putsch of 1923, he dictated *Mein Kampf* to Rudolf Hess. The eccentric Hess introduced Hitler to Haushofer and, on a number of occasions, the German geopolitician was Hitler's guest in jail. After Hitler came into power in 1933, Haushofer was appointed to the presidency of the German Academy for three years, and the Nazis furthered the work of the Institute at Munich. An important barrier between Hitler and Haushofer was the fact that Haushofer's wife was a Jewess. The leading German geopolitician was never, therefore, directly identified with the Nazi Party.

After the collapse of the Third Reich, Haushofer asserted to American questioners that his *Institut für Geopolitik* was really a department of geopolitics at the University of Munich, like a department in any American college. He claimed that he had very little to do with the Nazis, in fact, nothing to do with them, after Rudolf Hess, his only important Nazi friend, flew to Great Britain on May 10, 1941. He asserted that his books spoke for him and that the Nazis ignored his teachings. After the unsuccessful attempt to kill Hitler in the disturbance of July, 1944, Haushofer was detained at a concentration camp for a brief period by the Nazis. The geopolitician believed that his son, Albrecht, was killed because the Nazis considered him involved in the plot. After the war Haushofer's papers were collected at the American Seventh Army Document Center at Heidelberg. They revealed his great interest in Asia, especially in Japan, China, and India. The geopolitician himself was taken into the custody of the American army in Germany, but he was later released and allowed to return to his home. Early in 1946, however, both Haushofer and his wife committed suicide at their Bavarian home. At a previous interview the geopolitician had stated he lived in "perpetual fear" because Hess was no longer in Germany to protect him.[*]

An interesting bit of evidence was brought to light in Heinrich Himmler's library after the collapse of Germany. A particular book written by Haushofer, published in 1941 and sent to Himmler by the author, was found in the library. On a presentation card, bearing his full titles and his Munich address, Karl Haushofer had written in his own distinctive handwriting the following:

Please be so kind as to accept, with profound thanks for the incomparable help from your province in all Near Eastern matters both on land and on sea (*mit tiefem Dank für die unvergleichliche Hilfe aus Ihrem Bereich in allen V. A. Sachen über Land und See*), this study in the field of overseas, cultural, and power politics.

A number of passages in *Mein Kampf* reflect to a certain extent the influence of Dr. Haushofer. Hitler clearly indicated his belief in the need of Germany for living space in order to become a world power. In the chapter on "Eastern Orientation or Eastern Policy" the geographic ideas of Kjellén and Haushofer are evident in a number of places. For instance, Hitler asserted:

Only a sufficiently extensive area on this earth guarantees a nation freedom of existence. . . . State frontiers are man-made and can be altered by man. . . . Germany will either be a world power or will not be at all. To be a world power, however, it requires that size which nowadays gives its necessary importance to such a power, and which gives life to her citizens. . . . Never forget that the most sacred right in this world is the right to that earth which a man desires to till himself, and the most sacred sacrifice that blood which a man spills for this earth.[**]

[*] An interesting account of Haushofer's last days is found in the following article: Edmund A. Walsh, "The Mystery of Haushofer," *Life*, 21 (September 16, 1946), 107–120.

[**] Adolf Hitler, *Mein Kampf* (Reynal and Hitchcock, 1941), 935, 949, 950, 964. (By permission of Houghton Mifflin Company, proprietors of the copyrights on all American editions of *Mein Kampf*.)

On the other hand, the same chapter has statements that Haushofer could not have supported. For example, the comments of the Fuehrer on race reflected the influence of Alfred Rosenberg rather than that of Haushofer.

The influence of the studies by the Men of Munich on the geostrategy of the Third Reich cannot be ignored. The General Staff of Germany had been abolished by the Treaty of Versailles ending World War I. Through its studies on the various areas of the world the Institute of Geopolitics was the means of accumulating a wealth of material that could be utilized by a future general staff. Colonel Herman Beukema of the United States Military Academy at West Point has noted the importance of Haushofer's studies in Hitler's victories. The German generals of Hitler achieved many of their successes by a careful consideration of geography. For instance, while the men in Marshal Rommel's Afrika Korps were drilled in Europe, they lived in overheated barracks and ate a diet suitable for desert warfare. From a consideration of the terrain, Haushofer was convinced as early as 1939 that the British naval base at Singapore was vulnerable from land. Many of the ideas of the German geopolitician became a part of the global strategy of the Third Reich.

To a certain extent the Geopolitiker indirectly influenced the foreign policy of Germany, especially up to the time of the invasion of the Soviet Union. The publication, the *Zeitschrift,* skilfully predicted many events. Issues of this magazine have been devoted to certain countries that soon occupied the spotlight of European and even world attention. Predictions were based partly on geopolitical *manometers.* This term refers to certain geographic, political, and economic symptoms that were alleged to gage pressures and indicate probable events. Examples of geopolitical manometers are the change in the location of a national capital, the growth of urbanization, or a power field (*Kraftfeld*) where the drives of world powers come into conflict.

Haushofer believed that a country should not take the initiative of declaring war lest it incur the stigma of aggression. An official study made by Dr. Katharine Elizabeth Crane on the "Status of Countries in Relation to the War, August 12, 1945" in the *Department of State Bulletin* for August 12, 1945, reveals that in World War II Germany issued a formal declaration of war only in exceptional cases. The German declaration of a state of war (*Kriegszustand*) with the United States is the most striking exception. After Foreign Minister Ribbentrop handed the declaration of war to Leland Morris, the American Chargé d'Affaires ad interim at Berlin, the German minister exclaimed: *"Der Praesident Roosevelt hat den Krieg gewollt. Ihn hat er!"* (President Roosevelt has been wanting war. He's got it.) It is to be pointed out, however, that although Haushofer's opposition to declarations of war and Hitler's policy of not declaring war were alike, there is no proof that Hitler pursued this policy because Haushofer favored it. The chances seem to be excellent that Hitler would have pursued such a policy anyway.

Haushofer believed that geopolitics should teach the man in the street to think geopolitically and the leaders of Germany to act geopolitically. The Germans had been leaders in the study of political geography long before the emergence of Geopolitik. The German Embassy in Washington had a *Columbus-Gross Globus* showing the physical and political features of the world in 1938 and having a scale of 1:12,000,000. The Institute of Geopolitics at the University of Munich, the outgrowth of Karl Haushofer's seminar, was closely related to the educational system of the Reich. The German Peoples' Map Service (*Volksdeutscher Kartendienst*) was the agency of the Institute to publish and distribute maps and atlases at low prices for popular use. Albrecht Haushofer was head of the Geopolitical Seminar in the Institute of Politics in Berlin (*Hochschule für Politik*), which trained all men entering the foreign service of Germany.

WORLD POLITICAL OUTLOOK.* A design for world conquest was never written in any one document by the Geopolitiker. Published material, however, does present the general ideas of the German geopoliticians on the future of the Reich in the world. The first major objective was to be the consolidation of the political forces of the Heartland. This objective primarily concerned the Soviet

* For more specific treatment, see Russell H. Fifield, "Geopolitics at Munich," *Department of State Bulletin*, XII (June 24, 1945), 1152–1162.

Union; secondary were the control of Middle Europe (*Zwischen-Europa*) and Western Europe and the acquisition of African colonies. The struggle for the Heartland, it was known, might result in war and might become a test of land power. In this respect Haushofer definitely stated that the infantryman still decides the battle by taking possession of the space. The second major objective was the destruction of the sea power of the maritime states that opposed the Reich. This objective primarily concerned the Anglo-Saxon countries. Haushofer has realized the importance of sea power and noted that the conflict between oceanic and continental powers is a theme that runs through history. He stated that the most decisive of all political trends in the world is the drive of a country toward the sea. The Men of Munich believed that in the end world power was predicated upon both land power and sea power, implemented by air power.

The attitude of Haushofer toward the Soviet Union was motivated by a strong desire to form, under German leadership, a combination of powers, consisting of Germany, the Soviet Union, Japan, China, and India. Although he believed that the Heartland should be consolidated, he never wrote a final prescription for German policy toward the Soviet Union. The domination of the Heartland might be effected by "colonization, amalgamation, or conquest." He probably had his misgivings about the Nazi invasion of the Soviet Union on June 22, 1941, because his theories pointed up the fact that a country, having one sixth of the land area of the world and extending in an unbroken land mass for a distance equal to that from San Francisco to London, possessed defense in depth and could sell space to gain time. Napoleon's invasion of Russia was the most quoted case history in German geopolitics. Haushofer believed that Germany, located between the "pirates of the steppes" and the "pirates of the sea," should never undertake to fight on two fronts.

As a preliminary step to the consolidation of the Heartland, the Men of Munich thought that Germany must secure the military routes to the Soviet Union lying across the territory of Middle Europe from Finland to Greece. Trade agreements could be utilized to acquire political control. Otto Maull has said that complete economic penetration produces the same result as territorial occupation. This alternative might even be necessary. The mastery of the marginal lands of western Europe was also considered vital in the future position of the Reich. The German geopoliticians believed that the small western states, like Denmark, Belgium, and the Netherlands, were doomed to inevitable disappearance. France was the only obstacle in the west, but the military threat of the republic was discounted. France was considered a biologically and politically stagnating country in contrast to the renovating state of Germany. Likewise, the Geopolitiker placed small stress on Italy, whose geographical foundations limited her to very little freedom of action. The acquisition of colonies was also desired, chiefly in the colonial areas of Africa. Two numbers of the *Zeitschrift* in 1939 were devoted to the colonial question (*Kolonialfrage*) and a new branch of geopolitics was advocated—*Kolonialgeopolitik*.

In the eyes of Haushofer the Pacific was the most important geopolitical area in the world. He wrote in the *Zeitschrift* in January, 1925: "An enormous space is growing before our very eyes with potentialities that are quietly awaiting the dawn of the Pacific era which shall be the successor of the aging Atlantic and the aged Mediterranean and European period." Across the Atlantic, President Theodore Roosevelt had a similar idea in 1905. He wrote: "I believe that our future history will be more determined by our position on the Pacific facing China than by our position on the Atlantic facing Europe." *

From his days as a military observer in the Far East, Haushofer remained partial to Japan. He noted with approval the success of the Japanese leaders in convincing their people that they were suffering from population pressure. He once admitted that it was impossible to determine whether a country was overpopulated, but that population pressure could become a valuable propaganda asset in the struggle for expansion. The Men of Munich realized that Japanese imperialism would clash with the resisting power of China. They saw the dangers of a Japanese attack on China, and after the outbreak of open hostilities in 1937 they asserted that only

* Tyler Dennett, *Roosevelt and the Russo-Japanese War* (Doubleday, Doran and Company, Inc., 1925), 3.

an energetic strategy of annihilation could bring success to Japan. They also believed that Japan should have struck first against the colonial empires of Great Britain, France, and the Netherlands in the Pacific. Haushofer advocated a close relation between Japan and Germany. He based his idea partly on the fact that the Western powers in World War I had ejected Germany from the Pacific. The Germans in Europe and the "900 million southeast Asiatics" were considered "comrades of destiny." Haushofer also favored cooperation between the Soviet Union and Japan, so that the Anglo-Saxons would be less able to impose a policy of divide and rule.

The Men of Munich did not ignore the role of the United States in the Pacific. As early as the summer of 1938 the German geopoliticians counted on the eventuality of an attack at Pearl Harbor. In July of that year Klaus Mehnert in the *Zeitschrift* spoke of the easy conquest of the island of Oahu by an attacking naval force that had acquired air superiority. The German geopoliticians also believed that the Philippines and Hawaii had no organic connection with the United States. The presence of the Japanese minority in the Hawaiian Islands was stressed; the East Asiatics were reconquering the area anthropogeographically. In the minds of some of the Geopolitiker was the belief that the final war for world mastery would come in the Pacific realm.

Since the second major objective of the German geopoliticians was to be the destruction of the sea power of the leading maritime states, the Anglo-American countries were given attention on that score. With the consolidation of the Heartland under the Germans and with the aid of the Japanese, the defeat of the Anglo-Americans could be planned. However, Germany would have to gain sufficient sea power to supplement her land and air power. The German geopoliticians looked upon the British Isles as the basic representative of sea power. Hitler in *Mein Kampf* advocated an alliance with England in order to pursue an aggressive Eastern policy. Until the outbreak of war between Great Britain and Germany in 1939 Haushofer was guarded in his statements about the British. Most of the geopoliticians were convinced that the British Empire was in a state of gradual disintegration. The British Empire interfered with the "pan"-concept that had been discussed by the Men of Munich. The "pan"-concept of the German geopoliticians was considered a device for organizing the world into larger geographic units. Haushofer himself wrote a book entitled *Geopolitik der Pan-Ideen.*

The United States was not given marked attention by the German geopoliticians. The *Zeitschrift* devoted less time to the Western Hemisphere than to the Old World, with Colin Ross writing much of the material on the New World. Haushofer himself was more interested in the World-Island and in the Pacific than in the Western Hemisphere. He studied the "Pacific face" of the United States more than the Atlantic. In the development of American foreign policy he has praised the Monroe Doctrine as a brilliant application of geopolitical principles. The Geopolitiker also expressed an interest in the economic, political, and social institutions of Latin America. Haushofer was especially interested in the Pacific state of Chile. However, few maps on South America were published in the *Zeitschrift,* and little material has appeared on Latin America in comparison with the studies on the Old World.

Recent American Geopolitics

Nicholas J. Spykman. Probably the leading student in the development of American geopolitics was the late Nicholas J. Spykman, director of the Yale Institute of International Studies and professor of international relations at Yale University. Spykman defined geopolitics as "the planning of the security policy of a country in terms of its geographic factors." * He believed that the study of the location of the state in the world was essential in understanding the foreign policy of the country. He frankly recognized the aspect of power as a means of preserving the future peace. Only the great powers have the means of enforcing the peace. As a student of international relations, he noted that geopolitics revealed a picture of forces relative to a given frame of reference at a given time. A region from a geopolitical viewpoint was determined by the factors of geography and by the dynamic changes in the power centers.

* Nicholas John Spykman, *The Geography of the Peace* (Harcourt, Brace and Company, 1944), 5–6.

Geopolitical analysis was by its very nature dynamic and not static.

Spykman had carefully studied the ideas of Mackinder. He questioned the validity of the thesis of the English geographer relative to the pivot area, or the Heartland, as expressed in 1904 and 1919. He doubted whether the Heartland would be, at least in the immediate future, a center of world power potential, pointing out that climatic conditions and agrarian productivity, the distribution of coal, iron, oil, and water power, and the geographical obstacles along the north, east, south, and southwest boundaries of the huge pivot area tended to lessen the validity of Mackinder's thesis. The position of the central Asiatic regions of the Soviets would be less important if China and India were themselves more industrially developed than these areas of the Soviet Union. Spykman generally believed that Russian power would remain primarily west of the Urals and not in the central Siberian region.

Spykman also considered the "rimland" of Eurasia as more important than the Heartland. Occupying the intermediate region between the Heartland and the marginal seas, the "rimland" specifically included all of continental Europe except Russia, Asia Minor, Arabia, Iraq, Iran, Afghanistan, India, southeastern Asia, China, Korea, and eastern Siberia. All this area was considered largely a buffer zone between sea power and land power. He stated his thesis as follows: "Who controls the *rimland* rules Eurasia; who rules Eurasia controls the destinies of the world." *

Continuing his analysis of Eurasia, he considered Great Britain and Japan as political and military centers of power outside the rimland, off the shores of western Europe and eastern Asia, respectively. Africa and Australia were off-shore continents, with Africa related to the southwestern shores of Eurasia by the European Mediterranean Sea and Australia to the southeastern shores of Eurasia by the Asiatic Mediterranean Sea.** The state that controlled the seas would determine largely the position of Africa and Australia. The power potential of both these continents was restricted.

Spykman pictured the United States as surrounded by the land masses of Eurasia, Africa, and Australia. All of these areas together were about equal in energy output to the New World, but they had a population ten times and an area two and one half times that of the New World. He did not believe to any great extent in the development of the Arctic Mediterranean as a leading transit zone. The United States was separated from the power centers of Europe and Asia by the Atlantic and Pacific oceans. He asserted that the leading political objective of the United States in peace and war should be to prevent the unification of the power centers in the Old World against the United States. He believed that the North American Republic should not let any overwhelming power develop in Europe and the Far East.

Spykman wanted to see the closest American cooperation with Great Britain, which was a possible base for future action. He believed that France was not a land power strong enough to restrain Germany. On the other hand, Russia would be the strongest land power in Europe. A unified rimland would be a menace to Russia as well as to the United States. As a consequence of these factors, he advocated an alliance of the United States, the Soviet Union, and Great Britain to preserve the peace. A peaceful world based on the balance of power in Eurasia and the cooperation of the United States, the Soviet Union, and Great Britain in an effective security system were the main objectives of Nicholas J. Spykman.

Conclusion

Geopolitics has served to stress the importance of geography in international relations. War and peace may come and go, but the environmental factors in geography remain relatively constant. The Rhine still flows to the sea regardless of what state maintains the historic watch over it in days of peace or whose blood stains its waters in days of war. Man may mold the resources of the earth to produce a golden age in civilization, or perhaps man is destined to use the resources of the earth to destroy himself, to make civilization an historic intermission. In either case, however, one thing is certain: as long as international relations exist in the world, geography will remain an important consideration and influence.

* *Ibid.*, 43.
** The Asiatic Mediterranean Sea refers to the water bodies separating Australia from southeastern Asia.

PART TWO
The World Powers

THE real bases of national power are men, space, and natural resources. These three basic geopolitical factors are transformed into actual national power whenever a government safeguards human welfare, encourages the proper utilization of its space, and promotes the industrial use of its resources. War often destroys these means of achieving power and hence many nations hope to avoid war, but its avoidance involves relinquishment of total sovereignty. No strong state is willing to relinquish or even diminish its own sovereignty, but instead seeks peace by diminishing the influence and sovereignty of other states, while enhancing its own. Thus a continuing struggle known as power politics is engendered amongst the nations.

Never before in the world's history have there been so few Great Powers, and never has the list of Powers been restricted merely to political units of gigantic size. A close examination of the structure of these remaining Powers suggests that the day of the single national state as a Power is almost past, that to reach powerhood today requires a supranational state. For instance, the U. S. S. R. is a federal grouping of sixteen national republics. The United States is a federal union of forty-eight states. The British Commonwealth and Empire is an association of Great Britain with four self-governing dominions (or eight dominions if Eire, India, Pakistan, and Ceylon be included).*

If China and France be listed among the Great Powers, the same principle seems to hold true. China is at present a loose confederation of thirty-five semi-independent provinces. France is in process of reconstruction, but if she retains powerhood, it will be because she succeeds in welding metropolitan France,* Tunisia, Viet Nam, French West Africa, French Equatorial Africa, and Madagascar into a viable commonwealth or French Union—an achievement which is at present not at all certain.

Great Britain is an insular country of intermediate size, lying adjacent to the European continent. Its restricted area and island situation combined to favor early consolidation into a strong national state. From this firm home base the British people expanded over the seaways, colonizing certain areas, extending political and commercial sway over others. The colonized regions have matured into self-governing dominions, the remaining areas have been integrated into a globe-girdling empire. In order to effect that expansion and to guard the resulting empire, Great Britain built up immense naval power. This procedure was in sharp contrast to the European continental states, which developed military power and fought amongst themselves for control of the land.

From the home islands the main seaway, often called the British Lifeline of Empire, runs around western Europe, through the Mediterranean Sea, across the Indian Ocean, to the Orient. A second seaway crosses the North Atlantic via a great circle route to Canada. A third loops around Africa and swings across the Indian Ocean to Australia. A fourth cuts obliquely through the North

* The future status of India and Pakistan and of a former dominion, Newfoundland, is not clear at the present time.

* Including Algeria.

35

Atlantic to the Caribbean, passes through the Panama Canal, and runs on to New Zealand and the South Seas.

This geopolitical pattern was evolved when naval power was preeminent. Any one of the European states might have built such a pattern, but only Great Britain managed to accomplish it. Having done so, the British have long possessed a power advantage; but that advantage has, during recent years, been seriously diminished. With the rise of air power the British sea lanes can be cut at a dozen or more points. Also the British homeland itself, being near Europe, is vulnerable to devastating aerial attack. Moreover, being small, it offers no possibility of defense in depth. Further, being an island with limited resources, it also offers no opportunity for industrial and population expansion. This great Commonwealth and Empire containing about one fourth of the world's land and one fifth of the world's population has already begun to show some apparent signs of decline and break-up. There are, however, amazing strength, genius, and vitality still embodied in this great power structure.

Quite unlike the British maritime structure is the huge continental state known as the Union of Soviet Socialist Republics. It contains nearly one sixth of the world's area, and almost one tenth of the world's inhabitants. Its tremendous size gives it many of the attributes of the ideal state. It has vast fertile lands, immense mineral resources, abundant fuel, and one of the world's greatest areas of timber. In size of population it is exceeded only by China and India. Its area is so huge as to offer maximum defense in depth during time of war.

As a serious drawback to any maritime ambitions, its great area lies in such a high latitude that its coasts are largely ice bound; exit from the few ice-free ports has been strangled by Turkey, Japan, and the countries of North Europe. Many of its frontiers are unprotected by physical barriers. Its expanse is so huge that adequate transportation and communication have been, until recently, beyond the reach of the Russian peoples. With

industrialization, mechanization, urbanization, universal education, and the construction of a huge net of transportation, the Soviet Union is just now on the threshold of its full strength.

The United States of America is a young giant among the Powers. In part its position resembles that of the Soviet Union, since it stretches across a continent. In other part, its maritime interests resemble those of the British Commonwealth and Empire: its eastern and western coasts are washed by the Atlantic and the Pacific, respectively. Its southern shores face the Middle American sea, and its Alaskan outpost looks into the Arctic Ocean. Its small island dependencies and areas of influence extend from Liberia in Africa more than halfway around the world to the western edge of the Pacific. Although including only one fifteenth of the world's land area and possessing a population of less than 150,000,000, the United States has rich natural resources and uses one half of the mechanical energy of the world. Through its effective efforts it produces a surplus of both raw goods and manufactures, and its economic strength is larger than that of any other nation.

As a result of locational and other environmental factors, Great Britain has long been the paramount naval power, but her military land power has been almost negligible. During the war against the Axis the Soviet Union developed what was probably the greatest army ever seen on earth, a fairly strong air force, but a negligible navy. Under the stress of world war the United States with unmatched industrial capacity built the world's mightiest air force, a navy surpassing that of Britain, and an army second only to that of Soviet Russia. Since the end of hostilities the American army has been disbanded, the air forces largely dismantled, and only the navy retained in relatively undiminished strength. Today the Soviet Union remains the paramount power on land; the Anglo-Saxon nations share control of the seas. Control of the airways remains to be decided in the future, with all three Great Powers in relentless competition.

| CHAPTER 4 | # Geographic Foundations of Continental United States |

FOR many decades to come no nation will have greater economic and political influence on the future of the world than the United States. In the last analysis the basis for this influence is the fundamental strength the country possesses through its advantageous location, its enormous resources, its vast industrial empire, and its large number of educated and skilled people. The following discussion, which presents a brief survey of the major factors underlying this strength, provides a basis for the comprehensive political analysis in the next chapter.

Territorial Expansion

Original area and growth of the continental base. Permanent settlement of our original territory began with the arrival of the Jamestown colonists on the east coast in 1607. There the first representative assembly was set up in 1619. During the following hundred years many small isolated communities were established and expanded until they formed a continuous string of settlements along most of the Atlantic seaboard. By the time independence from England was attained near the end of the eighteenth century the settled area had also spread inland as far as the Appalachian Mountains, then a formidable barrier to human movement. Nevertheless, the population actually occupied only a small proportion of the 830,000 square miles that made up the original area of the United States. Although the United States was destined to increase its holdings as it expanded toward the Pacific Ocean, it possessed even at its beginning as a nation a land base richer in quality than that of any European

country and greater in area than that of any European country except Russia. And only twenty years later the Louisiana Purchase (1803) doubled the size of the nation (see the map directly below). That outstanding his-

UNITED STATES
TERRITORIAL ACQUISITIONS
1783-1853

toric event added a vast extent of choice agricultural land and many scattered deposits of valuable minerals. The acquisition of Florida from Spain by treaty in 1819 completed the nation's control over the Atlantic coast and a large portion of the Gulf coast.

In the short period of eight years between 1845 and 1853 Texas was added by annexation, the Oregon Country by treaty, the Southwest by cession from Mexico, and finally, the Gadsden area by purchase. These territorial additions, four times as large as the combined area of the then-powerful England and France, brought the United States to its present size—2,977,000 square miles. By that time the continental area was far larger than the entire continent of Europe, excluding Russia. However, the political and economic strength of the country lagged behind

37

its territorial growth and was not to be fully realized until the close of World War I, when the United States emerged as the greatest of the world powers. This preeminent position was further accentuated in World War II. But at this time Russia's great and rapid strides indicate that she may some day challenge the American nation for first place.

Acquisitions outside the continental base. By the middle of the nineteenth century the period of territorial expansion for the United States appeared to be definitely over. Northern and southern frontiers had been stabilized and the great westward movement had spanned a distance of continental proportions to reach the Pacific. But the United States moved forward again, purchasing Alaska in 1867, partly in order to prevent Russia from keeping a menacing foothold on the North American continent. Though this acquisition represented a departure from the former type of expansion within the continental base, it encountered little opposition from Americans; by those acquainted with international power politics it was regarded as a worthwhile safeguard against future difficulties. Still later, as a consequence of the struggle with Spain in 1898, the United States acquired additional territory far beyond the continental limits of the country. The new possessions, which included the Philippine Islands, the Hawaiian Islands, and Puerto Rico, amounted to a fair-sized empire of approximately 700,000 square miles (see map on page 63).* About the same time, through the Platt Amendment, the nation also obtained a considerable measure of political control in Cuba. After having secured an empire in both the Atlantic and the Pacific it needed a canal to connect the two oceans so vital to national interests. In a political maneuver the United States recognized Panama, which had rebelled against Colombia, and in turn received control in 1904 of the strip of land now called the Canal Zone (see map on page 57). As a result of World War II the country also acquired many other outposts and military bases at points along the routes of possible attack from aggressors in Europe or Asia.

On April 2, 1947, the Security Council of the United Nations approved a strategic area

* For a more complete discussion of United States possessions, see Chapter 5.

trusteeship of the former Japanese Mandated Islands under the United States. The new "Territory of the Pacific Islands" consists of the Carolines, Marshalls, and Marianas (map, page 385). At that time the disposition of the Ryukyus, Volcanoes, Bonins, and Marcus, integral territory of the old Japanese Empire, still awaited the peace treaty with Japan.

From an economic standpoint Alaska alone among the acquisitions outside the continental base has represented an unquestionable profit. In revenue from fish, furs, gold, and timber it has returned many times its cost, and at the same time its ownership has prevented many probable difficulties by keeping Russia out of North America. A number of the other territories secured have been of doubtful economic value. As has been shown in World War II, however, some of the distant possessions have offered protection from aggression by serving as defense outposts. Though the United States did not realize the worth of the Hawaiian Islands when they were secured at the end of the nineteenth century, they proved of inestimable value during World War II by preventing the American mainland from becoming a part of the battle zone.

Boundary Problems

The boundaries of continental United States, almost evenly divided between land and sea, have remained practically unchanged since the Gadsden Purchase in 1853. The military advantage of the compact shape of the United States is partially offset by the fact that the country is vulnerable to attack by sea from two sides. This exposure eventually necessitated the construction of the Panama Canal and the maintenance of a large navy as a first line of defense. With Britain, the only other great sea power, as a reliable ally the nation felt reasonably secure prior to World War I. In recent years, however, great technological progress in the development of new implements of war has made it vulnerable along with all other nations of the world, and furthermore, made it vulnerable not from one or two but from all directions. The country does, however, have a degree of advantage over most other countries in that any attacking power would find thousands of miles between the outer fringe of its defenses and the heart of the country.

Ocean boundaries. In the past the Atlantic Ocean on the east and the Pacific Ocean on the west have served as ideal boundaries for the United States. During the nation's early history these water bodies tended to hold at arms length all nations powerful enough to threaten its growing strength. In those days of slow and cumbersome transport the width of the oceans was enough of a handicap to discourage aggressors. Not until the second decade of the twentieth century had technology progressed to such an extent that aggressor nations might cross these oceans and inflict serious damage on the United States. By that time, however, the nation had become so strong that it no longer needed to depend entirely on the oceans for protection. Today, however, with the introduction of more and more advanced types of weapons, even the greatest water barriers have ceased to be any real source of security. To be sure, this resultant insecurity works both ways: if the oceans no longer protect the United States, neither do they serve as obstructions to an effective attack on any enemies beyond the opposite shores of those oceans.

Land boundaries. The line between the United States and Canada is generally held up as the classic example of an international boundary separating good neighbors who get along so well that not even a boundary fence is necessary. These thousands of miles of international frontier now cause but little friction, partly because they were established long before the area was well populated and partly because there are no economic, political, or racial conflicts of serious concern to either government. Even more important to the preservation of peace has been the sensible attitude of the two countries—a result of their common heritage and a recognition of their common interests—which has led to peaceful settlement of difficulties as they have appeared. Along that boundary, which is approximately half land and half water, there have arisen a number of problems that might under other circumstances have proved troublesome. For example, the northeastern boundary of Maine cuts squarely across the fertile St. John Valley, hardly a satisfactory line of demarcation. As another instance, many problems relating to the Great Lakes and St. Lawrence River have arisen in regard to fishing, navigation, the diversion of water, and the development of hydro-electric energy. As still another example, overcrowding in the Detroit area has resulted in large numbers of people crossing from the United States into Canada to seek homes; where trans-border passage becomes so frequent, many complications arise involving collection of duty, smuggling, identification of citizenship, and similar problems attendant to international rules and regulations. Likewise, on the West Coast the Strait of Juan de Fuca between Washington and British Columbia serves as a common channel for entrance to both American and Canadian ports.

In contrast to the Canadian border, the Mexican boundary with the United States has presented a number of small annoyances and sources of friction potentially more dangerous in their implications. Had these taken place between nations of more nearly equal strength, they might well have had serious consequences. Many of the troubles along the Mexican border have in part been the result of a lack of understanding and friendly feeling that developed out of the Mexican War, and in part the result of the indefiniteness of the boundary itself in some places. The Rio Grande, serving as an international barrier from El Paso to the Gulf of Mexico, affords an unreliable line, for its course changes laterally and unpredictably shifts the location of people from the domain of one country to that of the other. The determination of water rights for irrigation, complex at best, has also led to difficulties. Fortunately, because of the great distance between the densely populated portions of Mexico and its northern border and the minor character of most of the difficulties, peaceful solutions have been reached on all disputes growing directly out of this boundary line.

In general, the differences arising from the geographic and ethnic problems associated with the land boundaries of the United States have been relatively simple, and their solution has caused a minimum of friction between the United States and Mexico and almost none between the United States and Canada.

World Location

In a sense the United States might be thought of as a great world island (see map on front inside cover). On the west it is bounded by thousands of miles of ocean; on the north, except for a narrow strip of habitable land, by a vast extent of uninhabited wilderness of Canadian forest and tundra; on the east and southeast, by a second vast ocean; and on the southwest, by the deserts of northern Mexico. In the past these areas have provided an encircling zone of almost perfect protection against all enemies. In times of peace the oceans have been highways, but the land areas have acted as barriers. Today, too, this relative isolation continues to protect the country in a certain measure; but with the tremendous innovations in science, including atomic energy, jet propulsion, rockets, and other devices capable of potential "push-button" destruction, its whole concept of security must be changed to one of international cooperation. In place of countermeasures against attack, prevention has become the only dependable means of defense for the United States.

A glance at the country's position in relation to the great masses of the people on earth shows Europe to the east, with about one fourth the world's population, and the coastal countries of southeastern Asia, including Japan, China, and India, with one half the people of the world, to the west. Thus on one side the nation faces densely populated Europe with its great cultural and technical heritage, and on the other side Asia with its huge potential markets and vast sources of raw materials. Although Europe is far more important to the United States today, perhaps Asia will be the land where will lie its greatest opportunity tomorrow. To the north are found only eleven and one half million Canadians, but their proximity, advanced culture, and extensive resources have resulted in their being ranked near the top of the list of those with whom international trade and cultural relationships are maintained. To the south are one hundred and thirty million Latin Americans with whom Americans are interested in fostering trade and sharing cultural achievements. These southern neighbors are a part of the New World with which the United States is closely linked and upon which the country depends for hemispheric solidarity. Their wide variety of cultural and economic developments to a great extent complements the national existence of the

United States rather than competes with it. This relationship holds true especially with the tropical and subtropical countries.

The strategic location of the United States in the world has received special recognition in the decision of the United Nations to locate the seat of the organization in the United States. Selection of the eastern part of the country represented a compromise between those European states desiring Europe and those Pacific states wanting the western part of the United States as the site.

Physical Factors

Size, shape, and depth. Despite its size the United States is by no means the world's largest nation. The Soviet Union occupies a land area nearly three times as large; China, Canada, and Brazil each are slightly larger; and Australia is about the same. Even with its possessions the United States encompasses far less territory than either the British Commonwealth-Empire or the French Empire. As has already been stated, however, continental United States has an area greatly exceeding that of all the nations of Europe combined, exclusive of Soviet Russia.

The almost rectangular shape of the United States makes for compactness and gives considerable depth to the country, factors that in the past have been great military assets. Its compactness, preventing any part of the country from being far removed or isolated from other parts, has greatly facilitated development of the country as a whole, and materially enhanced its political and economic unity and strength.

Relief. The general pattern of relief in the United States is a key to the development of its national economy. The distribution of mountains and lowlands has logically influenced the superimposition of human activities. Fortunately a large portion of central and eastern United States is lowland well suited topographically to agriculture. Fortunately also much of this area is favored by a mild moist climate. Although the Appalachian Mountains loomed as a barrier to the early westward migration of the people along the Atlantic coastal lands (see map on the facing page), this restriction was actually an advantage; it forced them to develop a more closely knit political union than would have been possible had the population been widely scattered. With this more carefully inte-grated national development came greater political strength and stability. Today the mountains of the east no longer serve as effec-tive barriers though, due to the additional cost of materials and labor that they impose, they still act as a retarding force in the con-struction of roads and railroads.

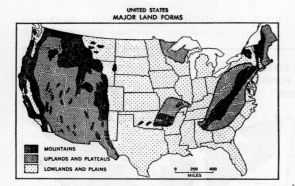

UNITED STATES
MAJOR LAND FORMS

MOUNTAINS
UPLANDS AND PLATEAUS
LOWLANDS AND PLAINS
0   200   400
MILES

The mountains of the West, oriented north-south, are not only higher and more continu-ous than those in the eastern part of the coun-try, but they present a series of major barriers. Starting at the western margin of the great interior lowland, the first of these is the mighty Rocky Mountain chain and the last is the equally mighty Cascade-Sierra Nevada range. Not only do these multiple moun-tain ranges constitute great barriers to east-west transportation, but they cut off the moisture-bearing winds from the Pacific, with the result that there are vast areas of desert and semiarid climate in the western half of the United States. Strategically the western mountains and deserts offer tremendous ob-stacles almost immediately to any invaders who might attempt to move eastward toward the heart of the country. In contrast the re-lief features of eastern United States offer no great handicap to invasion from the coast it-self to the Appalachian Mountains; and once these ranges were crossed, no other natural obstacles of major significance would keep an enemy out of the nation's deep interior.

Lakes and rivers. Although the United States possesses many mighty streams, such as the Mississippi, Missouri, Ohio, Columbia, Colorado, and Hudson, they have in some re-spects played a less significant role in the country's national life than have the rivers of most countries. Perhaps a leading explana-tion for this lack of importance is that the major streams flow generally from north to south, the wrong direction for world trade. Also, when the country was expanding and developing, the railroads, which competed as a means of transport, experienced a tremen-dous building expansion; during the same pe-riod relatively little development of river and canal transport took place. With but few exceptions the use of these inland waterways has greatly declined in importance, as evi-denced by the many unused river facilities and abandoned canals. The one waterway in the country that has retained its early impor-tance is the Great Lakes–Mohawk–Hudson system. Not only does this continuous chain of navigable waters offer favorable orienta-tion, that is east-west, but it taps the exceed-ingly rich iron ore deposits and grain-growing regions of the north central part of the coun-try. Although the Hudson-Mohawk portion has declined in significance because of rail-road competition, the Great Lakes are today more valuable than ever.

The use of rivers for irrigation, hydro-electric power, and industrial purposes has been more significant than their use for trans-port. Such western streams as the Columbia, Colorado, Sacramento, and Rio Grande have supplied both power and irrigation water. In the east, where precipitation is for the most part favorable, the streams have proved useful primarily as sources of power and water for industrial plants.

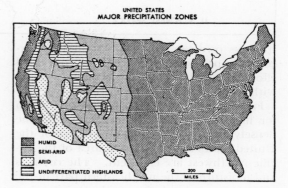

UNITED STATES
MAJOR PRECIPITATION ZONES

HUMID
SEMI-ARID
ARID
UNDIFFERENTIATED HIGHLANDS
0   200   400
MILES

Climate. The climate of the United States is one of its greatest assets. Vast portions of the country are sufficiently temperate and moist to be highly productive agriculturally (see the map above here). Moreover, the variations in temperature and moisture are such that a great variety of staple products can be grown, ranging from the wheat raised on the cool semiarid lands of North Dakota and Montana to the rice cultivated in wet, warm Louisiana and Arkansas. The great extent of land that is ideal climatically for agriculture gives the United States a higher degree of self-sufficiency in food than that possessed by the great majority of countries. Only in tropical and certain subtropical products is the country inadequately supplied

moreover, the natural climate exerts a decided influence on workers during their hours outside the factory.

Natural vegetation. Except in the more arid parts of the West, where the ax and the plow have not taken their toll, most of the natural vegetation of the United States has disappeared. The extensive forests that once covered a large part of the country were a great asset during the first two and a half centuries of colonization and settlement, for

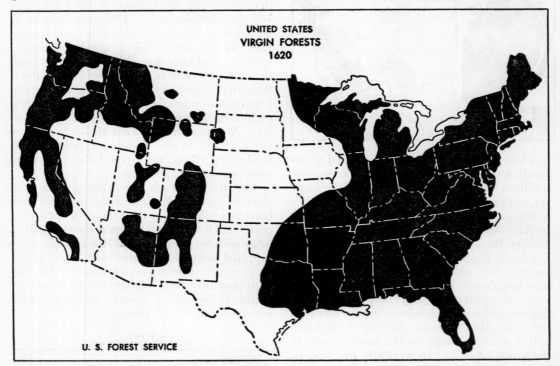

UNITED STATES
VIRGIN FORESTS
1620

U. S. FOREST SERVICE

from its own lands, a shortcoming that accounts in part for the government's continued efforts to establish a close economic tie-up with Latin America.

From the point of view of climatic optimum for mental and physical vigor, most of the densely populated northeastern part of the United States and the coastal area of the Pacific Northwest are excellent. The coolness and moisture of the northeastern part of the country are stimulating to human energy, with the result that they greatly facilitate the manufacturing industries. Although outdoor temperature and humidity undoubtedly have less effect today on factory production than in the past because of the possibility of air-conditioning, this process is expensive;

the colonists and pioneers depended upon wood for shelter, heat, and implements. By the time settlements had reached the great grasslands of the Mississippi Valley the exchange economy of the country was sufficiently advanced to insure the wood that was needed. Moreover, the settlers could to a large extent depend on iron for tools and coal for fuel. Although large tracts of forest land still exist in the northwest and in some regions of the south, the country has become increasingly dependent upon Canada for much of its wood (see maps above and on page 43).

Economic Factors

Natural resources. The natural resources of the United States and their utilization in an economy with a tremendous industrial capacity constitute the keystone of its national might The country's disproportionate share of the world's wealth and its weight in international affairs are based on its ability to produce goods in a manner and volume never before accomplished by any nation. Since World War I the United States has taken a lead role in furnishing food, money, arms, and other items to countries needing but less capable of supplying these items

often prove highly productive when irrigation facilities are available, as in many western states. If properly cared for through sound conservation practices and judicious use of fertilizers, these soils should continue indefinitely to yield crops suitable for a well-balanced agricultural economy.

MINERALS. Mineral deposits are of paramount importance in providing a country with the margin of wealth needed for a strong domestic economy and for world

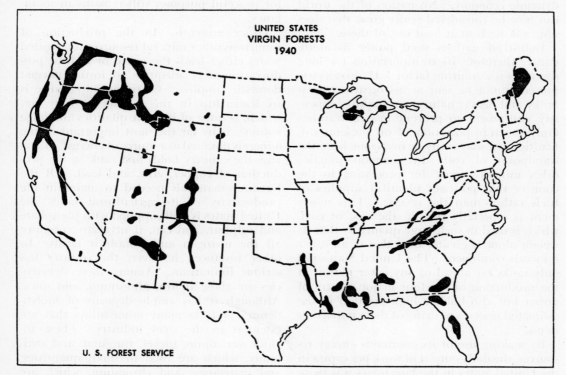

UNITED STATES
VIRGIN FORESTS
1940

U. S. FOREST SERVICE

themselves. In order to have a clear picture of the origin of this physical wealth one must keep in mind that soils and minerals constitute the basic natural resources of any country.

SOILS. The most valuable resource for the sustenance of a political area is soil. Vast areas of land in the United States have soils that rank among the best in the world. Aside from the mountainous regions and the more arid lands of the West, all sections of the country afford soils suitable in varying degrees for agricultural production. This generalization needs to be qualified by pointing out that submarginal lands appear within many otherwise fertile regions, whereas arid lands

power. Valuable minerals may be concentrated in great quantities within a small area —a characteristic not equally true in the case of other resources. The importance of individual minerals also varies greatly. Some minerals, such as coal, are not only extremely vital but are also required in vast quantities. Others, although equally essential, may be used only in small quantities.

In respect to mineral deposits the United States is exceedingly fortunate because of its many remarkable concentrations. The significance of the country's mineral wealth is augmented by the fact that only about six per cent of the people of the world live in the United States, a condition that gives our stock of minerals a relatively high per capita value. For example, the United States each year normally produces over 1,000 tons of pig iron per thousand population. In comparison, the United Kingdom produces around 820 tons, Italy around 100 tons, and India around 25 tons.

Fuel and power. Coal, petroleum, natural gas, and running water are the four outstanding minerals needed for power, consequently they are extremely important to a dynamic economy. No nation of the world can now be considered really great that does not rank high in at least one of these.

Industrial nations need power in abundance; therefore its transportation for long distances is a limiting factor. Hydro-electric power cannot be sent across oceans; coal is bulky and heavy; natural gas requires expensive equipment to prevent loss in transfer. Only the transportation of oil presents difficulties that may easily be overcome from the standpoint of cost. In common practice other minerals move for processing to the country that possesses plentiful supplies of fuels rather than the reverse. This movement is especially true in the case of coal, which is used in such large quantities that its weight alone is greater than that of all other minerals combined. The United States not only ranks far ahead of any other nation in the production of the four major sources of power but also holds a high position in the estimated reserves of many of these important items.

By making use of its enormous energy resources, the daily output of work per capita in the United States in the late 1920's was twice that of Great Britain or Germany, three times that of France, eight times that of Japan, fourteen times that of the U. S. S. R., and twenty-seven times that of either India or China. Today the country's relative position is even better, although the positions of the U. S. S. R. China, and India are improving. Further, not only have those of Germany and Japan declined, but they will almost certainly remain low for some time. The pre-eminent position of the United States in the production and utilization of energy resources is an expression of the dynamic force in the country, one of the factors that determine its industrial capacity.

The position of leadership held by the United States in the development of atomic power deserves special mention. At least for the present, uranium is the mineral basis used in the splitting of the atom, and the United States possesses supplies of this mineral. Atomic energy was harnessed in bombs dropped on Hiroshima and Nagasaki in 1945 during World War II. Although vast sums are being spent on research both in the United States and abroad, the use of atomic energy for peaceful purposes still remains in its infancy.

Other minerals. In the production of numerous other mineral resources the United States either leads the world or at least produces amounts adequate to insure normal domestic supplies. Of prime importance is its leadership in the mining of iron ore, which, because of its basic qualities and huge volume, is by far the most important of the minerals not used as a source of energy. Likewise the country holds first rank in the production of copper, zinc, and lead. Of the fertilizer materials needed to maintain the productivity of its agricultural lands the United States is well supplied with phosphate and sulphur, and can, if necessary, produce all the nitrogen and potash it needs. In other instances, however, the country has serious limitations. Among these deficiencies are those in tin, aluminum, and mica. Although it has ample deposits of molybdenum, it lacks many other alloys that are essential in the steel industry. These include vanadium, nickel, tungsten, and antimony, which are used in small quantities, and manganese and chromium, which are demanded in large amounts.

Of the minerals that the country lacks entirely, those that cause most concern are manganese, tin, aluminum, chromium, and mica. In peacetime they can be obtained from other countries without much difficulty, but in time of war acquisition of these minerals becomes a problem of paramount importance. Thousands of miles separate the United States from the deposits of Malayan tin, Indian and Russian manganese, Russian, Turkish and Rhodesian chromium, and Indian and Madagascan mica. As the lack of these essential minerals during war periods inevitably proves to be a serious handicap, they rank high on the country's list of strategic materials.*

Agricultural production. The United States is the only nation in the world that has worried more about too much agricultural production than about too little. So bountifully has nature supplied the country with agricultural land and productive climate and soil that it must constantly be on the alert lest so much be produced as to depress the market (see the chart directly below). Para-

whelming odds of high unit costs and low returns. Conservation practices will also have to be employed, so that it will be possible to maintain the productive capacity of the land.

The trend toward industrialization in the United States has gone so far that, in spite of the enormous production of agricultural commodities, only about one fifth of its gainfully employed people are engaged in agriculture, forestry, and fishing combined. To-

LAND AREA OF CONTINENTAL UNITED STATES BY MAJOR ECONOMIC USES, 1929

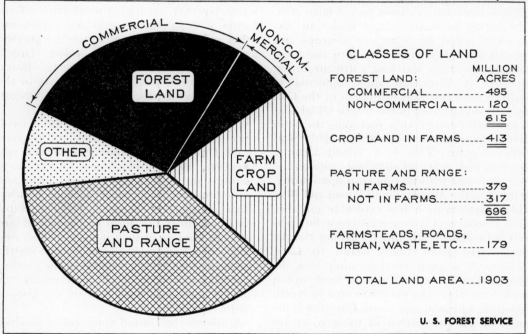

CLASSES OF LAND

	MILLION ACRES
FOREST LAND:	
COMMERCIAL	495
NON-COMMERCIAL	120
	615
CROP LAND IN FARMS	413
PASTURE AND RANGE:	
IN FARMS	379
NOT IN FARMS	317
	696
FARMSTEADS, ROADS, URBAN, WASTE, ETC.	179
TOTAL LAND AREA	1903

U. S. FOREST SERVICE

doxically, this possibility of overproduction does not mean that Americans have taken good care of their land and maintained it in a high state of productivity. Rather, productive land still exists in spite of the very poor care given it. If the United States is to solve these problems, it will have to adjust its production of the various commodities to the needs of the home and export markets. Poor, or marginal, land will have to be removed from cultivation in order that farmers, except in brief periods of great demand, will not have to struggle constantly against over-

gether they contribute approximately one tenth of the national income. Around fifty per cent of the land of continental United States is classed as farm land, seventeen per cent as grazing land, and twenty-four per cent as forest land. Farms on the average are large, and agricultural techniques in most regions involve the use of machinery, a development that greatly decreases the amount of hand labor.

AGRICULTURAL REGIONS. Agricultural activity in the United States varies markedly from place to place, largely as a response to variations in climate, soil, relief, transportation facilities, and markets. In a belt extending from Minnesota to Maine and reach-

* Strategic materials are those procurable in whole or in substantial quantities only from outside the national limits of the affected country.

ing as far south as the latitude of northern Illinois is a region of comparatively poor agricultural land. Devoted for the most part to dairying, the region has scattered through it several "islands" of special crops, such as fruit in Michigan and potatoes in Maine. The intensive nature of dairying, the many large cities, and a cool, moist climate favorable to grasslands have helped to make this an excellent milk-producing area. The Corn Belt, which extends through the midwest from the eastern parts of Nebraska and Kansas to the Appalachian plateau of eastern Ohio, is the country's most famed farm area. The highly productive land found in this region is noted for a variety of crops and animals but is best known for corn and hogs, with forage crops and beef cattle in strong support. A transition zone immediately south of the Corn Belt but north of the Cotton Belt sweeps from northeastern Oklahoma to southern Pennsylvania, including the Ohio River valley and the Appalachian Ridge and Valley region. This is a mixed farming country, with many of the same crops as the Corn Belt but with no one crop dominating. In much of the Appalachian Plateau and Blue Ridge Mountains a less favorable environment discourages commercial crops but permits subsistence agriculture. Along the Atlantic coast from Long Island to Cape Hatteras is a great truck-farming area developed largely because of the huge urban markets nearby. An extensive area in North Carolina, Virginia, and South Carolina is devoted to the production of tobacco, as are also favorable sections in Kentucky and Tennessee. The Cotton Belt, internationally more famous but less prosperous than the Corn Belt, has concentrated largely on cotton production. This region extends south from North Carolina and across the continent as far as west central Texas, excluding Florida and the immediate Atlantic and Gulf coasts. In addition, however, it now raises many other crops, such as corn, legumes, fruits, and vegetables. The Gulf coast from Mexico to Florida produces a series of crops that include citrus fruits, vegetables, rice, and sugar cane. Florida is especially famous for citrus fruits and early vegetables grown for northern markets.

In north central United States, centered in North Dakota, lies the great spring wheat country. The winter wheat area converges from adjacent states into Kansas. A third, less important, wheat area, located in eastern Washington, produces both spring and winter varieties. Most of the Great Plains country, the park lands of the Rocky Mountains, and the semiarid lands of the West consist largely of ranches given over primarily to the raising of animals. In many localities west of the wheat country irrigation farming is important, but except for these restricted areas the productivity of most of the land is very low. The valleys of the West Coast states, however, are highly productive. California, with its fruits, vegetables, grains, and other crops, has become one of the greatest agricultural states in the union, largely through extensive irrigation projects. Dairying and mixed farming predominate in the mild but wet Pacific Coast areas of Oregon and Washington.

Degree of self-sufficiency. The agricultural and grazing lands, forests, and fisheries of the United States supply most of its needs. However, the country must import large amounts of rubber, coffee, wood pulp and paper products, sugar, and silk, and somewhat lesser amounts of bananas, furs, vegetable oils, wool, hides, fish, meat products, and burlap. In the case of such items as rubber and silk, which have normally been high on the list of imports, recent progress in the production of synthetic materials may render the country almost independent of the outside world.

Although the United States could produce many commodities in exportable surpluses, the competition from countries with cheaper land and labor is exceedingly keen. As a result, with the exceptions of cotton and, to a lesser extent, tobacco and wheat, manufactures and minerals constitute the chief exports today. This ratio has not, of course, been true in the past, for through much of the country's history it has exported mostly agricultural, forest, and fishery products.

Industrial production. The United States reaches the apex of her tremendous strength in the industrial world. Under a politically stable government the nation has created a colossal industrial capacity through a fusion of its huge supply of capital, its wealth of raw materials and power, and its technical ability. The United States stands head and shoulders above the U. S. S. R., its nearest rival in industrial production, though in time the competition between the two countries promises to become much keener. So conclusively was its great industrial strength demonstrated during World War II that none can challenge its present position (see the following chart). Many decades will pass be-

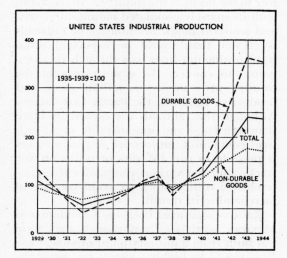

fore any of the other nations catch up, if indeed any ever does.

Despite a total population not nearly so large as that of any one of several other nations, the United States nevertheless has the greatest reservoir of scientists, the largest group of imaginative entrepreneurs, and the greatest supply of educated, skilled workers of any country. Coupled with enormous natural wealth and a progressive stable government, these advantages make the country the technological and scientific center of the modern world. Approximately one fourth of the gainfully occupied population of the United States is engaged in manufacturing, and this group accounts for one fourth of the national income. In the field of international trade, finished manufactures account for about seventy per cent of all its exports. This development is relatively recent, however, for as late as the early 1930's the percentage of finished manufactures in export trade amounted to only a little over forty per cent.

Approximately four fifths of the manufacturing in the United States is concentrated in the northeastern part of the country. Specif-

ically, the area is encircled by a line running from Minneapolis south to Kansas City, thence east to Norfolk, north to Portland, Maine, and west to the starting point in Minneapolis. Most of the remainder is concentrated in the piedmont area of North Carolina, South Carolina, and Georgia; around Birmingham, Alabama; and on the West Coast area in the Puget Sound–Willamette Valley and the San Francisco and Los Angeles metropolitan districts.

The position of the United States in manufacturing is unique in that it dominates the world completely in most of the heavy manufacturing industries that require enormous amounts of power, raw materials, and capital, and large numbers of scientists, entrepreneurs, and skilled laborers. These manufactures, which include iron and steel, industrial machines, railroad cars and locomotives, ships, electrical machinery, textile machinery, agricultural implements, machine tools, tractors, automobiles, and aircraft, represent the backbone of any great industrial nation. With Germany's decline the country's keenest competition in many of these fields has ceased to exist. The chemical, synthetic fiber, rubber, textile, and leather industries, as well as many others of importance, have also attained their highest development in the United States.

An enormous home market and the constant development of new labor-saving devices have made its workers the most efficient producers in the world. It is not because Americans have so much greater inventive ability than other progressive peoples that they have produced so many more labor-saving devices but rather because during the course of the country's industrial development the people were forced by shortage of labor to do so. It has been a case of the proverbial "Necessity is the mother of invention." In the heavy industries, in spite of high wages, the country can undersell other countries, but in the manufacture of such goods as textiles the country finds it exceedingly difficult to meet competition from lands of extremely low wages, such as Japan, India, and China.

EFFECTS OF THE INDUSTRIAL AGE. Industrialization has revolutionized the pattern of American life. The Machine Age has permitted workers to enjoy leisure time and an increased income; young men and women are insured the possibilities of an extensive education. This opportunity has been fundamental in creating the broadened horizons and advanced social thinking of the American people. Leisure time has also made recreational activities possible; in some instances so intense that sports and entertainments, such as football, basketball, baseball, tennis, golf, horse racing, and motion pictures, have become institutions. The surplus energy expended in hard play can be converted in time of emergencies to productive efforts amazing in their results. Moreover, the very fact that a people play hard is a good indicator of national vigor and well-being.

Through industry the American housewife has been relieved of much drudgery, for she has been supplied with such things as washing machines, refrigerators, electric irons, pressure cookers, and canned and frozen foods. The automobile and the telephone especially have been instrumental in widening the sphere of American life. One measure of the degree to which the people have advanced technically is found in their use of the telephone. Commonplace to Americans, this instrument is still a wonder to most of the people of the world. The United States alone has one half of the telephones of the world! New York alone has as many as all of either Latin America or Asia. As another illustration, three fourths of all the automobiles in the world are owned by the people of the United States. Since food and the manufactured products discussed above are accepted criteria of high living standards, Americans are, with the possible exception of one or two small countries, the most fortunate people in the world.

Transportation facilities. The transportation system of the United States is more complete and better integrated than that of any other large country. All types of modern transport facilities—railroads, roads, waterways, airways, and pipelines—are extensively utilized throughout the country.

RAILROADS. National, political, and economic unity would have been impossible in the United States had the nation not been knit together with an elaborate pattern of integrated railroad systems. Forming a grillwork of north-south and east-west lines, more than 235,000 miles of railroads have their most intensive development on the low-

lands but also penetrate or cross mountainous areas. Main axes, such as transcontinental or coastal lines, are supplemented by a complete network of connecting lines, with most traffic flowing east-west and immediately parallel to the two coasts. The density of the railroad lines conforms rather closely to the distribution of population and therefore to the needs of the country. In the West, with its sparsely populated mountain, desert, and semiarid lands, the mileage of railroads is greater than would be expected; seven transcontinental lines pass through these expanses to connect the eastern part of the country with the metropolitan areas and productive valleys of the Pacific Coast states. Although the railroads are owned by more than 150 large and innumerable small railroad companies, uniformity of gauge makes it possible to run any cars or trains on any tracks, and the various companies freely interchange rolling stock to avoid transfer of merchandise in transit.

Railroads parallel both the Canadian and Mexican borders. Even though they were not built from a military point of view, these lines would be highly strategic for use in deploying troops should the unlikely happen, that is, were some nation to strike at the United States through Canada or Mexico.

HIGHWAYS. The American system of highways, which is the most modern and complete found anywhere in the world, is constantly being improved. Nevertheless, the United States lacks carefully engineered arterial highways on which traffic can move at a maximum speed and efficiency with minimum danger. One of the country's greatest problems today is to engineer its highways and motor vehicles, so as to reduce the appalling number of traffic accidents that take place. Actually, the technical improvements of the automobile have moved considerably ahead of the highways available to the cars.

Highways parallel some of the trunk railroads, but the highway pattern also supplements and complements the railroad in many areas. Bulky materials can be hauled long distances over rails to greatest advantage, whereas the highways lend themselves to shorter hauls and less bulky commodities. Great trucking concerns, however, interconnect most of the country's large cities and offer serious competition to railroad freight interests. Railways are unable to outstrip this competition from highway transportation as they did that from river and canal transportation a century ago; witness 32,500,-000 automobile registrations in the United States on the eve of World War II.

Along with the railroad, the highway and the automobile are at the head of the list of factors that have affected the cultural pattern of the United States. As highway development continued its advance, even the remotest sections of the country were tapped and Americans were brought closer and closer together. The results, still in process, have enhanced tendencies toward national uniformity, complete utilization of the country's reservoir of potential human energy and ability, and a rising standard of living for Americans in general.

WATER ROUTES. With the exceptions of the Great Lakes and the coastal waters, improvements of the waterways of the United States have failed to keep pace with those for land transport. The only modern river and canal transport routes that carry appreciable amounts of traffic are the Ohio, the lower Mississippi, the Illinois, the Black Warrior–Tombigbee, and the Tennessee. Even these streams carry only bulky commodities of low value. As pointed out earlier in this chapter, two major reasons account for this failure of the river and canal system of transport to attain widespread development. First, the streams generally flow north-south, whereas most traffic flows east-west. Second, as the country was expanding and feeling the need of transport facilities, the railroads were coming into their own; from the very start they formed the backbone of its transport system. In contrast, however, the Great Lakes provide a tremendous artery of traffic for iron ore, coal, coke, petroleum, stone, sand and gravel, wheat, and other commodities flowing east-west. Also there is a considerable amount of coastwise traffic on both the Pacific and Atlantic-Gulf coasts. With the opening of the Panama Canal, the Pacific and Atlantic-Gulf coasts were commercially linked; shipments by this route between the east coast and the west coast come under the heading of "coastwise traffic."

AIR ROUTES. The air routes of today in the United States are increasing so rapidly that anything said about them will soon be out of date (see the map on page 50). In 1926 a large number of small air transportation companies formed an inadequate and unplanned network of air routes over the continental United States; planes were small, schedules generally infrequent and for short distances, and services not too dependable. On the eve of World War II a much smaller number of large commercial airlines, several of them transcontinental, had greatly expanded the network and were flying more than twenty-five times as many miles as were the commercial planes of 1926.

From 1942 to 1945 commercial aircraft "went to war," carrying military personnel and supplies at the expense of civilian traffic. In the latter part of the war period, however, when victory seemed assured, expansion of the domestic air pattern was again resumed. At the close of the war the airports of about 300 cities or combinations of cities were on regular commercial air routes, some air terminals handling more than one hundred scheduled incoming and outgoing passenger flights each day. During the postwar period air transportation has continued to grow, and is presently a "big business"—air travel is as firmly established an American institution as is rail or bus travel.

The above picture by no means takes into consideration the many aspects of commercial aviation other than the regular scheduled operation of the major airlines. The Civil Aeronautics Board (government bureau controlling commercial aviation) has approved air service into numerous small cities by means of "feeder" lines. The same board has also granted the right to hundreds of companies to fly non-scheduled (charter) flights for both passengers and cargo. Further, air cargo is eating into the high value–low bulk express and freight business of the railroads and trucking lines, and air mail is consistently becoming more and more popular for distances of 300 miles or more. Beyond the authority of the Civil Aeronautics Board, small intrastate airlines are carrying modest numbers of passengers, and will doubtlessly thrive when a small, economical airliner is perfected.

Commercial air transportation is only one phase of modern air travel; there is also civil aviation, which has grown by leaps and bounds as the result of the flying experiences of thousands of men during World War II and the increased emphasis on the building of relatively low-priced private planes. Because of the importance of commercial and civil aviation to the country's future military security, the aircraft industry has taken on political as well as economic and cultural significance. Except to call attention to the trends, it is as impossible to attempt any forecast of future developments in aeronautical science as it would have been for the would-be

further expand the pipeline system. The network is becoming nation-wide rather than concentrated around only the principal petroleum producing, refining, and consuming centers.

Population

Number and distribution. The 139 million population of the United States (1945) is surpassed only by that of China, India, and Soviet Russia. Of these, only Soviet Russia

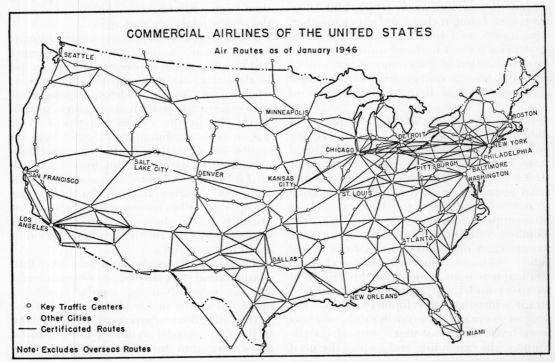

prophet of 1910 to have foreseen the millions of automobiles upon the roads of the United States during the following decades.

PIPELINES. As a highly specialized means of land transportation, pipelines play an integral part in the American pattern of industrial distribution. These carriers supplement tankers and tank cars in moving the nation's petroleum and petroleum products from the oil fields to the refineries and consuming centers throughout the country. During World War II the already extensive system was greatly expanded because of the tanker shortage brought about by submarine losses and by the need for so many tankers to haul oil to the fighting fronts. Since the end of the war plans have been developing to

is today a great power. China and India with their enormous numbers of people are overpopulated in relation to their productive facilities. As a result they are greatly handicapped, not only from the point of view of their own economic well-being but also from the point of view of fighting ability in time of war. In contrast to these latter two countries, the United States, despite its sizable population, has an adequate geographical base for an even larger population. During World War II the nation was not only able to put more men on the fighting fronts than any great power except Soviet Russia, but was able to do the essential work on the farms and in the factories that helped to feed and supply the fighting men of all the country's allies as well as to meet all of its own needs.

The people of the United States are unevenly scattered over the country, creating a density pattern of considerable variety (see the map below). The number of persons

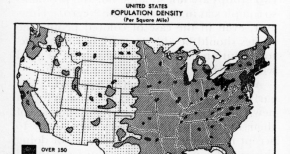

UNITED STATES
POPULATION DENSITY
(Per Square Mile)

OVER 150
10 – 150
LESS THAN 10

per square mile is greatest in the northeast, and becomes less toward the south and west. The mountains and arid regions of the west have few people, but the rich valleys and basins of the Pacific Coast states are well populated. In most areas throughout the country the population distribution has become adjusted to the ability of the land and industry to support the people. However, especially in the south, inefficient use of the land and lack of industrialization have led to inadequate living standards for large numbers of people in many regions.

The character of the population. Until recently the population of the United States grew rapidly, but at present the rate of increase is tending to decline. It is estimated that the total population will level off before the optimum number of inhabitants for the country is reached. One factor limiting population increases is the disproportionate growth of urban over rural dwellers. Statistics show that urban and industrial areas are today the regions of lowest birth rate. Urban dwellers are gaining at the expense of the rural population; in the 1940 census more than half the people of the United States were classified as urban, that is, they lived in communities of 2,500 or more people. However, without the constant flow of young people from the rural areas, these urban centers would decline in total population. Another factor in the slowing up of national population growth is the shift in the number of people within each of the various age groups. For many decades younger groups predominated, but more recently older people have constituted a relatively large proportion of the total population, a condition that characterizes lands with more mature economies. Still another factor responsible for a lower rate of population increase is the negligible immigration in recent years in contrast to the vast influx from other countries that formerly took place.

Cities. The 1940 census classed nearly 75 million Americans as city dwellers, living in approximately 3,450 separate communities. Large cities, that is, those with 100,000 or more population, accounted for more than half the urban population, and, in turn, for more than a fourth the total population of the United States. There are ninety-two such cities scattered through thirty-three of the forty-eight states. The greatest concentration of large cities, however, appears in the northeastern part of the country, with Massachusetts, Ohio, New York, and New Jersey alone accounting for twenty-nine of them, or approximately one third of the total number. Of the fifteen states in which no such cities are found eight are in the arid or semiarid regions of the West, three are in the South, and three are in northern New England—all on the periphery of the most intensively developed industrial regions or the more productive agricultural areas.

The largest cities of the United States * are highly complex. Their present size can be explained by taking into account a wide variety of factors, among them an early start, access to raw materials, a gateway position to adjacent regions, a commercially strategic position, a center for governmental functions, and a vigorous will to growth. No large city owes its entire importance to any one or two factors alone, but in some instances an urban area may enjoy a tremendous advantage because of a single factor or a combination of related factors. Illustrative are New York's excellent harbor at the eastern end of a water

* The ten largest cities of the United States and their 1940 populations are as follows: New York, 7,455,000; Chicago, 3,397,000; Philadelphia, 1,931,000; Detroit, 1,623,000; Los Angeles, 1,504,000; Cleveland, 878,000; Baltimore, 859,000; St. Louis, 816,000; Boston, 771,000; and Pittsburgh, 672,000. The U. S. Census also recognizes metropolitan areas, whereby entire urban areas, or clusters of cities, are counted as individual units.

level route to the interior of the United States; Chicago's position at the convergence of transportation routes near the southern end of Lake Michigan; Denver's location as a gateway to the Rocky Mountain area; New Orleans' location near the mouth of the Mississippi River; Los Angeles' enticing climate; Washington's function as the national capital.

Language and religions. No language or distinct dialect problems, such as those that appear in the Balkan states or in China, beset the United States. To be sure, there are localized groups of immigrants in a number of the larger cities who speak the language of their native countries. Nevertheless, such a small minority of the people fail to use or understand English that it is not merely the official language but actually the only one of any consequence.

In the matter of religion, complete freedom of worship exists in the United States. With more than 250 religious bodies, almost every one of the religions of the world is practiced by at least a few Americans, and any prohibition or repression of the establishment or free exercise of any religion is specifically forbidden by the Constitution of the United States. Of the people who are church communicants, about 40,000,000 belong to one of the Protestant groups, 20,000,000 to the Roman Catholic Church, 4,500,000 to Jewish Congregations, 500,000 to Eastern Orthodox Churches, and the others to one or another of the many smaller religious groups.

The admixture of many nationalities in the United States has for the most part been beneficial in giving its people the advantage of many cultures. However, the large numbers of Negroes in the South and to a lesser extent Orientals on the West Coast and Jewish people in the eastern states have created many problems of racial and religious intolerance that have developed largely because of economic competition and social prejudices. The unfortunate conflicts arising because of dislike or resentment felt by others for the Jewish and Oriental people in our country may well be eliminated with time, patience, and understanding, for these two groups are not so large nor the problems so complex as in the case of the Negro. However, even in the case of colored people the whites should be able to work out a satisfactory solution through the application of good will, patience, and intelligent planning.

Attainments of the American people. The early settlers in America came in search of a new life. Dissatisfied with many aspects of their European cultures, they were ready to accept new ideas and different ways of doing things. Their vigor and enthusiasm found expression in a utilization of the natural wealth they discovered in the new land. Old ways and traditions brought from Europe amalgamated with others developed in the new country to form what Americans today delight in calling "the American way of life." The infant culture permitted the rapid evolution of a new pattern of living. Abundant natural resources and freedom from the traditional European class system served as strong incentives to progress. Concurrently with industrial growth and mechanization, the American people have prospered. The measure of their strength as a decisive element in providing national defense was satisfactorily tested by World War II. With the possible exception of a few small countries, such as New Zealand and Sweden, the United States outranks all nations of the world in health and vigor, income per capita, superior diet, medical care, inventive genius, and widespread education.

America still has the urge and the ability to strive for a better world. On the threshold of a new era, there are before her people atomic energy, the research laboratory, and conservation of human resources as challenging frontiers.

CHAPTER 5 | The United States as a World Power

THE preceding chapter presented some of the basic geographic factors contributing to the strength of the United States. In particular, stress was placed on the historical, economic, and cultural aspects of the country in relation to its physical make-up, so as to permit proper evaluation of its geopolitical development. In turn, this chapter is designed to show something of the position of the United States and its operations as a political entity in a world subject to the constant change engendered by international politics.

Historical Background: Nineteenth Century

The Continental Republic. During most of its history the United States has not been obliged, amidst the strife of nations, to keep its potentials mobilized for outward thrusts of power. The supreme problem of American foreign policy during the nineteenth century was to keep the continent unblocked by foreign power, while the nation expanded through to the Pacific Ocean and preserved the Union. Thanks to the country's separation from Europe and Asia during that century, and to the continual wars and rivalries of the nations of the Old World, the people were able to achieve this goal without maintaining a large army or navy.

Since the fulfillment of that really exalted manifest destiny, the task of American diplomacy has been to secure the Continental Republic against aggression from without. Such security first involved the safety of the North American continent and the place of the United States in it, and next the safety of the whole New World and the place of the new nation in that. Maintaining the security of the New World—and of the United States—in the twentieth century, has involved maintaining a balance of power against the forces of aggression in the Old World. In our day this objective requires a standing military force measured in terms of that of other world powers, until all are ready to merge their power in a reliable system of collective security.

Canada the hostage. During the nineteenth century the only power that could have thought of attacking the United States successfully was Great Britain. Another war after 1815 was "unthinkable" if only because of the enduring kinship of culture, institutions, and ways of living that continued to bind the two peoples in the best of worlds. Back of that pleasing apposition lay the position of Canada. In any Anglo-American conflict, Canada must be either neutral or belligerent. Neutrality would be tantamount to secession from the Empire; perhaps annexation to the United States. Belligerency against the United States would mean invasion, conquest, certain annexation. So Canada served as a continual hostage, even if no hostage were needed, for the good conduct of the British navy toward the vulnerable coastal cities of the United States. It is still the "linchpin," as Canada's Prime Minister Mackenzie King put it, of Anglo-American relations. And let it be remembered that if any real power other than Britain were north of the Forty-ninth Parallel, Canada would not be a hostage but a springboard.

The New Frame of World Politics: Twentieth Century

Definition of world power. A world power is a nation that has the strength to make itself felt internationally in major dispositions of power and politics. Such a world power may choose to throw its weight in only one region. Even so, it causes major repercussions in world politics for better or for worse, for example, the United States in the New World, Japan in the Far East (in a recent epoch), and Germany in Europe.

Power in world politics consists first of military strength (army, navy, air forces), or a potential of military strength that can be mobilized unmolested in times of necessity. That strength is, in turn, based on favorable geographical location, natural resources, man power, civil organization, national unity and morale, and to some extent financial means (for a detailed discussion of the prerequisites to major powerhood, see pages 7–8). The United States has had all these requirements of world power since it became a Continental Republic.

Three new world powers. The happy position of continental isolation began to change with the advent of our times. For a portentous phenomenon occurred at the turn of the last century: the birth of three new world powers, the United States, Germany, and Japan. The appearance of one world power in the international firmament is a spectacle of tremendous significance. It is certain to cause major perturbations in the orbits of the other world powers. A triple birth of world powers was unprecedented in history. This triple birth was followed by the world-shaking convulsions of 1914–1945. The immediate effect was to bring forth a new frame of sea power and world politics in which the strategic position of the United States would no longer be foolproof.

The other two world powers confronted the United States, one across the Atlantic in Europe, the other across the Pacific in Asia. Each had a formidable army; each set about building a formidable navy. Either could threaten one of the populous seacoasts of the United States. Neither had a hostage like Canada to guarantee its benevolence. North America gradually became an island-continent menaced by hostile potentials of power. The British Empire became a world archipelago threatened by the nearby hostile continents of Europe and Asia. The new picture caused the United States and Great Britain to look more and more to each other for the security of their own destinies. Great Britain was first to feel the significance of the new order of power. The United States did not realize it fully until World War I.

Birth of the United States as a world power. Historians generally accept the year 1898, that is to say, the events of the Spanish-American War, as marking the emergence of the United States as a world power. The cause of that war was the Cuban Question, but behind the Cuban Question lay the Isthmian Question, that is, the question of the Isthmus of Panama.

THE ISTHMIAN LIFELINE. Ever since the completion of the Continental Republic, American opinion had focused increasingly upon the project of an Isthmian canal to connect the commerce and defenses of the two seacoasts. The new frame of sea power made such a waterway indispensable for national security. Without a canal two navies would be required. With a canal one powerful navy would be enough. A single fleet could be passed back and forth through the Isthmus to protect either coast as circumstances might require. Nobody dreamed, in the early decades of the twentieth century, that the United States might have to fight a two-ocean war.

RESULTS OF THE SPANISH-AMERICAN WAR. The Cuban Question lay conveniently at hand for the statesmen of the period—the Mahans, the Roosevelts, the Lodges—who wished to embark upon a "large policy" of securing control of the Isthmus and its maritime approaches from both oceans. The United States emerged from the Spanish-American War sovereign of Puerto Rico, protector of Cuba, and mistress of the Caribbean, ready and eager to build, control, and fortify a canal across the narrow part of Central America. The necessary arrangements, technical and diplomatic, were quickly completed. Under the dictation of President Theodore Roosevelt, the Isthmian Canal Commission switched its preference from Nicaragua to Panama as the site of the proposed waterway. Thanks to the propaganda and lobbying of the French New Panama Canal Company, Congress voted, through the Spooner Amendment, to dig the canal across Panama.

Great Britain, eager for an alliance with the United States against the rising menace of Germany, recognized the new interest of the United States in Central America. She speedily agreed to annul the joint control of an Isthmian canal imposed by the Clayton-Bulwer Treaty of 1850.* When Colombia refused to ratify a treaty that her representatives had signed, giving the United States control of an Isthmian canal zone across the State of Panama, the United States intervened to protect the secession of Panama. The new republic promptly signed a treaty creating a canal zone in which the United States was to act as if it were sovereign. In return the United States agreed to protect the independence of Panama.

THE PANAMA POLICY AND THE ROOSEVELT COROLLARY. Once the canal was under construction the United States could not afford to see a European power establish a base close enough to jeopardize the lifeline. A test case occurred as the engineers prepared to begin work. In 1902–03 Great Britain, Germany, and Italy intervened by force in Venezuela to collect contract debts and damages of their nationals to whom the dictator of that state had refused justice. A similar intervention by Great Britain and France in Egypt twenty years before had left the British in control of the Suez Canal. Only the rising tone of American public opinion in the winter of 1902–03 led the intervening powers to back out and arbitrate their dispute with Venezuela. Then the Hague Permanent Court of Arbitration, in a decision handed down February 22, 1904, justified the intervention by allowing the intervening powers a priority of payment of damages as against similar claims of powers who had not resorted to the use of force.

The precarious internal condition of nearly all the other Caribbean states made them liable to intervention similar to that which had taken place in Venezuela. To meet this menace in the general vicinity of the Panama Canal, President Theodore Roosevelt evoked a "Corollary" to the Monroe Doctrine: that the United States would intervene in those countries in order to make it unnecessary for European governments to do so to protect the rights of their nationals. The series of American interventions that resulted established an imperialistic control by the United States in several countries within a strategic radius of the Panama Canal: Cuba, Dominican Republic, Haiti, and Nicaragua.* Such action undoubtedly staved off a worse European intervention. In this way the Isthmian lifeline was secured for the United States and, so it proved in the two world wars that followed, for the liberties of the New World. Meanwhile, the progression of events excited the animosity of the Latin American states against the "Colossus of the North." The series of protective interventions was climaxed by the outright purchase of the Danish West Indies (now known as the Virgin Islands) during World War I, lest they fall somehow to Germany. The Caribbean Policy of the United States, or Panama Policy (as it has also been called), was a natural and logical sequence of the "large policy" of Mahan, Roosevelt, and Lodge.

THE PACIFIC AND THE FAR EAST. In the Pacific, as a consequence of the Spanish-American War, the United States annexed the Hawaiian Islands, and forced Spain to sell, for twenty million dollars, the Philippine Islands and to cede Guam. The United States had already become a Pacific power in a small way during the nineteenth century by the acquisition of a number of guano islets in the 1850's, that is, Howland, Baker, and Jarvis. Midway was annexed in 1867 and Wake Island in 1899. Since 1889 the United States had been engaged in a quarrelsome cooperation with Great Britain and Germany for the administration of the Samoan Islands. In 1899 Great Britain got out of Samoa in return for compensation in other parts of the South Seas and in Africa. By a tripartite treaty arrangement the United States took over Tutuila with the harbor of Pago Pago, and the islets east of 171 degrees West Longitude, while Germany remained

---

* The Clayton-Bulwer Treaty of 1850 provided that neither the United States nor Great Britain would obtain or maintain for itself any exclusive control over any ship canal through any part of Central America.

* Further interventions in Cuba followed the original one of 1898.

sovereign over the remaining islands of the group.*

There was certainly common sense in the American acquisition of these small islands, including the Hawaiian group, as defensive outposts for the Continental Republic. Alaska became a part of the same general cadre in 1867. But before the Spanish-American War nobody in the United States had ever dreamed of acquiring territory on the littoral of eastern Asia. The acquisition of the Philippines was not demanded by American public opinion. It was neither natural nor logical. Nor was the scaffolding of Far Eastern policy that was built upon that unexpectedly acquired archipelago.

The American Colonial Empire **

As has been indicated, the unexpected acquisition of territorial possessions beyond the continental limits of the United States complicated American foreign policy. The great American defense triangle in the Pacific and the Caribbean defense strategy, protecting the Panama Canal and the approach to the United States from the southeast, incorporate nearly all of the country's possessions. The lack of any possessions in the North Atlantic caused considerable concern at the beginning of World War II, a situation remedied only by definite territorial arrangements in the land areas serving as approaches to the country from the northeast.

Alaska. In the North Pacific the Territory of Alaska guards the approach to the United States from the northwest. It is the apex of the American defense triangle in the Pacific, the Hawaiian Islands and the Panama Canal Zone forming the other two corners. Aside from this locational aspect, the Seward Peninsula of Alaska is only fifty-four miles from Siberia across the Bering Strait. In addition, the Alaskan Peninsula, together with the Aleutian Archipelago, extends 1,500 miles in a southwest direction to within 600 miles of the Kamchatka Peninsula in Soviet Russia. In a diametrically opposite direction, the Panhandle of the Territory runs along the western coast of Canada to within 500 miles of the United States

* In 1919 Germany renounced sovereignty; in 1920 New Zealand assumed a mandate of Western Samoa.
** See Chapter 30 for a discussion of the Philippine Islands.

boundary. Alaska and its islands thus serve as stepping stones (or operational air bases) to and from Asia. As the only American possession that extends into the Arctic region, it is figuring more and more prominently in an air age world of polar and projected polar routes.

In 1867 Secretary of State William H. Seward purchased Alaska from Russia for $7,200,000. With an area roughly equal to one fifth that of the United States, the Territory contains a number of regions with varying topography, climate, and resources. Since its acquisition by the United States, Alaska has attracted widespread attention; there has been spectacular and profitable economic exploitation, especially in gold, fish, and fur; transportation facilities, particularly in and along the coastal zone, have been established; and the advantages of location in waging the recent war in the Pacific were seized upon by American military commanders. But despite all this, Alaska remains as a frontier land with no evidence of compact, intensive development. In 1940 the total population amounted to only 72,000, of whom 32,000 were Indians, Eskimos, and Aleuts. The maintenance of military bases, the new Alaska Highway from Edmonton to Fairbanks, and the rapidly expanding air network in and to Alaska may have their effect in furthering the economic and cultural development of the Territory. In turn, this increased importance would be the means of furthering its political role as a measure of military security. Statehood is a distinct possibility in the near future.

Hawaiian Islands. The mountainous Hawaiian Islands are vital in the Pacific triangle of defense. As a group they lie some 2,000 miles from the western coast of the United States, just south of the Tropic of Cancer. An already strategic location in the midst of the Pacific Ocean is made even more advantageous by other island possessions that help to form stepping-stone routes to lands of the Eastern Hemisphere. Midway, Wake, and Guam lead westward to the Philippines and the east coast of Asia. American Samoa and a number of American islets lead southwest toward New Zealand and Australia.

Strung out for 400 miles in a northwest-southeast direction, the eight major islands of the Hawaiian group (Hawaii, Kahoolawe,

Maui, Lanai, Molokai, Oahu, Niihau, and Kauai) have a total area of 6,435 square miles. The permanent residents of the eight islands number about 420,000. Although Hawaii is considerably larger than all the other seven islands together, Oahu, with the naval base of Pearl Harbor and the capital city of Honolulu, is the best known and politically the most important.

The events of the Pacific War of 1941–45 have revealed the great strategic importance of the Hawaiian Islands. In 1946 the President recommended to Congress that the Hawaiians be admitted into the Union as a state.

Puerto Rico and the Virgin Islands. The location of the Caribbean possessions of Puerto Rico and the Virgin Islands in the West Indies makes them key points for the defense of the Panama Canal by the United States. Puerto Rico is the easternmost island of the Greater Antilles, and the Virgin Islands are the northernmost islands of the Lesser Antilles group. Together they form the juncture in the arc of West Indian islands, a point most ideally located as the entrance to the Caribbean Sea (see the map on page 445). Puerto Rico and the Virgin Islands are thus logical gateway points to the Panama Canal, or at least stand as sentinels in the outer circle of defense.

Puerto Rico is a densely settled agricultural island void of natural resources having any particular value to the economy of the United States. With one and three-quarter million people crowded upon 3,400 square miles of land, there is a population density of about 500 persons per square mile. The people are largely of Spanish descent, but Indian and Negro blood resulting from centuries of intermarriage is also common. The cultural pattern of the island is typically Spanish, with adjustments for the tropical sun.

Only forty miles to the east of Puerto Rico are the Virgin Islands: St. Thomas, St. Croix, and St. John. Formerly the Danish West Indies, the Virgin group is overshadowed in importance by larger and more productive islands to the west and south. Their value to the United States lies primarily in their location.

Canal Zone. The land area of the Canal Zone is incidental to the Panama Canal itself. It is a strip of land ten miles wide (excluding the cities of Panama and Colón), with the boundaries roughly five miles on either side of the center line of the canal (see the map directly below). Granted to the

PANAMA CANAL

United States in perpetuity by the Republic of Panama in 1904, the Canal Zone is actually "leased territory" and is administered by army officials. The two-ocean navy of the United States is dependent upon the continuous functioning of the Panama Canal; hence it is the keystone of defense, which must be safeguarded by every possible means.

American Foreign Policy in the Far East

Following the Spanish-American War the eminent publicist of that day, Captain Alfred T. Mahan, described American foreign policy in a three-point formula: in America, predominance; in Asia, cooperation; in Europe, abstention. We have already noted the predominance of the United States in the Caribbean.

Cooperation in the Far East. Before coming into the Philippines, the United States had relied upon a most-favored-nation policy for the rights of its citizens in China. In this way it had acquired all the privileges of residence, travel, navigation, and trade that the imperialistic powers of Europe had won for their nationals after their wars with the

Chinese Empire during the nineteenth century. It should be noted, however, that the United States never insisted upon compensating *cessions of territory, leaseholds, or "spheres of interest."* It had always preferred the integrity of China, if only because the loss of Chinese territory meant the loss of most-favored-nation privileges therein. After the acquisition of the Philippines, the United States expanded its China policy from one of most-favored-nation treaties with China to one of diplomatic understandings with powers other than China for the preservation of its own interests in that land.

The Hay Policy. Secretary of State John Hay announced the new policy. In the famous "Open-Door" notes of 1899, he proposed to Great Britain, Russia, Germany, France, and Japan that each power holding leased territory or "spheres of interest" in China should not discriminate against the commerce of other powers within its sphere, in matters of tariff dues, railroad charges, and harbor fees. Hay accepted the equivocal replies of the powers as assurance in principle. From the Open-Door notes of 1899 it was only a step to the Hay Circular of July 3, 1900, at the time of the Boxer Rebellion: The United States stood for the "territorial and administrative entity" of the Chinese Empire. A series of notes between 1900 and the outbreak of World War I further elaborated this policy of the Open Door and the territorial and administrative entity of China. It cannot be said that the policy was successful, although the precarious balance of power in the Far East gave an illusion of success until 1914.

THE "ACHILLES HEEL" OF AMERICAN DEFENSE. After the Russo-Japanese War (1904–05), and Japan's entrance into Korea and Manchuria, President Theodore Roosevelt warned his successor, William Howard Taft, that for the United States to maintain the Hay Policy would require a navy as big as the British navy and an army as large as the German army. The American people were unwilling to build up such forces to support that policy in a region of the world where they had so few vital interests. There was another deterrent to any active policy in the Far East. The vulnerable Philippine Islands served as a hostage of the United States to Japan, just as Canada served as a hostage of Great Britain toward the United

States. They were, as Theodore Roosevelt put it, the "Achilles heel" of American defense.

Concessions to Japan. In return for repeated pledges not to molest the Philippines, the United States gave more and more of a free hand to Japan in Korea, Manchuria, and contiguous portions of China (1905, 1908, 1915). The climax of these concessions came in the Lansing-Ishii Agreement of 1917 after the United States had entered World War I. It reiterated the principle of the Open Door and "territorial" sovereignty of China, but recognized that "territorial propinquity" created special relations between countries and therefore Japan had "special interests" in China.*

Effect of World War I on United States Far Eastern policy. The Far Eastern policy of the United States stiffened at the close of World War I. At that time it had a navy as big as Britain's and an army as big as Germany's. The resulting Washington treaties of 1922 marked the high point in the policy of "cooperation" in the Far East and the region of the Pacific Ocean. In return for a limitation of naval power and naval bases that left her supreme as against any other one power in Far Eastern waters, Japan agreed with the other powers not to take advantage of "present" conditions in China that would abridge the rights of subjects of other friendly states or to countenance action inimical to the security of these states. She also joined in pledges to observe the Open Door and the administrative and territorial integrity of China. Japan evacuated the Chinese province of Shantung and also eastern Siberia (occupied jointly with the Allies in 1918), but she retained special interests she had built up in China before the Washington treaties. The Lansing-Ishii Agreement was abrogated by mutual consent.

The Monroe Doctrine in Asia vs. in Europe. Some students of international relations saw in the contrasting attitudes of the

* A secret protocol to the Lansing-Ishii Agreement stipulated that neither Japan nor the United States would "take advantage of the present conditions to seek special rights or privileges in China which would abridge the rights of the subjects or citizens of their friendly states." In the Washington Nine Power Treaty of 1922, article 1, paragraph 4, this secret understanding was brought into the light of day in open treaty.

United States toward Asia and Europe a curious inconsistency, even perversion, of the Monroe Doctrine. The writer of that historic pronouncement had counseled abstention from intermingling in the wars and rivalries of European powers "in matters relating to themselves." Only when our own rights were invaded, or seriously menaced, said President Monroe, would we resent injuries, or make preparations for our defense. In the Far East, our interests were considered to be involved after the acquisition of the Philippines. So we "cooperated" by "all peaceful means" to maintain the Open Door, the integrity of China, and the balance of power. In Europe we "abstained" from taking any decisive step to maintain the balance of power. There, in the very front yard of international policies, we did not consider our rights to be invaded, or seriously menaced.

The United States and World War I

When the European conflict broke out in 1914, so unexpectedly to the United States, President Wilson proclaimed neutrality and enjoined his fellow citizens to observe it in thought as well as in act. But the sympathies, cultural background, wartime commerce, finances, and vital interests of the people of the United States soon became enmeshed in the cause of Great Britain and her allies. It was these countries who were maintaining the balance of power in which our own security was involved.

If the "Allies" won in war, the United States had nothing to lose by their victory, as proved by the event. If Germany and her allies won, the United States had much to fear, as was proved when Germany twenty years later managed to throw off the shackles of defeat. Woodrow Wilson, however, did not lead the country into war on the side of the Allies because he decided that a victory of Germany would upset the balance of power dangerously for the United States. Rather, it was his *choice* of neutral policy that led this peace-loving President against his will into World War I.

Wilson's choice of neutral policy. Wilson had two alternate choices of policy, both honorably within the realm of neutrality. At the outset he could have announced that all American citizens traveled at their own responsibility and risk under a belligerent flag. Or, he could have insisted upon protecting the undoubted rights of American citizens (as did the Swiss and Spanish governments for their subjects) against violations of international law directed against a foreign, or even a belligerent flag. He chose the latter course. It led to war in 1917 when Germany, with unrestricted submarine warfare, challenged his stand.

First crusade for world peace. Once in the conflict, Wilson tried to turn the war into an American crusade for world peace through collective security rather than through the "forever discredited" system of the balance of power. After the victory, after restoration of the balance of power in Europe, after the settlement of the problems of the Pacific and Far East by the Washington Conference—in short, when everything seemed safe again in North America and in the New World—the United States turned its back on Woodrow Wilson's League of Nations. The Republic reverted to the traditional isolation of its continental position. No political party again dared to stand on a League of Nations' platform. It did not seem essential to the security of the United States.

The "Washington Period," 1922–37

We may appropriately designate as the "Washington Period" the fifteen years of apparently perfect continental security that followed the Washington Conference of 1922. During this period Secretary of State Kellogg concluded the Pact of Paris (1928) outlawing war as an instrument of national policy. "Even without this treaty," the Secretary rhetorically asked the Senate Committee on Foreign Relations while defending the Pact, "does anybody believe that the present governments of Europe are in any position to attack any one of the South American countries and impose their form of government upon them?"

A five-point pattern of foreign policy. During the Washington Period, under the influence of a historiography of disillusionment, American foreign policy crystallized out of Mahan's three-point formula into a five-point pattern: isolation, anti-imperialism, disarmament, neutrality, and pacifism.

1. ISOLATION. Isolation was confirmed by the refusal of the United States to enter into

the League of Nations or to have anything to do even with its judicial organ, the Court of International Justice.

2. LIQUIDATION OF IMPERIALISM. The inherent anti-imperialism of the American people reasserted itself in a liquidation of the protectorates in the Caribbean and Central America. By the Clark Memorandum on the Monroe Doctrine (1929) the Department of State formally repudiated the "Corollary" of Theodore Roosevelt, which had sanctioned the Caribbean interventions. President Franklin D. Roosevelt perfected this non-interference policy and christened it with the happy appellation of the Good Neighbor. It was signalized by conclusion of a number of multilateral pacts with the other American republics elaborating a system of peace without the sanction of force, through conciliation, arbitration, and good will: the Inter-American System. Henceforth, the keystone of the system was the doctrine of non-intervention: "It is inadmissible for any one state to intervene directly or indirectly, or for whatever reason, in the internal or external affairs of any American state" (1936).

Another feature of the American policy of anti-imperialism was the Philippine Independence Act of 1934 (consummated on July 4, 1946), and the manifestation of a disposition to get out of the back yard as well as the front yard of European politics, that is, to withdraw from any active diplomacy in the Far East as well as in Europe. The United States did not lift a finger of resistance when Japan conquered Manchuria in 1931, later moved into North China, and finally began the conquest of all China in 1937. All it did was to join with the League of Nations in ineffectual pronouncements against the use of force. It was apparent that the Hay Policy was going by default into the diplomatic dump-heap; the American people were unwilling to use force to maintain the integrity of China and the Open Door. In fact, at that time they did not possess adequate or organized force, even had they been willing to use it.

3. DISARMAMENT. The policy of disarmament was unmistakably reflected in several ways: (1) in the demobilization of the victorious American army and the reduction by 1930 of standing forces to a total of 137,645 men and officers (plus 182,700 in the loosely organized National Guard); (2) in persistent efforts to further international disarmament on land and sea; and (3) in naval disarmament *by example*. At the time of the breakdown of international naval limitation in 1935 the most to which the United States aspired was a "treaty ratio by 1942."

4. NEUTRALITY. The policy of neutrality appeared in the legislation of 1935–39. In the foreshadow of a new European war, Congress, pressed on by the powerful historiography of disillusionment, completely repudiated the policy of Woodrow Wilson during World War I. The new neutrality laws one by one outlawed the issues that had brought the United States into that conflict. They all but renounced the ancient "American birthright" of freedom of the seas.

All these precautions, designed to keep the United States out of the next war, only served the Pickwickian purpose of keeping it out of the last war—a war that had already been fought and won, and the victory thrown away. The new legislation conveyed the impression to Germany and to Japan and to the would-be world power, Italy, that never again would the United States go to war to preserve the balance of power in the Old World. It thus incited them to aggression under the persuasion that next time their intended victims could not get succor and support from across the ocean.

5. PACIFISM. Inherent pacifism and anti-imperialism were the taproots of the entire foreign-policy program. The people of the United States desired peace because they already had what they wanted in the world. Pacifism permeated public opinion, through the schools, the pulpit, and the press. The preachers and the teachers and the editorial propagandists of peace excoriated our munitions-makers as "merchants of death," and nearly drove them out of existence, to weaken further the military potential of the nation. In the colleges young men were taking solemn oaths on May Day never to fight in another war, or at least never to fight on any soil other than that of their own country. Pacifism was another invitation to programs of aggression outside the New World.

Such was American foreign policy on the eve of Munich.

The United States and World War II

Germany again threatens the balance of power in Europe. During the thirties Germany, defeated and disarmed in 1918, was allowed to rise once more under Hitler. As a result, the European war had to be fought over again. In advance the United States proclaimed its intention to stay out, adopting the alternative of neutral policy that Wilson had rejected in 1914. Franklin D. Roosevelt proclaimed neutrality, according to law, but, avowedly, not according to the sympathies of his countrymen. But the neutrality laws did not keep the United States out of the new war. The balance of power in Europe and in the world, destroyed diplomatically at Munich in 1938, was overthrown in a military way during 1940 by the German conquest of Denmark, Norway, the Low Countries, and France. The island of Great Britain seemed next on the program, but Hitler made the fatal mistake of first attempting to destroy Russia. Meanwhile (September 27, 1940) he made a triple alliance with Japan and Italy to make war together if any one were attacked by an outside power, meaning, of course, the United States.

THE GREATEST PERIL IN AMERICAN HISTORY. It was apparent to anyone who stopped to consider carefully, that if Germany defeated Great Britain and seized the British fleet, Hitler could then organize the sea power, air power, and man power of Europe for an irresistible attack on the New World and the United States from the Atlantic, while Japan attacked from the Pacific. The pacifistic United States faced the greatest peril of its history. It became a matter of life or death to protect England against German conquest from continental Europe, and the British Empire against demolition by Japan in the Pacific. Notwithstanding the pledges of both major parties and their candidates, in the national election of 1940, to keep the United States out of Europe's wars, American neutrality, already shaken by the initial impact of the war, broke down completely in 1941.

THE COLLAPSE OF AMERICAN NEUTRALITY. Faced by the appalling crisis, President Roosevelt on his own responsibility sent arms to Britain. He also gave the British fifty destroyers out of the United States Navy in exchange for American naval and air bases in British possessions of the western Atlantic: in Newfoundland, Bermuda, the Bahamas, Jamaica, Antigua, Santa Lucia, Trinidad; and Georgetown, in British Guiana, on the northern coast of South America. These bases were the citadels long needed for the defense of the Atlantic Coast of the Continental Republic and its Isthmian lifeline. The Lend-Lease Act passed by Congress on March 11, 1941, overrode the neutrality acts of 1935, 1937, and 1939. It confirmed the President's policy of making the United States an "arsenal of democracy" for the defense of Great Britain and the British Empire. From the export, both private and public, of arms, ammunition, and implements of warfare to Great Britain, it was only a step to convoy, and from that only a step to shooting.

An undeclared war with Germany had commenced on the Atlantic Ocean by the autumn of 1941. On November 17, 1941, Congress repealed the most essential features yet remaining in the neutrality acts. Meanwhile a conscription act was passed, and the General Staff engaged in putting the nation on a war basis as rapidly as possible. Competent military authority had estimated in the autumn of 1940 that it would take at least two years to prepare to fight the war with a reasonable prospect of success. In the meantime it was necessary, at all costs, to bolster Great Britain and the British Empire, and (after June 22, 1941) Soviet Russia.

Japan overthrows the balance of power in Asia. What about the other war: the Japanese War on the other ocean? Up until 1940 the people of the United States were unwilling to resort to other than peaceful means for the preservation of the Open Door and the integrity of China. That attitude was apparent ever since Japan had torn up the Washington treaties in 1931 (conquest of Manchuria), 1934 (withdrawal from naval limitations), and 1937 (attack on China Proper). In 1941 the United States was loaning money and aviation personnel and sending military supplies to China to help in her defense against Japanese conquest. It was a challenging absence of American neutrality in the undeclared war that had been going on in the Far East since 1937. The United States was now championing not only the integrity of China, but also the integrity of French Indo-China, of British Malaya, and of the Netherlands East Indies, not to mention the Philippine Islands.

A TREMENDOUS HISTORICAL QUESTION. How does one reconcile the new American action in Asia with the traditional feeling that no vital interests in the fate of China required us to fight for its preservation? The answer to this question is that Japanese conquests in Asia were now threatening to break up the very British Empire that the United States was trying to keep intact, for its own security, in Europe. Japan, by the Triple Alliance of 1940, had stepped out of the distant Far East into the Atlantic area of American vital interests.

ROOSEVELT'S MOMENTOUS DECISION. Franklin D. Roosevelt decided to risk a war simultaneously with Japan and the European Axis powers rather than permit Japanese conquests to extend to Singapore, India, and Australia. This further expansion by Japan would have destroyed the British Empire in the Pacific while the United States was striving to preserve it in the Atlantic. In order to unite the people of the country he was willing to chance a "glancing blow" from Japan by insisting that her conquests in China and Indo-China be given up, and that she enter into an understanding with the United States. The latter was to be based on the inter-American principles of nonintervention and the peaceful settlement of international disputes, and on nondiscrimination economically. Instead of a "glancing blow" at the Philippines, the United States suffered a direct hit in the solar plexus at Pearl Harbor on December 7, 1941, the greatest humiliation in American history. But it united the American people in the formal war—that double war which was the nightmare of students of American foreign policy.

The United Nations. When war came, a world alliance of the United Nations against the Triple Alliance followed promptly. It invoked the hopes and aspirations for human freedom and self-government as currently expressed in the Anglo-American Atlantic Charter (August 14, 1941). Thanks to the policy of the Good Neighbor, the Latin American nations successively (Argentina not until 11:59½ o'clock) declared war against the enemies of the United States, huddling for security under the wings of the Colossus of the North (see the map on this page). They granted the strategical bases that made possible the defense of the Panama Canal from a hostile attack by land or sea and the defense of South America against a possible German

WAR DECLARATIONS AGAINST AXIS POWERS BY LATIN
AMERICAN REPUBLICS

jump-off from the western bulge of Africa. Brazil sent an expeditionary force to Italy, and gradually took over the patrol of the western South Atlantic against German submarines.

The Atomic Age

Disappearance of two world powers and rise of another. The complete victory of the United Nations followed a second tremendous phenomenon in the international firmament: the simultaneous extinction of two of the new world powers, Germany and Japan; the reduction of one old world power, France, from the position of world power to a second-rate European power; and the unexpected revival and speedy growth of a dormant world power, Russia. Victory created another new frame of world policy for the United States. It prevented the threatened encirclement of the New World. It annihilated the enemies' threat from either ocean. It left a grouping of only three world powers—the United States, Great Britain, and Soviet Russia—surging into the international vacuum created by the extinction of German and Japanese, not to mention the change in Italian, French, and Dutch, power.

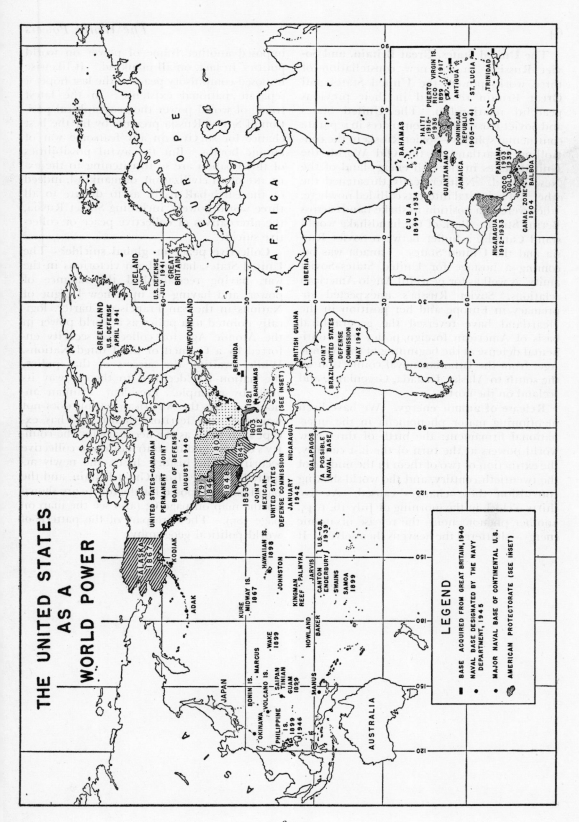

THE UNITED STATES
AS A
WORLD POWER

LEGEND

■ BASE ACQUIRED FROM GREAT BRITAIN, 1940

• NAVAL BASE DESIGNATED BY THE NAVY
  DEPARTMENT, 1945

● MAJOR NAVAL BASE OF CONTINENTAL U.S.

▨ AMERICAN PROTECTORATE (SEE INSET)

The United States, Great Britain, and Soviet Russia. In the new constellation of three world powers the United States and Great Britain remained in their previous peaceful relationship. The United States and Soviet Russia took their places in separate continental spheres—Soviet Russia in the controlling Heartland of the Old World, the United States in the rich energy-land of the New World. Neither really threatened the other. Their vital interests collided nowhere. They were in a position to shake hands across Bering Strait. Back of the handshake would stand Canada, a buffer between Soviet Russia and the United States. Canada was becoming a hostage for United States–Soviet amity, as well as for peaceful Anglo-American relations. Soviet Russia's unexpected supremacy in Europe and her position in the Heartland have reversed the geographical basis of American foreign policy and continental defense at the beginning of the Atomic Age: from the Isthmian naval connection on the south to Alaska, Canada, Greenland, and Iceland on the north.

Release of atomic energy. We have been mentioning major phenomena in the international firmament: the birth of three new world powers at the turn of the last century, the extinction of two of them in the middle of the twentieth century, and the world-shaking convulsion these changes caused. At five thirty o'clock in the morning of July 16, 1945, another phenomenon—the release of atomic energy—shattered the heavens themselves. It imposed another frame of power on world politics, in fact, on all mankind. It likewise imposed compulsory peace as the last hope of separate national existence. In the latest frame of world power the geographical position of Soviet Russia presents by far the best chance for survival in any fearsome war of atomic bombs. But the awful possibilities of this weapon are so threatening to the existence of all civilization, of mankind, indeed of the earth-ball itself, as to dictate to all three world powers, including Soviet Russia, the alternatives of collective peace or collective suicide.

Collective peace or global suicide? The United States, having been victorious in the war, having reestablished the balance of power, and having set up a new League of Nations in the San Francisco Charter, logically pointed to a policy as a world power in the Atomic Age for collective security enforced by a Council of the United Nations. While awaiting the success of that policy, the nation has declined to throw away its arms by example. President Truman announced that the American nation does not want any more territory than it now has, except such bases as are necessary for the country's defense and its contribution to collective security. The historic bases, the newly acquired war bases from Great Britain, and the naval bases proposed for the future are shown on the map on page 63 (also see the map on page 385). They are part of the pattern of world political geography.

CHAPTER 6

The Soviet Union:
A Land-Mass Power

AMONG the most significant results of World War II is the emergence of the Soviet Union as an undisputed and indisputable major power.* Whatever doubts existed in the pre-1939 period as to the strength of the Union of Soviet Socialist Republics among international powers were entirely removed between 1942 and 1945. The U.S.S.R. has come to the fore as the new great power, utilizing hitherto latent potentialities to emerge as a powerful state and shaking the other nations by her show of unexpected might. Therefore, if postwar problems are to be understood, it becomes imperative to know the geopolitical foundations upon which Soviet power rests.

This chapter purports to determine, analyze, and evaluate the internal geopolitical elements upon which the Soviet Union must maintain its new status.** However, within a single chapter only the major elements can be considered. Unfortunately the Soviet Union has provided neither the rest of the world nor its own people with any superabundance of factual data.† The prewar years are replete with exaggerations, omissions, and contradictions; the war years provide very scant statistical data of any variety. In quantity, material on and about Russia is far from lacking, but useful, authentic data are difficult to obtain. It may be that the controlling forces of the Soviet government have been too secretive in the dissemination of information, but the world-wide suspicion to which it has been subjected has fostered rather than diminished any original tendencies in this direction. As a result, non-Russian criteria and inadequate data must be utilized in any analysis, thus restricting the development of fundamental conclusions to the realm of generalizations.

As pointed out in Chapter 1, under "Factors of Powerhood," a number of prerequisites are essential if any country is to become a major power (see text on pages 7–8). The U.S.S.R. now possesses most of these power requirements, many of them having been dormant within the country for a long period. Only in recent years did internal development succeed in changing potentialities into actualities. The igniting spark effecting this transition was the awakening of national consciousness among the hitherto heterogeneous peoples that now comprise the Union.

In the discussion of the elements of major powerhood (Chapter 1) no attempt is made to list them in the order of their importance. Further, it should be obvious that the extent to which they are to be found in the Soviet Union, or any other major power, is both relative and variable. In the first two elements—natural advantages and resources and a numerous, energetic population—the U.S.S.R. ranks exceedingly high among the countries of the world; four other elements—an advanced technology, capital goods and credit, balanced economic development, and

---

* The terms U.S.S.R. (Union of Soviet Socialist Republics), Soviet Union, and Soviet Russia are used interchangeably. The term Russia and its derivatives are used to designate the pre-Soviet country, or in a general rather than strictly political sense, for example, *Russian power*.

** For an analysis of the international position of the Soviet Union, see Chapter 7.

† See George B. Cressey, *The Basis of Soviet Strength* (McGraw-Hill, 1945), p. 125.

internal political stability—can be accredited to it only with qualifications; and in the case of three of the elements—friendly relationships with other countries, a common language and historical background, and freedom of religion, education, and press—the extent to which the Russians qualify is controversial, with the result that they are ranked in various ways. In any event an understanding of Soviet position and power must be based upon a knowledge of these elements as they apply. And the extent to which they are developed further by the Russians will determine the ability of the Soviet Union to maintain its new status as a major power.

Historical Development *

European phase. As a political entity the present Russian nation has been in existence for some eleven centuries. The first unification of the Slavic tribes was accomplished in western Russia by a Varangian (Swede) called Rurik. Permanent settlements were established along the rivers that became the principal traffic arteries, and the abundant furs of the region became the chief article of value. Unity proved difficult to maintain, and various factions quickly developed. From among the numerous settlements established there evolved two centers of importance: Moscow, which held the key position, and Kiev, which held the secondary. These two principalities, although frequently in conflict with each other, acquired considerable surrounding territory and became the foundation of modern Russia.

TARTARS. Into the midst of these early Slavic consolidations swept waves of Tartar invaders from the east. Establishing a Russian base for their other European operations, they became the dominant element of eastern Europe from 1224 to 1480, when their power was finally broken. The area-control exercised by the Tartars was far greater than anything that had been held by the previous princes. The invaders also imparted an Asiatic veneer to this region, which to this day has not been dispelled. Beyond this influence, however, Tartar contributions offered little to Russian development.

* For a more extensive treatment of the historical geography of Russia, see George T. Renner and Associates, *Global Geography* (Crowell, 1944), Chapter 29, by R. L. Tuthill.

THE ROMANOVS. It remained for the House of Romanov to establish Czarist Russia and for Ivan the Third (1462–1505) to break the Tartar control and establish modern Russia. After the Czardom of Muscovy was set up, expansion policies were inaugurated, which continued, with few setbacks, for almost five centuries.

Absorption of peripheral regions constituted an ever-present challenge to the Czars, and because of their central position in the great Eurasian land-mass, unconquered area was plentiful. Ivan the Terrible (1533–84) pressed eastward against the receding Tartar territory and also turned westward into Lithuania and Poland. Succeeding Czars battled their way south into the Ukraine, southwest toward the Balkans, southeast to the Caucasus, and eastward over the Urals. Of the Romanov Czars, Peter the Great (1682–1725) was the most influential. During his reign unification of large areas, which had previously been Russian in name only, became a reality; the troublesome Scandinavians on the west were defeated and the historic "window on the Baltic" was annexed; St. Petersburg (Leningrad) was built; and of greatest consequence, there began the long, slow assimilation of Western ideas brought about by the influx of European culture. This interest in the West was continued by Catherine II, both by the partitions of Poland (1772, 1793, 1795) and by her interest in the French literati. The successful invasions of Poland were Russia's first truly imperialistic ventures, establishing a precedent for the recent incursion. No significant natural boundaries were reached; the land has little economic value; and there was raised a problem that continues to plague international relations. In the south the Russians had long been thwarted in their attempts to gain a major foothold on the Black Sea, but Catherine succeeded in taking the Crimea from the Turks in 1783.

The eastward movement. Continued pressure toward the east was a natural development following the defeat of the Tartars. As a movement it was abetted by several circumstances, the most notable of which was the entrance of Russia into the competitive world fur markets. After expanding to the Volga River and then to the Ural Mountains, the Czarist government sponsored the establishment of fur-trading posts in Siberia. The movement was spear-headed by the Cossacks, an unassimilated group of nomadic brigands from the region of the Don River whom the Czars had pressured into quasi-military service. The Ural Mountains proved no more of a barrier than did the Appalachian Mountains in our own country. A Cossack named Yermak launched a successful expedition over the Urals into Siberia in 1581, and within sixty-five years (1646) the entire continental expanse had been traversed. Again, as in the case of our own continent, the great rivers (the Ob, Yenisei, and Lena) and their tributaries were followed and drainage basins claimed by the Czar, though he had no concept of the tremendous size of the area involved.

As the Cossacks pressed eastward, Russian colonists, convicts, and escaped serfs followed slowly.* Even the Pacific Ocean, when it had been reached, failed to halt the movement. The wealth of fur to be had, first from the North Pacific islands, then from Alaska, and finally from our own Northwest, beckoned the Russian trappers onward. By 1840 the movement had overreached itself with colonies in northern California. The distance from Moscow was much too great at that time, and adequate controls from the government center could not be maintained. American and British competition grew to the point of friction, and a withdrawal was in order. With the sale of Alaska to the United States government in 1867, Russia's venture into North America ended, and thereafter a period of contraction on the Asiatic mainland was inaugurated.

The Russian Czars showed little active concern with their vast eastern domain. As the supply of immediately convertible, luxury resources declined, their interest waned. The basic resources of minerals, forests, and soils remained dormant and unexplored, and undernourishment and lack of capital goods and credit slowly undermined the unenlightened monarchy with its medieval system. So, with the Revolution of 1917, the Czarist realm disintegrated; each of the Nationalist groups initiated its own policies and re-unification became the first major problem of the Bolshevik Soviets.

* Hans von Eckardt, *Russia* (Knopf, 1932), p. 243. Population of Siberia: 1858, 4,000,000; 1897, 5,600,000.

Continentality of Russia

Of all geopolitical factors applicable to Soviet Russia those of continental size and location are the most fundamental. The U. S. S. R. is by far the largest single nation of the world. It occupies approximately one sixth of the earth's land surface, a total of more than eight and one-quarter million square miles. Such a huge area is difficult to conceive, for here is a country approximately the size of the entire North American continent. Although confined to the northern hemisphere, it stretches east and west almost halfway around the world. Great circle distances of over 5,000 miles can be traversed entirely within Russian territory.

The Soviet Union also constitutes about one third of the Eurasian land-mass—roughly, the northern third, for it stretches from the Bering Sea to the eastern half of Europe. Even more important is its centralized location in the midst of the land hemisphere. Such a world position has been considered by many political geographers as close to the ideal geopolitical location.* It must be noted, however, that Russia's location has not thus far been an unmixed blessing. This great expanse of generally undeveloped territory lies betwixt two great civilizations—the Oriental and Western European. For centuries pressures have been exerted on both the eastern and the western flanks of Russia, and in turn even greater pressures have been exerted in the opposite direction by the Russians. From an original European base we have seen how these internal pressures expanded control to the present great dimensions of the Soviet Union. It now remains to analyze this extensive territory.

The territorial limits of Soviet Russia have become generally delineated. The Arctic Ocean on the north, the Pacific Ocean on the east, and the great Himalaya chain together with the Turkestan deserts, the Caucasus Mountains, and the Caspian and Black seas on the south have provided natural boundaries to which, in the main, the Russians have adhered. Certain of these boundaries have been circumvented or temporarily breached and may be again. For obvious reasons this land-mass power has constantly, but as yet with inadequate success, sought

* This is the Mackinder "Heartland" theory.

access to the major oceanic trade lanes. Here again, central land-mass location has proved to be an inhibiting factor.

On the other side of the ledger for continentality may be listed many significant factors. Because of its great size, the large and rapidly increasing population of the Soviet Union has more than enough *Lebensraum,* or space for living. Size and location allow for great climatic diversity, which ranges through the various subtypes from semitropical to polar. A great variety may also be found in topography, soils, and in faunal and floral forms, further enhancing the national economy. In addition, a centralized location has enabled the Russians to draw selectively from both Oriental and European developments of all types.

To weld this huge area into a single nation has been a strenuous task; to hold it together will continue to be a problem. Transportation, which must constitute one of the chief bonds by which the component parts of the union are held together, is now inadequate. Over these millions of square miles the industrial potential must be so synthesized as to evoke economic unity. Throughout this land-mass must be engendered and maintained a single national consciousness. Thus, the continentality of the U. S. S. R. both facilitates and hinders Soviet development at one and the same time.

Internal Political Structure

The Czars, in spite of their long regimes and complete autocratic power, never were able to develop their vast domain into a first-rate power. In the eyes of the world the prestige of Soviet power has been conferred only by its achievements during the recent war. Undoubtedly credit for this achievement should go to the dynamic political and social system inaugurated by the Bolshevik Revolution in 1917 as well as to the natural environmental factors that made the feat possible.

The Czarist Empire collapsed completely in March of 1917. The radical Bolshevik revolutionary faction succeeded in taking over the government in November of the same year, after the Kerensky Government failed to gain the confidence of the Russian people. Bolshevik leaders realized that, if the new movement was to survive and carry out its unique economic and social theories, it must first reorganize the political structure in such a way as to reunite the many pieces into which the country had disintegrated. Actual reunion was accomplished by military force, although ostensibly it was achieved by a series of agreements entered into by the revolutionary governments of the various major regions. During the years from 1918 to 1940 a victorious Soviet Russia evolved from a defeated Czarist Russia.

Modern political units. Two principles were to be observed in the formation of the new union: first, autonomy for the numerous ethnological groups was to be maintained, and, second, economic regionalism was to be observed where it existed and established where it did not exist. With these two principles in mind the general political structure was established. A single national entity was derived from a union of the various nationalities into a supranational state known as the Union of Soviet Socialist Republics. Within the union the nationality principle was recognized by the establishment of major and minor territorial subdivisions conform-

Major Political Units of the U. S. S. R.

(Areas and estimated population as of mid-1941)

Name	Population	Area in square miles
1. Armenian Soviet Socialist Republic	1,346,709	11,580
2. Azerbaidzhan S. S. R.	3,372,794	33,200
3. Byelorussian S. S. R.	10,525,511	89,350
4. Estonia S. S. R.	1,120,000	18,050
5. Georgian S. S. R.	3,722,252	26,874
6. Karelo-Finnish S. S. R.	892,977	75,656
7. Kazakh S. S. R.	6,458,175	1,059,700
8. Kirghiz S. S. R.	1,533,439	75,950
9. Latvian S. S. R.	1,950,502	24,700
10. Lithuanian S. S. R.	3,134,070	22,800
11. Moldavian S. S. R.	2,321,225	13,680
12. Russian S. F. S. R.	114,337,428	6,322,350
13. Tadzhik S. S. R.	1,560,540	55,545
14. Turkmen S. S. R.	1,317,693	171,250
15. Ukrainian S. S. R.	42,272,943	202,540
16. Uzbek S. S. R.	6,601,619	146,000
Total	202,467,877	8,349,225

"The Soviet Union Today," *The American Russian Institute,* 1945, p. 10. Slight increases or decreases in area have taken place for some republics during the intervening years since this table was compiled. However, these changes, which have also affected the population figures, are relatively inconsequential.

ing to the ethnological pattern. The major divisions were designated either as Soviet Federated Socialist Republics or Soviet Socialist Republics (see the map on this page), and in turn these were further subdivided

been established since 1939.* The Polish acquisition of 1939 was incorporated as part of the Ukrainian and Byelorussian (White Russian) republics. The three Baltic states of Estonia, Latvia, and Lithuania were incor-

U. S. S. R.
MAJOR POLITICAL DIVISIONS

into oblasts, okrugs, krais, raions, and other units of a more local character. The minor national subdivisions, designated as Autonomous Soviet Republics and Autonomous Areas or Regions, were also internally subdivided in a manner similar to that of the major units.

Based upon the continued exercise of this principle, there are now sixteen major republics. Of these sixteen republics five have

porated as republics in the U. S. S. R. on August 3, 1940. Located between the power drives of the Germans and the Russians, they enjoyed independence only from 1920 to 1939. In 1934 they formed a Baltic Entente.

Integration of political units. The names of the various republics in the above table show the influence of nationality as the guid-

* Estonian, Karelo-Finnish, Latvian, Lithuanian, and Moldavian Soviet Socialist republics.

ing principle in the delineation of the major Soviet political units. Some fifteen other ethnic groups have been sufficiently strong to gain individual political equality with the Great Russians, who are the dominant population element both of the Russian S. F. S. R. and the U. S. S. R. This recognition and acceptance of national autonomy was the keystone to initial Soviet success. It is possible to be a Ukrainian or a Georgian or a Turkmenian and also be a Russian. Each of the republics warrants autonomy by virtue of an adequate population, homogeneity, and distinctiveness of culture. The great size of the U. S. S. R. enables each group to live with a minimum of territorial impingement upon its neighbors. Only the Great Russians and their kinsmen have spread widely over the U. S. S. R., and in the regions east of the Urals even these peoples have lost many of their original ties and have begun to develop a more cosmopolitan culture and economy. Yet it may be noted that natural environmental factors have facilitated the segregation process. The rugged Caucasus Mountains not only isolate the Georgians, Abkhasians, Armenians, and other nationalities of this general area from the Slavs, but also from each other; the Ukrainians continue to inhabit their plains; the Kirghiz, Turkmenians, and other nomadic tribes remain on the central Asiatic steppes; and the Uzbeks continue to live in the southern deserts. In recognition of this ethnic problem the Bolsheviks proposed, organized, and established a federation structure that united all of the national groups into a single nation without sacrificing traditional cultures or disrupting the local pattern of life. This was a major accomplishment.

Each republic is now represented in the supranational governing body known as the Supreme Soviet of the U. S. S. R.* This Supreme Soviet has two parts: the Council of Nationalities, where each republic has equal representation; and the Council of the Union, where representation is based upon population.** It is the general maintenance of this political structure with all of its subdivisions and intricacies that has enabled the economic and social revolution to carry out its func-

* Called the All-Union Congress of Soviets before 1936.
** See the 1936 Constitution of the U. S. S. R.

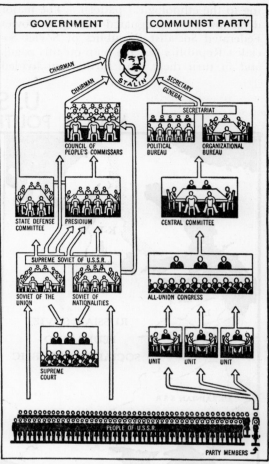

As stated in the 1936 Soviet Constitution, the USSR is a federal union of independent republics. The highest body is the Supreme Soviet (see chart), which holds exclusive legislative power. Its two chambers, which have equal rights, are elected for 4 years: the Soviet of the Union, chosen according to population, and the Soviet of Nationalities, chosen according to the regional and national divisions. The Presidium, elected by the two Chambers, convenes and dissolves the Supreme Soviet, interprets laws, arranges elections, rescinds decisions of the People's Commissars (now called Ministers), governs the high command of the armed forces, declares mobilization or a state of war, ratifies treaties, and appoints and recalls the country's foreign representatives. During the second World War the 8 members of the State Defense Committee, with Stalin as chairman, served as a war cabinet and held all government power in their hands. The administrative functions of government reside in the Council of People's Commissars, appointed by the Presidium and subject to removal by that body or the Supreme Soviet. The Council has a number of important and varied executive and supervisory duties. The Supreme Court is elected by the Supreme Soviet. As the Communists allow no organized opposition at the polls, the government is merely the agent of the Communist party. (Courtesy *Life*).

tions, even though most of the elaborate schemes have cut across the established ethnographical and national boundaries.*

LANGUAGE AND RELIGION. Quite naturally the many different languages spoken by the large number of ethnological groups in the republics of the U. S. S. R. compounded the problem of political integration. Nevertheless, the Soviet government encouraged retention of the traditional languages used by the inhabitants in each of the autonomous units. In this respect, as with native customs, dress, and literatures, the Communists regarded their continuance as a valuable phase in the task of winning united support for the federation. Though Russian is usually taught in the schools as an accessory to each native language, it is not compulsory in all regions. However, because of the prestige enjoyed by the Russian language, it has gained despite this nationalist emphasis.

Before the Bolshevik Revolution the Greek Orthodox Church was the state religion. Not only were there previously millions of dissenters but many others who opposed it solely because it functioned as part of the hated Czarist regime. After the Communist leaders, who were atheists, had achieved power, they disestablished the Church and appropriated considerable of its property. In time, however, this attitude softened, and today all religions are tolerated. Nevertheless, religion has only mild support; and among the younger generation, many of whom accept the Marxian philosophy, which precludes religion, the number of believers is small.

Internal Economic Structure

The Russian Revolution of 1917 was probably the most significant event in European history since the French Revolution at the end of the eighteenth century. In many respects it was a complete revolution—political, economic, and social. As the various experiments got underway, the movement gained increasingly popular support. It inaugurated a new era of exploration that is still going on. It reopened to investigation and experimentation every phase of Russian living. It threw open the natural environment of the entire country to planned investigation and experimentation, with results that

were revolutionary in themselves. Of even greater importance, all new experiments were conducted according to pre-established plans approved by the government. This application of planning on a national scale is of major significance.

Economic planning. Analysis of internal accomplishments during the past twenty-eight years indicates that more startling changes have been effected in the field of economic planning and experimentation than in either the political or social realms. The political structure, whether judged by the 1936 Constitution or by current events, includes only minor ideological innovations. Several of the major experiments initiated by the Communists in religion and social living already have been abandoned. The social changes that have taken place are significant mainly to the Russians and not to the world.

The Soviet Union has achieved its greatest successes in the field of economics, and its innovations have attracted world-wide attention. The initial step taken by the Communist leaders was the elimination of the capitalistic system and the establishment of government control and/or ownership. The low economic level of the Russian masses made this step feasible without serious upheavals or opposition except in the case of agricultural landownership, where a compromise was eventually reached. The temporary reversion toward capitalism that took place under the New Economic Policy eventually proved unacceptable to the Communist leaders. In consequence, after the death of Lenin, who had supported the compromises, there followed the inauguration of a series of tremendous experiments according to preconceived plans known as the *Gosplan*. Various proposals designed to reconstruct the national economy were carried out according to a series of five-year schedules, the first initiated in 1928, the second in 1933, and the third in 1938.

No phase of the country's social and economic life was left uncovered: electrification, light and heavy industries, agriculture, transportation, mail, communication, consumers' cooperatives, labor, public instruction, scientific research, health protection and social life, housing, and finance.* As a result of the

* See Eckardt, *op. cit.*, p. 459.

* Harry W. Laidler, *Social-Economic Movements* (Crowell, 1944), chapter 26.

campaign for compulsory school education, the literacy average for the country, which in 1897 was 24 per cent, reached 81.2 per cent in 1939, and with continued emphasis should go even higher. Plans were made for new techniques in agriculture, animal husbandry, mineral exploration, manufacturing, transportation and improved methods of utilizing all available resources. Great industrial combines were formed, tremendous collective and state farms were organized, arctic and desert agricultural experiments were inaugurated, new mineral areas were surveyed, air routes were projected to regions where no other transportation existed, and the resettlement of hundreds of thousands of people was planned. And these were but a few of the projects put into effect.

Never before had such large-scale, fundamental enterprises been undertaken at one time by any state. Progress was steady throughout the three five-year plans (starting in 1928), and it is certain that the interruption by World War II has been a source of much concern to the Russian people, who by 1938 could see many signs of real advancement. Despite the lack of factual statistical data by the Soviet government as proof of the claims of progress made, it is now evident to the world that Russian economic accomplishments were far greater than usually conceded. Even the astute German intelligence system seems to have underrated the Soviet economic position.

Soviet agriculture. During the last Czarist period agriculture was the chief economic activity, whereas industry played a very secondary role. Approximately half of the land was owned by either the nobility or the clergy, and the other half belonged to a relatively few wealthy landowners or to peasant communal groups. No more than serfs, the peasant workers constituted the great majority of the population. For the most part Russian agriculture was confined to the area west of the Urals. Agricultural specialization was largely limited to concentration on cash crops from which the peasant received no return. Considerable land-poverty resulted from forest "mining" and the plowing up of pasture land.

Although farming is now widespread throughout the Soviet Union, large-scale agriculture is most highly developed in a huge,

irregular triangle of land, the base extending from the Baltic to the Black Seas and the apex being at Lake Baikal. This area, on which has been developed one of the great cereal-producing regions, coincides with the largest belt of fertile *blackerth* soil in the world. There are also important agricultural tracts in Middle Asia and in the Caucasus areas.

REGIONAL DISTRIBUTION. The great size of the U. S. S. R. permits a diversified agricultural pattern on an enormous scale. In the European section of the Russian S. F. S. R. and in the Ukraine, grains, sugar beets, potatoes, and flax are the principal products. In the Caucasus, particularly on the north slopes between the Kuban and Don rivers, grains, fruit, livestock, rice, and cotton are the major crops; and along the Black and Caspian seacoasts there are tea, wine grape, citrus fruit, and some mulberry tree culture. In the Kazakh S. S. R. livestock farming holds a prominent position, and great emphasis has been placed upon dry-farming. Extensive and successful efforts have produced rich, irrigated farmland in the Middle Asian republics of Turkmen, Uzbek, and Tadzhik; although fruits of all kinds are grown, cotton of high yield is the main crop. The Ferghana Valley in Uzbek has been compared favorably with our own Imperial Valley as a major irrigation project. In Siberia the area extending north of the Trans-Siberian Railway from the Urals to Lake Baikal is devoted to grains, livestock, and dairying. In grain production this region ranked close to the Ukraine in 1938 and during the war became the chief Russian source. The Urals have also increased their production of the same products that are found in the Siberian area. The Far Eastern Provinces also produce a variety of agricultural commodities but chiefly for their own consumption. Grains, livestock, fruits, and vegetables make up the principal items.

AGRICULTURAL OBJECTIVES. To evaluate this agricultural productivity requires an examination of the Soviet agricultural aims as set forth in the *Gosplan*. The Russians planned (1) to develop their agriculture in such a way as to complement the proposed industrial development, (2) to utilize and master new agricultural techniques, (3) to increase the amount of arable land and the productivity of the existing land, (4) to increase the profitableness of farming, and (5) to consolidate agriculture. The results, as they are now known, show a development far beyond anything achieved under the Czars. In the establishment of economic regionalism, agriculture has been decentralized and diversified to accompany the development of new industrial regions and make them as self-sustaining as possible. Agricultural education has taught peasants to use tractors, to rotate crops, to study soils, and to select the best seeds. Scientific irrigation, dry-farming, and arctic agriculture are also being taught.

Between 1914 and 1940 the amount of arable land increased from 262,455,000 to 373,217,000 acres.* In addition, the productivity of existing farm lands and the value of crops have been tremendously increased. The use of virgin land, drainage of marshlands, and the practice of irrigation have been major factors in increasing acreage, but more scientific farming with consequent increased yields will tend to stabilize, if not actually result in a reduction in, the amount of land now under cultivation.

Techniques to achieve objectives. To facilitate these many changes the Communist leaders have evolved a system of agricultural collectivization. Farms are of two types: the collective farm, called *kolkhoz,* and the much larger state farm, called *sovkhoz.* At first an attempt was made to force all peasant farmers into one or the other of these two types, but rebellion broke out; now educational procedures and economic advantages have replaced force. In 1938 more than a million independent farmers cultivated approximately two and one-half million acres, but this area constituted less than one per cent of the total crop acreage.

The *kolkhoz* is a farm cooperative, averaging about seventy-five families, in which are pooled its resources. Such an organization is designed to eliminate the anathema of private property. On these farms machinery is for the most part rented from the government, the rent being paid in produce. Fixed quantities of each product must be sold to the government. After all expenses, including taxes, are paid, the remaining products and cash income go to the members in proportion to the type of work done and the amount of time invested. The law requires each member to work from 100 to 150 days

* Cressey, *op. cit.,* p. 139.

for the *kolkhoz;* the rest of the year he may work for himself. Incentives to increase collective working are numerous, and in 1939 there were approximately 242,000 of these collective farms.

By comparison there are but few *sovkhozes,* for they numbered slightly less than 4,000 in 1939. Of tremendous size, they are similar to government experimental farms in the United States. In Russia the *sovkhozes* have an organization comparable to the industrial soviets and employ their laborers just as do the manufacturing enterprises. For the most part they concern themselves with the production of high-quality seeds, the scientific breeding of livestock, and the development of specialized farming methods. They cultivate approximately ten per cent of the crop lands.

HANDICAPS AND ACHIEVEMENTS. Soviet agriculture faces a number of handicaps that cannot be solved by collectivism. Despite its great area, much of Russia's land is worthless. Large areas are too cold for cultivation, others too dry, and still others mountainous, infertile, or inaccessible. For the most part these inhospitable areas are beyond the limits of modern pioneering techniques. Good agricultural land, however, covers approximately a million square miles and enables the U. S. S. R. to be rated as one of the great agricultural countries of the world.

Soviet industry. As has been previously stated, development of the Soviet industrial potential was to be accomplished according to pre-established plans. These five-year plans fixed the objectives toward which all industrial activity must strive; set up specific criteria by which progress was to be measured; and formulated fantastic minimum quotas for Soviet workers to meet. The aim of converting decadent Czarist industry into modern competitive industry was in itself a tremendous undertaking; to do it on the time schedule as planned was impossible. Yet the workers have labored with great energy and zeal, and their accomplishments have been many.

INDUSTRIAL OBJECTIVES. In its proposals for industrial development the *Gosplan* set forth specific aims comparable with those advanced for agriculture. They may be summarized as follows: (1) to increase industrial output in proportion to population; (2) to increase the public wealth and advance social welfare;

(3) to advance the economic status of the nonindustrial populations; (4) to insure economic independence of the U. S. S. R.; (5) to evolve a more rational development and distribution of various types of industry; (6) to enable the modernization and collectivization of agriculture; (7) to reconstruct and reorganize the old industrial enterprises; and (8) to facilitate the development of self-sufficient economic regionalism throughout the U. S. S. R.

MINERAL RESOURCES. When the Czarist regime collapsed in 1917, there was little industry worth salvaging. In old Russia half of the country's industry was located in a triangular area with corners at Moscow, Gorki (Nizhni-Novgorod), and Leningrad (St. Petersburg). Another one fourth was located in Poland, and the remainder distributed through the Ukraine and the Urals. Feudalism had hindered any significant industrial growth as well as the accumulation of capital. The serfs had practically no buying power; resources had been skimmed for immediate profits; and there was much duplication of factories, with no regional distribution and no correlation of manufacturing and raw materials. Basically the Communists had to start from scratch. The planned economy, as developed by the Soviets, was supranational in scope; since the great majority had little or nothing to lose, the industrial proposals were quite readily accepted. However, new industrial developments could not be started until extensive, detailed surveys of raw materials had been made. The location and extent of these resources would determine both the location and the extent of the industries to be built. As Cressey has pointed out, such a planned economy is dependent upon the validity and adequacy of the basic resource inventories that are made.*

Industrialism, as presently constituted, is based upon metals and mineral fuels. More specifically, iron and steel and the minerals associated with their production were fundamental to the national industrial economy and economic regionalism proposed by the Soviets in the *Gosplan*. The quantity, quality, and distribution of these minerals determined the industrial pattern that had gradually become apparent. A summary of the Soviet resource position follows, but it must

* *Op. cit.*, pp. 126–127.

be constantly remembered that the industrial development is not restricted to commercially profitable resources, because such profitability is of no consequence within the Communist economic system. Unless this factor is taken into consideration, Soviet tabulations may be misleading.

By generalizing, it is possible to set up ten major regions of mineral resources: (1) the Kola Peninsula, in which there are large deposits of potash, nickel, and rare minerals; (2) the Moscow region, which has coal of inferior grade and iron ore deposits; (3) the Donbas (Don River) and Dnieper region, in which are some of the country's best deposits of coal, iron ore, and manganese; (4) the Ural region, considered the richest mountain range of its size in the world, which yields iron ore, manganese, copper, gold, platinum, asbestos, bauxite, chromite, nickel, potassium salts, and some low-grade coal; (5) the Caucasus region, in which are found manganese, lead, zinc, copper, and oil; (6) the Pamir and associated mountain region, little explored as yet, but known to be rich in minerals such as lead, zinc, and silver; (7) the Kazakhstan region, which contains coal, copper, manganese, tin, lead, and zinc; (8) the Kuznets region, from which are secured high-quality coal and, more recently discovered, small amounts of iron ore; (9) the Tunguska Plateau region, in which there are undeveloped coal fields in the north and some coal and manganese near Krasnoyarsk; and (10) the Far Eastern region, as yet only partially explored, which provides coal, iron ore, tin, gold, and the oil of Sakhalin Island. Despite immense intermediate areas that may be completely void of minerals, here is exceptional national wealth over a vast territory. Industrialism in the Soviet Union, as elsewhere, is predicated upon the ability to combine essential mineral ingredients; their mere existence does not insure their exploitation and development. The above enumeration of regions should be considered a very general, locative, rather than an economic, indicator of the Soviet mineral resource position.

Coal reserves. The 17th International Geological Congress (1937) estimated Soviet coal reserves as being in excess of one and one-half trillion tons, distributed through eighty-three fields from Moscow and the Donbas to Kamchatka. Approximately nine tenths of these reserves purportedly lie in Asia. In industrial importance, however, the Donbas, Karaganda, Kuznets, Ural, and Cheremkhovo (east of Irkutsk) coal fields are the leaders.

Iron ore reserves. Reserves of iron ore have been estimated at nearly ten billion tons, excluding certain known deposits as yet uncalculated. Krivoi Rog in the Ukraine and the Ural mountain area are the largest producers.

INDUSTRIAL REGIONS. The development of industrial regions is based primarily upon the strength of an iron and steel industry. In consequence, the brief mineral analysis given above furnishes the key to the industrial expansion and regional development promulgated by the five-year plans. There are now four major industrial regions and several minor ones in the U. S. S. R. In the major category are (1) the Moscow-Tula-Gorki triangle, (2) the eastern Ukraine, (3)

Oil reserves. Petroleum reserves were estimated in 1937 to be over six billion metric tons, with the greatest concentration in the Caucasus region. Grozny, Maikop, Baku, Krasnovodsk, and Sakhalin Island are all Russian place names associated with this industry. Unlike the coal reserves, most of the known petroleum is located west of the Urals. According to the U. S. Bureau of Mines, the U. S. S. R. is the second largest petroleum producer in the world and prior to World War II furnished about 80 per cent of the production of continental Europe and about 10 per cent of world production.

the Ural-Karaganda, and (4) the Kuznets industrial regions, all of which have witnessed the extensive development of heavy industry (see the map above here). Two of these, the Ural-Karaganda and the Kuznets regions, are entirely or in the main Communist developments, for during the Czarist period there was no real industrialization east of the Urals and only insignificant development within the Ural area itself. After 1933, greatly stimulated by the possibility of World War II, the normal trend for the location of industrial centers was toward the east. These new industrial empires within the U. S. S. R.

have shifted the country's economic balance, although how soon they will affect its economic position internationally cannot be predicted.*

Moscow-Tula-Gorki region. The importance of the Moscow-Tula-Gorki triangle as a manufacturing region is based primarily upon its historical development under the Czars and the existence of a large consuming population. The paucity and poor quality of natural resources in this region are limiting factors early recognized by the Communists. Although it will doubtlessly continue to be important as an industrial center, it will undoubtedly experience a restricted expansion and an inevitable decline in relative importance.

Eastern Ukraine region. Up to the time of German invasion, the eastern Ukraine

was the top industrial and metallurgical region of the Soviet Union. Possessing all the resources and facilities essential for an ideal production area it will probably be able to re-establish its pre-war pre-eminence.

In the eastern Ukraine iron ore is transported eastward by rail and sea to the Donets, and coal is carried west to the iron ore. Industrial cities in this region, such as Rostov, Stalino, Makeevka, Kharkov, Zaporozhe, Dnepropetrovsk, Mariupol, and Voroshilovsk, have become well-known (see the map on this page for major Russian cities). Further industrial expansion may well result in the inclusion of Kursk to the north and Stalingrad to the east as important cities in this region. In spite of the planned decentralization of industry, there is no reason at present for believing that Russian productivity in this region will be surpassed by that of any other.

Ural-Karaganda region. For several years

MAJOR CITIES OF THE UNION OF SOVIET SOCIALIST REPUBLICS

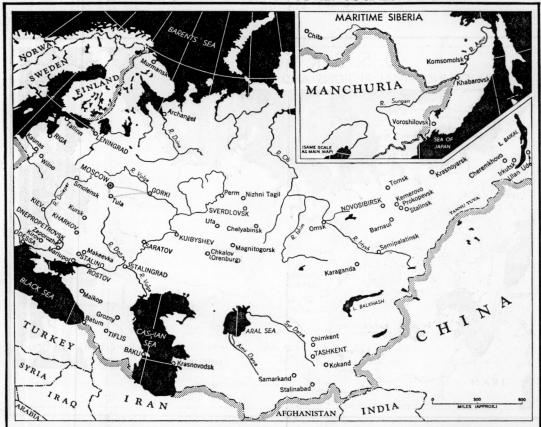

* C. I. Sulzberger, *The New York Times*, September 9, 1945, p. E5.

the Ural and Kuznets regions were considered together on the basis of the combine organized by the Soviet government to utilize their respective resources in a joint enterprise. The coupling of the regions was necessitated by the poor quality of the coal in the Ural area. Although the Kuznets coal was 1,200 miles to the east, a double-track railway carried it both to Chelyabinsk and Sverdlovsk. However, the discovery of coking coal at Karaganda, some 500 miles to the southeast of the Urals, changed the pattern. This discovery, plus the pressures of war production, led to the creation of the city of Karaganda (pop. 166,000) and its development as the major source of fuel for the Ural blast furnaces.*

Heavy manufacturing, as well as the existence of many minerals, has promoted this region to second rank in industrial importance in the Soviet Union. New cities have been developed and old towns have become new industrial centers. In the Ural region the following cities are of major importance: (1) Sverdlovsk (426,000), the center of Ural development; (2) Chelyabinsk (273,000), iron, steel, and tractors; (3) Molotov (Perm) (255,-000); (4) Ufa (246,000); (5) Nizhni Tagil (160,000), iron and steel; and (6) Magnitogorsk (146,000), newly created, iron and steel. The discovery and utilization of new resources, the central location, and increasingly good transportation make it evident that the Ural-Karaganda industrial region will increase in importance and contribute an even greater share to Soviet economic development.

The Kuznets Region. The most recent intensive industrial expansion has been around Kuznetsk (now called Stalinsk) and Novosibirsk. Here, as in the case of the Donbas and the Urals, are found the raw materials of heavy industry: coal, iron, manganese, and minor metals. Prior to 1920 the region contained no cities of importance, but the decision to utilize Kuznets coal for Ural metallurgy caused them to spring up rapidly. The railway westward to the Urals was double-tracked, new rail lines were built, and central Siberia was no longer merely a wilderness to be crossed en route to the Pacific. After carrying coal to Sverdlovsk and Chelyabinsk, empty railroad cars were filled with iron ore for the return trip, a plan that justified the building of blast furnaces and smelters in the Kuzbas. Newly discovered iron ore in the region now makes for independence from the Urals. Since 1925 six towns have grown to cities of over 100,000 population. In order of size they are Novosibirsk (406,000), Stalinsk (170,000), Barnaul (148,000), Tomsk (141,-000), Kemerovo (133,000) and Prokopyevsk (107,000).*

Minor industrial regions. It may be noted that of the four major regions three are in the Russian S. F. S. R. and one in the Ukraine.** There is no doubt that these will be the most important regions for many years to come and on them will depend Soviet Russia's industrial position. Yet vast areas of the U. S. S. R. are long distances from any of them. If the aim of self-contained, economic regionalism for the entire nation is to be fostered and if all nationalities are to share in the industrial advance, then minor industrial regions must be developed. This expansion has been undertaken.

West of the Ural Mountains are no less than eight industrial centers of considerable local significance. Leningrad, like Moscow, is an historic manufacturing and commercial center. Its present population of 3,191,000 might even justify listing the city and its surrounding area as a fifth important industrial region. Kiev (846,000), the third largest Soviet city, constitutes a comparable situation on a smaller scale. Important centers also have been developed around Murmansk (117,000) in the north; and at Stalingrad (445,000), Saratov (376,000), Kuibyshev (390,-000), Kirovo (143,000), and Chkalov, or Orenburg (173,000), all in the eastern part of

---

* The population figures used for Karaganda and for other industrial cities that follow illustrate the industrial development and present importance of urbanization in the U. S. S. R., especially in the more recently established centers in the Ural Mountains and in Siberia. According to the 1939 census the country had eighty cities with a population of 100,000 or more, as compared with ninety-two of that size in the United States. The ten largest cities of the U. S. S. R. are as follows: Moscow, 4,137,000; Leningrad, 3,191,000; Kiev, 846,000; Kharkov, 833,000; Baku, 809,000; Gorki (Nizhni Novgorod), 644,000; Odessa, 604,000; Tashkent, 585,000; Tiflis, 519,000; and Rostov, 510,000.

* Rank of these newly developed Kuznets cities in U. S. S. R. is as follows: 15th, Novosibirsk; 47th, Stalinsk; 55th, Barnaul; 61st, Tomsk; 64th, Kemerovo; 77th, Prokopyevsk.

** Karaganda, which supplies much coal to the Ural region, is located in the Kazakh Soviet Socialist Republic.

European U. S. S. R. In the aggregate these smaller centers make a significant contribution to the industrial total.

Of considerable importance has been the manufacturing development in the Tashkent area near the Afghan-Indian border. This region includes eastern Uzbek, western Tadzhik, and the extreme southern tip of the Kazakh Soviet Socialist Republic. The more important cities are Tashkent (585,000) and Samarkand (134,000), both of which are in the Uzbek S. S. R. Also important are the smaller centers of Stalinabad and Kokand in the Tadzhik S. S. R. and Chimkent in the Kazakh S. S. R. A remote location far from other industrial regions has made the development of light industry in this area advisable. Cotton, long grown in the region, is no longer sent to the spindles of Moscow but is being manufactured for national distribution near the source. This region bids fair to become a major textile center.

Between the Urals and Lake Baikal manufacturing industries are relatively rare. However, several small centers are being developed on the north shore of Lake Balkhash, about 200 miles south of Karaganda. There are also growing industries and considerable trading in the region of Semipalatinsk (110,000).

From and including the Lake Baikal region to the Pacific Ocean, all industrial development has followed the Trans-Siberian Railway. There are now five cities of more than 100,000 population in this area and several smaller developments of significance. The city of Irkutsk (243,000), always an important midway point on the railway, has taken on even greater significance since the discovery of iron ore near Cheremkhovo. Because of the railway junction and the discovery of iron ore near Chita (103,-000), Ulan-Ude (129,000), in the Buryat-Mongolian Autonomous S. S. R., is developing into a "competing" center with Irkutsk. The presence of coal and iron ore in the Amur River basin has aided the development of light industry between Khabarovsk and Komsomolsk. The former city (Khabarovsk), which has a population of 199,000, is also an important transportation center. The strategically located and politically potent city of Vladivostok (206,000) is a local industrial center as well as the eastern terminus of the Trans-Siberian Railway.

The development of these smaller centers is geopolitically significant to both the internal and external relationships of the Soviet Union. To facilitate their expansion many European Russians have been resettled in Siberia, Middle Asia, and the Far Eastern Provinces, thus making more effective the control of Moscow. At the same time the non-Russian peoples in these areas, having partaken of the new industrialism and with it the Communist doctrine, are experiencing a new and wider concept of national importance than they have ever known in the past. Such great nationalizing influences enhance the development and maintenance of a broad understanding among peoples of different environments and backgrounds and promote a strong national consciousness.

Soviet transportation. The entire gamut of transportational types can be found within the U. S. S. R. As the economic stages of development in Russia range from that of the Asiatic Indians, who are tribal hunters, to modern business executives of industrial combines, who fly from one factory to another, this wide range in methods of travel could be expected. Another significant aspect of Soviet transportation is its uneven distribution. In the main, this can be attributed to the irregularity of economic development and population distribution over Soviet Russia's tremendous area. Yet transportation was recognized by the early Communist planners as a crying need, and upon it many aspects of the *Gosplan* were directly dependent. Hence, in this field, as in both agriculture and industry, great strides forward have been made in the past twenty-five years.

RAILWAYS. Between 1913 and 1940 railway mileage increased 58 per cent (see the map on page 75). Despite a total of 62,500 miles, the U. S. S. R. is still a poor second to the United States, which has approximately four times this mileage. Of this total mileage, less than two per cent is electrified. In contrast to most European countries, the Russians have constructed broad gauge (five-foot) track, more suited than narrow gauge to the long, heavy haulage of Soviet industry.

The densest rail network is found in western U. S. S. R. South of Leningrad and west of the Volga River the railway pattern is entirely adequate. Again in the Urals the network is fairly heavy, but elsewhere through the nation rail lines thin out to form only a skeletal pattern. Most of the lines are single track. East of Chelyabinsk only the Trans-Siberian Railway is double tracked, the second track having been completed recently. The Communist-built Turk-Sib railway, as well as other lines, now connect Middle Asia with Siberia and European U. S. S. R. Industrial expansion in the Far East Provinces continues to stimulate railway building in that region. New railways will be an important phase of Soviet internal economic development, although reconstruction of the war-blasted western railway system will probably be an immediate postwar concern.

International railway connections are fairly numerous along the western European border, but across the long boundary from the Black Sea to the Sea of Japan pass only a few lines. Turkey and Iran are tapped through the Armenian S. S. R., and the Afghan border is reached at Kushka in the Turkmen S. S. R. and at Teruez in the Uzbek S. S. R. Another line runs southward from Ulan-Ude into the Mongolian People's Republic, and the Manchurian boundary is reached or crossed at five points.

INTERNAL WATERWAYS. The Soviet river and canal system is almost as long as that of the railways, but measured in terms of the weight of goods carried it is of much less significance. The Volga system, which can be traversed from the Caspian Sea to Lake Ladoga on the former border, is the most utilized of the waterways. Although inconsequential in ton-miles of freight carried, the Ob, Yenisei, and Lena rivers and their extensive tributary systems are the major means of transport north of the Trans-Siberian Railway. The Baltic-White Sea Canal is another important inland waterway. Actually, the Soviet government uses the Arctic Ocean as an internal waterway. It constitutes the only surface tie between the Soviet's Arctic ports and the rest of the Union. Some success has attended extensive experiments to prolong the open season for contact with this isolated coastline by means of icebreakers.

HIGHWAYS. Highways have never been of more than local importance in Russia. Of the existing mileage only a small percentage is even surfaced with gravel. Except in the Far East Provinces there are but few roads east of the Urals other than in cities. In European U. S. S. R. the much-publicized difficulty that confronted, bogged down, and harassed the invading German armies eloquently described the existing system; mud or dust seems to be the most outstanding characteristic. Notwithstanding all their progress in some directions, the Russian masses still lack the private automobile as a mode of travel. Passenger cars are rarely seen outside the larger cities, a condition that may well remain little changed for a long time. Trucks and tractors and, recently, tanks are somewhat more common.

AIRWAYS. Aviation, the newest form of transport, will certainly facilitate major transportation needs in the Soviet Union. Here is a method that overcomes the inhibiting aspects of continentality. Prewar statistics are of no help in evaluating the present or future Soviet system. Any additions to the entire air route pattern during the war were kept highly secret and are still unpublicized. Moscow has become a great national and potentially a great international air center. The larger cities of the west are all connected; Siberia has many air routes; and the Far Eastern Provinces and Arctic areas also are well acquainted with air services. Already the Soviet commercial airline, "Aeroflot," flies to the capitals of most eastern European countries; someday it may tap capitals and major cities throughout the world. As an outstanding example of its value, air transportation has now reduced the former nine and one-half day Trans-Siberian rail trip to but little more than twenty-four hours. And airports have been developed in previously inaccessible areas.

The young people of the Soviet Union are among the most air-conscious in the world and are daily being made more so by government-planned educational and recreational programs. It may also be assumed that the utility of aviation as a political and military, as well as economic, instrument is just as highly regarded by Soviet Russia as it is by the United States.

Geopolitical Problems

All countries have geopolitical problems, and certainly the U. S. S. R. is no exception. As such problems are deep-rooted, their solutions usually evolve only over long periods of time. Always there are partial answers, since it is natural for all groups to attempt to overcome their deficiencies or to maintain their advantages. So it is in the case of the new Soviet Union. All geopolitical problems involve the interrelated factors of natural environment, human adaptability, and political control; each country attempts to solve its problems by juggling these factors in such a way as to maintain internal solidarity on the one hand and to gain international prestige on the other. Both aims are basic to the nationalistic world of today. International unity is still an ideal toward which certain world leaders strive. World masses, however, still only hope for, rather than work for, that end. Even at this early point in the atomic era there may be serious doubt as to whether or not the intensely nationalistic populations can be frightened into actually working for international cooperation.

Although all geopolitical problems have international implications, direct or indirect, their foundations are often internal. At least five problems of this type can be found in the Soviet Union, namely: (1) achievement of military security, (2) maintenance of numerical superiority, (3) development of political stability, (4) augmentation of industrial capacity, and (5) domestic adjustment to international responsibility.

Military security. From the beginning of its history Russia has either pressed against or been pressed upon by peoples outside its borders. After defeats in 1905 and 1917 it was obvious to all intelligent Russians that their country was flanked by two covetous and vigorously aggressive neighbors—Germany on the west and Japan on the east. Both countries were inferior in size, population, and resources, but either, acting alone, could threaten Russian national security, or, acting collectively, could annihilate the Russian people entirely. Russians have had and still have a deep-rooted fear regarding these and other external threats to their national security.

It is, therefore, somewhat paradoxical that in 1904, at the time of the Russo-Japanese conflict, and again in 1918 at the close of World War I, a distinguished British political geographer, Sir Halford J. Mackinder, was pointing out to the world that the region of greatest military security on the globe was located in the very heart of Russia. He showed that Eurasia and Africa taken together constituted a "World Island" to which all other land is peripheral, and that the core of this island, called the "Heartland," lies roughly from the Volga River to the Lena River and from the Arctic Ocean to and including parts of Mongolia, Sinkiang, Afghanistan, and most of Iran (see the map on page 26).* So impressed did Mackinder become with this locative fact that he came to the conclusion that the power controlling the Heartland would command the World Island and, consequently, the world.** Like a good Britisher, Mackinder feared for the security of the British Isles should the aggressive Germans ever combine forces with the numerous, resource-wealthy Russians. This conclusion reverses the original idea from Heartland security to Heartland aggression. It is doubtful, however, whether the Russians were ever convinced of the security theory, and their present feeling concerning its aggressive possibilities is still unknown. Without question the Russians utilized their ability to withdraw toward the Heartland as a part of their strategy in the recent war, and without question they have expended much labor on its industrialization, but the physical existence of the Heartland cannot of itself be said to confer absolute security on the Soviet Union.

Cressey in his astute analysis has gone a long way toward disproving the Mackinder contention.† Security is relative; it was never more so than it is today. The future combination of air and atomic power contains the potential for changing all current ideas of security and balance of power. But even without these two new factors, Cressey has shown that, in terms of the Heartland, size is not enough: economic coherence is lacking; accessibility may be more desirable than not; progress is rarely achieved in isolation; the oceans are still the least expensive highways; total resource self-sufficiency exists for no nation, much less for a national region; optimum climate does not exist; and, finally, the people are as yet far from the cultural top. It is further pointed out that the United

* *Life,* December 21, 1942, pp. 106–107. Also R. H. Fifield and G. E. Pearcy, *Geopolitics in Principle and Practice* (Ginn, 1944), pp. 11–14.
** H. J. Mackinder, *Democratic Ideals and Reality* (Holt, 1919), p. 139.
† Cressey, *op. cit.,* chapter 10.

States and Canada have all the attributes assigned to Soviet Russia plus a few others, such as access to both the Atlantic and the Pacific Oceans. As a final factor relevant to the controversial problems, it might be noted in place of Mackinder's German-Russian combine, that America and Soviet Russia stand back to back across the North Pole. Here certainly is a combination that could not be beaten, for it is axiomatic that one country alone cannot stand against the combined force of the rest of the world.

Numerical superiority. Not merely is the U. S. S. R. by far the most populous of the major powers, but also, excepting the peoples of China and India, its population of approximately 200,000,000 is larger than that of any other nation. But in dealing with the U. S. S. R. it has already been noted that numerous nationalities have been brought together in its formation. A recent, valuable study lists forty-nine major nationalities and one miscellaneous group within the Soviet Union in 1939.* In that year, seventy-eight per cent of the population was Russian.**

This conglomerate population with many languages and an even greater number of dialects is in the process of amalgamation. Heterogeneity is being decreased by intermarriage, education, and increasing internal cultural and economic contact. The progress in that direction was indicated during World War II, which revealed an amazing development of national unity. The Soviet Union was able to place in the field the largest military force that the world has ever known, a numerical superiority that proved a most potent factor both in withstanding German invasion thrusts and in launching counter-offensives. Superiority of organized numbers has important psychological effects also. It is a source of security and of pride to the Soviet people, of worry to the other countries of Europe and those of the Middle East that have much smaller populations, and of attraction to certain Oriental groups.

During World War II Soviet Russia paid a terrific price in blood. The immense losses of man power both in conflict and through occupation have not yet been accurately calculated. They were probably greater than any official estimate given out; and, as in all wars, there was a heavy toll of young, vigorous lives. However, it now seems highly probable that of the warring nations the Soviet Union is among those best able to recoup their human losses, for the Russians are amazingly prolific. Natural increase before the war amounted to almost 3,000,000 annually. The Russian rate of natural increase is approximately 55 per cent greater than the Italians', 75 per cent greater than the Americans' and Germans', and 460 per cent greater than the English.* Should the Soviet Union continue its present rate of population increase, the war losses will soon be made up and the maintenance of numerical superiority over other major powers will be assured. It should also be noted that this high rate of population increase considerably perturbs most of the other nations of the world.

Political stability. Despite the democratic political organization set up for the U. S. S. R. in the Russian Constitution of 1936, the literate world constantly refers to the Russian "Dictatorship of the Proletariat." Only as its people progress toward a fuller realization of their democratic constitution can political stability be developed in the Soviet Union. This evolution is a long, slow process, readily recognizable to the American people from their own history.

The key to the skepticism concerning Soviet internal politics lies in the one-party system. Actually the organizational structure, which extends from the Supreme Soviet on the supranational level down to the individual, local, industrial or agricultural soviet, is more finely constituted than our own. But there is only one political party in Soviet Russia—the Communist party. Everyone over 18 years of age may vote, but Communists hold the majority of offices. Moreover, geographical distribution of Communists throughout the Soviet Union is carefully regulated, and in 1941 there were only two and one-half million members of the Communist party. Although there is no constitutional relationship between the party and the government, their connection is quite apparent.

There is no question that political stability

---

* A. Hrdlička, *The Peoples of the Soviet Union* (Smithsonian Institution, 1942), pp. 25–26.

** Great Russian, 58.41%; Lesser Russian, 16.56%; White Russian, 3.11%. Recent additions of non-Russians to the Soviet Union have, of course, somewhat reduced these percentages.

* Hrdlička, *op. cit.,* p. 2.

appears to exist within the Soviet Union. A
united front is presented to the world. Yet
the opposition has no medium of expression
from within. Just how strong a political
unity can be developed among forty-nine nationalities on this single-party basis remains
to be seen.

Industrial capacity. If the Soviet Union is
to achieve the ultimate aim of a competitive
position with Great Britain and the United
States, its present industrial capacity must be
augmented far beyond its present status. To
be sure, the Russian people have proved themselves excellent adapters of the industrial
techniques of other countries, and at the same
time have demonstrated that they possess industrial genius of their own. These factors,
combined with the availability of man power
and resources, provide all the necessary ingredients to noteworthy achievement. But such
development as is proposed will take considerable time—more time than the Russians
contemplate. Vast quantities of industrial
products must be produced for home consumption in order to lift the standards of the
Soviet peoples to a par with those of other
industrial populations. Further, quality of
production must be raised if competition in
world markets is to be successful. The Soviet
Union may well devote the next fifty years
to setting its own house in order. Thus far,
Russian developments have been spectacular, but much more remains to be done be-

fore their objectives can actually be realized.

The third of the five-year plans, which began in 1938, was cut short by the war, but in
February of 1946 a new (the fourth) plan for
the following five years was announced by the
Soviet government. Once again specifica-
tions called for a tremendous increase in basic
industrial production. The Russians aspire
to a production of iron and steel almost equal
to the prewar levels attained by that industry
in the United States. Since the Soviet government has quite consistently set its economic goals higher than could be accomplished, the complete fulfillment of these new
plans may be doubted. However, the world
will be much less skeptical than formerly concerning the progress that Soviet industry may
be expected to make.

International responsibility. With the attainment of major status in world affairs, acceptance of international responsibility becomes compulsory. No one who has lived
through the recent war and who follows current events can fail to recognize the international impact of Soviet action. Equal responsibility must be accepted by the people
of Soviet Russia. Gains in authority entail
increased responsibility. In the field of international relations the U. S. S. R. still must
meet this test.

The following chapter discusses these international relations and their attendant responsibilities.

CHAPTER 7 | The Soviet Union in World Politics

DESPITE the awe-inspiring significance of the Russian Revolution in modern world history, it would be an error to assume that the Soviet Union in her present international position or in her foreign policy can be considered apart from the foundation of the pre-Soviet past. The caprice of the Czarist autocracy was not sufficient to insulate it from the influences of geography and the facts of strategic position. Those same influences, in some instances enhanced and in others diminished, today exert their pressure upon the Soviet Union. No revolution enables its creators to escape the world in which they live or separates them wholly from the past history of the nation they have led into swift change. A revolution is but an episode in the organic growth of a society. A study of the growth and expansion of the Russian state reveals underlying physical stimuli to that growth and expansion and also discloses basic historic trends that are present today as factors in the Soviet Union's international position.

Russian Policy in the Pre-Soviet Past

The Russians, the most numerous branch of the Slavonic peoples, have devoted the past 1,100 years to the creation of the present gigantic Russian state (see the map on page 85). This state has been aided in its growth by the underlying geographical base of central Eurasia, compounded of a series of great plains, several widely scattered mountainous regions, and an extensive system of waterways, over all of which is superimposed the northern tundra, the coniferous forest belt, the vast steppes, and the southern deserts. Russian society represents a fusion of two cultural patterns derived almost entirely from the forest hunters on the one hand, and the nomads of the steppes on the other. The latter, particularly, came under the influence of the nomadic empires, especially that of the Mongols from the middle of the thirteenth to the middle of the fifteenth centuries. When these empires waned in power and contracted in area, the Russians from the forests and the steppes completed their social fusion and began their persistent march of conquest toward the lands and resources of central Eurasia.

A pattern of political power gradually took shape among the Russian peoples, a pattern in which the individual is subordinated to the group. Modern Russians are the natural heirs to this political attitude. Even more important than the influence of the nomadic peoples upon the Russians was the influence of Byzantium with its gift of Greek Orthodox Christianity, which in philosophy and organization became the matrix of early Western influences as well as authoritarianism in Russia. It was as Christians that the Russians in the fifteenth century moved outward and began to assert their hegemony over the vast reaches of central Eurasia. By the end of the eighteenth century Russia had come to occupy a pivotal position in European affairs. Especially during the Napoleonic era Russia was a key factor in the international picture. Since that time, despite periods of diplomatic and military failure, Russia has remained a strong force in international affairs.

Russian expansionist drives: TOWARD THE BALTIC. The Swedes remained dominant in the Baltic until Peter the Great was finally able to defeat them and by the treaty of Nystadt (1721) establish a Russo-Finnish border practically the same as that following the Russo-Finnish War in 1940. This treaty, by which Russia gained Ingria, Estonia, Livonia, and part of Karelia, gave her the access to the Baltic that she retained until 1918, when all these territories except Ingria were lost. For almost another century the basic conflict with Sweden continued, but the Russian conquest of Finland in 1809 forced Sweden to recognize the permanency of Russian power in the Baltic.

TOWARD CENTRAL EUROPE. In the eighteenth century Russian power began to creep westward toward central Europe. Poland more and more was forced to submit to Russian political influence although the impact of Polish culture on Russia increased. The three partitionings of Poland in the latter part of the century brought Poles and western Russians alike under the control of the Russian government and brought Russian power into the heart of Europe.* Thus, Russian interest in Polish affairs is of long standing; Russian influence upon Polish social relationships long antedates the Soviet period. As a modern medium of Russian penetration into central Europe, Poland is again playing an old role. In the same vein, western European alarm over Russian penetration is likewise an oft-repeated story.

TOWARD THE BALKANS. Russian relations with the Balkan area in the pre-Soviet period were the means of developing traditions of policy that exert great influence today. Since the spread of the Slavs into the Balkan peninsula in the seventh century, the Russians have been racially related to many Balkan peoples. The Russian drive here has been closely related to the one toward the sea through the Straits. Turkey, for centuries the sovereign or suzerain power in the Balkans, inevitably figures centrally in the problem of Russian expansion in this direction.

A series of Russo-Turkish wars brought Russian power southwestward to the Dnieper River in the latter part of the eighteenth century. In the nineteenth century Russian fortunes in the Balkans fluctuated. The Treaty of Tilsit between Alexander I and Napoleon and the settlement of the Congress of Vienna temporarily stalled the Russian drive.* By the Treaty of Adrianople in 1829, however, Russia procured the mouth of the Danube and increased her prestige in the Balkan countries. The Crimean War and the Congress of Berlin in 1878, by which Russia was denied many fruits of a war with Turkey in 1877–78, dealt Russia a severe blow in this area. Both Great Britain and Austria-Hungary feared Russian penetration. Although Great Britain was able to compose her differences with Russia after 1907, Austria, backed by Germany, remained a serious obstacle. This was a fundamental conflict among the many that engendered World War I.

TOWARD THE STRAITS. Much of the European history of the past three centuries, as well as of today, revolves around the conflict of political interests and ambitions centered at the Straits of the Bosporus and the Dardanelles (see the map on page 291).** The series of wars that Russia waged against the Turks was waged to establish Russian power at the Straits. This Russian thrust was in the main unsuccessful because of the military and diplomatic opposition of other major powers, especially that of Great Britain and Austria-Hungary. But Great Britain in an entente with Russia in 1907 relaxed her determined opposition to Russian penetration toward Constantinople (Istanbul). However, Austria, backed by Germany, continued to stand firmly in the way. Continuously frustrated for centuries in this drive, Russia retains today the tradition of ambition at the Straits and in the Eastern Mediterranean. This ambition is accepted as a major factor in contemporary world politics.

TOWARD THE CAUCASUS. The Caucasus and Transcaucasia have served as another avenue of Russian expansion. Here, too, Turkey has been the central obstacle. Major incentives to the Russian drive in this direction have been the desire to subdue the war-

---

* It is interesting to note that the boundary between the U. S. S. R. and Poland from 1921 to 1939 was almost the same as that which existed following the second Polish partition. See George Vernadsky, *A History of Russia* (New Home Library, 1944), p. 108.

* This generalization is valid even though Russia procured Bessarabia by the Treaty of Bucharest (1812), which terminated the Russo-Turkish War of 1810–12.

** For a detailed study, see James T. Shotwell and Francis Deak, *Turkey at the Straits* (The Macmillan Company, 1940).

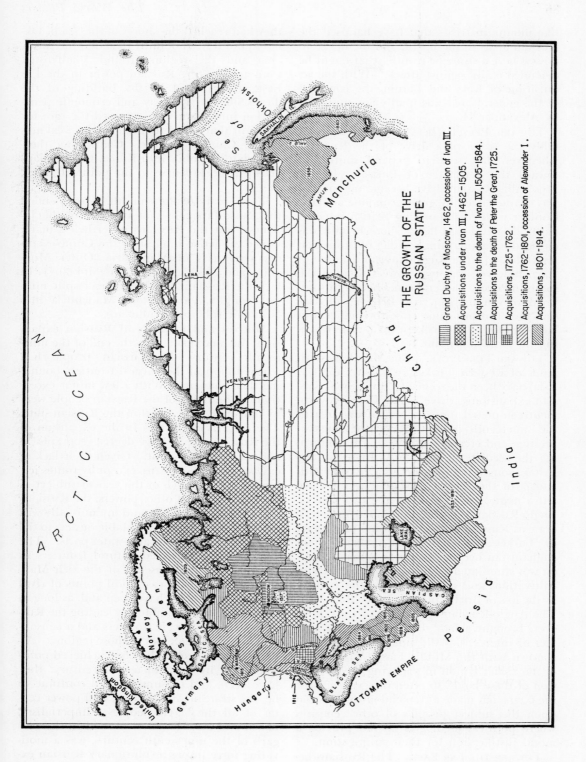

THE GROWTH OF THE
RUSSIAN STATE

Grand Duchy of Moscow, 1462, accession of Ivan III.

Acquisitions under Ivan III, 1462-1505.

Acquisitions to the death of Ivan IV, 1505-1584.

Acquisitions to the death of Peter the Great, 1725.

Acquisitions, 1725-1762.

Acquisitions, 1762-1801, accession of Alexander I.

Acquisitions, 1801-1914.

like mountain tribes that have harassed the Russian areas to the north, and the desire to possess here a strategic frontier that might be defended easily against attack. With the acquisition of Kars and Batum, the conquest of the general area was finally accomplished by Alexander II.

TOWARD PERSIA (IRAN). Persia is inevitably the scene of a drive of the Russians whenever they seek to expand southward toward the perimeter of Eurasia. In the 1890's this Russian drive became urgent and was characterized by great economic activity. Conflict with corresponding British interests naturally developed here, where Britain was engaged in maintaining a buffer of protection for India. In the Anglo-Russian Entente of 1907, however, the two powers divided the spoils in Persia. Several times before the outbreak of war in 1914 rival British and Russian imperialisms came close to conflict, but larger mutual interests kept them from reaching the breaking point.

TOWARD TURKESTAN. The Middle Eastern lands of western Turkestan (Soviet Central Asia) have been the scene of a traditional Russian expansionist drive. The Czar's government completed the conquest of the area in the nineteenth century, increasing Russian prestige and creating British alarm concerning the security of India. As early as 1869 Britain sought without success a division with Russia of the Middle East that would have left a neutral zone between the two powers. Anglo-Russian relations continued to deteriorate as Russian railroad building progressed in Turkestan and Russian pressure upon Afghanistan became greater. Russian interest was stimulated by the expansion of cotton cultivation, and at the turn of the century by the loss of British prestige in the Boer War. The Anglo-Russian agreement of 1907, however, brought a halt to the immediate conflict of interest but did not destroy Russia's concern with the Middle East. The success of the Soviet Union in pacifying the population of these lands, so often in revolt against the Czars, has made a tremendous impression upon the subject peoples of other empires where political ideologies do not provide a moral justification for their subjugation.

TOWARD THE FAR EAST. The Russians began the conquest of the vast expanses of Siberia in the sixteenth century. By the 1640's they had reached the shores of the Sea of Okhotsk, but it was not until 1860 that the Amur area and the region around Vladivostok were acquired.* Russian power in the Far East, strengthened by the building of the Trans-Siberian Railway and economic penetration into Manchuria, entered the race for spoils in that area promised by the weakness of the Chinese Empire. Continuing their imperialistic policy into Korea, the Russians alarmed the Japanese to the point of attack in 1904.

The Treaty of Portsmouth in 1905 ended the Russo-Japanese War in favor of the Japanese, but the Russians nevertheless maintained an active interest in the Chinese border territories of Manchuria, Outer Mongolia, and Chinese Turkestan (Sinkiang). In fact, the Russians and Japanese, despite military conflict, soon divided Manchuria into economic spheres of influence.

Motives and methods of Russian expansion: AREA CONCEPT. By the end of the nineteenth century the Russian people had reached most of the natural frontiers bounding their domain. With a few minor exceptions all branches of the Russian people were by that time united within the Russian state. The underlying factors in the expansion of the Russians are in large degree geographical and, as such, persistent. Given their lack of easy access to the oceans, except by routes icebound during much of the year or subject to the domination of other powers, the Russians inevitably have sought, and undoubtedly will persist in seeking, more suitable outlets to the sea and the control of warm-water ports. The lack of easily defended natural frontiers in the west and the presence of the rich Manchurian area in the east, focal points of rival national ambitions, have been and, as long as they exist, will remain forces leading the Russians to seek strategic frontiers and a consolidation of their defenses in those regions. Although the Russian Slavs had achieved political unity by the nineteenth century, they have been, and presumably will continue to be, the strategic, intellectual, and power center of all the Slavic peoples. Imperialism, naked and unashamed or dressed in the easy garb of the nineteenth century, was a motivating force in pre-revolutionary Russian ex-

* Robert J. Kerner, *The Urge to the Sea* (University of California Press, 1942), p. 78.

pansion. Motives of similar quality, cloaked with the moral rationalizations of Marxian thought, continue to move the Soviet Russians.*

POWER CONCEPT. From earliest times the Russians have been in search of new resources and natural wealth to enhance their position. As a socialist state, the U. S. S. R. has entered international competition for the same reasons. Balance of power motives lay behind the policy of Russia in the era of Napoleon; brought her into the alignment against Germany before 1914; guided her hand in meeting the danger of the Nazis in the 30's; and undoubtedly will influence Russian policy in the future. To supplement the balance-of-power policy, Russia associated herself with the collective security efforts represented by the post-Napoleonic Quadruple Alliance and the Hague Conferences. Similarly the U. S. S. R. has turned to other means of collective security when such a policy promised safety. And under both the Czars and the Communists there have been periods of isolation. A high degree of consistency between Czarist and Soviet foreign policy obviously exists, for the logic of history and geography is in some measure removed from the ability of men to manipulate.

Under the Communists, however, Russia has contributed some variants to traditional Russian policy. There has been a greater tendency toward isolationism based on suspicion of the aims of capitalist states. A peculiar type of opportunism has gone hand-in-hand with this isolationism, the two together calculated to prevent capitalist powers from combining their efforts against the U. S. S. R.** Finally, the Soviet state is the only power that has had political parties in other states working so consistently in its interest, providing reservoirs out of which to erect future Soviet regimes.

Soviet Foreign Policy, 1917–41

An analysis of Soviet foreign policy since the 1917 revolution must underlie any evaluation of the position of the Soviet Union in world affairs today. Such an analysis reveals persistent factors of importance for the future, factors conditioned by a largely unchanging physical environment.

The early struggle. The Bolsheviks signed a separate peace with Germany at Brest-Litovsk in March, 1918. Soon they were pressed on all sides by counter-revolutionary movements and interventions sponsored by the Allied powers, who were angered by the separate peace. Although the counter-revolutions and interventions subsided by 1920, the attempts in the same year of the Poles to revive the old Polish frontiers through war further deepened the Russian suspicions. To the surprise and dismay of the Bolsheviks, the national revolutions that they expected did not become widespread or permanent beyond the borders of Russia. The defeat of the Russians by the Poles in 1920 before the gates of Warsaw brought to an end Russian hopes for immediate world revolution. The Bolsheviks turned their attention to consolidating themselves at home and maintaining an uneasy *modus vivendi* with the capitalist world.

Uneasy international truce. Following the chaotic early period, the Soviet state sought to discover means of existing in an unfriendly world, particularly the world of the major European powers. Relations with Britain remained almost constantly irritated. In Russian official theory, Britain was the major imperialist power. In Russian strategic considerations, the continent-encircling British power repressed the Soviet state on all sides. From the British point of view, on the other hand, the Bolsheviks had become a symbol of anti-imperialist forces and a threat to the British Empire.* In spite of some improvement in Anglo-Russian relations in 1924, when a Labor Government was in power, British-Soviet interests remained in conflict in China and in the Near East during the entire interwar period from 1917 until June, 1941. Russian continental power has met and contested with British maritime and peripheral power along the whole southern fringe of Eurasia as consistently during the Soviet period as during that of the Czars.

Friendly relations, on the other hand, were quickly established between Russia and the German Weimar Republic. The Treaty of Rapallo of April, 1922, in which each gov-

---

* Cf. Charles A. Beard, *The Economic Basis of Politics* (Alfred A. Knopf, 1945), p. 87.

** See David J. Dallin, *Russia in the Postwar Period* (Yale University Press, 1935) for an excellent discussion of this policy.

* Dallin, *op. cit.*, p. 87.

ernment renounced claims against the other, was a major step in this rapprochement. Normal diplomatic relations followed, and measures were taken to improve trade. Russia desired a stronger Germany in order to rectify the European balance of power, which had been dangerously disturbed by the overwhelming victory of the Allies in 1918. German and Russian policy were complementary, therefore, until the advent of Hitler.

The Russian attitude toward France in the immediate postwar period was one of suspicion. The key to French policy was the League of Nations, which, in the Soviet view, was a front for the capitalist *status quo*. France, with the support of the states of eastern and southeastern Europe, represented both an obstacle to the revival of German power and a threat to the Soviet Union.

Collective security. The Nazi danger after Hitler's rise to power in 1933 was at first underrated by the Soviet Union, but soon the ominous implications of German policy became unmistakable. Germany rejected Soviet diplomatic overtures, and from 1934 through 1938 the Soviet Union became increasingly more friendly toward France and her allies. The Soviet goal was a formula of collective security that would restrain the potential aggressor. The foundation stones of the Soviet policy of collective security were cooperation with the League of Nations and pacts of mutual assistance signed with France and Czechoslovakia in May, 1935. Although the Soviet Union did not rule out the possibility of an agreement with Germany, the German-Japanese Anti-Comintern Pact and the outbreak of the Spanish Civil War in 1936 convinced the Russians that a great war was drawing near.

The Munich Pact, dated September 29, 1938, by which Great Britain, France, Germany, and Italy agreed to give the Czech Sudeten territory to Germany, tore to shreds the Soviet policy of collective security. Assuming that Britain and France were attempting to direct German aggression toward the east, the U. S. S. R., in order to avoid a war for which she was not prepared, sought to come to terms with Germany. This policy achieved success in a Soviet-German treaty of nonaggression, signed in August, 1939, a few days before the outbreak of World War II.

Preparation for war. From August, 1939, until the German attack on the Soviet Union on June 22, 1941, the latter feverishly engaged in internal and international preparations for war. Mutual assistance pacts were signed with the border states of Estonia, Latvia, and Lithuania in September and October, 1939. Polish territories were seized and incorporated in the White Russian and Ukrainian Soviet Socialist Republics. A short war with Finland resulted in a grant in March, 1940, of strategic territories to the Soviet Union. The alarming catastrophe in France in June, 1940, when the Nazis overran the country precipitated Russian incorporation of Bessarabia, northern Bukovina, and the Baltic States of Estonia, Latvia, and Lithuania.

Following the summer of 1940 Soviet-German relations began rapidly to deteriorate. A neutrality pact was signed with the Axis partner, Japan, in April, 1941, but the gigantic German attack on the U. S. S. R. followed shortly after. The Soviet state's great crisis had arrived. Russian nationalism, long subordinated to Marxian ideology, now came to the front in the fight against the army of the German Reich.

The Soviet Union in World War II

Simultaneously with the German attack on Russia in June, 1941, Great Britain and the United States announced their support of the Soviet war effort. Great Britain and the U. S. S. R. in a formal agreement of July, 1941, pledged themselves to render each other every military assistance; this agreement was followed in May, 1942, by a twenty-year mutual assistance pact providing for close collaboration during and after the war. Signs of strain, however, soon appeared as a result of the exigencies of the war. Suspicious of governments that might be consistent with the democracies of the West, the Soviet government sponsored groups in Poland and Yugoslavia more in conformity with its own aims. Only with the defeat of Germany in May, 1945, could Soviet Russia turn her attention to the Far East and Japan. In April she had denounced her agreement with the latter, in preparation for a declaration of war and an invasion of Manchuria a few days before Japan capitulated to the United Nations in August, 1945. The Soviet thrust into Japanese-controlled territory coincided with the devastation wrought on Japan Proper by atomic bombs.

The Soviet Position in the Postwar World

General Soviet position. It is important to reassess the position of the Soviet Union as it appears since the end of World War II. The U. S. S. R. retains unimpaired its domination over the vast continental reaches of central Eurasia. It retains its character as a power vitally concerned with global affairs. It has emerged from the period of uneasy isolation among capitalist powers into an era of tremendous responsibility as one of the three top ranking powers in a world in ferment. And yet its new status is conditioned by an amazing number of factors that have been persistent throughout Russian history.

Continuing factors in Soviet policy. It is apparent that the fundamental state socialism remains in the U. S. S. R. despite the modifications of earlier practice. The Soviet leaders cannot but hope that eventually other powers will be transformed into state socialisms within or friendly to the Soviet Union. Under its federal constitution contiguous noncapitalistic political entities may easily become incorporated into the Union. Whatever factors may indicate otherwise, the Soviet Union looks with satisfaction upon any revolutionary civil wars, even among allied powers, that might foretell a social change advantageous to its own political regime.

The persistent and traditional factors in Russian policy do not preclude the Soviet Union from participating in a program of cooperation with other powers. Like the United States, the U. S. S. R. may on one occasion emphasize a unilateral, on another a multilateral, approach to international problems. The United Nations offers an alternative to isolation for the Soviet Union. It is true that the organization has already shown discouraging signs of degeneration into a front behind which will be played the game of international big-power politics, but restored confidence in the organization may yet avoid the pitfalls of either isolationism or unilateral policy. Unfortunately the San Francisco Conference, which produced the Charter of the United Nations, and subsequent meetings of the Security Council exposed international conflicts in a manner that almost

from its inception boded ill for the future of the United Nations.

The alternative to international cooperation would be a renewal of Soviet isolationism and unilateralism. Western reaction to such a development would inevitably be an Anglo-American alignment closely associated with a western European bloc. The U. S. S. R. opposes a renewed *cordon sanitaire* behind which she sees a capitalist conspiracy, but it will be the inevitable result of a Russian zone of security proclaimed as a legitimate defense of the proletarian commonwealth. The only solution to this dilemma must be unselfish efforts on both sides to demonstrate good faith. The Soviet leaders must convince the Western powers that they are willing to let the non-Soviet world work toward sound economic and social ends through the medium of evolutionary democracy. In turn, the Western powers must convince the Soviet chieftains that the capitalist conspiracy against them is a myth.

Soviet Regional Foreign Policy

Since 1939 a Soviet regional foreign policy has become clearer in outline. This regional policy consists of a search for territorial settlements to safeguard the Soviet state should cooperative international efforts fail.

The drive toward strategic frontiers. As pointed out earlier, the U. S. S. R. does not possess natural frontiers in the west. Since 1939 there has been a consistent Soviet effort to rectify this condition by pushing the boundary line outward (see the map on page 91). Although in some cases historical justification for the Soviet policy exists, there are on occasion conflicts with the principle of national self-determination or the ethical views of major Soviet allies.

In the northwest the peace agreement signed between the Soviet Union and Finland on March 11, 1940, established a new boundary between the Soviet Union and Finland, which has the stated purposes of providing greater security for the city of Leningrad, for the port of Murmansk, and for the Murmansk railroad. Russia gained the Karelian Isthmus and the city of Viborg, which were joined to the Soviet Karelian district to form the Karelo-Finnish S. S. R., as a buffer against future attack from the direction of Finland. By the Russo-Finnish armistice of September, 1944, the 1940 boundary was reestablished, the territory around Petsamo in the north was incorporated into the U. S. S. R. to afford easier access to Scandinavia, and the Porkkala Peninsula near Helsinki was leased to the U. S. S. R. for fifty years in place of the former Hango lease.

In the summer of 1940 Premier Molotov announced to the Supreme Soviet that Lithuania, Latvia, and Estonia had been incorporated into the U. S. S. R. at the request of local legislative bodies. It was the Soviet claim that local obstructionists had made impossible the faithful carrying out of the Soviet mutual assistance pacts with the three small Baltic States. Mr. Molotov noted that this event reincorporated historic Russian territories that had been torn away by Western imperialism, restoring a much-needed ice-free port (Riga) in the Baltic. These territories were occupied by the Nazis during the greater part of World War II, but since the defeat of Germany they are again under Soviet administration.

After the capitulation of Germany, the Potsdam Conference in July, 1945, assigned to the U. S. S. R. a portion of East Prussia, including the historic city of Königsberg. Poland was compensated by receiving the remainder of East Prussia and territory in eastern Germany. These settlements were made pending a final peace treaty. By a treaty signed in Moscow on August 16, 1945, a Polish-Russian border was established. It followed the so-called Curzon Line, with slight deviations in favor of Poland (see the lower right map on page 238).

Soviet Russia also benefited from other territorial adjustments in central Europe. In June, 1945, Czechoslovakia ceded the Carpatho-Ukraine region to the U. S. S. R. Rumania in the armistice of September 12, 1944, had already agreed to adhere to the 1940 frontier, which yielded northern Bukovina and Bessarabia to the Soviet Union. Some of the territory returned to the U. S. S. R. had been Russian from 1812 until World War I. Although the armistice agreement was temporary, the final peace settlement did not alter this territorial arrangement.

Most of the border rectifications sought by Soviet Russia have been in Europe, where she is most vulnerable, but several were effected along her frontier in Asia. Recently Turkey has been pressed to make cessions in Transcaucasia of a strip of territory along the Black Sea southwest of Batum, 180 miles long and seventy-five miles wide. The incorporation in early November, 1945, of the independent People's Republic of Tannu Tuva was yet another sign of expanding Russian frontiers. The same indication held true of Stalin's announcement on September 2, 1945, to the effect that Russia had reacquired southern Sakhalin and the Kuriles.

Establishment of a security zone. It is clear that present Soviet policy is working toward a security zone of states bordering on or near the U. S. S. R. For the Soviet Union to seek friendly neighbors is normal, but the application of strategic pressure to force social revolutions and abnormal regimes on such states in possible violation of the principle of self-determination presents another problem. The Anglo-American world is particularly concerned lest this policy result in a widespread growth of Russian authoritarianism. Although the major motive underlying this Soviet policy is perhaps defensive, there are others of unquestionable significance. They include the desire for access to the sea, access to additional resources, and the extension of the Soviet system. To the degree that the present Soviet policy of building a security zone derives from doubt concerning the success of international cooperative efforts, the world can but hope that the record of future events will dispel such doubts.

GERMANY AND JAPAN. The states in the present or potential Soviet security zone may be conveniently categorized. They cannot in all cases, however, be grouped geographically, for their political status and international implications may cut across a strictly regional classification.

The first group consists of the two major defeated enemy states. The defeat of Nazi Germany has removed a major competitor of Russia on the continent of Europe. Administered and occupied in four zones by the U. S. S. R., the United States, Great Britain, and France (see the map on page 140), Germany stands at the crossroads socially, politically, and economically. More important, Germany is the testing ground of the cooperative spirit of the major powers. For the Soviet Union to seek immediately the development of a sovietized Germany would

SOVIET RUSSIA AND ITS PERIPHERAL SPHERES OF INTEREST

LEGEND

FRONT HELD BY GERMANS BY TREATY OF BREST–LITOVSK, MARCH 3, 1918.

FARTHEST ADVANCE OF GERMAN ARMY IN ATTACK UPON UKRAINE PRIOR TO TREATY OF BREST–LITOVSK.

SOVIET BORDER WITH UKRAINE, INDEPENDENCE OF WHICH WAS RECOGNIZED BY TREATY OF BREST–LITOVSK.

SOVIET BORDER FROM 1918 UNTIL 1940.

BOUNDARY OF POLISH TERRITORY TAKEN BY THE U.S.S.R. FOLLOWING GERMAN ATTACK ON POLAND, SEPTEMBER, 1939.

BOUNDARY OF POLAND ESTABLISHED BY POTSDAM CONFERENCE AND TREATY WITH RUSSIA.

TERRITORY ACQUIRED BY RUSSIA IN 1940: ESTONIA, LATVIA, LITHUANIA, BESSARABIA, NORTHERN BUKOVINA.

TERRITORY ACQUIRED BY U.S.S.R. FROM FINLAND IN 1940, REAFFIRMED IN ARMISTICE OF SEPTEMBER 1944.

CARPATHO-UKRAINE, ACQUIRED BY U.S.S.R. BY TREATY WITH CZECHOSLOVAKIA IN JULY, 1945.

TERRITORY ACQUIRED FROM POLAND, EAST OF A BORDER RUNNING GENERALLY ALONG CURZON LINE, BY TREATY IN 1945. EAST PRUSSIAN TERRITORY GIVEN TO THE U.S.S.R. BY THE POTSDAM CONFERENCE IN 1945.

TANNU TUVA, INCORPORATED BY THE U.S.S.R. IN NOV. 1945.

AREA ACQUIRED BY THE U.S.S.R. FROM JAPAN FOLLOWING THE DEFEAT OF THE LATTER.

STATES OR TERRITORIES ACTUALLY OR POTENTIALLY IN SOVIET SECURITY ZONE.

PETSAMO AND SURROUNDING TERRITORY CEDED TO U.S.S.R. BY ARMISTICE (SEPTEMBER 1944)

U. S. S. R.

MOSCOW

FINLAND

POLAND

GERMANY

CZECH.

AUST. HUNG.

RUMANIA

YUGOSLAVIA

BUL.

ALB.

GREECE

TURKEY

IRAN

AFGHANISTAN

SINKIANG

CHINA

MONGOLIAN PEOPLE'S REPUBLIC

MANCHURIA

KOREA

SAKHALIN

JAPAN

PACIFIC OCEAN

MERCATOR'S PROJECTION

be to overlook the Russian need for much German wealth for reconstruction purposes, the havoc wrought in Russia by the Germans, and the importance to Russia of cooperation with the other powers. These more immediate considerations must be weighed against the Soviet desire for a German barrier against western influence in central Europe.

Experience will gradually modify the implementation of policy in Germany. Much of the burden of occupation is felt by the U. S. S. R., whose citizens are needed at home for the work of reconstruction. The Russians, willing to use German officials under a rigid control, early established in their zone a twelve-department administration staffed with hand-picked Germans.

In the economic sphere the evidence presented during the early days of occupation was scanty. In Brandenburg, Saxony, and Mecklenburg, all in the Russian zone, a movement developed under government sponsorship for the breakup of the large landed estates into small peasant holdings. German reparations to Russia in the form of machinery and factories will have a deleterious effect upon German economy. But until the powers set forth and carry through a long-range policy concerning the German economy, the orientation of postwar Germany in Europe cannot be foretold, nor can the country's social and class relationships be predicted.

Japan, at the opposite extremity of the U. S. S. R., is likewise important in the Soviet strategic picture. The Russians cannot fail to be seriously concerned with the political settlements made in the Japanese Islands and in Korea—so close to the Soviet Far East (see the map on page 385). This concern was reflected in the opposition of the Russians to predominant United States control in Japan, where American policy insisted that final decision should rest with the Supreme Allied Commander. The Russians were of the opinion that American policy in Japan was not sufficiently stern nor adequately aware of the disguises that Japanese reaction can assume. Further, Soviet concern was not mitigated by the American creation of a ten-power Far Eastern Advisory Commission. Soviet Russia's determination to increase her control in Japan was shown in her refusal to be represented on the Advisory Commission and in the

reiteration of her demand for a Four-Power Allied Control Council to have headquarters in Tokyo.* There is no doubt that the U. S. S. R. will continue to seek a strategically favorable political settlement in Japan.

GREECE, TURKEY, IRAN, AND CHINA. Four states potentially in the Soviet security zone that actively, or through neutrality, supported the Soviet Union in the war—Greece, Turkey, Iran, and China—are now showing signs of resistance to inclusion in the zone. (Throughout the discussion (pages 89–95) of these and the following states peripheral to the U. S. S. R. continued reference to the map on page 91 will greatly assist in understanding the locational reasons for Soviet interest in these areas.) Although somewhat removed from the immediate zone of Soviet interest, Greece's proximity to the Straits makes her important to the U. S. S. R. Since her Mediterranean position also gives Greece an abiding importance to the British Empire, British influence in this southernmost Balkan state has been exceedingly powerful. There is, however, a sizable Communist organization that would welcome a pro-Soviet orientation.

Turkey remained neutral during most of World War II, but in most respects her neutrality worked to the advantage of the United Nations. In March, 1945, the U. S. S. R. requested the revision of the existing treaty of friendship and neutrality with Turkey. This reconsideration of treaty terms left the Russians free to press Turkey for cessions in Turkish Armenia and for bases from which they could dominate the general area of the Straits. Russian ambitions in this direction are almost as old as the Russian state, and the opposition of western European states is equally well established. In this area Russian proposals went beyond the concessions that Great Britain and the United States felt it safe to make.

The question of Iran in international politics is closely linked with that of Turkey. The Russian stake long antedates the Soviet period, and both Britain and the United

* In late December, 1945, Mr. Molotov, Mr. Bevin, and Mr. Byrnes anounced from Moscow the establishment of a Four-Power Control Council for Japan, representing Russia, Great Britain, the United States, and Japan. At the same time Russia joined the Far Eastern Commission.

States have interests in the area. During World War II Russian, British, and American military forces were sent to Iran to protect an avenue for lend-lease shipment to the U. S. S. R. The Iranians desired the withdrawal of these foreign troops as soon as possible. Although the Russians agreed to the withdrawal of their military forces by March, 1946, the Soviet army prevented the Iranian government from suppressing Iranian left-wing separatists and revolutionaries in the northern province of Azerbaijan. Later the pro-Russian regime in this province collapsed, and Iranian control was re-established. The Soviet interest in Iran is definitely linked to oil deposits and a desire for access to the sea through Iran and the Persian Gulf, possibly with a view to outflank the Straits and the entire Near East.

In China likewise there is resistance to Soviet influences. The Nationalists and the Chinese Communists have contended for power. At first consideration Moscow would be expected to give all available aid to the latter. The signing of an agreement in August, 1945, between the Nationalists under Chiang Kai-shek and the Russians indicated that larger considerations made it advisable for the Russians to seek a *modus vivendi* with the Nationalists, despite their lesser ideological acceptability. The agreement provided broadly for the re-establishment of the Russian position as it had existed prior to 1905. Joint Chinese-Russian ownership and management of certain Manchurian railways were established. Port Arthur was designated as a naval base to be used jointly by Russia and China. The agreement further called for general Russian-Chinese collaboration; the U. S. S. R. engaged to respect the sovereignty and territorial integrity of China—an old formula—and China practically recognized the independence of the People's Government of Outer Mongolia.

POLAND, CZECHOSLOVAKIA, YUGOSLAVIA, AND OUTER MONGOLIA. Another four states— Poland, Czechoslovakia, Yugoslavia, and Outer Mongolia—that supported the U. S. S. R. during the war appear to be safely within the Soviet security system, either under their wartime governments or new pro-Soviet regimes. In each case except that of Outer Mongolia these states are Slavic, and even though they may diverge in religious and so-

cial respects, they have a racial affinity for Slavic Russia. They are advance guards of the Soviet defensive scheme.

Of the three, Czechoslovakia, until February, 1948, successfully worked out a compromise between the demands of democracy and the demands of Soviet protectionist policy.* The Czechoslovak premier described Czech foreign policy in a speech before the parliament in October, 1945, as embodying a fundamental reliance upon cooperation with the Soviet Union and positive friendly relations with Great Britain and the United States. From the standpoint of Russia's allies, Poland under a pro-Soviet coalition and Yugoslavia under Marshall Tito represented failure in applying democracy to a full measure, except in the peculiar view of the Marxian left in which all parties right of the Marxists either are termed reactionaries or are allowed to participate in government on sufferance. In November, 1945, Yugoslavia for all practical purposes became a Federal People's Republic. In December, Great Britain and the United States recognized the new republic although the United States registered dissatisfaction with Yugoslav elections.

An almost complete blackout of information hampers an understanding of conditions in Outer Mongolia. Although it has enjoyed actual independence under Soviet sponsorship since 1921, the region is completely within the Soviet sphere of influence. This close tie was demonstrated when the Outer Mongolian government declared war on Japan on August 11, 1945, two days after the Russian declaration.

FINLAND, HUNGARY, AUSTRIA, BULGARIA, RUMANIA AND ALBANIA. Generally within the Russian zone are five states—Finland, Hungary, Austria, Bulgaria, and Rumania— that, as satellites of Germany, were at war with the Soviet Union. Albania, a satellite of Fascist Italy, could also be included as a sixth state in this category. Of them only Bulgaria is Slavic, which will be a factor working against the permanency of their pro-Soviet orientation. The Finnish position is inevitably overshadowed by the proximity of Russia, but there remain strong anti-

* On February 25, 1948, a Communist coup in Czechoslovakia revealed the temporary character of the loyalty given by Communists to the principle of coalition.

Communist forces at work to offset the 20,000 members of the Finnish Communist Party. Austria itself was divided into Russian, British, American, and French zones of occupation. Soviet influence was paramount only in the Russian zone. A coup d'état in Hungary during 1947 placed that country firmly in the Soviet orbit. In Bulgaria and Rumania pro-Soviet governments have been collaborating with the U. S. S. R., although there were parties in each country opposed to Soviet domination. The proximity of the Balkan Peninsula to Soviet Russia places these countries generally within the Soviet zone. Whether their organic development will be hampered by that situation is not immediately clear.

AFGHANISTAN AND CHINESE TURKESTAN (SINKIANG). Not readily classified as members of any group, two miscellaneous areas lie close to the Soviet security zone. One of them, Afghanistan, is in the path of a traditional Russian drive toward the sea and is also on the historic invasion route of India. Soviet-British conflict in the country developed early in the 1920's, with Afghanistan assuming importance as part of an Asiatic alliance projected by the Bolsheviks against British imperialism. The problems of Russian émigrés and escaped Indian rebels have given both Britain and Russia pretexts for interference.* The Afghans once remarked that their country was the unfortunate goat between the lion and the bear.

With the withdrawal of the British from India, Afghan-Soviet relations assume a new interest. A boundary controversy between the Soviets and Afghans was settled in 1946. The Kushk district in the Afghan province of Herat, where Iran, Afghanistan, and the Soviet Union meet, was claimed by both Afghanistan and Soviet Russia. In June, 1946, by the terms of a Soviet-Afghan treaty Kushk went to Soviet Russia. Significantly it is located within a hundred miles of the Tirpul oilfields in Herat province.

Chinese Turkestan (Sinkiang) in the center of Asia is surrounded by and has access to Russian Turkestan, Outer Mongolia, China Proper, and Tibet. It is of vital concern to both Soviet Russia and China. Russia desires internal tranquillity to facilitate

commercial intercourse. Civil disturbances frequently break out in Chinese Turkestan involving conflicts between the Moslem inhabitants and the Chinese administrators that have an indirect bearing on Russo-Chinese relations. In addition to the strategic importance of this land, it also has minerals and other resources of value.

OTHER AREAS OF SOVIET INTEREST. As a major world power, the Soviet Union obviously has global interests, in particular, wherever events give promise of social change favorable, or even unfavorable, to the U. S. S. R. For example, the French elections in October, 1945, in which the Communist party received the largest popular vote and the largest representation in the Constituent Assembly, had a direct bearing upon the Soviet position in Europe. The Catholic Mouvement Républicain Populaire and the Socialists together controlled the Assembly and, working in support of goals divergent from those of the Communists, qualified the Communist victory. The election results gave impetus to French discussion of a western coalition, initially comprising Britain and France, and, subsequently, other western European countries. France was particularly interested in modifying the domination of the Big Three, sponsored chiefly by Russia, which was so evident at the Foreign Ministers' London Conference in September, 1945, and in the meeting of the foreign ministers of Russia, Great Britain, and the United States in Moscow in December, 1945. France was likewise opposed to a central administration under Russian domination in Germany, at least until the Rhineland and the Ruhr were severed from Germany. On the other hand, Russia opposed the formation of a western European coalition that might menace the U. S. S. R.

In late 1945 defeated Italy was experiencing the pains of a great political and social transition, and the Italian Communist party was very active in this scene. The London Foreign Ministers' Conference failed to agree upon peace terms for Italy, but at the conference Russia proposed that Tripolitania, an Italian colonial possession included in Libya, be administered as an individual trusteeship by the U. S. S. R. under the United Nations. Commissar Molotov likewise indicated Russia's interest in the Italian

* Joseph Castagne, "Soviet Imperialism in Afghanistan," *Foreign Affairs*, XIII (July, 1935), p. 703.

colony of Eritrea on the Red Sea. Thus, Italy's internal conditions offered an opportunity for the establishment of a pro-Soviet or Communist regime, and Italy's international position offered the Soviet Union an opportunity to press for more widespread colonial opportunities. Of course, Russian interest in the Mediterranean was not new and was closely akin to the Soviet interest in a warm-water outlet at the Straits.*

In addition to the interest in Tripolitania and Eritrea, there are other Soviet concerns in the general area of the Mediterranean and the Near East. The U. S. S. R., which participated in the United Nations' decision in late 1947, to partition Palestine after Great Britain relinquished her mandate, has continuing interest in the future of that area. At a conference of the foreign ministers of the Big Four in 1946 Russia advanced her desire for bases in the Dodecanese Islands, off the coast of Asia Minor and strategically located with reference to the Straits. Greece, however, received the islands on February 1, 1947, with the provision that they be demilitarized.

Another area of Soviet interest is Scandinavia, which, located largely on the Baltic, is strategically important to the U. S. S. R. Soviet Russia has sought bases on the Norwegian island of Spitzbergen, ostensibly to enable her to carry out her obligations to the United Nations. This policy comes as part of the Russian desire to achieve naval, air, and colonial power commensurate with that of the United States and Great Britain. These Soviet ambitions have heightened British and American fears, for the Soviet Union as an already overwhelmingly strong continental

* A peace treaty for Italy was finally signed by the great powers on February 10, 1947. Ratifications, although delayed, were finally forthcoming. Italy adhered on July 31, 1947.

power would be immeasurably strengthened by these additions.

Finally, the Arctic is a region in which Russia has developed interests (see the map on page 513). In 1932 a Soviet ice-breaker completed a passage from Archangel to Vladivostok in a single season, a feat achieved only after years of study and effort.* Very soon after the Revolution the Soviet government started a program of Arctic exploration and exploitation. In 1932 the Central Administration of the Northern Sea Route was established, in which the army and navy were given considerable responsibility in its organization and operation. The Second Five-Year Plan appropriated a great sum of money to further its development. In November, 1924, the Soviet government laid claim to *terra nullius* between the Soviet Union and the Pole. Great strategic importance is attached to this region, and Soviet development of its potentialities made a contribution to the winning of the war, for the Soviet war effort received a surprising amount of supplies via the Arctic route from the east by the water route north of Siberia.

The Future

It is clear that Soviet Russia today has achieved a position of commanding importance. The vigorous national ethos of the Russian and associated peoples has contributed to this position. The Russians bring to their new eminence a social philosophy in many respects unique in man's history. It must be the earnest hope of all men of good will that the Russians will be able to live in peace and cooperation with their global neighbors who possess contrasting social philosophies that are equally valid historically and pragmatically.

* Bruce Hopper, "The Soviet Conquest of the Far North," *Foreign Affairs*, XIV (April, 1936), p. 499.

CHAPTER 8 | Great Britain and the Dependent Empire

IN STRONG contrast to the spacious continental land areas of the United States and the Soviet Union, the British Commonwealth-Empire is made up of a variety of widely scattered political entities (see the map on facing page). The island of Great Britain is the nerve center of a vast imperial domain, which includes dominions, crown colonies, protectorates, trusteeships, condominia, and other territory that falls under British sovereignty.*

About one fifth of the world's population live in the component parts of the British Commonwealth-Empire. Extending over a fourth of the total land surface of the globe the Commonwealth-Empire finds its strength in widespread coverage rather than in the intensive development of a large base area.** Only the British Commonwealth-Empire taken as a whole is a global power geograph-

* Many British terms refer to specific areas, or are used to designate certain political control. Following is a list most commonly used both in this chapter and at other points in which British areas are considered:
   Geographical areas: British Isles (made up principally of Great Britain, the larger island, and Ireland, the smaller).
   Political areas: England, Wales, and Scotland (political areas on Great Britain); Eire and Northern Ireland (political areas on Ireland); United Kingdom (Great Britain plus Northern Ireland).
   Political Control: British Commonwealth-Empire (present name of all areas under British sovereignty). British Empire (former name of British Commonwealth-Empire, also used in a general sense for the modern Empire). British Commonwealth of Nations (in 1946 the dominions of Great Britain and Northern Ireland, Canada, Australia, New Zealand, Union of South Africa, and Eire). Britain (general term referring to seat of British power in Great Britain).
   ** The dynamic forces now operating in the Commonwealth indicate that the membership is subject to change.

ically and a world power politically; Great Britain alone cannot fairly be ranked with the United States or the Soviet Union.

In this chapter brief consideration is first given to the entire British Commonwealth-Empire at the end of the recent world war. Following this treatment are more detailed discussions of the political regions of the British Isles and of the territorial and economic development of the British Empire. In Chapter 9 the dominions of the British Commonwealth of Nations in 1946, other than the United Kingdom and Eire are considered. Major areas of the dependent Empire in 1946 and significant postwar developments in these places are presented in regional chapters dealing specifically with these areas, that is, India and Burma, the African area of Britain, and British Malaya. The names and areas of British areas of less consequence are included in the table on pages 112–113, in which are listed all political subdivisions of the British Commonwealth-Empire. Several of the areas in this category are also taken up in conjunction with the more important political regions in their general vicinity, for example, Hong Kong in the chapter on China and Jamaica in the chapter on Caribbean America.

The Commonwealth-Empire as a Whole

Built up during the last four centuries, the British Empire came to be regarded as the ultimate expression of colonial development. British influence spread to the far corners of the earth, making itself felt in one form or another in all the continents and on all the oceans. Twice challenged in the present century, Britain survived both world conflicts,

BRITISH COMMONWEALTH–EMPIRE

JANUARY 1, 1946

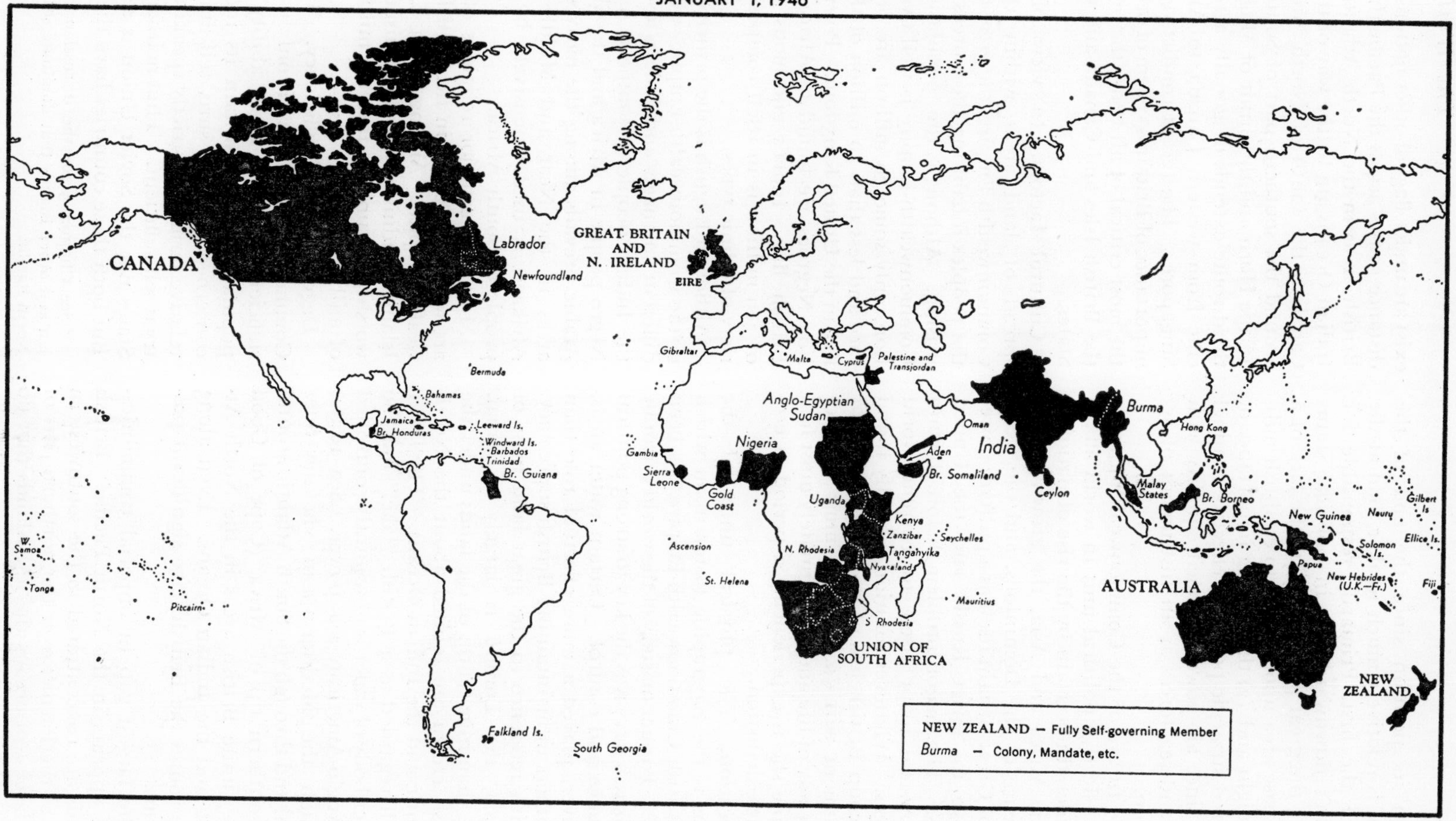

NEW ZEALAND — Fully Self-governing Member

Burma — Colony, Mandate, etc.

NEW ZEALAND

AUSTRALIA

Gilbert Is.

Ellice Is.

Fiji

Nauru

Solomon Is.

New Hebrides (U.K.–Fr.)

Papua

New Guinea

Br. Borneo

Hong Kong

Malay States

Burma

India

Ceylon

UNION OF SOUTH AFRICA

Mauritius

Seychelles

Zanzibar

Tanganyika

Kenya

Uganda

N. Rhodesia

S. Rhodesia

Nyasaland

Br. Somaliland

Aden

Oman

Palestine and Transjordan

Cyprus

Malta

Anglo-Egyptian Sudan

Nigeria

Gold Coast

Sierra Leone

Gambia

Gibraltar

Ascension

St. Helena

South Georgia

EIRE

GREAT BRITAIN AND N. IRELAND

Labrador

Newfoundland

Bermuda

Bahamas

Jamaica

Br. Honduras

Leeward Is.

Windward Is.

Barbados

Trinidad

Br. Guiana

CANADA

Falkland Is.

Pitcairn

W. Samoa

Tonga

though its position since the end of the second is relatively much weaker than at the end of the first. Primarily responsible for Britain's downward slip in political status among the great powers are (1) the lack of a great base area upon which to establish military might and (2) the waning importance of scattered strategic points as effective sentinel posts since air power assumed equality with land and sea forces as an instrument of aggression.

The future of the Commonwealth-Empire as an effective political unit in world affairs is rendered uncertain by the rise of nationalism in Africa and Asia, the growing independence of the Dominions, and the weakness of Great Britain itself as a military power relative to Soviet Russia and the United States. The major problem before Britain is how to adapt itself to current world changes. Whatever solution is finally found to recoup British loss of standing, no minor adjustment will do. Britain must discover a new way of life and unfortunately must find it while she is experiencing a period of economic exhaustion.

Location. The physical unity of the oceans is the geographic factor upon which the British Commonwealth-Empire has been based. Former mastery of the world ocean by the British navy was the key to strong political influence and control. Certain water areas, however, played a more effectual role than did others in maintaining British supremacy.

With reference to the great land mass of Eurasia, the Empire is largely marginal. More than nine tenths of the lands under the British crown are located about the North Atlantic and the Indian Oceans. The latter is still regarded as a British "lake," but the former body of water is now jointly controlled by Anglo-American sea power. Sea routes through the Mediterranean via the Suez Canal and through the South Atlantic around the southern tip of Africa (Cape of Good Hope) unite British areas in the North Atlantic and the Indian Oceans. Even along these routes the British have significant possessions.

The largest gap in imperial communications appears in the North Pacific. British islands are concentrated in the southwestern part of the Pacific; over the northern part of this largest of oceans the few islands that do

exist are under flags of other nations.* Long-distance routes across the Pacific that connect British areas in the North Atlantic and the Indian Oceans are by the way of the Panama Canal to the south of North America and around the southern part of South America (Cape Horn and the Strait of Magellan). A third route extends diagonally across the Pacific from western Canada to Australia or Singapore. The recent conflict revealed the importance of Britain's system of ocean routes, the most critical of all being the one between the British Isles and Canada and the United States.

Cultural factors. In view of the vast spread of land areas within the British Commonwealth-Empire, the great diversity in the peoples inhabiting these areas is not surprising. Although the population of the Commonwealth-Empire is well over 500 million, only some 70 million are of the white race and less than 50 million of these whites live in the United Kingdom. Possibly 50 million Negroes are found in Africa under the British flag. India's enormous population of 389 million is in itself composed of a variety of ethnic types.

Although English is the principal language of the Commonwealth-Empire, well over 200 different languages and dialects are spoken by the Indian people in southern Asia and the Negro people in Africa and the West Indies. Arabic prevails among the natives of British areas in the Near and Middle East, and Afrikaan is used extensively by the white people of South Africa.

Most of the major religions of the world are well represented in the British Commonwealth-Empire. Among them Christianity, Islam, Hinduism, and Buddhism each have worshipers running into the millions or tens of millions.

Degree of self-sufficiency. The British Commonwealth-Empire is only partially self-sufficient in so far as its ability to feed its population and maintain its industries are concerned. To be sure, self-sufficiency is a relative term and, strictly speaking, no country is self-sufficient. Thus neither the United States nor the Soviet Union is self-sufficient. But both these countries have the advantages

* See Chapter 5 for the discussion of the Hawaiian and other islands that dominate sea routes in the North Pacific.

of a large continental base, whereas the seas provide the unity of the British Commonwealth-Empire in peace and afford the inherent dangers to a maritime empire in war. As long as the seas remain open to commerce, the wheat and wool of Australia, the nickel and copper of Canada, the tin and rubber of Malaya, the oil of Trinidad—indeed, innumerable items essential to a balanced economy within a great political empire—may be exchanged. It is a well-established fact, however, that no single unit of the Commonwealth-Empire possesses the degree of self-sufficiency of either the United States or the Soviet Union.

Not only is the United Kingdom the political nerve center of the British Empire, but it is also a focal center for industrial wealth.

With the possible exception of coal it unfortunately lacks adequate supplies for the necessities of a mature industrial economy. Moreover, only one half of the annual food requirements for Great Britain is normally produced from home sources.

Like the United Kingdom, other major political units of the Commonwealth-Empire have their own particular problems arising from the presence or lack of domestic supplies of natural resources. Some attempt is made to correlate the economies of the various units, but the political structure of the Empire permits the development of independent economic regimes within individual units, especially in the case of the Dominions, which in many ways operate as separate countries.

GREAT BRITAIN

Geographic Background

The British Isles are separated from continental Europe by shallow seas. Although nowhere deeper than 600 feet, and only twenty-one miles wide at the narrowest point in the Strait of Dover, these waters form a natural line of defense. As a rich fishing region and as a link with the most distant corners of the globe, they have profoundly affected every aspect of British life.

Physical aspects. Although detached from the Continent, the British Isles in structure, climate, vegetation, and cultural and economic development are essentially European. This fact is obvious, but at the same time has too often been ignored by politicians in determining foreign policy and international economic relations. The climate, controlled by an insular location and further affected by the Gulf Stream Drift, is characterized by cool summers (July, 55° F. in northern Scotland; 64° near London) and mild winters (January, 44° along the west coast; 38° in the eastern section). Prevailing westerly winds and frequent cyclonic storms result in abundant rain, especially on the west coast uplands, where elevated areas have over 100 inches annually. The lowlands receive between 25 and 40 inches, rather evenly spread throughout the year, with the maximum in fall and winter, and the minimum in spring. Dull skies are a distinctive feature. On the average, clouds cover 62 per cent of the sky in spring, the brightest season, and 75 per cent in winter. This cool, humid climate resembles

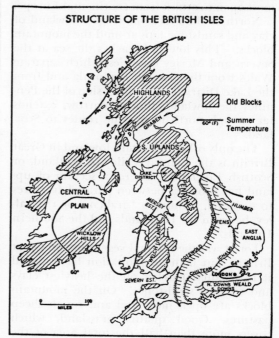

STRUCTURE OF THE BRITISH ISLES

that of the adjacent parts of Europe and has a close counterpart in North America along the coasts of Oregon, Washington, and British Columbia.

The structure of the two main islands of Great Britain and Ireland is similar. Both consist of isolated highlands of old hard rocks (granite, gneiss, schist, and slate) stripped of their surface soil by the ice sheets of the glacial age, and surrounded by lowlands of softer rocks (clays, limestones, sandstone, and chalk). The English lowland, which occupies one third of the area of Great Britain, is economically the most important section. Acting on many different rocks over long periods, erosion has produced a varied relief. Low unsymmetrical scarps, or ridges, of limestone and chalk alternate with clay and sandstone vales (see the map on page 99). In early times these ridges of porous rock formed fairly open breaks in the primeval forests that covered the lowlands, and here were the earliest sites of settlement. Today the principal significance of the limestone ridge lies in the iron ore deposits.

The lower Thames Valley between the Chiltern Hills and the North Downs, filled with clays, sands, and gravels, is the political focus of the whole island. Here stands London, guarding that stretch of eastern coast most open to attack from continental Europe.

North of the limestone ridge a lowland of clay and sandstone laps around the mountain blocks. This lowland reaches the sea at the Severn and Mersey estuaries, which separate Wales from the Cornish Peninsula and from the Lake District. On either side of the Pennines the lowland, though narrow, extends far enough north to provide routes to Scotland.

The only other important lowland in Great Britain is the Central Valley of Scotland, or Scottish Lowland. There, a section of upland has dropped between parallel fractures to sea level, forming a "graben," or rift valley, between the Highlands and the Southern Uplands.

Forest was the original vegetation on Great Britain, but man's exploitation has reduced it to residual patches on the heaviest clays and coarsest sandstones. On the mountain blocks are open moorland and rough sheep pastures. Good quality grassland, which covers more than half the total area of the west and central lowlands, forms the basis of an important dairy industry. Only the eastern coastal areas, with 25 inches of rainfall or less, are predominantly agricultural. East Anglia, the richest of these, is the principal wheat-growing region. But even there cattle

are numerous, fattened on root crops grown by rotation farming (for land use map, see directly below).

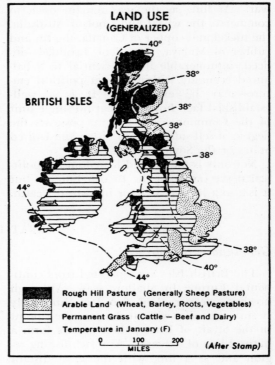

LAND USE (GENERALIZED)

BRITISH ISLES

Rough Hill Pasture (Generally Sheep Pasture)
Arable Land (Wheat, Barley, Roots, Vegetables)
Permanent Grass (Cattle — Beef and Dairy)
Temperature in January (F)

0   100   200
MILES   (After Stamp)

Economic aspects. Agriculture is of slight importance when compared with industry. Great Britain is essentially a manufacturing country, the primary basis of this industrial development being its coal deposits. The main coal fields are on the edges of the old mountain blocks, on the flanks of the Pennines, on the edges of the Welsh upland, and in the Scottish Lowland. All the coal fields are near the sea, and several actually on the coast, a factor conducive to the development of export trade. The major industries are located in the vicinity of the coal fields: cotton textiles in Lancashire, woolen textiles in Yorkshire, and pottery in Staffordshire (see the map on facing page). The iron and steel industry is concentrated in south Wales (tin-plating), Birmingham, Sheffield (cutlery), Northumberland, and Central Scotland. Because most of the coal-seam iron ore deposits are exhausted, these centers now rely on ore from the limestone ridge (Scunthorpe, Kettering) or on imports from abroad. Though some distance from coal, London is a manufacturing center to which secondary industries, especially clothing, boots and shoes, metal, furniture, and printing, have been attracted by the extensive labor supply and marketing facilities.

Historical Survey of Great Britain

A survey of Great Britain's history shows that three geographical factors have had great influence in the molding of the present political heart of the British Commonwealth-Empire. Briefly, these are:

1. Insularity—a position detached from Europe yet near enough to share in all cultural developments of the continent.

2. Favorable space relations—that is to say, an advantageous location for contact with the rest of the habitable world.

3. Uniquely located mineral resources.

These three factors that have influenced the growth and strength of Great Britain have not been equally important at every stage of Britain's development, nor indeed has the kind of influence they have exerted always been the same. Together, nevertheless, they account for many of the most distinctive features of British life.

The changing values of the three factors make possible a division of British history into three discernible eras.

From earliest times to the middle sixteenth century. During this era Britain lay in the outermost corner of the known world and its space relations were without specific advantage. In turn the era can further be broken down into two subdivisions.

FROM EARLIEST TIMES TO 1066. The period up to 1066 is one of cultural and racial immigration. The movement of people in Europe was mainly from east to west, controlled by migrations from the steppes of Central Asia. All major routes ended near Britain. Along the southerly route, following the continental coasts and the islands of the Mediterranean, came dark, long-headed Mediterranean folk seeking the tin and gold of Cornwall and Wicklow. They left dolmens and stone circles (Stonehenge) as evidence of their movement and of their cultural affinity with the people of the Mediterranean. Later, by the same route, came the Romans and, still later, Christian missionaries. Through the areas of light soils in Central Europe came several waves, ending just before the Roman conquest with the arrival of the Celtic tribes; from the coastal lowlands of the Baltic and North Seas came Angles, Saxons, Jutes, Danes, and Northmen.

For some time the political orientation of Britain was in doubt. Rome drew her to the south and Canute linked her with Scandinavia. But the North Sea was too wide for the latter affiliation and the link snapped; the Norman Conquest restored the southward orientation. By 1066 all the most important cultural elements had made their appearance on the then peripheral island.

FROM THE LATE ELEVENTH CENTURY TO THE MIDDLE SIXTEENTH CENTURY: *England and Wales.* During the centuries between 1066 and 1550 Britain advanced toward political unity. This advance was greatly facilitated by insularity, as a comparison of political conditions in contemporary Germany, Italy, or France will show. However, the personal ambitions of British kings delayed full exploitation of this advantage. In this period the local advantages of the London Basin were finally recognized. Political power was centered here, and gradually extended over the southeast lowland to the Irish Sea. In the face of this expansion of the English, the earlier inhabitants retreated until they were penned in by the western highlands. There, this folk with its early racial diversity preserved the Celtic tongue, and a Celtic culture zone came into being, linking northwest Scotland, Ireland, the Lake District, Wales, and Cornwall with Brittany in western France. Once in control of the lowland the English sought to subdue the people in the adjacent highlands. Cornwall and the Lake District were easily detached from Wales and absorbed, losing their Celtic culture in the process. Wales, more compact, offered greater resistance. But the relief of the country handicapped the defenders. Settlements clung to the edges of the mountain mass, and no central focus existed where resistance could be organized. The English, as the Romans had done before, drove along the northern and southern coastal plains and once in possession of the most settled areas quickly subjugated the whole. Nevertheless, rough topography and many isolated valleys protected the Welsh culture and today about 2 per cent of the population still speak only Welsh, and another 43 per cent are bilingual.

Scotland. Scotland, in marked contrast to Wales, had in the Central Lowland a natural organizing center. This area, like eastern Britain, was settled by Angles, who drove the Celts into the north and west and established an English-speaking nation. Distant from the London Basin and well defended by the bleak Southern Uplands, the Scots successfully repelled all attacks from the south and retained their independence until the peaceful union of the crowns in 1607.

Ireland. Ireland, despite dividing seas between it and Great Britain, was almost completely conquered between the twelfth and fourteenth centuries. An English-speaking aristocracy was established in control of all the island except the extreme western seaboard. During the Hundred Years' War and the Wars of the Roses, England was too much preoccupied to maintain control and contact was broken. But the Irish were too disunited to organize a single state and secure independence. Under the Tudors Protestant England began a second conquest. As Ireland had not been affected by the Reformation, this reconquest had all the bitterness of a religious war. English immigrants

again settled the conquered lands, and a large migration of Scots into Northern Ireland established a cultural minority that ever since has been a political problem.

Foundation of industry and overseas trade. In this phase of Britain's political development, separation from Europe reduced the danger of attack and was a distinct advantage. At the same time, proximity to the continent had significant results. Southern Britain faced Flanders, which was a node of medieval trade routes and the site of an early textile industry. English sheep pasturing on the chalk and limestone grasslands directly across the Channel from Flanders produced the finest wool in Europe. An export trade of this wool to the Flemish industry naturally began, and from this start flowed also to north Italy and the Hanse ports of northern Europe. Later the manufacture of woolen goods started in East Anglia (worsteds) and in the scarpface valleys of the Cotswolds (broadcloth and serges), and cloth replaced raw wool as the chief export. By the fifteenth century British cloth was without rival, and the Flemish industry became outclassed and moribund. Thus at the end of the first era Britain was well on the way to political unity, and the foundations of industry and overseas trade were firmly laid.

From the middle sixteenth century to 1914. The period between 1550 and World War I covers the rise of Imperial Britain. It can be subdivided into three parts:

FROM THE MIDDLE SIXTEENTH CENTURY TO AMERICAN INDEPENDENCE. The discovery of America transformed the space relations of Europe. Britain, till then tucked away in a corner of the Old World, suddenly found herself in the very center of the land surface of the globe. The long training of her people in seamanship, industry, and trade now bore fruit. British sailors explored the new seaways, colonies were planted in North America and the Caribbean, and trading stations were scattered at strategic points throughout the Orient.

All European countries with an Atlantic frontage shared the new opportunities, but not all had Britain's advantages. Spain and Portugal, first in the field, through overexpansion and an adverse combination of political, economic, and social factors, quickly lost their initial drive and became stagnant.

Holland, a more vigorous rival, was hampered by its small size and a long war against Spain. France alone offered serious competition to Britain, and a duel between the two powers lasted right up through the Napoleonic Wars. But the odds were with Britain. The loss of Calais in 1558 had freed Britain from continental ambitions and from the need of a large standing army. Thenceforward British energies were concentrated in the colonial field, and British wealth was devoted to the building of a large navy. France, on the other hand, could not renounce territorial claims in Europe so easily. Firmly embedded in the continent, the French frontier to the northeast was a constant source of danger from invasions as well as a lure to ambitious monarchs. With forces and interests in France so divided, Britain triumphed in both America and India, and the first Empire was won. It included half of North America, several Caribbean islands, and trading stations in India and the Far East. This Empire lasted only a few years before the secession of the American Colonies brought it to an end.

FROM AMERICAN INDEPENDENCE TO 1870. In the period after the fall of Napoleon in 1815 the world outside England was preoccupied with domestic problems. In India, China, the Near East, and Latin America large areas making up empires or segments of empires faced the problem of disintegration. European countries were absorbed in postwar reconstruction and the struggle for national unity. The United States was absorbed in its own westward expansion and the growing dissension between the North and the South.

Agricultural, industrial, and commercial advances. Without fear of competition in the political and military fields, Britain forged ahead. At home, agricultural and industrial processes were completely reorganized. New methods of cultivation, many imported from Holland as an example of cultural borrowing, had been widely introduced by the early eighteenth century. In the spread of agriculture open fields were enclosed, clover and roots in rotation replaced fallow, and marshlands were reclaimed (Fenns, River Humber). Attention was given also to the more efficient use of the land; the wet, heavy soils in central and western England gradually were turned over to permanent pasture, and arable farming was concentrated on the drier soils in the east. These changes continued through the first half of the nineteenth century until the present land-use pattern was established. In industry a more rapid and more far-reaching revolution took place. The use of steam-power made possible by the invention of machines designed for its use, drew industry from the rivers to the coal fields. Production expanded, foreign trade flourished, and overseas markets were staked out. The Industrial Revolution raised Great Britain to a most important position in the world of commerce and industry.

Imperial expansion. Abroad, expansion from early bases brought vast areas under the control of Britain. A second Empire arose on the scattered relics of the first. This new one embraced wide areas of temperate lands suited for white settlement to which a steady stream of emigrants moved—Canada, Australia, New Zealand, and South Africa. Almost against her will Great Britain took over general control of India from the decadent Mogul Empire. Trading ports along the African coast were expanded, and a foothold was acquired along the coast of China.

Protection of ocean lifelines. Ocean routes linking these territories were protected by island stepping stones and coaling stations. Particular attention was paid to those places where the routes converged on narrow straits, as is illustrated by the strategic development of Gibraltar and Malta in the Mediterranean. Ascension, St. Helena, Tristan da Cunha, Mauritius, Seychelles, Maldives, and Laccadives defended the route around the Cape of Good Hope to India; Malacca, Singapore, and Hong Kong guarded its continuation to the Far East. Later, when the Suez Canal was constructed, Britain secured almost half the shares of the Canal Company, and occupied Cyprus and Egypt at the northern entrance of the newly cut waterway. The southern outlet into the Red Sea was guarded by Aden, Perim and Socotra islands, and British Somaliland. Finally, the entrance to the Persian Gulf was made safe by the delimitation of a sphere of influence. In the New World, Caribbean holdings served as useful trade centers, and the Falkland Islands stood guard on the routes around Cape Horn.

Shaping the economy of colonial areas.
Political control gave Britain the opportunity
of shaping the economy of colonial areas to
fit that of her own pattern. The cloth industry of Northern Ireland had already been
killed; now the Indian trade in textiles shared
the same fate. First, tariffs to protect Lancashire's development destroyed the British
market for Indian calicoes. Next, when
Lancashire cottons invaded the Indian market, similar protection was denied the native
industry. Deprived of all chance of adjusting to the changed conditions the manufacture of cloth declined. Ever since then India
has had to rely too heavily on agriculture.
How to secure a better economic balance
through industrialization became and still remains one of that country's major problems.

Foreign policy. Foreign entanglements
would have impeded British development,
and so they were avoided. For some time
Britain had realized that her future did not
lie in continental Europe. As a result she exploited her insularity to the utmost and withdrew into "splendid isolation." From the
fall of Napoleon to the end of the nineteenth
century British foreign policy reduced to its
simplest form is seen to have been guided by
three cardinal principles:

1. The preservation of a balance of power in
Europe that would insure no single power achieving hegemony in that continent.
2. The safeguarding of the independence of
the Low Countries—that cockpit of Europe which
held by any great power would menace the London Basin and threaten British control of the narrow seas.
3. The maintenance of naval supremacy and
preservation of that freedom of the seas which
would allow British trade to expand peacefully.

A foreign policy based on these principles
proved successful. In general, peace was
maintained, and before any other country was
able to follow her lead Britain had achieved
great industrial and commercial strength and
a wide-flung empire.

FROM 1870 TO 1914. The year 1870
roughly marks the end of Britain's period of
uncontested expansion. In the half century
that followed, British imperial supremacy
was seriously challenged. Germany and
Italy were at last unified, and Austria had
found a temporary solution to her minority
problem. European and American indus-

trial resources were being exploited and developed, and rivals, benefiting by the experiences and mistakes of Great Britain, appeared in markets hitherto controlled by the
British. As trade expanded, political ambitions grew. When the new industrial powers
extended their attempts to carve out empires
of their own, the grab for Africa and the
loosely held parts of Asia ensued. Britain
took part in this drive for colonies and
emerged with additional territory equal in
area to one half that she already possessed.
The new acquisitions were for the most part
tropical lands, peopled by tribes existing at
a low level of culture. Effecting political
control over areas of this type raised serious
problems of colonial administration, most of
which are still unsolved.

Germany, more richly endowed than many
of her neighbors, soon outstripped all competitors. In expanding, she began to find
her interests everywhere clashing with those
of Britain. On the continent Germany threatened to upset the delicate balance of power;
in consequence, Britain was forced to leave
her splendid isolation and ally herself with
old rivals, France and Russia. Exports from
Germany were invading British markets all
over the world. The *Drang nach Osten* with
the planned Berlin-to-Baghdad Railway
threatened Britain's commercial and political
hold on the Near and Middle East, and the
naval race jeopardized British supremacy at
sea. By 1914 the situation was critical.
When at last the attack on Belgium threatened to establish Germany on the southern
shore of the narrow seas, Britain declared
war, not so much to protect a small nation
against a powerful aggressor as to safeguard
that basis on which for nearly three centuries
British political and economic life had rested.

The modern scene: 1914–45. The third
era is one of transition and brings us to the
consideration of the major problem facing
Britain—the search for a way of life more in
harmony with the modern world.

POPULATION. On the island of Great Britain live forty-eight million people, in an area
of slightly under 90,000 square miles, or less
than twice the size of Pennsylvania. The
density of population on Great Britain,
nearly 540 persons per square mile, is greater
than for that of the industrialized southern
New England states in the United States; Eng-

land alone has a population density exceeding that of either Belgium or the Netherlands, commonly considered the acme of industrialized settlement. A comparison of the map on this page with that on page 101 reveals the close relationship between industry and dense

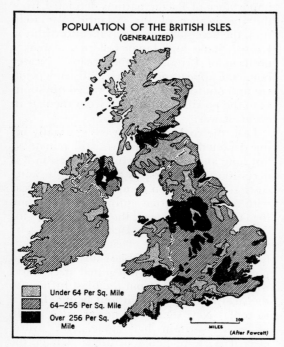

POPULATION OF THE BRITISH ISLES
(GENERALIZED)

Under 64 Per Sq. Mile
64–256 Per Sq. Mile
Over 256 Per Sq. Mile

MILES
(After Fawcett)

settlement. Although London, with eight million people, is by far the largest city in Great Britain, there are five other cities with a population of one-half million or more: Birmingham (1,090,000), Glasgow (1,088,-000), Liverpool (752,000), Manchester (685,-000), and Sheffield (509,000). Actually, 60 per cent of the people of Great Britain lives in cities or urban clusters with over 50,000 persons. This concentration of population in cities located mostly in the southeast lowland, the area closest to continental Europe, makes Britain particularly vulnerable to attack from across the narrow sea and enhances the strategic importance of the Strait of Dover.

ECONOMIC DEVELOPMENT. In 1914, despite Britain's position as one of the most powerful nations in the world, her unbalanced economy, that is, dependence on foreign trade, made her peculiarly vulnerable. The unbalanced economy arose in the following way.

About 1870 wheat from the farmlands of

the New World appeared on the world market. Wheat from this source was far cheaper than that grown in the cool, wet climate and leached forest soils of western Europe. Moreover, mechanized methods of cultivation were less difficult and less expensive to introduce in the pioneer lands across the Atlantic than on the small farms of western Europe. An agricultural crisis was precipitated. France and Germany protected their agriculture by tariffs. Denmark retained free trade and on the basis of imported fodder developed an export dairy trade. Britain had decided against agricultural tariffs in 1846 when the Corn Laws were repealed under pressure from the shipping firms and the northern industrialists. Both of these groups wanted a free import of foodstuffs, for that meant lower living costs and, therefore, lower production costs at home and greater competitive strength abroad. Free import of grain hit British agriculture badly, throwing large areas out of production. Some abandoned grain lands were left in grass; others became estates of the new industrial aristocracy. By 1914 acceleration in the drift of rural people to the towns had left only 7 per cent of the population engaged in agriculture (there were 31 per cent in Germany). More and more food was imported from abroad in exchange for manufactured goods. In 1910, for example, net exports were about $2,800,-000,000 and total exports $2,100,000,000, a comparison which reveals that Britain imported $700,000,000 worth of goods more than was paid for by exports.* The balance was made good by "invisible exports."

For many decades Britain had loaned other nations the capital with which to build railways, roads, and factories; by 1914 the total of such investments was about $20,000,000-000. Interest on such loans and repayment of the principal were part of the invisible exports received by Britain, which helped materially to make up the foreign-trade deficit. Furthermore, London, as the leading financial center of the world, earned large commissions for banking services, that is, floating loans and other monetary transactions. To this income was added the earnings of the

* In this chapter British monetary values are shown in dollars at the rate of $4.86 for each pound sterling. A uniform rate is used for comparative purposes, and all values are "round numbers."

British mercantile marine, which handled a substantial part of the world's trade. Mackinder gives the following estimate of British trade for the decade 1896–1906.*

Imports	Millions of dollars	Payment for imports	Millions of dollars
Imports	2475	By manufacturers (less raw materials used)	900
Less re-exports	625	Coal	120
	1850		
		Shipping services	440
		Interest on loans	315
		Banking services	75
			1850

The rough calculation above probably underestimates the amount of invisible exports. In most years they were sufficient to establish a credit balance.

World peace was essential for such an economy to function. War that interrupted foreign trade was a disaster, shutting off overseas markets and devouring profits normally used to increase investments abroad and maintain the flow of imports. War is inevitably more than a temporary calamity. It is a catalyst and, as such, speeds up changes that are slowly taking place in every economy; adjustment to these changes must be abrupt. For the four years of World War I former British overseas markets were forced to find other sources of supply. This they did, and when peace was restored Britain found previous sales outlets either in the hands of competitors or supplied by home industries behind high tariff walls. The British realized that drastic adjustment was imperative.

WEAKNESSES. From a re-examination of the three factors that had so marked an influence on the earlier stages of Britain's development (see page 101), the extent to which their importance had dwindled after World War I becomes immediately apparent. First, air warfare had reduced the strategic value of insularity, and economic separation from Europe had become a handicap. Ports, such as Liverpool and London, had far smaller hinterlands than their continental rivals, such

as Antwerp and Hamburg, which could tap the trade of regions much larger than the whole of the British Isles.

Second, in several ways the space relations of Britain were changed for the worse. Development of Pacific routes and the growing importance of Pacific nations detracted from the importance of the Atlantic. In addition, the acceptance of a naval ratio with the United States and Japan reflected a weaker position of Britain on the oceans. Nearer home the appearance of a virtually independent and not too friendly Eire raised questions as to the possibility of attack from the rear in event of war.

Last, the coal resources were gradually being depleted. Great reserves still remained, but long and often wasteful exploitation was necessitating deeper pits and raising mining costs at a time when competition from areas with newer and better equipment was becoming critical. Moreover, the world market for coal was diminishing. Demand was in part restricted by the more efficient use of coal, as for example, the use of blast furnace gas and powdered fuel in the integrated steel works where metal moved from the blast furnace to the steel rolling mills without being allowed to cool. New sources of power, such as oil, of which Britain had none, and hydroelectricity, were being utilized. Under the impact of such changes British coal exports fell from about one hundred million tons in 1913 to seventy-five million in 1930.

At the same time one must also remember the great expenditure on armaments and defense necessitated by the existence of the Commonwealth-Empire. From 1884–1931 Britain alone spent on armaments $53,000,-000,000, whereas the total value of colonial trade was only $89,000,000,000. Between 1921 and 1931 the average annual expenditure on arms was $590,000,000.*

STRENGTH. Despite an unfortunate setback in her international position Britain still had many assets. The first was the mo-

---

* Sir Halford Mackinder, *Britain and British Seas* (Oxford Press, 1925), p. 347. Note: British pounds converted to dollars: £1 = $4.86.

* In the year 1931 the $554,000,000 that Britain spent for armaments compares with other selected countries as follows (for the same year): France, $437,-000,000; Italy, $225,000,000; the United States, $705,-000,000; Soviet Russia, $1,180,000,000; and Germany, $213,000,000 (probably an underestimate). J. A. Hobson, *Imperialism* (G. Allen and Unwin, 1902, Revised 1938). See *Peace Year Books*, National Peace Council, London.

mentum attributable to an early start, which includes long industrial tradition and experience, well-equipped training and technical schools, accumulated knowledge of foreign markets, and many long-established commercial links. After World War I Britain still had over $15,000,000,000 in foreign investments, and her shipping had been increased by additions from the German mercantile marine.

A second asset was the Commonwealth-Empire. Within the limits of this great political structure one must distinguish between self-governing Dominions and dependent lands. In the interest of their own young industries the economically independent Dominions often followed high tariff policies. Nevertheless, they generally acknowledged Britain's political leadership for strategic reasons and shared defense costs. There was also a sentimental bond that connoted an economic influence. The Dominions tended to seek British capital and to use the London money market; in turn, British goods were given preferential tariff rates, and the large groups of citizens of English origin provided a ready market for old country products.

In the dependent Empire, such as India and the Crown Colonies, economic life was generally controlled to the advantage of Britain. This advantage held true even though Britain had long advocated an open-door policy in colonial territories, and with minor exception had applied it to her own. The use of English as the official language; the linking of the currency to sterling; and the tendency, other things being equal, to give public works contracts to British firms, all combined to preserve the favorable trade position between Britain and her dependent possessions. Moreover, the bulk of the trade between Britain and the dependent Empire was carried in ships flying the British flag. Thus the Empire was a great asset, important both for trade and reinvestment of capital.

BRITISH ECONOMIC DILEMMA AND METHODS OF CURE. British economy needed revitalizing to offset a weakened world trade position, stiff political competition, and heavy expenditures for defense measures. Two solutions could possibly alleviate the unfavorable situation.

First, there could be participation in world organization, entailing political and economic cooperation within the framework of the League of Nations and providing the initial step in the creation of a United States of Europe. This policy had many supporters, but the governing class, trained in the tradition of splendid isolation, viewed commitments in Europe as fraught with jeopardizing foreign entanglements.

Second, the solution might lie in the welding of the Empire into a self-contained economic unit, surrounded by high tariff walls. For a century British electors had consistently rejected tariffs, and as late as 1923 had defeated the Conservative Government on that very issue. But under the influence of the American high-tariff policy, Dominion pressure and Conservative policies combined at the Ottawa Conference in 1932 to impose protection on Britain under the euphemistic title of Empire Free Trade.

This particular type of policy, however, was geographically, historically, and economically impracticable. First, the Empire was not and could not be a completely self-supporting unit. Empire areas do not contain all things needed by the Empire, so trade with non-Empire areas will always be essential. Second, the Dominions, though eager to secure the British market for food and raw material, were too anxious to develop their own industries to remove all tariffs on British manufactures. Britain herself faced obstacles of greater magnitude. Only one third of her trade was within the Empire; the remainder was divided almost equally between Europe and the rest of the world. Immediate reorganization of a so widely distributed trade was impossible. Even had the Empire been able to supply all British needs for food and raw materials, higher prices would have been necessary to compensate for greater transport costs in bringing in products from distant points, for example, butter from New Zealand to replace that from Denmark or Canadian timber to replace that from Scandinavia. Moreover, tariffs on products from countries in which Britain had large investments would create difficulties in the payment of interest that normally entered as goods rather than gold. So clumsy a policy benefited the Empire little, if at all. The main result was that other countries adopted similar tariff policies. World trade became increasingly restricted within tariff-defended empires between which there was but little exchange of commodities.

Germany, with an industrial economy similar to Britain, had no political empire. In her efforts to secure markets she used the "blocked mark," that is, only bought food-stuffs and raw materials from producing areas on the condition that they took payment in German-manufactured articles. This device was a powerful weapon and, used unscrupulously, quickly brought the whole of southeast Europe into the economic grip of the Third Reich. Thus, in the attempt to solve the economic problem, Britain broke with tradition, but in a way that only sharpened economic conflict and speeded the drift to war.

GEOGRAPHICAL AND POLITICAL DANGERS. Changed conditions also forced Britain to devise new policies in the political field. Naval supremacy was forever lost. Even though friendly relations with the United States might be assumed, the naval programs of Japan and Italy were matters of grave concern. The lifelines of the Empire were menaced not only by the expansion of potentially hostile navies but also by the possibility of attacks by land-based planes.

The Mediterranean route especially was endangered. Gibraltar no longer stood impregnable, for attacks from the air had to be expected and there was little space for an air base. Nearby Fascist Spain was hostile and fiercely nationalistic; resentment at the British hold on The Rock was expressed even in official circles. Ceuta, across the Straits in Africa, would have given Britain a better defensive site, but even had an exchange been effected the city's minority of 60,000 Spaniards would have created serious difficulties. Almost surrounded by Italian territory, Malta also had its defensive strength curtailed by the fortification of adjacent Pantelleria. Britain's hold on the Suez Canal was threatened by the independence of Egypt and signs of growing hostility throughout the Arab world. This hostility was attributable partly to rising nationalistic feeling and the resentment of the grip Britain had on the economic life of the newly created Arab states, and partly to the Balfour Declaration, which accelerated the movement of Jews back to Palestine. Further, the hostility was sharpened by the intensive anti-British propaganda campaign inaugurated by Italy over conditions in the Near East. The Red Sea outlet, guarded by Aden, was menaced by the conquest of Ethiopia, which strengthened the Italian hold on the African shore. Altogether the Mediterranean route seemed so impossible to defend that one group of British strategists advised its complete abandonment in event of war and the re-routing of all trade from the East (about 50 per cent of the British total) around the Cape of Good Hope. Plans were made for redirecting traffic in this manner, but at the same time all Mediterranean possessions were strengthened for use as bases from which an enemy could be harassed. Events in World War II proved the wisdom of this latter policy.

Japanese aggression in China raised similar doubts about the safety of shipping routes in the Far East. There, Singapore and Hong Kong were the two British strongholds. A glance at the map on page 424 reveals the great strategic value of the site of Singapore. Not only did British strategists fail to anticipate Japanese tactics, but preparations for safe-guarding these bases were woefully inadequate. Whereas Malta held out through the entire period of World War II, Singapore and Hong Kong fell within a few weeks.

British policy in Europe was muddled and futile. The Treaty of Versailles had tended to "Balkanize" Europe, a result that at first seemed to simplify Britain's traditional task of preventing the rise of any overwhelming power. But with the spread of economic nationalism came the need for some form of international cooperation. The United States was not a member of the League of Nations. France, dominated by the age-old fear of the northeast frontier, was too occupied in keeping Germany weak. Britain was the most obvious nation to give the required lead. Traditional modes of thought proved too strong, however, and the geographical insularity of British thinking remained intact. "Storms sweep the Channel, the Continent Isolated"—headlines that appeared in the London *Times*—symbolically indicate how insular the British attitude still was. So Britain abandoned a strong European policy for one of greater Empire solidarity, and the way was open for the rise of the Third Reich. One might have expected that her old fear of one power dominating Europe would have driven Britain to act against Germany soon after the rise of Hitler. But fear of Bolshevik Russia was a compensating factor that succeeded in preventing such drastic action as an attack on the continent. British statesmen could not decide which menace was the greater; Nazi Germany was even welcomed by some as a possible anti-Bolshevik ally. Until it was too late Britain's leaders temporized, and then once again the nation fought to break German domination of Europe. Once again, probably for the last time, insularity saved her from defeat.

Future Outlook

Economic aspects. Though again victorious, and still ranking as one of the Great Powers, Britain faces a bleak future. The war has left her in an impoverished condition. Many of her foreign investments have been liquidated. Annual interest payments will be reduced by some $340,000,000 in prosperity and $630,000,000 in a slump. Britain also faces competition from newly developed industrial areas, such as those in Latin America, and from countries where industrial plants were expanded to meet war needs, such as Canada and the United States. Britain's carrying trade will meet even greater competition. In 1939 the size of the British mercantile marine was three times that of the United States. Following World War II it was only one half the size, with the likelihood that it may be further reduced to only one third. Thus the trade balance will be decidedly adverse. One estimate is as follows: *

	1936–38 (average)	Postwar (estimate)
	(in millions of dollars)	
Excess of imports over exports	1,885	1,945
Invisible exports	1,670	780
Debit	215	1,165

This estimate assumes moderate prosperity. A world-wide slump would increase the deficit to $1,700,000,000. How can this trade balance be adjusted?

By lowering her standard of living Britain could import less, but even if the wartime

* "Britain's Trade in the Post War World," *National Planning Association,* London, Pamphlet No. 9. See also Economic articles in *Bulletin of International News,* Royal Institute of International Affairs.

standard of living were maintained the saving in imports would amount to only about $500,-000,000 a year. If, in addition, Britain discontinued importing everything that could possibly be produced at home, another $300,-000,000 or $400,000,000 would be saved, but a deficit would still remain. The only real hope Britain has of solving the problem is to expand her export trade. This method will be possible only if there is prosperity and a high living standard in areas to which she might export, that is, the Americas, the Dominions, and tropical lands producing raw materials. At the same time there must be low prices for those raw materials required by her industries. These somewhat contradictory conditions could be created by the United States, producing, as it does, more than one quarter of the total real income of the world.

If the United States is prosperous, there will be a greater demand for British goods and services in the United States, and a still greater demand in those areas from which the United States buys, notably Canada, Latin America, and tropical lands. In that event, however, to prevent the high demand for raw materials from raising the level of prices, only the better soils and resources will be utilized and methods of producing commodities for trade will have to be improved. Any labor released as a result might be absorbed in industry and, if possible, in types whose products would not compete with those of Britain. An adjustment of this scope would require large amounts of capital. For the first time Britain cannot supply it, but the United States can. The solution of Britain's economic plight seems to depend on the ability of the United States to maintain prosperity at home and at the same time its willingness to follow economic policies abroad that are determined by international, rather than purely national, considerations. If American policies are not so designed, Britain might try to expand her trade by export bounties entailing a "blocked pound" and inflation methods recently used in Germany and Japan. But at best this technique could postpone ultimate defeat only by impoverishing the British at home and disrupting world trade.

It is now clear that Anglo-American relations must figure prominently in Britain's economic welfare of the future. To illustrate, on December 6, 1945, the United States and the United Kingdom signed an agreement whereby the latter would receive a loan of $3,750,000,000 and for which she agreed to relax import and exchange controls and to support a multilateral trade program.

Political aspects. Consideration of Britain's new space relations is necessary. In the postwar world two great centers of economic and political power are evident—the United States and the U. S. S. R. At least as long as India and, more particularly, China remain largely undeveloped and disunited, no other single nation, most certainly not Great Britain, can compete with these two great powers in wealth and influence. In order to counterbalance a lower rank in world position and retain something of her former power, Britain would have to organize a coalition. As in the interwar period there are again two possibilities. First, the Commonwealth Empire could be welded into a more cohesive unit that in world affairs would speak with one voice. Tending to favor great decentralization within the Commonwealth-Empire the Dominions would find this policy unpopular. Second, western Europe could be organized into a power bloc that, in addition to enhancing British prestige, might put a limit to the westward advance of Soviet influence. Though advocated by General Smuts of South Africa, and apparently favored by many leaders in the present government, such a plan could hardly be put into operation without further affecting Empire bonds, for the Dominions would hardly be willing to sanction a *purely* British policy on the continent of Europe.

The whole political importance of Great Britain depends upon continued coopera-

tion among the United Nations. If the United States and Soviet Russia fail to remain united and drift into opposite camps, two power blocs would divide the world, and consequently Britain would find herself in the uncomfortable position of a border state. In such an event, it seems probable that the Dominions would gravitate toward the United States because of proximity (Canada), sympathy (the United States would have more sympathy with South Africa's attitude toward the color problem than either Britain or the U. S. S. R.), or from a feeling that the United States could give security to their general way of life (Australia and New Zealand). Britain, likewise economically dependent on the United States, would probably swing her interests into the same bloc. Then the zone of tension where the spheres of influence of the two blocs overlapped would stretch across a belt of territory already politically unstable. Such a zone would cover (1) Central Europe, which Britain watches closely for any threat to her security; (2) the Near East, where Britain has economic interests and a concern for her air and sea routes to India and the Far East; (3) India, where Britain has $5,000,000,-000 invested; and (4) China, where Britain by insisting on her claims to Hong Kong seems anxious to re-establish her stake against United States and Russian competition. A renewal of power politics in this manner would be fatal to Britain and probably to the world as a whole.

If, however, the United Nations continues to function and forms the nucleus of a world organization more firmly knit than the old League of Nations, Britain and the Commonwealth-Empire could play an important intermediary role in world affairs.

EIRE AND NORTHERN IRELAND

Geographic Background

One third the size of Great Britain, or only slightly larger than West Virginia, Ireland consists of a central plain within a frame of mountains. The mountains of the island are detached fragments of those in western Britain, and support the same natural vegetation (see the map on page 99). The central lowland is formed of limestone over which lie impermeable glacial deposits. Absence of

slope and poor drainage cause the numerous bogs for which Ireland is noted. Although the drainage pattern is better near the coast and in the valleys of the highland rim, constant high humidity and cool summers favor grass rather than cereals. As a result, well over half the land of Ireland is in rough or permanent pasture, and forage crops in all parts support large numbers of cattle, horses, sheep, and pigs. These farm animals and their products are the main source of the country's wealth. Because lack of good communications has handicapped the dairy industry, beef cattle are more important than dairy herds. Of the few crops grown, potatoes and oats lead in production (see the land use map on page 100).

Ireland lacks important sources of power and has few industries. Despite the abundance of peat, or brown coal, in bogs about the Irish landscape, its inferior quality makes it unsuitable for industrial use in competition with English coal. Most of the industries that do exist are concentrated in Northern Ireland, linen (County Down) and shipbuilding (Belfast) being the two most important. Elsewhere, industries are confined to the processing of agricultural products —bacon curing, butter and cheese making, brewing, and grain milling.

The small population of four and one quarter million, in contrast to that of Great Britain, is mainly rural and widely scattered (see map on page 105). Of the total, about three million live in Eire and about one and one quarter million in Northern Ireland, which is a part of the United Kingdom. The density of population for Ireland as a whole is not high for western Europe, but much greater than that for states such as Indiana and Michigan. Each section has one large city approaching 500,000 in population: Dublin, capital of Eire; and Belfast, capital of Northern Ireland. Several secondary cities, all between 25,000 and 75,000 in population, lie along the seacoast: Cork, Limerick, and Waterford in Eire, and Londonderry in Northern Ireland. In 1846 the island of Ireland had a population of eight and one-half million, most of whom lived in the section now known as Eire. Thus, the present population is only half what it was in the middle of the nineteenth century. The decrease was primarily brought about by a great "potato famine." Because of heavy emigration to America the United States today has an Irish population four times greater than Ireland.

Historical Survey

Early in the Christian era Ireland consisted of five kingdoms—Ulster, North Leinster, South Leinster, Munster, and Connaught— each under its own ruler. In turn, these rulers acknowledged the overlordship of Ard-Ri, who lived at Tara. In the fifth century A.D. St. Patrick, who brought Christianity to the country, became its patron saint. By the seventh century the Irish had progressed to the point where they were the most advanced group in northern Europe. During the next several centuries thereafter the country suffered a long series of disrupting invasions, from which the native Celts received an intermingling of Saxon, Norman, Danish, and English blood. In the middle of the twelfth century the Pope gave all Ireland to the English Crown. Although Henry II became "Lord of Ireland" in name following this change in the sovereign authority, native sectional rule continued and English domination over the entire island became complete only in the seventeenth century. From that period down to the present century Irish Catholic tenant farmers bitterly opposed the injustices and oppression of the absentee British Protestant landlords. Added to the constant upheavals growing out of internal racial and religious cleavages was the continual struggle for freedom from the English Crown.

Recent political developments. In 1920 Ireland was granted home rule, with the status of a Dominion. At the same time six Ulster counties of Northern Ireland were given the opportunity to separate from the rest of the island politically and to remain in closer relations with Great Britain. The twenty-six counties of Eire accepted Dominion status "for the time being" in 1922, and consequently Eire is as independent of Britain as Canada or the Union of South Africa. Northern Ireland, which has a local government, has a governor appointed by Britain, a Senate, and a House of Commons. This local government legislates in all fields save those affecting foreign relations and a few reserved subjects, for example, stamps and postal service. In addition, Northern Ireland sends thirteen representatives to the British House of Commons.

The political division of the island of Ireland into Eire and Northern Ireland has a certain cultural basis. Eire is mainly Roman Catholic in religion (seven eighths of the total population) and agricultural. Northern Ireland is mainly Protestant (two thirds of the population) and more industrialized. These differences are intensified by the efforts of Eire to make Erse the national language,

Political Areas of the British Commonwealth-Empire

(at the conclusion of World War II)

Political units	Area in square miles
Europe	121,403
Great Britain and Northern Ireland	93,983
(England, Wales, Scotland, Northern Ireland)	
Isle of Man	221
Channel Islands	75
Eire	27,000
Gibraltar	2
Malta	122
Asia [1]	2,338,875
Cyprus	3,584
Palestine (mandated area) [2]	10,429
Transjordan (mandated area) [3]	34,750
Aden and the Protectorate	112,000
(including the Hadhramawt; and Perim, Socotra, Kuria Muria Islands)	
Arabian states (special relations with Great Britain)	96,000
(Muscat and Oman, Trucial Coast, Qatar, Bahrein Island, Kuwait)	
India [4]	1,581,410
(including Andaman, Nicobar, and Laccadive Islands)	
Bhutan (special relations with Great Britain)	18,000
Nepal (close relations with Great Britain)	54,000
Ceylon (including the Maldive Islands) [4]	25,332
Burma [5]	261,610
Federated Malay States [6]	27,648
Unfederated Malay States [6]	23,486
Straits Settlements	1,535
(including Christmas Island, Cocos Islands, and Labuan)	
Borneo, Brunei, and Sarawak	88,700
Hong Kong	391
Africa	3,780,866
Gambia	4,068
Sierra Leone	27,925
Gold Coast	91,843
(including Togoland Mandate) [7]	
Nigeria	372,674
(including Cameroons Mandate) [7]	
British Somaliland	68,000
Anglo-Egyptian Sudan	969,600
Uganda	94,204
Kenya	224,960
Tanganyika Mandate [7]	363,548
Nyasaland	37,596
Northern Rhodesia	290,320
Southern Rhodesia	150,354
Union of South Africa	1,083,696
(including the Mandate of Southwest Africa and the native states of Basutoland, Swaziland, and Bechuanaland)	
Zanzibar and Pemba	1,020
Seychelles and dependencies	156
(including Amirantes Islands)	
Mauritius and dependencies	809
(including Rodrigues Island)	
Tristan da Cunha	12
Ascension	34
St. Helena	47
America	3,732,285
Canada	3,462,103 [8]
Newfoundland and Labrador	154,734
Bermuda	19
Bahamas	4,404
Jamaica	4,674
(including Turks and Cayman Islands and Caicos Bank)	

Political units	Area in square miles
British Honduras	8,867
Windward Islands	820
(including Grenada, St. Vincent, the Grenadines, St. Lucia, Dominica)	
Leeward Islands	422
(including Antigua, Montserrat, St. Christopher, Nevis, Sombrero, the British Virgins)	
Barbados	166
Trinidad and Tobago	1,978
British Guiana	89,480
Falkland Islands and dependencies	4,618 [9]
(including South Georgia, South Shetlands, South Orkneys, Sandwich Group, and Graham Land)	
Australasia and Oceania	3,281,333
Australia and Tasmania	2,975,000
(including Norfolk and other islands)	
Papua (Australian)	90,540
Territory of New Guinea (mandated area under Australia, consisting of Northeastern New Guinea, the Bismarck Archipelago—New Britain, New Ireland, and the Admiralty Islands—and the former German Solomons—chiefly Bougainville) [10]	93,000
New Zealand	103,000
(including Cook, Union, and other islands)	
Territory of Western Samoa (mandated under New Zealand) [10]	1,250
Nauru Island (mandated to the British Empire) [11]	10
Fiji Islands	7,083
Pacific Islands (under British Commissioner)	11,450
(Gilbert and Ellice Islands Colony—including Ocean Island, Christmas Island, and the Phoenix Group—British Solomon Islands—including the Santa Cruz Islands—New Hebrides Condominium with France, Tonga, or Friendly Islands, Pitcairn Island)	

Antarctica (Great Britain, Australia, and New Zealand claim areas on the continent. Graham Land is previously mentioned).

[1] In the Near and Middle East certain areas are outside the Commonwealth-Empire but inside it in practice.

[2] In 1948 Great Britain withdrew from Palestine.

[3] Made an independent state in 1946.

[4] In 1947 the dominions of Pakistan and the Union of India (Hindustan) were created; in 1948, Ceylon.

[5] In 1948 Burma became an independent state.

[6] Organized after World War II into a Malayan Union and later into a Malayan Federation (without inclusion of Crown Colony of Singapore in Union or Federation).

[7] Changed into trusteeship under United Nations in 1946 but with same administrator.

[8] Land area. With water area Canada contains 3,695,189 square miles.

[9] Area given includes Falkland Islands only.

[10] Changed into trusteeship under United Nations in 1946 but with same administrator.

[11] Changed into trusteeship under United Nations in 1947 but with same administrator.

NOTE: Total area for the British Commonwealth-Empire, exclusive of the dependencies of the Falkland Islands, was 13,254,762 square miles at the end of World War II. For comparative purposes, this area is somewhat larger than the continent of Africa, but considerably smaller than the continent of Asia. Again, the United States and possessions are about 28 per cent as large and the U.S.S.R. is about 63 per cent as large as was the British Commonwealth-Empire at the beginning of the postwar period.

and relations between the two sections are not harmonious. Eire has never accepted the separation of Northern Ireland as permanent, whereas Northern Ireland on the other hand has steadily refused to consider a reunion. Britain supports Northern Ireland in its determination to maintain the *status quo*. No settlement acceptable to all parties seems possible within the near future.

During World War II Eire remained neutral, whereas Northern Ireland participated actively in the conflict. On July 17, 1945, Prime Minister de Valera of Eire told the Dail, "We are an independent Republic associated as a matter of external policy with the States of the British Commonwealth." Although Eire has a republican constitution (effective December 29, 1937) and was the only neutral unit of the Commonwealth in World War II, it has still not formally seceded from the British Commonwealth of Nations.

CHAPTER 9 | The British Commonwealth of Nations

THE three major Dominions of the British Commonwealth of Nations (other than the United Kingdom, made up of Great Britain and Northern Ireland) are the Dominion of Canada, the Commonwealth of Australia, and the Union of South Africa. Also important, of course, is New Zealand, a Dominion usually associated with Australia as a unit in Britain's Australasian lands. Likewise, Newfoundland, associated with Canada and formerly a Dominion, may be listed here because of the possibility of its reinstatement into the Commonwealth of Nations or of some other change in its government in the near future (see the map on page 97 for the Commonwealth-Empire). These Dominions and their dependencies are discussed in this chapter, complementing the preceding chapter that deals with the British Isles as the seat of Empire power and with various phases of the dependent Empire. Although a Dominion in practice, Eire occupies a special position with reference to the Commonwealth; and changes have come for India and Ceylon.

World Position of the Dominions

To understand the part that each of the three major Dominions plays in the economic and political relations of the British Commonwealth of Nations requires a glance at their position in the world plan. The globe may be viewed in an infinite number of ways, though the conventional way is to place the North Pole at the top. However, in this present age of travel by air there is much to be said for first considering the map of that hemisphere which shows the most *land*. Within this hemisphere is nearly nine tenths of the ice-free land of the world, on which live ninety-four per cent of the earth's inhabitants. Such a concentration of the land masses of the globe in part explains the favorable position of the British Isles, which lie practically in the center of the Land Hemisphere. Canada, especially its eastern portion, is not far from the center, but South Africa is on the margin of the Land Hemisphere. Australia is out of the picture—and indeed New Zealand is practically at the center of the Water Hemisphere. Thus from the point of land connections Canada is certainly in the most favorable position of the three great Dominions, and Australia is in the least favorable.

A shift in attention to the basic relief pattern of the three Dominions discloses that Canada and Australia adhere to a plan typical of continental structure. On their Pacific shores there are lately formed (that is, young, geologically speaking) but relatively high mountains. On the other coasts are low resistant granite plateaus (shields) covering large areas (see map on facing page). Between the two structural units in each case is a great interior lowland that, naturally, includes the chief rivers of the land mass. However, the principal mountain-building processes are to the east of eastern Australia, so that the eastern highlands of that continent are much lower than the Rockies in North America. In contrast, South Africa consists essentially of a resistant portion of the earth's crust, which has not been affected by folding. However, it has been lifted en masse to form the relatively elevated expanse that makes up the preponderant part of South Africa.

The three Dominions are widely different as regards their broad climatic characteristics. A glance at the diagram on this page, which shows not only continental structure but also indicates the best temperature belts in the Northern and Southern hemispheres, reveals the divergencies among these three environ-

United States, Europe, and North China seem to be the choice regions of the earth, and man's history supports this suggestion. Temperature conditions in Central Asia are also satisfactory, but the area has thus far proved too dry for successful settlement.

To return to the three Dominions with

THE MAIN STRUCTURES (SHIELDS, DOWNFOLDS, MOUNTAINS) OF THE WORLD
(SKETCH MAP)

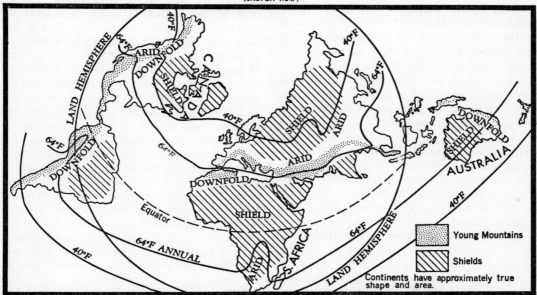

ments. The isotherm for 64° F. is near the optimum for physical work, and that for 40° F. is the optimum for the best mental work.* Thus the zone between the isotherms for 64° F. and 40° F. is probably the one in which civilization is likely to progress most rapidly. This zone covers large areas of land in the Northern Hemisphere. But, since the three main land masses south of the Equator taper toward the South Pole, there is not much territory in this favored zone in the Southern Hemisphere. On this basis the

which this chapter is largely concerned, Canada is seen to be rather too cold for satisfactory progress except along the southern margin. South Africa in general has acceptable temperature conditions but is too arid in the west to favor much development. Southern Australia (with New Zealand) is perhaps in the best position of the three with respect to temperature, and in addition has areas of rainfall sufficient to support agricultural productivity. South Africa and part of northern Australia are subtropical.

CANADA

Canada is roughly rectangular in shape. Having an area of about three and one-half million square miles, it is almost exactly the same size as Europe, and about the same as the United States together with its dependent ter-

* According to research by Ellsworth Huntington of Yale University.

ritories. In latitude it extends north to Ellesmere Island (83° North) and south to Lake Erie (41° North), a distance of 42 degrees of latitude. In longitude it ranges across 84 degrees, from the Atlantic to the Pacific oceans. Canada constitutes about 28 per cent of the total area of the British Empire.

Environment

Relief. As suggested in the diagram on page 115, Canada has four main topographic divisions. The largest consists of the Canadian Shield, an area of hard bedrock that forms a huge crescent around Hudson Bay and covers in all about two thirds of the whole Dominion. In the western third of the country are lowlands of softer material, drained by the Saskatchewan River in the south and the Mackenzie River in the north. In the extreme west the topography is high and rugged, forming a series of north-south ranges—the Canadian Rockies and Coastal Ranges—which are a continuation of those in the United States. Fortunately for Canada there is a fourth major topographic section in the southeast, a continuous belt of younger level-bedded rocks, which overlie the Canadian Shield between Lake Huron and the Atlantic shores of Nova Scotia. These constitute the farming lands of southern Ontario, southern Quebec, and the Maritime Provinces of New Brunswick, Nova Scotia, and Prince Edward Island.

The elevated portions of the Dominion, more than 2,000 feet in elevation, form a broken but discernible oval rim around the extensive lowlands in the interior of Canada. The center of the lowland area has been drowned to form Hudson Bay, and the broken northern rim forms the numerous islands of the Arctic Archipelago. East of the lowlands in the jagged peaks of the Torngats in Labrador the land attains an elevation of more than 5,000 feet. This rim extends southward along the western margin of Labrador to the Shickshock Mountains and the Appalachians in the southeast. There is also a fairly high rim just west of Lake Superior, which obstructs easy passage between eastern and western Canada. To the west the lowlands are bordered by the complex mountains of the Rockies and Coastal Ranges.

We may generalize somewhat and state that lowlands composed of relatively young sediments are more valuable to man than granite rocks such as those of the Canadian Shield—especially in the case of its eastern rim, where the rocks are considerably elevated. Mountain lands are usually of little value, though ancient "core-rocks" containing metals may be exposed in their valleys. In addition, the rugged nature of the relief provides an abundance of hydroelectric power in certain of the valleys.

NATURAL GATEWAYS. The natural gateways or corridors through the elevated rim surrounding the lowland will become of greater and greater consequence as settlement progresses. However, those that appear along the northern coasts of Canada need not concern us, since there is no settlement or trade of note in their vicinity. The most important corridor has always been that of the Gulf of St. Lawrence, through which medium-sized ships can now pass from the Atlantic Ocean to Duluth in the heart of North America, a distance of some 2,500 miles. This great corridor was of immense value in the French conquest of Canada from the Amerindians as well as later in the evolution of the Dominion. Some thousand miles to the north lie Hudson Straits, another wide entry to the heart of Canada. But this passage is closed by ice for nine months each year—a much longer time than is the St. Lawrence. Yet its use enabled the English to set up various settlements after 1670 that restricted the expansion of the French in the north just as early English settlements in New England, New York, and Pennsylvania checked them in the south.

Still another important gateway is that occupied by the Red River. This river rises in a "Valley Divide" at Traverse Lake about 150 miles northwest of Minneapolis. Here in the waning Ice Age vast bodies of water flowed south from Glacial Lake Agassiz into the Mississippi. Later, as the ice melted, the glacial lake drained away to the north. During the 1870's and 1880's thousands of new settlers traveled from the "end of rail" at Minneapolis northwestward into the fertile plains of Manitoba along the deep, wide valley made by the receding water.

The last notable gap in the rim is at Finlay Forks, where the Peace River cuts through the Rockies as it flows east from its source well to the west of the highest ranges. Here in the Peace River Pass the river is only 2,000 feet above sea level. This is much lower than the better-known railway passes to the south, which are traversed by the transcontinental lines of the Canadian National and Canadian Pacific railroads. Roads, and perhaps railways, will soon be constructed through this lower portion of the Rockies to link the fertile Peace River farms to the new agricultural lands being developed near Prince George. From this latter center a railway (but no continuous road) already leads west to the natural outlet at Prince Rupert on the Pacific Ocean.

Climate. Climate in Canada varies in detail from region to region but never departs markedly from the pattern peculiar to high latitudes and large land masses. Seasonal extremes are common to the entire country, although these are modified in the case of the

tional economy. As sources of wealth these latter are based, respectively, upon the great fishing banks off the Atlantic coast and 1,200,000 square miles of forest area.

In many mineral resources Canada is unusually well supplied. She has rich reserves of coal; she leads the world in the production of nickel; her deposits of gold, silver, copper, lead, zinc, and uranium are excellent; and petroleum reserves in the Dominion may exceed the meager estimates previously made. Canada is also endowed with valuable sites for the development of water power.

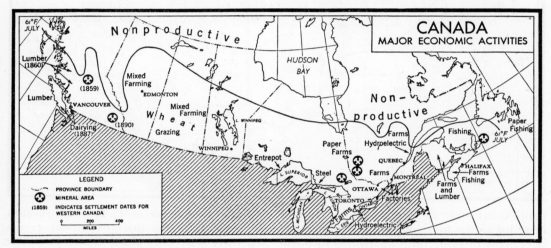

Pacific margin in British Columbia. In the north a short summer and long cold winter discourage most human activities. All the areas of settlement of note—except in Newfoundland and the Peace River region—are found in the south where the July temperature rises above 61° F. This isotherm, which separates the productive from the nonproductive regions, is shown in the map above.

Economic response. Although manufacturing is prominent in the cities of the southeast, the settled portion of Canada is largely agricultural (see the map on this page for major economic activities). In the prairie lands of the west grain raising is especially noteworthy. Successful fruit farming takes place in the regions protected from cold temperatures by the ameliorating effect of water bodies. Dairying, sheep raising, and fur farming lead in the Dominion's animal industries. Among nonagricultural activities fishing and lumbering (including wood for paper pulp) lend strong support to the na-

Internal Development

Migrations of settlers. Much of the initial interest of England and France in the New World centered in Newfoundland and Maritime Canada because of the economic advantages offered by that area. In 1497 Cabot took back glowing reports of the enormous numbers of fish in Newfoundland waters; and during the next century fishing fleets from Portugal, Spain, France, and England frequented the banks, or shallow seas, along the Atlantic coast. Trade in furs started with Cartier; and in 1597 the first post was built at Tadoussac on the Saguenay (see the map on page 118). Early permanent settlements were made by the French on the shores of the Bay of Fundy; Annapolis on an arm of the Bay of Fundy was founded in 1605, and Quebec on the St. Lawrence in 1608. In eastern Newfoundland the settlement of Cupids was founded in 1610 by Britishers from Bristol. The English have controlled Newfoundland ever since, although from about 1670 to 1800 they discouraged settlement there. Many skirmishes between French settlers at Placentia and English colonists on the east coast took place between 1660 and 1713, when England successfully declared her sovereignty over the whole island.

Although Newfoundland was noted chiefly for her offshore fishing grounds, the accounts of Radisson, a French explorer, about the furs

1745. Then three years later France regained them. In 1749 the British began the establishment of a strong naval port at Halifax, and ever since this has been a very vital focus of naval power. In 1758 a strong naval force from Halifax captured Louisbourg for the English again. On September 13th of the following year, the decisive battle of Quebec was fought, and as a result of the British victory, the French lost Canada.

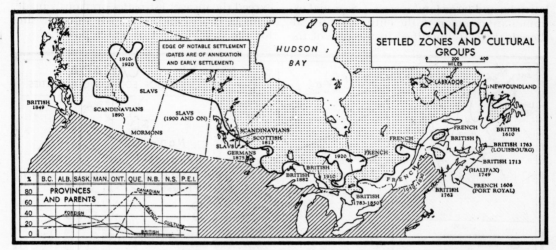

to be obtained in the region south of Hudson Bay led to the founding of the Hudson Bay Company in 1670. Still flourishing throughout northern Canada, this company for many years was represented by fur-collecting forts along the shores of Hudson Bay rather than by true settlements.

In 1642 the French settled Montreal, and from there explored all the large lakes to the west as well as adjacent rivers. In 1680–82 the French explorer LaSalle voyaged the whole length of the Mississippi. La Vérendrye founded many forts in the vicinity of Lake Winnipeg between 1731 and 1743. In the latter year his sons probably reached the Black Hills in Dakota. Hendry, starting in 1754 from the English fort on the Hudson Bay, seems to have reached Calgary and seen the Canadian Rockies.

Meanwhile, sailing from Boston in 1710, the English captured the French capital of Acadia (Nova Scotia) and named it Annapolis Royal. But the French still controlled the Isle of St. Jean (Prince Edward Island) and Cape Breton Island, and retained them until the forts at Louisbourg were taken in

Pattern of settlement: EASTERN SECTION. At the time of the British conquest (1759–63) there were only about 60,000 French in Canada, almost all of them settled on the shores of the St. Lawrence. As for the others, many "breeds" (half French, half Indian) were engaged in trapping around the Great Lakes, and, as pointed out, some fur traders had reached the Saskatchewan Basin and the distant prairies. Today people of French descent in Canada total nearly three million. Nearly all descended from the early French settlers, and in most cases are devout Catholics who have little cultural affinity with the modern population in France.

Aside from the region along the St. Lawrence, there were settlements in other portions of the Dominion of sufficient early importance to justify a rapid survey here.

During the War of Independence the French aristocracy and leaders of the church had little sympathy with the Americans revolting against British authority. The Quebec Act of 1774 gave religious freedom to the French Catholics, whereas many Americans were strongly opposed to the Catholic

Church. Carleton's wise rule in Canada also helped to save the newly conquered lands for Britain. Loyalist migrations from the seceding American colonies began in 1776, and many of the migrants helped to settle Nova Scotia. In 1783 large numbers of refugees from the United States founded settlements in New Brunswick. In the following year many loyal regiments took up land somewhat west of Montreal near Cornwall, in what is now Ontario. In 1794 Governor Simcoe moved the capital of Upper Canada (Ontario) from Niagara to Toronto.

In 1800 lumber men from the United States, interested in the exploitation of forest lands, arrived at Ottawa. About the same time an Irish officer, Colonel Talbot, began to induce settlers to clear the forests on the northern shores of Lake Erie.

In 1837 most of the settlers near Sherbrooke in southern Quebec were of English or American descent. Today, however, more than a century later, these "Eastern Townships" are occupied very largely by folk of French culture, for the prolific "habitant" is overwhelming the English stock in this portion of Canada.

WESTERN SECTION. Although La Vérendrye founded fur-trading posts in Manitoba as early as the 1730's, there was no true agricultural settlement until 1813, when Selkirk brought Scottish farmers to Winnipeg. These pioneers were isolated, and little in the way of crops was produced until after the Hudson Bay Company handed over control of the prairie regions to the Dominion in 1869. In 1875 many German Mennonites settled south of Winnipeg. Seven years later the first railway (Canadian Pacific) reached Calgary, passing through rather dry country settled by farmers mostly of British stock. When the northern railways were built through Saskatoon and Edmonton, large numbers of Slavs, Germans, Finns, and others settled on the mixed farming lands at the northern edge of the prairies. In 1900 Russian Doukhobor immigrants cleared farms near Saskatoon, and by 1908 farmers were occupying land in the Peace River Region. As a result, the population of the prairies increased from about 15,000 in 1870 to two million by 1921.

In British Columbia there was no important settlement until British rule became established at Victoria in 1849. The gold rush along the Fraser River brought many miners into British Columbia in 1858, but even today 93 per cent of the population is found in the southern quarter of the huge province and 70 per cent within one hundred miles of Vancouver.

Administrative pattern. Today the Dominion has nine provinces: Ontario and Quebec (old Upper and Lower Canada); Nova Scotia, New Brunswick, and Prince Edward Island (the Maritime Provinces); Manitoba, Saskatchewan, and Alberta (the Prairie Provinces); and British Columbia (the Pacific Province). To the north two territorial areas are Yukon and the Northwest Territories (Districts of Mackenzie, Keewatin, and Franklin). Ottawa, the capital of Canada, does not occupy a federal district like Canberra, the capital of Australia, or Washington, the capital of the United States.

Cities. Eight cities account for 44 per cent of the urban population of Canada, or nearly a fourth of the total population of the country. All but two of these are in the eastern third of Canada, concentrated in the St. Lawrence lowlands and along the northern shores of the eastern Great Lakes. Montreal (903,-000) serves as the metropolitan center for the entire country. Toronto (667,000), the second city of Canada, possesses a port and is tributary to rich agricultural land and productive mineral deposits. The next ranking cities in eastern Canada are Hamilton (166,-000), lake port and manufacturing center; Ottawa (155,000), national capital; Quebec (151,000), leading center of French-speaking Canada; and Windsor (105,000), virtually a suburb of Detroit across the international border. In western Canada the Pacific coastal area has Vancouver (275,000) as its regional economic center, and the prairie provinces look to Winnipeg (222,000), the focal point for a large agricultural region, as the gateway city to the east.

Aside from these eight largest cities there are numerous medium-sized cities that have important functions in the national economy. Illustrative are the seaboard ports of Maritime Canada, the agricultural centers scattered through the western prairies, and the secondary cities of the Ontario Peninsula north of Lake Erie.

Cultural pattern. The cultural (not racial) origins of the Canadians as recorded in the 1941 census in each province are as follows:

Canadian Cultural Origins (1941)

(Percentage in Canadian Provinces *)

Province	British	French	German	Ukrainian	Scandinavian	Dutch	Jewish	Indian
British Columbia	70	3	3	3	—	1	—	3
Alberta	50	5	10	11	8	2	—	1
Saskatchewan	44	5	14	12	7	4	—	2
Manitoba	49	7	6	13	2	5	—	2
Ontario	69	10	4	—	1	2	2	1
Quebec	13	81	—	—	—	—	2	—
New Brunswick	60	11	—	—	—	—	2	—
Prince Edward Island	82	15	—	—	—	—	—	—
Nova Scotia	80	11	3	—	—	4	—	—
Total	50	30	4	3	2	2	1	1

* It is inexplicable to the writer why the terms "English Race," "French Race," etc. are used in official reports. There are three European races: Nordics (tall, fair longheads near the North Sea), Mediterraneans (short, dark longheads), and Alpines (broadheaded and sturdy). All three races are found in France, and two of them (Nordic and Mediterranean) in Britain.

This table shows that folk of British stock are most numerous on the extreme coasts. In the Maritime provinces they date back to early migrations; in British Columbia they are more commonly recent immigrants from Britain. The French in Quebec greatly exceed other cultural stocks, and form important minorities in the adjacent provinces. The Germans, like the Scandinavians, are found chiefly in the western prairie lands; the Slavs, Dutch, and American Indians are somewhat more numerous in the eastern prairie lands. The 170,000 folk of Jewish culture live mostly in the eastern industrial provinces of Ontario and Quebec.

The graph inset in the map on page 118 is based on the number of folk having both parents Canadian-born, British-born, and so on, and supports the cultural distributions among the provinces described above. In 1947 the total population of the Dominion was estimated to be 12,360,000, and the density approximately 3 persons per square mile.

In spite of Canada's enormous area of close to three and one-half million square miles it is unlikely that its population will for many long years equal even those of such small countries as Great Britain, France, or Italy. Hurd and McLean suggest a figure of 20,700,-000 by 2300 A.D.; and in their opinion the population is likely to remain at that figure. The present writer thinks that when southern Alberta turns from ranches to factories—as her extensive coal supplies seem to warrant —and when the enormous third- and fourth-class lands capable of some agriculture north of Edmonton are occupied, the population may increase to forty or fifty million. But this development is a long way off.

LANGUAGE AND RELIGION. In keeping with the chief cultural origins, two languages— French and English—are widely spoken in Canada. Moreover, both these are recognized by the North America Act (1867) as official languages for the Dominion. At least 10 per cent of the people can speak both languages, and about four fifths of the remainder can speak only English, the rest only French. Because of the preponderance of French living in Quebec that province is truly bilingual.

As a result of the heavy French element in the cultural stocks, the Roman Catholic Church, which claims about 42 per cent of the people, represents the largest single religious group; and Protestant denominations, to which over half the population belong, include nearly all the remaining church affiliates.

Canada and the Outside World

The historical development of Canada into one state has assured her a voice in world affairs. The British North America Act of 1867 provides the federal constitution of a Canada capable of speaking in the councils of the world.

Strategically, the position of the Dominion had proved very favorable, since friendly relations with her only close neighbor, the United States to the south, have not been seriously threatened for a century or more. The British navy in the Atlantic protects Canada on the east, and on the west the broadest of all oceans separates her from the large Asiatic populations. Perhaps only in the northwest, where the U. S. S. R. comes close to North America, is there any possible threat. Here, however, Alaska intervenes as a mountain area guarded by the United States.

No doubt air travel makes distance of much less value as a protection against foreign aggressors, and it is to be noted that Canada is not far in flight-hours from the Soviet coasts. In northwesternmost Canada Aklavik is only about 1,000 miles from the nearest Russian shores, and the mouth of the Yenesei River in Siberia is 1,500 miles from Ellesmere Island, and about 4,500 miles from Winnipeg. Here is a potent reason why those who try to arouse dissension with the Soviet rulers should be deemed a menace to Canada. The atomic bomb is a strong argument for international peace, though the writer hopes that pessimistic forecasts of the destruction of civilization made with regard to this new weapon will be found to be in the same unfulfilled category as those that have marked the invention of torpedoes, dynamite, liquid air, and aircraft.

Canada has a special position among the Dominions of the British Commonwealth. Geographically she is swayed by somewhat the same motives as those that affect the United States, especially in regard to Pacific affairs. She has excluded all but negligible immigration of Chinese and Japanese laboring classes. The attitude of a minority in regard to the few thousands of inoffensive Canadian-born Japanese should not be allowed to imperil international relations. The Canadian Japanese complain with some justice that many folk of European culture give them the "cold shoulder," and then object to them as unassimilable. Only time and good will can solve such cultural problems.

For many years Canada spent but little on local armies or navies because, in the opinion of her leaders, transcontinental railways were sufficiently important in imperial defense to compensate for lack of armed strength. Today the increased size of the Canadian navy has provided a welcome addition to the Empire's forces, and in the future it seems likely that a Canadian air force of considerable strength will be maintained. During World War II Newfoundland was such an obvious point of attack from the east that the Americans maintained huge garrisons with artillery and radar along the Newfoundland coasts. However, Newfoundland has so far made no noteworthy effort to enter into closer relations with the United States. On the other hand, Newfoundland and Canada are likely to become more closely related in the future.

Canada's links with the United States are naturally strong. Three per cent of all Canadians were born in the States, and there are over one million Canadian-born in the United States.[*] Radio, the cinema, and American publications of all sorts tend to produce a similar culture on both sides of the unguarded frontier. A further potent link is found in the affiliation of Canadian labor unions with those of the United States. Commerce likewise shows close ties, about 82 per cent of her import trade and 39 per cent of her export trade in 1943 being with the United States. For trade with Britain the figures were 8 and 35 per cent, respectively. Moreover, tremendous sums of American money are invested in Canadian industries. Significantly enough, in 1946 a direct commercial air route was inaugurated between the capital cities of Ottawa and Washington.

In the Atlantic community of nations the Dominion of Canada has a significant role to play. Her position in the North Atlantic triangle of Great Britain, Canada, and the United States is indeed a vital one. As one of the British Dominions and as the great northern neighbor of the United States, Canada influences the foreign policy of both London and Washington.

NEWFOUNDLAND

In 1933 Newfoundland was forced by bankruptcy to yield its Dominion status. In December, 1945, Clement Attlee, Prime Minister of Great Britain, announced to Parliament that Newfoundland would vote the following year for an assembly of its own. As a consequence the determination of the political future of the island rested with the people.

The island of Newfoundland, discovered by John Cabot in 1497 and annexed to Great Britain in 1583, has an area of 42,734 square

[*] R. A. Mackay and E. B. Rogers, *Canada Looks Abroad* (London, 1938).

miles. And to the north Labrador, a dependency of Newfoundland, has an area of 110,000 square miles. The population of Newfoundland in 1947 was about 313,000 and of Labrador in the same year only about 5,000. The coast of Newfoundland is rugged, but good land is found near the shores and along watercourses. The mineral resources of Newfoundland are substantial, including iron ore, coal, copper, silver, and lead. Prevailing activities of the inhabitants are fishing, farming, logging, and mining. With a population of 43,000 (1941) St. Johns is both the capital and the only large city on the island. Internal transportation facilities

consist of 705 miles of government and 56 miles of private railroad. Recently commercial airlines have brought the island closer to Canada, the United States, and Europe.

Newfoundland occupies a strategic position in the North Atlantic. As a consequence of the "Destroyer-Base" agreement reached between Winston Churchill and Franklin Roosevelt in August, 1940, sites on Newfoundland were leased to the United States for military or naval uses. The island will undoubtedly continue as the ideal approach from the northeast to the densely populated industrial area of Canada and the United States.*

AUSTRALASIA

Australia, the largest of the component parts that together make up what is known as Australasia, has an area of 2,975,000 square miles, which is almost exactly the same size as the United States, but is somewhat smaller than either Canada or Europe. New Guinea covers an area of 312,000 square miles, but the western half, being under Dutch rule, is not herein included as part of Australasia. New Zealand has an area of 103,000 square miles, and the other large islands in the Pacific, near Australia and under Anglo-Saxon rule, range in size from New Britain (14,610 sq. mi.) down to Viti Levu (4,050 sq. mi.).

These foregoing units of Australasia exhibit contrasting environments that vary according to their latitude. Some are hot and wet, others warm and dry, and yet others cool and wet. In the following tabulation these are roughly classified in five divisions:

A. Wet Tropics . . . . New Guinea, New Britain and associated islands, New Ireland, Solomon Islands, New Hebrides, New Caledonia (French), Fijis, narrow northeast coastal fringe of Australia.

B. Dry Tropics . . . . North, northwest, and north center of Australia.

C. Warm Temperate—Dry . . Center and west coast of Australia.

D. Warm Temperate—Wet . . East, southeast, and southwest coasts of Australia.

E. Cooler Temperate—Wet . . Tasmania, New Zealand

The Environment of Australia

It is worth noting at the beginning of the description of Australia that the white settlers—who are 98 per cent of British origin—are endeavoring to develop a country that rather closely resembles the lands of North Africa. No part of this huge territory, if we exclude the island of Tasmania, is like any part of the British Isles, and very little of it resembles any part of Europe. Hence, the whole manner of Australian life is very different from that of the homeland. Moreover, although southern Australia has some similarities to the southern part of North America (see the map on page 115), little resemblance is found to the life in any part of the United States.

Relief. Australia tends to be oval in shape, with two well-defined breaks in the outline, namely, the Gulf of Carpentaria on the north and the Great Australian Bight on the south (see the map on facing page). Probably of all the continents Australia has the most uniform topography, for three fourths of the land mass lies in the form of a vast low plateau between elevations of 600 and 1,500 feet. Of the remainder there is a large lowlying area in the southeast comprising the Murray Basin, the Lake Eyre Basin, and some adjacent territory to the north, all of which is below 500 feet in elevation. The sole por-

* For a much more detailed study of this island, see the recent book by Griffith Taylor, *Newfoundland, A Study of Settlement* (Toronto, 1946).

tion of Australia that is really mountainous lies in the southeast corner, where there are considerable plateau-like areas over 3,000 feet in elevation. The highest point in Australia, which is only 7,328 feet above sea level, is a rounded boss on the southeast plateau, to

locally elevated plateau rather than a mountain range. The eastern scarp, which is close to the coast, receives heavy rainfall from the steady trade winds.

In northern New South Wales is the largest of these highlands, known as the New Eng-

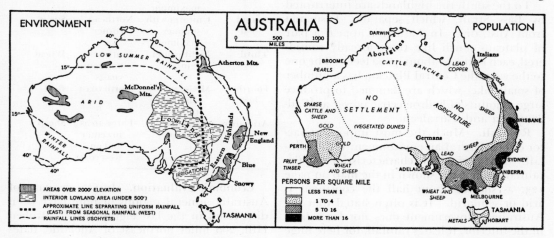

which a Polish explorer gave the name Kosciusko in 1839.

The continent consists of three main divisions: (1) the ancient shield that forms the extensive western plateau previously mentioned; (2) the eastern highlands along the coast, which culminate in the south in Mount Kosciusko; and (3) the shallow downfold between the shield and the highlands, which is mostly below 500 feet in elevation. It will be observed that the islands off the east coast of Australia extend like long festoons or arcs curving about the West Australian Shield. This particular type of formation is conspicuous in New Guinea, an area large enough to exhibit two parallel folds, and also in New Zealand far to the south. These folds extend in a general northwest to southeast direction; and if our map included Asia, we should see that they tend to join up with the numerous mountain ridges of Siam and Burma.

The Eastern Highlands of the continent are essentially made up of a series of plateau areas. In some instances these are separated by natural gateways, which provide entry from the coast to the interior of the continent. In the northernmost part of the Eastern Highlands is a notable elevation known as the Atherton Tableland. Although it attains a maximum elevation of 5,400 feet, it is a

land Plateau. Its general elevation is about 3,500 feet. On the south it is bounded by the well-defined Cassilis Gate. Not much above 1,000 feet, this gate has always been an important corridor for travelers and stockowners between the coastlands near Newcastle and the western plains. It is surprising that it has not yet been used by a railway.

South of the Cassilis Gate is located the well-known Blue Plateau, a relief feature locally known as the Blue Mountains. Essentially, however, the area is a gradual slope up from the coastal plain to a height of about 3,500 feet, and therefore does not agree with the usual concept of a mountain. The surface is generally flat when this elevation is reached; but it is cut into by rivers, which have produced some of the most spectacular wide canyons in the world. For example, Cox Valley is ten miles wide and 2,000 feet deep, but the gorge through which it empties into the coastal plain to the southeast is only a few hundred yards wide.

The Blue Plateau is separated from the Monaro Plateau to the south by the Lake George Gate. This natural gateway is not so well marked as the Cassilis Gate, but is much more used by lines of communication. It contains several small towns; and Canberra —the capital of the Commonwealth—lies just to the south. From the Lake George Gate to the Kilmore Gate behind Melbourne there is a regular series of plateaus at somewhat different levels. These seem to be arranged like a set of irregular bricks across a narrow path. Some are higher than others, but in all the long axis runs from north to south.

To the south the highlands are interrupted by Bass Strait, which separates Tasmania from Australia. In Tasmania appear a pair of plateaus much like those already considered, each rising to about 5,000 feet. The one to the west, the Central Plateau, has a number of small lakes which are dammed to produce large amounts of hydroelectric power at Waddamanna and Tarraleah.

Rainfall. Much the most important factor of the Australian environment is the rainfall. The principal characteristics of the rainfall regime are shown in the map on page 123; as shown, about half the continent is arid or semiarid. It is often stated that the Australian Government does not lease land in the interior, it leases rainfall, for here huge areas of land are without adequate rainfall and consequently are almost useless. The drier portion of Australia receives about 15 inches of rain on the northern edge, which falls wholly in the summer. The most arid region, around Lake Eyre, gets no more than five inches per year. The northern margin of Australia experiences moderate amounts of summer rain, and the south coast has a winter rainfall reaching 40 or 50 inches on the higher lands. The most satisfactory rainfall occurs along the east coast. Here it is distributed with fair regularity through the year, although there is a summer maximum in the north and a winter maximum in the south. This is the region labeled "Uniform" in the map on page 123; most of the important settlement in the continent is found in this region.

Along the east coast several factors give this country one of the most attractive climates in the world. From Brisbane south to Melbourne the temperatures are pleasant, neither too hot nor too cold. The trade winds bring good rains to the northern section, and in the south wandering low pressure areas (cyclonic storms) that often visit the coastline in the winter season provide good rains.

We may tabulate the various regions of Australia as regards season and value of rain as follows:

Evaluation of Rainfall Regions

Value	Season	General location	Typical agricultural products
Best rainfall	Uniform with winter maximum	Southeast corner	Sheep and wheat
Second best	Uniform with summer maximum	Northeast corner	Sugar
Third best	Light winter rainfall	Southwest and south coasts	Wheat
Fourth best	Moderate summer rainfall	North coast	Beef
Arid areas	(as defined earlier)	Large areas in center and on west coast	Sheep

Economic evaluation. In various parts of Australia mineral regions of note have been discovered in the last eighty years. Broken Hill, 260 miles northeast of Adelaide, dates from about 1885. Its rich mineral wealth, especially silver, lead, and zinc, led to the growth of a city of 30,000 in the semidesert. About ten years later Kalgoorlie started on the gold fields east of Perth, and it is still an important city. About 1915 the enormous deposits of brown coal at Morwell (80 miles southeast of Melbourne) were first exploited on a large scale. Now they are used in the production of electric power for much of southern Victoria. Hydroelectric power in Tasmania, based on the dam across the Great Lake, has in the last few decades changed Hobart into an industrial city. Local coal deposits at Newcastle gave rise to the growth of a remarkable steel industry—probably the largest in the Southern Hemisphere and one of the largest in the British Empire.

In a land where 87 per cent of the area has a rainfall below 30 inches per year, much attention is, of necessity, paid to extra supplies of water. Australia is fortunate in possessing the largest artesian basin in the world. This occupies 600,000 square miles in the northeast portion of the continent, which encompasses much of the lowland charted in the map on page 123. Here since 1885 about 7,000 bores have been put down to reach the porous water-bearing beds sometimes a mile or more below the surface. The water, led in narrow channels across the sheep ranches, is said to have doubled the stock-rearing capacity of the area. Such water is not, however, sufficiently abundant to be used to grow crops.

There is but little water available for irrigation, at any rate where broad plains suitable for such treatment occur. Almost all the downfold (see the map on page 123) is in arid country, and all the rivers are intermittent, that is, they flow only during a part of the year. However, the Murray River and some of its tributaries flow through arable plains, and here about 600,000 acres are irrigated. Many great dams have been constructed since 1906, such as the Hume Dam on the upper Murray and the Burrinjuck Dam on the upper Murrumbidgee River. They do not benefit desert lands because the areas of irrigation are mostly where the natural rainfall is about 15 inches a year; rather, they convert sheep ranches into regions where large crops of grapes, alfalfa, hay, rice, and other cereals are grown.

The soils along the north coast, where a heavy rain falls only in the three hottest months, are in general infertile; and no agriculture except a few acres of peanuts and coconuts has yet developed there. Thus in Australia, as in Canada, we observe that space alone does not mean power, and that careful geographical analysis is the best guide to planning the future of any nation.

Australian Internal Developments

Early spread of settlement. The continent was discovered in March, 1606, by the Dutch captain William Jansz. He sailed along the eastern shore of the large Gulf of Carpentaria a few months before de Torres, a Spanish explorer, passed through the straits that now bear his name in the same region. By 1644 the Dutch had charted the arid and tropical coasts, but it remained for the Englishman, Captain James Cook, to survey the fertile east coast in 1770. The first settlement in Australia was Sydney, founded in January, 1788, by Captain Phillip, leader of the British expedition that selected Sydney instead of Botany Bay for the settlement. This has remained the largest town ever since, except for a period during the third quarter of the nineteenth century when the great gold discoveries in Victoria resulted in a temporary superiority for Melbourne.

The young settlement at Sydney, hemmed in by the Blue Plateau to the west, grew in importance as the discovery and utilization of passes led to contact with interior areas. By 1820 the sheep owners had found the savanna woodlands of the western slopes, and the next fifty years were marked by steady expansions to the west and northwest, throughout the region of uniform rainfall (see the map on page 123).

Hobart in Tasmania, set up as a penal settlement in 1803, was the first outlying community established. However, the transportation of criminals from England ceased as the settlement grew. Perth in Western Australia was founded as a colony in 1827, but in both of these outlying regions populations increased slowly until valuable mines were discovered—about 1875 in Tasmania and 1890 in Western Australia. South Australia was created in 1835, and Colonel Light led a party of settlers to the Adelaide Plains in 1836.

A penal settlement was maintained near Brisbane for some years prior to 1842; then the district was thrown open to farmers. Queensland was declared a separate colony in 1859. The rich timber of the coast was soon cut down, and about 1862 cotton began to be grown in southeast Queensland as the result of the shortage in the United States. About the same time sugar cane came into production with Kanaka labor from the South Sea Islands.

Except for some of the cattle ranches of the northwest, almost all the better lands of Australia were occupied by 1870. Ranchers moved into the empty areas of the tropical lands during the eighties and nineties. There has been little new land of value occupied since that time, and the increase of population has been effected by closer settlement of lands already well known in 1870.

Modern political development. The federation of the Australian states came about in 1901,* but the choice of a capital site was delayed until 1908, when Canberra was chosen on the plains near the Murrumbidgee River in the midst of several sheep ranches. Construction of the new city was delayed by

* The states of the Commonwealth are Queensland, New South Wales, Victoria, South Australia, Western Australia, and Tasmania. In addition there are the Northern Territory and the Federal Territory on the continent.

World War I, and not until 1927 did it actually become the seat of government. In the meantime the parliament met in Melbourne. Nowadays about 7,000 folk live in or around the capital, which is surrounded by 900 square miles of Federal Territory. In 1911 Northern Territory was transferred from the state of South Australia to the Federal control.

Present population. In 1947 the population of the Commonwealth was estimated to be 7,485,000, almost entirely of British origin. Only in two small regions is there any concentration of population of foreign origin: the German settlements north of Adelaide, which date back a century, and the Italians, immigrants on the northern sugar plantations in Queensland (see the map on page 123). Sixty thousand aboriginals live mostly along the northern coasts.

In terms of the agricultural and industrial methods and requirements of the present-day world thirty millions is probably Australia's optimum population. This will be confined mostly to the eastern and southern areas, where a density of one per square mile has already been reached in an economy of extensive land utilization such as found in the western Great Plains of the United States. The best remaining areas are in central and southern Queensland, that is, the empty lands in the area of uniform rainfall.

In view of the huge populations at a low stage of culture in nearby Asia, the "White Australia" policy can be understood, even though it be declared somewhat selfish. After 1905 a test in "any prescribed language" could be used to exclude any alien. The large areas of useless or poor land in Australia refute the charge of a "dog in the manger" policy, for no part of the Commonwealth contains any large areas of rich, but unused, land.

Cities. Approximately half the total population of Australia is concentrated in the capitals of the five states on the continent. Only on the island of Great Britain itself does one find larger urban centers within the realm of the British Commonwealth than Sydney and Melbourne, Australia's two leading cities, with populations of 1,398,000 and 1,184,000, respectively. The remaining state capitals, Brisbane, Adelaide, and Perth, each count a population of between one quarter and one

half million.* Aside from these large urban agglomerations Australia has a few small and medium-sized cities, mostly agricultural and mining centers that relay economic goods between the key cities and the farming and mining areas.

Australia and the Outside World

The contrast between the external problems of Canada and those of Australia is profound. The southern continent is several thousand miles away from the friendly help of the United States and nearly twice that distance from Britain. Her neighbors are the vast populations of India, China, and Japan. This long distance from any powerful ally and the relative proximity of millions of folk of Asiatic culture have always affected Australia's attitude toward the outside world. Especially was this the case while Japan was a strong military and naval power. As a result, we may say that although Australia's foreign policy has in general been sympathetic with Britain's she has her own point of view with regard to Asiatic and Pacific problems.

In the matter of trade the exports from Australia (largely wool and wheat) go mainly to Britain. In 1936–37 shipments to Britain amounted to $300,000,000, whereas those to the United States in that year had a value of only one tenth that figure. In the same year Australia bought goods worth $165,000,000 from Britain, and two fifths as much from the United States. Just before the war Japan was her second-best customer, outranking the United States in that respect. Other adjacent lands, such as India, Java, and New Zealand, naturally ranked high in Australia's foreign trade.

In the early days Australia's dependence on Britain was natural. Self-government came gradually, and the power and position of the Governor in each colony, who was appointed by Britain, was at first somewhat indefinite.** Australia, always keenly interested in imperial defense, agreed as far back as 1907 to maintain a fleet "unit." Four hundred thousand Australians took part in World War I,

---

* Urban populations in Australia commonly refer to the total number of people in the general urban area, that is, suburbs are included. For example, the population of Perth includes that for its port city of Fremantle.

** *Cambridge History of the British Empire* (Cambridge, 1933), Vol. VII, Part I, *passim*.

and about a million in the recent war. The Japanese attacked her shores in the second war, and both Darwin and Broome were bombed by Japanese planes.

The Australian Dependent Areas

Australians have been greatly interested in political developments in Oceania. The French annexation of Tahiti in 1843 and of New Caledonia in 1853 caused uneasiness in Australia, especially after the latter island was made a penal settlement in 1863. From 1863 to 1872 there was much agitation against bringing in Kanaka labor from the South Sea Islands to Australia. In 1874 Fiji was annexed by Britain. Nine years later, in 1883, Queensland annexed the southeast portion of New Guinea called Papua, which was the area nearest Australia, having been stimulated to do so by German activities in that large island. In 1906 this annexed area of Papua became a Territory of the Commonwealth, and in 1920 the northeast section of New Guinea (formerly German) was mandated to the Commonwealth by the League of Nations. These two sections of New Guinea have a total population of about a million persons, of whom only 1,200 in Papua and 4,000 in the mandated territory are Europeans.

Australia's mandate is much larger than Northeastern New Guinea. The entire mandate, called the Territory of New Guinea, includes not only Northeastern New Guinea but also the Bismarck Archipelago (New Britain, New Ireland, etc.) and the northern Solomon Islands. In January of 1946 Australia offered to place her mandate under the trusteeship of the United Nations. However, like Papua, a number of small islands, such as Norfolk and Lord Howe, are direct dependencies of Australia and not trusteeships.

New Zealand

Environment. Although to Americans New Zealand seems quite close to Australia, it is a matter of four or five days by steamer travel to reach Wellington from Sydney or Melbourne. Thus, New Zealand is nearly as "distant" from Australia as England is from the United States. The group of three islands,* which is about 1,000 miles long, covers an area of slightly more than 100,000 square miles. The islands form the summit of a crustal-fold that extends northwest toward New Caledonia and Papua. The peculiar flora and fauna of New Zealand link it with these latter islands rather than with Australia to the west. The highest mountains are a range of peaks in the southern half of South Island, in which Mt. Cook rises to 12,349 feet.

Ancient granites containing some gold make up much of the mountainous section in southern New Zealand. In the north younger deposits account for several active volcanoes and numerous geysers. These as well as the occasional earthquakes show that mountain-building is still in progress. The climate is excellent; temperature and rainfall conditions are almost ideal in the lowlands. Unfortunately, however, areas suited for agriculture are not very extensive because of the poor quality of much of its soil and its rugged topography.

Internal developments. Although New Zealand was discovered in 1642 by Tasman, a famous Dutch explorer of the Southwest Pacific, there was no settlement until 1814 when foreign missionaries introduced Christianity. Timber for masts and the whales in surrounding waters attracted the early traders. For a time around 1840 the region was attached politically to New South Wales; but in 1841 it became a separate colony, and finally in 1907 was designated as a Dominion. Presently attached to New Zealand are the Auckland, Cook, Kermadec, and Union Islands.

In 1942 New Zealand had an estimated population of 1,639,000, including 63,000 of the Maori aboriginal tribes. It cooperates with Australia in matters of education and defense, but is quite independent in all other respects. The trade and interests of New Zealand are perhaps more centered in Britain than is the case with Australia.

The wheat-growing area is mainly on the Canterbury Plains on the east side of South Island. First exported in 1871, wheat became the leading item of trade, and about 1882 the much more important shipments of refrigerated foods started. In recent years the manufacture of machinery used in agri-

* New Zealand is made up of North Island, South Island, and the very small Stewart Island south of South Island.

culture has become of some importance. There is abundant waterpower, which is much used in butter and cheese factories. Industrial development centers in the two large cities of Auckland and Wellington, both on North Island. The latter, with a population of 173,500, is the capital of the Dominion; but the former, with a population of some 260,000, is larger.

Western Samoa. In the consideration of New Zealand the islands of Western Samoa are of interest. The group was first occupied by soldiers from New Zealand in 1914. This control continued until 1920, when the League of Nations granted New Zealand a mandate over the islands. An Administrator aided by a native Council controls the internal affairs of this group, whose capital is Apia. There are about 30,000 Polynesians living in Western Samoa.

New Zealand was among the first states to offer to place a mandate, that for Western Samoa, under the trusteeship of the United Nations. The Dominion also has an interest in the island of Nauru, rich in phosphates, which was mandated to the British Empire after World War I. New Zealand, Australia, and Great Britain, have agreed to place this mandate under the trusteeship of the United Nations.

UNION OF SOUTH AFRICA

In 1910 the four colonies of the Cape of Good Hope, Natal, Orange Free State, and Transvaal were united to form the Union of South Africa. The total area is 472,550 square miles, and all of it except the northern fringe of the Transvaal lies south of the Tropic of Capricorn. Hence the Union has a temperate climate suited for settlement by sion, that is, to one general level. During the world's last major phase of mountain-building this peneplain was elevated and tilted, with the result that much of the southeast section of the Union is 5,000 feet above sea level; and on the borders of Natal the Drakensberg Scarp rises to 10,000 feet above sea level (see the map directly below).

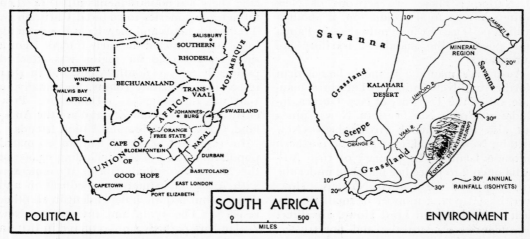

SOUTH AFRICA

POLITICAL   ENVIRONMENT

folk of European ancestry. In general its conditions of temperature are superior to those of either Canada or Australia. In addition, the elevation of South Africa gives it a more invigorating climate than that usually found in its latitude, which is 30 degrees.

Environment

The whole of Africa south of the Equator consists of an ancient land mass that has been worn down to a peneplain by continued ero-

Physical landscape. Almost all the Union of South Africa except the portion near the coast rises more than 3,000 feet above sea level (see the map above here). Because of this elevation, temperatures are about 10° F. lower than at the same latitude elsewhere, so that conditions in the interior, even during the summer, are usually quite pleasant. Thus, Pretoria, the capital city, lies at latitude 25° South; but the hottest month has an average temperature of only 71.7° F., and the coldest month falls to 51.7° F. At Capetown the hottest and coldest months are 69.7° F. and 54.8° F., respectively.

As in Australia, the major factor determining settlement in South Africa is the rainfall. The Union lies in the belt swept by the easterly trade winds, and hence its western portions are arid. Indeed, the 10-inch line of rainfall extends north and south, almost bisecting the south of Africa. Thus the western half is a dry steppe, whereas the eastern half is almost wholly grassland. Only along the Natal coast is the subtropical forest bordered on the west by thorny scrub (*Thorn-Veld*). Near Capetown, however, the rains fall in winter; and so we find here a development of flora characterizing a Mediterranean type of climate, that is, evergreen shrubs, bulbs, tussock grasses, and other plants that are able to withstand the desiccating effect of summer drought.

Economic evaluation. To a large extent the distribution of agricultural activities depends upon rainfall conditions. Thus, crop lands for the most part are limited to areas of heavier rainfall. On the other hand, stock-raising is the major industry in much of the Union because of the great expanses of steppes and grasslands. Maize is grown very largely in the east, especially in the Vaal Basin, Natal, and near East London. Cotton grows near the 30-inch line of rainfall (due north of Durban), and in somewhat wetter districts than those producing the main maize crop. Wheat is not important except in small districts near Capetown and Pretoria. Sugar is grown largely in the hot, wet coastal section of Natal; and vines and oranges flourish in the small area of winter rains in the southwest. Among the animals raised, sheep are the most important, their greatest concentration being in the region northeast of the Cape of Good Hope.

Cultural Development

The spread of settlement. The Cape of Good Hope was discovered by Diaz in 1487, and Da Gama passed along the coast of Natal in 1497. Although the Portuguese occupied Sofala in 1506, it was not till 1652 that the Dutch, under Van Riebeek, established a settlement at Capetown. In 1688 many Huguenots arrived from France, and their descendants are numerous in the neighborhood of Capetown. For a century and a half the region was under the despotic rule of the Dutch East India Company. After 1700 many settlers trekked into the interior and to the east; and indeed in 1795 some of the burghers in the eastern settlements drove out the officials of the Dutch Company. Cape Colony was occupied by the British in 1795, and again in 1806. In 1814 the Dutch formally ceded the colony to Britain.

The first natives with whom the Dutch came into contact were the Hottentots and Bushmen, but these were never very numerous or powerful. Later the warlike Bantu Negroes of the wetter portions of South Africa were encountered; and in 1780 the Great Fish River was adopted as the boundary between the Dutch and the Bantu. Today the great majority of the Negroes are to be found in the eastern part of the Union of South Africa (see the map on facing page).

During the first half of the nineteenth century white settlement became pronounced. In 1820 four thousand English emigrants founded Port Elizabeth. In 1836 began the great trek of 7,000 Boers who were dissatisfied with British rule. They migrated north beyond the Vaal River into the Transvaal. Natal became a British colony in 1845, and about this time many Boers settled in the Orange Free State. This was temporarily annexed in 1848, but was restored later to the Boers; and in 1852 the Transvaal was also relinquished to them.

In 1869 and 1870 the gold fields and the diamond mines in or near the Transvaal began to be worked, and this development led to a great influx of settlers who had little patience with the conservative views of the Boer pastoralists. The conflicts with the warlike Zulus hindered progress, though the latter were crushed at Ulundi in 1879. The Transvaal area had again been annexed by Britain in 1877, but in 1880 the Boers revolted against British rule and won several victories, as at Majuba Hill in 1881. In 1884 the Transvaal Boers were granted self-government under British suzerainty.

In 1886 Johannesburg was founded on what has become the richest gold field in the world. Conflict between the powerful newcomers (*Uitlanders*) under Cecil Rhodes and the Dutch authorities led by Paul Kruger was almost inevitable. The Jameson Raid in January, 1896, was abortive, and the raiders were imprisoned. The Boers were unwilling to extend the franchise to the large non-Boer population, and in 1899 the Boer war broke out, lasting for more than two years. The two Dutch Republics were formally annexed in 1900, but guerrilla war continued until the peace of May, 1902.

Peoples. In South Africa—unlike Canada and Australia—there was a dense population of tribes of primitive culture long before European settlement began. Today about 70 per cent are Negroes, and only 24 per cent are Europeans. Of the remaining population many are Chinese and Indians who were introduced to work in the mines and plantations. Thus the color question, which is almost nonexistent in Canada and Australia, is a burning question in South Africa.

In 1946 there were estimated to be 11,250,-000 people living in the Union, of whom 2,335,000 were European, 7,735,000 Bantu Negroes, 280,000 Asiatics, and 900,000 of other cultural groups. The predominating cultural group is made up of slightly more than 50 per cent of the Europeans, who belong to the Dutch churches. The Dutch population, which is almost wholly rural, lives mainly in the two former "free states." Many landless Dutch, known as "poor whites," drift from the "back-veld" into the mining towns, as do thousands of Bantu from Mozambique and elsewhere. There are also nearly 200,000 Indians (largely from Bombay) in Natal, where they are now about as numerous as Europeans. They are not allowed to vote or to buy land.

Between Natal and East London are the Transkei Reserves, where the Bantu occupy regions capable of close settlement not available to Europeans. Since 1913 the Bantu have not been allowed to purchase land outside of the reserves, nor are they permitted to undertake skilled trades. To the unprejudiced observer this treatment of the Bantu does not redound to the credit of the rulers of South Africa. The native areas of Swaziland, Basutoland, and Bechuanaland, geographically inside the Union of South Africa, are administered by Great Britain.

The Union of South Africa is not as highly urbanized as either Canada or Australia. Johannesburg, with 324,000 inhabitants, is the only city with a population exceeding a quarter of a million. Capetown, seat of the legislature and famed port on the sea route around the Cape of Good Hope, is second in the Union with 214,000 people. Pretoria, seat of the administration, and the seaport of Durban each has a population of 125,000. All other cities have less than 75,000 inhabitants.

South Africa and the Outside World

South Africa had a dominant strategic position in the early nineteenth century, as it guarded the sea routes to India and Australia. After the Suez Canal was opened in 1869, the importance of this region diminished. But Britain felt a special responsibility for a colony so near Portuguese territories. Moreover, the warlike natives inhabiting the area needed careful supervision. At first the British people of South Africa did not seek self-government, but with the close of the century there arose a feeling of colonial nationalism. At various Colonial and Imperial Conferences pressure for self-government was exerted, and in 1910 Dominion status was gained. A mild form of compulsory military service was adopted, and in recent years South Africa has played an important role in plans for Imperial defense.[*]

Following World War I the Union of South Africa received German Southwest Africa as a mandate. Previously the British had owned Walvis Bay on the coast of Southwest Africa as an enclave. Economically the area suffers from being located partly in the Kalahari Desert. Of considerable importance, however, is the production of diamonds, vanadium, and tin.

During World War II the Union of South Africa participated in the conflict, especially in the African phase leading to the destruction of the Italian Colonial Empire. South Africa opposed, after the recent war, changing Southwest Africa into a trusteeship.

[*] E. A. Walker, *Cambridge History of the British Empire* (Cambridge, 1936), Vol. VIII, *passim.*

PART THREE

Europe

ALTHOUGH Europe is practically the same size as Canada, it contains forty-five times as many people. Also, although most of Europe lies in the same latitude as Canada, it is for the most part climatically much milder. For instance, temperate marine England lies in the latitude of Hudson Bay; the sunny Italian Riviera is closer to the North Pole than is Toronto; Paris is about as far from the Equator as is Winnipeg.

Strictly speaking, Europe is not a continent, because it is in no real sense a separate land mass. Rather, it is merely a big peninsula thrust westward from the huge continental mass of Asia. However, as people have long mistakenly regarded Europe as a continent, it is now impossible to correct the error. Geographers usually employ the name *Eurasia* to denote the entire land mass of Asia and Europe.

Europe is the smallest of the continents, with the exception of Australia, which some geographers prefer to regard as a very large island. Its 3,781,000 square miles of area are less than one fifth that of Eurasia's total of 20,-275,000. It is less than one fourth the area of Asia, about one third the size of Africa, less than one half the size of North America. Further, this little pseudo continent is only two thirds as large as the Antarctic ice cap, and but 804,000 square miles larger than the United States.

Despite its small size Europe is geographically the most important continent. Its power and mineral resources are noteworthy. One half of the coal production and a sizable fraction of the petroleum output of the earth come from Europe. It ranks low among the continents in potential waterpower, but high in percentage of developed waterpower. One half of the iron ore and bauxite, and most of the potash and mercury come from this continent.

Germany, Britain, Russia, France, and Poland lead in Europe's production of coal. The principal oil fields lie along the Caucasus Mountains in Russia and along the Carpathians in Poland (now mostly Russian) and Rumania. The principal sources of iron ores are the Lorraine "minette" deposits of France, the Krivoi Rog and Ural ores of Russia, the Kiruna deposits of northern Sweden, and the Bilbao ores of Spain. Lead and zinc come from Poland, copper from Russia and Spain, and platinum from Russia. Among the vital ferro-alloys, tungsten from Portugal, chromium from Greece, and nickel and manganese from Russia should be mentioned.

Even though Europe comprises but one fifteenth of the world's land surface, it contains one fourth of its people. With 524,-000,000 inhabitants, it is the most densely peopled continent, averaging 140 per square mile. Western Europe, indeed, constitutes one of the earth's four great areas of population concentration. The little continent is able to support this huge population because of its unusual progress in agriculture, manufacturing, and trade.

One half of the world's wheat, barley, oats, milk, grapes, apples, and olives, one third of the sugar, and four fifths of the rye, potatoes, and flax fiber are produced there. From the rough lands of northern Europe and from the mountains and hill country of the central parts of the continent comes one half of the world's lumber and wood pulp. The European Manufacturing Belt stretches from Britain and Flanders eastward to the Urals. Industrial centers are especially concentrated upon the coal fields of the English Midlands, the Ruhr Valley, the Saar Basin, Silesia, and the Donets Basin. Here about half of the world's manufactures is fabricated, and this production is in turn distributed over Europe's fine systems of railroads and waterways. Many of the products of mine, farm, forest, and factory are consumed locally or regionally, but large amounts move into international and even intercontinental trade. Normally, about fifty-two per cent of world commerce is European.

Despite its quite complicated physical make-up, the continent consists of three general parts. The first of these is the North European Plain. From the rolling surfaces of the London Basin and the Paris Basin, this great lowland stretches eastward across Germany, Poland, European Russia, and into Siberia, growing wider toward the east. The English Channel thrusts a break across it, and the Ardennes Upland nearly pinches it in two in the Low Countries, but, nonetheless, it is one of the greatest plains on earth. In ancient times the North European Plain served as a corridor of human migrations. More recently it has been a highway of military passage and repassage, and four recent great wars in Europe have seen decisive battles —Waterloo, Sedan, Verdun, and the Ardennes "Bulge"—fought in or near the wasp-waist of the plain.

Southern Europe, by way of contrast, consists of many separate hilly blocks and mountain spurs, all interspersed with river valleys, deltas, and small coastal plains. These are broken into islands, peninsulas, and littoral strips by the various arms and bights of the Mediterranean Sea. Within this great fragmented region, the Mediterranean has been a major unifying factor. The Mediterranean Basin was an ancient cradle of civilization and, later, a nursery of human progress. During recent centuries, however, it has been merely a cultural back eddy.

The mountain core of the central part of the continent separates northern and southern Europe. This extends from the Pyrenees eastward through the Auvergne, Alps, Carpathians, and Caucasus Mountains; thence it continues on into Asia as the Elburz-Pamir-Himalaya system. Although this highland core forms a barrier between north and south Europe, it is breached at intervals by the St. Bernard, St. Gotthard, Simplon, Brenner, Rosul, and Tartar passes and the Rhone-Doubs, Main-Danube, Moravian, and other gateways. Through these have trickled goods, men, and ideas from Neolithic times to the present.

Europe was long ago populated by wave after wave of peoples from Asia. Today the inhabitants of Europe fall mainly into three racial types: the narrow-headed, dark-eyed, brunet Mediterranean or Iberian peoples in southern Europe; the broad-headed, gray- or hazel-eyed, fair to parchment-skinned Alpines in central and eastern Europe; and the medium-long-headed, blue-eyed, blond Nordics of northern and western Europe.

Despite this racial simplicity the continent of Europe is broken into so many valleys, basins, mountain blocks, littoral strips, and other separate topographic units that an immensely complicated pattern of languages and cultures has developed. There are no less than 5 linguistic stocks. These may be subdivided into 16 language groups, and these in turn into 82 major languages—all of them in current use. Within these appear probably 200 minor languages and several thousand dialects. With regard to cultural traits other than language, the pattern is also complex. In religion, Europe is principally Christian, being Protestant in the north, Roman Catholic in the south, Greek Catholic in the east, and mixed in the central areas. Nevertheless, large areas in the Balkan, Caspian, and Caucasus areas are Mohammedan, and the Pechora Basin is Animist. Also considerable numbers of Buddhists live in the Volga Delta, and Jews are found in most city areas.

As a result of physical, linguistic, religious, and economic diversity, the number of political units in Europe is greater than in any of the other land areas. Indeed, it is so great that the little continent is in a state of perennial tensions and intrigues. It is doubtful whether the world can ever have peace until much or all of Europe has been unified.

CHAPTER 10

The German Reich: European Pivotal Area

THE area of present-day Germany is somewhat different from that of the Third Reich, which crashed in defeat in May, 1945. The postwar country, according to the best estimates, will occupy about three fourths of the area of Hitler's Germany.* The major portion of the territory lost by Germany is in the east, where a radical boundary change places the new Polish border along the Oder and Neisse rivers (see the map on page 238). Among other things the westward shift of this boundary eliminated East Prussia, the detached German area east of the troublesome Polish Corridor. Elsewhere boundary changes will be far less radical, although prior to the final peace treaty of World War II the question of the Rhineland will remain a critical issue. Its rich industrial potential makes it a matter of international concern.

From the standpoint of area, the Germany of 1937 will be considered in this chapter. The boundaries at that date were "official," and it was according to them and previous boundaries that the political geography up to the present day evolved. Nevertheless, the reader should keep in mind the general

* The following ratios of postwar Germany to prewar Germany have been evaluated as follows (based upon 100% for the prewar area, as of January, 1938):

Area	76%
Population	86%
Rural population	80%
Urban population	90%
Industrial population	90%
Industrial output	93%
Steel production	97%

L. A. Hoffman, "Germany: Zones of Occupation," Department of State *Bulletin*, XIV (April 14, 1946) pp. 599–607.

postwar area and its relation to prewar Germany as discussed on the following pages.

The Historical Factor

Before unification. Germany was the last great power of Europe to achieve political unity and national existence. In contrast to the early unification of France and the development of a different yet no less cohesive England, Germany's history until after the middle of the nineteenth century is one of internal dissension and strife. Nominally it is the oldest empire of Europe, claiming its descent from the Holy Roman Empire, which in the words of Voltaire was neither holy, nor Roman, nor an empire. It lost its weak claim to the title of Roman with the ascent of the Habsburgs in 1273, and its very foundations were shaken by the Reformation. The final blow of the French Revolution and the Napoleonic victories struck at only an empty shell. When Francis of Habsburg in 1806 relinquished his title as Emperor of the Holy Roman Empire, he merely rationalized a political actuality of long standing.

The dissolution of the Empire left the numerous German states in a chaotic condition that could not have remained unchanged. Germany, a geographical expression, was eventually to become a national state. Since the cosmopolitan Habsburgs of polyglot Austria were unable to unify Germany, a German dynasty and state were to serve as the nucleus of modern Germany. That dynasty was the Hohenzollern family; and the state, Prussia. Ever since Emperor Sigismund entrusted the Electorate of Brandenburg to the Hohenzollern family in 1415, the members of that house had been identified with the idea of German conquest. Not only did they hold successfully that important eastern outpost of Germandom, but step by step they conquered and Germanized the plain east of the Elbe at the expense of its Slav settlers. They ultimately reached their goal by the complete division of Poland, eliminating that buffer state between the expanding Teuton and Russian realms.

In contrast to the Habsburgs, who became increasingly cosmopolitan in culture and in politics and remained Catholics, the Hohenzollerns were German in both culture and in politics, and embraced Protestantism in religion. Thus, their family and state evolved as the representative of the German ideal. When the question of leadership in the German Confederation, formed after the fall of Napoleon in 1815, could not be settled, German Prussia in 1866 decisively defeated polyglot Austria, which at the moment was torn by internal dissension. So the long Habsburg rule of Germany ended in utter defeat at the hands of the Hohenzollerns. With Austria excluded from the German sphere, Otto von Bismarck sought a suitable occasion to create a modern state with Prussia as its nucleus. Such a unification of Germany had been anticipated as early as 1834, when the foundation for the coming Empire had been laid by the establishment of the German *Zollverein,* or customs union. The suitable occasion was finally provided in the Franco-Prussian War of 1870–71. At its victorious conclusion in 1871, the German princes and kings declared the founding of the German Reich, with the Hohenzollern king, William of Prussia, as its emperor. The dream of a German Empire became a political reality. The hitherto centrifugal forces that had retarded the political development of the people gradually become subordinated to the new, cohesive, geopolitical reality, the Reich.

Political unification. With the millennial internal division terminated, a unified Germany appeared at a momentous time. On the continent no powers were left to match her. Defeated Austria, wedged between the Slavic pincers and *Italia irredenta,** needed

* *Italia irredenta* (unredeemed Italy) referred to areas, primarily controlled by Austria and adjacent to Italian territory, in which the population was mainly Italian.

the Reich to maintain her very existence. Centuries of war and attempts at the domination of Europe had bled France and temporarily checked her power. Russia possessed a vast expanse of land, which for the time being was more of a handicap than an advantage except in the case of hostile invasion. Being inhabited at that time by a mass of backward, suppressed, inert humanity, she was no threat to Germany. Britain could be counted as a potent foe, but her attentions were focused for the most part upon the economic and political consolidation of her vast empire, which had been enlarged and made secure by the defeat of Napoleon's militant European unity in 1815. Across the Atlantic the United States had just emerged from a destructive civil war. With apparently limitless undeveloped lands and resources, she was mainly preoccupied with her internal problems of reconstruction.

The Reich was thus born into a world void of any real global power, although potentially Great Britain qualified for that position. As long as these conditions prevailed, the world remained at peace and there was an era of general material progress and prosperity hitherto undreamed of. During these times the nations of the world turned to developing their lands with the aid of the great inventions and innovations that had been produced by the Industrial and Agricultural Revolutions.

The belated unification of Germany, however, proved to be a handicap in the economic and political evolution of the Reich. This fact is an important geopolitical factor in the shaping of world events. The Reich's access to the North Sea was limited to a narrow zone between the base of the Jutland Peninsula and northern Holland. Furthermore, Germany could not gain control of the outlet of her master stream, the Rhine. Finally, by the time the Reich began to attempt colonization outside of Europe, much of the suitable land had been staked out by the early colonial powers. All these factors played an important role in the subsequent political history of the Reich and the world.

During the four decades following the unification of Germany, tremendous changes took place in the world. Great Britain, still a leading power, had to yield and share her dominance of world trade, industry, and finance with the rising economic power of Germany, the United States, and Japan. Mechanical civilization and its dependence upon coal and metallic minerals, especially iron, changed the basic resource pattern of the nations. In this age of steam and steel the latent resources of the Reich could be fully utilized for the development of an industrial nation of first rank.

The physical setting of the region occupied by Germany, of course, has not changed materially since our earliest knowledge of the area in Roman times. The natural environment remains the same. Against this unchanged background stands the dynamic expansion of man's cultural environment, which results in the necessity of a reappraisal of the region's resource base and in a continuous readjustment to both natural and cultural factors in the light of our expanding perceptions of the forces of nature. So, in the case of Germany, the various geographic factors of the natural environment played different roles in the successive stages of its evolution, the sum total of which brought about her present conditions.

The Location Factor

As explained at length in Chapter 2, the implications of any country's location are multifarious. Location affects the natural environment, primarily through its relationship to climate. Furthermore, placement of a country in the neighborhood of other countries and people, and relative to land masses and bodies of water, affects the economic and political possibilities of the nation. From this factor of location Germany has derived much of its potency as a political area in international affairs.

Latitude. The latitudinal location of Germany between 47° N. and 55° N. places it in a medium high latitude. The map on page 136 shows how this position with respect to the Equator compares with selected areas on other continents. The large German cities have no latitudinal counterparts along the east coasts of either North America or Asia. New York (41° N.) and Tokyo (35° N.), for example, are 7° and 13° farther south, respectively, than is Munich (48° N.), Germany's most southerly large city. Along the west coast of North America, Germany would occupy a territory adjacent to Puget

Sound and the British Columbian archipelago. Of the land masses in the southern hemisphere only South America reaches into latitudes equivalent to that of Germany.

From these comparisons it is evident that Germany is about 10 to 15 degrees farther away from the Equator than the similarly developed areas in North America. In the case of Asia and of South America, the difference in location of development is even greater. In the high latitude the summer days are long and the nights short. Thus the expected decrease in insolation * due to lower elevation of the sun is counteracted, and the farmers can raise a variety of crops. The shortness of the winter days, however, necessitates the use of artificial illumination for longer periods than in the United States.

This latitudinal location would place Germany in the general zone of cold temperate climate, like the one we find in Canada. This condition, however, is greatly modified by other factors that offset the influence of a high latitude. Being situated near the western edge of the largest land mass of the world, in the belt of the westerly winds and near the coast washed by the warm Gulf Stream Drift, renders the climate of Germany relatively mild and favorable, particularly in the western sector of the country. Therefore, Germany's specific location on the continent not only mitigates the climatic consequences of its latitudinal position, but also accounts for a climate that approaches the optimum for human efficiency under our present stage of civilization.

Continental relief. The second complex of the location factor is related to the physical features of the continent. First, with reference to the Eurasian continental land mass, most of Germany occupies the western extension of the great interior lowland that stretches unbroken from the heart of Asia to the Atlantic. This lowland is separated from the Pacific lowland by a narrow zone of highlands in Siberia, which are roughly 5,000 feet in elevation. The lowland belt skirts the mountainous central cores of both Asia and Europe and, also, the low but excessively dry area of Turkestan. Consequently, this lowland, offering the least resistance to the movement of people, had become one of the chief

---

* Insolation: Amount of solar energy reaching the surface of the earth.

avenues of westbound migrations. Wave after wave of migrants have pushed over this wide route into Europe.

No serious barriers on the lowland route appear until the North Sea and the Atlantic had been replaced by various Slavic folks. The North Sea was only a temporary check, and several waves of migrants crossed it to conquer the British Isles. Most of these invaders moved from the plain; only the Nor-

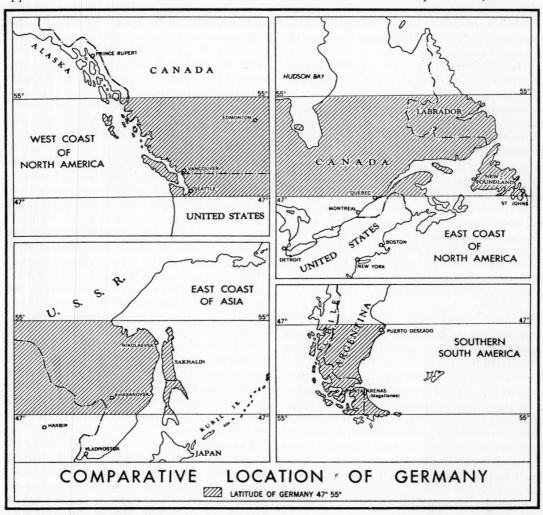

COMPARATIVE LOCATION OF GERMANY

LATITUDE OF GERMANY 47° 55°

are reached. The Romans, fortifying the natural lines of defense of the central mountain core, formed a man-made barrier against the onslaught of the barbaric hordes. Neither the natural nor the constructed barriers proved to be permanent, however. First, those made by man collapsed under the pressure of the Germanic tribes, and in a short while the whole western Mediterranean basin was overrun by the barbarians. By the time the southern regions were finally more or less filled with people, the Germanic tribes had evacuated the lowland east of the Elbe and

mans came from a region of ancient hills. Even the strong Atlantic barrier was surmounted, once temporarily by the Norsemen and the second time by Columbus and his successors. By the middle of the thirteenth century, with the ebbing of the Tartar-Mongol invasion, a reversal of population movement occurred that resulted in the slow re-conquest of the plain east of the Elbe by the Germans, culminating in the third partition of Poland in 1795.

The eastward progress of the Prussians, which is comparable on a small scale with the

Russian conquest of Siberia, suffered a set-back in 1918 with the restitution of Poland, only to be obliterated temporarily by the Hitlerian conquest. At present we are witnessing an attempted expansion of the Slav territory westward to the Oder, the limit of its extent during an earlier time. If carried out, this movement may prove to be a repetition in modern form of the history of the Völkerwanderung, when people being pushed out by their eastern neighbors in turn displaced their western foes.

Land and water bodies. The third group of influences deriving from location pertains to Germany's relationship to the seas and its position with reference to the core of the continent. Germany's location with respect to the ocean is less fortunate than that of Great Britain, for its access to the open sea can easily be blocked at either the Strait of Dover or at the northern narrows of the enclosed North Sea. The thalassic character of Germany's location is further intensified by the fact that its longer shore borders on the bottled-up Baltic. Mainly to overcome this handicap, the Germans built the Kiel Canal in 1895, cutting through the narrow land at the German-controlled base of the Jutland Peninsula. In its strategic significance, though on a smaller scale, it is comparable to our Panama Canal.

With reference to the physical continent of Europe, Germany's location is somewhat peripheral. On the other hand, if we consider the present cultural concept of Europe, which centers around the North Sea, it is decidedly central. As long as the cultural center remained in the Mediterranean Basin, however, Germany was a marginal region both physically and culturally. In contrast, neighboring France, being in part a Mediterranean country, came under the full civilizing effect of Rome much more thoroughly than did the southern fringe of Germany that was also within the bounds of the Roman Empire. Thus, France, because of more impressive Roman contacts, developed more rapidly than Germany. As evidence of the importance of Roman influence, the early centers of Germandom were in the south and west. From these regions, which were once Roman provinces, expansion proceeded slowly north and eastward along the plain.

By its marginal location Germany con-trols the most convenient Atlantic outlet of Czechoslovakia, Austria, and Hungary, thereby being in a dominant position in the foreign and transit trade of these truly central European states. On the other hand, by reason of its extension southward into the Central Highlands, Germany has easy access to the north Mediterranean trade and considerable influence over it. The political phase of this condition expressed itself in the endeavors of the medieval Holy Roman emperors to conquer and hold at least northern Italy. Later it reoccurred in the Austrian control of Lombardy in the Po Valley and even of Venice on the Adriatic Sea.

Surrounding countries. The final problem of location resolves itself in the question of neighbors. To the north Germany faces the North Sea, the Baltic Sea, and Denmark. Two small nations on the west—Belgium and the Netherlands—bar her from the sea across which lies England. Also in the west are Luxembourg and France; on the south are Switzerland, Austria, and Czechoslovakia; and on the east is Poland, completing the list of actual neighbors. Nevertheless, Italy and the Danubian and Balkan states, together with the U. S. S. R., form an important outer ring of neighbors. Local geographic and cultural conditions favored the consolidation of both France and Great Britain in a much earlier epoch than was the case with Germany. And the external policy of the two great powers successfully prevented the effective unification of Germany for three centuries. In contrast, it was partly through the help and aid from London and Paris that Holland and Belgium were able to attain nationhood, both culturally and politically before Germany. The Low Countries in the hands of a hostile power, whether it was Spain, France or Germany, are such a threat to the very existence of Britain, for example, that she has to prevent such an event by all means. With the development of modern war, the security of Britain called for an even wider zone of protection, which has been expressed officially by the phrase "England's frontiers are on the Rhine." The rapidly increasing range of airplanes, however, has caused this expression to become quite meaningless. Any protection afforded by the *cordon sanitaire* of the Low Countries, in reality, is merely a minor obstacle in the way of an aggressive power, as has been illustrated by the past war.

In contrast to the powerful western and southwestern neighbors, Germany's neighbors to the south, the southeast, and the east are

sulted in the country's absorption by the Third Reich. In Central Europe and the Balkans stretches a varied land of great possibilities but often retarded economic development—an ideal field for economic ex-

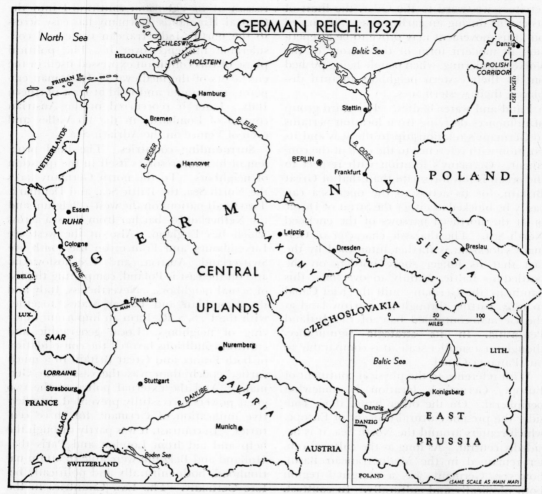

GERMAN REICH: 1937

weak. An independent German Austria may infinitely more than the Low Countries be the creation of the Western Powers. As such it has been and may again in the future become a contested prize in international intrigue. Bohemia, with Moravia, which two form the Czech part of modern Czechoslovakia, had been a component part of the Holy Roman Empire. Later the area became an integral part of the Habsburg Austria. The strategic significance of this area is great, and according to a historic axiom *he who controls Bohemia controls Germany.* This was very near the belief of Hitler and re-

ploitation. Furthermore, when considered with Asia Minor, it is a land bridge to the oil-rich Near East and to fabulous India. Hence the *Drang nach Osten* policy of the Kaiser * and its instrumentation by the Turkish alliance and the construction of the Berlin-to-Baghdad Railroad.

In the boundless Eurasian plain to the east lies four-times divided Poland, while on beyond lies Russia. Hemmed in on the west, often handicapped on the south, and not en-

* Loosely translated as "push toward the East," the *Drang nach Osten* policy signified the German ambition to extend its influence eastward via a *land route.*

ticed by the north, Germany wanted the vast grain fields of the steppe and the forest and minerals of lowland and mountains lying to the east in the Russian domain.

The cardinal tenet of Bismarck's understanding with Russia was discarded later in favor of a *Lebensraum* theory that definitely included at least the Ukraine in the German economic and, if possible, the political realm. The organization of an independent Ukraine around the end of World War I was an abortive German attempt to realize this idea. Within less than thirty years Germany has been involved twice in war with Russia. The second time the involvement resulted in the worst defeat in Germany's history.

The Site Factors

In contrast to the location factor of Germany, which influences the external relationships of the Reich, the site factors affect the possibilities of internal development. In this fashion the location factor represents a set of circumstances that are either augmented or counteracted by the site factors, and the resultant conditions will represent man's adjustment or maladjustment to both sets of circumstances.

Size, shape, and boundaries. Germany, including the Saar, which rejoined the Reich by an overwhelming vote during the plebiscite in 1935, had slightly over 180,000 square miles in 1937 (see the map on page 138). It was one of the largest European countries, but only two thirds the size of Texas. Whereas the Reich counted as a large state in Europe, in world relations it was a small country. The future seems to belong to large units like the United States, the U. S. S. R., or empires in which the mother country has become the metropolitan area of large, far-flung colonial possessions. In this modern sense Germany is a small country.

The size of the Reich has affected its economic and political growth. The ultimate limitation of the country's internal development is determined by its size and by the resources within its area. The realization on the part of the German leaders of the limitations imposed upon the state by its small area in comparison to that of other world states and empires led them to demand *Lebensraum* for Germany.

The shape of Germany was not ideal.

First, it consisted of two discontinuous parts separated by Poland. Second, Czechoslovakia formed a wedge pointing towards the vulnerable Elbe Valley. Third, the politically divided Rhine graben * opened up that much-invaded valley to possible attack. Not only the shape but the frontiers of the Reich were unsatisfactory to the Germans. Neither on the east nor on the west was there a satisfactory natural boundary. Even in the southeast the Bohemian mountains have been penetrated by German ethnic groups. The international boundary between Austria and Bavaria is of long standing, but it has little justification unless Austria were to become a member of a Danubian federation. The Swiss frontier, even if not an ethnic boundary, is cultural and thus definite. The Franco-German frontier is one of those constantly shifting boundaries so common to Europe. With the general historical background, ethnic perplexities, economic interests, and strategic considerations found in Europe, none of its countries can hope for perfect boundaries. Therefore, the real problem is to find such boundaries as are the least unjust for the two countries involved. Once these boundaries are established, both parties should be persuaded to acquiesce to the solution.

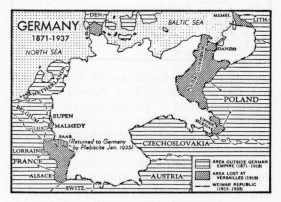

The territorial extent of Germany under the Empire (1871–1918) is indicated by the map above here. As a consequence of the Treaty of Versailles made in 1919, Germany relinquished Alsace-Lorraine to France, Eupen and Malmédy to Belgium, part of Schleswig to Denmark, a portion of Upper

* Graben: A depressed area bounded on two or more sides by faults and generally of considerable length as compared to its width.

Silesia to Czechoslovakia, Memel to the victorious powers (annexed by Lithuania in 1923), the greater part of West Prussia and Posen and a part of Upper Silesia and East Prussia to Poland, and the area of Danzig, which was made into a Free State under the League of Nations. The territorial extent of Germany under the Weimar Republic (1919–33) is indicated by the same map. In 1938 Hitler began the territorial revisions of the Treaty of Versailles that culminated in World War II and the Germany mastery of the greatest part of Europe. However, the Third Reich of Adolf Hitler (1933–45) perished in the ruins of the "New Order" in Europe. The occupation zones of Germany are indicated by the map directly below, with the probable eastern

boundary of the Reich shared with Poland and the partition of East Prussia between Russia and Poland. In mid-1948 the western boundaries of Germany were still unsettled, although no great changes were anticipated. The possibility existed of refusing Germany the right to control parts of her highly industrialized west. The French were in control of the Saar, with its coal, and wanted to see an international Ruhr and an independent Rhineland. Austria and Czechoslovakia have regained their independence, with possible boundary rectifications for the latter with Germany. Belgium, the Netherlands, and Luxembourg are also concerned with the future boundaries of the Reich.

Topography. The German land is dominated by two great European topographic features. Northern Germany forms a part of the broad Eurasian plain, whereas central and southern Germany occupies a considerable portion of Europe's central uplands. The plain is relatively simple both in structure and in surface features, sloping gently toward the Baltic and the North Sea. One of the most significant factors in shaping the present topography of the plain was the recurrent continental glaciation. The advance and retreat of the ice sheets resulted in the formation of several lines of moraines.* In crossing these belts of moraines, German rivers (for example, the Weser, Elbe, and Oder) were forced to flow in an east-west direction before finally emptying into the North Sea or the Baltic. The result is that the present river pattern in this region has a number of definite elbow turns. The rivers with their lateral valleys and tributaries were easy to canalize, a possibility that enabled the Germans to construct a complete, modern inland waterway system paralleled by few if any others in the world.

The glaciated surface of northern Germany, particularly of the Baltic Zone, is dotted with lakes and has extensive heath and marshes. These, combined with dense forests, presented formidable barriers to the movement of an enemy and often served as a refuge for displaced people. The strategic significance of such areas was brought out well during World War I when Hindenburg enticed the Russian steamroller into Masuria in East Prussia to be literally bogged down in the mire of the marshes and drowned in its lakes. With this brilliantly executed maneuver Hindenburg not only delivered Berlin from a Russian attack but also broke the real striking power of his Russian adversaries. Later, during World War II, the gently undulating and rolling areas of the glacial Baltic plain extending into western Poland proved excellent terrain for mechanized warfare.

The marshy and wooded character of much of the land in northern Germany, along with the poor quality of the sandy soil, has greatly retarded the development of intensive agriculture. The area was more suitable for exploitation by large estates than by small peasant holdings. With modern methods of drainage and cultivation, most western

* Moraine: An accumulation of surface material by glaciation; deposited by the melting of glaciers.

marshes have been rendered tillable and intensive truck production and dairying have spread over the former waterlogged waste lands.

COASTAL AREA. The physical features of Germany's North Sea and Baltic shore lines have both facilitated and handicapped the development of the country. In the main the coast suffers from extensive sand areas, many of which contain shifting dunes. The North Sea coast is characterized by postglacial submergence, forming deep estuaries * like those of the Weser and the Elbe. These estuaries permit passage by ocean-going vessels; consequently, the chief ports like Bremen and Hamburg are far inland from the actual seacoast. The Baltic coast is not so fortunate as the North Sea shore, since there a number of barrier beaches, lagoons, and submarine sandbars impede navigation. The climate is severe, and the brackish, shallow water freezes at relatively high temperatures. In addition to these local handicaps, the Baltic ports lack an active hinterland like the one served by the North Sea coast. For example, Stettin, the port of Berlin at the mouth of the Oder, was the leading Baltic port of Germany; yet it had only one ninth of the tonnage of Hamburg.**

The low isthmus of Schleswig-Holstein has about the most level land and the best soil along the Baltic. Agriculture is well developed along intensive, modern lines. The Kiel Canal was cut across this low area. The main consideration in its construction was naval strategy, but in reality it has achieved great economic significance as well. The number of boats using the canal exceeded 50,-000 annually, of which more than half were not flying the German flag.† Thus, what was originally intended to be a naval convenience turned out to be a valuable economic asset. In 1890 Germany acquired from Great Britain the strategic island of Helgoland, important in the defense of the future canal. This important naval fortress was demilitarized after World War I. Under Hitler, however, it became Germany's Gibraltar. To prevent any such development in the future,

in 1946 Helgoland was doomed to obliteration. The fortifications and naval base facilities were actually destroyed April 18, 1947.

Before the shift of the main field of economic activities beyond the scope of the enclosed seas took place, the coasts of the North Sea and the Baltic saw the great flourishing of the Hanseatic League. Rich fishing grounds and the abundance of wood, other forest products, and amber stimulated trade; the estuaries and lagoons provided sheltered harbor sites; and the long streams furnished access to the hinterland. These factors produced the growth and prosperity of the Hansa towns, which spread from London to Novgorod and from Cracow to Bergen, with the German North Sea and Baltic ports as nuclei. As a political advantage, the lack of a strong central authority greatly aided the independence of these trading cities. As time went on and conditions changed, the Hansa trade suffered an eclipse. The catch of fish fell off considerably; accessible forests became depleted; and many harbors, like those of Bruges and Ghent, became silted up.* The steadily expanding Atlantic trade overshadowed in importance the commerce of the enclosed seas upon which the prosperity of the Hanseatic League was based. Political pressure over the free towns increased. Finally, suicidal wars shattered the hinterland, resulting in the closing of the Rhine and the Schelde estuaries. In these conflicts the continental influences became supreme, and not until after the rebirth of the Reich in 1871 did the maritime factor assume an important role in guiding Germany's destiny.

INTERIOR AREAS. Southern Germany occupies the central portion of Europe's upland core consisting of a complex region of mountains, valleys, plateaus, and basins. Modern Germany includes only a fringe of the Alpine system to the south, being confined mainly to the outer ring of older highlands that extends from the Central Plateau of France through southern Germany to the Bohemian Plateau of Czechoslovakia. It continues in the low hills of the Lysa Gora in southern Poland, ultimately merging into the Russian steppe.

The part occupied by Germany is the most complex of the system. Among its major subregions the rift valley of the Rhine and the Rhine Gorge have been significant in the

---

* Estuary: A drowned river mouth, caused by the sinking of the land near the coast.

** Samuel Van Valkenburg and Ellsworth Huntington, *Europe* (John Wiley & Sons, 1935), p. 485.

† George D. Hubbard, *The Geography of Europe* (D. Appleton–Century Company, 1937), p. 610.

* Van Valkenburg and Huntington, *op. cit.*, p. 346.

historical development of Germany as well as that of all of western Europe. These two Rhineland areas formed the cradle land of the Germans. Together with the Rhone-Saône Valley, the Rhine Valley was the main avenue through which civilization spread from the Mediterranean into Europe.* These two north-south corridors are linked by the low Burgundian Gate, and through the Dijon and Basel gates they have access to the Paris Basin and the Bavarian Plateau, respectively. Another significant subregion was the Alpine, or Bavarian, foreland dominated by the Danube. The Brenner Pass, leading northward to Innsbruck in Tyrol and hence to Munich, was the chief link between the Mediterranean world and the German highlands.

POLITICAL AND HUMAN IMPLICATIONS. The great diversity of the German area, caused by the physiographic structure of the land, tracts of infertile soils, dense forests, and the fourfold drainage system of the Rhine, Danube, Weser, and Elbe, tended to divide human interests. In addition, being centrally located between the North Sea-Baltic lowland, the Po Valley, and to a lesser degree the Rhone-Saône Valley, the early rulers of the highland tried to control all these lands. This ambitious plan, however, failed and resulted only in their loss of control of the Mediterranean ports and in their diminished authority within the German realm. These losses were augmented by the numerous campaigns undertaken to control the outlying territory, which entailed a heavy drain of expense and depletion of material resources. Not only was the highland area incapable of supplying leadership sufficiently strong to consolidate the Empire, but it also lost its truly Alpine territories. Of these, the strategic cockpit of crossroads became independent Switzerland. The Habsburgs fell heir to the remainder, and in addition held the Bohemian folk fortress and Hungary and, upon occasions, parts of northern Italy within their realm.

The political separation of the true Alpine region from the Reich does not mean that it is not inhabited to a considerable extent by German people. Starting roughly from a line drawn from Basel to the Simplon Pass and extending eastward, the people of the

northern and central Alps are Swiss-German and Austro-German. This belt of population continues as far as the Danube Gate between the Alps and the Carpathians in the northeast and the Dolomites and the middle Drava Valley in the south. Thus, German ethnic groups control the Simplon, St. Gotthard, and Brenner Passes leading to the northern Mediterranean. To the east they control the Vienna gateway on the Danube and the foothill route leading along the eastern edge of the Alps through the Peartree Pass into the Adriatic basin. The acquisition of the southern portion of this outlet by Italy and Yugoslavia in 1919 terminated the last vestiges of Germanic rule in the Mediterranean realm. To the west, ever since the emergence of the French nation, German control of important passes and gateways on the country's borders has been on the wane. During the gradual dissolution of the Empire, first the Rhone-Saône Corridor and later the Burgundian Gate and Alsace-Lorraine came under the control of France. Even the control of the Rhine graben had to be shared with France except when the latter was in a political eclipse as it was following the Franco-Prussian War. In Switzerland the Geneva-Lyon, the Lausanne-Vallorbes, and the Neuchâtel–St. Sulpice gates are within the orbit of the French ethnic group.

These changes evidence a gradual displacement of German political and ethnic influences from the Mediterranean realm that, in reverse, somewhat parallels the German expansion beyond the Elbe. Such a shift naturally affects the relative strength of the two contrasting regions of Germany. Whereas Urdeutschland (German homeland) centered in what is now southern Germany, especially the Rhineland, during the later days of the Holy Roman Empire, the center shifted to the Habsburg domains of the Alpine lands. The unifying core of modern Germany, however, has evolved on the lowland, with Brandenburg as its heartland. Either by a slow process of peaceful acquisition or by conquest in war, the lowland became unified. The ultimate aim of the Nazi rule was the continuation and completion of this process by a final unification of the Reich through a radical reorganization of the internal structure of the country. Hitler reduced the federal states of Germany into merely admin-

* Griffith Taylor, *Environment and Nation* (The University of Chicago Press, 1936), pp. 64, 97, 189, 199, 206, 288, 316.

istrative units. By this move the last vestiges of medieval, feudal disunity were to be eliminated. This reorganization, coupled with the attempted inclusion of all contiguous ethnic groups of Germanic people outside the Reich, would have achieved the organization of an all-inclusive, complete Germany.*

The first goal of the Nazis, which was quite comparable to the administrative reforms of the French during their revolution, did not encounter serious internal or external criticism. The second, however, provoked strong opposition on several scores. First, several of the outlying ethnic groups had during the centuries acquired a strong nationalistic feeling, and concurrently they were strongly influenced by democratic ideas and ideals that were contrary to the philosophy of the Third Reich. These people resorted to arms and, when overpowered, organized effective resistance movements, as in the case of Holland or of Belgium, where the Germanic Flemish make up over half the population. Second, the incorporation of the nonresisting Austrian and the more than willing Sudeten Germans involved the almost unsolvable problem of Bohemia and of the Czech ethnic island. Third, such a consolidation of Germandom in an efficient, aggressive, modern state would have created such an overwhelming predominance of power for the Reich in Europe, and ultimately in the world, that its successful consolidation had to be prevented by the other powers of Europe as a measure of self-defense, even at the cost of a world conflagration. In the past, external forces merely intensified the centrifugal influences of Germany's site factors, thereby preventing or at least postponing the Reich's consolidation. After unification had been largely achieved through internal growth at a time of external disunity and dissension, the threatened nations once more rallied and united in a bloody war to crush the aggressive militarism of the Third Reich.

Climate: TEMPERATURE. The climate of Germany as a whole is stimulating and favorable for the development of a high level of civilization. As pointed out in the discussion of the location factor, on the basis of her latitudinal situation alone Germany's climate would be quite severe. This severity, how-

ever, does not exist. The January positive anomalies of temperature in Germany amount to from less than 10° F. to over 20° F., with most of the country having more than the lower of these values.* The narrow North Sea coast and the Schleswig isthmus have anomalies of more than 20°, whereas the Alpine foreland has less than 10°. As a result the German winters are relatively mild. Because of the same marine influences that cause these positive winter anomalies in western Europe and Germany, the winter isotherms ** run north and south along the meridians instead of east and west along the parallels as would normally be expected.

With the exception of Pomerania and East Prussia, all of Germany (1937 boundaries) has an average January temperature of 30° F. or higher. Hence much of Germany has a winter temperature not unlike that of the Ohio River valley of the United States—a latitudinal difference of ten or fifteen degrees. In southern Germany the higher elevation offsets its lower latitude. Thus Munich, on the Bavarian Plateau, is on the average 4° F. colder in January than Berlin, which is four degrees farther from the Equator in latitude.

Aside from the degree of coldness prevailing during winter, the next important climatic factor is the length of the cold season. In this respect the difference between western and eastern Germany is greater than the difference in temperature. Along the western margin of Germany the frost period is about 70 days; at the eastern extreme it is 150. This contrast is particularly significant in agricultural production. The longer growing season in the west permits the growth of valuable crops that would not ripen within the shorter growing period of the east. Here, then, the climatic factor enhanced the stimulating influences of the strategic location of western Germany and permitted the evolution of an intensive truck farming and dairy industry.

Since water transportation plays an important role in Germany's economic life, the effect of freezing temperatures upon navigation is of great consequence. The North Sea

---

* Adolf Hitler, *Mein Kampf* (Reynal and Hitchcock, 1939), p. 601.

* Temperature anomaly is the deviation from the normal expected at any given latitude. Thus a place with a positive anomaly is warmer than would be found on the average for that latitude.

** Isotherm: A line passing through points of equal temperature on the earth's surface.

coast is never frozen, but Hamburg, situated rather deeply inland, requires ice breakers to keep the harbor open. With the greater severity of winter, the Baltic ports are icebound: Lübeck for 32 days, Stettin for 61 days, and the inner harbor of Memel for 142 days (Stettin now in Poland and Memel in Russia). Similarly the icebound period of the Rhine at Cologne is 21 days, of the Oder at Frankfurt 80 days, and of the Memel at Tilsit 134 days. Although the Danube is farther south, it flows at a higher elevation and is closed to navigation for 37 days each year.*

During the summer the isotherms assume their normal east-west trends in accordance with latitudes. Almost all of Germany lies between the July isotherms of 70° F. and 64° F. Only a small area between the estuaries of the Elbe and the Oder has a July average below 64° F. Inland temperatures on the average are higher during the summer, a condition that explains the greater annual ranges of temperature for points away from the coast. In comparison to those of North America, the German summers resemble those of Oregon, Washington, and southern British Columbia. The positive summer anomaly of Germany is considerably smaller than during the winter, but with respect to the east coast of North America it is still discernible.

PRECIPITATION. The amount and distribution of precipitation indicate similar signs of marine versus continental influences, much like the ones found in the case of temperature. The amount varies from about 40 inches in the west to 20 in the east. In the west the distribution is rather uniform throughout the year, with a high percentage of cyclonic precipitation. Toward the east a steady decrease in the percentage of precipitation in winter accompanies a decrease in the proportion of the cyclonic type. Since the ultimate productivity of the land depends upon the available water, the decreased precipitation in the east is a potent factor in restricting the agricultural productivity of soils. Thus, from the agricultural point of view, the east is less favorable than the west, mainly because of the shorter growing season and the decreased amount of precipitation. On the other hand, the greater concentration of rainfall during the growing season tends to offset

its smaller amount. However, the greater and more frequent deviations from the average rainfall, both in amount and in time of occurrence, cause greater variations in crop yields in the continental east than in the west where the climate, under the equalizing effect of the sea, is much more dependable.

HUMAN IMPLICATIONS. As far as the effect of climate upon the people is concerned, Germany lacks the harmful results attributable to being too hot, too cold, too wet, or too dry. Furthermore, it has enough seasonal variations to render it necessary for people to work hard, at least during the growing season. Hubbard has stated that the German winters are harsh and compel the people to seek refuge in their homes. These circumstances may develop a family sentiment, deep feeling, and a contemplative mind leading to the study of science and philosophy.*

To this possible effect of the climate may be added another consideration. The southern German in the areas where grapes grow, which were held mainly by Rome, leads a somewhat easier life in a more cheerful climate than his northern brother. His mind turns to the lighter subjects of music and poetry, to the "Wein, Weib, und Gesang" attitude. As Taylor points out, in Europe at the close of the Renaissance period the Catholic south excelled in the arts and other humanities, whereas the Protestant north concentrated more and more on the sciences.** This observation is equally applicable to Germany proper, and the general inclination for literature and music in the south and for science and industry in the north may be explained in part at least on a climatic and religious basis.

Natural vegetation. The influence of soils and natural vegetation is not so significant today as it was in the past. Where man lives in great numbers, as in Germany, little surface area of the land remains untouched by human activities. The modern white man prefers the type of environment in which forests flourish, particularly the broadleaved deciduous forest or a mixed forest of broadleaved deciduous and coniferous trees. The Germanic people were forest dwellers. As time passed, they cleared more and more land, so that in modern Germany practically

---

* W. G. Kendrew, *The Climates of the Continents* (The Clarendon Press, Oxford, 1927), pp. 254, 258.

* Hubbard, *op. cit.,* p. 607.
** Taylor, *op. cit.,* pp. 208–209.

nothing remains of the natural vegetation. The tracts of timber that do exist are a part of the man-made economic environment. Forestry in Germany has long been a science, and with the exception of some swamp-woods the forest lands have been cultivated as have some of our orchards.

Soils. On the whole, German soils are mediocre or poor. In only limited areas could they be rated as favorable from the standpoint of natural fertility. In the glacial regions of the north are found some fine glacio-lacustrine loams and clays, and in other areas there are stretches of fine-grained, fertile loess soils. Wherever they were available, these better soils were the first choice for crop production. Certain crops do better on certain soils, and some will not grow at all on unfavorable soils. In general, however, the type of production depends to a much greater extent upon climate and economic conditions than upon soils. Such practices as the rotation of crops and application of fertilizers have been the means of increasing the productivity of the land, thereby offsetting the handicap of inferior soils. Hence soils affect not so much the type of production in Germany as its cost.

The increase of population and the heavy concentration in urban areas of people who could afford to pay high prices for agricultural products caused shifts both in areas and in the type of production. In order to meet the increased demand, as agricultural areas expanded, second- and even third-rate soils had to be brought under the plow. Concurrently agriculture became highly intensified. This intensification spread to animal industries and finally to silviculture.

The general weak quality of much of the soil was a handicap that had to be overcome. The German scientific mind turned early to the study of soils. Some of the basic discoveries in soil chemistry, the use and application of natural and commercial fertilizers, and new techniques in agricultural production were made in Germany. As a result, German agriculture, even in the face of the handicap of mediocre and poor soils, became among the most productive in the world. Due to the liberal use of fertilizers prior to 1914, crop yields could be maintained at a more satisfactory level in Germany than in the other belligerent countries of Europe during

World War I. This fact was probably responsible in great measure for the continuous efforts of the Third Reich to increase crop yields by improving methods of agricultural production.

The soils east of the Elbe are definitely the poorest, and here also the climate becomes gradually less favorable. Thus soil and climate, along with economic factors, combined to retard the development of this area. In addition to these conditions, there was the early ethnic problem of Slav minorities ruled by German overlords, an underlying cause for the evolution of the large and extensively utilized estates held by the military caste, the Junkers. Much of the soil has such low productivity that it is necessary to hold it in large units to render it profitable. Any plan formulated to break the power of the Junkers by the establishment of small peasant holdings would not work except in pockets of better soils; at least such attempts did not succeed in the past. The area east of the Elbe was settled under the "new law," according to which the land was transmitted undivided, in contrast to the "old law," which required division. The free peasants who moved in gradually sank to the level of serfdom, for on their small holdings they could not produce enough on which to live and pay rent.* This eastern area, therefore, became the nucleus and stronghold of the militant Prussian Junker class that slowly gained the leadership over the more cultured and less chauvinistic southern German people.

Minerals. The problem of mineral resources was for a long time one of the leading international questions of the Reich. In 1937 Germany was fortunate in having control of a large share of the carboniferous belt of Europe lying just at the outer edge of the uplands, extending from Belgium through Germany into Poland and Russia. The most important coal fields of Germany were in the Ruhr-Rhine region, the Saar Basin,** and the Upper and Lower Silesian fields. Aside from these, Germany had large deposits of lignite, inferior to bituminous coal because of a low carbon content. This low-grade fuel as-

* Derwent Whittlesey, *The Earth and the State* (Henry Holt and Company, 1939), pp. 182–184.

** From 1919 to 1935 the Saar was under the jurisdiction of the League of Nations, and the mines were under French control.

sumed a greater importance in Germany than in any other industrial nation. Here lignite was for the most part used only locally for generating electricity. Of the coal fields, the Ruhr region was by far the most important. Because of its excellent, strategic location on the Rhine and at the edge of the upland, access to the sea, to the plain, and to the Lorraine iron ore farther up the Rhine were all easy. Its location coupled with its coal mines has made the Ruhr district the most highly industrialized spot in the world.

With the exception of potash, Germany was deficient in other mineral resources. The Reich of the Weimar Republic produced three fourths of her zinc requirements, about one third of her iron ore and lead consumption, and inconsequential amounts of copper, phosphates, and petroleum.* Nitrates were produced on a large scale from the free nitrogen of the air. This production was carried out by means of the Haber process, a typical German ersatz invention necessitated by the blockade of World War I. The most serious loss incurred through the Versailles Treaty of 1919 was that of the Lorraine iron ore deposits, which left the iron and steel industry of Germany overwhelmingly dependent upon foreign ore. The difficulty was mainly economic in nature. In an age of economic nationalism and high protective tariffs, the purchase of foreign raw materials may become well-nigh impossible due to exchange restrictions and other monetary handicaps. Furthermore, no nation can buy from the world if the world refuses to accept its products in exchange. The general lack of mineral resources has been a cardinal point in determining Germany's foreign economic and political policy. In final analysis the German *Lebensraum* represented an economic and political realm, within the framework of which the German people would have been assured an economic independence comparable to that of the United States or the British Empire.

The Human Factor

Location and site factors are purely physical in nature. They are mostly unalterable and have shown few changes during human

* Frank H. Simonds and Brooks Emeny, *The Great Powers in World Politics,* New Edition (American Book Company, 1939), pp. 207-212.

history. The greatest alterations have occurred where man has changed. Although the location of the land that is now Germany has not changed since long before the time of the Roman conquest, the shift in the foci of man's activities turned the relative position of Germany from a peripheral to a nodal location. In final analysis it is man who, by building up his society, synthesizes the influences of nature and expresses the sum total of environmental influences and their human responses in his national culture.

The German people. In the physical environment of the Germany of 1937 lived 67,000,000 people, of whom only two per cent were not German. Thus the population was homogeneous. Yet there are definite differences among the various groups of which the nation is composed. The most striking is the difference between the south German and the Prussian. The cleavage is revealed in cultural traits, in religion, and in racial descent. The Prussians are military-minded, Protestant, and Nordic; the south Germans are more easy-going, literary-minded, Catholic, and of the Alpine race with some admixture of the Mediterranean. South Germany belonged to Rome, whose influence upon the culture and civilization there is discernible even today.

Throughout the country the density of population was high. On the average it amounted to 360 persons per square mile, with the industrial areas exceeding 500 and the Baltic glacial belt ranging between 60 and 125 persons per square mile. The dense population exerted a heavy pressure upon the resources. Only by the most frugal use of their resources and in a world of unhampered trade could the German people really hope to profit by their industry. The disciplined mind of the middle class turned to the problems with vigor. Science, research, and education flourished. Entering the field of economic development somewhat late, the German economy profited from the experience of others. To be able to compete with established industrial nations, Germany could not venture into haphazard undertakings; rather, her strategy had to be planned. The Anglo-Saxon principle of free enterprise underwent some modification in the interpretation of the German school of economics, and in a relatively short time there were definite evidences of success. German goods penetrated world markets, and the flag of the German merchant marine could be seen in all the ports of the seven seas.

A new Germany emerged and also a new German—the "Westerner." Reared in great industrial centers like the Ruhr, or in humming ports like Bremen or Hamburg, he reflected the spirit of the bygone Hansa. International, often cosmopolitan, in his attitude, he was the antagonist incarnate of the provincial, narrow-minded Junker. He was the force behind democratic Germany; he backed Stresemann and the pact of Locarno. His downfall came with the great world-wide depression. Some "Westerners" backed Hitler in the vain hope of ultimately gaining the upper hand of him. Some hoped to profit at least temporarily by the Nazis' ruthless methods of economic penetration. Some even shared the dream of world domination. A few balked at Hitler and sought refuge in foreign countries. But all found their calculations in error; they came to see their industrial empire laid waste, their proud cities leveled, most of their factories destroyed, and the once most efficient transportation system of the continent crippled beyond imagination.

With their national disunity preserved long after other nations developed into strong cultural and political entities, the German people were bound by conflicting loyalties. In the minds of some of the cultivated, there survived the idea of the universal Reich of German spiritual leadership, the incarnation of the ideal Christian state—the country of Goethe, Schiller, and Kant, of Bach and Beethoven, of Charlemagne and Barbarossa, of Luther and Melanchthon. But to the great masses who previously were called again and again to defend their righteous ruler and their sacred soil against the aggressive Austrians or Prussians or Bavarians or Saxons, the idea of German unity was somewhat perplexing. They had to learn that they were all brothers—that is, almost all of them. To the Bavarian, the distant East Prussian probably appeared more like a stranger than the close kin Austrian, despite the fact that the latter was legally a foreigner. However, the sectional division slowly submerged into a national loyalty, and the unity and existence of the Reich became an accepted fact. This birth of modern nationalism did not, of course, remain confined to the boundaries of the political Reich. It demanded the complete unification of all Germans into one national and political entity. The "Grossdeutsch" idea spread beyond Germany and assumed considerable strength even before 1918, particularly in Austria. The prohibition of the peace treaties against the union of the two German states received severe and serious criticism, especially since both the Germans and the Austrians considered such a prohibition a flagrant violation of the Wilsonian principle of national self-determination.

These politico-psychological factors led to a feeling of frustration among the German middle classes and gave rise to an almost defeatist attitude. It seemed to them that the League of Nations—in fact, the whole world—conspired to prevent the Germans from achieving those accomplishments that other great powers had possessed for centuries. This sense of frustration intensified the discouraging effects of the economic depression. In disgust and desperation the German nation turned to the one man who openly defied the world and promised to lead Germany to the pinnacle of power and prestige. His method was not the way of culture and enlightenment but over a road of iron and blood. The depth of desperation to which the German nation descended can be measured only by the meekness of their acceptance of the physical violence and the spiritual depredations that followed in the wake of the birth of the Third Reich.

Adolf Hitler justified his early foreign policy with the contention that common blood belonged in a common Reich. The ten million Germans of Austria, Sudetenland, and Memel were acquired without war. Danzig, the Polish Corridor, and Upper Silesia represented the irredentist cause for Germany in Poland. After the outbreak of war in 1939, Hitler continued the creation of an empire in Europe that rivaled that of Napoleon. Areas like Danzig, Eupen, Malmédy, and Luxembourg were annexed to the Reich. Early in 1940 Germans were urged to leave the South Tyrol, the Baltic states, and the Soviet Union and return to the Greater Reich. This Hitlerian idea underwent some transfiguration in the hands of the victorious Allies. After the collapse of Germany in May, 1945, it was deemed advisable to eliminate

German minorities to prevent recurrence of German irredenta. For this reason plans were made to transfer 3,500,000 Germans from Poland, 2,500,000 from Czechoslovakia, 500,000 from Hungary, and 150,000 from Austria into the four occupied zones of Germany (see the map on page 140), by August 1, 1946. What economic and political repercussion such an influx of population into an already heavily populated area will bring about is hard to tell.

Economic Factors

Industries. Utilizing their human and material resources and taking advantage of their pivotal location, the Germans after their unification in 1871 built up a strong industrial civilization that seriously challenged the economic world domination of Great Britain. The expansion of manufacturing was based mainly upon resources found within the confines of the country. Great coal fields served as the bases for the expansion of the iron and steel industry, especially in the Ruhr, the Saar (under League of Nations control, 1919–35), and in Upper Silesia. This basic industry supplied the material for the machinery industry, for the manufacture of rails and rolling stock, for ship building, and for other constructional industries. Of course, after the rise of Hitler, the manufacture of armaments became the paramount heavy industry.

The second development came partially from the utilization of the enormous potash deposits, largely as a source of fertilizer materials and partially from the chemical industry, in which Germany had until World War I a very strong, monopolistic position. The lack of the so-called critical resources forced the German chemical industries into trying to find domestic substitutes. They developed a number of ersatz materials and subsequently became leaders in synthetics. The dearth of resources was not necessarily a drawback. In the United States millions of tons of coke were produced by a process that wasted the by-products. In Germany every bit of the material was recovered. In fact, a substantial proportion of the chemical industry was based upon the use of the materials that in the United States were lost for good. The textile industry has a long history, but its importance in the international field came

about chiefly as a result of the rapid development of the chemical dye industry, which depends to a large extent upon the by-products of the coking industry.

Because of the desire for efficient use of the lignite deposits, which could not stand the cost of transportation, lignite was used to generate electricity locally and the current was distributed by a system of interlocking transmission lines. Germany became electrified to a large extent as a response to this technique, and a high-ranking electrical industry developed.

Two industries using local agricultural raw materials that rose to international significance in Germany are sugar refining and brewing. The German sugar industry was mainly responsible for the interregional sugar war that came to an armistice at the Brussels Convention in 1902. World Wars I and II both played havoc with the production of European beet sugar, thus materially aiding areas of cane sugar production elsewhere in the world. The German sugar industry, however, never regained the international importance possessed before 1914. Beer is the national drink of Germany, and German breweries have long been internationally famous. *Rathauskeller* (city hall cellars used for restaurants) and *Biergärten* are essential appendages of a German city's social and political life. Many a sinister plan was brewed in Munich's ill-famed *Hofbräuhaus* by a neurotic ex-corporal and his fanatic cohorts.

The rise of the industrial power of Germany, based as it was on insufficient local resources, was more the result of the skilful and frugal use of meager resources and the determination of the people than of purely geologic factors. The Germans themselves have known this, which, unfortunately for them and for the world, led some of their number to believe that they were superhuman—a master race destined to rule their inferiors. It was not their possession of heavy industries nor their skill and ability in organizing their economic life that led to their destruction, but the philosophical conclusions that they so fallaciously drew from these experiences. These led them to aggression, conquest, and finally to utter defeat.

Cities. In 1939 there were sixty-two cities in Germany having a population of 100,000 or more. Although a number of urban areas were largely or partly destroyed during World War II, and the economic organization of the country severely disrupted, the size and distribution of cities in prewar Germany indicate the normal pattern of urban settlement. The following list of ten cities, all over one-half million population, is proof of the degree to which Germany had developed a highly industrialized and commercialized economy:

river's resources, and to regulate navigation on the Rhine.

Besides the facilities for inland navigation, Germany built a strong merchant marine. Her first commercial fleet was badly decimated by World War I, partly by Allied sinking but mostly by reparations. So republican Germany rebuilt it, and for a time the sister ships *Bremen* and *Europa* were the fastest luxury liners afloat. With her merchant marine, Germany created a threat to

City	Prewar population	Location	Primary functions
1. Berlin	4,332,000	North German Plain	Capital and leading metropolitan centre
2. Hamburg	1,682,000	North German Plain —lower Elbe Valley	Leading German port
3. Munich	828,000	Bavarian Plateau	Bavarian capital and leading city of southern Germany
4. Cologne	768,000	Rhineland	Transportation center
5. Leipzig	702,000	Saxony	Trading and publishing center; fairs
6. Essen	660,000	Ruhr District	Steel (Krupp Works)
7. Dresden	625,000	Saxony	Rail center and Elbe River port
8. Frankfurt	547,000	Rhineland	General manufacturing
9. Dortmund	542,000	Ruhr District	Industrial center
10. Dusseldorf	541,000	Ruhr District	Industrial center

NOTE: Breslau (625,000), Silesian industrial center, is presently located within Poland.

Transportation. Germany's industrial development could not have taken place without an excellent transportation system. The importance of this has been well demonstrated in the negative during World War II. When the superior air force of the Allies destroyed the German transportation and communication system, the country collapsed. The system had been developed by careful coordination of water and overland routes. There were 6,000 miles of rivers or canalized rivers and 1,400 miles of canals proper in use. During normal times one fifth of Germany's merchandise, consisting largely of iron ore, coal, and coke, moves on waterways.

The most important waterway, of course, is the Rhine, its normal traffic exceeding that of the entire Mississippi-Missouri system. Outside the Great Lakes of North America there is no other single fresh waterway quite comparable to the Rhine. This river is a perpetual problem for international study. The International Commission of the Rhine River, which has functioned since 1868 except during war periods, held its first postwar meeting at Strasbourg, France, in December, 1945, to re-establish the international machinery, to encourage the development of the

Britain and the competition led to disagreements.

Germany's railroad system was excellent. The density of railroads and the per capita mileage were among the highest in Europe, indicating the intensity of their development. The fastest train in the world was a streamliner running between Berlin and Hamburg. However, much of Germany's 36,000 miles of railroad was destroyed in the recent war. With the ever-increasing use of the automobile, the truck, and the airplane, it is possible that not all of the trackage destroyed will be restored.

Roads were of secondary importance. Really large-scale road building began only with the ascent of the Nazi power. Most of the roads were built for military purposes, but they were excellent and without doubt will have an important part in the reconstruction of the shattered German economy. The use of trucks, buses, and passenger autos was relatively high among the countries of Europe but greatly below that found in the United States.

After the end of the Versailles restriction, the Germans were pioneers in air transportation. Even during the ban period, experiments were carried out with gliders. Later, commercial airlines formed a network over the Reich, reached most of the capitals of Europe, and extended across the South Atlantic to South America and southeastward into Asia as far as Iran and Afghanistan.

Agriculture. Generally speaking, German agriculture was intensive, scientifically conducted, and productive, especially in the west where natural and economic conditions were most favorable. Along with manufacturing, it was unquestionably one of the basic industries of the country. About two thirds of the land was devoted to agriculture, the remainder being chiefly in forests. Of the agricultural land, about three fourths was under cultivation and one fourth in pastures and meadows. The chief crops of Germany were forage, grain, and root crops. A third of the arable land was devoted to hay and another fourth to rye, chiefly in northern Germany, where soils are poor and sandy and the climate cool, wet, and cloudy. Wheat and barley were leading crops in southern Germany. Germany led Europe in the production of potatoes, using them principally for the manufacture of industrial alcohol. The cool, wet climate and sandy soils of northern Germany are ideal for potatoes. Germany's most productive field crop was sugar beets, in which she led the world. Minor crops included hops, tobacco, grapes, and fruits.

Foreign trade. The picture of German economy would remain incomplete without a brief discussion of her foreign trade. Germany's imports consisted mainly of raw materials and foodstuffs, which normally constituted 80 per cent of the total. The remainder was made up of manufactured goods. Of these, cotton goods, iron manufactures, and wool yarn were the most important. Exports were dominated by manufactures, which represented 80 per cent of the total. Raw materials, chiefly coal, followed with almost 14 per cent. The rest consisted of food products, mainly sugar. Under these conditions the whole prosperity of Germany hinged on her foreign trade. When her trade dropped off due to the depression and also to the high tariff philosophy of the world, German economy almost collapsed. The resultant insecurity of the masses was instrumental in raising Hitler to power.

During the prewar days a concerted and serious effort was made to expand German foreign trade, practically under state direction. This trade expansion was particularly conspicuous in the Danubian countries and in Latin America. As a result of this economic penetration Germany was able to exert a disproportionately strong political influence, particularly upon the small Central European and Balkan countries. Hungary, Rumania, and others in this category were forced to realign their internal economies to suit Germany in return for the dubious advantage of having a rather secure market for their products.

Conclusion

Since the proclamation of the German Empire in 1871 in the Hall of Mirrors of the Palace of Versailles, more than three quarters of a century of momentous events have gone into the pages of history. Germany has been a leading figure in three wars: the Franco-Prussian War (1870–71), World War I (1914–18), and World War II (1939–45). The constitutional status of Germany has reflected the vicissitudes of the times: the German Empire (1871–1918), the Weimar Republic (1919–33), and the Third Reich of Adolf Hitler (1933–45). Germany has gone from victory in 1871 to defeat in 1918, from triumph in 1940 to disaster in 1945. A unified Reich under Prussian military leadership represented such a combination of power that the security of Europe and of the world has been threatened. Only a grand alliance of most of the powers of the world has been able to defeat Germany in two world wars. Now the Reich lies in ruins equal only to the destruction after the Thirty Years' War ending in 1648. With the fall of Hitler a German government ceased to exist, but the German nation was not extinguished. Today a peaceful, democratic Reich is needed for the peace and prosperity of Europe since, regardless of the state's boundaries, the people will always have an important role in international relations.

CHAPTER 11

The Low Countries between the Great Powers

THE Low Countries are located at the mouths of one major European river, the Rhine, and two minor rivers, the Meuse and the Schelde (see the map on page 153). Napoleon is supposed to have remarked, as an argument in favor of his virtual annexation of the Low Countries, that both the Netherlands and Belgium really are nothing but the alluvial deposits of "these three French rivers." The fact that the Meuse and the Schelde both have their sources in France lends a modicum of truth to this statement. The largest part of the courses of these two rivers, however, lies in the Low Countries, and the Rhine, though it drains Alsace-Lorraine, can hardly be called a French river, since most of its drainage basin is located in Germany and Switzerland. As to the land itself, only the smaller portion of the Low Countries is composed of the recent delta deposits of these rivers; the larger part lies well above the present delta level.

In English usage the term *Low Countries* frequently applies to the territory of both the Netherlands and Belgium. The French version, *Les Pays-Bas*, is occasionally used for both, sometimes for Belgium, but more frequently for the Netherlands. This last use is the most fitting because the official name for the latter, *Nederland*, means low land.*

Despite the implication of the name three

* Belgium was named after the old tribe of the Belgae. The term *Holland* is often used, by the Dutch themselves as well as by others, for all of *Nederland*, but it is not an official designation. Originally, and even yet within the country, it refers only to that portion which has long been the most important politically and economically, the present provinces of North-Holland and South-Holland.

fifths of the Netherlands lies above sea level. Many sections have an elevation of more than fifty feet above sea level and in the southeast the land rises to a height of over 300 feet. However, if there were no protecting dikes, the remaining two fifths of the Netherlands would be inundated by the high tides of the North Sea or the overflow from the rivers. In comparison, Belgium has relatively little land that lies below high tide and high stream levels. Its average elevation is considerably greater than that of the Netherlands, as the entire southeastern half of the country lies well above 300 feet, rising to over 2,000 feet in the Ardennes near the German border.

Thus it would be entirely erroneous to imagine the Low Countries as a flat, monotonous delta region, akin to the delta of the Nile. Within the 12,680 square miles of the Netherlands and the 11,780 of Belgium (together equivalent to about half the size of the state of New York) there is a great deal of natural diversity.

Physical Aspects

Diversity. Within surprisingly short distances in the Netherlands and Belgium there are sharp contrasts of relief and soil. From the poor, forested highlands of the Ardennes it is scarcely one hundred miles to the low, rich, rather bare plains around Ypres; and from the high sandy hills north of Arnhem, covered with pine woods and heather, it is less than forty miles to the fertile, flat, open polder landscape west of Utrecht. There are six major natural regions, and each one differs basically from all the others.

Man has created even greater contrasts.

He found some regions, such as the marine clay lands of North-Holland, South-Holland, Zeeland, and the northern Netherlands; the alluvial clay lands of Gelderland and Utrecht; or the rich loamy plains of central Belgium, to be exceedingly fertile (see the map on page 155 for provinces). These lands he settled densely and changed profoundly. He found other areas, such as the sandy heaths of Belgian Brabant and Dutch North-Brabant and the moor lands of the northeastern Netherlands, to be very poor in their natural state. These regions yielded only slowly to his techniques of development. Here population density is considerably lower, and the process of converting the natural landscape into a cultural landscape has not yet been, and may never be, completed. In various parts of the Low Countries man discovered locations favorable for trade and manufacturing or provided with mineral resources; these became urban and industrial areas of high population density.

As a result of these geographical, and of historical and sociological factors, the cultural landscape varies greatly from region to region and with it the local economic, social, and political problems. The Low Countries should not be thought of as a small area with simple problems. Many problems of foreign relations as well as many domestic problems of these countries cannot be resolved without recognizing the reality of this great diversity.

Natural regions. The following paragraphs present thumbnail sketches of the six major natural regions of the Low Countries. A study of the basic characteristics of each region should help in understanding the relationship of the component geographic parts of the countries to principal political, military, and economic problems (see the map on page 153).

THE POLDERS. Without protection by an intricate system of engineering works, among which dikes (levees) are the most important, the northern and western parts of the Netherlands, the westernmost part of Belgium, and low-lying lands along the Rhine, the lower Meuse, and the Schelde would be exposed to flooding each high tide of the sea or each period of slightly above-normal river level. Large areas would even be flooded at low tide. Thus most of this land has had to be drained artificially, by means of hundreds of large and small Diesel, electric, and steam pumps. Here and there old-fashioned windmills can still be found, but for the most part they are passé. The entire area is intersected by thousands upon thousands of ditches, small drainage canals, and larger canals, the latter also suitable for navigation purposes.

The network of dikes, which range in size from very small to very large, is intricate. In general, the dikes along the seacoast and along the rivers are the largest. For example, the main dike that closes off the old Zuiderzee, the present Ijselmeer, has a base 280 feet wide and a height of about 24 feet. Hundreds of locks keep the water at different levels, a system made necessary by the fact that some sections are farther below sea level than others, and that therefore the water in their drainage ditches is at a lower level than that in adjacent, slightly higher sections. Each minor land area constitutes a cell, called a "polder," with its own water level, drainage ditches, and canals, operated by its own pumping facilities and protected by its own dikes. This polder landscape stretches from northern France across the Low Countries into northwestern Germany.

The polders contain some of the most fertile land of the Low Countries. Their reclamation has cost tremendous effort and maintenance expenses are high, but they yield abundantly under an intensive and scientific system of agriculture. Quite early in history these fertile lands were capable of supporting relatively high densities of population. With the tremendous growth of urban centers since the middle of the last century, population in many of these polder areas has increased beyond the food-supplying capacity of even the most fertile land. Average density of population in the province of Zeeland (which contains no large cities) is over 350 inhabitants per square mile. In urbanized North-Holland and South-Holland it is respectively 1,400 and 1,700 per square mile.

For hundreds of years the major rivers, the semi-abandoned delta branches, the tidal streams, and the older canals provided the polderland and adjacent areas with a network of cheap lines of transportation at a time when elsewhere in western Europe transportation of goods over poor and muddy roads was laborious and costly. During the same period these waterways as well as the

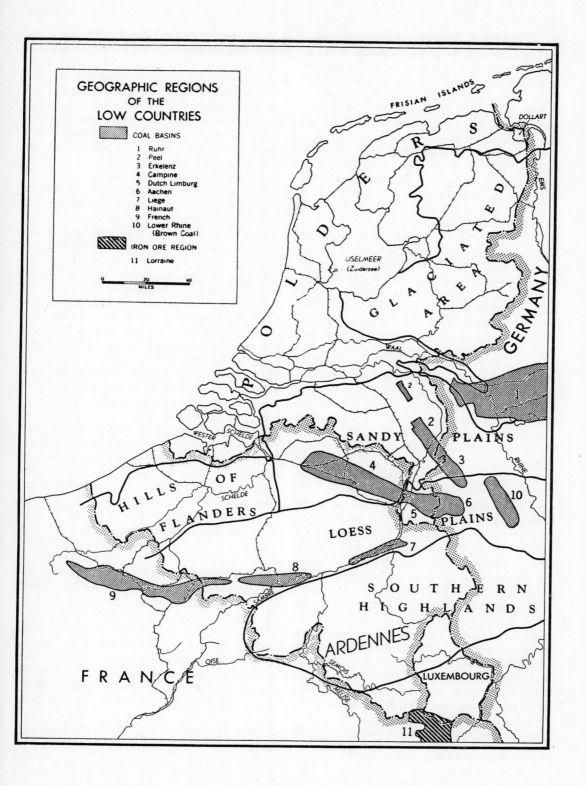

GEOGRAPHIC REGIONS
OF THE
LOW COUNTRIES

COAL BASINS

1   Ruhr
2   Peel
3   Erkelenz
4   Campine
5   Dutch Limburg
6   Aachen
7   Liege
8   Hainaut
9   French
10 Lower Rhine
    (Brown Coal)

IRON ORE REGION

11 Lorraine

0   20   40
        MILES

FRISIAN ISLANDS

DOLLART

P O L D E R S

GLACIATED AREA

EMS

GERMANY

IJSELMEER
(Zuiderzee)

WAAL

SANDY   PLAINS

RHINE

WESTER SCHELDE

HILLS   OF

SCHELDE

FLANDERS

LOESS

PLAINS

SAMBRE

S O U T H E R N

H I G H L A N D S

FRANCE

OISE

ARDENNES

SEMOIS

MEUSE

LUXEMBOURG

153

low polders have also afforded effective protection from attack to the valuable heart of the Netherlands—the present provinces of North-Holland, South-Holland, and Zeeland with their flourishing trading emporia, such as Amsterdam, Rotterdam, Dordrecht, Vlaardingen, Enkhuizen, and Middelburg, all along on near the coast.

Except for a few major entrances the west coast is difficult of approach to all but amphibious enemy forces. The sea is shallow, the beach is sandy, and beyond lies the belt of dunes that guard part of the polderland against flooding by the tides of the North Sea. At the eastern edge of the lowlands of North-Holland, South-Holland, and Utrecht a line of defense was once established, based upon the flooding of a belt of polders from near Amsterdam via Utrecht and Gorkum to the major mouths of the Rhine and the Meuse. This line, the famous *Hollandsche Waterlinie,* though effective in the past is now outmoded. Its principal weakness is not so much military as economic. The so-called "Fortress Holland," the entire region to the west of this defense line, could be held only briefly, because the present dense population could not be fed adequately for any length of time. Its large cities without possibilities for strong underground defenses are much too vulnerable.

THE GLACIATED AREA. The higher sandy lands east of Utrecht and north of the low country between the lower Meuse and the Rhine constitute an area where most of the present surface features are due to the effects of the next-to-the-last glacial period. Principal features are extensive sandy to loamy ground moraine plains, and sandy terminal moraine ridges. The latter rise to 150 feet * and occasionally to over 300 feet above sea level; the former lie from 50 to 80 feet. The result of the poor drainage, a condition frequently found with glaciated lands, has been the formation of moors, or "high peat bogs." Although much of the land is now in agricultural use, the morainic ridges are very poor and usually covered by heather or by

* When over one hundred feet or so in elevation these morainic deposits become "mountains." The Dutch topographic sheets are full of such mountains, gently rising piles of sand, such as the Trompenberg near Hilversum (80 feet), the Grebbeberg near Wageningen (130 feet), or the Galgenberg near Arnhem (350 feet).

planted pine forests. The land is much less fertile than in the polders and supports a lower density of population. But even here average densities are extremely high in comparison with those in the United States. In the province of Drente, for example, which has a predominantly agrarian economy, the density is 247 persons per square mile, compared to a density of 45 per square mile in rich, agrarian Iowa. On and near the German border these moor areas have long formed a protective belt against attack from the northeast. In addition, they have constituted a cultural divide.

THE SANDY PLAINS. South of the Meuse lie the extensive flat and sandy alluvial plains of North-Brabant, northern Limburg, and the Belgian Campine. Elevation increases imperceptibly from near sea level to about 250 feet in the south. Several sections have poor drainage, and here, as in the glaciated lands, exist moors, such as the Peel moors between North-Brabant and Limburg, long an effective belt of cultural separation but a scene of heavy fighting during the German invasion in 1940. Originally most of this plain was covered by heather, pines, and low sand dunes, but with the aid of modern artificial fertilizers large sections have been converted into pasture and cultivated land. Although the general relief offers little hindrance to modern military methods, the Peel long constituted a fairly good flank protection for North-Brabant.

THE HILLS OF FLANDERS. To the west of Antwerp and Brussels lie the low hills of Flanders. The relief is gently rolling except where interrupted by the wide flood plains of the Schelde and Lijs. Somewhat higher, individual hills, such as Mt. Kimmel of World War I fame, rise above the general level of the land, and numerous little valleys and scattered woods still further vary the landscape. In many places the soil is sandy, and in a number of spots small heath areas survive as a testimony of infertile land. Parts of the region have a cultural landscape that closely resembles the well-known *bocage* of Normandy.*

THE LOESS PLAINS. The Loess Plains of Belgium and the Netherlands are part of a

* The Normandy *bocage* of invasion fame is an area of small plots of land, surrounded by dense hedges that often are set upon low earth ridges.

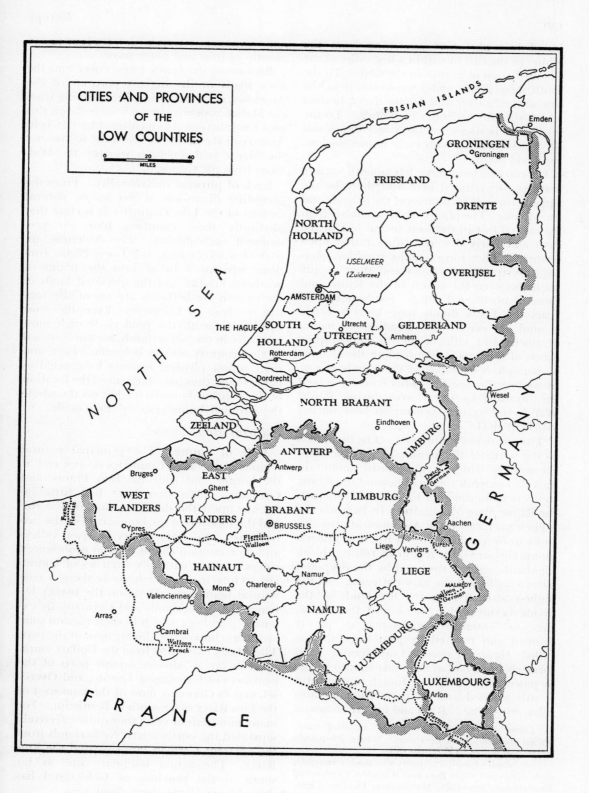

CITIES AND PROVINCES
OF THE
LOW COUNTRIES

0   20   40
MILES

FRISIAN ISLANDS

Emden

GRONINGEN
Groningen

FRIESLAND

DRENTE

NORTH
HOLLAND

IJSELMEER
(Zuiderzee)

OVERIJSEL

NORTH SEA

AMSTERDAM

THE HAGUE   SOUTH
HOLLAND

Utrecht
UTRECHT

GELDERLAND

Arnhem

Rotterdam

Dordrecht

Wesel

NORTH BRABANT

Eindhoven

LIMBURG

ZEELAND

ANTWERP

Antwerp

Bruges

EAST
FLANDERS

Ghent

LIMBURG

Dutch
German

WEST
FLANDERS

BRABANT

BRUSSELS

Aachen

Ypres

FLANDERS

Flemish
Walloon

Liege   Verviers   EUPEN

French
Flemish

HAINAUT

Namur

LIEGE

Mons   Charleroi

MALMEDY
Walloon
German

Valenciennes

NAMUR

Arras

LUXEMBOURG

Cambrai
Walloon
French

GERMANY

LUXEMBOURG

Arlon

German

FRANCE

French

155

broad belt of loess,* stretching from the Rhine in the east to within a few miles of the Channel coast of France in the west. To the south these plains end approximately at the line of the Sambre and Meuse rivers, beyond which rise the Ardennes highlands. To the north they border upon the Sandy Plains and the Flanders Hills with their numerous low, wet flood plains.

Deposits of loess have left smooth surface features, interrupted here and there by the upper valleys of tributaries of the Schelde and the Meuse. The plains, which are fairly high (from 150 feet in the west to 450 feet in the east) and fairly dry, constitute rather open country. They form a major corridor, offering easy transit to armies and their supply trains between the plains of the Rhine and those of northern France. For hundreds of years the Loess Plains have been a battle ground *par excellence*. Reading the names of towns and villages on the topographic sheets of the area is like reading the chapter or paragraph headings of the annals of war in western Europe.** This corridor served the invading German forces during World War I, and again a generation later during World War II.

THE SOUTHERN HIGHLANDS. The highlands to the south of the Sambre-Meuse line form the western wing of an extensive mountain area that extends eastward beyond the Rhine to the neighborhood of Kassel and Frankfurt, the Rhine Slate Mountains. In Belgium the highest part, called the Ardennes, attains altitudes of over 2,000 feet. It is not so much a mountain area as a region of rolling, bleak highlands, sharply dissected by the deep and narrow valleys of the major streams. At the highest altitudes, on the flat lands of the divide between the Meuse and the Rhine, there are extensive regions that are poorly drained and covered by peat bogs, the so-called *Hautes Fagnes*. Considerable land formerly in forest has been turned into tillage or pasture, but from one fourth to one third is still wooded and its population remains relatively sparse. Rain and fog are common,

* Loess: Deposits of fine-grained material transported by wind from dry areas. Where adequately watered, it makes an excellent soil.
** Students of military history will readily recognize such names as Quatre Bras and Waterloo, Landen and Neerwinden, Ramillies, Malplaquet, Fleurus, Ligny, Enghien, Mons, Fontenoy, and many others.

and winters are severe, with from four to five months of frost and much snow.

Because of the heavy forest cover and the poor roads in the highest portions of the Ardennes, particularly in a belt running from the Malmédy district to the Semois River, this area has functioned as a cultural barrier belt. As a result the divide between the Rhine and the Meuse still separates roughly the Walloons from the Germans.

Lack of physical individuality. From the preceding discussion of the major natural regions of the Low Countries it is clear that physically these countries have no pronounced individuality. The Ardennes are part of a larger area, the Loess Plains continue without a break into the plains of northern France, and the glaciated lands of the eastern Netherlands are essentially similar to those in Germany. Even the most striking element, the polders, though most extensive in the Netherlands, are not confined to that country and to Belgium. Here and there minor physical features have acted as barriers and thus have influenced the location of the political boundaries, but on the whole the national boundaries are man-made.

Political Boundaries

Role of nature. The principal natural regions of the Low Countries do not end at the border, but continue into France and Germany. Thus they have had little influence upon the determination of the size and the location of the boundaries of the two countries. No large rivers or river valleys and no mountain chains or even pronounced ridges coincide with any stretches of boundary. Only in the northeast is there a true natural boundary. Here, on the border between the Netherlands and Germany lie extensive peat bogs, which in their natural state are nearly impassable during most of the year. These bogs, extending from the Dollart southward as far as Almelo, occupy parts of the provinces of Groningen, Drente, and Overijsel, and in Germany most of the land west of the Ems River as far south as Bentheim. For many hundreds of years they quite effectively separated the northeastern Netherlands from the adjacent German lands beyond the Ems River. The actual boundary line as far south as the province of Gelderland has changed very little since about 1300.

This belt of peat bogs has only rarely been challenged by military forces. In recent decades, however, reclamation and drainage of large areas of peat bog on the Dutch side of the border and the construction of modern roads have greatly impaired the protective value of the belt.

Farther to the south, between Aachen and Arlon, the Belgian border cuts across the Ardennes-Eifel highlands. Stretches of this boundary are natural, especially where the line runs through the peat bogs on the divide between the Meuse and Rhine river systems.

The lower reaches of rivers emptying into the North Sea present two important boundary problems: one in the Ems estuary in the northeast, and the other in the tidal waters of the Wester Schelde in the extreme southwest. In the lower course of the Ems no agreement has been reached as to the exact location of the Dutch-German boundary. In the case of the Schelde, Belgium and the Netherlands have long clashed: the latter claims historical rights over the deep waters of the Wielingen, the main southwestern entrance to the Schelde, the former claims these same waters under the "three miles" clause.

Role of man. Most parts of the boundaries of the Netherlands and Belgium are the outgrowth of two human factors: the feudal system and war. Although the former has been defunct in both countries since the end of the fifteenth century, its after effects are still visible in many places.

The eastern boundary of the Netherlands south of the province of Overijsel is the result of the consolidation and complete or partial incorporation of a number of small, semi-independent feudal holdings during the period from the fifteenth century to the fall of Napoleon. Though later modified by war, the southern boundary of Belgium was originally determined, for the most part, by the accidents of feudal inheritance. Until the middle of the seventeenth century the boundary was located as far south as Boulogne, Arras, Cambrai, and the upper Oise River. Evidence of this earlier boundary is still visible today: the southern and western limits of the Flemish language lie in northern France, while Walloon, the Belgian variety of French, reaches almost to the western and southern boundaries of the French *Département du Nord*. The present boundary was largely fixed by the wars of conquest of Louis XIV during the period 1650 to 1680.

The existing boundary between the Netherlands and Belgium is essentially the result of the War of Independence fought by the Netherlands, the "Seven United Provinces," against Spain (1568–1648). At that time most of what is now Belgium was held by the Spanish armies and the center of resistance was located in the present provinces of North-Holland, South-Holland, and Zeeland. To safeguard the heartland of the new republic of the "Seven United Provinces," it was considered desirable to hold an area south of the Schelde and lower Meuse.* Scattered portions of the present Dutch province of Limburg were likewise acquired at that time. Consolidation of the holdings in the latter area, however, did not take place until 1815, when, after the fall of Napoleon, the Netherlands and Belgium were united as one country by the great powers.

Recent problems. In November, 1946, the Netherlands officially requested rectification of the Dutch-German border: reduction of its total length of 325 miles to 220 miles and the addition of 675 square miles of land to the Netherlands. Establishment of this new border would eliminate four bulges between Emden and Aachen, although these two cities were not requested by the Dutch. Approximately 120,000 people in the area in question would be allowed to acquire Dutch citizenship.

Belgium likewise made territorial claims against Germany in November, 1946. In the region of Monschein a railroad repeatedly crosses the Belgo-German boundary, and Belgium wishes a minor frontier rectification to bring the entire rail line within her domain.

Divergence in Development of the Netherlands and Belgium

Historical factors. Throughout the Middle Ages most of the Low Countries was *de jure* a part of the German Empire (the "Holy Roman Empire"), a situation that continued until the Treaty of Muenster, signed by a number of European states in 1648. However, for hundreds of years previous to that date, this legal tie had ceased to have any practical meaning. During most of the

* The part of Zeeland south of the Wester Schelde and North-Brabant.

fourteenth and fifteenth centuries the great feudal lords of the Low Countries were completely independent of the Kaisers, being oriented toward France rather than Germany both politically and culturally.

The accident of feudal inheritance finally brought the Low Countries under the rule of Spain, a far-away and alien power. The oppressive policies of Philip II of Spain and his attempts to drown the Reformation in blood led to the War of Independence (1568–1648), which made the republic of the "Seven United Provinces" politically and economically strong, and which for two centuries reduced the present Belgium to a completely passive area politically and a *quantité négligeable* economically.

Religious differences. The War of Independence left the Netherlands a strongly Protestant country—Calvinistic, not Lutheran as was northwestern Germany—the only exceptions being the southern areas, North-Brabant and Limburg, where the population remained almost entirely Roman Catholic. In contrast, Belgium remained a Roman Catholic area where, under the Habsburgs, the power of the higher clergy and the local Catholic aristocracy was strong. This religious difference became a major source of friction when during a brief period (1815–30) the Netherlands and Belgium formed one state. It still is an important political factor. The lack of enthusiasm in the Netherlands for a union with the Flemish in northern Belgium is partly due to the fear of thus re-enforcing the Roman Catholic contingent within the Dutch borders. Since the present-day Roman Catholic political party (*Roomsch-Katholieke Staatspartij*) is a powerful factor in Dutch internal politics, such a fear on the part of non-Catholics is, perhaps, understandable. The active mixing of religion and politics on the part of both Roman Catholic and Protestant groups today may make a closer union between the two countries more difficult.

The Dutch nation. Isolation of the Netherlands from the Reich, and later political separation from the Burgundian and other French lands to the south, gradually developed among the people not so much a feeling of "belonging together," as one of being different from the other groups of people in northwestern Europe.

As a separate "high" language, Dutch grew from the Frankian dialects spoken throughout the western and southern parts of the Netherlands. The War of Independence helped to mold the Dutch into a separate group and began the effacement of some of the sectionalism that long survived feudalism. The succeeding period was one of republican government—even though that government was essentially commercial-oligarchic —of free contacts with all parts of the world as the result of a far-flung trade, of free admission and gradual absorption of dissident groups from elsewhere, and of a comparatively generous measure of freedom of thought. All these factors furthered development of the Netherlands into one of the freest, most advanced, and enlightened countries of the seventeenth and eighteenth centuries. The period of French occupation from 1795 to 1813 finally welded the Netherlands into a distinct national unit.

MINORITIES. The country has few minority problems. There are really no non-Dutch speaking groups within its borders. The only possible exception is Frisian, which is still spoken in all but the southeastern part of the province of Friesland, especially in the country districts. It might be called a dialect that stands a little closer than Dutch to the Anglo-Saxon elements in the English language. It might also be considered a language, as it does have a literature. Once the area in which it was used was much larger than at present. In recent decades, under the spur of rampant nationalism, a revival of Frisian has taken place. This revival even gave rise to ill-advised demands for cultural and perhaps economic autonomy for Friesland within the Netherlands.

The only really "young" Dutch territory is the province of Limburg. During the Republic this province consisted of a nearly inextricable mixture of holdings—Dutch, German, Spanish (later Austrian), and Liégois. Out of these a new province was molded in 1813. After World War I Belgian extremists agitated unsuccessfully for the annexation of most of the province.

The Belgian nation. The southern part of the Low Countries was not sufficiently strong to liberate itself from Spanish overlordship as did the Netherlands in the War of Independence. With the exception of the bishopric of Liége it remained in the hands of the Habsburgs; first, the Spanish branch, and, after 1713, the Austrian branch. In essence it was an area passively ruled by an alien power, inhabited partly by Flemish people and partly by Walloons. The Flemish speak dialects akin to those spoken to the north, and have a written language nearly identical with Dutch. The Walloons of the country districts speak a French dialect; those in the cities speak French. Under the Spanish and Austrian regimes the local ruling groups came from the Walloon aristocracy and higher clergy, and to a smaller extent from the upper bourgeoisie.

In 1830, after a brief war with the Netherlands for which the Dutch showed little enthusiasm, Belgium started its life as an independent country, though hardly as a nation. The new country immediately came under the rule of the Walloon upper classes. With the support of the largest part of the higher clergy and the aristocracy, the ruling groups attempted to continue conditions of government as they had existed under the Habsburg regime. The Flemish part of the population soon began to resent the lowly position of their group and of their language. A long internal struggle followed between the powerful Walloon minority and the Flemish majority, lasting until the early 1930's. Regardless of these internal troubles Belgium gradually has become such a distinct unit that at present there seems to be very little likelihood that it might separate into its constituent parts.

MINORITIES. Flemish and Walloon minorities still exist in neighboring northern France, although the presence of these groups has never given rise to any active demands for boundary changes. In view of the disparity in power between the countries concerned, the lack of friction is, of course, quite understandable.

Along the eastern border there are several small regions of questionable nationality. The Arlon area has a predominantly Luxembourg population. Immediately to the north lie two sections annexed from Germany after World War I: Eupen and Malmédy. In the latter the population is partly Walloon and partly German; in the former it is mostly German.

Cultural outlook. The cultural outlook of both the Netherlands and Belgium has been toward France, especially in the case of the latter country. There the Walloon aristocracy, which ruled in the past, maintained close contacts of a cultural nature with France throughout the Spanish and Austrian regimes. In the Netherlands also French cultural influence has always been strong. There was a period during the seventeenth and eighteenth centuries when official or other formal Dutch documents often were interlarded with French words and expressions. Even the period of French occupation (1795–1813), though much resented by the Dutch, did not cause any abrupt change in this cultural orientation.

After the middle of the last century German influence grew slowly, largely as the result of closer economic ties between the two countries. This influence was particularly marked in the fields of science and engineering. To the Germans this trend seemed so pronounced that the late Kaiser is reported to have remarked, *"Holland annektiert sich selbst"* (Holland will annex itself). German obtrusiveness was counteracted, however, by a pronounced development of sympathy for and interest in English culture, a trend rudely interrupted by the Boer War, but resumed later.

The Changing Role of Geographic Location

Geographic location is a relative concept. In many cases it pertains primarily to the relationships between a specific area and larger surrounding areas via certain easy routes or approaches. As the routes or the approaches change in importance, or as there are basic changes in the economies or in the political strength of the surrounding regions, the effects of geographic location will vary. The Low Countries serve as an excellent example of the changing role of geographic location.*

Changes in political effects. The War of Independence of the Netherlands was conducted against the most powerful country of that time: a Spain flushed with the success of its colonial wars of conquest that had become enormously wealthy and that could hire large armies for the execution of its ambitions.

* Other examples of this principle are discussed elsewhere in this chapter.

During this war the Netherlands were supported—though intermittently and meagerly, and often only morally—by England and France, both of which distrusted the political designs of Philip II of Spain. Thus the Netherlands served as a bulwark against Spanish imperialism.

After the Treaty of Muenster in 1648, France succeeded Spain as the aggressive power of western continental Europe. The Dutch therefore preferred having the present Belgium held by a weak Spain to its division with France. England had somewhat similar interests. It did not want French territory across from the estuary of the Thames River, nor did it relish the idea of a possible occupation of the Belgian coastal area by the Dutch. In consequence the Spanish Netherlands became a Dutch-British barrier against the ambitions of the French kings to expand their dominion northward. By the Peace of Utrecht in 1713 the Spanish Netherlands became Austrian, but the Dutch retained the right to keep garrisons in a number of towns along the southern border in order to guard against a French attack.

Throughout this period little effort had been made by the Netherlands to protect its eastern boundary. There was not much necessity for such a move, since only a number of small, rather harmless German princedoms lay beyond the border. There were Dutch garrisons in Emden and a few neighboring small towns; other garrisons, such as those at Wesel and Emmerich, were located near the route around the "riverbelt" (the Rhine-Meuse lowland of Gelderland). However, only rarely did danger threaten from these directions. Friction with Prussia, however, began to develop as early as the first part of the eighteenth century. During the latter half of the century, however, the Netherlands, aware that she was becoming relatively weaker, being still afraid of France, and resentful of British inroads upon and limitations of its trade, attempted to improve her relations with Prussia.

After a period of French occupation during the Napoleonic regime, the great powers, on the initiative of Great Britain, made the Netherlands and Belgium into a single state —a kingdom—which was designed to function as a strong barrier to a possibly renewed French expansionism. However, subsequent events proved that the period of French aggressiveness was largely past. Instead, with the growing strength of Prussia during the second half of the nineteenth century, the Netherlands and Belgium became true buffer states between the great powers, the latter between France and an expansionist Germany on land, and the former between England and an expansionist Germany on the sea. This role did not last long. World War II seems to have proven conclusively that with modern methods of warfare neither country has sufficient depth to serve effectively as a buffer state.

Changes in economic effects. As economic changes often bring political changes in their wake, the effects of economic shifts upon the Low Countries must be considered briefly. The geographic location of Belgium and the Netherlands is economically important in two respects: first, their position at the mouth of three European rivers gives fairly easy access to the hinterland; second, their position on the western European coast, approximately midway between the northern and Baltic waters on one hand and the southern and Mediterranean on the other, has stimulated overseas commerce. The second position has long been the more important.

During the Middle Ages the main trade centers of the Low Countries were the ports of Bruges and Antwerp, with smaller ports and trading centers located in the northern part of the area. When Antwerp was retaken by the Spaniards in 1585, the Dutch took possession of the southern side of the Wester Schelde, thus cutting off all trade from the city, a measure that was made necessary for combined military and economic reasons. Much of the trade of Antwerp moved to the free north, to Dordrecht, Rotterdam, and especially to Amsterdam, greatly enhancing the commercial importance of these cities. Antwerp ceased to be a trading center until the end of the Napoleonic period, for the Dutch exercised the right given them by the Treaty of Muenster to keep the Schelde closed. The resultant bitterness in the south added to the difficulties of the Low Countries when in 1815 they were brought under one regime.

During the sixteenth century the commercial interest of the Low Countries was primarily focused upon trade with coastal areas to the north and south. From the Baltic came grains, timber, ships' supplies, and flax, the latter one of the major textile fibers of the time. From the southern lands of France, Spain, Portugal, Italy, and the Levant (eastern Mediterranean) came such goods as salt, wines, textiles, silk, and tropical products. Some of these items were destined for consumption in the Netherlands, but much of this commerce was carrying trade to and from the countries concerned. After the Dutch started sailing independently to the East and the West Indies (about 1600) tropical products were distributed directly from the Netherlands, especially from the port of Amsterdam.

From the late Middle Ages to the middle of the nineteenth century the immediate hinterland of the Netherlands was of relatively little importance. After the fall of Antwerp some goods went via Dutch ports to what is now Belgium. Other goods were carried up the Rhine River. In both the Spanish (Austrian) Netherlands and Germany, however, river traffic was greatly impeded by numerous tolls and duties, many of which persisted until the end of the eighteenth century, and a few as late as 1850. The German hinterland was primarily agricultural, exporting such products as wine, grain, and lumber and in turn importing moderate quantities of other goods.

Thus from an economic point of view during the sixteenth, seventeenth, and eighteenth centuries the location of the Low Countries at the mouths of the Rhine, the Meuse, and the Schelde was of subordinate importance, whereas their location in the approximate middle of the western European coast was of primary importance. Political relations—and political troubles—were with other west coast countries; Spain and Portugal, France, England, and some of the more northerly countries.

Only after 1850 did the German hinterland begin to play a more important role. Industrialization of the Ruhr and adjacent regions was accompanied by a steady rise in Rhine-borne traffic. The increase in economic activity reached phenomenal proportions during the twenty-five years before World War I, and the steady upward trend was resumed in the middle 1920's. In 1936 the Rhine-Westphalian industrial region embraced an area of about 1,250 square miles

with a population of four million. The area contained over three fourths of all of Germany's coal reserves, produced two thirds of the coal mined, three fourths of the coke, and seven tenths of the pig iron and steel. This small district on the Rhine became an enormous market for iron ores, mineral oils, lumber, textile fibers, tropical products, grains, vegetable oils, and a large variety of other foodstuffs, such as potatoes, vegetables, and fruits. Beyond the Ruhr the industrialized German hinterland extended as far south as the Swiss border and as far east as Bavaria.

While some goods moved via Emden and other German ports, the bulk of the imports and exports moved by water via Rotterdam; by rail; and to a smaller extent by water through Antwerp.* As German industrialization developed, the Netherlands, and to a lesser degree Belgium, gradually became more strongly oriented economically toward Germany. At the same time the rivalry for trade with Germany between Rotterdam and Antwerp became keen, and sometimes even bitter. Antwerp felt that its water connections with the lower Rhine were insufficient because the location of the Dutch province of Limburg prevented the construction of a huge Belgian canal to the Rhine that would be able to divert traffic from Rotterdam. The Dutch, quite naturally, were not in favor of such a canal and considered it to be less economical than the natural waterway of the Rhine and Waal rivers. They also resented Belgian subsidies of its waterborne traffic to the Rhine via Dutch tidal streams and rivers.

At present the welfare of the Low Countries is partly dependent upon that of the German hinterland, a condition not consonant with any policy that would severely limit the industrial capacity of the Ruhr Basin and adjacent regions. It is an ironic situation that a strong Germany tends to create political trouble for the Low Countries, and a weak Germany creates economic trouble.

Present Economy of the Low Countries

Relative importance of industry versus agriculture. The Netherlands and Belgium are both primarily industrial and secondarily

---

* Amsterdam also participated in the Rhine trade, but remained more oriented toward the Dutch colonies.

commercial countries. By comparison, agriculture occupies only a subordinate role: in the Netherlands the proportion of persons employed in agriculture is less than twenty per cent of the total number of employables; in Belgium it is less than seventeen per cent. Nevertheless, agrarian densities are exceptionally high. In the Netherlands there are 180 rural inhabitants per square mile of land in agricultural use; in Belgium, 190. However, the percentage of the population engaged in agriculture is declining steadily. Of every 100 workers by which the population of the Netherlands *increased* during the first three decades of this century, 46 went into industry, 30 into trade, transportation, and communications, and only 5 into agriculture.

Agricultural resources. Reclamation of land is approaching its economic limits. In the Netherlands only ten per cent of the area remains agriculturally unused. Much of this consists of unreclaimable dune areas and very poor sandy lands. Even the costly reclamation of the Zuiderzee polders will not satisfy the land hunger of the Dutch farmer. In Belgium twenty per cent of the land is not used for agricultural purposes, but much of it should remain in forest. With the aid of modern science and large applications of labor, however, even normally infertile soils are made to produce well. Yields per acre of grains and other crops are among the highest in the world.* The most intensive aspects of agriculture are dairying, the raising of hogs and poultry, and the production of vegetables, fruits, and flowers.

These extremely intensive and highly remunerative types of agriculture depend upon easily accessible, densely populated, and relatively well-to-do market areas, such as the German, Belgian, Dutch, French, and British industrial districts and cities. They also presuppose a trade unhampered by protective tariffs and other restrictive measures. Obviously the agriculture of the Low Countries was very vulnerable to the extreme protectionism that ran amok in the decade before World War II.

As agriculture in the Low Countries be-

came more specialized and as population density increased, it became necessary to import ever greater quantities of food, such as grains, vegetable fats, and meats. The animal industries also required the importation of large quantities of general and special feed stuffs.* Even with fundamental changes in the agricultural economy away from livestock and the utmost efficiency in production, it is highly doubtful that the agriculture of the Low Countries could adequately feed the present population.

Power resources. What makes the wheels of industry turn in the Low Countries? The relief is too flat to make possible the development of much water power, and the prospects of finding oil appear to be scant.** Fortunately, however, both countries are well provided with good coals of bituminous quality or better.

The coal deposits are a part of the great western European coal field that—with a few minor interruptions—stretches from northern France to the eastern tip of the Ruhr Basin. West of Namur lies the Belgian Hainaut basin, which continues into the coal basin of northern France. An extensive system of railroads, roads, and canals connects the two, and intricate economic relationships have developed across the border. Other fields are the Liége basin, the Dutch Limburg basin, the Belgian Campine, and the Peel-Erkelenz region. The Campine Basin is only in the first stages of development, and the Peel-Erkelenz region has hardly been touched. Total production in Belgium amounts to about 27 to 30 million metric tons per year, and in the Netherlands, 12 to 14. The older Belgian basins produce a surplus of domestic and industrial grades but are short in gas and coking coal, whereas the Campine has more of the latter types than of the former.

Coal reserves in the old basins along the Sambre and Muese rivers are estimated at three billion metric tons. Much of the coal, unfortunately, is rather folded and faulted and lies deep. The Campine reserves are estimated at four billion tons at a depth of

---

* Average wheat yields in the Netherlands are from 42 to 55 bushels per acre, and in Belgium from 38 to 46, in contrast to about 13 in the United States. For potatoes the figures are, respectively, 250 to 425, 270 to 335, in contrast to 110 to 125.

* After the occupation of the Netherlands by the Germans, it was necessary to slaughter part of the livestock for lack of imported feed.

** It is reported that during the war a producing well was opened up near Coevorden in the northeastern Netherlands.

from about 1,500 to 4,000 feet, and another four at greater depth. Dutch reserves in South Limburg are about two and one-half billion tons, with a similar amount in the Peel region.

Economic relations within the entire coal area are complex. Normally, for example, Dutch coal production equals consumption, but the bulk of the Limburg coal is exported to neighboring areas, and similar quantities are imported from the Ruhr and Great Britain. Also Belgium both imports and exports coal.

Mineral resources and other raw materials. The Low Countries are poor in metallic and nonmetallic minerals. There are deposits of salt, of sands for the manufacture of glass, of marl and stone for that of cement, and of clay for brick and tile. But the zinc and lead ores of Belgium are exhausted, and the country owns only an insignificant portion of the great iron ore deposits centering in Lorraine and southern Luxembourg. Thus both countries, and especially Belgium, must import large quantities of raw materials for their metallurgical and metal-working industries. Iron ore for Belgium comes from Luxembourg and France; for the Netherlands from a variety of sources. Belgium has built a zinc and lead smelting and refining industry of international importance, now based upon imported raw materials As a result of the exploitation of the mineral deposits of its Congo colony, it has also become an important copper refiner and a major producer of a number of rare metals. The Netherlands has become an important tin smelting country on the basis of the tin deposits in the Netherlands Indies.

In addition to their importation of these ores, the Low Countries have had to import large quantities of cotton, wool, and flax for their textile industries. The majority of other raw materials must also be brought into the countries, including hides and leather, tobacco, wood and woodpulp, fertilizer minerals, unfinished precious stones, and vegetable oils.

Thus manufacturing in the Low Countries, their major economic activity, depends only to a minor degree upon the materials available or produced within the countries, such as beets for the sugar refineries, potatoes for starch and alcohol factories, milk for but-ter factories, and straw for strawboard plants. Other raw materials, such as rice, cacao, vegetable oils and oil seeds, rubber, tobacco, copper, and tin, come from the colonies. Since many other raw materials must come from elsewhere, the Low Countries are to an unusual degree dependent upon a free world economy.

Industrial development. In the Netherlands 40 per cent of the population is engaged in industry; and in Belgium nearly 42 per cent. These percentages represent groups larger than those in any other economic activity. Moreover, industry—together with transportation and trade—must absorb most of the annual increase in the available labor supply.

The major types of large-scale manufacturing industries in Belgium are the metallurgical and metal-working industries and those engaged in the fabrication of textile products. In the Netherlands metallurgy is less highly developed, although along with textile manufacturing it stands high among the country's industrial activities.

The major regions of heavy industries in Belgium nearly coincide with the old coal basins. The area of greatest concentration is a narrow, densely populated belt that runs from west of Valenciennes in France via Mons, Charleroi, and Namur to Liége and Verviers. The textile industries are largely centered in Flanders. Highly diversified industries mark Brussels, Antwerp, and their environs.

In the Netherlands manufacturing is not quite so concentrated as in Belgium. The most highly industrialized sections lie on the poor, sandy lands of Overijsel and North-Brabant, where textile and shoe manufacturing and electrical industries predominate. The coal basin of southern Limburg thus far has not become a center of industrial development. In the Rotterdam and Amsterdam-Zaandam districts industry is diversified.

On the whole, since the domestic supplies of essential raw materials are somewhat limited, the industrial development of the Low Countries is based primarily upon its own coal resources and access by cheap water transportation to the coal of Germany, France, and Great Britain; upon good trade relations; and upon the availability of an abundance of efficient labor.

Industry has become the major pillar in the

economic structure of the Low Countries. Any events, be they political or economic, that prevent the full utilization of the industrial capacity of the two countries are apt to affect directly and indirectly large parts of the population. The impact of a decline in industrial activity would be serious because a temporary return of the workers to the land during a depression period offers a much less feasible solution than, for example, in the United States, where there is a greater margin for potential development.

Cities. Belgium and the Netherlands each have two cities ranking high among those of northwestern Europe. In each case the larger is the capital city—Brussels (1,205,000 with suburbs) in Belgium, and Amsterdam (800,000) in the Netherlands—and the second-largest is the leading port of its country—Antwerp (769,000 with suburbs) in Belgium, and Rotterdam (636,000) in the Netherlands. In addition, the Low Countries have nine other cities with 100,000 or more inhabitants each, of which seven lie in the Netherlands. Of these secondary cities the Hague (521,000) is by far the largest. It is the seat of the Dutch government, notwithstanding the fact that Amsterdam serves as the national capital city. Four other cities are noteworthy: in Belgium, Ghent (421,000 with suburbs) manufactures textiles, and Liége (265,000 with suburbs) is an iron and steel center; in the Netherlands, Utrecht is a rail center, and Haarlem (155,000) lies in the midst of the country's famed tulip-growing area.

Population problems. The population of the Low Countries has increased greatly during the last century. In Belgium it grew from 3,785,000 inhabitants in 1830 to about 8,300,-000 in 1940; during the same period the population of the Netherlands increased from 2,600,000 to 8,925,000. Though the birth rate has been declining in both countries, the death rate has fallen more rapidly. The result has been a natural increase during the period 1920 to 1930 of over 100,000 per year for the Netherlands and nearly 70,000 for Belgium. In recent years the increase has slowed down a little, to about 20,000 in the latter and about 90,000 in the former country. Population density is among the highest in the world: 736 per square mile in the Netherlands and 710 in Belgium, which is nearly twice that of prewar Germany, but less than the 750 persons per square mile in England. Pressure of population upon the means of subsistence is therefore great, but as both countries are small, they cannot hope to satisfy their need for *Lebensraum* by a military expansionistic policy.

Up to the present time emigration has taken care of only a very small part of the annual increase. The immigration quotas of the more attractive countries are quite small; and because of their tropical environment, neither the Belgian Congo nor the Dutch colonies are important outlets for population.

Though unemployment was exceedingly high during the 1930's, the labor needs of industry, trade, and transportation thus far have been able to take care of the additions to the population of working age. It is doubtful, however, whether these occupations can continue to absorb surplus workers.

The Low Countries in the European and the World Economy

The degree of self-sufficiency. The economic life of the Low Countries is closely integrated with that of the world as a whole. The small size of the countries, dense population, and deficiency in certain resources forbid any attempts at autarchy. Ever since the last century Belgium has been an importer of foodstuffs and raw materials and an exporter of semimanufactured and finished goods. The Netherlands, though noted as an exporter of specialized agricultural products, must import more foodstuffs than it exports, and is completely dependent upon the importation of raw materials from abroad for many of its industries.

Both countries generally have an excess of imports over exports on the basis of value. This deficit is made up in the case of Belgium by the returns from investments in the Belgian Congo and elsewhere, and by the revenue from the heavy transit trade. In the case of the Netherlands, returns from investments in the colonies and abroad, receipts from the transit trade, and income from services rendered by the Dutch merchant marine to other countries help to equalize the balance of payments.

Colonial empire. Both Belgium and the Netherlands possess large colonial empires. The Belgian Congo is a huge area of over

900,000 square miles in the equatorial part of Africa. Although it and Ruanda-Urundi are together approximately eighty times larger than the mother country, the total population is small, probably not over 15,000,-000. This colony is still in the first stages of economic development.* The Netherlands has colonies in both the Old and the New World. The Netherlands Indies occupy an area of about 735,000 square miles, nearly sixty times the size of the motherland, with a population of about 71,500,000. Java is densely populated and economically well-advanced, and Sumatra is partly developed, but the remaining islands play relatively unimportant roles in the economic life of the Indies. The other Dutch possessions are located in the Western Hemisphere: Dutch Guiana (Surinam) and several Caribbean islands. Dutch Guiana is not of much economic significance other than for the production of bauxite, but the island of Curaçao is an important trading center of the West Indies.**

Main currents of trade. Their colonial empires are of great importance to both Belgium and the Netherlands. Belgium obtains increasing amounts of raw materials from the Congo, and the Netherlands not only has large long-term investments in the Netherlands Indies, but obtains large quantities of raw materials from and sells many finished products to her colonial possessions. The loss of the Netherlands Indies would be an event of catastrophic proportions for the Netherlands.

Despite the interchange of goods with their colonies, trade with the surrounding regions is of paramount importance to both the Netherlands and Belgium. Just before the war nearly half of the imports of the Netherlands came from Germany, Belgium, Luxembourg, the United Kingdom, and France, and well over half of the exports went to those countries. Import and export trade with the Netherlands Indies constituted not more than about seven to eight per cent of the total value. A similar condition existed for Belgium; over

* For map and discussion of Belgium's colonial lands see Chapter 27.
** For maps and a more detailed discussion of the Netherlands Indies see Chapter 29, "The Malay Archipelago and Oceania"; of the Netherlands West Indies and Dutch Guiana see Chapter 31, "The Caribbean."

one third of the imports came from France, Germany, the Netherlands, and the United Kingdom, and over half of the exports were directed to those countries. Imports from the Belgian Congo constituted about six per cent of total imports, and exports to that region less than two per cent of total exports.

Trade with Germany, both direct and transit, had become vital to both countries. In Belgium, Antwerp participated in this trade because of its excellent port and good railroad connections with the German hinterland. The bulk of the transit trade, however, moves via the Rotterdam port complex. In quantity of goods, the total transit trade through the Netherlands normally amounts to about one and a half times the combined imports and exports of the country. Raw materials to be reshipped from the port of Rotterdam made up the bulk of this transit trade, such as iron, manganese and other ores, grains, petroleum and petroleum products, coal and coke, lumber, vegetable oil seeds, and chemicals. Part of the profits of this trade accrues to the Netherlands, though exactly how much is difficult to evaluate.

Conclusions

World War II has resulted—at least temporarily—in reducing the political power potential immediately to the east of the Low Countries to zero. However, Soviet Russia is stronger and has come nearer. Thus, for the time being, the Low Countries and northern Germany constitute a buffer zone between an eastern empire growing in strength and the heartland of a British Empire that reached its zenith of power some time during the last century. To the south France, weakened by three major wars in three quarters of a century, does not provide a strong power potential.

Economic productivity of the German hinterland of the Low Countries has been seriously impaired by the ravages of war—exactly for how long is difficult to foresee. This fact will have inevitable repercussions upon the economies of the Low Countries. Unless the world returns shortly to a much freer international economy than existed in the decades before World War II, economic integration may have to be sought with larger neighboring regions, both industrial and agricultural. In 1947 Belgium, the Netherlands, and Luxembourg (the Benelux countries) formed a customs union.

Fear of another Germany rampant is strong.

Perhaps an economic integration with France and the Germanic lands tributary to the Rhine lies within the realm of possibilities.

LUXEMBOURG

After a long period in the German Zollverein, the Grand Duchy of Luxembourg entered into a customs union with Belgium in 1922. As a result Luxembourg oriented itself economically more and more toward Belgium and France. A wide strip of territory along the southern border is part of the Lorraine iron ore basin. It is well-developed industrially, and has important iron and steel plants that are integrated with the French industries across the border. Iron ores from Luxembourg are exported to Belgium, as are a number of manufactured products.

The 300,000 inhabitants speak German, though both French and German are used for official purposes. Cultural relations with the adjacent French-speaking areas have been maintained for hundreds of years, and to the same extent as with the purely Germanic regions east of the border.

During the fifteenth century the duchy extended far into Belgium, France, and Germany, but its present area is only about 1,000 square miles, less than that of Rhode Island —much too small for a completely independent existence.

CHAPTER 12

France and Its Geographical Setting

THE position of France is unique in that it has important coastlines on both the North Atlantic and Mediterranean. Just how important these frontages have been can be seen from a study of Western history over a period of more than three thousand years.

From the time of early recorded history well into the Middle Ages the Mediterranean was the main avenue of commerce and the heart of Western life. Then in the fifteenth and sixteenth centuries came the age of exploration, a period of transition during which the Atlantic coastal area gradually became the center of the world's Western pulse. Throughout these successive periods in the development of Europe as we know it today France served as a "corridor" for many generations of adventurous migrants and marching men. She has rightly been called a "crossroads," for here northwest-southeast movements of people have intersected southwest-northeast movements. In recent centuries France has acted as a "gateway" to (and from) continental Europe, where trans-Atlantic forces come to have their repercussions in the Old World. And, finally, the country lies athwart the major political and commercial axis of communication between northwest Europe and India and the lands bordering the western Pacific.

France need not rely solely upon a strategic position for political importance. The country itself is productive from the standpoint of both soils and mineral resources, and the climate is favorable to human activities. Further, as the second largest country in Europe (1937), France has an area at least commensurate with her past political ambi-

tions. Finally, a compact shape is optimum for purposes of defense as well as for effective international policy.

The vitality of the French people has made itself felt not only in the Mediterranean and on the margin of western Europe, but throughout the world. During the era of exploration French explorers went both east and west. And when it was the hour to stake out empires, French colonizers were in Africa, the Americas, and the East. (See table, page 179, for list of French possessions.) The fortunes of France may rise and fall in international rank and prestige, but her past history indicates with some certainty that the French will undoubtedly long continue to play a forceful role within the world's political framework.

The History and People of France

French-speaking people have dwelt for many centuries on the land that is now France, bound together as have been the inhabitants of few countries in Europe. In no small measure this unity exists because of the integration of the land. Region by region the component parts of France and their inhabitants may differ rather markedly, one from another, but between the parts there is easy communication. This ease of contact has been of inestimable value in fostering cooperation and understanding. In contrast, intercourse between France and all neighboring lands (except Belgium) is more difficult.

The spirit of freedom found among the French has remained strong since the days when the old Gallic chieftains resisted Rome and proclaimed liberty a vital necessity. In modern times this spirit has been reflected in the unwillingness of the French to permit the regimentation of their numbers. In spite of their bloody setting, the flaming watchwords of the French Revolution, "Liberty, Equality, and Fraternity," have highlighted the position of France since 1789 as a leader of the common people in Europe. Guizot names three qualities of the French spirit that underlie their civilization and progress: clarity of expression, sociability, and sympathy.

Early events. Three thousand years ago the people of the land consisted of tribes grouped around chiefs better known for their prowess in battle than for their economic or political judgment. Some centuries later Caesar stated that Gaul was divided into three parts, but history shows that these three parts contained about eighty tribes, differing one from another in many respects.

Starting about 900 B.C. Phoenicians and Greeks from the eastern end of the Mediterranean visited the land of the Gauls for commerce rather than for conquest. Marseille, a Greek city on the Rhone delta, flourished, and there resided Greek scholars as well as traders. About the middle of the first century B.C. Caesar conquered the Gauls tribe by tribe. From that time on, Gaul, a tribal country, slowly but steadily evolved as France, an emerging entity among European groups.

From the time of King Clovis late in the fifth century through the Carolingian regime in the eighth century and on to the thirteenth century France was either united and powerful or weak and broken—as its leadership was able and unified or petty and jealously divided. Early in this period appeared the first indications of what became the long-drawn-out conflict between the nobility and the kings. Out of this struggle came, first, the manorial system and, later, the gradual flowering of feudalism in all its aspects. With the passage of governmental powers into the hands of nobility, government became localized rather than general. This change, which furthered the expansion of feudalism, proved a seriously disintegrating factor.

After the Hundred Years' War (1337–78 and 1413–53) feudalism gave place to an absolute monarchy governing the country. But for the next 300 years, from 1453 to 1753, France was never free of religious and civil intrigues and international conflicts. Yet during these three centuries the French learned to pull together. Under farseeing but unscrupulous statesmen and despotic kings France became a power abroad, even though the vast majority of the people lived in abject poverty and misery.

The Revolution and after. The French Revolution, called by many the greatest event of modern European history, came in two waves: the civil phase from 1789 to 1792, and the international phase from 1792 to 1799. It may have opened in an economic crisis, but its roots sprang from conditions and practices that were as much responsible for the economic crisis as for the Revolution. Although the Revolution did not put an end to the economic difficulties, it did liberate the common people and mark the beginning of the First Republic. In effect, the French Revolution marked the culmination of centuries of growth of a freedom-loving people, and the beginning of popular national self-expression such as no other European people had enjoyed. Situation, environment, and national spirit combined to stimulate the people to grapple with their internal problems and to meet any external pressure by challenge—Germanic or English, enemy or ally. Under Napoleon France for a brief period controlled the European continent. The victories and crushing defeats of Napoleon left France with military traditions and a historic enmity with the Germans, her nearest strong neighbors, that has found expression in the Franco-Prussian War (1870–71) and in the two world wars of the present century. The struggle between coast country and partially landlocked interior became also a battle of economics; between the so-called "haves" and "have-nots." Further, the struggle developed into a contest of ideologies, wherein individualism directed toward international cooperation clashed with regimentation controlled by a will to rule.

The decades of the nineteenth century saw not only the increasing industrialization of France but also the vast expansion of a colonial empire. Nevertheless, political instability was reflected in the many changes of government: the First Empire (1804–14); the restoration of the House of Bourbon (1814–30); the reign of Louis-Philippe of the House of Bourbon-Orléans (1830–48); the Second Republic (1848–52); the Second Empire under Louis Napoleon (1852–70); and the Third Republic (1870–1940). The Third Republic of France survived World War I but collapsed in the more recent one.

Physical characteristics. No clear-cut "type" of Frenchman exists, but from early

and the Basques in the western end of the Pyrenees. The Basques are as easily distinguishable from their neighbors by their non-Aryan language as by any physical characteristics, but the Celts speak an early Aryan tongue. These two small groups are well

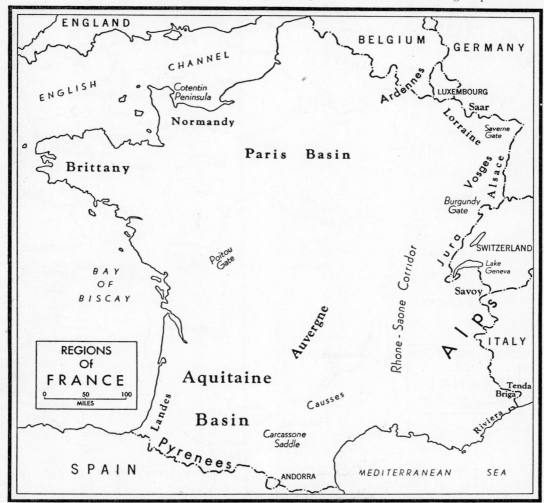

European racial stocks have come a number of characteristics generally associated with the modern inhabitants of the country. In southern France the dark, long-headed Mediterranean race prevails; in the north the fair, long-headed and long-faced Nordic people greatly predominate; and along the eastern side are mostly folk of the Alpine stock. In addition, there are two smaller groups descended from early races in western Europe: the Celtic people in Brittany, kinfolk of the Celts in the rougher lands of the British Isles;

differentiated physically, probably because of their separation in hilly lands from their neighbors in the plains. All types are mixed, however, particularly along their borders, until at present race does not represent pure blood characteristics.

Language and religion. Aside from the Basques the people of France speak Latin branches of the Aryan tongue. The language of the north and that of the south, Provençal, were in conflict for centuries; but ultimately the northern branch with many southern idioms and words became the true French language. Its lucidity, precision, and beauty express the logic of French thought and have given it a strong attraction for cultivated minds. For many years French served as the court and diplomatic language of Europe.

tribes of Gaul, was the prevailing religion. The Catholic religion and its spiritual hold upon medieval craftsmen were responsible for the many inspiring, well-built Gothic cathedrals scattered throughout the cities of France.

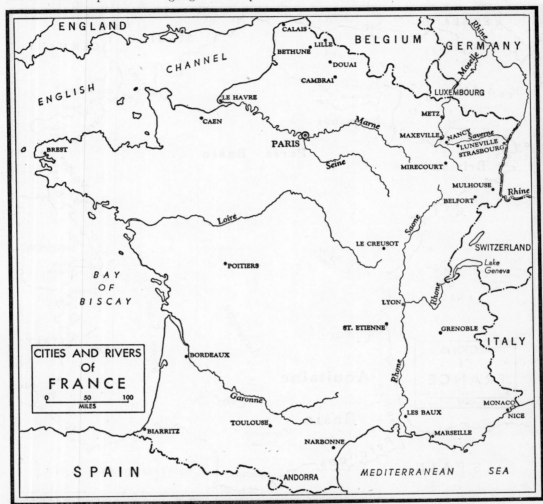

CITIES AND RIVERS
Of
FRANCE
0   50   100
MILES

Church and state are separate in France. Although the country is dominantly Roman Catholic, Protestants enjoy freedom of religion. In all, approximately two and one-half per cent of the population adheres to beliefs other than Catholic. Catholicism was introduced in France by the Roman legions in the Christian era that followed Caesar's invasion of Gaul. Its spread was promoted by the civic unity that obtained under Roman rule. Previous to this time Druidism, which replaced the pagan beliefs of the early

Physical Aspects

The relief and geologic structure of France present a maximum diversity. Four areas belong to the old Variscan Mountain range (Vosges, Ardennes, Brittany, and Auvergne), and three areas belong to the young Alpine system (Pyrenees, Alps, and Jura). Between these seven highland areas lie connecting plains and valley lowlands. The southern coastal plains border the Mediterranean Sea; the Aquitaine plains border the Bay of Biscay and reach back into France to the advanced mature topography of the volcanic Auvergnes; the Paris Basin, largest of the physical regions, lies between the Vosges and Ardennes on the east, the hills of Brittany and Normandy on the west, and Auvergne on the south. (See the map on page 169 for major regions and relief features of France.)

A fortunate system of connecting valleys or saddles links the plains or lowland regions and at the same time provides breaks or passes between mountainous areas. Flowing out of Switzerland through Lake Geneva, the Rhone River separates the Alps from the Jura Mountains. Together with its tributary, the Saône, the Rhone connects the Mediterranean lowlands with the Paris Basin. The Carcassonne Saddle, a broad gateway, leads from the Mediterranean to the Aquitaine Basin. The Poitou, or Orléans, Gate connects the Aquitaine and Paris basins. In the northeastern part of France the Saverne Gate lies between the Ardennes and the Vosges and the Burgundian Gate between the Vosges and Jura, the latter connecting the Rhine River valley with the Rhone-Saône Corridor. Through these gateways rivers or canals provide water transportation and through them also run the busiest railway lines of France (see the map on the facing page for rivers).

Natural regions. As part of the understanding of French economic and cultural life, one must recognize the dominant contributions made by her major physical regions. The *Auvergne Plateau* (Central Massif) is sometimes known as the "poorhouse" of France. Nevertheless, its ancient crystalline rocks contain excellent building material and are interspersed with a little coal and meager metallic minerals. In relatively recent but wholly prehistoric time vulcanism was rife in the central part, and even now heats ground water sufficiently to create mineral and thermal springs. Some Auvergne soils composed of decayed volcanic rocks are rich and productive; others consisting of schists (a form of crystalline rock, such as mica) are poor and only suitable for use as pasturage for sheep, goats, and cattle, or as ground for forests. Infertile sandy soils on the southern slopes of the plateau support chestnut groves, yielding nuts as a rich, nutritious food and bark for tanning purposes. Closely identified with soil resources, deposits of excellent kaolin clay in the region have made Limoges one of the most noted porcelain-manufacturing centers in Europe.

The relatively rough surface of the Auvergne Plateau presents a barrier effect to travel, handicapping, though not stifling the transportation pattern in this part of France. Gorges carved in the plateau require high viaducts for the roads and railroads. During World War II Auvergne Plateau received considerable notoriety when the Nazis designated it as the nucleus of "Free France." Here was the most isolated part of the country, where opportunity for initiative on the part of the French population would be at a minimum.

Two rocky peninsulas, Brittany and Cotentin with their connecting bases, make up the *Armorican Peninsula.* Craggy headlands challenge the stormy sea, while inland valleys, developed on folded limestone and sandstone, furnish much good soil and nourish vegetable gardens for the Paris market. Apples and cider, cereals, and pasture lands for meat and dairy products are also characteristic of this region. Although a little lead is found, this area, just as in the case of the Auvergne, but unlike many parts of these old Variscan mountains, is not rich in minerals.

In northeastern France are the *Vosges* and the *Ardennes.* Rising from the Rhine River valley the rocks of the Vosges are now carved into beautiful, old hills given to forests, grazing, and terraced agriculture. From the northern Vosges red sandstone is quarried and sent down the valleys. The Ardennes consist of rocks folded into intricate wrinkles and eroded into wild, rocky mountains. Only a fringe of the Ardennes spills southward across the French-Belgian border to add to the variety of French scenery and building resources.

The *Jura,* a crescent-shaped area of young strata folded into simple mountains, are structurally a part of the Alps. The people of the Jura valleys, who are organized into cooperative societies, make Gruyère cheese, butter, toys, clocks, watches, pipes, glass, horn, celluloid, and wood articles, products involving much labor and little material. Silk manufacture and vine-growing for wine are also active industries.

The *Alps,* much more lofty, forbidding, and complexly folded and carved than the Jura, extend from Lake Geneva to the Mediterranean Sea. Their crests form the Franco-Italian boundary; in France they attain a width of almost 100 miles, pouring powerful and abundant waters down the Durance and Isère rivers to the Rhone. Both these rivers furnish hydro-electric power (the French "white coal") for the small iron and steel industries clustered around Grenoble and for a variety of other plants located up the valleys far back into the southern Alps. Bauxite, or aluminum ore, from the southern and western foothills is obtained and manufactured near the lower Rhone.* Spurs of the Alps between scenic valleys reach the sea at the Riviera and add their charm to those of the climate and the coast.

The *Pyrenees* make up another lofty mountain structure similar to the Alps, but less complex. If supplied with minerals, they are not sufficiently eroded as yet to reveal much of value. Forests, particularly in the well-watered western half, and sheep pastures interspersed among fields of cereals and vineyards suggest the main products. The altitude and ruggedness of the Pyrenees handicap transportation so that many of the communities on the northern slopes of the range are in many ways virtually isolated from the rest of France.

The *Aquitaine Basin* in southwestern France is a rich agricultural district. Two rival cities, Bordeaux and Toulouse, process and export the principal products of the region; the former specializing in wines, and the latter in cereals. The Landes, a sandy area along the coast south of Bordeaux, has in recent years been planted with coniferous trees, restricting the former picturesque grazing industry. Biarritz and other nearby coastal towns are pleasure resorts that do a thriving business in normal times.

The *Mediterranean Plains,* with a subtropical climate, irrigation water, and alluvial soils, grow grapes, peaches, cherries, olives, almonds, vegetables, and flowers, partly for northern markets. Manufactures include sea-lagoon salt, chemicals, ceramic products, and aluminum. To the east, close to the Italian border, is the Riviera (French "Côte d'azur"), winter playground of international repute.

The *Paris Basin* in some ways resembles a stack of shallow dishes, the upturned edges of which form a series of fragmentary, encircling ridges. The basis for this roughly concentric structural arrangement is a series of rock layers underlying the region, which in the center are warped downward. At their outer edges they bend upward toward the Ardennes, Jura, and Auvergne highlands. The resulting ridges form natural defense barriers for the French defense of Paris, and present obstacles that must be surmounted by any invaders from the east and north. The plains between the ridges are vast vineyards, gardens of fruits, vegetables, and flowers for Paris; and the ridge slopes are clothed with pasture, wheat fields, deciduous forests, and newer pine forests. The north slopes of the plain facing toward Belgium lack the ridges and are cropped with cereals, sugar beets, flax, hops, and feed for poultry and dairy stock. Many industries, often in the old hand-machine stage, are overshadowed by the modern steel and iron mills and textile plants of the Lille district.

Corsica is a mountainous but rich island bathed by the warm Mediterranean waters and well-supplied with rain.* Its forests have been little worked; its plains are covered with subtropical fruits and vegetables; and its hills yield a wealth and variety of building stone, slate, clays, mineral waters, and a few metallic minerals. Since pirating along the Mediterranean coast has ceased, Corsicans have made considerable progress in their economic development and are finding more or less political security.

International aspects of location. Location with reference to other nations has meant much to France. Greeks developed commercial cities on the Mediterranean coast before the tribes of the interior had so much as thought of a great nation. Centuries later the Romans not only came to the coast but progressed inland; following the Rhone-Saône Corridor northward, and then over the Carcassonne Saddle to the west and the Burgundian-Belfort and Saverne gates to the east toward Germany. Their sojourn in France was sufficient to teach many generations of the people the fundamentals of settled government, legal justice, art, science,

---

* The name "bauxite" comes from the little town of Les Baux, near the site of France's major aluminum ore deposits.

* Corsica is a part of Metropolitan France, being one of the country's ninety administrative departments.

religion, reason, discipline, philosophy, the value of unity, and roads for commercial intercourse. But if France benefited by Roman penetration, she also was touched by Saracen influences from Africa. Leading contributions from this direction were the high types of dry-climate agriculture, the Moslem religion, and style of architecture. The two latter never really took root in France, but agricultural techniques advanced by introduction of crops, plants, and methods of cultivation.

As Romans could go entirely across France from the south, so the culturally retarded "barbarians" could make inroads on the country from the north and northeast. The same gateways and lowland routes were utilized although the direction of approach was different. Apparently the Teutonic invaders outnumbered the remaining Romans and thus gave a strong Teutonic cast to the stature and complexion of the people in northern France. They likewise promoted trade with the fisher folks, foresters, and livestock men in the north, who carried home ideas of religion, government, and methods of living learned from the French. This limited yet continuous mingling and intercourse in early days with neighbors on every side held the germ of French political cosmopolitanism.

Size, shape, and depth. From Caesar's time to the present France has been nearly the same size. Hovering around 200,000 square miles, the country was larger when Alsace and Lorraine were a part of it, and smaller when they belonged to Germany. Corsica with an area of 3,367 square miles adds to the total. Despite some changes in boundaries along the Italian, Spanish, and Belgian frontiers, there has been less shifting of area through the 2,000 years of its existence than for almost any other European nation. Through short periods France has been included among the great empires, and at times she has imposed her power over large adjacent territory; but when adjustments have come, a France practically unchanged in size and shape, about five times the size of Ohio, has reappeared. Manner of life, means of subsistence, and standards of living have gradually improved and become exceptionally uniform, and by means of better geographic adjustments this strong area

has come to support several times as many people as in the early centuries—about 40,000,000 in recent decades.

The form of France is roughly hexagonal, with the angles near Calais, Brest, Biarritz, Narbonne, Monaco, and Strasbourg. Only peninsular corners like Brittany or Cotentin, the island of Corsica, and a number of indentations on the Alpine frontier prevent the country from being extremely compact, or block-like, the optimum shape for defense. Little except Corsica is more than 400 miles from Paris, even though the capital city is well north of the country's center.

Climate. France is favored by an oceanic climate that is most nearly pure marine along the Atlantic coast (marine type). The influence of the sea becomes much less effective in the eastern parts, where continental influences are responsible for wider ranges and greater extremes of temperature than near the coast (continental type). Northern France is continually in the belt of the westerly winds and their succession of high and low pressure areas, the latter partly responsible for frequent storms and heavy rainfall. As a belt the westerlies shift to the north in summer and to the south in winter, and when far south bring a rainy season to these parts during the winter months. Their northward shifting in summer permits the dry high-pressure belt of descending air to move poleward from subtropical latitudes and brings to the Mediterranean Plains and the Riviera the sunshine and dry weather so characteristic of the summer there (Mediterranean type).

Three factors are important in the climate of France: (1) latitude, which accounts for the position of the westerlies and cyclonic storms; (2) relation to sea and land, which insures sufficient moisture from the sea and a moderate range of temperature; and (3) relief, which causes increased precipitation, lower temperatures, and stronger winds as altitude increases. The Alps and Pyrenees are lofty enough to attain that balance of snowfall and coldness conducive to many mountain glaciers.

Because the Mediterranean Sea retains its summer heat in the cold season, it tempers the winter of the south and offers long periods of sunshine and warmth to the tourist. Open houses and an outdoor life are common in that region, whereas in the north, glass, sometimes in roofs of porches, transmits the sunshine, which is conserved by stone walls and insulation. In the Mediterranean Plains evaporation is sufficiently high to promote a lively salt industry in lagoons along the seacoast. In the Rhone Valley and in areas cut off from rain-bearing winds by the Cevennes, however, irrigation and dry farming are necessary.

Resources. As the result of a diversity of structure and rocks, France has a wide range of rocks, minerals, ores, and soils. Ancient crystalline rocks in the four old mountain areas provide marble, slate, gneiss, and granite for architectural needs. The vulcanism of the Auvergne adds to the variety of igneous rocks, and black basalt is much used here for the construction of houses. In both mountains and plains appear a large variety of shales, limestones, and sandstones useful in the ceramic industries. In addition to these sources of building materials, forests are so well cared for that, while there is not much wild game, there is a perpetual though limited supply of timber for lumber. Thus the country is fortunate in its possession of an abundance of construction supplies that are widely distributed and of excellent quality.

Iron ore of fine grade in the northern part of the Auvergne and the enormous reserves in Lorraine supply the steel plants of St. Étienne, Le Creusot, and the Moselle towns of Nancy, Maxeville, and Bouxiere. The exchange between the Saar Basin and Lorraine of coking coal from the former and minette iron ore from the latter provides each with the materials needed for steel manufacture. Lesser iron resources are worked near Caen in Normandy, in the Ariège Valley of the Pyrenees, and near Grenoble, where hydroelectric furnaces reduce the ores to metal. Coal is mined in Douai, Béthune, and Cambrai south of Lille; in the Ardennes; and in the upper Loire Valley. Nevertheless, the total production is only about seventy per cent of domestic needs. Of salt, potassium, nitrate, gypsum, talc, aluminum, antimony, and pyrite for sulphur, France has an abundance. Gold, silver, lead, manganese, and zinc are mined, but in amounts insufficient even for domestic needs. Tin, petroleum, radium, uranium, tungsten, mica, arsenic, copper, nickel, chromium, cobalt, and coking coal are largely

lacking and must be imported. Much of France's heavy industry rests on expendable resources found within the country's borders, such as metals and coal. Most of the light industry is based on skill and tradition rather than on a strong inventory of raw materials.

Coal is supplemented by hydro-electric power developed in the foothills and mountains of the numerous highland districts. In total, electricity furnishes a fifth as much energy as does coal. Within Europe, France is exceeded in the utilization of waterpower by only Italy and Norway. Soils are the greatest of the natural resources. They are usually mature, rich, and warm, and very little disturbed by glaciation. Fisheries in both the Atlantic and the Mediterranean are abundant and varied.

France has much to attract the tourist in natural scenery. Its picturesque mountainous topography, rivers, coastal areas, and other phenomena of the landscape give the country a regional diversity holding charm and appeal to visitors. Adding to the attractiveness is the superimposition of a human culture, uniquely colorful and traditionally rich.

Political and Social Aspects

France has experimented with many forms of government. Since the days of feudalism there have been kings, emperors, republics, and a Commune. The legislative, executive, and judiciary machinery savor of ancient Rome, the Grecian city state, and later the United States, but the blending, harmonizing, and implementing are peculiarly French. The present regime is the outcome of postwar innovation. On October 21, 1945, a French electorate chose the members of a constituent assembly to draw up a new constitution and establish the Fourth Republic of France. On May 5, 1946 the new constitution was rejected in a referendum, and during the next month an election was held for another constituent assembly to draw up a new constitution. In a plebiscite held October 13, 1946, the French people approved their new constitution.

Administrative units. In Napoleon Bonaparte's time the land was subdivided into 83 *départements,* a number now increased to 90. These are further divided into *arrondissements,* of which there are over 300; into *cantons,* of which there are around 2,900; and finally, for each *canton,* into about a dozen *communes,* comparable to American townships though much smaller, averaging in the neighborhood of six square miles in area. The *département* is headed by a *préfect,* the *arrondissement* by a *sub-préfect,* the *canton* by a justice of the peace, and the *commune* by a mayor and a municipal council. The *canton* is an areal rather than an administrative unit. The total administrative plan appears quite simple, standard, and serviceable; but it is only the latter. The tremendous number of units prevents simplicity, and notable differences in topography and population density make the units far from standard. Shiftings of local political boundaries cause variations in numbers of small divisions.

Social structure. Classes in communities seem to be more differentiated than in America. The "nobility," whose titles are no more than tokens of courtesy, are the proprietors of lands. Usually estates are not large but to own land is significant and socially desirable. Peasants, or *paysans,* are those who work on the farms, in the forests, or engage in other rural activities. As a class they are decreasing in number and probably account for no more than thirty-seven or thirty-eight per cent of the total population of France today. Prior to the Revolution they were subject to feudal chiefs, but by 1848 all were freed. This liberation was the work of the middle classes, impelled by political, economic, and social motives. The *paysans* are now entering politics as a class.

As a class apart from the *paysans,* artisans are mechanics, craftsmen, architects, and operative workmen; not artists as originally interpreted. This group makes up about forty per cent of the populace. The *bourgeois,* who constitute the middle class, account for about twelve per cent of France's inhabitants. They are shopkeepers and townsmen in distinction from *paysans,* or country people. They, like the artisans, are between the "nobility" and the "people." They may be further described as the small capitalists forming a class well developed in France but a very small class until recent years in many other European countries. "Proletariat," which is a more general class term, includes all people who depend for subsistence on their earnings from daily labor, that is, they are not property owners. The remaining eight to ten per cent of the population are in the professions and the public service.

As in the case of all social institutions in France, religious life has been thoroughly patterned into a hierarchy harking back to early traditional conventions. The Roman Catholic church is organized into seventeen archbishoprics and sixty-eight bishoprics. Sees, corresponding roughly to *départements,* are divided into deaneries, and these into parishes, the working units. Although the church has no official political standing, it may and does initiate social movements for progress and order.

Modern Protestantism is chiefly Calvinistic, introduced from Britain by members of the Baptist, Methodist, and English Reformed churches. Influences and migrations from Germany and Switzerland have resulted in a number of Lutheran churches in the northeastern part. Protestants number about 1,000,000. The Jewish faith, which is largely limited to the cities, is organized into "cultural associations." Small groups of Mohammedans of North African origin are found in and near Paris.

Population. The average population density of France is about 190 persons per square mile, a low figure for a long-settled, productive land like France. Areas of high population density are widely scattered: along the Mediterranean coast from Marseille eastward; inland from the same coast in an arc extending from the Rhone to the Pyrenees; through most of Alsace; along the coast of Brittany; the Channel coast of France north of Le Havre; the lower Saône River valley; Paris and environs; Lille and its coal towns; and around a few other large commercial and industrial cities not included in the above regions, for example, St. Étienne and Grenoble. These all exceed at least 250 persons per square mile, and in many instances have more than double this number.

Areas of low density are the sandy and pine-covered Landes along the Bay of Biscay coast; a larger area in the southern Alps; the relatively barren *causses* of the Auvergne Plateau; broad areas in the upper Marne and Seine valleys; and scores of *communes* of rougher country from the Pyrenees to the Ardennes. Here the density of population is less than 100 persons per square mile. More than half of France has from 100 to

250 persons per square mile: over the plains and low hills from Toulouse in the south to Brittany and Calais and throughout the plains of the Rhone, upper Saône, and upper Moselle. These are the great farming lands with their hundreds of towns and villages interspersed throughout.

In 1700 the population of France was about 19,000,000. By 1866 it had doubled, and since that date the birth rate and the death rate have fluctuated at about the same relative ratio. In general, the birth rate now shows a gradual though uneven decline. In recent decades only a small emigration has taken place, and this has been far more than offset by a large immigration. As a result two and one-half to three million foreigners were permanent dwellers in the country up to the start of World War II. Augmenting the native population in times of peace, thousands of tourists flood the country each year. In many instances these visitors remain a long time, staying in the various cities and spas, or even buying villas for their prolonged period of residence.

There is little pressure of population, such as is found in several other European countries, either within or from without. For forty years there has been a relatively stable population, which the educational and health programs and the uniformity of living standards have fashioned into a strong, intelligent people. As in any country that has such a population, France has a relatively higher per cent of employables, although there is a tendency toward an increasing proportion of older age groups.

MINORITIES. In France a minority problem scarcely exists except in Alsace-Lorraine. There, however, high feelings have been raised as the result of four transfers of the region between Germany and France within a century. From 1871–1918 and again from 1940–44 the Germans controlled Alsace-Lorraine. Although the people of that region speak a German dialect (many are bilingual), they look culturally to France. The territory is justly a part of France, but consideration of local problems is essential to a satisfactory national determination in an area as complex as Alsace-Lorraine.

Many people other than French live in France. Basques and Celts have already been mentioned, but they have no feeling of being minorities. Algerians and Negroes are numerous in the south; Belgians have entered along the north side; Germans have come into the northeast part; many Italians live in the southeast; Spanish are present in the south; and Jews are scattered over all France in the cities. Probably thousands of families in each of these groups have lived in France for a generation or more; but they have attained such a fortunate status that they do not cry out as minorities. Aided by French tolerance and democratic spirit and, in most instances, by Latin-derived languages they have tended to mingle healthily with more strictly French people and become absorbed linguistically and socially.

Boundaries

In many sectors French boundaries have needed no apologies, but the Rhine and Vosges as borders and the resulting Alsace-Lorraine problems have long vexed the French as well as the Germans. When boundaries were for protection, the ridges of the Vosges were far superior to the Rhine. When friendly intercourse and trade gained priority over defense, the Rhine became a natural point of contact between the two countries. But when potassium salts near Mülhausen, salt for chemical industries near Nancy and Lunéville, iron ore near Metz, coal in the Saar Basin, and the forests of the hills became known and their values understood, both France and Germany coveted Alsace and Lorraine. Treaties were not enough restraint; both nations broke them repeatedly by insidious penetration and by actual conquest. The problem has been complicated by the fact that there is no ethnic line of any sort through this district. The people are mostly Alpines over the whole area and many are bilingual, though often slow to admit it.

Luxembourg also presents a boundary problem. Its ruling house had a German origin, and at different times it has been in the German, French, and Belgian customs union. Strongly industrial, it uses its own iron ore but must import coal from the Saar Basin and limestone from the Ardennes to complete the list of basic resources essential to heavy manufacturing.

The Belgian-French boundary has no physical or ethnic justification, and the distributions of coal, iron, agriculture, and industry have been no respecters of nationalities. In past centuries the line has been drawn more with reference to the positions of contending armies at the time of an armistice than with reference to anything local. In some instances the line follows rivers, giving it a zig-zag effect. As a result there are French protuberances extending into Belgium and Belgian protuberances into France.

The continental boundaries of France on the east reflect the great zone of transition between western and central Europe. From the Low Countries and Luxembourg in the north the belt extends southward through Alsace-Lorraine to Switzerland and the Maritime Alps. After both world wars of this century the French were eager to have the Saar with its important coal mines under their political—or at least economic—control. In the Rhineland the French have wanted to see an independent unit separate from Germany, and in the industrial Ruhr they have favored international control. On the Italian border they acquired the pass and enclave of Tenda and Briga in 1947. France also secured minor border rectifications in the areas of Little St. Bernard Pass, Mt. Cenis Pass, and Mt. Thabor and Chaberton. The map on page 196 shows the new boundary changes favorable to France on the Franco-Italian frontier.

Monaco and Andorra. The boundaries of France also reach the microstates of Monaco and Andorra. Monaco, a famous principality of 370 acres on the Mediterranean coast, nine miles east of Nice, is surrounded on land by French territory. Not only does it have the same customs duties as France but also the language is French. Here Prince Louis II rules over a population of about 20,000. Monte Carlo, one of the three communes and a famous gambling resort, offers the only feature of interest in the eyes of many tourists.

Andorra is a semi-independent state between the eastern and central Pyrenees on the border between France and Spain. This group of mountain valleys has an area of 191 square miles, and a population of about 5,200. It has its own spoken language, Catalan, but both Spanish and French currency are used. Since 1278 Andorra has been under the joint suzerainty of France and the Spanish bishops of Urgel. The official title of Andorra is "les Vallées et Suzerainetés."

Commerce

Domestic trade. The physical units of France, component parts of a long-established national entity, contribute heavily to the support of one another. Among the various regions there are exchanges of mineral resources, or products of the soil, and of commodities coming from the forests and pasture lands. The result is that rural and industrial areas supplement each other; coast and mountain regions interchange their specialties with plains areas; and commercial facilities stand ready to effect the exchange of these mutual benefits by an efficient nation-wide transportation and communications pattern. There is a fine system of rivers, which is inherent to the country, and this has been augmented by canals and canalized rivers. Of greatest import, however, are the dense networks of rail lines and highways extending into every part of France. Only in a few of the more rugged areas are there points farther than ten miles from a railroad. Normally French railroads carry seven ninths of the country's goods, highways carry another ninth, and the inland waterways the remaining ninth. In relatively recent times air transportation has further strengthened the contact among the regions of France, although for the most part airlines are used to reach points beyond the nation's borders. Despite the disruption of this entire scheme of economy during the German occupation, the system is being rapidly restored and no doubt will return to and surpass its accustomed functioning.

Foreign and colonial trade. French foreign commerce is quite another matter than its internal trade. Although trade with the colonies has been important, it has not been so significant as it might have been. The North African units trade through Marseille, sending in wheat, barley, oats, wine, olive oil, dates, cork, lumber, sheep, goats, and cattle. Among these items the livestock furnish meat, hides, wool, and hair. Phosphate rock for fertilizers has also been a large import item from across the Mediterranean. The balance of trade is maintained by exports of machinery and manufactured goods and by large investments in roads, harbors, mining, and loans to increase production in the colonies.

France has large colonies in West and Equatorial Africa, where different climatic conditions make possible the production of goods that would do much to supplement the home country. Nevertheless, although fibers, fruits, starch foods, lumber, and gold and other ores are imported to some extent, vastly more could be done in these African colonies to produce for the homeland and to furnish markets for home products. With France as with all highly developed countries in the middle latitudes, the trade potential with equatorial lands is as yet only lightly tapped. Off the east coast of Africa, France has Madagascar, an island possession larger than the mother country. Its leading economic advantages are mineral resources and a rich subtropical vegetation yielding forest wealth. Farther afield is French Indo-China, subtropical like Madagascar, but with a location in the Far East introducing other differences that could well promote trade.*

Foreign trade between France and other leading industrial countries outranks colonial trade in value. In the years before World War II imports from Germany and the United States were greatest, with those from Great Britain and Belgium next in rank. Exports run in somewhat different order: Germany tops the list of those receiving outgoing commodities, followed by Great Britain and Belgium; next comes Switzerland, which outranks the United States. Argentina and Brazil show up well on both export and import lists. Because France's foreign trade has been greatly disrupted by the effects of the war years, no up-to-date evaluation can be provided. One can only guess that this trade will become larger than in the decade prior to World War II and that relative positions of countries in that trade will almost certainly be altered. Negotiations and treaties are already under way in various fields and directions.

Stimulating both foreign and colonial trade France had a large mercantile marine that during the thirties ranked sixth in the world in tonnage (3,000,000). Much of this was destroyed during the war, but the basis of maritime activity remains as an incentive to the rapid rebuilding of the commercial fleet. Likewise, air transportation service, which reached the Far East, Madagascar, Equatorial

*For more detailed discussions on French colonies, see Chapters 25, 27, and 31.

Africa, and South America during the prewar years, is being rapidly rejuvenated. "Air France," the French national airline, now skirts the southern coast of Asia to French Indo-China, has a fairly complex route network over the French part of Africa, and reaches New York in its initial transatlantic service. Its routes in western and central Europe and the Mediterranean region are much like those in the thirties, linking Paris with the capitals of other countries.

Cities

Paris, the capital, is the only city in France exceeding 1,000,000 in population. In fact, it exceeds in numbers the combined population of the next sixteen largest cities of the country. The city proper numbers 2,725,000 and Greater Paris nearly 5,000,000. From an ancient settlement on the *Ile de la Cité* the city grew along two great meanders of the Seine until it now covers not only the land within the loops but far beyond. Today it is rich in points of interest, both ancient and modern. Within the greater city are several large suburbs, each significant for some group of industries or items of commerce. A large forest tract and many parks, one an old quarry, lie within the immediate environs of Paris. As the railroads that come into the city from all directions terminate at about ten separate stations, passengers through the city must transfer from one station to another; however, freight can be sent from any road to another on the inner or outer belt railroad without unloading. The city also has a huge subway system, with an aggregate length of double track in excess of seventy miles, that carries in normal times an average of over 2,000,000 persons daily.

The city began as a fortification of an island to guard a ferry. On a fertile open plain in the heart of the great Paris Basin, and within reach of the coast by river, its location attracted local and national trade. Gradually it became the center of France's web of transportation. One wall after another, each of greater circumference than its predecessor, was built to enclose the growing city. Today the walls, obsolete before modern machines of war, have been replaced by boulevards, and the city has expanded far beyond the outermost of the former walls.

Paris is not only the political capital of France but also the commercial, financial, educational, religious, and cultural center. Although one hundred miles from the sea, figures show it to be the leading port by virtue of its location on the navigable Seine and one of the world's chief ports.

Marseille, with a population of 636,000, is the second city of France and the nearest rival to Paris in commercial importance. As a Mediterranean port it dominates French trade with North Africa and the East. Lyon, located at the junction of the Rhone and Saône rivers, is the third city of France, with a population of 571,000. The great popularity of its commercial fair, held each March, testifies to a convenient central position and easy access. Another port, Bordeaux, is the fourth city. Its importance rests more with its position as distribution and assembly point on the Gironde River at the edge of the extensive Aquitaine Basin than as a commercial port depending upon foreign trade. Nice, famous for its location along the French Riviera, ranks fifth. Both Bordeaux and Nice hover around the quarter-million mark in population.

Twelve other cities in France exceed a population of 100,000 (see the map on page 170 for the principal cities). These cities, along with many smaller ones, are noted for some specific industry or product. French cities, more than those of other countries, seem to have this characteristic of specialization. As examples, the relatively large city of St. Étienne (approximately 175,000) is a center of heavy industry, and the small city of Mirecourt in the eastern part of the Paris Basin specializes in the manufacture of violins.

The French Colonial Empire

The colonial empire of France is nearly twenty times as large as the homeland and carries a population nearly fifty per cent larger, but the people are in the main on a much lower standard of living. The following list affords comparisons of the units of the present colonial empire of France with Metropolitan France scattered over or near all of the world's habitable continents and in the Pacific, Atlantic, and Indian oceans.

France and the Colonial Empire (French Union)

Continent or ocean	Year of acquisition	Area in square miles
EUROPE:		
France and Corsica	Corsica (1768)	212,681
Andorra (special relations with France)		191
Monaco (special relations with France)		(370 acres)
AFRICA:		
Algeria	1830–1902	847,500
Tunisia	1881	48,313
Morocco	—	213,350
French West Africa (including Togoland Trusteeship)	1637–1919	1,840,591
French Equatorial Africa (including Cameroons Trusteeship)	1884–1919	1,125,745
French Somaliland	1864	8,492
INDIAN OCEAN:		
Madagascar and Comoro Is.	1643–1896	241,884
Réunion Island	1643	970
ASIA:		
French Indo-China	1862–1893	286,000
French India	1679	196
PACIFIC OCEAN:		
New Caledonia and dependencies (including the Loyalty Islands)	1853	8,548
New Hebrides (condominium of Great Britain and France, 1906)	—	5,790
French Establishments in Oceania (including Society Islands with Tahiti, Marquesas, Tuamotu group, Leeward Islands, and Gambier, Austral and Rapa Is.)	1841–1881	1,520
Clipperton (small atoll)		
AMERICA AND THE ATLANTIC:		
St. Pierre and Miquelon	1635	93
Martinique	1635	427
Guadeloupe	1634	688
French Guiana	1626	65,041

NOTE: Syria and Lebanon, former mandated territories under France, are now independent; Kwangchowan has been returned to China.

Postwar France

Internal problems. The well-balanced economy and cultural adjustment of France have contributed in the past to the welfare of the nation. Internal economic problems have often arisen from general shortcomings or instances of stagnation on the part of certain industries or groups of people. The question of the decreasing birth rate (discussed previously) is closely related to the insufficient supply of labor, which as a problem is only partly solved by the extensive immigration, also mentioned earlier. Mechanization of agriculture, lumbering, and heavy construction, such as harbor, road, and railroad building, have tended to ameliorate difficulties growing out of the labor shortage.

If French industry is to develop further and absorb rural labor released by mechanization, imports of raw materials for industry must increase. Although France exports food and beverages, she also must import many types of food, in a raw state, which are then processed. The mineral shortage, which is sufficiently pressing to call for extensive planning, may be eased, at least in part, by colonial and other importation.

The France of the Fourth Republic suffers from a number of large political parties leading to unstable coalition governments. On many occasions the internal stability and international position of the country are impaired by cabinet crises. The Fourth Republic of France will have to face this important issue of government.

External questions. The main problems of France with respect to the outside world fall into two categories: commercial and political. The former category refers to the routine of maintaining a stable national economy. In the past efforts in this direction have yielded results ranging from intolerable to satisfactory. Without the pressure of population, French economy would seem to have the potentialities for a standard of living unattainable by her neighbors. However, the political problems have been instrumental in embroiling the country in most of the major political and military issues of Europe, and even the world. As a result, France has indeed had a tumultuous history.

Closely knit with the supply of raw materials for home industries is the question of trade balancing. For decades France has not sold enough exports to pay for her necessary imports. Further, her exports are in large part of the luxury or semi-luxury class—artificial flowers, perfumes, jewelry, toys, works of art, highly finished fabrics, and hundreds of knick-knacks to please the eye or catch the fancy or taste of a fastidious, discriminating class constantly changing in its interests. These exports offer an excellent opportunity for the small manufacturer, for the cultivation of individual skills and inventiveness, but because of this specialization a substantial proportion of French exports has a somewhat fictitious and even precarious basis. To be sure, agricultural products, such as wines, brandies, vegetables, dairy and poultry products, flowers, seeds, nuts, and some fruits are also exported, with England as the largest market. But the combined exports of luxury items and agricultural products are not enough to balance the essential imports.

That balance was formerly attained, partly by foreign investments, foreign banking, and insurance, but these were declining before the last war and France was seeking to stay the slump. By restoring waning foreign business and increasing the legitimate tourist intake she has sought to balance her books.

Colonial administration has usually been along paternal lines and not so exploitive as that of some nations, but the colonies cost more than they return. Some plan to promote financial solvency will be mutually advantageous. There are such vast differences between the homeland and the colonies in climate and products that there should be no insurmountable difficulties to the development of some economic plan of cooperation.

One other external element greatly hampers France. Her position and success have often kindled the jealousy of neighbors. Her foreign policies have aggravated the relationship, and her declining birth rate, which makes her appear to be a labor market, has brought to her domain large numbers of foreigners. Although France has lost much of her strength, she is still a valuable potential ally to any power. In the interests of peace, growth, and service, real statesmanship is required in France to maintain a foreign policy commensurate with her advantages of position, resources, and cultural leadership. France, no doubt, will prove capable of maintaining herself in a key position in European affairs and, together with her colonial territories, of occupying an important if not leading place in world affairs.

CHAPTER 13 | # Switzerland: A Successful Neutral

THE Swiss were the first Europeans to demonstrate that peoples of different race, religion, language, culture, and tradition can live side by side in peace and unity if the rights of all are treated with tolerance and respect.

Switzerland came into being on August 1, 1291, when the three rural cantons of Uri, Schwyz, and Unterwalden through chosen delegates formed a political and military alliance to maintain mutual independence against all outside influences. The remarkable document concluded on that date contains most of the essential principles of later Swiss constitutions. However, the two basic principles of the present Constitution, internal democracy and external neutrality, were not formulated until 1848.

The maintenance of these two principles has not always been easy. Many times during its historical development, Switzerland has been called on to make vital decisions, and although the Republic has occasionally faltered, it has never lost sight of its goals— democracy and individual freedom. Today the twenty-two cantons of Switzerland are welded tightly into a country that assures a common governmental policy and essential liberty, without jeopardy to local culture and tradition.

Geographical Structure

Boundaries. Switzerland has both natural and artificial boundaries. In the south the Italo-Swiss border follows the crests of mountain ridges or crosses them with no regularity. At one point it reaches as far south as the northern slopes of the Po River basin; and Lake Maggiore, one of the famous Italian lakes, is partly in Italy and partly in Switzerland. From the junction with the Italian border to the Rhine River the Austro-Swiss boundary runs irregularly across mountainous terrain in a general east-west direction. Northward to Lake Constance Switzerland and Austria meet in the Rhine Valley except for a wedge that makes up the tiny Principality of Liechtenstein. Turning westward where it meets Germany the border is open and follows the middle of Lake Constance and the Rhine River to Basel except where Canton Schaffhausen forms a Swiss salient north of the Rhine. The Franco-Swiss boundary turns southwestward and for the most part follows the crest of the Jura Mountains from Basel to Geneva. From Geneva to the Italian border the common boundary with France first follows the center of Lake Geneva and then the crest line of the French Alps.

Although seventy-five per cent of Switzerland's boundaries are mountain crests, they are not well suited to defense. As the prime handicap, the mountainous stretches of boundaries are broken by many lakes, rivers, and open valleys. From the politico-geographical viewpoint the weakest part of the Swiss boundary is that of the north facing Germany.

Routes and passes. In the central part of the Alps is a mountain knot known as the "Gotthard Massif," which geographically and militarily is the most important center of Switzerland. The Reuss, Rhine, Tessin, and Rhone rivers have their origin in this high mountain area, and each flows in a cardinal direction: north, east, south, or west. Together the valleys of the Reuss and Tessin rivers form a north-south route of travel leading over the famous St. Gotthard Pass. This is the shortest and quickest connection between Germany and Italy. Perpendicular to this natural arterial north and south, the Rhine and Rhone rivers occupy deep longitudinal valleys that are oriented essentially east-west and separate the Alps into two more or less parallel mountain chains. Traversed by a continuous rail line, the two valleys serve as arterial routes of travel in an east-west direction (see the map on page 183 for rail pattern).

Because Switzerland is a transit country between north and south Europe, her many mountain passes, including the Great St. Bernard, Simplon, St. Gotthard, and several others of lesser importance, have played an important role in the history of Europe. In addition to the movement of goods across them in earlier times, they were used by such military figures as Hannibal in his march against Rome, by the Germans in their many expeditions to the south, and by Napoleon in his wars against northern Italy and Austria.

With the advent of railroads and technical developments in the field of engineering, tunnels have pierced the mountains. Today the Gotthard Massif is penetrated by the St. Gotthard tunnel, and the Lötschberg tunnel passes through the Berner Alps and leads directly to the Simplon tunnel, which in turn pierces the Walliser Alps for a distance of over twelve miles. These tunnels provide direct rail passage between Switzerland and Italy. As a result, the mountain passes have decreased in importance.

The Jura Mountains of northwestern Switzerland consist of parallel ridges and valleys trending in a northeast-southwest direction. A few transverse valleys serve as routes of travel for highways and railroads leading into France. The Paris-Rome express trains that maintain the fastest schedules run through the valleys of the Jura.

Major physical characteristics. Although the greater part of the Alps has elevations that range from 5,000 to 10,000 feet, many mountain peaks rise well over 13,000 feet.* As a

* The highest point in the Alps is Mont Blanc in France (15,782 feet), but several Swiss peaks approach this elevation: Weisshorn (14,804 feet), the Matterhorn (14,780 feet), Jungfrau (13,671 feet), and others.

result of the extreme elevations much of the Alpine highlands is snow-covered throughout the year. Not only is this perpetual snow an attraction essential to the country's large tourist trade, but also it is a source of water supply that has made possible many important hydro-electric plants.

The Swiss Plateau, between the Alps and the Jura, extends from Lake Geneva to Lake Constance. Ranging from 40 to 50 miles in width and approximately 180 miles in length, it varies from 1,200 to 1,800 feet in elevation. Although called a plateau it is a region of rather high relief with many hills, lakes, and entrenched rivers. On the Swiss Plateau the winters are cold, cloudy, and often foggy, but the summers are warm and rainy. Most of Switzerland's limited agricultural and industrial development as well as her urban and transportation facilities center in this region. It is the economic heart of the country and has always been the core area.

Completely different from either the Alpine lands or the Swiss Plateau, the Jura Mountains are of intermediate elevation. The highest points reach 5,000 feet, but the crests are so regular in outline that they lack the scenic appeal of the Alps. Within the mountainous region are numerous valleys and hillside slopes that support agricultural activities, especially the dairying industry widely known for its production of milk chocolate and cheese. Because of isolation and long winters the inhabitants have established home industries in various crafts, such as wood carving and watch making, in which they have acquired specialized skills.

Historical Development

Throughout its long history Switzerland has been inhabited by many peoples and has been under the rule of several nations. Each of these has left its impress on the country in one way or another.

Prior to the Swiss Confederacy. Among the first of the early inhabitants in the Swiss area were the Helvetians, a branch of the Celtic race, who had established themselves in the region between the Alps and Jura Mountains. During the time of Caesar these people were conquered but not expelled from their homes by the Romans, who moved across the Alps into northern Europe. At that period Switzerland became a Roman province

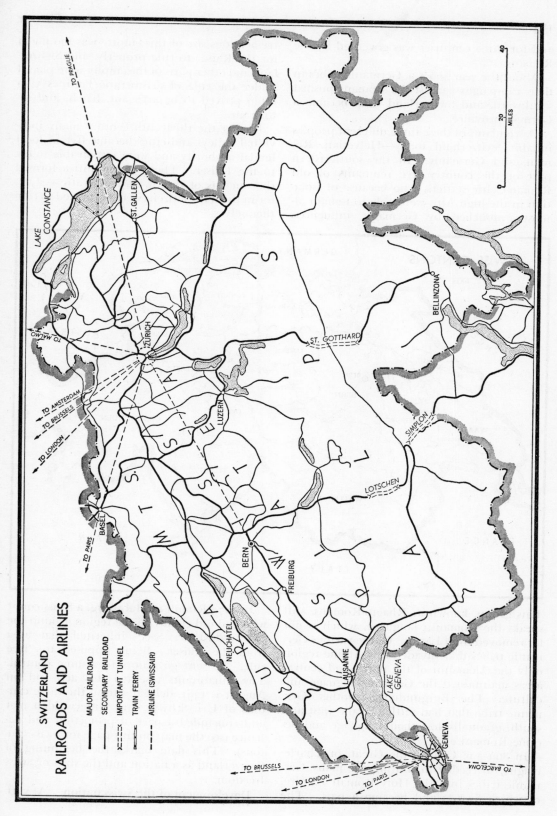

SWITZERLAND
RAILROADS AND AIRLINES

MAJOR RAILROAD
SECONDARY RAILROAD
IMPORTANT TUNNEL
TRAIN FERRY
AIRLINE (SWISSAIR)

LAKE CONSTANCE

TO PRAGUE

ST. GALLEN

A L P S

TO MALMÖ

ZÜRICH

ST. GOTTHARD

BELLINZONA

TO AMSTERDAM
TO BRUSSELS

TO LONDON

LUZERN

SIMPLON

S W I S S   T A B L E

LOTSCHEN

TO PARIS

BASEL

BERN

FREIBURG

NEUCHATEL

J U R A

LAUSANNE

LAKE GENEVA

GENEVA

TO BRUSSELS

TO LONDON

TO PARIS

TO BARCELONA

MILES
0   20   40

and for three centuries was governed by the Romans.

About the year 400 A.D. Germanic tribes in their campaigns against the Romans pushed southward, and Switzerland then became a German province.

Descendants of these three different peoples inhabit Switzerland today—Helvetian, Roman, and Germanic. In the southeastern part of the country live remnants of old Roman-Celtic settlers, who because of isolation in the high Alps were able to remain almost untouched by Germanic influences.

tremendous size of this empire was too much for the Kaiser to rule properly, and Switzerland and other parts of the empire were placed under the rule of aristocratic families who often proved to be arrogant, harsh, and intolerant.

During the thirteenth century many individual valleys and cities became free of local feudal authority and were responsible solely to the Kaiser. These communities formed the nucleus of the Swiss democratic system, for in them the citizens were permitted to rule themselves.

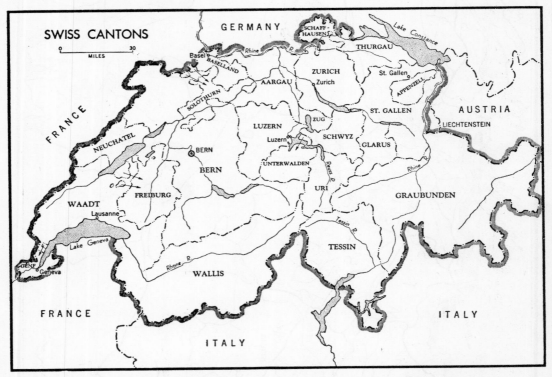

This group, known as Rhaeto-Romans, still speaks the Romansh language, which is not far removed from Latin. Of the various Germanic tribes that invaded this Alpine region only the Alemanni of the north and central areas maintained the German language and culture. The Burgundians, another Germanic tribe that had settled in the west and south, gradually lost their language and became Romanized.

In 800 A.D. Charles the Great, or Charlemagne, succeeded in uniting the many Germanic tribes into the Holy Roman Empire, of which Switzerland became a part. The

In 1273 Rudolf of Habsburg, a Swiss count who had old claims on the region around the "Vierwaldstätter See," inherited that area from the Kaiser. Being opposed to "free rule," he sent governors to assume control. The inhabitants resented this act, and on August 1, 1291, delegates from the three cantons of Uri, Schwyz, and Unterwalden met and concluded a pact of protection and defiance (see the map on this page for Swiss cantons). This date marks the beginning of Switzerland as a nation and the start of Swiss freedom.

Development of the Swiss nation. At various times during the next three centuries after the initial establishment of the Swiss Confederacy, other provinces joined the three original cantons. Luzern was fourth, followed by Zürich, Zug, Glarus, and Bern.* Later Freiburg, Solothurn, Basel, Schaffhausen, and Appenzell joined the Alliance, so that by 1513 the Swiss Confederacy embraced thirteen cantons known as the "Thirteen Old Districts." Some of the later cantons to join the Confederation were city areas that became rather powerful politically. The ensuing conflict between rural and city cantons extended into the nineteenth century and almost led to civil war.

During its early existence as a nation Switzerland was forced to defend itself at intervals. In 1515 it suffered its first severe defeat at the hands of the French, which resulted in the breaking of Swiss power in north Italy. But later, in their wars against the Germans, French, and Italians, the Swiss acquired more territory, which was added to the Confederacy as the subject areas of Aargau, Tessin, and Waadt. Still other cantons were added as allied or associated areas. The cantons of Graubünden, Wallis, and Geneva were of this type. Their inhabitants were free, but in the Swiss state they did not have equal rights with the "Thirteen Old Districts." The lack of uniformity in government in the various cantons led to confusion. A firm central government was almost entirely lacking; and each canton was more or less independent, had its own money and its own rules, and could do almost anything it desired.

Religion along with military prowess became a keynote in the sequence of Swiss political history. The Reformation of Martin Luther strongly influenced Switzerland. In the city of Zürich the former priest Zwingli became the spiritual leader of the Swiss Reformation, which by 1523 had spread over most of the city cantons. Some years later Geneva became even a greater center of the Reformation than Zürich, and from this city the doctrines of the French reformer Calvin emanated to England. Out of the teachings of these two great reformers grew many religious quarrels among various sections of

Switzerland. A severe military defeat by the French at Marignano (1515) and the loss of Swiss unity through the Reformation so weakened the country that it was forced to withdraw from European politics and become a small, neutral country. Formal independence from the Holy Roman Empire came in 1648.

In 1798 Switzerland was conquered by Napoleon and made a French vassal state. Napoleon's invasion of Switzerland, although resented by the Swiss, ultimately proved beneficial, for Napoleon abolished the subject cantons and gave equal rights to all. The internal strife that had weakened the country for centuries gradually ceased, and Switzerland became revitalized to the extent that it was able to free itself from French control in 1814. After a period of confusion the adoption of a constitution in 1848 served to unify the country.

Present administration. There are now twenty-two cantons, all having equal rights and united to one another by an elastic rule. In internal politics the cantons are autonomous, but in foreign policy they have surrendered all rights. The Constitution of 1848 was revised in 1874, but the basic principles—complete internal democracy and absolute external neutrality—remained the same and are still in operation today.

Switzerland has a bicameral legislature: a State Council, to which each canton sends two members; and a National Council, with membership elected according to population. However, the execution of laws is in the hands of seven Federal Councilors who are elected by the parliament for a term of four years. Each of these Councilors is the head of a special department of the government. Further, a member serves as President for a period of one year, during which time he holds no special power conferred by this position. In order to represent all language groups proportionately it is customary to elect four German-Swiss, two French-Swiss, and one Italian-Swiss Councilor. Since there are two major religious groups within the country, Protestant and Roman Catholic, it is also customary to see that both groups are properly represented. In this way no minority language or religious group has reason for complaint, and all parts of the country are treated equitably.

* For the sake of uniformity the German names of Swiss cantons are used in this chapter. The only exception is Geneva (Génève in French; Genf in German).

Human Factors

Population. Switzerland with an area of slightly less than 16,000 square miles has a population of more than four million people unevenly distributed over the country. The most sparsely populated section is the broad Alpine region, south of a line drawn between the eastern ends of Lakes Geneva and Constance (map, page 184). Although this region comprises three fifths of the total land area, adverse physical and economic conditions limit the population to one fifth the total for the country.

The average density of population in the mountain cantons is about 25 persons per square mile. In the cantons of the Jura, where physical conditions are less severe, the population density is between 25 and 125 persons per square mile, and on the Swiss Plateau there are between 200 and 600 persons per square mile.

Cities. Switzerland has four cities of over 100,000 population, and twenty-three others with a population above 10,000. Most of these lie in the plateau region. Several of the cities are well known either as educational centers or as the seats of institutions that have national or international interest. In many instances they are high in tourist appeal, such as those that have attractive locations along the shores of Switzerland's picturesque lakes.

Bern (130,000), the capital, lies close to the German-French language boundary. It is the only national capital in Europe that is greatly outranked in population by other cities in the same country. *Zürich* (336,000), the largest city, is the metropolitan center of German-speaking Switzerland. Because of its size and strategic location it is a focal point for railways and is the country's leading air transportation center. As an educational city, it has the country's only technical university. *Basel* (162,000), which formerly was the home of the Bank for International Settlements, is the leading port of entry (Rhine River) for goods consigned to Switzerland. Its position in the Rhine Valley also makes it an important railroad center. *Geneva* (124,000) was the site of the League of Nations and the International Labor Office. Just as Basel is a gateway city to Germany, so Geneva is a gateway to France. The city's location in French-speaking Switzerland adjacent to France gives it a cultural life more closely akin to Paris or Lyon than to Zürich or other German-speaking Swiss cities. *Lausanne* (93,000) houses the Supreme Court of Switzerland. *Luzern* (55,000) which is located on Lake of Luzern, is the administrative center of Swiss railways. It has the reputation of being one of the most beautiful of Swiss cities.

Of the seven universities in Switzerland, four are located in the predominantly French-speaking cities of Geneva, Lausanne, Fribourg, and Neuchâtel. The remaining three are located in the predominantly German-speaking cities of Zürich, Bern, and Basel.

Since each of the large cities in the various sections of the country has a particular distinction, urban and sectional friction is greatly reduced.

Languages. The Swiss are a multilingual people, reflecting the diverse ethnic groups from which they have descended. Approximately seventy-two per cent of the population speak German or Germanic dialects; twenty per cent, French; six per cent, Italian; and one per cent, Romansh. All four languages are official. German is spoken by the inhabitants of the north, east, and central parts of the country. French is spoken in the western part, and Italian mainly by the inhabitants of canton Tessin. Some 45,000 inhabitants of the mountainous and relatively isolated southeastern canton of Graubünden speak Romansh (see the following map for

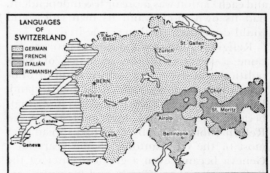

language distribution). The Swiss government is trying to preserve this language, and in 1937 it was made the fourth national language of the country. In some places the French-German language boundary is surprisingly sharp. This is especially true in the city of Fribourg, where the lower part of the town is German-speaking and the upper part of the town is French-speaking. All cities along this boundary line use both a German and a French name.

In spite of the four languages the Swiss state constitutes a strong political unit. No language is legally more important than the others. All laws and public notices are printed in three languages, and in parliament each speaker may use his native tongue. In order to maintain this equality of languages, all Swiss children must learn in school at least one language other than that spoken in his home. In addition to native languages many Swiss have become familiar with English in order to facilitate the tourist industry. Signs of interest to foreign visitors frequently are printed in German, French, Italian, and English.

Religions. There was never any real conflict between the people of Switzerland over the question of languages, but for a time there was much strife over religious differences. For three centuries, from the early 1500's through part of the 1800's, bitter quarrels and civil wars during certain periods almost caused the disintegration of the Confederacy. Only the desire for freedom from external influences enabled it to survive. Since the adoption of the Federal Constitution of 1848, however, which included the guarantee of full religious liberty, harmony has prevailed.

There is no correlation between language and religion. Many German-speaking cantons are dominantly Roman Catholic, and many French-speaking ones adhere to Protestantism. (See the map directly below and

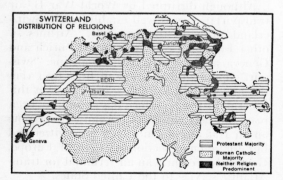

SWITZERLAND
DISTRIBUTION OF RELIGIONS

Protestant Majority

Roman Catholic
Majority

Neither Religion
Predominant

compare with the map on page 186). Protestants, who comprise approximately fifty-seven per cent of the population, in general, inhabit the cantons of the Jura Mountains and the Swiss Plateau; and the Roman Catholics,

who compose forty-one per cent of the population, are dominant in the cantons of the Alps. However, no canton is completely Protestant or Catholic, and over a period of time there has been much intermixture of faiths, with resulting shifts in the religious zones.

Foreign groups. A perennial problem confronting the Swiss is the large number of foreigners within the country. At one time the ratio of foreigners to citizens was one to seven, and although it has gradually declined to about one to ten it is still one of the highest in Europe. Germans, Italians, French, and Austrians form the larger foreign groups. These alien groups are most numerous along the border cantons. In certain cities they make up as much as one third of the population, and in several valleys of Tessin they actually form a majority. Despite the belief by many Swiss that the alien problem is a political, economic, and social danger, it is well to remember that in Switzerland people are quickly assimilated.

Economic Development

Agriculture. Approximately twenty-five per cent of the area of Switzerland is unproductive. Adverse climate, poor soil, and steep slopes have made it necessary to leave about ten per cent of the total land area in forest growth and forty-five per cent in Alpine meadows and grasslands. Of the three broad regions of Switzerland, the relatively low Swiss Plateau has the lowest percentage of waste land, and it is here that agriculture is most intensively developed.

For the country as a whole less than twenty per cent of the land is arable. Other than on the Swiss Plateau the raising of crops is largely confined to several low-lying valleys of the Jura Mountains and the Rhone Valley, where the most favorable conditions appear. Dairying and forestry are the dominant activities of the people in the Jura, although there are many vineyards on the southeastern slopes. Dairying, forestry, and a great tourist industry distinguish the Alpine region.

Before the period when grain could be imported cheaply, Switzerland grew more than it does now. Vineyards have also been reduced, but these reductions in acreages of grain and grapes have stimulated an increased production of vegetables, fruits, and dairy products that has resulted in a better balanced agricultural economy for the country.

Pastoral activities are common to all regions in Switzerland, but contrary to general belief the greatest number of dairy cattle is in the plateau region. The interesting practice of driving cattle up the mountain sides in spring and down again in autumn (called "Transhumance") enables the Swiss to utilize pastures on the Alpine slopes during the warm season when they are free from snow.

In the production of potatoes, fruits, vegetables, and dairy products Switzerland is almost self-sufficient, but about one third of the required grain must be imported. There is also a serious deficiency of meat, since the greater proportion of Switzerland's cattle consists of dairy breeds. During World War II Switzerland was forced to create a merchant marine to insure the flow of foodstuffs from abroad. The registry of the vessels was at Basel on the Rhine.

Industry. The major resources that make an industrial economy possible for Switzerland are the abilities of its people rather than the possession of a bountiful physical landscape. Skillful workmanship, ingenuity, and boundless energy are the mainstays of the country's enviable reputation in manufacturing ability and quality production.

Small deposits of coal are remotely located and of such poor quality that they are of little importance except in extreme cases. The country also lacks other useful minerals or metals with the exception of building stone, sand, and clay. Her greatest physical resource for industry is a plentiful supply of potential waterpower, made available by heavy precipitation, snow-covered mountains, steep slopes, lakes, rivers, and streams. Thus Switzerland seemed destined to a predominantly agricultural economy. Nevertheless about forty-five per cent of the people are engaged in industry, and in relation to its area and population it is one of the leading industrial (and commercial) nations of the world.

Because nine tenths of all raw materials are normally imported, the Swiss cannot produce cheap goods requiring much raw material in their manufacture. They must produce articles having a high value per unit of weight, and thus sell their skill. As a result, Switzerland is famous for the manufacture of fine watches, beautiful silk textiles, high-grade cotton textiles, exquisite embroidery, electric motors, and even steam engines. Possession of the skills needed for the production of these goods is an outgrowth of the consistent policy of neutrality since the sixteenth century. This course led to the influx of refugees from neighboring countries who brought with them various crafts, such as watch making and silk weaving, for which Switzerland has become now world famous. Most of the country's manufactured goods are made for export, which is of primary importance to Switzerland in order to approach a balance of trade.

Transportation. Railways, about ninety-five per cent of which are electrified, form the backbone of Switzerland's transportation system. Because of topography and economic development, the railway network is best developed in the plateau area. Between Lake Geneva and Lake Constance main lines operate to link western with eastern Europe. Many transverse lines tie in most of the towns and cities of the plateau. Elsewhere, rail lines are less numerous because of difficult topography. Main through-lines joining northern Europe with southern Europe follow transverse valleys, climb over passes, and wind through tunnels. Over these railways Switzerland imports her food supplies and raw materials, and exports her manufactured goods. Where railroads are lacking, the Swiss have constructed highways connecting one valley with another, so that no town or village, even in the high Alps, is really isolated except during the winter season of heavy snows.

Although disrupted by World War II, air transportation was well established in Switzerland prior to that struggle. Airlines of other European countries served Zürich and Geneva, and the Swiss national airline, "Swissair," operated a network of lines over central and western Europe. Since the war this general air route pattern has essentially been re-established, and Zürich promises to become an air traffic center not only for Switzerland but for a large section of Central Europe. Geneva is presently an air terminal for trans-Atlantic service to the United States.

Trade. Since Switzerland must import so much food for her people and raw material for her industries, the country normally has an unfavorable balance of trade. Value of imports generally exceeds value of exports by thirty per cent. However, this unfavorable condition is partly offset by interest from foreign investments and by the tourist industry. The latter is so well developed that it normally attracts tens of thousands of visitors, who leave behind over a hundred million dollars annually.

Political Factors

Price of neutrality. Switzerland's inland position inflicts great hardships upon the people during time of war. Unfortunately, all four nations with which the country has a common boundary have been embroiled in the last two major world conflicts. As a neutral, her deficiency in food production and a lack of minerals and metals place Switzerland in a precarious position, for her entire economic structure is based on foreign trade.

During World War II Switzerland increased the area of land under cultivation to a slight degree, with the result that the country was nearly self-sufficient in the production of potatoes, fruits, and vegetables. Nevertheless, even with a slight increase in grain production and a reduction in caloric consumption per person, about one third of the grain supply still had to be imported. There was also a sharp shortage of meat. By means of commercial agreements with Germany, Switzerland was able to obtain from German-dominated Europe and through German-occupied ports, the necessary goods to keep its people alive. Using her newly created merchant marine, she secured coal from Germany, ore from Sweden, and foodstuffs, especially grain, from overseas. In exchange for these imported goods, Switzerland, with permission from both belligerents, shipped part of her domestic production abroad. These exports consisted mainly of watches, textiles, shoes, and millinery.

Switzerland, like other neutral countries of Europe, was subjected to German pressure, and although she was not able to maintain strict neutrality, she did her best to adhere to the principle. In order to do this the Swiss government reserved the right to approve all German orders for goods. Sometimes orders were altered in order to live up to at least the letter of neutrality. For example, the Swiss could refuse to process German leather into soldiers' boots, but agree to manufacture it into children's shoes, or refuse to repair tanks or army trucks, but agree to repair German automobiles.

Defense of the country. In 1815 Russia, Great Britain, Prussia, Austria, and Portugal guaranteed the inviolability and neutrality of Switzerland. On various occasions since then, the great powers of Europe have acknowledged the neutrality of Switzerland, but in time of war there need not be a just cause for the invasion of a country as long as it is advantageous to the aggressor nation.

Switzerland, situated entirely within German-dominated Europe, for one reason or another was always faced with the possibility of invasion during this most recent conflict. Evidently it was not advantageous enough for Germany or any other country to violate the neutrality of this small, mountainous republic. If she had been attacked, Switzerland, in spite of her small size, would have defended herself not only with words, but with action.

Switzerland has a militia rather than a standing army. Each Swiss youth is obliged by law to start rifle practice when a schoolboy and at the age of twenty to enter military training for about three months. He must then serve for a period of two or three weeks each year for several years, with his liability of being called to the colors for active duty during the time he is between eighteen and sixty years of age.

Each militiaman keeps his military equipment at home and can be mobilized very quickly. In peacetime the active Swiss army consists of nine divisions of about 16,000 men each. In addition there are four mountain brigades, each consisting of about 12,000 men. Men of the mountain brigade are trained especially for high mountain fighting to prepare them for the defense of strategic positions in the Alps. The Swiss mobilization of 1939, which called up 650,000 men, was completed in two days.

Switzerland has expended huge sums of money on fortifications in the Alps, Jura, and along the Rhine frontier. During World War II, anti-aircraft batteries were scattered all over the country and fired on both Axis and Allied aircraft. Tunnels, mountain railroads, and strategic places were mined, and barbed-wire entanglements were erected around lake shores to aid in fighting off possible lake landings.

As a successful neutral, Switzerland has

for years been a haven of refuge in war. During the past two major European wars many humanitarian services were rendered to the unfortunate victims of the strife. Wounded prisoners of war were cared for, and their exchange was effected. Prison camps were inspected. Thousands of children from war-torn countries were cared for, and a haven was provided for thousands of war refugees from neighboring countries. Switzerland serves as headquarters for the International Red Cross, and following World War I the city of Geneva was selected as the home of the League of Nations.

Switzerland and Neutrality are synonymous.

LIECHTENSTEIN

Liechtenstein, a tiny remnant of feudal Europe, is closely associated with Switzerland and the two have a customs union. This independent state, with an area of sixty-five square miles, lies between Switzerland and Austria. Most of the 11,000 inhabitants are German in origin and speech and embrace the Roman Catholic faith. Although much of its terrain is mountainous, its interests are chiefly agricultural.

The Principality of Liechtenstein was founded in 1719 and formed part of the Holy Roman Empire. From 1806–15 it was included in the Rhine Confederation and later was part of the German Confederation.

Since 1866 the little state has been independent, and since 1867 it has had no army. Until 1919 Liechtenstein was closely allied with Austria, but in 1921 it adopted Swiss currency, and since 1924 it has been included in the Swiss Customs Union. Today Switzerland administers both its postal and its telegraph systems.

Lacking resources in any appreciable amount, and not on or commanding any strategically-located territory, the Principality attracted no special attention during World War II. For all apparent purposes it was a part of Switzerland rather than a unit in Fortress Europe during the conflict.

| # Italy in the Mediterranean

THE position of Italy on the central of Europe's three great southern peninsulas is one of the most significant in the world. Together with insular Sicily and Sardinia the Italian peninsula thrusts southward into the central Mediterranean, virtually dividing this million-square-mile sea into two basins. The long western coast of Italy is in a position to dominate the 328,000 square miles of the western basin. In turn, the Adriatic and Sicilian coasts are well placed to control the 644,000 square miles of the eastern basin. All east-west transit in the Mediterranean must funnel through the Sicilian Channel or the strategic Strait of Messina (see the maps above and on page 198). Moreover, this region of narrow seas, known as the Mediterranean "Waist," is the only approach or "near bridge" between Europe and Africa in the central Mediterranean. The gateways at Gibraltar and Suez are approximately a thousand miles distant to the west and east respectively.

From this central position in the vast Mediterranean Sea rose empires and imperial domination. In one era Rome dominated all of the known Western world. At another

ITALY AND THE MEDITERRANEAN

time Venice and Genoa extended vigorous control over part of the sea and its encircling shores. Of more recent date modern Italy, from Cavour to Mussolini, sprang to imperial position. In the interval between the imperial domination and sway of ancient Rome and modern Italy, many a nation about the Mediterranean and in Europe has sought and fought for a position on, or control of, the Italian peninsula and the strategic lands immediately beyond. In early historic periods

191

Phoenicia, Carthage, Greece, the Saracens, and Germanic tribes invaded Italy from the north or south or from both directions. Later on, the Turks, Spanish, and French had their day on and about Italian lands. In modern times states like Great Britain, France, Germany, Yugoslavia, Albania, and Greece have shared in the holding of strategic positions about the Italian lands, and most recently Soviet Russia has made a determined bid for a foothold in Tripoli.

The close proximity of Europe and Africa to Sicily and the southern tip of Italy has long oriented north-south movements of armies and peoples. As late as World War II the Mediterranean "Waist" was bridged first by the Germans in their North African desert campaigns and then by the Allied forces in their initial penetration of Fortress Europe.

The Italian People

Italy was first inhabited by dark-skinned native tribes. From one of these tribes, the Itali, came the name for the peninsula and nation. Subsequently, Italy was subjected to many folk migrations that terminated in the peninsula, and from these came part of the present stock. These migrants were mainly Germanic peoples who for the most part found homes in northern Italy. Although many later military invasions swept over the peninsula from nations both to the east and west, they had little effect on the Italian race.

While the Italians are evolving toward ethnic unity, they already have achieved two marked cultural uniformities that have gone far toward making them a strong people: a common language and a common religion. Except in several small areas near the border Italian prevails throughout the country. Further, Italian is the dominant language in certain regions beyond the national territory, such as parts of Switzerland, Alpine districts in France, and the Trieste area. Roman Catholicism is the almost universal religion (99.6 per cent of the population), but other creeds may be freely practiced without interference. The presence of the Holy See in the Vatican City exerts a strong spiritual influence over the state. Both language and religion will continue as dominant factors in maintaining Italian unity, and under a more

generous geographical environment might well have helped to foster a powerful state.

Historical sequence. Historically, Italy rose from legendary Rome. The Roman Empire, by virtue of its vigorous people and geographic advantages in the Mediterranean world, successfully challenged all rivals and became one of the few great empires of history. Until about the fifth century A.D. Rome dominated the nations of the Mediterranean and her influences extended over many of the peoples of Europe and the Near East.

Rome fell because of social degeneracy within, and the invasion of active barbaric tribes of the north and east. From the fall of Rome until 1870 the Italian peninsula was unable to achieve political unity and was subjected to constant strife, both from the invasions from almost every nation of the Mediterranean and from feudal states that sprang up in the peninsula itself. In the Renaissance, however, Italy made an outstanding cultural contribution.

Although such powerful city states as Venice and Genoa succeeded in dominating large areas of the Mediterranean, they were bitterly opposed to each other and made no progress whatsoever toward restoring unity. Finally, favored by the struggles, jealousies, and recurrent conflicts among the great powers of Europe, Italy completed the steps of unification in 1870.

Despite her defensive alliance with Austria and Germany, Italy elected to enter World War I in 1915 on the side of the Allies. Following victory in 1918 her requests for control of strategic Mediterranean positions and colonial expansion were largely ignored at Versailles. Italy nursed her resentment at being thus snubbed internationally. This grudge was a contributing factor in the launching of a nationalistic program of growing intensity under the leadership of Mussolini, beginning in 1922 and continuing until 1943. At first the Fascist state was fairly tolerant and cooperated with the League of Nations. Later, however, encouraged by the indecision of the Allied Powers, the growing weakness of the League of Nations, and the patronage of Germany, the Fascists spurred on by Mussolini became ruthlessly imperialistic.

Entering World War II in 1940 as an ally of Germany, Italy in 1943 surrendered to the

Allies while a large part of the country was still occupied by the Germans. As a result, both Sicily and the Peninsula became battlegrounds. Italy, like her Axis partners, had neither the size nor natural resources for prolonged modern warfare. Recovery from the disasters of World War II will be mainly a matter of material reconstruction and rehabilitation. At the same time the Italian people will not need the conversion and reconversion so necessary for the German Nazis and Shintoistic Japanese.

Population. There are about fifty-five million Italians in the postwar world. Forty-five million are in Italy; almost ten million are in other countries, especially France, Tunisia, Argentina, Brazil, and the United States; and almost seventy thousand are in the former Italian colonies in Africa. Between the world wars no real irredenta (certain neighboring regions that, though largely Italian in population, were subject to other governments) existed beyond her boundaries. Italians in other nations such as the United States have, by their thrift, culture, and industry, been of great service both to their adopted country and to Italy. The major share of Italy's international income (income from abroad) has come from those Italians who emigrated to other lands of opportunity and sent their savings home.

Another aspect in Italian population has been its rapid growth. Beginning with twenty-eight million people in 1881, shortly after the unification of the nation, the population rose to about thirty-three million in 1901, thirty-five million in 1911, thirty-eight million in 1921, and nearly forty-four million (estimated) in 1940.* In addition, about ten million had emigrated to other lands. This leaves a burden for Italy proper of an average of about 388 people per square mile. Such a population density greatly exceeds that of other Mediterranean nations, including France, Spain, Yugoslavia, Turkey, and Greece.

The huge population, its steady growth, its congestion in plains and cities, and its major dependence on the land for subsistence constitute Italy's greatest national question and one which has repercussions in the international field. It has been charged that the re-

* About one and one-half million of the 1921 population was added by peace treaty adjustments.

strictions placed on Italian emigration shortly following World War I were one of the many causes leading toward World War II. Italy may be criticized for the prewar measures she took to provide for her people, but the only attitude taken by other nations was negative.

Three constructive measures are possible in order to help Italy in the postwar world. First, there are many nations where there is room for Italian emigrants, and they could be allowed and encouraged to emigrate. The Italians make valuable citizens, and in many lands they currently make up a thrifty and industrious segment of the population. Second, every feasible opportunity for trade could be given Italy. Third, Italy herself could seek to develop occupations other than farming; this move should be facilitated in order to divert a part of the present rural population into industry.

Space Relationships

Area. Italy's national area is about 117,000 square miles, or approximately equal to the combined areas of Ohio, Kentucky, and Indiana. Among the Mediterranean nations, Turkey with 296,000 square miles, France with 213,000 square miles, and Spain with 195,000 square miles are all much larger. Owing to Italy's naturally defined area in Europe there was no great change in her size after World War I, and she was not greatly changed in the adjustments following World War II. In her national unification program between 1848 and 1870, Italian ambitions were mainly limited to consolidation within the peninsular area south of the Alpine divide and in Sicily; and, succeeding largely in the accomplishment of this goal, the political area has been relatively stable ever since.

Prior to World War II, Italian statesmen referred to their national territory as relatively small when considering their huge population and comparatively small when pointing out other of the larger countries of Europe, especially Spain, France, and Germany. They considered this small size in formulating their policy toward trade, emigration, and colonial expansion. Economically speaking, however, Italy's size is not her primary restricting factor. Her limitations in mineral resources, a high percentage of mountainous land, and adverse climatic conditions all precede restriction in area as handicaps to the achievement of a stronger national economy. Nevertheless, from the modern military point of view, Italy's small area makes her extremely vulnerable. Of major import is the fact that as a peninsula she lacks depth, that is, distance from boundary to center. In large part because of her position, form, and size, she was selected as the first of the Axis nations to be invaded in World War II.

Generally common to small size is a marked feeling of insecurity in *national consciousness,* but this reaction does not appear to have affected the masses in Italy. Their maritime contacts have been adequate to overcome in large measure any worries about the limitations of small size. As is often true in pelagic (sea-located) nations, the Italian people tend to be broadminded and cosmopolitan. Furthermore, they never were wholly overcome by the intense nationalism that so bitterly afflicted many of the smaller nations. Neither have they entirely succumbed to the feeling of inferiority in relation to other countries.

Form and boundaries. The geographer considers Italy a geographical entity. In form the country is a peninsula, and her political land boundaries in the north are often exclusively mountain divide. The objectives in the national unification of Italy between 1848 and 1870 were thus largely defined by nature, which has influenced her boundary policy in Europe.

Italy has 2,400 miles of Mediterranean coastline. This equals one mile of coast for every fifty square miles of national territory. Such a high proportion of maritime frontage has on the one hand made necessary a naval policy for Italy; on the other it has freed Italy from many of the vexing problems of land boundaries, both from the military and diplomatic angles. Even though the number of ports and harbors is limited by the nature of this coast, ready contact with the sea has been of great value to Italy in trade, fishing, recreation, and resorts, and is a stimulating influence on the character of the Italian people. Some of the small islands along her coast are famous: Elba, the first exile of Napoleon; Capri, of tourist renown; and the Lipari Islands, historically used for penal establishments.

On her land boundaries Italy is separated from her neighbors by the high crest of the Alps. This natural border has favored Italy in at least one respect: fewer minority group problems than in most European countries have existed to obstruct progress toward national unification. Although the Alps constitute a definite natural boundary, they are at the same time breached by passes that have always permitted trade or travel and exchange of ideas with the rest of Europe. Likewise, numerous invasions by foreign armies and folk movements prove that the Alps are not an absolute protective barrier.

Through the use of coastal plains, river valleys, passes, and tunnels, Italy has established numerous railway contacts between it and adjacent European countries (see the map on facing page for railroads). Two trunk railroad lines extend westward into France, one along the coast via Nice and the other over the Alps via the Mont Cenis tunnel. To the north, railroad routes reach Switzerland via the Simplon and St. Gotthard tunnels, and Austria by way of Brenner Pass. The eastern contacts to the Balkan Peninsula and the Danube plains are made easier by passes through the Julian Alps and Carso Plateau, much lower than the high Alpine passes and tunnels to the north. Three railway lines breach the mountain barrier on the old Yugoslav boundary. The historically famous Pear Tree pass (elevation 2,897 feet) connects the Mediterranean with peoples and countries of central and eastern Europe.

In the northeast Italy finds her most serious land boundary problem. Here trade and military routes from the Danubian plains and the Balkans lead over an easily traversed route to the year-round warm waters of the Adriatic (see the map on facing page). From the days of the Roman Empire this border has presented a constant hazard to national and international stability. Central Europe, and even Russia, have sought access to this trade outlet. Here the Slav peoples of central and eastern Europe reached through to settle in Italy and later gave the unified country an annoying minority problem in the province of Venezia Giulia (the Istria area), where they became around one-half million strong.

Just how this strategically, ethnically, and commercially important boundary of Italy would be stabilized was a problem for the statesmen. After World War II Italy was prepared to cede Fiume and Zara to Yugo-

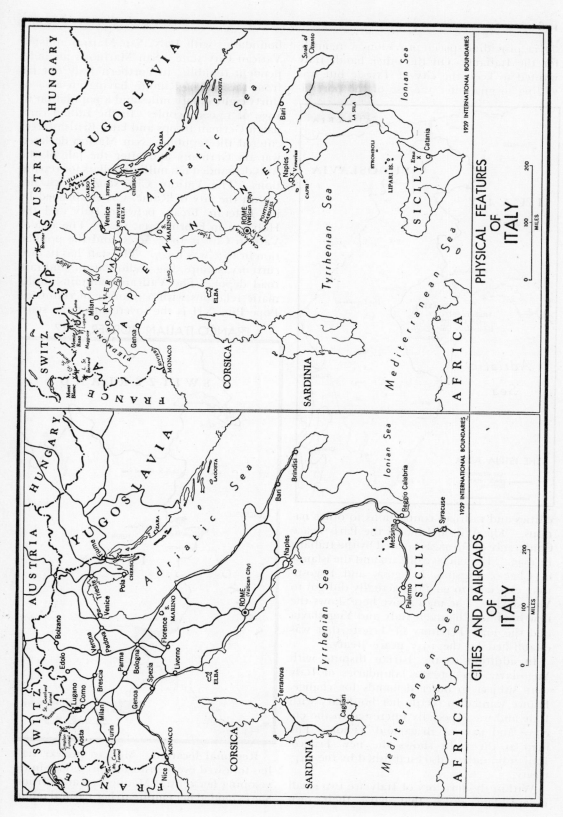

PHYSICAL FEATURES
OF
ITALY

1939 INTERNATIONAL BOUNDARIES

CITIES AND RAILROADS
OF
ITALY

1939 INTERNATIONAL BOUNDARIES

195

slavia, providing special provisions were made for the Italians. On the other hand, Italy wanted to keep the city of Trieste but was willing to guarantee the use of the port fa-

THE ISTRIA AREA

----- 1937 BOUNDARY
——— PEACE TREATY BOUNDARY

0   10   20
MILES

cilities and railroad connections to other nations. The Wilson Line of the Paris Peace Conference of 1919 was favored by the Italians in 1945. The enclave of Zara and the islands of Cherso, Lussino, Pelagosa, and Lagosta were expected to go (and actually did go) to Yugoslavia. The map above here shows the new boundary between Italy and Yugoslavia and the Free Territory of Trieste that was established by the 1947 peace treaty.

In addition to the Istrian dispute with Yugoslavia, the prewar boundaries of Italy were subject to other demands for change. France wanted to rectify her boundary with Italy and was especially interested in the enclave and pass of Briga and Tenda. The map at the right shows the new Franco-Italian boundary also established by the 1947 treaty.

Within the territory of Italy are two small independent states that have their own

boundaries with Italy: San Marino and the Vatican City state. San Marino is an independent republic, in northern Italy not far from the city of Rimini, having an area of thirty-eight square miles and a population in 1939 of 14,000 people. In the Italian campaign German troops and later British forces entered the republic. San Marino declared war on Germany and after the fall of the Axis demanded ten million dollars for reparations. The Vatican City state, which lies within the city of Rome, was established by the Lateran Treaty between Italy and the Holy See on February 11, 1929. The area of Vatican City is 108.7 acres, and the population in 1932 was 1,025. The state has its own currency, stamps, flag, radio station, and railroad depot. The Vatican maintains diplomatic relations with a number of countries. Pope Pius XII is the sovereign of the state.

FRANCO-ITALIAN BORDER, 1947

Territory ceded to France by Italy at the Peace Treaty, 1947

0 10 20 30 40 50
MILES

Regional location. Modern prewar Italy has followed every historical precedent in developing her central Mediterranean position. She extended her empire to her natural **moun-**

tain boundaries in Europe and toward Africa and Asia. She repeatedly challenged British and French imperial positions at Toulon, Ajaccio, Bizerte, Tunis, and Malta, and sought to control the Adriatic coast, disputing it with Yugoslavia, Albania, and Greece. She fortified strategic positions, built naval bases, and developed harbors at Genoa, Spezia, Naples, Messina, Brindisi, Venice, Trieste, and Pola. Pantelleria near Malta in the Mediterranean was also fortified, as were the Pelage Islands of Linosa and Lampedusa in the same general vicinity (see the map on page 198). Furthermore, the Italians built a navy that by 1939 ranked fourth among the nations of Europe; constructed a merchant marine of 1,336 vessels of 100 tons or over that ranked fourth among the great merchant fleets of Europe; and raised a huge army in an effort to protect their peninsular corridor and empire. It is significant for the future that as early as 1925 the military aspects of this imperial program cost the Italian government 3,611,000,000 lire as against 2,902,000,000 spent during the same year for the combined program of public works, social betterment, and public instruction. It was inevitable that Italy's enormous financial expenditures and imperial activities involve her in difficult international problems of finance and aggression.

In the present and foreseeable future there will be no diminution of the importance of the Italian position in the Mediterranean. This country with its 45,000,000 people is now, and will continue to be, a national and international problem of primary importance.

Count Antonio Cippico asserted in the 1920's about his country:

But unlike any other great Mediterranean Power, Italy is stretched like a bridge in the very center of that sea; its waters bathe all her coasts. Not only her liberty but her very life depends on the good will of those who hold the keys of Gibraltar and Suez, of those who have installed themselves, for imperial, not national needs, in Malta and Cyprus. More than forty-one millions of Italians could be starved in a few weeks if those who hold the gateways of the Mediterranean were suddenly to decide on hostilities and close those gates to the imports of grain, coal, fuel oils, and iron, of all the raw materials, in short, essential to the life of a modern civilized nation. In view of her geographical position, which makes her a pris-

oner in her own sea, her almost complete lack of raw materials, and her ever-expanding population, Italy is today the gravest problem of the Mediterranean.*

In like vein, Dino Grandi wrote in 1934:

Ours is a vital problem that involves our very existence and our future, a future of peace, tranquillity, and work for a population of 42 million souls, which will number 50 million in another fifteen years. Can this population live and prosper in a territory half the size of that of Spain and Germany and lacking raw materials and natural resources to meet its vital needs, pent up in a closed sea beyond which its commerce lies, a sea the outlets of which are owned by other nations, while yet others control the means of access . . . ?**

In the light of these statements concerning the regional location and the resultant foreign policy of Italy, it is not illogical to assert that had the other Allied powers been as considerate of Italy's position at Versailles at the close of World War I as they were of their own interests, a major cause of World War II might have been avoided. As to the present and future, this exposed location points to a number of essential lessons concerned with ways of serving the best interests of Italy and international stability.

(1) Proximity to the strategic positions about the "Waist" of the Mediterranean dictates that Italy's interests should be considered first concerning their control (see the map on page 198). The past indicates that it is natural for a state to seek control of both sides of neighboring straits as well as any strategic islands that might strengthen that control. At Malta British interests come into close proximity with those of Italy; at Tunisia French interests do likewise. At these places, where overlapping spheres of influence might jeopardize international harmony, there is need of accord through the medium of the United Nations. For Great Britain to state openly that her position in the Mediterranean is primarily to protect her imperial interests and to hold an advantage over potential European enemies cannot but provoke the Italian people and invite discord in international affairs.

* Count Antonio Cippico, *Italy,* Lectures at the Institute of Politics, New Haven (Yale University Press, 1926), p. 32.
**Dino Grandi, "The Foreign Policy of the Duce," *Foreign Affairs,* XII (1934), p. 566.

(2) It will eventually be necessary for the United Nations to arbitrate proportionately the rights and interests of the coastal nations about the Adriatic. This long channel reaching farthest into central Europe at the lowest breach of the Alps is of international importance as well as vital to the immediate interests of Italy, Yugoslavia, Albania, and

THE MEDITERRANEAN WAIST

Greece.   Between the world wars of this century Italy obtained control of the Adriatic: she acquired Venezia Giulia in the Treaty of St. Germain with Austria in 1919; received the enclave of Zara in Yugoslavia, and the islands of Cherso, Lussino, Lagosta, and Pelagosa in the Adriatic in the Treaty of Rapallo with Yugoslavia in 1920; gained possession of the strategic island of Saseno across the Strait of Otranto guarding the entrance to Valona Bay in Albania; annexed Fiume in the Agreement of Rome in 1924; and seized Albania on Good Friday, 1939.   In a quarrel with Greece over Corfu, the Greeks retained the island. The Adriatic is an important outlet for all of central Europe and in the future cannot fail

to escape attention by the Soviet Union.

(3) The facts that from two thirds to three quarters of Italy's maritime commerce passes by Gibraltar and that the Italian merchant marine is a heavy user of the Suez Canal argue for Italian participation in the control of these outlets. Internationalizing such strategic waterways will go a long way in quieting fears and satisfying national pique and pride.

From an international point of view, Italy should be allowed and encouraged to take full advantage of her geographical location: first, by continued development of a merchant marine; second, by participation in a commercial aviation program; and third, by being relieved of the huge cost of military forces maintained in order that she might hold the balance of power in the Mediterranean.

A strong position in commercial aviation is assured by the fact that within a very few hours' flight from cities of the Italian Peninsula there are at least 130 European cities of 100,000 or more inhabitants, with a total population of nearly 60,000,000 people. In view of the attractions of Italian climate and her development in valuable specialized products that can be carried by air transport, this advantageous position can be calculated as an invaluable source of revenue and trade. Within a year after the close of World War II rapid strides were being made under the auspices of Allied nations toward the inauguration of an internal airline. By July, 1947, seven such airlines were operating; and, later, restrictions against any international routes were removed.

Physical Factors

Relief.   Italy, like the state of California, has numerous types of surface features. Rough to rugged terrain is most characteristic of the landscape, however, for no part of Italy is without mountains or strong mountain influences. Hills and mountains make up seventy-nine per cent of the country, whereas plains amount to only twenty-one per cent of the surface features. With the exception of the broad Po Valley in the north the plains not only constitute a very minor percentage of the total surface, but they are small and detached.

REGIONS.   With such a topographic variety, generalizations are meaningless. However, four major divisions can be readily discerned by studying the map on page 195: the minor distinctions in each can be related to the major division. These divisions are, first, the Alps, in a huge crescent that, with the Carso Plateau in Venezia Giulia, completely established the northern boundary of Italy before World War II; second, the Po Valley and related basin lands; third, the Apennine chain extending the entire length of the peninsula and ending in the La Sila Plateau, the toe of the boot; and finally, the perimeter of coastal plains extending more or less narrowly about the entire seaward margin of the peninsula. The central mountain areas of Sicily and Sardinia may be considered with the Apennine chain; the coastal plains of these islands may be classed with the coastal plains of the mainland.

Alps. The Alps have magnificent relief rising directly from 600 feet in height on the floor of the Po basin to crests and peaks from 10,000 to 12,000 feet and over in height everywhere except in the east. Towering peaks of 14,000 feet are common, and such giants as Mont Blanc and Monte Rosa exceed 15,000 feet. This abrupt wall enclosing Italy on the north is a powerful climatic barrier against cold air masses from the north. It is prevented from being an exclusive barrier economically and strategically only by numerous glacial and stream-carved valleys. These valleys have cut natural highways and trail routes toward relatively low passes between the perpetually snowbound and impassable peaks.

Brenner, St. Gotthard, and Simplon passes, the latter two undercut by long railway tunnels, are well known, but numerous other passes (among them, Great St. Bernard, Little St. Bernard, Mt. Cenis, St. Genèvre) provide breaches for penetrating or traversing the Alps. Near the base of the Alps in some of the river valleys are the world-renowned Italian lakes, formed, in part, by the gouging action of glaciers that once moved down from Alpine heights. The largest and most beautiful of these lakes are Garda, Como, Lugano, and Maggiore.

At first glance these rugged mountains would appear to be an unmitigated handicap to Italy. Naturally they do limit farming and hinder transportation, and the isolation and severe climate of the higher elevations exclude settlement altogether. On the other hand, however, unpopulated crests provide a natural and little disputed boundary for Italy. As an area of scenic grandeur, with an invigorating climate in summer and snow sports in winter, the constant recreational appeal of the Alps provides world-wide metropolitan contacts and a needed source of international income for Italy. And as a source of hydroelectric energy and water supply to the densely populated Po basin, the Alps are an economic asset of immense value. Further, soil material from the upper reaches of the Alpine streams is deposited as alluvium on the Po River lowlands.

The Alpine mountain land itself is not wholly useless. Grazing, forestry, dairying, and tree crops are upland enterprises of considerable value carried on by mountain folk in a wholesome environment. The southward facing warm slopes permit the growth of such hillside crops as grapes, olives, and figs. Mulberry trees occupy some of the lower slopes, providing the base for valuable silk production. On the east, however, the Alpine barrier breaks down to the lower Julian Alps and the low Carso Plateau. As this plateau is of limestone and has underground stream systems and many caves and sinkholes blocking its surface, its usefulness for any purpose is limited.

Po Valley. In striking contrast to the Alps is the productive and densely populated Po Valley. With but fifteen per cent of the total area this region holds nearly forty per cent of the Italian population, for the country's agricultural and industrial economies both have their greatest development here. Although toward the Po River delta to the east swamps handicap land use, few areas are more intensively and effectively farmed. Two lines of large and important cities parallel the Po, one on the Alpine and one on the Apennine side of the stream. Here they take advantage of the nearby sources of hydroelectric energy. Over the level surface is spread an efficient railway net. Augmenting the land transportation pattern, rivers and canals furnish additional means of transportation, provide relatively pure water for domestic use, and serve as a system of sewage disposal.

The Po basin may be broken down into two rather distinctive subregions: the lowland valley proper, and the piedmont uplands on either side at the base of the Alps and Apennine mountains. The piedmont,* while not high in elevation, is nevertheless more healthful than the valley lowlands, being free from foggy, chilly weather in winter.

Apennines. Like the Alps, the Apennines are a climatic, political, and economic divide and barrier, though on a smaller scale. Generally, they range from 2,000 to 5,000 feet in height but attain more than 9,000 feet in places. The western slopes of the Apennines have more rainfall, longer and larger river valleys, and are more heavily forested than the more arid eastern slopes. The political divide between provinces runs along the crest of the chain except in the extreme south, where Lucania and Calabria are almost wholly mountainous and the political division is more arbitrary.

Passes through the mountainous backbone of Italy have been formed by rivers and streams cutting their way back from both the east and west. As in the Alps, these low passage ways are utilized as connecting links between the Mediterranean and Adriatic coastal lands. At intervals, railways follow the more open valley routes and lower passes across the peninsula, tunnels and bridges being used wherever needed.

The northern Apennines are like the Alps in their value for water power, forestry, grazing, and slope agriculture. These possibilities decrease with the increasing aridity toward the south. On the average the Apennines have a relatively sparse population and are very limited in both industry and farming. Nevertheless, their slopes are intensively used compared to many other mountainous countries. Terracing and contouring are practiced to permit the production of such slope crops as grapes and at the same time prevent excessive erosion.

Sicily and Sardinia both have large mountainous areas associated with the Apennine chain, yet those of the former island are extensively used whereas those of the latter are not. Sicily has fertile limestone soil capable of storing water, and in contrast the soil of Sardinia does not prevent rainfall from running off rapidly or being absorbed to depths beyond the reach of crop roots.

Coastal plains. As north-south corridors of communication the coastal plain on each side of peninsular Italy is followed by rail and highway routes. On Sicily and Sardinia it also functions as an aid to the transportation pattern, but on a more limited scale.

The coastal plain is intensively used for farming along the drier Adriatic side, but because of swampiness it is intensively developed only at two places along the Tyrrhenian coast: the valley of the Arno from Florence to Livorno and the Campania plain around Naples. As the good drainage of former Roman times is being restored in the Pontine marshes and the valley of the Tiber about Rome, these areas are again being developed. The coastal margins of Sicily are among the most densely populated parts of Italy, but this is not true of Sardinia.

Notwithstanding a long and fairly irregular coastline, good natural harbors are not numerous in Italy. There has been little incentive in the limited hinterland of the peninsula or the islands to overcome coastal limitations by building better harbors except for strategic purposes.

VOLCANOES. Among special physiographic features the volcanoes and volcanic areas deserve mention. Throughout Italy's history they have periodically spelled calamity, but their provision of fertile and productive soil material and of tourist attractions has offset their destruction. Vesuvius at Naples has been the most distinctive in all three respects. Mt. Etna at nearly 11,000 feet has been a striking scenic feature but has not supplied the surrounding area with fertile soil material. Stromboli, outside the Messina straits, has been called the lighthouse of the Mediterranean because of the beacon-like glow from its fiery crater.

Climate. Italy's climate can conveniently be divided into three general types that are primarily dependent upon location (or exposure) and relief: first, an *Alpine type* prevails in the high Alps and high northern Apennines; second, a *continental type* characterizes the Po basin; and, third, a *Mediterranean type* marks the balance of the peninsula and the islands of Sicily and Sardinia.

REGIONAL CHARACTERISTICS. The low temperatures and very heavy precipitation of the Alps nearly exclude economic activities at the higher elevations but show their importance

---

* The term "piedmont," used here in reference to relief in general, is not to be confused with "Piedmont," a province of northern Italy located in the higher land of the upper Po basin around Turin.

as a source of water for the great rivers of Europe. Much of the precipitation is in the form of snow, which melts slowly and thus maintains a constant stream flow throughout the year. This dependable source of water supply and power is of inestimable value to the Po system with its many tributaries reaching up into Alpine heights.

As illustrative of the Po basin, Milan shows temperature and precipitation almost identical to stations of mid-continental United States, such as Indianapolis, with cool to cold winters and long, hot summers. This climate is ideal for corn, cereals, fruits and forages, vegetables, and animal husbandry. The long growing season, warm summer and fall temperatures, and abundant water enable rice to be produced and the mulberry to thrive for silk production. In winter the low-lying Po basin is actually colder than the sunny south-facing Alpine slopes to the north, for the rays of the sun strike them at a sharper angle.

Except for the higher Apennines and adjoining Po Valley, peninsular and insular Italy is truly Mediterranean. In many ways the area is similar to the coastal ranges and valleys of central and southern California. The summers are hot and dry, requiring irrigation for all but hardy crops and diminishing the water supply for other purposes. The winters are mild and rainy, except in the higher elevations of the Apennines, permitting winter vegetables to grow and the hardy cereals, such as rye and wheat, to thrive and mature for a spring harvest.

Although temperatures on the peninsula generally increase toward the south, the total annual rainfall not only decreases in this direction but is less effective because of higher evaporation. Rainfall is also less on the east side of mountains because the prevailing wind is from the west. In summer, under the influence of the high pressure of the horse latitudes, rainfall is everywhere light.

OTHER CHARACTERISTICS. Northern Italy is subject to strong winds from the Alps in winter. One of these winds, called the Bora, blows with great force down the Po Valley and on into the Adriatic. Southern Italy has a hot, dusty wind, known as the Sirocco, from the African deserts. It brings temperatures so high that readings of 95° F. have been observed at midnight.

Generally, however, the climate of Italy is stable and dependable, being free from exceptional extremes and destructive storms. Its superiority over the rest of Europe in the amount of sunshine is one of its most attractive features. Over the year there is an average of seven hours of sunlight a day. Even though winter months have far less sunshine than summer months, they are sunny compared with those in central and northern Europe. Because blue skies and bright days attract people to Italy from all over Europe, tourist revenue from places like the Italian Riviera attains considerable significance.

National Economy

Present conditions. For years to come, any discussion of Italy's economy must take into account the terrific disruptions of World War II. As one of the major battlefields the effects of the conflict were intensified in the country because of its dense population, its normal deficiency in many natural resources, and the loss and destruction of life and property associated with a small area subjected to the combat and looting attending war. Further, because of her central position in the Mediterranean, Italy suffered from both Allied and Axis invasions.

Before the war Italy had achieved, by great effort, about ninety-four per cent self-efficiency in food stuffs. During the war crop yields were greatly reduced, and since the war recovery has been handicapped by (1) the decrease in soil fertility, particularly in the matter of phosphates, imports of which were cut off; (2) the increase in plant diseases and pests that resulted from inability to procure insecticides and fungicides; (3) the decline in supplies and sources of breeding stock and good plant seed; (4) the loss of the country's market for specialty products; (5) the destruction of farm equipment and loss of draft animals; and (6) the lack of adequate labor and breakdown of labor morale. These are exemplary of the items suggesting the specific nature and seriousness of the early postwar situation in the field of agriculture, a condition that will affect Italy's geographic adjustment and political conditions for years to come.

In Italian industry the picture is even more confused. Before the war Italian manufacturing had come to depend upon hydroelectric energy to produce up to ninety per cent of its power. During the conflict many installations of motive force were either unavoidably or wantonly destroyed. With her geographic deficiencies in raw materials (and therefore machinery) Italy is at a handicap in any program of self-recovery. Moreover, help from outside sources can only be slow because of the world-wide need for the existing limited surpluses of raw materials and equipment and the available shipping space to transport them. Serious political issues, both national and international, will develop in a country of 45,000,000 people crowded into an area of about 117,000 square miles, suffering cruelly from the effects of war, if outside aid is not extended.

An analysis of Italy's national economy in the Mediterranean and the future prospects of the country, however, should not be solely based on the present near-chaos and confusion. This discussion will, therefore, now turn to Italy's normal methods of supporting herself as they influenced the country's welfare and progress up to World War II. Opportunities for the Italian people in the future are mainly based upon their ability to pick up the broken threads of this past economic pattern and weave them into an even stronger design.

Efficiency of land use. Italy's material standard of living is far below that of the United States. On the other hand, she is supporting an immense population within a small area at standards far above the wretchedness prevailing in many other countries, such as India and China. This record indicates that on the whole she is an efficient user of her domain. Considering the net results in per cent of land used and people supported, she far exceeds the efficiency of the United States in degree of utilization. Moreover, considering the handicaps of surface, climate, and soil fertility, Italy equals the best in Europe in the use of her land. To be sure, she has inherited bad practices from the past, particularly in land tenure, and her dire need has in many instances led to serious problems in soil erosion from deforestation and overgrazing. These shortcomings, however, are common to most nations.

Regardless of mountainous terrain ninety-two per cent of Italy's land is used in enterprises that are productive to a greater or lesser degree; only eight per cent is totally unproductive. More than two fifths (42 per cent, or 32,000,000 acres) is classed as arable and available for cropping. Special wooded growths, such as vineyards and orchards, occupy another seven and one-half per cent. For a land of such predominance of slope surface, the large per cent of cultivated land is significant and is accounted for only by such practices as swamp reclamation, terracing, contouring, and cultivation with hand tools.

AGRICULTURE. Farming engages the efforts of about half the workers, and approximately nineteen million of the country's total population of forty-five million depend directly upon the land for a living. In variety of crops Italy equals any nation in the world, regardless of size, and in many instances is among the leading nations in total production of certain crops.

Wheat, corn, and potatoes provide the bulk of Italy's total yield in food crops. Prewar wheat production was normally close to 300,000,000 bushels, and this great yield at times equaled or exceeded that of France, which is frequently second in European wheat production. Even with this world-sized figure, wheat is so important in the Italian diet that Italy had to import quite large amounts. Corn and potatoes are important in supplementing the starch food supply, each providing over 100,000,000 bushels yearly. Other crops are far less in amount, but rice and oats at about 40,000,000 bushels are far from insignificant in the food supply. In the regions having a Mediterranean climate, fresh fruits and vegetables are produced in tremendous quantities, and previously several million dollars' worth were sold annually to the winter market of central Europe.

Italy is one of the world's leaders in wine and olive oil production and exports. Because of inadequate water supplies the bulk of the immense wine production of over one billion gallons is consumed at home, only a relatively insignificant forty to fifty million gallons being exported. This almost exclusively domestic use also holds true of the olive oil production. Olive oil and wine products, like wheat products, are major and indispensable elements of Italian diet.

In animal enterprises Italy's position can scarcely be understood by farmers in the United States. Farm work is still mostly done by draft animals, two thirds of which are draft cows and oxen, a practice that gives rise to a situation almost inconceivable to machine-minded Americans. The total of 3,600,000 draft animals provide 65 per cent of the total power used on the farms and do 87 per cent of the total work. There are, in comparison, only 182,000 motor units (tractors, engines, and pumps). This condition keeps Italy in the pioneer stage of farming according to American standards. Moreover, the feed for these animals uses the resources of a considerable amount of land that might be utilized for the production of more efficient and desirable food-producing animals.

Italy's agriculture is regional in character. The Po basin produces most of the wheat, corn, and animal products, and all of the rice, silk, and sugar beets. The Peninsula and Sicily produce all of the olives and citrus fruits, and many of the grapes, potatoes, and winter vegetables. Wheat is a major crop over the entire peninsula. Dairy cattle occupy the Alpine pastures in both the Alps and northern Apennines, and good herds are kept in the Po basin. Sheep and goats in large numbers utilize the rugged lands, including the more arid and less desirable pastures of the southern Apennines, Sicily, and Sardinia.

Agricultural problems. Probably the biggest problem in Italian agriculture is the great amount of work done by man and beast in relation to the returns. This condition is a direct reflection of the limited amount of productive land available because of rugged terrain, arid summers, lack of commercial fertilizers, and a number of social, economic, and political factors. Additional land has long been an important objective for the Italians, and in their homeland since 1870 they have reclaimed land to the extent of one sixth of their present farm area.

Low soil fertility presents another difficult problem. Italy's soil is generally poor, for only two soil materials have any measure of natural fertility. These are the alluvium of the Po and minor basins and the volcanic deposits in a few scattered areas. A soil map of Italy shows that the more fertile soil areas coincide almost identically with the areas of dense population. Every effort is made to improve soil fertility or maintain that which exists, but the problem is difficult. Italy lacks deposits of phosphates, potash, nitrates, and other minerals, such as coal and oil, from which fertilizers and soil restoratives can be extracted.

How to substitute mechanical power for the draft animals in a rough land of small farms is an exceedingly tough nut to crack. Such substitution has not been done too well anywhere in the world. Irrigation, terracing, and contouring are techniques upon which the Italians have spent prodigious labor, but the physical limits of the land may have been reached in these respects. However, a survey may show that such related problems as overgrazing and deforestation, if solved, will improve the water supply and reduce erosion. It must be emphasized that correcting these conditions will not change Italy's climate, but, rather, will alleviate adverse climatic effects.

Uneven distribution of land ownership, ranging from holdings that are much too large to be efficient, down to plots of ridiculously small size, offers one of the most critical problems in Italian agriculture. The following excerpt illustrates the evils of the problem:

In the long period of evolution of Italian agriculture, uneconomical systems and patterns of land tenure have developed. Large feudal estates called *Latifundia* are still prevalent. On the other hand, more than a third of the holdings are less than 3 acres in size. In intensive farming, holdings may be excessively small. At Aosta 3 acres of garden land were divided among 1,000 owners.

Another problem lies in the "dispersion" of a holding. In dispersion a farmer will have his farm in scattered and detached plots. In Umbria there is a farm divided in 12 widely scattered tracts located in three different townships and again in Aosta a 55 acre farm is made up of 315 separate tracts.*

Such old land tenure patterns aggravate the problem of best adjustments to the physical potentialities of the land.

Forestry and fishing. A relatively small number of Italians are engaged in lumbering and fishing. Lacking extensive forest resources for wood products, Italy has built from stone and clay and other nonmetallic minerals of which she has an abundance. Architectural types, even in humble homes,

* Victor B. Sullam, *Foreign Agriculture*, VII, No. 12 (December, 1943), p. 278.

are made to conform both to the building materials available and the climate. Large amounts of fish foods are imported, even though the Italian fishermen supply a considerable catch, particularly of the tuna fish.

Industry. Italian industry has developed to second position in number of people employed in Italy, in spite of handicaps in raw materials and power. Beyond mercury, sulphur, zinc, aluminum, and stone, she has little or none of the minerals. Having little iron and no coal or petroleum is a terrific handicap in both domestic development and international competition. Hydroelectric power, developed largely along the base of the Alps where the water supply is steady and adequate, is the only power resource of any significance. Electric power has great possibilities in northern Italy but is of little importance in central and southern Italy because of the erratic water supply.

Lack of cotton, an insufficient wool supply, and almost no coarse fibers are further serious deficiencies for a large population requiring large amounts of these commodities. Warm clothing for a people with cool to cold winter weather and inadequate heating facilities in their homes is a prime essential. Italy's import of raw cotton in 1938 was double any other commodity except coal and coke.

The largest industry is the manufacture of textiles and clothing, with machinery, foodstuff processing, construction materials, and paper and wood products following in order of importance. Italy's industrial development is inadequate to supply her people, provide alternative occupation to relieve the load on the land, or meet international competition in armaments.

Trade. In foreign commerce Italy purchased annually, before World War II, more than a half billion dollars' worth of goods ($593,000,000 in 1938). These imports were largely raw materials and machines. The two largest groups, of about equal value, were the raw materials for fabrication—fibers, wood pulp, rubber, and paper—and coal and oil and their products. Together these two groups accounted for about half of the imports. The next group, metals and machines, accounted for about one fifth of the imports, and the following group, foods, accounted for about one eighth the total. Of the numerous remaining items, phosphate and commercial fertilizers were prominent. Politically, Italy will in the future be very much interested in the countries and areas that can provide these products so necessary to her livelihood.

Italy's exports are made up largely of two groups. The first of these consists of subtropical fruits, their products, and vegetables grown in winter. The subtropical fruit products are principally those derived from grapes, olives, nuts, and citrus fruits. The second group includes a great variety of skillfully wrought manufactured articles ranging all the way from hats to automobiles. In prewar years these exports totaled around a half billion dollars ($552,000,000 in 1938). Any deficit in Italian foreign trade was usually more than compensated by savings sent home from Italians abroad, tourist receipts, services rendered by the merchant marine, return from investments in foreign countries, and payment for the services of skilled and talented Italians employed by other countries.

Before World War II, Italy's largest trade was with Germany, with the United States second. From the latter she secured a variety of raw materials to meet her deficiencies. In return the United States bought special foods and wines and a variety of specialized manufactured products.

Postwar trade, however, is necessarily adjusting itself to a different pattern of world commerce. Efforts of the United Nations will be of great import in the role Italy can be expected to play.

Transportation. Italians, like the most of mankind, still carry a large part of their burdens in primitive fashion by donkey, oxcart, and by hand. However, modern means of transportation along principal travel arteries attained some prominence before World War II, both within the country and between Italy and countries with which she had common boundaries. Mainline trains were considered good by European standards and some tracks were electrified. Some of the finest de luxe passenger ships crossing the Atlantic Ocean flew the Italian flag. "Ala Littoria," the principal Italian airline, not only spread an aerial network of routes over most of Europe and over Italian Africa, but also inaugurated a line to South America. In part these efforts were genuine signs of progress, but in part they were "show" for the purposes of national prestige and were not typical of the basic transportation program of the country.

The railway pattern of Italy deserves some attention, for upon it was placed the burden of interregional and international commerce (see the map on page 195). The country's 14,450 miles of track compare favorably with the mileage in other European countries and, considering the handicaps to be overcome in construction, are a noteworthy physical achievement. Most of the railway mileage is in the network of lines in the Po Valley and the trunk routes following the coastal plain around the entire perimeter of the peninsula. Short transverse lines cross the peninsula to connect the major cities on either coast of the peninsula. Italy's ratio of one mile of railway to every nine square miles of territory is better than that of the United States, which has a ratio of one to twelve. On the other hand, the United States has more miles of railroad per 1,000 population than does Italy.

Just what part geographic factors play in handicapping the effectiveness of the railways would be a difficult problem to answer, but that they exert a significant influence will be readily admitted. Mountain curves and grades not only present engineering problems, but remain constant hindrances to effective railway operation. Mountain climate, too, in particular, the frequent disrupting effects of snow and landslides, reduces effectiveness. Despite the efforts to create an effective railway pattern over Italy, however, many mountainous sections of the country remain relatively isolated.

Cities. In this modern era cities play a dominant role in the life of a nation out of proportion to the number of people in them. Large cities usually occupy key positions geographically: they frequently are transportation centers; they often are important industrial areas. Politically they are governmental nerve centers where national issues get under way and where national disintegration is first apparent. Their importance was emphasized by the extent to which they were targets in World War II. Italy has a number of cities ranking high in both national and international importance. Rome, Milan, and Naples each have near a million

or more inhabitants. Twenty-one other cities have populations of 100,000 or more, and over half the people of Italy live in cities of 10,000 or more (see the map on page 195 for important cities).

Rome, capital of Italy, is a monument for its country and the world alike—the "Eternal City." Milan is the metropolis of the Po basin and Italy's leading industrial center, and Turin, another large industrial city, also is located in the upper Po Valley. Genoa and Naples are the two leading ports, the former ranking as the second greatest port in the Mediterranean (after Marseille). Florence and Venice represent art centers to the entire world. Bologna, on the edge of the Apennines in the Po basin, and Palermo, on the north coast of Sicily, which complete the list of Italy's greatest urban centers, are busy commercial cities.

Colonies *

Italy's colonial policy to date has been of no value in solving her acute population and economic problems. Moreover, her 1935 colonial expansion into Ethiopia involved her in a difficult international situation. Italy's colonies did not generally attract Italian immigrants and also did not yield products or provide resources to pay for their development. Consequently, their possession entailed a drain on national resources rather than a contribution. In her acquisition of colonies Italy as a new nation was forced to take the leavings of other nations whose colonial policies were well developed and who had already selected the best lands for their imperial domains. Even before World War II Italy's colonial possessions were modest compared with the British and French.

After World War II Italy lost her colonial possessions in Africa and the Mediterranean. The Dodecanese were yielded to Greece. These thirteen islands have a strategic location in the Aegean Sea, especially with regard to the Straits. They have an area of 1,000 square miles and a population of 105,000, largely Greek. Castelrosso, the thirteenth island of the group, is a special case. It is geographically separated from the others, and was taken over by Italy, not after the war with Turkey in 1911–12, but after World War I.

* See Chapter 27, page 405, for a more complete discussion of Italian colonies in Africa.

The island of Saseno, ceded by Italy to Albania, which was freed from Italian control during World War II, is an addition to this small Balkan nation. Ethiopia in Africa has been returned to Haile Selassie. Eritrea, Somaliland, and Libya (which includes Tripolitania in the west and Cyrenaica in the east) became the object of power politics. In 1947 a type of trusteeship seemed the probable solution.

International Policy

Italy has always followed a "balance of power" policy, seeking diplomatically to advance her position at opportune moments when other greater powers were in a mood to make concessions because of their absorption with more pressing problems of their own. Militarily she has maintained an army and navy large enough to defy her weak Mediterranean neighbors and to invite alliances with great powers.

Italy should be relieved of this necessity to maintain a large military force by a United Nations organization both strong enough to give her the protection her position demands and at the same time willing to allow her a share in the responsibility of her own protection. Specifically, Italy should be given a share in policing the Mediterranean befitting her national pride and need. This recognition of her position in the Mediterranean would at once alleviate complete dependence on other nations and make unnecessary the overwhelming cost of a future military organization that might be considered essential to protect her interests in an imperialistic world.

Sumner Welles has an excellent statement for a constructive international attitude toward Italy in the following words:

Since "Glory" is gone, the waste of money on army, navy, and bogus public works could go into education, rebuilding, and farm machinery. Italy requires capital and the services of experts. Her colonies are important neither for her nor for any other country; their disposition is almost a psychological matter of Italian pride. . . . Italy was, until the Fascist sham, a liberal country, almost first in the world in humane penology, social science, and intellectual maturity. She was always a decent member of the family of nations. She can resume that position tomorrow.*

When Italy assumes "that position tomorrow," another marked step will be taken toward world stability.

* Sumner Welles, *An Intelligent American's Guide to the Peace* (Dryden Press, 1945), p. 88.

CHAPTER 15

Spain and Portugal: Powers of the Past

ALTHOUGH the great powers of the present have a dominant influence on contemporary world events, the powers of the past have contributed substantially to the political pattern of today. Spain and Portugal were once leading world powers with the largest empires on the surface of the globe. Although they no longer count among the great powers, their activities still influence international affairs. The history of Spain and Portugal since 1930 proves this statement. Growing out of the overthrow of the Spanish monarchy and the proclamation of a Second Republic in 1931, the Spanish Civil War from 1936–39 became a dress rehearsal for World War II. After World War II the existence of Generalissimo Francisco Franco as the only fascist dictator remained a problem for the Spanish people and the United Nations. Across the boundary in Portugal the *Estado Novo* constitution was adopted on March 19, 1933, while Dr. António de Oliveira Salazar guided the destinies of the country. Although Portugal under his leadership remained neutral during World War II, the Azores became bases for Anglo-Americans in the Atlantic and Japanese occupied Portuguese Timor in the East Indies.

Location

Spain and Portugal have their homelands within the Iberian Peninsula, westernmost of the three great peninsulas of southern Europe. A part of Europe at the threshold of Africa, the Iberian Peninsula has been a principal point of contact for peoples of the two continents. Facing the Atlantic, yet a Mediterranean land, the peninsula has fostered maritime activity out on the open ocean after the benefit of experience within the protecting shores of enclosed seas. Venturing first southward along the west coast of Africa and later rounding the Cape of Good Hope, crossing the Atlantic to the West Indies and later to the northeastern coast of Brazil, Iberian adventurers and explorers ushered in an age of world-wide exploration and colonization. Thus the Iberian Peninsula became a center from which Spanish and Portuguese culture and influence were carried to most parts of the world.

The peninsula gets its name from the Iberians, the people who inhabited the area prior to and at the beginning of the Christian era. Probably the name should be applied only to those people who dwelt in the basin of the Ebro River, called Iberius by the Greek writer Scylax. The peninsula is the most southerly of all lands of peninsular Europe, extending approximately half a degree south of Greece and two degrees south of Italy.* It also has the most westerly position of continental Europe, the longitude of Cape Roca in Portugal being approximately 9° 30′ West. In that respect it has a westerly terminal location comparable with that of Ireland, which lies more than six hundred miles to the north. In the United States the latitudinal range of the Iberian Peninsula, 36° to 43° 30′ North, would extend from Cape Hatteras to Portland, Maine, along the Eastern Seaboard or from Santa Fe, New Mexico, to Boise, Idaho, in the western part of the country. Because

* The island of Crete, which belongs to Greece, extends about one degree farther south than does the Iberian Peninsula.

of Spanish and Portuguese associations in South America, it is interesting to superimpose the same latitudinal range on that continent. Thus, in latitude, Spain and Portugal extend from one degree south of Buenos Aires poleward to northern Patagonia, or the northern extremity of the Chilean Archipelago. Despite their low latitude among European countries, Spain and Portugal are thus farther from the Equator than the capitals of any Latin American country that they colonized.

The Pyrenees Mountains isolate the peninsula from the rest of Europe. Although France is the next-door neighbor across the Pyrenees, it has little in common with the Iberian countries. Spain and Portugal have had closer relations with Africa than with Europe. The Sierra Nevadas of southern Spain and the Atlas Mountains of northwestern Africa have handicapped contact with interior regions, but the harbors of the two adjacent continents have minimized the water barrier, especially in the Strait of Gibraltar.

Although Spain and Portugal are often classed as Mediterranean countries, they never dominated the Mediterranean as did the nations to the east, such as Phoenicia, Crete, Greece, Carthage, and Rome. Being at the western end of the Mediterranean, the Iberians were the last to feel either beneficial or detrimental effects from eastern Mediterranean trade and culture. And the absence of land routes across Spain and Portugal from the Mediterranean to the Atlantic prevented the easy dissemination of eastern Mediterranean culture across and through the Iberian Peninsula.

Historical Development

Growth. The Spaniards are a combination of peoples who became strongly unified during their successful struggle to expel the Moors from a substantial part of the Iberian Peninsula in the eleventh and twelfth centuries. Although the Moors were driven out, their contributions were utilized by the Spanish in their ascendancy to world power. The Spanish fleet, which had been built up by the Moors, became the major factor in Spanish world power. Of almost equal significance were the study of navigation and the training of navigators, each actively con-

tributing to the voyages through uncharted seas. Two port cities in the Andalusian Plain of southwestern Spain, Cádiz and Seville, served as the nuclei of empire building.

Portugal, an outgrowth of old Spain, developed from a group of Iberians who had taken refuge in the northwestern part of the peninsula at the time of the Moorish invasion. In 1095, as the Moors lost territory and moved farther south, the county of Portugal in the northern part of the present nation was granted to Henry of Lorraine. The rulers of Portugal steadily increased their holdings and thereby gained sufficient strength to maintain a government and authority separate from that of the counties of León and Castile, two of the strongest neighboring provinces. Finally, Count Alfonso Enriquez assumed the title of King of Portugal and was recognized as such by the King of León and later by Pope Alexander III. As the Moors retreated southward, the King of Portugal extended his kingdom to the Tagus River and later to the South Atlantic coast. The eastern boundary between Spain and Portugal in the northern section has remained unchanged for more than 675 years.

A number of factors contributed to the rise of Spain and Portugal to the status of World Powers. Probably their position at the western extremity of Europe was the most important of these. Certainly from this position both nations had a better opportunity than did other nations of continental Europe to send ships to the west. Their coastline on the Atlantic also offered the countries of the Iberian Peninsula an advantage over other Mediterranean lands. The mountainous coast of southern Portugal and southern Spain, together with the Guadalquivir River, provided a number of small, well-protected ports for the small ships that at that time were the largest afloat. The cutting of the trade routes at the eastern end of the Mediterranean by the European invasion of the Turks gave added impetus to a western, Atlantic outlook.

The study and research in navigation that had been encouraged by the Moors and the discovery and control of the islands along the northwest African coast stimulated western oceanic exploration. In three groups and at not great distances from the mainland, these islands served as stepping stones to more distant exploration (the Madeira, the Canary, and the Cape Verde Islands). In addition, the Azores lay to the west of Spain and Portugal. Finally, the adventurous spirit of the peninsular men cannot be disregarded, for the daring that these men had to have in order to gain power, glory, and wealth certainly carried the flags of the two nations far beyond the limits that a timid people would have reached. Of prime importance to world political history were the initial exploratory trips of da Gama, Columbus, and Magellan. Vasco da Gama's trip around Africa to India in 1498 was a major milestone in navigation and world history for Portugal. Columbus' discovery of America in 1492 and the circumnavigation of the globe by the Magellan expedition in 1522 were Spain's major contributions to the new era in political history.

It is rather significant in the history of colonial development that Portugal turned to the east while Spain projected her energies westward. Even so, considerable rivalry developed between the two nations for the control of new lands and the establishment of colonies and stations therein. Since both were Christian nations, the argument for control was settled first by a declaration of the Pope in 1493. A Line of Demarcation was established at a point 100 leagues west of the Azores. Later the line was changed by the two powers to 370 leagues west of the Cape Verde Islands. New lands west of the line accrued to Spain, and those on the east were assigned to Portugal. At the height of its power Spain controlled much of the Americas and the West Indies and carried her realm across the Pacific to the Philippines. Portugal, on the other hand, established her main strength in Africa and the East Indies. The location of the Line of Demarcation made it possible for Portugal to establish one strong colony in the Americas, namely, Brazil. The importance of Brazil in the Portuguese Empire was reflected by a transfer of the royal court from the mother country to the colony as the center of the empire (1807–21).

Decline. Of the two nations, Spain lost her territories the more rapidly. Most of the Spanish colonies in America sought and gained their freedom following the independence movement by the English colonies and the establishment of the United States in

1783. This rapid decline was brought about partly through Spain's lack of manpower for such an empire, but primarily through her squandering of American riches in trying to become a dominant political power in Europe. Spanish wealth was used to pay soldiers, to buy supplies, and to pay interest to other European nations on loans made to her. Portugal did not fare as badly as Spain, but she was unable to compete for long with the northern European countries in establishing colonies. She lacked the area, the resources, and the human and political power to maintain a leading world position. However, Portugal preferred to cast her lot with England rather than to compete against the growing maritime power to the north, and thus was able to maintain most of her colonies.*

At the present time the location of the Iberian Peninsula no longer bolsters the external strength of the countries occupying it. Moreover, Spain today does not completely control all of her former share of the peninsula, Gibraltar being a strong bastion of Britain's empire route through the Mediterranean (see the map directly below). Despite the posi-

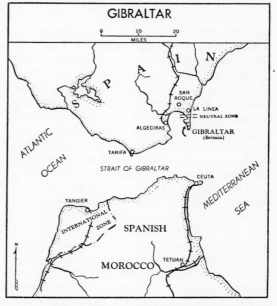

GIBRALTAR

tion of the Iberian Peninsula as the most southwesterly extension of Europe, it did not become the steppingstone from Europe to the most actively growing sections of North

* The present-day possessions of Spain and Portugal are discussed in the final part of this chapter.

America; instead, the Great Circle route from Europe to North America received preference for transatlantic travel from the British Isles.

The Environment

Climate. The climate of the Iberian Peninsula plays a dominant role in influencing the economic activities of its people. In its latitude, between 36° and 43°, the sun bears down almost vertically in the summer months and shines quite obliquely in the winter months. Thus, between summer and winter there is a pronounced difference in the length of days and also in the amount of insolation. Its intermediate latitude also places the Iberian Peninsula under the influence of the moisture-bearing prevailing westerly winds in winter. During the summer months, however, wind belts shift northward and except for northwestern Spain and northern Portugal the entire peninsula is dominated by the dry horse latitudes, a fact accounting for the marked contrast between north and south in summer.

Because of its plateau character the peninsula has a climate unique to southern Europe. During winter months the relatively high interior lies in the influence of a cold air mass that extends westward from the Asiatic continental high pressure area. Cyclonic storms carried by the westerlies usually move across the Aquitaine Basin of France, north of the Pyrenees, or eastward in the vicinity of Gibraltar to enter the Mediterranean. Seldom do the stormy low pressure areas cross the plateau itself. During the summer months the central part of the peninsula becomes extremely heated. Inflowing air from the surrounding water areas rises over the edge of the plateau toward the interior and results in some precipitation on the slopes and in high towering cumulus clouds over the plateau. The relatively high altitude of the peninsula causes the temperature to be cooler than would be normally expected for the latitude. Some of the mountains are high enough to cause a noticeable increase in orographic precipitation,* especially where the moisture-bearing winds from the Atlantic can reach them.

* Rainfall resulting from winds blowing upward because of topography is known as *orographic*. Ascending air becomes cooler and is able to hold less moisture, hence loses it in the form of precipitation.

A final factor influencing the climate of the peninsula is the presence of almost encircling water. The Atlantic bathes the shores of the north and west coasts, thereby keeping temperatures mild. Along these coastal margins the summers are cool and favorable for summer resorts, such as those in Portugal and San Sebastián in Spain, just across the border from Biarritz in France. The waters of the Mediterranean keep the temperature of the southeastern shores mild during the winter months and moderate during the summer months. Thus the Balearic Isles off the east coast also have a most inviting climate.

CLIMATIC REGIONS. Controlled by the four principal factors just identified (latitude, winds and cyclonic storms, relief, and relation to water bodies) the climate of the peninsula may be subdivided for convenience into five types. First, the Cool Marine, or Marine West Coast, type exists in the northwestern part of the peninsula and on the northern slopes of the Cantabrian Mountains. Here the winters are cold and have the maximum precipitation. The summers are cool with less rain, the months of July and August having a delightful temperature. As in other Marine West Coast climates, there is a great amount of cloudiness—more than in any other part of the peninsula. Here the people build their houses more substantially, are greatly concerned with heating facilities, and utilize a large amount of wool for their clothing.

Second, a Continental type of climate prevails over the plateau, which includes most of the peninsula. The extremely cold winters have some rainfall brought by occasional cyclonic storms, but in general the area is dry and dusty. Summers are hot and dry, for the westerlies migrate northward beyond the plateau. Such moisture-bearing winds as do approach lose their precipitation on the plateau slopes.

Third, a typical Mediterranean, or Dry Summer Subtropical, climate predominates in the southeastern part of the peninsula. Winters are mild, with from ten to fifteen inches of precipitation, primarily the result of passing cyclonic storms. The summers are hot, dry, and sunny, slightly moderated along the coast. Occasionally the Sirocco, a hot, dry wind from Africa, sweeps across the southern part of the peninsula, evaporating moisture and causing the vegetation to wither.

The remaining two types of climate are transitional, found between the three major types just enumerated. For instance, most of Portugal and of southwestern Spain experience climatic conditions between those of the Marine West Coast and the Mediterranean. In other words, the winters are cooler than in southeastern Spain and warmer than in the Galician hills of the northwest. In summer this area has a more comfortable temperature than southeastern Spain and is always dry, even though it faces the Atlantic. This climate approximates that of the southern California region. In northeastern Spain, between the Continental and Mediterranean types, is a modified Mediterranean type having more rain than southeastern Spain and a less prominent summer drought.

Most of the peninsula is a land of abundant sunshine, with an estimated average of one thousand hours more sunshine per year than in the British Isles. This great amount of sunshine increases plant growth, assists in the curing of crops, and contributes to more highly flavored fruits. It also encourages a great amount of outdoor life and recreation.

Relief and structure. The dominant relief feature of the peninsula is the Spanish Meseta, a plateau that occupies sixty to seventy per cent of the area (depending on the boundary criterion selected). Most of the Meseta lies between 2,000 and 5,000 feet elevation, although some small areas drop below the lower point in this range. Within the broad plateau are three large basins in which alluvial deposits cover the old resistant rock of the Meseta: Old Castile basin, drained by the upper Douro River between the Cantabrian Mountains and the Sierra Guadarrama; the basin of New Castile, drained by the upper portion of the Tagus and the Guadiana Rivers between the Sierra Guadarrama and the Sierra Morena; and finally, the Ebro Basin, drained by the Ebro River. A triangular area formed by the Pyrenees, the Catalonian hills, and higher land to the southwest, the Ebro Basin cuts deep into the Meseta—dropping to below 500 feet elevation in the southeast. (See the map on page 212 for major relief features of the Iberian Peninsula.)

The mountains are the second prominent feature of the peninsula. The northern mountain range consists of three different groups. In the west are the Galician hills, which have a worn-down and subdued topography developed on old crystalline rocks. Eastward the highlands continue as the Cantabrian Mountains, which have a more irregular topography. Still to the east are the Pyrenees, the most rugged of the three northern ranges, and among the most lofty in Europe. In this range the more recently folded rocks (in contrast to old worn-down formations) culminate in peaks reaching altitudes of 10,000 and 11,000 feet. Rising abruptly from the peninsula the Pyrenees form a boundary-barrier between Spain and France. Difficult to cross, they contribute to the isolation of the peninsula from the rest of Europe. Passage by rail from France to Spain is limited to lines that follow the Atlantic and Mediterranean coastal zones or pass through two tunnels deep in the interior of the mountainous region. The presence of both the Galician hills and the Cantabrian Mountains so close to the coast creates a large number of small harbors, which have encouraged the fishing industry in the northwest.

The central Sierras extend eastward from central Portugal to the vicinity of Madrid. The northern range consists primarily of old crystalline rocks that are rather important from the standpoint of minerals. The Sierra da Estrella, in east central Portugal, is reported to have the most extensive deposits of wolframite (tungsten ore) in Europe. The Sierra de Gata, across the border in Spain, also contains some wolframite deposits. The principal range of the central Sierras is the Sierra Guadarrama north of Madrid, which separates Old Castile from New Castile. Included with the central Sierras, but located primarily at the south edge of the Meseta, is the Sierra Morena, which rises abruptly from the low Andalusian plain. This is the principal range for minerals.

The southern ranges are the most alpine of the peninsula. They are much like the Alps of Switzerland in that the Sierra Nevadas are extremely folded and rise to a height of 11,-420 feet in Mt. Mulhacén. A less folded area along the northern border is similar to the Jura Mountains in northern Switzerland. The ridges of the Sierra Nevadas, extending in a northeast-southwest direction, have constituted a barrier between the interior plateau and the Mediterranean coast, as well as between the plateau and continental Africa.

Bordering the plateau, except where mountains predominate, are the slope lands ascending from sea level to the Meseta. These slope lands are widest in Portugal, where the

Irregularly spaced around the coast of the peninsula are several lowlands of varying areas, each with conditions more favorable to human activity than the slopes separating them from the interior. Two of these lowlands face the Atlantic, one bordering Setúbal

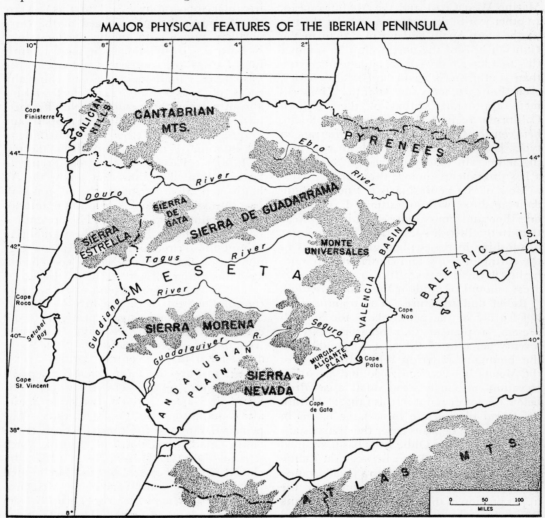

MAJOR PHYSICAL FEATURES OF THE IBERIAN PENINSULA

greater precipitation of the Atlantic has carried erosion more rapidly eastward. Both the northern and southeastern coasts rise abruptly from sea level to the adjacent mountains. These abrupt ascents on the northwest and southeast have handicapped communication between the coastal areas and the interior. From the standpoint of land utilization, it is significant that coastal lowlands are absent in both these parts of the peninsula.

Bay and drained by the Tagus River, and the other extending into the Andalusian lowland drained by the Guadalquivir River. Seville and Cádiz are the two cities most significant in the latter area, and Lisbon is the focal point for the former. Along the east coast there are three coastal lowlands of sufficient area to support large cities. The most narrow of the three is in the north where Barcelona, Spain's largest city, is wedged between the coast and the highlands of Catalonia. In the central coastal area the Valencia Basin is the largest eastern lowland, its key city of Valencia ranking third among Spanish cities. The Murcia-Alicante plain to the south extends inland by means of the Segura River valley and provides a breach into the Meseta.

Vegetation. Since vegetation depends so intimately on climatic conditions, the different types of Spanish and Portuguese vegetation can be closely related to the diverse climatic regions found within the limits of the Iberian Peninsula. Deciduous forests and prairie park lands of northwest Spain develop under the heavy rainfall and cool temperatures that predominate there throughout most of the year. This is the real timberland of the peninsula, and it has supplied oak, chestnut, beech, and ash lumber for dwellings and boats since earliest recorded history. On some of the higher land there are stands of softwoods. Cultivated fruits include the apple, pear, and cherry, typical of middle latitude climates.

The Mediterranean evergreen, broadleaf but not coniferous, is associated with the Mediterranean, or Dry Subtropical, climate of southern Portugal and southeastern Spain. Olives, evergreen oak, tropical palms, and citrus are the major trees. Also typical to the region is a scant but hardy vegetation, known as *maquis,* made up of broadleaf evergreen shrubs that thrive and flower in spring but become lifeless during the summer drought period. This is the land of irrigated tropical and subtropical products, such as dates, citrus, grapes, sugar cane, and rice.

On the Meseta, where extremes of the Continental climate with its negligible rainfall prevail, steppe and bunch grass are general. True steppes exist in three major areas: the Ebro Basin, the basin of New Castile, and the southeastern coastal lowlands in the neighborhood of Valencia. The latter two areas contain much esparto grass, definitely a steppe type, which makes excellent pasturage and is also widely used for cordage, shoes, baskets, and paper. Smaller areas of steppe grasses lie in the basin of Old Castile, in Catalonia, and in the Andalusian basin. During many generations alpine grasslands on the slopes of the Cantabrian and Pyrenees mountains, together with those on the central highlands, have provided summer pastures for countless millions of sheep that have spent the winter months in the lower valleys of southern Spain. Much of the Meseta, however, is a combination of scrub and bunch grass, rather than the characteristic steppe that one is likely to associate with the Spanish plateau.

As in the sequence of climatic regions, the vegetation passes through a transition zone from one major type of vegetation to another. Central Portugal has some deciduous and some evergreen broadleaf trees. The grape and the cork oak, a broadleaf evergreen, are the most dominant species in this area. The northwest Meseta displays a gradual change from the grass and scrub of the plateau to the deciduous timber of the Galician hills. In northeast Spain subtropical trees, ranging from the olive to characteristic beech timber, mark the transition from Mediterranean type vegetation to the broadleaf deciduous trees of northwest Europe.

Mineral resources. Since ancient times the mineral resources of the Iberian Peninsula have attracted foreign peoples. Phoenicians, Cretans, Carthaginians, and Romans all sent expeditions there for ores and metals. Even at the present time many nations are interested in the metal stores to be found in the mountainous regions of Spain and Portugal. The Cantabrian Mountains in the north are the principal iron ore producers of the peninsula. During normal times iron ore production about equaled that of Germany and was about one half that of Great Britain or Sweden. Most of the iron ore is exported to industrial nations by way of Bilbao and Santander, ports on the north coast of Spain. Scarcity of coal on the peninsula, plus the lack of energy and of capital, has prevented the development of a large iron and steel industry in Spain. The province of Asturias, however, does have some significance as a coal producer. Coal beds vary in thickness from sixteen inches to as much as six and one-half feet, but the folded character of the Cantabrian Mountains means that the beds dip steeply, thus making mining difficult.

Previous mention has been made of the very important wolframite deposits in the Sierra da Estrella of Portugal and in the Sierra de Gata in western Spain, resources for which the industrial nations bid highly during World War II. Some ores of tin, zinc, and mercury are also found in these regions.

Toward the south the old folded rock formations of the Paleozoic Age in the Sierra Morena region are shot through with metalliferous veins, many of which contain silver. Here is the world-famous Rio Tinto district, which has yielded copper and tin since long before even the Phoenicians sought tin for bronze. Equally famous is Almadén, known for its deposits of mercury, which in normal times produces about one third of the world's total annual output. Linares, in the upper part of the Guadalquivir valley, is the principal center for lead production. Although the Sierra Nevada region is the highest and most Alpine of all Iberian regions, it is the least significant in the production of minerals. The only metal obtained in notable quantities is iron ore inland from Málaga and Almería.

Since the larger portion of the peninsula is underlain by sedimentary rocks, a type yielding oil and gas in other localities, such mineral fuels may exist. Only recently has exploration for such deposits been undertaken. A past deterrent to possible exploitation of any such wealth has been the fact that both Spain and Portugal lack scientifically trained personnel for an up-to-date survey of mineral resources and for a program of systematic development.

Water resources. Water resources in Spain are probably the most important environmental factor influencing the location of the people. Located on the windward side of the Iberian Peninsula, Portugal is less critically affected. Practically all the water resources utilized are surface supplies. The well-distributed rainfall in the northwest provides abundant run-off water, and there is little need for conservation. However, the lack of surface water throughout the remainder of Spain handicaps practically all activities. Springs or man-made wells provide common watering places in some localities, a single source often supplying an entire community. Agricultural progress is retarded by the concentration of field workers in villages clustered around such water supplies. Being dependent on oxen for power, the farmer must move out to the field very early in the morning and back in the evening. Much time is thus consumed with slow-moving oxen, for the fields are on an average of one to three miles from the village. Some

agricultural villages have as many as 10,000 to 15,000 inhabitants.

Besides the use of surface water for domestic purposes and watering livestock, water power and irrigation also utilize a portion of the supply. Irrigation requires water from the highlands, which is diverted to slope lands and alluvial terraces and fans. This practice makes possible the utilization of soil that would otherwise be left for pasture or scrub timber. Introduction of irrigation by the Moors permitted more intensive farming than had been previously undertaken and thereby encouraged a larger population.

Each of the two nations of the peninsula has approximately two million horsepower of hydroelectric energy available. Spain, with a much larger area and much less rainfall, has developed about twenty per cent of her estimated potentialities, whereas Portugal has utilized less than one fourth as much as Spain. With the exception of the northwest in which the rainfall is evenly distributed, the peninsula in general suffers from the lack of rainfall, which handicaps irrigation and the development of water power as well as limits the domestic supply of water.

Subsurface, or ground, waters have scarcely been touched. The formation of the rock structure is such that water can be transported by filtering through porous subsurface strata (known as "aquifers") from highland regions of abundant rainfall to interior basins where surface water is scarce. The exploitation of such underground sources of water would stimulate progress. Individual wells for private homes would eliminate the necessity for concentration of agricultural workers about common watering places and thus permit settlement comparable to that in the prairies and Great Plains of the United States. Larger wells would provide better watering facilities for livestock and thus improve the grazing industry. Where the ground supply was sufficient, large wells would also make possible the reclamation of more slope land and alluvial soil for agricultural purposes, the irrigated garden lands of the peninsula being limited primarily by the availability of water.

Peoples of Spain and Portugal

The Iberian Peninsula, slightly larger than France, has a population of about 33,500,000.

The resulting density of 145 persons per square mile is similar to that of the Balkan Peninsula in southeastern Europe. The population of Spain is much greater than that of Portugal—26,000,000 as compared to 7,750,000—but in density of population the position is reversed—220 persons per square mile in Portugal and only 130 in Spain. Within the two countries, however, population distribution is extremely uneven. On the one hand, several areas favorable to human activities, such as the coastal lands of Portugal, the Catalonian coast, and the Valencia Basin, have in excess of 250 persons per square mile. On the other hand, mountainous regions and the more barren parts of the Meseta drop to below 25 persons per square mile.

Influence of early invaders. The Iberians are generally accepted as the people who dwelt in the peninsula at the time of Phoenician trade and colonization. Their background is rather obscure, but probably they were descendants of early Cro-Magnon people who later intermingled with Mediterranean and Celtic immigrants. The Basques of today, living in the western Pyrenees, are descendants of some one of these early inhabitants.

The earliest definite foreign commerce is recorded by the Phoenicians, who sent expeditions to the peninsula to obtain tin and copper from the deposits in the vicinity of Rio Tinto. Evidently the Phoenicians had heard of these deposits previously, for the Iberians were known to have begun the use of bronze from 1,000 to 2,000 years before the reported coming of the Phoenicians in the eleventh century B.C. Chapman reports that the Phoenicians probably gave the name Spain to the peninsula by referring to it as "Span" or "Spania," interpreted to mean "hidden (or remote) land." * The principal Phoenician settlements were at Málaga, Seville, Cádiz, and Cartagena. Later the Phoenician colony of Carthaginia traded with the Iberians, the exchange being principally in minerals. The Greeks attempted to have a share in the Iberian trade, but resistance from the Phoenician settlers and Carthaginian traders restricted their commerce to the northeast coast. It

is only in this area that any influence of Greek culture remains.

By 206 B.C. the Romans had taken over control of the peninsula and dominated government and trade for over six hundred years. The first touch of modern culture and western civilization in the Iberian Peninsula can be traced to the Romans. The principles of Roman law and government were established, and Christianity was thus introduced to the peninsula. As in other Roman colonies, the building of roads, bridges, aqueducts, and other public improvements stimulated economic progress to a greater degree than ever before. Some of the Roman structures are still standing and in use today. Formal education of the population was also begun, but much of the progress accomplished was lost in succeeding centuries.

Modern Spaniards also reflect the influence of Nordic blood. Such tribes as the Suevians, Alani, and Vandals successfully invaded Spain from the north, and each in turn reached the southern part of the peninsula. Later the Visigoths appeared and advanced over eastern Spain. Not only did education suffer, but the loss in wealth and resources, the disruption of legal and government procedures, and the massacre of the best of the male population all retarded the growth of Spain.

Moorish influence. Moorish blood was the last great addition to the Iberian people. In 712 A.D. the Moors conquered the Visigoths, and although failing to subdue the whole peninsula, they dominated much of the life there until the thirteenth century. The most noticeable contribution of Moorish blood is the light-hearted character of the descendants of the Moors, now living in Andalusia and southeastern Spain. In other ways the Moors contributed as much to the development of Spain and Portugal as did the Romans. They introduced Asiatic irrigation and such new crops as rice, sugar cane, dates, oranges, figs, and almonds; improved livestock by selective breeding; built up the fleet and introduced the study of navigation; purchased paper manufactured in the Orient for the publication of books; and introduced particular skills in leather and metal making. Moslem architecture is still visible in southeastern Spain, the most outstanding example being the famous Alhambra Castle in Granada.

* Charles E. Chapman, *A History of Spain* (The Macmillan Company, 1918), p. 10.

The general characteristics of modern Spanish peoples began to emerge noticeably during the period of Moorish control. At this time the surviving remnants of the Christian peoples took refuge in the northern mountains, where the Moors were unable to penetrate. Later these Christians, with outside help, drove the Moors southward. As they advanced, three definite political groups developed. First, the northeastern Christians of Aragon and Catalonia, who had been under the influence of France, moved south along the eastern coast. There, finding it difficult to associate with the central people because of the intervening slope lands, they developed into the modern Catalonians— democratic, energetic, and progressive. Second, the people who had taken refuge in the western Pyrenees and Cantabrian mountains moved southward over the Meseta and became the Castilians. They were more aristocratic and more steeped in the culture of the past than the Catalonians, as is evidenced by the prevalence of the Castilian language and literature. They tried to unite the peoples of Castile and Aragon by Isabella's marriage to Ferdinand in 1469. However, even after almost 500 years, the two peoples today are not strongly unified. Third, the Galician hill men drove the Moors southward along the western coast. At the same time they established the country of Portugal in what is now North Portugal, and thus provided the foundation of the modern nation.

At the zenith of Portuguese power, the nation was unable to man the industries and ships with native citizens and therefore imported many Negroes from Africa to serve as slaves. The subsequent racial intermingling explains the darker skin and the greater amount of Negro blood in the present-day Portuguese than in the Spanish.

Languages. Fundamentally the Spanish and Portuguese languages began with the Roman invasion, when Latin was introduced by the Romans and a widespread system of education was begun. This Roman influence survived during the Nordic invasion, and the Christian people preserved it at the height of Moorish power by taking refuge in the northern mountains. For four or five hundred years these refugee Roman Christian peoples maintained their individuality in the mountain valleys.

As indicated in the development of the modern peoples, three definite language groups emerged with the expulsion of the Moors. The western group, finding refuge in the Galician hills and probably influenced by the old Suevian culture, developed the modern Portuguese now spoken all along the western coast, even though Galicia is a part of Spain. The central group developed the kingdom of Castile and fused the dialects of the Spanish Meseta into modern Castilian, the accepted language of Spain today. The northeast group, having found refuge in Aragon and in southern France, were influenced by the French-Provençal. The latter group, accompanied by many French Crusaders, advanced southward along the coast in the expulsion of the Moors. As they did so, they developed a dialect that was distinct from Castilian due to the isolation of the coastal lowland from the plateau. This dialect is the basis for modern Catalan, used almost exclusively in the province of Catalonia.

Apart from the three prevailing languages of the peninsula, the Basques in the west end of the Pyrenees have maintained their own tongue. Under the modernizing influence of transportation, commerce, and tourist industries, however, the distinctiveness of this language is gradually giving way to French on the north side of the border and to Castilian Spanish on the south. Thus Spain is handicapped by having three major languages (Portuguese, Castilian, and Catalan), while Portugal benefits by having only one.

Religion. Both Spain and Portugal are recognized Catholic countries today. Following the introduction of Christianity by the Romans, active support was given to the Christians in Iberia by the Roman emperors in the fourth century A.D. At the church council in Toledo in 400 A.D., Christians were unified on the basis of the Roman Catholic creed and succeeded in overcoming minor faiths. Although the Christians suffered under the Nordic invasion, they converted a large number of the northern intruders. Thus, despite the later invasion of the Moors, Christianity was strong enough to survive. As previously indicated, many of the Christians sought refuge in the mountain valleys, and some became Moslems in order to save their lives. With the expulsion of the Moors, Roman Catholicism was again superimposed on the peoples of the peninsula, and at that time many Moors were converted to Christianity.

During the period of the Inquisition much unjust accusation was directed against those who were not devout Catholics, and much fear was spread among the poor and uneducated peoples. Many non-Catholic elements migrated from Spain in order to survive, and others were expelled. Although the kings of Spain were loyal to the Pope, they were very jealous of Papal authority over the Christians both in Spain and in the American colonies.

Economic Factors

The estimate that more than seventy-five per cent of the population depends directly or indirectly on farming indicates the importance of agriculture in the Iberian Peninsula. Industry has never been developed beyond that required for the more common needs of the Spanish and Portuguese people. With few exceptions exportable surpluses come from the soil, forests, mines, and the surrounding seas rather than the factory. In turn, many of the nations' complex wants must be imported. Athough the peninsula was once the granary of the Roman Empire, a present weakness of the national economies of Spain and Portugal is that great quantities of cereals and some other foods must be imported to meet the needs of the population.

Agriculture. There are two distinct types of agricultural activities: intensive cultivation of terrace lands and irrigation areas, and extensive farming in most of the semiarid country. Intensive agriculture and the great number of tropical and subtropical products, both introduced from Africa, were primarily responsible for the great progress made in culture and wealth during the period of Moorish control. Today some of the irrigated land is held by small individual farm owners, who are making further progress in agricultural techniques. Much of the irrigated land, however, belongs to large estates, and the tillers of the soil do not benefit from the profits of intensive culture. Most of the large estates are in the semiarid country, where the laboring population devote their energies to cereal culture and grazing. And many of these large estates have long supported the landlord in aristocratic leisure, while the laborers, receiving low wages or a small share of the crops, have experienced conditions of poverty.

Over the peninsula as a whole little improvement has been made in methods of cultivation or in crop diversification. Yields are as low as or lower than they were ten centuries ago. There is little chance for the farmers to get ahead. Since the preponderant proportion of Spanish population is dependent upon agriculture and the majority exist under poor living conditions, it is not difficult to see the reason for economic instability. The Spanish Civil War intensified the economic hardships of the people.

Even though agriculture is the chief industry, it will always be handicapped by three environmental conditions. First, the insufficiency of rain and its uncertainty handicap the extensive culture of cereals and limit the use of irrigation. Second, much of the land surface is rocky and infertile; and even if water were available, the ground would not be suitable for cultivation. Third, the relief of the peninsula handicaps transportation, which in turn hinders the distribution of surplus agricultural production. A non-environmental factor that can be remedied, however, is the existence of extremely backward methods of cultivation. The kind of machinery used in the United States to farm the prairies and plains of the Mississippi valley is unknown to the farmer of the Spanish plateau.

In addition to cereals there are large numbers of orchards or groves of olives, citrus fruit, dates, and almonds. Hundreds of vineyards spread over the slope lands, especially in Portugal. Almost fifty per cent of Spain's exports consist of olive, citrus, grape, and almond products. Portugal has won world renown for its export of grape and cork oak products.

Grazing is an industry older than crop farming on the Iberian Peninsula. Sheep have been produced for centuries, both Rome and Greece, for example, having obtained wool from Spain. The early Iberians were more interested in herds than in sedentary agriculture. As war drew close, they could move their flocks to safety, whereas they had to leave their agricultural products to the invading armies. Moreover, the semiarid climate and the vegetation of the Meseta are more suitable for grazing than for crop agriculture. A heavily fleeced type of sheep, known as the "Merino," was developed on the plateau, and later was adopted by wool-producing regions throughout the world.

Early Spain was dominated to a great extent by the Mesta, a powerful organization of sheep men who were concerned with the maintenance of freedom of passage for sheep, northward in the spring and southward in the fall. In later years, as the inhabitants of the villages and cities fenced off the cultivated areas and had sufficient power to resist the Mesta, the significance of that organization dwindled. Goats are raised in large numbers, for they browse well on the shrub-like vegetation of the plateau and provide about the only source of milk. Herds of cattle also range the steppe lands. The most lucrative phase of the cattle industry is the raising of bulls for the bull fights. Small indeed is the Spanish city without an arena for this type of entertainment. Much of the peninsular demand for meat is met by the slaughter of hogs, fattened primarily on acorns and other edible items found on the floor of forest lands. Other animals are mules and horses, which, together with oxen, are the principal beasts of burden.

Industry. The mining industry has been discussed in conjunction with the mineral resources. It is necessary to point out here that most of the mines are owned and operated by foreigners. This is an unfortunate situation, for the profits leave the nation and only the wages of laborers remain as a benefit.

Manufacturing industries are primarily geared to supply local needs. The only exception of significance is the processing of certain crops or local resources for export. Winemaking is associated with vineyard areas. Sawmills are limited to timber areas in the west. Brick-making and quarrying for building purposes are widespread. Meal and flour mills, depending primarily on wind or mule power, are scattered everywhere over the peninsula. Leathermaking, a heritage from the Moors, is centered in Córdova, which is known for its cordovan leather. Portugal converts much of its cork bark into cork products. Only two real centers manufacturing goods of a complex nature exist, and both of these are in Spain. The coal and iron in the Cantabrian Mountains have led to the development of some heavy industry in the cities of Oviedo, Bilbao, Santander, and Irún. The hydroelectric power in Catalonia, together with the energy of the Catalonian people, has fostered a second industrial area centered in Barcelona.

The minor industries are commerce and fishing. It is rather strange to think of two nations that were once world powers now having only skeleton merchant fleets. Portugal has only a small number of sailing vessels, and Spain has less than two per cent of the world's merchant marine. Many small boats go forth from the innumerable small harbors in Portugal and northwestern Spain to catch tuna and sardines, the principal fish products. Nevertheless, the industry does not supply the demand, and large quantities of fish must be imported from the North Sea area.

Cities. Despite the fact that Spain is not highly industrialized, large cities are numerous in the country, especially along the Atlantic and Bay of Biscay coasts in the northwest and the Mediterranean coast in the southeast. Between 1932 and 1946 the number of Spanish cities with 100,000 or more people jumped from ten to twenty. Six of these cities exceed a quarter million inhabitants each: Madrid (1,171,000), in the center of the Spanish Meseta, is the governmental, financial, and cultural heart of the nation; Barcelona (1,125,000), in Catalonia, serves as chief port to Spain and specializes in textile manufacturing; Valencia (544,000), in the rich Valencia basin, manufactures silk and handles agricultural commodities; Seville (370,000), on the Guadalquivir River in Andalusia, is a regional center well known for its wine; Zaragoza (284,000), on the Ebro River at the northeastern edge of the Meseta, serves the Aragon region; and Málaga (271,000), on the southern Mediterranean coast, is a seaport.

In Portugal only two cities are comparable in size to those of Spain. Lisbon (709,000), capital and leading seaport, has recently become an air gateway to continental Europe. Oporto (262,000), which is a seaport, has given its name to the port wine produced in Portugal.

Transportation. The relief of the peninsula makes surface transportation extremely difficult. The abrupt climb from sea level to the Meseta handicaps contact between the coastal areas and the plateau. Furthermore, there is no centralizing river system with converging tributaries to direct and facilitate the building of roads and railroads over relatively low land free from heavy grades (see the map directly below). Political considerations have also interfered with railway building. In order to make progress Spain needed to look toward the Atlantic with its great trade lanes, and the way to do that most conveniently was to look across Portugal. Formerly Portugal frowned on the movement of products across her territory. Now, realizing the advantage of cooperation, Portugal allows goods to move more freely between the Meseta and the Atlantic coast. Even here the rivers do not help surface transportation, for the gorges are too deep and narrow for railroads to follow. Another handicap to railroad

transportation is the lack of a standard gauge: railway cars that shuttle freely through most other European countries cannot be brought south of the Pyrenees.

Highways were not considered essential until the need arose for bus transportation.

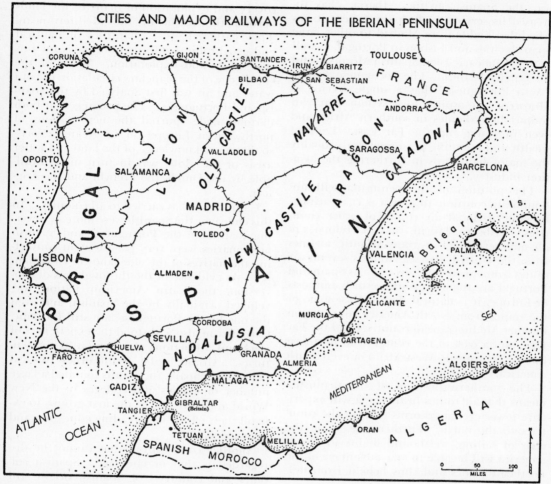

CITIES AND MAJOR RAILWAYS OF THE IBERIAN PENINSULA

The importance of automobiles and international contacts encouraged the building of highways, with most of the improvements coming in the 1920's. Some of the new highways are equal to the best in Europe, but many old ones are little better than trails. Plenty of material exists for the manufacture of cement; the principal handicap to highway improvement is the lack of motor cars, a condition that may be remedied by increasing the purchasing power of the population.

Airline transportation offers the best means for getting over the rugged country. In both

Spain and Portugal, however, poor airfields and facilities indicate the infancy of their airlines. Before World War II both countries had national airlines, although their route patterns were much more limited than those of most countries to the north. Since the war the Spanish airline, "Iberia," has increased its service to the point where it has scheduled flights from Madrid to other large Spanish cities and Lisbon in Portugal, as well as to the Balearic Isles, Spanish Morocco, and the Canary Islands. The Portuguese airline, "Aero Portuguesa," has a single service to Morocco, but aspires to a system that will contact her colonies in southern Africa and even in India and the Far East. Lack of wealth and scientific personnel are probably the major handicaps in furthering the aviation industry.

The position of the peninsula will undoubtedly continue to play a part in attracting international air routes of other countries. Lisbon, Madrid, and Barcelona are already terminals of trans-Atlantic airlines from the United States as well as several air routes from northwest Europe. As Spain and Portugal are the most southwesterly outposts of Europe, it is natural that at least some of the routes from North America continue on to other Mediterranean countries and the Far East, and a part of the routes from northern Europe continue to West Africa or even South America.

The southern position of the peninsula means that air routes in this area will experience fewer cyclonic storms than in the countries to the north. Furthermore, as in the days of sailing, westbound flights to North America will be able to take advantage of the northeast trades and thus benefit from tailwinds.

Much improvement needs to be made in communications within the peninsula. Some improvement was effected in 1924 when the International Telephone and Telegraph Corporation of New York took over the telephone system in Spain. Phones were rapidly installed all over the country, and several hundred new telephone exchanges were established. In the long run such an improvement in communication will have a very great influence in unifying the peoples of the peninsula and stimulating them to greater achievements in international contacts.

External Factors

Contributions. It is rather difficult to enumerate the specific ways in which Iberian peoples have contributed to the progress of civilization and to Western culture. Certainly they must be given credit for the discovery and exploration of many of the lands beyond the realm of the Mediterranean. They gathered great quantities of nautical and geographical information, bases for further study and exploration. Much of the knowledge of the planetary circulation of both water and air was first analyzed by the Spanish and Portuguese. The progress that both nations made spurred the new nations of northwestern Europe on to greater efforts, so that more knowledge of the land and water areas of the globe was in turn made available by the Dutch, the French, and the English.

Catholicism was carried to all colonies. In this endeavor the Spanish were more persevering than were the Portuguese, and Spanish missionaries were very persistent in converting the natives of the new lands to Christianity. As evidence of the thoroughness of conversion, the Latin American nations developed originally by the Spanish, and even the one by the Portuguese, are still Catholic. Catholicism also withstood the experiences of wars and attractions of other faiths for centuries. Although the Jesuit order was expelled from Spain, the Jesuits founded a large number of schools and colleges in the New World and were one of the first groups to expand their efforts in spreading education and knowledge.

Another contribution that cannot be disregarded is that of language. Spanish colonies and countries of Spanish origin still speak Spanish. Portuguese is the official language in Brazil and in the Portuguese African colonies. The almost universal acceptance of the Spanish language in eighteen Latin American countries is reflected in the increased study of Spanish in the North American schools and colleges today.

Colonies. The colonial empires of Spain and Portugal are but remnants of what they formerly were. Most of the remaining colonies are of doubtful value to the national economies of their respective countries, although in general they offer a certain potential worthy of development. The Canary Islands in the Atlantic and Spanish Morocco in Africa are two of Spain's most valuable possessions, the latter a dependency (over which Spain exercises a protectorate) and the former two provinces of Spain. Other territory belonging to Spain includes Guinea (Rio Muni and the islands of Annobon, Fernando Po, Corisco, and Elobey), Rio de Oro on the African coast adjacent to the Canary Islands, and the enclave of Ifni in French Morocco. As a province of Spain the Balearic Islands are strategically located in the western Mediterranean. They have an area of almost 2,000 square miles and a population of around 425,000. Ceuta, a fortified post in northern Africa, directly across the Strait of Gibraltar from southernmost Spain, is a part of the Spanish province of Cádiz.

Portugal has more extensive holdings on the continent of Africa than does Spain, with Portuguese Guinea, the islands of Principe and São Thomé, and the large areas of Angola and Mozambique (see the map on page 399). She controls the Azores, the Madeira Islands, and the Cape Verde Islands in the Atlantic. Toward the East Portuguese possessions include part of the island of Timor in the East Indies, the small trading territories of Goa, Damão, and Diu on the coast of India, and Macao opposite Hong Kong on the Chinese coast. Under her colonial policy, trade and commerce have been increased between Portugal and her colonies, thus adding to the value of trade in the mother country.

Importance today. The location of Spain and Portugal is still a factor in the relationship of these nations to the rest of the world. The Iberian Peninsula cannot help being a stepping stone for commercial air transportation between America and the Near and Far East and between northwest Europe and South America and West Africa to the south. Passengers and flights funneling through Portugal and Spain to and from other nations will help to maintain world contacts. Although both nations have been handicapped by the restriction of trade during the two world wars, they have benefited to some extent by improved commercial relations with some of the victorious nations. Both nations still maintain influence in their colonies and original settlements where the mother language is spoken. As evidence of this influence, one may examine the strong trade ties between Brazil and Portugal.

In order that the peninsula may fulfill its share of responsibility in providing a home and a livelihood for its peoples, it is necessary that both nations fully utilize their resources. Up to the present neither has reached its limit in the exploitation of its climate, soils, and natural vegetation. Although minerals and water supplies may be limited, neither nation has made a scientific survey to judge these limitations accurately. Perhaps Spain and Portugal may be considered backward countries; yet it is safe to say that neither nation has stepped backward. The contrast with the north European nations shows only that they have not kept pace. Besides their responsibilities to other nations, both Spain and Portugal have responsibilities to their own people. Education must be improved so that all may know of better things—the improvements, the problems, and the accomplishments of other peoples. The majority of people must be helped to better themselves, particularly with respect to living conditions, health, and sanitation. National pride, rather than being founded on the decadent past, can be restored to a stimulating position in the present by the people's exploration and development of their own resources.

CHAPTER 16 | # The Five Fenno Scandic Countries

As A politico-geographic region the Fenno Scandic area * derives its unity from a number of similarities in race, language, religion, and social institutions operative in lands in close geographic proximity and in a geographic environment that, although varied in detail, possesses many common features. Historically, the people of these lands have been explorers, colonizers, and conquerors. In recent years they have won international respect from the successful application of advanced social and political ideals. Moreover, their products are needed by most of the industrial nations of the world, especially those of Europe. Collectively, the Fenno Scandic countries could raise a large armed force, but the scattered locations of their core areas and the demands of modern warfare for a strong inventory of strategic resources would not permit them much hope for victory.

General Considerations

Peoples. The peoples of Fenno Scandia include the largest single nucleus of the Nordic race. They represent the descendants of

* The term Fenno Scandia is used here to include Denmark, Norway, Sweden, Finland, Iceland, and their possessions. Broken down into its component parts, the term Fenno Scandic (or Fenno Scandia, used elsewhere) refers to Finland (Fenno) and Scandinavia (Scandia). The term is used rather arbitrarily in this chapter, for the Scandinavian Peninsula includes only Norway and Sweden. However, in a more general sense, reference to the Scandinavian countries frequently implies the inclusion of Denmark because of the latter's location with respect to Norway and Sweden and because of the cultural association that the three countries have in common. Until 1944 Iceland had the same king as Denmark; hence its inclusion in the group of Fenno Scandic countries.

the people who crossed the European plain from Asia and, using the Jutish Peninsula and the Danish Islands as embarkation points, moved across the narrow seas to what is now Scania (southernmost region of Sweden) and up through Southern Sweden to the Central Lowlands. Later some of the migrants moved by sea through the Åland Islands into Finland, and others sailed to Norway and Iceland.

The Finns, who are probably of Mongolian origin, are shorter, broader, and of even lighter complexion than the fair Swedes. However, they have adopted most of the social forms and ideals of Sweden, a nation that ruled them for over six hundred years and left such an indelible stamp that more than one hundred years of Russian rule could not erase it.

General cultural level. The Scandinavian countries, together with Finland, rank among the leading European nations in cultural accomplishment. Excellent schools, advanced medical science, high literacy, and much interest in the arts, as well as relatively high real incomes, are conspicuous. Finland, last to have the opportunity to develop these characteristics, was improving rapidly when World War II halted its progress.

The need for careful, scientific use of their resources and a keen desire for the greatest freedom of the individual through voluntary cooperation have combined to help the peoples of Fenno Scandia adopt the latest technical and social ideas to improve their way of life. Geographic environment, though far from uniform, possesses enough similarity to create many reactions in individuals and groups that lead to social responses differing but little from one country to another. For example, the dependence on forest products encourages the latest methods of forest management in Norway, Sweden, and Finland. Again, the need for scientific methods of farming in a rigorous environment stimulates the people to work together, resulting in the development of the cooperative system for which the region is well known.

The high cultural and economic level of these countries has certain geographic foundations. Historically, the early settlers and pioneers were subjected to a severe process of natural selection as they moved northward from the plains of Germany. The rugged land, dense forests, and storm-swept seas permitted only the strongest to survive. Settlements were scattered and farms small because land suitable for cultivation was to be found only in patches. Each family and each small colony were encouraged to develop a high degree of independence. When adaption to the physical environment was accomplished, wars between the different groups further eliminated weaker individuals, whether they were Danes, Finns, or Swedes. In early times these people fought almost continually—among themselves, or as conquerors on the continent, or as raiding Goths and Vikings far from their homeland.

Language and religion. In the Scandinavian countries there is very little overlapping of languages from country to country. Despite some similarities, Denmark, Norway, and Sweden each have their own distinctive tongues. Many of the inhabitants of these three countries however, are multilingual, speaking not only Danish, Norwegian, and/or Swedish, but either or both English and German, which are important in the commercial world. The Icelanders, reputedly the only country in the world enjoying one hundred per cent literacy, speak only their own language. Oddly enough, Icelandic has a pronunciation much like English, although its vocabulary and grammar differ radically. Only in Finland, where there are a variety of racial stocks, do any appreciable language problems appear. Here Finns, Swedes, Germans, and Russians all speak their own tongues, making a single official language less effective than is the case in the other Fenno Scandic countries.

In each of the Fenno Scandic countries Evangelical Lutheran or Lutheran Christian is the established state religion. However, complete tolerance of worship exists throughout. From 97 to more than 99 per cent of the total population of each country adhere to the Lutheran Church. Other religions, never amounting to more than about one per cent of the total population in any one of these countries, include Roman Catholic, Greek Orthodox, and Jewish. It is obvious that such religious unity, both internally and between states, definitely contributes to the overall cultural unity of the five countries.

Regional location. Although in area Norway, Sweden, and Finland are among the largest nations in Europe, they have surprisingly small populations. Rugged topography, snowfields, and large areas where the climate or the type of soil discourages farming limit the arable land to a small proportion of the total landscape. Nevertheless, the scientific use of forest and farm lands and careful adaption of manufacturing industries to natural and human resources yield high in-

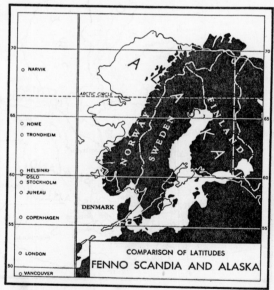

COMPARISON OF LATITUDES
FENNO SCANDIA AND ALASKA

comes for the persons who live in the more favorable parts. Population density is more in accord with the natural environment than is the case throughout much of the remainder of Europe.

The maintenance of a relatively high living standard in the Fenno Scandic countries is by no means accidental, as evidenced by the relatively retarded economic and social progress found in Alaska, a region that lies in the same general latitudes and has much the same type of environment (see the comparison map for

the windward side of a continent is fortunate (see the map on this page). Solar heat is supplemented by warm, moist winds from the sea. The North Atlantic Drift, extension of

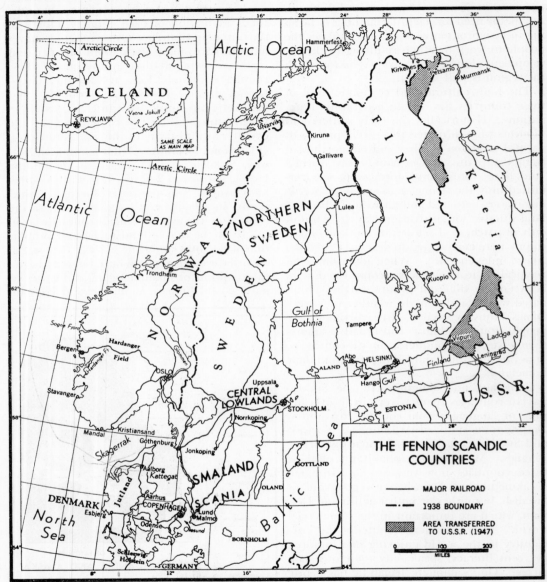

THE FENNO SCANDIC COUNTRIES

MAJOR RAILROAD

1938 BOUNDARY

AREA TRANSFERRED TO U.S.S.R. (1947)

0   100   200
MILES

the two areas on page 223). To take care of an increasing population it became evident that the optimum utilization of natural resources required hard work, education, co-operative action, and intelligent legislation. The willingness and ability to work hard and wisely were encouraged by a climate excellent for physical and mental vigor.

The location in northwestern Europe on

the Gulf Stream, flows parallel to the coast of Norway and prevents the winter from being as long and cold as would be suggested by the high latitude of these northern countries. This combination of factors permits the growth of forest and farm crops for which there is always a ready demand in nearby densely populated European countries. At the same time proximity to highly industrialized western Europe insures access to the ideas and techniques of some of the world's most progressive countries. Couple these conditions with cheap water power, several highly important minerals, adjacent fishing grounds accessible from innumerable harbors (which are also the home ports of a significant proportion of the world's merchant fleet), and one finds many of the fundamental requirements for an advanced civilization.

International stability. Despite possession of the elements requisite for an advanced civilization, the prosperity of Scandinavia is relatively recent. Additional factors should be detailed to account for this development. The geographic separation of Norway and Sweden from the wars of Europe for the last hundred years or so before World War II helped to keep peoples who believed in peace out of war.* Up to World War II the many years of peace and the small size of the armies kept military expenditures low as compared to those of other nations. As a result, more of the national income was available for the welfare of individuals. Also there was less need for tariffs and bounties to protect war industries. Hence, prices were lower for many goods. At the same time when farmers demanded and needed higher prices for their products, protective tariffs enabled them to be secured easily because home production only partially met the demand. These factors were especially significant in lands where so large a percentage of the population was composed of farmers.

Thus these Fenno Scandic lands, where 17,-500,000 people live and work in latitudes much farther north than most of the world's population, are looked upon as leaders in cultural and economic fields because they have succeeded in working out economic and social systems adapted to their environment. How the people in each nation have done so will be shown by studying in turn, first, agricultural Denmark; second, forested Finland; third, unarable Norway; fourth, a diversified and relatively more important Sweden; and, as a fitting climax, remote Iceland.

DENMARK

Denmark proper comprises the Jutish Peninsula and the islands to the east as far as the Öresund between Copenhagen and Sweden, plus the island of Bornholm. The country is separated from Norway by the Skagerrak and from much of Sweden by the Kattegat (see the map on page 224). As an overseas colony Denmark possesses Greenland, and the Faeroes are still subject to Danish sovereignty. The 4,045,000 Danes live in a land a little larger in area than that of southern New England—16,500 square miles.

Physical Characteristics

A low-lying land with maximum elevations approaching only six hundred feet, Denmark has as its structural backbone a series of clay hills extending north and south through eastern Jutland. To the west are sandy plains or clay lowlands covered with heather and pasture that extend to the sand dune coastal area which borders the North Sea and the Skagerrak. Dunes and sandy surfaces similar to those of Cape Cod in Massachusetts extend the Jutish Peninsula northward to form Skagen. On the west coast waves have maintained water passageways through the dunes. Not only has the lack of natural harbors in this section discouraged trade, but shifting sands and fog have proved additional handicaps. The improved harbor of Esbjerg dominates the western coast land.

The thirty per cent of the area of Denmark that is composed of islands contains more than half of the population. In economic significance and leadership the insular portion carries even greater weight. Island hill tops, often covered with beech woodlands, and valleys with rich farm lands form a characteristic setting for the low, white farmhouses surrounded by trees. In some instances the valleys have, in geologic times, submerged to become waterways that now separate the islands.

Economy

Denmark is the most highly developed agricultural country of Fenno Scandia. Best known are its butter, bacon, and eggs, but

---

* These facts apply to a lesser extent to Denmark and Finland. The latter, adjacent to Russia, was in a less fortunate position. The former is such a small country that it maintained neutrality for the most part through its buffer character.

there is also an extensive production of cherry brandy, beer, Diesel-engined ships, bicycles, and potteries based upon kaolin from the island of Bornholm. Conspicuous by their absence are wood products, minerals, and water power. A much larger percentage of the land is better suited to farming than to forests, in direct contrast to the other countries of the Fenno Scandic region.

Farming. Among the Scandinavian countries Denmark has a distinctive agricultural economy, its lack of mineral wealth forcing dependence upon farming activities. It offers an outstanding example of how farming may be the basic economic activity of a nation and yet may give it an income sufficiently high to permit a rank among the leading nations of the world in terms of cultural attainment and high living standards. This unique agricultural achievement has been possible because of the remarkable levelness of the land. Further, the soils of Denmark are capable of giving heavy crop yields under latest scientific farm practices. Still another factor is a climate that provides a long growing season and a relatively mild winter, permitting animals to remain in pasture for most of the year. In addition, the Danish farmer possesses the ability to cooperate in the use of machinery, buying of seeds and stock, and in the grading, financing, and marketing of products. The nearness to Britain, a market that demands the best in butter, bacon, and poultry, has proved still another asset.

Danish farming was not always intensive. The change has come in the last forty years. Up to the end of the last century, wheat and livestock were produced mainly on large, landed estates. However, decreases in domestic yields and competition from new grain lands in the Western Hemisphere encouraged the change to smaller farms, accompanied by the significant shift to specialization in animal products rather than grain.

Cities. Copenhagen (Köbenhavn), meaning "merchant's harbor," has a population of 927,000 and accounts for more than a fifth of the total for Denmark. It is the capital of the country and also the leading manufacturing and trade center. The location of the city makes it a focal point for lines of transportation that serve all of Denmark. On the eastern edge of the most populated section of the country, the port of Copenhagen is the best site for ships to stop on their way through the Skagerrak and the Kattegat. Its importance decreased in 1895, however, when the opening of the Kiel Canal permitted ships to bypass Copenhagen and go between the Baltic and Atlantic by a more direct route (see the map on page 138). First in prewar years and now in the postwar period Copenhagen is an air transportation center, with routes connecting it with other traffic centers of western and central Europe. Railroads are somewhat handicapped by the island location, but a system of train ferries permits efficient operation between Copenhagen and the rest of Denmark and between the insular part of Denmark and Germany. The city dominates all forms of Danish economic, political, and cultural life.

Other than Copenhagen only one city in Denmark exceeds 100,000 in population: Aarhus, a shipping and commercial center. The next ranking cities are Odense and Aalborg, each with between 50,000 and 100,000 inhabitants. Like Aarhus, the latter two are medium-sized commercial centers and seaports, accounting for a small proportion of the agricultural exports.

World Relations

Danish power. Denmark's location and its peninsular shape, extending northward from the European plain and separating the Baltic from the North Sea, destined her to play an active part in European history. In the distant past, when northwestern Europe was being settled, Denmark was a base from which people of the European plain could go to Sweden. The journey was by land except for a short overwater crossing. At the same time a central position between the North and the Baltic seas was an important factor in making her a leading power. In addition, Danish land was relatively more fertile and prolific than that of her northern neighbors.

Early in the eleventh century the Danish King, Canute the Great, conquered England, and he and his son after him ruled over both England and Denmark until their deaths. (After the son's death England's rule was again taken over by Anglo-Saxons.) In 1397 Norway, together with Iceland, Greenland, and the Faeroe Islands, which were all under Norwegian rule, became part of the Danish Empire. Iceland, an independent republic from 930 to 1264, had joined Norway in the latter year. Greenland, discovered and settled by the Norwegian, Eric the Red, in the tenth century, had remained a republic until 1261, when the colonists swore allegiance to the king of Norway. In 1814 Norway separated from Denmark, but as neither Iceland, Greenland, nor the Faeroes were mentioned in the dissolution, they were retained by Denmark. In 1918, however, Denmark acknowledged Iceland as a sovereign state united with Denmark only in that the Danish King, Christian X, was also King of Iceland. Then in 1941 the Icelandic parliament voted to cancel the union with Denmark, and in 1944 the people formally voted to sever their ties and establish an independent republic. In 1946 the assembly of the Faeroe Islands * also proclaimed their independence after a referendum had voted in favor of the action. However, the decision did not become final, and the subject was under negotiation in Copenhagen. Greenland still remains an outright possession of Denmark.

During the fourteenth and fifteenth centuries, when the Hanseatic League ** functioned, the central position of Denmark between the two "Hanseatic Seas" gave her three Hanse towns. The Danes continued the Hanseatic League custom of charging tolls for entry into the Baltic, a practice abandoned only in 1857.

The strategic position of the country is reflected today in the significance of Copenhagen as a port, called by some the "Gibraltar of the North." For many years Denmark's neutrality was assured in part by her strategic position, which no great power would long permit another to control. Hence, Denmark became a buffer state.

Boundary problems. Denmark has a common land boundary with only one country— Germany. Consequently, territorial conflicts have been limited to Schleswig-Holstein at the base of the Danish Peninsula. After German power had increased, Denmark could not extend to the bank of the Elbe River in order to encompass the entire Jutish Peninsula.

In 1864 Austria and Prussia defeated Denmark in a short war and deprived her of Schleswig-Holstein. After World War I a plebiscite in a northern zone of Schleswig awarded that area to Denmark, and a plebiscite in a southern zone awarded it to Germany. Although Schleswig still remained a problem area for future consideration, Holstein became a German area, no longer questioned by the Danes.

World War II events. Denmark was occupied by the Nazis on April 9, 1940. The repercussions were significant, not only in Denmark but in the North Atlantic. Danish colonial areas were strategically located along the highly important supply route between the United States and Great Britain. During the course of World War II Greenland was protected by American forces; Iceland was occupied by British and later American troops; and the Faeroe Islands, which were still a Danish possession, were occupied by the British. In the last days of the Third Reich the Russians occupied the Danish island of Bornholm, but they later evacuated it.

In the Danish homeland there was interest after World War II in a possible future plebiscite in the northern part of German Schleswig to determine whether the boundary should be changed in favor of Denmark. The Danes were also concerned with the British settlement in Schleswig of German refugees from Russian-occupied areas and with the future status of the Kiel Canal, strategic in the commerce and politics of the Baltic. The location of Denmark has certainly made the kingdom very important in international relations. The economic and political future of Denmark is largely dependent upon the attitude of the great powers.

FINLAND

Finland, with an area of about 117,000 square miles, is only slightly smaller than the

* The Faeroe Islands have an area of 540 square miles and in 1945 had a population of 29,200.

** The Hanseatic League was an association of Germanic cities and towns whose objectives were the securing of greater safety and privileges in trading and mutual defense against foreign aggression.

British Isles, but has only 3,900,000 people. This nation can claim the distinction of having its major population concentrations in cities and industries and on farms farther north in the world than any other large group of persons with an advanced economy. The Finns are confronted with the problem of deriving a living from a land composed largely of lakes and swamps, and a soil more suitable to forests than farming. In addition, they face the problem of adjusting their economy to long winter nights, a short, cool growing season, and harbors blocked by ice for many months of the year. The lack of fertile farm land is reflected in the small population living in the relatively large area. Only ten per cent of the land is in cultivation or pasture; seventy-five per cent, in forest; and the remainder, in marsh, bog, lakes, and other unproductive surface covering.

Physical Features

The Finns live in an elongated land extending from 60° to 70° North Latitude. More than one fourth of the country is north of the Arctic Circle, a location not unlike that of Alaska. The basic physical structure of Finland is a plateau rising from 500 to 2,000 feet above sea level and extending north and south through the greater part of the country. Overlying some of the oldest rock areas in the world are materials left by the continental ice sheet. The melting of the ice caused clay and gravel hills to be deposited in a crescent shape at an elevation roughly five hundred feet above sea level. These deposits mark the boundary zone between the lake region and a coastal margin some fifty to one hundred miles wide, extending along the Gulf of Finland and the southeastern shores of the Gulf of Bothnia. Central Finland, with its lakes, swamps, and forests, contrasts sharply with the coastal areas, which are lower, have few lakes, and offer more soil suitable to farming. On the inner edge of the coastal margin, where streams flow from the lakes, water power is developed. The seaward edge has many harbors and numerous islands, which in some places form small archipelagos. Eastward from the head of the Gulf of Bothnia the land is higher and lakes are fewer. The northern part of the country is occupied by forests and tundra and is unsuited to farming.

Economy

Finland's resources are limited on two counts: they are meager and they lack variety. As a consequence the national economy is based on developments of a specialized nature. The Finns have shown a remarkable initiative in exploiting to best advantage those resources that they do possess.

Farming. Agricultural activities are limited by lack of arable land and severity of a high-latitude climate. The sands and clays sufficiently fertile and well-drained for crops are used to grow rye, oats, barley, potatoes, and hay, and to support natural pasture. As a result, dairying and its products are most characteristic of Finnish agriculture. However, the rigorous environment causes yields to be smaller and costs higher than in Denmark. The Finns have formed cooperatives but were never able to capitalize on them sufficiently to earn the high incomes typical in Denmark. Two primary handicaps in Finnish agriculture are the scattered location of the farming units and farming techniques less efficient than those of the Danes. Nevertheless, at least fifty per cent of the people are classified as farmers. The majority live on small, scattered farms and in villages and derive a marked share of their income from lumbering.

Forests. The feature most characteristic of the Finnish landscape is the thousands of lakes and streams in their forest setting. It is therefore natural that forest products dominate the economic life of the nation. They comprise from seventy-five to eighty-five per cent of the country's exports, and the manufacture of these products furnishes a livelihood to fifty per cent of the nation's gainfully employed. Climate and soil combine to grow timber conducive to the production of good lumber, fifty per cent of which is pine. Lakes and streams furnish means of transportation to move the lumber as well as the power to mill it. European countries, England and Germany especially, provide an excellent market for these products. Finland, which has greater access to western Europe than has Soviet Russia, exports lumber, veneer, wood pulp, paper, and matches. Modern methods of forest management, the latest milling devices, and cooperative marketing are techniques that have been coming to the fore. Continued improvements in these practices are essential to Finnish prosperity in the future if the nation is to compete with the greater experience of Sweden and the vast resources of the Soviets.

Minerals and manufacturing. Although the kind of rocks found in Finland indicate possible resources in metallic ores, there is little mining or fabrication of metal products. Small amounts of iron ore exist between Åbo and Helsinki and between Kuopio and Viipuri, but the nickel of Petsamo is the only mineral of international importance. The Petsamo area and the region around Viipuri were ceded to Soviet Russia as a result of World War II.

Cotton textiles have been a significant manufacture in the Finnish economy, although the total output cannot compare to that of Europe's more industrialized nations. Textile mills are concentrated at Tampere, at which point water power and access to cotton-importing ports facilitate the industry.

Cities. The larger proportion of Finland's population lives in the southern coastal areas, and here are located most of the cities. There is no important city on the Gulf of Bothnia. Åbo (Turku), located at the southwestern corner of Finland and facing the Åland Islands, was the main Swedish town in Finland during the period when Sweden ruled Finland. Åbo, which has a population of 77,000, is still important as a Finnish port and shipbuilding center, and has two universities. Located squarely on the southern coast is Helsinki, which has a population of 328,000, the capital of Finland and without question the commercial, financial, and cultural center of the country. Between Åbo and Helsinki lies the small city of Hangö, the Finnish port most easily kept free of ice blockades during the wintertime. In the southwest interior of the country Tampere with 84,000 inhabitants is a manufacturing center for textiles and paper.

International Politics

Location and history. Finland's location east of Sweden, easily accessible by water from western Europe, and her common boundary with Soviet Russia account in great measure for her social and political objectives as well as her major political problems. The Swedes gained control over Finland in the twelfth and thirteenth centuries and held it until 1809. During this period the Finns were impregnated with Swedish ideals and cultures. The ideals of individual freedom and democratic forms of government were so strong that Russian control from 1809 to 1917 could not greatly change them. When a republic was declared in 1917, these forces quickly came to the fore. By the time Soviet Russia and Finland clashed in the early part of World War II, Finland had successfully adopted many social and political ideas already highly developed in Sweden.

Minorities. The accessibility of Finland to Sweden, their similarity in resources, and the long period of Swedish control over Finland have all been instrumental in creating a minority group. The majority of Swedes and their descendants live on the west and south coasts. Thirty per cent of the Finnish population speaks Swedish, and in many areas there is a distinct bilingual effect. The Swedes are strong politically in proportion to their numbers because of their wealth and control of economic activity, and they cause some internal friction. Additional trouble from minorities arises from the several thousands of Germans and Russians living in the southern part of the country. On the other hand, the more than one thousand Lapps living in the northern part have created little, if any, problem.

After World War I the Åland Islands at the entrance to the Gulf of Bothnia were claimed by both Finland and Sweden. Finland finally received the islands under guarantees to respect the rights of the inhabitants as a distinct group. A neutralization convention signed in 1921 by the Baltic powers replaced the earlier convention of 1856.

Results of war. Soviet Russia's desire for ice-free ports led to acquisitive action toward Finland. Her attempts to satisfy this aspiration were reflected in her acquisition of the lease of Hangö in the 1940 peace treaty between Russia and Finland and the later exchange of the lease for a base on the Porkkala Peninsula near Helsinki in 1944. On the other hand, the need of Finland for an ice-free port on the Arctic when she became independent after World War I motivated her successful attempt to secure ownership of the Petsamo region for access to the Arctic and North seas. However, Finland ceded Petsamo and the nickel mines to the Soviet Union as a result of her defeat by that country in 1944, and returned in general to the 1940 borders drawn after her defeat by the Soviets in the Russo-Finnish War of 1939–40. At that time she also gave up Viipuri, much territory in Karelia, and all the shores of Lake Ladoga to the Russians (see map on page 224).

NORWAY

Norway, more than any other Fenno Scandic country, reflects the geography of a land closely bound to the sea. This fact was evidenced in the early days by maritime discoveries and raids of the Vikings, and in more recent times by a large merchant marine and an important fishing industry.

About three million people live on Norway's 125,000 square miles. Why does one of the European countries that is relatively large in area possess such a small population? Causes are based primarily upon an inhospitable terrain. Percentage-wise the surface of Norway is calculated as being nearly seventy-five per cent unproductive tundra, bare rock, snowfields, and steep slopes; about twenty-three per cent forest; and but little more than two per cent in arable land. No other European country suffers from such an adverse land surface. It is little wonder that as a source of relief from Norway's inhospitable environment, a large number of people have emigrated to the United States.

Physical Geography

Norway is an elongated north-south country comprising most of the rugged western part of the Scandinavian Peninsula. Because of the prevailing westerlies and the North Atlantic Drift, which are both effective in keeping minimum temperatures relatively high, its climate is unusually warm for the high latitudes. Although nearly one third of the country extends north of the Arctic Circle, ice does not form in any of its harbors. Lacking the disadvantage of frozen ports for a part of the year, the coastal areas and the Trondheim Depression form a band of economic activity and a line of communication that extend the length of the country. Even the Glommen Valley and Oslo, in the lee of the interior highlands, benefit from the marine modifications of what otherwise would be a rigorous, high-latitude climate. Unfortunately, most of that part of Norway exposed to the warm westerly winds cannot derive much benefit from their ameliorating effects because of high elevation, lack of soil due to glacial scouring, expansive snowfields, and poor soil drainage.

To illustrate the effect of Norway's position with regard to climatic factors, the marine climate extending along the whole west coast gives mild winters (coldest month temperatures, 25°–35° F.), cool summers (warmest month temperatures, 55°–65° F.), abundant rainfall (25 to 85 inches per year), heavy snows on the higher land, and a great deal of mist and fog.

The interior highlands of the Scandinavian Peninsula are essentially a plateau area of old, hard rocks worn down nearly to sea level and then uplifted. In the process the plateau was tilted eastward, presenting an abrupt, sharp western edge toward the Atlantic. The steep plateau face, or scarp, is broken by numerous fjords, that is, river valleys scooped out by ice moving seaward often along faults, from interior glaciers, so that they are U-shaped in cross section. In places the fjords reach for many miles into the plateau, in one instance coming within eight miles of the Swedish border. Parallel to the coast are islands of all sizes, from one to several of them usually lying across the mouth of each fjord. Through these rocky islands, called "Skerryguards," channels form an inland passage of relatively calm water, not unlike the "Inland Passage" of southeastern Alaska. The protected waters served as a cradle in which Viking sailors learned to set forth on more hazardous ventures. Today the fjorded coast is renowned for its scenic beauty. Moreover, from a practical standpoint in Norwegian economy, it provides sites for fishing villages and small farms, the latter lying in low spots where soil has collected. On the southern coast the plateau front is less steep and is farther back from the shore. In the Trondheim Depression, erosion of softer rock has provided lower and gentler relief suitable for farming. In the Oslo area the plateau is lower, and the rocks have been eroded into valleys with gentle slopes and rolling lands.

Over this generally forbidding land surface, people live in three areas of comparatively dense population (for Norway): first, the region around Oslo, the adjacent shores of the Skagerrak, and the Glommen River valley; second, the Trondheim Depression; and third, the southwestern and western coastal lands and islands.

Economy

Farms and forests. Soils best suited for farming and forestry lie in the Oslo, Trondheim, and southern coastal areas. Here fields of hay and pasture dominate the landscape, but oats, barley, and potatoes are produced as staple crops. Dairy cows, swine, and sheep are also numerous. In the vicinity of Oslo stone walls, pastures, cows, and farms remind one of New England. Agriculture engages more than half the population in Norway, and many of the fishermen and lumbermen are part-time farmers as well.

Much of Norway's forest is in southeastern Norway. Of the country's total stand of timber about seventy-five per cent is composed of conifers and twenty-five per cent of hard woods, such as elm, beech, oak, and birch. Lumber, wood pulp, and paper are exported, but timber for construction is imported.

Water power. Norway is a land of abundant water power. Deep snows and lakes on the plateaus, numerous waterfalls, and ease of dam construction in resistant rock formations provide very cheap, accessible hydroelectric energy. Moreover, the nearness of this water power to seas and fjords open to ocean ships the year around facilitates the export of manufactured products. This combination of factors has encouraged the production of aluminum and calcium carbide, chemical industries requiring large amounts of low-cost electricity. Foreign capital is prominent in the development of these industries.

Minerals. Norwegian minerals are neither abundant nor diversified, but in a few instances deposits of comparatively valuable ores warrant exploitation for world commerce. Near Mandal some seventeen per cent of the world's molybdenum is produced for export, and magnetite is mined on Syd Varanger near Kirkenes in the far north. Of greater geographical and political importance is the port of Narvik, which serves as an outlet for Swedish iron ore from Kiruna and Gällivare. This port makes possible the continued shipment of ore during winter months when the Gulf of Bothnia is frozen.

Attraction of the sea. Norway's rugged plateau topography discourages communication between Sweden and south and southeastern Norway except by way of the Glommen Valley to Trondheim. The rail line from Oslo to Bergen (Norway's second city) must twist, turn, and tunnel to get over the Hardanger Fjeld. Such difficulties, plus the inhospitable nature of the land, have turned the people toward the sea. Norway faces the Atlantic and Arctic oceans, also the North Sea and the Skagerrak.

In no other European nation do the sea and coastal margins play such a large part in the life of the people. As population increased in the early days of the nation, the small farms scattered along coastal valleys or clinging to narrow terraces, or on the deltas at the heads of the fjords, provided insufficient food. Nearby fishing grounds were used more and more. The stormy waters and the scattered, isolated farms early bred a spirit of independence in the people. Only the hard workers on the land and skilful sailors and fishermen on the sea could achieve success. Journeys to Iceland, Greenland, and even North America were only a series of longer voyages after these hardy Nordics became accustomed to fishing. Five centuries before Columbus Eric the Red sailed the seas to "Vinland." The Vikings also operated southeastward as far as Athens and participated in the founding of many kingdoms.

The attraction of the sea and the difficulty of earning a living at home in a country with three fourths of its land unproductive are still evident in Norwegian life. In proportion to her population Norway has the largest merchant marine of any country. Her whaling fleet is the most modern, and she catches and packs a substantial proportion of the fish caught in European waters. Norwegian fishing vesssels also make their way to the Antarctic Ocean to supplement the supply of a commodity so important to the population.

Cities. Although the cities of Norway are not large when compared to those characteristic of the more highly industrialized sections of northwest Europe, a number of them are important to her economy. Most of them are ports, and all serve as regional commercial centers for assembly and distribution of goods to the more remote sections of the country.

The capital city of Oslo, which has a population of 289,000, is the nation's nerve center and occupies the heart of the most highly developed region. The country's meager rail network centers here, and the city is the air terminal for NDL (the Norwegian national airline) as well as for other European—and one American—airlines.

Bergen, with slightly more than 100,000 inhabitants, lies on a narrow shelf of the mainland on the southern part of the fjorded, isle-studded west coast. The city was chosen as a depot by the Hanseatic merchants. Being near Hardanger and Sogne fjords, it served as a pivot to North Sea trade. Today it continues to hold its place as a commercial port, fish harbor, shipbuilding center, and tourist haven.

Trondheim, market city for the "Depression" of the same name, with a population of 56,000, was the last heathen capital of Norway, for it lay farthest from the warring Danes. The city also became the nation's first Christian capital. Its importance arises from its port, fishing industry, and timber.

Smaller cities, with populations of less than 50,000, include Stavanger, a seaport and fishing center on the southwestern coast. North of the Arctic Circle are Narvik and Hammerfest, the former a terminal for the railroad from northern Sweden's iron ore region, and the latter considered one of the most northerly cities in the world (nearly 71° North Latitude).

Implications of Location

The position of Norway at the northwest extremity of continental Europe has been sufficiently remote to keep her from directly participating in the more or less continuous pressure of power politics common south of the Baltic. On the other hand, it is close enough to other European powers to be occasionally embroiled in some of their struggles. The exact nature of the locational factor goes a long way toward explaining much of Norway's external history (see the map on page 224). From 1397 to 1814 she was under the Danish Crown. The softer rock and milder climate of the Trondheim Depression and its extension into Sweden facilitated her falling under Swedish rule, and in 1814 the King of Sweden became King of Norway. In 1905 the union of the two countries was dissolved. In World War I Norway succeeded in maintaining neutrality; but on April 9, 1940, early in World War II, the Nazis invaded and conquered the kingdom, thus involving an unwilling people in that struggle. The Germans took full advantage of the physiographic aspects and weather conditions of the country to insure a rapid defeat from which Norway won relief only after the defeat of the Third Reich in 1945.

Norway's most noteworthy overseas possession is Spitzbergen, or Svalbard, halfway between Norway and the North Pole. Spitzbergen, accessible by sea four months in the year, has the coal Norway lacks. There are also fisheries and whaling associated with the economy of this far northern island group. Norway has asserted her right to the islands periodically since 1261, but her claim was recognized only in 1920. Norway also possesses Jan Mayen Island, which is about 300 miles north of Iceland; Bouvet Island in the South Atlantic; and Peter I Island in the Antarctic Ocean.

SWEDEN

Sweden differs from Norway, with its characteristic oceanic orientation, in that Sweden's past has been more closely tied to the Baltic Sea than to Atlantic waters. Historically, its central position in the heart of the Fenno Scandic region has led to its control at various times over parts of Norway, Finland, and the states along the southern shores of the Baltic. In the past the Swedes flowed out from the Central Lowlands, their centrally located Baltic coreland, as conquerors. Today from that same center come progressive ideas of economic cooperation, regulation of industry, and increased governmental ownership.

Contrasts with other countries. Sweden, with 173,500 square miles of territory and more than 6,500,000 people, has an area and population considerably larger than those of Norway, Finland, or Denmark. However, it is not so intensively developed as the latter, which has an area approximately one eleventh the size of Sweden but is occupied by more than half as many persons. On the other hand, it is not so sparsely peopled as Norway or Finland. Swedish economic life is similar to that of Denmark in the farming phase, with dairying the chief type of agriculture. It is comparable to that of Finland, in that forests and their products loom large as exports. As in the case of Norway, a peninsular shape and a location adjacent to cool shallow seas have made fishing an important activity. Like Norway, too, Sweden has a large merchant marine. Sweden differs from the other three countries in the great importance of its mines and in the manufacture of metal products and machinery.

Location. Although Sweden covers the same general range of latitude as Finland and Norway, it should be noted that it extends as far south as most of Denmark and that the northern two thirds of the land, north of 60° Latitude, is not so high in elevation nor so rugged as adjacent Norway. Neither is it so poorly drained or scraped clean of soil by glacial action as Finland. Coastal areas of Northern Sweden and nearly all of the country south of the Sixtieth Parallel are below 600 feet in elevation. The southern area of lower altitude, which contains most of the farm land and a large proportion of the population, has milder winters and longer growing seasons than much of the rest of Scandinavia except Denmark and the western coast of Norway, both of which are more marine. Although the warming effect of the westerly winds from the Atlantic is diminished in much of Sweden as compared to western and southern Norway in winter, and there is a lower annual rainfall, a deeper soil cover in Northern Sweden encourages forest growth.

Natural Regions

Sweden by no means has physical uniformity throughout her enormous north-south extent. From south to north four distinct regions, each with the basis of an individual economy, are readily distinguishable: Scania (Skåne), Smaland (Småland), the Central Lowlands, and Northern Sweden (Norrland).

Scania. Largely a limestone area on which beech forests once thrived, Scania is the Swedish province from which the term "Scandinavia" is derived. Its extreme southern location on the peninsula subjects it to the influence of ameliorating marine winds. Wheat, cattle, and sugar beets are raised on the level to rolling land. The rural landscape resembles that of Illinois because of the large, well-kept farms and farm houses, as well as the use of more machinery than is customary in other countries of Europe.

Malmö, third city of Sweden, which has a population of 171,000, dominates the commercial life of Scania. It is only an hour's steamer or ferryboat ride across the Öresund from Copenhagen. Near Malmö is the small city of Lund, in which is one of Sweden's two leading universities.

Smaland. To the north of Scania is the higher and more rugged region of Smaland. Its hard rocks wear a thin mantle of rocky soil except in some of the coastal valleys, which are more fertile. Forests of conifers and aspen dominate the landscape in Smaland. A world-renowned product, the safety match made from aspen timber, is produced here, with Jönköping as the center. The islands of Öland and Gottland fall within this region. Their soils derived from limestone rather than from hard rocks permit some grain production, and rocky limestone pasture lands favor the grazing of sheep.

Central Lowlands. Extending from Smaland northward to approximately 60° Latitude, the Central Swedish Lowlands are the historical core of the country. The region also represents the present commercial heart of Sweden, for it has the country's two leading cities, most of the manufacturing, an excellent transportation pattern, and a large percentage of the farms.

The Central Lowlands present a surface that nowhere reaches great height. Within the region are the large interior lakes of Sweden. Submergence of the lake belt has been the source of marine clay deposits advantageous for farming. The total area of soils suitable for farming, however, is limited by rock surfaces, gravel ridges, lakes, and swamps. Forests are extensive, and some of the area's manufacturing importance is attributable to timber products. Among the mineral resources of the region, non-phosphoric iron ore was the means of establishing quality metallurgy in medieval times when charcoal was the only fuel used. Water power likewise contributes to the industrial activity of the region. The central location, domestic markets, and ports for foreign trade are other factors responsible for the concentration of economic activity in this part of Sweden.

Northern Sweden. Occupying approximately two thirds of the country, Northern Sweden is by far the least developed part of the country. At the same time it offers the greatest potential for future development.

The surface of Northern Sweden slopes eastward from the Norwegian border, which roughly coincides with the crestline of the Peninsula's mountainous backbone. Many rivers flow into the Gulf of Bothnia, and long, finger-like lakes occupy their upper courses. Glacial soil of fair depth covers the interstream areas and is in turn covered by forests except at higher elevations and in the very northerly portion where tundra prevails. A small amount of agriculture, rich stands of timber, and high-grade iron ores in the north form the basis of the region's present economy.

Industrial Development

In addition to agriculture, which predominates in the economic pattern as a whole, Sweden is favored with enough natural wealth to foster industrial development of a specialized nature. Rich deposits of iron ore, heavy timber stands, and the extensive development and use of hydro-electric power enable the energetic population to produce commodities that have a demand in industrial countries throughout the world.

Northern iron ore. Tremendous reserves of iron ore high in metallic content (60–70%) lie in the far north of Sweden. Kiruna and Gällivare, town names identifying the location of these deposits, are well known wherever iron and steel are discussed. This ore cannot be profitably smelted in Sweden because of her lack of coal, and high phosphorous content discourages its use by Britain under peacetime conditions, but it has proved desirable for a large German steel industry.* Large quantities of the ore normally move to Germany by way of Luleå and the Gulf of Bothnia in months when the latter is free of ice. The delay in shipment resulting from ice blockage led to the construction of a railroad through Norway to the port of Narvik, which is free from ice in winter because of the warm North Atlantic Drift. The attack

* Iron ores with a high phosphorous content could be utilized in the German iron and steel industry with greater facility than in the English industry. The German equipment, being newer, was adapted to handle ores with a high percentage of phosphorous content. In contrast the British ore was high in phosphorous and imports needed to be relatively free from such impurities in order that they could be mixed with British ore to improve the quality.

by England on Narvik during World War II in which the port facilities were wrecked was designed to decrease the amount of iron ore that could reach Germany.

Forest products. Fifty-five per cent of the land in Sweden is covered by forests, most of which are pine and spruce. As a result, wood and wood products provide upward of forty per cent of the exports of Sweden. This trade ties Swedish industry tightly into the commercial trade of Europe. The many lakes and streams assure low-cost transportation of timber to the mills, and cold water prevents rotting and maintains the quality of the wood. The cold climate makes for slow growth, which insures lumber of superior texture. When properly dried, machined, and selected, the wood is excellent for items of house finishing, such as doors and sashes. Much of the wood is also well suited for pulp and paper. In recent years wood cellulose has provided raw material for rayon, cellophane, and other products of this general class.

Sweden, unlike Alaska, which is in a similar physical location, has distinct advantages accruing from a rich experience in manufacturing techniques, especially those pertaining to wood. It lies near a ready market and will likely continue to make a profit in the utilization of its forests.

Special steels. A distinctive feature of Sweden's economic structure during the last sixty years has been a marked trend toward industrialization. Outstanding in this development was the important rank attained by metal and machine products, especially those made from steel. From Central Sweden comes iron ore high in metallic content and exceedingly low in phosphorus and sulphur, providing the basis for steel of exceptionally fine quality. During recent years armament manufacturers have demanded Swedish steel for use in heavy plate on battleships, edging tools, and ball bearings. The high quality results from the low content of phosphorus, sulphur, and copper, which are difficult to remove from the ore. As Sweden lacks coking coal, she uses charcoal in her blast furnaces. As a result, the impurities that would be added from coke but are not found in charcoal do not form a part of the end product, steel. Also, since charcoal furnaces must be small, for this light fuel cannot hold up so heavy a charge of ore as coke, closer control of the process can be maintained. Electric furnaces permitting excellent control of temperatures are used for some of the products. The resultant product is high in value and scarce in amount and caters to special markets. Hence, Sweden has of necessity developed highly trained metallurgists and uses her quality production in the manufacture of specialized finished products.

Cultural and Political Aspects

Cooperatives. Sweden has attained international fame because of her cooperatives and her success with government regulation and ownership of iron mining, forestry, and public utilities. Partly responsible for Sweden's rapid strides along these lines is an environment necessitating economy in the use of her natural wealth. Stimulating the efforts was the demand for iron ore by stronger nations. Also significant in Sweden's success is the fact that government participation in certain key industries carried youthful enterprises through early periods of development. This sustained support on the part of the Swedish government is in contrast to practices in some countries where state control of industries comes only when businessmen have failed or in cases of emergency.

Core areas. Sweden's Central Lowlands, with Stockholm and Gothenburg at the eastern and western ends respectively, present a picture similar to the Glommen Valley in Norway, with Oslo and Trondheim at either end. Only Scania to the south can be considered as a supplementary core area in the political and economic structure of the country.

Long the political and cultural pulse of the core area, Stockholm has been the capital and religious center of a succession of Swedish regimes. Located around the seaward end of Lake Mälar the city is built on a group of islands between lake and sea in the forward area of Svealand. It has a location that is marine, yet far enough inland to insure fairly easy protection. Although Gothenburg has

become the commercial capital, Stockholm, a city of well over 650,000 persons, maintains its former influence and prestige as the political capital. Having an excellent river harbor, Gothenburg, a city of 315,000 people, is an import and export center for the Central Lowlands. It is also an important fishing, manufacturing (textiles), and tourist city, as well as a center for financial interests. Two other cities add to the importance of the core area at the eastern end of the Central Lowlands: the industrial and regional center of Norrköping, fourth largest city of Sweden with 78,000 persons; and the small city of Uppsala to the north of Stockholm with 30,000 persons, well known for its university established in 1477. Stockholm, Gothenburg, and Malmö form a triangle upon which is based the Swedish rail network. All three are port cities and have excellent air transportation facilities.

Foreign relations. Sweden has not fought a war for over 130 years, but prior to this long period of peace she was frequently in conflict. Svealand and Gotland, located in the rugged area south of the Central Lake District and easy to protect, formed an excellent fortress from which to attack in all directions. The Goths fought their way from Sweden to Novgorod and on to Kiev in what is now the Ukraine. Although the Danes once ruled Scania, the Swedes drove them out by 1658. Sweden has controlled various parts of the coast of the Baltic Sea for many years in her history.

During the two world wars of this century, Sweden maintained her neutrality. In the last great conflict she found herself surrounded by belligerents, the only neutral state in Scandinavia. The decline of German power in the Baltic and the ascendancy of Soviet Russia are certain to affect the future policy of Sweden. Although Sweden is no longer the leading Baltic power, she is the strongest of the Fenno Scandic countries. Any efforts to establish a political or economic bloc among the countries will see Sweden in a key role.

ICELAND

Iceland, fourth largest island in the North Atlantic, has only 130,000 people in an area of 40,000 square miles. Of these people more than one third (46,000) live in the capital city of Reykjavik. Seventy-five per cent of the land is uninhabitable because of lava flows, ice fields, rugged rocky topography, and a largely tundra climate. In favored spots a cool marine climate permits the grazing of sheep and the growing of root crops, such as turnips and potatoes. Cod fisheries provide the remainder of the food supply and exports.

Located in the path of early Irish and Vi-king routes, Iceland has for centuries been a democratic country governed by intelligent people. Its strategic position in an air age, indicated by British and American army occupation during World War II, guarantees her an important place in international relations in the future, especially in view of the increased possibilities in polar flying.

GREENLAND

By far the largest island in the world, Greenland with an area of 837,500 square miles, extends through some twenty-four degrees of latitude. Thus, in spite of its Arctic position, the southern portion reaches into a temperate, marine zone. Along the coast of this southern section, where the land is not covered by the great ice cap that spreads over eighty-five per cent of the island, most of the population of 18,000 live. Greenland has the world's only large deposit of cryolite, a mineral used in electrolytic manufacture of aluminum, opal glass, and enamel. Except for this mineral, trade is a monopoly of the Danish crown.

The strategic importance of Greenland, like that of Iceland, stems from its location in the North Atlantic in an air age. On April 9, 1941, the United States and the Danish Minister in Washington signed an agreement in which the United States assumed the responsibility of the defense of Greenland. Throughout World War II a number of bases served to aid American ships and planes. Both the Nazis and the Americans realized the meteorological value of Greenland in a study of the weather of Europe, for over this island pass many of the storms that later pound upon the continent of Europe. The future of Greenland is closely related to the security of the Anglo countries on either side of the Atlantic.

CHAPTER 17

Poland: A Perpetual Problem

For a thousand years Poland and the Poles have been a problem for Central Europe and for themselves, for Slavdom, and for Teutonic and Mediterranean neighbors. Geographic, economic, religious, and linguistic factors are such as to perpetuate this problem or at least to prolong it for some time to come.

The national boundaries of Poland have been shifted over and over in response to the political and military pressure of neighboring countries. At some periods recognized boundaries as such ceased to exist, and only the will of the Polish people marked the location of a Polish nation. In 1938 the western boundary of Poland centered on Longitude 18° East, bulging at one point to within 100 miles of Berlin. Following World War II Poland found its political boundaries again shifted, this time well to the west of those that marked the country of post-World War I (see the maps on page 238). The new German-Polish border along the Oder and Neisse Rivers is generally west of Longitude 15° East, and at one point it approaches to within forty miles of Berlin. Among other things this new line gives the rich German industrial district of Silesia to Poland. (See introductory pages of chapter on Germany for more details on this boundary shift toward the west.)

Complementary to this westward gain, a wide strip of Eastern Poland was lost to Soviet Russia. As a result, the Polish capital, Warsaw, is now in the eastern rather than in the western half of the country. Notable boundary changes for Poland have also taken place to the north. The troublesome Polish Corridor has been eliminated, and Poland now has a wide strip of the Baltic coast, occupying what was German Pomerania, the Polish Corridor, the Free City of Danzig, and a part of East Prussia (the remainder of East Prussia, including the capital city of Königsberg, is now a part of Soviet Russia).

In area, Poland has lost more than she has gained. The area of the country from 1919 to 1938 was 150,290 square miles, but the area today is only 120,000 square miles. On the other hand, development of the land to the west is markedly advanced over that to the east, with the result that the new territorial gains are of greater economic value than are the losses. Add to this benefit the advantage of a substantial frontage on the Baltic Sea, and it would seem that from a physical standpoint, at least, Poland is in a position to take strides forward in advancing her status as a strong political entity.

Poland as discussed in this chapter does not, except in a general way, conform to the new boundaries just reviewed. It was the Poland of the 1920's and 1930's that shaped the political destiny of the nation that emerged from World War II. Before that, it was the Poland *without* political borders that gave rise to the creation of physical delineation following World War I. The reader is therefore urged to keep in mind the fluid character of Poland's historical borders in order to appreciate fully the implications of the politico-geographic factors. In effect, fluctuating boundary lines are in themselves a potent factor in the political geography of any country possessing them.

Historical Evolution

Long ago Poland shared with the rest of Europe the race migrations and settlements that eventually established the Nordic, Alpine, and Mediterranean races over a large part of the continent. Of these the Alpine, so-called because they lived largely in mountains, spread north and east over the plains and became in part the Slavs. In turn the Slavs are divided into three principal groups: eastern (Russian), western (Poles and Czechs), and southern (Yugoslavs).

the Netze, barred their access to the Baltic Sea.

The first Polish empire, organized under Mieszko I (962–92) with the capital at Gnesen (Gniezno), established its rule northwest to the mouth of the Oder, then southeast over eastern Galicia and southwest over Silesia. In addition, the expanding empire gained a strong foothold on the Baltic and acquired the Slovak country on the south. Poland was then a well-organized political unit with an absolute monarchy and a strong feudal system, adapted alike to its position, cultural heterogeneity, and stage of development.

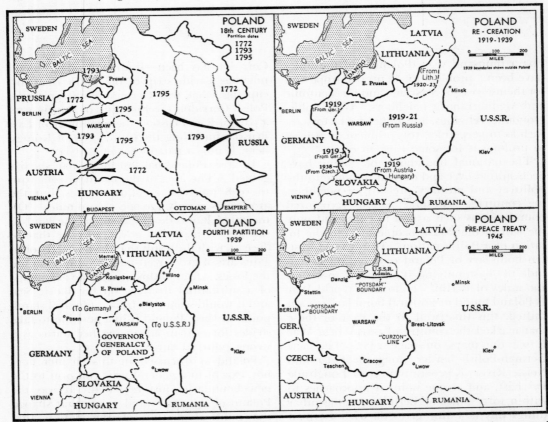

Early checkered career. Poland's history of expansions, contractions, alliances, and antagonisms is a continual expression of aspects of Poland's problem. A thousand years ago the first Polish nation emerged as a small interior people occupying lands between the Oder and Vistula rivers and south of the Netze River (see the map on page 241 for these rivers). Pomeranians and Prussians, who occupied the morainic plains north of

Following 1025, however, the empire started to crumble. Divisions within and pressure from without cost Poland most of her acquired lands. The pattern of future political history appeared when the jealousies of neighbors saved the empire from collapsing entirely. Neither Germans nor Czechs (Teutons and Bohemians) would let the other completely annihilate Poland. The country repeatedly rose and fell in power and extent as leadership was strong or weak, and adjacent powers waxed and waned.

The partitions. Pressure of the Germans over the feeble western frontiers, of Russia over equally open eastern boundaries, and of the Turks from the south, as well as the threats of Austria, presaged the temporary end of Poland's checkered history as a separate state. Despite the valiant and generous help of the Poles in defeating the Turks, the gratitude of her neighbors soon evaporated; and in 1772 about one fourth of Poland was divided among Russia, Prussia, and Austria. Twenty-one years later (1793) Russia and Prussia took additional slices, and in 1795 the partition of Poland among these three adjacent powers was completed (see the map on facing page).

For 120 years these three nations at one time or another vied in the invention of schemes to break the Polish spirit by introducing their respective languages and ideologies, by imposing many economic and social restrictions, by colonizing, and by hampering local self-government. When World War I broke out, Poland's long-repressed nationalism burst into flame. Following this conflict, with the indorsement of the victorious Allies, the new Polish state was constituted with an area a little different from any previous outline. Included were the valleys of the Vistula (basis of the Polish Corridor) and Bug rivers, most of the valley of the Warta River, Galicia to the Carpathians, and the mid-Niemen to the Dwina on the northeast.

The New Republic. The new Polish Republic dates from Armistic Day, 1918, when Marshal Pilsudski, who had escaped from Magdeburg prison, returned to Poland. He built an army, hastened the disarmament and evacuation of German-Austrian armies, and developed a growing civil service. The latter had been a gift of the Regency Council, set up in 1917 by Germany and Austria to hold Poland for them. The unconquerable vitality of the Polish populace was expressed quickly in national unity and government.

The Paris Peace Conference in 1919 established western and southern boundaries somewhat along ethnic lines, in general, dominantly Polish on the one side and dominantly German and Czechoslovakian on the other. A plebiscite area, which was left in Upper Silesia, became a subject of controversy. After a dispute between Czechoslovakia and Poland over Teschen, the area was divided between them. In recognition of the need for sea outlets, the delineation of the republic granted Poland a corridor to the Baltic; Danzig was made a Free City; and the Vistula was internationalized. The treaty of Riga in 1921 fixed the eastern boundary between Russia and Poland, none of which could be wholly ethnic because of mixed populations on plains with no definite physical boundaries.

The New Republic thus consisted of Russian, Prussian, and Austrian Poland (see the map on facing page). Russian Poland had received little encouragement to progress and had experienced many hindrances. However, in the latter part of the last century, industries were developed, but for a largely rural land it was overpopulated, especially since agriculture was primitive and crop yields were low. Western Poland later did much to strengthen backward agriculture and education in the east, but the expenditure of effort was unequal to the task. There was little commercial or industrial call for railroads under the Russians, and the few built were of Russian gauge (5 feet), wider than that of the Austrian and German systems (4 feet, 8½ inches). Emigration to the United States and Germany (partly seasonal) was heavy. Prussian Poland centered on the city of Posen. This section was relatively progressive, somewhat industrialized, and decidedly westward-looking. Its textile industries had nearly doubled since 1900. Austrian Poland had developed much mineral wealth in and north of the Carpathians and built many miles of railroads to facilitate its movement and manufacture. This particular part of Poland, however, teemed with illiterate, primitive Ruthenians.

Land systems, in general far too feudal, were diverse in the three areas. A Polish General Land Office was later established and given authority to buy, divide, and sell large private estates and government lands—a program that has done much for agriculture and rural life.

One of the problems of the new Poland was to unify her three peoples, who for more than a century had been given such different treatment and outlook. Their differences ranged from social customs and creeds to standards of living and equipment for work. But an ingrained unconquerable vitality and nationalism were effective in producing a growing unity, particularly offensive to Germany with her sharp turn toward National Socialism. On September 1, 1939, Poland was the victim of the first German blitz, and from then until Germany's surrender in May, 1945, her history was that of a war-ravished country.

Importance of position. Poland, no matter how large or small her area, has always been on the western border of Slavdom. This position linked her commercially with the Hanseatic League and pulled her into close commercial relations with other Baltic and with Atlantic peoples. It gave her the Roman Catholic rather than the more formal Orthodox branch of Christianity. It brought her closer to the politically progressive influences of the West, as expressed in the Low Countries, France, and England (and at times in Germany), than to those of the more autocratic Russia and Near East. This position also brought Polish peoples into contact with the liberalizing literature of Bohemia, with the Reformation in Germany, and with the music and theology of western Europe. Nevertheless, Poland touched the East and was not sufficiently affected by western influences that it advanced farther politically than to a transition stage.

West Slavic core. In language as well as position, Poland is West Slavic. Her political authority has repeatedly reached far beyond the outposts of Polish language, religion, and national character. An ethnographic map of central Europe between the two world wars shows a Polish core around Warsaw in the Warta and Vistula valleys. A circular line of 150 miles radius delimiting this core area would reach East Prussia, lead across the Vistula near Thorn, swing west and south around Posen into Silesia, extend to the mountains south of Cracow, curve east around Przemyśl and Lublin, follow the Bug fifty to sixty miles west from Brest-Litovsk, and finally turn northeast to East Prussia. In this more or less circular area the Poles constitute 98 per cent of the population in the south, 85–95 per cent in the central part, and 75 per cent in the vicinity of Posen. An outlier of population away from the main body is located around Wilno and another west of Danzig, in each of which the Poles slightly exceed 50 per cent of the total. Poland has many times reached far beyond these limits. Her traditional nationalism constantly impels her to recover her maximum territorial limits. Conversely, when blocs of Germans or Russians have been taken into the Polish political unit, instability and friction have followed. Poles are too nationally minded to absorb immigrants or conquered people.

Physical Aspects

Location. As an ethnic group the Poles have never reached the sea. They are dwellers in the plains and do not have any of the characteristics of a sea-going people. Although the Baltic Sea has been from time to time the northern boundary of Poland, it was for centuries of little economic consequence to the great majority of the population. In years to come, as industry increases and international commercial relations develop, the sea and even the ocean probably will become an essential adjunct to the Polish economy.

Geologic location may be more important to Poland's welfare than relation to the sea. Ancient sedimentary and crystalline rocks are mantled by glacial drift over most of the country, and by rich loess deposits, spread by winds, over the southern plateaus and their bordering mountain slopes. This extensive covering of finer soil materials is reflected in the agricultural nature of the country's economy and in the small percentage of non-arable land. Below the drift but covering the ancient rock structure in places are younger deposits of sedimentary rocks. These include limestones and sandstones of geologic mid-age as well as younger Mesozoic and Tertiary sandstone and shale. The oldest rocks here and there protrude toward the former Russian border south of the Pripet Marshes. They constitute the buried roots of an old mountain chain, most of which was eroded away before the Carpathians made their appearance. Mid-age and ancient rocks are the mineral bearers; the more common younger rocks furnish sands for glass and limestone and shales for cements; and in rocks of all geologic ages are resources for a wide range of other ceramic industries. In recent geologic time some of the younger rocks were slowly folded into the Carpathians and are as valuable for stone and ceramic materials here as they are farther north. In addition, broad folds contain the petroleum deposits of the Galician fields (now largely Russian).

extending east and west as morainic plains in the north, higher plains or plateaus in the central part, and mountains in the south. Increasing altitude toward the south neutralizes any latitudinal tempering of the climate.

POLAND
PRIOR TO WORLD WAR II

1937 International Boundaries

Surface features. In contrast with other countries of Central Europe, Poland has a relief lacking much diversity. Glacial plains and moraines with many lakes and lake beds comprise most of Poland. The Carpathians, which cover approximately five per cent of the area, give the country its only mature mountainous topography. This area is far from being waste. It is splendid for forests and grazing, and in the comparatively level valleys agricultural utilization is high.

The geologic patterns in Poland are linear,

North of the mountains the topography continues east and west of Poland, unchanged at the borders. The Carpathians reach no farther west than through Poland, but in the east they continue in a large arc across Rumania and back to the Iron Gate of the Danube. Structurally and genetically the Carpathians are closely related to the Alps, which lie to the southwest.

Most rivers of Poland rise in and near the southern mountains and flow nearly north to the Baltic (see the map on this page). The

Vistula with its right-side branches (Dunajec, San, and Bug, and a Bug tributary, the Narew) is truly a Polish river, navigable for a long distance and improvable much farther. The Warta rises near Cracow and flows by great turns north and west, serving Posen, and empties into the Oder. The Netze is one of the streams in a channel formed by glacial action, connecting the Vistula and Oder; hence, with the Bydgoszcz (Bromberg) Canal it helps to form an easy continuous link between Polish and German areas. An exception to this general river pattern, the Pripet River, a branch of the Russian Dnieper, has among its several headwaters the Pripet Marshes. In this area glacial deposits, which are strewn abundantly, interfere with drainage and the movement of man and goods.

Many lakes in the northern plains aid navigation and are valuable as fishing grounds. Some have disappeared and their peat or clay deposits are valuable in Polish industries. The Royal Canal, which makes use of both lakes and marshes along its route, connects the Bug and Pripet rivers—linking Polish and Russian areas. The Augustów Canal connects the Narew and Niemen rivers; the Królewski Canal between the Vistula and the Dnieper connects the Baltic and Black seas.

Boundaries. The great European plain is continuous from the heart of Russia westward entirely across Germany. Nothing could be more transitional in climate, vegetation, and crops than the portion of this plain occupied by Poland. Here many of the physical and cultural aspects characteristic of eastern Europe merge into those characteristic of western Europe. Yet from its early beginnings Poland has maintained a surprising ethnic and linguistic entity. As would be expected, there have been ethnic and race mixtures that have infiltrated from both the east and the west sides because of the lack of topographic barriers, a lack that has encouraged the relatively free movement of trade and people, the building of highways and railroads across the plain, and the unfortunate tramp of armies and pillagers, and has repeatedly rendered Poland an avenue between east and west.

The northern and southern boundaries have been perhaps as movable as those in the east and west, but they are marked by real physical barriers. The Baltic Sea on the north, despite its ofttimes sandy beaches and broad inlets, is bordered all the way by intractable morainic lands. These minor obstacles of relief to hostile incursions are balanced on the south by the mature Carpathian Mountains. The latter are nowhere lofty, rugged, and ice-covered as are the Alps, but their contrast with Poland's plains is sharp. Rounded summits of 5,000 feet are not rare; passes are usually less than half as high. The barrier quality of the Carpathians is indicated by the low density of population and the paucity of towns as well as by the sparse pattern of roads and railroads.

As suggested in the opening paragraphs, the political frontiers of Poland have been changed often (see the maps on page 238). This instability of boundaries is to be expected in areas where no physical barriers are present, and has precipitated intense political crises with a people who have kept to themselves enough to maintain so pure a core. Frequent oppression over these same defenseless frontiers has nurtured a nationalism that under strong leadership pushes outward, and, when restricted, aspires to recover all lost territory. Here are the clues to some of Poland's major problems.

When the republic appeared as a new European country after World War I, it was given a remarkably compact shape, though disproportionately large on the east. Extending northward from the block-like area were two corridors. By this time Poland had increased her industries and commerce beyond any previous volume. To accommodate a greater volume of trade the Polish corridor was opened to the Baltic across drift plains, although at least fifty per cent of the occupants in the area were Germans. In previous centuries a similar corridor had been used more than once, but never with as good reasons. A compact outlier of Poles around Wilno, which was mentioned earlier, was also eventually incorporated within Polish boundaries; and this additional territory created the second corridor within the boundaries of the new republic. It thrust the boundary of Poland to Latvia between Soviet Russia and Lithuania, antagonizing both of the latter nations. Corridors have constituted another Polish problem.

Polish ambition has been the means of spurring the political occupation of territory beyond the substantial Polish core. However, the greater this marginal area becomes the greater become Polish minority problems. Given Poland's topography and her nationalistic spirit, this type of problem must be ever present.

Climate. Po'and has indeed a very diversified climate. Located at a latitude squarely in the belt of the prevailing westerlies, she receives much of her weather from the west. Nearly all precipitation is from this direction, especially in the warmer half of the year, when the westerlies are stimulated by the continental low pressure area of central Asia and its inward-moving masses of air. With the westerlies come air masses from the North Atlantic and southwest Europe. The succession of low and high pressure areas bring their characteristic weather; local electric storms, mists, rains, clear sunshine, and soft, wet snow move eastward across the country. At such times the weather is said to be English.

Lying on the flank of the great Eurasian continent, Poland is subject in winter to masses of cold air that have descended over north central Asia. Frequently rolling west and south over her lands this cold air wraps the country in the severities of a true continental winter climate. Characteristic are cold winds and fine, sifting snow or still, steady cold with no precipitation for days at a time. This type is called Russian weather.

The latitude of Poland gives her a short growing season resembling northern Montana and Manitoba. The July isotherm of 65° and the January line of 25° intersect within her borders, showing that the temperature range, while not unusually wide, is considerably greater than found in the countries of western Europe. Rainfall is ample, seasonable, and well-conserved in all the more level land.

Resources. The fundamental relationships of Polish resources to her geologic structure have already been described under "Location" on page 240. With the exception of the Teschen area and Upper Silesia, Poland's boundaries have rarely been drawn with the strategy of minerals in mind. Iron ore and coal are sufficient in the west and south, and iron ore occurs also in the Carpathian slopes. Salt for domestic and industrial uses is plentiful in undisturbed beds near Cracow and in the folded Carpathian strata in the west. Potassium salts in the east encourage fertilizer and chemical manufacture. Iron ore and limestone in combination with the coal of Silesian Poland plus imported coking coal from Czechoslovakia and more iron ore from Germany form the base of a heavy steel industry extending from Silesia to Cracow. Lead and zinc in the southwest add to the mineral supplies, but copper, gold, silver, tin, aluminum, and other basic materials of modern use must be imported. Sulphur is recovered from the smelting of lead and zinc, and in part is converted into sulphuric acid. Abundant nonmetallic minerals, particularly in and north of the Carpathians, provide the raw material for the fabrication of brick, tile, pottery, chinaware, glass, and porcelain.

Soils in Poland are more diversified than is the relief. In the northern two thirds of the country they are in large part glacial, but in many places young and heavy. Where supplied with humus they are rich and productive. The foreslope of the mountains in the south, often called "loess plateau," has light, rich, mature, calcareous soils favoring wheat production. Carpathian soils are generally residual; about half are covered with valuable forests typical of a higher latitude. In the other half diversified farming and stock raising furnish meat, oats, root crops, and dairy products.

Except in winter when frozen, much of the Vistula, Warta, Netze, and many miles of the Bug rivers are navigable. Not all these rivers have been so well improved as would be possible, but all are useful at present. River water supply, supplemented by some lake water, meets many domestic and industrial needs. In addition, wells tap deep-lying strata that slope gently from the Carpathians. Land north of the mountains is rarely over 1,000 feet in altitude; hence, streams are more valuable for navigation, water supply, fishing, recreation, and scenic interests than for power. In the Carpathians water power is abundant in unfrozen seasons.

Forests are predominantly deciduous, with oak, chestnut, elm, ash, and maple; but coniferous trees mingle with the hardwoods in many places and become more and more prominent to the north. Twenty-three per cent of prewar Poland was forested, and nearly one third of this was government owned. The forests supply pulpwood and a variety of lumber for the building trades. Lumber is used extensively for houses in rural regions and towns, but stone and brick greatly predominate in the northwest, where forests are scarcer and fireproof construction is deemed more essential.

In addition to her lack of certain metals Poland suffers other limitations. Insufficient fuel or water power has prevented the realization of complete industrialization in the past. Many crops, such as cotton, silk, maize, citrus fruits, grapes, and rubber, cannot be grown. On the other hand, flax, hemp, wheat, oats, barley, stone fruits (except peaches), apples, pears, sunflowers, sugar beets, and potatoes were abundant prior to World War II.

Poland has a splendid opportunity to use her satisfactory central location, from a physical standpoint wide open to cross-country transportation. Trade reciprocity with neighbors is suggested by domestic products, industries, and needs with respect to surrounding countries. Lódz, Posen, and Warsaw manufactured large quantities of cotton and woolen goods in pre-World War I days and shipped them to Russian cities. The Polish textile industry was then largely in Russian Poland, though carried on by Poles. This is a normal outlet dictated by geography. In return, flax and flax products and minerals should flow west from Russia to Poland. Between the world wars, however, these textiles moved to Germany and stimulated the return of coal, iron ore, and food products from that country.

Human Aspects

For thousands of years the Poles have occupied the plains called Poland. In their language the word "Pole" means plain or field and the word "anie" means a dweller. Thus, a polian (polanie) is a dweller of the plains or fields, and Poland the country of the polians or polanie. Upon this physical landscape, devoid of sharp relief, has grown up a human culture characteristic of the Polish people.

Population. Population in Poland had been increasing since the establishment of the New Republic, and in 1939 was estimated at about 32,390,000, sixth among European nations. Postwar Poland, however, is esti-

mated to have only 24,000,000, the reduction partly attributable to a smaller area (about one-fifth smaller than the 150,290 square miles of prewar Poland) and partly to the loss of life during World War II. European Russia had three times as many people as prewar Poland and Germany nearly twice as many. Relative man power of neighbors and friends as well as potential enemies proved significant in the battles of World War II.

Because Poland has less waste land and more inviting topography, her density of population exceeded that of France. However, there were but seven cities larger than 100,000, whereas France with only twenty per cent more people had seventeen such cities, and Germany with less than twice Poland's population had seven times as many cities in this class. Less than one tenth of Poland's people were concentrated in these seven cities, a strong indication of the country's rural nature. Postwar Poland has lost Lwow and Wilno to Russia, but has gained the former Free City of Danzig and several large industrial cities from German Silesia, including Breslau.

Although Poles are a prolific people, the increase of population among them has been less than among the other Slav groups or among Jews. Increasing industrialization and intensification of agriculture between the world wars absorbed a substantial part of the population growth. Also twenty years of emigration to Brazil, the United States, and France have amounted to about 3,000,000 persons, equal to approximately half the normal increase for that period.

DISTRIBUTION. Between the two recent world wars the people of Poland were very unevenly distributed. The varying density in different regions was an outgrowth of several factors: topography, soils, climate, and degree of industrialization. Dense clusters appeared in the industrial west, southwest, and south sections; to the east and north the population became increasingly sparse. Average density was 230 persons per square mile. Province Polesie in the east had seventy-five persons per square mile, whereas Silesia in the southwest had ten times this number. From 1939 to 1945 approximately 5,000,000 Poles were slain by the Nazi invaders, and the areas of dense population suffered most.

Social progress. Poland has for many years valued education, and the country has produced noted musicians, painters, statesmen, poets, historians, and scientists. Beginning in 1921 the country greatly improved its school system, even in German Poland, and reduced illiteracy in Silesia by more than one third. There were about fifteen universities, including polytechnic, commerce, and mining colleges, operating in Poland between the two world wars. Higher education advanced rapidly, and the number of students and teachers increased greatly up to World War II.

Public health programs made phenomenal growth in the new Poland. Workable legislation pertaining to health insurance, hospitalization, municipal and rural sanitation, and control of diseases was enacted. Competent medical education, hospitals, clinics, sanitaria, a radium institute, and special care for the treatment of tuberculosis and other communicable diseases were provided. Probably no more advanced or scientific health program than Poland's existed in Slavdom in the late 1930's.

Religion. The fact that the Poles are Western Catholic in religion, whereas the Russians on their eastern border were Orthodox, called forth in the closing years of the sixteenth century the peculiar Uniate Church. More Greek Orthodox than Roman, it still succeeded in recognizing the supremacy of Rome. It drew many on the eastern border out of Russian influence, but at the same time preserved the Eastern ritual and the Slavonic liturgy. Since Polish Roman prelates looked down upon the Uniate Hierarchy, it tended strongly to become a peasant church.

The Reformation was never strong in Poland, spreading slowly long after its great impetus had roused Germany and other countries to the west. Nevertheless, since Poland was close to Germany, a strong Lutheran church did develop, and this growth was followed by a more varied and extensive Protestantism. As neither form was able to cope with Roman Catholic strategy and strength, however, they are represented only by small groups.

Language. Polish is a western branch of the great Slavic stem of the Aryan tongue. Like the Czech language, it has been westernized to a marked degree, far beyond the Russian dialects. Like Russian, it was originally written in the Cyrillic alphabet, which was invented in the ninth century to replace a more primitive Slavonic form. Cyrillic was superseded in Poland by the Roman alphabet through Latin influence introduced by the Roman Catholic Church in the late tenth century. Much of the literature in the eleventh and twelfth centuries was written in Latin.

Minorities. Poland's minorities, thirty per cent of the people before the recent war, grew out of her ill-defined eastern and western boundaries, her repeated expansions and contractions, her invitations to Jews and Germans to aid in business, and in recent decades invidious infiltrations of Germans. Ruthenians, comprising about fourteen per cent of the population, dwelt in East Galicia, an area formerly in the Austria-Hungarian Empire. They were given autonomy in local affairs but were not satisfied. White Ruthenians and Russians farther north constituted four per cent scattered among Poles. Jews, who made up about eight per cent of the population, came for centuries from Germany and Austria and were never expelled by the Poles. Although they received many privileges, they were burdened with onerous restrictions as to trades, businesses, and locations; yet before Hitler's onslaught they flourished everywhere, particularly in cities. They constituted eighty-four per cent of the merchants, fifty-one per cent of the educators, and twenty-four per cent of the physicians, but only two per cent of the farmers, miners, and factory workers. Their lack of national feeling—not disloyalty—made them a problem. They sought religious liberty, but scarcely political equality. The whole Jewish question has changed with the murder of over two and a half million of them by the Nazis. Germans, who formed another minority of about three per cent, in many cases crowded over their borders along lines of transportation and in areas of industry. They retained citizenship in Germany even when living permanently in Poland. Lithuanians, amounting to about three per cent, were only partly assimilated, but these were not a restless or serious group, and many are now in Soviet territory because of the recent boundary shift. A Polish minorities treaty signed in 1919 granted Polish citizenship, if desired, to all bona fide inhabitants except recent German colonists. The conditions of the treaty also provided for the use of their own language and institutions, and primary instruction in their languages wherever there were groups large enough for such schools. On the whole Poland has been generous to her minorities.

Economic Aspects

Agriculture. Agriculture in Poland, as in most countries of eastern Europe, has been the primary basis for her economic life, although the exploitation of mineral resources has given rise to a considerable amount of industrial activity. Especially in the southern two thirds of the country the tilling of the fertile soil normally brings abundant harvests of northern grains and root crops, such as sugar beets, turnips, potatoes, and onions. In the poorer lands of the northwest grazing and dairying form the primary activities, and flax and hemp replace cereal crops.

Fuel. Before World War II Poland ranked as high as third in the annual output of coal in Europe. The richest fields lay in Upper Silesia and the Cracow area. Oil, developed in part by foreign capital and experience, was produced in the Carpathian area in East Galicia (now largely Russian). Although this region had the largest production of any oil field in Europe outside of Russia and Rumania, it yielded only a small fraction of the output of either. Polish industries depended in part upon these fuels and in part upon the country's forest resources and its localized water power.

Manufacturing and commerce. The textile industries of prewar Poland exceeded all others in value. Imported cotton, silk, and jute added to native wool, flax, and hemp made possible a large cloth, yarn, rope, embroidery, and clothing production. Normally, chemical and ceramic industries are important. Sixty to eighty refineries, varying in number with the size of the beet crop, produced enough sugar to give Poland fourth rank in Europe. Other food industries processed rye, wheat, barley, meat, and potatoes for domestic use. From the forests came pulpwood for paper as well as timber for lumber and wood products.

While under foreign control, from 1795 to 1919, all three parts of Poland (Russian, German, and Austrian) were hampered because

transportation was subservient to military rather than to economic interests. After World War I, railroads, the port at Gdynia, and several canals came under government control. Conscious of her transportation shortcomings, Poland forged ahead in the construction of railroads and waterways. Many miles of existing railroads were relaid in order to unify their gauges and make them of real value for domestic trade. Rivers, which were in part internationalized and granted a toll system, were to be maintained in usable condition by Poland. In 1929 the national airline, "LOT," was inaugurated, and soon established an air network connecting Warsaw and other Polish cities with large centers in other countries in eastern and central Europe. World War II and resultant boundary changes have again disrupted the country's transportation system.

Even during much of the partition from 1795-1919, foreign trade was healthy for Poland, for Russia took large quantities of textiles and Germany bought and sold goods freely. Despite the loss of Russia as a market at the close of World War I, Germany continued much as before. Great Britain became more prominent, both in importing and exporting goods, and was credited with about seven per cent of Poland's total trade. Trade agreements were written with a score of nations. Exports were cereals, sugar, flax, dairy products, forest products, textiles, coal, iron, steel, petroleum, and chemicals. Imports consisted of fertilizers, farm equipment, machinery, raw materials (for many industries), fish, fats, cocoa, and other food stuffs not obtainable by domestic production.

In World War II tremendous damage was done to homes, to small business, to manufacturing, and to transportation facilities. Whole towns were completely razed, and great areas of cities, docks, warehouses, and farms were blasted to destruction. Foreign trade was almost annihilated and home trade stagnated. Recovery is just as possible as it was after World War I, but such rehabilitation presents another major problem for Poland and her people.

Cities. Before the recent war Poland's large cities could be classified as commercial, industrial, and administrative. Each individual city tended to stand out as one or another of these, the exception being Warsaw.

As the largest city, with a population nearly as large as that of the next three Polish cities combined, Warsaw embraced all three classes. With a prewar population of about a million and a quarter the city occupied a fine site on the Vistula a few miles above the mouth of the Bug. During the period from 1813 on to 1919 Warsaw was a local capital of Russian Poland. After World War II it was reinstated as the national capital of the new Poland and became a railroad center and international air terminal, and had many fine business blocks and attractive residences. Many industrial enterprises flourish: textiles, machinery, food-processing plants, paper, printing, and the banking system.

Old capitals were Cracow and Lemberg, and both have retained a certain amount of importance; the latter, however, is now in Soviet Russia. In the twentieth century they became industrialized. Cracow, with a quarter of a million inhabitants, became known for its textiles, their reputation being based upon skillful handicraft. Lódz, the woolen center for 1,000 years, is now the principal city in a group of four industrial towns on the northern edge of the upland. It manufactures cotton, wool, silk, and mixed fabrics, chemicals, beer, and machinery. As a result of its industrial expansion, the city in seventy-five years grew in population from 50,000 to over 600,000.

Commercial cities associated with Poland's access to the Baltic are Danzig, the old delta city on the Motlau, and Gdynia, the new seaport on the Baltic sea coast in the former Polish Corridor. Danzig was an important trading center in Hanseatic days, and its importance has persisted through six centuries to the present time. At various times in its history it has been a part of Germany, a part of Poland, and the basis of a free city state. It had this latter status at the outbreak of World War II in 1939, at which time it contained a population exceeding 400,000. Danzig is advantageously situated with respect to the Vistula River, which drains the heart of Poland. Like most large rivers the Vistula divides in its delta into many distributaries, of which Motlau River is the westernmost. These distributaries are connected by canals, so that most of the commercial city is served by waterways as well as by streets. Old warehouses on the water's edge, many with pulleys in their gables, still are in service. The city's amber market, known in prehistoric days, is still active. The railroad and airplane reach its modern business life, and its waterways are kept dredged to serve ocean vessels.

It is not natural to think of Danzig as being separate from Poland, but at the close of World War I it was made a Free City with surrounding delta territory embracing in all 791 square miles, some thirty villages, and several coast towns. Although Danzig was within the Polish customs unit, it remained in practice a territory closely allied with Germany. As might be expected, since the city lies adjacent to East Prussia, more than ninety per cent of its population was German. As soon as Danzig became a Free City, Poland began to build Gdynia on the coast of its corridor, about twelve miles northwest of Danzig. The dredging and building continued during the 1920's and 1930's until harbors of thirty-five feet depth, thousands of feet of piers, warehouses, grain elevators, and full harbor equipment were installed. Gdynia became both a commercial seaport and a naval base on the Baltic Sea within the Polish domain. Before the recent war intercepted its growth the population of the city had grown to about 113,000.

Problems of the Future

Poland has the advantage of a long historical and strong cultural homogeneity coupled with an intense patriotism and a feeling of unity. The latter is geographic in its implications, founded upon the basin of the Vistula. Although these factors form a sound basis for entity, it remains necessary for the people to solve a multitude of problems before they may establish a strong state.

Internal problems. The desire of the Poles to annex all the lands they ever possessed, regardless of the approval of the present inhabitants, has often proved a political blunder. On the other hand, Poland's religious diversity has been handled well in its constitutional period. Continued tolerance and cooperation in religious and social work will do much to foster a healthy spirit within the governmental framework. Internal differences nurtured by long partition still exist, but the best inheritance in each experience can be shared by all three parts if at the same time there be tolerance when conflicts of interest or biases appear.

In many respects the state has taken a commendable attitude toward its minorities. Their origins are historic, and the Poles are responsible for many of them. In the interest of national peace and strength the necessity for careful study of their rights and obligations is evident.

Overpopulation has been serious in Poland and will be so again as the scars of war disappear. Probably some emigration is wise as long as the people remain so prolific, but a stable population is devoutly to be desired. With the flight or transfer of most of the Germans to points west of the Oder-Neisse line, Poland plans to ease her problem somewhat by populating the newly acquired area with Poles.

External problems. The first external problem facing Poland is the exact determination of her boundaries. Under the terms of the Potsdam Agreement, August 2, 1945, the frontier with Germany is tentatively placed east of the Oder, and, above Grieg, east of the Neisse. This new border places nearly all the mineral wealth of Upper Silesia in Poland. The northern frontier is the Baltic coast meander, beginning in the vicinity of Swinemuende and extending through Danzig to south of Königsberg in former German East Prussia. Poland acquired the German city of Stettin on the west bank of the Oder. East Prussia is divided between Poland and Soviet Russia, the latter keeping Königsberg.

In August, 1945, Poland and Soviet Russia agreed approximately on the Curzon Line as the international boundary to separate the two countries. This line gives Poland a short boundary with Soviet Lithuania from East Prussia to just beyond the Niemen. Between Poland and Soviet Russia the new border follows ethnic distributions in such a way as to divide Poles from Russians reasonably well. Wilno, Pinsk, and most of the Pripet Marshes are left out of Poland. From Brest-Litovsk the boundary follows the Bug River south. The southern boundary with Czechoslovakia lies as before the last war and leaves possession of the Teschen area for later settlement by the two nations.

As neighbors are a part of a nation's environment, it is important that any national administration and its people shall adjust to their neighbors near and far. Poland needs to approach hers as modern world problems, not historical ones; to see them objectively, not subjectively. Russians and Germans present the great problems; with Lithuanians the Polish people have much history in common and their predominant religions are similar; and in the case of the Poles and the Czechs both groups are Western Slavs, both have been interior nations, and both are well supplied in their mountainous regions with natural resources. Poland could make profitable use of the Moravian Gate across Czechoslovakia to nations southward and the Mediterranean. Nations in western Europe may sometime again be valuable friends and allies. Such has been Poland's relationship with France, and such was the influence that brought England to her side when the Reich marched onto her soil in 1939. Treaties based on real needs are good politics. A transitional state, if in healthy relations with its neighbors, is bound to be a buffer state, but need not be a cockpit.

| # The Lesser Countries of Central Europe

CZECHOSLOVAKIA, Austria, and Hungary form a small cluster of countries in the heart of Europe throughout which the factors of political geography have a number of elements in common (see the map directly below). All

LESSER COUNTRIES OF CENTRAL EUROPE

three states are strongly affected by the great Danube River, which flows in a general southeasterly direction through the interior of the continent.* All three have been subject to multifarious outside influences and pressures. A highly centralized position has given them dynamic contact with western, northern, eastern, and southern Europe. From all directions have come peoples and ideas, each of them making its contribution to the political, cultural, and economic patterns of the region.

As an expression of mutual political de-

* Rumania, Yugoslavia, and Bulgaria, countries that also have territory in the Danube basin, are considered in the next chapter. The term "Danubia" has by some writers been used to designate the countries closely associated with the Danube. In this book the term is employed only in a general sense.

velopment, Czechoslovakia, Austria, and Hungary together make up a predominant proportion of the area that previously formed the realm of the old Habsburg monarchy and, later, the Austro-Hungarian Empire. Because of its location, large size, and considerable population, Austria-Hungary played a significant role in European politics prior to World War I. After the defeat of the Central Powers the three countries were organized as separate political entities. As national groups, however, the inhabitants of each country had long occupied the same general areas delineated by the international boundaries formulated at Versailles. World War II saw their participation, willing or unwilling, as a part of Nazi Germany's "Fortress Europe." In the postwar world each of the trio is receiving a second chance (though somewhat restricted by the Great Powers) in less than a half century to make its own way as a minor power in a continent dominated by major powers.

Influence of the Danube River

The location of Czechoslovakia, Austria, and Hungary along the Danube, one of the longest European rivers, has been of supreme importance historically (see the map on page 250). The most favorable direction for a military entry to central-eastern Europe has always been along the Danube, whether the invasion was from downstream (east) or upstream (west). From the dawn of history peoples and empires have struggled to obtain mastery of the Danube or to exclude others, the attacks producing disunion and confusion and the confusion inviting fresh attacks.

Basic Danubian communications. Several connections lead to the ancient Danubian line of communications. These permit entry to the historic corridor from the east as well as the west. First, the northern route to the Danube basin from the west, which was fol-

verse nomadic tribes, provides access to the Danube through the Gateway of Moravia. Using that route were the Huns, the Avars, the Magyars, and the Tartars—Mongolians who either fought one another or went forth to plunder in the fertile lands of the Danube,

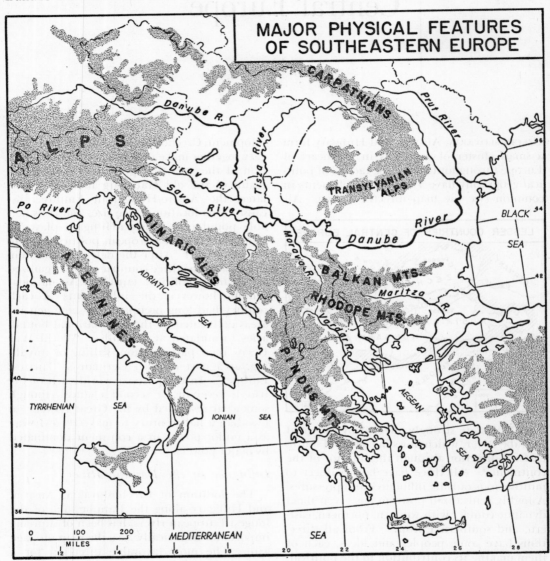

lowed by the Germans who came from the Rhine Valley and from the area east of the Rhine, starts in the Germanic forests north of the Alps. Second, a southern route from the west, which was used by the Romans in ancient times, leads from the Apennine Peninsula south of the Alps. Third, the northern route from the east, which was used by di-

in the Balkans, and in Italy. Long known as the "Amber Route," this passage also links the Baltic Sea with the Adriatic via the low-lying Danube basin. Fourth, a southern route from the east, which was used by the Ottoman Turks at the opening of the modern era, leads from Asia Minor via the Balkan Peninsula.

It is significant to note that these four historic routes lead to the Danube from four widely different directions, each offering an avenue of invasion. The northern and southern routes from the west to the Danube basin are separated from each other by the Alps. In a somewhat similar manner the northern and southern routes from the east are divided by the Black Sea.

The middle Danube—kernel of routes. Points of origin for these trade and military routes to the Danube basin are diverse—the Apennine Peninsula, the Balkans, the Rhineland, the Elbe valley, and the middle reaches of the Dnieper. But the points of destination are confined to the stretch of the upper Danube between its confluence with the Enns on the west and the Ipel on the east. This portion of the Danube between the Enns and the Ipel, some 300 miles in length, thus represents the main military crossroads in central-eastern Europe. Important centers of communications have arisen in this sector of the Danube, among them Vienna, Bratislava, and Budapest. Vienna is a junction not only for communications from west to east in Europe but also from north to south. In modern times the Orient Express runs precisely along the old Rhine-Danube line of communications. The old "Amber Route" from the Baltic to the Adriatic is likewise followed by a railway, including the strategic gateway section between Bohumín in Silesia and Přerov in Moravia (see the map on page 261).

In the beginning of the Christian era, Danubian Europe north of the crescent was inhabited in the west by the Germanic and in the east by the Slavic tribes. On the Hungarian Plain in the tenth century there appeared new nomads—the Magyars. Their incursions into Germany along the Danube and via the Gateway of Moravia forced the Slavs in the north to join forces with the Germans. The Turks pushing up through the Balkans to central Europe along the Danube brought many Germans, Slavs, and Hungarians (Magyars) together under the Habsburg monarchy by 1526.

Starting in the seventeenth century, the imperial forces of the Habsburgs, supported by the Poles and Croats, slowly pushed the Turks back to the Balkans. Then in the eighteenth century the Turkish thrust, which for three centuries had been directed northwestward along the Danube, was replaced by German pressure exerted in precisely the opposite direction. Furthermore, two other thrusts were destined: one from the southwest along the old Roman route, represented by the gradual Risorgimento of Italy; and the other along the old Mongolian routes from the Russian steppes, where the Russian Empire started searching for "the window in the west."

During the nineteenth century, Austria (Austria-Hungary after 1867) became a more definite object of three pressures from the Danubian periphery: Italian, Russian, and German (the German Empire). After the formation of the Dual Alliance in 1879 between Austria-Hungary and Germany, the former was in reality only a German *Ostmark* on an enlarged scale. Germany, as the strongest state in central Europe, used the docility of Austria-Hungary to insure connection with the Balkans and, across the Dardanelles, with Asia Minor. Her efforts to dominate the Hamburg-Basra axis helped to produce World War I.

The Birth and Rebirth of the "Lesser Countries"

As a result of World War I the geopolitical picture of the Danube basin changed markedly. The Slavs and other dissatisfied members of the Austro-Hungarian monarchy

FORMER AUSTRO-HUNGARIAN EMPIRE

——— International Boundary (1937)   ░░ Area Taken From Austria-Hungary

0   100   200
MILES

revolted against German and Magyar domination, and Austria-Hungary as an empire fell to pieces. Austria and Hungary emerged as separate states. Czechoslovakia, Poland, Yugoslavia, Italy, and Rumania acquired the remaining portions of the Habsburg crown lands (see the map on page 251).

The next two decades were characterized by the efforts of Italy and then of Germany to replace French and British influence in the Danube basin and the Balkans.

The appeasement policies of England and France, culminating in Munich (1938), released the Nazi flood of conquest that swallowed Austria, Czechoslovakia, and Hungary and, until 1945, incorporated them into German-controlled Europe. With the defeat of Germany in May of that year, the somewhat different forms of these three states reappeared again in the Danube basin—this time generally dominated by policies favorable to the Soviets. The smashed Germanic thrust into the Danube basin had been replaced by that of Soviet Russia.

CZECHOSLOVAKIA

Physical Aspects

The "new" Czechoslovakia that appeared on the map of Europe in 1918 consisted of the so-called "historical lands" of Bohemia,* Moravia, and part of Upper Silesia, the constituent parts of the one-time Kingdom of Bohemia; and of Slovakia and Ruthenia (annexed by Russia in 1945), both of which territories formerly belonged to Hungary. The historical lands were slightly increased further at the expense of Germany by the assignation of the district of Hlučín to the new Republic, and at the expense of Austria by the allotment of the districts of Valtice and Vitoráz. To the east of the historical lands, by the decision of the Council of Ambassadors of July 28, 1920, the western part of the Duchy of Teschen (Těšin) was also transferred to Czechoslovakia. Ruthenia was incorporated in the Republic as an autonomous territory. At no point did the component parts making up Czechoslovakia touch the sea; therefore the country was landlocked. This handicap obviously lends importance to its position on the Danube waterway.

The total area of Czechoslovakia (1920-38) was 54,000 square miles, comparable in size and in its elongated shape to Florida. At present the area amounts to about 49,000 square miles. From north to south, the country has dimensions suggestive of Belgium or Holland. From west to east, however, it was (when it included Ruthenia) as long as the island of Great Britain or the peninsular part of Italy (see the map on page 263).

In western Czechoslovakia appear characteristics typical of the whole northwest of Europe—an intensive and highly specialized industrial development, intensive and rationalized agricultural practices, and a concentration of the population in urban communities. But as one progresses from west to east, the regions and the life become more and more rustic, picturesque, and primitive, until in the extreme east one can walk through primeval forests, which 2,000 years ago blocked the path of the Roman legions on their way northward. Here the frontier of southeastern Europe's region of wine, maize, and tobacco extends to the very threshold of the north. It is the country of the workers and peasants, of people bound to the land and to the sources of production.

Climate. Although Czechoslovakia's position places her in the temperate zone, a typically continental climate and a variety of relief features cause differences in temperature between her northern and southern borders. Between the districts at her extreme western and eastern ends temperature differences are much more marked, for the influence of the Atlantic Ocean is noticeable in the west and fades out to the east. Generally speaking, the warmest parts are the plains and the coldest are the mountains. A remarkable minimum of temperature is recorded in deep highland valleys (especially in Slovakia), into which the cold air pours from the surrounding mountains. Sheltered from the north wind by the mountains on her

---

* Originally, the name pertained to the Bohemian Kingdom of the Middle Ages. After the Hussite Wars (1419-34) and the defeat of the Bohemians at the Battle of White Mountain (1620), many nationals of the vanquished kingdom were scattered through Europe. Names of principal politico-geographic regions used in this chapter (Bohemia, Moravia, Slovakia, etc.) are shown in the map on page 263.

frontiers, there are vine-growing districts in northern Bohemia. The seasons are clearly differentiated, a wet spring and autumn alternating with a comparatively dry summer and winter. Lacking climatic extremes for the most part, the country does suffer from destructive hail storms.

Economic Evaluation

Farm and forest. Agricultural development in Czechoslovakia, particularly in the west, has benefited from intelligent legislation and an energetic population. The intensive methods of land cultivation and cattle breeding were facilitated by a reasonable distribution of land ownership introduced by the Czechoslovak Land Reform acts of 1919 and of subsequent years. From 1934 on, the State Grain Monopoly, representing producers, merchants, millers, and consumers, regulated the supply of home-grown and imported grain. The intensity of cultivation decreases from west to east. The grain-bearing zone comprises the greater part of the Republic, the main crops being barley and wheat, with rye and oats being pushed into the higher regions. In the sugar beet zone wheat and barley are important secondary crops. Maize thrives in the fertile plains in southern Slovakia. Regions producing grain and potatoes have numerous distilleries and starch factories concentrated in the areas.

Forests occupy nearly one third of the total area in the country and provide a valuable source of income. In contrast to agricultural land, the proportion of the area in forest increases from west to east.

Industry. Many of Czechoslovakia's industrial products have an international reputation for quality. Techniques common to the manufacturing districts of northwest Europe and east central North America are employed, including mass production. The individual items manufactured cover a wide range, but in total indicate a type of production suitable for people with a high standard of living. High-speed steel, machines, and machine tools give evidence as to the complexity of the industrialization. In the textile and ready-made clothing categories are cotton and woolen goods, shoes, knitted wear, hats, stockings, linen, and gloves. Other items include toys, glass, earthenware, china, fancy goods made of glass and leather, bent-wood furniture, malt, beer, ham, and sugar. The natural bases of Czechoslovakia's industrial production are her deposits of pit coal and lignite, certain iron ores, timber, kaolin, and glass sand. On the whole, however, the natural resources of the country are not abundant, and the industrial economy must necessarily rest on free interchange with other regions.

In prewar Czechoslovakia, occupational groups were numerically well balanced. According to the census of 1930, a little more than one third of the population lived by agriculture, forestry, and fisheries; an equal proportion by industry and crafts; an eighth by commerce, transportation, and finance; and about a sixth by the professions and public service. There was a trend toward industry and commerce at the expense of agriculture, but not so marked as in many countries. The western provinces of Bohemia, Moravia, and Silesia are much more industrialized than Slovakia or former Czechoslovak Ruthenia in the east.

Cities. The diversity of the geographic regions within Czechoslovakia has facilitated the development of numerous cities as regional centers, each serving the interests of the particular type of economy within its region. Only the capital city of Prague, with 924,000 persons, stands out as having extensive nationwide interests. Brno, in western Moravia, and Ostrava, in the Silesian district, are both industrial cities, ranking as the second and third Czechoslovakian urban centers, with a population of 269,000 and 176,000 respectively. Bratislava (formerly Pressburg) on the Danube, in southern Slovakia, and Pilsen (Plzeň), in western Bohemia, are the only other cities in the country exceeding 100,000 in population; the former the only Danubian port in Czechoslovakia and the latter the home of the famous Škoda iron works.

Transportation. Czechoslovakia is no exception to the majority of European states that consider the telegraph, telephones, and railways state services just as essential as the post office. They are owned by the state, together with several hundred bus routes and the commercial air transportation of the country. Street railways and electric, gas, and water services are owned and operated by municipalities, or as cooperatives in country districts and villages. Inheriting the communication system built on the more extensive needs of old Austria-Hungary, Czechoslovakia tried very hard to build and maintain roads that would be geared into international communication. The basis of the inland waterway system is formed by the Elbe with its tributary, the Vltava, which connects Czechoslovakia with the North Sea; the Danube, which forms the southern boundary of the state for 106 miles and links the country with the Black Sea; and finally the Oder, which connects the region with the Baltic.

Geopolitical Implications

Historical background. Westernmost outpost of the Slavic world, Czechoslovakia has always been a relatively isolated ethnic region almost entirely surrounded by a threatening German force. Time and again the mountain ranges at its borders acted as barriers against enemy pressure. The Czechs have lived since the sixth century under constant Germanic pressure for expansion, exerted under the guise of the need for *Lebensraum,* or space for living. As a result, Czech history is a history of constant wars against the Germans or the Austrians. Every generation of Czechs had to fight, either with sword or spirit, against Germanic aggression. The Slovaks, on the other hand, were conquered in the eleventh century and subjected to de-nationalization by the Magyars, who separated Slovakia from Bohemia-Moravia.

When World War I began, the Czechs and Slovaks initiated their revolt against the Austro-Hungarian monarchy. Professor Thomas Garrigue Masaryk and Dr. Eduard Beneš, together with General Štefánik, organized the Czechoslovak movement abroad and secured the support of the Allies for the formation of an independent Czechoslovak state. The new Czechoslovak republic, headed first by President Masaryk (1918–35) and then by President Beneš (1935–38), prospered. The late 1930's produced the Munich agreement, wherein Czechoslovakia was abandoned to Hitler. Again, as in World War I, Beneš (this time without Masaryk) escaped abroad and organized Czechoslovak resistance against the oppressors of his nation. His government was recognized by all members of the United Nations. He returned in 1945, when the country was liberated by the Russians and the Americans.

Minority problems. Czechoslovakia's outstanding problem in the interwar period was that of minorities. In a total population in 1938 of 15,250,000, Czechoslovaks predominated to the extent of 64 per cent, or a total of 9,750,000. Other nationalities were Germans (23 per cent), Hungarians (or Magyars) (5 per cent), Jews, Poles, Rumanians, Yugoslavs, and a few others (each one per cent or less).

The Republic of Czechoslovakia signed a minorities treaty providing for the fair treatment of minorities by the Czechoslovak government and, according to unbiased reports, executed the provisions of the treaty in a democratic and tolerant manner.* The problem of the Sudeten Germans proved to be the most difficult. Contrary to the popular conception, Czechoslovakia did not acquire the Sudeten Germans from modern Germany. From the twelfth to the fourteenth centuries, Germans settled in Bohemia at the invitation of the Bohemian rulers as artisans, miners, and priests.

At the end of World War I, Czechoslovakia chose to include the Sudeten area on the grounds that its inclusion strategically strengthened the frontier between Germany and Czechoslovakia. But the Sudeten Germans, reduced from a position of dominance to that of a minority, naturally resented the new setup and welcomed Nazi political advances after 1933. Konrad Henlein, Hitler's agent, organized the pro-Nazi Sudeten Germans. After Munich, these Germans were delighted to become members of the Greater German Reich. During World War II they fought on all fronts with unbounded enthusiasm. Czechoslovakia planned to deport, over a period of several years, the Sudeten Germans who were considered disloyal. In 1945 and 1946 many were shipped into the American zone of occupation in Germany.

The Slovak problem. As in the case of the Sudetenland, Hitler made use of a section of Slovak dissidents to aid in the dismemberment

---

* For more details, see Joseph S. Roucek, "Czechoslovakia and Her Minorities," Chapter IX, pp. 172–192, in Robert J. Kerner, Ed., *Czechoslovakia, Twenty Years of Independence* (Berkeley, Cal.: University of California Press, 1940).

of Czechoslovakia. The religious issue was in part responsible for difficulties that existed between Czechs and Slovaks. Of the Protestant Czechs who came to Slovakia as teachers and administrators some offended the religious feelings of the Slovak peasantry, who were predominantly Catholic. The opposition to the Czechs was led by Father Hlinka, a Roman Catholic priest who exercised great influence over the Slovaks. After Hlinka's death in 1938, his place was taken by Father Tiso, also a priest, who until 1945 headed "independent" Slovakia under Hitler. The watchword of this Hlinka party was "Autonomy for Slovakia." This party, although numerically the strongest of all Slovak factions, had a bare majority of the Slovak votes. Considerable opposition to old patterns of government existed in the Slovak part of Czechoslovakia, until they were abolished in the Communist *coup d'etat* early in 1948.

The "new" Czechoslovakia. During World War II the country was not devastated as were the neighboring countries. Nevertheless, the problem of feeding the population and of restoring the economic foundations of the state was enormous. The population of 14,200,-000 at the end of the war amounted to about a million less than the maximum prewar number.

LANGUAGE AND RELIGION. Languages in Czechoslovakia roughly correspond with the racial stocks living in that country. Before the forced migrations that took place after the end of World War II, about 70 per cent of the people spoke Czechoslovak, another 24 per cent spoke German, and almost all the rest spoke Magyar. Ruthenian was virtually eliminated as a national language when Ruthenia became Soviet territory in 1945.

The majority of the population in modern-day Czechoslovakia is Roman Catholic—nearly 70 per cent, according to a 1947 estimate. The remainder of the people belong to the Czechoslovak church (which broke off from the Roman Catholic in 1920), or are Protestants, Jews, Orthodox, or those without confession.

TERRITORIAL PROBLEMS. After World War II the old problem of Teschen stood as one of the leading issues in the final settlement of Czechoslovakia's boundaries. Czech Teschen had been seized by Poland at the time of Munich, and its restoration became a matter

of prime concern. As previously stated, this vitally important portion of the old Duchy of Teschen was assigned to Czechoslovakia by a decision of the Allied Council of Ambassadors in July of 1920. From November, 1918, until the spring of 1920, Czechs and Poles had argued—even fought—over a zone containing many coal fields and the area including the railroad junction of Bohumín and the line running south from Bohumín. The area in dispute, in 1948 as in 1920, was actually inhabited by Czechs, Poles, and Germans. Any line of demarcation will do some ethnic injustice to Czechs and Poles alike. The 1920 frontier, which followed rather closely a line proposed by American observers, was drawn in such a way as to give Czechoslovakia the major portion of the coal fields and the railroad line, which was and is the principal west-east line connecting Bohemia-Moravia with Slovakia. Poland exported coal between 1920 and 1938 and might have encountered great difficulty in marketing her own output had it not been for the approaching European war and the German war industries, which absorbed what was expected to be an unmarketable surplus.

Ruthenia, or Carpatho-Ukraine, is now Soviet territory by agreement of Czechoslovakia and the U. S. S. R. as of June, 1945. This territory was independent for a few hours at the time of Czechoslovakia's dissolution (March, 1939) and then was seized by Hungary. In the period between the two wars some of its very few leaders were rather unhappy in Czechoslovakia. It must be admitted that the province was always an economic drain upon the Czechoslovak State; of the four major divisions in Czechoslovakia it was the most backward on virtually every count. For Russia, however, possession of this region offers the distinct advantage of providing direct access to the Hungarian Plain (see the map on page 259).

A portion of the Hungarian Plain within Slovakia was seized by Hungary in the days of Munich. Czechoslovakia has now not only regained this territory from Hungary but also has acquired a small area of land from the same country to allow the enlargement of the Danube port of Bratislava. In the peace treaty with Germany, Czechoslovakia expects the rectification of her boundary with the Reich.

AUSTRIA

The Republic

The Republic of Austria emerged from the wreckage of the Austro-Hungarian monarchy in November, 1918 (see the map on page 251). After World War I Austria was completely surrounded by a group of countries anxious to sell their exports and exceedingly reluctant to take Austrian exports in exchange. Few could imagine that this little remnant of the Empire would survive as long as twenty years. Formerly the metropolis for much of Austria-Hungary, the great capital city of Vienna with its two million people alone accounted for nearly one third of the population of the "beheaded" state containing only 32,000 square miles. Vienna's 1946 population estimate of 1,407,000, however, shows an appreciable reduction in the number of inhabitants. The second and third Austrian cities, Graz with 208,000 persons and Linz with 128,000, were more closely adjusted to the regional economy and its commercial needs.

Resources. Deficient in food-bearing soil, and particularly lacking in wheat-growing areas, Austria was forced to export to buy foodstuffs and raw materials, such as cotton, wool, and coal. In the inter-war period the small republic harnessed water power to replace coal that had formerly come from the Empire, developed basic agriculture, and furthered the development of the textile industry. Despite the most drastic restrictions on imports, the country suffered steadily from a large adverse balance of trade. Repeated borrowing from abroad provided relief from more than one economic crisis.

Cultural Aspects

History. For many centuries Austria was the core of the Holy Roman Empire and, until 1918, the heart of the multi-racial Habsburg state. During the latter regime it was threatened both by the Slavs under Russian influence and by the newly united Prussianized Germans. After World War I Austria favored a union with the German Republic, but the Allied Powers refused to allow it. In 1934 Nazi forces precipitated an uprising in Austria, and in March, 1938, annexed the Republic. In a "bloodless blitz" Austria's absorption in this fashion was a prelude to Munich and World War II.

People. Before World War II Austria had approximately 6,650,000 inhabitants. Of this number, 6,500,000 spoke German and the remaining 150,000 consisted of small minorities, chiefly Croats, Slovenes, Czechs, and Magyars. The strongest minority was that of the Yugoslavs (88,000), formed in part by the Croats, concentrated in the former western Hungarian province of Burgenland, and in part by the Slovenes, settled to the south in Carinthia. Nearly 100,000 Czechs represented the remnants of a once much more numerous body inhabiting Vienna and the adjacent districts of Lower Austria. A small group of Magyars lived in Vienna and in Burgenland. In addition, Southern Tyrol, annexed by Italy, had an intermixture of Italians and Germans. Less than three per cent of Austria's inhabitants were Jews, of whom more than ninety per cent were concentrated in Vienna.

In general, the workers of Vienna and of the industrial area, running as far south as Wiener-Neustadt, were militantly anti-clerical. On the other hand, both the peasant and the landowning groups in the rural areas continued their historic allegiance to and support of the Roman Catholic Church.

There were some who had believed Hitler's empty promises and had been dazzled by the glitter of the might of a "Greater Germany." After a year or so of the Nazi regime, however, all but a small minority desired the departure of the Germans. "Go-slow" movements in the factories, grumbling, and critical jokes were quite universal.

By 1944 under the Nazis there was nothing Austrians could call their own. Their industries were under the control of a few huge German monopoly combines; their banks were all but nominally branches of the German Big Five; their savings were frozen in German state bonds; and their cities, especially Vienna and Linz, swarmed with armies of Nazi officials, Gestapo agents, profiteers, and evacuees from the Reich. Further, much of their forests had been cut down; their iron ore, magnesite, and oil were being fed to the German war machine; and even their milk and butter were going to the Reich. Even worse, the country's man power had been bled white on the battlefields of Russia. In short, the Austrians under German imperialism enjoyed a status little if any better than slaves.

The Rebirth of Austria

Liberated in 1945, Austria was placed under the military control of France, Great Britain, the United States, and Soviet Russia. More than two years later no progress toward unification of administration had been made in the Allied Control Council, nor had there been any implementation of the declaration issued at Moscow in November, 1943.

Territorial problems. The postwar boundary of Austria is likely to remain substantially the same as before the recent war. Austria has been refused a request to annex the South Tyrol, which was ceded to Italy in 1919. Marshal Tito of Yugoslavia, who has strong Russian support, has claimed a part of Carinthia from Austria; but the Americans, British, and French are opposed to the claim.*

* See page 270 for a more detailed discussion of this territorial controversy.

HUNGARY

Between 1920 and 1938 Hungary lay just south of Czechoslovakia. Of the two countries Hungary was somewhat smaller in size and much more compact in shape. Prior to 1920 old Hungary, the eastern half of the dual Austro-Hungarian monarchy, was a large basin surrounded by mountains on every side except the south. The new boundaries, drawn up after World War I, were natural only along the Danube in the northwest and the Drava in the southwest. Elsewhere the borders had no physical basis, for in the northeast and in the east they ran south of the Carpathians, and in the south they cut through the southern section of the great Hungarian Plain.

Geographic Aspects

Area. The Treaty of Trianon (1920) reduced Hungary to a little less than 36,000 square miles, approximately a third of its former area (see the map on page 251). Excluded from the newly formed Hungary were rich mineral resources and extensive timber lands. The core of the country was, and presently is, the great Hungarian Plain, lying in the eastern half of the country and reaching from the Czechoslovak frontier on the north to that of Yugoslavia on the south. Its greatest length is traversed by the Tisza (Theiss) River. Its undulating surface is marked with salt marshes, sand dunes, and rows of mounds. Broad roads and railways form a cultural pattern over formerly lonely tracts. Occupying a substantial proportion of the area, immense pastures provide forage well suited for cattle, horses, sheep, and swine.

Economy. Trianon Hungary was almost devoid of mineral resources, and agriculture was the basis of Hungarian life. Of the entire population, slightly over 50 per cent were engaged in agricultural work, as compared with 30 per cent in industrial and commercial activities. Of the total area, 60 per cent was arable, 18 per cent meadowland and rough pasture, and 12 per cent forest. Next to Russia, Hungary was the biggest wheat exporter in Europe. The cultivation of vines, fruit, and garden produce also was a significant feature of the Hungarian economy. More than half of the vineyard area is in the drift sand districts, which are immune from Phylloxera.* The extensive grasslands in the western part of Hungary have been developed as a cattle-raising region.

In 1938–39 the partitioning of Czechoslovakia by the Nazis restored mountainous Ruthenia and the fertile farm lands of southern Slovakia to Hungary. By the end of 1940, nearly half of Transylvania, with its wealth of gold, silver, lead, copper, and zinc, and its natural gas, had also been returned to Hungary by Rumania under Nazi pressure. In 1941 Hungary occupied the fertile border lands of Baranja and Bachka, awarded to Yugoslavia at the close of World War I.

As a dominantly agrarian country Hun-

* Phylloxera, plant lice deadly to the vine, wiped out entire areas of vineyard in some sections of Europe, including southern France.

gary is not highly urbanized. The only city of great size is Budapest with a population of more than a million. Situated on the navigable Danube and at the edge of the broad Hungarian Plain, the city serves as the political, commercial, and cultural heart of the nation and is also the leading manufacturing center.* Elsewhere in Hungary, cities are little more than rural communities of local significance, although three of them, Szeged, Debrecen, and Miskolc, each exceed 100,000 in population.

Land reform. The Hungary of the interwar period was primarily a land of large estates. Over half the farm land was in the hands of the landed gentry. The remainder consisted of minute to small peasant holdings averaging around eight acres per holding. Landless laborers, numbering several millions, were paid in kind, and often before the end of a winter were without resources. Such land reforms as the Hungarian Parliament passed made the lot of the peasants even more difficult. The inarticulate misery of the farmer was exploited with some success by the Arrow-Cross Movement, an anti-Semitic group with Nazi connections. This group attempted to convert the peasant to a nationalistic program of land reform.

Political Aspects

History. The exact origin of the Hungarians, or Magyars, is a matter of involved dispute. The accepted opinion is that they are a Mongolian people—like the Huns and the original Bulgars—whose earliest homes were on the eastern slopes of the Ural Mountains. They first appeared at the foot of the Carpathian Mountains in 894. Although not the last to invade central Europe, they were the last invaders to stay there until the present. Aside from the Finns they were also the only people of Mongolian origin who, although adapted to European influences, maintained themselves as a national body. They formed a permanent wedge between the northern and the southern Slavs.

During the tenth century Christianity began to permeate through Hungary, and finally the Magyar leader, Duke Géza, accepted the

Western form. During his reign, however, Christianity did not spread far beyond the court. In 1001 A.D., during the reign (997–1038) of Stephen I (St. Stephen),* the Pope recognized Magyar nationality by endowing the ruler with the famous Holy Crown of Hungary. The peak of Hungary's medieval power came during the reign of King Louis the Great, of Anjou, whose dominions touched the Baltic, Black, and Mediterranean seas. In 1526, at the Battle of Mohács, the Turks conquered the Hungarian army and killed King Louis II. The Habsburg Archduke Ferdinand of Austria thereupon laid claim to Hungary and Croatia, of which Louis had been king. Near the end of the seventeenth century the old frontiers were recovered and the country reunited under Leopold I, of Austria, the Turks having been driven out and Transylvania reincorporated. After the 1848 revolt against Habsburg rule, led by Kossuth, was crushed, the dual monarchy of Austria-Hungary was established in 1867 and Francis Joseph installed as ruler.

After its collapse at the end of World War I, Hungary went through a liberal revolution and then a communist dictatorship, both of short duration. These ephemeral regimes were followed by a counter-revolution that reconverted the country into a kingdom, but with a vacant throne from 1919 to 1945 and Admiral Horthy ruling as regent until toward the end of the kingdom. Horthy benefited from his friendship with Hitler, who awarded him a large part of Slovakia (1938) and Sub-Carpathian Ruthenia (1939) and then northern Transylvania (1940). But, in return, Hungary's forces bled on Russian battlefields. With the Allied victories on the horizon, Horthy announced in October, 1944, that he had asked the Allies for an armistice. While Budapest was undergoing its death agony, a Russian-sponsored government was formed at Debrecen from the democratic and pro-Allied parties. It announced a program of democratic and social reform, the restoration of the old liberties suppressed by the previous tyrannies, the repeal of the anti-Jewish laws, and the introduction of a radical land reform and other urgent social measures. War was declared on Germany, and the Allied armistice terms pledged Hungary to denunciation of

---

* Budapest is actually two cities, made up of Buda on the hilly west bank of the Danube, and Pest on the low-lying east bank.

* St. Stephen was the great grandson of Arpád, the original leader of Hungarians in the area.

whatever temporary gains of territory she had made at the expense of the United Nations.

Nationalities, minorities, and religions. Pre-1918 Hungary was a polyglot country of many peoples whose unity was merely political. Taking the population of old Hungary proper at eighteen million, the Magyars were in a minority, totaling only some seven to eight millions. The postwar situation in 1920 was very different: out of a population of approximately nine million, Magyars formed 87 per cent of the population, Germans 5.5 per cent, Slovaks 1.2 per cent, Yugoslavs 0.7 per cent, and Rumanians 0.2 per cent. The most important language is Magyar, but German- and Slovak-speaking groups make up small segments of the population. Many Magyars resided beyond the boundaries of Hungary outlined in the Treaty of Trianon. Nearly two thirds of the population belong to the Roman Catholic Church, but the remainder are widely scattered among a number of faiths. Those representing one per cent or more of the population are Helvetian Evangelicals, Augsburg Evangelicals and Greek Catholics.

Territorial problems. Revision of the restrictive treaty forced on the country after World War I became the dominant note of Hungarian foreign policy between 1920 and 1938. During that period Hungary was always on the side of the dissatisfied states of Europe. Restoration of much of the lost territory (southern Slovakia, Ruthenia, and Transylvania) did not become an accomplished fact, however, until between 1938 and 1940.

In April, 1941, when Germany invaded Yugoslavia, Hungary received Baranja and Bachka.* This region, once the frontier zone against the Turks, has been inhabited over the centuries by many national groups. In general, it is the transitional zone between Magyars and Serbs. Due to the complex ethnographic pattern, no good line of demarcation has been found, especially in the two eastern parts, Bachka and Banat. Baranja, in the western portion, presents a different ethnographic picture, for the population is largely Magyar with a Croat minority. The

Yugoslavia Magyars, although dissatisfied with their political lot, were economically well off in the inter-war period. The present boundary between Yugoslavia and Hungary is the same as that existing after World War I.

Czechoslovakia has now acquired the northern rim of the Hungarian Plain, which was seized at the time of Munich. This region is occupied by 200,000 Slovaks and some 800,000 Magyars. There has been some discussion of an exchange of minorities in the area to lessen the friction in the northern Hungarian Plain. As previously noted, Hungary ceded after World War II a small area of land near Bratislava to Czechoslovakia (see the map directly below).

Two changes have taken place in the region of Hungary's eastern frontier: Ruthenia, held by Hungary during the war, has been ceded to Russia; and Hungarian Transylvania, reacquired by Hungary in 1940, has been returned to Rumania to compensate for the loss of Bessarabia.*

Future. Hungary, now a republic having an area, boundaries, and total population almost the same as after World War I, faces a difficult task. Its conduct between 1938 and 1941 antagonized neighboring states. The republican form of government, the reforms of the republican regime, and the degree of industrialization achieved during the war may be promising signs for the future. On the other hand, Hungary shares with Czechoslovakia and part of Austria the serious drawback to democratic processes of being within the Soviet orbit.

---

* Baranja and Bachka, along with Banat, are three units of the southern Danubian plain (see the map on page 263).

* Consult the next chapter for the presentation of the Transylvania question. The Ruthenian problem is discussed in more detail earlier in this chapter under "Czechoslovakia."

CHAPTER 19

The Balkan States: Peninsular Rivals

THE Balkan Peninsula occupies roughly the southeastern section of Europe, between the Black and Aegean seas on the east and the Adriatic Sea on the west. There is no complete agreement as to the northern boundary, but in general it may be taken as the Danube River and its great tributary, the Sava, thence west along an imaginary line to the Adriatic Sea. The southern boundary is, of course, the Mediterranean. The Balkan states are Yugoslavia, Albania, Greece, Rumania, Bulgaria, and European Turkey (see the map on this page).*

Geographic Factors

Physical features. Uneven terrain has been responsible for a strong diversity among the several Balkan States (see the map on page 250). No symmetry of relief, such as parallel mountain ranges or uniformity of coastal plains, exists to match one country with another or to simplify the landscape pattern—the whole Balkan Peninsula is little more than a topographic jumble. As a result communications are handicapped from one country to another; indeed, within each of the countries themselves.

Travel across the Balkan Peninsula, particularly in an east-west direction, is blocked by a succession of mountain barriers. Especially prominent are the rugged ranges of the Dinaric Alps in Yugoslavia, the Pindus Mountains of western Greece, and several finger-like peninsulas jutting from Greece into the Aegean. The Rhodope massif separates

* Turkey in Europe is treated in Chapter 20 except in instances where its political geography is associated with the states of the Balkan Peninsula.

these rugged western mountain ranges from the great east-west arc of the Balkan Mountains from which the Peninsula's name is derived. The latter curves from the Iron Gate of the Danube to the Black Sea.

Variety of climate ranges from the cold win-

THE BALKAN STATES

ters and warm summers of the north to the typically mild Mediterranean winters and dry, hot summers of the south. These two general climatic types have their approximate counterparts in the United States, the former in the states of the Ohio Valley, and the latter in southern California.

Agricultural base. Nearly as large as France and Great Britain together, the Balkan countries before World War II supported a population of more than forty-three million. Between 70 and 80 per cent of these inhabitants lived directly from the produce of the soil. Although large areas in the Balkan Peninsula are unsuited for cultivation, agricultural products formed three fourths of the total exports. Apart from cereals, important exports normally included oil and lumber from Rumania; attar of roses, tobacco, and silk from Bulgaria; pigs, copper, and timber from Yugoslavia; wool, hides, and furs from Albania; mineral ores, tobacco, and currants from Greece.

In the first years after World War II war-ravaged farms, depleted livestock, the lack of seed, and the years of undernourishment for their peoples presented obstacles too great for the Balkan countries to overcome. As one result, crops planted and harvested in the 1945 season fell far below the normal yields. In 1946 UNRRA lent considerable help to certain of these regions that formerly produced agricultural products in excess of their normal needs. For the coming years there is the prospect of greater agricultural production and also better distribution of the crops that are raised.

Basic routes. History has never been kind to the Balkans. Wave after wave of invaders has overrun the region, destroying the political and social institutions of the countries of the Peninsula, imposing an alien culture upon the resentful victims, and adding new racial groups to the already inextricable mixture existing there.

Invaders have entered by three traditional routes that have Belgrade as their focal point: (1) the land route and waterway along the Danube Valley; (2) the line through Nish, Sofia, and Adrianople (now followed by the transcontinental railway from western Europe to Istanbul); and (3) the route through Nish and Skoplje (Uskub), along the valleys of the Morava and Vardar to Salonika, thence by sea or by the ancient coastal route to Constantinople (Istanbul), capital of the Byzantine and Ottoman empires (see the map on this page). Salonika has the distinction of being the best Aegean port for the whole interior of the Peninsula because of two major land routes converging there: the north-south furrow indicated by the Morava and Vardar rivers and the route from Istanbul to the Thracian lowland. The importance of the

Morava-Vardar Gorge is augmented by the railroad line that follows it from Belgrade to Salonika by way of Nish and Skoplje. Istanbul, on the bridge between Asia Minor and the Balkan Peninsula, is connected with Belgrade from the Morava Valley by way of the Nišava tributary. Eastward the route then crosses passes to the basin of Sofia and henceforth continues into the Maritsa Valley, from

which Istanbul is reached. Belgrade, Salonika, and Istanbul are the three nodal points on the northern, southern, and eastern margins of the Peninsula, all being important because of the land and water routes converging upon them. Likewise, each of them is a focal center for trunk rail lines of southeastern Europe.

Cultural and Political Factors

Racial mixtures. History and geography together have mixed the diverse racial elements in the Balkans and scattered the blend throughout the Peninsula; at the same time these factors have led to the segregation of various stocks into groups isolated by natural barriers and resulted in national boundaries drawn according to the numerically superior strains in each section.   Thus, Yugoslavia is largely peopled by Serbs, Croats, and Slovenes; Rumania by Rumanians; Bulgaria by Bulgars; Albania by Albanians; Greece by Greeks; and Turkey by Turks.   However, smaller groups of these people and their cross strains are widely distributed all over the Balkans, and frequently give rise to troublesome minority problems.

It is impossible to understand the Balkans without remembering that Turkey ruled the whole region until slightly more than a century ago.   Though the army and the tax-gatherers of the Turk are now gone from the Balkans, an unmistakable legacy remains.   It is apparent in the Oriental notions of pomp, splendor, and luxury that still prevail in the upper classes of the whole peninsula; it lingers in the widespread contempt for the man who works with his hands; and it is seen in the low standard of education, which is a sore and pressing problem.   Murder—or assassination, if one chooses—is often regarded as a constructive political act in the Balkans, especially among the Macedonians.   The reason is not too deeply buried in the past.   The Turk was a Moslem, and between him and his Christian subjects was a wide religious gulf that led each to look upon the other as "infidel."   In all parts of the Balkan lands this view has, at times at least, been regarded as full license for murder.

Heritages of foreign imperialism.   The impositions of foreign imperialism upon the Balkans have been manifold.   There is no more striking relic of a crime than the despoiling of Macedonia and old Serbia, where the Turks for centuries robbed the native population.*   The poverty of all Bosnians and Herzegovinians, except the Moslems and the Jews, is quite as ghastly an indictment of both the Turks and their successors, the Austrians.   Dalmatia was picked clean by Venice.   Croatia was held back from prosperity by

* Because of a diverse geographical setting and a complex political history numerous areas on the Balkan Peninsula have become identified with specific regional names, i.e., Macedonia, Serbia, Bosnia, Herzegovina, Thrace, Bessarabia, etc.   The more important of these politico-geographic regions are featured in the map on the facing page.

Hungarian control in countless ways that left it half an age behind its western neighbors in material prosperity.   Never in the Balkans has empire meant trusteeship.

International crosscurrents.   European relations in the fifty years preceding the outbreak of World War I were closely bound up with Balkan problems.   Of major import were the disruption of the Turkish Empire and the rise of Balkan statehood, both of which precipitated a conflict of interests among the great powers.*

Since Turkey controlled the Dardanelles and the eastern Mediterranean, the onslaughts that weakened the ports of these areas were of pivotal importance for Russia, posing as the natural protector of the Slavs as well as the Orthodox Christians in the Balkans.   Austria, anxious to control the Danube as far as its mouth and the Dardanelles as the outlet for the Danube commerce, was deeply concerned over the possibility of having strong Slavic states under Russian mentorship at the backdoor of the Habsburgs.   German jingoes were devoted to fostering the "Berlin-to-Baghdad" dream envisaging a great empire along the "transversal Eurasian Axis."   England, eager to keep Russia out of Constantinople, doggedly worked for the safety of her route to India.   France, accustomed to regarding herself as the defender of Christianity in the Mediterranean orbit, found her claims contested by upstart Italy.   Each of the great powers had its own protégés among the Balkan nations.   In turn, each Balkan state sought to obtain territorial gains, including an outlet to the sea, without regard to the consequent incorporation of national minorities into its domain.   The Balkan wars of 1912–13 led both directly and indirectly to World War I.

World War I stopped Germany from achieving the "Berlin-to-Baghdad" dream.   In the first postwar decade, Italy tried to replace France and Britain as the influential power in the Balkans, at that time in a state of seething unrest.   In the second decade German interest in the Balkans definitely manifested itself, first economically and then politically.   But the course of World War II, which

* Joseph S. Roucek, *The Politics of the Balkans* (McGraw-Hill Book Co., 1939), Chapter IX, "Balkan Foreign Policies," pp. 152–64.

brought Germany's armies to the Aegean, resulted in Germany's defeat and the liberation
of the region by the Russian forces.   In 1948
the Balkans—with the exception of Greece

German *Führer* and his Italian henchmen,
but by Soviet Russia after a long debate with
Britain and the United States as to the extent
of her influence.   The Truman Doctrine to

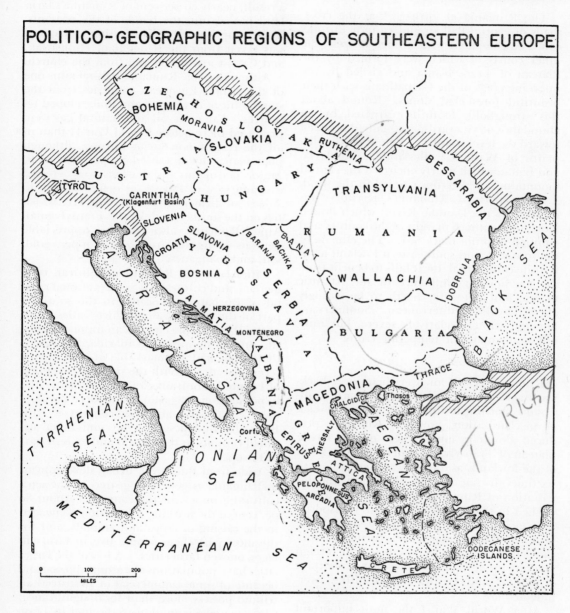

POLITICO-GEOGRAPHIC REGIONS OF SOUTHEASTERN EUROPE

—were under the direct and indirect domination of Soviet Russia. A "new order" was
finally being worked out for the Balkans as
Adolf Hitler predicted; the great difference,
however, was that it was planned not by the

support Greece and Turkey and to limit the
spread of Communism has brought the United
States more actively than ever into the politics
of the southern Balkans and the eastern Medi
terranean.

RUMANIA

Geographic Background

The Rumania of 1919–39,* at the cross-roads of central-Balkan and eastern Europe, could be compared with a huge fortress, the inner courts of which were formed by the Plateau of Transylvania and girded by the imposing crags of the Carpathians with their beautiful forest-clad slopes. Round about this stronghold, foothills, carpeted by an abundance of vineyards, gradually descended toward the level country. Below, on the rich plains of Wallachia, Bessarabia, Moldavia, and Banat, which nearly encircled the central mountains, ample crops rippled in the wind. A large part of Rumania's territory was drained by the Danube River, which flowed along the southern margin of the country and emptied into the Black Sea. The climate of the southern and southeastern lowland areas is quite continental, for it fails to benefit from the ameliorating influence of the Atlantic Ocean, and is too far north to be strongly affected by the Mediterranean. Summers are hot and winters relatively severe, but rainfall is adequate for temperate crops.

National Economy

Rumania is still an overwhelmingly backward agricultural country trying hard to introduce machine techniques. Despite its lack of mechanization, however, Rumania produced almost as much wheat on the fertile plateau of Transylvania and on the black soil of the lowlands as did prewar Germany with six times the population. Moreover, the distribution of Rumanian products was accomplished in the face of inadequate transportation facilities. Between 1930 and 1938 the problem of the peasantry was further complicated by exceptionally low prices in foreign markets for agricultural products, a shortage of capital and credit, and resulting over-indebtedness.

After World War I the most important move of the government was to distribute the

---

* Prior to World War II Rumania touched six other European countries (U. S. S. R., Bulgaria, Yugoslavia, Hungary, Czechoslovakia, and Poland). At the present time only four countries have common boundaries with Rumania (U. S. S. R., Bulgaria, Yugoslavia, and Hungary).

land more equitably among the people. As a result, nearly 90 per cent of Rumania's farm land passed into the hands of the peasants. To accomplish this redistribution much land was taken from the Rumanian, Hungarian, and Czarist aristocrats and from the church.

Although poor, Rumania still remains one of the richest European countries from the standpoint of developed and undeveloped resources. Far more oil and natural gas were produced there before World War II than in all the rest of non-Soviet Europe, although poor management wasted 75 per cent of it. Major petroleum installations were erected east and west of Ploești (as is well known to American airmen of World War II), which lies on the southern side of the Transylvanian Alps. Rumania also contains appreciable deposits of lignite, iron, zinc, copper, gold, salt, and manganese.

Cities. Key to Rumanian political, commercial, and cultural life is the national capital of Bucharest. Located in the southern part of the country, about thirty miles north of the Danube, the city has an unimaginative site on the steppes of Wallachia, but nevertheless has had a remarkable growth during recent decades. With the possible exception of Istanbul it outranks all other Balkan cities in population (985,000) and modern development. Rail and air lines connect it with Belgrade, Budapest, Prague, and other national capitals in the central and eastern part of Europe.

Aside from Bucharest, urban development in Rumania is generally geared to the agricultural economy of the country. About 80 per cent of the working population is engaged in the raising of crops and animals, and for the most part these people live in farm villages, or even farm cities. A few of the larger cities have populations of around 100,000 and because of some commercial or industrial attribute possess more than local significance: Cluj (111,000) is an industrial center in Transylvania; Jassy, or Iasi (109,000) is the leading trading center of Moldavia; Timișoara (108,-000) is a western commercial center; Ploești (105,000) is an oil center 35 miles north of Bucharest; Galați (93,000) is the chief Danube port. Somewhat smaller is Constanta, principal port on the Black Sea coast of Rumania.

Historical Background

The fortress of colossal mountains and surrounding dense forests and wild ravines were for hundreds of years the refuge of the Rumanian people. The history of Rumania began in 101 A.D. with the colonization of Dacia by the Romans. From the sixth century onward, however, the territory was so trampled and exploited by barbarian conquerors and by invaders from other regions that today the people are a conglomerate mixture of Alsatians, Armenians, Bulgars, Cumans, Dacians, Goths, Greeks, Gypsies, Hungarians, Huns, Jews, Petchenegs, Poles, Romans, Saxons, Scythians, Slavs, Tartars, Thracians, Turks, and Ukrainians. All these strains are combined in the people who now speak the Rumanian language. Likewise, many religions are represented in the modern country, although two thirds of the people belong to the Greek Orthodox Church.

Transylvanian problem. At this point it is important to notice the ancient controversy over Transylvania. Because Transylvania had been an integral part of ancient Dacia, conquered by the Roman Emperor Trajan, it follows that its population is of the same Latin stock as that of Moldavia and Wallachia, the two regions that eventually became Rumania. Thus, the arrival of the Magyars in Transylvania in 1003 signified the subjugation of an old established people of Latin, albeit intermixed, stock by an Asiatic tribe. Nonetheless, the majority of the Transylvanian population preserved their racial and linguistic characteristics despite centuries of Magyar domination. The Magyars, however, always desirous of keeping Transylvania or having it returned to them, have maintained that the region was settled by themselves first. According to the Magyar argument, it was not until later that the Rumanian element infiltrated.

Formation of modern Rumania. In 1411 the Turks took Wallachia, and in the sixteenth century, Moldavia, although both regions retained semiautonomy. After the Russo-Turkish War of 1774 they went under *de facto* Russian protection. In 1858 the Convention of Paris nominally united the two provinces, and Alexander Cuza was elected Prince of Moldavia and Wallachia. At the time of his forced abdication in 1866, Cuza was succeeded by Prince Charles I of Hohenzollern-Sigmaringen, who became Carol I. In 1878 the Treaty of Berlin included the recognition of the country's complete independence, and in 1881 the principality advanced to a kingdom. From that time until 1914 Carol I ruled as king. He was succeeded by his nephew, Ferdinand.

In World War I the Rumanian armies were defeated by the Germans. But as the Rumanians were allies of the winning nations and good bargainers, Rumania nearly doubled its size through the peace treaties of 1919–20, becoming the largest Balkan state. Her spoils included Bessarabia, Northern Transylvania, Bucovina, and part of Banat, a Hungarian area that was divided with Yugoslavia. After this territorial aggrandizement the area of Rumania was nearly 114,000 square miles; prior to 1940 its population had increased to slightly above 20,000,000.

Between World Wars I and II. In the period following World War I Rumania tried to make secure her new possessions. The ever-present menace of a Hungarian or a Russian *revanche* (the first claiming Transylvania and the latter Bessarabia) caused Rumanian statesmen to orient their foreign policy in favor of a guarantee of the *status quo*. In 1926 Crown Prince Carol renounced his rights to the throne; and at the death of King Ferdinand, Carol's son, Michael, became king under a regency. In 1930 Carol, however, returned from exile to become King Carol II. Early in 1938 he abolished the democratic constitution of 1923. As World War II approached, the Rumanians found themselves in the path of Nazi Germany's *Drang nach Osten*.

World War II and after. Soon after the dismemberment of Czechoslovakia at Munich (1938), Rumania started losing steadily on the political front. In June, 1940, the country was reorganized along fascist lines, and the fascist Iron Guard became the nucleus of the new totalitarian party. Almost immediately thereafter Soviet Russia took Bessarabia and Northern Bucovina. When Germany invaded the U.S.S.R., those territories were returned to Rumania, but the repossession was not destined to be permanent. In the meanwhile, by manipulations of Hitler, the king dissolved

Parliament, granted the new premier, Marshal Antonescu, full power, and then abdicated. His son, Michael, who succeeded him, continued Antonescu in power as dictator. Cessions of land to Hungary (forced on Rumania by Hitler's Vienna award of August, 1940) and to Bulgaria (by the agreement of September, 1940) were compensated by occupation of Russian areas between the Dnieper and Bug rivers. Yet Rumania paid heavily in oil and in men for its expansion. Not only did Germany receive one third of its fuel oil from Rumania during World War II, but also this unfortunate Balkan country contributed the largest number of satellite troops to the *Wehrmacht,* and lost the most. Following the invasion of the country by the Russians and the overthrow of Antonescu in a *coup d'état* led by King Michael, Rumania appealed to the Big Three for an armistice. Signed in the Kremlin in September, 1944, the armistice, which provided that Rumania go to war against Germany and Hungary, promised, among other things, the restoration of Bessarabia and Northern Bucovina to Soviet Russia. Thereafter came the period when the Russians sponsored pro-Russian cabinets, and in recognition of Rumania's cooperation allowed Bucharest, in 1945, to re-acquire Northern Transylvania. Near the end of 1947 King Michael signed abdication papers presented to him without choice by the Russian-dominated government.

Political Problems

Prewar minorities. Scattered among Rumania's prewar population of 20,000,000 were more than 5,000,000 people who by ancestral habit spoke one or another of eight languages other than Rumanian.* No nation had a wider or a more dangerous variety of minorities than Rumania, even though Poland had a greater total number. The diverse groups made an imposing array: 1,425,000 Magyars, who once ruled Transylvania (and did briefly again during World War II); 155,000 Turks, who once governed all Rumania; 582,000

* In Rumania, as everywhere in eastern and Balkan Europe, groups of people have lived side by side for hundreds of years without agreeing upon a common language. Villagers may never in a lifetime leave their native village. The language of the cabaret girls—French in Rumania—meant nothing to these peasants.

Ukrainians, who once ruled Bessarabia; 367,000 Bulgars, who once ruled Dobruja (the southern part of which was returned to them during World War II); 745,000 Germans, who read Nazi newspapers and became fifth columnists during the last war; 728,000 Jews, most of whom disappeared or were slaughtered during World War II; some 22,000 Tartars and Gypsies; and an unknown number of mountain Macedonians.*

Rumania's minorities were not, however,

TERRITORIAL CHANGES IN RUMANIA AND BULGARIA BY PEACE TREATIES, 1947

CZECHOSLOVAKIA — U. S. S. R. — Bukovina — HUNGARY — R U M A N I A — YUGOSLAVIA — Bucharest — BLACK SEA — 1920–39 Boundary — 1947 Boundary — Southern Dobruja — BULGARIA — Sofia — 0 50 100 200 Miles

citizens in quite the same sense that Rumanians were. The treatment of these minorities and the anti-Semitic tendencies of certain Rumanian groups attracted unfavorable attention in Rumania and in the outside world.

Current situation. As a defeated nation, Rumania's postwar future is problematical. Occupying one of the key positions in central-Balkan Europe, the country must learn how to provide better government for its peasant masses, who, as elsewhere in the Balkans, are undernourished and suffering from a high birth rate and death rate. So far Rumania has suffered from the abuses of pseudo-democracy, which allowed the peasantry no voice in the government and permitted the squandering of the nation's resources. Internationally Rumania will have to continue to cooperate, probably more than she would like, with Soviet Russia, and at the same time worry about such items as free elections with

* After World War I the Rumanian government invited back to Rumania groups of Macedonians who had emigrated to the United States and settled them on Rumania's frontier, facing Bulgaria. There they built neat villages on the American plan.

their influence on the United States and Great Britain.

The present area of Rumania is 92,000 square miles (about the size of Illinois and Indiana together), and the present population slightly over 16,000,000. The density of population is 178 persons per square mile, exceeding that of other Balkan countries, but slightly under that for France. As noted earlier, the Rumania that emerged after World War II had ceded Bessarabia and Northern Bucovina to the U. S. S. R. and Southern Dobruja to Bulgaria (see the map on page 266). The latter settlement was made with the mutual consent of Rumania and Bulgaria and, according to reports, has been the practical solution of a less pressing problem.

Northern Transylvania, acquired by Rumania from Hungary after World War I, was returned to Hungary in August, 1940, and given back to Rumania in September, 1945. Any line of demarcation would leave numerous Rumanians in Hungary and large groups of Magyars in Rumania, including almost a million of the so-called Czeklers living in the southeast corner of Transylvania. Since no satisfactory ethnic solution is possible for Transylvania and its independence is untenable (Transylvania would never be a viable economic entity), the problem of the area continued to tax the diplomats.

YUGOSLAVIA

Internal dissension in Yugoslavia, which divided the country between World War I and II, as well as at the conclusion of World War II, is nothing new to that unhappy land. Although the country as we know it was a creation of the peace treaties following World War I, the regions lying within its present boundaries have for centuries been torn by external as well as internal strife. Like the other Balkan countries, Yugoslavia has long been a pawn in the hands of the major powers of Europe and has figured prominently in the wars of the past. Significantly, the "incident" that started World War I took place in Sarajevo, which is now located within the country's boundaries. There, on June 28, 1914, Archduke Francis Ferdinand of Austria was assassinated by Serbs who sought to bring about the downfall of the Austro-Hungarian monarchy and to increase the power of Serbia.

The complexity of Yugoslavia's political status is augmented by common boundaries with all of the other Balkan countries on its eastern and southern sides, with the central European countries of Austria and Hungary on its northern side, and with Italy (and the Free Territory of Trieste) at the extreme northwest. Because of its position and extent Yugoslavia shares with other countries the political problems of the highly important Danube Valley, the strategic head of the Adriatic Sea, and the mountainous interior of the Balkan Peninsula itself.

Geographic Factors

Roughly occupying the northwestern third of the Balkan Peninsula, Yugoslavia, about the size of Oregon or the United Kingdom, is larger than any of its immediate neighbors other than Italy. In total the country represents a striking diversity of regions, peoples, religions, and customs. Much of the area is fertile agricultural land, although the mountainous sections west and south are generally rocky and unproductive except for intervening river valleys. Bold buttresses of the jagged Dinaric Alps rise abruptly from Yugoslavia's rocky Adriatic coast facing Italy, the in-and-out length of which is almost 1,200 miles. Catching the moist winds from the Adriatic, these steep slopes have a heavy rainfall—in fact, the rainfall record for Europe is in the Dalmatian coastal mountains. Top-ranking spectacle of the coast is the Gulf of Kotor, which cuts 30 miles into the land where peaks soar almost 6,000 feet directly out of the sea. Gray, sterile karst topography (limestone pitted and tunneled by water) lie behind the coastal ridges. There rivers flow from subterranean streams in the mountains, often to disappear back into the earth after a few miles along the surface. Northeastward, the country slopes down into the broad, productive Danubian plain drained by the large Sava and Drava tributaries as well as the Danube itself. In the southeast is a rumpled land of hills and small plains through which flow the Morava and Vardar rivers.

With about 17,000,000 inhabitants on more than 97,000 square miles, Yugoslavia supports about 175 people on an average square mile, compared with 500 for the United Kingdom and 23 for Norway. Natural barriers of mountains and rivers and the history of former political divisions have helped to keep the diverse elements of the population apart.

National Economy

Farming, stock raising, and forestry are leading occupations in Yugoslavia. More than half the land is suitable for cultivation, and of this area 80 per cent is normally devoted to grains. Before the recent war the country produced quantities of grapes for wine and more plums, both fresh and dried into prunes, than any other European country. The annual output of honey ranged around 7,000,000 pounds. A fine quality of tobacco came from valleys in the south. Great surpluses of foodstuffs formed the backbone of Yugoslavia's foreign trade; in 1939 hogs led the nutritive export list, followed by wheat, fruit, lard, cattle, and eggs. The most valuable single outgoing item, however, was timber.

In prewar days Yugoslavia was Europe's leading copper producer. Mines also yielded substantial quantities of coal, iron, lead, chromite, antimony, and bauxite (aluminum ore), a production that established the land as one of Europe's richest mineral regions. Handicapping the exploitation of resources, however, was the inadequacy of the country's railroad communications. Partially making up for this deficiency, the Danube was available as a commercial traffic artery, and half the boat and barge tonnage on the river sailed under Yugoslavia's flag.

Yugoslav economy does not revolve around a single great metropolitan center, for the country is actually a composite of a number of politico-geographic regions (see the map on page 263). Located in the broad Danube plain in the northern part of the country, Belgrade, with a population of 267,000, functions as the national capital, although it is not closely tied with the regions in southern Yugoslavia. The second city of the country is the Croat commercial center of Zagreb, with

186,000 people. The next ranking cities, which are much smaller in size, serve largely as regional centers.

Historical Background

Human element. Almost half the prewar Yugoslavs were Serbs; more than a quarter were Croats; only a fourteenth were Slovenes. Although all three groups are Slavs, the Croats and Slovenes use the Roman alphabet, whereas the Serbs write in Cyrillic. The ·Yugoslav state recognizes three languages: Slovene, Macedonian, and Serbo-Croat. Moreover, the Croats and Slovenes, being Roman Catholics, received their inspiration from Rome, but the Serbs, being members of the Orthodox Church, had their roots in the Byzantine Empire. Further, belonging to the "western" cultural zone, both Croats and Slovenes have been convinced that their civilization stands as an "older" and "higher" one than that of the Serbs and have long resented the political domination of Belgrade.

Making up the remaining population within the boundaries of 1937 Yugoslavia were 550,000 Macedonian Slavs, 450,000 Magyars, 450,000 Albanians, 230,000 Rumanians, about a million Germans, and a considerable sprinkling of other minorities. Among these people Serbian Orthodox was the principal religion, but there were also Roman Catholics, Greek Catholics, Moslems, Jews, and Protestants. After the change of the Italo-Yugoslav border, following World War II, Yugoslavia acquired a notable minority of Italians.

In but few states of the world was the prewar birth rate as high as in Yugoslavia. However, the rate of mortality was likewise high. These conditions were closely related to the high rate of illiteracy. The prevailing low standards of education also made the peasant ignorant, superstitious, and provincial, and unwilling to employ modern methods of cultivation. Overshadowing the masses of peasants, as elsewhere in the Balkans, was found a small, select group of foreign-educated individuals, living in the cities, imitating the Parisian or Viennese dress, maintaining a western European standard of living, and keeping a marked social distance from the people of the lower economic brackets.

Political areas. The inhabitants of present-day Yugoslavia were living under six different governments before World War I. This heterogeneous political pattern, which accounts in a large measure for the constant friction and strife of the area, including that of the present, makes it difficult to trace the country's history. Serbia, the nucleus of the new state, was itself once a powerful European nation. However, in 1389, after the Battle of Kosovo, Serbia became a vassal principality of Turkey, and so remained until 1878.

Throughout the period of Turkish domination, only two small sections of the Yugoslav lands practically retained their independence: Montenegro, which, cut off in its barren mountains, kept up a continual struggle and developed a tradition of heroism; and the Republic of Dubrovnik (Ragusa), which became rich through its trade and was a flourishing center of Yugoslav art and literature.

In 1878, after several insurrections, Serbia was established as an independent kingdom under the terms of the Treaty of Berlin. Unable to expand northward into the rich plains inhabited by the Croats and Slovenes under Austrian rule, Serbia continued its expansion southward at the expense of the Turks. The Balkan Wars of 1912–13 established the southern frontier much as it was following World War I. In 1918 the Kingdom of the Serbs-Croats-Slovenes was formed under the Karageorgevitch dynasty. It was principally the union of the old kingdom of Serbia with Montenegro and the former Austro-Hungarian areas of Croatia, Slovenia, Bosnia, Herzegovina, Dalmatia, and the Voivodina.

Independent Yugoslavia. The unification of the variegated country has been the main problem ever since its formation. The Croats demanded autonomy and a federal system (which was introduced by Tito at the end of World War II). Also in the years after 1918 the intra-Serbian quarrels caused much trouble. Things came to a head when Raditch, leader of the autonomist Croatian Peasant Party, was shot by a Montenegrin deputy in the Yugoslav Parliament (June, 1928). King Alexander I dissolved the Parliament, established a dictatorship, and changed the name of the state to "Yugoslavia." At that time the country was divided into nine "banovinas," or provinces, the boundaries of which cut across the borders of the old regions of Serbia, Croatia, and Slovenia. All parties were dissolved, and in 1931 a new constitution created a parliamentary system which kept the dictatorial power of the king intact.

When King Alexander was assassinated by a Macedonian during a visit to Marseille on October 9, 1934, Crown Prince Peter was proclaimed King with a regency of three members, the most important of whom was Prince Paul, named to serve until Peter became of age. Under Regent Paul Yugoslavia's foreign policy was re-oriented, the former strong ties with France were loosened, and an increasingly pro-Axis trend drew the country toward Italy and later toward Germany. Dr. Maček, leader of the Croat dissidents, joined the government in 1939, and Croatia was granted a considerable measure of autonomy. But in 1941, when the Regency agreed to join the Axis, a national uprising overthrew Prince Paul, thereby inaugurating King Peter's rule. Following this came the invasion by Germany (April 6, 1941) and Hungary. Italy, Germany, Hungary, and Bulgaria took slices out of the country, and Montenegro and Croatia were recreated under puppet regimes. Serbia was reduced to its pre-1918 proportions. The government of King Peter carried on, however, in exile, and from the underground two leaders arose: General Mikhailovitch, leader of the royalist Serbian forces; and Marshal Tito, who organized the Partisans—the democratic forces favored by Soviet Russia. In 1945 Yugoslavia was liberated and the regime of Tito installed. Late in 1945 this regime repudiated King Peter, declared Yugoslavia a republic, and established a form of federal union, which was an attempt to solve the troublesome "South Slav" problem. The federal union consisted of six republics: Serbia, Croatia, Slovenia, Montenegro, Macedonia, and Bosnia-Herzegovina.

Territorial Problems

Outstanding territorial problems involving Yugoslavia relate to Trieste, Carinthia, and Macedonia.

Trieste. The territory at the head of the Adriatic Sea to which Yugoslavia laid claim is often described as Istria, though the former Austrian province of that name made up less than half of the critical area. The Italian-Slav nationality frontier marked the point at which Slav incomers were intercepted in the seventh century as they tried to advance onto the Italian plain. Trieste itself was an "artificial" town, a creation of the railroad age and of German plans for European domination. An obscure fishing port of no trading importance until the 1840's, it began to be built up by Austria as the principal imperial outlet to the world. Because of its access to the Mediterranean through the Adriatic, it became the chief port for the maritime trade of Austria, of Bavaria, of Hungary, of northern Yugoslavia, and, to a considerable extent, of Czechoslovakia. In contrast, Italy's traffic with Trieste in 1913 was but 3 per cent of the port's total. The Austrian census of 1910 showed that the Istrian countryside was solidly inhabited by Croats and Slovenes, but that the towns were Italian "islands." When Italy entered the war in 1915, the Treaty of London recognized Italy's claims to Trieste, and the Treaty of Rapallo granted Italy all her demands apart from Fiume except the coast of Dalmatia. By this accession of territory Italy brought under her rule more than 500,000 Slovenes and Croats in what was called Venezia Giulia. After World War II, however, the Italian boundary was moved westward to the advantage of Yugoslavia, and the Free Territory of Trieste was created (the map on page 196, in the chapter on "Italy in the Mediterranean," shows the new boundaries).

Carinthia. Yugoslavia has advanced definite claims to a part of Austrian Carinthia, the so-called Klagenfurt Basin, lying northeast of the boundary junction of Austria, Yugoslavia, and Italy. Unquestionably the area was once the cradle of Slovene nationalism and had strong cultural ties with the southern Slavs. Unfortunately, the only outlets to the south and to the land of their brother Slavs are two passes over the high mountains and the Rosenbach tunnel of the Trieste-Vienna railroad line. These inadequate connections have always made it necessary for the commerce of the Klagenfurt Basin to move northward to Austrian markets. Inhabitants of Carinthia, mindful of the economic factors and aware that the basin was an economic unit, elected to join Austria rather than Yugoslavia at the close of World War I.

In fact, the Austrian census of 1934 revealed a marked trend among the Klagenfurt Slavs away from Slavic ties. It is possible that the trend has been reversed and that many Slovenes in the area may now prefer union with Yugoslavia. It appears likely, however, that the boundary between Austria and Yugoslavia will not be changed.

Macedonia. Yugoslavia has a vital interest in Macedonia, an area that is difficult to define. In general, the physical extent of Macedonia can be roughly determined by drawing a semicircle with a radius of about 150 miles around the port of Salonika (see the map on page 261). During the last half century this historically prominent region has been a source of political friction. Embittering Yugoslav-Bulgarian and Greco-Bulgarian relations, the quarrel over the disputed territory has helped the Balkans to maintain their reputation as the "powder-keg" of Europe.*

Successive Slav empires contended with the Byzantine Empire for dominion over Macedonia. With the breaking up of that empire, Macedonia first came under Bulgarian rule and subsequently, in the fourteenth century, was incorporated into the Serbian Empire of Stephan Dushan, an outstanding empire builder of the Balkans. From 1430 to 1912 Macedonia was under the Turks. In modern times the Bulgarian case for the possession of Macedonia rests on the limits given to the ecclesiastic jurisdiction of the Bulgarian Church and on the Treaty of San Stefano between Russia and Turkey in 1878, although the latter never actually came into operation. In 1893 the dreaded Internal Macedonian Revolutionary Organization (*IMRO*) was organized, headed by Bulgarian and Macedonian refugees. One branch desired the incorporation of Macedonia into Bulgaria, and the other advocated federation with Bulgaria accompanied by a certain degree of autonomy for Macedonia. Both groups were responsible for the chronic state of unrest and disturbance during the first decade of this century.

The *IMRO* and its *comitadjis* (Macedonian rebels) helped to drive Bulgaria into war with Serbia in 1913 and with the Entente

* For more details, see: Joseph S. Roucek, *The Politics of the Balkans* (McGraw-Hill, 1939), Chapter VIII, "Macedonians," pp. 138–51.

Powers in 1915. After World War I, raids by *comitadjis* based in Bulgaria against Yugoslavia and Greece led in 1922 to a joint protest from Yugoslavia, Greece, and Rumania to Bulgaria. Later an exchange of the Greek population of Anatolia and the Turkish population of Greek Macedonia was carried out to the mutual satisfaction of both nations. However, it also led to a considerable influx of Slav Macedonians into Bulgaria, thus further increasing the numbers of the possible disturbers of the peace collected there.

During and following World War II the situation in Macedonia again became a matter for concern. In April of 1941, Bulgaria, without any declaration of war, seized possession of the whole of Yugoslav Macedonia and of Greek Eastern Macedonia as far as the Struma, but was forced to give up her spoils when Nazi defeat appeared on the horizon. After the war Yugoslavia pressed the idea of a united Macedonia within a possible Balkan federation. Yugoslav Macedonia itself became one of the federal units of Yugoslavia, and voices were soon heard in Belgrade accusing Greece of mistreating the Macedonians in Greece—an indication that Macedonia could become again an explosive element in the international relations of the Balkans.

BULGARIA

Geographic Factors

Bulgaria is situated near the gateway between southeastern Europe and Asia Minor, within a few hours' journey by rail from Istanbul. In the southern part of the Balkan Peninsula its eastern edge touches the dead-end trade channels of the Black Sea, but fails by less than twenty miles to open on the Aegean Sea directly south. Land boundaries give immediate contact with Rumania in the north, Yugoslavia in the west, Greece in the south, and European Turkey in the southeast —a position that places it deep in the cockpit of the Balkan world. The strategic nature of this location is suggested by numerous battles fought on Bulgarian soil by conquerors of bygone days. Bulgaria's location is also a handicap, however, as it borders on the politically turbulent but trade-starved waters of the Black Sea, and not on the Aegean Sea, where Bulgaria has desired a seaport.

National Economy

The transverse Balkan Mountains extend from west to east through Bulgaria and divide the main agricultural area into two parts. Genuine plains occupy less than one third of the country's 42,800 square miles, which is a total area about equal to that of Tennessee. Over 89 per cent of the inhabitants of Bulgaria gain their livelihood by agriculture and the manufacture of agricultural products. The major portion of the cultivated land is devoted to wheat and corn, the former normally exported in part and the latter a staple item of diet within the country. Other crops include barley, potatoes, lucerne, sugar beets, rice, cotton, vines, mulberry trees for silk production, and roses from which the well-known perfume base, attar of roses, is extracted. Notwithstanding this wide variety of crops the overall agricultural economy is stagnant because of primitive methods of cultivation, ignorance of scientific implements, and excessive subdivision of land. Moreover, not only is a lack of capital evident, but also transportation and communications are still inadequate.

Bulgaria has some of the prerequisites essential for the development of industry, but as yet any marked progress toward this end has been limited. Agricultural products, especially wool and sugar beets, are the principal basis of the industry which does exist. The chief minerals are coal and copper, which are exploited only in a small way. Extensive forest areas and falling water for hydroelectric power, along with an energetic population, complete the list of factors that favor an increase in industrial advancement.

The national capital, Sofia, has a population of 401,000, making it the country's largest city. But despite this rank a location near the western edge of Bulgaria on a plateau 1,800 feet in elevation prevents it from serving many of the country's commercial functions. With populations ranging from 35,000 to 100,000 several other cities have key roles in the nation's economy: Philippopolis (Plovdiv), a commercial center on the Maritsa

River; Ruščuk (Ruse), a Danubian port; and Varna and Burgas, Black Sea ports.

Historical Background

In Roman times Bulgaria was occupied by a population of Thraco-Illyrian origin, which was expelled or absorbed by the great Slavic migration at the beginning of the sixth century. The first Bulgarians were a Tartar tribe that crossed the Danube from the north in 679 A.D. and took the province of Moesia from the Eastern Roman Empire. They adopted Slav dialect and customs and twice conquered most of the Balkan Peninsula between 893 and 1280. Under Simeon the Great, for instance (893–927), the Bulgars created the first Bulgarian Empire, including Serbia, Thrace, Macedonia, Thessalonica, Epirus, Albania, Wallachia, and part of Hungary—a substantial portion of the entire Balkan Peninsula. After the Serbs subjected their kingdom in 1330, the Bulgars gradually fell prey to the Turks, and from 1396 to 1878 Bulgaria was a Turkish province. In 1878, after the Turks cruelly suppressed a Bulgar revolt, Russia forced Turkey to give an enlarged Bulgaria practical independence, but the other European powers tempered this to make a much smaller Bulgaria autonomous under Turkish sovereignty. Autonomous Bulgaria, as sanctioned by the Congress of Berlin in 1878, included only the area north of the Balkan Mountains and the Sofia Basin. Eastern Rumelia, in the Maritza Valley, remained under the Turks until 1885, when a *coup d'état* united it with autonomous Bulgaria. The independent kingdom of Bulgaria came into being in 1908 under Prince Ferdinand of Saxe-Coburg-Gotha, who was elected ruler in 1887 and became czar in 1908.

From that point on the story of Bulgaria is a sad one. In 1912, 1913, 1915, and again in 1941 Bulgaria went to war, emerging unsuccessful in the last three instances. As a result of the Second Balkan War (1913), Bulgaria lost most of the booty gained in the First Balkan War (1912). Losses amounted to part of Macedonia going to Serbia and Greece, and Southern Dobruja to Rumania. In World War I Bulgaria joined Germany, Austria-Hungary, and Turkey. This time Bulgaria lost some territory to newly created Yugoslavia, the so-called Aegean extension in Thrace to Greece, and, once again, Southern

Dobruja to Rumania. On October 3, 1918, Czar Ferdinand abdicated for his son, who became Czar Boris III.

From 1920–23 was the period of the "green dictatorship" of Premier Stambolisky. He improved relations with Yugoslavia, and dreamed of south Slav unity under peasant leadership. But in 1923 he was executed by the army and bourgeois and Macedonian leaders. An era of civil disturbances followed, with continuous terror, bomb plots, and murders. The Macedonians, always a powerful factor in Bulgarian politics again became active. In 1935 King Boris took over dictatorial power and steered a course that took Bulgaria into World War II, again on the side of Germany, in the hope of acquiring Macedonia. In the course of the war, Bulgaria was given Southern Dobruja by Rumania (1940). After the German invasion of Greece and Yugoslavia in 1941, Bulgaria occupied all of Yugoslavia's Macedonia, Greek Western Thrace, part of Eastern Macedonia, and the districts of Florina and Castoria. Late in 1941 she declared war on the United States and Britain, but in less than three years had to declare war on Germany and conclude an armistice with Soviet Russia that again deprived her of most of her spoils.

The Bulgars and the Postwar Era

The Bulgars, like the Yugoslavs, belong to the Slav race. In religious faith they are predominantly Greek Orthodox. The minorities problem in Bulgaria is less serious than in any of the other Balkan states, for the Bulgars constitute an exceptionally uniform people. The postwar population, including Southern Dobruja, was a little more than 8,500,000; and the average density per square mile around 200.

Bulgaria is the only Axis satellite in Europe during World War II that managed to emerge from the conflict with no loss of prewar territory and even to gain some additional territory, namely, Southern Dobruja. Moreover, supported by the Soviets, the Bulgars demanded land from Greece that would give them access to the Aegean. However, the Greek-Bulgar boundary remained the same after World War II as before the conflict. Bulgaria was securely inside the Soviet orbit in the years that followed the fall of Hitler.

GREECE

By reason of a strategic geographical position Greece has a unique place in history. For many centuries it has stood at the crossroads between East and West. The currents of humanity passing from one region of the world to another—among them hordes of Persians, Romans, Goths, Slavs, Moslems, and Venetians—had to pass through Greece. It was in Greece that the onrush of the Persians and the ambitions of Venice came to a halt. It was Greece that served as a springboard for the Crusades, the military expeditions undertaken by Christian powers in the eleventh, twelfth, and thirteenth centuries, to recover the Holy Land from the Moslems. And in our times it was Greece that early in World War II irrevocably set back the Axis timetable for the conquest of the Middle East.

Geographic Factors

Greece is a composite of irregular mainland and innumerable islands. The largest island is Crete, about sixty miles southeast of the mainland, but the greatest concentration of them is found in the Aegean Sea to the east. In the Ionian Sea the island of Corfu has in the past acted as a sentinel to the west. Macedonia, in the north, is the largest mainland division. The southern end of the irregular peninsula that Greece thrusts into the Mediterranean is the Peloponnesus, which in turn has its own smaller peninsulas. Although bounded by water bodies on three sides the country touches four others (Albania, Yugoslavia, Bulgaria, and European Turkey) along its 500-mile northern border. Prior to World War II the total area of Greece, including the islands, amounted to 50,000 square miles, a size about the same as that of New York state. Postwar Greece is unchanged except for the addition of the Dodecanese with their 1,000 square miles.

Mountains roughly parallel the coasts of Greece in their north-south extent, angling eastward through Macedonia and Thrace into Turkey. Heights range up to the 9,730-foot summit of Mt. Olympus, mythical home of the gods. Mountain spurs extend in all directions, almost reaching the sea in places; these "compartmentize" the country into many small communities and make communication difficult. Fertile valleys lie between the ridges, as in Thessaly and Arcadia. The Vardar River, rising in Yugoslavia and flowing across northeastern Greece into the Gulf of Salonika, has particular importance because it provides access to the upper territory of the Balkan Peninsula.

While hot winds sweep in from Africa, cold blasts of air descend from the mountainous areas to the north. The lowlands escape heavy frosts and snows. Rainfall is heaviest in the west and lightest in the east; in both areas, however, dry summers accentuate the need for irrigation. In the drier eastern half severe droughts dry up streams and blight the countryside.

National Economy

Not being a land of extensive resources, Greece has never been overrun by invaders seeking wealth. As a further deterrent to attempted conquest its rocky and eroded soil and its dry climate do not make it a prosperous agricultural country capable of supporting a large population. There are few local resources to permit the creation of industry. Shipping and commerce were and are important sources of livelihood. The search for trade opportunities and the invasions from East and West scattered the Greeks along the coasts and sent them into colonies away from home—in Marseille, in Sicily and southern Italy, in Asia Minor, and on the Black Sea.

Figs, almonds, oranges, lemons, and melons grow well without much care in the scattered fertile pockets. Currants from vineyards around the Gulf of Corinth were a staple in prewar foreign trade. Olives grew on the dry slopes and provided oil for export. The best of the tobacco leaf that was grown went to American buyers. Extensive mountain areas suitable for grazing enable Greece to count her sheep and goats by the million. While the fishing industry in no way compares in importance with that found in the North Sea countries, the seas do support active fisheries. Although commerce and, particularly since 1931, industry are not negligible, the mainstay of the people remains agriculture.

Three cities in Greece have a population exceeding 200,000. Foremost is Athens, celebrated since ancient times for its cultural achievements and classical architecture. As the national capital it serves as the focal point for all Greek life. The fortunes of the city have risen and fallen through the centuries, resulting in great fluctuations in population. In 1930 the population was around 500,000 but a decade later the number had dropped to less than 400,000. Associated with Athens is its port city of Piraeus, with a population of 284,000.* In northern Greece the seaport of Salonika (Thessalonika), with 237,000 people, is the commercial outlet for Macedonia.

The relief and coastal configuration of Greece handicap roads and railroads. Athens is the terminal point of a rail line extending northward through the Balkan countries to central and western Europe, but nothing resembling a railroad network exists within Greece. In air transportation, however, the country is more fortunate, for the location of Athens on global trunk routes ties it directly with the United States, western Europe, the Middle East, and India. Further, Greece has its own airline which connects Athens with Salonika and with the Greek islands of Crete and Rhodes.

Social aspects. Over 60 per cent of the 7,778,000 inhabitants, estimated to have been living in Greece in 1946, made their living as farmers. The great majority are small landholders cultivating their fields with the help of members of the family. The density of population is about 10 per cent higher than the average for all Europe—155 per square mile. Scarcity of arable land, however, makes the land far more overpopulated than the statistics would indicate. Furthermore, the system of land tenure still shows extensive traces of feudalism. In spite of expropriations of state and church lands and of much privately owned property, decreed during the period 1920–30, only 50 per cent of the agricultural area has been redistributed. Holdings are uneconomically small; thousands of peasant farmers do not own more than a little over an acre, an animal or two, and a wooden plow.

Greece, too, has been cursed by the chasm between the intellectuals and the wealthy on the one hand and the masses of peasants and workers on the other. The cleavage between

city and village is widened by the peculiarities of the Greek tongue. The written language is used in official, scientific, and legal documents, which the uneducated Greek cannot understand. Moreover, the constant struggle between rural and urban standards has been intensified by the influx of 1,500,000 Greeks from Asia Minor. Settling in the cities for the most part, they brought a temporary and modest prosperity as a result of a refugee loan from the League of Nations, as well as new industries (carpet-making, coppersmithing, silk, and glassmaking).

Historical Background

Although excavations have carried the beginnings of ancient Greece back to the third or fourth millennium B.C., the recorded history of Greece proper is often considered to begin at the time of the first Olympiad (776 B.C.). The country reached the peak of its glory and power in the fifth century B.C. By the middle of the second century B.C. it had declined to the status of a Roman province. After many years of Roman domination Greece became a part of the Byzantine Empire, which, saturated with Greek ideas, remained the heart of civilization for many centuries. In 1204 Constantinople, the capital of the Eastern Roman Empire, fell to the Crusaders, and later the Empire was in almost constant jeopardy from the Turks. Finally, in 1453, the Turks under Mohammed I captured Constantinople and took it over as the new capital of their Moslem realms. With the fall of Constantinople, Greece soon became a Turkish province.

Although under Turkish rule from 1460 to 1821 except for the Venetian interlude from 1699–1715, Greece was still able to preserve contact with Western civilization. The revolution of 1821 rose on a tide of sentiment friendly to the Greek cause, which swept Europe and America. The intervention of Great Britain, Russia, and France culminated in the Peace of Adrianople of 1829, proclaiming Greece an independent state. Three years later Prince Otto of Bavaria was recognized as king. Because of his religion, his taxation, his use of German officials, and the interference of his wife an insurrection arose, forcing him to grant a constitution (1843), and a revolt ousted him in 1862. Prince William of Denmark, as George I, succeeded him. In 1863 Britain gave Greece the Ionian Is-

---

* In some instances the population of Piraeus is combined with that of Athens. By this method of computation Athens could be said to have a population exceeding 650,000.

lands, and in 1881 Thessaly was added. As the result of the Balkan Wars, Greece received Crete, Southern Macedonia, Salonika, part of Epirus, and a number of Aegean islands. In World War I Greece entered on the side of the Allies, but, making the mistake of continuing the war against the Turks in Asia Minor, was ejected from that region. After World War I Greece received Western Thrace and some more Aegean islands.

During much of the period between the two world wars the politics of Greece was dominated by the towering figure of Venizelos, who had identified himself with the grandiose scheme of a Greater Greece—with unfortunate results. He was bitterly opposed by the Royalists. The King, George II, returned in 1935, and General Metaxas became premier the next year. Shortly thereafter the king dissolved parliament and authorized Metaxas to set up a dictatorship, which was maintained until the German invasion of April, 1941. Then George II fled, and with him went a group of ministers who formed a government-in-exile.

Nationality. Up to the time of the two Balkan Wars (1912, 1913), the population was almost exclusively Greek. These and the subsequent world wars gave Greece territories generally inhabited by Greeks, but also containing minority groups. A far-reaching change was wrought by the Greco-Bulgarian and Greco-Turkish population exchanges, the first organized in 1919 and the second in 1923. All Turks left the country—save those in West Thrace—and in addition Slavs emigrated under the agreements. Their places were taken by Greeks from Asia Minor, East Thrace, and Bulgaria. All in all, the homogeneity of Greece is extraordinary. So is the religious composition of the people, 96 per cent being Greek Orthodox. On the whole, the Greeks have not been too friendly to the remaining Slav minorities in Macedonia and Thrace, which is comprehensible in view of the bloody record of the *IMRO*. Periodic complaints have come also from Tirana regarding the treatment of the Albanian minority in Greece.

Greece under the Nazis. Following their successful invasion of Greece, the Germans apportioned outlying districts to their several allies: the Bulgarians received Western Thrace, Eastern Macedonia to the Struma River, and the islands of Thasos and Samo-

thrace; the Italians annexed the Ionian Islands; the Albanians extended their frontier to include three Greek provinces in the Epirus area; and the Germans themselves retained central Macedonia, with its strategic port of Salonika, and most of the Aegean Islands. An unhappy torso, consisting of the Peloponnesus, Attica, and Thessaly, was left to the "Quisling" Greek governments. On the eve of liberation, inflation had reached the point where the drachma was officially valued at 159 million to the American dollar; a pound loaf of bread cost 18 million drachmas.

Postwar Status

The Greek resistance movement so affected the thought and outlook of the bulk of the Greek population that the years 1941–44 have come to represent a great divide in the course and direction of Greek politics. The largest and most effective resistance organization in the war was the *EAM* (National Liberation Front), with its military arm, *ELAS* (National Popular Liberation Army). Most of the other groups consisted of army officers, usually of Metaxas and royalist persuasion.

After the war the primary political task was that of finding a basis for cooperation between the supporters of the rightist (royalist) government-in-exile and the leftist (resistance) units. Trouble developed at the time the newly established government in Greece attempted to disarm the resistance forces. British troops, called upon to preserve order, actually had to fire upon demonstrating groups barely two months after they and the returning ministers landed in Greece. Later, in a plebiscite held in the country on September 1, 1946, a majority of the voters wanted the return of King George II. Returning to his country in September, 1946, the king died in April, 1947, and was succeeded by King Paul I.

At the same time the Greeks have experienced keenly the price of war. According to Greek government estimates more than 500,000 Greeks were slain or died of privation during the occupation of Italian and German forces, and about 30 per cent of the nation's wealth was destroyed. Apart from the immediate relief requirements, there are certain long-term economic problems that date from the prewar period and for which some solution must be found if Greek economy is to function properly in the postwar period.

Outstanding among these is the enormous public debt, which in 1940 claimed 9.25 per cent of the Greek national income (as compared with 2.98 per cent in Bulgaria, 2.32 per cent in Rumania, and 1.68 per cent in Yugoslavia). The addition of the Dodecanese did not materially change the postwar picture of Greece. The little country needs long-term loans at low interest for a long-range program of rehabilitation and renewed industrialization.

The end of extensive British aid in 1947

made necessary by Great Britain's financial difficulties in the postwar period was followed by an American program of economic support and military advice. Beset by economic troubles and by political disturbances involving civil war, the Greek government also faced the necessity of trying to maintain the integrity of Greek boundaries to the north from encroachments by Albania, Yugoslavia, and Bulgaria, all within the Soviet sphere of influence. Greece was surely in the spotlight.

ALBANIA

By far the smallest of the Balkan states, Albania lies along the mountainous Adriatic coast. It is a wedge between Yugoslavia and Greece, with an area of only 10,500 square miles, a size equal to that of Maryland. During historical times Albania has served as a corridor into the Balkan Peninsula, although natural obstacles impair the way and prevent it from being an effective gateway. The most significant aspect of its position is domination of the narrow water gate between the Adriatic and the Ionian seas.

Geographic Factors

Wild and rugged, with some of its mountains more than a mile high, Albania offers only a difficult and precarious livelihood to its 1,100,000 inhabitants. There is little for the great majority of them to do other than farm and raise stock. Alluvial plains are topped with a fertile soil suitable for raising corn, rice, wheat, barley, tobacco, and cotton. In the mountainous areas lower slopes are utilized for vineyards and tree crops, and much excellent pasturage lies at elevations above those devoted to tended farm lands.

Methods of agriculture, however, remain primitive and no more than one eighth of the country's total area is under cultivation. Rivers are unreliable as sources of needed water, drying up in summer and becoming raging torrents in winter and spring. The coastal plains have large swampy areas handicapped by the problem of malaria.

Albania possesses a few valuable mineral resources but vigorous development of them is retarded by transportation difficulties and a general lack of security in the country. In 1938 Albania ranked sixth among Europe's

producers of oil. A 45-mile pipe line brought oil from inland Petrolia, named for its petroleum deposits, to the port of Valona for shipment. Mines in the mountains of the north were in 1940 producing copper at a rate of 40,000 tons a year.

Albania, in contrast to most European nations, has no large metropolitan center representing the political, commercial, financial, and cultural heart of the country. The capital city of Tirana, with a population of 31,-000, is close to the geographic center of the country, but with no railroads and lack of a radial road pattern it cannot maintain close contact with other Albanian communities. In the northern part of the country, close to the Yugoslav border, Scutari (Shkodër), with 29,000 inhabitants, serves as a regional trading center. Of the remaining cities and towns only two have more than local significance, the small ports of Valona in the south and Durazzo in the central part of the Albanian coast.

Historical Background

Anciently a part of Illyria and, later, of the Roman Empire, Albania was ruled in theory by the Byzantine Empire until 1204 A.D. It served as a direct route to the east for Roman legions, who sailed from Brindisi to Durazzo and trudged inland to reach Greece over the *Via Egnatia,* a Roman road still used in the twentieth century. As part of the Roman Empire, Albania learned early the significance of being the country closest to the heel of Italy's boot. At the mouth of the Adriatic Sea, the two lands are separated by only forty-seven miles of water, the Strait of Otranto. To Tirana from Brindisi, southern Italian port at which Italy's troops concentrated just before invading Albania in 1939, is a distance of 105 miles—less than that from New York to Albany.

Acquiring its independence in 1913 after more than four centuries under Turkish rule as a fragment of the old Ottoman Empire, Albania set out to make a fortune of its own. Its population of 1,106,000 is made up mainly of Ghegs in the north and Tosks in the south, comprising the two language groups of the country. Two thirds of the inhabitants are Moslems, whom muezzins from mosque minarets call to prayers before the same Allah as that of Asia Minor. Among the remainder of the people around 200,000 are Orthodox Christians and 100,000 Roman Catholics.

Invaded during World War I, Albania fell into a state of anarchy. After having its independence recognized by membership in the League of Nations in 1920, the country tried to live as a free state. A republic, set up in 1925, continued for three years. Then Albania reversed the contemporary historical procedure by changing its system of government from a republic to a monarchy. The turn-about occurred when Ahmed Zogu, who had been premier in 1922–24 and President from 1925–28, became King Zog I. In 1939 the Italian army at Mussolini's direction invaded weak Albania, and rapidly conquered it. During World War II the country served as an important source of certain supplies for the Axis Nations. After the war Albania became a republic under the leadership of Enver Hoxha who led the country into the Soviet orbit.

Boundary problems. The major territorial problem confronting Albania after World War II was the future status of Northern Epirus. This area, long a bone of contention between Albania and Greece, was claimed by both countries. Lying to the north of Greece and in the south of Albania it extends from the Adriatic Sea on the west to Greek and Serbian Macedonia on the east. The Greeks estimate that it has about 250,000 settlers, of whom about 130,000 are Christians and about 120,000 Moslems. The population is quite mixed in geographic distribution and largely bilingual. A veritable campaign for and against the cession of Northern Epirus to Greece has been waged in the United States, where there are many politically active groups of Greek descent and the largest Albanian colony outside of Albania. However, the prewar Greek-Albanian boundary appears certain to remain. The only territorial gain of the Albanians from World War II was the island of Saseno, formerly under Italian sovereignty, which dominated the Albanian harbor of Valona.

PART FOUR

Asia

AMONG the continents Asia is a giant—containing one third of the land surface of the globe and harboring well over half of all the human inhabitants of the planet Earth. Despite this pre-eminence, the direct influence of Asia upon modern world history has apparently been small. This is because the precocious industrial and maritime civilization achieved in Europe has tended to eclipse the achievements of Asia. Indeed, the industrialized and superbly armed modern western Europeans have invaded southern and eastern Asia by way of the ocean lanes, and have held a large part of Asia vassal for over three centuries. Simultaneously, the eastern Europeans invaded by land, and have colonized and Slavicized the northern half of Asia.

Evidence exists, however, that the exploitation of Asia by Europe is nearing an end. The Soviet Union has wiped out all boundaries between Asiatic and European Russia, and has erased all human caste lines. Mongolia has won its independence (at least on paper), China has seen the end of the extraterritorial rights of the European nations on her soil, and Japan, although defeated in the recent world war, has succeeded in seriously impairing the prestige of the European in the Far East. Siam has regained its freedom. Indo-China and Korea are demanding self-government. Burma and India have forced Britain to vacate the southern portion of the continent. Turkey has emerged in modernized form, and the Arab States are becoming extremely vocal in the southwest section. It would seem that Asia is now assuming more geopolitical significance in world affairs.

Throughout most of historical time Asia and Europe have been militarily vulnerable to each other. Europe has seen the invasions of Genghis Khan, Tamerlane, Attila, and the Ottoman Turks. Asia has been invaded by Macedonians, Romans, Crusaders, and Slavs. With the rise of modern European sea power, however, the maritime states of western Europe flung a naval cordon around two sides of Asia, leaving Arctic ice to guard the north side. Among the states Great Britain achieved naval supremacy and accordingly riveted a steel ring of sea power about the whole of Eurasia. Scapa Flow, Gibraltar, Malta, Cyprus, Alexandria, Aden, Socotra, Ceylon, Singapore, Hong Kong, and Wei-hai-wei became known as the British lifeline of Empire. Britain further strengthened her position by her sponsorship of Portugal, Greece and Turkey; her special position in Iran, Oman, India, Burma, and Arabia; her diplomatic relations with France, the Netherlands, and the United States; and her former mandates in Palestine and Transjordan. Thus British naval power has long bottled up all Eurasian military land power inside its great line of ships and naval bases. Outside its cordon lay only Britain's daughter nation, the United States, with whom Britain eventually shared control of the oceans. France, Germany, Turkey, Czarist Russia, Italy, and Japan have at various times tried to break out of the Anglo-Saxon rings of naval power, but each attempt has ended in failure.

World peace has thus rested uneasily upon a delicately balanced set of global geographical relationships. Until quite recently these turned upon the following three facts: (a) Great Britain was industrially strong enough to maintain a pre-eminent navy; (b) no country in Eurasia was strong enough to consolidate the vast interior regions into one great military nation; and (c) if such a great land power had arisen, it would have had no means of driving British sea power away from the shores of Asia.

All three of these former facts have now ceased to be facts. First, two world wars and an economic "depression" have so weakened Britain that, even with American financial help and diplomatic backing, she is presently unable to maintain enough power for world control. Second, Soviet Russia has consolidated her hold upon practically all of interior Eurasia, using the modern instruments —railways, automobiles and good roads, commercial planes, and means of communication —to accomplish national unification. Moreover, airpower has given Soviet Russia a potential means for attacking and driving navies away from the Asiatic continent.

Thus the new geographical relationships have altered the entire power equation of the world. Indeed, Britain, being a small island near the continent of Eurasia, is so vulnerable to future aerial attack as to find her position practically untenable. Even more significant, much of the interior area in which the Soviet Union lies is situated behind a wall of mountains—the Caucasus, Elburz, Hindu Kush, Himalaya, Khingan, and Stanovoi systems. Other protective features are the frozen Arctic, the huge Tibetan Plateau (the so-called Roof of the World), and the invasion-absorbing 2,000 miles of European plain on the west. Were naval and amphibious invasions to penetrate all the margins of Eurasia, there would still remain an impenetrable core as large as North America in inner Asia. Into this Asiatic core, or Heartland, only air power might be able to penetrate, and in that event the advantage would lie with the interior-defending nation rather than the exterior-attacking forces, if anything approaching equal industrial strength for the opposing states is assumed.

In conclusion, with Britain unable longer to blockade Eurasia tightly and having a geographic situation well-nigh untenable under sustained aerial attack, and with the United States far away and having her attention spread over the whole earth, British and American leaders have a vital obligation to appraise changing geographic relationships promptly and accurately.

To continue to keep Soviet Russia in Asia from breaking out to the warm seas, or to keep Arabo-Iranian oil, the Kurile fisheries, or the empty lands of northern Manchuria out of her hands may prove to be well-nigh impossible. It would likewise appear that the attempts to prevent the Soviets from achieving their own "hemispheric solidarity," or at least their own continental hegemony, may result in a world-wide struggle frightful beyond belief. The spotlight of political geography is focused squarely upon Asia.

CHAPTER 20

Turkey and the Straits

By REASON of its location Asia Minor, now occupied by the greater part of Turkey, has had thrust upon it an all-important role in the geopolitical strategy of many nations. In a narrow sense any interpretation of the location can be focused upon the region in terms of its importance as the intersection of the land route between Europe and Asia and the water route connecting the Black Sea with the Mediterranean. Modern Turkey commands this "crossroads of the world," about which a continuous succession of international agreements and treaties has been enacted. In a broad sense, however, an analysis of the setting of Turkey must be dispersed over large areas on three continents. As the political heart of the huge Ottoman Empire, Turkey for more than six centuries controlled the tri-continental bridge that makes up the nucleus of the Middle East. It was Old Turkey that stood in the gap between West and East and forced Spanish and Portuguese navigators to put to sea in search of an unobstructed route to the Spice Lands. In both world wars Turkey figured prominently, not as a great power, but as a keystone on the route to the riches of the Middle East.

Turkey is separated into two natural divisions by the historic waterway formed by the Dardanelles, the Sea of Marmara, and the Bosporus. Although the Turkish Republic, covering 296,100 square miles, thus embraces territory on two continents, the area of the European portion is less than one thirtieth that of the Asiatic (see the map on page 282). This European area, about the size of New Hampshire, is the wedge-shaped segment of the Balkan Peninsula east of the Maritsa

River. With frontage on the Black Sea, the Aegean Sea, and the connecting Straits, European Turkey has land boundaries in common with Greece and Bulgaria, sharing the politico-geographic region known as Thrace with the former (see the map on page 263).

The area of Asiatic Turkey (Anatolia) is coextensive with the Asia Minor peninsula.* More than one half of the boundary is water, formed by the Black, Marmara, Aegean, and Mediterranean seas. In the east, however, Turkey is blocked in by Soviet Russia on the north, Iran on the east, and Iraq and Syria on the south. Although the latter three countries are independent, they have represented spheres of influence held by Western Powers and conflicts of interests among these powers have from time to time resulted in border friction. The most recent actual change in the boundaries took place in June, 1939, when Alexandretta (Hatay) was taken from Syria—this country was subject to a French mandate—and given to Turkey by France as payment of a twenty-year-old Turkish claim and as a token of friendship in an atmosphere of war tension. Russian territory northeast of Turkey consists of the Soviet Republics of Armenia and Georgia. In 1945 Soviet Russia agitated for territorial control of Turkish Armenia and the Trebizond area, which are adjacent to Armenia and Georgia respectively, but without success.

The study of the political geography of

* Asia Minor is poorly defined in its southeastern extremity, with the result that Syria, Lebanon, Palestine, and Transjordan have sometimes been included as a part of the peninsula. The term *Anatolia* is frequently used in referring to Asia Minor but some geographers apply it to the upland areas only.

Turkey falls naturally into two major divisions. On the one hand, the breakdown of the extensive Ottoman Empire and the emergence of the modern Turkish Republic deal *tegic location*. Obviously, the two divisions of study are closely related, but each is primarily related to a different set of operating principles. The remainder of this chapter

MODERN TURKEY

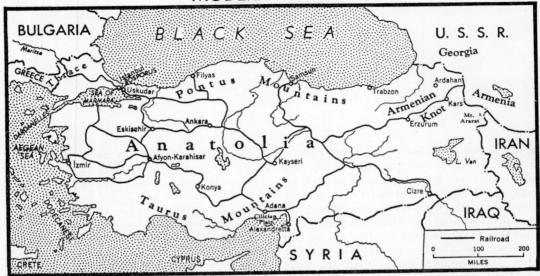

principally with factors of the *political area*. On the other hand, the history of incidents related to the highly strategic Straits region with their international implications and resulting repercussions has mostly to do with a *geostra* is divided in accordance with this arrangement, in order that the discussion may be pointed more clearly toward each of the two prime issues of political area and geostrategic location.

THE TURKISH NATIONAL STATE

Historical Evolution

An understanding of modern Turkey is impossible without first considering the great Ottoman Empire that dominated the Middle East from the late thirteenth century until the early part of the twentieth century. Taking its name from the ruling house descendent from Osman I, the Ottoman Empire was founded on the dynamic Moslem religion and thrived by virtue of military prowess. At the zenith of its power in the sixteenth century the sprawling and loosely knit empire bore very little resemblance to the compact and highly nationalistic Turkish Republic of today. Yet it was out of the residue of Ottoman territory, as it cracked to pieces, that the Turkey of today emerged as a state possessing a vitality that startled the world and at the same time demanded its respect.

The Ottoman Era. The Ottoman Turks first appeared in history early in the thirteenth century. Driven from their homes in Central Asia by the Mongols under Genghis Khan, a horde of several thousand persons settled in Asia Minor under the protection of the Seljuk Turks, to whom they acknowledged sovereignty. About 1299 Osman, who succeeded his father as leader of the tribe in 1288, declared his independence from the Seljuks and assumed the title of emir. Accordingly, the foundation of the Ottoman Empire is frequently dated from this event. Throughout his reign Osman continued to expand his dominions through conquests. His son Orkhan, who succeeded him at his death in 1326, continued to wage aggressive war. Among the remarkable achievements of Orkhan's reign are the capture of much territory in Asia Minor and southeastern Europe previ-

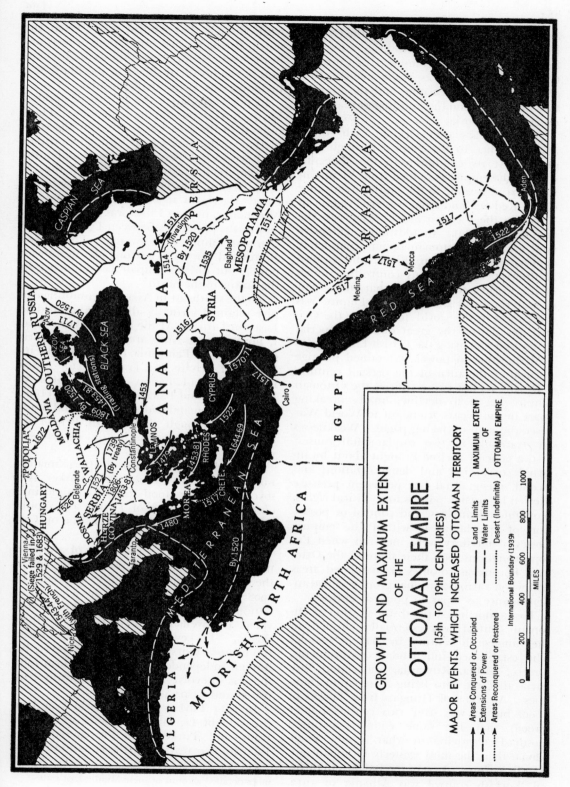

GROWTH AND MAXIMUM EXTENT
OF THE
OTTOMAN EMPIRE
(15th TO 19th CENTURIES)

MAJOR EVENTS WHICH INCREASED OTTOMAN TERRITORY

Areas Conquered or Occupied — →
Extensions of Power — – →
Areas Reconquered or Restored ····→

International Boundary (1939)

Land Limits
Water Limits
Desert (Indefinite)

MAXIMUM EXTENT
OF
OTTOMAN EMPIRE

MILES
0   200   400   600   800   1000

ously held by the Seljuk Turks or the Greeks, the organization of the Janissaries, a force of intrepid mercenaries composed of captured Christian boys raised as Mohammedans, the encouragement of learning and the foundation of schools, and the building of roads and other public works.

For 200 years after Orkhan each sultan added further to the empire through conquests. At its maximum in the sixteenth century the empire extended from Vienna in the heart of Europe to the southern entrance of the Red Sea and from western Algeria in Africa to the Caspian Sea in Asia (see the map on page 283). In addition to extensive land areas, the Ottoman regime completely dominated the Aegean, Black, and eastern Mediterranean seas, thus controlling much of the world's commerce at that time. For several centuries the Ottoman Empire was the largest in the world (excluding the Orient), postdating the great days of Imperial Rome and predating the British Empire. As a Mediterranean power it retained prestige until after the turn of the present century.

During its last two centuries the Ottoman Empire began to decline, finally breaking apart in the events attendant to World War I (see the map on facing page). Weaknesses are traceable to two fundamental causes: first, a general decline brought about by internal corruption and demoralization; and second, the gradual but persistent pressure exerted by outside powers for political rights, economic advantages, and control or possession of specific areas within the empire. Losses of territory were incurred when European nations took their share of the Ottoman Empire as colonies or mandated areas and when various national groups gained independence as separate political entities.

To the northwest the disintegration of Ottoman control was essentially effected in the nineteenth century by Balkan peoples who established independent governments. Greece, Serbia, Rumania, and, later, Bulgaria all came into being as separate countries. Austria took Hungary from Turkey in 1699, but it was over two centuries later (1908) that the same country acquired Bosnia-Herzegovina in what is now Yugoslavia, then the most westerly Ottoman outpost in Europe. Last of the Balkans to throw off Turkish control was Albania in 1912,

weak though that control was. From the north, Russia pushed into Ottoman territory in the eighteenth century and secured possession of the northern shores of the Black Sea, including the Crimean Peninsula.

In northern Africa the British penetrated Egypt, forcibly occupying it in 1882. Their interest in the area was spurred by the completion of the Suez Canal through Egyptian territory—a link between England and growing empire interests in and beyond the Indian Ocean. Farther west the French secured Algeria in 1830 and Tunisia in 1881. Much later, in 1912 Libya was given to Italy, and in 1914 final ties between Egypt and the Ottoman Empire were severed. These losses eliminated Turkey as a strong Mediterranean power, but did not impair her influence in the Straits to the north.

To the southeast in Asia the crumbling empire retained virtually all of Arabic Middle East until 1918. At the close of World War I, however, the Arab areas, except in parts of the Arabian Peninsula, came under the influence of Britain and France, victor Allied nations. Syria-Lebanon was mandated to France; Iraq and Palestine, including Transjordan, were mandated to Britain; and much of Arabia, though tinged with British influence, was already working out its own salvation.*

Stripped in this fashion of approximately nine tenths of its former area, Turkey as a sovereign power stood ready to topple into obscurity. The birth of Turkey as a republic is a striking sequel to the decline of Turkey as an empire.

The Turkish Era. Evidences of a rejuvenated Turkish nation appeared long before the Ottoman Empire finally expired. In 1908 a revolution, fomented by a group of nationalists known as the Young Turks, activated a movement best described by their slogan, "Turkey for the Turks." Fifteen tumultuous years were to pass, however, before an independent Turkey on a firm footing was to evolve in an area politically frustrated and weary of war.

In 1914 Turkey entered World War I on the side of Germany. Results were disastrous, and Turkey paid the consequences. In 1920, two years after the cessation of hos-

* See Chapter 21, "The Arab World," for a much more detailed account of these Middle East states.

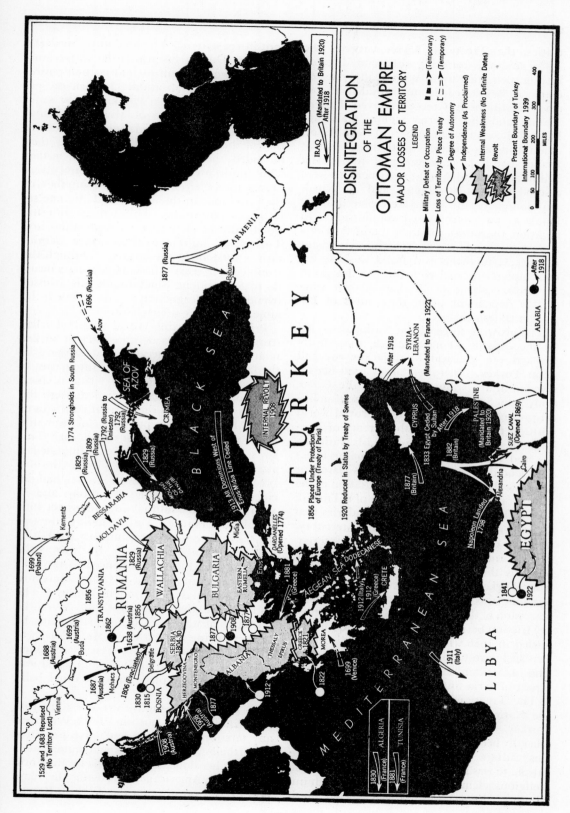

DISINTEGRATION
OF THE
OTTOMAN EMPIRE
MAJOR LOSSES OF TERRITORY

LEGEND

Military Defeat or Occupation
 ▬▬▶ (Temporary)
Loss of Territory by Peace Treaty
 ═══▶ (Temporary)
Degree of Autonomy
Independence (As Proclaimed)
Internal Weakness (No Definite Dates)
Revolt

Present Boundary of Turkey
International Boundary 1939

MILES
0   50 100   200   300   400

IRAQ (Mandated to Britain 1920)
After 1918

ARABIA — After 1918

1696 (Russia)

1877 (Russia) — Batum — ARMENIA

T U R K E Y

SEA OF AZOV

CRIMEA

B L A C K   S E A

1774 Strongholds in South Russia

1792 (Russia to Dniester (Russia)

1829 1809 (Russia) (Russia)

1829 (Russia)

MOUTHS OF THE DANUBE

BESSARABIA

MOLDAVIA

Kements

1699 (Poland)

1688 (Austria)

1699 (Austria)

Vienna

Buda 1856

TRANSYLVANIA

RUMANIA

1829 (Russia)

WALLACHIA

1638 (Austria)

1687 (Austria)

Mohacs

1806 (Evacuated)

1815

1830

Belgrade

SERBIA 1804-30

BOSNIA

HERZEGOVINA

MONTENEGRO

1878 (Austria)

1908 (Austria)

1877

1912

ALBANIA

1829 (Russia)

BULGARIA

EASTERN RUMELIA

1908

1877

1878

1881 (Greece)

THESSALY

EPIRUS

GREECE 1821-29

MOREA

1699 (Venice)

1822

Enos

DARDANELLES (Opened 1774)

Midia

1913 All Dominions West of Enos-Midia Line Ceded

1856 Placed Under Protection of Europe (Treaty of Paris)

1920 Reduced in Status by Treaty of Sevres

INTERNAL REVOLT 1908

AEGEAN SEA

DODECANESE

1912 (Italy)

1912 (Greece)

CRETE

1911 (Italy)

M E D I T E R R A N E A N   S E A

ALGERIA 1830 (France)

TUNISIA 1881 (France)

L I B Y A

EGYPT

Cairo

Alexandria

Napoleon Landed 1798

SUEZ CANAL (Opened 1869)

1882 (Britain)

1833 Egypt Ceded by Sultan

After 1918

PALESTINE (Mandated to Britain 1920)

CYPRUS

1877 (Britain)

SYRIA-LEBANON (Mandated to France 1920)

After 1918

1841

1922

1529 and 1683 Repulsed (No Territory Lost)

285

tilities, the Treaty of Sèvres between the Allies and the tottering sultanate directed further penalties upon an already crushed empire. Besides earlier territorial losses (already mentioned) Greece received Eastern Thrace and the Smyrna region; Italy was handed the southwestern part of Asia Minor, amounting to about one fourth the total area; France got a large segment of south Asia Minor adjacent to Syria; the Armenians were assured their independence, and the Kurds autonomy; and the Straits were placed in the hands of an international commission. In addition, the Sultan was to be retained strictly as a puppet, and even the remaining remnant of Turkey, in northern Anatolia, was divested of complete internal control. At this point the future status of Turkey seemed completely dependent upon the whims of European statesmen.

The growing force of the Nationalists, led by the capable Kemal Ataturk, successfully revoked the political humiliation wreaked upon Turkey. In 1922 Turkey used her revived military strength to drive the Greek army from Smyrna. A resurrection of political prestige won Turkey an improved world position in the terms of the Treaty of Lausanne in 1923 between the Turkish Nationalists and the Allies. Here the major issues represented the ambitious nation's claim for an honorable existence: (1) repudiation of the Treaty of Sèvres; (2) recognition of a Turkish Nationalist Government; (3) boundaries that did not rob Turkey of "rightful" territory; and (4) correction of the evils of interference in internal affairs. With but few exceptions these issues were settled favorably from Turkey's point of view. Discord over territory was limited to continued Italian possession of the Dodecanese Islands, a boundary friction between Turkey and Iraq (finally settled in 1926 with the Mosul oil district of British interest going to Iraq), and the question of Alexandretta (retained by France as a part of Syria until 1939).

The Treaty of Lausanne set the stage for the Nationalists to take over completely in Turkey. In the same year the Turkish state officially became a republic. One year earlier the Sultan had been deposed, but the caliphate was not abolished as an undesirable (religious) element in the new government until 1924. Kemal Ataturk was elected presi-

dent in 1923, an office he held until his death in 1938. During his regime he carried out an extensive program of reform, modernization, and industrialization. In fact, the period 1919–38 in Turkey is known to some historians as the "Era of Mustapha Kemal (Ataturk)." His career is inseparable from that of the Nationalists, for as early as 1908 he aided their cause as a military leader. The multilateral Montreux Convention, drawn up in 1936, abrogated a number of the provisions in the Treaty of Lausanne relating to the Straits, abolished the international control of the Straits, and authorized Turkey to militarize the former demilitarized zone along the Straits. Through the troubled war years following Ataturk's death in 1938 President Ismet Inonu, his faithful friend and colleague, carried on in much the same vein as his predecessor.

Prior to and during World War II Turkey strove to maintain a delicate balance in her relations with two great armed camps. In the late 1930's the country was automatically thrown toward Germany by virtue of Nazi economic tentacles that reached through the Balkan Peninsula to the natural resources of Asia Minor. In preparation for war the Reich's need for war goods made her Turkey's best customer and thus stimulated a program of industrialization. Before the outbreak of hostilities, however, Turkey had decided against the aggressor nations, and in 1939 concluded a mutual assistance pact with Britain and France. During most of the war she skillfully enforced a neutrality with "two million bristling bayonets." In this way the cause of the Allies was enhanced by the closing to Axis troops of a possible intercontinental land passage through Turkey. The policy more than offset for the Allies the deliveries of war goods to Germany made by Turkey during the first war years. Finally in 1945, having previously broken off relations, Turkey declared war against the Axis nations —thus taking her place with the other belligerent Allies.

By virtue of having thrown her weight on the winning side, postwar Turkey escaped any territorial losses or restrictive penalties. Nevertheless, new problems were immediately thrust at her door; Soviet Russia on the north and British-American interests on the south now exert a pressure on the Turkish Republic certainly no less critical than those pressures of prewar years.

Physical Landscape

The natural environment of Turkey is generally inhospitable, though not sufficiently so to preclude material advancement by an energetic people. Adverse surface features seriously impede human development over large areas; cultivated land amounts to but little more than one tenth the total area of the country.

Long serving as a land bridge beween the cultures of Europe and Asia, Anatolia nevertheless offers poor overland travel conditions between continents—hence the success of the water route to the south. The climate is harsh, but with hampering rather than intolerable temperature and precipitation factors prevailing over the greater part of the land. Mineral resources are present in appreciable quantities, but they demand intelligent exploitation before a successful regional economy can be secured. Since the establishment of the Republic, however, the Turkish people have made rapid strides in the task of utilizing their resources for the benefit of the nation as a whole.

Relief. Topographic structure in Asiatic Turkey generally conforms to an east-west alignment. Lowlands, mountain ranges, an extensive plateau, and a massive mountain knot give a discernible pattern to surface features. The elongated central portion of Anatolia is a well-defined treeless plateau, averaging around 2,500 feet in elevation in the west and more in the east. On the north the Pontic Mountains and on the south the Taurus Mountains effectively separate the plateau from the Black and Mediterranean seas respectively. Elevations reach 8,000–9,000 feet in the Pontic and 10,000–11,000 feet in the Taurus mountains. On the east these two mountain systems fuse to form the Armenian knot, which makes the entire eastern fourth of the country preponderantly mountainous. In the extreme eastern part of Turkey, near the point at which Soviet Russia and Iran meet, is the culminating altitude of Mt. Ararat (16,916 feet). On the west the Pontic and Taurus ranges do not converge to enclose totally the central plateau by a mountain rim, but rather extend finger-like projections into the Sea of Mar-

mara and the Aegean Sea and help to form the Bosporus and the Dardanelles. The Anatolian Plateau likewise drops to the sea in the west, forming an irregular zone of hill lands along its Aegean Sea margin.

European Turkey is hilly country drained by the Maritsa River and its tributaries. On the west it is well forested and only thinly inhabited; on the east near the Maritsa the land is fertile and more intensively utilized.

Around the entire coastal margin of Asiatic Turkey are lowlands, although they do not form a continuous belt. In many places the mountains descend abruptly to the sea, and at irregular intervals areas of flat land usually are identified as the lower sections of river valleys. The most extensive of the lowland areas are along the western shores, but the clearly delineated Cilician Plains in south central Turkey at the northeastern corner of the Mediterranean also deserve mention. These peripheral flat areas are focal points of human activity.

The nature of the relief gives the country a dual physical environment. First, the fertile marginal lowlands, including the Straits area, are easy of access and have been subjected to conflicting cultures over the centuries. For example, the Aegean region of Asia Minor became Hellenized. Second, the relatively barren plateau and isolated mountain areas have retained a distinctive cultural unity from historical era to historical era. The Turkish peasant, beneath his twentieth century veneer lives much as he did under the Ottoman Sultans. Even in the face of the Westernization of modern Turkey, Turkish people look to the Anatolian Uplands as their traditional home.

Despite the economic advantages offered by coastal regions, the real Turkish coreland —at least politically—is on the Anatolian Plateau. Here the Ottoman Turks first banded together to found the Turkish Empire in the thirteenth century, and here remained the Turkish "homeland" throughout the pulsations of strength that carried in all directions and swept over much of southwestern Asia, southeastern Europe, and northern Africa. The toughest soldiers of the Ottoman Empire traditionally came from the Anatolian highlands. Transferring the Turkish capital from Istanbul to Ankara in 1923 was an attempt to bolster national independence, by an appeal to the deep-seated love of the people for the source of their heritage.

Climate. The climate of Turkey, which shows wide variations, matches relief as a factor in helping or hindering human development. The Anatolian Plateau is steppe-like in its climatic characteristics, closely related in this respect to the semiarid lands of Soviet Central Asia. Icy winds sweeping southward from Russia make the winters bitter cold. Snow covers most of the area for three months or more each year. In stark contrast, the summers are hot, and their dryness reflects the scant annual rainfall of less than ten inches. Cultivated agriculture is limited to irrigable areas, and the prevailing occupations are pastoral, based upon the native grasslands. The continuous search for adequate grazing lands long ago established nomadism as a leading activity of the plateau.

A pure Mediterranean type of climate typifies the southwest coastal section of Turkey. Elsewhere the coastal sections are also Mediterranean, but modified in one respect or another by exposure to winds, availability of moisture, and degree of continentality. Rainfall over most coastal lowlands ranges from 20 to 30 inches per year, but along the eastern part of the Black Sea coast it exceeds 100 inches. The Black and Marmara sea coasts are subject to cold winds, which may come either from the north or sweep down from the plateau and mountain areas of Turkey itself. Compared to the barren aspects of interior Turkey, the coastal plains favor most lines of human endeavor.

People

A common racial background is not responsible for the national unity of the Turkish people. In fact, the term *Turkish* is generally conceded to be linguistic rather than ethnological in its implication. Citizens of modern Turkey trace their ancestry to a wide variety of European and Asiatic peoples, including Armenians, Mongols, Arabs, Greeks, Albanians, and Circassians. Racial distinctions are thus much less effective in the identification of Turkish people than are religious factors, a single language, and a common feeling of national consciousness, all the result of a unique historic and cultural evolution. Beyond the frontiers of Turkey the homogeneous characteristics of the population cease to exist in one or more respects, thereby setting off the people of the nation from those of neighboring states and at the same time justifying the international boundaries of the modern Turkish state. Existing minorities do not seriously affect the political stability of Turkey, although they give rise to problems in certain districts, principally in the periphery of the country.

Cultural aspects. The religious pattern of modern Turkey is simple and offers no political complications of import. More than 98 per cent of the population are Moslems, with Christians and Jews predominating among the remaining less than 2 per cent. During the six centuries of the Ottoman Empire, however, religion served as a dynamic factor in political functions. The basic philosophies of both Islam and Christianity not only entered strongly into the composition of the Empire but infiltrated into its relations with outside powers. The Sultan also carried the title of Caliph (successor of Mohammed). His dual temporal and spiritual role made the peoples of the entire Moslem world his potential subjects, although the long-visioned dream of a great Pan-Islam was never actually realized. After the Sultan was deposed (1922) and the caliphate abolished (1924), the new state divorced itself from Islam as a device of political control although the people retained their Mohammedan faith. Illustrative of full cleavage between state and church in the Turkish Republic was the total prohibition of the fez as a religious, spiritual, and political symbol.

Languages and minorities. Minorities within Turkey are best indicated by the distribution of language groups. People speaking non-Turkish languages as their mother tongue are largely concentrated in the eastern part of the country. These language minorities make up 14 per cent of the total population, of which a dialect of Kurdish alone accounts for 9 per cent.* The second largest linguistic minority, forming about one per cent of the population, speak Arabic. Smaller language groups include Lazis, Circassians, Armenians, Georgians, and Jews.

Of these minorities only two have created serious internal pressure on Turkey since the establishment of the Republic. The Kurds, as the first group, are essentially backward

* Turkish language statistics from the 1935 census.

mountaineers and nomads concentrated near the Iranian and Iraqi borders. Motivated by their Moslem fanaticism, they revolted against Ataturk's strong nationalization program. The Armenian people, a second, though smaller, group, have survived from ancient times as a race without a state. Their dream has long been a country of their own —a fire recently fed fuel by the Russians for purposes of their own.

In the early 1920's the minority problem was substantially reduced by a Turko-Greek agreement to exchange national population groups. The repatriation of an estimated 1,500,000 Greeks from Turkey to their own country amounted to a reduction of about 10 per cent of the Republic's entire population. In turn, Turkey received roughly half a million Turks from Greece. In Turkey the industries suffered by virtue of their having been manned in large proportion by Greeks.

As a nationalistic measure in the early days of the Republic, President Kemal Ataturk enforced the use of the Latin alphabet in the Turkish language. Both educational and modernizing, the underlying motive was to purify the state language of foreign words, especially Arabic because of its Moslem implications. Arabic characters had been used for centuries, and the instance of an entire people relearning its own language in another vehicle of writing testifies to the vigor of a determined leader and the enthusiasm vested in the Turkish population.

Census characteristics. The 1945 population of Turkey totaled 18.9 million. In decided contrast the population of the area once held by the Ottoman Empire at its peak *now* contains 140 million.* The latter figure is roughly comparable to the population of the entire United States, whereas the former is only equivalent to that of New England plus Pennsylvania. The population density for Turkey as a whole slightly exceeds 60 persons per square mile, about one and one half times that of the United States but much less than that of most European countries. The people are unevenly distributed over the land, for approximately one half live in the narrow coastlands and the other half on the spacious Anatolian Plateau.

In addition to differences in population

* 140 million represents an estimate based upon latest prewar census statistics.

densities, the coastal and plateau environments reflect marked contrasts in the living habits and standards of the people. The heavier concentrations of population along the coasts, especially in the west, have been relatively susceptible to Western ideas and techniques and have had the direct advantages of world commerce. Despite attempts at modernization the more isolated interior, with its large proportion of semi-nomadic population, has tended to be self-sufficient.

Over the country as a whole about one fifth of the population lives in urban centers of 5,000 or more persons. Along the coastal zone in Asiatic Turkey this ratio increases somewhat in favor of the urban dwellers, and in European Turkey the proportion goes up to over one half. Of the four cities exceeding 100,000 in population, three (Istanbul, 845,000; Izmir, or Smyrna, 200,000; Adana, 100,000) are on the coastal lowlands. As previously mentioned, the capital city of Ankara (227,000) is located deep in the interior on the Anatolian plateau. Six other cities exceed 50,000 in population: one (Bursa) on the lowlands not far from Istanbul, and five (Eskisehir, Gaziantep, Konya, Kayseri, and Erzurum) scattered about the plateau as regional centers. Other than Istanbul, European Turkey has no large cities.

National Economy

The advances of Turkish economy since the establishment of the Republic have been accelerated by the elimination of "extra-territorial rights" for foreigners. Known as *capitulations,* these rights worked against Turkey during four centuries of Ottoman rule. In principle, they meant that Turkey had no political jurisdiction or economic control over subjects of outside countries who lived or traveled in the Ottoman Empire. In practice, the capitulations meant that foreigners exploited Turkey unmercifully to their own advantage, and virtually strangled any semblance of an economy that the Turks themselves might have effected. Some foreign governments went so far as to operate their own post offices on Turkish territory, and the entire transportation pattern of the country was developed in accordance with designs such as foreign powers might hold for enlarging their own empires in the Near or Middle East. France, Britain, Germany,

Austria-Hungary, and Russia were leaders in the abuse of extraterritorial rights in Turkey. The assumption of responsibility for their own economy in the early 1920's was a major step in making it possible for the Turkish people to throw off the shackles of an unfortunate heritage and to undertake reforms that have proved of material benefit to the rejuvenated state.

Bases for an economy. Always a mainstay in Turkish economy, agricultural production has come to hold even greater importance within the last two decades and today engages about two thirds of the population. Governmental encouragement, including the introduction of scientific methods, has doubled and even trebled agricultural production in certain instances. Attention is divided among staple cereal crops, commercial specialty crops, and animals and animal products. Wheat and barley lead in acreage, but tobacco, cotton, sugar beets, olives, figs, grapes (raisins), and filberts enter trade channels and so are better known. Lowland areas in the vicinity of the Aegean Sea and the Sea of Marmara are the greatest centers for commercial crops, many of which are exported. Sheep, goats (ordinary and Angora), cattle, horses, mules and asses, and buffaloes are numbered in the millions, for animals rather than crops support the bulk of the population on the Anatolian Plateau. Besides supplying local needs, the pastoral industries furnish mohair, wool, skins, and hides as surplus commodities.

Turkish ambition to industrialize the country goes far beyond the installation of equipment for heavy manufactures. It involves the scientific utilization of available resources, and the fabrication and processing of innumerable types of lesser complex consumers' goods. As illustrated above, agriculture can supply some of the essential raw materials needed for industrial production, for example, cotton for ginning and spinning and figs for packing. Thousands of factories, most of them relatively new, are pouring out everyday items in quantities sufficient to satisfy domestic demand. These products include various items in such categories as glass, paper, chemicals, cement, and household utensils, as well as foods and textiles. An iron and steel industry was activated in 1939 near the coal region in the north central

part of the country, and production continues on a modest scale.

Large reserves of certain minerals augment the Turkish economy. Coal, copper, and chrome exist in substantial quantities, although poor transportation facilities in many instances handicap exploitation. A recent move on the part of the government has been to open up coal fields in the northern mountains by constructing railroad spurs to them. Molybdenum, lead, zinc, manganese, antimony, mercury, gold, silver, borax, emery, arsenic, and meerschaum are also present in amounts justifying production. Turkey holds important world status in the production of chrome, meerschaum, and emery, although in tonnage the latter two amount to but little. There are two known reserves of iron ore, one in the Meander River valley and the other in the Cilician Plains; and oil has been struck in eastern Turkey adjacent to the Iraqi border.

Transportation. In addition to adverse surface conditions, political jockeying on a wide international scale gave the new Republic of Turkey a poor start in a serviceable transportation pattern. Interest was centered in the Constantinople-Baghdad rail line, stemming from the Prussian project to drive a railroad from Berlin through to the Persian Gulf in order to compete with Britain's lifeline to the south.* Started late in the 1880's, the railway reached Ankara in 1892, but not until World War II was Europe (and Turkey) linked to Baghdad and the Persian Gulf at Basra. Ironically, it was the British who finally completed the project —to use against the Germans.

This trunk line of international intrigue, plus a few auxiliary lines mostly of foreign design, left much to be desired from the standpoint of serving Turkish needs. With the riddance of foreign intervention (the capitulations) Turkey has been able to add numerous railway lines to the skeleton network inherited by the Republic in the early 1920's.

* Known as the "Berlin-to-Baghdad" railway project the idea was originated by Austria-Hungary to block Russia in the Balkans, and subsequently taken over by the Prussians in order to build an empire. Eliahu Ben-Horin states, however, that the slogan *Drang nach Osten* (drive to the East) had only one meaning in German politics, namely, *Drang nach Turkei.* Eliahu Ben-Horin, *The Middle East—Crossroads of History* (W. W. Norton, 1943), p. 26.

Manufacturing centers, Black Sea ports, and northern coal fields are now accessible to major rail termini, such as Istanbul, Ankara, Izmir, and Adana.

Supplementing the railroads are a number of "feeder" highways. In addition several roads, some of military importance, are of international importance, for example, one from Istanbul to the Bulgarian border and another from Trebizond to the Iranian border. In general, however, Turkish roads are classed as "terrible" by American travelers.

A Turkish State Airway interconnects most of the larger cities within, but in no place extends beyond national boundaries. The Istanbul-Ankara service is excellent, with multiple daily schedules. When European air routes were being pushed to India and the Far East in the 1930's, Turkey refused to grant right of air transit over its territory, but presently an American airline flies into Istanbul.

THE STRAITS

Importance of Location

A series of deepwater passages—the Dardanelles, the Sea of Marmara, and the Bosporus—collectively make up the Straits. Separating Asia Minor from Europe, this 200-mile sea passage forms a narrow but highly strategic link between the landlocked Black Sea and the international waterway of the Mediterranean (see map directly below).

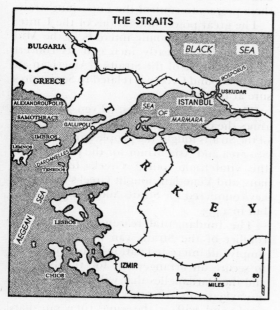

Along with the Suez and Panama canals, it is one of the three most important waterlinks in the world, and consequently has had a tremendous bearing on relationships among nations throughout history. Control of the Straits has fallen to the lot of Turkey, attracting to a single nation an undue share of political limelight and international tension.

Physical aspects. From a physiographic standpoint the Dardanelles and the Bosporus are drowned river valleys. They are suitable for vessels of every type and draught. At some points the narrows are only a mile wide, but in the interconnecting Sea of Marmara the maximum width exceeds forty miles. Solely because of the geological incident of subsidence in the Straits, the Black Sea is not landlocked as is the Caspian.

The Straits have enhanced strategic significance because no other water transit road exists between the Black Sea and the Mediterranean. The Suez and the Panama canals are of utmost world importance, but vessels normally using them could ultimately reach their destinations by other, though more devious, water routes. From global shipping lanes the Black Sea can be reached only through the Straits.

The Balkan and Anatolian regions form a continuous highland area from Europe into Asia, interrupted only by the depression in which lie the drowned river valleys and intermediate sea. In fact, the restricted width of the Straits has long made this region a natural land bridge between Asia Minor and Europe, similar to the bridge between North Africa and Europe formed by the Strait of Gibraltar.

The Straits area served also as a bridge for the exchange of goods and ideas between the peoples of central and southeastern Europe and southern Russia to the north and east, and the Middle East to the south and east. As a specific example, it proved to be a commercial gateway to the fertile, mineral-rich region that lies between the Ural and Carpathian mountains. The excellent river system of this vast European plain served even in ancient times for transporting goods from the Baltic Sea to the Straits. It is thus inevitable that as a focal point for widespread commercial activity the Straits would have great strategic, political, and economic value.

Istanbul. The strategic and trade importance of the Straits is expressed by the great city and port of Istanbul. A population of 845,000 makes it not only the leading metropolitan center of Turkey, but the largest city on the Balkan Peninsula. Moreover, there is no other city so large in any of the countries in southwestern Asia. Located at the southern end of the Bosporus on the European shore, the city's site was originally selected about 658 B.C. as a trading post by a Greek named Byzas.* Even in ancient and medieval times the port city of Istanbul served as an important center for trade. Merchants from many lands came with their goods, such as amber, skins, and hides from Russia; metals and grain from central and western Europe; and slaves from Africa.

With increased world trade during the latter part of the nineteenth century, Istanbul played an important role as a modern trade center. Although Austria-Hungary shipped most of her commodities to the Near East via Trieste and Germany used the port of Hamburg, the Danube River carried bulk commodities from central Europe to Istanbul, where cargoes could be transferred to larger vessels. During the period of 1870–1914 Russian import and export trade dominated commercial activity in Istanbul, although British, French, Austro-Hungarian, and German vessels were utilized in conveying most of the traffic. Trade in and through the Straits was hard hit by the dismemberment of the Austrian and Turkish empires. The establishment of numerous national states in the Danubian region split trade into many individual units, and each state sought a port best fitted for its particular needs. Russia's shrinking export and import trade after 1919 also had much to do with the fact that Istanbul ranks third behind Salonika and Piraeus as a commercial city.

The commercial position of Istanbul will undergo new changes. The future of Trieste, the stability of northeastern Greece and its port of Salonika, and the predominant political and economic influence and interests of Russia in the Danubian countries will materially affect traffic through the Straits. Moreover, industrialization and reconstruction within Russia may increase that nation's import and export trade and, in turn, influence Istanbul and the Straits.

Political Issues *

The crux of the Straits problem is that in this proximity the interests of two of the world's most powerful states clash. Even though other states also have interests in the area, Great Britain and Soviet Russia will remain principals in any possibility of conflict as long as the Straits question is unsettled. Soviet Russia's desire to move in and out of the Black Sea undisturbed in time of peace and war and Britain's dependency on an uninterrupted lifeline through the Mediterranean and the Suez Canal underlie the efforts of these powers to control the important straits.

The great power obligations of the United States and its economic interests in the Middle East have greatly increased its concern with the future of the Straits. American aid to Turkey and Greece is related to Soviet pressure at the Straits.

The balancing powers. Even in ancient times the people from the Mediterranean side of the Straits fought the people from the Black Sea area and Asia Minor for the possession of this vital trade route. Greeks fought Trojans, and Venetians fought Greeks until Turkey conquered the Straits and occupied Istanbul in 1453.

The fundamental reason for the age-old conflict of the Straits can be stated rather simply: all interested nations constantly strive to secure an arrangement for the Bosporus and the Dardanelles that will assure freedom of navigation satisfactory to their commercial needs and will at the same time safeguard their strategic interests. Any decisions regarding the Straits have been of critical interest to two powers: first, to Russia, with her important agricultural and industrial terri-

---

* The original name of Istanbul was Byzantium. Constantine, the Roman Emperor, decided to use the city as his new capital and named it Constantinople, by which it was known until the establishment of the new Republic of Turkey.

* Part of the material dealing with the political aspects of the Straits has been adapted from an unpublished manuscript by George W. Hoffman.

tory and her historic interests promulgated under the guise of security and such jingoisms as *Pan Slavism* and *defender of Christianity;* second, to Great Britain, with her lifeline through the Mediterranean to the Red Sea and her important interests in the Middle East. In addition, at one time or another, France, Italy, Greece, Germany, and Austria-Hungary have also showed strong interest in the problem of the Straits. The United States is a relative newcomer in discussions and negotiations relating to this area.

RUSSIA. From the time of Peter the Great the issue of an outlet to an open, warm sea has played a dominant role in Russian foreign policy. One of the great geographic deficiencies of the gigantic country has been the absence of such an outlet, and its acquisition has always been a paramount goal. It is therefore inevitable that Russia has in the past used and is still using every means possible to obtain control of this important outlet, giving her a free passage to and from the Black Sea for commercial and naval ships at all times. Passage through the Straits is important to Russia for geographic reasons because all important Russian rivers flow south and because the Caspian and Black seas, except for the Straits, are landlocked. Thus, the richest regions of Russia—the Ukraine, the Don Valley, the Crimea, the Caucasus, the Baku oil fields, and the new industrial combinats east of the Urals—are condemned to a kind of continental imprisonment.

Throughout history Russian rulers have used various methods of approach to strengthen their position with regard to the Straits. At times they did not desire actual occupation and incorporation of the water passage and Constantinople within Russian boundaries. The principal objective was always to open the Bosporus and Dardanelles to Russian shipping. Only once in history have Russian troops set foot upon Straits territory, and that was to protect the Sultan from an Egyptian rival. The resulting treaty of Unkiar Skelessi (1833), drawn up as an expression of friendship and alliance, benefited Russia but aroused the hostility of Great Britain.

In 1911 the Russian government proposed an alliance with Turkey along lines similar to the treaty of Unkiar Skelessi. In the meantime, however, Turkey had drawn close to Austria-Hungary and Germany and consequently refused. During World War I Russia obtained a promise from Britain and France for cession of Constantinople and the Straits, but it was never fulfilled because of the new Russian government and altered postwar circumstances. The new Soviet regime, fighting for its life, could not at first be concerned with historic claims and sea passages. It was not long, however, before geographic necessities and century-old historic claims again made themselves felt in the determination of Russian national aspiration and resulting foreign policy with respect to former interests in the Straits.

New Russia under Lenin and new Turkey under Ataturk were close friends for a brief period. Russia supported Turkey during the immediate postwar period, first in the war against Greece, and later at the Lausanne Conference. At this conference Turkey obtained important modifications of the Treaty of Sèvres signed with the Sultan in 1920. Although the shores of the Straits were demilitarized, Turkey received permission to keep warships at Constantinople. In the main the Lausanne Conference sought to maintain the principle of freedom of the Straits and to safeguard the position of Turkey by a separate agreement signed by Britain, France, Japan, and Italy, in which these nations promised to protect Turkey from any untoward consequence. Turkey signed the Lausanne Convention of 1923, but she was not entirely satisfied with the regime it established and expressed her claims for its abrogation and for the establishment of a new regime that would recognize Turkey's complete control over the Straits. Russia opposed the Convention, for she felt that it gave no consideration to her special interests as a Black Sea power. However, she became a party to the Convention on August 4, 1923.

In the following decade Russia participated in the Montreux Conference of 1936, which brought about satisfactory agreements, at least on paper, for Russia, Britain, and particularly Turkey, which was allowed to fortify the Straits. As a nonbelligerent, Turkey was permitted to stop the passage of armed vessels belonging to belligerents, with the exception of those going to the assistance of a victim of aggression to whom Turkey might be bound by a mutual assistance pact within the framework of the League of Nations or with the exception of those warships acting under the collective security provisions of the Covenant of the League of Nations. The Soviet Union, Britain, and the United States, as well as Italy and Germany, found the use of the Straits barred to their warships in World War II as long as Turkey upheld her neutrality.

At the end of the recent war Soviet Russia demanded a revision of the Montreux Convention, pointing to her strengthened position and increased interest in the Straits question. The Big Three agreed at the Potsdam Conference to submit proposals for changes. Soviet proposals contain five points: (1) The Straits should be open to merchant vessels of all nations at all times and (2) to warships of the Black Sea powers only. (3) They suggest the passage of warships of non-Black Sea powers only under certain circumstances, and (4) demand that all future arrangements must "constitute the competence of Turkey and Black Sea powers only." (5) There shall be "Joint means for the defense of the Straits in order to prevent their use by other states for purposes hostile to the Black Sea powers." * These proposals together with expressed claims to the territory of Kars and Ardahan on the Turkish eastern border and the area of Trebizond on the Black Sea, show that Russia actually has not appreciably changed her aims through the centuries.

GREAT BRITAIN. As the principal rival of Russia, Britain maintained a policy dictated by her anxiety to maintain the safety of communication lines with her empire in the East, to insure the security of the Suez Canal, and to protect her economic interests in the Middle East. In pursuance of this policy Britain early opposed Russia's entry into the Mediterranean and sought to close the Straits or to at least demand the principle of equal treatment for all nations by the Ottoman Empire.

The principle of intervention for preservation of the balance of power is the main reason for Britain's participation in the Crimean War waged against Russia. As the result of this war, Russia was forbidden to have military establishments in the Black Sea area. Later, Britain's rigid policy toward Russia slowly relaxed, a change occasioned partly

* *Christian Science Monitor*, August 15, 1946.

by her acquisition of financial control of the Suez Canal. Although she still desired no unfriendly power in Constantinople and the Straits, there was no further pressure for the integrity of the Ottoman Empire as long as peaceful arrangements could be made beforehand to distribute Ottoman territory as the empire broke apart.

For some years Britain pursued a policy of "splendid isolation." Realizing her untenable position, especially after the outbreak of the Boer War (1899–1902), Britain started discussions with Germany, Russia, France, and Japan, hoping to consolidate territorial gains previously made and thereby end the period of isolation. Allying herself with Japan, Britain again used pressure to forestall opening the Straits for the passage of Russian warships during the Russo-Japanese War (1904–05). In 1905 new governments came to power in Britain and Russia, thus opening the way for a settlement of many outstanding issues.

With the outbreak of World War I, Turkey, fearing Russian-British common goals, sided with Germany and Austria-Hungary. Britain, realizing the need to strengthen the Russian government after 1915, for the first time made definite promises to support Russia in the acquisition of Constantinople and the Straits.

At the Lausanne Conference of 1923 the prewar positions of Great Britain and Russia were reversed. Whereas before the war Russia had sought freedom of passage for its warships and Britain had refused to grant any such concession, a weakened Russia now wanted to close the Straits to warships of all foreign powers except Turkey. The new Russian government renounced all ambitions toward the Straits and agreed to bottle up the Russian fleet in the Black Sea. Moreover, since the interests of Turkey and Russia coincided, they set up a close working relationship, which was maintained for the next few years.

During the Italo-Abyssinian War of 1935–36 the British government entered into a series of mutual assistance agreements with Mediterranean powers directed against Italy. Among other diplomatic gestures Britain sought Turkish support and in return promised a benevolent attitude with regard to Turkish claims for a revision of the Lausanne agreement. At the Conference of Montreux, called in 1936, it was agreed to discontinue the Straits Commission working under the League of Nations and to permit Turkey to refortify the Straits. Such an arrangement proved satisfactory for a while to the powers.

AUSTRIA-HUNGARY AND GERMANY. The appearance of the Austro-Hungarian and German empires in the question of the Straits coincides with Austria's growing interest in the Balkans. Russia's predominant influence in the new Balkan principalities established after 1877 brought her into headlong collision with Austria. Considering the newly formed Bulgaria a Russian vassal state, Austria feared the presence of countries under Russian control so close to her empire. On the other hand, Germany under Bismarck had no interest in the Ottoman Empire; close relationship with Austria became the cornerstone of her foreign policy.

When the German Emperor, Wilhelm II, came to power, however, he not only continued the previous efforts to increase Germany's influence in Austria but also looked toward the backward land of the Ottoman Empire as a good field for the economic expansion of growing German industry. The economic penetration soon was followed by closer political ties between Germany and Turkey, a move that aroused the suspicion of Russia as well as that of Great Britain.

Until the end of World War I, both Austria and Germany supported Turkey in upholding her rule over the Straits. Further, both countries vigorously encouraged Turkey to refuse an offer of alliance with Russia and even went so far as to promise help in case of war.

SUMMARY. From the above it can be seen that two closely linked questions always remain: first, Russia's commercial and strategic interests in the Straits and, second, Britain's interest in the land route to the Persian Gulf and her seaway to India. It is also clear that the United States will be vitally concerned with any policies involving the Straits. With a decreased number of powers formulating a balance in this area, the United States has a special position to maintain in helping to guide the destiny of so important a focal point of international stress and strain.

Role of the Straits in the Atomic Age

In final analysis it is necessary to evaluate the strategic position of the Straits with relation to new weapons. Whereas the Straits were formerly the only passage between the Black Sea and the Mediterranean, planes can now cross this zone at will. Rockets lessen the distance between the Black Sea nations and the Mediterranean. The atomic bomb can quite possibly make the Straits of but little value in time of war. Because of these developments the position of Turkey as guardian of the Straits has radically changed. In addition to new complicated weapons, an increase in Turkish industrial establishments and a consequent increased dependency upon a steady flow of raw materials weaken her position today more than ever in the long history of struggle for control of the Straits.

Any new balance that will prevent Turkey from becoming a victim of regional interests must rely upon outside influences. Either a strong United Nations Organization or the United States in the role of arbitrator could conceivably maintain a proper working balance.

CHAPTER 21 | The Arab World

DURING past centuries the Arab World fluctuated both in importance and territorial extent, but always its main strength stemmed from the Arabian Peninsula and adjacent land areas to the north, from the shores of the eastern Mediterranean to the Persian Gulf. Today the political nucleus of the Arab World comprises seven independent states and a number of small political entities largely populated by Arabs but controlled externally by Britain, all near or within the confines of this peninsula. The Arab states are Saudi Arabia, Egypt, Iraq, Syria, Lebanon, Transjordan, and Yemen. Also of tremendous importance is Palestine, whose political future presents a serious world problem. Forming a more or less continuous string of quasi-political units in a chain around the southern and southeastern periphery of Saudi Arabia are the dependent areas of Aden Colony and Aden Protectorate, Muscat and Trucial Oman, Qatar, Bahrein, and Kuwait (see the table on page 311 for summary and details of the various political units of the Arab lands). In many instances exact boundaries between political divisions in the interior desert areas of the Arabian Peninsula are poorly defined or virtually non-existent.*

Set off as it is from other regions, the Arab World forms a more or less natural unit (see the map on this page). Topography and climate on the physical side and a common cultural background on the human side foster

* The Arab World actually extends across northern Africa to the Atlantic, but as yet independence has not been achieved by the large Arab countries west of Egypt. Libya, Tunisia, Algeria, and Morocco are discussed in Chapter 27. Likewise, Egypt as a geographical part of the continent of Africa is touched upon in the same chapter.

unity within the region. In these lands—among the earliest to be inhabited—Phoenicians, Hittites, Babylonians, Egyptians, and Hebrews have made history. In turn, these people were followed first by Persians and Kurds and later by Greeks, Romans, Mongols, Arabs, and Turks.

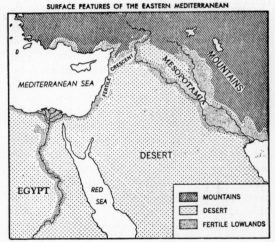

SURFACE FEATURES OF THE EASTERN MEDITERRANEAN

The importance of the Near East today can be expressed in terms of environment, culture, and tradition. First, its strategic location between East and West and its lines of intercontinental communication make the area one of importance and interest to every great power. Second, its unique historic role in the world of religion has significance for Christians, Jews, and Moslems alike. Third, from an economic standpoint, the development of oil and the increasing importance of rapid transportation make the Near East of vital interest to all industrial nations. Great Britain has long been interested in the area, as evidenced by her continuous political and military maneuvering in Egypt since 1882. Russia views the Near Eastern region as her southern doorstep and has for many years been involved in the great changes that have taken place in the area. The interests of the United States, which are of a more recent

tolia in Turkey and the Iranian Plateau in Iran and the latter two are largely desert or wasteland, the borders offer a considerable measure of natural protection against invaders. Elsewhere the Arab lands under consideration are bounded by water bodies: the Mediterranean Sea, the Red Sea, the Gulf of

THE ARAB WORLD

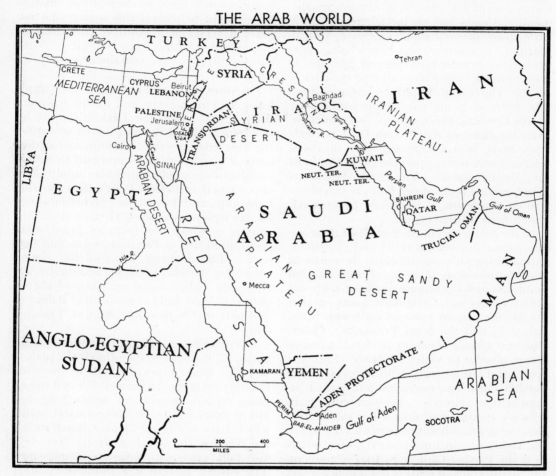

date, have developed as a result of significant discoveries of oil in the Near East, the rising position of the Arab units in international relations, the question of Palestine, and the region's important role in global air transportation.

Analysis of Environmental Elements

The heart of the Arab World as delimited above has land boundaries in common with only four outside countries: Turkey and Iran in Asia and Libya and the Anglo-Egyptian Sudan in Africa. As the former frontiers roughly coincide with the mountains of Ana-

Aden, the Arabian Sea (Indian Ocean), the Gulf of Oman, and the Persian Gulf. The constrictions in the narrow seas at the southern and southeastern extremities of the Arabian Peninsula and that formed by the Suez Canal constitute highly strategic water passages to and through the Near East.*

* The term *Near East* as used in this chapter is in the traditional sense and appears in a new authoritative work on the region: E. A. Speiser, *The United States and the Near East* (Harvard University Press, 1947). As a geographic region, the Middle East includes more territory than does the Near East; for example, Turkey and Iran are a part of the Middle East but not in the Near East.

Frequently characterized as "the desert and the sown," the Arab World is for the most part a forbidding desert irregularly interspaced with oases and river valleys (see the map on page 297). Areas such as the Syrian Desert, the Arabian Desert (in Egypt), and the Great Sandy Desert of Arabia are virtually empty except for wandering nomads on the occasional oases and on the fringes, where a little grass permits some extensive animal grazing. In contrast, the "sown" may support many hundreds of persons per square mile, as in the Nile River valley or some parts of the Tigris and Euphrates river valleys. The latter areas are part of the well-known Fertile Crescent, which extends in a semicircle from the head of the Persian Gulf through Iraq, Syria, and the greater part of Palestine, and terminates upon the eastern coast of the Mediterranean. The Arab World as here bounded is about one half the size of the United States and is inhabited by approximately forty million people.

In the entire area of the Near East there are few great variations in relief and elevations. Culminating altitudes are along the southern and southwestern margins of the Arabian Peninsula and in extreme northern Iraq—all under 10,000 feet. Highland areas parallel the Mediterranean coast in Lebanon, Syria, Palestine, and the Sinai Peninsula. Otherwise the terrain tends to be level, whether desert plateau or valley lowland. Even the great Arabian Plateau, which slopes to the Persian Gulf, has no significant surface irregularities. However, adequate rail facilities are lacking, and only a few roads exist. Because of the almost uniformly level ground, the laying of pipelines from the oil districts near the Persian Gulf or in Iraq to ports on the Mediterranean coast is not a difficult task from the standpoint of rugged topographic barriers.

Although rainfall is more plentiful along the Mediterranean coast and on nearby mountain slopes and in the Yemen highlands, annual rainfall in Near Eastern countries with but few exceptions is under twenty inches, most of which falls intermittently between November and May. As a result, irrigation in most regions is the rule. Representative crops are cereals, sorghum, corn, beans, cotton, and sugar in Egypt; vegetable oils, olives, and citrus fruits in Lebanon, Syria, and Pales-

tine; and dates in Iraq. Of these, cotton, citrus fruit, and dates are produced especially as cash crops for export. Where there is water the land is highly productive; in the Fertile Crescent originated the Bible stories of the beauty of the Garden of Eden and the land of milk and honey. In prehistoric, early historic, and even modern times nations have sought to control this stretch of land; today it serves as a multiple core area for five Arab countries, but several Western nations still strive to retain their special privileges.

Palestine, Syria, and Lebanon. Geographically, Palestine, Syria, and Lebanon form a single unit. Under the Turkish Empire before World War I the entire area comprised the two vilayets (chief administrative divisions or provinces) of Aleppo and Damascus and the three sanjaks (districts or subdivisions of a vilayet) of Beirut, Petit Liban (Smaller Lebanon), and Jerusalem. Sometimes used for this region is the term "Greater Syria," the concept of which also includes Transjordan and Iraq as well as Palestine, Syria, and Lebanon. The drainage areas of the eastern end of the Mediterranean Sea and the Jordan-Dead Sea Valley make up parts of the republics of Syria and Lebanon, all of Palestine, and part of the new Kingdom of Transjordan.

Palestine has no natural frontiers on the north. The heart of Palestine is the plateau of Judea, flanked on either side by lowlands. On the west is the fertile, well-watered coastal plain, approximately 100 miles long and fifteen miles wide. On these coastal plains, which have a rainfall of over thirty inches, are thriving cities such as Haifa, Tel Aviv, and Jaffa, ports with a variety of industries. The eastern margin is a pronounced scarp that leads to the Ghor, the flat-bottomed depression of the Jordan River and the Dead Sea, the latter more than 1,200 feet below sea level. This scarp, the home of the Bedouins, is a rocky belt of land early known as the wilderness of Judea. Eastward beyond the Ghor is the Syrian Desert, broken in three places by tracts of higher, better-watered country.

Palestinian agriculture centers on citrus growing. Enclosed by the highlands of Palestine, which consist of lonely rocky areas and deforested hillsides, are fertile valleys and basins where cereals are grown. In addition, olives, vines, and fruit trees thrive on tiny terraced strips. The plateau of Judea ordinarily has enough rainfall for limited agriculture. The rolling desert in the east is grassy near the margin of the plateau, but parched farther inland. The center of the plateau has broad fields and fertile valleys, and here are found the principal inland cities of Jerusalem, Bethlehem, and Hebron. By contrast the Negeb, in the southern part of the country directly south of the plateau, is a desert land, uninhabited except for a few permanent villages supported by wells. Vast stores of salts (common salt, bromide, and others) that are associated with the Dead Sea area are now being exploited.

In Syria and Lebanon, as in Palestine, topographic belts extend north and south parallel to the coast, even though they are less distinct in the north than in the south. The principal economic products are barley, millet, maize, wheat, and olives. Tobacco is grown around Latakia, Aleppo, Beirut, and Damascus; and wine is commonly produced in Lebanon. An important difference between Syria-Lebanon and Palestine is the more heterogeneous composition of the people of the former area. Prior to the influx of Jewish immigrants Palestine was for centuries primarily an Arab country, but in Syria and Lebanon many minorities found protection in the secluded mountainous areas. Today they are represented by such groups as the separate Moslem tribes in the Jebel Druz and the mountains of Latakia in Syria, and Christian Maronites in the Lebanon highlands. In addition, the Turks have extended their control southward along the coast to include Alexandretta. The Kurds live in the northeast, and various other groups can also be found in this region. The important coastal towns of Beirut (Lebanon), Tripoli (Lebanon), and Latakia (Syria) form an important link between the Mediterranean lands and the plains of the Tigris and Euphrates rivers in Iraq.

Transjordan. Transjordan is the junction between the Haifa-Baghdad west-east and the Mecca-Damascus north-south routes. Its western frontier extends along the Jordan River, the Dead Sea, and a line southward to the Gulf of Aqaba. The tableland east of this line permits extensive crop raising, especially in the northern and middle portion; but still farther east, where rainfall drops sharply,

nomadic tribes find only a poor living. Amman, the capital and only large city, lies in the northwestern part.

Iraq (formerly Mesopotamia). Core area of the Fertile Crescent, Iraq is largely an area of rich soil stretching from the Persian Gulf in the south to the mountains of the Armenian massif in the north. It is watered by the Tigris-Euphrates rivers and their tributaries. The valleys of these rivers are often spoken of as the "Cradle of Humanity"; historians point to the early historical records of the Sumerians, Hurrians, and Semites who lived there. Modern Iraq, which inherited the culture of Mesopotamia, also embraces parts of the Syrian Desert. Wedged in between Iran and the eastern Mediterranean states, Iraq occupies a key position on the land routes of the Middle East, and is sometimes called the continental bridge to India.

Northern and northeastern Iraq differ radically from the rest of the country. They are mountainous regions comprising the foothills of the Armenian Taurus range and the Zagros Mountains. Irrigated mountain valleys are well suited for the raising of wheat and tobacco. This area, which has sufficient rainfall for agricultural needs, is essential for the food supply of southern Iraq. The population is made up exclusively of Kurds, who have lived in this area since ancient times. They now constitute approximately fifteen per cent of the total population of Iraq. Along the Zagros Mountains lie the important Mosul oil fields of the Iraq Petroleum Company.

Dates, the most important crop of Iraq, provide eighty per cent of the world's production. They are also the most widely used food of the local Arabs. Rice that is poor in quality but high in yield ranks second. In parts of the Mosul area the amount of rainfall permits wheat and barley. In addition, irrigated corn, tobacco, cotton, fruits, sesame (from which oil is obtained), and the olive are likewise grown. With the exception of petroleum few minerals are available.

Leading cities are Baghdad, the capital, with a population of 400,000, and the port of Basra, now connected with the Persian Gulf by a canal eight miles long. Originally the Tigris and Euphrates rivers had separate mouths, but the two streams are now united because of river sediments deposited at the head of the Gulf, which extended the land area southeastward for a distance of about 150 miles. On this newly built alluvial plain, built up as a delta, the two rivers coalesced. Mosul and Kirkuk are medium-sized cities in the Iraq oil district.

The Arabian Peninsula. The Arabs often refer to the Arabian Peninsula as the "Island of the Arabs." Occupying the major portion of the area is the Kingdom of Saudi Arabia. To the extreme south stretches the highland, occupied by the Kingdom of Yemen, and along the south and east coasts appear the British colony of Aden and six semi-independent principalities (Aden Protectorate, Muscat and Trucial Oman, Qatar, Bahrein, and Kuwait), which are British protectorates, but virtually autonomous in their internal administration (see the table on page 311 and the map on page 297).

Despite the desolate terrain of the Arab desert lands, tribesmen have roamed its vastness for centuries and recognize provinces based more or less upon natural regions, even though the exact border between them is not always sharply defined. The southern part of Saudi Arabia, a large and virtually uninhabited desert, is called the Empty Quarter (al-Rub'al-Khali). The Hijaz is made up of a 700-mile coastal plain on the Red Sea. This lowland, which varies in width from ten to forty miles, includes the port of Jidda and the holy city of Mecca. South of Hijaz is Asir, which extends to the mountains of the Kingdom of Yemen. Mountains along the eastern edge of these two provinces rise to over 9,000 feet at the southern end of Asir and to 4,000 feet east of Mecca.

Najd, a plateau in the heart of Arabia, ranges from about 4,000 to 6,000 feet in height. In this province, the original home of King Ibn Saud, present ruler of the Kingdom, is located the national capital of Riyad, deep in the desert heart of the peninsula. The province of Hasa stretches from Trucial Oman along the Persian Gulf to Kuwait. Major oil fields have been found in this province; the one at Dhahran has been most developed. The famous Hufuf oasis also lies in the area.

Agricultural crops in the peninsula include dates, sorghums, and some wheat, and rice. Dates, the most important of these, are raised in a majority of villages below 4,500 feet.

The highly-prized "khilas" dates come from Hasa on the lowlands close to the Persian Gulf. Coffee from Asir along the Red Sea, and bananas, figs, citrons, pears, potatoes, and okra from various regions are among the minor agricultural products. Important livestock raising includes camels, sheep, goats, poultry, and horses; of these, the camel undoubtedly makes the greatest contribution to the lives of the people because of its vital service to every Bedouin family. Fishing, pearling, and rug weaving furnish other economic occupations. Today, however, all these fields of economic endeavor are overshadowed by the oil industry.

The two best-known cities in Saudi Arabia, and the most significant to the Arabic population, are Mecca, birthplace of the Prophet Mohammed, and Medina, the tomb of the Prophet. Other cities and communities of national or regional influence include Jidda, the main Red Sea port, with a population of about 35,000, which is located approximately 700 miles south of Suez; Yenbo, with a population of 10,000, in Hijaz province; Taif, a summer capital not far from Mecca; Abha, capital of Asir; and Hufuf, the fertile oasis, where over 150,000 people live, approximately 30,000 in the city itself. In recent years, the newly developed city of Dhahran and oil port of Ras Tanura have sprung into the economic limelight. Overland transportation is by camel because there are few roads. The most important road is from Mecca to the Saudi Arabian capital city of Riyad by way of Taif, thence to the city of Dhahran, the highway thus serving as a trans-Arabian trunk line of communication. A new Saudi Arabian airline likewise follows this route across the country.

Yemen is the only other independent state on the Arabian Peninsula. Situated in the southernmost part of the peninsula adjacent to the Red Sea, its highlands have adequate rainfall for numerous crops. Coffee growing, which is the chief industry, has brought worldwide acquaintance with the city of Mocha, near which the industry centers. Otherwise, grazing is the chief means of livelihood. San'a, with a population of from 20,000 to 25,000, is the capital of this state of three and one-half million people.

Approximately seventy-five square miles of the peninsula are under outright British control. This area, located at the southern entrance to the Red Sea, and two islands— Perim, in the Bab-el-Mandeb Strait between Arabia and Africa, and Kamaran, approximately 200 miles north of Perim—are together known as Aden Colony. This small area, with approximately 50,000 people, owes its importance to its strategic position on the important water route to India and the Far East. Its hinterland, known as Aden Protectorate, which stretches toward the state of Oman and includes the Shaykdom of Hadramawt, is approximately 100 miles long.

The other political units, among them the Sultanates of Muscat Oman and Trucial Oman, which reach from Aden Protectorate on the southern coast to the Gulf of Oman and along the Persian Gulf, are under British protection. The mountainous area has numerous oases producing wheat, barley, millet, tobacco, and dates; the capital of Muscat was once an important Arab shipping center. The exploitation of oil resources has enhanced the economic status of the areas of Bahrein and Kuwait, and may augment that of Trucial Oman and Qatar.

Egypt. Although Egypt belongs geographically to Africa, politically it is closely affiliated with the Arab countries in the Near East. Throughout history most of her contacts have been with neighboring Asia. Of the country's 383,000 square miles, 13,600 are in the Nile Valley, the delta, and oases; the remainder (more than 96 per cent) is desert. The Nile River, with its long narrow valley, is one of the most densely populated regions in the world (1,045 persons per habitable square mile). Crowded into the Nile Valley, approximately 900 miles long, are most of Egypt's seventeen million people. Employment is largely determined by the yearly floods of the silt-laden waters of the Nile. Its valley averages approximately thirty miles in width; on the desert margins high cliffs form a natural boundary. Cotton, wheat, flax, corn, rice, and oils from cotton seed are the main products of the land. With the exception of manganese, and possibly petroleum, Egypt lacks important mineral resources other than in the Sinai Peninsula. Also lacking forests, she looks toward Lebanon for timber.

Of twelve cities in Egypt with a population of 50,000 or more each, four are well known far beyond the borders of the country.

Cairo, the national capital, has 1,320,000 persons, ranking it not only as the chief metropolitan center of Egypt, but the largest city in Africa as well. At the head of the Nile delta its site is centrally placed in relation to the Egyptian population. Internationally it has a strategic commercial location near the junction of the three major Eastern Hemisphere continents. In the modern world, as terminal for nineteen airlines, Cairo may be rightly regarded by most of the Western world as the air "gateway" to eastern Africa, the Middle East, India, and the Far East. Alexandria on the Mediterranean coast, with 685,000 people, is the second city in Egypt and also the second in Africa (from the standpoint of population). It serves as a naval base and leading seaport for the country. Port Said lies at the northern and Suez at the southern end of the Suez Canal, with populations of 125,000 and 50,000 respectively (see the map directly below). As a port of call for all ships

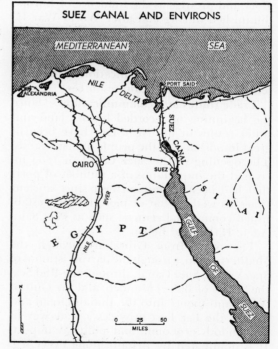

SUEZ CANAL AND ENVIRONS

passing through the Suez Canal between Europe and Asia, the East Indies, Australia, and East Africa, Port Said developed into one of the world's most notorious bazaars, with every known device to extract money from the unwary traveler.

Five other cities, ranging from 50,000 to

100,000 in population, are scattered about the Nile delta as regional trade centers, offering but little in the way of interest to the outside world (Tanta, Mansûra, Mahalla, Damanhûr, Zagazig). Still three other cities of this general population range (Fayûm, Asyût, Minia) have sites along the Nile, upstream from Cairo. On a definite route leading toward the plateau of East Africa and on to Capetown, this trio of river ports is known to many travelers.

Economic and Strategic Elements

Even in ancient times, when the political boundaries of the world were only vaguely defined, the Near East was a great center of political and economic activity. During the Roman conquests it largely lost this position. With the rise of powerful western European countries between the seventeenth and twentieth centuries the region was again overshadowed, but regained some of its earlier glory and prestige as the influence of Europe diminished during and after World War II. The role of the Near East in international affairs is destined to increase during the next few years because of its favorable location in relation to world communications and its extensive supplies of natural resources.

Trade routes and communications. Since the beginning of recorded history land and water routes in the Near East have been of great importance to the people of many lands. The opening of the Suez Canal in 1869 increased the importance of a number of ports that had been prominent ever since ancient times, as well as that of more recently established commercial centers, such as Port Said, Aden, Haifa, and Beirut.

The route from Gibraltar through the Mediterranean, through the narrow isthmus of Suez via the Suez Canal, through the Red Sea, the Straits of Bab-el-Mandeb, and the Gulf of Aden, and thence into the Indian Ocean and toward the Far East provides a waterway of tremendous economic and political import. It is dominated by Britain along every segment. Another vital route, especially before the opening of the Suez Canal, was that through the Persian Gulf to the city of Basra in Iraq, where this route converged with the important land route across Syria and down the valleys of the Tigris-Euphrates.

The land routes of the Near East have long been important ties between Occidental and Oriental cultures. Even in ancient times the land route from the Mediterranean coast through Mesopotamia and into the Persian Gulf was of utmost importance to the trade between East and West. Toward the end of the nineteenth century Germany became interested in building an unbroken railroad line from Germany across the Near East, part of which would run along the ancient caravan trail across the mountains of the Taurus range to Aleppo and the Syrian Saddle into the Fertile Crescent. As a project, it became widely known as the Berlin-to-Baghdad Railroad. The railway line between the Bosporus and Basra near the Persian Gulf was completed only in 1940, at which time the first direct train reached Ankara from Baghdad (see page 290 for further details). Today other railway lines have been built, among them the important north-south connections between Aleppo and Cairo via Damascus, Haifa, and the Sinai coast, and a parallel railway line from Damascus to Maan in Transjordan. Egypt has also built an important railway reaching up the Nile Valley as far as Aswân.

Though rail and sea routes are of great importance and are still the main arteries of communication, the automobile has introduced a new and more flexible means of transportation. The main automobile route goes across the Syrian Desert from Damascus to Baghdad, and fast schedules are maintained between the Mediterranean and Iraq on large buses, especially equipped for desert travel. Highways lead south from the Mediterranean to the holy cities of Mecca and Medina in Saudi Arabia, over which many Arabs travel on pilgrimages. To expand the highway systems even further, several modern roads are now under construction in the Near East, and it should be possible in a few years to travel to every important city in the Arab World by automobile over the relatively smooth terrain and with stops at oases. Out of these improved communication lines will come increased trade, more pilgrimages, and enlarged tourist traffic.

Since the first regular air-mail flights in 1921, service expansions now embrace most large centers in the Near East. Out of the last war came large increases in the number as well as the size of airports. Cairo and

Baghdad are today key air centers in the global network of American and British airlines. Dhahran in Saudi Arabia is directly con-

for traffic and operational stops for global routes between Europe and Asia, Australia, and Africa.

OIL CONCESSIONS

nected with the United States by several weekly flights—about forty-four hours from New York, of which about thirty-seven are flying time. Today the Near East is a hub of air transportation, with suitable facilities

Resources: OIL. The Near East today possesses the earth's richest petroleum deposits. Proven crude oil reserves run to approximately twenty-six billion barrels of oil and the potential reserves may reach 150,000 billion.

In the near future the oil from this area will not only supply much of the Far East but most of Europe, which previously received its supplies largely from South America and the United States. In comparison, the oil reserves of the United States are only twenty-one billion barrels and but few new discoveries are being made. Clearly, Near East oil will play an increasingly important role in the strategic pattern of world politics (see table on facing page and map on page 303).

The production of most Near Eastern oil (and Middle Eastern oil from Iran) comes from three areas: Iran, where the British occupy a dominant position but face Russian demands for participation; Iraq, where the British, Dutch, French, and Americans all have interests; and Arabia, including Bahrein, where the Standard Oil Company of California and Texas Company have drilled on a large scale. Recently the Standard Oil Company of New Jersey and the Socony Vacuum Company have collaborated in the development in Arabia, and plans are now under way for additional large-scale developments and the building of a long pipeline to carry oil from the fields to a Mediterranean terminal. One pipeline in the Near East already carries oil from Kirkuk in Iraq to the port of Haifa, a distance of approximately 600 miles. A branch line leads from Haditha, Iraq, to Tripoli, Lebanon. Production of the Arabian-American Oil Company in Arabia, which was approximately 9,000 barrels per day in 1939, is now well over 200,000 barrels per day. A large oil refinery has been built on the Persian Gulf. Further, Iraq plans to increase its production, a move that will bring the total Near Eastern (including Middle East Iran) production to approximately 750,000 barrels per day. Moreover, other plans are under way to bring this total to approximately 1,500,000 barrels per day in the near future. Private United States investments in the countries of the Near East total about $250,000,000, of which ninety to ninety-five per cent has been made by a small number of oil companies.

OTHER RESOURCES. In addition to oil, the Near East has other natural resources, though they are of small economic importance in comparison to oil. Wherever water is available in lowland areas, the soil is productive and is the mainstay of the various national economies for the bulk of the population. Grains that supplied most of the Mediterranean world in ancient times have been supplanted by cotton, especially in Egypt. When England was forced to find a new source of supply of cotton for its mills during the War between the States, Egypt successfully experimented with the long-staple fiber. In 1938 Egypt was producing over 1,900,000 bales of cotton annually and ranked sixth in the world production of raw cotton. England is one of the main markets for Egyptian cotton, a condition that partly explains the tight hold England has so long held on Egyptian economy and politics. Today cotton comprises seventy to eighty per cent of the country's total export. One twelfth of the world's olive oil supply comes from Syria and Palestine; and tobacco, wheat, wool, sesame seed, oranges, dates, and barley, are produced in relatively smaller proportions.

International competition in the marketing of these agricultural products is heavy, but even in the face of a poor outlet for her goods the Near East must export in order to buy such items as steel, machinery, automobiles, drugs, and timber. The economy of the Near East is becoming more and more diversified; and new resources, such as the chemical deposits of the Dead Sea and the manganese of Egypt, are gradually being developed.

Historical and Social Elements

People living in what are now Arab lands have been an active force throughout history. They built the first large empires associated with the West, their religion later became the basis of our faith, and their culture became the foundation of Western culture. Historians divide the progress of the Near East into four phases: (1) the preliterary period, covering at least 3,000 years, for which our information is relatively scanty, all of it limited to the discoveries and deductions of leading archaeologists; (2) the centuries of ancient history, beginning about 3000 B.C.; (3) the period of Western influence introduced by Hellenistic political and cultural missionaries; and (4) the rise of Islam, which today includes more than 300 million Moslems in various regions from the Atlantic coast of North Africa to the Philippines.

Two contrasting modes of life exemplified by Egypt and the Fertile Crescent have been

Oil Production, 1946

Concessionaire	Location	Bbls. per year status	Transportation	Refineries	Approximate annual crude output
Standard-Vacuum (Std. N. J., Socony Vac.)	Egypt	Exploration			
Standard of Calif.– Texas Co.	Egypt	Withdrew 1945			
Anglo-Egyptian (Royal Dutch Shell)	Egypt	9,200,000	Pipeline to Suez	Anglo-Egyptian Oil Refinery Egyptian Gov't. Refinery	12,000,000 bbls. 500,000 bbls.
Anglo-Iranian (British Gov't. 55.9%; Royal Dutch Shell 22.3%; Individuals 17.8%)	Iran	146,500,000	Pipelines	Abadan Refinery	146,000,000 bbls.
	Iraq	750,000 (domestic)	Pipelines	Kermanshah, Iran	750,000 bbls.
Gulf Oil 50%	Kuwait	6,900,000	Pipeline	Loading dock for crude	
Iraq Petroleum Co. Anglo-Iranian, 23.75% Shell, 23.75% French, 23.75% Std.-Vac., 23.75% Gulbenkian, 5%	Iraq	35,000,000	Pipelines to Haifa and Tripoli	Haifa Refinery Tripoli Refinery Alwan Refinery, Raq	23,000,000 bbls. 650,000 bbls. 2,500,000 bbls.
	Qatar	Shut in	⎰ Pipeline ⎱ under con- struction		
	Oman Trucial-Oman	No develop- ment			
Arabian-American (Standard of Calif., Texas, Standard of N. J., Socony-Vacuum)	Saudi Arabia	60,000,000	Pipeline under discussion	Ras Tanura Refinery	32,000,000 bbls.
	Bahrein	8,000,000	Pipeline to refinery	Bahrein Refinery	43,500,000 bbls.
Petroleum Development Ltd. (Iraq Petro- leum Co.)	Transjordan	Test drilling, 1947			

1946 Production: British Control— 176,950,000 bbls.
U. S. Control— 88,450,000 bbls.

(Compiled by Dr. W. T. Buckley, Indiana University, Bloomington, Indiana, June, 1947.)

studied at great length by E. A. Speiser.* He contrasts the contributions of the Sumerians of the fourth millennium B.C. in the Fertile Crescent in regard to a "social order based on the rights of the individuals, embodied in a free economy, and protected by the supreme authority of the law, which applies to ruler and subjects alike," with the Egyptian concept that the "king was a god and as such the absolute ruler of all he surveyed." The art of writing grew out of this former concept. The Sumerians also introduced the system of reckoning whereby the circle is divided into 360 degrees and the hour into 60 minutes or 3,600 seconds.

A new phase of cultural consciousness was introduced by the conquests of Alexander the Great, when for the first time the whole area of the Near East was occupied by a European power. But the ideas and traditions of Hellenistic culture did not penetrate deeply enough to have any really lasting effects. In contrast, Near Eastern culture had lasting effects on the Greeks. Ancient Near East tradition was defended by Hebrew culture, and its effect can be seen in the extent to which Christianity—the early Christians were all Jews—has adopted the basic factors of the old Mesopotamian law and order and the relationship between God and man.

The Hellenistic era was eventually followed by Islam, the Arab version of Near East culture and tradition. The symbol of the Crescent penetrated the whole of the Near East in a relatively short time; and even after the conquest of the Turks, Islam grew steadily, mainly because it adapted itself so well to the basic environmental pattern of the whole area. For almost fourteen centuries now it has been gathering widely diversified people into a similar cultural pattern. This culture is best exemplified by the Arabs, who have one basic language, one tradition, and one religion. Only a few of the present-day Arabs are direct descendants of those originally inspired by the teachings of Mohammed. Egypt, Palestine, Syria, and Mesopotamia were not Arab originally; and many of the present-day problems stem from the diversities of people, tradition, and dialect that deviate from the principal pattern.

Early Arab conquests swept across the

* E. A. Speiser, *The United States and the Near East* (Harvard University Press, 1947).

whole of northern Africa and over the Strait of Gibraltar into Spain. In the other direction parts of Inner Asia, the East Indies, and the Philippines were penetrated.

Egypt was conquered in 1517 by the Ottomans, who moved the Caliphate from Cairo to Constantinople. Realizing the strategic location of the country, Napoleon led an expedition into Egypt in 1798, but was defeated by the British with the help of the Turks. Britain, because of her interests in India, could not permit a strong power to occupy the shortest route to India; instead, she preferred a weak Turkish power. During the Napoleonic conquests a young Albanian officer with the Turkish Army, Mehemet Ali, made himself master of Egypt. In that capacity he fought in Arabia and Syria until the British intervened and restricted his power to Egypt. In 1841 his rule was made hereditary for the country, and his heirs are still the Kings of Egypt.

The Turkish position was weakened before World War I; but the Sultan, in his capacity as Caliph, retained his ecclesiastical powers. As part of their policy of imperialistic expansion, both France and Britain acquired territories or extensive interests in the Near East itself. In 1860 France, defending the Christians of Damascus against Druz attacks, temporarily occupied Syria. In 1864 Lebanon was declared semiautonomous under a Christian governor. Britain, mindful of her interest in India, in 1839 captured the port of Aden, which guarded the southern entrance to the Red Sea, and penetrated the southern fringe of the Arabian Peninsula eastward toward the Gulf of Oman into the Persian Gulf area. Then in 1882 increasing unrest in Egypt caused Britain to occupy that country.

Arab nationalism was gradually emerging, manifesting itself in two ways. In Egypt the main emphasis was on independence. In other Near Eastern areas this movement followed ethnic lines and resulted in a demand for home rule from the Turks.

With Turkey taking the side of the Central Powers, contacts with the Allies for Arab independence were established shortly after the beginning of World War I, and in June, 1916, led to the proclamation of the Arab revolt. Within this period falls the controversial correspondence between the British High Commissioner of Egypt, Sir Henry McMahon, and the Arab leader, Husayn, the **Grand Sharif** of Mecca. The British then became the logical ally of Arab independence.

A new era began in the Near East with the armistice of Mudros ending hostilities between the Allies and the Turkish Empire in October, 1918, and with the abolition of the Ottoman Caliphate in 1924. The policies of the Western Powers became a greater threat to Arab independence than Ottoman policies ever were. A serious conflict started over Western promises, pledges, and future plans, a conflict that is still unsolved.

Problems of the Present and the Future

Forces within the Near East: THE ARAB LEAGUE. Although minority groups, such as the Jews and the Kurds, predominate in certain local areas today, Arabs far outnumber other racial groups in the Arabian Peninsula, Egypt, Syria, Palestine, Transjordan, and Iraq. As in many other racial centers of the world, religion and language constitute strong factors in the ethnic unity of these people. In religion, almost all Arabs are Moslems. Despite the many adherents of Mohammedanism found from the Atlantic Ocean in French Morocco to scattered sections of Australasia, many of whom are not Arabs, a concentration of the followers of this religion in the Near East makes it the center of Islam. The Arabic language, common to the people of this area, also binds them together.

The existence of the Arab League indicates an organized movement toward Arab independence. After Arab nationalism had been aroused by Napoleon's invasion of the country, Mehemet Ali, leader of a band of Albanian soldiers, became Pasha of Egypt in 1805, founding the present line of rulers. Early efforts of the new Pasha were directed toward the creation of an Arab empire. With British help the Sultan repressed such nationalistic ambitions, and as a result Mehemet Ali was confined to Egypt. Later the leadership of the Arab nationalist movement passed to Syria and Lebanon, where Christian Arabs who were educated in the American University in Beirut (founded in 1866) assumed important roles. The entrance of Turkey in World War I on the side of Germany in November, 1914, spurred the Ottoman Empire to suppress dangerous Arab revolts in Syria. The Arab revolt of 1916 was called by the Sharif of Mecca. Great Britain, trying to take advantage of this situation within the heavy burden of the war, obtained relief by making promises to the Arabs (correspondence between Husayn and Sir Henry McMahon mentioned earlier), to the French (the Sykes-Picot agreement of 1916), and to the Jews (the Balfour Declaration, November 2, 1917). At the end of the war, the peace treaties left Arab nationalists frustrated and disgruntled, and nursing a strong feeling of grievance against both France and Britain. Although most of the Arabian Peninsula became independent, the area included in the Fertile Crescent was divided into League of Nations mandates; Great Britain receiving Iraq and Palestine, and Syria and Lebanon going to France. Despite having gained additional freedom, Egypt still remained under British protection. Complications arising from overlapping promises by Britain and France, Zionist ambitions, and Arab bitterness made the regime of the mandates extremely difficult. Rebellions in Iraq and Syria hastened the termination of British and French mandates.

After World War I internal quarrels as well as external difficulties beset the Near Eastern countries. Fighting broke out between the forces of Husayn, Sharif of Mecca, and the supporters of the royal family of Saudi Arabia. During a war in 1924–25 Ibn Saud defeated Husayn and occupied Hijaz and the holy cities of Mecca and Medina. Leadership of the defeated family was taken over by Faisal, son of Husayn, who in the meantime had become King of Iraq. Faisal and his brother, Abdullah, then Emir of Transjordan (later King) signed an agreement with Ibn Saud in the interest of Arab unity. Difficulties also arose between King Faruq of Egypt and Ibn Saud. Further, King Abdullah's plan for a Greater Syria, uniting Syria, Lebanon, Palestine, Transjordan, and Iraq, met the opposition of either Faruq or Ibn Saud, and it was not well regarded by the republics of Syria and Lebanon.

During World War II discussions were held among the seven Arab states of the Near East —Egypt, Saudi Arabia, Yemen, Transjordan, Iraq, Syria, and Lebanon—which led to the signing of the Arab League Pact in Cairo on March 22, 1945. The League's goal was "to strengthen the relations between member states and to coordinate their policies in order to safeguard their independence and sovereignty." The agreement also called for closer cooperation among the member nations on economic, social, cultural, and legal problems. Arab leadership, which shifted to Iraq until Faisal's death in 1933, was gradually taken over by Egypt.

Two outstanding aims were in the minds of members of the League at the end of World War II: the departure of foreign troops from Syria, Lebanon, and Egypt; and the formation of an independent Arab state of Palestine. However, only a measure of success was reached in attaining these objectives. British and French troops left the independent republics of Syria and Lebanon in 1946. Although British forces have left Alexandria and Cairo in Egypt to consolidate in the canal zone, Egyptians resented foreign troops even in the latter area. The Palestine problem continued to arouse the Arab League, as the members bitterly opposed any Jewish state in Palestine.

It is difficult to predict the future of the Arab League, but its impact is felt at international conferences and at the meetings of the United Nations, where members of the League act as one. With Russia showing considerable interest in the Near East, Great Britain weakened by two wars, and the United States becoming actively interested in the problems of this area, the contributions of the Arab League as a whole, and of each individual country in particular, to the security and peace of this important crossroads of three continents can be immense.

PALESTINE. The Holy Land is not only a problem of the Arab League but also of the world. During World War I Lord Balfour made the famous declaration stating: "His Majesty's Government views with favour the establishment in Palestine of a National Home for the Jewish People, and will use their best endeavours to facilitate the achievement of this object . . ." Although the Arabs, then our allies, protested this statement, promises were made by the British that Jewish settlements in Palestine would not interfere with the "political and economic freedom" of the Arab population. Moreover, Sir Henry, the British High Commissioner in Egypt, promised Husayn the ter-

ritory claimed by the Arabs, except for certain portions. No agreement has ever been reached as to the exact British promise. These assurances issued by the British during World War I laid the groundwork for the difficulties surrounding the Palestine mandate.

Today the area is occupied by more than 648,000 Jews and more than 1,300,000 non-Jews, overwhelmingly Arabs. The Jewish immigrants have succeeded in bringing large stretches of barren desert into production, have built new cities like Tel Aviv, have established industries, and have constructed roads. Although they occupy most of the productive lowlands, Jewish settlements have also been founded on the Judea Plateau, in the southern Jordan Valley, and in the desert area of Negeb. The only hope of the Jews in obtaining a majority in the country is through further immigration, a solution opposed bitterly by the Arabs.

In contrast, Arabs, who have lived in this area for many centuries, have a much lower standard of living than the Jews, but they are progressing slowly. It should not be forgotten that they have always been dominated by an outside power. The struggle over Palestine in our day is actually Zionism versus the Arab World. The Arabs are against partition and against further sale of land to the Jews. They concede the Jews minority rights, but feel that Palestine was, is, and should remain Arab country.

During the last twenty years many commissions have surveyed the future of Palestine. So far it has never been possible to find a solution mutually agreeable to both Zionists and Arabs. The American-British Cabinet Commission of 1946 favored a trusteeship for Palestine under the United Nations. Britain has suggested a partition with certain areas internationalized and the southern portion of Palestine (the Negeb) used for Britain's defense needs.

In considering the future of Palestine it should be remembered that the country has had three contestants, the British, Jews, and Arabs, and that each group has had special interests. Although the British still remain interested in the region, they placed the future of Palestine in the hands of the United Nations in 1947, and withdrew in 1948. In November, 1947, the General Assembly of the

United Nations recommended the partition of Palestine into Jewish and Arab states with a special international regime for Jerusalem (see the map directly below). Any solution

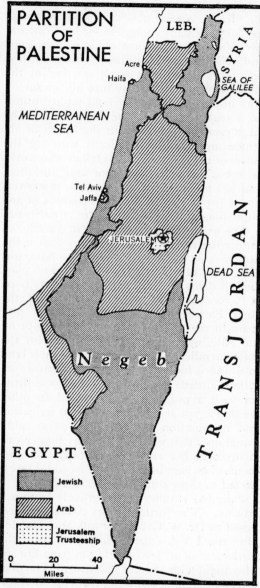

PARTITION OF PALESTINE

LEB.

SYRIA

Acre

Haifa

SEA OF GALILEE

MEDITERRANEAN SEA

Tel Aviv
Jaffa

JERUSALEM

DEAD SEA

N e g e b

TRANSJORDAN

EGYPT

Jewish

Arab

Jerusalem Trusteeship

0   20   40
Miles

backed by the genuine sentiment and power of a majority of all nations might solve the problems of this land.

Forces from without. That the Near East was of great strategic importance has been recognized by the British government since the conquests of Napoleon. The British policy has been that no European power be allowed to dominate the area. Britain also engaged in long-range economic and political maneuvers, even using the force of arms, to preserve her lifeline from the Mediterranean to India and, more recently, to insure oil to the British navy. The aggressive expansionist policy of Russia in the past few years, her nearness to the Arab World, and her powerful interest in the general area have in combination all led Great Britain to redouble her past efforts to win the friendship and support of the Arab peoples.

With the end of World War II a readjustment of political rights in the Near East was necessary. In addition to a reconsideration of the status of Palestine, Britain granted Transjordan her independence, her motive being to create a friendly feeling with the Arab states. Although Egypt is an independent kingdom, the Anglo-Egyptian Treaty of 1936, which provided for British military, naval, and air bases on Egyptian territory or in Egyptian waters, has caused political unrest and anti-British demonstrations. The future status of the Anglo-Egyptian Sudan, a condominium between Britain and Egypt, is complicated by the desire of the latter to incorporate this strategic area within its boundaries and by the opposition of the former to outright Egyptian annexation. Because of their opposition of interests in these matters, postwar negotiations between Egypt and Britain have been long and bitter.

Russian interest in the Near East has already been pointed out in this chapter and is stressed in the chapter on Turkey and the Straits. To these earlier discussions should be added the observation that Britain's complete retreat from the Near East would leave a vacuum in this area; and a possible Russian advance that might follow because of her position as the nearest of the great powers would not please the Zionists, the Arabs, or Anglo-American interests.

Initial contacts between the United States and the Near East go back to 1820, when the first American missionaries visited the Levant. The aim of establishing educational institutions represented our chief interest in the Near East; in these schools many of the present-day Arab leaders were educated. American archaeological activities likewise stimulated interest in Near Eastern lands. Later the Wilsonian principle of self-determination evoked much response in the Near East. Realizing that our interests were only economic and cultural, the Arabs on the whole welcomed the Americans. Until our participation in the distribution of Iraq's oil in 1924, trade with the Near East represented but a small percentage of our total exports and imports. The United States really discovered the Near East during World War II. Following the joint Anglo-Soviet occupation of Iran in 1941, the American Persian Gulf Command was established in 1942, through which a large percentage of Russian Lend-Lease supplies was handled after their arrival overseas. This new relationship was evidenced by the meeting of President Roosevelt with the heads of Saudi Arabia and Egypt after the Yalta Conference, by our attempts to assist in settlement of the Franco-Syrian dispute of 1945, and by our participation in talks on the future of Palestine.

The need to insure adequate oil supplies for the United States has increased our interest in the Near East. The route of the new oil pipe line leading from the Saudi Arabia oil fields is an important question to be decided jointly by private companies and government officials.

The strategic location, the oil, and the air communications of the Near East will all affect the future security of the United States. The future of such areas bordering on the Near East as the Straits, Iran, and the waterway through the Mediterranean to India will also play a part in this country's future security. Therefore a close coordination should exist between any plan for the Near East or any part of it and the over-all commitments and general foreign policy of the United States.

Future possibilities. As the Near East region is one of great contrasts, largely inhabited by nomad tribes and sedentary farmers, but including modern cities, its future is difficult to predict. Plans call for large-scale irrigation dams, power plants, and the further development of mineral resources. Perhaps such a development will ultimately help to change the balance, which is now weighted on the side of farming and animal raising. Except for oil in certain countries, ninety-five per cent of the exports of the region normally fall within the class of agricultural commodities. Thus, the three outstanding factors that will determine the ultimate prosperity of the Near East are the future life of the peasant, development of irrigation, and the utilization of minerals.

Max J. Wasserman discusses the plight of the fellah (peasant): ". . . who although free, owes so many charges to the landlord and government in the form of rents, fertilizers, and irrigation fees, equipment charges, tithes, and taxes that but a small fraction of the farm income finds its way into his pocket." * Any improvement in the land tenure would be a real progress in the Near East. The large estates are usually in the hands of absentee and wealthy landlords who are the rulers of the country. The fellah who works on these estates is very poor and unskilled, and has few modern implements; moreover, under present conditions, the chances of any improvement in his situation are virtually nil.

The second important factor to consider in evaluating the future of the Near East is the decisive role the few rivers, like the Nile, Jordan, and the Tigris-Euphrates, may play. Only if dams are built can there be any hope of favorable development in many of the Near East states. The dam-building program in the Sudan upstream from Egypt on the Nile, which has provided water for the cotton syndicates who in turn lease their land to workers, has under ideal land tenure conditions already demonstrated the possibilities for such a program if effectuated in other areas. Egypt also operates several irrigation and reclamation projects, and plans additional ones that will undoubtedly render vast changes in her economy. Similar developments elsewhere in the Near East could be expected to show comparable results.

Palestine is suffering extensively from soil erosion. The Jordan Valley Authority, proposed by Dr. W. C. Lowdermilk and modeled after the T V A, expects to make feasible the settlement of all Jewish refugees from Europe who might wish to enter Palestine. The plan calls for bringing salt water from the Mediterranean to the Dead Sea. The desired goal involves control of the Jordan River, provision for irrigation facilities, and creation of hydroelectric power for industrialization. The materialization of the project would contribute much to the improvement of the fel-

* Mordecai Ezekiel and Associates, *Toward World Prosperity* (Harper, 1947), p. 248.

Political Divisions of the Arab World

Country or political entity	Area in square miles	Population	Form of government	Ruler	Minorities	Capital
Syria	73,000	2,800,000	Parliament, Republic	President for five years	Various Moslem sects Greek Orthodox	Damascus
Lebanon	3,600	1,100,000	Parliament, Republic	President for six years	Moslems	Beirut
Palestine	10,000	1,950,000	Arab and Jewish states in transition		Jews 650,000 Others 100,000	
Transjordan*	34,750	350,000	Monarchy	King Abdullah	10 per cent Greek Orthodox	Amman
Iraq	117,000	5,000,000	Constitutional Monarchy	King Faisal II	Kurds Jews Various Christian sects	Baghdad
Egypt	386,000	17,000,000	Constitutional Monarchy	King Faruq I	Copts, Greeks, Italians, French	Cairo
Arabian Peninsula						
Saudi Arabia	597,000	4,800,000	Absolute Monarchy	King Ibn Saud	—	Riyad
Yemen	75,000	3,500,000	Absolute Monarchy		Jews	San'a
Muscat Oman	82,000	800,000	Sultanate	British control of foreign affairs	Negroes in coastal region	Muscat
Trucial Oman	—	110,000	Sultanate and Shaykdoms	British control of foreign affairs	—	
Qatar	8,500	30,000			—	Doha
Kuwait	1,950	50,000			—	
Bahrein (Island)	210	90,000			—	Bahrein
Aden	75	50,000	British Colony	Governor	—	Aden
Aden Protectorate (including Shaykdom of Hadramawt)	112,000	600,000	British Protectorate	British Governor	—	Aden

* Kingdom since 1946; previously, part of the Palestine mandate.

NOTE: Christian minorities include Maronites, Greek Orthodox, Gregorian Armenians.
Moslem or pseudo-Moslem sects include Druzes, Ansariyah, Alawites, Ismailians, Shi'ites, Wahabis.

lahin throughout the Jordan Valley in Palestine and Transjordan, and insure the satisfactory immigration of many additional people from other areas.

Iraq has irrigation plans similar to those of Egypt. Ultimately the irrigation canals will be modernized to shut off the harmful silt of the Tigris-Euphrates rivers.

A sufficient water supply, the development of modern port facilities, and the building of power plants and dams present the major problems for Saudi Arabia. During the war the United States Government started an agricultural experimental station at Al-Khary, and successfully provided food for a large number of Americans. It has been reported that over 2,000 acres of desert are now producing wheat, alfalfa, lettuce, tomatoes, cabbages, and other crops. Plans to increase the water supply at Jidda and the holy cities are in an advanced stage. Other plans call for the use of the rainfall in the mountains of the provinces of Hijaz and Asir, as well as the use of ground water and the mechanization of existing wells. In addition, King Ibn Saud hopes to develop better ports. For example, Jidda, the only large port in Saudi Arabia, has no facilities for direct loading and unloading. All commodities and passengers have to be transferred by lighter two miles outside the harbor. Moreover, despite the value it would have, no major port exists at the present time along the Saudi Arabian coast in the Persian Gulf.

The third important factor to consider in any evaluation of the future development of the Near East is a possible increase in the output of mineral resources. Oil is now the most important resource, and every one of the Near Eastern countries is vitally interested in the further expansion of production facilities. Gold is now being mined in Saudi Arabia, Syria, and Lebanon. Manganese in amounts averaging 85,000 tons for the last few years has also become an important export. Some 600,000 tons of salt are annually exported.[*] These and other resources should help to develop industries in the Near East and thus to some extent balance the unequal distribution between agricultural and industrial production. Although oil has a decisive influence today on the cultural, economic, and political position of Iraq and Saudi Arabia, some of the other important resources should make substantial contributions to the future development of the region.

[*] Ezekiel, *op. cit.*, pp. 255–6.

CHAPTER 22

The Middle East States of Iran and Afghanistan

IN SOUTHWEST Asia, Iran and Afghanistan represent transitional lands between the Near East and the Far East. The two countries make up a section of the Middle East not embraced in the subdivision of that area known as the Near East.* As one moves eastward toward Iran, little of Western culture appears and even the influence of the eastern Mediterranean has made little impression. Conversely, Afghanistan lies west of cultures generally attributed to India and the Orient. In order to find the key to an important aspect of Iran's and Afghanistan's positions, one must look to the north, particularly to the northeast. From this direction came the forces that since prehistoric times have given Iran and Afghanistan important places in the affairs of man.

For thousands of years these two countries served as a locale of the routes followed by the movement of people surging outward from the heart of the Asiatic continent. Large hordes of pastoral people seeking a passageway from the central plateaus chose to trek through Afghanistan and Iran, probably because the alternative land routes north of the Caspian were dry and cold. South of the mountains that extend from the Mediterranean to the Himalayas the temperatures are higher, and as long as the migrants kept close to the ranges they were never far from forage and water. Because people moved slowly in

bygone centuries, migrations while en route to their final point of settlement often left behind a definite imprint of culture. As a result, despite their contact with the modern world, both countries have customs and traditions harking back to their early role as a nomadic corridor.

In more recent times the region has lost ground as a focal point of human movement. With the political development of Eurasia, great continental migrations have become negligible, for seaways to the south of Asia's coast have by-passed old land routes. But the advent of the airplane is again bringing Iran and Afghanistan into the political limelight, in large part because of their being "on route" from Europe to India, the Far East, and Australia. Iran has already been the object of much international bickering over landing rights for commercial aircraft.

Afghanistan and Iran today are not well known to the Occidental world partly because they have not in the past produced large quantities of raw materials needed by Western civilization. Afghanistan still has little to offer. However, Iran has in recent years proved to be an important source of petroleum, and hence is rapidly becoming involved more deeply in world politics. Today Great Britain controls the oil. A second major British interest in the country of much longer duration centers around the desire to protect her lifeline to India and her Far Eastern possessions, a route that passes through the Indian Ocean to the south of Iran. At the same time Russia has for many centuries been gradually spreading outward. Sometimes slowed up or even stopped, she always

* The *Near East* and *Middle East* are terms frequently used but seldom sharply delineated (see footnote on page 297 for full explanation). More and more, however, the Middle East is used to designate territory around the eastern end of the Mediterranean as well as the countries dealt with in this chapter.

comes back for more, looking not only for additional resources but also for routes to warm seas. During World War II she obtained partial fulfillment of this desire.

Because of these various concerns, the power politics of the postwar world will inevitably continue to involve the states of the Middle East.

IRAN

Physical Features

Location. Iran lies between 25° and 40° North Latitude. A line drawn from the southeastern extremity to the northwestern corner of the country covers a distance of 1,400 miles—as far as from the Black Hills of

due east of Indianapolis, and much of the south has a latitudinal position similar to that of southern Florida.*

Five major political units and three water bodies touch Iranian territory (see the map on facing page). On the north is the Russian border, split in two parts by the Caspian Sea.

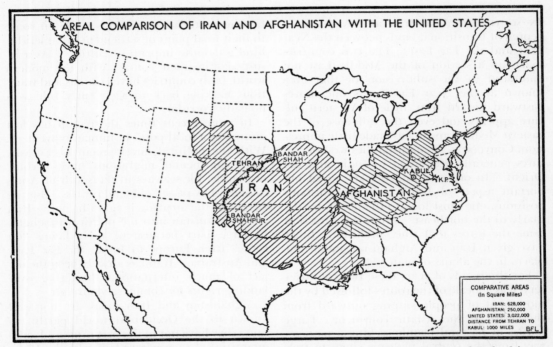

AREAL COMPARISON OF IRAN AND AFGHANISTAN WITH THE UNITED STATES

COMPARATIVE AREAS
(In Square Miles)
IRAN: 628,000
AFGHANISTAN: 250,000
UNITED STATES: 3,022,000
DISTANCE FROM TEHRAN TO
KABUL: 1000 MILES

South Dakota to New Orleans. If a map of Iran is superimposed on that of the United States, its area—628,000 square miles—extends from eastern Wyoming to about the longitude of Chicago, and from central Iowa to the Gulf of Mexico (see the map on this page). Tehran, the capital of Iran, is approximately 1,000 miles west of Kabul, capital of Afghanistan, a distance greater than from Tehran to the Mediterranean. Extending over approximately fifteen degrees of latitude, Iran has a climate ranging from temperate to subtropical, with modifications caused by topography and continental position. The northern portions of the country are about

On the east are Afghanistan and Baluchistan, formerly in India; the latter now a part of Pakistan and the former a declining sphere of British influence. Great Britain makes the most use of the Gulf of Oman and the Persian Gulf, which together form the southern boundary. To the west of Iran is Iraq, a sphere of British activity despite its status as an independent kingdom. Finally, also to the west and north of Iraq, lies Turkey, a country that at times has been closely allied with Britain. It can be said that Iran is virtually bounded by

* The map on this page comparing the area of Iran (and Afghanistan) with that of the United States does not show latitude comparison.

the U. S. S. R. and by areas greatly influenced by Britain.

Topography and climate.   The position of Iran on the margin of a great continent is instrumental in the control of its climate. If the country were a region of level land at low elevation, the low pressure area of Asia during the warmer months would cause des-

miles.   Many of its peaks reach 12,000 feet; Mount Demavend north of Tehran, is almost 19,000 feet.   (2) The Kurdistan Mountains extend southeastward but continue as the Fars ranges along the Persian Gulf.   This highland mass then becomes the Siahan Mountains, extending nearly to Pakistan. Together, the three parts of this mountain

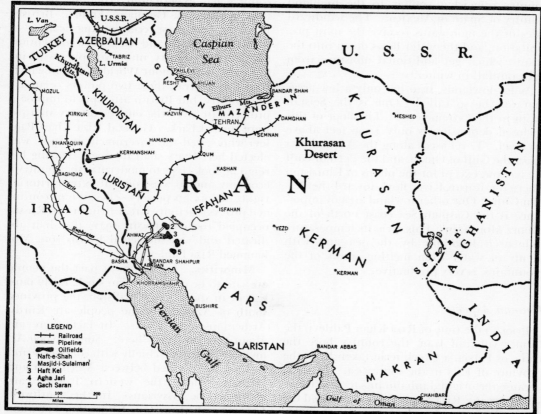

iccating winds from the direction of Africa and result in dry, hot summers.   In winter, cyclonic areas from the west would pass over the region, bringing rain with temperatures low in the north and somewhat modified in the south.   These conditions actually prevail, but their effect is varied because almost all of Iran is more than 1,000 feet above sea level, and numerous mountain areas are much higher.

On the northwest a high plateau known as the Armenian Knot diverges toward Iran into two ranges of mountains: (1) The Elburz Mountains swing in a big arc around the southern end of the Caspian Sea, forming an almost unbroken range for more than 650

chain serve as a barrier into the country from the south.   Much of the drainage of the southern mountainous region goes into enclosed basins to the north and into longitudinal depressions within the mountains themselves.

A series of interior basins, all more than 5,000 feet above the sea, forms a corridor from northwest Iran to Pakistan.   Between this corridor and the Khurasan Desert, a large area 800 miles long and from 100 to 200 miles wide in central Iran, are the Kerman ranges or plateaus, parts of which are 14,000 feet high.

Northeastern Iran is separated from the steppelands of Russia by the Kopet Dagh range, a continuation of the Caucasus on the eastern side of the Caspian depression. Along the eastern border of the country are the Khurasan Mountains, serving as one of the barriers that have seriously handicapped overland travel eastward from Iran.

Iran is commonly spoken of as a plateau, but it is better described as a basin and range country somewhat similar to the highland country of Spain or Mexico. The windward sides of the mountains receive the most precipitation, and the water flows down into the basins, which get additional moisture from light rainfall in winter.

As for lowlands, Iran has only a few areas that can be so called. One is the Seistan Basin in the extreme east. The floor of this enclosed depression is only 1,500 feet above sea level. Level areas along the Arabian Sea coast, the Gulf of Oman, and the Persian Gulf are narrow, except for the plains of Khuzistan where the Karun River flows toward the Persian Gulf. One other lowland area of importance is the Caspian Sea coast north of the Elburz Mountains. This area, its temperature influenced favorably by the sea and with plenty of water from melting snows of the mountains, is very productive.

Human Aspects

Prior to the time of Riza Khan Pahlevi, the former ruler of Iran, the country bore the name of Persia, a Greek term taken from the province of Fars in the southwest. In 1935, because the original inhabitants termed themselves Aryans, Riza Khan Pahlevi changed the country's name to Iran and that of the approximately 15,000,000 people to Iranians. This gesture was a declaration of national selfhood, for the new name was to recall the independence of past ages.

Historical background. The history of Iran is a long one of rising and falling rulers. At the beginning of the sixteenth century B.C., the Aryans, moving out from their original home in Eranvej, a region between the Oxus and Jaxartes rivers in Central Asia, penetrated Iran and India. After periods under Assyrian and Median rule, Persia rose to the position of a great empire under Cyrus the Great, extending at its zenith in 500 B.C. from the Indus to the Nile. Defeats were inflicted by Alexander in 331 B.C., by Seleucus in

312 B.C., and by the Parthians in 129 B.C. About 226 A.D. a native Persian regime arose. This was undermined by conflicts with the Turks, and in 636 fell to the Arabs. Then in the thirteenth century the Mongols assumed rulership over Persia, and early in the eighteenth century the Turks and Russians overran the country. In modern times the country has experienced economic penetration by Italians, Germans, French, British, Russians, and, most recently, Americans.

In 1907 England and Russia in a convention divided the country into two spheres of influence. Throughout World War I, in which Iran was neutral, these two powers occupied the country, but British attempts to impose a protectorate over the entire country in 1919 were turned back. General Riza Khan Pahlevi who seized the government in 1921, was elected hereditary shah in 1925. During his reign he took steps to modernize the country's economy and to wipe out all extraterritorial rights of foreign powers. Because of continued pro-Axis activity Great Britain and Russia occupied the country in 1941; the shah abdicated and was succeeded by his son, Mohammed Riza Pahlevi.

Minorities. For the most part the people are said to be of old Iranian stock, fairly pure except in spots. In Kurdistan, the province south of Azerbaijan, the people are Kurds, Armenians, and Turks. In fact, there are about 800,000 Kurds here. Some 50,000 Armenians, occupied chiefly with commerce and finance, are divided between Azerbaijan and Isfahan. Along the western frontier are about 25,000 Assyrians. In the southwest, Kermanshah, Luristan, Khuzistan, Fars, and Laristan provinces contain some admixture of Arabs. Khurasan, in the northeast, has many Turkomans. Baluchis inhabit the Seistan Basin. Jews are few in number, the great majority having almost entirely blended with the native population. About 95 per cent of the people are of a Moslem sect, official religion in Iran.

Population distribution and cities. The relief and availability of water in Iran rather rigidly control the distribution of population. Favored areas are marked by urban centers or farming communities (often oases), but over the remainder of the land only more extensive types of occupations are practiced. More than 1,500,000 Iranians live in large cities;

2,000,000 are semi-nomadic; and the others live in small towns and villages scattered among the basins along the lower portions of mountain slopes where they can get water for crops or find forage for their livestock. The greatest density of population is in the Caspian provinces of Gilan and Mazanderan, where there are 80 to 100 persons to the square mile. Azerbaijan, a northwestern province, has 40 or 50 per square mile.

Tehran, the capital, with nearly 700,000 people, is the largest city and quite cosmopolitan. One can say that it is modern along Oriental lines. The shops, of one or two stories, are run by Jews, Armenians, and Syrians. The bazaar, like a Mexican market, sells everything. The side streets often go by trades—one for copper-smiths, another for bakers, a third for clothiers, and so on. Although there are schools, hospitals, and the Iranian University, this city has no sewage system and the water supply flows through gutters of the principal streets.

Tabriz and Isfahan are the next ranking cities of Iran, each with slightly more than 200,000 inhabitants. The former, capital of Azerbaijan, is the commercial center for northwestern Iran and lies on a rail line from Tehran to the U. S. S. R. The latter is the largest of a number of regional oasis cities in the interior basins and lies on the route between Tehran and the Persian Gulf.

Meshed, a Moslem shrine and the chief city in Khurasan, with 175,000 people, is the meeting place of the tribes of Asia. Through its streets pass Afghans, Baluchis, Indian traders, Caucasians, Turks, Tartars, and others. As in Mexico or Spain, however, the life of the people is more clearly seen outside the large cities. On the highways are the pack trains of donkeys and camels bringing goods to town. Beside them walk men, women, and children. Whole families engage in road work. Western dress is the rule in the large cities, but it is probable that the peasants have neither the inclination nor the money to obtain other than the types of clothing adapted to their cold winters or dry, dusty summers.

Three other cities exceed 100,000 in population: Shiraz, on high land but near the Persian Gulf; Resht, on the narrow coastal plain of the Caspian Sea; and Hamadan, on the plateau between Tehran and Baghdad.

National Economy

Agriculture. In a country of mountains and basins, with much interruption of the free movement of winds that have not had much chance to pick up water vapor, it is natural to find people vitally concerned with their water supply. The Persian name for an estate means "walled garden that has its own water." Much of Iran consists of areas where precipitation is too light for agriculture but suitable for winter grazing. During the summer animals are driven into higher mountain pastures where rainfall is heavier and grass more plentiful. Most areas do not provide sufficient forage for cattle and hogs, but camels, sheep, and goats are adaptable. Where the streams from the mountains debouch into the basins are lands underlain by a water table fairly close to the surface. As these areas provide spots for irrigated farming, they are densely populated.

Winter wheat is produced in the provinces of Azerbaijan, Khurasan, Isfahan, Khuzistan, and Kermanshah.* Because of its short growing season, barley is a common crop. Rice in substantial quantities is raised on the slopes of the Elburz Mountains in Gilan and Mazanderan. Other staple crops are maize, millet, peas, beans, and lentils. In the vicinity of Isfahan, melons, lemons, oranges, and pomegranates are common. Dates are produced in the southwest. In the Caspian area about 600,000 kilos of tea are produced annually. Cotton and mulberry trees for silk are cultivated in Gilan. Tobacco, sugar beets, and grapes for wine are also important products for domestic use. The agricultural surplus of the country is represented by wool, cotton, fruit, nuts, rice, hides and skins, leather, opium, silk cocoons, and sausage casings.

In the past, crop yields have been poor and methods of cultivation primitive. Centuries ago the Achaemenids and Sassanids were noted for their irrigation works, but that was before the arrival of the Mongols, Huns, and other barbarians. The backward condition of agriculture in the more recent past has been greatly influenced by high taxes, land ownership, and the fact that much of the best land was in the hands of the nomadic hill

* In Iran a province and the leading city within it may have the same name. Examples are Isfahan, Kermanshah, and Hamadan.

tribes, who might have gotten more from it but never stayed long enough in one place. The land was owned either by absentee landlords or by the state. The peasant tenant had to give most of his produce to his landlord, retaining only about a fifth for himself.

Today the government is tackling these problems seriously. The wandering tribes are settled in villages. Land ownership abuses are being modified. Many of the state lands have been broken up for settlement, and foreign-owned land has been expropriated. The general principle being applied is that land is likely to become more productive in the hands of private enterprise. Illustrative of this, an act was recently passed giving the government powers to nationalize and sell land and irrigation works belonging to religious foundations.

Although there is still distress resulting from ineffective distribution of foodstuffs, the situation is improving. Ambitious irrigation schemes have been developed, and prices for agricultural products, varying according to the standard of living in each region, have been set up. A state-controlled agricultural bank provides long-term credit for farmers.

Tobacco and tea are two new agricultural products, the former a government monopoly with rapidly increasing production. Large tea plantations have been established at Lahijan under the control of Chinese experts. Cotton is increasing in importance, and beet sugar, silk, and wine industries have government support.

There is an agricultural school at Lahijan devoted to the tea industry, one at Kharkun given over to forestry, and another in the marshlands at Shadegan in Khuzistan. Locust prevention is receiving extensive research, and plant diseases are being studied. All these activities are under control of the Department of Agriculture. An ambitious five-year plan, which was launched in 1940, provided for an increase in crops, erection of fertilizer plants, more irrigation projects, importation of merino sheep, and extensive reforestation.

Mineral resources. Iran may have important mineral resources, but so far with the exception of oil they have been little developed. To be sure, a low grade of coal is mined at Zirab in the Elburz Mountains north of Tehran, iron at Semnan, and copper at Ab-

basabad, but petroleum is the only important mineral development. In 1937 Iran produced more than 78,000,000 barrels. The main fields are in Khuzistan near Masjid-i-Sulaiman, Haft Kel to the southeast, Agha Jari near Behbehan, at Gach Saran about seventy miles farther southeast, and also to the northwest of Masjid-i-Sulaiman (see the map on page 315). All these fields are connected with the main refinery at Abadan, south of Khorramshahr. One other field, which is really a part of the Khanaqin area of Iraq, is at Naft-i-Shah, west of Kermanshah. The oil of the latter field supplies the needs of Iran; that of the other fields goes into foreign commerce. The Anglo-Iranian Oil Company controls Iranian production.

Manufacturing. Iran's indigenous industries are mainly of the handicraft class, carpet-making being the most outstanding example. Much of the work is done in Tabriz, Kerman, and Kashan. Isfahan is the center of the "arts and crafts," that is, metal work, embroidery, lacquer, wood-carving, and textile printing. Hamadan produces blue, glazed earthenware.

The light industries include cotton, woolen, and silk textiles, sugar, tobacco, cigarettes, canned and dried fruits, macaroni, leather goods, shoes, vegetable oils, paper, gums, dyes, and matches. Iran is trying to carry to the consumer stage as much of its raw materials as possible to eliminate the necessity of importation.

Among the country's modest development of heavy industries are shipbuilding at Pahlevi, iron foundries and blast furnaces in Mazanderan, aircraft and munitions factories, and repair shops for locomotives, machinery, and motor vehicles. The chemical industries produce tar products, soap, candles, and stearine; and plans have been drawn up for construction of creosote, rubber, carbon, soda, and hydrochloric acid plants. All factories are owned at least in part by the state.

Iran has a factory act that controls both employers and workers and could well serve as a model at least on paper for industrial regions in other countries.

Transportation: RAILROADS. For many centuries Iran was an area where travelers and goods were carried by camel and mule caravans at the rate of ten or fifteen miles a day over rough trails. Today a standard-gauge railroad extends from Bandar Shah on the Caspian to the Persian Gulf deepwater port of Bandar Shahpur (see the map on page 315). The 892 miles of line, built between 1927 and 1938, were financed by a tax on tea and sugar and completed without indebtedness to western financiers. During the late war Americans took over and practically rebuilt and equipped the line in order to transport supplies to Soviet Russia via Bandar Shah and Baku.

The former shah, Riza Khan Pahlevi, under whose direction the line was initiated and built, carefully kept his railroad away from those of Iraq, Turkey, Soviet Russia, and India. To expedite the movement of munitions, however, the Iranian system was connected with Russian railroads via Kazvin and Tabriz to the Soviet republic of Armenia, where lines lead to Erivan and Baku. A connection was also built between Ahwaz and Khorramshahr across the Shatt-al-Arab from Basra, the terminus of the Iraqi lines. Plans now exist to extend the rails to Meshed, but construction has not proceeded beyond Damghan.

From a strategic viewpoint the Trans-Iranian railroad is valuable for the movement of troops and supplies between Mazanderan and the south via Tehran, the capital. Economically it links the northern and southern provinces. Now products of Mazanderan are available to the rest of the country, and that province is less dependent upon the Soviet Union for supplies and markets. In spite of the purpose for which it was built, this railroad provides a route from the U. S. S. R. to the warm waters of the Persian Gulf and rendered enormous assistance to that country when it was badly needed during World War II. It will be of world interest to observe future incidents along this route, especially since it opens into that carefully guarded passageway, the British lifeline to the Far East.

HIGHWAYS. The Iranian government has also pushed highway construction. Several roads now run northward from Tehran to the Caspian. The Tehran-Isfahan-Bushire route is usable the year round, as is also the road from Isfahan through Yezd, Kerman, and Bandar Abbas. Both routes connect the capital with the southern coast. A good road links Meshed with Zahidan (the terminus of the Indian railway from Quetta), and Tabriz with Mosul in Iraq and Trabzon in Turkey (on the Black Sea). Iran has over 15,000 miles of highways, and hopes to build 1,000 additional miles each year.

WATER. Although Iran has two coastlines, water transportation is not very important. Bandar Shahpur is the chief port on the south, and most of its traffic is in petroleum. A long railway jetty makes it possible for the largest ships to tie up alongside. However, the Persian Gulf is a backwater extending 800 miles away from world routes. If it ever becomes important in normal times, petroleum will be the base. Bandar Shah, the northern terminus of the railway, is the chief Caspian port, but Pahlevi still handles most of the trade with the Soviet Union.

The foreign trade of Iran has little significance as such things are regarded today, and the country is trying to reduce its imports. However, the most progressive countries are those that have the largest trade. Therefore, to continue her progress, Iran will need to increase both her selling and buying.

AIR TRANSPORTATION. Planes of Imperial Airways (forerunner to present British Overseas Airway Corporation) were the first to land at various termini along the Persian Gulf on their way to India in 1928. Later, this route was transferred to the southwestern side of the gulf, but the Iranian coast continued to be served by Dutch and French airlines. During World War II much new airport construction was carried on. Nearly every large town now has a landing field, but few of them are in good repair. The Anglo-Iranian Oil Company maintains its own airport at Abadan and others in its properties. Several postwar air routes in, to, and through Iran have been put into operation. Included are two Iranian airlines (Iranair and Iranian State Airways), which serve most of the larger cities of the country, with Tehran as their principal terminal.

Political Aspects

Government. Although Riza Khan Pahlevi was responsible for the efforts at modernizing his country, he, unlike Kemel Ataturk in Turkey, never broke completely with the past. He did aim for an independent nation that would take its place in world progress.

A national consciousness was cultivated; Communism, class antagonism, and disruptive ideas were suppressed; and Islam was permitted only in so far as it exerted a unifying force. Ideas of Western progress were exploited but with determination to place economic and cultural tools in the hands of the Iranians in order that they might meet the world on equal terms.

The Crown Prince, now Mohammed Riza Pahlevi, Shah of Iran, was educated in Switzerland and was active with his father in initiating the reforms. The Queen was one of the first prominent women to appear unveiled at a public ceremony. Riza Khan Pahlevi, the former ruler who abdicated in September, 1941, built up a good army with which to subdue unruly tribes. The goal was reform rather than punishment of the tribes; it was accomplished by building roads and villages in the Bakhtiari, Khorramshahr, and Kurdistan districts in which the nomads were induced or compelled to live. The regular army is maintained by conscription of men at the age of twenty-one for a two-year period. University and secondary school students may enter officers' training schools. No workman can obtain a job unless he can show a certificate of completion of or exemption from his military service.

The Constitution of 1906, with minor amendments, still stands. It established a National Assembly (Majlis), whose members represent constituencies throughout the country. These members are elected for two-year terms by secret ballot, and every male citizen with a few exceptions is allowed to vote. The work of government is symbolized by the Shah but carried on through a cabinet presided over by the Prime Minister, who is appointed by the Shah but responsible to the Majlis. The cabinet consists of the Prime Minister and the various ministers in charge of the government departments. The Constitution also provides for an upper house, although it convenes only at times when the Assembly for some reason cannot meet.

In 1938 the country was divided into twelve districts, each under control of a governor-general. These are further subdivided, but the authority of the Shah reaches from top to bottom of the organization.

Position in world affairs. As pointed out previously, Iran's location establishes it as part of a transition zone between Eastern and Western cultures. It has always lain in the path of world conquerors and world commerce, a pawn among pawns. It is a poor country, lacking the materials modern nations use to gain power. Centuries of instability have weakened the ambitions of the people to a degree where, however able the leadership, it will take a long time to develop a nation capable of vying for the best of the world's goods. Conditions beyond her borders will largely mold her destiny.

The most significant influence at the geographical borders of Iran is now the Soviet Union, with a long-standing aspiration for direct access to warm-water ports. The opening between the Black Sea and the Mediterranean is in the hands of Turkey, and Iran offers a parallel avenue of approach to warm water. In carrying forward a policy of expansion, Soviet statesmen use various techniques; a favorite method is, when blocked at any given point, to apply pressure in a different place along the borders of the U. S. S. R. Iran at different times has been subject to this pressure. During World War II Russian, British, and American forces found it expedient to occupy Iran, their forces to remain in the country only as long as necessary. After the hostilities ceased, Britain and America wished to withdraw, but Soviet Russia stated that by a former agreement she could not get out of Iran before the spring of 1946.

East of Turkey is the fertile Iranian province of Azerbaijan. In December, 1945, the Azerbaijanians revolted, with the declared purpose, according to news reports, of setting up an autonomous republic. Troops of the U. S. S. R. blocked any effort on the part of the Iranian government to suppress the revolt. An Azerbaijanian republic would, of course, tend to be sympathetic toward its protector. At about the same time, propaganda statements appeared in the news of the world that the people along part of the Black Sea coast in Turkey should really be joined with their kinsmen in the Soviet areas across the border. Although Azerbaijan in 1946 lost out to Tehran in its attempts to secure autonomy, northern Iran and northeastern Turkey still remain trouble spots.

The location of Iran remains a vital factor in the maintenance of unchallenged transportation routes to the south and east. Great

Britain's economic existence depends upon the uninterrupted flow of commerce between the various parts of her empire. No British statesman, regardless of political views, dares ignore this fact. Britain's sea route to the East skirts southern Iran. Britain has large investments in the territories that border Iran on the west, and, of course, India lies to the southeast. Britain's logical land and air routes can never be far removed from Iran; her best interest demands that no other major routes come close enough to cause serious inconvenience.

Today we have the situation as of old, seemingly brought closer to a critical stage than ever before, of Russia's straining southward and Britain determined to maintain her eastward course free from encroachment. If the United Nations really functions, the position of Iran will be respected. Otherwise, her sovereign rights may receive but slight consideration.

AFGHANISTAN

Physical Features

Location and area. Lying between 30° and 38° North Latitude, Afghanistan is in southwest central Asia, an interior country in the world's largest land mass. On the north

is the Soviet Union, south and southeast is Pakistan, and on the west, Iran. At a point high in the Pamir Mountains, which jut into the northeastern corner of Afghanistan, the U. S. S. R., the subcontinent of India, Greater China, and Afghanistan almost meet, but so inhospitable is this elevated region that few human beings could ever successfully survive there.

If one crossed Afghanistan from the extreme northeast in the province of Wakhan to the Seistan Basin in the southwest, the distance would be equal to a trip from New York City to northern Mississippi. Again, from Khyber Pass near eastern Afghanistan to the central portion of the Iranian border is as far as from Lynchburg, Virginia, to Cairo, Illinois, and from north to south is equal to the distance from Toledo, Ohio, to Atlanta, Georgia (see the maps here and on page 314). The area is 250,000 square miles, which is larger than that of France and equal to that embraced by Ohio, Indiana, Illinois, Michigan, Wisconsin, and Kentucky. Afghanistan has, according to a recent estimate, about 12,-000,000 people, whereas the American area just mentioned contains more than four times that number. In viewing the whole country, Afghanistan appears sparsely populated (density per square mile: 48). In some areas the density of population is relatively heavy, far above the average for the country, these compact regions depending upon accessibility, water supply, tillable soil, pasturage, workable mineral resources, and other factors that permit a concentration of people in a country not having a well-developed and advanced economy.

Topography. The elevation of almost all of Afghanistan is above 1,000 feet, and much of it exceeds 6,000 feet. The great Hindu Kush mountain system, rising in the Pamirs, spreads southwestward with ranges that extend over a large portion of the country; the main body splits into two parallel ranges that decrease in height as they come down to the vicinity of the city of Herat (farming center of 85,000 inhabitants) in the northwestern part of the country. In the southwestern third of the country is a series of interior basins like those in the central part of Iran.

Much of the northern boundary of Afghanistan follows the Oxus River from its source in the Pamirs to a point west of Kilif about the center of the northern border, where it turns north toward the Aral Sea. The section of this boundary where the upper Oxus is known as the Ab-i-Panja is mountainous, but westward the river border passes through the plains of Bactria, in which lies the important city of Balkh.

In northwestern Afghanistan, where the Hari River emerges from the outlying ranges of the Hindu Kush system, is another fertile land surrounding the city of Herat. To the south the Helmand River and its tributaries drain an area of more than 100,000 square miles. Rising in the Hindu Kush mountains between Kabul and Bamian, this river emerges from the lower slopes in the vicinity of Kandahar (trading center with 60,000 people), then flows in a steep-sided valley most of the way to Lake Helmand in the Seistan depression.

Near eastern Afghanistan is the famous Khyber Pass, India's only easy outlet to the northwest. Despite the region of towering mountains surrounding the pass, its maximum elevation reaches only 3,000 feet. The route utilizing Khyber Pass follows the Kabul River, which rises in the Hindu Kush west of Kabul (capital city, population 120,000), and flows eastward between mountain ranges into the Indus River. This is the pass through which moved the soldiers of Alexander the Great, the hordes of Genghis Khan, and numerous other warriors on their way into India. In the other direction modern troops under the British flag have marched through Khyber Pass into Afghanistan.

From one point of view, Afghanistan may be considered a mountainous region separating the civilization of the Euphrates from the civilizations of the Oxus and the Indus. It may also be regarded as a region of caravan routes joining central Asia to the plains of India. The cities of Kabul, Herat, and Kandahar are frequently described as the keys to India.

Climate. Lying at a considerable distance from any large water bodies, Afghanistan has a climate that is generally dry. The precipitation that does occur is brought during the winter and spring by low pressure areas entering from the west. Frequently northwest winds follow the storm areas, bringing low temperatures. High mountains cause an updraft of air that results in rain or snow, beginning at some point along the upward slope. This precipitation furnishes a source of water, and the melting snows of early summer give rise to many intermittent streams.

Except at the higher altitudes summer temperatures are hot. During this season maximum temperatures exceed 100° F. and are rendered even more uncomfortable by dust storms. Due to lack of humidity the daily range of temperature is ordinarily high; the nights are always cool to cold. Although winter temperatures rise considerably above freezing during the day, this season is cold.

Cultural Aspects

People. The inhabitants of Afghanistan are called Afghans, although a number of individual groups make up the composite national population: Afghans (proper), Pathans, Ghilzai, Tajiks, Hazaras, and Kaffirs. Among these peoples considerable admixture has taken place, yet each group retains outstanding characteristics.

The dominant people of the country are the Afghans proper, who call themselves *Durani*. Afghan tribes along the northwest frontier of Pakistan are organized on a tribal system. They are really Pukhtuns, generally termed "Pathans" by Europeans. Ethnographically they are related to India. The Ghilzai, believed to be of Turkish descent, now occupy the plateau of Kandahar. The Tajiks, who are the aboriginal Persians, probably once occupied all the fertile areas of the country before the Afghans moved in from the eastern mountains. Where the Afghans have seized lands, the Tajiks remained as their tenants. The Hazaras in Afghanistan, who came from the east with the army of Genghis Khan, have Mongolian features but speak Persian. The Kaffirs of the country claim to be Greek in origin.

Religion and languages. Despite the racial diversity, the predominant religion of Afghanistan is Islam. A minority of about a million Shiah Mohammedans does exist. Prevailing languages spoken in Afghanistan are Persian and Pushtu, although Turki dominates in some of the northeastern parts of the country.

National Economy

Agriculture. Afghanistan for the most part is a barren, treeless country. This fact alone would indicate lack of rainfall. The position of the country in the Asiatic land mass, considered in connection with its topographic features, is further proof that human activities would have to be adapted to dryness and degree of accessibility. Agriculture furnishes the chief means of livelihood for the population: extensive cultivation of crops that do not need much water; intensive farming in spots where there is adequate water, or irrigation. Finally, the animal industries utilize the thousands of square miles of pasture lands.

Staple food crops include wheat and other grains, and also fruits, which can be produced in great variety where water is available. Kabul, at an elevation of 6,000 feet, lies in a valley of terraced cultivation, where walnuts and apricots are raised in large quantities. Fruit raised around Kandahar is shipped in quantity to India via the railhead at Chaman. Herat is an important trade center for caravans carrying hides, wool, dried fruit, pistachios, and walnuts to the Russian railhead at Kushk.

The policy of the government has been to reduce imports by growing cotton and sugar beets. Factories for the manufacture of cloth and sugar were established by the government-owned Ashami Company, but the government later decided to sell them to private entrepreneurs.

Camels, sheep, and horses graze on the plains. Badakhshan and Afghan Turkestan are famous for horses. Fat-tailed sheep are valued for their meat and fat, and their wool and skins are used for the manufacture of the pustin or skin coat, a common article of clothing. The leading export of the country is karakul lamb skins, normally about four or five million dollars worth annually. Thus, Afghanistan is primarily a pastoral land, with scattered areas of irrigated agriculture.

Mineral resources. Although good deposits of copper, lead, coal, and iron are reported, mining has not been developed to any extent. Coal of poor quality is produced in the vicinity of Kabul. Traces of petroleum have been found in the neighborhood of Herat, but due to the small local demand and the expense of constructing a pipeline to the Indian Ocean, nothing has been done about it. Afghanistan is known for the lapis lazuli of Badakhshan and the alabaster-like stone of Kandahar.

Political Aspects

Recent developments. Prior to the 1920's Afghanistan did not welcome foreigners. In later years changes began taking place. King Amanulla and his queen visited Europe, where they absorbed many new ideas, especially during their stay in Turkey. The king and queen lived a monogamous life in a polygamous country. The queen started the fashion of going without the veil, and European dress and headcoverings were prescribed for all. Girls were forced to attend school without the consent of their parents, and it was ordered that marriages should not occur unless the bride-to-be was willing.

In Turkey Kemal Ataturk was successful in breaking his subjects away from old customs because his people were ready to follow his direction after he had saved their country from division among the great powers, and had lifted the burden of oppression long suffered under former rulers. Amanulla did not have all these supporting forces to back him up, but he attempted to put into effect reforms even more forceful than those initiated by Ataturk. Many of his subjects lived in secluded valleys where fierce independence is almost necessary for survival. The Moslem leaders also exercised more power than he realized. A revolution resulted in 1928, and for a short time a former bandit chief controlled the country. However, the ruler of Afghanistan must have the royal blood of the ruling houses of the Durani tribe, and this the usurper did not have. A few months later Nadir Khan, a royal descendant, overthrew the bandit chief and became Nadir Shah. Like Amanulla, he believed in modernization but recognized the necessity of effecting changes gradually. In 1932 he issued as his policy the doctrine that the government should be founded on the principles of the law of Islam. Further, there were provisions for absolute prohibition of alcoholic beverages; establishment of a military school and an arsenal for manufacture of weapons; maintenance of diplomatic relations and development of commercial intercourse with foreign countries; repair of telephone and telegraph communications and reconditioning of highways; collection of revenue in arrears; and reconstruction of the old Council of State and appointment of a Prime Minister.

In 1933 Nadir Shah was assassinated, and his son Zahir Shah was proclaimed king. Educated in Europe, Zahir Shah speaks both French and English. With his uncle, Sirdar Hashim Khan, he is studying Afghanistan's problems. Sirdar Hashim Khan understands his countrymen, and the two have a chance of success in advancing their country. Education is being pushed, with English as the medium of instruction in the higher levels.

An effort is being made to improve the roads, bringing cities closer to one another and strongly facilitating the spread of civilization. Although there are no railroads in Afghanistan, there are today passable highways linking Kabul, Herat, Kandahar, and Balkh with each other and with cities and railheads in Pakistan, Iran, and Soviet Russia. The postal service now runs six days a week between Kabul and Peshawar.

With the spread of law, order, and education in Afghanistan, it is probable the improvement in the way of living of the formerly independent lawless elements will follow the pattern observed in Turkey and Iran. Raiding, feuding tribesmen see others better cared for under stable conditions and grasp the idea that such a situation might be better for themselves.

Position in world affairs. Like Iran, Afghanistan is an old, old country that felt the thrusts of foreign invaders for many centuries. The results of those experiences still show in the manners and customs of the people. Afghanistan has existed in the more recent past because it has served as a buffer state between two ambitious powers—Russia and Britain. The withdrawal of the British from India, however, is changing this relationship.

Afghanistan became an independent state ruled by a capable monarch for the first time in 1747. Before that time it had been variously a group of small states under nominal Arab rule, or part of Mongol empires, or a region broken into areas divided among India, Persia, and the Uzbeks. As late as the second quarter of the nineteenth century, the boundary of Russia in Central Asia ran from the mouth of the Ural River to Orenburg and thence east to Omsk and Semipalatinsk, skirting north of the great Kirghiz Steppes.

A zone 1,400 miles wide separated Russia from Britain's sphere of influence. By 1849 the British controlled the Punjab. Five years later the Russians had the Aral Sea area and the Kirghiz Steppes and, by 1868, Tashkent, Bukhara, and Samarkand. In 1873 Russia agreed with Britain on the northern boundaries of Afghanistan and declared that the country lay outside her sphere of influence. By 1884 she had gained Khiva, Kokand, and Merv. In 1875 the British took Quetta. In 1885 the Russians picked up Panjdeh Oasis, and in 1893, the provinces of Roshan and Shignan on the north side of the Oxus. Afghanistan did get the Wakhan—the small end of the bargain—in exchange. About that time, the northern boundary of the Afghan state was stabilized for the most part. By 1896 the southern boundary was fixed; seven years later the Persian-Afghan border was determined. In 1907 Britain and Russia entered into an agreement whereby Russia for the second time affirmed that Afghanistan was outside her sphere of influence. In 1946 a treaty between Afghanistan and the Soviet Union provided that the Kushk district in Herat, where Iran, Afghanistan, and the Soviet Union meet, should go to the latter.

Today Britain is primarily concerned with the maintenance of her routes to the East. But to the north remains the threat from the U. S. S. R. It is said the Afghans mistrust the Soviet policy and abominate its atheism. Before modern developments in aviation, Kabul was protected from northern invasion by the lofty double ranges of the Hindu Kush. Even then, however, Badakhshan and her other Oxus Valley territory could not have been defended against Russian encroachment. The Russian railways run from the north to the Oxus and from the Caspian via Merv to Kushk. Recent warfare has shown that modern armies can overcome difficulties previously considered impossible. Distance and terrain are no longer insurmountable, and since the advent of air power Afghanistan could not defend itself either from the north or the south. Thus, it is the difficult and delicate task of the ruler to hold a balance in the world politics of today.

Afghanistan must surely hope for the success of the United Nations.

CHAPTER 23

The Complexity of India and Burma

No COUNTRY in the world presents a politico-geographical pattern of greater complexity than India,* and no part of the Orient contrasts more sharply with the Western world. In a physical setting of great variety India developed over many centuries as a heterogeneous collection of political units, with varying degrees of dependence upon Great Britain.

Often referred to as a subcontinent, this huge country presented Great Britain with many grave problems. It is not primarily size that made the task of ruling India so difficult, but the extreme complexity of Indian life, which through centuries of conquest and infiltration has become a veritable maze of races, languages, creeds, and customs. Prior to British assumption of control, India was the scene of almost constant conflict between the rival peoples and ruling families. In spite of great diversity in the cultural pattern, however, a number of strong geographical factors tend to unify the country.

The great mountain wall of the Himalayas on the north effectively separates the country from the rest of Asia and allows overland passage through only a few restricted passes. Bordered by the sea on the other sides, the great subcontinent forms a compact geographical unit. The coastline is unbroken by penetrating seas such as have favored the development of numerous nations in Europe, thus preventing any section of India from becoming the focal point of commerce at the expense of other sections.

There is also a small degree of unity, in some cases easily apparent and in others obscure, underlying the diversity of Indian culture. Centuries of living together and intermingling have given the various races and religious groups a community of interest that is characteristically Indian. The major problem is whether the unity is great enough to overcome the forces of division and allow the discordant groups to live peaceably within the frame of India as a free and independent society.

Until it was separated in 1937, Burma was one of the provinces of British India. The separation was a logical step because the two countries are fundamentally different in race, religion, and language, and they represent different stages of economic and political development. Burma is much less complex than India, and her problems are of a much simpler order. There is no population pressure on the land; the religious problem is much less acute; and Burma's minority groups, although sometimes in conflict, are of less potential danger to the state.

INDIA

The Indian peninsula occupies a dominat-

* India is treated in this chapter as a subcontinent, but consideration is given to the division of India in 1947 into Pakistan and Hindustan or the Union of India (see page 334).

ing position at the head of the Indian Ocean and projects southward to within 8 degrees of the Equator. Located between two distinctly different types of country—the semiarid pastoral lands of southwestern Asia on the west and the rice-producing, wet, monsoon lands of Farther India on the east—India exhibits characteristics of each. Her position on the

ment will be linked most closely with the countries of southwestern and southeastern Asia, southeast Africa, and Australia.

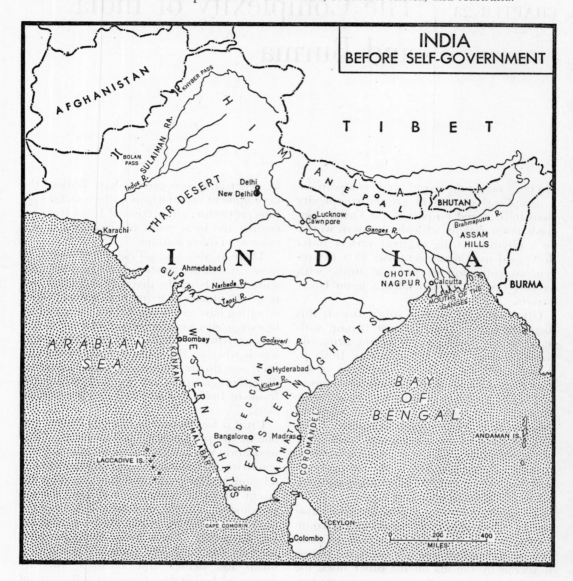

INDIA
BEFORE SELF-GOVERNMENT

main trade route between Europe and the Far East via the Mediterranean, the Red Sea, the Indian Ocean, and the Strait of Malacca, provides favorable commercial connections with the rest of the world.

Flanked on the north by the world's highest mountains, the country is protected from the winter cold of the north, but it is denied easy overland contact with Inner Asia. Hence, it seems likely that India's future develop-

Physical Framework

Comprising a compact, wedge-shaped area of over 1,500,000 square miles, India is approximately seventeen times the size of Great Britain and as large as all Europe without Russia, thus ranking as one of the very large areas of the world (see the map on this page). The maximum dimensions from the northwestern to the northeastern border and also from the northern border of Kashmir to Cape Comorin in the south are each roughly 2,000 miles. It is not surprising that in a country so large there should be diversity.

Topography. Within the mountain frame in India are four major physical divisions: the mountain wall in the north, the great lowland of the Ganges and Indus valleys, the peninsular plateau, and the coastal belts of the peninsula. Each of these major divisions contains a number of distinct subregions.

The northern mountain wall includes the high, snowcapped mountains of the Himalayas and the associated ranges, stretching in an unbroken sweep for 1,500 miles across northern India; the densely forested, moderately high mountains on the northeast between India and Burma; and the moderately high, moderately forested Sulaiman and Kirthar ranges on the northwest between India and Afghanistan. The high mountains directly north of India constitute a formidable barrier because of their general elevation and because of the great height of even the few passes. It should be emphasized that the northern mountain wall is complete and that landward connections with neighboring countries are limited. The weakest part of the wall is in the northwest, where four main routes traverse the barrier—the Khyber, Bolan, and Gomal passes and the Makran coastal route. Until World War II all of India's land invaders came by way of the northwest passes or along the Makran Coast of Baluchistan. British and Indian statesmen have always concentrated on the defense of the northwest frontier, neglecting the northeastern frontier. About the same number of passes cross the mountain frontiers in the northeast as in the northwest, but the routes in the former offer more formidable barriers because of the dense vegetation, the floods (during the rains), and the incidence of malaria. As a result the northeastern frontier should present no danger of invasion in the near future.

At the foot of the mountain wall, the extensive lowland, known as the Hindustan Plain, extends eastward for 2,000 miles from the Arabian Sea to the head of the Brahmaputra Valley near the Burma border and averages 150 to 200 miles in width. This plain is characterized by its flatness and by the sharpness of the dividing line between the plain and the mountains on the north. The Hindustan lowland is divided into two major sections by a low watershed near Delhi. To the west is the Indus Valley, largely dependent upon irrigation for its agriculture. To the east is the Ganges-Brahmaputra Valley, which receives enough rain during half the year for crops. These two sections have, respectively, the least and the greatest concentrations of people in all India. Also within the lowlands of Hindustan, to the east of the Indus Valley, is the Thar, or Indian, Desert. As one of the driest and hottest places on earth, it presents an odd contrast to the intensive utilization practiced elsewhere on the plains of India.

Most of peninsular India consists of a plateau, which slopes eastward toward the Bay of Bengal. The western edge of the plateau forms a high escarpment known as the Western Ghats, and the eastern edge consists of disconnected highlands known as the Eastern Ghats. These two highlands join in the south to form the high Nilgiri Hills. Separating the Nilgiris from the Cardamon Hills still farther south is the Palghat Gap, which connects the plain of the Malabar Coast with the Carnatic, or southeastern part of the peninsula. A line of highlands stretches across the peninsula between the latitudes of 21 and 24 degrees North Latitude, forming the dividing line between the Aryan and Dravidian peoples.

The plateau is flanked on both sides by relatively narrow coastal belts, the western belt including three sections. In the south is the plain of the Malabar Coast with its famous lagoons and plantations; in the middle section around Bombay is the Konkan, made up of a series of plains and hill spurs; and in the north is the Gujarat Plain, which has connections with the interior via the Tapti and Narbada river valleys. Along the Coromandel Coast on the eastern side of the peninsula are a number of large river deltas separated by narrow belts of rolling to hilly land.

Only two regions of India lie outside the mountain frame—the barren plateau of Baluchistan in the westernmost part of the country and the high country of Kashmir along the northern frontier.

Climate. Nowhere else in the world is the tropical monsoon climate so well marked as in India, and nowhere else are the people more dependent on climatic conditions. To a country so dominantly agricultural, the rhythm of the monsoons is of vital importance.

Throughout most of the country there are four seasons: the "cold" season from December through February; the hot season, March through May; the season of general rains, June through August; and the season of retreating monsoon, September through November, when rainfall is decreasing everywhere except in the Carnatic, along the east coast in Madras province.

The country alternates between luxuriant green during the rains and drab brown in the dry season. India's huge population is distributed according to the rainfall possibilities except as the extreme pressure of population on the land has caused many to settle on the climatically marginal lands where rainfall is very uncertain. Here are the areas of India's terrible famines. These conditions have been somewhat alleviated by irrigation, which has greatly increased the productive lands in these climatically unproductive areas, and by modern transport facilities, which have made possible the rapid movement of supplies into famine zones.

Coasts and islands. India's 4,000 miles of coastline are so regular that no penetrating seas extend marine influences inland (see the map on page 326). Except for Bombay, the ports either have artificial harbors or are located far up river channels difficult to navigate. Thus, the coasts of India have not lent themselves to the development of a maritime nation. The only important islands near India are Bombay, a small island on which the great port city is built, and Ceylon, the new British Dominion at the southern tip of the peninsula. Although politically separate from India, Ceylon is geographically very similar to the nearby mainland.

Historical Background

Before recorded history began in India, a race of unknown origin widely occupied the country. These people were driven into the scattered hilly regions, where their purest descendants are still recognizable, by the Dravidians, a race of a higher type, that entered from outer Asia. Largely out of contact with the rest of the world, these invaders developed a civilization of their own over a long period. Then a great invasion of Aryans, who migrated to India from the northwest between 2400 and 1500 B.C., drove many of the Dravidians southward into the peninsula, where they still form most of the population in a large block of territory. The lighter-skinned Aryans settled in northern India, and the racial blends that matured there developed the religious organization that gave rise to the complex Hindu caste system of today. During the sixth century B.C., Buddhism and Jainism were introduced. Buddhism had considerable influence on India for a time, but it finally faded out.

In 327 B.C. Alexander the Great invaded India, conquered the Punjab and Sind, and founded a Greek kingdom. Many other invasions followed, and numerous independent kingdoms were set up, their chief occupation being constant war with one another. Beginning in the eighth century A.D. Islam appeared in India, and, beginning about 1000 A.D., rapidly expanded. In 1398 came the Mongol conquest under the leadership of Tamerlane. In 1526 Babur, the fifth in descent from Tamerlane, invaded India, conquered the chief ruling monarch in the north, and founded the Mogul Empire, the most brilliant in Indian history. The decline of the Mogul Empire began in 1707, although it endured in name until 1857.

The first Europeans on the Indian scene were the Portuguese, who visited the country under the leadership of Vasco da Gama. They established a trading port at Goa in the sixteenth century and held a virtual monopoly of all Oriental trade for a hundred years.* They were gradually expelled from almost all their territorial possessions by the Dutch. In turn, the Dutch were driven out in the eighteenth century by the English, who had established the British East India Company in 1600. In the ensuing struggle for dominion between the British and the French, who also attempted to found an empire in India, England won; and all that remains of French power in India are a few small enclaves: Pondichéry, Karikal, Yanaon, Chandernagor, and Mahé.

Until 1858, the year after the Indian Mutiny, India was ruled by the British East India Company. In that year power was transferred to the British government. Since

* The Portuguese still hold Goa, Damão, and Diu, possessions that make up Portuguese India.

then, there has been a gradual process of putting Indian officials into responsible government positions and a transfer of certain powers to Indian legislatures. A constitution for India, issued in 1919, provided for a greater proportion of elected members in the provincial councils, and another in 1935 gave India a federal form of government and a measure of self-rule. An important step taken by the British government in 1942 was the unaccepted Cripps offer of self-government under certain specified conditions. In 1947 after extended negotiations between British officials and Indian leaders, India was divided into two dominions, Pakistan and the Union of India, each having the right to secede from the British Commonwealth of Nations.

The Economic Strength of India

Agriculture. The predominance of agriculture in India's economy is shown by the fact that three quarters of her population are dependent upon the soil for their living. With an agricultural population already dense (in some places over 2,000 per square mile and an average density of more than 246), India's problem of feeding her people is made more difficult by a yearly increase of over 3,000,000 people. About twenty per cent of its 260,000,000 acres under cultivation depends upon irrigation. Although this practice has relieved the pressure on the land in the past, the limit in reclaiming dry lands has been reached, or soon will be. A third of the total cropland is devoted to rice, of which India grows one fourth of the world's total. Cotton, grown especially in Bombay and the Central Provinces, is the big money crop, and represents about fifteen per cent of the world's total. Bengal grows a large proportion of the world's jute; wheat, tea, and sugar cane are also important crops. A crop found everywhere is a mixture of groundnuts, sesame, rape, mustard, and linseed, which yields seeds for vegetable oil. Corn, barley, tobacco, and indigo are also grown. Any marked increase in production of food crops in the future will be made at the expense of cash crops. Reduction of population growth, greater industrialization, and more scientific agriculture—the three most obvious solutions—are all difficult of achievement. It appears likely that the second solution—increased industrialization—may have the most success, although during the last fifty years industry has failed to reduce appreciably the pressure on agricultural land.

One of the chief agricultural handicaps is the fragmentation of land holdings. Upon the death of a landowner, the lands are divided and subdivided among all his heirs, with the result that most individual holdings are far too small to support a family. It has been estimated that the area under cultivation averages less than one acre per capita.

The per-acre yield of most crops is much below world averages due to poor methods of cultivation, poor seed, and exhaustion of the soil. Crops are taken from the land year after year and nothing added to maintain fertility. Cattle, and in some localities water buffalo or camels, are used for plowing and hauling. Much has been done to improve the lot of the Indian farmer, but there yet remains a tremendous task to change old methods, raise the buying power, and otherwise encourage progress on the vast agricultural lands of the country.

Mineral and forest wealth. Generally speaking, India is not outstanding in mineral wealth. However, there are significant deposits of coal, iron ore, limestone, copper, mica, and manganese in the country, largely concentrated in the uplands west of Calcutta. These have given rise to an iron and steel industry of considerable proportions. Nevertheless, the importance of mining is not impressive when compared with agriculture, for only one tenth of one per cent of the people are in mining as against seventy-five per cent in farming.

The estimates of coal reserves throughout India range from 52 to 80 billions of tons, of which only a small part is suitable for coking. Fortunately, practically all the coal can be used for industry and transportation, since almost none is needed for the heating of homes. Eastern India supplies most of the domestic needs and also exports considerable amounts to Burma for use on the Burma railways. Western India has to import coal from South Africa.

Petroleum production is negligible, and India is forced to import. Most of Burma's production normally goes to her.

Iron ore is widely distributed, but concentrations of economic value in modern exploitation are found near Madras and in the northeastern peninsular provinces of Bihar and Orissa. These fields compare favorably with the Lake Superior fields of the United States in both tonnage and quality of ore and constitute one of the best reserves in all Asia. Other concentrations of high-grade ore are in Mysore in the southwest and in Portuguese Goa.

India is the world's second largest producer of the highly strategic alloy metal, manganese. Although widely scattered, the deposits are mainly in the Central Provinces, Bihar, Orissa, and Madras. Only about one tenth of the production is used in India, the other nine tenths going to England and France. More than 75 per cent of the world's supply of sheet mica is produced in Bihar and Madras and is of excellent quality. Other mineral products of less importance are gold, ilmenite, saltpeter, chromite, monazite, diamonds, magnesite, zircon, silver, graphite, tungsten ore, and sapphires.

Although roughly 20 per cent of India is forest land, much of it is in the relatively inaccessible hills and mountains. Three quarters of the forested area, classed as "reserved," is controlled by the provincial governments and intended to be permanently maintained as a supply of timber or to protect the water supply by preventing a rapid run-off of rainfall. Forest products include timber of teak, conifers, and sandalwood, and bamboo, fibers, gums, resins, and firewood. In the more settled parts of the country commercial timber is largely lacking; hence imports (especially teak and pyingado) from Burma supplement domestic woods.*

Manufacturing. Some 39,000,000 people, of whom less than 2,000,000 work in modern factories, are engaged in manufacturing industries, and in the sheer bulk of manufactured products India ranks relatively high among the industrial nations of the world. However, as her industries have grown, her population has also increased. The result is that even now only 10 per cent of her people make their living from manufacturing, and it has not lifted the general standard of living in the country to any appreciable degree.

Many Indian Nationalists believe that their country's great hope is in industrialization. Gandhi, on the other hand, encouraged and fostered handicrafts and home industries in an attempt to get away from European-type, large-scale industry.

Most of the manufacturing today is confined to the processing of agricultural products, chief among them cotton yarn and cloth, jute, and cheese, and, to a certain extent, minerals. The formerly well-developed handicrafts and household industries have suffered under British rule because they were unable to compete with goods produced more cheaply by machine methods in England. Without any permanent plan on the part of British political leaders to foster in India the production of raw materials and the importation of manufactured products, that is what actually took place. There is little evidence, however, that this development would not have resulted even if the country had been independent.

India has many of the requirements for industrial progress. In addition to her mineral production, she is the world's largest grower of cotton, jute, and sugar cane. She is the number one producer of lac and of hides and skins, and is number two in the production of tea. Counteracting the advantages of raw materials for manufacturing and processing is a lack of adequate power resources. To a certain extent, however, hydro-electric energy supplements the modest amounts of good coking coal.

The number of modern factories in India is not large, being estimated at about 10,000 in 1936. They are concentrated in a few cities, such as Calcutta, Bombay, Ahmedabad, Cawnpore, Jamshedpur, and Madras. At Jamshedpur was established the largest steel plant in the British Empire.* The development of much of India's modern manufacturing was accomplished during the two world wars, when India became a sort of eastern arsenal for the Allies.

Trade. Practically all of India's foreign trade moves by sea, passing through the ports of Calcutta, Bombay, Karachi, and Madras. Although there is a large total export trade,

---

* For a detailed account of India's forests, see H. G. Champion, "Preliminary Survey of the Forest Types of India and Burma," *Indian Forest Records*, New Series I, No. 1 (1926).

* The Jamshedpur plant, Indian Nationalists point out, is entirely under Indian management and gives proof of India's ability to develop her resources and become a highly industrialized nation.

the per capita amount remains unimpressive. Raw materials and food products account for approximately three fourths of the entire exports. Most of the jute and tea is produced in the hinterland of Calcutta and is shipped from that port. The greater part of the cotton goes through the port of Bombay; wheat and barley through Karachi.

Transportation. In India the railways are the chief means of transport. Some 43,000 miles of track, although consisting of different gauges, serve to knit the country together. The main lines radiate from the four major ports, especially Calcutta and Bombay. Only one railway crosses the traditional Indian boundary into a neighboring country—the line from Baluchistan to Duzdab in Iran. The areas with the greatest density of rail net correspond rather closely to those with the greatest density of population.

India has four main motor highways, but the road net is inadequate for the needs of the country, particularly since water transport is not highly developed.

India's central position on the south coast of Asia makes it a strategic transit zone for global air routes. Calcutta, Bombay, Karachi, and Delhi are all termini on airline routes between Europe and the Far East. Two internal air transportation companies connect most of the large cities of the country, one radiating from Calcutta and the other from Bombay. It must be understood that this modern means of transport does not directly affect the great masses of population, but it does advance the overall economy of the nation.

The People

Pressure of population. The population of India has grown from 100,000,000 to 389,000,000 in the last 350 years. These millions are crowded into an area less than two thirds the size of the United States. About one half live in the plains of the north on one fifth of the total area of the country.

The greatest population densities are in a wide belt along the Ganges Valley, in narrow belts along both coasts, and in a broad area in the southern part of the peninsula. Many parts of the Ganges Valley have densities of over 1,000 per square mile and, in some places, 2,000. Cochin, in the south, has 4,000. Other places, such as the Thar Desert and the rough lands of the Chota Nagpur Plateau in the northeastern part of the peninsula, are almost empty.

The strikingly rural character of India is shown by the fact that 90 per cent of the people live in towns of 5,000 or under. There is great concentration on the alluvial lands, wherever water is obtainable, as would be expected in an agricultural country.

Despite the fact that Indian population is preponderantly rural there are numerous cities, some of which have attained considerable size. Calcutta has more than 2 million inhabitants, Bombay has nearly a million and a half, five other cities exceed one-half million,[*] and still fifty-one others have more than 100,000 persons.

Religion. Religion is of tremendous importance, affecting the attitudes of the people toward all economic, social, and political problems. There are nine major religions and many religious sects, but two groups are of outstanding importance—the Hindus and Moslems. Roughly seventy per cent are Hindus, and twenty-two per cent Moslem, with Christians, Sikhs, Jains, Buddhists, Parsis, and Jews making up most of the remainder.

HINDUS. Numbering more than 250,000,000 (including 51,500,000 of the Scheduled Classes) the Hindus are the dominant group throughout most of India. Hinduism is not only a highly complex and mystical religion, but a code of life. Its rules are interpreted and enforced by the top caste, the Brahmins.[**] According to the book of Manu, Hindu society has four main castes: the Brahmin (priests), Kshatriya (warriors), Vaisya (traders), and Sudra (servants). The first three are twice-born and occupy a much higher social position than the Sudras. As mentioned above, however, the real power lies with the Brahmins. With the passage of time, other castes or sub-castes developed until there are now some 2,000. When a person is born within a certain caste, he must remain within it; there is no way out. Apparently based on color, race, and occupation, caste is a permanent fixture in Hindu society.

[*] Madras, 777,000; Hyderabad, 739,000; Lahore, 672,000; Ahmedabad, 591,000; Delhi (including New Delhi), 522,000.

[**] For more details see Lord Meston, *Nationhood For India* (Yale University Press, 1931).

Outside of caste are the 51,500,000 Depressed or Scheduled Classes, whom Brahmanism has refused to admit into Hindu social life. In some parts of India, particularly in the south, they have become so numerous that they are in political control of large areas. Hinduism has lost many of these people to Christianity and Islam because under these religions they can obtain a recognized social status.

The caste system of Hindu India was one of the great problems facing the British and Indian leaders in their attempt to work out a satisfactory basis for Indian political freedom. Britain hesitated to relinquish power in India until the various groups were adequately represented.

MOSLEMS. The second strongest religious group is the Moslem, comprising about 95,-000,000 persons, or nearly one quarter of the total population of the country. Originally entering India from the northwest, the stronghold of the religion is still in northwestern India, although there is a secondary concentration in Bengal. Mohammedanism has never attained great strength in peninsular India except in small isolated localities.

Islam has been modified in India by the influence of Hinduism. In fact, many members of each religion practice some of the forms of the other. In spite of this interrelation, however, there is a basic antagonism between the two that periodically flares into riots and constitutes a permanent threat to the peace of the country. It is impossible to say definitely at this time whether the two groups can work out a basis for cooperation. Massacres coincident with and following the establishment of Pakistan and Hindustan have not spoken well for the future.

Moslems, recalling that they were once the ruling people in India, firmly believe that, with the help of their kinsmen in southwest Asia, they could again rule India. It should be noted in this connection that although the Hindus are much more numerous in India, they are virtually alone in the world. The Moslems, on the other hand, have at least the moral support of the entire Mohammedan world from North Africa across the Near East to India and beyond.

Many people believe that Britain has in the past intensified the quarrel between Hindu and Moslem in order to retain power for herself. They use the arguments that Hindu-Moslem rioting seldom occurs in the Indian states and that it did not occur before the British came to India. The most logical answer to the first is that their natural antagonism is intensified now, as they see Britain's withdrawal, and as they each struggle for power. In pre-British times there was war until the control was definitely in the hands of one group—the Moslem—and then the other was obliged to accept it.

OTHER RELIGIOUS GROUPS. Sikhism is an offshoot of Hinduism and represents an attempt to purify the Hindu creed by eliminating idolatry, religious pilgrimages, and polytheism. Beginning as a pacific sect, it was changed into a militant body by the political persecutions of the Moslems and the social tyranny of the Hindus. Comprising a group of more than 5,000,000, the Sikhs are strong enemies of the Moslems. Although the Punjab is the Sikh stronghold, they have spread widely into other parts of India. The recent division of the Punjab between Pakistan and Hindustan split the homeland of the Sikhs.

Another offshoot of Hinduism, the Jain religion, has about 1,500,000 followers. They comprise a small but fairly wealthy group, concentrated largely in trade and banking. Since they accept most of the principles of Hinduism, they should be regarded as a Hindu reformed sect.

Beginning as a branch of Hinduism, Buddhism evolved into a very different religion. It is free from caste and does not accept idolatry and sacrifices. The essence of Buddhism is moderation, and it is much less mystical and complex than Hinduism. It was for a time the state religion, but it is now almost entirely non-existent in India. It has had particular appeal for the Mongoloid peoples of eastern Asia.

The other religions of India are not large in numbers. The Parsis are Zoroastrians and are concentrated mainly in the Bombay area. The Jews number about 25,000. Christianity has made considerable progress, but it is significant that this has been mostly among the animists and the outcaste Hindus, who have no status in the indigenous religions. Estimates of converts run as high as six million.

It is difficult to over-estimate the influence of religion on the daily lives of the Indian people. Religion largely dictates the food they eat, the clothes they wear, and the thoughts they have. The power of religion over the people is not made weaker by the great gulf between Hinduism and Islam but is intensified in the two groups, and here lies the great danger to India.

Language. There are over 200 languages in India; and, of these, twenty are spoken by more than one million persons each. English has been the official language throughout the country, but in each political unit at least one indigenous language was also declared official. The *lingua franca* of northern India (other than English) is Hindustani, a combination of Hindi and Urdu. In total, Hindustani tongues account for 33 per cent of the population, more than double that of any other language group. In southern India, Tamil is perhaps most widely understood.

The pattern of language in India is extremely complex, crossing racial, religious, and political boundaries. However, the dividing effect of religion is so much greater than that of language that the latter has had no great politico-geographical importance.

Political Framework under the British

Political units. India was divided into two main administrative parts (see the map on page 335). British India, comprising roughly three fifths of the country and containing a population of 295,000,000, was annexed to the British Empire and governed directly. The Indian states, with 93,000,000 people and two fifths of the area, had local autonomy but were under the suzerainty of Britain.

The division of the country into British India and the Indian states did not follow geographical boundaries. Rather, it was the result of historical accident and represented, in general, the political units as they existed at the time Britain assumed control. The two major political areas were not units distinctly set apart, but were fragmented and interspersed throughout the country.

The only difference between the Indian states and British India was political. The political units were not cultural units. Linguistic, religious, and ethnic lines cut across the political boundaries and formed an extremely complex pattern.

BRITISH INDIA. British India included most of the coastal states and those of the major river valleys. A glance at the map on page 335 shows that British territory almost surrounded the Indian states and agencies, affording sea power control of the entire peninsula.

The major provinces of British India were Bengal, Bombay, Madras, the Punjab, the United Provinces, Assam, the Central Provinces, the Northwest Frontier Province, Bihar, Orissa, and Sind, each under a governor and a legislature. The Laccadive Islands, about 200 miles off the Malabar coast, were attached to Madras Province. There were several other British units, such as Delhi, Ajmer-Merwara, Coorg, and British Baluchistan, which were ruled by commissioners. The Andaman and Nicobar islands in the Bay of Bengal, occupied by the Japanese in 1942, were administered by the Governor-General of India through a Chief Commissioner.

THE INDIAN STATES. The organization of that part of the country outside British India was very different. In contrast to the small number of provinces in British India, there were 562 Indian states varying in size from Hyderabad, nearly as large as France, to small areas the size of a private estate. The relations of these states with the British Crown were based on individual treaties and agreements and presented a great variety of working arrangements. All, however, recognized Britain as the "Paramount Power" and turned foreign affairs over to her. The rulers of the states were autocratic, but their absolutism was restricted by tradition, religion, and the power of the state nobles. Britain had considerable influence on the Indian states, either directly through her political advisors or indirectly through the example set in British India. Many of the large states adopted the British Penal Code and organized local administration along the lines of that in the districts in the provinces.

India in the British Empire: BOUNDARIES AND DEFENSE. A unique geographic periphery has facilitated the defense of the subcontinent of India. A large part of India's land boundaries are undemarcated, such delineation being unnecessary because the frontiers lie in the areas of rugged, relatively unsettled land where there is normally little intercourse between the people on either side. Both sea and land frontiers present great difficulty to an invader, except in the northwest where mountain passes, chiefly Khyber Pass, offer an avenue of approach.

BRITAIN'S PROBLEMS. Great Britain stated in early 1947 that she would hand over political control of the subcontinent to a United India or to Pakistan and Hindustan, one dominion or two being established, whichever the Indians might determine prior to their final decision whether or not to stay in the British Commonwealth. There were a number of obligations that Britain felt she should discharge satisfactorily before she relinquished control. First of all, Britain desired to see some scheme worked out that would provide for the defense of India against external attack. Britain also felt that since she had been responsible for peace within India so long, she should be certain that civil war would not break out upon her withdrawal. At the same time the British were determined to leave India, even though its division into Pakistan and Hindustan might result in a weakening in its strength.

Second, Britain wanted some agreements worked out by a responsible Indian government or governments fitting the Indian states into the new governmental structure. Some system of law would have to take the place of treaties and agreements between the British government and the individual Indian states. Actually the Indian states were finally required to join either Pakistan or Hindustan.

Third, and most important of all, was the safeguarding of the various minority groups, which were guaranteed justice by the British government. As stated before, the greatest rift in India was that between the Hindus and Moslems. It must be remembered that the Moslems would form a minority in an all-India federation. Since 1940 they had demanded that India be partitioned and that they have Pakistan (northwestern India and northeastern India) as their national home, completely independent and separate from the rest of India. The Sikhs, who form a militant minority in India, also needed consideration. Another group meriting protection was the Scheduled Classes. Further, there were large numbers of people in the "backward" areas of India who should receive consideration. Some of these areas could easily be fitted into the pattern of an Indian federation or of a partitioned India. Others,

such as the Assam Hill tracts, might require separate treatment.

Fourth, Britain owed an obligation to the military services and to the All-India Civil Service personnel. And finally Britain had the obligation to work out some scheme with the future Indian government or governments to safeguard investments made in India by both Indian and British people, as well as to agree on a general overall financial settlement. India's debt in the past was of two kinds: (1) the "sterling debt," raised mainly in Britain, and (2) the "rupee debt," raised mainly in India. The former was liquidated during the war, however, and therefore presented no problem. Britain, in fact, at the time of partition in India owed an amount roughly equal to British investments there.

INDIA'S PROBLEMS. The Indian nationalist movement began in 1885 with the organization of the Indian National Congress. At first the idea of the Congress was to gain dominion status for India, but later under the leadership of Gandhi, it began working for complete independence. On the other hand, the great rival organization of the Congress was the Moslem League under the leadership of Jinnah, who since 1940 had recommended the partition of India.

The Indians themselves had to decide whether they wished to form a federation, partition the country, or form a unitary state. In the case of federation, they had to decide what kind of central and local governments they would have. In the case of partition, they had to decide along what lines the partition would be. Here were involved the economic basis, political basis, religious basis, and so on. The Indian situation was not just a case of a nationalistic attempt to overthrow alien rule, it was the case of a country deeply divided along many internal lines.

Pakistan and the Union of India

In August, 1947, the subcontinent of India was divided into the dominions of Pakistan and Hindustan or the Union of India (see the map on page 336). Initially within the framework of the British Commonwealth of Nations both dominions were free to leave the Commonwealth or to remain within its folds. Most Indian states of the subcontinent joined either Pakistan or the Union of India,

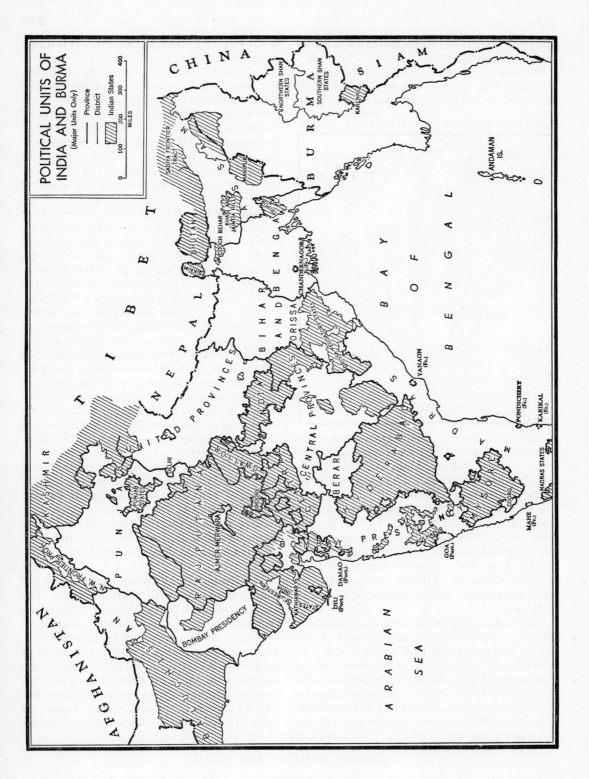

POLITICAL UNITS OF
INDIA AND BURMA
(Major Units Only)

——— Province
——— District
▨ Indian States

MILES
0   100   200   300   400

although Hyderabad still remained aloof from both at the end of 1947.

Pakistan. At the end of 1947 the area of Pakistan was 300,000 square miles, located partially in northwestern and partially in

EARLY STAGE IN PARTITION OF INDIA

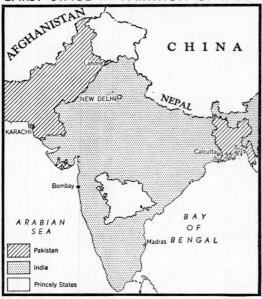

northeastern India. Key areas within Pakistan are eastern Bengal, part of Assam, Baluchistan, western Punjab, Sind, and the Northwest Frontier Province. The interim capital of the new state is Karachi.

The population of Pakistan is estimated at about 70,000,000, 72 per cent of which is Moslem. In terms of population this new political division is now the largest Islamic state on earth. It is also estimated that a minority of some 19,000,000 Hindus and another of some 1,600,000 Sikhs live in the newly created dominion.

Pakistan is poor in mineral resources and industry but rich in agricultural land. Wheat and cotton are leading crops and jute is produced for its fiber. The country has a good network of roads and railroads but communication between east and west Pakistan is across the Union of India. The three leading cities of the state are Karachi and Lahore

in the west and Dacca in the east. It is significant to note that in population these three cities ranked 5th (Lahore), 12th (Karachi), and 20th (Dacca) in India before partition.

The constitution of Pakistan will be based on Moslem law as expressed in the Koran and on the Moslem religion. The strong man of the country is Ali Jinnah, leader of the Moslem League, president of the constituent assembly, and governor-general of the country. In the fall of 1947 Pakistan was admitted into the United Nations.

Union of India (Hindustan). The area of Hindustan is well over 1,200,000 square miles, occupying the greater part of the subcontinent. The Union includes most of the 562 Indian states and all the great Hindu provinces of India. The capital city is New Delhi, which was the British capital for all of India.

Well over 300,000,000 people live in the Union of India, including a large minority of some 38,000,000 Moslems and another of some 3,900,000 Sikhs. Religious strife has been serious in both the Union of India and Pakistan since the partition despite efforts toward conciliation on the part of the leaders in both states. It has been estimated that possibly 10,000,000 people have crossed boundaries in an effort to be in the country in which their religion predominates.

The Union of India has the best mineral resources of the subcontinent and the leading industrial centers. Most of the important ports and cities of India, including Bombay, Madras, and Calcutta, are found in the Union. Transportation facilities in the country are good from the standpoint of the existing economy.

The Union of India plans to adopt a democratic constitution with a bill of rights. The leading political party of the Union is the Congress party whose leader, Jawaharlal Nehru, is also premier and foreign minister. The late Mohandas K. Gandhi, a member of the Congress Party, who led the independence movement in India for many years before his assassination, was always opposed to the partition of the subcontinent. The future of India divided into two states is unpredictable.

CEYLON, BHUTAN, AND NEPAL

Three other Asiatic areas are geographically and politically related to India: Ceylon, Bhutan, and Nepal, listed in the order of their ties with Great Britain. The island of Ceylon, a new British dominion, is at the southern extremity of India. In area it covers a little over 25,000 square miles; in 1943 it had a population of 6,000,000. Colombo is the capital of a people who embrace Buddhism and Hinduism. The island produces paddy, tea, cacao, cinnamon, rubber, and mica. The Maldives are now under Great Britain. The British have given Ceylon self-government since the end of World War II.

Bhutan is a semi-independent country in the eastern Himalayas between India and Tibet. The country is mountainous with deep valleys. The area is about 18,000 square miles, and the population is about 250,000.

In a treaty with the British in 1910 Bhutan agreed to follow the advice of Great Britain in external affairs, but the latter agreed not to interfere in internal affairs.

Nepal is an independent kingdom and like Bhutan lies between India and Tibet. The area is about 54,000 square miles, including part of Mt. Everest, the highest mountain on earth. The population is about 5,600,000, with some 110,000 living in the capital city of Kathmandu. The Gurkhas of Nepal rendered valuable service to the British in the recent conflict. Although Nepal is independent, her relations with the British are intimate.

BURMA

Probably the most important single geographic factor in Burma's development is her isolated location. Lying almost 700 miles north of the main east-west shipping lanes, Burma remained for centuries in a commercial backwater. Tucked away in a corner of southeastern Asia amid great mountains and valleys, the country was little known to the outside world until construction of the Burma Road (the Allies' vital supply line to China) drew world attention to her.

Although influenced by the great population groups of India and China, relations with them have been hindered by the lack of land communication and trade among the three countries. The persistent landward isolation of Burma may be attributed to several causes. Among the more important are: the rugged terrain of the border country, the small trade with China, which did not warrant the building of expensive transport facilities, the fact that trade with India could be carried on more cheaply by sea, and the fact that the "back door" of Burma adjoins the "back doors" of her neighbors.

Physical Factors

Size and shape. Comprising an area of 261,000 square miles, Burma ranks as one of the large countries of the world. For example, although slightly smaller than Texas, it is larger than any European country other than Soviet Russia. The main body of the country is nearly rectangular in shape, and the old capital of Mandalay is almost in the ex-

act geographical center (see the map below).

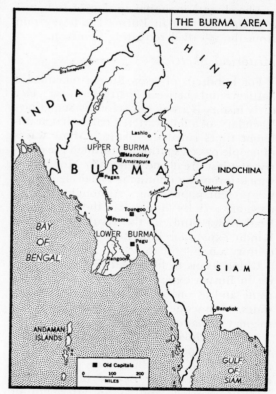

THE BURMA AREA

The comparatively large size of the country, coupled with the sparse population and backwardness of economic development, creates a problem of unifying the various regions with adequate means of transportation. Because it has enough space to support a considerably larger population, Burma has been very attractive to Indian and Chinese immigrants.*

Topography and climate. Great topographic variety characterizes the Burmese landscape. Although more rice could be produced if the central valley and delta were larger, the general economy of the country would be even more unbalanced if this were the case.

The chief politico-geographical factor regarding the physical features of the country is the "insulating" effect of the mountain borders. Like the other states in Farther India, Burma is essentially a valley "compartment" separated from adjoining countries by rugged mountains. The north-south alignment of these mountains and valleys has caused Burmese life to flow in that direction, with the result that east-west movement is still restricted.

The climate is similar to that of India except that no area in Burma has heavy rain from the so-called retreating monsoon.

Historical Sketch

For hundreds of years Burma remained a battleground between petty princes. Her early history is a series of accounts, sometimes legendary, of a few scattered tribes that at different times ruled the plains. Many waves of people passed southward through the country, the last great one being the Mongolian, which forms the dominant racial element in the present population. Although the Burmese are racially Mongolian, their early civilization was Indian, the result of a great Hindu expansion into Burma in the third century A.D.

China seems to have had very little interest in Burma except as a very limited trade route and as one of her nebulous tributary states. Consequently, her influence was not so great as that of India.

In the eighteenth century the inhabitants vigorously repelled the efforts of the British and French to establish trading posts on the eastern shores of the Bay of Bengal. The British persisted, and as an aftermath of three Anglo-Burmese wars (1823–26, 1852, and 1885–86) annexed Burma to the British Empire and joined it with India.

Under the various Burmese rulers the capitals (Prome, Pagan, Pegu, Toungoo, Amara-

* L. D. Stamp, "Burma, An Undeveloped Monsoon Country," *Geographical Review*, XX (1930), pp. 86–109.

pura, and Mandalay) were all inland, the last ones being situated in the tribal heartland of Burma, the central dry zone. The capital established by the British was Rangoon, reflecting their dependence on sea power.

Burma differs from India in race, religion, language, density of population, and almost every other respect. In 1937 this fact was given political recognition, when the British separated the two countries and set Burma up as a colony with its own legislature and a British governor.

Economic Aspects

Agriculture, forestry, and mining. Burma is predominantly an agricultural country, with a commercial one-crop system in the delta of Lower Burma and a subsistence type of agriculture in Upper Burma and the Shan States. About one and one half million acres are under irrigation. Rice is by far the most important crop, occupying 75 per cent of the cultivated area. Burma's main economic weakness is too great dependence on this one crop. A number of other crops are produced, such as sesame, millet, cotton, and groundnuts, but all in Upper Burma and in relatively small amounts. Other minor crops include tobacco, fruit, vegetables, and cereals. In the delta the water buffalo and in other areas the small humped oxen serve as the beasts of burden.

Approximately one third of Burma is covered with forest, one third of which contains valuable timber. The government has placed in reserve a large part of the forest lands to prevent uncontrolled private exploitation and attendant waste. Teak is the most important timber and has a wide variety of uses.

Mineral resources are considerable but to a large degree undeveloped. These include tungsten, tin, zinc, nickel, lead, silver, cobalt, copper, gold, iron ore, molybdenum, coal, rubies, sapphires, and jade. Perhaps the factor that made Burma most valuable to Great Britain was the petroleum deposits. The fields in the central Irrawaddy Valley were the main source within the British Empire until they were recently exceeded by those in Trinidad. Although the total output is less than one per cent of the world total, Burma's oil has political significance out of proportion to the amount produced.

Manufacturing, trade, and transport.
Burma is in only the beginning stage of industrial development. There is no heavy industry due to the lack of workable deposits of coking coal and iron ore. Industrial units are small, and the Burmese people have not yet organized large-scale manufacturing enterprises. Such industries as exist, other than handicrafts, have been developed with European capital and management.

Rice milling accounts for approximately half the factory workers and provides fairly steady employment. Other large industries are oil refining, silk weaving and dyeing, and wood carving. There is the same cry from the nationalists of Burma for industrialization as there is in India, but Burma has far to go before she is as highly industrialized as India.

Burma's trade is typical of relatively undeveloped countries. Her exports are largely raw materials; imports are manufactured goods. Roughly 85 per cent of the foreign trade passes through the port of Rangoon. The foreign trade of the country is linked very closely with India, since one third of the exports go to India and about one half of the imports come from there. Burma's trade position remains weak because of her great dependence on the export of rice.

Unlike India, the roads and waterways in Burma are complementary to the railways. There is a well-developed system of transport on the internal waterways, but the road net leaves much to be desired. Most of the transport lines follow the valleys in a north-south direction, and east-west lines are very few.

The famous Burma Road, extending from Kunming in China to Lashio in Burma, connected with the railroad from Lashio to Rangoon. The Stilwell Road from Assam in India through northern Burma to the Burma Road, built during the war, has already been abandoned.

The People

Burma's population increased during the decade 1931–41 from 14,500,000 to 16,800,000, a growth of almost fifteen per cent. Like India, Burma is a country of villages. Only two cities have populations of over 100,000: Rangoon (500,000), the capital and chief port; and Mandalay (150,000), river port and commercial center of Upper Burma.

The density of population is low for southeast Asia, being 64 per square mile. Most of the people are concentrated in the delta and valley of the Irrawaddy. Highland barriers retarded large-scale migration overland from India and China, and the population was largely indigenous until the sea route came into use and large numbers of Indian laborers were brought into the country for work in the rice fields.

Of the racial groups in Burma, four are estimated to make up three quarters of the total population: Burmans, Shans, Chins, and Indians (non-indigenous). Other stocks include Kachins and several non-indigenous peoples (Chinese, Indo-Burmans, Europeans, and Eurasians). The Burman group is by far the most important, with nearly two thirds of the total population, and is the most active politically.

Foreign groups have taken the lead in the economic development of the country. Excluding the Europeans, who have been responsible for most of the large-scale economic enterprises, the Burmans have seen Indians and Chinese take most of the good jobs in industry and commerce until very recent years. The Chinese constitute no minority problem except in the delta where their economic importance is out of proportion to their numbers, but even here they offer no such problem as the Indians.

Indians are concentrated mainly in the towns and along the waterways and railways. They present a minority problem because their money-lending class now owns much of the rice land in the delta. Also, the Indian laborer is willing to work for less than the Burman, and thus displaces him in the labor market.

Religion plays an important part in the economic, political, and social life of Burma and in some cases is the cause of severe racial strife. More often, however, it is the excuse given when the main causes are economic. The leading religion is Buddhism, incorporating 84 per cent of the population. Religious minorities include Animists, Mohammedans, Hindus, and Christians. There is considerable friction between Hindus and Moslems and, on occasion, between Burman Buddhists and the Indian group. On the whole, however, there is much less religious trouble than in India.

The Political Framework

Political units under the British. Political units in Burma under the British were much less complex than in India, but even so the pattern was somewhat similar (see the map on page 335). The principal administrative division of the country was into Upper and Lower Burma. Historical in origin, the division involved several differences in law and administration, although the recent trend had been to establish uniformity throughout the country.* From an economic viewpoint Lower Burma (south of Toungoo), with conditions favorable for commercial rice growing, has developed a one-crop agricultural economy and a high degree of tenancy. Upper Burma, on the other hand, has a diversity of crops, and the small landholdings are largely owned by the cultivators themselves. These two systems, each of which has attendant problems, bring about a certain cleavage in the political policies of the two parts of the country.

The most advanced part of the country was divided into seven Commissioner's divisions, which in turn were subdivided into districts, circles, and townships. Divisional Burma, which was under the Burma legislature, had a considerable degree of self-government. The more backward Shan States, in the highlands of eastern Burma, formed a federation directly under the Governor, who was represented by the Commissioner. Here the legislature had no control except in cases where the Governor proclaimed a law that was applicable to the Shan States as well as to Burma proper.

In addition there were other relatively large areas that were excluded either partially or entirely from control of the Burma legislature due to their lower degree of development. These areas were for the most part in the mountain border lands of Burma, although some were scattered throughout the country in the more rugged sections. The only part of Burma not annexed to Britain was the little group of Karenni States east of Toungoo. These particular areas corresponded to the native states of India. They were not British

*J. L. Christian, *Modern Burma* (Berkeley, University of California Press, 1942).

soil but surrendered the management of foreign affairs to Britain.

Independent Burma. In January, 1947, a conference in London between British and Burman leaders resulted in the decision to call a constituent convention in Burma to draw up a constitution for the country and to determine the future status of Burma, either as a dominion in the British Commonwealth or as an independent state in southeast Asia. The constituent convention adopted in August, 1947, a draft constitution calling for a Union of Burma including Burma proper and three autonomous frontier states: Shan, Kachin, and Karen. The Union of Burma is designed to be an independent sovereign republic outside the British Commonwealth. In 1948 Burma celebrated her independence.

Boundaries. There have been numerous disputes over the Indo-Burma boundary, one disagreement leading to the First Burmese War. Although now apparently settled and peaceful, the boundary is undemarcated on the ground throughout much of its length. No trade or travel of any consequence crosses the frontier in peacetime, and there is little likelihood of friction.

For a long time the British and French had rival claims in the Upper Mekong Valley. Each thought that this valley was the key to Yunnan and the Lao states, and the dispute reached a pitch out of all proportion to the economic and strategic value of the area. Finally, the boundary between Burma and French Indo-China was settled along the mid-channel of the Mekong.

The boundary in common with Siam was reconsidered and settled in 1941. Siam gained some 1,600 acres as the result of a shift in the channel of the Meh Sai River, a tributary of the Salween. In 1943 Japan, who was in occupation of Burma, ceded two of the Shan States—Kengtung and Mong Pan—to Thailand. At the close of World War II Siam renounced the cession.

China has advanced some rather far-reaching claims to territory in northern Burma. The boundary in the extreme northeast appears differently on different maps and is not demarcated north of 26° 45′ North Latitude. South of this point the boundary seems to be settled.

CHAPTER 24

The Foundations of Modern China

CHINA as a whole is encircled by countries currently in the political spotlight. In the northeast the U. S. S. R. maintains a common boundary with China. To the southeast and east are strong United States' interests expressed by a half century of ties in the Philippines and recently by participation in the Pacific Theatre of World War II. Also to the east is insular Japan, exhausted by military defeat but still capable of economic and political recovery. To the south and southeast the colonial powers of Britain and France rest their territorial interests against, or even on, Chinese soil. Only in the western and southwestern periphery do geographical barriers appreciably separate China from dynamic neighbors.

Reflecting the modern importance of a marginal location on both the world's largest continent and the largest ocean body, China occupies a centralized position in the Far East. Its bulky area, comprising nearly one fourth of the giant Asiatic land mass, dominates the eastern coast of that continent. Moreover, because of its long, middle latitude coastline, the same great area dominates the western Pacific.

Political Framework of China

As a political region the name *China* may refer to either China Proper or Greater China. *China Proper* is the name generally applied to the original eighteen provinces south of the Great Wall, whereas *Greater China* corresponds roughly to the old Chinese Empire of the Manchu Dynasty, including China Proper, and the four dependencies of Manchuria, Mongolia, Sinkiang, and Tibet before

1878 (see the map on this page). Although China Proper, which is nearly twice the size of the United States east of the Mississippi, comprises less than one half the area of Greater China, it contains over 400,000,000 inhabitants, or nearly ninety per cent of the total population of the larger region. The cul-

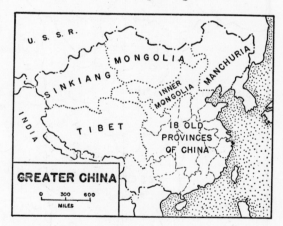

tural, economic, and political aspects of Chinese life stem primarily from the compact region of China Proper, even though repercussions from incidents in any of these fields may be acutely felt in the outermost reaches of Greater China.

The internal boundaries of China as a whole have been in a state of flux since 1878. The nation today has actual or nominal control over thirty-five provinces and the one territory of Farther Tibet (see the map on page 342); how long before these limits are again changed only time will determine. In addition to the eighteen provinces of China Proper prior to 1878, ten new ones were created between 1878 and 1928 from the old Manchu dependencies of Greater China; in 1878 Sinkiang, or Chinese Turkestan, was raised from a dependency to the rank of a province; in 1903 Manchuria was divided into three provinces; in 1928 Inner Mongolia was separated into four provinces, and also Nearer Tibet was divided into two provinces.   The

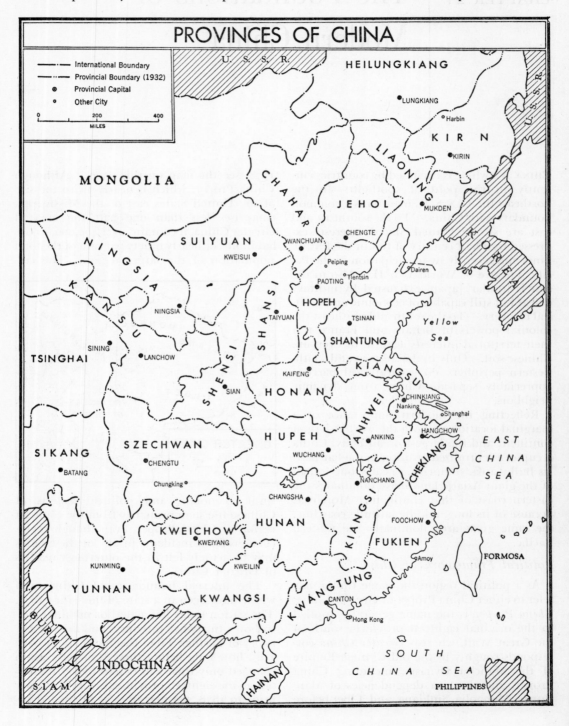

PROVINCES OF CHINA

International Boundary
Provincial Boundary (1932)
⊗ Provincial Capital
• Other City

0   200   400
MILES

number was later raised to thirty-five by the subsequent further division of Manchuria into nine provinces and the addition of Taiwan (Formosa) after World War II. With the possible exception of the Northeastern Provinces in Manchuria and the island of Taiwan these more recently created political divisions actually resemble territories because of their sparse population, great expanses of uninhabitable land, and remoteness from the economic heart of China. For the purpose of discussion in this chapter China Proper refers to the eighteen traditional provinces.

Recent territorial changes. Since World War I the "official" area of China has undergone several major territorial adjustments. In 1921 Outer Mongolia was divided into the Mongolian People's Republic and the Tuvinian People's Republic, both under the control of the Soviet Union. Nevertheless, China still possessed sovereignty in name over all of that area for nearly a quarter of a century thereafter. In 1945, however, Outer Mongolia became independent of China in name as well as in fact. China recognized the independence of the Mongolian People's Republic, and the Tuvinian People's Republic was incorporated into the Soviet Union. Following the military capitulation of Japan to the United Nations in August, 1945, the Chinese took over Taiwan and the Pescadores—areas they had lost in the Sino-Japanese War of 1894-95.* After the surrender of Japan, Britain and Portugal failed to relinquish their territorial rights in Hong Kong and Macao respectively, but France restored its leased territory of Kwangchowan to China.

Boundaries. China's inability to maintain a tight political control over its outlying regions because of its great size and unsettled government has not been conducive to the maintenance of fixed international boundaries. Through the centuries the limits of Chinese political domination have fluctuated with the strength of its centralized government. As national power waned, encroachment by tribesmen or foreign powers became easy. On the other hand, when the internal government was strong, it extended its influence at the expense of the invaders. As a result, boundaries in China other than coastlines have largely been zones. In and around Mongolia, for example, sharp border lines existed only on a map. Actually, the contact area between dominating political and military influences provided the "boundary" at any particular time. This same varying boundary line also existed between Free and Occupied China in the recent war, when China and Japan were generally deadlocked across combat zones and areas of guerilla warfare.

Historical Background

China has had a long and eventful history. Inscriptions, shells, and other relics dating back to the period before the earliest written records give evidence of a relatively advanced culture. Prehistoric inhabitants built fortifications and utilized tools and weapons. From these early times to the fall of the Manchus in 1911, China's history is usually divided into an account of the great dynasties, each with its period of stability and progress during which Chinese culture advanced. Between the fall of one dynasty and the rise of the next there were usually periods of great chaos and civil strife, frequently marked by incursions of nomadic tribesmen from Inner Asia. Shih Huang-ti, who became emperor of China in 246 B.C., first united the warring feudal states. His reign is usually taken to mark the end of feudal and divided China. In 228 B.C. he began construction of the Great Wall of China against the Huns in Mongolia and large areas of northern China.

The Great Wall of China is an emblem of historical demarcation. Its construction aimed to prevent wandering and warlike nomads from descending upon settled farmers. Even though the wall extended for more than 1,500 miles and represented a tremendous effort it failed to accomplish the desired result. When the rainfall outside the Great Wall increased to the extent that crops could be

---

* The return of Taiwan (Formosa) and the Pescadores to China was promised in the Cairo declaration of President Roosevelt, Prime Minister Churchill, and Generalissimo Chiang Kai-shek. Taiwan is historically Chinese, and the population of over six million is almost entirely Formosan-Chinese. Taiwan is an island of 13,840 square miles, important in the production of sugar, tea, and camphor. The only large island possessed by China after the loss of Taiwan in 1895 was Hainan, fifteen miles south of the China coast and one hundred miles east of French Indo-China. In the South China Sea the Chinese have laid claim to the Paracels and have been interested in the Spratly Islands.

grown, colonists from China pressed into Mongolia for more than a hundred miles while the nomads retreated to grasslands farther north. As the climatic cycle progressed and the rains failed, the farmers retreated southward and nomads seeking grasslands invaded the area inside the Great Wall.*

Following a civil war at the death of Shih Huang-ti came the establishment of the Han dynasty, which lasted from 206 B.C. to 220 A.D. Under this dynasty the empire greatly expanded beyond the two river valleys of the Hwang Ho and the Yangtze, the Huns were effectively restrained, and Chinese overland travelers brought acquaintance and trade with other civilizations in India, Persia, and the Western world. The Han emperors also set up a uniform system of education and of literary degrees throughout China that has continued the intellectual solidarity of that great and expanding country into modern times. Despite many changes in the political fortune of China since the Han days, these have not affected her basic character; despite divisions she has always recovered her unity ultimately; despite conquerors she has always absorbed and assimilated the victor eventually.

During the period in which Europe was emerging from its limited medieval world and entering an era of exploration and colonization, China continued to develop its own culture and remained virtually untouched by the developments of Western civilization. Overland and maritime expeditions from Europe did succeed in reaching China in search of Oriental luxury goods, such as silk, tin, and porcelain, but they were too infrequent to be commercially significant on a large scale or to leave any lasting impressions. Until the establishment of regular ocean trade routes China faced Inner Asia, where through the Jade Gate outside contact was maintained by caravan. The Pacific Ocean served only as a little-used back door.

The Chinese closely restricted foreign activities, and at the end of the eighteenth century European traders had access only to Canton and the Portuguese port of Macao. In the nineteenth century, however, China began to play an important part in the interna-

tional politics and commerce of the West. The Europeans, anxious to expand their colonial and mercantile frontiers, began to make regular appearances in the Far East.* After the Anglo-Chinese War of 1839–42 they succeeded in opening China to foreign trade. This penetration was the general signal for Western nations to make inroads upon China politically as well as commercially. The technique of controlling Chinese trade was through treaties that extended special commercial and political privileges in "treaty ports." By this method a country obtained an area in a Chinese port in which all control was outside the jurisdiction of Chinese law. Concessions and extraterritoriality were largely responsible for much of the later friction between China and other countries. At the close of the Sino-Japanese War in 1895 there followed an increased scramble for Chinese leases, concessions, and cessions by European countries that led to the Boxer Rebellion in 1900, which was suppressed by an international force.

In addition to the threat of the Western Powers who participated in Chinese trade, there was the menace of a growing and militant Japan in the late 1800's. Japan exerted pressure on China, not only for trade concessions but for political control as well.

From the Sino-Japanese War until the end of World War II the Japanese tended to expand their power over China. In 1931 Manchuria was seized. In 1933 the border province of Jehol was cut off as a buffer area. Finally Japanese attempts to seize China's five northern provinces precipitated resistance by Chiang Kai-shek, who had rallied most of China to his support, and resulted in the Sino-Japanese conflict that began in 1937.

Meanwhile, partly as a result of the policies of the Manchu rulers, agitation increased for the overthrow of the monarchy. In 1911 a revolution broke out in Wuchang, and on December 27 Dr. Sun Yat-sen became the first President of the Provisional Chinese Republic. However, a republican government in China failed to produce political unity; many

---

* The Great Wall of China is said to be the only work of man on the face of the earth that could be viewed from Mars.

* During the sixteenth century Spanish and Portuguese traders visited the Far East in appreciable numbers, and in the early part of the seventeenth century English and Dutch traders followed. These movements, however, were sporadic, and did not succeed in establishing permanent commercial routes between Europe and the Orient.

of the provinces were governed by practically independent warlords. In 1926 the Kuomintang, the party of Dr. Sun Yat-sen—the leadership of which had fallen to Chiang Kai-shek after Dr. Sun's death the previous year—began the northern military drive from Canton that ended in 1928 with the capture of Peking by the Kuomintang forces. Chiang Kai-shek still remains in power in China despite an inefficient, graft-ridden government, a shattered economy, and constant pressure in the north from Chinese Communist armies.

Physical Features

China is continental in its dimensions. With an area of more than three and three-quarter million square miles Greater China is larger than continental United States and Mexico together. In terms of latitude on the continent of North America China reaches from south of Mexico City to the southern part of Alaska. The great cities of Peiping, Shanghai, and Canton are comparable in latitude to Philadelphia, Jacksonville, and Havana, respectively. No part of China Proper, however, extends farther north in latitude than New York City. Although the maximum east-west extent of Greater China is roughly equivalent to the continental width of the United States, the country's axis of general activity trends north and south parallel to the Pacific Coast. This direction of activity is in vivid contrast to the east-west trends of the United States and the Soviet Union.

Relief. The great diversity of land forms in Greater China is a fundamental influence in the cultural and economic life of the country. Knotty mountainous regions, broad plateau areas, expansive lowlands, and narrow river valleys play equally important roles in the physiographic history of the area. Nevertheless, the complex nature of surface features does not prevent a division into broad topographic regions, each with its own distinctive type of terrain and its accompanying cultural response.

MAJOR TOPOGRAPHIC REGIONS. The inaccessibility of the Tibetan region, location of the fabulous Shangri-la, acts as a rigid barrier to trade and transportation as well as to cultural diffusion. High plateaus in Tibet and encircling mountain ranges dominate the southwestern part of Greater China. In this area, known as the "roof of the world," elevations range from 12,000 feet above sea level to peaks more than twice that height, and average 16,000 feet in elevation.

North of the high, rugged Tibetan area, in the northwestern part of Greater China, the terrain merges into a relatively low but barren plateau interspersed with hills and mountains. Rather than forbidding elevations, vast distances and extensive desert or semi-desert stretches restricted the development of Chinese overland commerce to long, thin caravan trains into and through the area. Somewhat like the plateau country of the American west between California and Colorado, this type of relief makes up the great bulk of Sinkiang and Mongolia.

The entire area of southeastern China is preponderantly mountainous, but its elevations, typically from 4,000 to 6,000 feet, are much lower than those of the Tibetan highlands to the west. Despite the rugged relief, the provinces of southeastern China are well peopled. River valleys and small coastal plains provide some level land capable of intensive utilization. The largest lowland area is the valley of the Si Kiang, which flows into the sea past Canton and Hong Kong.* Regions of dense settlement, however, are usually isolated from one another by any modern mode of transportation except the airplane.

The central and northern parts of China Proper consist of mountain chains trailing seaward from the massive Tibetan highlands. Relatively high and complex in the west, these chains divide and sub-divide as they extend eastward, decreasing in altitude to the point where they lose their identity before reaching the coast. The rough Shantung Peninsula projecting seaward is the only marked exception to this pattern. Flowing between mountain chains the Yangtze Kiang and Hwang Ho reach the sea in valleys that become spacious lowlands near their mouths. Tremendous populations, including many of China's great cities, are clustered in these valleys and lowlands.

The last of the broad physical regions of Greater China, Manchuria, is a huge lowland plain in northeastern China extending north and south between mountainous borderlands. It has no dominating river like the Yangtze or Hwang, but otherwise resembles a great val-

* In Chinese "Kiang" and "Ho" mean river. Thus, Si Kiang is equivalent to saying Si River.

ley, with a chain of important cities extending along the longitudinal axis.

The pattern of relief in China, as is discussed later, influences the agricultural pattern, the population pattern, the transportation pattern, and the commercial pattern. The political pattern with its far-reaching zones of influence has been less directly affected by the terrain, but actual military conflict on Chinese soil never failed to be oriented by the factor of relief, upon which was based successful or unsuccessful defensive or offensive action. In this connection guerrilla warfare by Chinese soldiers in hilly regions prevented the Japanese in World War II from fully occupying sections in which they had but little trouble in capturing the lowland areas.

Climate. The second great physical feature of China is climate, which combines with relief to help or hinder human activity and ambition. Great size and the diversity of relief in combination give Greater China a wide variety of climates. The latitudinal range from south of the Tropic of Cancer to the northern part of the temperate zone provides broad temperature differences, and the tremendous east-west extent affects the influence of the ocean as a source of moisture for rainfall. In turn, the elevations of mountainous regions bring about lower temperatures and may likewise influence the rainfall because of exposure to moisture-bearing winds. Cyclonic storms and monsoon winds, both laden with great quantities of moisture, tend to strike the southern rather than the northern coastal sections, with the result that the amount of rainfall decreases from south to north as well as from east to west.

In southeast China the continuous warmth and copious rainfall give the lowland areas a high and dependable agricultural utilization. Along the extreme southern coast the average temperature for the coldest month of the year stays above 60° F., and the total rainfall may exceed 80 inches on the more exposed slopes. To the north and west the climatic factor becomes steadily more adverse to the Chinese farmer. The winters are longer, limiting the growing season to one crop per year north of the Yangtze Valley in comparison to two, and even three, crops during a single growing season in the south. Rainfall not only diminishes toward the north and in the interior,

but becomes more undependable. In the North China Plain droughts accompanied by famines are common, and, on the other hand, unusually heavy rainfall during some years causes floods fully as devastating to food crops and in the loss of life.

Throughout the interior of China the moderating effect of the ocean is missing, making the summers hot and winters cold. Of greater import to human development, however, is the lack of rainfall. Beyond the western margins of China Proper the landscape is semiarid at best, and often arid to the point of being totally inhospitable to man's quest for a livelihood. Only isolated pockets in which irrigation water is available present exceptions to the sparse populations that prevail in the expansive interior reaches of Greater China.

Natural resources. The total inventory of physical resources possessed by China includes soil, natural vegetation, and minerals. In total quantity many items, such as millions of tons of coal reserves, or thousands of square miles of arable land, sound impressive. In terms of resources per capita, however, the situation is less fortunate. In addition, the inability of the Chinese in many instances to efficiently utilize their mineral resources definitely limits their economy. As an example, China, exclusive of Manchuria, produced in 1936 around six pounds of iron ore per inhabitant as compared to over 850 pounds produced per person in the United States during the same year.

For centuries the Chinese have utilized to the fullest extent their precious soil, and have almost denuded the timber and other natural plant growth from accessible regions. Only mineral resources remain as the potential that holds any real promise of further development on an appreciable scale.

Chinese and foreign interests alike have made numerous surveys and estimates as to the existing quantities of coal, metals, petroleum, and water power. Coal reserves are tremendous; China ranks fourth in the world in this source of power. Although coal deposits are scattered throughout the Chinese provinces, about 80 per cent of them are concentrated in Shensi and Shansi. In iron ore the future holds less hope, for the most careful estimates place total reserves at only about one twentieth those of the United States. It is now mined principally in the lower Yangtze Valley where the ores are not extensive but among the richest in the world. The large deposits in southern Manchuria, although actively exploited by the Japanese during their occupation of that area, are low in metallic content. Tin, mined in Yunnan and southwest Szechwan, is the major export mineral under normal conditions. Of some of the more rare minerals, notably antimony and tungsten, China is normally the world's leading producer. Other minerals of which China has deposits being mined are manganese, mercury, copper, lead, zinc, gold, silver, bismuth ore, uranium, molybdenum, and salt. Estimated petroleum reserves are modest, although oil-bearing shale in Manchuria and the possibility of making synthetic gasoline from coal brighten the picture. Oil wells on a small scale are now worked notably in Kansu Province. Potential hydroelectric energy is most abundant in the more rainy mountainous areas of southern China.

In most instances actual production of Chinese mineral resources is negligible when compared to the existing deposits. Only Japanese exploitation in Manchuria and the extraction of metals from a few accessible deposits in China Proper have dug deep into China's stock of mineral wealth.

Economic Pattern

Agriculture. About four fifths of the people of China look to the soil for their sustenance. For countless generations the intensive cultivation of arable land has been the means of supporting hundreds of millions of people. The agricultural economy is based upon the family unit whereby a small parcel of land, which at best furnishes a precarious living, is handed down from generation to generation.* Floods, famines, wars, and taxes combine with the scarcity of land, primitive conditions, and large families to prevent the emerging of China as a strong modern power except by a long, slow, uphill climb. Occupations other than farming primarily concern foreign powers in their economic penetration of China, but the effects of the country's major activity cannot be escaped. Impoverished agricultural conditions find na-

* The average Chinese farm contains around four acres.

tion-wide expression in low living standards, low buying power, and poor means of transportation.

Crop types and agricultural techniques vary considerably from place to place throughout China. Rice, wheat, and millet, which are the three most important food crops, occupy more than two thirds of the cultivated area. North China with its low rainfall and short growing season is primarily a land of wheat and small grains, such as millet, kaoliang, and barley. Corn, beans, and peas are also items of local diet. In the semiarid area to the northwest dry farming and animal husbandry take precedent over intensively cultivated crops. However, such animals as goats, poultry, and especially pigs are not localized; they may be found throughout China on even the smallest farms as a modest supplement to the money income or as additional food items.

South China, including the Yangtze Valley, is known broadly as the rice region. Heavy rainfall and a long growing season, however, permit a wide diversity of crops. Supplementing rice as the great staple of the area are many temperate and subtropical products used as money crops or for subsistence. Tea, the chief beverage, is grown mainly on the central uplands and coastal ranges. Silkworm culture, practiced widely and especially in the Yangtze Valley, yields over 200,000 tons of cocoons in a normal year. Cotton, the major purely industrial crop, may run as high as four million bales a year. Soybeans are of ever increasing importance. Other crops include sugar, indigo, tobacco, sweet potatoes, cereals, legumes, and fruits. South China can produce more per unit of land, but it also has a greater population density to support.

Transportation. Physical barriers and great distances common to the western frontier along with little early Western trade along the Pacific seacoast severely limited adequate contact with the Western world. Except for a selected few port cities China has remained rather well isolated even from neighboring countries. Occupation of the coastal zone cities by Japan in the recent war could result in nothing other than a huge blockade for China. Outside aid by helpful allies became dependent upon a small number of western approaches in the form of caravan trails, supply highways, and freight airways.

These emergency supply roads had their counterpart in the Middle Ages, before the advent of ocean trade routes, when nomadic trails and silk and jade caravan routes from Siberia and Central Asia skirted the desert stretches of the Gobi and Sinkiang. In modern times, when Chinese commerce first became stifled along the coast by the Japanese, help from Russia trickled along these historic western roads by auto caravan, pack train, and to a lesser extent, by air. More positive help came from the United States over the world-famous Burma Road. Built by the Chinese government between 1937 and 1939, the road stands as a masterpiece of engineering over terrain cut by deep gorges. Streams of trucks winding over the tortuous highway carried much needed goods from the Burma railhead at Lashio to the leading centers of distribution for Free China; Kunming, Chungking, Chengtu, and Suifu (Suchow). The Japanese, however, succeeded in closing the road in their conquest of Burma in the spring of 1942. The Burma Road was replaced by transport aircraft operating over "the Hump" between southwest China and northeast India and also later by motor caravans transporting equipment and fire-power over the newly constructed Ledo Road (renamed Stilwell Road) from Assam across North Burma to a northern sector of the Burma Road. Early in 1945 the Burma Road was reopened to convoys carrying military supplies. It was the airways, however, that proved the lifelines of China during the war period; only they were able to span China's great distances and link its far-flung parts with themselves and with the outside. As an example of air service from outside, at the close of the war in 1945 about 75,000 tons of supplies per month, most of it from the United States, were being flown into Free China over "the Hump" air route to the Chungking government.

One of China's great handicaps in achieving the status of a world power can be traced to poor transportation facilities. The nation cannot hope to capitalize on its favorable location, its natural wealth, and its colossal population without an efficient method of interregional exchange for distribution and assembly of goods, and without ease of personal travel. Likewise, transportation is the key to political control, if only evidenced by the successful inroad of foreign powers in their bid for trade concessions. Granted that China has progressed to a tremendous degree since the days of the Manchus, the benefits of any progress have failed to reach the preponderant mass of population (see the map on page 349). Primitive methods have prevailed in providing a means of transport throughout most of the country. Human porters, crude two-wheeled carts, and tiny river and canal craft all reflect the extent to which mechanical power is lacking. Even animal power is at a premium, and the average Chinese coolie or peasant has no choice than the use of his own body to carry out his meager transportation needs.* Calculation of miles per day instead of per hour typifies the average Chinese conception of travel involving any considerable distance.

Only in the country's few commercial areas, especially those developed by foreign enterprise, are there semblances of modern transport. Concentrated largely in North China and Manchuria and in the lower Yangtze basin, China's railroads, highways, important waterways, and airways tend to radiate only from these centers of external influence. Most notable are Shanghai and Hankow, in the rich valley of the Yangtze Kiang; Tientsin and Peiping, in the North China Plain; Canton and British Hong Kong, at the mouth of the Si Kiang; and Harbin, Mukden, Changchun, and Dairen, in the plains of Manchuria. These modern facilities, as limited as they are for China's great population, stand as the nuclei for future development of Chinese communications both internal and external.

RAILROADS. The rail pattern of Greater China is largely limited to the northeastern part of the country (see the map on page 349). Manchuria alone has about one half of the 15,000 miles of railroads, and the bulk of the remaining mileage serves the North China Plain and the lower part of the Yangtze Valley. Southern China has but a few isolated lines and western China is entirely without railways. Trans-China rail travel has been non-existent, although interior railheads,

---

* Primitive means of transportation must not be under-rated, however, for it was by human effort that the Chinese people were able to move their government, education facilities, and a large proportion of their industry westward to the interior of the country where a stand could be taken against the Japanese penetration in the east.

such as those at Paotow and the Sian area, have served as "jumping off" places for long hauls into the western regions of Greater China. The major portion of the traffic is normally between cities strong in foreign in-fluence. Prewar statistics (1936) show that the five heaviest traffic segments were from Shanghai to Nanking, Shanghai to Ningpo via Hangchow, Peiping to Hankow, Tientsin to Nanking, and the southern section of the

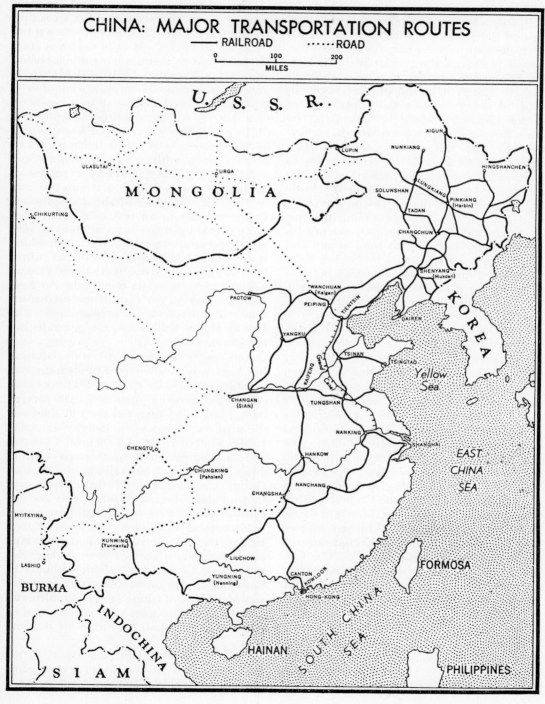

CHINA: MAJOR TRANSPORTATION ROUTES
—— RAILROAD   ······ ROAD

0   100   200
MILES

Canton-Hankow line. These exclude the Manchurian railways, which were built by Japanese and Russian as well as Chinese interests and which were intensively developed by the Japanese after their penetration of the area in 1931.

In only a few instances do rail lines extend beyond the political borders of China. An alternate route of the Trans-Siberian Railway crosses the central Manchurian plain via Harbin between the border town of Manchouli and the eastern terminal of Vladivostok in maritime Siberia. This short cut, south of the Siberian border along the Amur River, reduces traveling time between Moscow and the Orient. Two rail routes cross the Manchurian border into Korea, both leading to Fusan, where overnight steamer service across the narrow straits to Shimonoseki closely linked Japan with those cities on the mainland that were in her sphere of influence until 1945. In the south the French extended a narrow gauge railway line from Hanoi and the port city of Haiphong in French Indo-China to Kunming, over 300 miles into the plateau country of South China. This project strengthened the French position in southern China, but it also provided an outlet to the landlocked economy of Yunnan province.

The lack of railroads in the interior and western part of Greater China accentuated her plight in the Sino-Japanese conflict between 1937 and 1945. Of the 7,500 miles of railroads in China (excluding Manchuria), only 450, or six per cent, were not lost to Japan by capture or destruction. Of an additional 1,175 miles built by the Chinese during the war, only 295 miles, or twenty-five per cent, remained in their hands intact. The French-built line from Kunming to French Indo-China was destroyed by the Chinese in their sector in 1940 to prevent its falling into enemy hands in usable condition. This self-inflicted sabotage left China entirely without rail connections with the outside world. The Chinese have a special post-war interest in the re-establishment of this railroad between Kunming and the French Indo-China coast, for it provides Yunnan province with a commercial outlet.

ROADS. In addition to the important supply highways of western China already discussed, there are extensive road systems in the eastern and central provinces. The total

of 50,000 miles for the modern highway system sounds impressive; but since good paved or all-weather roads are not extensive, the highway pattern does not exert a strong unifying influence over the nation.

WATER TRANSPORTATION. An extensive coast line, one long river, and flat areas suitable for canals have all fostered water transportation in China. Most of the great cities of China owe their size to port development, and countless rural and village dwellers rely upon the waterways as the sole means of moving themselves and their goods from one place to another. An outstanding example of a Chinese waterway is the Yangtze Kiang, which has some 200,000,000 people living within its basin. Along with tributary streams and canals, this gigantic water highway represents the lifeline of travel from Szechwan province to the coast, a distance of about 2,000 miles. In the summer ocean vessels of 10,000 tons can navigate upstream as far as Hankow (630 miles) and smaller steamers reach Chungking (1,427 miles) and beyond. Shanghai, which in its location within easy reach of the Yangtze has long been the major port in the Far East, accounted for 50 per cent of the total maritime customs revenue in prewar days. The Hwang Ho, or Yellow River, is generally not navigable.

AIR TRANSPORTATION. Air transportation in China, a relatively recent innovation, had significant prewar development. The network established between 1929 and 1937 covered more route miles than did the rail lines (see the map on facing page). Service extended to the western cities of Lanchow, Chengtu, and Chungking, and the southern city of Kunming, none of which had rail connections with Chinese coastal cities. Scheduled flights over most of the routes were infrequent and because of the high cost of air transport, only a small number of Chinese benefited. Nevertheless, the groundwork was laid for a type of transportation that could span long distances and tap remote regions without the laborious mile-by-mile construction of surface routes. Many of China's major problems attributable to poor internal transportation facilities can be solved by future air development.

China is scheduled to play a part in the global air pattern that is presently being formed. World War II interrupted the establishment of around-the-world air service through China. The British Colony of Hong Kong was tapped by both Pan American Airways and British Imperial Airways, the latter from London along the southern periphery of Eurasia, and the former from the United States across the Pacific. With transoceanic flying now far beyond the experimental stage,

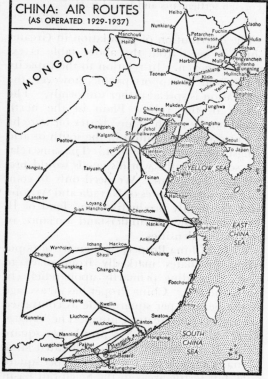

CHINA: AIR ROUTES
(AS OPERATED 1929-1937)

the favorable position of China's large commercial cities in eastern Asia makes them suitable termini along far-reaching air routes from other continents. Within two years after the close of World War II in the Pacific regular air schedules had been initiated between China and the United States.

Commercial and industrial capacity. Sharp differences of opinion exist as to whether or not the Chinese Republic will ever become a powerful industrial nation. A large area, fair natural resources, and hundreds of millions of people as a labor supply and market suggest a strong potential. Nevertheless, the development of large-scale industries up to the present time has been negligible. Lack of political unity, backwardness of the great majority of population,

and totally inadequate transportation facilities are perhaps the prime shortcomings that have hindered industrial advancement.

Certain large cities in prewar China, including Shanghai, Nanking, Hankow, Canton, Tsingtao, Tientsin, and Mukden, were nuclei of industrial districts. Rather than resembling Pittsburgh or the Ruhr Valley of Germany, these districts were largely known for the manufacture and processing of products for local consumption. Coal, cotton textiles, cement, salt, flour, and cigarettes were typical commodities. In Manchuria the Japanese went a step further and expanded an iron and steel industry capable of bolstering their military machine.

Export trade was for a time largely limited to tea and silk; later it included numerous unprocessed agricultural items such as textile fibers, animal and animal products, and spices. Frozen eggs and hog bristles exemplified two specialties from China that became well known in Europe and the United States, the latter as a base for brushes and the former as a cheap ingredient in manufactured foods. Imports depended upon simple needs, such as kerosene, raw cotton, yarn and thread, cotton cloth, matches, sugar, dyes, paints, paper, chemicals, and other basic commodities universally needed and not too expensive to be purchased by relatively large numbers of people. Almost all goods of complex manufacture utilized in the country were also imported.

The existing type of industry and commerce will definitely not permit the Chinese to assume the role of a great power in the postwar world. An enlightened policy toward internal economy is a prerequisite toward the building of a strong country. The Kuomintang party, organized on the principles of Dr. Sun Yat-sen, sought the economic development of the country as well as a solution for strictly political problems.

In the past the Chinese have suffered from two major political ills that have markedly decreased any opportunity for economic stability or maturity. First, foreign commercial infiltration tended to delegate Chinese-owned and -operated interests to less important roles in their own country. American and European interests largely controlled commercial and industrial development for economic gain, but the Japanese sought extensive control in every way possible as a part of their plan of conquest and expansion. Second, disunity, friction, and armed disagreement between various regions and groups within China have undermined the execution of any constructive programs that have been initiated. The evils of war lords as a drain on the countryside have long operated as a deterrent to the development of China's economy.

The Human Element

Few journalists can refrain from the use of the expression "teeming millions" in writing of the population of China. The hundreds of millions of people living in China represent between 20 and 25 per cent of the earth's inhabitants. When properly directed, a large population may be the basis of national strength, or, when the peoples are not welded into a cohesive unit, as in the case of China, it may present some of the most weighty unsolved problems facing a nation.

The average Chinese worker struggles to eke a living from the tiny bit of soil allotted him or from his meager share of the country's other resources. In total, the problems of the individual become the problems of the nation. These problems can be solved only when a national pattern of economic existence and security converts the small population units, such as the family, or the community, into productive units of the total economy. In other words, solution to these serious problems must come from the top—the government. At least until today no ruling body has proved itself capable of coping satisfactorily with these problems.

Population. Because the number of people living in China has never been accurately determined, estimates or sample counts must replace census statistics in any population study. The estimate of the total population of Greater China varies from source to source, but the most authentic sources approximate a figure of about 455,000,000, excluding Outer Mongolia. Latest estimates regarded as moderately reliable cover the period from 1936 to 1940. The following table gives in round numbers the population of the various political regions that made up Greater China during the early years of the war with Japan. It should be used for comparative purposes

rather than as a source of accurate population data: *

China Proper (18 traditional provinces south of the Great Wall)	412,000,000
Five outer provinces	7,250,000
Manchuria, including Jehol	43,250,000
Outer Mongolia and Tannu Tuva ..	1,000,000
Sinkiang	4,250,000
Farther Tibet	1,500,000
(Foreign settlements and leased territory)	4,500,000

The distribution of population in Greater China as seen from the above table is extremely uneven. In relation to the capacity of the land to support people, however, the population is spread rather uniformly. The farmer of the Yellow Plain in the north would not be much, if any, better off were he to go to crowded Canton in the south or arid Ningsia province in the west. The same relative scarcity of the world's goods would prevail at either point. We need only to compare our desert wastes of Nevada and Arizona with the highly productive crop land of Illinois and Iowa to understand variance in population densities.

Within China Proper, the density of population fluctuates markedly from place to place, depending primarily upon relief, climate, and soil. China Proper has an average of 180 persons per square mile as contrasted to only 105 for Greater China. The Yangtze River valley supports 847 people per square mile. If one considers only cultivated land, China as a whole has 1,485 persons per square mile, but fertile areas in the Szechwan Basin have more than 3,000 per square mile. These figures plainly illustrate why average Chinese farms must support about two persons per acre.

The total population of China steadily increases despite numerous checks that take incredible toll of life. Disease, starvation, floods, earthquakes, and wars all stimulate the death rate, but never sufficiently to overtake the high rate of birth. Even the estimated loss of five or six million lives during the recent war, while appalling as a casualty list, only represents a little over one per cent of the total population. Based upon past demographic records, the China of the year

* Totals based upon best available figures as given by George Cressey in *Asia's Lands and Peoples* (McGraw-Hill, 1944), pp. 42-46.

2000 will have a population approaching one billion, or nearly one half of the earth's present population.

Cities. China has a number of large cities despite the preponderance of rural dwellers.* Shanghai, estimated to have nearly three and a half million people (including suburban areas), stands among the ten greatest cities in the world. Nanking, the present day capital, and Peiping (formerly called Peking), the capital prior to 1928, each contains more than a million and a half inhabitants. The great northern port city of Tientsin, only sixty miles distant from Peiping, has a million and a quarter people. Three other cities, Canton (southern port), Hankow (middle Yangtze port), and Mukden (Manchurian metropolis) have populations ranging from three quarters of a million to a million or more. Chungking and Chengtu, because of their influx of wartime populations, were estimated to have reached one million or more people each during the war period. Although not in Chinese territory, Hong Kong, situated about ninety miles south of Canton, likewise has a population of more than a million (see the map on this page).** Most of the provincial capitals are metropolitan centers for the political areas they serve. Several of these, including Changsha, Hangchow, Kweilin, and Tsinan, have populations that put them in the "one-half million" class.

A direct relationship can be traced between the size of Chinese cities and the transportation facilities at hand. Most of the larger cities have coastal or river sites that encouraged port development. In some instances the junction or crossing of land routes stimulated the growth of commercial centers. The only appreciable exception to this correlation between urban population and means of

* Population figures for Chinese cities are likely to be undependable. Those presented in this discussion, although taken from the most authentic sources, are only rough approximations. Further, shifts of population because of wartime conditions and postwar disruption have frequently swollen or deflated the number of inhabitants in many of China's urban centers.

** The British Crown Colony of Hong Kong includes the thirty-two square mile island of Hong Kong as well as territory on the mainland (Kowloon, 3 square miles, and the "New Territories," 356 square miles). The true urban center is the city of Victoria located on the island of Hong Kong. The term Hong Kong is popularly used to designate the city of Victoria rather than the island or the entire British Colony.

transportation lies in the population impetus given to cities selected as capitals, either national or to a lesser extent provincial.

Racial characteristics. The difficulty of reaching Chinese territory before the advent of modern transportation prevented racial mixture on a large scale. In the heart of China Proper the ethnological uniformity is remarkable in the light of the number of people involved. Although many types of Chi-

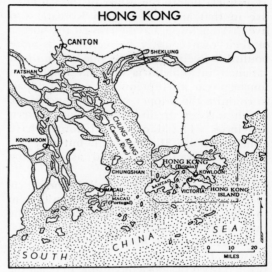

nese cultures sprang up in the various provinces, homogeneity with respect to human nature, philosophical ideology, a consistent written language, and certain physical traits remains easily recognizable throughout. Only in the western regions of Greater China, in the southwestern part of China Proper, and in Manchuria are there significant numbers of non-Chinese peoples—possibly a total of around twenty-eight million.

If the non-Chinese peoples of Greater China are considered as minorities, they do not present the racial problems commonly associated with minority groups in Europe. Internecine wars in China reflect political rather than ethnological differences.

The natives of Mongolia, Tibet, and Sinkiang consist of varied racial stocks, including Mongols, Tibetans, Mongol-Turks, Turkic-Tartars, and Tungans, but their interests as well as their remote location have resulted in their being virtually independent from direct Chinese political control. In the hill and mountain regions of southwestern China

Proper live the Lolo, Miao-Tye, and other non-Chinese aborigines. Although actually outnumbering the Chinese in some areas, they occupy the more backward sections where they were evidently driven by the Chinese. Ruled for the most part by tribal chieftains, they are semi-independent in relation to the government of China.

More than a million Manchus, remnants of the racial stock dominating the region of Manchuria before the influx of the Chinese, live in that area. A million Koreans also live in Manchuria, having crossed the border of their own country in search of a more bountiful livelihood. The one-half million Japanese in Manchuria were the result of a fourteen-year attempt on the part of Japan to colonize the puppet state of Manchukuo, which was set up in China's Northeastern Provinces. The Manchus and Koreans have remained politically dormant, but the Japanese immigrants were used as a "flying wedge" in assailing China.

Language. Common to all Chinese people, the single written language would seem to offer the advantages of unification. The inherent difficulties of a language with 40,000 characters, however, have made it almost impossible for the Chinese to distribute the printed word in sufficient volume to reach the mass of the population. It is also likely that the inability to properly utilize the written language contributed to the growth of the many dialects, especially in the more remote mountainous areas.

The most important dialect spoken in China is the so-called Mandarin, basis for the modern "National Language," which covers China Proper in and north of the Yangtze River valley. Thus, it is spoken by about three hundred million people. In various other parts of Greater China occur about 45 dialects, including those used by non-Chinese peoples. In the southeastern provinces, where communities are frequently separated by topographical barriers, inhabitants in neighboring towns or cities may not be able to understand each other. An interesting linguistic device used for carrying on business along Chinese coastal areas has been "pidgin English," consisting principally of a few basic English words arranged in the Chinese word order.

Religion. The three indigenous religions of China are (1) Confucianism, with its outward practice of ancestral worship; (2) Buddhism, which actually came from India; and (3) Taoism, which copied most of the ritual of Buddhism. Most individual Chinese, strangely enough to those of the Western world, do not consider it inconsistent to be devotees of and to profess all three of these religions. One reason for this apparent anomaly is that the Chinese tend to consider Confucianism and Taoism as political philosophies rather than as religions. Mohammedanism, introduced into China from western Asia is estimated to have about 48 million followers, located largely in Sinkiang, Yunnan, Szechwan, Shensi, Shansi, Kansu, Shantung, Honan, and Hupeh. Christianity has grown in China in the last decades, having been spread by missionaries of many branches of the religion.

National stamina. A good part of this chapter has dealt with the handicaps facing China—factors both geographical and political that have operated to prevent the nation from ranking as a major world power. Topographical barriers, droughts, floods, pressure of population, lack of transportation facilities, industrial backwardness, and internal political strife are but a few of the handicaps that have long choked the modern concept of progress in China. More recently, eight years of a life-and-death struggle against Japan have left in their wake a trail of physical devastation, economic chaos, and political dissension. Instead of collapsing completely under these seemingly overpowering factors, the nation is now slowly showing signs of making a bid for a place in the sun. Possibly this intangible quality to survive and benefit from disaster can be attributed to the people themselves as an expression of their "National Spirit." Evidences of a "New China" come largely from the spirit displayed during the war years. Most symbolic was the gigantic migration of patriots to the central and western provinces where the unoccupied portion of the country continued successfully to represent the interests of the entire nation. This great accomplishment turned the attention of the world to some of the areas of Greater China peripheral to its original economic heart.

*Politico-Geographic Aspects of
Greater China*

The four great dependencies of the Manchus—Manchuria, Sinkiang, Tibet, and Mongolia—located outside the historic eighteen provinces of China Proper have been subjected to a combination of internal and external factors that have created special conditions peculiar to the political balance in each area. On the one hand, the Chinese have in some cases created provinces from all or parts of these outlying areas, quite possibly as an attempt to solidify national unity at a time of strong foreign pressure. On the other hand, the influence of foreign powers has in all cases been significant in the development of Greater China.

Manchuria. This land has been an arena of conflict among China, Russia and Japan. Possessing an area of more than three times that of Japan Proper and a population of about forty million, Manchuria by her strategic location is a focal point of attention in the international politics of the Far East. Resources in coal, iron, and foodstuffs, such as wheat and soybeans, have likewise attracted surrounding nations.

Urban and commercial life in Manchuria has as its axis a north-south chain of large cities extending from Harbin in the north central plains region to Dairen, southern gateway to the region (see the map on this page). This longitudinal string of cities includes Mukden, with an estimated population of about a million, and Changchun, the traditional Chinese provincial capital. Associated with Dairen is nearby Port Arthur, ice-free naval base of historic interest, which was controlled by Russia between 1898 and her war with Japan in 1904–05.

After the Soviet Union declared war on Japan in the summer of 1945, Manchuria was quickly occupied and the Japanese puppet regime of Manchukuo collapsed. After fourteen years of control by Japan, Manchuria reverted to China, reverting to its previous status as the Northeastern Provinces. In the Sino-Russian agreement of August, 1945, the Soviet Union agreed to respect Chinese sovereignty over Manchuria. Port Arthur became a Russian naval base for thirty years, but the Chinese navy had theoretical access to it.

Dairen, the commercial port, was theoretically shared on equal terms by China and Russia. The Soviet Union and China became co-owners for thirty years of the Chinese Eastern Railway and the South Manchuria Railway, terminating at Vladivostok and Dairen, respectively. After the end of the Pacific War in 1945 Manchuria became a battleground

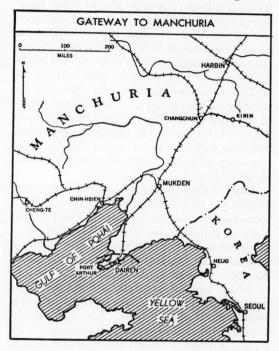

GATEWAY TO MANCHURIA

between Chinese Communist and Chinese Kuomintang armies.

Sinkiang. Chinese Turkestan, or the "New Borderland," is expressed politically as Sinkiang. Its area is about 700,000 square miles. Historical interest in the area has centered in the command of low-level routes through Inner Asia between the East and the West. Strings of oases along both the northern and southern slopes of the high Tien Shan range fostered the caravan trails that once provided China with its primary contact with the Occidental world.

The economy of present-day Sinkiang is focused upon the oases, for otherwise the region is largely barren. Cotton, wheat, millet, kaoliang, rice, beans, tobacco, and fruits all flourish when irrigated by water from the streams or underground channels of the oases. Away from the desert oases in the less arid stretches grasslands support pastoralism as the second most important agricultural industry. Mineral resources of Sinkiang are not yet adequately surveyed, but it is known that gold, iron, copper, coal, and petroleum are present in some quantity. Much of the world's jade comes from this region.

Although Sinkiang is a Chinese province, Russian influence was dominant from 1933–43. In the latter year the Soviets withdrew completely and in 1945 they formally expressed political disinterestedness in Sinkiang. However, Soviet influence in northwestern Sinkiang was increasing in 1948. With the end of the Sino-Japanese war in 1945 the Chinese may be more interested in the China of the Pacific coast than in the China of Inner Asia. If this possibility proves to be the case, Sinkiang will have to rely upon its own initiative or upon the Soviets for economic advancement.

Tibet. Largely a plateau between the lofty Himalayas in the south and the Altyn Tagh mountain system in the north, Tibet is perhaps as remote from the paths of modern civilization as the interior of the Arabian Peninsula or the frozen wastes of the Polar North. The area of the region, large sections of which are unexplored, is 800,000 square miles. Great altitude has preserved isolation from the rest of the world. Lhasa, capital of Farther Tibet and center of Lamaism with its priest rulers, is almost legendary because of its inaccessibility. Locally, however, the city is the hub of the road system that does exist in Tibet. For the most part the country is desolate and void of vegetation; only in a few favorable places of relatively low elevation can people successfully live by grazing or simple agricultural activities. Such trade as exists is largely with India.

Politically, Tibet is divided into Nearer Tibet, made up of two Chinese provinces, and Farther Tibet, a territory that in many respects is independent. The latter is not recognized as being fully independent and Chinese sovereignty remains, although in practice British influence is strong and Russia has interest in the area. It is likely that Farther Tibet will eventually gain formal independence from China.

Mongolia. The former Manchu dependency, which has an area of about 800,000 square miles, has been divided into Outer and Inner Mongolia. The latter is made up of four modern Chinese Provinces, but the former is now lost to China. After a plebiscite in October, 1945, revealed a vote of 483,-291 to 0 for independence, China recognized the independence of the Mongolian People's Republic. Actually, the republic was established in the early 1920's with a capital at Ulan Bator, after which time it was paradoxically within the Chinese border but under Russian influence. Tannu Tuva, the northwest portion of Outer Mongolia, was annexed to the Soviet Union in 1945.

Geographically, Mongolia is best described as a true nomad land. The area is large and the population sparse, for the landscape ranges from barren desert to semiarid grasslands. The areas most favorable to pastoral activities are the steppes that rim the margins of the uninhabitable Gobi Desert. Here sheep and cattle provide food, and horses and camels afford transport. Like Sinkiang, important historic routes cross the area. Of significance is a north-south route passing through Ulan Bator, connecting Inner Mongolia with Siberia.

Problems Facing the Chinese Republic

A major need facing modern China is undoubtedly that of a strong domestic economy. Around it revolve multifarious problems ranging from those that affect the welfare of the average Chinese individual to those that are concerned with the country's critical international relations. A desperately low standard of living has been a sign of weakness in China; it has kept the peasant and the coolie on the verge of starvation, and allowed the nation as a whole to be duped by almost any other country that chanced to sail its shores. Any improvements that bolster the internal exchange economy of China will add to the nation's commercial stability and therefore discourage the inroad of foreign interests.

Since the collapse of Japanese power in China, one of the great problems of the Chinese has been the relations between the Kuomintang and the Communists. The leadership of the latter is allied with the U. S. S. R. and in the area under their control, there is a population in excess of 100,000,000. In the area now under their rule the Chinese Communists have inaugurated some reforms; lower rents, lower tax rates and lower interest rates. They practically maintain a separate state, economically, politically, and militarily; and in doing so, they collect their own taxes, make their own laws, issue their own paper money and maintain their own army.

Unity among all Chinese factions is the key to China's future as a great power. If this can be accomplished, the nation will go forward in achieving economic reform for the individual, in developing its natural resources, in acquiring a degree of self-sufficiency, and in putting into operation the principles of Dr. Sun Yat-sen, which will bring democracy to the people.

China is old in many ways, but she can begin a rebirth in a new industrial era; China is weak in many respects, but she can become strong by coordinating her people, her resources, and her future relations with the world. China's future will not be decided, in the final analysis, by anyone but China, and this the Chinese themselves must realize.

The late President Franklin D. Roosevelt's one desire in the Far East was to see China unified on a democratic basis in order that she might become the bastion for peace in Asia. It is to be hoped that such will be the ultimate result, especially in view of the suffering China has endured. The time is at hand when she has an unprecedented opportunity to assume her logical place in the modern family of nations.

CHAPTER 25 | # Korea, Indo-China, and Siam: Historic Asiatic Buffers

KOREA, Indo-China, and Siam are located on the margins of China.* These peripheral locations have resulted in their subjection in varying degrees, at different periods of their history, to the political, ideological, and economic power of China. To be sure, each of the three countries is separated from China by a mountain barrier, partially counterbalancing the effect of proximity. Moreover, Korea, Indo-China, and Siam have each been independent political entities at various times in their history. Nevertheless, the important part that proximity to China has played in the political geography of each country justifies linking the study of the three countries (see the map on this page).

With China a weak power in the last few decades, Korea was annexed to Japan; Indo-China became a colonial dependency of France; and Siam alone, by adroit political maneuvering, retained its independence. During World War II all three countries were

* The translation and romanization of Oriental names often lead to confusion. The names of the three countries about which this chapter deals fall into such a category. The name of Korea was derived from the French and Italian pronunciation of the Chinese name for a dynasty that once ruled part of the Korean Peninsula. The Koreans in their own language have used most commonly in recent centuries the word Choson. The Japanese pronounced the characters as Chosen and sometimes romanized it as Tyosen. The Chinese used the words, Peaceful South, or Annam, for Indo-China. The French called it French Indo-China. The present nationalists there prefer the name Viet-Nam. The Siamese call their land Muang Thai. In the nationalistic era of recent years they were able to have a translation of this name, Thailand, adopted in foreign countries. However, since the end of World War II they have gone back to the use of Siam for foreign consumption.

a part of the Japanese Greater East Asia Sphere. With the end of the war, Korea started on the difficult road toward independence; Indo-China again came under French

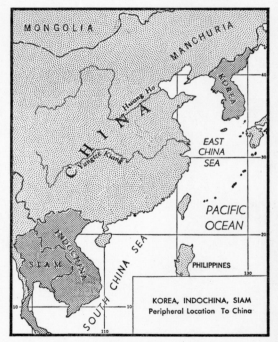

KOREA, INDOCHINA, SIAM
Peripheral Location To China

control, though armed revolt led to a more independent status than previously; and Siam resumed its place among the sovereign nations. As conditions in each country are still in a state of flux, the ultimate outcome is still uncertain.

The three countries have internal geographic and cultural similarities. Common to each are the expanses of mountain and hill lands and the limited areas of plains, where the people, densely crowded, carry on intensive agriculture. Farming is tuned to the demands of rice, favored as each country is by the seasonal rainfall of the monsoonal climate. In each land local differences result, of course, from latitudinal location and historic development. Common also to the three countries, much of the culture and racial stock has come from China, though each of the three has succeeded in developing its own national traits.

The political life of each country has been strongly influenced by Confucian political ideas derived from Chinese contacts. Westerners, trained in European concepts of international law and relations, are often at a loss to understand these Confucian concepts or their manifestations. However, these ideas are important in understanding Far Eastern political geography. The Confucian concept embodies an approach to moral order and social stability through the channel of manners. Regulations of an elaborate etiquette governed every relationship and action, even to the food eaten by different classes of people, the separation of males and females on the street, the size of coffins, and the shape and position of graves. As part of the old political basis of the teaching of Confucius, the world is a unit, centered around China, the Middle Kingdom. The sovereign of China, who rules under the Mandate of Heaven, provides an example for his subjects. The people strive to live in correct relationships with each other and with nature. When man and nature are in accord, individual and world peace and happiness result.

Outside the Middle Kingdom are barbarians, who, when they are taught by example the principles of correct conduct, will then voluntarily submit themselves to the sovereign power of China, the superior nation, and its ruler, Heaven's chosen instrument. Obviously, such idealistic concepts have not always prevailed, but they have had an important influence in the past political scene of eastern Asia.

In the frame of Chinese political thought, Korea was considered as a "younger brother." The kings of Korea and Annam, which became a part of Indo-China, obtained investiture from the Chinese Emperor. The Siamese rulers also borrowed some of their political concepts from China, though Indian influences were strong.

The future political geography of the Far East will reflect much of this political background. This prediction does not imply that China will become an imperial power, guided by Confucian doctrine. If a strong China emerges in the Far East, however, Korea, Indo-China, and Siam, along with other regions of eastern Asia, will be drawn closer to the Chinese political and economic orbit.

Prior to World War II these three countries were potential danger spots in an unsettled Asia. In the postwar world Korea and Indo-China have remained as focal points of tension involving outside countries and Siam has suffered from internal dissension. The detailed discussion of each country will bring a more complete understanding of the problems they face.

KOREA

The buffer position of Korea in the Far East dominates the political geography of that peninsula. With China, Japan, and Russia surrounding it, Korea always has had an uneasy independence or has been under the political control of one of its neighbors. Historically, however, it has learned its arts from China and considered itself in a subordinate position in the Confucian system. Korea has nevertheless maintained a separate and distinct nationality in the Far East because of its physical geography and its people: it is a peninsula cut off from the Asiatic mainland by a broad mountainous base, and its population forms a unique cultural and economic group. Today, freed from Japan, its latest aggressor, it faces an uncertain future.

Physical Factors

The land. Korea is a land of beauty. This beauty has always made a lasting impression on all Koreans. Today the insecure and fast-changing economic and political world has greatly enhanced the traditional love of the Koreans for the sparkling streams and high mountains of their land.

The peninsula extends south 600 miles from a broad continental base. With the Sea of

Japan to the east, the Korea Strait to the south, and the Yellow Sea to the west, Korea has some insular characteristics like Japan. About 500 miles of its northern frontier lie along Manchuria, but a few miles touch Siberia. This wide attachment to the large continent of Asia makes Korea a continental rather than an insular land (see map immediately below).

KOREA

HIGHLANDS

MILES

Much of the 85,000 square miles, an area about equal to that of Minnesota, is mountainous or hilly; only a fifth can be used for agriculture. On the small areas of plains and lower hill slopes the more than 24,000,000 people are most densely crowded.

The mountains and hills have complex relief and structure.* In the north there is a block of ancient rock, extending into Manchuria, which has been overlain with lava. The whole block has been raised in the south and east by movements of the earth's crust, giving it a gently northward tilt. Into this block the Yalu and Tumen Rivers (forming part of the northern boundary) and their tributaries have cut deep, winding courses. On the southeastern edge of the same block the escarpment is quite sharp; on the southwestern edge, not so abrupt.

Another major structural block makes up central and southern Korea. In geologic time long past the complex rock formations were leveled by erosion and then uplifted by a major crustal disturbance. The crest of the upthrown block is the mountainous ridge along the Sea of Japan. The major streams, which were entrenched, flow westward to the Yellow Sea. In southern Korea a series of parallel ridges branch from the major block to the southwest, cutting the relief up alternately into plains and hills or mountains. The southwest corner of Korea is a veritable maze of islands, peninsulas, and bays, where mountain spurs have been cut by structural lines and the lower areas submerged.

The complex structure of Korea has been subjected to stream erosion and has been built up by stream deposition. Headwaters of rivers and streams are cut back into the hills, and along the lower courses extensive flood plains with deposits of fertile alluvium have been formed. Subsequent uplift has developed some areas of diluvium now used for dry crops. Erosion varies with rock structure and vegetation cover.

The climate. Just as relief is important to the farmers of Korea, so is the climate. The location between 33° and 43° North Latitude puts the peninsula in the belt of westerly winds and cyclonic storms. Modifying this climatic control, however, is the position of Korea on the eastward fringe of the world's largest land mass; the heating and cooling of

* For a more detailed, though still generalized, discussion of the relief of Korea, see Arthur H. Robinson and Shannon McCune "Notes on a Physiographic Diagram of Tyosen (Korea)," *Geographical Review*, XXXI, No. 4 (October, 1941), 653–658.

the Asian land mass cause seasonal drifting of monsoon air, oceanward in winter and toward the continent in summer. The deep Sea of Japan and the shallow Yellow Sea on either side of the peninsula exercise additional climatic controls. Naturally the variations of elevation due to the mountainous land form also lead to variations in the climate.

Multiple controls result in regional differences in the climates of Korea.* The dominant contrast is between the north and south. The northern interior of Korea, cut off from the moderating influence of the sea and at a higher elevation, has long, bitterly cold winters and short, warm summers. In contrast, the southern third of the peninsula has hot, moist summers and relatively mild winters, so that double cropping can be practiced. The northeast coast is influenced by cool currents, so that the summers are not so warm, though the winters are cool rather than severe; fogs are common phenomena there. The northwestern and central parts of Korea have cold winters and hot summers. All of Korea has sufficient rainfall for agriculture except during occasional years when droughts occur. Although the southern part has considerable winter rain, the maximum rainfall of the peninsula comes in the summer months. The climatic differences from place to place, in part a result of the topography, result in variations in the fertility of the soil and profuseness of the vegetation. Of even more importance to the economy, however, are the limits that the climate puts on the crops that may be grown.

Economic Pattern

Korea has several mining regions, the best of them in the north. Among the most important of the minerals are gold, silver, copper, and coal. Others are tungsten ore, iron ore, graphite, lead, alum stone, zinc, pyrite ore, and kaolin. Although steps have been taken in recent years, especially during the period while the country was under Japanese domination, to exploit its mineral wealth, much of it still awaits development.

* A series of monographs on the climatic regions of Korea have been prepared by Shannon McCune, *Research Monographs on Korea*, Series B, No. 1–4, Series E, No. 1–11, Korean Research Associates, 1941 and 1945. A brief account of these regions is in Shannon McCune, "Climatic Regions of Korea and Their Economy," *Geographical Review*, XXXI, No. 1 (January, 1941), 95–99.

For several centuries ravages of insect pests, wood-hungry farmers, and, in recent years, Japanese exploitation stripped the natural vegetation cover in some sections of southern Korea and serious erosion has resulted. Considerable areas of extremely valuable forests remain, however, especially in the north.

During the last years of Japanese rule the country experienced considerable expansion of its industrial facilities. Most of this development took place in the northern part of the country. The leading industries in terms of output were iron and steel, light metals, chemicals, food, textiles, beverages, and tobacco. New factories for cotton spinning, cotton, silk, and rayon weaving appeared. Also constructed were large chemical fertilizer plants, oil refineries, hydroelectric plants, and works for the manufacture of cement, paper, pottery, electric bulbs, and enameled ironwares.

As Korea remains predominantly an agricultural nation, its farm production is important. The areas of level land and an adequate supply of water for paddy fields are the determining factors in the distribution of agricultural land. The mulberry tree thrives there, and thousands of acres are devoted to it. With the encouragement of the Japanese, expansion of silkworm culture and improvement in the quality of the cocoons have provided high silk production. As in other Far Eastern countries rice is an important crop. Tobacco raising is also fostered. Included among the other important crops are barley, grain, sorghum, millet, rye, wheat, soybeans, cotton, and apples. The medicinal root ginseng is also cultivated.

The Japanese strengthened land communications for strategic reasons, with several thousand miles of railway lines and many more of highways. A considerable fleet of rather small steamships and sailing ships also exists.

The People and Culture of Korea

Koreans constitute a distinct national group but the racial origins of the people are veiled in antiquity. Definitely Mongoloid in racial character, they probably were the result of mixtures between successive waves of migrants out of Central Asia, Manchuria, and North China. Although Koreans today are distinct from both Chinese and Japanese, they do have dark straight hair, dark oblique eyes, and a tinge of bronze in the skin. In height they are intermediate between the two races.

The distinct ethnic character of Korea is reflected in the language. It is a polysyllabic language similar to the Altaic languages of Central Asia. Although Korean is different from Chinese in its grammar and speech, it has borrowed many Chinese words. Since Chinese was considered the classic language of Korea, the court and scholars in olden times became skilled Chinese linguists. In modern decades Japanese was learned by many Koreans. The common people, and in recent times the scholars as well, developed and used a simple alphabet of brief symbols with which they can signify all the Korean sounds.

Korean culture has been greatly changed in the past few decades by the encroachment of Western habits and customs modified by the Japanese. The old culture, largely modeled after the Chinese, has fallen into decay, and the present cultural life is a weird hodgepodge of the old and new. Under the rule of Japan many drastic steps were taken to force the Koreans to follow the Japanese cultural pattern.

Historical Development of Korea

The Koreans trace their mythology back to the time of Tangun, 2333 B.C., who established a dynasty that lasted more than one thousand years. However, their written history usually begins with Kija, a Chinese sage, who came to Korea in 1122 B.C. He and 5,000 of his followers settled among the uncultured natives and brought the benefits of the superior agricultural civilization of China. His dynasty ruled until 193 B.C. From this earliest recorded contact until three quarters of a century ago, Korea received almost all its culture from China.

During the early centuries of written history a series of petty kingdoms were set up in different parts of the peninsula and the adjoining areas of Manchuria. In reality these kingdoms were tribal organizations, forming various alliances amongst each other and constantly shifting in power. At the start of the Christian era there were three major kingdoms in Korea: Silla in the southeast, Pakche in the southwest, and Koguryo in the north. Among these kingdoms Silla gained the ascendency by 668 A.D. and ruled over most of the

peninsula until 918. At that time Wanggun seized power, unified the peninsula under the name Koryu, established Songdo as the capital, and made Buddhism the state religion. This kingdom borrowed heavily from China, copying the civil service examination system and other governmental practices.

Invasions of Korea. All was not peace and quiet, for the Tartars moving off the steppes of Asia conquered China. They invaded Korea in 1011 A.D. and forced the Korean kings to submit to their suzerainty. Two centuries later another nomadic group, the Mongols, under the leadership of Genghis Khan, spread out from the steppes and seized the throne of the Middle Kingdom. The Koreans sided with the defeated groups in China, and thus were subjected to another invasion in 1231. Almost as serious as that invasion in the dislocation of economic life on the peninsula was Kublai Khan's use of Korea as a base for attempted invasions of Japan in 1274 and 1281.

The revolt against the Mongols and the establishment of the Ming dynasty in China was followed by a revolt and establishment of a new dynasty, the Yi, in Korea in 1392. The capital was moved to Kyongsong (Seoul) and the name of the country was changed to Chosen, the "Land of the Morning Calm." For two hundred years the nation enjoyed a comparative calm, broken only by the coastal raids of Japanese pirates. The gentle arts flourished, though Buddhism was suppressed as an aftermath of the undue temporal power gained by the monks in the preceding dynasty. One unfortunate aspect of the period was the growth of a party system among the court nobles. These political parties were not formed on the basis of fundamental issues, but were separated only on personal and trivial grounds. Bitter battles were waged for the favor of the king. The welfare of the common Korean was neglected. This old party system is presently reflected in the divisive nature of Korean political leadership. Korean political activities have long been strongly marked by bitter party rivalries.

In neighboring Japan the warring feudal clans were finally united under Hideyoshi by 1590. Two years later, partially as a relief to internal pressures, Hideyoshi attempted an invasion of Korea with the ultimate objective of subjecting China. Once more Korea was invaded and overrun, but in this case not conquered. The last invaders of Korea until modern times were the Manchus, who overthrew the Ming dynasty in China and invaded the peninsula in 1627 and 1631 in order to stop any aid from Korea to the Mings.

Korea now believed that the only safeguard against more invasions, with their attendant suffering, was isolation. Foreign contacts were kept at a minimum, limited largely to exchanges made by Chinese envoys, periodical fairs held on the northern border of Korea, and restricted trading with the Japanese at Fusan. During this period of isolation sharp cleavages were made between the educated noble families and the common people. Within the ruling classes political parties carried on feuds. Thus Korea was a weak nation when the isolation was broken by foreign treaties with the Japanese in 1876 and with other nations during the following decade.

Loss of independence. The internal weakness of Korea became apparent as the country served as a pawn in the game of power politics. Two wars were fought over the peninsula: the Sino-Japanese War of 1894–95 and the Russo-Japanese War of 1904–05. Both resulted in victory for Japan. The first supposedly clarified the status of Korea as a state independent of China. In 1897 the official name was changed from Chosén to Dae Han, and the Korean king became an emperor. The second war resulted in Japanese military occupation of Korea in 1904, followed by the establishment of a protectorate in 1905, and by outright annexation in 1910. The Korean royal family was cared for by Japan; Korea as an independent nation disappeared.

This historical sketch has omitted many of the details of intrigue between the different neighbors of Korea and between groups within Korea. It does, however, reveal how difficult political independence has been for Korea. With her political destiny so closely tied to China it was during the periods of Chinese weakness that Korea most keenly suffered.

Modern Korea

Under Japanese domination. Under the Japanese Korea made considerable material advances. The amount of arable land was increased; extensive erosion control and reforestation were instituted; and rice production and that of other crops, notably cotton, were increased. Industrial progress included the building of railroads and roads; greatly increased mineral production, especially that of gold, iron, copper, and coal; and development of large-scale hydroelectric projects. New industries were mostly of the basic heavy type, for the aim of the Japanese program was to make Korea an integral part of the economy of Japan, which itself was pointed toward war.

Modern cities in Korea show a tendency toward this industrialization and commercial activity. The chief city is the capital of Seoul, or Keijo (935,000), with its industrial suburbs and port gateway of Jinsen (102,000). Heijo (286,000) in the northwest and Taikyu (111,000) in the southeast are regional centers that are showing industrial progress. On the southern coast lies Fusan (250,000), a seaport that long handled traffic to and from Japan. Newer, but as yet much smaller, seaports are being developed along the northeast coast of the country. Among these, Rashin is one whose importance is growing.

The Japanese naturally dominated the political and economic life of Korea. Most Koreans were allowed to hold only minor posts in government or business. The lack of true self-government or any political self-expression prevented political maturity. Though the Koreans abroad kept alive the flame of independence, this activity was coupled with discouraging disunity among the refugees. Thus it was only natural that Korea was only promised independence "in due course" by the Cairo declaration of December, 1943.

Postwar era. At the end of hostilities in the recent war Korea was divided into two zones, separated by the 38° parallel, for the avowed purpose of disarming the Japanese. The Russians had the responsibility in the northern half and the Americans in the southern half. This artificial division was very poorly chosen, for by slight changes a similar division could have been drawn along established provincial lines. According to the abortive Moscow Declaration of December, 1945, Korea was to be administered under the joint trusteeship of Soviet Russia, the United States, Great Britain, and China until Korea was ready for political independence. The trusteeship period, it was anticipated, would not be longer than five years. However, the Americans and the Russians could not agree on an initial Korean government. The arbitrary division along the 38° parallel remained in force, and the Russians and the Americans set up different systems of government within their zones, thereby greatly damaging Korea's opportunity for peaceful growth and unified independence.

The prospects for Korea in the postwar world are only as bright as are the prospects of peace. If the larger nations that surround Korea are at peace, then Korea will be at peace. There is a great advantage in having Korea as a peaceful buffer nation, not under the dominance of any one nation. There are myriad internal problems that must be faced in Korea: the large number of tenant-farmers living on a semi-starvation status, the need for continued large-scale development of mineral and water resources, the development of consumer goods industries, the necessity of free trade with surrounding areas, the redirection of cultural development, and the growth of political maturity. Externally there are minor boundary problems in northeastern Korea, but more significant is the problem of knitting the economy of the peninsula of Korea into that of the whole Far Eastern region.

In November, 1947, the General Assembly of the United Nations approved an American resolution to establish a United Nations Commission to supervise elections in Korea, scheduled for May, 1948, and to help set up a Korean government. The Soviet Union, which unsuccessfully sponsored a resolution calling for the evacuation of American and Russian troops in Korea by January 1, 1948, stated that it would boycott the United Nations Commission.

INDO-CHINA

Like Korea, Indo-China has throughout its history had close ties with China, developed in part because of the nearness of Indo-China to southern China. Indo-China differs from Korea in its recent history by having been under the political rule of a European country—France—whereas Korea was under an Oriental people—the Japanese. Just as Korea, Indo-China may become more closely allied with a strong China in the future due to the geographical propinquity, the cultural affinity, and the modern Chinese economic infiltration.

Physical Factors

The land. Indo-China has an area of 286,000 square miles, which is more than that of Texas. However, its hilly and mountainous character makes much of the land unsuitable for use, and, in all, only fifteen per cent is utilized. The main mountain area is in northern Indo-China, but extending south from this massif is the Annam chain, which effectively separates the two deltas of the country: the Tonkin, or Red River, Delta in the north, and Cochin China, or the Mekong River Delta, in the south (see the map on facing page). These lowlands areas are by far the most important regions of Indo-China. The Tonkin Delta and its associated deltas are small and geologically old. Within them are sharp local differences between the sterile sand dunes along the coast, the levees and leached alluvial plains, and the small areas of relatively unleached recent alluvium. The Mekong Delta is large and, though some areas of older alluvium have poor laterite soils, much of it is covered with fertile newly-deposited material.

Climate. Not only do the two deltas differ in land form, but in climate, for the Annam chain acts as a climatic barrier. The southern delta has a simple equatorial climate with uniformly hot temperatures. Saigon, for example, has an average monthly range from 79° to 86° F. Rainfall is heavy; 77 inches is the yearly average at Saigon, with very dry winters and very wet summers. The northern delta does not have such equatorial conditions. Despite yearly averages of temperature that are only slightly lower, the average monthly range is greater—63° to 85° at Hanoi. Also the annual rainfall of 60 inches is more evenly distributed throughout the year. Though the summer months are still the rainy season, winter rains are usually sufficient to enable double cropping. When a period of ten days without rain during the critical season of rice growth occurs, however, disaster results. Likewise, heavy rain storms, usually coming during the fall typhoon season, cause equally disastrous floods.

Human and Economic Factors in Indo-China

People on the land. Four fifths of the 24,000,000 people of Indo-China live on only

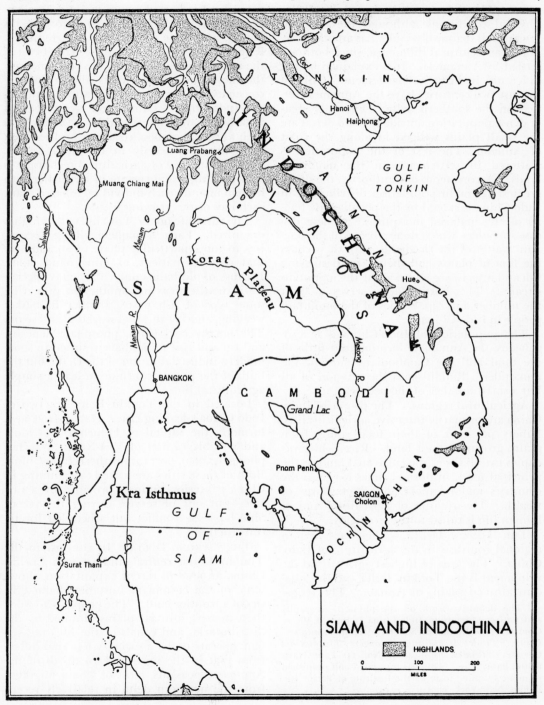

SIAM AND INDOCHINA

HIGHLANDS

0   100   200
MILES

one eighth of the land area. The great crowding is generally restricted to the deltas. However, the Mekong Delta with its average density of 410 persons per square mile contrasts with the Tonkin Delta with a density of 1,100. This difference is not primarily due to physical conditions, although the contrasting rainfall regime obviously has an influence, nor to any cultural difference, since both are settled by Annamese. It is explained by the difference in historical settlement. Only in the last two centuries have the Annamese settled on the southern delta. The only areas of dense population outside the two deltas are the small plains wedged in along the coast of Annam. The rest of the population is scattered in settlements in the mountain lands. According to one authority, the single greatest factor in population distribution in Indo-China is caused by the peculiar life habits of the malarial mosquitos.* These disease spreaders, which do not breed in the stagnant waters of the rice fields, with their choking film of plants and their larva-destroying fish and insects, are found along the mountain streams. This hostile factor serves to limit the number and capabilities of the mountain people in Indo-China.

The population of Indo-China is heterogeneous, the Annamese forming four fifths of the total and the Cambodians most of the remainder. Buddhism is the religion of all but a small number of the people.

Agricultural regions. The people of Indo-China are primarily intensive agriculturalists. Ninety per cent of their food comes from grains grown on their land. Rice, which occupies five sixths of the cultivated land, is the principal food; in normal times it is also the country's major export and chief source of wealth. The rhythm of agriculture and of human life is tuned to the rice fields.

THE TONKIN DELTA. There are certain regional contrasts in the agriculture of Indo-China. The area of highest agricultural development is the Tonkin Delta and the adjacent alluvial plains of Annam. The irriga-

* The definitive work on the physical geography and native economy of Indo-China is that of Pierre Gourou, "L'Utilisation du Sol en Indochine Francaise," *Centre d'Études de Politique Étrangère, Travaux des Groupes d'Études,* Publication No. 14, Paul Hartmann, Paris, 1940. This was translated and published in mimeographed form by the Institute of Pacific Relations, New York, in April, 1945.

tion system, developed over the centuries on the Red and other river deltas, is extremely important. An estimated 16,000 fields are divided among many small owner-cultivators; and, in addition, about one fifth of the cultivated land is owned communally. Tremendous amounts of hand labor by the owner, his family, and some day laborers are required. Rice, occasionally double-cropped or grown in the winter season, demands the best land and the most care. The rice is almost entirely consumed by the dense population of northern Indo-China. Other food crops, such as potatoes, beans, and vegetables, or cash crops, such as corn, bamboo, coconuts, and tobacco, are cultivated mainly in the drier season. The infinite care of agricultural technique is shown by the usual custom of fertilizing with human manure each individual tobacco plant each day of the growing season.

The rural life on the Tonkin Delta is highly organized. Each Annamese village specializes in some particular phase of an industry that requires patient, exacting hand labor. Because of old habits one village may specialize in textile weaving, another in preparing some type of fish paste, another in basket weaving, another in wood working, and so on. The nearby coal fields, phosphate deposits, and tin and zinc mines have resulted in some modern industrialization of the Delta, but the bulk of the people continue to lead a simple agricultural life.

Located in the Tonkin Delta are two of Indo-China's leading cities: Hanoi (149,000), formerly the capital of French Indo-China, and possibly capital of Viet-Nam; and Haiphong (97,000), port for northern Indo-China. Both of these cities are linked to Kunming in China's interior Yunnan province by a rail line—put out of service during the recent Sino-Japanese conflict but scheduled for reconstruction.

THE MEKONG DELTA. In contrast to the Tonkin Delta, central and western Cochin China, an area of recent exploitation, shows some of the customary unstable characteristics of a frontier land. The people who work the extensive alluvial plains, drained by the distributaries and canals of the Mekong system, operate under a social system that differs from that in the north. Two thirds of the Annamese peasants, most of whom migrated from the northern delta in relatively recent times, are landless and rent four fifths of the rice fields. The rents average seventy per cent of the harvest. Everyone in the area is either a debtor or a lender. Feeling no tie with the land, the peasants tend to gamble excessively. Landlords receive more of their income from interest on loans and advances than from profit on crops. Rates of interest are exorbitant; a one-day loan, surprisingly common, demands an interest of ten per cent. Such conditions, growing worse rather than better in recent years, have led to instability of population and have reduced the intensity of land use.

Rice occupies nine tenths of the cultivated land. Three fourths of the rice is a single crop, grown in the rainy season. From this region comes the rice used for export. The rice trade is almost completely in the hands of Chinese merchants centered in Cholon (207,-000) and Saigon (190,000), twin industrial cities about which the economic life of Cochin China revolves. Secondary crops are not important, although the production of sugar cane and coconuts is increasing.

CAMBODIA. Adjoining the Mekong Delta to the northwest is Cambodia. Here the Cambodian farmers, racially and culturally slightly different from the Annamese, use even less care and exploit the land less intensively than in Cochin China. There is a dominance of small owners, who lead an easy life and often get into debt to Chinese merchants. Irrigated rice is the main crop; secondary crops, except for corn raised on the levees, are but little developed. The only city of consequence in Cambodia is Pnom Penh (103,-000), in the interior but located on the west bank of the Mekong River. The Grand Lac is the fishing center of Indo-China, but the industry is in the hands of Annamese and Chinese rather than Cambodians. This lake, which has a fluctuating level, provides not only excellent fishing grounds but also lands on which floating rice can be grown. The outlet of the lake, by the way, is that unique stream that, depending on the flood stage of the Mekong River, flows part of the year in one direction and the rest of the year in the opposite direction!

MOUNTAIN LANDS. The mountain lands of Laos and parts of the neighboring civil divisions of Indo-China are for the most part forested; agriculture is limited by the preva-lence of malaria and the poor soils. A large part of the agricultural personnel is migratory. Patches in the forest are cleared by fire, and crops are then planted at these points for one or two years. The nomadic agriculturalist then moves on to another patch. The common crops grown under this wasteful system by the malaria-ridden primitive tribes are upland rice and corn. On the abandoned land grow poor secondary forests, not economically valuable for teak or other forest products.

Overall commercial view. Indo-China has not thus far developed an exchange economy of any complexity. As has been pointed out, the people live close to the land in the various sections favorable to human settlement; and, among other factors, lack of a unified transportation pattern has worked against any concerted effort toward national economic strength. The country is largely an exporter of raw materials. Its factories, which are small, process goods for local consumption or agricultural and forest products for foreign markets. Most important commercial items are rice and timber, although cotton and silk textiles, sugar, matches, and paper also enter trade channels. In addition to valuable hardwood timber, the mountain forests yield bamboo and lacs.

Political Factors in Indo-China

Development of Annam. Closely paralleling the situation in Korea, Annam, or the "Peaceful South," was for generations under the political influence of China. Waves of Chinese emigrants brought Chinese culture to less civilized nomadic tribesmen, who had perhaps been earlier migrants from Central Asia. On the plains of Tonkin, therefore, there developed a group of sedentary farmers. This group, called the Annamese, in later centuries pressed toward the south. The native groups living on the Mekong Delta were pushed back into the mountains or on to the less fertile plain areas. The Annamese did not conquer by ideological infiltration as did the Chinese, but left ruins in their wake. The recently discovered temples and dwellings of Angkor Vat in Cambodia are mute symbols of a highly developed civilization, perhaps surpassing that of the Annamese.

Among the Annamese there were struggles for power, though in 968 A.D. they united and freed themselves from direct Chinese rule. Throughout the succeeding centuries, under the Confucian philosophy of government, the kings of Annam received investiture from the Chinese Emperor. Sometimes these ceremonies were long delayed because of the difficulties of travel. Occasional revolts occured; French soldiers of fortune were involved in the 1780's. In 1801 a new dynasty on its establishment received Chinese permission to change the name of the country to Viet-Nam.

Development of French Indo-China. As the protective power of China decreased in the eighteenth and nineteenth centuries and as the internal struggles for power weakened the country, Indo-China fell prey to other nations. Before the French arrived, the Portuguese and Dutch traders and missionaries had some contacts with the country. However, the French, through Catholic missionaries and adventurers and through the French East India Company, gained eventual control over Indo-China. This was a slow process, involving intrigues among groups of Annamese and periodic invasions of certain areas by French naval units and troops. The Annamese and Cambodian rulers either ceded territory outright to the French or retained only nominal control over parts of their kingdoms.

China quite naturally came to the defense of her satellites, but the poorly equipped Chinese could not withstand the French, especially when the military operations included a blockade of the Yangtze River. A treaty signed between France and China in 1885 gave the French a free hand in Indo-China. During the following years the French "pacified pirate bands" within Indo-China and by 1897 were masters of the whole country. The form of conquest resulted in a union of native states and French colonies. However, the differences in governmental administration in the five parts of Indo-China —the colony of Cochin China, the protected kingdoms of Annam and Cambodia, and the protectorates of Tonkin and Laos (including the kingdom of Luang Prabang)—were academic rather than real.

FRENCH POLITICAL POLICIES. The French colonial policy in Indo-China has been somewhat different from that of Japan in Korea or of other European nations in other parts of the Orient. The French policy has called for

somewhat strict regulation by law. In the early days, when only parts of the land were under the rule of French military forces, the policy was definitely one of subjection. In the following period attempts were made to assimilate the Indo-Chinese into the French Empire. Neither of these methods suited natives, accustomed to Confucian political philosophy, with its emphasis not on law but on interpretation by moral administrators. The final period has seen, though not continuously, a policy of association between the natives and the French administrators. According to this cooperative policy the Indo-Chinese were allowed considerable freedom and responsibility in certain internal affairs.

After the defeat of France by Germany in World War II the Japanese exerted pressure upon Indo-China, and the French administrators became virtual Japanese puppets. In March, 1945, the Japanese finally took over the colony of Cochin China and encouraged the native states to proclaim their independence. Following the collapse of Japan the French were faced with the delicate problem of regaining control and esteem. Such an accomplishment was complicated by the Chinese occupation of northern Indo-China for the purposes of demilitarizing the Japanese and by the rise of strong Indo-Chinese nationalism. In March of 1946 the French recognized the Viet-Nam Republic, holding northern Annam and Tonkin as a free state within the proposed Indo-China Union, and promised a plebiscite to determine whether that state would also include southern Annam and Cochin China. The Chinese troops withdrew, and the French troops moved into northern Indo-China, but with the understanding that all French troops would be withdrawn from Viet-Nam within five years. These concessions were in part the result of the wave of nationalism in southeast Asia and in part the result of the more liberal elements that came into power in France. Fighting, however, continued in Viet-Nam as a result of disagreements over the implementation of the 1946 agreement and the status of Cochin China.

The grand plan of the French for Indo-China at first called for an Indo-China Union or Federation consisting of Viet-Nam (Annam, Tonkin, and possibly Cochin China), Cambodia, and Laos, all within the framework of the French Union. Discussions later were held to permit the units of Indo-China to be members of the French Union without resorting to the formation of an Indo-China Federation.

FRENCH ECONOMIC POLICIES. The economic policy of the French has been as confused and difficult as their political policy. At-tempts were made to tie Indo-China into the Empire economy. Though Indo-China was a potential market for some French manufac-tures, France was not a major market for Indo-China's rice. Therefore, there has been some emphasis on the production of corn, silk, rub-ber, spices, and coffee in Indo-China for ex-port to France. Coal, zinc, tin, and phos-phate deposits in northern Indo-China have been exploited by the French but not ex-ported to France in large quantities.

The Chinese. Chinese merchants have complicated the economic situation in Indo-China. China, particularly the Canton area, is an importer of Indo-China's rice. In order to stimulate trade Chinese merchants have acted as petty capitalists, money lenders, and merchants. Rice warehouses, rice mills, and transportation facilities on the canals were developed by the Chinese. They have gained economic control over the rice trade of south-ern Indo-China and have exploited the natives by usury and other sharp practices. The fact that they aided in the establishment of the Viet-Nam Republic may enhance their eco-nomic strength in the future.

The Japanese. In the first years of World War II the Japanese were able to move some commodities out of Indo-China, for example, rice, rubber, corn, coal, zinc, and phosphates. The Japanese were also instrumental in the construction of a railroad paralleling the en-tire east coast of the country. Such a rail line fitted into the plan of a north-south land route through a newly acquired empire. But as the available Japanese ship tonnage decreased and the American air forces reached positions that enabled them to attack targets in Indo-China and adjacent waters, the Japanese advocated a self-sufficiency program in Indo-China. This change worked a hardship on the coun-try because of its previous dependence upon an export market. The Japanese, by keeping French officials in nominal charge much of the time, made the French the scapegoats for this economic hardship. In some cases the Japanese replaced the Chinese banking and exporting circles. It is doubtful, however, that the Japanese will be able to play any future economic role of significance in Indo-China.

The future. For postwar Indo-China the economic situation is as difficult for its people as the political situation is for the French. The Chinese will probably reassert themselves and maintain a strong economic position. France, weakened by war, is not in a position to devote the necessary capital, skilled admin-istrators, and industrial and communication equipment to bring Indo-China to high eco-nomic prosperity. The native people of Indo-China, through the lack of political training or economic strength, will probably not gain complete independence. Thus, Indo-China does not face a very happy future and is a threat to peace in southeast Asia.

SIAM

Siam differs from Korea and Indo-China in two major aspects of political geography: First, though in close proximity to China, the Confucian ideas of political life have had only an indirect effect on Siamese political concepts. Second, through clever political manipulation Siam has been able to keep its national sovereignty. These developments are in large part a result of the geographic position of the country. Siam is separated from China by a mountain barrier and faces toward the south and west rather than to-ward China. Actually, the modern bounda-ries of Siam and China are not contiguous, for Indo-China and Burma meet along the Chinese border and squeeze out Siam. In the days of European encroachment in southeast Asia, Siam aided by its sheltered position played the British off against the French and maintained its independence.

Partially because of its orientation Siam gained much of its culture from India and Burma. The ruling clan originated in the Yunnan region of southern China; but, as it came south, adopted Hindu ideas, including that of Divine Kingship. Under the later Buddhist influence, also derived from India, the idea was changed to thinking of the king as a potential Buddhist deity. The concept was further modified, in part by the impact of European political ideas, during the bloodless revolution of 1932, when the constitutional monarchy was inaugurated. Some Confucian concepts reappeared at that time, especially the principle that if the king did not rule with justice, the people had the right to revolt. At the present time 95 per cent of the people of Siam are Buddhists with Mohammedans and Christians making up most of the remainder.

In actual practice, however, these political trends and theories have had only small bearing on the simple agricultural life of the common man in Siam. Either under the absolute monarchy or under a constitution, the people have had a minor voice in the government. In common with their neighbors in Asia, the Siamese in their daily life have maintained a close tie with their land and have little concern with affairs outside their immediate and limited sphere.

Thais make up the preponderant proportion of the population of Siam, but in addition there are nearly a million Chinese, and two million more people with some Chinese blood. The Chinese handle much of the domestic commerce of the country and are also prominent in the import and export business. The Chinese form the only important minority group in the country, which in the past has been involved in racial antagonisms.

Physical Regions and Human Occupance

In size Siam is relatively large, its 200,000 square miles amounting to about three fourths the area of Texas; in relief it is varied (see the map on page 365). Although four fifths of the 15,750,000 people are engaged in agricultural pursuits, Siam has small deposits of many important minerals and some precious stones. Of these, however, only tin, gold, and tungsten are commercially produced. Next to agriculture in value of products rank fisheries—sea and river. For the sake of easier description of its geography and agricultural production, the country may be divided into four geographic regions, the northern, eastern, southern, and central sections of Siam.

In *Northern Siam* high mountains contrast with flat-floored valleys. In the isolated mountain regions, where national borders mean little, tribes of hill folk carry on migratory agriculture. The parallel-flowing rivers deposit alluvium on the valley bottoms during their flood stages. On these irrigable and fertile lands sedentary farmers, the Lao or northern Thai people, have their fields. Rice, the dominant crop, is used primarily for local food. Tobacco, cotton, and opium poppies are also grown for the needs of the two million people in this region. Because of its interior location, rainfall averages only 35 inches a year on the plains and slightly higher on the mountain slopes. The mountains are forested, but the only commercial timber is teak.

The relatively level land of *Eastern Siam,* or the Korat Plateau, contrasts with the topography of Northern Siam. The slightly tilted sandstones and shales are drained by a tributary to the Mekong. Because of interior location and its topographic features the region receives small rainfall, which fluctuates in amount from year to year. Both floods and droughts are common. The soil on the plateau is leached and generally infertile. On the small valley floors around the edges of the plateau most of the region's five million people find only a poor living in their self-sufficient economy. The drainage is into the Mekong, but because of the rapids on the river, the small trade of the area normally goes to Bangkok. Parts of this border region have been in dispute between Siam and Indo-China.

Siam extends south along the Malay Peninsula for six hundred miles. This area of *Southern Siam* is mountainous land with small coastal plains. The sea modifies the climate, resulting in a smaller range of temperature than elsewhere in Siam. The usual equatorial monsoon regime brings heavy rainy seasons. The east coast receives its maximum rainfall in December; the west coast, in June.

Although the mountains average about three to four thousand feet in elevation, they do not present a continuous barrier. Cut through the mountains are some transpeninsular routes. Some of these were utilized by the Japanese in supplying their troops in Burma during World War II. Probably the greatest single engineering feat of the Japanese during that war was the railroad built between Siam and Burma. The road, constructed at the cost of the lives of thousands of Allied prisoner-of-war laborers, may be important in knitting together the countries of southeast Asia. One transpeninsular route, the scheme of a ship canal across the Kra Isthmus, has been fine grist for political propaganda mills, but will not stand sober engineering and economic analysis. However, the treaty between Britain and Siam signed on January 1, 1946, included the clause that no canal "linking the Indian Ocean and the Gulf of Siam should be put across Siamese territory" without the consent of the British.

The valleys of this peninsular area are important as a base for agriculture. Rice and palms along the coast provide food for the native people. Small amounts of rice must be imported into the region, however, for the tin and tungsten mining communities.

By far the most important region is *Central Siam*, the heart of the nation. This is the large alluvial plain and rapidly advancing delta of the Menam Chao Bhraya, commonly, though incorrectly since the word means river, called the Menam River. The monotonous plain teems with human life. Convectional rainfall during the monsoon season on the rich delta soil favors the intensive cultivation of rice, which occupies three fourths of the crop land. In those fields that are subject to floods rice is sown broadcast, though most of it is grown in orthodox paddy fields on the delta. Rivers and canals provide the main arteries of transportation. Villages hold to precarious sites along the levees. Around the edges of the plain are low hills, which are covered with forests and in whose shelter other villages are located. Bangkok, the capital and largest city in Siam, with 685,000 people, between 4 and 5 per cent of the nation's population, lies in the heart of the region. The nation's meager rail pattern is made up of narrow gauge lines which radiate from the city. Since it is located up the winding and silt-laden river some fifteen miles, new port facilities have been built down river and on islands in the bay. However, Bangkok remains the commercial, religious, and political hub of Siam; no other city in the entire country approaches it in size or importance.

Political Factors in Siam

Independence. The land of the Thais has been the only nation in southeast Asia other than China to maintain its sovereignty. The difficulties have been great and success has come in part through clever opportunism. Political independence has not, however, been coupled with economic independence. Especially strong in the economic life of Siam has been the hold of Chinese skilled workers and merchants. Their position can be attributed to their own efforts, to the lack of Siamese commercial acumen, and to the country's dependence upon an export rice economy.

In 1932, with the establishment of the Thai constitutional monarchy, strong efforts were made to create economic independence. Conservative groups interpreted some of the original plans as communistic and therefore shunned them. However, the urge toward nationalization and independence from foreign control continued and was in part realized. Colonization plans to settle people on new lands were formulated and partially executed. Unfortunately, these plans failed to solve the problems created by the increasing pressure of a rapidly expanding population. The ownership of transportation facilities and the shipping of rice were put largely into the hands of Thais. The development of new resources and the encouragement of more diversified agricultural production have made some headway. Nevertheless, the long road to economic independence can only be shortened by a change in the indifferent attitude of the average Thais.

The Japanese in Thailand. Both before and during World War II the Japanese found in Siam a good base for operations. One of the early Japanese moves was to back the Thais in their territorial claims against the French in Indo-China. They forced the cession of territory along the border between Thailand and Indo-China. After the fall of Malaya, the Japanese allowed the Thais to incorporate some Malayan states into Siam. All these gains, including some from Burma, have since been renounced by the Siamese, although they endeavored for many months to keep some of the Indo-Chinese territories.

Postwar independence. During the war the Japanese kept up the figment of Thai independence. Some Siamese actively aided the Japanese, others played a double game and helped the Allies in the small ways that were possible. Thus after the war, the Siamese, by renouncing their ill-gotten gains, by pointing to the help they had given, and by agreeing to the concepts of the victorious nations, restored their country to its former position among sovereign nations.

Siam suffered economically during the war with the loss of the export market for rice. But this loss may have been a blessing in disguise, for it forced them to diversify their economy. Despite the emergence of Siam as an independent nation, some of its resources have been put into the British economic orbit, under the terms of the peace treaty between Britain and Siam. Moreover, the Chi-

nese are hoping and may be expected to strive to regain their strong economic position in the country.

The prospects for Siam, to which the Thais have changed back the name of their country from Thailand, are not too bright. Of major importance, the country lacks the raw materials to build a strong, well-rounded economy. Partly because of this deficiency and partly because of its geographic position Siam will remain a weak buffer nation. However, in the country as a whole the people can continue to carry on a simple existence without a high standard of living.

CONCLUSION

Korea, Indo-China, and Siam occupy distinctive positions in the political geography of the world. The three nations, without great resources of land or people, cannot become world powers. They will have to be content either as small cogs in a united world machine or as satellites of some larger power in a world of great powers. Perhaps, because of their geographic location and historical development, they will become satellites to a strong China. If there is peace in

the world, they will be at peace; if there is war, they will suffer along with their neighbors. As a result of their strategic locations and weaknesses, it is likely that they would be among the heaviest sufferers in the event of a world conflagration. Recognizing this threat, their peoples and their leaders will probably bend their efforts, if necessary through concessions, to do what they can to maintain peace throughout the world and, especially, southeastern Asia.

| # The Japanese Isles

DYNAMIC political and military activity during recent decades has closely associated the islands of Japan Proper with the entire western Pacific region. Because of this association the nodal position of the Japanese Islands relative to other maritime areas of eastern Asia deserves close attention. China, Korea, the Philippines, French Indo-China, Siam, Malaya, the East Indies, and many other areas suffered from the aggressive military expansionist activities that stemmed from the strategically located home islands of Japan. Even the maritime margin of Soviet Siberia was long a zone alerted to military action. So severe was the destructive quality of the culminating struggle in the Pacific Theatre of World War II that the effects will be projected into a postwar period of many years duration.

In the future Japan will inevitably continue to influence the existence of her neighbors in the western Pacific. Relations, however, may be friendly, based upon an exchange economy permitting Japan to harness her high energy and productive capacity toward constructive rather than destructive objectives. Physical, historic, human, and economic factors all contribute to the evaluation of Japan's politico-geographic role—a dynamic role that the nation will continue to play in its external as well as internal affairs.

Physical Factors

Grouped off the eastern coast of the Asiatic continent the four main islands of Japan Proper—Honshu, Hokkaido, Kyushu, and Shikoku—extend north and south from about the 45th to the 30th parallels. In latitude

this position is equivalent to that of the east coast of the United States from southern Maine to northern Florida. The principal island of Honshu is virtually the "mainland" of the Japanese group, making up nearly sixty per cent of the total area, containing the bulk of the population, and including the great metropolitan centers. Of the three remaining islands, Kyushu and Shikoku lie to the south and Hokkaido to the north of Honshu (see the map directly below). Altogether, the

THE JAPANESE ISLANDS

four islands total only 148,000 square miles, less than the area of our second largest state, California. Both distances and areas in the Japanese Islands are small when contrasted to those usually associated with the great Asiatic land mass and the expansive Pacific Ocean. Thus, no point in Japan is far from the sea.

The insular nature of Japan gives it definite national boundaries, which have remained virtually inviolate since the settling of the islands by ancestors of the present population. Even military defeat in World War II did not affect the fixed coastal boundaries of the Japanese homeland. A shoreline configuration giving easy landing access to the islands, however, has confronted the Japanese with strategic defense problems. Presumably a coastline of 18,000 miles * prompted the acquisition of outlying territory to serve as a protective screen. Prior to World War II the Japanese military authorities carefully fortified strategic coastal areas, such as those guarding the entrance to the Inland Sea between Honshu and Shikoku and the entrance to Tokyo Bay with its great naval base of Yokosuka.

Relief. Surface features have been instrumental in orienting human development throughout Japan Proper. The surface of the main islands consists largely of mountains separated by narrow valleys, and rimmed by narrow coastal plains. There are eighteen active volcanoes, and earthquakes are frequent. The northern islands are a continuation of the Russian Karafuto chain running down through Hokkaido and into Honshu. In the southern islands appears a continuation of the mountain range found in China, the ranges from the north and west meeting in the Japanese Alps in the heart of Honshu. In this area is a vast transverse fissure crossing from the Sea of Japan to the Pacific, within which rises a group of volcanoes, mostly extinct or dormant. Here the sacred mountain Fujiyama, sixty miles west of Tokyo, lifts its peak to an altitude of over 12,000 feet.

So moutainous are the islands that only one sixth of the area is sufficiently level to permit normal agricultural utilization. The total arable land, including lower hillside slopes which are customarily terraced, amounts to

* Estimated length of the coastline around the four main islands of Japan Proper plus some 500 small fringing islands.

an area smaller than the state of West Virginia. Urban areas with their industrial cities, like agricultural activities, are for the most part restricted to level land. Only the development of hydroelectric energy and certain activities involving the extraction of minerals and the utilization of forest products have attracted industry to rough terrain.

Lowlands of Japan are largely limited to river or stream valleys and coastal plains. Here are the core areas of the country, in which are concentrated the preponderant proportion of the population, the greater share of industry, and the leading channels of commerce. In turn, the core areas may be interpreted as the country's critical areas, for political interest is naturally centered on those places suited to the creation and maintenance of the national economy. The power of the state springs from such areas, and, quite logically, these same areas must receive maximum protection in defensive measures and provide maximum power in offensive action.

Three lowlands areas stand out as being somewhat larger and more important than the rest. They all face the irregular southern shore of Honshu with its excellent harbor sites. The great urban centers of Japan are clustered within these lowlands, which, in addition, support high densities of agricultural population. First, the Kwanto Plain with its 14,000,000 inhabitants provides the immediate hinterland for Tokyo and its port city of Yokohama. Second, the Kinai Plain at the eastern end of the Inland Sea contains Osaka, Kobe, and Kyoto, all cities exceeding a million in population. Third, the centrally located Nobi Plain around the great city of Nagoya supports a rural population density even heavier than do the other two plains.

Climate. Fewer restrictions have been placed upon the Japanese people by climate than by relief. The islands benefit from a marine location at the margin of a continent squarely within the mild po.tion of the temperate zone. Temperatures are generally stimulating with pronounced, but not extreme, seasonal changes. North of Tokyo winters tend to be more severe than those at similar latitudes on the east coast of the United States. Heavy snowfalls are frequent on the Japan Sea slopes of the mountains of Hokkaido and northern Honshu, whereas the

Pacific side, by which flows the Japanese Current, enjoys relatively pleasant winters. A warm growing season permits the culture of rice as far north as the middle of Hokkaido. Much more detrimental to human life in Japan than any climatic catastrophes, however, are the earthquakes attributable to the many fault lines present in the rock structure underlying the mountainous archipelago.

Resources. Japan does not possess the physical resources essential to the development and maintenance of a powerful world state. Soils require the most careful and intensive utilization to provide minimum sustenance for so many millions of people. Grazing lands have never figured prominently in Japanese economy, with the result that fish from the surrounding seas furnish the protein demanded in the national diet. Disputes with Soviet Russia and the United States over fishing rights reflected the concern of Japan relative to this important source of food.*

In terms of mineral resources Japan with but minor exceptions has neither enough to export as surplus commodities nor to develop heavy industry. At best the home islands supply only a few of the prime essentials for current peacetime needs. For the manufacture of iron and steel, eighty per cent of the iron ore is normally imported; the low-grade Japanese coal must be supplemented by special coking varieties; and in nearly all instances the minerals used for steel alloys have to be brought into the country. Only in copper and sulphur could Japan be classed as self-sufficient. Deposits of other minerals are negligible or completely lacking except for limited quantities of chromium and manganese. The poor quality of the coal and a totally inadequate supply of petroleum are partially offset by the use of the hundreds of tumbling mountain streams to provide power. These streams, which are short, swift, and often unruly, are of little value for transportation, but they offer a vast although as yet little developed supply of hydroelectric power.

Scarcity of resources at home and their availability in other countries of the western Pacific encouraged military aggression.

* Fishing forays off foreign shores provided Japanese Naval Intelligence the opportunity of studying waters from the standpoint of military operations.

Japan's development of an iron and steel industry in the puppet state of Manchukuo and seizure of oil and rubber in the East Indies were but two instances of supplementing meager stocks of domestic resources.

Before completing an inventory of Japanese resources we must turn to the human factor as expressed first by the historical development of the country and next by the characteristics of the population itself. An appreciation of the national economy and political role of a state rests upon far more than the physical constituents of a landscape.

Historical Factors

The sharp influence of Japan's geographic environment has been apparent throughout the historical period and is reflected even in the mythology of the country. Of external importance were the sea and an off-shore location—nearness to the vast continent of Asia on the one hand and remoteness and self-imposed isolation from the Western world on the other. Of internal importance were the paucity of natural resources and the extremely mountainous terrain, the latter limiting free movement and the former restricting choice of economic opportunity within the narrow confines of the home islands. It is easy to establish the connection between these geographic influences and recent Japanese activities of international significance, such as the development of a strong navy, the quest for raw materials not found domestically, and the attempt to obtain foreign markets all over the world. Similarly, political events of more remote periods may be interpreted in the same light.

For the sake of convenience Japanese history may be broken down into three ages: the ancient, very roughly up to 600 A.D.; the middle, from 600 to 1853; and the modern, after 1853.

The ancient age. Present knowledge of the ancient age embodies much more of mythology and legends than it does of history. These nebulous concepts were related to an insular location, for according to Japanese mythology the very islands of Japan were supposed to have been created from the drops of water that fell from the spear of Izanagi, a god, as he plunged it into and withdrew it from the sea. Myths and legends have furnished a potent background for modern Japanese propaganda.

Early foreign relations of Japan were limited to those with Korea and China. The peninsula of Korea lies only about 125 miles from Japan, and at the nearest point China is less than 500 miles away. These countries on the mainland of Asia possessed the only significant civilization accessible to Japan.* It was just as natural a phenomenon for the people of Japan to make their initial contacts with this continental land mass as it was for the people of the British Isles, who occupy a complementary position with regard to the European continent, to have had their earliest dealings with Europeans rather than American Indians.

Except for the probability of a very early migration of population to Japan from or through Korea, the first relations between the two countries were effected during several hundred years immediately before and after the time of Christ. In this period the Metal Age seems to have been introduced to Japan from Korea, and also from China through Korea. Making use of metal weapons, the Japanese surged into Korea in an effort to subdue the country. Thus, Japan appeared early determined to dominate the geographical "dagger" pointed at her heart. Finally driven out of Korea in 663 A.D., they did not return for a millennium.

There are records of Sino-Japanese relations in as early a period as the first century A.D. From that time on, it is a story of Japan's receiving its first rather highly developed civilization from China. Of foremost importance in this connection was the formal adoption of the Chinese written language, probably early in the fifth century A.D. Prior to that the Japanese had possessed no written language. Buddhism also came from China through Korea about 552 A.D., and with it, as well as afterward, came scholars and artists of various kinds, bringing all the appurtenances of the advanced Chinese civilization.

Of some political interest is the fact that the sun, the importance of which was widely recognized by early peoples throughout the world, seems to have been taken over for the Japanese flag about the seventh century from the sun on the imperial banner of China.

From the very start of national existence a significant feature in the history of Japan has been the adoption of those attributes that were considered best in other civilizations. It has also been common practice for the Japanese to attempt during certain periods to dominate the home areas of these civilizations, especially should there be the opportunity of deriving political and economic benefits therefrom.

The middle age. The factor of relief noticeably affected the internal political development of Japan during its middle age. A mountainous terrain was partially responsible for making very difficult the subjugation of an aboriginal people known as the Ainu. Not until the sixteenth century were the Japanese, coming from the south, able to occupy the southern portion of Yezo (the present island of Hokkaido). Mountains also make communication and governmental organization difficult, probably contributing in no small measure to the historic, decentralized political system. The lack of a powerful central authority has persisted, in fact, until very recent times, and has had to be combated by modern military propagandists. Significant in this connection, the national flag referred to previously was not finally adopted until 1859, after the re-opening of Japan by Perry.

Relief and relation to the coast were factors quite probably taken into consideration in the selection of Yedo (the present Tokyo) as the capital, first by the shoguns and later by the emperor, when the institution of the shogunate was abolished.* It is located at the head of a bay, and mountains not too distant

---

* The importance of the location of the Japanese Isles with reference to China is clearly indicated by the Chinese origin of the name "Japan." This and the Japanese "Nippon" or "Nihon," the "Zipangu" of Marco Polo, the "Cipangu" for which Columbus sought are merely corruptions of the name given by the Chinese to the country *east* of them: JIH (日 sun), PEN (本 rising, origin). The suffix "gu" is a corruption of the Chinese KUO meaning country.

* The location of other Japanese capital cities from the middle age until the present time may also be associated with relief and relation to the coast, but to a lesser extent than Yedo. The first of these imperial capitals of centralized authority was established in the eighth century at Nara, a small city just to the east of Osaka. Later in the century it was moved a few miles north to Kyoto, where it remained until taken to Tokyo in 1869. In the early seventeenth century Tokyo (then known as Yedo) had become a shogunal capital of strong political power, and continued as such until the arrival of the Emperor (as pointed out above).

in the rear make approach somewhat difficult from that direction.

In view of the obvious importance of sea power to an insular people, it is surprising that the Japanese did not seem to possess an extremely strong navy. The fact that the Japanese Islands were never successfully invaded from the time they became anything resembling a nation until 1945 cannot be attributed to their sea power alone. Although their fleet did eventually succeed in driving off a tribe of Manchurian pirates in the eleventh century, it did not prevent the invaders from landing in northwestern Kyushu. Again in the thirteenth century during two attempted Mongol invasions the Japanese fleet could only partially ward off the blows. Even though their light craft performed effectively at close quarters, the Japanese had excellent land defense as the principal human factor to thank for the defeat of the Mongols.

The military lesson to be learned from the above-mentioned incidents is that though insularity provides a certain measure of protection, it should be supplemented with sea power (in the present and future, air power would logically come into the picture as well).

Weak on the defensive, the Japanese fleet likewise failed to secure control of the sea in an offensive campaign. Late in the sixteenth century the shogun Hideyoshi's attempts to conquer Korea and China proved unsuccessful. With supplies from the homeland unavailable the Japanese army in Korea, across the Sea of Japan, was powerless to wage an effective attack.

The efforts of the Mongols to invade Japan from Korea and the abortive Japanese invasions of Korea and China illustrate the reason for the concern of Japan about the Asiatic mainland both in terms of defense and offense. In modern times this concern of Japan for the mainland became very largely offensive, both morally and strategically.

In contrast to the efforts to repel attacks from the Asiatic mainland, or their machinations toward it, there arose the intense desire on the part of the rulers of Japan, especially during the sixteenth and seventeenth centuries, for absolute security from opposition within their domains. These rulers, called shoguns, were military dictators who from the twelfth century on had actually exercised the powers of the emperors. To check any possible opposition from within, the shoguns saw to it that friendly lords were assigned lands that dominated important highways and towns, or that threatened the flank and (or) rear of potential shogun enemies. In short, the shoguns in Yedo were isolated from easy communication, both by geographic location and deliberate lack of transportation facilities.

First contact with the West came about 1542, when three Portuguese traders arrived. By 1613 Portuguese, Spanish, Dutch, and English traders had all visited Japan, and Jesuit missionaries had settled there. But in 1636 suspicions about the missionary attempts to Christianize the people and aroused fear of foreign interference in Japan caused the shogun to expel all foreigners except the Portuguese and the Dutch. In 1638 the Portuguese were expelled, and three years later the Dutch were restricted to Nagasaki. In turn, the Japanese under severe penalty were forbidden in 1636 to leave the home islands. Thus Japan's insularity and her extreme geographic remoteness from the Western world were emphasized by law. The effect of these checks on political and economic development was to postpone the normal processes of cultural diffusion for over 200 years until the reopening of the country by Perry.* This self-inflicted isolation from the stream of forces brought about a very provincial type of civilization, rather well unified and nationalistic.

The modern age. At about the mid-point of the nineteenth century the sea influenced the history of Japan in an exceedingly profound manner. The occasion for the reopening of Japan to the outside world, after more than two centuries of self-imposed seclusion, arose from a sequence of maritime incidents. The mistreatment of American sailors shipwrecked upon Japanese shores and the need of a source of supplies for whaling vessels operating in the area constituted two of the main reasons for the visits of the American Commodore, Matthew Perry, to Japan in 1853–54. These visits and the treaty arising from them ended Japan's exclusion-of-foreigners policy.

Once more in contact with the outside

* However, a very thin stream of Western learning did enter Japan because of minor deviations from the policy of seclusion.

world the Japanese were aware that Western civilization had been developing at a rapid pace while their own domestic advancement had progressed sluggishly, if, indeed, it had progressed at all. They were, then, very ready to use force to try to make up for their having failed to secure valuable colonies at the time some of the Western states were securing them. It was their misfortune that when they did begin to use the weapons of the Western world the use of those weapons was beginning to be frowned upon by the colony-satiated states.

Human Factors

Although the Japanese are originally of a mixed racial make-up, they stand today as rather uniform in physical appearance. There has been little intermixture of blood with other peoples during historic times. The only inhabitants living in Japan who could be considered as a racial minority group are the Ainus, gradually pushed northward onto the island of Hokkaido by the surge of Japanese expansion. They presently number no more than twenty thousand and live quite apart from the Japanese.

The Mongolian racial strain predominates among the Japanese, with the usual physical characteristics including black hair, short stature, and an epicanthic fold of the eyes. There are some strains from the South Seas and from islands off the southeast coast of Asia. Some authorities claim that there is no positive way of distinguishing a Japanese from a Chinese on the basis of physical traits alone.

Having no written language of their own, the Japanese borrowed Chinese ideographs around the third century A.D. These pictorial symbols proved so awkward in use that they later developed a syllabic system of signs of their own, made up of whole or parts of Chinese characters. The resulting variants have made the Japanese language one of the most difficult in the world. Cultural differences between Japan and the West are undoubtedly magnified because of the linguistic element.

Japan has been able to maintain great secrecy within the country because of a difficult Oriental language. Government documents and other printed matter in Japanese were relatively immune to scrutiny by foreigners, a fact accounting for the ability of the government to execute policies without the world in general knowing about their promulgation.

State Shinto, the national religion for many decades, has played an important part in the governmental as well as the cultural life of the Japanese. Literally translated as the "way of the gods," Shintoism associated the worship of countless deities to matters of the state. The people were taught that Japan is transcendent among nations of the world; that the Japanese race possesses divine attributes, based upon their unbroken imperial line of rulers; and that the fulfillment of their god-given obligations rests in unwavering obedience, matchless loyalty, extraordinary courage on the battlefield, and other manifestations of reverence to the state. Patriotism was thus instilled into the Japanese mind by extolling the virtues of national glory in the form of religious beliefs dramatized by religious rituals. Since 1868, state Shintoism was utilized as a deliberate effort to further the totalitarian spirit of Japan. The excess of political implication, bound up in the religion in its accepted form, prevented its standing as a pure form of worship.

Despite the official sanction given to state Shintoism until after Japan's defeat in World War II, Buddhism continued to persist on a large scale. It was introduced into Japan during the sixth century from Korea, which in turn had received it from China. Forty million Japanese are still classified as Buddhists. Moreover, there is nothing to prevent one person from being both a good Shintoist and a good Buddhist; Buddhism is more of a philosophy than a form of religion as commonly accepted in the Western world. Although Shintoism and Buddhism seem to Westerners to present certain fundamental contradictions, these do not disturb the Japanese because the two religions serve different functions. Shintoism represents a belief in the past; Buddhism one in the future. The former is traditionally conservative, whereas the latter is progressive, being often associated with social progress and advances in education, arts, and crafts.

Population. Close governmental control over the lives of Japanese people plus the definite delimitation of the country by fixed water boundaries has worked to make population statistics surprisingly complete. Since the middle of the Tokugawa Era, early in the eighteenth century, census counts have been remarkably frequent and apparently reliable. From a population of about 25,000,-000 at that time, the number of people in the Japanese Islands increased only 2,000,000 by the time Perry visited Japan in 1853, more than a century and a quarter later. Oppression of the peasant by the ruling classes and a restriction of commercial enterprise while Japan was isolated from the rest of the world were largely responsible for this lack of population growth.

At the beginning of the Meiji Restoration in 1868, the total population stood at the 33,-000,000 mark. Since that date the increase has been extremely rapid, correlating perfectly with Japan's need for an increased population to enable her to carry out her desire to adopt certain phases of Western civilization. Methods of government administration, techniques in scientific agriculture, and ways of carrying on commerce and industry all enabled the Japanese to support additional millions in a land previously impeded by narrow customs, underdeveloped potentialities, and shackled energies. An official census of 1940 gives a population of 73,114,000, ranking Japan among the six most populous countries of the world. After the repatriation, forced on the Japanese in Greater East Asia after the recent war, is completed, the population of Japan is expected to be 78,000,000.

INCREASES. In the two decades before Japan went to war with the United States her annual population increase had reached the incredible rate of nearly one million. During the same period the United States with its much greater total population increased only around 900,000 per year. An industrial revolution, similar to but much later than that in northwest Europe and the United States, deadened the immediate economic repercussions of the tremendous population increase. It is reasonable to assume that the population curve will tend to level off in postwar Japan; even before the war there was evidence that the total number of people was *increasing at a decreasing rate*.

URBAN VS. RURAL POPULATION. The recent population increase has been chiefly reflected in the growth of cities. In 1893 the rural population amounted to about five sixths of

the total, but by 1940 the urban population had increased to the point where only about one half of the people of Japan lived outside the cities. Some rural areas have actually lost population within the last decades. On the other hand, the number of urban dwellers increased from six and a half million in 1893 to more than thirty-six million in 1940. Cities of 100,000 or more population numbered only six in the Japan of 1893, whereas forty were to be counted in 1940.

Six Japanese cities stand out as great metropolitan centers, the smallest of which has nearly a million inhabitants:

Tokyo	7,100,000	Kyoto	1,177,000
Osaka	3,395,000	Kobe	1,006,000
Nagoya	1,249,000	Yokohama	866,000

These six cities are strung out along a 275-mile stretch of the Pacific coast of Honshu between Tokyo Bay and Osaka Bay, a region now somewhat resembling the eastern seaboard of the United States between New York and Washington with its concentration of large cities (see the maps on page 381). Other than these cities, Japan has none with a population greater than one third of a million people.

POPULATION DENSITY. In justification of her colonial aspiration, Japan has emphasized the crowded conditions of her homeland, frequently employing authentic statistics to strengthen her case. The population density amounts to about 500 persons per square mile, but the Japanese point out that a more accurate measure is the 3,100 persons per square mile of arable land. This latter type of evaluation does not take into account the advantages of nonarable lands in supplying hydroelectric energy and forest resources; the fishing banks in the surrounding seas; nor the small amount of area actually needed for industrial development. Neither does it explain Japan's nation-wide campaign to stimulate interest in and even demand large families of every married couple.

Her large population poses a serious problem for postwar Japan. The solution, however, may be less difficult than commonly supposed if the new regime of the future devotes the national economy to peaceful rather than military pursuits. Elimination of a military regime that demands unprofitable heavy industries and exorbitant taxation of the agricultural classes should do much toward easing the burden of the Japanese people. Since population problems of a country actually spring from economic pressure, attention is next turned to the Japanese economy.

Economic Factors

The keynote of prewar Japanese economy was an industrial superstructure based upon the traditional agricultural pattern common to Oriental countries. Nearly one half of the people eked a living out of the soil. Crowded two or three to each acre of tilled land, the debt-ridden farmers and their families not only had to provide for themselves, but nurture the nation's program of expanding industrialism as well. Without adequate resources, many phases of the resulting economic development were subsidized outright, and it was inevitably the farmer who paid the bill.

An ever-growing proportion of the population manned the machines that brought Japan into being as a world power. Little better off than their country cousins, these wage-earners were in essence the "resource" of human labor that enabled Japanese goods to compete on the world market with countries richly endowed with raw materials and with long-standing industrial experience. At the same time farmer and wage earner alike shared the lack of any popular participation in government affairs.

Directing the energies of these millions were the ruling factions, who were united in their effort to maintain supremacy. Often there were differences among leaders as to the exact course the empire was to follow, but from 1868 until 1945 the national economy never failed to support the state at the expense of the individual. Among the foremost of those at the helm were the industrialists and the military cliques, making the decisions which ordained that Japanese economic strength be used to generate armed force.

Postwar economy must follow the broad pattern of prewar functions from the standpoint of resources, industrial capacity, lines of commercial development, and type of foreign trade. It is necessary to look at these established functions before attempting to understand the adjustments needed to convert a wartime economy into one suitable for permanent peacetime operation.

Agriculture. Fully half of the cultivated land of Japan is normally given over to rice production. Yielding more than 2,400 pounds per acre per year, the rice crop almost literally feeds the nation (supplemented by fish as a source of protein). The government vigorously controlled rice production and trade in an effort to stabilize agriculture and assure the country a dependable food supply. The importation of rice never reached significant proportions in amount, although as the "critical margin" foreign or colonial rice sharply affected the price structure of the commodity. The per capita consumption of rice is regarded as the best measure of the standard of living within Japan. Other grain crops, vegetables, and fruits are raised as supplementary food items, but not in the variety commonly found in an environment so capable of diversified agricultural production.

Beyond supplying food for seventy-odd million people, Japanese farmers have found it desirable to augment their income by certain cash crops. Most important among these is silk, a crop based upon cheap labor and the raising of mulberry leaves for feeding the silkworms. Before the war Japan produced nearly four fifths of the world's silk, most of it coming from the central part of Honshu. Other cash crops include tea, tobacco, flax, hemp, pyrethrum, and peppermint.

Compensating for almost complete lack of a livestock industry as a source of meat, the extensive fishing banks surrounding the Japanese Islands figure prominently in the national economy. From three to four million persons depend upon the fishing industry as a means of livelihood. Not only are fish products consumed throughout Japan, but in prewar years canned fish was a valuable export item. Fishing interests were largely concentrated around the coastal areas of Japan itself, but frequently vessels and floating canneries operated in waters thousands of miles from their home base.

Industry. The Westernization of Japan has been expressed through manufacturing. Before 1868 industry consisted almost entirely of the handicraft trades, such as weaving, ceramics, and the production of cutlery. Following the Meiji Restoration machine methods came into being, at first with foreign and later with domestic equipment. Until the 1930's, emphasis was placed upon the manu-

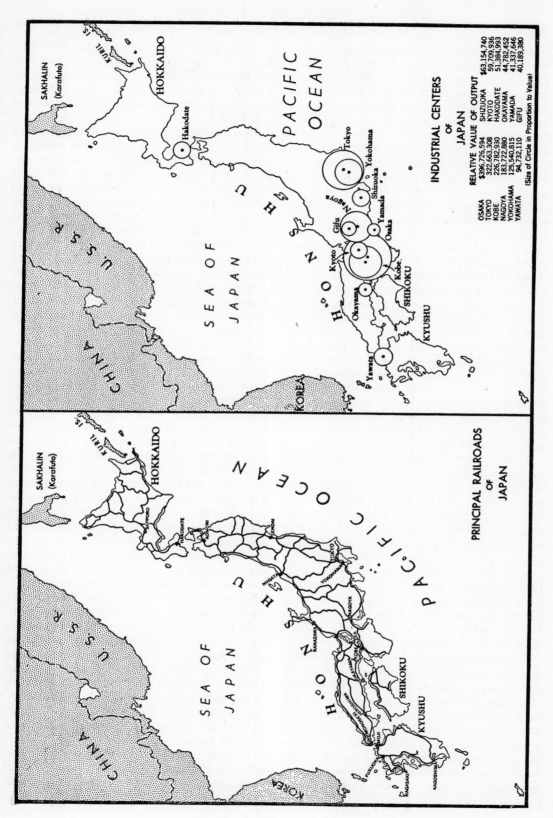

INDUSTRIAL CENTERS
OF
JAPAN

RELATIVE VALUE OF OUTPUT

OSAKA	$396,726,594	SHIZUOKA	$63,154,740
TOKYO	322,663,308	KYOTO	59,709,936
KOBE	226,782,930	HAKODATE	51,384,993
NAGOYA	183,722,880	OKAYAMA	44,782,452
YOKOHAMA	125,540,815	YAMADA	41,337,646
YAWATA	94,732,110	GIFU	40,189,380

(Size of Circle in Proportion to Value)

PRINCIPAL RAILROADS
OF
JAPAN

facture of foreign-type consumer goods that could be sent to markets all over the world. Japan's great specialty was textiles, although the technique of fabricating more and more complicated types of wares added to the list of export items and catered also to a growing home demand. There was a distinct carry-over from the more primitive pre-industrial era, however, in that two thirds of the workers were employed in very small shops or engaged in piecework in their own homes.

It was with manufacturing that Japan made a bid for world importance in foreign trade. If raw materials were not to be found within the country, they were imported. Japan could depend primarily upon an extremely cheap and fairly efficient labor supply to keep costs down. In addition, managerial skill, a strategic commercial position with respect to world trade routes, and a willingness on the part of the government to subsidize industry aided in the production of low-cost commodities. Low-income groups abroad, especially in eastern Asia, were willing to buy inferior products if they were "dirt cheap." Eventually tariff and quota restrictions inflicted by other manufacturing nations interfered with the forceful Japanese policy of economic imperialism.

An urgent need for heavy industries became apparent as Japan developed plans for her "Greater East Asia Co-Prosperity Sphere," and prepared for a major military conflict. Despite insufficient resources, a program of iron and steel manufacturing was pushed ahead to supply the armaments necessary to back up a mighty army and navy. Territorial acquisitions were to provide raw materials lacked by the homeland. In fact, coal and iron ore from Manchukuo and Korea, cotton from China, tin and rubber from southeast Asia, and oil from the East Indies partially fulfilled Japanese needs before final military defeat.

Transportation. In her attempts to establish and maintain an industrial economy Japan required both internal and external lines of communication. The small size of the country and the limitation of intensive development to a relatively small number of lowland areas greatly simplify internal transportation needs. Further, the highly irregular coastline abounds with harbors conducive to coastwise trade. A favorable maritime position in the western Pacific has become a focal point for ocean shipping lanes that link the Japanese Islands with trans-Pacific lands, with Europe via the Suez Canal, and with every important economic region in Asia and Australia.

By a system of trunk lines the rail network of Japan efficiently ties together all major industrial and urban areas (see the maps on page 381). Less important railways filter along the more remote coastal plains and through the valleys, providing excellent contact to all areas that support large numbers of people. Continuous interisland rail service is maintained by the use of fast ferries operating from Honshu to Hokkaido and Honshu to Shikoku, and a tunnel that connects Honshu with Kyushu. Railways greatly overshadow roads from a traffic standpoint, although the latter have local importance.

Although several hundred ports actively support coastwise shipping, only a few were ever developed for large-scale international trade. Before the war the ports of Kobe, Yokohama, and Osaka accounted for more than four fifths of the foreign trade of Japan. In registered tonnage Kobe ranked third among the ports of the world. Large liners from Britain, France, Germany, Italy, the United States, and Canada called frequently at Kobe and Yokohama, and equally large Japanese ships covered every important port in the world. In addition, smaller vessels and tramp steamers from many nations crowded the waters of leading Japanese ports.

Commercial air service in prewar Japan was little more than a prelude to aerial combat and the transportation of personnel and supplies to areas of conflict and military control. As early as 1929 an airline operated regularly between Tokyo and Osaka. With this meager start, air transportation routes by 1941 extended from Japan to Korea and Manchukuo; to north, central, and south coastal China; to Formosa and the Mandated Islands as far eastward as Jaluit in the Marshall Islands; to French Indo-China and Siam in southeast Asia; and to Portuguese Timor in the East Indies.

Postwar airlines will not simulate the pattern of Japan's wartime system. Global routes from North America and Europe will first contact Japan, and regional lines in eastern Asia will be based upon traffic needs of a commercial rather than a political or military nature.

Economic problems. Shorn of the empire built up over a period of years and powerless to force economic control upon unwilling neighbors, Japan must still find sustenance for its huge population. Agriculture must always remain as the mainstay of the domestic economy. The fishing banks and the forests can supplement the soil in meeting basic wants. In addition, however, the assets of a favorable trade location and a bountiful labor supply will be able to stimulate industry directed toward the manufacture of goods desired by the mass markets of eastern Asia. Without a war machine to maintain, the Japanese people should be in a position to benefit from an economy that permits them to best utilize those resources at hand.

Most essential to the realization of such an economy will be the dissolution of the great commercial and industrial monopolies. Operating as holding companies and based upon family partnerships, fifteen of these monopolies controlled more than three fourths of Japan's business, both internal and foreign. The Mitsui family alone is said to have transacted about one seventh of the country's total business! These huge concerns were very much integrated with the governmental machinery of militant Japan. The farmers and the wage earners can never enjoy the fruits of their labor if they continue to be subjected to crushing influences that do not recognize the rights of the laboring classes.

Several pertinent questions in Japanese postwar economy relate to external factors. Will national interests of other countries suppress any honest efforts that Japan may make to establish legitimate trade relations abroad? Will China, India, and other Asiatic countries turn to manufacturing themselves and supply cheap commodities for their own mass markets? Can Japan hold her own in a world that may rapidly turn toward the use of synthetic goods as a substitute for unevenly distributed resources? Already the silk industry is in grave danger of being overwhelmed by the encroachments on its former market by the manufacturers of nylon and other synthetic fibers.

Aggressive Expansion

With the physical, historical, human, and economic factors operating in and upon Japan clearly in view, there is now the opportunity to examine why and how those factors were blended into a program of attempted domination of eastern Asia and the western Pacific. Over a period of approximately three quarters of a century Japan expanded her territory. This expansion lasted from the early part of Emperor Meiji's rule in the late 1860's until the country's defeat in World War II. During this period the Japanese Empire grew from the original home islands to a large domain stretching up and down the Pacific margin of Asia and eastward into the Pacific Ocean (see the table on page 388 and the map on page 385). Even though each Japanese action was relatively brief during this expansion, the cumulative effect amounted to a continuous building up of power.

If Japan is used as an example, it is possible to learn to recognize the motives and methods of a government or a people contemplating a career of territorial aggrandizement. Motives for aggressive expansion may be classified into three basic types: economic, psychological, and political. The economic motives are rather clearly defined, but the psychological are to a certain extent intangible, and the political have a number of ramifications that involve both internal and external forces.

Economic motives. The history of industrial development in Japan revealed the inherent lack of domestic raw materials and the need for markets for manufactured goods. Scarcity of resources in relation to the population of Japan has often been presented as a justification for looking beyond the area of the home islands for national sustenance or possible avenues of immigration. So effective has been this type of propaganda that other nations have at times closed their eyes to or even lauded Japanese acquisitions. Nevertheless, the plea for more colonial "living space" as fields of investment, sources of raw materials, and markets for goods is no more valid than that of any highwayman who claims he needs more of the world's goods.

Psychological motives. The feelings and beliefs of a people, however right or wrong they may be, play a large part in determining whether the foreign policy of a state will be peaceful or warlike. Many of the Japanese people were led to believe that their emperor was a direct descendant of a sun goddess and that they as a people were destined to rule the world. This belief made the motive of revenge all the more powerful whenever they found themselves treated as an inferior racial group by the peoples of the West.

Political motives. The political impetus for aggressive expansion may be broken down into two principal subtypes, one revolving around defensive strategy, the other around offensive strategy. As an underlying motive, the lure of power has added its weight to all Japanese political activity having international objectives. Since the Meiji Restoration every important political move in Japan has been attuned to external conditions.

DEFENSIVE STRATEGY. Japan was fortunate in securing excellent insular defenses. The geographic factors making this possible were that the nations actively or potentially opposed were either primarily continental or were remote from the areas in which Japan became interested. During the last half of the nineteenth century, in a period peculiarly propitious for that undertaking, the Japanese saw the value of neighboring islands as outposts in the western Pacific.

None of the islands secured offered any particular hazard to Japanese occupation. The Volcano Islands and Marcus Island were practically uninhabited and virtually waiting to be occupied. The Kuriles and Bonins were also sparsely populated and no serious difficulty was encountered in acquiring them. Formosa, the Pescadores, and the Ryukyu Islands (Liukiu) were taken from China, the first two as a result of Japanese victory in the war of 1894–95. Karafuto, the southern part of the Island of Sakhalin, came into Japanese hands from a Russia defeated in 1904–05. The Carolines, Marshalls and Marianas were taken from Germany in 1914.

By virtue of the proximity of her home islands to a great continental land mass, however, geography provides the greatest defense worry of Japan.* Japan's attempts throughout modern history either to control Korea, or

* Compare Britain's concern over Germany's march through Belgium in World War I and control of the coast opposite in World War II.

to prevent its control by other states, are a case in point. For many years the same strategy has also been followed with regard to China. And Russia, possessing mainland territory opposite Japan, qualified automatically as the object of Japanese fear and suspicion. The Russo-Japanese War of 1904–05, fought over Korea and Manchuria, was a result of this basic Japanese strategy, and Russia's demonstration of military power in World War II so concerned Japan that she kept a large army during the war in the puppet state of Manchukuo south of the Siberian boundary.

OFFENSIVE STRATEGY. Japan's geography presented her governing powers, including industrialists and offensive-minded strategists, with the knotty problem of whether to expand on the continent or insularly. On the one hand, the continent possessed important natural resources owned by a weak China and impotent Siam, and lands controlled by states too remote to exert protective power easily. French Indo-China and British Malaya exemplified colonial possessions especially helpless during times when the mother countries had troubles at home. On the other hand, there were insular storehouses of great natural wealth to the south. In this category were the Netherland East Indies, owned by a weak, remote state, and the Philippine Islands, in close proximity to Japan but remote from their protector. The ocean road to these rich island groups was easy for a state possessing sufficient naval and air power to dominate it. When the Japanese strategists surveyed the factors that they considered favorable to them in 1941, they decided that they could attain both continental and insular objectives simultaneously despite the conflict in China that had been going on for four years.

Once the desired objectives of the country were clearly in view, the final problem was to determine how to achieve those objectives.

Tools and techniques of policy. The economic, social, and political tools and techniques, including the strategical and tactical, seemed excellently suited to their purpose. As a basis for war, the economic system of Japan was ideally organized, that is, concentrated in the hands of a select few, hence pliable. Also, the Japanese took great pride in thinking that they had overtaken the West

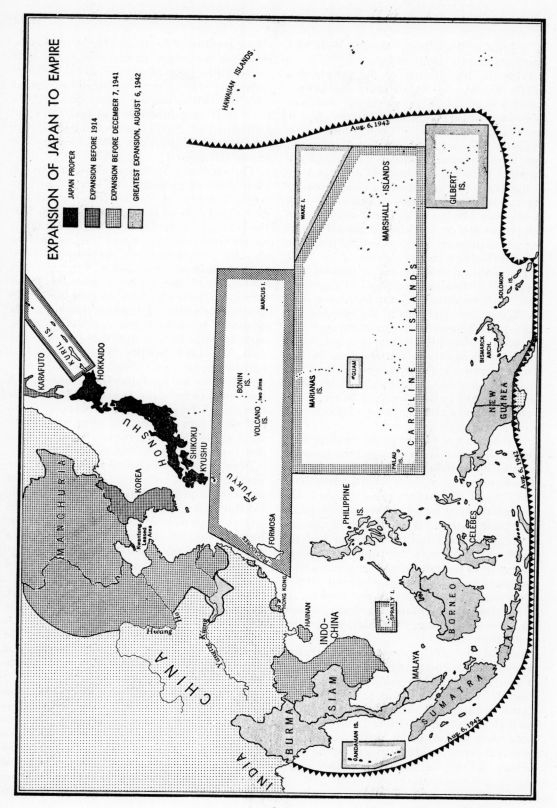

EXPANSION OF JAPAN TO EMPIRE

JAPAN PROPER
EXPANSION BEFORE 1914
EXPANSION BEFORE DECEMBER 7, 1941
GREATEST EXPANSION, AUGUST 6, 1942

in industrial "know-how," despite their late start after Perry's visit in 1853.

With the background of the people distinctly feudal, the opportunity for propaganda was good. The militaristic class had demanded respect since feudal times when it was known as *Samurai*. When volunteers or conscripts were taken into the army and navy, they were indoctrinated with the code of the Samurai, known as the *Bushido*, or "The Way of the Warrior." Qualities inbred by exacting training in the tenets of this code, such as absolute obedience to one's superior, development of a certain kind of mental endurance, and frugality, were especially desirable in conditioning a people for war.

The political institutions of Japan were peculiarly adapted for purposes of aggressive war. Although many countries possess dual or "figurehead" elements in the political systems, Japan's government was saturated with them. For example, the emperor has always ruled Japan *in theory*, but from the twelfth century until 1868 the shogun (referred to in the discussion of the historical factor in Japan) actually ruled—and in turn his powers were sometimes taken over by still other officials.

In 1868 the real powers of the emperor were supposedly returned to him, and the Japanese constitution of 1889 later vested all the powers of sovereignty in him. Parliament (the "Diet") and the cabinet were merely imitations of Western forms of government rather than their essence. The military clique and the leading industrialists of Japan had tremendous influence in the country, although the extent of power of the latter group varied with the time. Various provisions as to governmental finance assured the cabinet, or rather those groups that controlled it, of having the necessary money to function regardless of the Diet.

In final analysis the governmental structure in Japan was orientated toward the realization of strictly nationalistic ambition by those in control. During the latter part of the nineteenth century and until the end of World War II the military clique "built up" the emperor in the people's minds as a sacred, all-powerful ruler. Then along with other groups, shifting in importance, this clique merely ruled through the exalted throne.

To further insure their control, the military clique combined the state religion of Shintoism with patriotism in order to make men more willing to go to war and to die for their emperor. The men were thus indoctrinated with the belief that the surest way to have one's spirit worshiped was to perish on the field of battle. Soldiers were also assured that they would be tortured and killed by the enemy if captured.

The civilian population also came in for their share of guidance and control by governing factions. A very active police watched over the people to see that they did not harbor "dangerous thoughts." Steps were taken to see that no one heard foreign radios, thereby accentuating the geographic isolation of an insular location.

Outside of the Japanese Islands various techniques were employed to gain favor with prospective victims or frighten them into submission. Impressive and deceptive phrases, such as "Asia for the Asiatics" and "Greater East Asia Co-Prosperity Sphere," served as bait for the unwary. Native puppet governments were set up following invasions. A type of psychological warfare, which first threatened the people and then attempted to lull them into a feeling of security, was utilized against foreign groups. Sometimes the order of this procedure would be reversed.

Many basic principles of a strategic nature were employed, oftentimes involving long and careful preparation. Treaties were violated in order to fortify certain islands as defense screens or points for attack; landing rehearsals were staged on tropical shores of a type thought to be impenetrable; and shipments of oil and scrap metal were secured from the United States for military stockpiles. The principle of opportunism was observed, for the Chinese giant probably would not remain asleep much longer and Germany was keeping the Western Powers occupied in Europe. The bombing of Pearl Harbor was an example of the principle of surprise accompanied by systematic espionage.

With the thoroughness of preparation represented by all of the above in mind, it is not difficult to understand why Japanese military leaders adopted an arrogant "how can we lose" attitude. They did lose, however, because they made a wrong estimate of the situation, especially in underestimating the material power and the quality of leadership of the Western Powers as well as the endurance of the Chinese people.

Problems of Postwar Japan

Japan's postwar problems may be divided into two major classifications. Initially the country is concerned with recovery from the war. Over a longer period, Japan must look to a role of reform in what should be for her a new world.

Recovery. A rapid recovery from material losses is, without qualification, Japan's first desideratum. The fundamental basis of the country's existence and vitality lies in its physical possessions. The physical destruction to Japan has very probably shaken her more than the loss of man power, which was not very great from the military point of view. Cities especially were hard hit, huge metropolitan areas having in many cases been reduced to rubble. However, because of the relatively low standards of living to which the Japanese people are accustomed and because of their unquestionably industrious nature, reconstruction of cities should prove to be no insurmountable handicap.

Reform. The keynote to progress in Japan must be both internal and external. A complete economic, social, and political revolution is required from within, and at the same time a genuine, sincere policy of peaceful relations with the rest of the world must be effected. The undesirable aspects of her life—obvious to the readers of this chapter—must be completely wiped out. The new Japan must welcome the intellectual and moral as well as the material contributions of the West and of China.

General Douglas MacArthur, the Supreme Allied Commander in Japan after the termination of World War II, made great strides in helping the Japanese to pave the way to progress. His directives opened many new paths toward the establishment of a democratic, peaceful state. The whole psychological framework for the rule of Japan by an oligarchy in the name of the emperor, and for military aggression, was vigorously attacked by the abolition of state Shinto and the elimination of all ultranationalistic and militaristic teaching in the schools. The emperor's own denial of the militarists' claim of his divinity helped to disprove the existing code for imperial veneration.

General MacArthur also precipitated an economic revolution of a sort. His attempts to discourage the control of large landholdings by absentee owners and to better the lot of the many Japanese farmers in various ways may be construed as an endeavor to lay an economic basis for democracy. Likewise, he has tried to break up the great family control of industry and labor unions have been given the right to organize.

In political matters democracy has been given its first real chance to gain a foothold. The civil liberties of speech, press, and assembly have been assured and the obnoxious "thought control" police have been eliminated. Leaders responsible for terrorism in Japan and for her former militaristic policies are barred from public office. There exists a freedom of political party organization. The suffrage has been made universal, with the earliest age reduced to twenty. A new constitution went into effect in 1947. To facilitate this progress, MacArthur, in his directives, insured a minimum amount of confusion and trouble of any kind to his occupying forces by the use of gradual, step-by-step methods.

Two important measures are necessary to safeguard as far as possible the security of the world from future Japanese aggression. The first of these requires that a real, permanent democracy under the right kind of leaders be realized. There is obviously a very great danger that early withdrawal of occupation forces from Japan will jeopardize the establishment of any such regime. It may well take at least a generation of supervision (25 or 30 years) to undo the harm of centuries of militarism and autocratic rule. In general the early cooperation of the Japanese is excellent, but one must beware lest this has been merely a ruse to hasten the departure of the occupying forces. The other necessary measure must be one from without. Security is probably best insured by the cooperation of all peace-loving nations in the maintenance of bases, international "watch-towers," or other means of control over territory in the vicinity of Japan itself.

Finally, two factors of a broad geographic nature stand out that augur well for the future of Japan as a modern nation. First, the victorious powers have expressed no great desire to restrict Japan's access to, as dis-

The Japanese Empire—December 7, 1941[1]

Name	General location	Area in sq. mi.	Population	Military significance	Date of Acquisition	Status in 1948
Japan Proper	Off east coast of Asia	148,756	73,000,000	Small area formerly protected from mainland by water	(Original area of state)	Largely American occupation
Bonin Islands	500 miles south of Japan	27	5,000	Defensive screen	1861–76	American occupation
Kuril Islands	Arc from northern Japan to Kamchatka Peninsula	6,150	4,400	Cuts U. S.–U. S. S. R. communications near Japan	1875	Russian
Ryukyu Islands (Liu Chiu)	Arc from Japan to Formosa	935	455,000	Defensive screen	1875–79	American occupation
Volcano Islands	710 miles south of Japan	10	1,200	Strategic outposts	1891	American occupation
Formosa (Taiwan)	Island off southeastern coast of China	14,000	5,315,000	Naval bases; air bases; practice area for warfare in tropics; springboard to Philippines	1895	Chinese
Pescadores	Group of small islands between Formosa and Chinese coast	49	70,000	Associated with Formosa	1895	Chinese
Marcus Island	1,200 miles southeast of Japan	1	—	Strategic outpost	1899	American occupation
Karafuto	Southern part of island of Sakhalin; north of Hokkaido	13,935	332,000	Check against maritime provinces of U. S. S. R.	1905	Russian
Kwantung Peninsula (leased area including Dairen and Port Arthur)	Tip of Liaotung Peninsula; southernmost part of Manchuria	1,435	1,657,000	Base for penetration into Manchuria; has ice-free outlet in winter	1905	Chinese (with special Russian interests
Korea (Chosen)	Peninsula of Asiatic mainland; 125 miles west of Japan	85,206	24,324,000	"Dagger pointing at the heart of Japan"; offensive base against Manchuria or the maritime provinces of the U. S. S. R.	1905–10	Transition area before independence
Japanese Mandated Islands (Carolines, Marianas, Marshalls)	From 700 to 3,300 miles east of the Philippines	829	124,000	Stepping stones to penetration southward	1914 (conquest)	American strategic trusteeship
Manchuria * (Manchukuo)	Northeastern Provinces of China	503,013	36,933,000	Base against U. S. S. R.; reservoir of important materials	1931–32	Chinese
Jehol	Chinese province adjacent to Manchuria on the southwest	74,297	2,184,723	Entering wedge into China to the south and base for operations to the west	1933	Chinese
More of China (including Hainan)	Coastal city areas and much of northern China	500,000 (estimate)	185,000,000 (estimate)	Control limited chiefly to cities and lines of communication; important resources	1937 on	Chinese
Spratly and Paracel Islands	In South China Sea	5	—	Small bases	1939	Latter in dispute between France and China
French Indo-China	Southeastern Asia; south of China	286,000	24,461,251	Main base for invasion of southeast Asia	1940–41	French

* Manchuria was set up as the puppet state of Manchukuo from 1931–32 until the end of the war in 1945, but was never officially designated by the Japanese as a part of the "empire." In practice, however, it was as rigidly controlled as were Korea and Formosa which were claimed as parts of the Japanese Empire.

388

tinguished from control of, raw materials. A future in world trade need not be limited in view of the acknowledged Japanese capacity to maintain commercial relations with other countries. Second, the isolation of Japan from the Western world, which has so frequently been mentioned in the preceding pages of this chapter, stands to be rapidly broken down. A chief means by which to accomplish this feat lies in the New Air Age, bringing Tokyo and other Japanese nerve centers within hours of Occidental capitals and commercial areas. Both factors offer the advantage of facilitating the recovery of the Japanese Isles as well as hope of a respected position in the world.

PART FIVE
Africa and Australasia

AUSTRALASIA and Africa represent merely overseas extensions of Europe. In Australasia, the process of casting off European political control is now under way; in Africa it has scarcely begun. These two areas, therefore, afford an excellent study in imperialism and in the geography of dependent colonial areas. Since the indigenous cultures of Africa and Australia have made negligible contributions to the world community, they are of little moment. The natural resources of these two areas are immense. Questions of who shall own, develop, and use those resources are so important as to have produced a long series of geopolitical tremors, severe enough to be felt throughout the world community. Moreover, repercussions from these realms promise to increase rather than decline during the near future.

Australasia has been variously described as an "island continent," as an "oceanic continent," and as the "archipelago of southern Asia." None of these designations is quite accurate. It is actually a huge island realm, wherein seven per cent of the earth's land area is scattered over twenty-seven per cent of the water surface of the globe. Physically, it consists of some three parts: First, there is the very large subcontinental island of Australia, closely associated with which is the island of Tasmania to the south and the two islands of New Zealand to the southeast. Second, there are, to the northwestward, the East Indies, which stretch from Australia to Asia. They consist of the five large islands—Papua, Borneo, Sumatra, Celebes, and Java, and the three great island groups—the Moluccas, the Lesser Sunda Islands, and the Philippines.

Third, there are the almost countless atolls, small islands, and swarms of islets, composing Oceania. These extend 2,000 miles northward, 4,000 miles northeastward, and 6,000 miles eastward, from Australia.

When first discovered by Europeans, this vast realm contained some four types of inhabitants. In Australia, Papua, and the islands stretching from the Bismarcks to the Fiji Islands, the inhabitants were generally black-skinned and frizzy-haired folk. For that reason Papua and the islands to the eastward are still called Melanesia (black islands). In the islands stretching westward from Papua the peoples were generally of the short, brunet, Malay, or East Indian, type. These islands, therefore, carry the name Malaysia or Indonesia (Indo-islands). New Zealand, Hawaii, and Easter Island each form one apex of a colossal triangle enclosing many scattered groups of islands collectively known as Polynesia (many islands). The Polynesian people are tall, well-formed folk, who show characteristics somewhat similar to those of brunet Europeans. North of Papua, stretch several swarms of tiny islands, the Palaus, Marianas, Carolines, Marshalls, and Gilberts—collectively termed Micronesia (small islands)—whose people exhibit mixed Polynesian, Malaysian, Negroid, and Mongoloid traits. Finally, there were the Philippines, whose many thousands of islands were a veritable museum of human types.

After the Portuguese, in search of spices, discovered this great realm, a scramble for ownership of the islands occurred. Portuguese, Spanish, Dutch, British, French, German, American, and Japanese at various times established title to parts of the region. For 450 years the flood tides of imperialism have washed over the islands. The Spaniards colonized the Philippines and Guam, the British settled Australia, Tasmania, and New Zealand, the Americans colonized Hawaii, and the Hollanders to a limited degree settled Java.

Colonialism at its worst and its best has been seen in Australasia. Australia and New Zealand typify it at its best. British people settled these lands, establishing seven inauspicious colonies. From them have grown two of the most socially and politically advanced nations of the earth. In contrast, the Japanese record in the Philippines and the Portuguese in Timor is imperialism at its worst. The Philippines have seen all kinds. Manuel Quezon, first president of the Philippine Commonwealth, stated it thus: "We have had three masters, the Spaniards who brought us *churches,* the Japanese who brought us *brothels,* and the Americans who brought us *schools* and trained us for self government." The Indies have a colonialism that contains both good and bad elements. The Dutch have developed the islands, making Java, for instance, the most productive and densely populated spot on earth, but they have undoubtedly neglected the social and political development of the area (at least, the Indonesians consider that to be the case, and consequently desire to be rid of their overlords). At present, British,* French, Dutch, Portuguese, and Americans retain dependencies in Australasia. What will be the ultimate disposal of their holdings can scarcely be forecast at the present time.

Africa repeats with variations the story of colonial exploitation in Australasia. Nearly everything else regarding Africa is, however, very unlike the latter. Africa is next door to Europe, not at the Antipodes. It is the most compact among the continents, not the most maritime portion of the earth. It has long been known to Europeans, not one of the last areas to be discovered. And, finally, Africa possesses thrice the area and twice the population of Australasia.

Africa is a huge triangle, whose short side lies adjacent to Europe and whose long apex points toward the South Pole. The continent is a block of land so compact that entry be-

* Including the Australians and New Zealanders.

yond the coastal areas can be made only by small river boat, spur line of railway, caravan, or safari. Once inside, half of the continent is seen to consist of desert and tropical forest. Most of the remainder is high plateau.

The continent of Africa has unbelievable riches in forest products, wild game, and minerals. Its waterpower is the greatest on earth, and there are huge areas of productive soils and native grasslands. So unfavorable are the coast zone and the surface configuration, however, that Africa is the most backward of the continents, and its 11,530,000 square miles support a mere 163,000,000 persons.

At one point Africa is connected with the continent of Asia. There, Egyptian civilization arose in Neolithic times, and flourished through the Bronze and Early Iron Ages. After that, it stagnated in tyranny and intellectual reaction. Nowhere is there any industrial or political power in Africa today.

From the fourteenth to the nineteenth century the European nations gradually appropriated the African coasts. During the late nineteenth and early twentieth century, they overran the interior. After 1914 there were struggles among the European masters, with the elimination of all but the British, French, Portuguese, Belgian, and Spanish.

None of the original African states have retained their independence except Ethiopia.* Egypt, long a protectorate of Britain, seems to be in the process of regaining full sovereignty. The so-called Arab states of Morocco, Algeria, Tunisia, and Libya are now agitating for independence.

Despite the long term of European domination, less than 4,000,000 Europeans have colonized the continent. These include about 2,000,000 Dutch and British in southern Africa, 1,000,000 French and others in Algeria, and less than 1,000,000 French, Belgians, Germans, Italians, and others in the rest of the continent. The British and Dutch of South Africa have been welded into a dominion of the British Commonwealth. Algeria has been annexed to metropolitan France. A handful of American Negroes were colonized on the Guinea Coast, where they formed the Republic of Liberia. Elsewhere colonialism of the exploitative type is well-nigh universal.

* This was overrun by the Italians for a time, but has been restored.

| # Africa: A Study in Colonialism

Among the world's seven continents, Africa is second only to Asia in size. In population, however, it stands fourth, and in civilization it should be rated near the bottom, probably next to uninhabited Antarctica. The relatively low status of Africa strongly suggests that certain conditions of the natural environment in that continent are, and probably have always been, comparatively unfavorable to human endeavor along geonomic and socio-geographic lines. Politico-geographic development, in turn, has been greatly retarded, with the result that Africa for long remained a "dark continent." It is, of course, no longer unexplored and unknown, but its political control has passed almost wholly into the hands of outside powers. As a consequence, Africa is today a vast study in imperialism.

At first glance, many of the natural characteristics of Africa would seem to favor human occupance. It is located near the center of the land mass of the world; indeed, it is connected with Asia at the Isthmus of Suez and almost connected with Europe at the Strait of Gibraltar. It possesses large areas of relatively level land and a small proportion of mountainous terrain. It is well mineralized. It contains some of the world's mightiest rivers—the Nile, Congo, Niger, Zambezi, Limpopo, Orange, and several others. Its wealth in waterpower and wild game exceeds that of any other continent. Moreover, it contained human inhabitants at a very early date in prehistoric times.

Closer examination, however, brings to light several serious disadvantages. First among these is the shape of the continent.

Like the silhouette of a huge lop-sided pear Africa has remarkably smooth and regular outlines and no major coastal indentations. For instance, its area is about three times that of Europe, and yet its coastline is less than half as long as that of the latter.

Physical Characteristics

Surface configuration. The surface of most of Africa is that of a vast tableland or plateau separated from the sea by a rim of coastal plain, which in most places is very

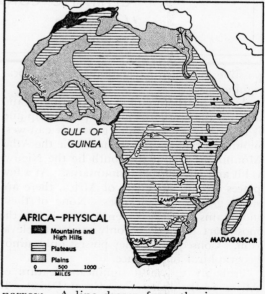

AFRICA—PHYSICAL
- Mountains and High Hills
- Plateaus
- Plains

0   500   1000
MILES

narrow. A line drawn from the inner corner of the Gulf of Guinea to the southern end of the Red Sea would divide Africa into halves. South of that line the plateau aver-

393

ages 3,000 feet above sea level; north of that line, it averages about half that (see the map on page 393).*

Most of the rivers of Africa descend from the interior tableland by a series of falls or rapids that make it impossible to reach the interior by ship from the ocean. The Congo, Nile, Niger, and a few other rivers have eroded great lowlands in the plateau and on some of their interior reaches, navigation is

across. It is such a formidable barrier that it effectively separates the continent into two unequal portions. Africa north of the Sahara, is, and has always been, essentially a part of the Mediterranean realm of southern Europe and the Asiatic Near East. This "oneness" among regions of the Mediterranean, including North Africa, is clearly revealed in the historical geography of the area. Africa south of the Sahara is in its effects a vast "is-

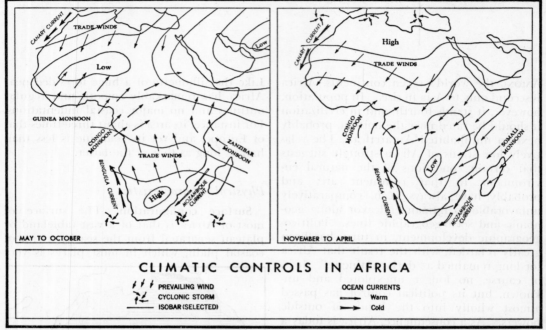

CLIMATIC CONTROLS IN AFRICA

	PREVAILING WIND		OCEAN CURRENTS
	CYCLONIC STORM		Warm
	ISOBAR (SELECTED)		Cold

possible; but such navigation is of only local significance.

At the northern end of the continent, and again at the southern end, the plateau upland is replaced by a system of generally east-west mountain ranges. At the north lie the Atlas Mountains, and at the south lie the Nieuwveldt and Drakensberg mountains. At a few places around the edges of Africa, there are small groups of volcanoes. None of these mountains is very extensive, and for the most part they are of only moderate elevation. Consequently they possess only minor geographical importance.

Probably the most significant feature of Africa is the Sahara, or Great Desert. It stretches unbroken from the Atlantic to the Red Sea and averages more than 1,000 miles

* Geologically speaking, Africa is a block of old rocks of the Archaean and Paleozoic ages, peneplaned, uplifted, and partially redissected.

land" isolated from the great land mass of the Old World.

Climate and natural vegetation. The earth's Geographical Equator lies across the middle of Africa, and the continent stretches from latitude 37° North to about 35° South. Thus, most of Africa is distinctly tropical, with only the northern and southern extremities being subtropical. Rays of the noonday sun fall vertically on some part of Africa every day in the year; and on no part of the continent do they fall at a very oblique angle. Consequently Africa receives more heat from the sun, proportionately, than does any other continent.

Because of the simplicity of Africa's surface configuration, its pattern of climates and natural vegetation zones (see the map on page 395) follows the prevailing wind system more closely than on any other continent (the map above shows the major climatic controls that operate). For this reason, Africa is the world's best example of regional symmetry.

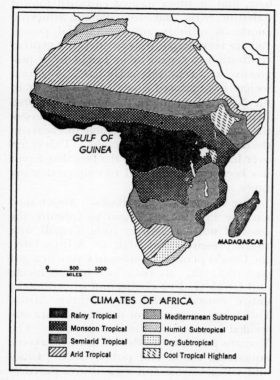

GULF OF
GUINEA

MADAGASCAR

0   500   1000
      MILES

CLIMATES OF AFRICA

Rainy Tropical   Mediterranean Subtropical
Monsoon Tropical   Humid Subtropical
Semiarid Tropical   Dry Subtropical
Arid Tropical   Cool Tropical Highland

In the equatorial regions most of the land receives rain throughout the year, and accordingly it supports a heavy cover of tropical forest. To the north and south of the equatorial regions are broad belts where there is a long wet season and a short dry season, and where the natural vegetation is savanna. These in turn are paralleled on their poleward margins by zones of tropical grassland where the season of rainfall is short and the season of drought is long. At about latitude 18° North and South, these grassland zones fade out into arid regions, marked by tropical desert vegetation. Unfortunately, the widest part of Africa lies squarely in one of these arid zones. Accordingly the Sahara is the largest desert in the world. In southern Africa the Kalahari is complementary to the Sahara but only a fraction as large.

Owing to the annual north-south migration of the wind system, the extreme northern and southern ends of Africa are, during their respective winter seasons, freed from the grasp of the dry trade winds (see the map on page 394). This absence of dry trade winds in the winter allows the cyclonic storms of the middle latitudes to bring a moderate winter rainfall to these coasts. The result is a Mediterranean, subtropical climate and a landscape of evergreen woodland, giving way to steppe vegetation inland. On the extreme southeastern part of the continent there is a small area of subtropical forest.

Native Races

By the layman, Africa is often believed to be inhabited mainly by Negroes. This is far from being the actual condition. The *native* races of that continent (exclusive of European colonists and their descendants) range all the way from Negritoes to Nordic types. The Negroes proper occupy only a small fraction of the total area, being limited to the forests of the Guinea coasts, the Sudanese savannas from the Senegal River eastward to the upper Nile, and a portion of the central Sahara. The somewhat similar Bantus occupy the Congo forest region and the savannas and grasslands of southern Africa. The pygmy Negritoes occupy several areas in the central African forest zone. These three very brunet races (Negritoes, Negroes, and Bantus), however, inhabit only about half of Africa (see the map on page 396).

Within the remaining half of the continent, the Kalahari and the Cape region are the home of Bushmen, Hottentots, Strandloopers, and other primitive peoples—mixtures of Negrito, Mongolic, and Mediterranean strains with varying amounts of Bantu blood. On the big island of Madagascar the inhabitants are of Malay and mixed Bantu-Malay origin. The Mediterranean coast of northern Africa is inhabited by large numbers of people of the Mediterranean (so-called Hamitic) race. In the Atlas Mountains, there are a few areas of Kabyles, which show generally Nordic racial characteristics. The Sahara and the eastern Sudan are about equally divided between Mediterranean and Semitic peoples, the latter going under the general name of Arab.

Historical Backgrounds

Early African civilization: THE NILE VALLEY. One of the seats where civilization first arose in the world was the delta and valley of the lower Nile. There, between five and six thousand years ago, human society achieved a state of social integration and material advancement which is usually associated with the adjective "civilized." This old Iberian civilization of Egypt may have been a colony

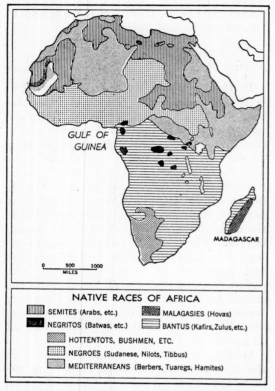

GULF OF
GUINEA

MADAGASCAR

0   500   1000
        MILES

NATIVE RACES OF AFRICA

SEMITES (Arabs, etc.)   MALAGASIES (Hovas)
NEGRITOS (Batwas, etc.)   BANTUS (Kafirs,Zulus,etc.)
HOTTENTOTS, BUSHMEN, ETC.
NEGROES (Sudanese, Nilots, Tibbus)
MEDITERRANEANS (Berbers, Tuaregs, Hamites)

of a somewhat older civilization in Mesopotamia, or it may have arisen independently (see the map on page 296). Certain it is that the Nile Valley offered all the major environmental inducements for the invention of a civilized way of life. The desert afforded natural protection, and the annual wetting and fertilization of the soil by the seasonal rise of the Nile taught man his primary lessons in systematic agriculture. Moreover, the sharply delineated valley strip anchored large numbers of men to one locality long enough for custom, ritual, barter, and superstition to become thoroughly transformed and institutionalized into law, religion, commerce, and science—recorded in writing, measured in mathematics, and rationalized in philosophy. Unquestionably, the unremitting demands of irrigation routinized human toil and enforced social cooperation. Unfortunately, it also bred a high degree of despotism in government.

This ancient civilization, therefore, flowered at an early date, overflowed its valley base, and at times washed eastward toward Palestine, Syria, and Mesopotamia, achieving enormous military and commercial power. But its very despotism caused this Egyptian civilization to crystallize and cease to be progressive at a relatively early date. Civilized society has endured down to the present in the Nile Valley, where the ways of farming, living, and thinking by the fellahin are essentially the same as those by their forebears in the days of the earliest Pharaohs. This carryover has occurred despite the fact that Egypt has been conquered and reconquered many times.

THE MEDITERRANEAN BASIN. About 1000 B.C. the Phoenicians began to colonize the coast of northern Africa from Tripoli west to the present site of Algiers. A little later, the Greeks planted colonies in Cyrenaica just west of Egypt. By the efforts of Phoenician and Greek traders, civilization spread to the entire coastal section of northern Africa. Following 146 B.C. all of northern Africa was welded into one civilized community. The Romans put down wells and built reservoirs, aqueducts, roads, and public baths. Cities and villages arose and agricultural practices became more widespread. In Roman times the term Africa was applied only to a limited portion of the region (see the map on the facing page).

In the fifth century A.D., as the Roman Empire was breaking up, the Vandals and other barbarians from eastern Europe settled the northwestern coast of Africa. During the seventh century the Moslem Arabs washed across northern Africa, and for several centuries that region was united under the Caliphate. Gradually, however, it split up into minor caliphates, and out of them grew the modern Moslem states: Egypt, Tripoli, Barca, Fezzan, Tunisia, Algeria, and Morocco. These have survived up to the present day, but have passed under European control.

Contacts between northern and southern Africa: EARLY CONTACTS. From earliest Egyptian times on down to the beginning of modern history, northern Africa had little contact with the larger portion of the continent lying south of the Sahara; and what contacts were made, were of short duration. The earliest seems to have been when Necho, an

Egyptian Pharaoh, sent a fleet of Phoenician ships from the Red Sea around Africa about the end of the seventh century B.C. Later a party of Greeks from Cyrenaica crossed the Sahara. About 520 B.C. the Carthaginians sent a fleet under Hanno westward and southward to the Gulf of Guinea. There, a number of trading towns were established on the Guinea Coast. In 400 B.C. the merchants of Carthage sent a caravan overland to West Africa. Several centuries later, the Romans

The Opening of Africa

The real importance of the African continent to the outside world began in the fifteenth century. Starting in this period, many European nations showed a live interest in the dark continent. Around its coasts and into its interior went the exploration parties, the trading expeditions, and later the armies which were to produce a scramble for African colonies and the eventual division of most of

ROMAN EMPIRE IN AFRICA

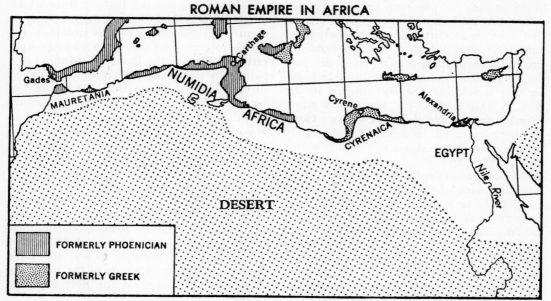

are reputed to have sent several expeditions southward across the desert.

MEDIEVAL CONTACTS. Somewhen near the end of the tenth century A.D. Mohammedan missionaries appeared in the western Sudan region; and by the beginning of the thirteenth century most of the Sahara and the Sudan had been converted to Islam. Meanwhile, many parts of Africa south of the Sahara were rapidly evolving out of the small tribal stage, and native states were emerging. Most of them were on the order of petty kingdoms, but a few were veritable empires. All of them seem to have been cursed by constant warfare and slave-raiding on a huge scale.

In the early fourteenth century French merchants from Dieppe sailed to the Guinea Coast. Between 1346 and 1413 they planted trading posts along the coasts of what are now Gambia, Portuguese Guinea, Sierra Leone, and Liberia. War in France, however, soon put an end to these voyages.

Africa into possessions of Portugal, the Netherlands, Britain, France, Spain, Germany, Italy, and Belgium.

The Portuguese in Africa. The coastal explorations of the Portuguese were the first of a long series of operations that finally put Africa under the domination of Europe. These early voyages were instigated by Prince Henry of Portugal, who bore the honorary title "the Navigator." Prince Henry sent out his first expedition in 1415. In 1434 Gil Eannes passed Cape Bojador; seven years later Nuño Tristam reached Cape Blanco; and in four more years, 1445, Diniz Dias attained Cape Verde. Soon the Guinea Coast was reached; and a lucrative traffic in gold, ivory, pepper, and slaves sprang up.

Continuing the procession of explorational voyages, Santarem passed the Bight of Biafra by 1471, Diogo Cam reached the mouth of the Congo in 1482, and six years later Bartholomew Dias rounded the Cape of Good

Hope. Finally, in 1497–98, Vasco da Gama turned the Cape, crossed the Indian Ocean, and reached India.

After 1488 Portugal laid claim to the entire coast of Africa south of Morocco. This claim was confirmed by the Papal Line of Demarcation in 1493 and the Treaty of Tordesillas in 1494. Portuguese trading settlements were early planted on both the east and west coasts of Africa, two of the earliest of these being on the Gold Coast in 1482 and in the Mozambique in 1505 (see the map on facing page).

The first modern nation to explore Africa, therefore, was Portugal. The Portuguese paid little attention to colonizing, however, because their primary interest lay in developing a trade with India and the Indies. Later on they developed a second interest in the African slave trade. The Portuguese established slave markets along the Guinea Coast and for a century they exercised a monopoly in supplying Negro slaves to South America and the West Indies.

In South Africa the Portuguese encountered difficulty with the natives and thereafter avoided the area. Instead, they developed a trade route across the southern interior from the Angola highlands to the Zambezi River. On the east coast the Arabs drove the Portuguese traders to a position south of Cape Delgado; and on the west coast the Dutch, British, French, and even the Danes and Swedes drove the Portuguese out of most of their possessions. The British, in carrying out their Cape-to-Cairo scheme, also managed to drive a wedge through Portuguese possessions in southern Africa. The only Portuguese territorial gain in World War I was the "Kionga Triangle," formerly a part of German East Africa.

At present the African holdings of Portugal consist of the following:

Possession	Area (sq. mi.)	Population
Azores Is.	922	254,000
Madeira Is.	314	212,000
Cape Verde Is.	1,557	162,000
Portuguese Guinea	13,944	415,000
St. Thomas and Prince's Is.	590	60,000
Angola	481,226	3,485,000
Mozambique	297,654	4,996,000
Total	791,207	9,584,000

The Dutch in Africa. The entry of the Netherlands into Africa was interwoven with the activities of Portugal. Dutch merchants had gradually come to act as distributors of the Oriental goods that the Portuguese brought to Europe from India.

Shortly after 1580, through a curious mischance of history (Philip II of Spain seized the Portuguese throne and was crowned king of Portugal when King Henry died without any heirs), the Netherlands found itself at war with Portugal because of the latter's tie with Spain, with whom the Netherlands was fighting. Soon the port of Lisbon, from which the Dutch procured their goods, was closed to them. In 1602, to meet this situation, the Dutch government chartered a trading corporation of its own, the Dutch East India Company. In the naval and trade war that ensued, the Dutch almost drove the Portuguese out of Africa. They captured the Gold Coast in 1637, but long before this they had superseded the Portuguese in the slave trade.* In 1641 they also seized part of Angola.

Shortly thereafter, in 1652, the Dutch planted a settlement at the Cape of Good Hope to serve as a way-station to the Indies. Subsequently, they were joined by French Huguenots and by settlers from other nations. For a time the Dutch were left alone and their colony grew rapidly. In 1814, however, the Netherlands was obliged to sell the Cape Colony to Britain as a part of the peace settlement which followed the defeat of Napoleon.

THE DUTCH DAUGHTER REPUBLICS. In 1833 slavery was abolished by law in the British Empire. When the British Minister undertook to enforce this and other laws, some ten thousand rebellious Dutch farmers (Boers) trekked with their wagons and livestock to a new area north of the Orange River. There they set up the Orange Free State. Other Dutchmen trekked eastward and founded the Republic of Natalia. A few years later many Boers migrated still farther north and organized the Transvaal Republic.

Britain promptly annexed Natalia in 1845. In 1867 diamonds were discovered in South Africa, and in 1884 a rich gold field was opened up. These developments led to an enormous influx of British settlers. The resulting friction between Dutch settlers and British immigrants led to the Boer War

* It was a Dutch vessel which, in 1619, brought the first slaves to Virginia.

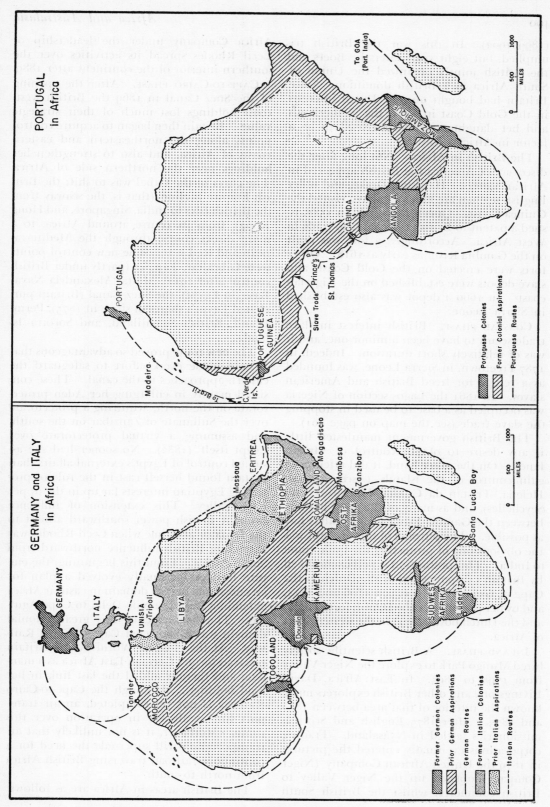

PORTUGAL
in Africa

To GOA
(Port. India)

MILES
0   500   1000

MOZAMBIQUE

ANGOLA

CABINDA

Prince's I.

St. Thomas I.

Slave Trade

PORTUGAL

Madeira

C. Verde Is.

PORTUGUESE
GUINEA

To Brazil

Portuguese Colonies
Former Colonial Aspirations
Portuguese Routes

GERMANY and ITALY
in Africa

MILES
0   500   1000

GERMANY

ITALY

TUNISIA
Tripoli

Tangier

MOROCCO

LIBYA

TOGOLAND

Lome

KAMERUN

Douala

ERITREA
Massaua

ETHIOPIA

Mogadiscio
SOMALILAND

OST-
AFRIKA

Mombasa
Zanzibar

SUDWEST
AFRIKA

Lüderitz

Santa Lucia Bay

Former German Colonies
Prior German Aspirations
German Routes
Former Italian Colonies
Prior Italian Aspirations
Italian Routes

(1899–1902). In this war the British triumphed, but eight years later the Boers and the British jointly organized the Union of South Africa as a British dominion. Since Britain had bought out the Dutch interests in the Gold Coast in 1871, the Netherlands and her daughter republics ceased to be a factor in African politics.

The British in Africa. Not long after the discovery of America the British appeared in African waters. Hawkins, Drake, and other English seamen are known to have visited the Guinea Coast. Queen Elizabeth, in 1588, issued a patent to British merchants to trade in West Africa. Accordingly, a fort was built on the Gambia River as early as 1618. Other forts were erected on the Gold Coast, and slave depots were established on the Nigerian coast. In 1660 a depot was also established in Sierra Leone.

COASTAL PHASE. British interest in slave trade seems to have been a minor one, and it was of relatively short duration. Indeed, in 1787 Freetown, in Sierra Leone, was founded as a refuge for freed British and American slaves. In 1861 the Lagos section of Nigeria was occupied as a base to be used in stopping the slave trade (see the map on page 401).

The British government manifested little if any desire to obtain control of African lands. On the other hand, it did attempt to gain control of the islands (Ascension, St. Helena, Tristan da Cunha, Mauritius, and Seychelles), and as many of the good harbors between the Gambia Estuary and Walvis Bay as possible. The purpose of this attempt was the obvious one of protecting the trade route to India. This precaution is well exemplified by Britain's dispossession of the Dutch at the Cape of Good Hope between 1806 and 1814, and by her purchase of the Danish forts (1850) and the Dutch posts (1871) in the western part of Africa.

INLAND PHASE. A British scientific society hired Mungo Park to explore the Niger Valley from 1795 to 1805. In East Africa, David Livingstone and other British explorers made known the interior of that area between 1850 and 1873. After 1875 English and Scottish missionaries settled in Nyasaland. Trading corporations eventually entered the picture; in 1879 the United African Company (Niger Company) opened up the Niger Valley to British commerce, whilst the British South Africa Company under the leadership of Cecil Rhodes spread its activities over the southern interior of the continent after 1889.

CAPE-TO-CAIRO PHASE. After the opening of the Suez Canal in 1869 the British west-coast holdings lost much of their strategic value. Britain then began to acquire control points along the northeastern and eastern coasts of Africa, and also to strengthen her holdings near the northern side of Africa. The effect of the Canal was to shift the British Empire lifeline (that is, the seaway from the British Isles to India, Singapore, and Hong Kong) from its course around Africa, to a more direct course through the Mediterranean and Red seas. The new control points were Gibraltar, Tangier (partly under British control after 1912), Malta, Alexandria Naval Base (in Egypt), the Suez Canal (Britain purchased Egypt's shares of stock in 1875), Perim Island, British Somaliland, and Socotra Island.

The new route proved so advantageous that Britain made every effort to safeguard the eastern approaches to the canal. These consisted mainly in enlarging her Aden protectorate on the north, acquiring a protectorate over the Sultanate of Zanzibar on the south, and assuming a virtual protectorate over Egypt itself (1882). No sooner had she assumed control of Egypt's external affairs than Britain found herself cast in the role of protecting Egyptian interests far up in the upper Nile Valley. This extension of influence brought British power southward almost to the Equator at a time when Cecil Rhodes was extending British influence northward from South Africa. From this beginning, the empire builders gradually evolved a plan for an enormous British domain in eastern Africa extending from the Nile Delta to Cape Agulhas. The backbone of this great colonial domain was a projected Cape-to-Cairo Railway. At the close of World War I Britain received former German East Africa as a mandate and thereby added the last link in her land holdings. Although the Cape-to-Cairo Railway is not yet completed, an air transport line is already in operation over this route. Moreover, it is not unlikely that air transportation will supersede the need for a continuous railroad traversing British Africa from north to south.

The British areas in Africa are as follows:

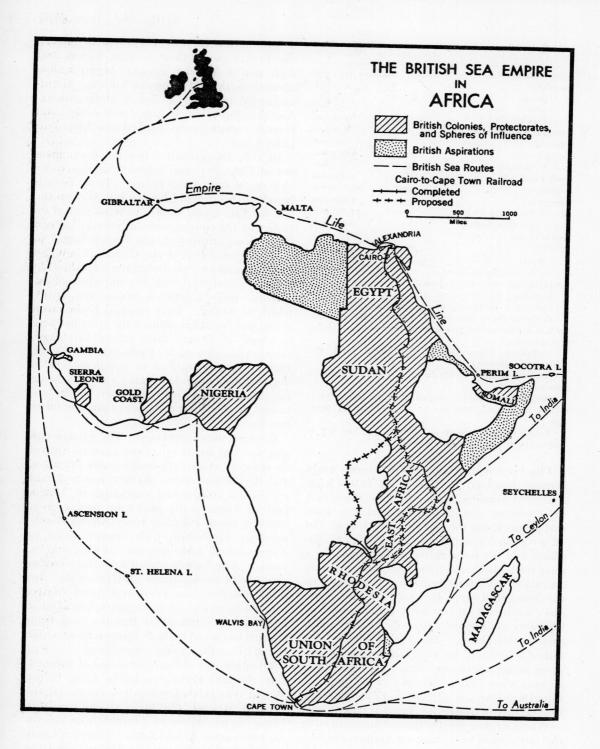

THE BRITISH SEA EMPIRE
IN
AFRICA

British Colonies, Protectorates, and Spheres of Influence

British Aspirations

British Sea Routes

Cairo-to-Cape Town Railroad
Completed
Proposed

0   500   1000
Miles

Empire

GIBRALTAR

MALTA

Life

ALEXANDRIA

CAIRO

Line

EGYPT

GAMBIA

SUDAN

SIERRA LEONE

GOLD COAST

NIGERIA

PERIM I.

SOCOTRA I.

SOMALI

To India

SEYCHELLES

ASCENSION I.

EAST AFRICA

To Ceylon

ST. HELENA I.

RHODESIA

MADAGASCAR

WALVIS BAY

To India

UNION   OF
SOUTH AFRICA

CAPE TOWN

To Australia

Political Unit	Area (sq. mi.)	Population
Tristan da Cunha	12	165
Ascension	34	155
St. Helena	47	4,680
Seychelles	156	32,000
Mauritius [1]	809	432,000
Zanzibar and Pemba	1,020	235,000
Gambia	4,068	200,000
Sierra Leone	27,925	1,769,000
British Somaliland	68,000	345,000
Gold Coast [2]	91,843	4,092,000
Nigeria [3]	372,674	21,511,000
Rhodesia [4]	440,674	2,812,000
British East Africa [5]	720,308	14,242,000
Anglo-Egyptian Sudan [6]	969,600	6,343,000
Union of South Africa [7]	1,083,696	10,522,000
Egypt [8]	383,000	17,626,000
Total	4,163,856	80,166,000

[1] Including small dependencies.

[2] Including the Togoland trusteeship.

[3] Including the Cameroons trusteeship.

[4] Both Northern and Southern Rhodesia. The latter has a responsible government and is approaching dominionhood.

[5] Including Kenya-Uganda, Nyasaland, and the Tanganyika trusteeship.

[6] An outstanding example of a condominium in government.

[7] Including the native states of Bechuanaland, Basutoland, Swaziland, and the South-West Africa mandate.

[8] Egypt regards herself as independent but she is within the British sphere of influence.

The French in Africa.

The French early became involved in the India and China trade. Accordingly, they became interested in obtaining way-stations in Africa as control points along the route to the Orient. In 1642 a French company built a fort on Madagascar and for some thirty years carried on a slave trade there. A little later, trading posts and slave sheds were built near the mouth of the Senegal River. In 1700 a French post was established on the Ivory Coast. France, however, manifested little official interest in these undertakings. In 1830 the French obtained a foothold in Algeria in order to suppress piracy there, and nine years later laid a somewhat vague claim to Gabon in Equatorial Africa. In 1849 Libreville was founded as a refuge for freed slaves.

When France finally turned in earnest to the business of obtaining an African empire, it was inspired largely by a desire to recoup her own pride and to restore her international standing after the disastrous defeat at the hands of Germany in 1870–71.

FRENCH EXPANSION. From North Africa, the French, with their foreign legion and their native Algerian cavalry, began a slow advance southward across the Sahara. Simultaneously, in 1875, De Brazza undertook extensive explorations in Equatorial Africa, and French conquest was pushed northward to Lake Chad.

In 1887 the French drove the Portuguese out of Dahomey, and renewed their activity in Senegal and Cote d'Ivoire. Thus, French North Africa, the old French holdings on the Guinea Coast, and Gabon were all linked together by the conquest of the Sahara. When this was accomplished, the French began to push eastward from Lake Chad. They also strengthened and expanded their foothold in French Somaliland with the intention of extending their conquests across the entire width of Africa. They reached Fashoda on the upper Nile and planted the tricolor there in 1898. A British army under Kitchener, however, advanced to Fashoda, and so the French were compelled to withdraw. This disappointment ended France's grand scheme for dominating Africa, but even so she obtained more of that continent than any other nation.

GEOGRAPHICAL PATTERN. The French empire was not based upon any plan to control the seaways, as were those of Britain, Portugal, and the Netherlands. Rather, it was a land empire—a continental extension of Metropolitan France. Its backbone was a great caravan route running from Algiers southward to Timbuktu, with branches east to Abeshr, south to Bingerville, and west to St. Louis. The French planned to reinforce this route with motor roads and railroads. Indeed, a railway has been built from Algiers into the desert as far as Tuggurt, from Dakar and St. Louis inland to Bamako, and from Djibuti westward halfway across Ethiopia (see the map on the facing page).

Owing to the difficulty and cost of this railway project, France took the lead, before World War II, in developing commercial airlines in Africa. The main airway ran from Marseille to Algiers to Timbuktu to Save to Ft. Lamy (near Lake Chad). From Ft. Lamy it branched to Brazzaville, Djibuti, and the island of Madagascar.

The possessions of France in Africa are as follows:

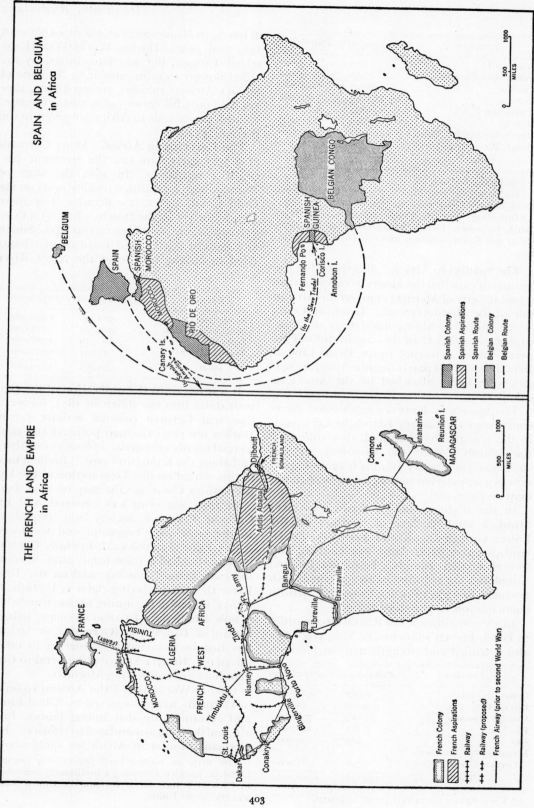

SPAIN AND BELGIUM
in Africa

BELGIUM

SPAIN

SPANISH
MOROCCO

RIO DE ORO

Canary Is.
(to Spanish
America)

(to the Slave Trade)

Fernando Poo
SPANISH
GUINEA
Corisco I.
Annobon I.

BELGIAN CONGO

0   500   1000
MILES

Spanish Colony
Spanish Aspirations
Spanish Route
Belgian Colony
Belgian Route

THE FRENCH LAND EMPIRE
in Africa

FRANCE

Algiers (FERRY)

MOROCCO   TUNISIA

ALGERIA

St. Louis
Dakar
Conakry

Timbuktu

FRENCH   WEST   AFRICA

Niamey

Bingerville
Porto Novo

Zinder

Ft. Lamy

Bangui

Libreville

Brazzaville

Djibouti
FRENCH
SOMALILAND
Addis Ababa

Comoro
Is.

Tananarive
Reunion I.
MADAGASCAR

0   500   1000
MILES

French Colony
French Aspirations
Railway
Railway (proposed)
French Airway (prior to second World War)

403

Possession	Area (sq. mi.)	Population
Réunion I.	970	313,000
French Somaliland	8,492	44,000
Tunisia	48,313	2,606,000
Morocco	213,350	7,094,000
Madagascar [1]	241,884	3,798,000
Algeria	847,500	7,235,000
French Equatorial Africa [2]	1,125,745	5,940,000
French West Africa [3]	1,840,591	15,725,000
Total	4,326,845	42,755,000

[1] Including Comoro Is.

[2] Including Gabon, Middle Congo, Ubangi-Shari, Chad, and the Cameroons trusteeship.

[3] Including Senegal, French Guinea, the Ivory Coast, Dahomey, French Sudan, Mauritania, Niger, Dakar and its surroundings, and the Togoland trusteeship.

The Spanish in Africa. Shortly before the Spaniards expelled the Moors from Spain they seized the city of Melilla (1470) on the African side of the Mediterranean. Later on, Ceuta (1580) and the Alhucemas (1673) were occupied. Farther than this, Spain did not go, partly out of deference to the Papal Line of Demarcation and partly because Spanish energies were being absorbed by the American colonies.

The Spaniards, however, established sovereignty over the Canary Islands in 1479, and, in the century that followed, they colonized the islands. After the discovery of the Americas, the Canary Islands became important as a way-station to the Caribbean (see the map on page 403).

In the Bight of Biafra, Spain owns Rio Muni, a small enclave of territory on the Lower Guinea Coast, and Fernando Po Island, together with Annobon, Corisco, and several smaller islands. Fernando Po and Annobon were acquired in an agreement with Portugal in 1778 in order to permit Spanish participation in the slave trade.

In 1885 Spain annexed Rio de Oro in order to check French influence in Morocco. She also extended and strengthened her holdings

Possession	Area (sq. mi.)*	Population
Canary Islands	2,807	564,873
Rio de Oro	109,000	30,000
Spanish Morocco	13,125	750,000
Rio Muni	9,454	120,000
Ifni	965	20,000
Fernando Po, Annobon, Corisco, Great Elobey	795	24,000
Total	136,146	1,508,873

* These figures are merely rough estimates.

in northern Morocco at various times between 1904 and 1937. During World War II she seized Tangier, but was later forced by the allied powers to relinquish it.* As none of Spain's African colonies are profitable, they are held only for reasons of national prestige. Spanish possessions in Africa are given in the preceding table.

The Germans in Africa. Many Germans at a very early date saw the economic possibilities of Africa. In 1681 the State of Brandenburg established trading posts on the Gold Coast, but a few decades later these were absorbed by the Dutch. In 1861 a Prussian explorer traveled extensively in the Sudan and eastern Africa, and German merchants tried to obtain a share of the Niger River trade.

Colony	Area (sq. mi.)	Population
Tanganyika	380,536	8,946,000
Southwest Africa	323,725	315,000
Kamerun	200,570	3,386,000
Togoland	34,934	1,072,000
Total	939,765	13,719,000

It was not until the unification of the German states into the Reich in 1871, however, that real German colonial activity began. Within ten years German political and commercial agents were active in Southwest Africa and along the Kamerun Coast. Bremen merchants settled on the Togo section of the Upper Guinea Coast (see the map on page 399).

In 1884 Kamerun was annexed, and the German Colonial Society was organized. In the same year Togoland and Southwest Africa were annexed. Meanwhile, German traders, who had become firmly established on the coast behind Zanzibar and on the Tana River Delta, were laying claim to Uganda, to Kenya, and were beginning to penetrate what is now Rhodesia. In 1890 Germany gained control of Tanganyika (German East Africa), but Britain thwarted her program in other quarters. In 1911 France put an end to German hopes of controlling Morocco.

During World War I the African colonies of Germany were conquered by Allied forces and eventually divided among France, Britain, and Belgium as mandated territories. For German colonies in Africa see table above.

* In 1945, an international regime was re-established in Tangier, following a preliminary conference in Paris of France, Great Britain, the United States, and the Soviet Union.

The Italians in Africa. Like Germany, Italy was late in becoming unified into a modern nation. As a consequence, her advent into the arena of colonialism was delayed until about 1870. What colonies the Italians did obtain were largely desert or semi-desert and of relatively low economic value.

In 1882 Italy gained a foothold in Eritrea and, soon after, in eastern Somaliland. A few years later the Italians tried to link up the two colonies by annexing Ethiopia. The Italian army was almost annihilated at the battle of Adowa in 1896, and the scheme was temporarily abandoned (see the map on page 399).

After Italy had reached an agreement with France, an Italian army invaded Tripoli, Fezzan, and Barca (Cyrenaica) in 1911. After their conquest these areas were combined to form Italian Libya. In the territorial settlement following World War I, Italy received small additions to Libya and Somaliland. These gains were so small, however, that the Italians became greatly dissatisfied. As a consequence, Italy defied the League of Nations in 1934, and during the next two years conquered and annexed Ethiopia. Moreover, in 1940 she joined Germany in World War II. This policy led to disastrous defeat for Italy and loss of all her African possessions.

The disposal of the Italian colonies in Africa, except Ethiopia, presented the chief territorial problem of that continent after World War II. The Charter of the United Nations provides for trusteeship over territories under certain conditions. These territories may be areas detached from the Axis as a result of World War II, or territories that were mandates under the League of Nations, or areas voluntarily placed under trusteeship. Strategic areas in the trusteeship system are placed under the Security Council of the United Nations, but nonstrategic areas are under the General Assembly and the Trusteeship Council of the Organization. The British, Belgians, and French in 1946 placed their African mandates under the trusteeship of the United Nations as nonstrategic areas. However, the Union of South Africa was eager to incorporate Southwest Africa into its territory. The Italian colonies in Africa presented greater problems. The Russians, as a step in their drive to the Mediterranean, have expressed an interest in the Italian colonies; the British are concerned with the

security of their communications through the Mediterranean to the "Empire east of Suez"; Americans are interested in the stability of the Mediterranean areas which were so vital in the recent conflict; the French are vitally concerned with any territorial change in Africa; and the Italians desire to regain their African empire.

The Italian colonies in Africa (except Ethiopia) were:

Possession	Area (sq. mi.)	Population
Eritrea	45,754	601,000
Italian Somaliland	194,000	1,300,000
Libya	679,358	888,000
Total	919,112	2,789,000

The Belgians in Africa. When the final scramble for African colonies began shortly after 1870, Leopold II, King of the Belgians, decided to enter the arena. And so, in 1876, Leopold convened an international "geographical" conference in Brussels. At that meeting the basis of a future Congo Free State was established and the International Africa Association hired Henry M. Stanley to explore it. By somewhat devious means the Belgian king and his financial advisers obtained complete control of the Association, which owned and administered Congoland. Indeed, he considered the latter his own personal colony (see the map on page 403).

The king and his officials set out to exploit ruthlessly the natural wealth of the region. Since this is the richest part of Africa, an immense personal fortune was amassed by Leopold. Conditions became so scandalous that world indignation was aroused, and so in 1908 the Belgian parliament took control and annexed the area. At the end of World War I an area of German East Africa was added to the Belgian Congo as the mandated territory of Ruanda-Urundi.

Today the Belgian Congo covers some 922,-617 square miles and has a population of approximately 14,000,000. The territory, which occupies an area seventy-nine times that of the mother country, is a veritable storehouse of resources. During World War II it became the leading producer of cobalt and radium, and one of the chief sources of copper, gold, industrial diamonds, tin, and manganese. The production of zinc, palm oil, wild rubber, silk, and even certain small manufactures increased rapidly. Its exports rose to a value of more than 5,000,000,000 francs. This extracted wealth, however, merely scratches the surface of Congoland's potentialities.

come a vast frontier of Europe. Nevertheless, a few native states, such as Zanzibar, Morocco, and Tunisia, retain a shadow of autonomy. Egypt bids fair to achieve real

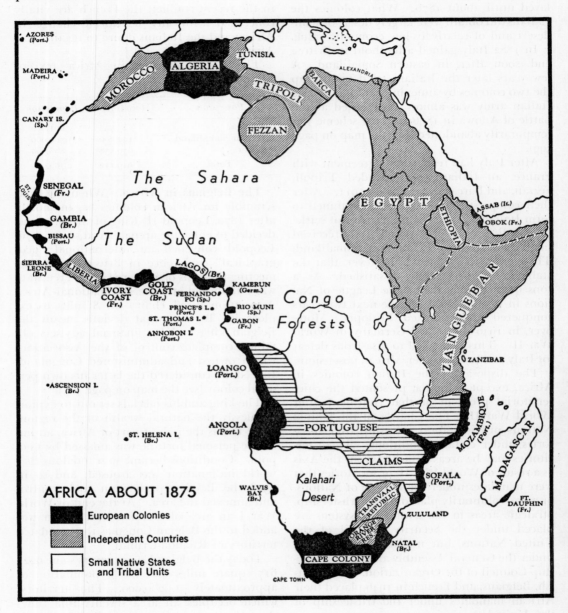

AFRICA ABOUT 1875

■ European Colonies

▨ Independent Countries

□ Small Native States and Tribal Units

Independent African States

Since 1870 Africa has changed from a rim of small coastal holdings about a huge unknown interior (see the map on this page) to a veritable patchwork of European colonies, protectorates, and dependencies. It has be-

nationhood under a minimum of British control. The Union of South Africa has grown from colonial beginnings to dominionhood. However, only two states, Liberia and Ethiopia, possess complete independence.

Ethiopia. Ethiopia has had a long and

venerable history as an independent state. The core of its population seems to be Mediterranean in race with some Semitic admixture, and consists of several Amharic tribes. These inhabit the high, temperate, well-watered Abyssinian Plateau. This plateau averages more than a mile high, and hence its inhabitants are healthful and energetic, albeit generally backward.

In modern times these plateau peoples have extended their military rule over large areas of arid and semiarid lowlands populated with Hamitic and Negroid peoples. The area of Ethiopia is some 350,000 square miles, and population estimates range widely —from as low as 5 million to as high as 12 million.

Until recent years the only avenues into Ethiopia were a few caravan routes through Italian or British territory, or the French railway from Djibuti. Exports from the country consist of hides, skins, coffee, grain, wax, and a few other articles. The plateau has steep, almost precipitous marginal slopes, and hence the Ethiopians have been able to defend their liberties. In 1935, however, the Italians employed aerial and poison gas warfare, and the primitive defenses soon crumbled. Ethiopia's independence has now been restored, but her former isolation is necessarily of the past. Several Ethiopian cities are presently on air routes, which bid fair to stimulate the country's economy.

Liberia. The small Negro republic of Liberia lies on the Guinea Coast. It has an area of about 43,000 square miles, and a population of one and one-half million or more people. The little state owes its origin to the American Colonization Society founded in 1817. The Society procured a tract of land in western Africa and began settling American Negroes in 1820. For the most part these were ex-slaves from Virginia, Maryland, and Georgia.

In 1847 these Americo-Liberians issued a declaration of independence. A "White House" was erected, a Congress elected, and a President chosen. The little country is annually in financial arrears, but the United States has loaned it money from time to time. France and Britain nibbled off some of its frontier areas in the early days of the republic, but the United States has put an end to that type of menace.

Liberians of American descent do not exceed 15,000, and the total civilized population numbers only about 50,000. For the most part these are concentrated in the coastal towns of Monrovia, Greenville, Grand Bassa, Harper, and a few others; or they are in small villages scattered along the rivers, such as White Plains, New York, Coontown, and Louisiana.

In 1925 the Firestone Company leased a million acres of potential rubber-plantation land in Liberia. During World War II the United States obtained air bases in the republic. These might offer valuable springboards for future American participation in African affairs, if they were retained.

CHAPTER 28 | A Strategic Appraisal of Africa

ALTHOUGH Africa is relatively unimportant in terms of its own human geography, its significance in the geopolitics of Europe and Asia (and indirectly of the whole world) is considerable. Moreover, its locational relations to Europe and Asia are such, that under certain political conditions, it could assume a decisive position in the strategy of world control.

Africa in Early Times

The Nile Valley—cradle of early civilization. The land bridge at Suez has always made Egypt, in one sense, a part of the Near East of Asia. Accordingly, the Nile Valley became one of the old fluvial cradles of civilization, which developed in that area during prehistoric times. Long before the birth of Christ Egyptian civilization in turn, along with those of Crete, Phoenicia, Troy, and Israel, mothered the later and more extensive Mediterranean Basin civilization. South and central Africa contributed almost nothing to this cultural advancement.

Mediterranean civilization. In the civilization of the Mediterranean Basin, all of North Africa and not merely Egypt was involved. The Greeks colonized the shores of the eastern Mediterranean and became politically dominant in the entire half-sea. The Carthaginians (western Phoenicians) similarly colonized and became dominant in the western Mediterranean. (For this entire region see the map on page 397.) In neither case was any distinction made between the European and the African shores. In any circum-sea civilization, continental distinctions lose their meaning, and all the margins of the unifying body of water tend to become equally important.

Neither Greeks nor Carthaginians, however, were ever able to achieve control of the whole Mediterranean Basin. That role fell to the Roman Republic located near the center of the Mediterranean, in the year 146 B.C.* After that event Rome rapidly became the base for an empire extending entirely around the shores of the great inland sea. It retained its imperial power as long as no other peoples were able to break in and establish themselves upon the shores of the Mediterranean.

Eventually, other peoples did break in. Wave after wave of Goths, Franks, Vandals, and other folk poured into the Mediterranean area; the Empire was weakened and eventually split into halves—a Western or Roman, and an Eastern or Byzantine. Thus disunited, the Mediterranean world was successfully invaded from the southeast by the Mohammedan Arabs. During the seventh century, they swept across northern Africa. Then using the southern and eastern shores of the Mediterranean as a base, they spilled across into Spain and the Balkans and began the conquest of Europe. They were ultimately defeated and turned back.

After the lines were more definitely drawn between the Moslem and Christian Mediterranean, the sea became a "moat" separating the rival armed forces of Christian Europe and Mohammedan Asia and North Africa. During the eleventh, twelfth, and thirteenth centuries a series of religious wars and pil-

* In that year Rome destroyed Carthage, thus ending the Third Punic (Phoenic) War.

grimages, known as crusades, to recover the Holy Land from the Moslems, were conducted by the Christian world against Islam. Although these were unsuccessful, they served to widen the breach between the two cultures.

Thus North Africa, instead of continuing to develop as an integral part of Europe, as it had during Greek, Carthaginian, and Roman times, has for a thousand years been culturally a part of Asia. Divided into two antagonistic areas, the Mediterranean realm declined commercially and politically, and it has never recovered its former importance.

Africa in the World-Ocean Age

Decline of North Africa. Probably the decline of the Mediterranean, more particularly that of the African half, was inevitable. Civilization was spreading northward across Europe, and a new center of culture was arising rapidly in the lands about the Baltic and North seas. The net result was that both northern and southern Europe began to feel an urge toward commercial expansion. This tendency became all the more marked when the Turks overran the Arab world, and began to interfere with the ancient trade routes that extended from the Mediterranean to the Orient. Even before the Turkish conquest of Byzantium in 1453, several nations were already on the high seas looking for new trade routes.

With the discoveries of Da Gama, Columbus, Cabral, and Magellan, the era of world commerce began, and the great world ocean was soon transformed into man's most important highway. Geopolitically, this meant the beginning of the Age of Seapower, epitomized successively by caravels, frigates, and steel battleships.

This great era of exploration and world commerce changed the geographical status of Africa completely. Prior to 1492 Mediterranean Africa was the only important part of the continent. Africa south of the Sahara remained unknown and untouched by civilization. After 1492 northern Africa went into a rapid cultural and commercial decline, and soon its harbors were merely the seats of petty traders, local fishermen, and pirates.

The rise of coastal Africa. As Mediterranean Africa was going into a decline, the remainder of Africa was assuming enormous importance; not for its own sake, but because

of its bearing upon man's main objective in this period of world commerce. That main objective was, of course, the carrying of goods back and forth between the two ends of the great land mass of Eurasia. The Portuguese explorations demonstrated that the continents of Europe and Asia were one great body of land, so huge as to deserve the name of "World Island." At the eastern end of this land mass lay the wealth of the Indies, Cathay, Zipangu, and Golconda. At the western end lay the growing economic might of western Europe. The Spanish discoveries made known a second land mass to the westward, but demonstrated the impracticability of establishing trade routes to the Orient in that direction. The belt line of trade, therefore, soon ran from the ports of western Europe, down the Atlantic coast of Africa, around the Cape of Good Hope, and across the Indian Ocean to India, Indonesia, the Philippines, and China. All the important maritime nations of western Europe—Britain, Portugal, France, the Netherlands, and to a lesser extent Spain—became interested in this seaway.

The detour around Africa. Unfortunately, this trade route was a circuitous rather than a direct one. Africa is in reality a giant peninsula projecting southwestward from the "World Island" and attached to it only by the slender Suez Isthmus (see the map immediately below).

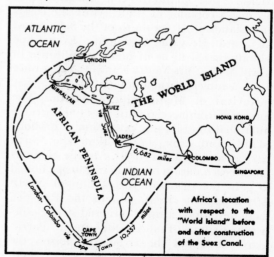

Africa's location with respect to the "World Island" before and after construction of the Suez Canal.

Because of these circumstances, the only way a nation could guarantee its participation in the circum-Africa trade was by seizing control of strong points along the way. This move would provide it with watering and victualing stations on the long, slow trip, sites at which needed ship repairs could be made, and bases from which naval operations could be conducted. Accordingly, all the small islands along the way were soon in the hands of one European power or another. One by one the better harbors along the African coast also came to be occupied. By the last of the eighteenth century, practically the entire coastline of Africa was in European hands.

Strategic South Africa. Along the whole Europe-to-Orient trade route, the extreme southern tip of Africa was the most strategic locality. As early as 1652 the Dutch began actively to colonize that area. In 1806, however, the British occupied this Cape Colony; and after 1820 a fairly large British immigration commenced. Meanwhile, almost the entire interior of the continent remained unknown to European man.

The Suez Canal. Because the sea route around Africa was long and time-consuming, man at a relatively early date began to discuss the feasibility of digging a canal through the Isthmus of Suez (see the map on page 301). Such a feat was finally accomplished by an Egyptian-French corporation in 1869. When completed, the canal instantaneously changed the geopolitical complexion of Africa. The Mediterranean Sea once more became a corridor of trade, while the coasts and islands of Africa south of the Sahara lost their strategic value overnight. Even Cape Colony ceased to be of much significance in world terms, but Mediterranean Africa once more assumed paramount importance.

Revival of Mediterranean Africa. The European commercial nations at once became interested in obtaining possession of harbors, islands, and strong points along the North African and Red Sea coasts. In the Mediterranean each nation of southern Europe hoped to gain possession of the section of North Africa opposite itself, and in the Red Sea there developed a three-cornered struggle between Britain, France, and Italy. Particularly keen was the rivalry to possess the "bottlenecks" along the new seaway—Gibraltar and Tangier in the west, Suez in the center, and the Strait of Bab-el-Mandeb in the east.

The scramble for North Africa. The contest for possession of Mediterranean Africa consumed the better part of a century and required a considerable amount of bitter fighting to overthrow what remained there of Moslem power. France first gained a foothold in Algeria in 1830, and by 1847 had completed the conquest of the Algerian coast. After the opening of the Suez Canal, however, her interest was renewed in the area, and she undertook the conquest of the Algerian interior. This was completed by 1901, after which (1904–22) she sent more than half a million colonists to the area. In 1881 France established a protectorate over Tunisia. The following year Britain occupied Egypt. In 1904 France undertook the control of most of Morocco. A few years later, Spain began a quarter of a century of conquest in northern Morocco. In 1911 Italy occupied Libya and began the colonization of Tunisia. Between 1905 and 1911 Germany made several unsuccessful attempts to gain a foothold in Morocco. In 1925 Tangier at the western gateway to the Mediterranean was placed under international control. Meanwhile, along the Red Sea coast of Africa, France obtained a foothold at Obok in 1862, Italy at Assab in 1882, and Britain at Berbera in 1884 (see the map on page 406).

Other changes in Africa. In the remaining part of Africa, Belgium obtained the Congo Basin, South Africa slowly grew into a self-governing commonwealth, and Germany was (during World War I) eliminated as a colonial power. Aside from these changes, the African colonies of Britain and France developed steadily, whereas those of Portugal and Spain have retrogressed through exploitation and neglect.

Africa in the Amphibian and Air Age

Africa's importance. World War II was a global conflict in the real sense of that term. As a result, Africa became a theater of conflict and a significant factor in the strategy of that war. For the first time since Roman Empire days, Africa assumed military-geographic significance to Europe. Moreover, it also became highly significant in a strategic sense to America. The primary reason for this importance was Africa's geographic location in relation to the great "World Island" of Eurasia.

Strategy of the Axis in World War II. World War II represented a plan by some leaders in the Axis countries (Germany, Italy, and Japan) to seize the entire "World Island," convert it into a colossal fortress and arsenal, and use it as a base for global conquest. First, Germany and Italy subdued all western Europe and fortified its coasts. Second, Japan subdued nearly all of eastern Asia and fortified its coasts and islands. Third, Italy and Germany undertook the subjugation of northern Africa. The fourth step would have been for Japan and the Italo-German Axis jointly to subdue southern Asia, and slowly compress Soviet Russia and China to death. Had this over-all plan been accomplished, it would have left Britain, Australia, the Americas, and Africa south of the Sahara to assail the Axis-held "World Island" from the outside. Had the Axis strategy been completed, the Sahara would have served as an almost perfect defense on the southwest; the sea entrances at Gibraltar, the Skagerrak, Murmansk, and the sea passages through the East Indies and Kuriles could have been easily closed; and land-based aircraft could have driven off attempted amphibious invasions. Under such a handicap, the United Nations might never have won the war.

The Axis plan failed, not because of any inherent impossibility, but because the German army undertook to strangle the Soviet Union *before* North Africa had been cleared of British armies. As matters turned out, the Germans, unable to use their full force against Soviet Russia, dissipated their energies in eastern Europe, and delayed their attack on the British army in Egypt. This delay enabled the United States to bring up tanks, guns, and other matériel to the British via the Red Sea. This support, in turn, brought the Italo-German drive to a standstill, and gave America time to land its new armies on the Moroccan coast outside the Mediterranean, and to spatter additional landings along the Algerian coast inside the Mediterranean. The presence of American troops on the Atlantic coast posed a threat to the forces of fascist Spain, which were poised behind Gibraltar ready to fall upon the flank of the British sea lines. Eventually, the Italo-

German army was squeezed to destruction in Tunisia between the British army in the east and American–British–Free French armies in the west. Thus the entire Mediterranean side of Axis-held Europe was stripped bare of its outer defenses. Regardless, therefore, of subsequent moves in the great war, it may be stated that the defeat of the Axis was forged in northern Africa (see the map on page 412).

Strategic significance of Africa. In these facts there is an important geographic principle for statesmen and military leaders to note. It is almost axiomatic that if any real threat to America arises in the future, it will originate in some part of Eurasia, whether it be posed by a resurgent Germany, Japan, or Italy, or an estranged Russia or China, or a hostile Pan Arab League, or an anti-liberal unified Europe, or a mass Asiatic movement, or whatever. In the event of conflict with any such hypothetical enemy, Africa is apt to assume primary strategic importance. This is true because it lies against the great "World Island" without being a part of it. At least, Africa-south-of-the-Sahara is not part of it.

No power or combination of powers in the "World Island," therefore, would be secure until it had conquered and fortified Africa against invasion. But it could not conquer southern Africa until after its consolidation of Eurasia was completed. Obviously, therefore, one of America's first steps toward future global defense should be to utilize and strengthen its position in its unofficial colony of Liberia, to exploit its relations in Ethiopia, and to make a close alliance with the Union of South Africa. Even though atomic-power warfare seems to be in the offing, the role of the part of Africa lying south of the Sahara still remains as a military-geographic approach to, and threat against, Eurasia. Moreover, even in an era of atomic-power warfare, Africa has area enough to provide "defense in depth" and possesses large sparsely-populated spaces in which certain war industries might be hidden. It is idle to assume that an atomic-power war will consist solely of long-range reciprocal operations conducted by aerial fleets based in North America and Eurasia. Such an assumption would be as unrealistic as was the massing of the American fleet in Hawaii, the seaward orientation of all the British guns at Singapore, or the placing of the French army behind the Maginot Line before World War II.   Such

Reduction of Africa's value by appeasement. Even though American and British leaders did use Africa as a "point d'approche"

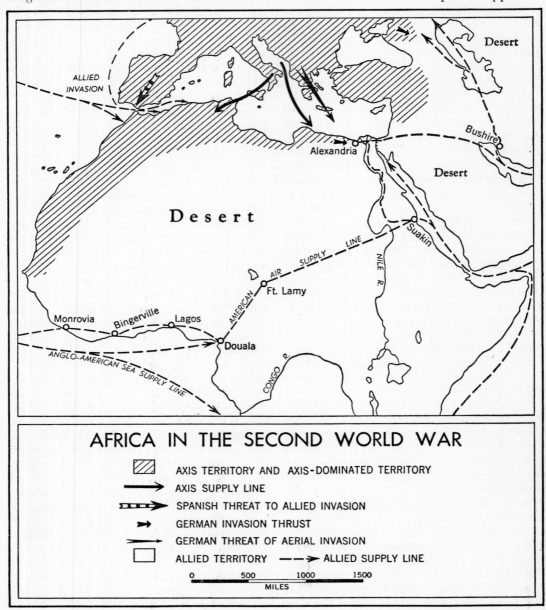

AFRICA IN THE SECOND WORLD WAR

▨ AXIS TERRITORY AND AXIS-DOMINATED TERRITORY

➝ AXIS SUPPLY LINE

⬛⬛⬛➤ SPANISH THREAT TO ALLIED INVASION

➤ GERMAN INVASION THRUST

➝ GERMAN THREAT OF AERIAL INVASION

☐ ALLIED TERRITORY ----➤ ALLIED SUPPLY LINE

0   500   1000   1500
MILES

mistakes were very nearly the undoing of the democratic allies between 1939 and 1942. Underevaluation of Africa's role in world strategy might conceivably be the undoing of America in any future major conflict.*

* This discussion is postulated upon the assumption that no real sovereign global government will be created—a super-government that alone would possess monopolistic control of war-making facilities.

to the Axis-held "Fortress Europa," and apparently appreciated fully its geographical virtue as a base of counter-operations, its usefulness was greatly reduced by prior mistakes in their thinking.   What our leaders do not seem to have realized is that the geography of any given region is contingent upon the geography of other areas—some of them far removed from the region in question. In other words, in the geography of war (and of diplomacy as well) the usefulness of region A depends to a surprising degree upon one's policies and actions in region B or C or D.

For instance, the use of North Africa by America and Britain was far less effective than it should have been. One specific example was the British position in Egypt and the Near East. Egypt contained the vital Suez Canal; the adjacent Near East contained oil for the British navy. After World War I Britain had eagerly accepted a mandate over Palestine, where she had made an earlier agreement to establish a Jewish Commonwealth. However, with one eye on the Canal and the other on the oil fields of Iraq, Britain adopted a policy of vacillation, indecision, and indirection, and finally one of direct appeasement of anti-Jewish Arab sentiments. She faced her crucial test against German power at El Alamein with an unfriendly Arab world (made confident by long years of appeasement) at her back. She might instead, have had a pro-British, democratic Jewish Commonwealth with an army of 200,000 well equipped soldiers ready to quell any pro-Axis disturbances.

Similarly unwise was the failure of Britain, France, and the United States to check Italian aggression against Ethiopia in 1935 and 1936. This mistake compelled Britain to wage war in northern Africa with a hostile Italian force, entrenched within a great natural fortress, upon her left flank. Eventually, a difficult and costly campaign by South African and British troops was required to subdue the Italians in Ethiopia. This at a time when the Empire badly needed its strength elsewhere!

The appeasement of the Axis puppet government of Vichy-France, by Britain and the United States, also seriously reduced the strategic value of Africa to these two nations during World War II. The port of Dakar at Cape Verde in western Africa was at that time the naval and aeronautical gateway to the Americas. Had the United States moved promptly and taken over the port of Dakar immediately after the fall of France in 1940, she could have undoubtedly accomplished that occupation without opposition. In that event, all of French Africa might have sided with the Allies, and the later costly American invasion might have been rendered unnecessary. Instead, the United States allowed the Vichy puppet government to become firmly entrenched along the African coast from Senegal to Tunisia.

Most costly of all was the policy of conciliation and semiappeasement which Britain, France, and the United States pursued toward fascist Spain. This began with a nonintervention pact during the Spanish Civil War,* continued as recognition of Dictator Franco's government by Britain, France, and the United States in 1939, and culminated in a long series of concessions and conciliatory gestures during World War II.

Spain repaid the democracies by permitting their enemies to use submarine bases in her Balearic Isles from which to attack British shipping in the Mediterranean; she seized the international port of Tangier; and she amassed troops behind Gibraltar in an effort to seal the western entrance to the Mediterranean. In 1940, when the French defenses broke under the German attack, the French government and army quickly disintegrated. Had there been a democratic government in Spain, a large section of the French army would undoubtedly have retreated across Spain and eventually reached North Africa, there to join the allied cause. Hemmed in between Nazi Germany and Falangist Spain, however, it could only collapse utterly. This debacle in turn required an American invasion to reopen North Africa.

When the American invasion did come, it faced the threat of hostile Spanish forces mobilized on its flank. The invasion, therefore, had to be planned and executed cautiously rather than boldly. That cautious campaign began late in 1942, worked slowly across North Africa, and then bogged down until the following year in the mud of the rainy season. During this halt, the Germans reinforced and supplied their African forces via Tunisia. In the spring of 1943, therefore, the Americans and their Allies faced an

* This pact was consummated by a number of democratic powers despite the known fact that both Germany and Italy were actively aiding the Spanish Falangist rebels. It can be explained either as the result of the inability to perceive the politico-geographic implication of the whole situation, or else as a Bourbon attitude on the part of the leaders of the democratic countries. Certainly that mistaken policy was paid for, many times over, by the democracies.

enemy well braced for a last stand. There ensued one of the bloodiest campaigns of the war, one lasting until the middle of May, 1943. With a friendly democratic Spain on the left flank, an assault might have been made directly upon the "geopolitical bridge of Tunisia" (see the map on page 412) and the war in Africa could have been brought to a successful close within a few weeks.

Geography is relative and cumulative. Perhaps the conclusion to be drawn by the student of geography and history from the part played by Africa during the war against the Axis is threefold: First, international relations and most other geopolitical phenomena, whether they be those of war or those of peace, are largely man-made, but are invariably conditioned by the character of the natural environment and by man's geographic relations to that environment. Second, geopolitical situations in any given area are contingent upon other man-made, environment-conditioned situations in other regions, both near and far. Thus, politico-geographic decisions are literally far reaching. Third, geopolitical mistakes and geopolitical achievements are cumulative over a period of time. That is, geopolitics as it is manifested in diplomatic relations, trade policy, or war is a long-range rather than a short-term social science.

Africa in the Atomic Power Age

Military bases and control points. The record of historical geography shows clearly the politico-geographic significance of Africa during the early age of River Valley Civilization, the Mediterranean Inland Sea Age, the World Ocean Seapower Age, and the brief Amphibian and Airpower Age.* But the significance of Africa in the coming Aeronautical Atomic Power Age is difficult, if not impossible, to foresee. From the geographer's standpoint, however, a few points are fairly clear. For one thing, the Suez Canal as a strategic control point will be of little value. British efforts, therefore, to keep the Soviet Union out of the Mediterranean, and more specifically to prevent her from acquiring Libya as a colony, are largely meaningless in military terms. The international control point at Tangier promises also to be of doubtful value. The petroleum fields of the Near

* Approximately from 1918 to 1945.

East, with their African Moslem ramifications, promise to be equally meaningless in future strategy. The world stands upon the threshold of the development of synthetic fuels on a scale that promises to make the present limited supplies of petroleum not worth the risk of distrust and enmity among the great powers.

As long as the threat of global war hangs over mankind, however, Africa does possess considerable geographic value as a base for offensive and defensive operations by the United States and any allies against the "World Island" (see maps below and on page 409).

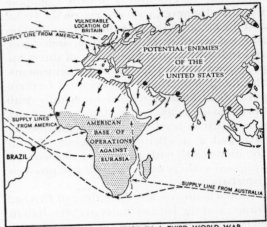

STRATEGIC VALUE OF AFRICA IN A THIRD WORLD WAR

In the event that there is created a real World Government endowed with a monopoly of military force, two points in Africa do possess strategic value in global terms. These points are Dakar, the aerial gateway to South America, and Bizerte, the aerial gateway to southern Europe. These might well be Africa's contribution to the list of possible control points to be used by a world peace patrol.

Raw materials and man power. As a source of raw materials, Africa has long been of great value to the colony-holding nations of western Europe. Cotton, gold, diamonds, zinc, tin, phosphates, wool, rubber, hides, graphite, vegetable oils, cacao, and timber are but a few of the materials essential to a strong industrial economy. What is not so well known, however, is the fact that the African continent has also become a vital source of military man power for the European nations.

Much of western Europe has reached a condition of relative saturation in human terms.

The rates of population growth in many western European countries are already beginning to taper off. Moreover, the populations of this region are coming to contain a larger and larger proportion of old people. Modern war, however, demands great numbers of young men for its successful prosecution. Without a reservoir of native African man power on which to draw, France could no longer be considered a military power. In both world wars she has used great numbers of Spahis or Berber cavalry soldiers, and Senegalese or Negro infantrymen. To a certain extent all of the colonies have helped to man the French armies.

Similarly, Spain draws upon Morocco for some of its soldiers, Belgium upon Congoland, and Britain upon Gambia, Nigeria, and East Africa. Britain, in addition has a large source of both white and Negro troops in South Africa.

White colonization in Africa. Some importance attaches to Africa as an outlet for European settlement. The Netherlands and Britain have colonized South Africa, and the white population there now numbers about 2,000,000. France has planted nearly a million settlers in Algeria, Morocco, and Tunisia. Italy has sent some 200,000 colonists to Tunisia, Eritrea, and Ethiopia. There are some 70,000 Europeans in Rhodesia. Large areas of cool, healthful uplands lie in Kenya, Tanganyika, Angola, and elsewhere; and these might readily accommodate several million Europeans. Their settlement has been slow, however, because it is contingent to a great extent upon large-scale organization and governmental enterprise. In turn, this type of sponsorship has been retarded because the energies and resources of the European governments have been largely absorbed within modern times by a series of ruinous wars interspersed with periods of feverish reconstruction.

Perhaps an even more significant factor regarding white colonization has been a general doubt regarding the future political status of Africa. The native peoples are everywhere manifesting the stirrings of nationalism and political consciousness. Egypt has achieved semi-independence and now demands complete freedom. All of Moslem North Africa is becoming restive. In South Africa, where blacks outnumber whites four to one, bitter problems of race relations are becoming serious. Even the native peoples of tropical central Africa are no longer entirely docile under European overlordship.

CHAPTER 29

The Malay Archipelago and Oceania

BETWEEN the long, slender, southeastern tip of Asia and the island continent of Australia lies one of the largest groups of islands on earth, the Malay Archipelago. Strung along the Equator for about 4,000 miles (from northwestern Sumatra to eastern New Guinea), this archipelago has been the scene of almost continuous international rivalry for many centuries. During the recent conflict with Japan, the people of the United States became vividly aware of the strategic significance of this area and its resources as well as those of Oceania to their everyday life.

THE MALAY ARCHIPELAGO

The area making up the Malay Archipelago is composed of the Netherlands Indies,* the British-controlled section of Borneo, Malaya, and Eastern (Portuguese) Timor (see the map on this page). Malaya, which includes the prewar Straits Settlements and the Federated and Unfederated Malay States, is considered within this area despite its physical attachment to continental Asia, mainly because of its many environmental and cultural similarities to the Netherlands Indies. Eastern New Guinea, the Solomons, and the Bismarck Archipelago are excluded owing to their political ties for the most part with Australia and their relative commercial and political isolation from the rest of the archipelago.

The total land area involved, including small islands, is approximately 875,000 square miles, equivalent to almost one third the land area of the United States. The table on page 417 presents a statistical summary of the principal territorial divisions and their population before World War II.

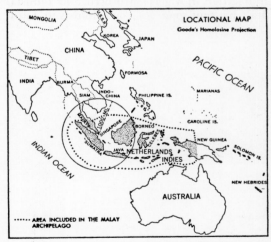

cipal territorial divisions and their population before World War II.

Should the amount of land area prove surprising to the reader, the combined land and water area will be even more striking. If a map of the Malay Archipelago were superimposed on a map of Europe of the same scale, the northwestern tip of Sumatra would fall on the west coast of Ireland; the northern tip of Borneo would touch the south coast of the Baltic Sea; and the long, southern arc of the

* Netherlands Indies is the official name of the area sometimes designated as Netherlands East Indies or Dutch East Indies. In the agreement at Linggadjati, Java, on November 15, 1946, however, provisions were made for the formation of "The United States of Indonesia," this change to go into effect by January 1, 1949.

Netherlands Indies would cross southern France, northern Italy, and the Balkan Peninsula, with the center of New Guinea lying in the northeastern corner of the Black Sea.

gone more strain in the last fifty years than during the previous six centuries. These discordant forces represent the natural clash of powerful cultures introduced into an area that

Population and Area of the Territorial Divisions of the Malay Archipelago

Division	Area (in thousands of sq. mi.)	Comparable area	Population (in thousands) *	Population per sq. mi.
Netherlands Indies	734.9		60,726	83
Neth. Borneo	208.2	Calif. and Ariz.	2,169	10
Sumatra	164.1	California	7,678	47
Neth. New Guinea	159.4	California	314	2
Celebes	72.9	New England	4,232	58
Java and Madoera	51.0	Alabama	41,718	818
Molucca Islands	32.3	Maine	579	18
Timor Archipelago	24.5	West Virginia	1,657	68
Riouw-Lingga Arch.	12.0	Conn. and Mass.	298	25
Bangka and Billiton	6.5	New Jersey	279	44
Bali and Lombok	4.0	Connecticut	1,802	450
Malaya	52.6		4,388	86
Straits Settlements	1.5	Delaware	1,147	765
Federated Malay States	27.6	West Virginia	1,713	62
Unfederated Malay States	23.5	West Virginia	1,528	65
British North Borneo	29.5	South Carolina	270	9
Sarawak	50.0	Alabama	490	10
Brunei	2.2	Delaware	30	14
Portuguese Timor	7.3	New Jersey	464	63

* All population figures are from latest official census statistics. Netherlands Indies figures are from the 1930 census; Malayan figures from the 1931 census; British Borneo figures are for 1931; Portuguese Timor figure is for 1936.

NOTE: Supplementary to the above population census statistics are the following most recent estimates from government sources (in thousands): Netherlands Indies, 71,534; Malaya, 5,560 (Straits Settlements, 1,436; Federated Malay States, 2,212; Unfederated Malay States, 1,912).

The most continuous land area in the archipelago lies along the southern, or outer, arc. From the northwestern tip of Sumatra through Java and the Lesser Soendas to Eastern Timor—a distance of approximately 2,400 miles—the largest water gap is only about twenty miles wide. East of Timor the island stepping stones are slightly farther apart, but even here the gaps do not exceed seventy miles. The water gaps between Borneo and the Philippines and between New Guinea and Australia are only short distances for native boatmen. It is not surprising, therefore, that despite the great diversity of native races, there is a noteworthy homogeneity of native culture * in the more settled parts of the archipelago. As the result of disruptive social forces that have become interwoven throughout the political geography of the area, this Indonesian culture has under-

* The term *culture* as here used signifies the association of customs, habits, tools, and techniques identified with a particular way of life.

hitherto had accessibility within itself, but which was more or less isolated from the rest of the major world cultural groups by distance and physical barriers—oceans, deserts, mountains, and tropical forests.

The Locational Factor

The outer reaches of southeast Asia. In many respects the Malay Archipelago is the outer bastion of southeast Asia. To the southwest the Indian Ocean has few islands. The heavy seas that pound the coasts of Sumatra, Java, the Lesser Soendas, and Timor from that direction often originate in gales near the margins of Antarctica and sweep unchecked to their destinations. Farther east, to be sure, Australia lies nearby, but the dry, sterile interior of that island continent and the dense, wet forests of Queensland, its northeastern tip, are formidable barriers effectively isolating the more habitable areas farther south. The waters that lie to the northwest and northeast of Australia are no less inhospitable, particularly from November to April, because of typhoons, or "willie-willies," as these destructive storms are called in Australia. Torres Strait, separating New Guinea and Australia, is one of the most dangerous stretches of water on earth for ship navigation. For 300 years the sea-going natives of this islet-studded strait successfully defied the white man, secure in their knowledge of the maze of reefs and shoals. They probably were no more hospitable to visitors before the coming of the whites. Although the natives now are friendly, the Strait still is seldom used by major steamship lines. The Solomon Islands mark the eastern end of the Malay Archipelago. From here toward the east and northeast, the relatively empty reaches of the Pacific are the frontiers of Asia.

During the recent war, the importance of the Malay Archipelago as a natural outer defense line for east Asia was recognized by the Japanese, who developed it as such for the first time in history. The great outer arc of the archipelago offers enormous natural defensive advantages for the nation that controls the sea and air to the north. Fortunately for the Allied Powers, Japan did not have quite enough time to secure the eastern flank. If any nation in the future decides to dominate east Asia, it undoubtedly will again make the archipelago part of its outer and strongest line of defense in global strategy—unless, of course, future military tactics negate the value of advanced bases.

Where East meets West. The Malay Archipelago not only lies between two continents; it also lies between two oceans. The shortest route for ships passing from Europe to western Pacific ports is through the Strait of Malacca (see the map on page 421). This narrow body of water ranks with the Strait of Gibraltar, the Suez and Panama canals, and the English Channel as one of the foremost foci of world shipping routes. International rivalry to secure domination of these straits dates far back into the early years of the European era. The specific site of the control point has not always been the same. Singapore is the present one, but Malacca, Palembang, and Djambi (the latter two are river ports in eastern Sumatra) at one time or another have controlled shipping through the straits.

Commercial powers naturally have by far the greatest interest in shipping lanes. When one commercial power is far more formidable than all of its rivals together, control of shipping is a monopolistic venture carried on to enhance its commercial strength and to decrease that of its rivals. Such was the policy of the guardians of the Strait of Malacca in early years. In more recent times monopolies of sea lanes cannot be accomplished without global domination, mainly because there are many strong commercial nations. Instead, the vital foci of world shipping routes are in the hands of guardian powers, who, in return for accepting the responsibility of insuring an equitable use of the foci, receive certain commercial advantages. Britain's interest in Singapore, for example, lies not so much in the dominance of the straits as in the business advantages accruing from service charges in handling ships and cargoes (the *entrepôt* function). In return she must defend the straits adequately against monopolistic control and must be able to defend her own commercial functions either alone or with the aid of friendly nations.

The mutual trust of the British and Dutch has been an important factor in the political geography of the area. After 200 years of active rivalry in the archipelago, the two nations settled their political and commercial disputes by the London Treaty of 1824. The Dutch acceptance of English commercial advantages at Singapore resulted in much lower Dutch expenditures for defense, withdrawal of English territorial claims in the East Indies, and, as is being proved today, a support for Dutch commercial and political interests in the Netherlands Indies. A strong Singapore is a necessity to British commercial interests and to Dutch sovereignty in the area.

Airways. It is not too early to define the general location of the archipelago in relation to postwar international air routes. First of all, a British trunk airway passes within the area, its planes stopping at Singapore enroute from Europe to Australia (as did British Imperial and Dutch KLM before World War II). Plans also provide for the area to be served by a southern trans-Pacific route linking eastern Asia to the Western Hemisphere. In addition, the Dutch are renewing regional and connecting air lines in the area (KLM). Although many of the military air bases developed in the area have deteriorated, enough of them remain to provide ground facilities for air transport throughout the archipelago.

Physical Setting and Human Settlement

Similar to other lands near the Equator that have both plains and mountains, the Malay Archipelago has a wide variety of environmental conditions (see the map on page 421). Climatic conditions change abruptly. Tropical rain forests are within an hour's drive of desert cacti (as in Eastern Timor), and fertile tropical plains lie at the foot of cold, fog-shrouded mountain peaks. Some soils are among the world's richest, whereas others are among its poorest.

This is an area where descriptive generalities often may be misleading. Java commonly is used as an example of a fertile, tropical island crowded with native farmers; yet there is a considerable part of the island that is devoid of human habitation. In the heart of the Sumatran mountains there are small basins where the density of population rivals that of the rice-plains of China. Large cities are unusual in equatorial regions; but Singapore, practically astride the Equator, has a population of more than 750,000, with boulevards, multiple-storied office buildings, and traffic policemen. The sharp contrast between areas teeming with humanity and vast untouched wildernesses merits closer attention.

The unused areas. By far the larger part of the total area is unattractive for human settlement. These empty lands include steep, rugged areas (not always mountainous), poorly drained swamps and marshes, wide expanses of equatorial rain forest on infertile soils, and a few areas where dry conditions prevail.

STEEP SLOPES. Mountain ranges extend throughout the archipelago. Many of them have peaks exceeding 10,000 feet in elevation, and the highest, located in western New Guinea, reaches over 16,000 feet. Many of the higher peaks in the Netherlands Indies are volcanic cones, sources of the ash and lava that have produced rich soils on adjacent lowlands. Most of the rugged areas, however, are at intermediate elevations of from 1,000 to 5,000 feet. Heavy equatorial rains falling on upland areas near the sea carve the land into a maze of ridges and steep-sided valleys. Only where thick volcanic deposits have been laid down recently, or where islands have recently been uplifted from the sea, are there upland areas of even relief.

SWAMPS AND MARSHES. The rivers of Malaya and the Indies carry heavy loads of sediment as they descend from the mountains toward the coast. As a result, many of them have laid down broad, flat deltaic plains. During high water periods they overflow their banks and spread broad sheets of water over the flat terrain. The resultant swamps and marshes are wholly unsuited for settlement and act as significant barriers to the development of coastal highways and railroads. Such poorly drained coastal areas are common on all of the islands of the East Indies, as well as in Malaya. Many individual swamps are several thousand square miles in area. Even on Java, swamps and marshes form an almost continuous narrow strip along the northern coast.

EQUATORIAL FORESTS. With few exceptions, the sparsely settled parts of the archipelago are covered with dense forests. These forests occupy the steep lands and the wet lands, and other areas of infertile soils. The well-drained, fertile soils are the only originally forested areas that have been cleared and kept for permanent settlement; but even on many of these, the difficulty of transforming virgin tropical forests into productive farm land has prevented complete utilization. The forests have also proved one of the main obstacles to road and railroad construction. It is far easier to use coastwise shipping despite its slowness than to construct highways through the forests. This handicap has tended to discourage the development of interior areas unless they are served by navigable rivers.

DRY LANDS. In keeping with the variety of environmental conditions, there are areas in the archipelago where drought is a powerful deterrent to human settlement. Desert-like conditions are rare, but there are appreciable areas where soil moisture conditions are deficient for normal agricultural demands set by prevailing cultural standards. Many of the Lesser Soenda Islands, much of Timor, parts of eastern Java, and a sizable part of southern New Guinea have long dry periods. In these areas rice cultivation, one of the primary bases of Indonesian culture, is not possible except in a few localities favored by available water for irrigation. Subsistence agriculture, based mainly upon corn, seldom has supported dense populations in the drier areas. The principal exceptions are the island of Madoera and parts of eastern Java, where a corn economy supports a noteworthy concentration of people; and here drought conditions are not quite so pronounced.

Densely settled areas: THE RICH LANDS. Concentrations of population were developed centuries ago on the areas that had fertile soils capable of producing large yields of rice. The rich soils are mainly of two types: first, volcanic soils derived from fresh basic lavas or ashes that have not had their nutrients dissolved; secondly, river-laid loams and silts that are not too wet. Among the areas blessed by the addition of volcanic detritus are the ash plateaus and basins within and bordering the axial mountain ranges that extend along the outer rim of the Netherlands Indies from northern Sumatra through Java and the Lesser Soendas, thence northward through the Moluccas toward the Philippines. The northeastern arm of Celebes (Minahasa) and the famed spice islands of Ternate and Tidore are part of the northward swing of the volcanic belt. The southwestern peninsula of Celebes, on which the soils were derived from the ash of the extinct volcano Lompobatang, has a rich agricultural district. Malaya, Borneo, Timor, and New Guinea do not lie along the main "circum-Pacific belt of fire," although relatively small volcanic deposits occur in each.

Not all river-laid soils are fertile, and only a small percentage of the alluvial soils in the archipelago are intensively utilized. The best of them occurs where well-drained alluvium is derived largely from volcanic soils. These comprise the tobacco lands near Medan in Sumatra, the rice and sugar plains of northern and eastern Java, and large parts of the rice areas of Bali and Lombok. Other good alluvial soils are those along the natural levees of the larger rivers, which seldom are inundated. They explain the ribbon-like strips of settlement in southeastern Sumatra and parts of Borneo.

REGIONS OF SPECIALIZED PRODUCTION. Not all of the concentrations of population are based on highly fertile soils. A number of areas have dense populations mainly because of particular conditions of environment favoring the production of commercial specialties. Rubber can be grown on widely different soils, but it demands certain conditions of rainfall and good drainage. The labor supply is another critical factor in its location. The west coast of Malaya (above the wet plains and below 1,000 feet in elevation), the Lampongs district of south Sumatra, many lower volcanic slopes in Java, the northwestern coast of Borneo, and the Barito River area of southeast Borneo all carry dense populations based mainly upon rubber production.

Tin mining has resulted in dense populations in the areas around Ipoh and Kuala Lumpur in Malaya. On Bangka and Billiton, however, tin mining is highly mechanized and never attracts much unskilled labor. Oil production and refining, because of their demand for relatively small numbers of highly skilled workers, have stimulated the development of small, compact, modern cities, such as Balikpapan and Miri on Borneo and Palembang and Djambi on Sumatra, but seldom have led to dense settlement in the areas about these centers. Most urban centers owe their size and importance to commercial functions and have well-settled environs.

The possibilities for the development of new areas of dense settlement appear to lie largely in specialized crops adapted to certain types of environment, or in some new form of semi-self-sufficient economy in which the principal food base would be a crop more tolerant of drier conditions and less demanding of fertility than rice. The Lesser Soendas have not reached their maximum productive capacity. Some parts of New Guinea appear now to have excellent possibilities for settlement, once inaccessibility is alleviated. This seat of possible future expansion holds especially true for some of the north coastal districts. The reclamation of delta plains by flood control possibly could add considerable agricultural land.

Most of Borneo, central and southern New Guinea, central Celebes, and east central Sumatra probably always will remain relatively empty of population. The soils of the rainy tropics generally are notoriously infertile. Despite the small areal extent of the good lands in the archipelago, their productive capacity is unique in all the world. As

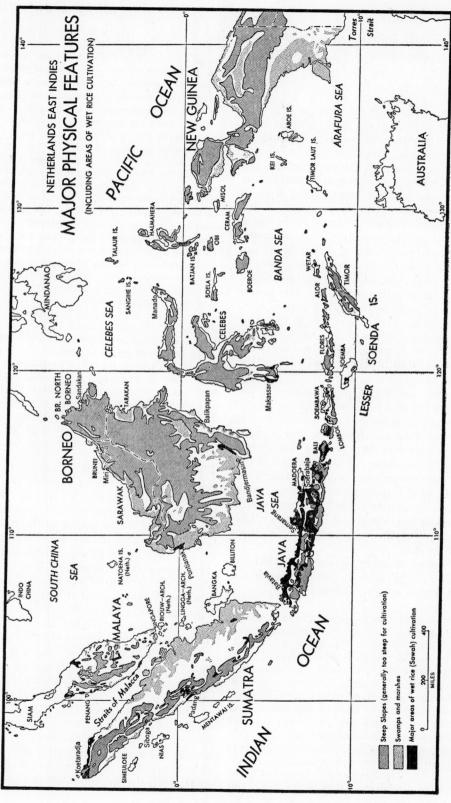

NETHERLANDS EAST INDIES
MAJOR PHYSICAL FEATURES
(INCLUDING AREAS OF WET RICE CULTIVATION)

Steep Slopes (generally too steep for cultivation)

Swamps and marshes

Major areas of wet rice (Sawah) cultivation

MILES
0   200   400

a home for human beings, they continue to be a source of amazement even to experts in demography.

The People

Diversity of race. It is not surprising that this area between oceans and between land masses has experienced wave after wave of racial migrations. With the flow of peoples back and forth through the archipelago, the widely differing environmental conditions tempted certain racial elements to stop at sites that were particularly enticing. With every successive wave of visitors, there was a corresponding intermingling of racial types. At present the main mass of the native population is an almost indescribable confusion of racial characteristics, with the latest pre-white arrivals as the dominant strains. The purest racial stocks include the oldest inhabitants, who have maintained themselves in the most inaccessible parts of the area. Some of these peoples (mostly Negrito), recently observed in New Guinea, are scarcely beyond a Stone Age culture.

Dominant culture groups. Despite the wide variation of racial stocks in the archipelago, there are relatively few culture groups in the settled areas. Each one, for various reasons, wields a certain political force, and the interplay of these interests promotes the internal strains on the political structures. The cultural and political strains are evident and impelling only in the settled areas, which form a small fraction of the total area. The largely empty lands are interesting mainly as ethnic museums.

Thumbnail sketches of the principal social and political traits in the four dominant cultural groups are given below:

Indonesian: The native peoples, sometimes inaccurately termed Malays. Predominantly rural-minded; village dwellers; rice cultivators. Religion is Islamic; hence they have a fatalistic conservatism. Slow and deliberate, they constantly rationalize work. Generally have a great respect for authority, but can become fanatical rebels. City dwellers mostly are laborers and coolies. As a class they have not gained materially in standard of living under colonial administration. Distribution: the predominant culture group in numbers in nearly all parts of the archipelago.

Chinese: The dominant merchant class throughout the area; the laboring class in tin mines and cities of Malaya. Often a buffer group between natives and whites. Originally from southeast coastal China. Few Chinese coolies outside Malaya. In Malaya a large percentage of the Chinese coolies are migratory laborers. Hard workers and thrifty. An extremely homogeneous group, but generally loyal politically to their adopted country. Strongest political pressure is in Malaya, where they form the largest group in population centers. Communistic leanings among the transient coolie class in Malaya. In the Netherlands Indies main power of the Chinese is economic. Distribution: mainly in cities and towns of Netherlands Indies, where they form about 1.5 per cent of the population; throughout settled Malaya, where they form about 50 per cent of the population.

Europeans: Administrators, plantation owners, professional groups, commercial entrepreneurs. Small minority in numbers, but political control is usually in their hands. Relative standard of living (at time of writing) is far higher than in home country. Throughout the area they are envied by the natives, not so much for their wealth and prestige as for their "gadgets of modern civilization." Distribution: almost entirely confined to urban centers of the archipelago.

Indians: Almost wholly a transient, contract-labor class confined to rubber areas of Malaya. Appreciable numerically in Malaya but of little political significance. A restless group affected by the nationalist movement in India has started labor uprisings occasionally. Most of the Indians are Tamils from southern India.

The most dynamic cultural group is the Europeans. The glitter of Western civilization is bright in the eyes of all the others. The strength of the Western Powers commonly is misassociated in the minds of the native and Chinese laboring classes with the tools and material objects of European culture. Thus arises a great desire to obtain these tools, even when they cannot afford to purchase them. The most complacent Indonesian peasant often is willing to sacrifice considerable personal security for "tailor-made" cigarettes, tinned foods, and an occasional "movie."

CONFLICT AMONG THE CULTURE GROUPS. The internal political frictions of the archipelago are understandable but difficult to solve. To be sure, plural societies are present in almost all nations—the United States has dozens of them. Colonial Southeast Asia, however, lacks one important ingredient essential to harmony between widely different culture groups—an accepted sense of common social will, the inalienable need of a person as a member of a state society. In Southeast Asia and the archipelago, there are no universal demands; there are only demands within each culture group. Complicating the situation is the fact that, owing to the geographic patterns of position and resources, each group is economically dependent upon the others for material progress. In this area where commercial raw materials rank so high in the productive capacity, economic motives play a great role in social and political behavior. The usual reaction to the political impasse is generally a hue and cry for nationalism by the more ambitious native classes.

Economic Structure

Economic considerations rank foremost among all the factors that influence political ties and frictions. Nearly every important nation in the world has some economic stake in the archipelago, mainly because of the variety of industrial raw materials and staples produced there. The map directly below

to withstand new competing areas, new methods of production, the heavy burden of interest on investments, changes in industrial demands, the discovery of synthetic substitutes, or the vagaries of international price levels. The Netherlands Indies have seen many a product wax and wane in importance, and the adaptability of the Dutch colonial officers has been a credit to their administration. Although European countries were fighting among themselves as early as the seventeenth century for economic dominance in the archipelago, none of the four leading products listed in the table of exports on page 424 was at that time an appreciable item in commerce. Rubber and petroleum shipments belong entirely to the twentieth century. Bloody struggles between the Dutch and the Portuguese were fought over control of the spice trade in the early colonial period; now spices are among the lesser important products. Coffee, which at one time was the leading export from the Netherlands Indies, now is far down on the list of exports, despite

COMMERCIAL PRODUCTION

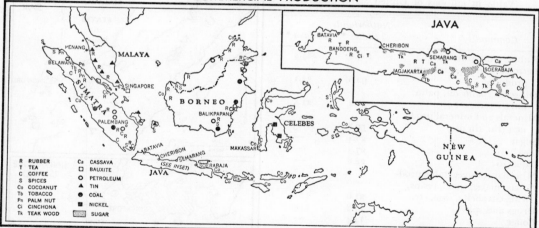

shows the location of the principal producing areas, and the table on page 424 lists the leading exports. A few items—rubber, petroleum and petroleum products, oil seeds, and tin—stand out far above the others in value.

Commercial development. In any area specializing in staples and raw materials, world-wide competition is a harsh master. Many prospering corners of the world have fallen into oblivion because their inhabitants could not adjust their productive capacities

the fact that more is being shipped than ever before. Sugar has had its troubles owing to tariff schedules and world economic depressions. It is remarkable, for example, that the total value of exported sugar in 1937 was almost exactly the same as it was in 1875, though the tonnage in 1937 was six times that of 1875.

Production and export statistics for the period just before World War II reveal a number of interesting facts. Among these are:

1. Production of nearly all items showed sizable increases in volume.
2. Values of staples and raw materials showed only moderate increases and some decreases, indicating close correlation to low international price levels.
3. Natives were supplying a constantly increasing share of the exports, although they dealt through middlemen (Chinese, Europeans).
4. Percentages of exports to the mother countries decreased with corresponding increases in east Asiatic and U. S. trade.
5. In the Netherlands Indies, the value of exports from the Outer Provinces had since 1925 overtaken and greatly surpassed that of exports from Java.

The changed conditions represented by several of these items have entailed significant political repercussions. The fact that the native population in the Indies was entering more and more into the field of commercial production at a time when the entire area was suffering from depressed prices made the problem of production regulation by the government more difficult. It also indicated increased open economic competition between culture groups.

No part of the Malay Archipelago is far from the coast. As a result innumerable cities and small communities abound along the thousands of miles of shore lines of the East Indian islands and Malay Peninsula, normally handling much of the trade springing from the region's commercial activity. Only in southern Malaya and in Java, however, are there urban centers exceeding 100,000 in population: the great commercial center and British base of Singapore (769,000 people on Singapore Island), at the southern tip of the Malay Peninsula (see map directly below); the rubber center of Kuala Lum-

Exports for 1937

(Value in millions of United States dollars)

Commodity	Netherlands Indies *	Malaya **
Rubber and gutta percha	165.6	284.4
Petroleum and petroleum products	92.6	33.1
Oil seeds (palm oil, palm nuts, copra, etc.)	58.2	21.5
Minerals and mineral products (tin, tin ore)	50.8	116.3
Sugar	28.4	—
Tea	27.3	—
Tobacco	22.8	—
Miscellaneous vegetable products: maize, wood, resins, rice, citronella, sago, etc.	21.0	18.0
Drugs and spices	14.8	11.9
Coffee	14.4	—
Fibers (mainly kapok)	13.0	—
Tapioca	10.5	1.1
Animal products	7.5	4.3
Miscellaneous (bullion, etc.)	3.0	30.7
Totals	529.9	521.3

* Indisch Verslag (Indies Report), *Statistisch Jaaroverzicht van Nederlandsch-Indie over het Jaar 1937* (Statistical annual abstract of the Netherlands Indies for the year 1937), II (Batavia, 1938), p. 330.

** U. S. Department of Commerce, Bureau of Foreign and Domestic Commerce, *Foreign Commerce Yearbook* (Government Printing Office, 1938), pp. 343–344.

NOTE: The figures for Malaya include a considerable number of re-exports.

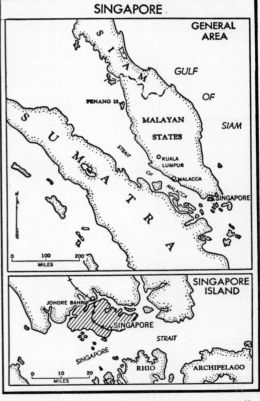

pur (138,000), on the peninsula 200 miles northwest of Singapore; the Dutch colonial capital of Batavia (254,000), on the west end of the north coast of Java; the trading center and seaport of Soerabaja (192,000), at the east end of the north coast of Java; and the trade and plantation center of Surakarta (134,000), in the interior of Java. In the less densely populated parts of the East Indies, such as Borneo, few cities have a population of more than twelve or fifteen thousand.

Regional aspects. Java is still the political center of the Netherlands Indies, although the commercial interests are shifting more and more to outlying areas. In most colonial areas a large surplus of exports over imports is needed to pay the interest on capital investments. The position of Java is rapidly changing in this respect. During the economic depression of the 1930's the island imported more than it exported, a situation certainly not normally associated with that of a colonial area. It is becoming the service center for the Outer Islands—a transshipment point for the products destined for world shipping lanes, the administrative center, and the distributing point for manufactured goods. It is even beginning to develop con-

producing areas and the smaller number of producing units. The main interests of Britain in Malaya are rubber plantations, huge commercial investments, and a rigid control of international policy. In the past the British have held most of the higher administrative posts, but shortly before World War II they were relinquishing many of these to specially trained natives.

In the Netherlands Indies the Dutch population includes a large number of resident plantation owners and managers. Dutch nationals are also found throughout the governmental organization; many are in professional services; some live in the area on their own incomes; and others are in industry. In 1930, for example, there were about 208,000 Dutch in the Indies. In 1940 there were only about 20,000 British subjects of white origin in Malaya.

Population Employed in Occupational Groups: Netherlands Indies—1930
(in thousands) *

Occupation	Natives		Europeans		Chinese		Other Orientals		Totals
	No.	%	No.	%	No.	%	No.	%	
Production of raw material	14,193.2	70.6	18.8	22.0	144.9	30.8	7.0	19.4	14,363.9
Industry	2,105.1	10.3	4.7	5.5	93.9	20.0	5.0	14.0	2,208.7
Transport	290.7	1.3	10.9	12.9	12.7	2.7	1.7	4.7	316.0
Commerce	1,090.9	5.3	11.4	13.2	171.9	36.6	19.0	52.8	1,293.2
Liberal professions	150.2	0.7	11.3	13.2	7.2	1.5	0.8	2.3	169.5
Public administration	491.9	2.3	20.7	24.3	3.0	0.7	0.5	1.4	516.1
Others	1,957.6	9.5	7.4	8.9	36.1	7.7	2.0	5.4	2,003.1
Totals	20,279.6	100.0	85.2	100.0	469.7	100.0	36.0	100.0	20,870.5

* *Indisch Verslag,* II (Batavia, 1938), 64.

siderable manufacturing of its own. The pressure of population on the land has limited native participation in commercial production on Java. On the other islands, where land is cheaper, the native is less handicapped by these restricting factors and has greater economic possibilities. Consequently, economic restrictions do not play a particularly strong role in delineating culture groups on less crowded land.

Malaya differs from the Netherlands Indies economically, mainly because its commercial production is limited to two major products—rubber and tin. There is not the wide range of plantation products common to the Dutch in the Indies, and the natives have little opportunity to enter into commercial production. Regulation of production is much easier because of the compactness of the

Strategic raw materials. Several of the principal products of the area have a political significance that transcends normal economic processes. Among these are petroleum, rubber, tin, nickel, and bauxite. Although the area produces only about nine per cent of the world's supply of petroleum, this output is by far the largest source of supply in east Asia. The importance of this supply to the Japanese army was well illustrated during the recent world conflict. A growth of industrialization in China and India would place new demands on this source. Imperialistic designs in the future by any east Asiatic power certainly would necessitate the acquisition and use of this raw material that is essential in modern warfare.

Experience in the recent struggle also demonstrated that modern warfare cannot be carried on without an adequate supply of rubber. Synthetic rubber production reduced some of the strategic significance of plantation rubber, but possession of the latter still is a great advantage. The Malay Archipelago (including Malaya) normally produces over nine tenths of the world supply of natural rubber.

By virtue of the limited sources of supply throughout the world both tin and nickel are strategic minerals. Before the war Malaya was the world's largest producer of tin, supplying three fourths of the United States' requirements. Its only close competitors are Bangka, Billiton (close neighbors south of Singapore), and Bolivia. Nickel is found in commercial quantities in only a very few places in the world. The determined efforts of the Japanese to develop and protect the nickel deposits of southeastern Celebes during the recent war indicated their dependence on this source.

One of the largest single sources of bauxite (aluminum ore) for the Japanese war machine was the small Dutch island of Bintan, south of Singapore. Japanese interests also operated the bauxite mines of Johore state in southern Malaya.

The virtual world monopoly of quinine production held by the Dutch on Java placed the Allied Powers in a critical position for a time following Japanese conquest of that island. The mass production of atabrine and the development of other synthetics represented some of the great triumphs of science during the war. The postwar influence of these new synthetic substitutes undoubtedly will be felt seriously by the cinchona growers.

Native self-subsistence agriculture. The internal political strains have their strongest expressions wherever Indonesian, Chinese, and European cultures are in closest proximity, as in the cities and in the areas where European-owned or -managed plantations predominate.

A comparatively large part of the native population, however, has little or no direct interest in commercial production. In the case of many Indonesians, their economy is based primarily on the cultivation of rice supplemented by a few other food crops. These people live in village communities and tend their tiny outlying fields with infinite care. They have little or no cash income, and their political horizon seldom transcends village affairs. Both the English in Malaya and the Dutch in the Indies have done much to improve native agriculture. Probably nowhere has a colonial power done as much as the Dutch in providing expert agricultural advice to the common farmer. Partly because of this aid, the Javanese are among the world's most efficient farmers. Efficiency in native agriculture, combined with favorable environmental conditions, has been largely responsible for the density of population on Java. However, the increase of population (which has expanded from about 4,500,000 in 1800 to 41,000,000) has absorbed the increased productive capacity of the rice lands, so that as a result the standard of living of the typical Javanese peasant has not noticeably increased.

In recent decades there has been a growing tendency toward individual ownership of land in the areas of permanent rice cultivation. This is in direct contrast to the long-standing cultural tradition of the Indonesians, whereby the community (social group or area) has the right of disposal over land within its jurisdiction. Individual ownership, with its increased economic responsibilities, almost always fosters a greater appreciation of current political policies. It likewise sharpens "business wits." The Indonesian native is not so naïve as to refuse an opportunity for a profit. If he can obtain a greater real income by raising cassava or jute on his tiny piece of land with an equivalent amount of work, he generally does so; and when international price levels fall, he usually goes back to cultivating rice again. Once in the field of commercial production, he is likely to be a fervent believer in economic nationalism for the Indonesian.

In the sparsely settled parts of the archipelago, self-subsistence agriculture also is practiced, but in a form entirely unlike the *sawah,* or wet-field rice cultivation. Here the cultivated land is almost entirely in dry-crop cereals, such as upland rice and maize, or in yams, sago, sweet potatoes, or cassava. Land ownership means little, as cultivation shifts periodically with depletion of fertility or for superstitious reasons. Village communities are the basic units in this migratory agricultural (*ladang*) system as they are in *sawah* cultivation, but their political significance is slight, largely because they lack permanence of location.

Major Political Trends

By virtue of its productivity and its strategic position astride one of the major highways of world commerce, the Malay Archipelago commands a prominent place in any plan of geostrategy. It is one of the few equatorial regions that contain appreciable areas of fertile soils, and it is well supplied with available labor to work commercial plantations specializing in tropical products. It likewise is particularly blessed with several mineral resources that rank high in the demands of modern technology.

Its political and economic status has been predominantly colonial, effectively controlled until recently by western European nations. These nations hold control as a heritage of long-past military achievements. Until comparatively recent years economic exploitation in the area has been a sad example of ruthlessness. Shortly before the turn of the present century, however, the colonial policies of both Britain and the Netherlands in the area changed abruptly to a kind of benevolent, paternalistic bureaucracy. Since that time, both British Malaya and the Netherlands Indies have had efficient, progressive governmental programs conforming to the newly-found international code of ethics for colonial administrations.

The government of the British areas in this part of the world was extremely complex. At the outbreak of the Pacific War the British Governor of the Straits Settlements was High Commissioner for the Malay States and the State of Brunei in Borneo and, in addition, was British Agent for the states of North Borneo and Sarawak. In the Malay Peninsula the British had three general political divisions: first, the Straits Settlements, a Crown Colony, consisting of the Settlements of Singapore (including the Cocos Islands and Christmas Island in the Indian Ocean), Penang (including Province Wellesley), Malacca, and Labuan, an island off northwest Borneo; second, the Federated Malay States of Perak, Selangor, Negri Sembilan, and Pahang; and third, the Unfederated Malay States of Johore, Kedah, Perlis, Kelantan, and Trengganu. In Borneo, British North Borneo was a Protected State administered by the British North Borneo Company under a Royal Charter granted in 1881; Brunei had a British Resident and a local Sultan; and Sarawak was a Protected State with a white Rajah, Sir Charles Brooke.

In January, 1946, the British Secretary of State for Colonies announced in Parliament a plan for a "Malayan Union and Singapore." The Malayan Union would consist of the four Federated Malay States and the five Unfederated Malay States and the Settlements of Penang and Malacca. Great Britain would exercise supreme jurisdiction in all the Malay States. The Crown Colony of Singapore would include the Cocos Islands and Christmas Island in the Indian Ocean south of Sumatra. A governor general would head the Malayan Union, the Crown Colony of Singapore, and British Borneo. British Borneo itself would consist of Sarawak and British North Borneo in addition to Brunei and the island of Labuan. Both Sarawak and British North Borneo would receive the status of crown colonies in 1946. Although strong opposition developed among the Malay sultans over the British plans in Malaya, they were carried into practice later in the year. Continued opposition, however, led to a subsequent decision to change the Malayan Union into a Malayan Federation and grant more consideration to the native sultans.

At the outbreak of the Pacific War the Netherlands Indies were governed through "provinces" and "governments"; the former had a representative body and the latter did not yet possess one. West Java became a province in 1926; East Java and Madoera, in 1929; and Central Java, in 1930. In 1938 the Outer Islands were divided into the three governments of Sumatra, Borneo, and the Great East.

The political status of the Netherlands East Indies remained in flux for a long period after the end of the Pacific War. The struggle centered between the nationalists on Java and Sumatra, who had created the Indonesian Republic, and the Dutch, who were eager to maintain some control over their rich colonial empire in the Far East. In November, 1946, the Linggadjati Agreement was reached providing for the establishment of the United States of Indonesia by January 1, 1949 as an equal partner under the Dutch Crown. The United States of Indonesia as then planned would consist of the following three major divisions: The Indonesian Republic, comprised of Java, Sumatra, and Madoera; Dutch Borneo; and the Great East, comprised of Bali, the Moluccas, the Celebes, the Lesser Soenda Islands, and possibly Dutch New Guinea. Fighting, however, broke out in July, 1947, over disagreement on the actual interpretation of the Linggadjati Pact. The Security Council of the United Nations at once tried to end the conflict. The formation of a United States of Indonesia depends upon a lasting peaceful settlement of the difficulties between the Dutch and Indonesians.

With the increased opportunities for education and participation in commercial production on the part of the Indonesians and other laboring classes, and the increased borrowing of European tools and techniques, the right of European authority is certainly being challenged in this part of the world. There is little doubt that the white man's prestige is rapidly shrinking and that today he is on the defensive, as is true throughout all of east Asia. The Dutch and British have not been oblivious to the pressure for increased native participation in governmental affairs, and both took preliminary steps in this direction prior to the Pacific war.

The relative importance of Malaya and the Netherlands Indies to their respective mother countries is much different. Britain would certainly lose but little of its total political strength by relinquishing administrative control in Malaya, provided it could still retain control over the foreign policy, enjoy preferential commercial advantages, and maintain a strong military base at Singapore. The

Dutch, however, would lose more by such a step in their possessions. The Netherlands Indies are the largest and wealthiest part of the Kingdom; without them, the Netherlands is but a minor European state.

In any event, colonies are rapidly becoming the outmoded relics of an earlier era in world affairs. During the past century many forces have been at work for the betterment of subject peoples. This trend will probably continue unless a single nation achieves global domination and imposes unbridled imperialistic policies on its conquered masses.

There are definite advantages for the people of British Malaya and the Netherlands East Indies in retaining some connection with Britain and the Netherlands. The international good will of these two nations is a powerful asset, as was illustrated in World War II. The experience of years of colonial administration must be borrowed and used to avoid serious errors. Naïveté in international, political, and commercial techniques is an open invitation to disaster. Other nations besides Britain and the Netherlands have economic, social, and military interests in the area, and the factors of distance and time mean little today. The migratory Chinese or Indian coolie in Malaya and the typical Indonesian rice farmer still have a long way to go before they can justifiably accept all the responsibilities of an independent state. At the same time the archipelago is too richly endowed with natural resources and has too large an indigenous population to remain as an heirloom for successive generations of Europeans.

OCEANIA

Extending largely beyond the Malay Archipelago is the vast region of scattered islands and island groups known as Oceania, or the South Seas. Although the actual land area amounts to only 400,000 square miles, the islands are spread across one sixth of the earth's surface.* The political geography of the area, like that of the continent of Africa, has reflected the expansion of colonial powers,

* The area of New Guinea alone (usually considered as a whole in Oceania) is 312,000 square miles, therefore the thousands of islands making up the remainder of Oceania (Fijis, Gilberts, Marianas, Marshalls, Carolines, Solomons, Hawaiians, New Caledonia, Nauru, etc.) total only about 88,000 square miles, an area but little more than one half the size of California.

as various countries went ever farther afield to acquire new possessions and strengthen their world position with strategic outposts and supplementary resources.

The South Seas may be divided into Polynesia, extending in a triangle from Hawaii to Easter Island and New Zealand; Melanesia, stretching south of the Equator from New Caledonia and Fiji to Timor and the Moluccas; and Micronesia, extending north of the Equator from the Gilberts to the Palaus.

Geographic aspects. Approximately 360,000 Polynesians live on widely scattered islands, including Hawaii, that cover about 10,000 square miles; almost two million Melanesians live on islands, including New Guinea, the second largest island on earth, that cover about 388,000 square miles; 110,000 Micronesians inhabit islands that cover an area of only 1,200 square miles. Before World War II white settlers in Oceania numbered about 33,000 exclusive of Hawaii, and over half of these were in French New Caledonia. About 13,000 Chinese had entered the South Sea Islands, the largest concentration being at Rabaul on the Australian island of New Britain. Some 80,000 Japanese civilians had settled in their Pacific mandate, and about 105,000 British Indians had migrated to Oceania, chiefly to Fiji.

The islands of Oceania, united by the common highway of the sea, are more important from a strategic than from an economic viewpoint. The route of Japanese expansion in the South Seas and the Allied road to Tokyo involved the strategy of island hopping. Warships can utilize important bases in the South Seas, like Guam in the Marianas, Manus in the Admiralties, Truk in the Carolines, Noumea in New Caledonia, and Pago Pago in American Samoa. In an air age many of the islands of Oceania also afford excellent bases for commercial and military aircraft crossing the long distances of the world's largest ocean.

The natives of Oceania are essentially self-supporting in their tropical oceanic climate. Copra, rubber, sisal, and palm oil are products of the area that have failed to survive stiff competition from other areas. Traders are now more interested in the nickel and chrome of New Caledonia, the gold of New Guinea and the phosphate of Nauru, Ocean, and Angaur islands.

Political aspects. Before the war the political administration of the South Seas was divided into eighteen units under the flags of Great Britain, Australia, New Zealand, France, the United States, the Netherlands, Japan, and Chile. As would be expected, colonial governments in the vast dependent area of Oceania reflected a wide divergency in form. The New Hebrides were a condominium of France and Great Britain; Nauru was a joint mandate of Australia, New Zealand, and Great Britain; Samoa was divided between the United States and New Zealand, which had a mandate over her share; the Southern Solomons were a British protectorate, but the Northern Solomons were

part of the Australian mandate; New Guinea was divided between the Netherlands and Australia, with the western portion of the island a part of the Netherlands East Indies; Fiji was a British Crown Colony under a governor who was the British High Commissioner of the western Pacific, and Tahiti was a French island in the Society group under the "French Settlements in Oceania"; Canton and Enderbury in the Phoenix Islands were under the joint control of Great Britain and the United States; the Carolines, Marshalls, and Marianas were a mandate of Japan, but Guam in the Marianas was a possession of the United States and controlled by the American navy; Tonga was a British protectorate under a native Polynesian queen, and Easter Island was a dependency of Chile.

The end of the Pacific War has brought many political changes to the islands of the South Seas. The Japanese have now been repatriated from their Pacific mandate, and henceforth the United States will wield paramount influence in the Carolines, Marshalls, and Marianas. The Australian and New Zealand mandates in the South Seas have now become trusteeships under the United Nations. Hawaii is approaching statehood in the United States with the approval of President Harry S. Truman. The French possessions in the Pacific are becoming a part of the French Union, and the political status of the Netherlands East Indies is under revision.

The problems of the South Seas in general were the subject of an international conference called by Australia and New Zealand. In 1947 the United States, Great Britain, France, the Netherlands, Australia, and New Zealand discussed ways to promote the welfare of the natives and to spur economic development in the islands of the South Pacific. A regional organization, like the Caribbean Commission, was brought into being, and was named the South Pacific Commission. Meanwhile, Australia and New Zealand have been pressing for a general regional defense agreement involving a zone extending from the Cook Islands and Western Samoa in the east to the arc of islands north of Australia. The defense of this zone would primarily concern the powers with possessions in this area. In January, 1944, Australia and New Zealand signed the Canberra Agreement, wherein they agreed to pursue a common policy on Pacific questions.

CHAPTER 30 | The Philippine Islands

FERNANDO MAGELLAN, the Portuguese navigator in the service of Spain, discovered the Philippine Islands in 1521. Twenty-one years later a Spanish exploration party named them in honor of Prince Philip, later Philip II of Spain. During the next fifty years several Spanish expeditions gradually overran most of the important islands in the group and established many permanent settlements. By 1600 the Spaniards were in peaceful possession of nearly all the Philippine archipelago.

Authentic accounts indicate that, long before the islands were known to Europeans, Chinese trading voyages to the Philippines took place at least as far back as the tenth century, probably earlier. Also Hindus, who presumably came by way of the Malay Peninsula, influenced the people, probably in the early centuries of the Christian era. One evidence of this Hindu influx is found in the many Sanskrit words in the languages and dialects used by the natives when the Spanish arrived.

The islands lie off the coast of southeast Asia, directly across the South China Sea from Hong Kong and Saigon, 500 and 600 miles, respectively, to the west (see the map on inside of front cover). As an approach to the continent of Asia, however, the Philippines have never figured prominently. Unlike the situation of Japan to the north, nearness to the Equator prevented their location on an important Great Circle route across the Pacific to North America. Another consideration relative to their location is that the island group is on a part of the vast archipelago that rims the coast of southeast Asia and

thrusts southward toward Australia and eastward into the central Pacific. Hence, the Philippines do not have a unique position, although in certain instances they have figured in the military strategy of the general area. Rather than a strategic location, they are best known for their natural wealth and their productivity. In the years ahead their potential economy may be realized if and when resources are properly exploited and developed. In short, the Philippine Islands are important in themselves and may hope to become even more so.

Spain, which brought Christianity to the Philippines, is responsible for its religious advances, but that country's interest in exploitable products retarded genuine economic progress. Monopolistic policies and high export taxes on the part of the Spanish prevented successful competition with either the West Indies or the Netherlands East Indies. The latter carried greater favor in the European markets, and the former were less remote than the Orient.

Although the Moros in the southern islands continued to harass the Spanish until 1850 and several other European nations tried to secure part of the trade or to capture part of the islands at various times, Spain retained fairly undisputed sovereignty until the Spanish-American War. At the conclusion of that brief struggle the United States acquired sovereign rights in the Philippines by virtue of the Treaty of Paris (December 10, 1898). Under American guidance have come educational and medical progress, economic development, and finally full membership in the family of nations. The Filipinos have attained their present political status through peaceful cooperation, rather than through violence and bloodshed, a development that has been watched with great interest by other subject-peoples of the Far East.

Physical Setting *

The Philippine Islands form an archipelago that extends over sixteen degrees of latitude, a distance of more than 1,100 miles (see the map on page 433). If a map of the Philippines were superimposed upon a map of the United States, on the same scale (irrespective of matching latitudes), the islands would extend from the Gulf of Mexico to the latitude of Minneapolis. If Manila were placed at St. Louis, Aparri in northernmost Luzon would lie on the Illinois-Wisconsin boundary about sixty miles west of Lake Michigan, and the southeastern tip of the same island would lie within Tennessee. Davao, the chief city of Mindanao, would be at the southeastern corner of Alabama; New Orleans would be covered by the Island of Jolo, the largest of the Sulu group; and Palawan would extend southwestward almost to Dallas, Texas. Relative to distance from the Equator, however, the Philippine Islands have about the same latitude as Central America and southernmost Mexico.

There are 7,083 islands in the Philippine group, of which 463 have an area of more than one square mile. The total area of the islands, 114,400 square miles, is about equal to the combined area of New York, Pennsylvania, and West Virginia, and each of the eleven largest islands has an area greater than the land area of Rhode Island (1,058 square miles). These eleven islands contain about ninety-five per cent of the total land area, but approximately two thirds of the archipelago's surface is made up of the two principal islands: Luzon (41,000 square miles) and Mindanao (37,000 square miles), which are, respectively, approximately equal in size to the states of Ohio and of Indiana. Recently the Philippine Islands have claimed sover-

eignty over the Shinan Gunto islets, 200 miles west of Palawan, and over Turtle Island off northeast Borneo, additions that would increase their area slightly.

Relief. In the Philippines the relief and its underlying structure are complex. The islands have a highly irregular configuration and consequently an extremely long coastline. Rugged mountains, folds, fault blocks, and volcanic ranges form the backbone of the islands and trend roughly in a north-south direction. Mountain ranges in general parallel the coast and are separated from it by narrow, interrupted coastal plains. The principal intermontane lowlands are the Central Plain of Luzon and in central Mindanao. In the central part of the island group many of the synclinal basins * are below sea level and form the bays and straits that separate the principal Visayan (central) Islands.

Climate. Rainfall regime rather than temperature differences determines climatic regions in the Philippines. The mean annual range of temperature varies from one to eleven degrees; only in the extreme north is there a noticeably cooler season.** Altitude exerts a greater influence than latitude. Along the west coasts there are three seasons: a mild dry period from November to mid-March with average temperatures in the low or middle seventies; a shorter hot, dry season lasting until mid-June with considerably warmer days, although the absolute maxima rarely reach 100° F.; and the rainy season, from June through October, which is accompanied by cloudiness and a high relative humidity.

The east coasts have maximum precipitation in the cooler months, but no dry season in summer. In the south rain is somewhat uniformly distributed throughout the year. In all regions interior valleys receive less moisture than coastal stations. The central and northern islands may experience typhoons anytime from April to December, although most of them occur between July and October. Their high winds and torrential rainfall may cause heavy damage to coconut plantations, sugar cane, and abaca crops, and also interfere with coastwise shipping.

---

* Much of the material in this section and in the section on economy, pages 435-36, is an adaptation and revision of paragraphs from Alden Cutshall, "The Philippine Islands and Their People," *Journal of Geography,* XLI (1942), 201-211.

* Synclinal basin: A topographical depression caused by a downward fold of the rock structure on all sides.

** In contrast, Kansas City has a mean annual range of 50° F.; Miami, 14° F.

Vegetation. Forests cover almost three fifths and *cogonales* (man-made artificial grasslands) occupy about one fifth of the total area in the Philippines. Twenty-two per cent is in farms, but only eighteen per cent is actually cultivated (1938). The forests include both virgin timber, much of it relatively inaccessible, and worthless second growth. There are excellent tropical hardwoods; before the recent war, woods of the lauan family (Philippine mahogany), which constitute 75 per cent of the total stands and 90 per cent of the production, were exported to the United States, Japan, and China. The equatorial forests of the southern islands merge into middle latitude species in the higher altitudes of Luzon, but the more temperate oak thrives only above an altitude of 4,000 or 5,000 feet.

People and Culture

Despite a diversity of racial and language components, the Philippines are characterized by a unity of culture. The cultural heritage, however, results from a fusion of contacts and ideals. Upon a basic Malayan society, the Spaniards superimposed Christianity and a modified feudal system. American control introduced a veneer of Anglo-Saxon civilization and planted the seeds of democracy. Finally, Chinese and Japanese intercourse and immigrants have left discernible imprints on local communities or areas.

Racial characteristics. The original population of the Philippines consisted of the Negritos, a group of primitive, black pygmies with kinky hair, thick lips, and flattened noses. These people, of which only a few mountain tribes remain, were forced into the more inaccessible regions by the invasions of Mongoloids, known as Indonesians in the northern islands and as Malaysians in the southern islands. From the latter two groups emerged the basic racial strain of the modern Filipino. A substantial proportion of the inhabitants have mixed racial characteristics, part Spanish and part Filipino. These individuals are known as *mestizos,* the Spanish word for those with mixed blood.

For more than three centuries the Chinese have constituted the largest alien group in the Philippines, and their number nearly tripled between 1920 and 1940. Chinese interest in the islands results from geographical propinquity and commercial intercourse upon a large scale from the dawn of Philippine history. The pure Chinese, making up only a small percentage of the islands' population, are shop-keepers and traders. Much more numerous are the Chinese *mestizos,* totaling about 750,000.

In the years prior to World War II many Japanese immigrated into the Philippines. Although they settled throughout the islands, they became most numerous along the moist eastern coast, where the production of abaca prevails. In fact, this industry was largely taken over by the energetic Japanese, as the Filipino dislikes the strenuous hand labor required in the stripping operation. About half the 29,000 Japanese settled in Davao, where they practically controlled the province. In 1941 Davao city, in many respects a Nipponese center, was connected with Tokyo by regular steamship service.

Religious imprint. The term "Filipino" connotes neither physical nor cultural characteristics, although current usage tends to restrict its use to designate the more active and progressive peoples and usually those professing the Christian faith. Christian Filipinos make up more than ninety per cent of the population and are the representative peoples of the islands.* They are the ethnic composite of the early Negritos, the Indonesians, and the *mestizos.* Their culture is primarily a mixture of native, Spanish, and American customs and traditions in various stages of fusion.

The Christian inhabitants are divided into seven principal ethnographic groups, each possessing characteristics, including its own native dialect, which set it apart from the others. Of these groups, the three largest and most important are: (1) the Visayans, who inhabit the islands between Luzon and Mindoro on the north and Mindanao on the south; (2) the Tagalogs, who live in the provinces around Manila Bay; and (3) the Ilocanos, who occupy three narrow coastal provinces in northwestern Luzon (see the map on facing page for island locations). In recent years the latter have overflowed into nearby provinces and have also migrated to Mindanao

* For a more complete treatment of Filipinos and alien groups, see J. R. Hayden, *The Philippines: A Study in National Development* (Macmillan, 1942), or Herbert Kreiger, *Peoples of the Philippines* (Washington, Smithsonian Institution, 1942).

THE
PHILIPPINE ISLANDS

0   50   100
MILES

LUZON

Aparri

Vigan

San Fernando
Baguio

Lingayen
San Quintin
San Jose
Cabanatuan

MANILA

Batangas

PACIFIC

OCEAN

China

Sea

MINDORO

Sibuyan
Sea

Legaspi

MASBATE

SAMAR

Capiz

Visayan
Sea

PANAY

Iloilo

LEYTE

Leyte
Gulf

NEGROS

Danao
Cebu

Argao

CEBU

BOHOL

Surigao

Mindanao Sea

PALAWAN

Sulu Sea

MINDANAO

Zamboanga

Davao

SULU IS.

Celebes
Sea

433

and Hawaii. Many Ilocanos are business men, and they have been termed the "Yankees of the Philippines." This choice of vocation may not be entirely voluntary, since their home provinces are in the dryer, less-productive section of the islands.

The Moros, most of whom live in Mindanao and the Sulu Islands, are the most numerous of the non-Christian groups. Their origin probably differed little from that of the other inhabitants, but they came under Moslem influence sometime before the fourteenth century, and their chief characteristic is an almost fanatical adherence to that faith. They were among the last people to submit to American occupation, and in 1942 the Japanese found their attitude toward conquest by a foreign power no different than it had been forty years earlier. They occupy a position somewhat analogous to that of the American Indian a century ago in the United States. The central government has made concessions to these people, who possess a different religion, unconventional customs, and a distinct history of their own. However, the Philippine administration has also attempted to develop Mindanao and to assimilate the Moros. Both of these efforts have been opposed by the Moro population. The Moros are thought to be the largest single group that would have preferred that American control be continued.

Language. Despite the various languages and local dialects (eighty-seven are recognized), English has become the principal tongue. The leading Philippine newspapers and magazines are printed in English, but Spanish is still used locally, especially by the wealthier class. In 1937 Tagalog was chosen as the official language. As only slightly more than one fourth the population speak it, this selection caused some local dissension, and in 1948 the language question was reopened for consideration. Literacy is slightly less than fifty per cent, but this statement is misleading for the average length of school attendance is less than three years, not enough time to attain permanent literacy in any language.

Population. As shown by the following table, the population of the Philippine Islands has more than doubled since Spain relinquished control:

Philippine Population

Year	Number of inhabitants
1903	7,635,425
1918	10,314,310
1930	12,583,066
1940	16,000,303
1945 (estimate)	17,000,000

The distribution of population throughout the islands is far from uniform. In some parts there is not enough land for the farmers to cultivate; other areas have large tracts of virgin domain. Of the larger islands, Cebu has 558 persons per square mile, but isolated, rocky Palawan has only 10 per square mile; Rizal province on the central plain of Luzon has a density of 564 but on the northeastern margin of the plain rugged Neuva Viscaya province tallies only 30 per square mile. To encourage a more uniform distribution, the National Land Settlement Administration has sponsored migration from central Luzon and the more densely populated Visayan Islands to agricultural colonies in the sparsely populated alluvial areas of Mindanao.*

Cities. Although the urban population amounts to almost 4,000,000, there are only a few large cities in the islands. Manila (1939 population: 623,500), the capital and largest city, is also the leading port and has ninety per cent of Philippine manufacturing. Although Cebu (1939 population: 145,000), on densely populated Cebu Island, is the leading city of the middle islands, it has in some respects been surpassed by Iloilo (90,000), whose rise somewhat paralleled the increase in sugar production on Panay and Negros, for which it served as the principal outlet. In Mindanao, Davao (95,000) and Zamboanga (70,000) are the most important centers.** Secondary cities on Luzon, the most highly urbanized of the islands, are Legaspi, Batangas, Lingayen, Vigan, Aparri, and Baguio (see the map on page 433). Baguio in the highlands, 125 miles north of Manila, is the summer capital. In a comparatively short

* For an excellent treatment of governmental-sponsored resettlement in the Philippines, see Karl J. Pelzer, *Land Settlement in the Asiatic Tropics* (American Geographical Society, 1945), 127–159.
** Population figures in each case are for the chartered city, which for Davao and Zamboanga includes considerable territory outside the urban area.

time it has grown from a village of pine shacks and Igorot huts to a modern city of 25,000 permanent residents.

Government and Politics

The Philippines are organized as a political democracy with a liberal constitution and no legally privileged class. This organization has not coincided with actual practice, however, for the government has been dominated by the wealthy landholding class. Lack of a large middle class has helped these landholders to become more and more entrenched in the life and welfare of the nation. Before the war a single party, the *Nacionalista* party of Manuel Quezon and Sergio Osmeña, dominated all elections. At times the Quezon and Osmeña forces engaged in major political warfare, but in 1935 the rival factions adjusted their differences to present a united front for independence. The Commonwealth government was established in November, 1935, under the provisions of the Tydings-McDuffie Act of March, 1934, which provided for a commonwealth period prior to independence. The government and the people worked diligently to prepare for independence, which was granted as scheduled on July 4, 1946.

Minority political groups in the Philippines have found survival difficult. The old *Democrata* party was probably the strongest prewar minority group but could never offer successful competition to the *Nacionalista* party at the polls. During the period of Japanese occupation, organized guerrilla groups, for the most part made up of landless peasants, fought the enemy and fostered truly democratic ideals. After the Japanese had been defeated, some of these groups and their successors campaigned for agrarian and other socio-economic reforms, opposing, in part, the policies of President Osmeña and especially Manuel Roxas, the *Nacionalista* leaders after the death of President Quezon. Of these groups, the Democratic Alliance, a progressive group organized in central Luzon in 1945, had the greatest strength; but it is doubtful whether it will ever become a significant party in Philippine affairs. After the 1946 split in the old *Nacionalista* party, the Alliance joined forces with the Osmeña faction in an unsuccessful attempt to defeat the so-called liberal wing of Roxas. This is representative of Philippine politics, for the history of Philippine political parties is one of fusion, mergers, and absorption of minorities. Strong new parties and the end of one-party rule may never materialize.

Economy

Agriculture. The economy of the Philippines prior to World War II was predominately agricultural, with nearly seventy per cent of the population dependent upon agricultural pursuits. Most of them were small landed proprietors or tenants, or were laborers on the larger sugar, abaca (Manila hemp), tobacco, and rice estates. In 1938 about four million hectares * were cultivated, almost one half of that area being devoted to rice culture. Roughly another one third of the cultivated area was used for the production of export crops (coconuts, abaca, sugar, and tobacco). Although beneficial to a few plantation owners, processors, and exporters, this emphasis on cash crops in a state that has consistently imported foodstuffs has failed to benefit the Philippine masses. A relict of the Spanish regime, the semifeudal character of the agrarian system does not take into account the necessity of a well-balanced production satisfactory to the domestic demand. Even though there are many small landowners, the proportion of landless people is extremely high for an overwhelmingly agricultural country in which there is little industry and only one metropolitan center. Less than forty per cent of the 3,144,000 families own both house and land. A little over forty per cent own homes on rented sites.** Most of the farms, to a large extent concentrated in the fertile valleys and coastal areas, are small, averaging about ten acres each.

The islands occupy a latitude that, except in the higher altitudes, has a 365-day growing season. Thus two or more of a wide selection of crops may be grown during the year, and forage and shelter for livestock do not present significant problems. An insular position permits more moderate temperatures than are characteristic of larger land masses and, in addition, insures ample precipitation over

* One hectare equals 2.47 acres.
** *American Chamber of Commerce Journal,* II (October, 1940), 8.

most of the area. Even in the regions that have a dry season of several months, there is still sufficient time to produce adequate food crops during the wetter months. Because of regional differences in climate and soil, a variety of crops can be grown: rice and tobacco in the fertile river valleys, coconuts on the sandy coasts, corn on the coralline soils of the central provinces, abaca on the moist eastern slopes, sugar cane on the fertile coasts of Negros and in the valleys of Luzon, and sweet potatoes on the more rocky uplands. Rubber and pineapples offer commercial possibilities, although two rubber plantations in Zamboanga province and a single pineapple plantation, also on the island of Mindanao, are the only significant examples of these particular products.

In 1898 crude methods of cultivation were widespread and scientific knowledge even less utilized. Since American occupation, and with American assistance, there has been a constant and rapid improvement in farming methods. Contributing factors included the initiation of agricultural experiment stations, the introduction of foreign plants and new strains of existing cultivated crops, the establishment of rural credit associations and agricultural schools, and the passage of liberal homestead laws.

Mining and forestry. Recently mining and lumbering have become important industries, and in 1941 each occupied a significant role. The value of Philippine mineral production doubled between 1931 and 1936; then the 1936 figure was tripled by 1940. Around 1930 the value of lumber products was about equal to that of minerals, but up to World War II the increase, although significant, has been considerably less rapid than that of mineral production.

About a quarter of a million people depended upon mining for their living before the war. Gold production amounted to four fifths (83 per cent in 1940) of the total value of the mineral products. It exceeded that of Alaska, and in the United States only California had a greater production. Iron ore reserves at Surigao in Mindanao have been estimated at 500 million tons, making it one of the major ore bodies of the world. The Zambales chromite deposits, north of Manila, are estimated at ten million tons; in 1940 the islands supplied about one fourth the United

States chrome imports. Silver is associated with most of the gold ores, and the value of manganese, copper, lead, and zinc follow in that order.

The principal deficiency of Philippine mineral resources is fuels. There are petroleum seeps, but no producing wells. The drilling of test wells was interrupted in 1941 by the hostilities of World War II. Coal deposits are widespread, but the beds are thin and oftentimes broken by movement of the earth's crust. Moreover, the coals are young, and there is no coking variety on the island.*

Internal Problems

The future success of an independent Philippines hinges in part upon the action taken by the United States Congress in early 1946 pertaining to reconstruction, rehabilitation, and trade relations.** More important to the Philippine populace, however, is action taken by the Philippine administration, reinforced until July 4, 1946, by the assistance of the American High Commissioner and his staff, to alleviate socio-economic unrest. This action, centering around farm tenancy, even though far from adequate, has lessened internal dissension and partially appeased the resistance groups of debt-saddled tenants and underpaid laborers, who could have caused even greater embarrassment to the government. The Democratic Alliance deserves a major share of the credit for the agrarian reform and related progressive (liberal) action. Its leaders called mass meetings and conferences, thereby forcing a cautious Osmeña government to face some of the true issues before the 1946 national elections and independence. When Osmeña was defeated, however, almost open warfare resulted between the agricultural factions of the Central Plain and the new Roxas administration.

After three and one-half years of warfare and resultant oppression by a rigid Japanese military regime, the people of the islands suffered from physical debilitation as a result of

* For a more complete treatment of mineral resources, see William F. Boericke, "Future of Philippine Mining," *Far Eastern Survey*, XIV (1945), 300–303; or Alden Cutshall, "Mineral Resources in the Philippine Islands," *Scientific Monthly*, LIV (1942), 295–302.
** The Philippine Rehabilitation Act (Tydings Bill) and the Philippine Trade Act (Bell Bill) both were adopted by the United States Congress in April, 1946, only a few weeks before Philippine independence.

improper diet, destruction of housing, inadequate medical care, and war casualties. Nearly every family throughout the islands was affected either directly or indirectly. The people possessed neither the adequate strength nor the facilities to reconstruct a normal economic life or reinstate the cultural progress on which the national existence is based. A well-organized educational system, which increased literacy from almost nil to almost fifty per cent in forty years, was mentioned with pride in 1941. Its restoration alone presents a major problem in rehabilitation.

Economic rehabilitation: AGRICULTURE. The islands must have a realignment of agricultural production. An independent Philippines must compete with other nations without the benefit of the continuous tariff protection granted the islands when they were a colonial dependency. Sugar and coconuts are thus destined to occupy a less significant role in the insular economy: sugar, because it can be grown and marketed more cheaply in Cuba and other areas than in the Philippines; and coconuts, because the principal product, coconut oil, must compete with other vegetable oils. In the years up to World War II the United States purchased most of the Philippine copra and coconut oil; as a result of the increase in American soya bean acreage since that time the coconut industry may never permanently regain its prewar position.

This loss of a foreign market for agricultural products may not handicap the Philippines so much as it would first appear. In recent years the islands have never been self-sufficient in foodstuffs. The release of sugar lands should mean an increase in rice acreage and the removal of rice from the import list. Increased production of corn and other grains and an expanded animal industry may result from the lessened emphasis on catering to an export market. Regardless of the basic cause for any shift in agricultural production, these modifications, plus the encouragement of a modern poultry and vegetable program, should result in a higher standard of living, a more stable economy, and a firmer basis for a new nation that must fight for its place in world trade.

MINING. Reconstruction of the mining industry is more difficult. The principal markets for Philippine minerals were the United States and Japan. Since Japanese manufacturing has been restricted to nonmilitary products, Japanese industrialists can normally obtain sufficient minerals from areas within or nearer Japan Proper. The United States will continue to import Philippine minerals or mineral concentrates but probably in smaller quantities than in the immediate prewar years, especially since higher quality manganese and chromite are available in other parts of the world. A further handicap to immediate recovery of the mining industry stems from lack of Philippine capital. Among all known Philippine mineral resources the rehabilitation of chromite mining will be easiest.* Deposits are near the surface and, other than transportation, no major technical problems are presented. Gold mining will probably regain its former position, but not for several years until American capital is invested in Philippine mining interests in greater quantities than heretofore.** Iron, manganese, and copper mining face special marketing problems as a result of the war, and their future is problematical.

TRANSPORTATION. In any archipelago transportation and communication are not easy. Insular isolation, rather than unity, prevails. In the Philippines the interisland steamers were the most prevalent method of communication before World War II, yet only one steamer of the interisland fleet was repaired and in service six months after cessation of military hostilities. Except for short private lines in the sugar districts of Negros and Panay and a short coastal line on Cebu, the only railroad is on Luzon. Wanton destruction during the war left it only partially serviceable. Air service connects the principal islands and links the more remote areas with the capital and major ports. A revived interisland steamer fleet for bulky commodities and an air net for passenger, mail, and fast freight service can provide adequate facilities and a national communication system unsurpassed in insular areas.

INDUSTRIES. At no time have the islands had significant industries other than those of a service type or those engaged in elementary

---

* Boericke, *loc. cit.*, p. 303.
** It is interesting to note that the stringent regulations by the Filipino government pertaining to investment of American capital have been rescinded.

processing of agricultural, timber, or mineral products. Destruction of plants and equipment and the loss of foreign markets between 1941 and 1945 caused even these manufacturers to begin almost entirely anew. However, the Philippine Islands have a great industrial potential. A major asset is the large and increasing population with a relatively high degree of literacy. A great majority of the inhabitants are trained to work for a common goal and to frugal living as a matter of pride. A variety of minerals, agricultural products, and forest resources provides ample raw materials. The hydro-electric power potential partially offsets a deficiency in mineral fuels. Finally, a geographic proximity to possible new markets in Asia permits the insular manufacturer an advantage of lower transportation costs over his Occidental competitors.

Cultural and social problems. Several problems unrelated to direct economic needs should receive the continuing attention of the new government. A national language has been suggested repeatedly, but there has been no concerted effort to find a solution. The Philippines are not likely to become a multilingual Switzerland or a bilingual Belgium. A single language should do much to promote tolerance and internal unity. Minority groups have not been a pressing point of friction, but the Moro problem has never been satisfactorily solved. With the population increasing in Mindanao, the home of more than half a million Moslems traditionally hostile to the Christian Filipinos, serious friction is probable. Illegal entrance of aliens, particularly Chinese, will always be a problem, for it is physically impossible to patrol the coasts of all the islands.

Foreign Relations

American ties with the Philippines will continue to be extremely close. Economically, politically, and militarily the two countries will share many common interests. The United States has continued to maintain bases in the islands. For eight years from the time of independence major Philippine products are to be admitted free to the United States on a quota basis, but thereafter five per cent of the normal duty is to be added annually until the full American tariff has been reached. Congress has also approved a grant of $625,000,000 in cash or supplies to lighten the burden of the war damage in the islands.

If Philippine independence is not a success, then the government of the United States has failed in its responsibility. We fostered the islands' independence and guided their destiny through a transitional period of semi-self-rule; nevertheless it can be argued that the United States has a further moral responsibility to the Philippines. Moreover, the American government has pledged itself to protect the security of the islands. It was not possible to defend the islands in 1942, and as a consequence they suffered large human and economic losses. Subsequent legislation partially reimbursed the Filipinos for their economic losses, but no simple act of Congress can atone for the loss of human life, for the mental suffering of the survivors, for the loss of foreign markets, or for the disintegration of an established business.

Ties with the United States are rooted in the past, and branched toward the future, for the United States did not sever itself completely from the Philippines on July 4, 1946. By mutual consent an associate-nation relationship has evolved, and our government is permitted to retain military and naval bases in the islands. It is not intended that these bases or their personnel be used to police the islands; rather, it is planned that the islands have at least some protection from outside aggression. The United States can scarcely be responsible for preservation of Philippine independence without some influence over agreements or commitments the islands may make with other nations. Hence, the essentiality that the conduct of Philippine foreign relations be assisted at least for a while by American personnel or agencies in the interests of the future security of each nation. Tariff concessions, granted for the early years of the new republic, are being removed only gradually, in order that abrupt competition in the world market may not stifle initiative. As a result, adjustments in insular economy will be transitional and less painful.

For nearly a half century the Philippine Islands have looked eastward to the United States as an outlet for her commodities and as a source for her needs. Prewar Philippine economic dependence upon the United States is illustrated by the fact that about eighty per cent of all Philippine exports was sold on the American market, and normally seventy per cent of her imports was supplied by this country. The islands must increase their commerce with the states of the western Pacific to compensate for the normal decline of exports to and imports from the United States. If a united China becomes a reality, and if Chinese trade increases to the point where it is commensurate with the natural wealth of the huge country, the Philippines are advantageously situated to share this trade. In any case, foreign relations in the Far East, both political and economic, are most likely to hinge on developments in China.

Compared with the Philippines, the Netherlands East Indies have a somewhat similar heritage and many similar problems. Even as economic competitors these two insular lands might, however, establish close political ties. Japan, Korea, and the Northeast Provinces of China—middle-latitude areas of eastern Asia—are the natural markets for products from the Asiatic tropics. A north-south rather than an east-west trade, if encouraged, might become the dominant one. Likewise, relations between the Philippine Islands and middle-latitude Australia and New Zealand have potentialities, although the smaller population in the South Pacific and the possibility that its limited needs for tropical products may be supplied by nearer islands and northern Australia itself lend emphasis to the thesis that the economic destiny of the Philippines is directly aligned with continental east Asia. The Philippines have historical and political ties with the United States because this country laid the foundation for a democracy, but geographically the islands are a part of the Orient.

PART SIX

Latin America

LATIN AMERICA is a designation for those parts of the Western Hemisphere in which the peoples speak languages of Latin derivation. Traditionally it has been customary to divide the Western Hemisphere into two continents —North America and South America—with the dividing line drawn between Panama and Colombia. Such a division has no meaning in human terms, however, because, culturally, the boundary between the United States and Mexico is the dividing line between two unlike realms—Anglo America and Latin America.

Latin America thus includes the continent of South America and those parts of its northern neighbor known as Caribbean America. Physically, therefore, it consists of two immense triangles and a chain of islands. The larger triangle is South America, the corners of which are Cape São Roque, Cape Horn, and Point Gallinas. The first looks toward Africa, 1,700 miles away; the second stretches toward Antarctica, 600 miles southward; the third points toward Florida, 1,000 miles northwestward. The smaller triangle consists of Middle America. Its short side adjoins the United States at the Rio Grande. Its long sides face the Atlantic and Pacific oceans, and its southern corner touches South America just south of the Gulf of Darien. Through the narrowest portion of this second triangle the Panama Canal has been constructed. Three other canals have been proposed—in Mexico at the Isthmus of Tehuantepec, in Nicaragua at the lake district, and from Buenaventura to the Atrato River in Colombia. The chain of Caribbean islands, that is, the West Indies, includes three groups:

(a) the Bahamas; (b) the Greater Antilles (Cuba, Haiti, Puerto Rico, and Jamaica); and (c) the Lesser Antilles (Virgin Islands, Northern Leeward Islands, Southern Leeward Islands, and the Windward Islands). Enclosed by South America, Middle America, and the West Indies is the Caribbean Sea, the so-called American Mediterranean.

The area of Latin America is approximately 8,600,000 square miles and its population (1940) was 134,000,000. The area and population (1940) of Anglo America were 8,200,000 and 144,000,000, respectively. Notwithstanding these general similarities in area and number of inhabitants, there are great political differences between the Americas. Anglo America consists of two self-governing, national states and a few colonies, whereas Latin America comprises twenty independent republics and a considerable number of colonies.

Latin American countries fall into three language groups. The official language of Brazil is Portuguese, that of Haiti is French, and that of the remaining eighteen republics is Spanish. Thus, in 1940, Portuguese and French were the official languages of about 48,000,000 persons in two republics, whilst Spanish was used by some 86,000,000 in the other republics.

The populations of Latin America are derived from three diverse sources. First, there are the indigenous Amerindians, who are apparently of several basic racial types.* Sec-

* The Ges were of the Australoid type, the Tupi were of the Mediterranean type, the Arawaks showed some Nordic characteristics, and the Caribs and the highland tribes were generally Alpine-like.

441

ond, there are the conquering and later immigrant Europeans.* Third, there are African Negroes, who were brought in as slave laborers. In some states, as, for instance, in Uruguay, Costa Rica, and perhaps Cuba, Spanish blood is dominant. In Argentina, because of prolonged immigration, Italian elements now preponderate. At the other extreme, in Bolivia, Peru, Mexico, Guatemala, and Ecuador, the Amerindian stock is strong. The peoples of Chile, Paraguay, Colombia, Venezuela, Honduras, El Salvador, and Nicaragua are mestizo, or mixed Spanish and Amerindian. Negroes predominate in Haiti and in the British, French, and Dutch colonies, and are very numerous in Brazil, Panama, Puerto Rico, and the Dominican Republic.

As a cultural realm, Latin America is almost wholly unlike Anglo America. For one thing, it originated from wholly different political premises: the former was a military conquest, which resulted in the settling of a conqueror cast upon subject peoples; the latter was a colonization of the land by a free people. For another thing, the two areas were developed under wholly different ecclesiastical premises; in Latin America the clergy of what was officially designated as the only true church accompanied the military in a program designed to produce religious uniformity. By way of contrast, there is in most parts of Anglo America, a strong tradition of religious freedom and equality before the law. For still a third distinction, a difference has arisen out of the different status of the common man, based upon unlike concepts of the worth of the individual in British and Hispanic society, unlike degrees of experience in self government, and unlike commitments to the ideal of universal education. For a fourth contrast, the Latin American realm, when discovered by Europeans, contained large nations of barbarous or semi-civilized indigenous peoples. These were conquered but not exterminated. In Anglo America practically all native peoples were in a low stage of Neolithic culture. They either died out or were later confined to small reservations. Finally, much of Latin America has

an unfortunate attitude toward labor. The Negro, a descendant of slaves, sees little or no virtue in work. The "Indio," member of a conquered and broken people, performs his labor all too often in an apathetic manner. The Spaniard, descendant of the Castilian Conquistadores, usually disdains hard manual labor.* Only the Brasileiros, the Japanese, and the Italian and other European immigrants regard work as an unmixed blessing.

Added to an unfortunate social and political heritage, therefore, most of Latin America is considerably less advanced and progressive than its rich equipment in natural resources, space, and locational advantages would seem to promise. Moreover, the northern three fourths of the realm lie within the Tropical Zone and hence does not provide optimum conditions for European man. Throughout the tropical portions of the realm there are many pleasant and healthful highland areas suitable for Europeans, but these are badly isolated from the outside world, from one another, and from the lowland regions within the same political units. The sum total of these negative qualities has produced twenty nations instead of four or five, disunity and provincial differences within individual nations, and poverty, ignorance, and general lack of economic development in the tropical lowland portions of the realm. Only in Uruguay and perhaps Cuba is there true progress and liberalism. Only in Mexico, Argentina, and Brazil is there any real economic and political power.

The states of Latin America still retain many of the economic traits of colonies even after more than a century of independence.** Moreover, the cultural influences of Spain or Portugal are still strong in nearly all parts of Latin America. Despite this latter tie with Europe, most of the states of the realm have found many or all of their markets in Anglo America and have therefore gravitated into the political orbit of the United States.

* The attitude in Costa Rica, which is Gallegan rather than Castilian in heritage, is generally an exception to this.

** Cuba is an exception, having had political independence only half a century, and Panama only won independence in 1903; Puerto Rico has yet to achieve it.

* Mostly Mediterraneans or mixed Mediterranean-Nordic types.

CHAPTER 31

The Caribbean: An American Mediterranean

SIXTEEN flags fly over the Caribbean, the Mediterranean of the Americas. In addition to those of the twelve independent Latin American nations, the flags of Britain, the United States, France, and the Netherlands appear over colonial territories (see the map on page 445).

As a region, Caribbean America is rather well defined except in Colombia, where it merges into the Andean region facing the Pacific. It encompasses the entire area south of the Rio Grande down to and including the north coast of South America.* The Caribbean Sea is the unifying influence that justifies classifying this large area as a single geographic region. Most of the lands are in close proximity to this sea, although El Salvador has a coastline only on the Pacific Ocean, and extreme northwestern Mexico is more than 2,000 miles from the nearest Caribbean water. Economically and politically, as well as physically, all the lands in general face the Caribbean and the neighboring Gulf of Mexico.

The region can conveniently be separated into three major subdivisions: Mexico and Central America, the West Indies, and the north coast of South America. The Republic of Mexico is the only Caribbean land that has territory contiguous to that of the United States. In Central America there are the six republics of Guatemala, Honduras, El Salvador, Nicaragua, Costa Rica, and Panama; the colony of British Honduras; and the Panama Canal Zone, territory leased to the United States.

The West Indian Archipelago forms a huge arc of islands partially enclosing the Caribbean Sea on the north and east. The western part of the chain (known as the Greater Antilles) is composed of four large islands, on which there are the Republics of Cuba, Haiti, and the Dominican Republic, and two colonial possessions: Puerto Rico, belonging to the United States; and Jamaica, belonging to Great Britain. The island made up of Haiti and the Dominican Republic is known as Hispaniola, although it is also called Haiti and, less frequently, Santo Domingo. The string of small islands curving clockwise from Puerto Rico to the coast of Venezuela (known as the Lesser Antilles) is divided among four countries. Britain owns most of them, of which Antigua (in the Leeward Islands); Dominica, St. Lucia, St. Vincent, Grenada (all in the Windward Islands); and Barbados and Trinidad are the largest and best known. At the northwestern extremity of the Lesser Antilles are the Virgin Islands, belonging to the United States. France owns two significant islands, Guadeloupe and Martinique, located in the heart of the group. The Dutch still have a few small islands in the northern part of the Leeward Islands. Associated with the West Indies are also several Dutch islands off the coast of Venezuela. Curaçao and Aruba, not far from the oil-rich Maracaibo basin of Venezuela, are the only ones of significance, largely on account of their petroleum refineries. North of Cuba, extending from the coastal waters of Florida to those of Hispaniola, are the Bahama Islands, owned by

* The term "Middle America" is used to designate the same region minus the north coast of South America. "Latin America" is the Americas south of the Rio Grande, complementary to Anglo-America, which lies north of that river.

Britain, bringing British colonial soil to within sixty miles of southern United States.

Along the north coast of South America, but reaching far into the interior of the continent, are the republics of Colombia and Venezuela and the possessions of three European nations: British Guiana, Surinam (Netherlands Guiana), and French Guiana. As Colombia and Venezuela have in them the northern termini of the Andean ranges, they are also physically related to Ecuador, Peru, Bolivia, and Chile—Pacific states of South America. Colombia has a Pacific as well as a Caribbean coastal frontage and its position introduces an unavoidable overlap of regional divisions (see Chapter 34, "Pacific South America").

Whether the Caribbean be considered from the standpoint of strategic location, physical characteristics, commercial development, or political relationships, the region is a tremendously important part of the world. Further, its political geography is closely interwoven with that of the great powers of western Europe in addition to all the countries in the Western Hemisphere. In particular, a considerable amount of interest and concern from the United States is focused upon the political areas in and surrounding the Caribbean (see the table on page 456).

Space Factors

Location. A most significant feature of the Caribbean is its location. For more than four hundred years the area has been a busy highway of transport to and from the Western Hemisphere. Here lay the romantic-sounding "Spanish Main," in the days when the area attracted pirates along with legitimate adventurers, traders, and representatives of European crowns. The Isthmus of Panama, about fifty miles wide, served as a portage for transshipping goods from the Spanish colonies bound for Europe—treasures tempting to marauders of the sea. Later, the opening of the Panama Canal made the Caribbean one of the world's greatest trade routes. Presently the area supports a network of crisscrossing routes which both serve the region and connect the United States with republics of South America to the south.

Like the position of the Mediterranean, that of the Caribbean has made it one of the dominant strategic spots of the world. In the light of the respective economic and political importance of these two regions, growing out of similarity of their positions in relation to neighboring continents, it is natural to draw comparisons between the two areas. Beyond a few primary traits in common, however, such an analysis immediately discloses that many significant differences exist between the regions in climate, natural resources, and population. Another noteworthy distinction between them is the fact that in place of the single narrow Mediterranean entrance of Gibraltar from the Atlantic, there are many and wide passages into the Caribbean. The most frequently used of these entries are the Florida Straits (100 miles wide) leading into the Gulf of Mexico, which in turn is connected with the Caribbean by the broad Channel of Yucatán; the Windward Passage between Cuba and Haiti (45 miles wide); the Mona Passage separating the Dominican Republic and Puerto Rico (60 miles wide); the Anegada Passage east of St. Thomas (70 miles wide); the routes between Martinique and St. Lucia; and those north of Trinidad (see the map on page 446).

Size. The oval-shaped Caribbean is about 400 miles wide at its narrowest part in the east and about 700 miles between Panama and Cuba. From east to west it measures approximately 1,500 miles. Its total area of about 750,000 square miles, not including the Gulf of Mexico, is approximately three fourths that of the Mediterranean.

Land areas of the Caribbean countries amount to more than 2,000,000 square miles. The twelve republics range in size from Mexico, which has 760,000 square miles, down to Haiti with 10,000 square miles. Intermediate are Guatemala and Cuba, each roughly comparable in area to Ohio or Pennsylvania. Of the colonial possessions British Guiana with 89,000 square miles, about twice the size of Pennsylvania, is the largest; all of the islands in the Lesser Antilles except Trinidad are much smaller than Rhode Island.

Boundaries. The Caribbean area is relatively free of important boundary problems or disputes. Primarily responsible for this situation are two factors, one natural and one cultural. First, a large proportion of the international boundaries of the region are water. Cuba has no land boundaries, and most of the other countries have extensive water

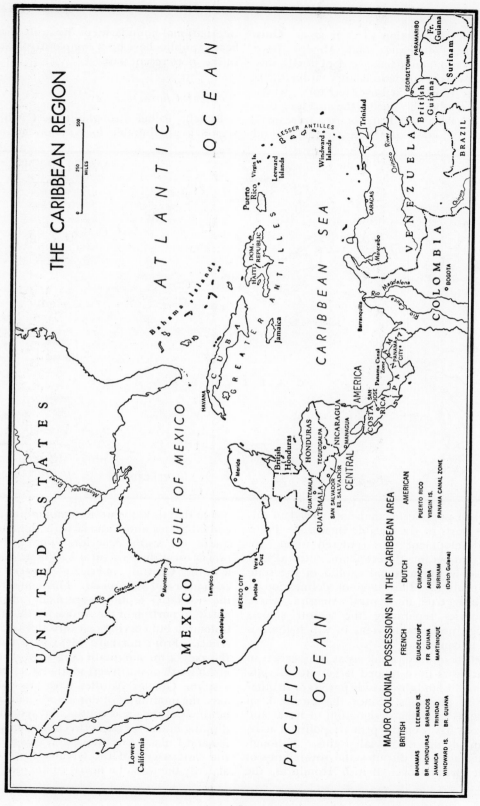

THE CARIBBEAN REGION

MAJOR COLONIAL POSSESSIONS IN THE CARIBBEAN AREA

BRITISH	FRENCH	DUTCH	AMERICAN
	LEEWARD IS.	GUADELOUPE	CURACAO	PUERTO RICO
BAHAMAS	BARBADOS	FR GUIANA	ARUBA	VIRGIN IS.
BR HONDURAS	TRINIDAD	MARTINIQUE	SURINAM	PANAMA CANAL ZONE
JAMAICA	BR. GUIANA		(Dutch Guiana)	
WINDWARD IS.				

boundaries in relation to their area. Only Colombia, Venezuela, and Mexico have lengthy land boundaries, and of these only Colombia has experienced international friction since World War I over territory—where its southern border touches the area long contested by Peru and Ecuador (see page 487). Second, national states were created around

international boundaries of the twelve Caribbean republics have been comparatively stable in the more recent past.

Physical Characteristics

Relief. Relief throughout the Caribbean region is attributable to a major mountain

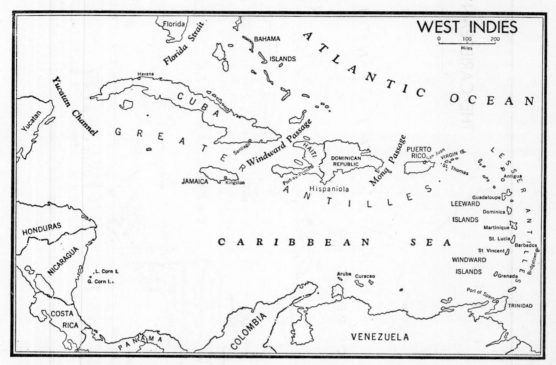

nuclei of population that had settled in different parts of the Caribbean world. Political development thus centered upon core areas that became the economic, cultural, and ultimately the national capital of the state that evolved. This type of delineation is especially true in Central America, where boundaries separating the countries pass through undesirable areas in which there is little to contest.

Such boundary problems as have arisen in recent years have related largely to the possession of islands by outside powers or to other colonial questions. Since the outbreak of World War II the designation of naval and air bases has been the primary political activity involving territorial rights. Although Guatemala still disputes the sovereignty of Great Britain over British Honduras, the

system that links the western mountains of the United States and Canada with the Andean chains of South America. The principal ranges form the structural backbone of Mexico, the Central American countries, and Colombia and Venezuela. The mountains of the two latter republics are made up of the northern portion of the Andes, north-south in Colombia but curving eastward through Venezuela. From northern Mexico to Panama the axes of the mountain ranges are generally north-south or northwest-southeast, but to the east the Greater Antilles have an east-west axis; the mountains of this island chain are an off-shoot of the great continental system after dipping under the sea between southern Mexico and Cuba. Curving southeastward from the eastern end of the Greater Antilles are actually the tops of a nearly-submerged chain of mountains that continues to the Venezuelan coast.

The generally mountainous nature of the Caribbean region provides all of the political divisions, other than the smaller islands, with highly complex topographical patterns. Rugged mountains, plateaus, low-lying coastal plains, and narrow valleys make up the preponderant proportion of the Caribbean land area. Despite this variety, however, the several countries have many features in common. For example, Mexico, Guatemala, Honduras, Nicaragua, and Costa Rica each have a rugged interior, with habitable plateau areas, and two coastal plains—Pacific and Caribbean (or Gulf of Mexico).

REGIONAL CHARACTERISTICS. Mexico is for the most part a lofty plateau, which becomes wider and lower in altitude as one approaches the northern border. The compound Sierra Madres, bordering the extensive plateau area on either side, unite south of Mexico City to form one range that continues into Central America. Coastal plains are in all places relatively narrow except for the peninsula of Yucatán, about 55,000 square miles in area (Illinois: 56,400 square miles). Yucatán's unique location with respect to the rest of Mexico somewhat isolates it. In the northwest the mountainous peninsula of Lower California, extending for 760 miles south of the Mexico–United States boundary, is even more isolated than Yucatán.

Elevations in Mexico are generally high. The heart of the Mexican plateau lies above 7,000 feet and many peaks exceed 12,000 feet in altitude. Mt. Orizaba, the highest, with an altitude of 18,206 feet, is higher than any point in the United States or Canada. Dotting the plateau and mountain landscape of Mexico are numerous volcanoes, some of which have recently been active.

In Central America the mountainous backbone makes up most of the total land area. The western coastal strip is very narrow. Parts of the eastern coastal plain are also quite narrow, but in Nicaragua and Honduras it attains an appreciable width. Northern Guatemala and British Honduras extend onto the Yucatán Peninsula, therefore have moderate to low elevations. As in Mexico, the Central American countries count many volcanic cones, some of which are presently smoking. Allied to the volcanoes are earthquakes, which are common to this type of landscape.[*] In modern times three Central American capitals—Guatemala City, San Salvador, and Managua—have been severely damaged by earthquakes. One of the strong arguments against building a canal in Nicaragua is the persistent danger of recurring earthquakes and volcanic eruptions.

The Caribbean coastal lowlands of northern South America are in general narrow; in Colombia, however, the lowlands extend far inland up the Magdalena and Cauca river valleys. Also, the oil-producing center of Venezuela, the Maracaibo Basin, is an important lowland. In the Guianas most of the population lives on the coastal flats, the interior Guiana Highlands being extremely inaccessible.

The four major islands of the Greater Antilles have a mountainous structure, but each one is rimmed by a coastal plain and cut with valleys to the extent that each has proportionately more low-lying level land than the Caribbean countries on the mainland. Cuba, especially, has large areas of level or rolling land suitable to agricultural production, related geologically to the peninsula of Yucatán. High relief in this largest of the West Indian islands is for the most part localized in a range in the eastern part of the island parallel to the southern coast. The highest elevation in the Antilles is in the Haitian part of Hispaniola, towering up to over 10,000 feet. The Bahamas and most of the Lesser Antilles are low in elevation although volcanic peaks are present here as in all other parts of the Caribbean. The eruption of Mount Pelée on the island of Martinique in 1902 killed more than forty thousand people.

One of the principal handicaps of the Caribbean region in general is the lack of level land in an area with so many millions of people. Moreover, much of the available flat land is not used because of poor drainage, malaria, and worn-out soils. As a result fields are often planted on extremely steep slopes simply because not enough level land is available for essential agricultural needs.

[*] The same forces within the earth's crust that produce volcanoes are also responsible for the instability of rock formations, causing earthquakes.

Terracing, however, which is so widely practiced in China, Japan, and the East Indies, is virtually unknown in the Western Hemisphere.

Climate. With the exception of northern Mexico and the northern Bahamas, the Caribbean region lies within the tropics. Southernmost Venezuela reaches to within about fifty miles of the Equator and a segment of southern Colombia lies in the Southern Hemisphere. Within the confines of tropical and subtropical latitudes a great variety of climatic types exist. Differences in elevation, location with respect to northeast trade winds, and the influence of ocean waters all result in widely divergent temperature and rainfall conditions. In general, despite significant modifications due to topography, the low-latitude location of the area causes high temperatures throughout the year. The amount of rainfall varies according to location in respect to mountains and winds. Rainfall contrasts between windward and leeward sides of mountain ranges are sharp; semiarid conditions caused by a scarcity of moisture may prevail but a few miles from lush vegetation nurtured by heavy precipitation. The varying temperature of the Caribbean waters is another important factor in coastal areas. For example, there is a sharp contrast between the wet east coast of Central America with warm waters offshore and the dry north coast of Venezuela and Colombia with cold waters.

CLIMATIC ZONES AND REGIONS. The highlands in Mexico, Central America, and northern South America affect temperatures so sharply that a unique classification has been assigned to dominant climatic zones: *tierra caliente,* or "hot land," at elevations generally below 3,500 feet (coastal plains, valleys, and lower slopes); *tierra templada,* or "temperate land," between elevations ranging from about 3,500 to about 7,000 feet (intermediate slopes and plateaus); and *tierra fria,* "cold land," normally at elevations above 7,000 feet (highland areas). A fourth classification has also been recognized; *tierra helados,* or "frozen land," at elevations perpetually barren and frigid. Thus, temperatures vary from place to place, according to the relief, even though at any given point the season to season changes may be insignificant because of the low latitude.

Mexico, extending through 18 degrees of latitude and 30 degrees of longitude, has wide variation in rainfall amounts and in temperature. Frontage on two large water bodies and highly diversified relief cause sharp deviations from the normal to be expected in the country's location with respect to latitude. Annual rainfall totals range from only 2 inches in the northern desert to 185 inches along the southern Gulf coast. In the southern part of the Central Plateau, where most of the people live, the average annual rainfall is moderate. Here the temperature is very uniform, ranging from 50° to 70° F. throughout the year.

All of Central America lies within 18 degrees of the Equator, but the effects of strong insolation are to some extent modified by high relief and by the proximity of the Pacific or Caribbean (or both) to all parts of the area. The bulk of the population lives in the relatively healthful subtropical *tierra templada.* Here the distribution of rainfall depends primarily upon location in relation to moisture-bearing winds.

Hot and oppressive, the Caribbean coast of Central America has an extremely heavy rainfall as a result of the moist trade winds that blow directly onshore from the northeast. Along the Pacific coast temperatures are also high, but precipitation is considerably less and there is a pronounced dry season.

As in the highlands of the mainland, the climate of the West Indies is subtropical. Most of the islands lie near the outer edge of the tropics (Cuba is within 20 miles of the Tropic of Cancer), and further, the entire archipelago has a distinctly ameliorating marine influence. To be sure, temperatures are moderately high, but there are no great extremes. The ranges between the warmest and coldest months are 10 degrees at Havana and only 4 degrees at Bridgetown in Barbados. The northeast trade winds, which blow steadily throughout the year, cause great differences in amounts of rainfall on the windward and leeward slopes of the mountainous islands. A most striking example of this contrast is found in Jamaica, where the exposed mountain slopes of the northeast receive more than 200 inches of rain, while only thirty miles away at Kingston on the south side, the average annual rainfall is less than 30 inches. In late summer and fall the northern islands frequently have tropical hurricanes. These tropical storms, bringing high winds and large amounts of rain, often do great damage.

The low-lying coasts of Colombia and Venezuela, under the influence of the trade winds, are very hot and in general quite arid. These conditions are also found on the Dutch islands of Curaçao and Aruba, located off the Venezuelan coast. In contrast, the Guiana lowlands are extremely wet as well as hot. The climate there, similar to that of the Caribbean coast of Central America, has been described as a cross between a stream bath and a hothouse.

In the interior of Colombia, Venezuela, and the Guianas extensive lowlands (close to the Equator) are hot and humid and inhospitable to human habitation. But the highland areas are similar to those in Mexico and Central America and here are found pockets of heavy population.

PHYSIOLOGICAL EFFECT OF CLIMATE. Most people think of the Caribbean region as having a uniformly hot, humid, and enervating climate. This belief holds true only for certain coastal lands and interior lowlands in northern South America. Actually most of the people of the Caribbean live in areas having quite pleasant climates. The tradewind-swept West Indies have uniformly warm temperatures, which do not appreciably lower the working capacity of the population. On the mainland the highland regions have an "eternal spring" type of climate that is not only pleasant but also is quite stimulating. These highland climates, however, lack the changeable weather characteristics of the spring season in the mid-latitudes. Despite certain adverse factors, however, it is certainly misleading to think of the tropical climates of the Caribbean as monotonously alike throughout the region and with generally debilitating effects on the energy of the population.

Regional Economy

Basic resources and occupations. Tropical foodstuffs and industrial raw materials are the chief commodities of the region. The hot and wet coastal lowlands are covered by tropical rain forests, which yield valuable hardwoods, rubber, balata, and medicinal products. Where the forests have been cleared, the land offers opportunities for the cultivation of bananas, cacao, rice, and other crops demanding a hot, humid climate. In areas where rainfall is less, such as in Yucatán, henequen is important. The West Indies have long been important sugar producers. Highland areas on both the mainland and the islands grow coffee, tobacco, and agricultural products similar to those of more temperate lands.

Although the region produces a wide variety of commodities, specialization in one or two crops within a given area is common. This limitation is only natural where physical and economic conditions are almost ideal for a particular crop. Thus, in Cuba, for example, sugar dominates the economy of the entire island. In Honduras, bananas make up the bulk of the country's exports, and in a number of the highland countries coffee is all-important. The prosperity of these countries fluctuates with the world market prices for their special products.

In addition to tropical crops, the area is an important producer of minerals. The most significant mineral asset is petroleum in Venezuela, Colombia, Trinidad, and Mexico. Venezuela ranks high in world production, closely rivaling Soviet Russia. Within the country the Lake Maracaibo district is the chief center of production. Nearly all the oil is shipped out by shallow draught tankers to refineries on Curaçao and Aruba. Some of the Colombian oil fields are located 350 miles up the Magdalena River, necessitating transportation by pipe line. In addition to an appreciable production of petroleum, Trinidad is a heavy producer of asphalt from its famous Pitch Lake. The Mexican oil industry, once very important, has declined rapidly because of the exhaustion of wells and the lack of proper administration since the expropriation of foreign oil properties.

Surinam, or Netherlands Guiana, and British Guiana are important in the mining of bauxite, the ore of aluminum. Tremendous expansion of bauxite mining operations in Surinam during World War II was of material aid to the United States, which has a limited supply of this strategic ore.

A large variety of other minerals also exists in the Caribbean world. Manganese, chromite, and copper are mined in Cuba; silver, gold, vanadium, lead, antimony, mercury, graphite, and copper in Mexico; gold in Venezuela; and gold and platinum in Colombia. The other countries produce small amounts of many minerals. Coal deposits, however, are few and of poor quality, but Mexico, Colombia, and Venezuela have a limited quantity of this all-important source of power. Water power potential is widely distributed but little used.

The large-scale production of critical and strategic tropical foodstuffs and industrial raw materials has given the Caribbean an important place in the economic and political affairs of the world. It is necessary to examine the means by which they are distributed.

Transportation and commerce. Transportation has been the keynote to the commercial development of the Caribbean world. The moving of goods and people about the region has faced enormous natural handicaps. Mountains, swamps, deserts and semideserts, dense vegetation, and long distances between important centers have all stifled the development of an efficient land transportation pattern. Except where capital supporting large-scale commercial enterprises entered the region, the means of transportation remain primitive and backward. Human porters and pack animals continue to serve great masses of the population. It is a paradox that modern commercial aircraft in large numbers fly directly over the slow-moving peasants, carrying great quantities of air cargo as well as heavy passenger traffic.

Most of the republics have railways, but only Cuba and Mexico can claim nation-wide systems. Mexico now has 20,970 and Cuba 4,880 miles of railroads. Even these two systems give scant coverage to their respective countries. Many of the rail lines are spurs from the coast to the interior, or provide a highland capital or commercial center with an outlet to a seaport. Colombia is so rugged that the railroads are nothing more than a score or more short lines scattered about the country offering local service. Even the major cities of that country are not inter-connected by rail; and continuous travel by train from the capital to either the Caribbean or Pacific coast is impossible.

Highways in the Caribbean region fall into about the same category as railroads, although the Pan American Highway may some day provide an all-important traffic artery connecting North and South America and tap all the Caribbean countries with the exception of the islands and the three Guianas.

From the standpoint of regional economy, water transportation has been the most important means of unifying the Caribbean. Travel by ship originally opened up the area to the outside world and was largely responsible for the present commercial pattern. Steamship lines have as ports of call cities on the coasts of every country and every colony. Oil tankers, banana boats, lumber vessels, general freighters, and de luxe passenger ships all ply across and along the shores of the Caribbean and the Gulf of Mexico, and up and down the Pacific Coast of Mexico and Central America. It is interesting to note that this maritime trade is largely between the region and the outside world; very little international trade within the region exists because of the similarity of the commodity types from one country to another.

In recent years air transportation has begun to play an important part in the commercial life of Caribbean countries. The very handicaps that prevented the development of surface transportation have stimulated air travel. Airfields are much easier to build than roadbeds, tunnels, and bridges for rail lines or highways. Too, airlines hold a distinct advantage over the steamship in that goods or passengers do not have to be transferred from one type of carrier to another in order to carry them to interior points. In Colombia six days are required to travel by surface from the coast at Barranquilla to Bogotá, the capital; the plane covers the distance in about three hours. Pan American World Airways and several other American lines connect points throughout the Caribbean to leading American cities. In addition, a number of local lines add their routes to the complex network that covers the area from Lower California on the west to the easternmost of the West Indies and the Guianas. Facilitating air transportation, the Caribbean lands serve as stepping stones for planes enroute between traffic centers in temperate North America and subtropical and temperate South America.

Of commercial significance to the Caribbean region, many Americans look southward to the tourist lure of sunny skies, spectacular scenery, and, to them, quaint habits and customs. Before the war there was much interest in cruises through the Gulf of Mexico to the lands that rim the Caribbean and in rail and highway travel to nearby Mexico. Such pleasure trips are becoming more popular than ever in the postwar era, and air transportation is competing for its share of vacation travel. Tourist receipts have been and will doubtlessly continue to be an important source of revenue to these lands depicted so attractively on travel posters.

People

Racial traits and cultures. The Caribbean world is noteworthy for its great admixture of races. The original Indian population was extremely diverse and had cultural standards decidedly different from place to place. The Mayas of Yucatán had reached a stage of civilization exceeded in the Western Hemisphere only by the Incas of South America; but along some of the hot humid coastal lowlands were primitive tribes that hunted and fished for their livelihood. The Spaniards were the first immigrants, followed by countless Negroes from various parts of Africa. Whites from European countries other than Spain and, in more recent times, Orientals have added to the cosmopolitan nature of the population.

In the West Indies, the native Indians (Caribs and Arawaks) were quickly exterminated, as they could or would not adapt themselves to the toil in gold mines or on sugar plantations. Consequently, a dependable labor supply became the prerequisite for successful exploitation of the New World. Negroes from Africa proved themselves superior to any other available laborers, with the result that the West Indies are now predominantly Negroid.

In most of the British, French, and Dutch islands, the proportion of blacks is well over three fourths. In former Spanish colonies, like Puerto Rico and Cuba, the percentages are not so high, because slave importations were fewer.

After the abolition of slavery in the nineteenth century, a large number of Negroes refused to work on plantations. Agricultural labor was considered by many Negroes as a continuation of slavery. In desperation, plantation owners, looking for additional labor supply, brought in white workers from Portugal, the Azores, and Ireland. Orientals from India, China, and Java swelled the labor ranks, particularly in Trinidad, Surinam, and British Guiana. As a result, the population of these colonies is more mixed and cosmopolitan than elsewhere. White, black, brown, and yellow people live side by side, with little hostility compared to the racial relations often found in other parts of the world.

On the mainland, from Mexico through Venezuela, the Indians are still very important, and in certain parts of Guatemala and Mexico they form a majority of the inhabitants. In Mexico as a whole 30 per cent of the people are pure Indian, 55 per cent mestizo (Indian-white), and 15 per cent white. South of Guatemala, except in white Costa Rica, a mestizo population is more numerous. The original high-standard Indian cultures of the Mayas of northern Guatemala, the Aztecs of Mexico, and the Chibchas of Colombia had great and lasting influence in these respective areas. The old Mayan civilization was noted for the skill of its people in mathematics, astronomy, and architecture. The advanced Indian groups were not systematically eliminated as were the original inhabitants of the United States and Argentina. Brought in initially as plantation laborers, Negroes form a significant proportion of the population in the coastal lowlands of the Caribbean side of Central American and northern South America.

Many of the Spanish obviously came to the New World to get rich and then return to Spain. However, most of them stayed and intermarried freely with the native Indians, giving rise to a steadily increasing mestizo population. Under Spanish rule, immigration was restricted to Spanish citizens; therefore, Spanish blood is the predominate European type added to the racial composition.

Religion and language. As in the case of racial heterogeneity within the Caribbean, so is there a mixture of religions. Roman Catholics, Protestants, Buddhists, Mohammedans, Voodoo worshipers, and many other religious types are found in the region. Quite naturally the most important religion is Roman Catholicism, which was first introduced at the time of Columbus by Spanish priests. Even though the Catholic church has been criticized for exerting powerful political and economic influence, its work has nevertheless been beneficial in many ways. The church has borne the major responsibility for humanitarian and educational progress.

The prevailing language of the Caribbean area is Spanish; official in all of the republics other than Haiti, where French has remained as a result of the former control of France over that country. In the colonial areas the British, French, and Dutch use their respective tongues, although the natives do not in all cases adhere to this practice. Puerto Rico is virtually bi-lingual, with Spanish as the prevailing native language and English instruction obligatory in the school system. In the American Virgin Islands English is used by government officials and the majority of the natives alike.

Population. In comparison to the Mediterranean the Caribbean region is not densely populated. In the total Caribbean world there are roughly 55,000,000 people, giving an average density of about 30 persons per square mile (see the table on page 456 for the population of the individual countries and possessions). For the region as a whole the population density is considerably less than that of the United States (45 per square mile). Most of the islands, however, are crowded with people. Puerto Rico has a density of 545; and Barbados, the most thickly settled, 1,225 per square mile. The mainland states are sparsely inhabited except for El Salvador, which has 155 persons per square mile. On the lower end of the scale, Panama has only 22, and Venezuela less than 12 persons per square mile. Mexico, the largest country of the region, has a population of 22 million and a density of almost 30 persons per square mile.

Although large numbers of people live in the highlands, where the climate is more salubrious than in the lowlands, many of the more productive coastal areas are also thickly settled. Following the same pattern, many of the important cities are located at appreciable altitudes (Mexico City a mile and a half above sea level and Bogotá even higher!), but many important commercial centers are ports along the coast. Because of the more stimulating marine climate of the islands, all of the larger cities have grown up at the water's edge, where transportation facilities to and from foreign countries are immediately available.

Cities. With few exceptions each republic and colony in Caribbean America has one city that stands out prominently in the regional economy. In practically every case this prime city is the national or colonial capital and represents the cultural heart of its particular political area. In addition, the more populous republics and colonies have relatively large secondary cities.

In total, the Caribbean region has nineteen cities with a population of more than 100,000.* Of these, four are in Mexico, four in Central America, eight in the West Indies, and three on the mainland of South America. Again, fifteen are in independent states and four are in colonial possessions. Still another classification, ten of the nineteen cities are ports and nine are interior cities, most of which lie in highland areas. The latter type of city must depend upon relatively distant ports as commercial outlets—a factor favoring the continued development of air transportation.

By far the largest city of the entire Caribbean region is Mexico City (called simply "Mexico" in Mexico), with a population approaching a million and a half. The only other city exceeding a half million is Havana, the capital and well-known metropolis of Cuba. Other leading cities include Caracas (269,000), capital of Venezuela; Guadalajara (228,000), manufacturing and distributing center of western Mexico; Barranquilla (183,000), leading port of Colombia (when considered along with Puerto Colombia on the Caribbean coast, 15 miles distant); Guatemala City (177,000), capital and only large city of Guatemala; San Juan (169,000), Puerto Rican political and economic center, and largest colonial city in the Western Hemisphere; San Salvador (157,000), capital of populous little El Salvador; and Managua (132,000), capital of Nicaragua.

Many of the key cities of colonial areas are extremely small in actual population, but they are nevertheless bristling little commercial centers of regional importance. For example, Bridgetown is the economic focal point for the entire island of Barbados, but has only 14,000 inhabitants.

Some of the Caribbean cities are rich in historical tradition, dating back to the period

* Three cities in highland Colombia (Bogotá, Medellín, and Cali), discussed in Chapter 34, "Pacific South America," are omitted from this enumeration.

when European explorers and adventurers searched and fought for treasure and territory in the New World. The walled cities of Havana, San Juan, and Cartagena were Spanish strongholds. Acapulco, on the west coast of Mexico, was a transfer point for goods moving across the Pacific from the Far East toward Europe. Santo Domingo (now Ciudad Trujillo) on the island of Hispaniola was founded before the year 1500 as the result of initial explorations in the New World, including those of Columbus.

Historical Background

Before independence. European settlement in the Americas had its beginnings in the Caribbean world. Columbus established the first Spanish colony on Hispaniola. For more than a century following the discoveries of Columbus, Spain had complete control of the area. Cuba and Hispaniola for a long time were the headquarters for Spanish colonists, who established control over a mighty empire stretching from California to Cape Horn. The conquest of Puerto Rico began in 1508 under Ponce de León. Balboa pushed across the Isthmus of Panama, and the city of Panama was founded in 1519. Mexico was subjugated by Cortéz between 1519 and 1521. The forces of Montezuma at first offered no opposition to Cortéz but later tried in vain to drive him from Mexico. It was not until the seventeenth century that the Spanish monopoly in the Caribbean region was disputed. In 1627 the British took possession of Barbados, and in 1655 Jamaica also fell into their hands. This infiltration represented what was up to that time the major break in the Spanish control of the region. Then in the same century the French and Dutch also acquired possessions.

Independence. In the nineteenth century the oppressive Spanish rule was broken. In 1821 Mexico threw off the Spanish yoke and established independent rule after a revolt under Hidalgo failed in 1811 and another under Morelos in 1815. Simón Bolívar led the fight for freedom in Venezuela and Colombia and helped the fight for independence in five countries from Venezuela to Bolivia. He hoped to hold Venezuela, Colombia, and Ecuador in one great state; but Venezuela seceded in 1829, and Ecuador the following year. Bolívar, the father of Pan American-

ism, called the first conference of American states in 1826 at Panama. Haiti, under the rule of France since 1697, was the first colony in the Caribbean to revolt, ending French rule at last in 1804. The entire island was taken over by the Haitian government in 1822 but in 1843 the Dominicans in the eastern part formed their own republic. Today the island is the only one in the world containing two sovereign states and Haiti is the only Negro republic in the Western Hemisphere. Independence did not come to Central America until 1821, when a revolt started in Guatemala. At first a union with Mexico was tried. When that attempt failed, the "United Provinces of Central America" was established in 1823 with five provinces, consisting of Costa Rica, Nicaragua, El Salvador, Guatemala, and Honduras. The union shortly broke up into five separate nations. Frequent efforts have been made to create a Central American federation but they have failed. Puerto Rico and Cuba, lacking the power to secede, remained in Spanish hands until the Spanish-American War in 1898, when Cuba won independence and Puerto Rico passed to the United States. Panama, the youngest republic, became a separate state in 1903 after a successful revolt from Colombia.

After achieving independence, the separate republics began the task of putting their houses in order. They soon discovered that, lacking capital and technical capacity, foreign assistance was needed to prime the economic machine. Capital, managers, and technologists were imported, with the result that the countries became debtor nations whose economic affairs were controlled by foreigners.

Disorder has marked the political history of the republics. Dictatorships have been customary in most of the states, although in name they are democratic republics. Revolutions against corrupt dictators have been frequent. Petty international wars, usually provoked by aggressive dictators, have been all too common, and such strife has often led to foreign intervention. In a number of cases desperate groups have invited foreign aid and protection. Selling national assets to foreigners has been more prevalent than in many other parts of the world. Ruthless tyrants were willing to cede military bases or grant mineral, land, or transportation concessions in exchange for foreign aid. The "Trojan horse" so eagerly invited in often led to further foreign intervention.

The history of Mexico since independence reveals this general condition of political instability that has lasted for many years. A federal republic existed from 1824–34; a centralized republic from 1834–46; and a second federal republic from 1846–57. The Constitution of 1857 lasted until 1917; and the Constitution of 1917 is still in force. During this period of constitutional change, a war was fought with the United States from 1846–48, resulting in the loss of northern territory including Texas, New Mexico, and Upper California. From 1861–67 Mexico was occupied by French troops and a new empire of the Habsburgs was set up under Maximilian in 1864. The leading man of Mexico from 1876–1911 was Porfirio Díaz who ruled the country with a firm hand, gave peace to Mexico, and encouraged foreign capital. The revolution against Díaz led to the new Constitution of 1917. In the following years great estates were expropriated; communal villages were recreated; relations with the Catholic Church were severely strained; labor received practically a free hand; and the oil properties of seventeen British and American companies were seized in 1938.

The problems facing Mexico and other Caribbean countries on the domestic front are still many: the distribution of the land, the income of the farm workers, the role of labor, the standard of living of the people, the production and marketing of mineral resources, the fight against illiteracy, and the expansion of democracy.

The Caribbean and the United States

The general weakness of the Caribbean lands has always been disturbing to the United States, inasmuch as the national security of the country is partially dependent upon the political status of its southern neighbors. Hence, the United States gradually evolved a more or less permanent Caribbean policy, aimed to prevent domination of the area by any other strong power.

During the twentieth century, the United States has taken successive steps to insure its control of the Caribbean. At the beginning of the century it had just acquired Puerto Rico. In 1903 Guantánamo Bay in Cuba was leased by the United States as a naval base. Canal Zone rights were granted in 1903 by Panama after this country obtained independence from Colombia.

From the standpoint of geo-strategy the possession of the Panama Canal has extended the southern border of the United States to the Canal. This interoceanic lifeline between the Atlantic and Pacific coasts of North America is most vulnerable to attack in the Caribbean region; consequently, control of strategic bases by an aggressive non-American power cannot be permitted by the United States. This policy is particularly true at the present time, inasmuch as the airplane has brought the West Indies dangerously close to the Panama Canal and even to continental United States itself.

Nicaragua, in the treaty of 1914, leased to the United States Great and Little Corn islands. Shortly afterwards World War I was the means of influencing the United States to purchase from Denmark the Danish West Indies, renamed the (American) Virgin Islands.

Control over Key West, Guantánamo, Puerto Rico, the Virgin Islands, and the Panama Canal Zone gave to the Unites States a position of great power, which was considered adequate for our protection in this sector. However, the events of May and June, 1940, radically changed the situation. The fear of German and Italian domination of the colonies belonging to conquered European nations now became great. Submarines in the Caribbean region likewise proved a menace. Consequently, on September 3, 1940, in exchange for fifty small, over-aged destroyers, Britain granted the United States ninety-nine-year leases on bases in the Bahamas, Jamaica, Antigua, St. Lucia, Trinidad, and British Guiana along with bases in Newfoundland and Bermuda. In recommending the executive agreement to Congress, President Franklin D. Roosevelt described it as "the most important action in the reinforcement of our national defense that has taken place since the Louisiana Purchase." *

On November 23, 1941, the American position was further strengthened by an agreement with the Netherlands government, which permitted the occupation of Nether-

* Franklin D. Roosevelt, Official Statement, *New York Times*, Sept. 4, 1940, p. 1.

lands Guiana by American troops. An official White House statement issued at the time said in part, "Bauxite mines in Surinam furnished upward of 60 per cent of the requirement of the United States aluminum industry, which is vital to the defense of the United States, the Western Hemisphere, and the nations actively resisting aggression." * American troops were also stationed in the Dutch islands of Aruba and Curaçao to protect the oil refineries. The acquisition of British and Dutch bases greatly strengthened the position of the United States, particularly in the vulnerable southeastern approaches to the Caribbean. Also these bases provided vital links in the American air transport routes to Africa via the bulge of South America in Brazil.

In regard to British, French, and Dutch colonies, the United States has been interested in preserving the *status quo*. During the colonial era these possessions provoked many conflicts, chiefly because they were regarded as potential sources of wealth, especially sugar, which was in high demand at that time. The island of St. Lucia had seventeen changes in ownership; in 1763 Guadeloupe was considered by some statesmen to be more valuable than all of Canada. Today, however, nearly all the colonies are economic liabilities to their respective motherlands. The Guianas and British Honduras have never been extensively exploited because of their hot, humid climates and poor transportation facilities. Raising tropical agricultural crops, notably sugar, the island colonies face keen competition from areas better suited to large-scale production.

It has been suggested by some American politicians that the United States take over all of the European colonies in the Caribbean as payment of debts. Before taking any such rash step, which would certainly not promote international harmony, the government will need to remember that most of the colonies are "poor houses" similar to the Virgin Islands. Furthermore, it should be noted that the chief importance of the territories is strategic and that inasmuch as the United States already has a large number of bases, direct ownership of additional colonies would bring only economic and political problems.

The policy of the United States in seizing

* Franklin D. Roosevelt, Official Statement, *New York Times,* Nov. 24, 1941, p. 1.

more and more control of the Caribbean has been severely criticized. The United States has usually tried to obtain its objectives by diplomacy, but force and threat of force have been used when necessary. Although the country has taken a stand against imperialism, United States policy in the Caribbean has been aggressive. The most flagrant examples of such actions were the Panama Affair and the sending of marines to enforce "dollar diplomacy." It is not the intention of this author to condone such actions. However, it should be pointed out that our policy has not been so bad as it is usually painted. After all, no independent state has disappeared through absorption by the United States. Except in the cases of Mexico and Colombia, no nation has lost territory because of American influence. In order to compensate Colombia for the loss of Panama, the United States made a payment of $25,000,000 in 1921. Furthermore, the Monroe Doctrine has shielded the Caribbean republics from aggression by non-American powers. This protection is very important, inasmuch as all of the states are comparatively weak and insecure. Caribbean nationalists cannot fail to be conscious of their weakness if strong European powers threaten their countries. Nevertheless, the dominating role of the United States emphasizes the political inequality of Caribbean states and naturally causes some resentment.

Even the undignified Panamanian Affair has had its good results through the completion of the canal in 1914. This important waterway has been beneficial not only to the United States but also to the Caribbean area and to the whole world. Naval advantages of the canal chiefly benefit the United States, but commercial advantages are widespread. The canal is open to vessels of all countries on equal terms. The Isthmian Cut shortens sailing distances between many commercial areas. Of course, American trade benefits most from the canal. The water route between New York and San Francisco is 7,800 miles shorter by way of the canal; Callao, Peru, is 6,200 miles nearer New York; and San Francisco is 5,600 miles closer to Liverpool. Congress has been considering for some time the construction of another canal across Nicaragua and the renovation of the Panama Canal.

Country	Form of government	Area in sq. mi.	Population

I. MEXICO AND CENTRAL AMERICA

Country	Form of government	Area in sq. mi.	Population
Mexico	Republic	758,000	22,227,000
Central America:			
Costa Rica	Republic	23,000	747,000
El Salvador	Republic	13,000	1,997,000
Guatemala	Republic	42,000	3,284,000
Honduras	Republic	44,000	1,201,000
Nicaragua	Republic	49,000	1,095,000
Panama	Republic	29,000	632,000
British Honduras	British possession	8,867	63,311
Panama Canal Zone	U. S. control	553	51,827

II. WEST INDIAN ARCHIPELAGO

Country	Form of government	Area in sq. mi.	Population
Greater Antilles:			
Cuba	Republic	44,000	4,779,000
Haiti	Republic	10,000	2,719,000
Dominican Republic	Republic	19,000	1,768,000
Puerto Rico	U. S. possession	3,435	1,869,000
Jamaica	British possession	4,404	1,237,000
Turks and Caicos Is.	(under Jamaica)	166	6,133
Cayman Is.	(under Jamaica)	104	6,670
Lesser Antilles:			
Leeward Islands:			
American Virgin Is.	U. S. possession	133	24,885
British Virgin Is.	British possession	67	6,720
Antigua, Barbuda, and Redonda	British possession	171	40,970
St. Kitts–Nevis, including Anguilla	British possession	152	38,845
Montserrat	British possession	32	13,330
Guadeloupe and associated islands	French possession	688	304,240
St. Eustatius and associated islands	Dutch possession	29	4,585
Windward Islands:			
Grenada	British possession	133	90,585
St. Vincent and the Lesser Grenadines	British possession	150	61,447
St. Lucia	British possession	233	71,230
Dominica	British possession	304	53,200
Martinique	French possession	427	264,712
Barbados	British possession	166	203,410
Trinidad and Tobago	British possession	1,978	522,168
Dutch West Indies:			
Curaçao	Dutch possession	210	73,340
Aruba	Dutch possession	69	35,933
Bonaire	Dutch possession	95	5,725
Bahamas	British possession	4,404	68,846

III. NORTH COAST OF SOUTH AMERICA

Country	Form of government	Area in sq. mi.	Population
Colombia	Republic	440,000	9,390,000
Venezuela	Republic	347,000	3,951,000
British Guiana	British possession	89,480	341,237
Surinam, or Netherlands Guiana	Dutch possession	54,740	47,500
French Guiana	French possession	65,041	37,000

A swing away from American-Caribbean imperialism began during the administration of President Herbert Hoover. Diplomatic and military pressure against Caribbean republics was relaxed. The marines were withdrawn from Nicaragua, and plans for ending the occupation of Haiti were made. This new policy of restoring sovereignty to Caribbean nations, which was continued in force, blossomed during the Presidency of Franklin Delano Roosevelt, who called it the Good Neighbor Policy. The marines were recalled from Haiti, and special privileges in Cuba and Panama were foregone. The United States also pledged nonintervention at Pan American conferences. As a result, the attitude of Caribbean peoples toward the United States changed. Suspicion of the "colossus of the north" diminished and a spirit of friendship and good will steadily grew, even though the Latin American republics were not sure whether the new policy was permanent or temporary.

The importance of the Good Neighbor Policy in strengthening the United States' position in the Caribbean was tremendous. The attitudes of many of the countries were quite different in World War II from those manifested during World War I. For example, during 1914–18 many German agents operated quite freely in Mexico, and many Mexican nationals openly sympathized with Germany. In World War II, however, Mexico declared war on the Axis on June 1, 1942, and gave her full support to the war effort of the United Nations. She greatly increased her shipments of war materials to the United States, and Mexican planes and ships helped patrol Caribbean waters. All the Central American and West Indian republics showed that they were solidly behind the United States by their prompt declaration of war against the Axis following Pearl Harbor. Colombia and Venezuela severed diplomatic relations with the Axis, and later, both entered World War II (see the map on page 62).

The chief contributions of Caribbean lands to the United Nations victory were economic, not military. The strategic resources of these republics—oil, bauxite, rubber, manganese, silver, and others—were quickly mobilized. Without these materials, industrial production in the United States would have been severely handicapped.

Although all of the Caribbean countries have experienced serious political and economic difficulties, the future looks considerably brighter. At least the individual countries no longer need to fear intervention. The role of the United States in Caribbean affairs, which got off to such a bad start, has exhibited heartening progress and seems destined to ultimate success.

CHAPTER 32

The United States of Brazil

PORTUGUESE AMERICA, as distinguished from Spanish America, is encompassed entirely within the United States of Brazil, the largest Latin American nation and the fourth largest nation in the world. Nearly all of Brazil lies within the tropics. It is roughly a wedge-shaped land, broadest in the north along the course of the Amazon River and narrowing to a southern tip where it meets the northern boundary of Uruguay (see the map directly below). In the south Brazil is also bordered

BRAZIL
IN
SOUTH AMERICA

by Argentina and Paraguay; on the west by Bolivia and Peru; and on the north by Colombia, Venezuela, and the three Guiana colonies. Thus, the United States of Brazil touches every one of the other twelve political

areas in South America except Ecuador and Chile.

Because of its heritage Brazil is closer by tradition to Europe than it is to nearby Spanish America. Although contact between Brazil and the transatlantic continents is maintained over well-traveled sea routes centuries old, its relations with most of its American neighbors are along remote frontiers deep in the uninhabited continental wilderness. Hence, its settlements are centers of a culture developed during four centuries of relative isolation from the rest of Latin America. As a result, Brazil presents a race, language, and social pattern, and an economic life that are unique among the countries on the South American continent.

Brazil exceeds the size of the continental United States of America by a quarter-million square miles. For administrative purposes the country is divided into twenty states, a number of outlying territories, the present federal district of Rio de Janeiro, and a federal district in Goiaz selected for a future capital (see the map on facing page). Atlantic islands belonging to Brazil are Fernando Noronha, Rocas, and St. Paul, all northeast of the easternmost point of Brazil. A political map of Brazil, however, fails to indicate the distribution of population or degree of development from place to place within the country. Ninety per cent of the population lives on or close to the Atlantic coast. Within an hour's plane flight from the coastal margin the interior is sparsely peopled. The greater part of the savanna-scattered states of Mato Grosso, Goiaz, and Pará have not even been completely explored, and most of the settlement in the Amazon Basin is confined to the banks of the huge river and its tributaries. Along the coast there are no extensive plains; in some parts of the country mountains and dense forests confine the peopled area to a strip bordering the water's edge. Thus there is no natural focus of transportation. Every account of Brazil as a nation must take into consideration these restricting factors of its topography.

Historical Background

When navigators from Spain and Portugal began to lay conflicting claims to the territories discovered by Columbus and his contem-

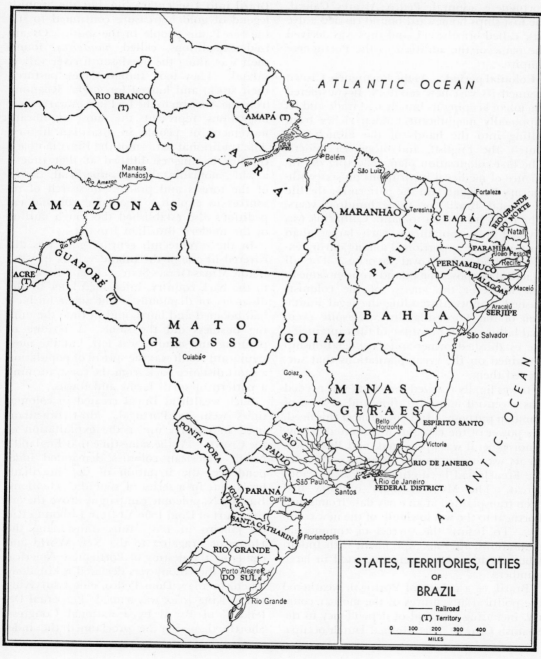

poraries, the New World was soon divided by agreement between Spain and Portugal. The Treaty of Tordesillas, drawn up in 1494 set the western boundary for Portuguese colonization at 370 leagues west of the Cape Verde Islands, which included the Atlantic bulge of South America. After the territory now called Brazil was discovered in 1500 by the Portuguese admiral, Pedro Alvares Cabral, the first ships homeward bound carried a dye base called brazilwood, and thus was derived the name of the addition to the Portuguese Empire.

Colonial period. As the Portuguese Crown scanned its vast new territory, it considered the job of keeping its brazilwood trade and its supposedly magnificent hidden riches from falling into the hands of the French, the Dutch, the English, and other sea raiders. The first colonization plan, reflecting the influence of medieval institutions on sixteenth-century Portugal, laid the pattern for the life of coastal Brazil for three hundred years. The coast from Pará to Santa Catharina was divided into captaincies, each larger than Portugal, and apportioned among daring explorers and other royal favorites. For all practical purposes the inland frontier came to rest wherever the energy of the colonists pushed it, notwithstanding the legal limitation of the Tordesillas line. Despite eventual failure of all but three of the captaincies, the established owner-and-slave relationship remained on the great plantations that succeeded them.

It was finally realized that what was needed was a central administration and a sense of common purpose. In 1549, to meet this need, the power of the captains was limited; a governor general was appointed; and Brazil was on its way to becoming a nation. By 1615 the French had been eliminated as a serious threat. The Moorish sugar industry had been transplanted at an early date from south Portugal to the wet lowlands of the new country. To insure the success of commercial plantations, after an experiment with Indian labor, African slaves were imported in large numbers.

Brazil, as a colony of Portugal, weathered the political adventures of the mother country, including a period of dependency to the Spanish Crown. Determined Dutch occupa-tion of the Brazilian coast was ended after Portugal won her freedom again in 1640. In these unsettled times the accepted frontiers of Portuguese influence in the New World were pushed far west of the original line of demarcation.

Quick sugar wealth gradually lured the restless Portuguese of the northeast coast of Brazil into a sedentary life, but the Spanish legend of golden treasure continued to stir the São Paulo people in the south. Organized expeditions, called *bandeiras*, found their way along the north-south river valleys inland. They took Indian slaves, pastured their stock, and looked for gold. Roaming from the Amazon to the La Plata estuary, their migrations represent the most significant movement of people in Brazilian history. The traditional pattern of the Brazilian back country became established at that time— a wide, nomadic, though superficial, survey of the forests and prairies in search of resources to exploit. The same colonial expeditions also established the rough outline of the modern Brazilian frontiers.

In the seventeenth century gold was discovered in one of the inland valleys in what is now Minas Geraes State. There was a rush to the back country, intensified later by the discovery of diamonds. The sugar business had boomed and burst, and in time the mining business did the same. A residue of planting and mining was left, but the most significant result was the spread of population a short distance back from the coast, forming a pattern of small farms and towns.

Such wealth as Brazil created in colonial times went to Portugal. Most Brazilians lived in poverty under the exploitation of the Crown. At the same time that England's North American colonies demanded independence, the irritation of the Brazilians broke out in a series of sporadic rebellions. But the Napoleonic campaigns drove the entire court of Dom João VI from Lisbon to Rio de Janeiro in 1807, thus transferring the House of Braganza to the New World and changing the destiny of Portuguese America. In 1815 the colony was declared a kingdom. Then, in 1822, Dom Pedro, eldest surviving son of King João, was named "Perpetual Defender" of Brazil by a national Congress. Shortly thereafter he proclaimed the independence of the country, and was then chosen as emperor.

Modern Brazil. When Dom Pedro I experienced continuing difficulties with the Congress, he abdicated in 1831 in favor of his young son, who became emperor as Dom Pedro II in 1840. Brazil reached political and cultural stature under his rule, which continued until 1889. Only the war in which Brazil, Argentina, and Uruguay broke the military dictatorship of Francisco Solano López over Paraguay disturbed this long period of peaceful development. Dom Pedro's statesmen developed a policy that relied on a tolerant exchange of viewpoints as a substitute for war. A competent federal administration was created. Slaves were freed; libraries were established; and health and social welfare became national projects. The courtesy and charm of the monarch made a deep imprint on all classes of society and came to be reflected everywhere. Dom Pedro's mark is still on the nation.

Dom Pedro was dethroned by a revolution in his old age, and Brazil became a republic without bloodshed. Until the advent of Getulio Vargas, Brazil developed along liberal democratic lines, usually free of the passion for personal dictatorship then sweeping many Spanish-American nations.

Vargas, an unsuccessful candidate for president, seized control of the government in 1930. In 1932 he defeated an armed uprising in São Paulo. His 1934 constitution sharply limited state's rights and emphasized a nationalistic policy. Then in 1937 Vargas proclaimed a new constitution and seized absolute powers. An authoritarian, he dedicated himself to create a modern state, streamline administration, hasten industrial development, and diversify the agricultural economy. He converted the Brazilian public health service into an instrument of assistance in the conquest of the tropical lowlands of the Amazon.

Under the Vargas regime Brazil was a leader in the establishment of an inter-American system designed to protect the Western Hemisphere against European aggression. In August, 1942, Brazil declared war on Germany and Italy, mobilizing an expeditionary force that fought in Italy, permitting the construction of strategic air and naval bases by the United States, and gearing up her output of materials for the United Nations war machine. She emerged from the war the greatest military power in Latin America.

In 1945 Vargas was overthrown. In the subsequent election, victory went to General Enrico Gaspar Dutra, who was the Vargas candidate. His administration was committed to many of the social and economic aims of the Vargas dictatorship. Meanwhile a constituent assembly prepared a new constitution, designed to return the nation to democratic legislative processes, which was adopted a few months after his inauguration in 1946.

Expansion. From 1851 to 1907 Brazil expanded in South America at the expense of all her neighbors except Peru and the Guianas. Territory was acquired from Venezuela in 1859 and 1905, from Colombia in 1907, from Ecuador in 1904, from Bolivia in 1867 and 1903, from Paraguay in 1872, from Argentina in 1895, and from Uruguay in 1851. This expansion, however, occurred in sparsely settled areas in the interior of South America where boundaries were largely indefinite. On October 1, 1943, an area of 200,000 square miles was taken from several Brazilian states bordering foreign countries and organized as five territories. The new territory of Amapá bordered the Guianas, Rio Branco bordered Venezuela, Guaporé bordered Peru and Bolivia, Ponta Pora bordered Paraguay and Argentina, and Iguaçu bordered Argentina. The older territories continued to exist: Acre on the Bolivia-Peru border and the island of Fernando Noronha in the South Atlantic (see the map on page 459).

Brazil has never permanently abandoned her tradition of orderly progress. She has solved most of her domestic problems without violence and has achieved important increases in her national territory largely by treaty and arbitration. However, before the establishment of Uruguay as a buffer between expanding Argentina and expanding Brazil, the Paulistas were engaged in border wars in the south.*

Economic cycles. The wild fluctuation of

---

* The southern plainsmen, the Paulistas of São Paulo, are traditionally the most aggressive and restless of the Brazilians. They constitute the *bandeiras* already mentioned.

the Brazilian economy has provided excitement that Brazilians have generally avoided in the political and international fields. The first Portuguese captains had no intention of living in Brazil. They were looking for quick riches for themselves and their royal sponsors and a life of luxury back home. They scoured the forests for exportable products. Impatient of these profits and unable to find gold equal to the treasures of the Inca in the Spanish west, they turned to sugar. Everybody planted sugar on a rising world market, which declined when other tropical countries produced it more cheaply. Cotton followed sugar; gold and diamonds followed cotton; rubber, cacao, and coffee followed gold. While others experimented with new crop methods, Brazilians planted and harvested as if they were playing a lottery. Very often land and workmen were exhausted, for the pace was fast and results were riches or ruin. The only products to survive this cycle, coffee and cotton, have to be supported by government subsidy.

Human Factors

Origin of the Brazilian people. By the year 1583 the three elements of what is becoming the unique Brazilian character were already clearly identified. At that time Brazil was a coastwise cluster of communities, in which lived a total of 57,000 civilized people. Back of these was an unknown interior peopled by about 800,000 Indians. From these forest tribes, 18,000 had been brought into the colonial community, and there were also 14,000 imported Negro slaves near Bahia. At the same time the total Portuguese population was only 25,000. Many Portuguese men took Indian wives or mistresses, and the result was a mixed race. Some of these settled on small plots of land near São Paulo; some became lone herdsmen; and others joined the *bandeiras* bent on plundering Indian tribes, searching for gold, and exploiting the resources of the interior forests. When the wild Indian came in contact with the Portuguese, he usually died soon of disease or overwork. But his mixed descendants were adapted to survival in the economic and social atmosphere evolving in São Paulo state and neighboring inland areas.

In the north the Negro proved himself the savior of the plantation system. The Bahian black man came from an African race noted for its fine physique, advanced civilization, and susceptibility to instruction. The result of the mixture of Portuguese and Negro blood was the mulatto, whose position on the early colonial scale was lower than that of the mixed Indian and Portuguese, the mameluco. The Negro and the Caucasian in Brazil are mixing rapidly by the process of intermarriage, and in some sections the Indian is disappearing as a recognizable type.

Although a new race is developing, the fusion is not yet complete. The northern Brazilian can usually be recognized as a type —short, heavy, and dark. In the south, where five million new immigrants from Europe are being absorbed, the Brazilian is taller and lighter, often blond. He still may show German, Polish, or Italian characteristics. The least assimilated immigrants are some quarter of a million Japanese settled in exclusive communities, but there are others of that race who intermingle more freely. Despite certain instances in which Negroes are not granted some privileges in the military and diplomatic professions, Brazil has no serious race problems.

Population. The population of Portuguese America is today estimated to exceed 45,000,000, roughly equal to that of all the Spanish-speaking nations of South America combined. About half the people are of European extraction. There are scarcely more than 2,000,000 full-blooded Negroes left as compared to the 12,000,000 originally brought in as slaves.

More than two thirds of the Brazilian population live in rural districts, and another tenth in suburban areas. The agricultural nature of the country has thus far limited urban growth to a few large metropolitan centers, which without notable exception are strung along the coast as seaports or lie on important waterways as river ports. Rio de Janeiro and São Paulo rank far ahead of other Brazilian cities, with around a million and a half and a million and a quarter inhabitants, respectively. São Salvador (Bahia), Recife (Pernambuco), and Belém (Pará) to the north and Porto Alegre to the south each have between a quarter and a half million people. Only six other cities exceed 100,000 in population (Bello Horizonte, Fortaleza, Maceió, Nictheroy, Curitiba, and João Pessoa), giving this country of forty-five million people only twelve urban centers of appreciable size.

Brazilian culture. The language of Brazil is Portuguese. The culture of old Portugal, with some frontier adaptations and modernizations, has become the culture of Brazil. Also, as in the case of the Portuguese, most Brazilians are Catholic. The individual Brazilian is usually temperate, courteous, and home-loving. Without the appearance of haste, he is likely to work hard under difficult dietary, climatic, and topographical handicaps. His public institutions often reflect a highly developed sense of government, and his private life frequently shows a devotion to the artistic and the intellectual. He is fond of music, conversation, and coffee, and unusually tolerant of other peoples and other ideas.

Generalizations applying to Brazil as a whole are often submerged in the distinct individuality of the regions of the country. Of these, the bright Arabic-African costumes and the Ibero-African music of Bahia are best known in North America and equally appreciated in their own country.

Transportation: Man vs. Space

The difficulty of moving men and goods from one point in Brazil to another is the greatest single handicap to national development. Underlying the unbalanced distribution of population and the primitive condition of the economy is a mechanical problem —transportation.

Less than four per cent of the land is under cultivation, and more than half is still covered with dense forest. Moreover, its mineral possibilities are largely unknown. As a consequence, the nation may have a tremendous reserve of potential wealth, largely unexploited.

Some parts of the vast inland are reached conveniently by train, car, or air, but many others are inaccessible, or reached only by river boat, muleback, or cart. In fact, some places are as remote from the small activated areas of Brazil as if they were on a distant continent. Although the cosmopolitan families of the coastal cities are familiar with Europe, the back country remains to them a legend of lost explorers and exotic tribes.

Water routes. With 4,000 miles of coast-line, Brazil was from the first a maritime nation. Coastwise shipping, which is still the most nearly adequate of all Brazil's transportation, is the only connecting link between the major economic centers, that is, the more-developed areas along or near the Atlantic margin. Three of Brazil's nineteen principal ports are situated inland on rivers—Belém (Pará), Manaus, and Porto Alegre; Manaus being 1,042 miles up the Amazon. River navigation was added to sea routes early in Brazilian history, and for centuries it offered the only practical method of spreading settlement into the interior. There are 23,000 navigable miles on the Brazilian river network, but the tremendous distances between settlements and bases of supplies reduce this to a very limited practical system. Although the Amazon has become a water highway, cataracts and falls block most of its tributaries. In southern Brazil the Uruguay handles commercial vessels, its entrance being through the La Plata estuary beyond Uruguay. The Paraná and the São Francisco also carry regular passengers and freight traffic to the interior (see the map on page 465).

The riverway system is also important because it carries the tiny craft by which the Indian and his successors penetrated deep into the wilderness. The flat-bottomed *montaria* developed from the Indian canoe brought the trade, the language, and the religion of Portugal into otherwise impenetrable jungles. Today this small boat is to the riverman what the horse is to the Argentine gaucho.

Overland transportation. Land transportation is an important factor only in the southeast, the Brazilian Coreland. The 21,000 miles of railway are largely concentrated in a network radiating out of Rio de Janeiro toward the farming and mining country of Minas Geraes and out of São Paulo through the coffee country and southward. There are also short lines inland from São Salvador (Bahia) and other northeast coast cities. More than 50 per cent of the railroad mileage is in three states (Minas Geraes, São Paulo, and Rio Grande do Sul), in which also are concentrated 40 per cent of Brazil's people. The state of Amazonas, more than three times the size of Germany, has only about three miles of rail. There is no east-west trans-Brazilian railroad, but a line from Rio de Janeiro and São Paulo continues southward through South Brazil to Montevideo in Uruguay.

The highway pattern is almost like the railroad pattern, largely concentrated in the same areas and serving the same centers of population. There are some good roads in the northeast, but no concrete highways connect the large cities. However, 170,000 miles of highway have been built in the last twenty years, and the increasing use of motor vehicles indicates that this amount will grow rapidly. Important cross-country roads are planned, with connections that will eventually bring international traffic into Brazil.

The development of airways in Brazil has already broken the traditional pattern of regional isolation. Numerous commercial airlines give service to every important community and, what is more important, cross Brazil in many directions. Many journeys have been reduced from weeks to hours with the building of an airport and installation of an airway. Brazilians have been quick to grasp the tremendous importance of flying for their country. But the great bulk of people and goods, landbound for many years yet, remains unaffected. Until air, land, and water transportation grow into an effective, coordinated system, the mule train, the oxcart, and the river boat will transport much of the nation's goods, and the great inland states must remain empty of farms and cities.

Regions of Brazil

The United States of Brazil is sufficiently large and varied to embrace innumerable physical regions. Even though there are no mountain ranges in the country comparable to the Andes or the Rockies, land forms contrast markedly from place to place. Temperatures all reflect the low latitude, but rainfall ranges from areas that are always wet and steaming to those where droughts are characteristic. Resulting soils and vegetation add to the regional diversity. Finally, the uneven distribution of mineral resources accentuates the regional aspect.

Without regard for local detail, Brazil may be conveniently broken down into four broad regions: (1) The Amazon Basin; (2) The Northeast; (3) The Brazilian Coreland (or Southeastern Heart of Brazil); and (4) The South (see the map on the facing page). Brief surveys of each illustrate the physical and economic factors that make up the overall national pattern.

The Amazon Basin. The Amazon River rises in the Andes within a hundred miles of the Pacific Ocean and empties into the Atlantic at the Equator. The heavily wooded inner basin of the Amazon, which covers 1,465,000 square miles, is the world's largest rain forest.

PHYSICAL LANDSCAPE. The Amazon watershed embraces almost all of northern Brazil —the states of Amazonas, Pará, and their adjacent territories, as well as the northern parts of Goiaz and Mato Grosso states and western Maranhão. Above the junction with the Rio Negro and the Rio Madeira, the river's plain widens to a distance of 800 miles between the highlands north and south. About 90 per cent of this surface is above flood basins, which are generally less than fifty miles in width and resemble the lowlands of the Mississippi. In the eastern parts of the state of Amazonas and down river into the state of Pará, the highland closes together toward the stream, giving the effect of a vast impenetrable jungle growing from the cliffs that line the flooded plains. Farther below in Pará, near the 150-mile wide mouth of the Amazon, the plains again widen along either side of the mouth of the river.

On the upland savannas and in the scrub forest, the soil is generally infertile; soluble minerals, humus, and fine topsoil are rapidly washed away. It is unsuited to the growth of shallow-rooted crops and lacks necessary mineral salts. The river plains, however, are filled with dense masses of equatorial forest vegetation, where luxuriantly leaved trees rise to a height of 130 feet.

From these dense forests the riches of the land must be taken. To the casual observer they create an impression of monotony, but actually there are many thousand species of trees and shrubs. Due to the lack of climatic change, each tree blossoms, bears fruit, and sheds its leaves in an individual cycle.

Although the rainfall of the whole Amazon area is heavy, only the upper part of the basin and the coast area have in excess of 80 inches a year. The rainiest season is from January to June. In that period the rain comes in true tropical cloudbursts, with intermittent cloudless, sunny skies, and clear, starlit nights.

In the lowland the temperature varies from 65 to 95 degrees, debilitating to man chiefly because of the lack of stimulating change zon Basin are many and varied. They include the babassu palm, which yields a fiber suitable for the production of acetic acid, char-

REGIONS AND RESOURCES
OF
BRAZIL

⊕ Rubber   △ Wheat   □ Lumber
◍ Coffee   ⊞ Oranges   ◮ Minerals
◖ Cotton   ○ Yerba Mate   △ Coal
▲ Cattle   △ Wax   ◪ Diamonds
■ Cocoa   ◑ Nuts   ◠ Sugar
▲ Rice   □ Tobacco   ⬚ Bananas

0   100   200   300   400
MILES

rather than the severity of the heat itself. The humidity is 80 per cent or more, which is made bearable, however, by easterly trade winds.

RESOURCES.   Natural resources in the Ama-

coal, and methyl alcohol, and whose nuts are a valuable source of vegetable oil; medicinal plants; gums and resins; skins of rare animals; balsa and cabinet woods; Brazil nuts; and carnauba wax, a unique Brazilian product used in shoe polishes, furniture waxes, and phonograph records.

In the lowland Amazon forest were found the first wild rubber trees. In 1827, 69,174 pounds of rubber were shipped from Belém. By 1853 this output had been increased to more than 5,000,000 pounds. There was an Amazon Valley land boom, which resulted in ruthless exploitation of native labor and natural rubber resources. Nevertheless, the yield per wild rubber tree is less than one third that of the planted, cross-bred Malayan variety. A single man, unsupervised, ill-equipped, and away from the necessities of life and access to a regulated diet, could scarcely tap more than 200 trees scattered through the forest. By comparison, the plantation worker, with experts available to guarantee maximum yield, could easily attend to more than 500 trees. Skilled labor, not to be had in the Amazon country, was plentiful in the East Indies. As a result, the plantations of British Malaya and Dutch Sumatra, which produced only 9 per cent of the world's rubber in 1910, were producing 60 per cent in 1914, and by 1924 their output had risen to 93 per cent. In the meantime, the rubber business and land values along the Amazon had collapsed.

In 1927, in an attempt to re-establish the rubber resources of the Amazon, the *Companhia Ford Industrial do Brasil* purchased 2,500,000 acres of land on the right bank of the Rio Tapajoz, 135 miles upstream from the Amazon. A modern town was built, and the tract was known as "Fordlandia." Over eight thousand acres of rubber trees were planted before tree disease, soil erosion, and the impossibility of using machines on the hilly ground made it necessary to exchange part of the tract for 600,000 acres in the state of Pará, 30 miles up the Tapajoz from Santarem. The newer area was known as "Belterra." In April of 1939, 12,500 acres had been planted by modern methods. Ford later sold the development and withdrew from what had proved to be an unprofitable venture.

The outer basin of the Amazon is a semicircle of higher land cut by the big river's tributaries. Where this plateau drops off to the inner lowlands, the sudden change in elevation causes a break (known as a "fall line"), which blocks river traffic. The high land is known to be more hospitable to man than the humid, jungle-grown floodland below, but it still includes tremendous unexplored areas in the heart of the continent. In the midst of the little-known wilderness is the state of Mato Grosso, divided between the northward-flowing Amazon tributaries and the watershed of the Paraguay River flowing south. Along the Paraguay are great cattle ranches, many owned by British or North Americans.

The Northeast. East and south of the Amazon's mouth, Brazil projects far into the Atlantic. First part of Brazil to be heavily settled, the Northeast retains many characteristics of the colonial empire. This region, steeped as it is in early Brazilian history, still exerts an influence on national life out of proportion to its economic and political importance. It includes the states of Piauhi, Ceará, Rio Grande do Norte, Parahiba, Pernambuco, Alagôas, Serjipe, Bahia, and most of Maranhão (see the map on page 459).

PHYSICAL SETTING. The Northeast is not a simple geographical unit. Nature has divided it into two contrasting areas—a strip of wet, tropical coast and a highland subject to disastrous droughts. Men have followed the division of nature, creating in the one a system of plantations owned by white families and worked by black laborers and in the other a free pasturage ranged by a particularly hardy and independent people.

ECONOMY. From Natal to São Salvador, in the state of Bahia, a series of streams come down to the sea. In their valleys is the fertile, well-watered land that attracted the first large-scale sugar planting in the Portuguese colony. April-to-July rains wet this coast but cease to be effective a few miles inland. The rain belt, and the resulting band of heavy forest, is much wider in the south at São Salvador. This was the original brazilwood forest; now it grows sugar, tobacco, rice, and other crops. From southern Bahia comes about 20 per cent of the world's cacao supply. Fishing, lacemaking, and other small-scale industries long have been established along the coast.

The interior highland flanks the forested coastal strip, sloping northward toward the coast west of Natal. This area will grow crops where irrigable, but in general it is utilized only as pasture. Rainfall is undependable; and when years pass without moisture, as is true in some localities, the land takes on the appearance of a desert. The vegetal covering that survives the peculiar cycles of disaster common to this country is a tangled scrub growth called caatinga.* It grows in a hard, sandy soil and in times of drought sheds its leaves, surviving by attrition.

In early times adventurous Portuguese drifted away from the lowland sugar plantations and, despite the forbidding character of the upland scrub area, established an important cattle industry. They have cleared large sections of the caatinga for better pasturage. The land imparted its toughness to the people who have learned to live on it. Although these pioneers established a definite boundary between their country and the coast, they retain a sense of unity with the plantation country of their origin. Within the *sertão* are tracts of cashew and carnauba (the waxpalm) from which nuts and wax can be gathered during favorable years.

Sugar cultivation has passed largely out of the hands of plantation owners to corporations with capital enough to construct modern mills. The sugar market is no longer world-wide but local, and even southern Brazil grows its own cane. Planted farther inland, back of the sugar cane land, cotton became an important crop a century ago, but the coast produces an inferior grade. By irrigation the *sertão* can be made to grow long staple varieties. The Northeast still produces about half of Brazil's cotton. Where the back country has been brought under irrigation, it has become thickly settled by small farmers, in contrast to the early pastoral tradition.

The Brazilian Coreland. The southeastern heart of modern Brazil is a complex, mountainous area stretching from the coast inland as far as habitation has penetrated toward the southern headwaters of the Amazon and the eastern watershed of the Paraná. Rio de Janeiro and São Paulo, Brazil's two metropolitan cities, are situated not far apart in the population center of this region.

The capital city of Rio de Janeiro, with a population exceeding 1,500,000, includes in its back country Rio de Janeiro state, the states of Minas Geraes and Espirito Santo, and the eastern part of São Paulo state. The rest of the southeast from the Paraná River to the coast is under the influence of São Paulo, a city only slightly smaller than Rio de Janeiro and growing rapidly.

In the southeast of Brazil were early developed small settlements, small holdings, and individual enterprise. In the first gold rush the southeast began draining population from the sugar plantations, a process continued into modern times. The spectacular rise of São Paulo coffee culture to a position of dominance in the Brazilian economy and in world trade made this the center of Brazilian agriculture. The climate, soil, and atmosphere of independence make it the most attractive section of Brazil for settlement and investment. These factors, coupled with the development of mineral resources, transportation, and power, have made it the industrial core of the nation.

TOPOGRAPHY AND CLIMATE. The relief of the Southeast is complex. The Great Escarpment rises in the form of a low mountain wall from southern Bahia almost to the Uruguayan border. It is the eastern rim of an interior highland, separated from the ocean by beaches and alluvial plains varying in width from a few yards to several miles. The coastal strip is cut by a deep bay at Rio de Janeiro. In the north two rivers, the Doce and the Paraíba, open flat valleys leading to the interior, a factor facilitating the settlement of the back country. In the north the Escarpment descends in a series of steps to the sea. South of Rio de Janeiro the coast of São Paulo state shows a continuous sloping wall nearly 3,000 feet high. The river Iguape cuts through the wall, emptying into a series of lagoons at Santos.

Above and behind the Escarpment rise the mountains of Espirito Santo and Minas Geraes, exhibiting a highly intricate surface and culminating in the highest point in Brazil, the Pico de Bandeira (9,462 feet). Back of São Paulo is a comparatively flat highland tilted westward and draining into the Paraná, which flows toward Argentina. This area is a broad sweeping country, broken by low mountains and wide, swampy valleys. Here are the rich red soils favorable for the growing of coffee trees. Further inland is

---

* Brazilians call their interior wilderness the *sertão*. Historically, this word was used to describe the back country of the Northeast. In this area one of the distinguishing features of the *sertão* is the harsh growth known as caatinga, green in the wet season, white in the dry.

the vast country of southern Mato Grosso and
Goiaz, ranging in relief from moderate plateaus to low swamp lands and offering but
little to the present economy of Brazil.

The climate of southeastern Brazil is more
favorable to sustained human activity than
the Northeast and the Amazon Basin—regions
deep in the tropics. The narrow strip of
coast is warm and moist in the north but becomes temperate in the south. As far south
as Santos, however, it is still warm. Rainfall
is heavy in the summer months in the north,
as much as 80 inches falling on the slopes of
the Escarpment, while up to 150 inches have
fallen between Santos and São Paulo.

The interior highlands are cooler and drier
than the coast, and the land supports wheat
and other hard grains. In the mountains of
Minas Geraes there is some frost, but tropical
crops grow in the lowlands. South of São
Paulo, inland frosts are frequent and regular
during the colder months.

Originally all the southeast coastline and
the valleys were covered with heavy forests,
becoming thinner in the high country.
Where settlement is heaviest, most of the
wood has been cut for fuel or cleared away to
make room for agriculture. The deep interior of Minas Geraes is savanna country characterized by thickets and scrub growth.
South of Rio de Janeiro the coastal forest is
still dense, but in the highlands thins out to
grassy glades. The basin of São Paulo was
originally a grassland. South of São Paulo
there is still heavy prairie grass, and farther
south and west are pine and oak forests.

ECONOMY AND POPULATION. The original
Paulistas were not court favorites but southern Portuguese, many of them infused with
Moorish blood. They came to Brazil looking
for an existence, not for soft living. At the
time that Negro labor was saving the tropic
north from decay and ruin, the Paulistas, too
poor to own slaves, were ranging the inland
mountains and establishing their own pattern of development. Early in the sixteenth
century they brought cattle from Europe to
found the extensive southern livestock industry.

With the discovery of gold the center of
population finally became fixed on the São
Paulo–Rio de Janeiro axis. The gold fields
were soon extensively populated, and the center of shipping activity moved from São Salvador to Rio de Janeiro, nearest port to the
mines. In 1763 the capital moved with it.
Brazilian enterprise, long spent on exploration, was brought to bear on the exploitation
of newly uncovered riches. The important
contribution of Minas Geraes was that it
joined the most enterprising of the north-
erners with the restless Paulistas to produce a
national spirit that broke away forever from
the plantation pattern.

Later, when popular interest shifted from
mining gold to planting coffee, São Paulo,
center of the new coffee district, soon filled
with European immigrants. Small shops and
factories and skilled labor, never before available in Brazil, prepared the way for modern
industrialization. After Rio de Janeiro had
become the administrative, cultural, and shipping center of the nation, São Paulo attained
stature as a banking and manufacturing city.

Modern São Paulo makes textiles, clothing,
metals, machinery, and a variety of other products in more than 10,000 factories. Its
growth can be compared with that of Chicago,
Detroit, and Cleveland.

São Paulo still depends largely on its back
country—the coffee district—for its capital,
its population, and its pre-eminence in Brazilian economics. A highly developed rail
system links the coffee port of Santos, the city
of São Paulo, and the hinterland. Rio de
Janeiro, on the other hand, cast itself off from
the influence of the immediate interior and
expanded independently. Its attitude is that
of New York, with rich cultural overtones.

The resources of the southeast coast are
varied, for forests and minerals supplement
the strong agricultural basis of the region.
The principal agricultural products are sugar,
oranges, rice, and bananas. Coffee, despite
its spectacular depressions and its recent
overproduction, is the backbone of São
Paulo's highland prosperity. Cotton, the second crop, represents about half of Brazil's
production. Livestock and forest exploita-
tions are important in the interior and in the
south. Inland, yerba maté is gathered to
make the native tea popular in the gaucho
country. Minas Geraes is rich in industrial
minerals, notably iron, and gold is still mined
on a modest scale.

The South. Southward the character of
the country changes. The three states of
Paraná, Santa Catharina, and Rio Grande do

Sul are being settled rapidly by farmers on small land holdings. Lowlands and valleys are notable in Brazil for agricultural self-sufficiency and stability.

The great coastal Escarpment, which is a feature of most of the southeast coast, breaks up in southern Paraná. Farther south swampy lowlands and park-like prairies reach into Uruguay. The climate is wet and mild, and upland winters are cool. Temperatures in the uplands are too cold for coffee, but sugar cane grows along the coast.

Paulistas made the first settlements in South Brazil, turning the grasslands into regions of large cattle enterprises. The Portuguese Crown originally settled the extreme south with immigrants from the Azores, to hold Brazil's southern flank against the Spaniards. Recent immigration has been German and Italian, the former establishing European-type farms and the latter vineyards. Low-grade coal is now mined near Porto Alegre and in southern Santa Catharina. Largely due to the presence of this fuel, Porto Alegre has become an industrial center, outranked in importance only by São Paulo and Rio de Janeiro.

Brazil in the Postwar World

Economic problems. Brazil is faced with a number of pressing economic problems that stand in the way of national development. Some are traditional; others were brought by the war. Until the depression of 1930, Brazilian goods were produced and exported for spectacular profits. As each commodity reached its price peak in world markets and declined, a new "wonder crop" was found to take its place. In 1930 coffee, the latest of the great crops, accounted for about 70 per cent of Brazil's export trade. Since then, Brazil has found that a modern state based on a modern, complex economy cannot afford a recurring "boom-and-bust" history. The object of Brazil's new program of diversification of agriculture, manufacturing, and trade is stability. At the beginning of the war, coffee had declined in relative importance to about 30 per cent of the Brazilian export trade, the result of a determined effort to broaden the base of Brazilian economy. First, cotton exports were increased. By 1942, leather, cocoa beans, wax, canned meats, lumber, and a score of other products,

including some manufactured and processed goods, were being shipped out. Wartime displacement of markets and shipping services increased the export of rubber, rare minerals, and other strategic materials and confined trade largely to the United States and Spanish-American countries. Re-establishment of widespread markets and the greater diversification of trade may require many years of effort. Meantime, the continuation of wartime inflation has presented the definite threat of an economic collapse before readjustments can be made.

With Europe on a peacetime basis and with transport again available, Brazilian coffee will enjoy an increased heavy demand. This turn back to specialization will tend to delay stability, but the trend toward diversification is expected to continue. For many years to come any variety of commodities in the export field will have to be largely confined to increased shipments of agricultural products —cotton, cocoa beans, waxes, nuts, oils, and rubber. Some of these items will respond to scientific planting and harvesting, now encouraged by the government. Others will disappear because they cannot meet outside competition. In the field of manufacturing, Brazil cannot expect to export until the heavy local demand for domestic-made goods is satisfied and until machinery, skilled labor, power, and transportation are more highly integrated. Nevertheless, industrial production is already the leading factor in the nation's economy. Its value is already two-and-one-half times as great as that of agricultural and animal products.

Industrial outlook. The war gave tremendous stimulus to the heavy metal industries, and it is in this field that the most spectacular development is expected. In Minas Geraes and other states there are ample reserves of iron, manganese, nickel, chromium, tungsten, aluminum, magnesium, tin, lead, copper, and the rare ores like zirconium and beryl. Under the pressure of war many new deposits were found, some far in the interior. South of São Paulo are significant coal deposits. The problems of getting power, ores, and skilled labor together in one place, and of finding capital for the construction of processing plants and shipping facilities for the finished product, are not easy to resolve in a country of vast, uninhabited spaces. The complete industrialization of Brazil, like its exploration and settlement, must be expressed in terms of generations. Nevertheless, steel production is increasing under government encouragement, as is that of aluminum and other metals. The manufacture of chemicals is likewise being augmented. Hydroelectric power is undergoing development on a large scale, particularly in São Paulo state.

The new Brazilian constitution is designed partly to nationalize the Brazilian economy and to keep it under close control. Industrialization and diversification are a part of a long-range national program. The geographical vacuums must be peopled, and adequate skilled labor and professional classes must be created. The *sertão* is still an immense wilderness supporting a pastoral, primitive people claiming almost nothing in common with modern Brazilians of the southeastern cities. Scientific farming and manufacturing processes must replace the old colonial methods. The wealth and industry of the Brazilian Coreland must be extended to the rest of the nation.

Political future. Although Brazil faces serious handicaps to immediate rapid growth and development, one of these—the inhos-pitable climate—is exaggerated. On the Ford rubber plantations it has been shown that the inner Amazon Valley is livable. The great unpeopled outer basin of the Amazon is high enough to be comfortable, contrary to popular belief. As modern medicine reduces the dangers of tropical lowland living and exploration reveals greater areas of moderate climate, this over-emphasized objection to settling the back country will disappear.

Brazil is in a fortunate strategic position. The size and location of the country make possible the domination of not only South America but the South Atlantic, a factor of increasing importance in world-wide communications. Its undeveloped resources are almost limitless, as is its capacity for supporting a population. Its political stability makes it attractive to immigrants.

In the course of time a higher standard of living, a population widely spread by area and closely knit by communications, and a diversified economy will make Portuguese America an important world power. Brazilian tradition and wholehearted participation in the United Nations indicate that the weight of Brazil will be used to further international cooperation.

CHAPTER 33

The States of the Rio de la Plata

ARGENTINA, Paraguay, and Uruguay are generally referred to as the states of the Rio de la Plata or as the River Plate countries.* This is a natural grouping, for all three countries are drained by one great river system, the La Plata–Paraná and its two major tributaries, the Paraguay and Uruguay rivers. In addition, the Paraná drains the highlands of southern Brazil; and a tributary of the Paraguay, the Pilcomayo, drains much of southern Bolivia. Rivers of the La Plata–Paraná system also serve as segments of international boundaries: the La Plata and the Uruguay between Argentina and Uruguay; the Uruguay between Argentina and Brazil; the Paraná between Argentina and Paraguay; the Paraguay and the Pilcomayo between Argentina and Paraguay; and the Paraguay between Paraguay and Brazil (see the map on page 472). In no other place in the world does a river system play such an important part in delineating borders of countries.

The three states of the Rio de la Plata occupy the entire southern part of South America east of the crest of the Andes. Aside from southern Brazil and the entire trans-Andean republic of Chile this region includes all of the temperate portion of the continent. Among South American countries Argentina ranks next to Brazil in size and population; Paraguay and Uruguay, along with Ecuador, are the smallest and least populous republics. Argentina has attained world importance, but Paraguay and Uruguay play roles that are secondary to their larger and more powerful neighbors.

ARGENTINA

Physical Characteristics

Argentina's 1,079,960 square miles slightly exceed one third the size of the United States. Argentina extends some 2,500 miles in a north-south direction, from 22 degrees South Latitude near the Tropic of Capricorn to 55 degrees South Latitude at the southern tip of South America. In the North American continent, this extent would equal the distance from central Mexico to central Canada. Because of the comparatively narrow width of this part of the South American continent, however, and the consequent proximity of a large part of Argentina to oceanic influences, the extreme temperatures common to comparable latitudes in the North American continent do not appear. Nevertheless, the extensive range of latitude affords a variety of climates sufficient to support the growth of a diversity of temperate as well as tropical vegetation types.

Although Southern Argentina lies in the path of the prevailing westerlies, they lose their moisture on the Pacific, or Chilean, side of the Andes and hence bring that part of Argentina very little rainfall. On the other hand, the northern part of the country is in the path of the southeast trade winds, which

* The Rio de la Plata, or River Plate, is actually the estuary of the Paraná River. As a breach it extends 200 miles into the continent of South America and thus exerts a significant geographical influence upon the countries of the area.

encounter no high altitudes to draw off their moisture as they pass from the Atlantic Ocean to eastern and northern Argentina. As a result, annual rainfall decreases from about 60 inches in the north to generally less than 10

inches in the south and west. However, since lower temperatures in the south result in less evaporation, this small amount of rainfall is considerably more effective than the same amount in an area of higher temperatures.

Regions and Resources

For convenience in describing the geographic patterns of Argentina, most authorities recognize four or five major regions: (1) Pampa; (2) Andean, or Arid West; (3) Patagonia; (4) Chaco; and (5) Mesopotamia. The last two (Chaco and Mesopotamia) are sometimes combined and designated the North Region (see the map on the facing page).

The Pampa. The Pampa region, which reaches roughly from 30 to 40 degrees South

Latitude, occupies most of the broad, grassy plains extending westward from the Atlantic coast toward the arid land that lies in the rain shadow of the great Andean range. Although international boundaries intervene, almost all of Uruguay also lies within the same natural region. The soil is deep and rockless. The lack of rock and gravel is favorable to soil cultivation, but the scarcity of these materials for building roads, fences, and general construction is a great disadvantage. There are surprisingly few rivers in the Pampa proper. The Paraná drains the northern border, and to the south is the Rio Colorado system, which empties into the Atlantic Ocean at Bahia Blanca.

The climate of the Pampa is generally favorable to human activities, especially those related to agriculture. The average annual rainfall ranges from 20 inches in the west to 40 inches in the east. In the west rainfall is somewhat unreliable in character, and severe droughts occasionally cause crop failures. Fortunately, most of the rainfall occurs during the growing season. Temperatures are generally mild in the Pampa. As December, January, and February are the summer months in the Southern Hemisphere, the mean January temperatures at Buenos Aires are comparable to those of New York in July. However, winters are milder and growing seasons longer in Buenos Aires than in New York. The truck farming area near Buenos Aires normally supplies the city market with fresh vegetables throughout the year, and grazing and some agricultural activities are possible during most of the year. In the Pampa the growing season varies from five to six months in the southwest to ten or more in the northeast. The warm, humid, and rather depressing winds from the north are called *Norte*, and the clear, cool, dry, and somewhat invigorating winds from the southeast are called *Pampero*.

The Pampa region is well known for its production and export of grain and livestock and the numerous by-products of these two major agricultural industries. The richest natural resource in Argentina has been, and is likely to continue to be for some time, the deep, fertile soil. A factor increasing its value is its combination with other characteristics highly suitable to cultivation, especially adequate moisture and a long growing season.

The greatest hazards to farming are periodic droughts, grasshoppers, and locusts. A serious problem of the grazing industry is the hoof-and-mouth disease. Because of this disease, the United States government has a quarantine law that excludes the importation of fresh or frozen beef from countries where the hoof-and-mouth disease is prevalent. Many Argentinians have interpreted this law as intended discrimination against Argentine trade.

The Andean, or Arid West. The Andean,

PROVINCES AND REGIONS
OF
ARGENTINA

0   250   500
MILES

or Arid West, which occupies the eastern slopes and foothill zone of the Andes Mountains, forms the westernmost part of Argentina north of 40 degrees latitude. The mountain streams, consisting chiefly of the Rio Colorado system, carry large quantities of sediment to the desert plains, where they are deposited to form rich alluvial fans. Irrigation projects have transformed these fans into green oases of intensified agriculture and regions of relatively dense population.

A wide variety of crops are grown in these fertile oases, but fruit production is the most important commercial enterprise. The provinces of Mendoza and San Juan are often referred to as the California of Argentina, and they have given Argentina a place of international importance as a fruit-producing nation. Of recent importance in the region is a rapidly growing dried-fruit industry. Alfalfa, however, occupies more land in the oases than do the fruits. As a forage crop it is used for fattening cattle in the region and also for supplying seed for the alfalfa ranges in the Pampa region. Most of the people not engaged in oasis agriculture raise goats, sheep, and some low-grade cattle.

Despite rich mineral deposits in the Andean region, mining has not become an important industry. Some low-grade coal is mined, and two districts produce petroleum. There was considerable exploitation of minerals during World War II, and some were exported. Because of high relief and mountain precipitation this region is rich in potential water-power resources.

Patagonia. The coldest region of the country, Patagonia extends approximately 1,200 miles south from the Rio Colorado to the southern tip of the continent. Made up of the territories of Rio Negro, Chubut, and Santa Cruz, this elongated region comprises nearly a fourth of the area of Argentina but includes less than one per cent of the population. There is an average of less than two persons per square mile, consisting largely of English, Scotch, and Welsh herdsmen. The climate is cool, arid, and stormy, and the land forms are plateaus alternating with canyons that extend east-west. Scattered farms and sheep ranches occupy the wide canyon bottoms, where rich alluvial soils, availability of water, and shelter from the boisterous winds are important advantages. Argentina's

major petroleum-producing district is at Comodoro Rivadavia on the coast in southeast Chubut. Kaolin (China clay), which was recently discovered in the Patagonian region, is being used in the manufacture of bathroom fixtures and insulators.

The Chaco. The Chaco region in northern Argentina is a portion of the vast and undeveloped lowlands that extend into Paraguay, Brazil, and Bolivia. It is an alluvial plains area of alternating patches of savanna and scrub forest. The climate is subtropical, with dry winters and warm, humid summers. The annual rainfall decreases from 60 inches in the northeast to 20 inches in the west. Temperatures are high and sometimes reach 120° F. The lowlands are frequently in a flooded condition during the rainy season, and the rivers become braided and often change their courses.

The Chaco produces both agricultural and forest products. The agricultural products include cotton, cane sugar, tobacco, rice, castor beans, and numerous fruits and vegetables. The most important forest product of this region is extract from the quebracho tree, which enters into world commerce as the material most widely used for the tanning of leather. Limited to the general region, the quebracho forests normally supply about two thirds of the vegetable tanning extracts used in the world.

Mesopotamia. The region of Mesopotamia between the Paraná and Uruguay rivers includes two provinces and one territory. In southern Entre Rios are flood plains; in Corrientes are gently rolling plains and innumerable streams; and in the territory of Misiones are highlands, an extension of the great Paraná Plateau of southern Brazil This region is more humid than the Pampa, and crops are more dependable. It is an important grazing and agricultural region, and the Paraná flood plains in Entre Rios form Argentina's chief linseed-producing area. Yerba maté—a popular South American tea—tobacco, and tung nuts are also important commercial products of the Mesopotamia region. Rapeseed is another important oil seed.

Claims to other territory. In addition to the five major regions, Argentina claims the Falkland Islands as Argentine territory and deeply resents the British occupation of them. These islands, located in the whale-fishing region, are strategically placed, for they command the entrance to the Strait of Magellan (see the map directly below).

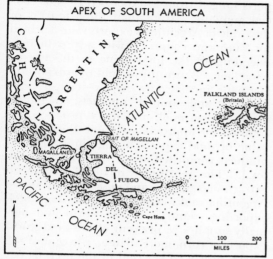

APEX OF SOUTH AMERICA

Also, the dispute with Chile in 1847 over the ownership of the Strait of Magellan and adjacent territories has not been completely settled to Argentina's satisfaction. A partial settlement was mediated by the United States in 1881, and in 1902 King Edward VII acted as arbitrator. The Strait of Magellan, Cape Horn, and Magallanes (Punta Arenas) went to Chile, and Tierra del Fuego and the Beagle Channel were divided between the two countries.

Principal urban areas. Despite the dominant agricultural nature of Argentine economy, about two thirds of the people live in cities having a population of 100,000 or more. This proportion of city dwellers is comparable to the situation in Australia, also a land specializing in the production and trade of agricultural commodities. Large cities are units in the commercial channels that handle and finance the many items of Argentine trade.

THE EASTERN CITIES. Without exception the large cities of eastern Argentina depend upon commercial traffic for their importance, and for the most part are associated with the Rio de la Plata and the Paraná. Buenos Aires, in addition to being the capital, is by far the most important commercial and industrial center in Argentina and one of the major ports of the world. Situated on the River Plate, it has a population of about 2,500,000

and its metropolitan area has some 3,500,000. About two thirds of the total value of Argentina's foreign trade moves through the port of Buenos Aires, imports greatly exceeding exports. The city is also the most important railway and airway center in Argentina. Railways fan out to all large cities and important regions north of Patagonia and to points in all countries that border Argentina.

Rosario, which, with a population in excess of 500,000, is the second largest city in Argentina, is located on the Paraná River 200 miles above Buenos Aires. It is the chief city in the province of Santa Fé and the most important grain-exporting port in Argentina, normally handling about 40 per cent of the total cereal production of the country.

La Plata, which has a population around 250,000, is a port city about thirty miles below Buenos Aires. Meat packing is the most important of its numerous industries. Bahia Blanca (360,000) owes its importance as a port to its location at the natural southern outlet for the agricultural products of the Pampa region. Santa Fé (150,000), upstream on the Paraná from Rosario, serves as an outlet for varied products of Northern Argentina.

THE WESTERN COLONIAL CITIES. The cities of the Andean region are much older than those of eastern Argentina. Some of them were founded during the latter half of the sixteenth century, when trade with Chile and Peru comprised the chief economic activity of the country. Located in the arid or semiarid part of the country, these cities depend upon water from the Andes. They are primarily agricultural oases.

Salta, with a present population of only 43,000, was an important distributing center for livestock, chiefly mules, destined for the Chilean desert nitrate-mining region. When this industry declined, Salta lost its importance as an entrepôt. Tucumán (present population, 150,000) was the chief "outfitting" city for traffic to and from Salta and the important Spanish settlements in Peru. Late in the nineteenth century it became the nation's sugar center.

Colonial Mendoza was destroyed by an earthquake in 1861, but it was rebuilt and is now the center of the Argentine wine industry. A large percentage of its 80,000 people are Italians, who are engaged in growing grapes and making wine.

National Economy

Foreign trade. The national economy of Argentina strongly reflects its foreign trade. Imports have been mostly complex manufactures, which are presently the country's greatest insufficiencies in a modern world. Exports have long been strong but highly specialized. Predominate are raw and processed agricultural materials, but recent foreign trade trends indicate a considerable expansion of industrial facilities in the country.

IMPORTS. In the years preceding World War II the average annual value of goods imported by Argentina amounted to roughly $400,000,000. Europe was the source of about 60 per cent of this amount; the United Kingdom supplied 22 per cent. In the Western Hemisphere the United States was the most important source of Argentina's imports, accounting for 15 per cent of the overall total. Brazil's share was only 5 per cent, and all other Western Hemisphere countries together supplied less than 8 per cent. Even Japan sent more goods to Argentina than did her Latin American neighbors.

About one fourth of the value of all imports consisted of textiles. Machinery and vehicles, iron and steel products, coal and petroleum, foods, chemicals and drugs, lumber, newsprint and paper products, sand, cement, glass, tile, rubber, radios, electrical apparatus, oil-drilling equipment, tobacco, and musical instruments (in approximately that order of importance) accounted for most of the remaining three fourths of Argentina's prewar imports.

During World War II Argentina's foreign trade pattern changed with respect to both sources and markets. The three chief sources of Argentina's imports became the United States, the United Kingdom, and Brazil. Purchases from other American Republics and from Sweden showed enormous increments. The belligerent countries of continental Europe were largely cut off but now have reentered the Argentina market with their industrial goods.

Argentina's imports from the United States reached a high of $109,000,000 in 1941. In the face of wartime shortages and the United States' economic and political sanctions directed against the regime in Argentina, imports from the United States dropped to less than $30,000,000 in 1944.

EXPORTS. Prior to World War II total exports ranged from $400,000,000 to $700,000,000 annually. More than three fourths of the value of Argentina's exports were destined for European countries, with approximately one third of the total going to the United Kingdom. Between 1935 and 1939 exports to Germany increased by nearly 100 per cent. Animals and animal products, including meats, hides, wool, and dairy products, accounted for approximately one third of the value of total exports, and grains and grain products comprised about three fifths of the total. The remainder included quebracho extract, sugar, fruits, and miscellaneous items. Argentina ranks as one of the leading food-exporting countries of the world and normally supplies 75 per cent of the total world exports of corn, more than 25 per cent of the wheat, nearly 70 per cent of the beef, 90 per cent of the linseed, 90 per cent of the quebracho extract, and 25 per cent of the mutton.

During World War II Argentina profited by the increased demand for her exportable surpluses at high prices, especially of meats, fats and oils, hides, and many strategic materials. Her favorable balance of trade reached the highest figure in Argentine history. There is a noticeable increase in Argentine exports of industrial commodities, most of which go to neighboring republics. On the whole, Argentina's trade with her neighbor republics has increased tremendously, especially with Brazil. Her trade with Chile and Colombia is five times greater than before the war.

Although Argentina was the last of the Latin American states to break with the Axis and did not contribute to the United Nations in a military way, she was an important source of raw materials and foods. The United Nations were supplied with the much needed meat, grains, vegetable oils, quebracho, leather, hides and skins, tungsten, zinc, mica, hog bristles and horsehair, feathers and down, glycerine, casein, beryllium, and a number of other raw materials. Argentina became one of the most important sources of fats and oils, both industrial and edible. A decade earlier she had imported nearly three fourths of her own requirements of edible vegetable fats and oils. The United States government sent special representatives to Argentina to encourage increased production of foods and other strategic commodities, particularly the fats and oils. Pre-emptive agreements or contracts were concluded, whereby Argentina was guaranteed a market and a price for her surplus production. The result was that by 1944 the total annual value of Argentina's exports to the United States amounted to $176,-000,000, an increase of 400 per cent over the figure for 1938.

RECENT TRENDS. Every effort is being made by Argentina to promote trade with other South American countries. Her Export Development Committee investigates new possibilities for promoting increased trade between Argentina and other Latin American countries, with a view to creating a nearby foreign market for Argentine products and obtaining raw materials for her expanding industries. The majority of recent trade treaties have been with neighboring republics and are of the most-favored-nation type, with reciprocal duty concessions. Several agreements have been signed with Bolivia, one of which involves Argentinian loans for building a railroad, for oil exploration, and for the construction of oil pipe lines. Other agreements with Bolivia include a protocol to the boundary treaty of 1925, a plan for promoting increased tourist traffic between the two countries, and provisions for appointing an international commission to plan the utilization of the waters of the Pilcomayo River. A recent agreement with Paraguay provides for establishment of a foreign exchange fund to aid in Paraguayan monetary stabilization. Brazil, Cuba, Colombia, and Chile have also signed recent commercial agreements with Argentina. One with Chile makes provision for Chilean iron, copper, coal, and nitrate to be exchanged for Argentine wheat.

Industry. Prior to World War I manufacturing was limited largely to the processing of foodstuffs. At that time new industries were established, and later, as a result of the world-wide economic depression, domestic industries received another impetus due to exchange restrictions, high import duties, and the increasingly protectionist policy of the government. World War II brought shortages of manufactured products, shipping problems, and blockades, all of which combined to stimulate industrialization in Argentina. Manufactured articles now occupy a greater portion of Argentine exports, and her industrial expansion has created a demand for a wider variety of imports. Meat packing, wool and cotton textiles, leather goods, flour milling, sugar, dairy products, tobacco, edible oils, and yerba maté are the leading industries (in value of finished products). Most of these items, however, are based upon agricultural production. Of especial significance, butter, cheese, and canned milk output has greatly expanded.

After the outbreak of World War II castor-oil-base plasticizer, for use in the manufacture of paint and varnishes, and dehydrated eggs were introduced and quickly sprang into importance as industrial products. Probably one of the most interesting war-born industrial developments in Argentina is the industrialization of fish products. The most important of these is shark liver oil (for vitamin A), which has found a profitable world market, particularly in the United States. Argentina is now the second largest producer of vitamin A in the world. The shark-fishing activities are concentrated in the Atlantic near Buenos Aires. The industry started as a result of the need for a substitute for dried cod fish, a popular food item in Argentina, which was formerly imported from northern Europe.

Argentina's 1,650 miles of Atlantic coast line are rich in marine life. The Patagonian shelf, similar to that off the British Isles in the North Sea, is believed to offer great fishing possibilities. However, whale and seal fishing are at present the most important activities in the southern waters. In the large rivers of Argentina there is a wealth of shad, trout, and other edible species. The annual output of canned fish in Buenos Aires and Mar del Plata has increased considerably in the past decade.

In general, the industries that are expanding are rather elementary manufactures. Argentina's industrial growth, particularly in the heavy industries, is limited because she is almost entirely dependent upon imports for both coal and iron. Artificial inducements, such as protective tariff and subsidies, may prove an expensive experiment to the national economy. Nevertheless, many of the lighter industries, especially those using locally produced raw materials, can be expanded. With better quality and improved methods of production and distribution, these industries should produce a better-balanced economy for the nation as a whole.

Communications. All types of communication developments are expanding. This growth is reflected in the increased railway and highway facilities to neighboring countries, building of new bridges, improved harbors, and increased airline service. Air transportation should help to diminish internal sectionalism, mitigate to a large extent Argentina's remoteness, and, in general, help to promote better foreign relations. The country has a dozen airports of customs entry, about forty public airdromes, three hydroplane bases, and numerous landing fields. The government sponsors a Department of Aeronautics, which has a National Meteorological service. A new international airline, *Flota Aera Merconte Argentina* (FAMA), or Argentine Merchant Airfleet, has been established by the government and maintains regular flights from Buenos Aires to cities in western Europe. This line offers competition to a number of European airlines which cross the Atlantic between West Africa and Northeast Brazil to link Buenos Aires with traffic centers in the Eastern Hemisphere.

National problems of surplus. The major problem in Argentina's economy is the recurring surpluses of agricultural and other commercial raw materials. During the early years of World War II millions of tons of surplus wheat, corn, linseed, and other grains were burned for fuel, as coal shipments from the United Kingdom were virtually stopped. The government is encouraging the building of underground granaries and other storage facilities for the purpose of storing grains in surplus years and selling in the lean years.

Recognizing the problem of wheat surpluses, the four major wheat exporting countries—the United States, Argentina, Canada, and Australia—in 1942 formulated an agreement dividing the world market on a percentage basis and arranging for future price agreements. By this means Argentina was allocated one fourth of the world wheat market.

Other agricultural surpluses in Argentina

are less pronounced than grain, but nonetheless existent. The meat problem is complicated by the system of land ownership. Some fifty patrician families own more than eleven million acres of grazing land in the Buenos Aires province alone. These owners, normally well represented in the government, tend to encourage inflation and oppose any attempt to reduce the price of meat or make other adjustments. Shortly before World War II the United Kingdom, Argentina, Uruguay, Brazil, Australia, and New Zealand formed an International Marketing Agreement for the purpose of regulating quantities and prices of meat exported to the United Kingdom. Production of oil seeds was enormously increased as a result of high prices and unusually large demands by the United Nations during the war. In the face of lowered consumption in the postwar era and competition from other areas, Argentina may find it necessary to reduce production or find new uses and new markets for her surplus oil seeds.

Solution of the problems of commodity surpluses requires careful domestic planning and international cooperation, plus increased world consumption. The latter is largely dependent upon the general prosperity of all consuming countries.

Another major problem that now faces Argentina is the large surplus of gold and foreign exchange accumulated during the war, resulting from the enormous excess of exports over imports. Most of this gold and foreign credit is held by the Central Bank of Argentina, which issues currency against it. This practice, coincident with the scarcity of consumer goods, has caused serious price inflation in the country. On the other hand, this surplus has enabled Argentina to repatriate a large part of the sterling loans.

Historical Background

Colonial period. In 1516 a party of Spanish explorers under the leadership of Don Juan Diáz de Solís discovered the Rio de la Plata. Argentina remained under Spanish domination from that time until early in the nineteenth century. As a Spanish colony, Argentina was not permitted to engage in commerce with other countries, and in order to prevent smuggling the Spanish viceroyalty forced Argentina's exports to move westward and northward to such a well-established

Spanish stronghold as Lima, Peru, and up the west coast to the Isthmus of Panama and then by ship to Spain. Thus, the western piedmont regions rather than the eastern seaboard became the seat of early colonial development, the reverse of developments in the colonization of the United States. The people who occupied the western and northern interior regions came from Chile, Peru, and Paraguay and had a racial and cultural background quite different from that of the Europeans and Uruguayans who colonized the region around Buenos Aires. These western settlements became supply centers for the westbound traffic, which handled mules, wild cattle, and general supplies for Chilean nitrate miners, and for the north-bound export trade, which included traffic in hides, tallow, dried beef, cattle, and mules. They also served as local distributing points for imported products, which also were routed over the Andes. Locally produced wine, sugar, rice, and numerous handicraft specialties, such as leather goods, saddles, metal work, woolen ponchos, blankets, and other woven materials, were transported by oxcart trains to domestic markets as far away as Buenos Aires. The economy of the piedmont, however, was more closely linked to Chile and Peru than to eastern Argentina.

The early republic. By the beginning of the nineteenth century, the Argentine militia had successfully repulsed two British attempts (1806–07) to occupy Buenos Aires and the River Plate area; and, encouraged by the American and French Revolutions, San Martín (the George Washington of Argentina) and his followers set up a local government on May 25, 1810. The revolution of 1810 led to the formal independence of Argentina in 1816 and thus opened the port of Buenos Aires to European markets. This event marks the beginning of the political rift between the capital city and the interior provinces, a rift that has continued to be a major factor throughout Argentina's turbulent political history.

The capital city and the province of Buenos Aires grew rich on the lucrative trade with Europe. The west could not compete with imported goods—French wines and British woolens and manufactures. Consequently, east-west and north-south commerce decreased, profits in sales and services dwindled,

and the inland country sank into poverty. The cattlemen had supported the revolution to break Spanish monopoly, but the Constitution of 1819 failed to unite the prematurely born nation. San Martín lost his command, and until Rivadavia became president in 1826 there was no real national government. Rivadavia vigorously encouraged immigration and capital investments, and English bankers responded to the appeal for investments. From this start the British continued to control the major portion of Argentina's railroads and other utilities until the revolution of 1943. Public land was offered as collateral, and between 1822 and 1829 some 546 speculators bought up more than 20,000,000 acres of rich land. The result was the well-known feudal system of land utilization, which never has been conducive to a diversified economy nor to a democratic way of life.

In an attempt to force the province of Buenos Aires to share its wealth with the poverty-stricken interior, Rivadavia proposed to nationalize the tariffs, virtually the only source of the nation's wealth. In this way other provinces might get their rightful share of the national income. But the province of Buenos Aires, dominated by a landed oligarchy whose back was turned to the interior as its greedy hands reached out to Europe, opposed this policy of the government and organized a provincial party that defeated Rivadavia. The nation continued to be torn by intersectional strife and civil wars in which governors of the various provinces attempted to dominate the nation. The governor of Buenos Aires province, Colonel Juan Manuel de Rosas, won in this struggle, and the period from 1829 to 1852 was known as the "Bloody Rosas" era.

Rosas was the strong man, the dictator, of the nation. He was cruel, ruthless, cunning, and clever, with a peculiar ability to analyze the psychology of the various classes, to understand the mentality of the illiterate, and to use this knowledge in attaining power, wealth, and loyalty. He was defeated in 1852 in a civil war skirmish with the opposition and fled to England. The following year a federal constitution was adopted.

The Argentina constitution was patterned after that of the United States, and the division of authority and power resembles that of the United States government except that the President has greater powers and may intervene in provincial governments. There are now fourteen provinces having a limited autonomous form of government, one federal district, and ten national territories, which are administered by officials appointed by the President. Several territories are qualified for provincial status, but none has had the opportunity to avail itself of this privilege.

The new constitutional congress of 1853 abolished the transit duties and inter-provincial tariffs that had so hindered domestic commerce. The province of Buenos Aires revolted against this act and seceded from the confederation. The federal government under the leadership of Urquiza established the national capital in the city of Paraná, in the province of Entre Rios. Urquiza made free navigation treaties with the United States, England, and France to preclude any move by Buenos Aires to prevent navigation up the Paraná and Uruguay rivers. The major foreign powers, including the United States, recognized Urquiza's government. In an effort to bring Buenos Aires into the confederation, Congress designated Rosario as the national port, and ships from abroad were required to sail directly to Rosario or pay a double tariff. Rosario prospered at the expense of Buenos Aires. In 1857 the first railroad was built, and by 1859 Buenos Aires joined the confederacy. Three years later Bartolomé Mitre became the first constitutional president. During the next thirty years a railroad net was established; immigration was encouraged; postal and telegraph systems were inaugurated; agriculture and industry expanded; and foreign trade was stimulated. It was during this period of development that the refrigerator ship was first used, and as a result Argentina's meat exports rapidly expanded.

From 1865 to 1870 Argentina, Brazil, and Uruguay joined together in a war against Paraguay. As her share of the spoils, Argentina was ceded the areas now comprising the territories of Formosa and Misiones.

The latter half of the nineteenth century was a period of extensive land grants, high immigration, railroad building, large British investments, and general financial boom. The new wave of immigrants that came in—Irish, English, Italians, Spaniards, French, Belgians, Germans, and Swiss—was largely of the middle class and became shopkeepers, traders, and workers. When the country was faced with the economic depression of 1890, this class gave birth to the Radical Party as an outgrowth of their persistent demand for universal suffrage and free elections. The agricultural aristocracy had never permitted general suffrage, and political opponents were kept from the polls either by fraud or sheer force. The Secretary of the Interior used his power to intercede in provincial affairs for the sole purpose of controlling elections.

The modern republic. After the turn of the century in 1900, Argentina ceased to be a nation in the making and took her place among the countries of the world. Experimentation in independence became a thing of the past, for a certain amount of political maturity had been attained. An agricultural potential assured economic rank among lands better developed industrially.

The boundary dispute in the north between Chile and Argentina had been settled in 1899, and the first trans-Andean railroad was completed by 1910. In 1916, during World War I, the Radicals won their first election and Irigoyen became President. His greatest political achievement was keeping Argentina neutral. Because the nation was so largely dependent upon foreign trade for its wealth, the agricultural industry was severely disrupted in the early years of the war; but soon the demand for raw materials for the Allies increased, and Argentina's exports rose rapidly while imports decreased. This favorable balance of trade made Argentina seem prosperous, and for the first time in her history she became an international creditor. As a result of the scarcity of imports, domestic manufacturing industries were developed.

In 1928, at the height of mounting inflation, Irigoyen was again President. Despite his lack of a democratic attitude, the memory of a prosperous neutrality kept him in office. He was by now past eighty years old and mentally senile. There followed two years of fraud and looting of the public treasury by incompetent and parasitic politicians, who took advantage of the President's apathetic attitude and dulled senses. Such was the government that faced the world-wide crisis of 1929 and 1930. Military revolution, led by General Uriburu and encouraged by the resentful and confused masses, ousted the whole Radical administration in September, 1930. Thus ended the "democratic" experiment. Uriburu planned to create a corporate form of government similar to the fascist state in Italy but did not succeed. Totalitarian election methods, however, continued during the following decade; the government was filled with bankrupt aristocrats who needed jobs for themselves and their relatives.

In 1933 the British maneuvered Argentina into signing the Roca-Runciman Treaty, which practically gave control of the export beef industry to Great Britain and forced Argentina to increase its imports from Britain in an effort to keep the British meat market. As a direct result of this treaty, imports from the United States were drastically reduced, much to Argentina's embarrassment and consequent resentment a decade later when Argentina begged for United States' manufactures. Factions in Argentina were able to use the Roca-Runciman Treaty as an example of foreign economic domination caused by foreign investments in their country. Partly as a result, Argentina's attitude during World War II was both anti-American and anti-British. There were pro-Nazi factions, especially in the military forces, anti-Jewish groups, and other minorities who were able to influence the foreign policy of the government.

In the military revolution of June, 1943, General Ramírez became Provisional President and canceled the fall election. The revolution was largely a culmination of resentment against the selfish rule of the landed aristocracy, combined with the intention of the previous ruler to name a successor detested by the masses as a feudal landlord. Nevertheless, the totalitarian regime of the past few years was a serious challenge to the principles for which the Inter-American System stood.

Effective action by other American governments was difficult because they were committed to a non-intervention policy. The Ramírez regime (June, 1943–February, 1944) was prematurely recognized by the United States and other American Republics. However, it was clear that the Argentine-Nazi clique planned to form a bloc of anti-Pan American countries in South America, and Argentina consistently refused to sever relations with the Axis. As new evidence of Argentine-Nazi complicity came to light and it became apparent that the Bolivian revolution in December, 1943, was being aided by Axis officials in Argentina the United States denounced Argentina and threatened political and economic sanctions. Ramírez immediately (January, 1944) severed relations with Germany and Japan. Because of pressure from pro-Axis officials in his administration, however, the break was only nominal.

In February of 1944 Ramírez was replaced by General Farrell. Farrell's regime was not recognized by most of the American republics. However, he ostensibly attempted to expel Axis missions from the country and to make certain nominal concessions to the United Nations. A few days after D-Day (June, 1944) Colonel Perón, a strong man of the Farrell regime, publicly stated that there would be no difference to Argentina between an Allied victory and an Axis victory and that Argentina would realize her national aspirations through a totalitarian government. However, war was declared on the Axis on March 27, 1945.

In October, 1945, an army *coup d'état* temporarily unseated Perón as Vice President and virtual dictator of the country, but he continued to be supported by Farrell as presidential candidate for the next election. Early in 1946 wages were increased about thirty per cent by decree of the Farrell regime, which appeared to be making a bid for the labor vote in the coming election. Colonel Perón was thus the chief beneficiary, and all commerce and industry in Buenos Aires closed its doors in protest. Perón was backed by the New Labor Party and by certain Catholic organizations, who opposed the Democratic Union party on the grounds that this party favored the separation of church and state. In the elections of February, 1946, Perón received an overwhelming victory for the presidency of Argentina.

Argentina and the United States

Political relations between the United States and Argentina have in general not been harmonious. Three major basic factors contribute to the lack of understanding between the two countries.

The first factor accounting for discord is that of location. Both countries are located in the temperate zones; thus they have similar climates and similar agricultural and grazing products for export, making them competitors in world agricultural markets. Furthermore, Argentina's remoteness from the major countries of the world has made it relatively unnecessary for most of them to seek her favor. During World War II, for example, the United States felt that it was necessary to supply Brazil with arms and equipment for hemispheric defense, since Brazil's proximity to Africa and Europe would make this a logical invasion point. Also, the United States continued to allocate relatively scarce manufactured products to Brazil in return for coffee, tropical products, and certain strategic raw materials needed in the United States. Argentina was not thus favored, and it was a source of great resentment.

The second basic reason for friction is racial and cultural. About 97 per cent of Argentina's 14,130,000 people are of European stock, chiefly from the Mediterranean countries, and some 20 per cent of these are foreign born. The remaining 3 per cent are Indian or non-Caucasian. Approximately 90 per cent of the total population are Catholics, who do not favor separation of the church and state. The people of Argentina whose official language is Spanish have continued to look to Europe, especially to France and Italy,

for cultural leadership; and their political philosophy is a combination of old Spanish dictatorship and modern totalitarianism.

The third factor is Argentina's intense desire to dominate the other South American countries, especially Chile, Uruguay, Paraguay and Bolivia. Lack of coal and iron prevents her from being an important industrial nation, and makes her dependent upon foreign trade for a large part of her national income. She would like to be in a better position to control this trade and make herself less dependent on other countries. In the world at large the Roca-Runciman Treaty between Argentina and Great Britain, which was signed by Argentina during the economic depression of the early thirties, resulted in Argentina's having to reduce imports from the United States in order to increase those from Britain. Consequently, World War II caught Argentina with a severe shortage of machinery, vehicles, rolling stock, and other heavy machinery normally imported from the United States. By the time the Argentines realized the need for imports from the United States, the latter had none to spare; and the Argentine government claimed that Argentina was being discriminated against.

PARAGUAY

Paraguay lies directly north of Argentina. It is a land-locked country with an area of 150,000 square miles, which is slightly smaller than the state of California. The Paraguay River divides the country into two major geographic regions, one east, the other west of the Paraguay River. In the first of these regions the land consists of an extension of the Paraná Plateau. This area resembles that of the territory of Misiones in northeastern Argentina, both in physical characteristics and in similarity of products. The plateau slopes toward the Paraguay River, giving way to a subregion of gently rolling hills and low, frequently flooded plains. In the second geographic region lies the Paraguayan portion of the great Chaco region of scrub forests and savanna, which is shared by three other countries and which has been the source of almost continual boundary disputes and costly wars, lately occasioned by new discoveries of oil.

The climate of Paraguay is similar to that described for the Chaco region of Argentina,

except that it is more subtropical in character. Average seasonal temperatures of Asunción, the capital, resemble those of Miami, Florida.

Economy

Agricultural production forms the basis of most of Paraguay's economic activities. Forestry ranks second in importance and together with agriculture provides the great majority of the commodities that enter channels of international commerce.

A wide variety of subsistence crops are grown, including corn, beans, manioc, oranges, pineapples, rice, and sugar cane. Approximately 40 per cent of the total value of Paraguay's exports consists of cattle and cattle products. Cotton of the long-staple variety comprises nearly one fourth of the total export value, and quebracho and yerba maté make up most of the remaining exports of the country. Other exports include tobacco, lumber, mercury, petitgrain oil (extracted from the leaves of the bitter orange tree and used in the manufacture of perfumes), and miscellaneous forest products.

Industrial growth is limited to elementary manufactures located in the city of Asunción, of which flour milling, meat canning, and extraction of essential oils are the chief industries. Paraguay is rich in potential waterpower resources but is lacking in most of the natural and economic factors necessary to industrial expansion.

The People

Some 97 per cent of the 1,140,000 people in Paraguay are *mestizo*. However, the small percentage of Europeans (principally Germans, Russians, and Czechs), most of whom have settled in Asunción (125,000), are politically and economically a very influential group. About 75 per cent of the people are illiterate, and the living standard of the masses is pitifully low. Spanish is the official language, but Guaraní Indian is also widely spoken both in business and in social circles. The Roman Catholic Church is the established religion of the state.

History and Foreign Relations

Asunción was founded in the sixteenth century by a Spaniard, Domingo Martínez de Irala, largely as a result of the attempts of Spanish immigrants to reach the riches of Peru via the Paraná-Paraguay River system. The hostile Indians on the grassy plains of Argentina prevented any attempt to settle there. Upon reaching the vicinity of present-day Asunción, the Spaniards found the friendly and easily dominated Guaraní Indians. In the southeastern part of the country (which later became Misiones in Argentina) Jesuit missions were established, and the Indians shared the prosperity of the productive land until the Jesuits were expelled from the country in 1767. The Indians then drifted toward Asunción, where they gradually were reduced to a state of peonage on the feudal estates there.

From 1811, when Paraguay won her independence from Spain, to 1864, the nation enjoyed relative prosperity. From 1865 to 1870 she fought the combined forces of Argentina, Brazil, and Uruguay in a senseless and futile war under dictator Francisco López. This war reduced her population of more than a million people to a mere 200,000, most of whom were women and children and old men. In addition, she lost to Brazil a large strip of territory between the Paraná and Paraguay rivers. To Argentina was ceded the regions now comprising the territories of Formosa and Misiones in northeastern Argentina. For many decades thereafter Paraguay made slow economic progress, constantly hampered by revolution, intrigue, and corrupt government. Unfortunately the war of 1865–70 failed to settle the boundary disagreement between Paraguay and Bolivia to the north, and the dispute continued until it culminated in another war (the Chaco War of 1932–35). A settlement was finally effected in October, 1938, as a result of the Chaco Peace Conference representing six neutral countries—the United States, Brazil, Uruguay, Argentina, Chile, and Peru. Paraguay gained considerable territory (three fourths of the disputed area), but the known oil fields remained on the Bolivian side of the boundary line.

During World War II Paraguay threw her sympathies in with the United Nations and broke relations with the Axis powers in January, 1942, in spite of the fact that her economy is dominated largely by Argentina. In return for increased production of foods and forest products needed by the United Nations, the United States loaned her money for the construction of health and sanitation facilities.

URUGUAY

The topography of Uruguay is generally rolling, and consists largely of grassy slopes and numerous wooded valleys and streams. In the western part of the country where the Rio Negro enters the Uruguay River, the forests are quite extensive. Ocean steamers navigate up the Uruguay River as far as Paysandú.

The climate of Uruguay is temperate. The average temperature of the coldest month seldom exceeds 50° F., which compares with the winter temperatures of southeastern United States. However, the summer temperatures are relatively cool and compare with those of the New England states. The rainfall is well distributed throughout the year, and Uruguayan agriculture is not seriously affected by droughts.

Uruguay, the smallest of the South American republics, has a total area of only about 72,000 square miles, which is slightly larger than the state of Washington.

History

Uruguay owes its independence to the fact that it is located between two rival powers, Brazil and Argentina, and is therefore a typical buffer state. Its position as a buffer state dates back to the rivalry between the Portuguese to the north and the Spaniards to the south. After the discovery of the Rio de la Plata by Juan Díaz de Solís in 1516, Uruguay later became a part of the Spanish viceroyalty for that region, and subsequently a province of Portuguese Brazil. In 1825 the Argentine army gained control of Uruguay. For commercial reasons the British, who had an economic interest in the River Plate region, opposed the idea of Argentina's controlling both sides of the Paraná-Plate River; and in 1830 they were a factor in establishing Uruguay as an independent state. After that time the population in Uruguay increased rapidly, partly because of increased British investments and partly because the Rosas regime in Argentina discouraged foreign immigration in that country. Although Uruguay has experienced constant pressure from Argentina and has been forced to make some concessions, she has remained one of the most democratic and progressive of South American countries.

Population

One large city, Montevideo, comprises about one third of the country's 2,200,000 inhabitants. It has no competitor as the economic, political, and social center of Uruguay. There are only two other cities of importance, Paysandú and Salto, both situated along the Rio Uruguay and each having less than 50,000 people. Despite the few cities of importance, Uruguay is the most densely populated of the South American nations. Thus, in the southern part of the country the density of its rural population runs as high as 125 persons per square mile. In the northwest, with a rural population of less than 10 per square mile, the population density is the lowest. The average density for the country is over 30 persons per square mile. As in Argentina, the major portion of the population is of European descent, with Italian and Spanish predominating. The *mestizos* of the regions remote from Montevideo comprise approximately 10 per cent of the total population. Spanish is the official language and Roman Catholicism the principal religion.

National Economy

Uruguay has had a relatively recent economic development. The wide Paraná-Plate River isolated Uruguay from the early Spanish settlements in Argentina, and its remoteness from the important Spanish establishments in Peru precluded any significant trade development in that direction. Consequently, it was only after cattle buyers from Argentina created a demand for livestock that the people in Uruguay became ranchers and landowners.

The major commercial products in Uruguay include wool, beef and canned meats, hides and skins, flaxseed, wheat, and wheat flour. In meat exportation Uruguay ranks second to Argentina. High-grade wool, mostly from merino sheep, comprises considerably more than one third of the total value of Uruguayan exports. Uruguay, like Argentina, is largely dependent upon foreign trade for her national income. The United States, Brazil, and Argentina, in that order, are her principal sources of imports; and the United States and the United Kingdom together buy more than 80 per cent of her exports. In general it can be said that Uruguay's prosperity is almost entirely dependent upon international market conditions, especially in the wool and meat trade.

Uruguay is making industrial progress in the production of woolen textiles, leather, and meat products, but her basic economy remains definitely pastoral.

CHAPTER 34 | # Pacific South America

PACIFIC South America includes western Colombia, Ecuador, Peru, Bolivia, and Chile, a region roughly coincident with the great Andean mountain system. Extending over 60 degrees of latitude, or about 4,500 miles, these lands necessarily have strong contrasts in physical situation, climatic and topographic features, soils, natural vegetation, mineral endowment, and economic products, as well as in population elements, culture, and political administration. Nonetheless, the entire area has enough in common to safeguard the concept of unity, even though one must at the same time take cognizance of the differences. At least it has a geographic personality that sets it apart from the Caribbean area, from the United States of Brazil, and from the Rio de la Plata lands. Following is an evaluation of the forces that work toward and against unity within Pacific South America.

Forces working toward unity:

1. All five countries had a common origin as colonies of Spain. Thus, in a figurative sense, they all "speak the same language"; that is, they have much in common, just as have the United States and Canada.

2. All of these countries won their independence in the early nineteenth century by a series of revolutions, and the same heroes fought in several of the countries.

3. In all five the official language is Spanish, and possibly nothing serves more strongly as a common bond to bring people together in national or even international unity. Yet Spanish is not used by all the people, as the masses of Bolivians, Ecuadoreans, and Peruvians are not a Latinized people to the extent that the Argentines and Uruguayans are.

Hence throughout the central Andes, populous communities retain their pre-conquest dialects.

4. Practically all whites and mestizos, as well as many Indians, are Roman Catholics. The existence of strong anti-clerical groups merely emphasizes the traditional Roman Catholic nature of organized society. Most of the Indians, however, even those professing Christianity, have a superstitious regard for the spirits of familiar objects—hills, rocks, and so on. At every high pass the Aymaras build tiny stone houses to the hill spirits, throw an offering of masticated coca leaves upon overhanging cliffs along the roads, and spill a bit of each drink of liquor in reverence to the Earth Mother.

5. All of the countries are still semicolonial in their economy, producing basic foodstuffs and raw materials for export. Especially characteristic is their heavy production and export of minerals, though not to the same extent from country to country. The region as a whole is dependent to a great extent upon Europe and North America for fabricated products.* Until the end of the eighteenth century Spain's economic machinery drew raw materials from the colonies and "like a pump, sent them back in a stream of finished products." Manufacturing was forbidden in the colonies so long as Spain was master.

6. Throughout the Andes heavy tribute must be paid to nature in transportation and communication by reason of the barrier effect of the continuous high elevations. Accordingly, common problems arise.

7. Most of the contacts with the outside world

* "You must become convinced that the Latin American countries are still colonial countries; that although we are independent countries in the political sense, we are not so in the economic sense." Enrique de Lozada, "Latin America: United States' Achilles Heel," address before the Chicago Council on Foreign Relations, November 22, 1940 (Mimeographed).

are made by way of the Pacific Ocean, although air transportation is decreasing this limitation.

A major error in the concept conveyed by words is that the expression *Latin America* denotes a unified area. Latin America must be considered a general rather than a specific term, and there is no such person as a typical Latin American. Each component part is an independent, vigorous nationality, well aware and jealous of its own individuality and its cultural and historical autonomy.

Forces working against unity in Pacific South America:

1. Topography. The countries run the whole gamut of terrain, from high mountains and lofty plateaus to low plains. Obviously the economic, political, and social problems of the dwellers of the high plateau are not those of their countrymen in the coastal area and the interior lowlands. Thus, the Andes virtually divide Peru against itself, and national unity is attainable only with great difficulty. Virtually the same statement may be made for Ecuador and Bolivia, although Bolivia lacks a coastal area. Separatism, therefore, characterizes most of the countries of the West Coast —separatism rooted in topographic differences. The building of railroads and roads is so very difficult and costly that, except for Bolivia, each country maintains its international contacts primarily by sea and air.

2. Climate. The truly tropical countries may have many diverse climatic characteristics by reason of differences in elevation. One could scarcely encounter greater contrasts than those between coastal Colombia (Buenaventura) and the high plateau (Bogotá), or between the high mountains and the Amazon lowlands of Peru.

Marked contrasts exist also in Chile, but here latitude is more important than altitude. Thus, Chile goes from a northern desert (so dry that not a plant—not even a lichen—grows there) to a mediterranean subtropical land (Central Valley), and thence to one of the rainiest regions on earth in the extreme south.

3. Intense nationalism. Viewed broadly, each country is determined to build itself into a strong, independent nation, to develop a more efficient economy, and to create new social institutions. The common objective of the politicians is to bring about a broader distribution of wealth and raise the standard of living for the masses.

4. The people themselves. The composition of the population varies greatly. Bolivia, Ecuador, and Peru are predominantly Indian, whereas Chile and Colombia are predominantly mestizo. In not a single Pacific country of South America is the white population numerically the most impor-

tant.* Although the color line is not drawn here as it is in the United States, there exists, nevertheless, a caste system. The bulk of the whites have little use for the Indian. By and large the Indian is ignorant, exploited, despised, and at the very bottom of the scale. His lot is little better than that of a domesticated animal. As Hudson Strode puts it, "The Spaniard considered the Indian a beast of burden and the mestizo a mistake of nature." Some mestizos gain places of prominence in business and politics, but many are only slightly better off than the Indians. Negroes are numerically important in the hot coastal areas of Colombia and Ecuador, but they are for the most part miserably poor and live under unbelievably bad conditions.

5. Contrast in wealth. Pacific South America, like Latin America as a whole, is characterized by the ostentatious wealth of the few and the biting poverty of the many. With most of the land in the hands of a few, nothing but a low standard of living is possible for most of the people. This is a major factor in the lack of political and economic stability. More than two thirds of the people of each nation are reported to be ill-housed, ill-fed, and ill-clothed. Hence, genuine political and economic stability is impossible until an honest attempt is made by those "who have" to bridge the gap between themselves and the masses.

Physical Setting

Area. The total area of the five republics of Pacific South America (including Colombia) somewhat exceeds one half the size of the United States, or nearly eight times the size of France (see the map on facing page). The largest of these republics is Bolivia, its area spread over the widest part of the Andes and far eastward onto the extensive lowlands of the interior of the South American continent. The 507,000 square miles making up Bolivia are nearly equal to twice the area of Texas. Slightly smaller, Peru with an area of 501,000 square miles includes a significant portion of the upper Amazon River valley within its boundaries. The 440,000 square mile area of Colombia ranks it third among the Pacific coast states of South America. (As much of that country faces the Caribbean Sea rather than the ocean to the west, its northern sector is discussed in Chapter 31, "The Caribbean: An American Mediterranean.") The coastline along the Pacific Ocean totals about 900 miles as compared to about 1,100 miles

* As a possible qualification it may be noted that in Chile nearly 25 per cent of the population is white and the mestizos are predominantly white.

along the Caribbean Sea. However, as Colombia reaches deep into the interior lowlands of South America, it would be difficult to determine any dividing line between Colombia's Pacific and Caribbean sectors. Con-

siderably smaller than its northern neighbors, Chile with an area of 286,000 square miles is still three times the size of Oregon. Its equivalent latitude in the Northern Hemisphere extends from south of Mexico City to south-

PACIFIC COUNTRIES OF SOUTH AMERICA

ern Alaska—a tremendous distance in any sense of the word. Smallest of the Pacific states of South America is Ecuador, wedged between Colombia and Peru. Nevertheless, its approximate area, believed to be in excess of 100,000 square miles,* is twice that of New York state.

Climate and relief. It is impossible to comprehend and appreciate the problems—local, national, and international—of these Pacific South American political areas without first taking into consideration the physical aspects of climate and relief. The natural environment contributes mightily to these problems. Except for parts of Chile, the area lies cartographically *within* the tropics; Ecuador and the southern segment of Colombia actually ride the Equator. Yet this tropical *location* does not mean that the entire area is tropical *climatically,* for altitude here results in temperatures ordinarily associated with much higher latitudes. The cold Peru Current also influences the climate of much of the coastal area; as a result of this cold water, the air temperatures from northern Chile almost to the Equator are considerably lower than would be expected for the latitude. Thus, the average annual temperature for Lima is 66.7° as against 76.6° for São Salvador in Brazil in the same latitude.

The Andes stand as a formidable barrier to east-west movement, but the aspect of these mountains is not everywhere the same (see the map on the facing page). Only from Cape Horn to the central part of Chile do they constitute a single range. In some places they are a confusing tangle, whereas in Bolivia they form an orderly array of gigantic ranges between which lie the floors of the lofty tablelands (the *altiplano*). Only in the Himalaya Mountains and in Tibet are there relief features of greater dimensions than those of the central part of the Andes.

Along much of the coast, the mountains rise almost out of the Pacific. The Andean system varies from 100 to 400 miles in width, is 4,500 miles long, and possesses few passes as low as 10,000 feet. In the extreme south the passes are lower, but even there they lie thousands of feet above sea level. Nowhere else on the globe does so long, so high, and so de-

* Although the frontiers, long in dispute, have now been settled, no exact figure for the area is yet available.

fiant a wall of mountains "challenge man to conquer it if he can." Were these mountains not rich in minerals, it is doubtful whether white men even now would be attempting the conquest of the most rugged portions.

Just as along the Pacific Coast of North America, a coastal chain of low mountains extends over much of the length of the continent. Only occasionally does it become a formidable barrier, but its naked slopes and summits give the west coast an inhospitable aspect for the 2,500 miles from southern Ecuador to Valparaiso, Chile.

Illustrative of great physical contrasts, Ecuador and Peru are each made up of three great natural regions (coastal area, mountain, interior lowland), so different one from another in climate, topography, soils, natural vegetation, and mineral resources that all human institutions are profoundly affected.

Physical handicaps. Unfortunately, as a result of the emergence of the ocean floor along about four fifths of the entire length of the coast, there are few good harbors.* The only sizable indentation is the Gulf of Guayaquil in Ecuador. Elsewhere, ports occupy small headlands or inbends of the coast, where they get some small amount of protection from winds and waves. Except in a few man-made harbors, large vessels are obliged to anchor a mile or so offshore and discharge and receive cargo and passengers by lighter.

Pacific South America's location has from the very beginning been a handicap. From the days of Francisco Pizarro, Spanish conqueror of Peru, down to the opening of the Panama Canal, its position virtually meant isolation; the region was off the beaten path. To reach the West Coast by ship meant a long, dangerous, and costly journey via the Strait of Magellan or around Cape Horn.**

The People

The more than 28 million people who live in the five Pacific republics of South America represent 30 per cent of the continent's total

* Buenaventura, Guayaquil, and Chimbote are exceptions.
** By a portage across the Isthmus of Panama, the circuitous sailing route around South America could be avoided. From about 1543 to roughly the last quarter of the eighteenth century this shorter but more awkward itinerary served as the official colonial trade route from Spain to Callao, Peru. From here, one route went further south to Chile; and the other overland to Buenos Aires via Tucumán and Córdoba.

PHYSIOGRAPHIC DIAGRAM OF

SOUTH AMERICA

By Guy-Harold Smith

The Geographical Press
Columbia University
New York

Small Scale Edition
1935
SCALE

By courtesy of Guy-Harold Smith

© G·H·S 1935

population. The most populous of these countries is Colombia (9,390,000); Peru (7,-023,000) ranks second; Chile (5,024,000) is third; and Bolivia (3,596,000) and Ecuador (3,086,000), the largest and smallest of the countries, stand last. Their combined population exceeds that of the westernmost seventeen states of the United States, an area almost identical in size with the five South American countries under discussion.

Composition of the population. The Indian, the mestizo, and the white man comprise the bulk of the total population, although locally the Negro predominates in several areas, and in a few communities Japanese are important.

THE INDIAN. The Indian occupied Pacific South America prior to the coming of the white man. It is believed, however, that he had not been in the New World very long, possibly having first trickled into Alaska from Asia about 25,000 years ago.*

Pacific South American Indians differed markedly among themselves in civilization, economy, political development, and density of population. In the high basins of the Cordillera Oriental of Colombia dwelt the civilized Chibchas; in the highlands of Ecuador, Peru, and Bolivia, along the coast of Peru, and in Chile and Argentina dwelt the peoples of the Inca Empire; in central Chile, south of the Maule River, lived the fierce, warlike, semi-nomadic Araucanians; and in the forests east of the Andes roamed numerous small tribes of savages.

Today the Indian element predominates numerically in Bolivia, Ecuador, and Peru. Most of the people in the altiplano are Indians.

THE WHITES. Spaniards were the first to arrive in Pacific South America. Coming as conquerors, they sought to obtain the natural wealth and utilize the native labor for the benefit of Spain and themselves. They were indisputably great conquerors and energetic explorers. With them came the Catholic clergy, who sought with zeal to civilize the Indian and to save his soul.

The whites of today reflect the ideas of the conquistadores. One of the latter said: "I came to gain gold with sword and shield, not to follow the plow like a peasant." Many whites still have the point of view of the landed aristocracy, looking down upon those who work with their hands or even upon those who make money through trade. Hence, throughout Pacific South America has developed an aristocratic caste civilization, with the white at the top, the Indian and the Negro at the bottom, and the mestizo frequently in between. However, the mixed blood is gaining in economic and political power and prestige. More and more the word *mestizo* is becoming synonymous with the words *Colombian, Chilean, Peruvian,* and so forth.

Though comprising only a small part of the population, possibly not more than five to fifteen per cent, the whites have possessed most of the wealth, have wielded the political power, and have enjoyed the educational and cultural advantages. In short, it has been they who have dominated. But in Pacific South America, as in Mexico, for example, they are losing their power. In many instances whites are being replaced by mestizos in politics.

THE MIXED BLOODS. The attitude of the Latin regarding mixed blood differs from that of the Anglo-Saxon. The Spaniard himself has highly mixed blood. In his veins flows the blood of Iberians, Celts, Phoenicians, Greeks, Carthaginians, Romans, Visigoths, Vandals, Moors, and Jews. Since most Spanish conquistadores did not come to the New World accompanied by their own women, they cohabited freely with Indian women and rapidly built up a mixed-blood population.

In Pacific South America the mixed bloods are mostly the product of the union of Spanish and Indian—the mestizo, commonly known as the *cholo.* The product of the union of Negro and Indian—the *zambo*—makes up a small but significant group in parts of the West Coast area.

The mestizo is the dominant element in the population of Chile and Colombia and is becoming so in Peru, but accurate data on blood strains are most difficult to obtain. In Colombia and Chile census takers do not inquire into race or color, first because of the difficulties involved in such heterogeneous populations and, second, because race prejudice has practically disappeared. Alberto Arca Parró, of the Peruvian Census, states that

* Harry L. Shapiro, "Ethnic Pattern in Latin America," *The Scientific Monthly,* LXI (November, 1945), 345.

. . . racial intermixture is going on at high speed and that out of it is emerging the new Peruvian race—the "mestizo." . . . The mixture is so strong that it is difficult if not impossible to count the whites as an independent group within the racial classification.*

Thus, Peru's last census (1940) classifies the population in four groups: (1) white and mestizo; (2) Indian; (3) Asiatic; and (4) Negro.

THE NEGRO AND THE ORIENTAL. Small and relatively unimportant (except locally) groups of Negroes and Orientals enter into the population picture of the West Coast. Negroes were introduced into the hot coastal areas as slaves to work on plantations, and in places, as the Buenaventura area of Colombia, they comprise the bulk of the population. Some 17,600 Orientals (Japanese) occupy land in Peru's irrigated coastal desert.

Distribution of population. A study of the distribution of population indicates two salient features. First, the bulk of the population lives in clusters either on the Andean Plateau or along the coast. Second, these clusters are separated one from another by thinly occupied territory. This population pattern is typical of all industrially underdeveloped countries. Thus in Peru five eighths of the population occupies the plateau area, one fourth the coastal plain, and less than one eighth the eastern slopes of the Andes (the *Montaña*). The population of the Peruvian portion of the Amazon Basin is small because of isolation, remoteness, insect pests, deadly diseases, a trying climate, and poor transport facilities. In fact, large areas have not even been explored by white men as yet. These are lands of the civilized Indian, who moves from place to place, accepting no rule except that of his own community.

In Chile ninety per cent of the people are clustered in a single region—Middle Chile. Northern Chile, one of the driest areas on earth, and Southern Chile, one of the rainiest, offer few inducements as habitats for large numbers of people. Middle Chile, unlike any other single part of the Pacific Coast countries, represents the economic, political, and social core of its nation. Moreover, racial homogeneity is an accomplished fact here.

* Alberto Arca Parró, "Census of Peru, 1940," *The Geographical Review*, XXXII (January, 1942), 14.

Population distribution from the standpoint of race is geographically important. In Colombia and Ecuador the white people are confined almost exclusively to the upper plateaus, between the approximate altitudes of 5,000 and 9,000 feet. In Bolivia, farther from the Equator, they live mostly in the many valleys that dissect the eastern Andes—valleys that lack the penetrating cold of the windswept altiplano. Here not only do the people adjust themselves better, but so do the European plants and animals that have been introduced. In Peru most of the whites occupy the irrigated valleys in the coastal region, which is a white man's land by reason of the cold Peru Current along the coast.

The Indian population for the most part lives on the high intermontane plateaus, although small numbers of nomadic and seminomadic tribes live in the rainy tropical lands east of the mountains and along the coast of Colombia.

The Negro population is concentrated along the coasts of Colombia and Ecuador. In the Colombian tropical rain forest Negroes are proving better able to survive than the native Indians whom they are displacing. Here they live in small clearings and practice a shifting cultivation of food crops. It has been reported that ninety-nine per cent of the population of Buenaventura, the only important port in the area, is black. Most of the placer gold and platinum miners of the Atrato area are Negroes. About fifteen per cent of the people of Ecuador are Negroes who, along with the mestizos, occupy the coastal area, particularly the northern part. Here, as in coastal Colombia, they engage in *milpa,* or shifting agriculture.

Cities

Capitals. The location of capital cities in Colombia, Ecuador, and Bolivia at high elevations far from the ocean is geographically, economically, and politically significant. Despite virtual isolation these cities are comparatively large.

Bogotá (395,000) in Colombia lies 8,560 feet above sea level; Quito (150,000) in Ecuador, 9,350 feet; and La Paz (300,000) in Bolivia, 11,910 feet. Completely shut off from other settled areas by physical barriers and by a distance of hundreds of miles, Bogotá is the most isolated national capital in the world.

Quito, lying in a basin on the plateau, was the northern capital of the Inca Empire. Although situated within twenty miles of the Equator, it enjoys a temperate climate. Although Sucre (30,000) is the legal capital of Bolivia, La Paz is the actual capital as well as the major metropolitan center of the country (ten times the size of the second Bolivian city). A less promising site for a large city would be difficult to imagine. The site was chosen by the Spaniards because of its nodal location: it combined accessibility to a major colonial trade route (a half way post between Cuzco and Potosí) with shelter from the cold winds. When centuries later railways were built, they were made to focus on Viacha, a junction in the highlands near La Paz.

Lima (625,000), capital of Peru (also the economic and social capital), is not a highland city but owes its founding in 1535 to the conqueror, Pizarro. The site combined two special advantages of importance to the Spaniards; (1) its location in the Rimac Valley, one of the larger irrigable areas in the coastal desert; and (2) the presence of an offshore island and a long gravelly promontory that faces the island from the mainland. This insular configuration of land permitted vessels to anchor in the nearby port of Callao, protected from the waves brought by prevailing southwest winds. Lima enjoys a cool climate by reason of the Peru Current.

Santiago (1,015,000), Chile's capital and also a lowland city, is situated only 1,700 feet above the sea in the Central Valley.

Ports. Since the great webs of transcontinental railroads that characterize the United States are lacking in South America, each west coast country must depend upon the sea as a means of international contact. Numerous ports were established long before the railroad era, for Spanish explorers as they advanced along the coast opened up ports at the mouth of almost every valley. Along that great stretch of coast that is desert, towns sometimes grew up at the landing places. More often, however, they were built a short distance inland, where water and fertile soil supported the settlers. Pairs of towns also developed—one a port, one inland—the two being linked by a road. Examples are Arequipa and Quilca (later Mollendo), Tacna and Arica, and Lima and Callao. Thus a large number of west coast ports grew up despite the dearth of good natural harbors.

The largest port city along the western coast of South America is Valparaiso (215,-000), second city of Chile. It is the commercial outlet to the rich Central Valley of the country. On the Pacific Coast of Colombia the port of Buenaventura is outshadowed in importance by Barranquilla on the Caribbean shore, outlet for much of the nation's production. Guayaquil, with a population of 160,-000, situated on the right bank of the Guayas River, is the principal port and the leading commercial center of Ecuador.

Other cities. Aside from the capitals and the port cities there are also a few other relatively large urban centers in the Pacific countries of South America. In the highlands of Colombia are Medellín (200,000) and Cali (100,000), the former a mining headquarters and cotton textile manufacturing city, the latter a coffee center. Arequipa, with 80,000 inhabitants, located in a valley just within the mountains, is the second city of Peru and the commercial center of the south. High on the eastern slopes of the Andes the Bolivian city of Cochabamba (60,000) is a leading commercial city. In total, the five republics (exclusive of the Caribbean region of Colombia) have eight cities exceeding 100,000 in size, two less than the three Pacific Coast states of the United States.

Historical Highlights

Pre-Columbian period. The outstanding Indian civilization in Pacific South America was that of the Incas. Their empire, the "Roman Empire" of pre-Columbian America, extended from northern Ecuador to Middle Chile and Argentina (see the map on facing page). Although essentially confined to the highlands, the Inca Empire also included the irrigated valleys of coastal Peru.

The Incas were farmers, cultivating not only the flatlands but also terracing many mountainsides. Their establishment of a permanent agriculture in the forbidding mountain and plateau habitat is considered one of the wonders of the world. The Incas learned all the essential elements of successful agriculture, that is, preparation of the soil, destruction of weeds, terracing slopes, use of fertilizers, irrigation, and selective breeding of plants. Among their contributions to world agriculture is the potato. They lacked the domesticated animals that we know, however; they had only the alpaca and llama, both limited in usefulness, but of inestimable value in the high mountains.

Another advanced group of Indian tribes was the sedentary agricultural Chibchas of

SOUTH AMERICA

PACIFIC OCEAN

ATLANTIC OCEAN

INCA EMPIRE
(MAXIMUM EXTENT)
0   500   1000
MILES

central Colombia. Their culture was not equal to that of the Incas, but they occupied large cities and had united formerly independent tribes into well-organized states.

The Araucanians, who occupied what is now Middle Chile, never permitted themselves to fall completely under the sway of the Incas. Even when dominated by them in the area near the present city of Santiago, they never lost their strong sense of independence and individual initiative. They had achieved a culture level much like that of the Iroquois of North America; they were hunters and fishermen, but they also grew some crops.

Spanish era. Into this Indian world in the early sixteenth century, the Spaniards came seeking gold. In a few years Spanish control extended from the Caribbean to Middle Chile. Indian homes and public buildings were demolished for what gold ornaments they contained. The Spaniards elected to

establish themselves wherever the native population was most concentrated and most advanced—that is, in the highlands. These natives were easiest to conquer and made the best slaves, and their women were the best cooks. They were also the best-knit politically. By taking over here, the whites merely substituted another exploiting class for the one with which the aborigines were familiar.

Those Indians who were unaccustomed to such a system rebelled. These the Spaniards either exterminated or drove into marginal or inhospitable areas. The Araucanians were such a people, and to conquer and hold their country cost Spain more in men and money than all her other New World possessions combined.

The Spanish Conquest brought great injury to the lands of the Inca and Chibcha. Large numbers of Indians perished through fighting, and many more were enslaved in mines and on coca plantations in climates ill-suited to them. New diseases, such as measles, smallpox, and tuberculosis, were introduced by the Spaniard and took a terrific toll. Many irrigation works fell into disrepair and ruin, and many terraces were abandoned. But the Spaniards made many contributions. They brought with them cattle, horses, goats and sheep; they introduced many crops, such as barley, wheat, and sugar cane; and they inaugurated many new farm practices. They also built cities, universities, and monasteries. The Spaniard was now supreme along the West Coast and wherever else he had gone.

From 1519 to 1821 was the so-called Spanish Colonial Period. In Pacific South America a viceroyalty had been set up in Peru, under a Viceroy from Spain. His rule was supreme, and he was responsible only to the Spanish Crown. Certain areas, among them Chile, were given the status of captaincies general, and the limits of the colonial administrative areas became more or less the basis of the national frontiers of the present-day republics. During these three centuries, the West Coast area was little more than a feudal appendage of the mother country. Spain systematically denied her colonies any chance at self-rule. The Spaniards were divided into two classes: (1) those born in Spain—the *gachupines,* for whom government posts were reserved and who came to the New World only temporarily; and (2) those born in the New

World—the creoles (also pure-blooded Spaniards), who were denied any real opportunities in administration. Rivalry naturally grew up between them, for the *gachupines* considered themselves to be superior.

In the early 1800's came revolutions, led largely by creoles. Most brilliant among the leaders were Sucre, O'Higgins, San Martín, and especially Bolívar. Bolívar fought the Spaniards up and down the Andes and finally drove them out of Bolivia, Colombia, Ecuador, and Peru in Pacific South America. The colonial system collapsed; Spanish political power cracked and died in the New World.

Independence. Independence was not a unified struggle undertaken simultaneously and with a common understanding; rather, it was begun as separate revolutionary movements in different areas.

When the struggle for liberation was over, no period of stability characterized the transition to a republican order. With no strong hand of authority to make the many factions cooperate, Pacific South America dissolved into the several republics. Mountain ranges, distance, and other geographical factors, as well as several non-geographical factors, particularly the loss of the monarchical myth that had bound Spanish America together, constituted formidable obstacles to unity. The spirit of *localismo,* or narrow local patriotism, is nurtured by the topography of Pacific South America.

Independence was followed by disorder, which resulted from political inexperience, social antipathies, geographical barriers, and sectional and/or personal ambitions.

The new republics, in a wave of idealism, adopted constitutions much like that of the United States. A form of government more ill-suited to the social structure, however, could hardly have been devised. Geography and social realities soon reasserted themselves over the paper constitutions, and after a period of anarchy there followed the political pattern of government by the *caudillo,* or military despot. At the present time there is less government by the *caudillo* than formerly. Democratic practices are evolving, even if slowly. Only in Chile among the West Coast countries is any considerable middle class evolving. Without a substantial middle class, it is difficult for a significant opposition party to develop. The illiterate masses have never shown allegiance to principles; instead, they have shown allegiance to persons.

Economic Developments

Unfortunately for its own economic welfare, each of the West Coast countries in South America specializes in a small number of commodities that it sends into world markets. The influence of this type of economic organization, traceable to the colonial period, has penetrated every phase of the national life of these countries; independence of action has been curtailed, and dependence on world markets has grown. To be specific, Colombia relies largely upon coffee and petroleum; Ecuador upon cacao, petroleum, coffee, balsa wood, and bananas; Peru upon petroleum, copper, sugar, and cotton; Bolivia mostly upon tin and several other minerals; and Chile upon copper, nitrate, and iron ore. Since the republics have a dearth of financial reserves, they must sell irrespective of market conditions. Hence, because of this lack of a varied economy, they are at the mercy of changing world markets over which they can exercise no real influence. Two world wars and the worst depression in history shook their economic life to its very foundations. The result has been genuine efforts to diversify products and to industrialize—efforts aided by the United States.

Agriculture. Since earliest times the Indians have tilled the ground, irrigated the fields, and planted and harvested their crops. It is around agriculture that their laws, governments, religions, and numerous social customs have grown up. Yet despite its importance, agriculture is limited in its possibilities by altitude, terrain, types of soil, and other factors. Yields, therefore, are not abundant in the cool climate and thin soils of the altiplano. Crops are actually insufficient to sustain the population, and some foodstuffs must be imported. The diminutive size of the land plots also intensifies the meager subsistence, for long ago the Spaniards seized most of the land to form their great rural estates.

In portions of coastal Ecuador and Peru, and in the Central Valley of Chile, agriculture differs markedly from the crude subsistence farming of the mountains and plateaus. In Peru, sugar cane is the predominating crop of the haciendas of the north—in the Chiclayo-Trujillo area; to the south, in the Huacho-Lima-Ica sector, cotton predominates. In Middle Chile most temperate and many subtropical crops flourish, although irrigation must be practiced in the northern section with its mediterranean type of climate. Throughout the Central Valley of Chile livestock is important.

Mining. For 400 years Pacific South America has been outstanding for its mineral production, and in the past century this has even far exceeded that of the previous three. Originally the treasure of the Incas lured the Spanish conquistadores to Pacific South America. At first attention was given almost exclusively to the precious metals—gold and silver; later to copper and tin. In more recent years the region has also produced copper, antimony, iron ore, lead and zinc, platinum, nitrates, bismuth, tin, and vanadium. Petroleum has been found over the full length of the Andes, lending credence to the belief that one of the world's greatest reserves may be located there. However, the forbidding aspect of the towering Andes has discouraged exploitation. Colombia and Peru, nonetheless, boast some of the world's most daring pieces of oil exploitation. Despite the inaccessibility of much of her oil in and beyond the Andes, South America is the world's second largest producer among the continents. Petroleum is produced commercially in the coastal area of northwestern Peru and southwestern Ecuador.

With the possible exception of Ecuador, mining has been of great significance to all the West Coast countries. It has supplied government revenues and paid a considerable aggregate of wages. Nevertheless, the benefits of mining have not been and are not now satisfactory to most of the governments, for outside interests come in for a large share of the profits. Discontent is leading to much nationalization of mineral resources. By getting the mining industry into their own hands, the leaders feel that their countries will be able to escape what they call their "colonial status." Yet there is another angle to this problem, regardless of what is said to the contrary. All investments by foreigners have not been for exploitation in the bad sense of the word, and all profits have not accrued to absentee landlords. Great chances frequently have to be taken, and profits have not always proved fantastic. Almost invariably the minerals are badly located; that is, they lie in high mountains, which impose all but insuperable difficulties to the building of railways, cheapest known means of transporting heavy commodities by land.

Most of the copper, tin, and vanadium mines lie 13,000 to 16,000 feet above sea level, where the air is thin. This rarefied atmosphere precludes the white man from performing much physical work. Only the Andean Indians, who have unusual lung development in abnormally large chests, are able to compensate for the lower oxygen content of arterial blood and are in a sense immune to mountain sickness, or *soroche*.

Manufacturing. To date, the countries comprising Pacific South America have not been a part of the industrial world upon which our modern age rests. They do not wish, however, to accept permanently the status of producers of foodstuffs, minerals, and other raw materials; they are convinced that the higher standard of living they desire so insistently for their poverty-stricken millions can be achieved mainly through industrialization. But the fact should not be overlooked that there are specific bases upon which industrialism rests and that wishful thinking —even a fiery determination—are not among them.* For the present, at least, Pacific South America lacks the combination of large population in juxtaposition to accessible and high-grade coal and iron-ore reserves, which appears to be necessary for the development of heavy industries. Hence, its evolution as a major industrial region seems unlikely to many students.** Others, however, believe that petroleum, water power, and electricity "may provide the basis for a future industrial development based on South American mineral resources, which will rival that of the United States." †

It it possible that *light* industries may grow and prosper within the region, for they are

* George T. Renner and Associates, *Global Geography* (Crowell, 1944), Chapter 18, pp. 311–333.

** C. Langdon White, "Is the Twentieth Century South America's?" *Economic Geography*, XXI (April, 1945), pp. 79–87.

† Mordecai Ezekiel, "Economic Relations Between the Americas," *International Conciliation*, No. 367 (February, 1941), p. 48. Carnegie Endowment for International Peace.

composed mostly of consumer goods and involve a minimum of marketing and distributing problems. This type of development, however, is a far cry from *heavy* industry, which normally nurtures most other types of manufactures. The United States and the industrial giants of Europe, for example, did not attain their manufactural status by developing *light* industries; they built up impressive concentrations of *heavy* ones.

In addition to physical handicaps, two human factors strongly suggest that marked industrialization in the region will at best be a slow process. First, the wants of the large nonwhite population are few and simple, and can be supplied by the primitive handicrafts already established. Second, the heavy production of minerals within the region is based upon export. Complex commercial channels once set up at huge expense are difficult to alter.

Trade. Trade *within* each country, trade *among* the West Coast nations, and international trade to countries *outside* the region all play a lesser role than is commonly believed. Throughout the plateau, in hundreds of villages, trade is conducted by exchanging one kind of goods for another. As in the days of the Incas, trade is a matter of barter; the Indians know little of the complications or benefits of money. People who go barefoot—and tens of thousands of highland Indians do—are scarcely those to carry on complex trade. Dearth of transportation also is a retarding factor.

Trade of the five nations with one another has never been important. In fact, intracontinental trade has until recently been almost totally neglected, partly as a result of the manner of trading during the colonial period and partly because of the poor land transport facilities connecting the various countries. Commerce between Chile and Peru is growing, however; and Bolivia, Chile, and Peru recently have been purchasing an increasing proportion of their imports from Argentina. Exports to neighboring countries on the other hand continue to be very small.

So far as general international trade is concerned, especially Pan-American trade (United States–Pacific South America), there long has been too much geographical romanticism. There is a tendency to overestimate the potentialities of the West Coast market. To be sure, United States trade with Pacific South America boomed during World War II, because that region possessed many critical and strategic materials the United States had to have in order to win the war.* The United States will probably continue to dominate this trade because of financial investments there and because of proximity, difference in climate, difference in natural endowment (minerals), and difference in the stage of economic development.

After the cessation of hostilities (World War II), buying and selling in the foreign trade of the United States centered in the Western Hemisphere rather than in Europe as before the war. But in the trade with Latin America, Pacific South American nations lagged behind Mexico, Cuba, and Brazil.**

Transportation. Any semblance of a rail or highway pattern is nonexistent in Pacific South America. High elevations act as barriers to most surface transportation construction. It is estimated that to ship freight from the Pacific port of Buenaventura to Bogotá on the plateau requires the equivalent of elevating each ton three miles in the air.

Several railways—one in Colombia, one in Ecuador, three in Peru, three in Bolivia (these last originating at Chilean and Peruvian ports), and four in Chile—penetrate the Andean highlands to interior points. The Central Railway of Peru climbs to 15,665 feet in the first 106 miles from the coast. La Paz lies only 500 miles inland, but the cost of transporting a ton of coal this distance is several times as high as the normal ocean rate from England to the port terminal of the railroad, an ocean distance of about 10,000 miles. Only in Chile is there a fairly effective north-south railway.

So much of the West Coast is rugged and sparsely settled that roads are relatively unimportant; terrain of the type found here

* In order to see at a glance what the five Pacific South American countries sell to and buy from the United States, see Wallace W. Atwood, "Graphic Summary of Trade between the United States and the Other Americas," *Economic Geography*, XX (April, 1944), pp. 107–110.
** "Why U. S. Export Trade Booms: Handicaps of War-Torn Lands," *United States News* (January 31, 1947), pp. 21–22.

presents stupendous engineering difficulties. Governments can, for strategic reasons, build and maintain roads, but West Coast governments are poor in capital, equipment, and technically trained men. Though much progress has been made on the Pan American Highway (see the map on page 487), there still remain large gaps that need to be completed. Several excellent roads have been built in recent years, and some are now being constructed across the Andean barrier.

Latin America as a whole has taken naturally to aviation without the traditional lag that characterizes so many things there. Outlying territories, which were long detached from the capitals and other cities, are, as a result of aviation, able to receive the amenities of modern civilization in spite of lofty mountains, swift rivers, or dense jungles. Thus aviation has brought civilization to areas that were dead or at least sleeping and abandoned to their fate and that had vegetated without illusions or hope of a better life. Efficient airlines now cover most of Pacific South America. Planes regularly deliver mining machinery into almost inaccessible places in the mountains. In one case delivery was made in twenty-eight minutes that would have required from seven to ten days by pack animal and trail.* Although the airplane is of supreme importance in solving the transport problems of mountainous countries so far as passengers and freight of high value are concerned, it must be supplemented by the railroad and the highway in handling freight that is bulky and heavy and of low value.

Political Relations

Conquest of the Inca Empire by Pizarro was facilitated by the fact that the empire had grown too large to be well administered. Equal in size to that part of the United States from Maine to Florida and from the Appalachians to the Atlantic, and with terrain much more diverse, the vast domain was suffering from disruptive forces, which were cracking the mighty fabric.

The Spaniards in a short time overcame the

Incas and the Chibchas. They cut across Indian settlements, merely superimposing their culture on that of the aborigines. Political boundaries and all they stand for were Spanish importations. If the boundaries of the West Coast countries should disappear tomorrow, the Indian communities would pay little or no attention. In fact, there are hundreds of thousands of Indians who do not even know they are Bolivians, Ecuadoreans, or Peruvians. Schurz, for example, states:

Bolivia and Ecuador, though in varying degree, still lack a real basis of nationality. They are afterthoughts of history, conceived with little regard to the factors that make of a country a nation. They have governments and flags and other trappings of sovereignty. On occasion their populations manifest a rather bellicose patriotism. But all these do not make them nations." *

In Ecuador the political center is situated in the midst of the Andean Indian country, whereas the economic center is located on the coast. To the capital city of Quito foreign relations, economic and political, seem remote; not so to Guayaquil, however, on a navigable river easily accessible to the sea. Preston James discusses the problems presented by the dual nature of the country's core area:

"This geographical separation of the political and commercial capitals and the fact that the contacts between highland Indian communities and the lowland settlements are not intimate are a major factor in the interpretation of Ecuador's internal difficulties." **

Bolivia became a state because men from Venezuela thought it would be a check to the possible expansionist ambitions of Argentina and Peru. Bolivia's future as a nation is still unpredictable. It has been said that Bolivia is militarily and politically the strategic key to South America, for it borders on Peru, Brazil, Argentina, Paraguay, and Chile. Two of these countries are attempting to get spheres of influence in Bolivia. For her part, she needs railroads—the technical organs of regional interrelationship. Markets for the crops, livestock, and oil of the eastern Andes

---

* For a thrilling account of how an airplane carried one million pounds of mining machinery into an inaccessible jungle valley to recover a buried Inca gold mine, read "The Lost Mine of Tipuani," *The Lamp*, XX (June, 1938), pp. 24-26.

* William L. Schurz, *Latin America* (Dutton, 1942), p. 110.
** Preston E. James, *Latin America* (Odyssey, 1942), p. 125.

must be made available, and this can be done only by constructing railways. Brazil is pushing a railway toward Santa Cruz; Argentina is planning one from the south to tap the rich petroleum area; and the United States is helping to finance a highway from Cochabamba to Santa Cruz.

Moreover, Bolivia needs a window upon the ocean. It is geographically wrong for a country so near the sea to be denied unhindered access to it. Bolivia has contact with the Pacific ports by three railways—through southern Peru to Mollendo and through northernmost Chile to Antofagasta and Arica. This lack of a frontage on the sea is a potential cause of international friction, for there is a geographical principle to the effect that any rich interior exerts pressure on the seacoast in order to gain a free outlet. Bolivia has long been politically restless for this very reason.

The following conclusions regarding national unity in the three predominantly Indian countries (Bolivia, Ecuador, and Peru) seem sound:

1. None can fully achieve national unity so long as the Indians will not cooperate, a situation for which the Indians cannot be blamed.

2. True national unity is damaged also by "political and economics rivalries between Guayaquil and Quito in Ecuador; by cultural and racial opposition between Cuzco and Lima in Peru; and by a bitter political and economic struggle against La Paz by Sucre and Cochabamba in Bolivia. The chasm between the Indian and the white man is being widened and deepened by the "love of the vernacular Indian language, Quechua, which is growing up all over the altiplano." *

Chile and Colombia have achieved national unity. Despite a pattern that on the surface would seem to offer little hope for coherence, Colombia has nevertheless achieved it—"an astounding victory of man over nature and of man over man." ** Chile, too, is unified; here the ocean binds together the three distinct parts of the long, narrow country. Unity has been further strengthened by construction of the Longitudinal Railway, which serves more of a strategic than a commercial purpose for the elongated country.

* Fernando de los Rios, "South American Perplexities," *Foreign Affairs*, XX (1941-42), p. 657.
** Preston E. James, *op. cit.*, pp. 115-116.

Cross currents. Following their successful independence revolutions, the states of Pacific South America faced the problems of finding a workable system of government. The leaders believed that "by borrowing the original ideology of the French Revolution and the machinery of American republicanism, they could rationalize and implement their dream of democracy." But the stabilizing influence of a middle class was wanting. Everywhere the large Indian group remained aloof—outside the political life of their nation—while an oligarchy of landowners and lawyer-politicians grew up. Thus *democracy* as practiced has been the game of a relatively few privileged individuals.

A strong nationalism characterizes Pacific South America. The corruption of public officials, incompetence of legislators, prevailing low standard of living, and exploitation of natural resources by foreign corporations have influenced nationalism. Especially are the leaders in some countries concerned over the United States—her demand for raw materials and air bases.

There can be no doubt that during the entire administration of Franklin D. Roosevelt relations between the United States and her southern neighbors were greatly improved. In the light of past experience, however, many consider that the Good Neighbor Policy is more a matter of words than of deeds. Possibly as typical a reaction of the Latin American as can be had is that expressed by the eminent Peruvian, Luis-Alberto Sánchez:

To achieve a common inter-American front . . . the United States must demonstrate that it is concerned with the welfare of the common man in Latin America. One wonders why so many sons of the rich and of government officials in Latin America have been chosen for scholarships. One wonders why so few North Americans who really know Latin America and speak its languages have been used in the program of cultural relations. Will we of the North and the South finally come to a fundamental understanding of each other? Yes, if the Pan-American movement is not too much dominated by the privileged classes, and the common people of the Americas are allowed to unite in their mutual desires for liberty and social justice." *

* Luis-Alberto Sánchez, *Un Sud Americano en Norte América* (Ediciónes Ercilla, Santiago de Chile, 1942), pp. 344-370.

Boundary Disputes *

Underlying causes. Sometimes boundary disputes grow out of ambition and sometimes out of ignorance. But in either event they are potential breeders of war. The best way to settle such disputes, however, is not by war but by peaceful means. In this respect Latin America has set a good example before the world nations in a number of instances.** Where boundary disputes that have led to conflict have occurred in South America, however, they have taken place among the West Coast countries more frequently than among the East Coast countries. The boundaries of Pacific South America have been highly unstable. In the majority of cases they represent a classic ignorance of geography.

Another cause of boundary disputes is the lack of space mastery. Not a single West Coast country is fully occupying its territory. This condition led to Bolivia's loss of her once rubber-rich Acre territory to Brazil; it caused the Chaco War between Bolivia and Paraguay; and it was a major contributory factor to the War of the Pacific (1879–83) † and the subsequent Tacna-Arica controversy between Chile and Peru.††

Settlement of disputes. For some of their boundaries the West Coast nations have mountains. Thus, the sky-reaching Andes form the boundary between Argentina and Chile for approximately 3,000 miles, and,

* For an extensive treatment on this subject, see Gordon Ireland, *Boundaries, Possessions, and Conflicts in South America* (Harvard University Press, Cambridge, Mass., 1938). Also see Raye R. Platt, "Present Status of International Boundaries in South America," *The Geographical Review,* XIV (October, 1924), 622–638; Stephen B. Jones, *Boundary-Making* (Carnegie Endowment for International Peace, Washington, D. C., 1945); and Alexander Marchant, *Boundaries of the Latin American Republics, 1493–1943* (Government Printing Office, Washington, D. C., 1944).

** See Chapter 36 of this text, "Boundaries in International Relations."

† In this war Chile fought both Bolivia and Peru; the primary cause was the nitrate deposits which were then the property of Bolivia in the Bolivian province of Atacama. As a result of the war, the nitrate deposits became the possessions of Chile and Bolivia was cut off from the sea. Peru also ceded the province of Tarapacá to Chile.

†† In the final settlement between Chile and Peru in 1929 Chile received Arica and Peru acquired Tacna. Both areas had belonged to Peru prior to the war.

superficially, would appear to be an ideal line of demarcation. Actually, however, this appearance is not upheld by the facts, for the question is whether the main crest of the range or the water divide should be the criterion; the two are not synonymous. In 1900 the two nations were on the verge of war over the interpretation of the treaty of 1881, which defined the boundary of Patagonia as the "crest and the watershed" of the high cordillera. It happens that the divide between the Atlantic and Pacific drainages in places lies not on the crest of the Andes but east of it. As neither country knew the terrain accurately, war was avoided only by resorting to an article in a former treaty, which stipulated that in case of a boundary dispute, the issue would be submitted to a friendly power. Both nations agreed to abide by the result of field investigations, and England's King Edward VII was asked to serve as arbitrator. The disputed zone was surveyed, the work being in charge of Colonel Sir Thomas H. Holdich, an officer of long experience on the borders of India and Persia. He applied the rule of "common sense," and the award proved satisfactory to both countries.*

Threat of war between Colombia and Peru in September, 1932, was engendered when the town of Leticia was seized and claimed by Peruvians. Leticia was included in territory that Peru had ceded to Colombia by a treaty ratified in 1928. After prolonged negotiations, the dispute was referred to the League of Nations by Colombia. Finally, on May 24, 1934, the two disputants signed a protocol wherein Peru admitted that the boundary could not be changed except by mutual consent; both governments renounced the use of force to settle disputes between them. Ratification of the protocol was achieved in September, 1935.

The boundary between Ecuador and Peru has been the subject of disputes and treaties for more than a century. Boundary treaties were signed in 1860, 1887, and 1890. The huge unmapped frontier region under dispute, however, proved difficult to handle. It had originally been subject to Spanish colonial law, cloaked in language hard to inter-

* For interesting geographical material on this dispute, read Bailey Willis, *A Yanqui in Patagonia* (Stanford, Stanford University Press, 1947), pp. 86–89.

pret. As increased explorations were carried forward and valuable natural resources became known in that region east of the Andes, increasing hostility arose between Ecuador and Peru. Finally armed conflict broke out in July and August of 1941. A settlement was made at the Rio de Janeiro Conference of Foreign Ministers in January, 1942. As a consequence, the area of Ecuador was reduced to about 100,000 square miles.

Social Problems

The social aspects of life in the West Coast countries of South America are significant and interesting.* One of the fundamental problems is that of land tenure. Sixteenth-century Spaniards, in colonizing the region, transplanted the semifeudal agrarian system that prevailed at that time in southern Europe. The Spaniards appropriated land and people alike in establishing their estates. This *encomienda* system enabled the landowners to exploit the labor of Indians. Unlike the application of the system in Europe, however, the Indians did not cluster around the mansion of the landowner but lived in their own villages.

As with the Chinese, Japanese, and Javanese, the Andean Indians have a strong attachment for the land. Most of the families have lived on their present holdings from time immemorial, and they will not leave for any reason. Even if, as often happens, the land is absorbed by an adjoining hacienda and passes repeatedly from one owner to another, the Indians remain—being transferred with the soil. Today these people comprise a great landless peasantry. Having suffered so long at the hands of white men, their land hunger makes them a factor with which to be reckoned. Over the Andes hangs the specter of agrarian revolution.

The biggest weakness in the population is the absence of a middle class (except in Chile). Reference has already been made to the thin veneer of whites and the great mass of In-

* Those particularly interested in this phase of the subject are urged to do additional reading: Charles C. Griffin, Editor, *Concerning Latin American Culture* (New York, Columbia University Press, 1940); William L. Schurz, *op. cit.*, Part VII, pp. 321–365; George Soule, David Efron, and Norman T. Ness, *Latin America in the Future World* (Farrar & Rinehart, 1945).

dians, mestizos, and Negroes. Until more Europeans emigrate to the West Coast or until a marked change occurs in the social and economic situation, there can be no middle class in the real sense of the word. Immigration other than to Chile is unlikely, for the European cannot, and therefore will not, try to compete with the Indian and the Negro or even the mestizo, all of whom have a lower standard of living. Moreover, he cannot adapt himself well to the high altitude of the altiplano.

Finally, there is no real cultural amalgamation between the Indian and the white, a situation attributable to the small number of Spanish settlers, the geographical barriers that lend to regional isolation, and racial and class antagonisms that arose from the exploitation of the Indian. Actually the Indian is an obstacle to the development of a homogeneous culture. As the Indian has found himself becoming increasingly exploited, his social solidarity has been concentrated in an effort of defense; and despite his loss of leaders, he has maintained his basic loyalty to the blood-group—the *ayllu* (clan). In Peru, he is emerging with sufficient vitality to give impetus to the recent movements for social reform.

Pacific Islands

The strategic Galápagos of Ecuador are located in the Pacific, 620 miles west of the mother republic and approximately 820 miles southwest of Panama. They were annexed to Ecuador in 1832. The sixteen islands and the numerous rocky islets have an estimated area of 2,868 square miles, limited chiefly to two islands—Albemarle (or Isabel) and Chatham (or San Cristóbal). The Galápagos have a number of excellent anchorages, which are important in the outlying defense of the Panama Canal. The islands were occupied by American forces during World War II.

Chile has a number of islands situated from 400 to 2,000 miles from her coast. The largest are the Juan Fernández group. Easter Island, 2,000 miles west of Chile, was sighted on Easter Sunday, 1722, and has the remains of a very interesting civilization. The Sala-y-Gomez group of islands in the Pacific, less than 2,000 miles west of Chile, also fly the Chilean flag.

Conclusion

Pacific South America has been treated in a single chapter. This would appear to imply regional unity. As has been pointed out, however, much diversity exists among the lands and peoples, and no simple generalizations can be used to describe the ways of living followed by the peoples of the five countries. Each has an independent, vigorous nationalism with increasing awareness of its own individuality and is quite disinclined to lose sight of its cultural and historical autonomy. Pacific South America is more complex than appears at first glance. The uniformity of a common history, a related language, and a spiritual tradition tend to obscure what has evolved during more than a century of independence, throughout which national lines have deepened, a national consciousness has been intensified, and a cultural maturity has been attained.

A new Latin America is in the making—a Latin America that refuses to be content as a feeder of raw materials for the great industrial nations of North America and Europe; a Latin America that no longer is willing to submit to mass unemployment and misery by being cut off from markets and needed goods every time there is a world war or a great depression. Rightly or wrongly, Latin America believes it can solve such problems by industrialization, and hence manufacturing facilities are being increased rapidly.

Finally, it has been noted that the principal problem in the West Coast countries is the lack of proper relations between man and the land and between men (the whites and the Indians). In each country vast areas abounding in potential wealth remain unproductive, while at the same time men die of want in other areas. In recent years, however, air transportation has done much to overcome the handicaps of vast distances and lofty elevations.

PART SEVEN

Some Special Aspects of Political Geography

In the study of political geography, or indeed in the study of any other phase of geography, two methods of approach are always possible. These are (a) the regional or areal, and (b) the topical or systematic. So far in this book, the treatment has been exclusively regional; in the five chapters of Part Seven that follow, some special aspects of world political geography, which do not readily lend themselves to the regional approach, are presented topically.

The first of these involves a consideration of the geopolitical implications of the oceans. These and the dozen or so major seas are of markedly different sizes and shapes, and they are fairly well demarked from one another. Despite these factors distinguishing them, they are connected to form one system, sometimes called the World Ocean, which comprises more than 70 per cent of the earth's surface. Throughout his early history man struggled to explore and develop skill in navigating the ocean expanses. During modern times the ocean has become a great highway of travel and trade, and under Anglo-Saxon dominance "Freedom of the Seas" has been a generally accepted world policy.

The margins of the oceans have had enormous political and military significance, and hence many states that possess coastlines have gradually pushed their control farther and farther out from the lands. Recently the United States has set a startling precedent by annexing all water areas out to the edge of the continental shelf. This suggests that the nations are becoming fully aware of the ocean's resources, as, for instance, the petroleum underneath the tidelands, the mag-

nesium and other minerals in sea water, the great abundance of plant and animal life that grows in the oceans, and the power resources in the waves, tides, and marine temperature gradients. From all evidence control of the oceans will also assume a crucial geopolitical importance in any air-naval warfare of the future.

The ocean boundaries of all maritime states are, therefore, presently in a state of flux, a condition that has long been characteristic of land boundaries. This state has been so characteristic, indeed, that the study of boundaries has always constituted an important aspect of political geography. In the past it has been the custom to distinguish between natural and artificial boundaries. The former included mountains, rivers, lakes, sea coasts, swamps, and even deserts and dense forests. The latter consisted of lines wandering aimlessly across a plain, or transecting a mountain chain or river valley, or dividing an archipelago or an area of hill country, or following the straight course of a parallel or meridian. Such a distinction is misleading, however, because all boundaries are artificial, that is, drawn by the hand of man.

Perhaps the only really satisfactory boundaries are those drawn so as to separate unlike ethnic groups under a "self-determination of peoples" principle. This type of division is closely approximated by the boundaries of certain states, but most of them depart from it widely, with the result that minority problems and irredentism are rife. Self-determination was adopted as a formula for state-making at the Versailles Conference but was largely discarded as unworkable. Were it applied rigidly, it would result in an intricate "Balkanization" of the political map of the world. This in turn would compel either political federalization or confederation on a large scale or widespread extranational economic unions.

Even if ideal boundaries could be achieved, they probably would not long remain satisfactory. Population increase, decrease, or stasis would eventually create land hungers and cross-boundary pressures. Population is both the substance and, in part, the strength of a nation. Trends in population, therefore, take on considerable significance. Indeed, population problems constitute one of the most pressing and controversial topics in political geography.

For example, the French government has been much concerned over the declining population rate in France. It has been equally concerned over the noticeable increase of human numbers in neighboring Germany and Italy. These latter countries have often cited their growing populations as arguments for the acquisition of colonies; but a study of colonialism suggests that, except for one debatable example,* emigration has never provided any substantial outlet for overpopulation. The present-day rate of population growth in Soviet Russia is occasioning considerable alarm in the capitals of western Europe.

Population growth and pressure are also used as arguments for political expansion and conquest of the territory of neighbor states. Nazi Germany, Fascist Italy, and Shintoist Japan were loud and voluble in their demands for territorial expansion during the decade just prior to World War II. Especially insistent was the German demand for *Lebensraum,* or life space. In this demand, and in the subsequent diplomatic reign of terror,

* Emigration has markedly reduced population in Ireland, but in the present writer's opinion only because of the thrust of severe potato famines.

and, finally, during the ensuing years of war, many of the Nazi arguments, programs, and strategies were drawn from the work of the German political geographers.

Actually, a good part of the war strategy developed by the German geopoliticians was based upon the politico-geographic theories of a Scot, Halford J. Mackinder. As finally evolved, German strategy was reduced to the following steps:

(a) An alliance, or Axis, with Italy was formed in order to sever Europe in two and render Soviet Russia inaccessible to the Western Powers.

(b) Striking westward, Germany overran France and drove Britain's navy away from continental Europe by land-based air power.

(c) An alliance was formed with Japan for the purpose of encircling the vast continent of Asia and slowly strangling Soviet Russia and China.

(d) After Asia should have been conquered, the Axis planned to transform it into a world fortress, from which a naval and aerial onslaught was to be launched upon the Americas and the outlying portions of the British Commonwealth and Empire.

The plan was somewhat nebulous but it nearly enabled an otherwise hopeless idea to succeed. It is possible that it might have succeeded had the German leaders not digressed from sound geopolitical principles and attacked Soviet Russia *before* North Africa and the Near East had been cleared of enemy forces. It might also have succeeded had Japan been a first-rate rather than a second-rate industrial nation.

Political geography is thus not only the basis of military strategy; it is also the key to the understanding of international relations and future world politics. In peace or in war no nation can ignore political geography. The time has come when the people of the United States can ill afford to be geographically illiterate.

CHAPTER 35 | Political Geography of the Oceans

IN THE preceding chapters the approach to political geography has been through the political area. The various political areas and regions of the world have been considered from the viewpoint of location, size, shape, relief, climate, natural resources, and the man-space-resources relationships that exist. In addition, the history, language, religion, race, nationality, population, and the political and social organizations of the several nations and areas have been detailed. The result has been the establishment of the relationship of the geographic factors to the political ideas, plans, and actions of the peoples living in such politico-geographical regions. Although the ocean is not a typical political area, it is a definite geographical entity. As such, it is a vital component of political geography, since the geographical factors of the sea have a bearing upon the geopolitical elements outlined in previous discussions.

The Science of Oceanography

The science of oceanography has been defined as the study of the world below the surface of the sea. However, according to present-day concepts, it is concerned with the characteristics of the water of the sea, the bottom and margins of the world ocean, the inhabitants of the latter, the contact zone between sea and atmosphere, and the physical, chemical, and biological relationships of the oceanic pattern. It does not include the treatment of political considerations arising from the influences of oceanography, although an appreciation of the physical nature of the influences is important in the establish-

ment of an understanding of the political considerations.

In terms of the modern understanding of the word, oceanography is a new science. Its birth may well date from December 21, 1872, when the "Challenger" put to sea from Plymouth, England, on an oceanographic investigating mission. In the last thirty years of the nineteenth century more scientific information was gathered on the world ocean than in all previous time. Since this era of accelerating investigation many scientific organizations and investigating groups have been formed for the purpose of furthering the study.

The advancement in the science of oceanography has exercised a direct effect upon the ocean fishing industry, nautical navigation, harbor construction, weather forecasting, radio and cable communications, and the knowledge of raw material availability in the world ocean. All these aspects have an instrumental effect on national policies, political actions, and world power. In short, an accumulation and utilization of the scientific facts of oceanography are of prime interest to any nation recognizing the importance of the world ocean in the field of geopolitics and political geography.

Unlike Mars and the Moon, the earth possesses a great amount of water. Its major relief features are the continents and the ocean basins, with the oceans overlapping the margins of the continents to the extent of some ten millions of square miles—the continental shelves, which comprise an area larger than North America. In all, about seventy per cent of the surface of the earth is ocean and only thirty per cent land. The relationship of land masses to the world ocean is clearly illustrated in the map on page 510. It is noted that the mean depth of the oceans is five times the mean height of the continents; and, on the average, the land surface stands about three miles above the bottom of the deep sea.

the character of the high seas above the continental shelf or enlarge the present limits of the territorial waters of the nation. Rather the proclamations of the President illustrated the political importance of the geography of the sea.

It is evident that an increase in the knowledge of oceanography, which is in many re-

Comparative Dimensions of Sea, Land, and Earth

	Area (square miles)	Average depth (feet)	Average depth outside the continental terraces (feet)	Average elevation above sea level
Whole earth	196,700,000	——	——	——
Whole ocean	141,000,000	12,000	12,500	——
Pacific	64,000,000	14,000	14,000	——
Atlantic	32,000,000	12,900	13,100	——
Arctic	5,500,000	4,100	10,000	——
Indian	28,500,000	12,900	13,100	——
Antarctic	5,700,000	——	——	——
Seas	5,300,000	——	——	——
Asia	16,500,000	——	——	3,150
Europe	3,800,000	——	——	1,115
Africa	11,500,000	——	——	2,460
North America	9,400,000	——	——	2,360
South America	7,000,000	——	——	1,935
Australasia	4,200,000	——	——	1,115
Antarctica, including ice-cap	5,400,000	——	——	6,000
All land	57,800,000	——	——	2,500

Such physical characteristics of the sea are not in themselves of importance in a study of the political geography of the sea. Their importance is in the fact that the shape, depth, margins, temperature, winds, currents, composition, tides, animal life, and industries pertaining to the sea have a profound influence upon the environment of man and in turn upon his thoughts and actions.

Illustrating this influence, the President of the United States on September 28, 1945, issued two proclamations "asserting the jurisdiction of the United States over the natural resources of the continental shelf under the high seas contiguous to the coasts of the United States and its territories, and providing for the establishment of conservation zones for the protection of fisheries in certain areas of the high seas contiguous to the United States." Geologists claim that parts of the continental shelf have important oil deposits. Ore mines extend under the sea bordering a number of countries, among them Chile and England. The action of President Harry S. Truman did not change

spects a geographical science, not only aids man in the formulation of economic and political policies but also serves to explain the underlying causes for certain existing environmental and political conditions. Further consideration will be devoted to direct influences of geographical factors of the sea upon man's actions and national policies.

History and the Sea

Ancient and medieval history. Throughout recorded history the ocean has been important to man in relation to his overall environment. In the poems of Homer there are various references to the sea, which when pieced together indicate that the then-known world consisted of the countries bordering the Mediterranean, the ancient world sea. The Babylonians developed the concept that a bounding ocean encompassed the habitable world and that the enclosing dawn in turn encircled the ocean. This picture of the world was accepted by the Greeks until approximately 750 B.C., when the poems of Hesiod began to describe mythical lands out in the bordering ocean where resided the peoples of Greek mythology.

Herodotus (about 450 B.C.) seems to have been the first student of oceanography. His writings contain references to the Atlantic Ocean, the tides of the ocean, the Indian Ocean, and the idea that Africa was surrounded by water. Plato referred to the Isle of Atlantis beyond the Pillars of Hercules (Strait of Gibraltar). Aristotle spoke of the earth as a sphere, but his idea of the oceans was vague and erroneous. With Pytheas' writings (325 B.C) the Atlantic Ocean came into accepted being, and the relationship of the moon and tides was noted.

At the beginning of the Christian era, Strabo, a Greek writer, wrote his famous book entitled *Geography*. Strabo took for granted that the earth was spherical and suggested the possibility of existing continents in the outer world ocean. Shortly thereafter the Roman, Pliny, in his *Historiae Naturalis,* acknowledged that people might be living across the world ocean and definitely associated the action of tides with that of the moon. We may conclude our survey of the ancients' knowledge regarding the sea with the *Guide to Geography* of Ptolemy, written in the second century. To Ptolemy is traced the popularization of parallels, meridians, latitude, longitude, and modern navigation.

Ptolemy's writings were a breaking point in the development of knowledge of the sea, since nothing more of scientific or other importance was discovered throughout the Dark Ages. In the eleventh century new inventions and discoveries came along with the introduction of the mariner's compass and attempts at longer voyages into the world ocean. In the eleventh century the nomadic Vikings first reached the continent of America. By the middle of the thirteenth century direct communication had been established between Latin Europe and the Far East. During the fourteenth century the islands of the Atlantic off Europe became known, and late in the fifteenth century the voyages of Columbus took place. The news of his crossing the Atlantic Ocean created an era of unprecedented exploration of the world ocean. Magellan started on his circumnavigation of the globe in 1519, and the results of that exploit revealed the true extent of the earth and sea and established the modern concept of world geography.* By these voyages, mankind swept the oceans free of the imaginary terrors believed to exist therein. The discoveries coincided with the Renaissance in Europe, and the subsequent development of knowledge of the sea is well known.

World's great navies. The term sea power, in its proper interpretation, must be considered to include not only the navies of nations but their total strength and interests in the seas, overseas bases and possessions, seaborne trade, and the extent of coastline. With this expanded meaning of the term the history of sea power actually includes an account of the great maritime nations and of their rivalry for trade, possessions, and power. Among the Western nations this rivalry has long been of dominant importance and hence exerts a strong influence upon national political policy.

The first naval power was founded by the Aegean islanders approximately in 1500 B.C. Their successors were the Phoenicians, whose trade area and strength extended throughout the Mediterranean and on to England. The naval battle of Salamis fought in 480 B.C. in the Graeco-Persian War was one of the decisive engagements of history and ended the Persian threat to European soil. This naval victory saved Greek civilization, which reached its zenith in the following eighty years.

More than two centuries elapsed between the Greek victory over the Persians at Salamis and the Punic Wars, a second naval struggle for Mediterranean control. The Carthaginians had replaced the Phoenicians in dominance of Mediterranean trade. With the rise of the Roman Empire it was inevitable that a naval conflict with Carthage would occur. In two naval engagements, Mylae in 260 B.C. and Ecnomus in 256 B.C., both in the First Punic War, the Romans gained victories that eventually gave them control over the western Mediterranean and opened the Roman road to Africa. Their victory over Egypt at Actium in 31 B.C. rendered the Mediterranean *Mare Nostrum* for the Roman Empire for a number of centuries. After Constantine had shifted the capital from Rome to Constantinople in 330 A.D., an Eastern Roman Empire

* For an illuminating description of the sea of ancient and medieval times, see H. A. Marmer, *The Sea* (Appleton, 1930), pp. 1–16.

naval power developed. The western Mediterranean naval supremacy then declined to the point that little defense was offered against the Teutonic and Gallic invaders of the fifth century. The major sea rivalry of the Mediterranean in Medieval times was between the Turks and the city-state of Venice.*

After the opening of the larger world ocean, naval power shifted to Portugal and Spain. In 1588 the English defeated the Spanish Armada and began a long rule of the seas. In the seventeenth century three wars involving naval conflicts occurred between the Dutch and the English. The might of the British fleet increased, augmented by the defeat of the French power and Napoleon, a victory that raised Nelson to British naval immortality. The battle of Trafalgar with the French in 1805 is one of the famous naval engagements of history. The War for American Independence and the War of 1812 provided the beginning of American sea power, which was gradually but not consistently augmented through the years until World War I. In the period between the two world wars Great Britain and the United States were recognized as the world's principal naval powers, with Japan in third place and France and Italy ranking lowest among the great sea powers.

World War II found the naval power of the Allies seriously threatened by German submarines and Japanese surface fleets in the earlier years of the conflict. By the end of the war, however, Allied naval might was overwhelming, and the center of world naval power shifted to the United States.

In a review of the development of sea power in world history the conditions and principles operating to either produce or retard the development of naval might (including commercial power) appear to be classified as: physical character of the nation, that is, such factors as climate, production, and naval facilities; geographical position; extent of world territory; number of population; inherent character of the people; and character of the state and institutions thereof.**

Strategic bases and passageways. The utilization of the world ocean for commerce and for sea power has created throughout recorded history a struggle for possession or control of certain strategic bases and passageways of the land pattern. The national policy of many governments has been to acquire and protect such points. A few examples from history adequately illustrate this influence of the ocean upon state power and policy.

In ancient history a conflict existed for control of the islands of the eastern Mediterranean, and during the first Punic War the Romans and Carthaginians fought bitterly for the control of Sicily and the adjacent straits. The selection of Constantinople in 330 A.D. for the seat of power of what became the Eastern Roman Empire was based partially upon the strategic location of the site of the Dardanelles.

The British Isles are so strategically located as to provide control not only of the English Channel but also of the entire naval approaches to the Atlantic shore of the European continent. In turn, the lifeline established by the British Empire to the Far East via the Strait of Gibraltar and the Suez Canal represented the vital national need for control of strategic bases and passageways in times of peace as well as war. The islands of Ceylon, Oahu, Hong Kong, Singapore, Malta, Truk, Guam, and the Philippines are further examples of the importance of strategic bases for the exercise of control of the seas, and it has been the national policy of naval powers to exert all possible efforts to retain ownership or control of such points.

The Panama Canal, probably the most important strategic passageway in the world, is considered a primary zone of defense by the United States. The Air Age has stressed countless additional points of national interest, such as Bermuda, Iceland, Ascension, Okinawa, Iwo Jima, and the Azores. The method of operating and controlling such strategic bases and passageways in the future is one of the most perplexing problems arising from World War II.

Sea power and political action. A significant point in reviewing the relationship of the sea to ancient and medieval history is the indication of profound influence that the mysterious sea has exerted upon the great thinkers of the time, upon actions of the state, and upon national character. Throughout the changing location and development of sea

---

* See W. O. Stevens and Allan Westcott, *A History of Sea Power* (Doubleday, Doran, 1942), pp. 1–68.

** A. T. Mahan, *The Influence of Sea Power upon History, 1660–1783* (Little, Brown, 1923), pp. 28–89.

power, it is significant that international trade, national prestige, and world power accompanied the possession of naval power. The presence of sea power has been a definite tool of national policy and action. In the postwar world sea power continues to be a strong political factor, although new weapons of war are altering traditional concepts of naval techniques.

World Ocean and Man's Environment

It has been stated that six principal geopolitical elements form the basis for the world power of a given state, namely, location, size and shape, climate, natural resources and industrial capacity, population and manpower, and social and political organization.[*] As is explained below, some of these elements derive a portion of their greatness from the sea and impart to the world ocean an important role in political geography.

Location. A significant aspect of a country's physical location is sea frontage. The sea has long played an important role politically in the determination of national boundaries.[**] The desirable land of the several continents is parceled out and claimed as the property of the various nations, but the sea is the common property of all—the open route to every land on its shores. History indicates that hardly any spirited people rest content with a national domain that does not touch upon the ocean or have ready access to it by means of coastal indentations. Only five countries in present-day Europe and two in the New World fail to possess a maritime border.

Nations covet and almost universally demand a border on the world ocean. The sea is the world's one common highway, and the state that it touches cannot be easily isolated. Every land on its shores is joined to every other by routes open to all except in times of war and sea blockade. Ships may freely come and go, and the commerce and culture of one nation are open to all nations. "The liberalizing influence of the sea" is one of the chief means by which civilization has spread itself over the world. Europe's rise in culture was

aided by its remarkably indented coastline. Aside from Russia there is no site in Europe more than 500 miles from the sea. The backwardness of the people of Africa is due partly to unfavorable climates and an unfortunate coastline. In an evaluation of the geographical locations that are advantageous to nations, frontage on the sea receives first consideration, because the sea expedites a lively exchange of goods and ideas.

Climate. Of all the geographical influences to which man is subjected, climate seems to be the most potent. Fortunately the earth as a whole has a limited range of temperatures created by (1) the almost perfect circle of the earth's orbit, (2) the rapid succession of night and day, (3) the atmospheric layer, and (4) the three-to-one dominance of water over land, coupled with the high specific heat of water and the existence of ocean currents. The influence of climate (a geographical factor) upon health, human wants, distribution of population, human progress, and, eventually, political beliefs and national concepts requires little, if any, elaboration. It is the role of the oceans in influencing world climate, therefore, that assumes considerable importance from the viewpoint of political geography.

The movement of the contents of the world ocean consists of waves, tides, tidal currents, and ocean currents. With respect to the ocean surface currents there exists in the three major oceans (Atlantic, Pacific, and Indian) a general flow of water from east to west in the equatorial regions. Between the north and south equatorial currents there is a narrow, and weaker, counter equatorial current flowing toward the east. The general scheme of the world's ocean currents is pictured in the map on page 510. These currents are caused by varying temperatures of ocean water, difference in salinity, atmospheric pressure variances, and prevailing winds.[*]

The Gulf Stream, with its modifying effect upon the climate of northwestern Europe, is perhaps the most famous ocean current. Its counterpart in the Pacific Ocean is the Japanese Current. The Peru, or Humboldt, Current brings about climatic conditions along western South America quite similar to those

[*] R. H. Fifield and G. E. Pearcy, *Geopolitics in Principle and Practice* (Ginn, 1944), p. 25.

[**] For a treatment of the sea as a national boundary, see Chapter 36 and various items in the bibliography supplementing that chapter on pages 600–01.

[*] For a scientific discussion of ocean currents, consult H. U. Sverdrup, *Oceanography for Meteorologists* (Prentice-Hall, 1942), pp. 155–222.

conditions brought about by the Benguela Current in Southwest Africa. Both climatic regions are caused by cold ocean currents flowing equatorward. Over these currents blow moisture-laden winds that form fog and upon striking warm land develop into clouds and subsequently drift toward the interior of the continent.

The circulation of the ocean waters with

oceans. The ocean lanes are valuable assets; consequently, the power to control the important trade routes is a political requisite of importance. The map on the facing page illustrates the world's major peacetime trade routes, most of which operated during World War II. It is significant to note that prior to World War II the annual dollar value of all ocean trade amounted to approximately $13,-

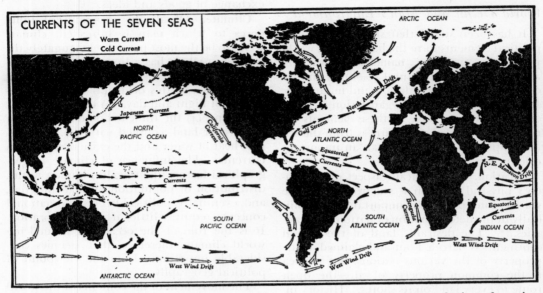

the resulting climatological effects upon both continental and maritime areas is a technical and involved study. It is sufficient to note that, in general, the circulation of the surface waters of the world ocean (and the accompanying prevailing winds) will modify the otherwise existing climate of the coasts and immediate hinterland. As an example, the current flowing along one coast may be abnormally warm and that along another coast abnormally cold. The influence primarily depends upon the character of the currents, which in turn is controlled by the prevailing winds and the processes of heating and cooling to which the waters of these currents are subjected.

Commerce and industry. The ocean is the world's most efficient medium of transportation and this factor is one of the reasons why nations desire frontage on the sea. The utilization of natural resources is markedly affected by the opportunities for trade. The full fruition of possessing valuable resources may come only with transport across the

000,000,000 in matériel, exclusive of services and equipment involved.

Foreign trade is an industry considered of such national importance as to be closely guided along lines of national policy by all governments regardless of political or social doctrine. The importance of foreign trade transported over the world's seaways to a nation's economy is such that a major power considers it prime national policy to protect its ocean trade interests often to the extent of entering into a state of war.

Population distribution. A study of the population distribution presented in Chapter 37 indicates that population density is largely dependent upon three principal factors, namely, climate, soil, and industry, or trade. Industrial areas are in part dependent upon natural avenues, such as oceans, inland seas, harbors, and navigable rivers, which provide access to world trade. According to the most recent prewar statistics there are forty-four cities of the world with populations of one million or more; twenty-five of these cities have frontage on the ocean; fourteen more are located on navigable outlets to the sea. In the future, however, although the world's areas of dense population will probably undergo but little change, the improvement in communications and transportation will tend to offset the geographical influence of the sea upon concentration of population in large metropolitan areas.

Food and health. In Medieval days it was the fashion among pseudophilosophers to speak of the sea as the *Primum mobile,* the

fected with disease-carrying insects and micro-organisms.

Each year man draws an enormous amount of human food from the sea. The Gulf of Maine yields annually approximately 500,-000,000 pounds of edible food; the Atlantic Seaboard catch amounts to 1,350,000,000 pounds yearly. The annual world yield of aquatic products (other than minerals) is more than 27,000,000,000 pounds in weight and $1,000,000,000 in value.

The world's primary fisheries, both shore

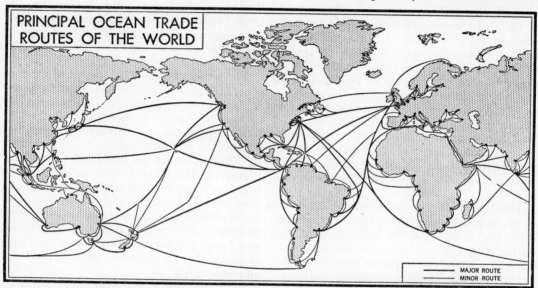

PRINCIPAL OCEAN TRADE ROUTES OF THE WORLD

MAJOR ROUTE
MINOR ROUTE

source of all human health, and, in a measure, of prosperity. Some of the guesses of the Middle Ages about the uses of the vast water surface of the globe have become the facts of our day; and as science extends her horizons, it becomes more evident that what we have of health on the land we owe to the "healing of the sea." The predominant influence of the sea upon the climate of the world has been noted previously. It is common practice for man to seek recreation and rest on the ocean beaches in the temperate and subtropical areas of the world. The refreshing winds and the salinity of the sea water impart an invigorating influence upon the health and well-being of vacationers and residents alike. Conversely, many low and swampy areas adjacent to the sea exert a detrimental effect upon the health of the local population, especially in those areas of heavy vegetation and hot and humid climate that are normally in-

estuarine and high sea, are found in four principal groupings, namely, the Asiatic Coast, the Atlantic Coast of Europe, and the East and West Coasts of North America. Major secondary commercial fisheries are located in the Antarctic Ocean, the East Indies, the Arctic Ocean, and in many other smaller areas along the world's coastlines. Local fisheries involving mostly primitive equipment without modern processing exist almost continuously along the ocean coastline and in the various lakes and seas of the world. The nations bordering the world's primary fishing banks consider the fishing industry as one of primary national importance, from the standpoint of both home consumption and foreign trade.

The food, general health, and mental welfare of any oceanic state population are derived in portion from the ocean. Hence, its physical geography must exercise an influence upon the national thoughts and actions of the state, thus further demonstrating the place of the world ocean in the concept of political geography.

National outlook. In so far as our discussion is concerned, the national outlook of the separate nations of the world may be classified into two categories—continental and maritime. The purely continental power or state is one having no physical contact with the sea and hence no prime interest in the use of the sea. Such would be a state with no seacoast, no merchant marine, and dependent in the main upon agricultural and limited manufacturing industries for national livelihood. A maritime state is one whose principal interests lie in and about the sea. Such would be a state occupying an island or peninsula with a long coastline of usable harbors, and possessing a merchant marine, and usually a naval force. Bolivia and Switzerland are examples of strictly continental powers, whereas England and Japan represent the maritime type. Most of the countries, however, vary in degree between these extremes.

The very existence of a maritime power seems to rest in part upon the effect of the ocean on the spirit of the individuals of the state. Ratzel in his famous writings on the sea stated that "the limitless horizons mold the great characteristics of boldness, perseverance, and foresightedness into the spirit and personality of maritime peoples." * He went further to expound the principle that the sea broadens the vista not only of the merchant but also of the statesman. Ratzel's teachings to the effect that the ocean is the most dynamic geopolitical force became one of the foundations of the Haushofer school of thought in Nazi Germany. The German government recognized the importance of expanding its control over the seas of the world, and despite the fact that the nation was not a maritime state, a coordinated plan of education was conducted for the purpose of following complete German land power in Europe with control over the seas of the world.

It has been advanced that the sea brings a unity of purpose and spirit into maritime

* Andreas Dorpalen, *The World of General Haushofer*, Selections from Friedrich Ratzel (Farrar and Rinehart, 1942), p. 114.

thought and actions. This same school of thought implies that the standards of living and welfare for maritime peoples tend to equalize and rest at a higher level than for continental powers. The existence of the sea does exert an influence in this respect but principally because of the locational advantages of the maritime powers rather than the effect of the ocean upon the thoughts and spirit of men. Maritime powers have developed and maintained many of the world's most vigorous and lasting cultures. The culture of ancient Egypt gradually passed to the lands beyond the Mediterranean whose people understood the medium of exchange of worldly goods across the then-existing world sea.

The national outlook of states and the concept of sea power have changed over the years. In ancient times it was not uncommon for nations to exert a tremendous influence in lands beyond the sea without first becoming established as a land power. The power of the Phoenicians of ancient history and later that of the Hanseatic League were primarily based on sea power. It gradually became evident that in order for a nation to exert influence on the sea it must of necessity first become a land power. The United States and Great Britain are examples of the latter category—"great powers" on land and sea and now in the air.

Both Mackinder and Haushofer wrote at length concerning the "call of the sea" and its relation to political geography. It is sufficient to note that throughout modern history the drive to the sea or across the seas has been an uppermost consideration for such nations as England, Germany, Russia, Japan, and even for the United States. In fact, Mackinder advances the theory of relating the basic causes of all world conflicts to struggles of "oceanism versus continentalism."

The advent of intercontinental air transportation on a large scale has been represented as decreasing the importance of the oceans in future world events. This advanced mode of traffic will serve primarily to speed up the tempo of international action to such an extent that no nation can safely consider the ocean as a protective barrier, either in war or peace, in favor of the national political principle of isolationism.

The Polar Mediterranean

Looking into the air age of the future, practical geopolitics may be partly concerned with the implications of the distribution of land and water in and around the Arctic Mediterranean (see the map on this page). Vilhjalmur Stefansson, famous polar explorer, and George T. Renner, professor of geography at Columbia University, have written on this subject. Actually the Arctic "Ocean" is an inland sea of the Atlantic Ocean. The Arctic was called an ocean because it appeared so large on a Mercator projection. The land mass of the Northern Hemisphere is essentially grouped around the North Pole.

The large extent of the northern continents and the small area of the Polar Mediterranean acquire considerable importance in the light of an air age. A great circle route

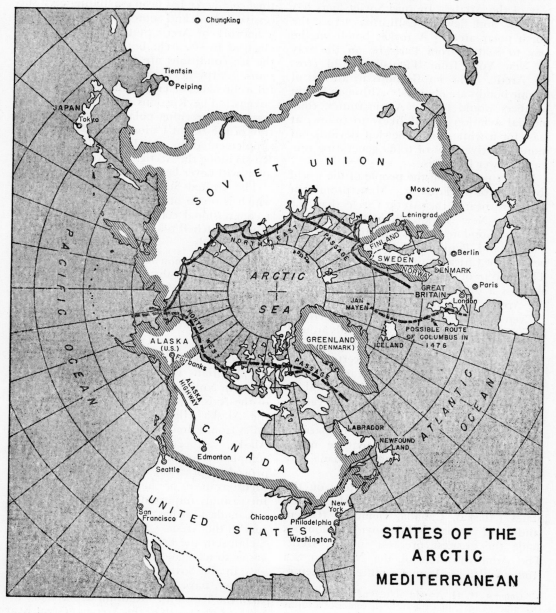

STATES OF THE ARCTIC MEDITERRANEAN

is the shortest distance between any two points on the globe. The great circle air routes from America to Eurasia pass over the Arctic. The shortest route from the United States to the Far East is north—not west across the Pacific. The Arctic Sea lies on the shortest route between the United States and China. The shortest distance from Chicago to Chungking, from Panama to Singapore, or from the North Cape to Des Moines is by way of the Arctic. In 1937 Soviet fliers left Moscow and flew to California across the north polar area.* A rocket bomb on the way to Seattle from Paris or on the way to New York from Tientsin would cross the Arctic. The implications in an age of atomic bombs are obvious. Although future bombers would fly the Arctic routes, commercial aviation is still likely to follow, at least for a while, the somewhat devious but more lucrative lines of traffic-generating centers of lower latitudes.

Ninety per cent of the people of the world live north of the Equator. Many prominent cities are nearer the Arctic Circle than the Equator—New York, Philadelphia, Washington, London, Paris, Berlin, Moscow, Tokyo, and Peiping. Actually, Moscow is nearer to Chicago than is Buenos Aires. The concept of the Western Hemisphere thus assumes a different complexion in view of the Arctic Mediterranean.

Events in recent history have revealed the importance of petroleum. The lands around the basin of the Polar Mediterranean may be rich in petroleum, especially certain areas in the Soviet Union, Canada, and Alaska. The Russians have already drilled for oil on the northern shores of Asia and in the valleys of the great rivers of Siberia. The American navy has an oil reserve at Point Barrow, Alaska, consisting of 30,000 square miles. The Mackenzie River valley of Canada may have rich oil reserves.

The polar states having territory on the Arctic Sea are the Soviet Union, the United States (Alaska), Canada, Denmark (Greenland), and Norway. The Soviet Union has made the greatest progress in the Arctic. The Administration of the Northern Sea Route, which was formerly centered at Lenin-

* General H. H. Arnold stated in an address on December 6, 1945, that the strategic center of a future war would be the area of the North Pole.

grad, has been moved to Moscow. This Administration controls an area of land equal to perhaps two thirds of continental United States. Vilhjalmur Stefansson has described the activities of the Administration as equivalent to a combination of the work of the Department of Interior in the United States and the Hudson Bay Company in Canada. The Russians have developed the Northeast Passage north of Eurasia through which maritime commerce has been expanding each successive August and September. Establishing a network of Arctic Stations the Soviet has engaged in research; both the weather and the ice conditions are forecast by the Russians. Airplanes for ice scouting and powerful icebreakers of 11,000 tons are used by the Soviets. The Russians are also engaged in research concerning polar flying. The location of the Soviet Union in the Heartland is supplemented by the location of northern Russia along the Arctic. However, the polar areas will never be a base for power per se.

The United States holds Alaska, part of which is north of the Arctic Circle. Before a congressional committee in 1935, General "Billy" Mitchell referred to Alaska in the following words:

Alaska is the most central place in the world for aircraft. And that is true either of Europe, Asia, or North America, for in the future I think whoever holds Alaska will hold the world, and I think it is the most important strategic place in the world.

The importance of Alaska was revealed during the Pacific War. Some of the islands in the Aleutians were the only American territory in North America occupied by any one of the Axis powers. As a war development, the Alaska Highway, extending for 1,671 miles from Edmonton, Alberta, to Fairbanks, Alaska, was begun in the spring of 1942 and completed in October, 1943, but it never proved of practical use then. In the Polar Mediterranean of the future, Alaska will be increasingly important.

Canada also has a large expanse of territory in the Arctic. According to Vilhjalmur Stefansson, the famous Northwest Passage is easier to navigate than the one to the northeast in the Soviet sphere. The Canadians, however, have utilized their passage far less than the Russians. Radium deposits are developed just south of the Arctic at Great Bear

Lake, and extensive copper deposits are found north from Bear Lake to the middle of Victoria Island.

Denmark possesses the vast area of Greenland, which is very strategic in the North Atlantic. During World War II American forces were landed in Greenland, where the Germans had established meteorology stations to study the weather conditions affecting Europe. Iceland, which in 1944 formally severed the union with Denmark, is not an Arctic state. Norway has the Arctic possession of Svalbard, whose coal mines were seized by the Germans during the recent war. The North Cape, which was strategic in the conflict, and the island of Jan Mayen, which Columbus possibly visited, are both Norwegian. Finland formerly possessed Petsamo with its nearby deposits of nickel. In 1944 the Russian government bought the nickel mines from the Canadian interests. In an agreement signed at Moscow on September 19, 1944, Russia acquired the Finnish territory of Petsamo and deprived Finland of an outlet on the Arctic. Sweden has territory north of the Arctic Circle but no land on the Arctic Sea. The famous iron deposits around Kiruna are in Swedish territory north of the Arctic Circle.

The theory of polar "sectorism" acquires more interest as a result of the developments in the Arctic Mediterranean. The theory is centered around the idea that each subjacent Arctic state has full jurisdiction over all the territory and air space within an area that has the pole as the apex, usually bounded by the territorial coastline of the state as the base, and the two meridians of longitude as the sides, rising from the longitudinal extremities of the coastline base and converging at the pole. The Arctic sectors would be five in number if they were based on the Arctic states of 1945, namely, the Soviet Union, the United States, Canada, Denmark, and Norway. Since 1926 a number of Russian writers have taken the leadership in defending the case of "sectorism" in principle. However, the Soviet sector decree of April 15, 1926, proclaimed only that all the lands and the islands north of the Soviet mainland between 32° 4′ 35″ East Longitude and 168° 49′ 30″ West Longitude belonged to the Soviet Union. No mention was made of the jurisdiction of air space.

Law of the High Seas

At the time when the concept of international law first came into being, most maritime states claimed sovereignty over certain seas. For example, England claimed dominion over the North Sea, the Channels (English, St. Georges, and North), and large areas of the Atlantic; Sweden and Denmark insisted on exclusive control of the Baltic; and the city-state of Venice considered the Adriatic a portion of the state domain. Such claims were often-times disputed, but the principle that sovereignty might exist over the ocean was not questioned. The modern theory that the open sea is free and common to all nations would historically not have been in harmony with the times. The state that claimed a portion of the sea often rendered a service to the world by policing the area against piracy. Ceremonial honors were sometimes required to be paid its flag; it might reserve the fisheries for itself or force other nations to secure transit licenses; it might levy tolls on the ships of such countries; and in some instances navigation was entirely restricted.

It was the abuse by Portugal and Spain in the sixteenth century of these established rights to control the open sea that prepared the way for a revision of the principle of such claims. These two countries claimed to divide the New World between themselves; Spain claimed the entire Pacific and the Gulf of Mexico; Portugal, the Indian Ocean and part of the Atlantic. Foreigners were excluded from these areas. In 1608 appeared the *Mare liberum* of Grotius, which maintained that the sea could not become the property of any state. As a result of the opposition to the document, the English replied with the *Mare clausum* in 1635, maintaining the original claims of the British. Gradually the claims of the various nations were dropped, and by the end of the first quarter of the nineteenth century the freedom of the open sea had been generally established. The question of distinction between "territorial" and "open" sea was not definitely settled and the matter is still frequently the subject of international concern.

Even though the principle of freedom of the seas is not absolutely established, the oceans could not be left unregulated by any law. There exist certain principles by which a state may extend its authority to the seas. Every state has jurisdiction over ships flying its flag on the high seas and consequently may apply its law, civil and criminal, to the occupants of such ships. It follows from this principle that a state may seize and bring into port any ship sailing under its flag without authority, and any such ship and contents may be confiscated in its courts. The right of "hot pursuit" is also recognized, whereby a foreign ship that has committed a crime may be pursued and taken on the high seas. Maritime treaties between nations, moreover, have provided for jurisdiction of ships in certain areas by a designated state. It is also recognized that any state may bring pirates to trial by its own courts on the ground that they are *hostes humani generis*. Furthermore, the principle of self-defense may justify the exercise of authority of a state on the high seas contiguous to its territorial waters. The concept of territorial waters, whereby the exclusive control of the state extends into the open sea to a fixed limit, has also been recognized in international law. In times of war the principles of exercise of authority on the open seas are divided so as to provide for the "rights of belligerents" and the "rights of neutrals."

Based upon these principles of freedom of the sea and international control of the open ocean, there exist certain more specific consequences that have a direct influence upon the action of individuals and the state. The right of free navigation carries with it the responsibility of preventing collisions by adhering to international communication arrangements, respecting signs and signals, and the right of passage. Freedom of fishing on the high seas, a right that can be limited only through an international agreement, has assumed more international importance in recent years than ever before. The fisheries on the North Sea are controlled by the Hague Convention of 1882; pelagic sealing in the Bering Sea is regulated in an international agreement. The fishing agreements between Japan and Russia formed an important part of the political warfare between Soviet Russia and Japan before the entry of the former into the Japanese phase of World War II. The control of the state over all mineral deposits in the continental shelf under the water adjacent to the state has been established and is now an accepted practice of international law. The more generally recognized dividing line between territorial waters and the open sea is a line three miles off shore, although current strategic considerations have discounted this legalistic conception.

In order that the principles of the freedom of the sea may be promulgated throughout the world, certain regulatory bodies and commissions have accepted at one time or another the responsibilities of expressing the subject in international law. Although not all are successful, international regulatory conventions and covenants represent attempts by peoples to settle by peaceful political means international problems created by the geography of the world ocean.

CHAPTER 36

Boundaries in International Relations

AN INTERNATIONAL boundary is a line marking an outer limit of the territory within which a state exercises its sovereignty. Since the boundary also marks the limit of a neighboring state's sovereignty, its location has in many cases been the subject of delicate negotiations and the cause of many disputes. Boundaries may conform to physical features of the earth's surface or to the distribution of various human elements, or they may have been drawn simply on the basis of geometrical lines. Often a boundary represents a combination of all these types. Different, and even conflicting, principles are employed in the choice of boundary types, and each state tends to apply the principles most favorable to its own supposed interests.

Marking the limit of the highest form of sovereignty, the international boundary is a bar, or at least an interruption, to the movement of persons, goods, and ideas. For purposes of military defense, police protection, collection of revenue, protection of the national industries and currency, and regulation of immigration, the state keeps close watch over its boundaries. In many cases the state attempts to prohibit the entrance of ideas considered harmful to its morals, religion, or governmental and economic system. Careful boundary surveillance may work hardship upon persons living near the line who must cross into the neighboring country in the normal course of their daily occupations unless frontier regimes are instituted that allow relatively unimpeded travel.

The kind and degree of regulation applied at a boundary determine the way in which that boundary functions. Boundary functions vary greatly from one frontier to another and affect a state's relationships with other states as much as does the problem of boundary location. The principal problems in international relations, then, so far as boundaries are concerned, have to do with the *functions* and the *placing* of boundaries.

Development of Frontiers and Boundaries

Core area and frontier of the state. A strong state tends to grow in area at the expense of its weaker neighbors. Such a state expands outward from a central *core area*. The core area is usually the original seat of the state and contains a population that may be more homogeneous culturally than other areas in the country. Here is often found the capital city, and here usually are the nerve centers of the nation's political and economic life. The state's authority may be more firmly established in the core area than elsewhere.

Beyond is frequently found a zone of more recently acquired territories, called the *frontier*. Here peoples speaking the national language and having the national culture mingle with those of other languages and cultures. The voice of the state's authority may be less firm here than at the center. Economically this frontier is tributary to the core area. In many cases communication with the core area is comparatively easy, but in other instances the frontier lies in a region where nature has raised serious obstacles to travel, for example, mountains, deserts, swamps, or jungles. Although this concept of a core area and a frontier cannot be applied to all states without discrimination, it is applicable in greater or less degree to states that have had a history of territorial expansion.

Development of the frontier. The frontier is likely to be a debatable land, for here the state in its outward expansion has been forced to struggle for supremacy with adjacent states. Weaker rivals may have been absorbed. If the neighbor is equally strong, frontier territories may have changed hands several times, or a deadlock and stability may have resulted. A small state may have been spared absorption in order to preserve it as a buffer between powerful neighbors. In some instances a frontier state has been more or less dependent upon a larger central state and has acted as a protective buffer or a vanguard for the larger state's expansion. In other instances a frontier state has enjoyed a high degree of independence. The frontier, then, is a zone of varying width on the periphery of a state's geographical area. The international boundary is a line laid down in this zone. It is well to keep in mind this clear-cut distinction between the frontier and the boundary.

In earlier times the frontier of a state was much more important than the boundary. Among more primitive folk there were no boundaries, various natural obstacles or simply uninhabited areas being sufficient to keep tribes and nations apart. The more powerful of the ancient states erected walls and supporting fortified works along their frontiers with unruly tribes. Thus, the several Roman walls across Britain and the several walls separating Chinese agriculturists from Central Asian nomads, of which the Great Wall was only a consolidation and extension, represented successive high water marks in the fluctuating frontier of civilization against barbarism. Advanced, well-organized states sometimes purposely kept their frontier zones depopulated. It is said that this policy, until rather recent times, was true of the frontier between Korea and the Chinese Empire.

Increased importance of the boundary. The boundary line of a state became more important as a result of several developments. Increasing population and more intensive utilization of natural resources made it undesirable to maintain empty areas of uncertain ownership in the frontier zone. In Europe at the end of the Middle Ages central governments became more powerful and better able to exercise close supervision over their frontiers. The medieval patchwork of territories gave way to the more compact areas of kingdoms and principalities, and these in turn evolved into modern national states. Improvements in surveying and cartography also made the accurate drawing of continuous boundary lines more feasible. The sixteenth and seventeenth century maps of France were rather indefinite as to boundaries, and an actual demarcation of French boundaries as a whole was undertaken only after 1815. Thus, Europeans were becoming more exact in their definition of boundaries by the early nineteenth century (see the map below).

BOUNDARY FLUCTUATIONS IN A FRONTIER AREA

As European states extended their control over Africa and Asia in the nineteenth and twentieth centuries, they carried with them the concept of exact boundary demarcation. Africa, mostly a vast congeries of tribal states divided only by native frontier zones until the 1880's, was partitioned at European council tables with scant regard for the geographic conditions of the continent. Boundaries were driven through jungle, swamp, and desert, in many cases dividing tribes and causing a reorientation of trade and communications. In Asia the European powers demarcated not only the boundaries of their own expanding territories but those of states, such as Afghanistan, that they allowed to remain as buffers between them. They were also instrumental in securing the demarcation of lines between strictly native states. Wandering herdsmen looked on with disapproval as a new line was cut through arid pastures claimed by both bordering states but hitherto left conveniently to the possession of the momentary occupant. At the same time the American states were bringing order out of the confusion of overlapping claims inherited from the colonial period.

Today there are very few international frontiers without definite boundary delimitations. However, snow-clad heights, burning sands, or vast jungles hinder a complete demarcation of many boundaries on the ground. In these areas the frontier retains much of its ancient importance as the true factor of separation.

Types of Boundaries

A fourfold classification of boundaries is based upon the locational factors, visible or invisible, used in determining the position of the line. The *physical types* of boundaries follow natural features in the frontier zone. *Cultural types* follow zones of separation between peoples of different language, religion, "nationality," economic ties, tribal affiliation, or other cultural characteristics, or some other feature resulting from human occupance of the land. *Geometrical types* of boundaries are defined in terms of straight lines, parallels of latitude, meridians, arcs of circles, lines parallel to some topographic feature, or other mathematically determined lines. *Complex types* of boundaries are based on a number of factors, including those listed under each of the above types.

Physical types. An older term for the physical type is "natural boundary." There is a widespread belief in the superiority of the so-called natural boundary over other kinds, based on the former very real defensive utility of a natural barrier frontier, and the excuse that this doctrine gives for expansion to some coveted natural feature. However, since the state itself is a man-made, artificial institution, its boundaries are artificial and cannot

be defined automatically by nature. Mountains, deserts, swamps, forests, jungles, and rivers have lost much of their usefulness for defense with the advent of modern methods of warfare. Nevertheless, they still retain value as boundary locations if they mark zones of separation between more densely inhabited areas, or if they are barriers to communication. In other words, natural barriers form good boundary locations if they reduce to a minimum the friction caused by contact between neighboring peoples. Deserts, swamps, forests, and jungles are generally so wide that the actual boundaries within these areas follow more restricted physical features or geometrical lines.

WATER BOUNDARIES. River valleys are likely to be important arteries of commerce and to contain centers of population. They are zones of unity rather than zones of separation. For this reason it is rather infrequent that boundaries have followed important rivers in the older areas of power and civilization. The Rhine and the Danube seem to be exceptions to this statement, but periods of valley unity on these rivers have been as significant as periods when they served as borders. On the other hand, in newer areas such as the Americas, large rivers are often used for boundaries because they may be the most prominent landmarks on the maps of a poorly explored region. Because of their unstable character many rivers serve poorly as boundaries. Changes in river course and changes in the main channel and banks cause frequent shifts in the position of the actual line. The Rio Grande between the United States and Mexico forms a boundary that is continually migrating.

The oceans form the most prominent frontier features of the planet. Once the object of exclusive claims by some states, they have long been accepted as free to all. Exclusive sovereignty of the individual state is now limited to the straits, harbors, and landlocked bays on its coasts and to the zone of "territorial waters" adjacent thereto. Many states accept three nautical miles, measured from low tide, as the width of this zone, but some states claim wider limits. Peaceful merchant vessels have the right of innocent passage even through these territorial waters. Some functions may be carried on by the state outside the territorial waters. The United States undertook to combat liquor smuggling outside its territorial waters. The Great Lakes and many other large boundary lakes are divided between the contiguous states by agreement and are considered as analogous to territorial waters, although the states may agree to use the lakes jointly for navigation and other purposes.

MOUNTAIN BOUNDARIES. In the tropics mountain ranges are apt to be centers of population and zones of unity. In this respect they are like many river valleys. In higher latitudes, however, the inhospitable character of large mountain areas makes them more suitable as frontier zones. Thus, the core areas of several tropical South American countries are in the Andes, but in the temperate south these mountains carry the long boundary between Argentina and Chile.* The boundary line in mountains may follow one or more of several courses: the waterparting between drainage basins, the generally highest land, an alignment of the highest peaks, points along the slope below the highest land, or the foot of the slope. The assumption by treaty makers that the line of waterparting and the line of highest peaks coincide has caused disputes between nations.

Cultural types. When new states were created in Europe along lines of nationality, especially after World War I, many of the boundaries followed roughly the zones of separation between cultural traits of the different nationalities. Language was the most prominent trait considered, but not the only one. Among others, a Polish state was erected, and the boundary between Germany and Poland was intended to separate areas where most of the population spoke the German language or wished to be considered as German, from areas containing a majority of persons speaking Polish or desiring to become Polish citizens. Cultural areas are usually not sharply defined, and the zones of separation where one cultural group merges imperceptibly with another are often rather wide, especially in eastern Europe. A boundary in such a zone must therefore be defined in detail with reference to villages, rivers, administrative boundaries, railroads, and other features of the terrain although the line as a whole may be intended to follow a language divide.

* See page 499 for a brief account of the boundary friction between Argentina and Chile and its solution.

Few cultural boundaries can be drawn that do not include minority groups of foreign culture or nationality within a state. In some cases these groups assimilate easily with the larger body of citizens, but in other cases they remain unreconciled to their status and may cause international difficulties. States may attempt to achieve cultural homogeneity by an exchange of minorities. Such an arrangement involving some 2,000,000 persons was made between Greece and Turkey following World War I, whereby Greeks in Turkey were sent to Greece and Moslems in Greece were transferred to Turkey. These movements are said to have improved relations between the two countries, but they caused misery for the emigrants and placed severe economic strains on both countries. Compulsory transfer of minorities on the one hand, or forced assimilation of minorities on the other hand easily become weapons of tyranny and are apt to create more problems than they solve.

Outside of Europe the development of the feeling of nationalism has been so recent that few attempts have been made to erect new states on this basis. Nevertheless, such cultural traits as religion and tribal affiliation have occasionally been considered in laying down Asiatic or African boundaries. Religious differences between Moslems and Hindus formed the basis for the division of India into the Dominion of Pakistan and the Dominion of India.

Geometrical types. Geometrical lines for the most part disregard the cultural and physical features of the landscape and are superimposed upon them. The use of geometrical lines in defining boundaries quite commonly denotes the negotiators' unfamiliarity with the region being divided, or the fact that the area is considered of small value. Thus, most geometrical boundaries are found in the more recently explored or settled parts of the world—in Africa, the Americas, and Australasia. One of the earliest examples of a geometrical line was the so-called "demarcation line" between the claims of Spain and Portugal, defined by the Pope in 1493 as a line 100 leagues west of the Azores. The longest geometrical boundary in existence today is probably that along the 49th Parallel of North Latitude between Canada and the United States. Boundaries defined as parallel to or at a given distance from a certain feature are to be found in Africa and elsewhere. The boundaries of the territorial sea are like this. It is practically impossible to lay down geometrical boundaries exactly as they are defined, but once demarcated they are perhaps less expensive to administer than, say, shifting river boundaries.

Complex types. Our discussion of boundary types has indicated that a boundary may be laid down on the basis of physical features, or on the basis of separating cultural areas, or it may be determined by mathematics. To attempt to follow one of these principles alone does violence to the others and, indeed, this method is rarely undertaken. The different factors of culture do not coincide, and a line drawn on the basis of language distribution frequently does not coincide with transportation lines and the flow of trade. The division of the Austro-Hungarian Empire into national states disrupted the railway system and destroyed the economic unity of the middle Danube region. Even high mountains seldom serve as divides between cultural groups. The Basques are found on both sides of the Pyrenees barrier between France and Spain. Peoples of German culture live in Italy south of the Alpine divide crossed by the Brenner Pass. Following the principle of the "natural," that is, the physical, boundary, and for reasons of defense, Italy secured southern Tyrol up to the Brenner in 1919, but many of the German-speaking inhabitants, not satisfied with Italian rule, wished to be reunited with Austria. The problem was complicated by the location in southern Tyrol of hydroelectric power plants of considerable value to Italy.

These conflicting distributional factors cause much boundary-making to be a compromise of the various principles involved. The boundary maker, if he attempts to be impartial, must strike a balance between the conflicting wishes of the frontier inhabitants, the requirements of circulation along roads and railways, and the location of prominent physical features. Viewed in their entirety, then, numerous boundaries are of the complex type, their short stretches being adjusted to first one factor and then another.

Boundary-Making

Establishing the location of a boundary requires a process in which we may distinguish three steps or stages: *territorial allocation, delimitation,* and *demarcation.* Territorial allocation takes place when a given area is assigned to a given state. Since the area may be described in terms of its limits, this arrangement makes necessary the second step, delimitation. This is the definition of the boundary line in general terms in a treaty or similar document drawn up by the parties concerned. The third step, demarcation, occurs when a mixed commission composed of representatives of the interested parties surveys and marks the line on the ground.

Territorial allocation. Allocation may involve areas only a few square miles in extent, or areas containing many thousands of square miles. The reasons for territorial allocation also vary greatly. A state may desire an area because it is a strategic military site, or because it contains a population of the state's own nationality, or because its land would support an overflow of agricultural population, or simply because its acquisition would represent an increase in national prestige and reflect credit on the government currently in power. Although this list of motives is not exhaustive, it is sufficient to indicate that territorial allocation is a matter of high politics, involving a state's general relationships with other states.

These general political relationships among states are part of the pattern of the *general situation,* a factor fully as important as the detailed merits in solving any boundary problem. The general situation is so important because the states concerned have usually been the final judges of their own cases for annexation of territory. A state can settle amicably the most complicated and persistent frontier problem or it can foment difficulty over the most stable and hitherto satisfactory boundary —depending upon its own motives and supposed self-interest. The history of the United States–Canada boundary, in contrast with the course taken by Hitler regarding the German-Czechoslovak boundary in 1938 are cases in point.

The two most time-honored and important methods of securing territorial allocation are war and negotiation. The practice of negotiating general territorial settlements, guaranteed by most of the principal powers after a period of warfare, became important in Europe in the seventeenth century and in recent times has spread to the whole world. Thus, most of the territorial arrangements at the end of World War I were made in the name of the Allied and Associated Powers. European states have generally been willing to settle questions of colonial territory among themselves by negotiation. With the exception of the Italian-Turkish War of 1911, the partition of Africa from 1880 to 1914 was accomplished without hostilities among European states, although the peoples being partitioned were not consulted, nor did they always submit peacefully.

In the present formative state of international law and order all methods of allocating territory involve war or negotiation. The application of the following methods requires prior agreement by the victors or the negotiators. Nevertheless, these methods are important in themselves and may point the way to eventual peaceful settlement of all territorial controversies. They include purchase, arbitral award or other quasi-judicial settlement, assignment by some international body, and plebiscite.

The principal areas subject to purchase have usually been colonial possessions of the vendor, having undeveloped or unexplored resources. The United States has been the outstanding country to expand by purchase of territory. The award of territory by arbitration or similar quasi-judicial process has been successfully employed on a number of occasions. An outstanding example is the part played by the League of Nations Council in settlement of territorial disputes, as its award of the Mosul district to Iraq during the latter's dispute with Turkey (1926). The assignment of territory by an international body is best exemplified by the mandates system of the League of Nations and trusteeships under the United Nations. Extra-European territories of Germany and parts of the old Ottoman Empire were assigned as mandates under the League to different Allied states. These states were in theory responsible to the League for fulfilling certain conditions in the administration of their mandates, and the eventual goal for many of the mandated territories was independence or some form of self-government.

The plebiscite is an election held in a disputed area to decide the national allegiance of its people. Its successful use at the end of World War I was an outgrowth of the Wilsonian principle of the self-determination of peoples. Formal plebiscites were held in several areas in the territories of Germany and the former Austria-Hungary, resulting in the confirmation to the previous owner of a number of the areas, and the division of others between the two states involved. In the case of Upper Silesia, one of the divided areas, the results of the plebiscite were so inconclusive that the final boundary was an arbitrary compromise line. A successful plebiscite can be held only in an area whose people have sufficient national consciousness and are well enough informed to vote intelligently. Public feeling regarding the issues at stake must be relatively calm, and the local administration must be under the control of an international authority powerful enough to prevent fraud or intimidation and able to insure an impartial count of the ballots. These stringent requirements necessarily limit the applicability of the plebiscite. It is difficult to visualize the holding of a fair plebiscite in an area where widespread displacement of population by warfare has recently taken place.

Delimitation. The way in which the line is delimited depends considerably upon the type of boundary, the physical and cultural features of the area, and the extent to which it is explored and mapped. In the case of some geometrical boundaries the treaty may give a complete definition, leaving very little to the discretion of the demarcators. In other instances only the major turning points of the line are named and the placing of the line between these points is left to the discretion of the demarcators. Definition by courses and distances, as in a surveyor's traverse, is sometimes used. Again, the treaty may provide that the line should be fixed on the ground leaving to Country A the villages 1, 3, and 6, and to Country B the villages 2, 4, and 5. Quite common is the stipulation that the boundary is to follow some topographic feature, such as a mountain range, waterparting, canal, or road. Finally, the line may be defined only "in principle," leaving the demarcators wide latitude of judgment. In such a case the demarcation commission might be instructed to run a line separating two tribes or leaving trade areas intact. Several of these methods of definition are generally found in one boundary treaty, different methods being used to define different sections of the line (see the map on page 525).

Most treaty delimitations are drawn up in a council chamber rather than in the field. The negotiators usually have little, if any, first-hand knowledge of the area they are attempting to delimit. The resulting treaty texts can be no more accurate than the maps and other technical data upon which they are based. If the region in question is poorly mapped or explored, all sorts of inaccuracies may creep into the definition of the line. Even in the thoroughly surveyed parts of Europe, maps and statistics of nationality or flow of trade, upon which delimitation might depend, are likely to be biased, inconclusive, or out of date. On numerous occasions the failure of treaty delimitations to conform to "geographical realities" has prolonged negotiations and strained good relations between states. The negotiators of the treaty of 1783, establishing independence for the United States, used Mitchell's map of North America as the basis for boundary delimitation. This was the most accurate map available at the time, yet between that date and 1925 the boundary from the Atlantic to the Lake of the Woods was the subject of at least sixteen treaties, conventions, and other instruments. Some of these were executed as a result of demarcation, but most of the earlier ones were necessary because of inaccuracies in the original treaty based on errors of the map.

Arbitration is often applied in disputes over boundary delimitation. For the period 1794 to 1923 one authority lists forty-three cases of arbitration between various countries, most of them relating to boundary disputes as such, but a few being questions involving allocation of appreciable amounts of territory. Cases have been submitted by the disputing parties to mixed commissions, the heads of third states, other officials or private citizens of third states, or some international body, such as the Council of the League of Nations. This has been a favorite method of settling the numerous disagreements over Latin American boundaries.

Wise boundary negotiators or arbitrators are not content to rely solely upon documentary knowledge of the area under discussion. They send commissions or individuals into the field to investigate at first hand. The Protocol of Rio de Janeiro of 1942 defining the boundary between Peru and Ecuador provided that the demarcators could grant reciprocal concessions to fit the line to "geographical realities." The defined line was indeed found to be inaccurate, but the two parties could not agree on concessions for all the points of difference. An arbitral award on the disputed points was made by a Brazilian officer after field investigation. More ambitious are the field investigations that take in not only physical terrain but such factors as the economy, ethnography, history, local administration, and political feeling in the area. Two famous investigations of this type were conducted for the League Council in the Mosul dispute between Turkey and Iraq and the dispute over the Iraq-Syria boundary. Much time and expense may be spared and international discord prevented if the investigations are made before rather than after the delimitation.

Demarcation. Demarcation is a highly technical job requiring surveying and mapping. Several demarcations in recent years have made use of aerial photography, and doubtless many more will do so in the future. Not the least important task is the erection of markers or otherwise making the line visible. Demarcation may involve negotiations in the field if considerable discretion is given to the mixed commission by the delimitation treaty.

When the work is completed, a final report is sent to the governments concerned, embodying a complete description of the line, perhaps a description of the numbering and location of markers, and maps of the boundary zone. The execution of a protocol accepting these reports by the governments frequently completes the boundary-making process.

Boundary and property line monumentation is a practice dating from remote times. The likeness of the Etruscan god Terminus, or some other deity, carved on boundary pillars, bore witness to the sacred character ascribed to these markers by the ancients. Modern international boundaries are customarily marked at intervals by cairns of loose stones and monuments of bronze, cement, or carved stone. The prairie section of the 49th Parallel boundary between the United States and Canada was formerly marked by sod mounds. It is customary to cut a boundary "vista" along the line in country that is forested or covered by undergrowth. This narrow cleared strip supplements the markers in making the line clearly visible. A ditch, or a ditch and bank, is another means used to mark a boundary.

Boundary Functions

Nature and types of boundary functions. The international boundary is the outward limit of the territory over which the absolute sovereignty of a state extends. Within its ring of boundaries the authority and functions of a state are limited only to the extent that the citizen body of the state itself cares to limit them. Outside its boundaries a state has no authority or functions except those that can be secured by the acquiescence of other states. Since each state exercises the highest temporal sovereignty within its borders, its boundaries could in theory be a sealed wall closing off all intercourse with the outside world. Such a boundary regime has been approximated on rare occasions in modern times, as in Japan until 1854 and on the Lithuanian-Polish boundary for some years after World War I. Nevertheless, the obvious advantages of trading in goods and ideas and the difficulties in preventing smuggling have all worked to give boundaries a considerable degree of permeability. A state allows intercourse across its boundaries to the extent that it considers this profitable to itself and its people and not detrimental to its safety or its political aims. The object of boundary *functions* is therefore to compromise the principle of absolute sovereignty with the conflicting principle of free intercourse. These functions are concerned with defense; the welfare of local frontier populations; the movement of goods, persons, and information in international intercourse; and the sharing of natural resources, including those in the frontier zone.

DEFENSE. Defense is one of the oldest functions of the frontier and the boundary. The successful performance of this function, however, has generally depended upon the strength and resources of the state backing up the frontier. The Alps, the Hindu Kush, and the English Channel served not as effective defense barriers but as highways for successful invasion so long as there were relatively weak states, unable to put up resistance, in Italy, India, and Britain. On the other hand, strong states have not been content to stop at the line of a natural barrier. The Roman Empire maintained a fortified area to the northeast of the Rhine and the Danube. Russia secured not only the peaks of the Caucasus but the territory to the southeast, where she planted military colonies. Such examples, together with the existence of dependent buffer states on the frontier, attest the long-standing recognition of the value of defense in depth.

With the development of mechanized three-dimensional warfare and combined air-land-sea operations, the principle of defense in depth along the frontier zone has lost most of its significance. In Soviet Russia the depth of frontier necessary to absorb the German attack in 1941–43 was about 800 miles. The atom bomb was dropped on Hiroshima by a Superfortress flying from Tinian, some 1,600 miles away. More recently military aircraft have made non-stop flights of many thousands of miles. British Prime Minister Attlee, speaking before the United States Congress in November, 1945, expressed the idea in this manner:

Defensive frontiers, mountain barriers, the seas, and even the oceans are no obstacle to attack. The old discontinuity of earth and sea has been replaced by the continuity of the air. . . . [and] the devastating weapons which are at present being developed may menace every part of the world.

CIRCULATION OF PEOPLE AND GOODS. Any boundary running through a populated region may disrupt the normal movement of persons and things. Farms may be cut in half, churches may be separated from their congregations, and electric power plants from their consumers. These difficulties are surmounted by the setting up of frontier regimes exempting the inhabitants of a zone of given width on either side of the line from the usual restrictions incident to boundary crossing.

In Europe, before the late war, long-established rights of access to mountain pastures or woodlands at some distance from the villages were respected in boundary treaties. Farmers, fire-fighters, and others could cross the boundaries in the pursuit of their occupations and could take stated amounts of produce or equipment with them duty-free, subject to certain restrictions as to time of day and season of the year that circulation was permitted.

BOUNDARY DELIMITATION AND DEMARCATION

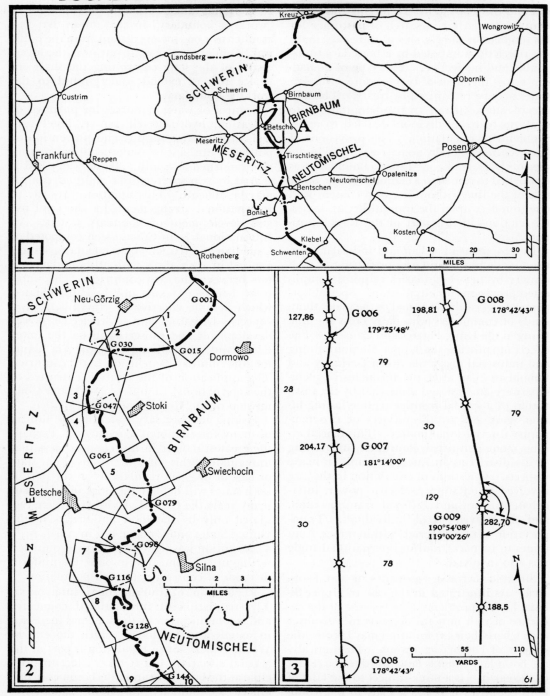

1. Portion of German-Polish boundary as delimited on map attached to Versailles Treaty, 1919.
2. Index map of German-Polish boundary as demarcated on ground, 1924. Rectangle A on Map 1 shows section covered.
3. Detailed diagrams of German-Polish boundary as demarcated, showing position of markers. Rectangle no. 1 on Map 2 shows section covered.

The severe environments of the Arctic tundra and the tropical desert, forcing the herdsman to wander far in search of pasturage for his reindeer or camels, sheep, and goats, make the restrictions imposed by a boundary undesirable and ineffective. This type of nomadism across the areas of two or more sovereign states may be recognized by treaty. The failure of most African treaty delimitations to conform to tribal divisions has led to many problems of circulation. The provisions of a convention whereby no native woman in the area of the Sierra Leone-Liberia boundary was compelled to return to a claimant on the other side of the line without her own consent lead one to reflect upon the tranquillity of domestic relations in this part of the Dark Continent.

Development of urban and industrial centers astride old boundaries or cutting of such centers by new boundaries requires complicated provisions for circulation. Special border-crossing cards are issued to the many thousands of commuters who daily cross the line between the United States and Canada. The effects of splitting the Upper Silesian mining and industrial district between Germany and Poland in 1922 after the inconclusive plebiscite were ameliorated somewhat by the institution of a special frontier regime lasting fifteen years and by the services of two temporary international bodies. This official arrangement permitted continued functioning of the district as an integrated unit in many respects. Questions of circulation in the case involved water supply, electric power, interurban railway and railroad transportation, and the movement of individuals. Transportation of raw materials within mines, from mines to furnaces, and in international trade was also involved.

SHARING NATURAL RESOURCES OF THE FRONTIER. As illustrated in the case of Upper Silesia, knotty problems arise because of the existence of rich mineral deposits in a frontier zone where their exploitation may become the subject of conflicting claims. Theoretically the boundary extends downward to the center of the earth. Is a mine subject to the laws of both countries if it has a shaft in one country, but follows an underground vein across the line into an adjacent country? In Upper Silesia some mines extending across the new boundary were closed off at that line, but others were allowed to continue operations

as before. In 1939 an agreement between the Netherlands and Germany provided for a "working boundary" in coal mines that was as much as 1,000 meters distant from the political boundary. For most purposes the sovereignty of the state controlling the shaft entrance was to extend underground to the working boundary.

Control of water resources for purposes of irrigation, hydro-electric power, flood control, urban water supply, and prevention of pollution can best be undertaken by treating the watershed as a unit. If the watershed is shared by two sovereignties, unity of control may be difficult. This situation gives rise to international arrangements for the joint use and development of boundary waters. An International Joint Commission composed of Canadian and United States members, first organized in 1912, deals with all boundary waters between the two countries. The water treaty between Mexico and the United States, which became effective in November, 1945, concerns irrigation and hydroelectric power development and conservation on the lower Rio Grande, the Colorado, and the Tia Juana, for the mutual benefit of both countries. The application of the treaty is entrusted to the International Boundary and Water Commission of the United States and Mexico.

Fishing in boundary waters is the subject of many international agreements. Perhaps the greatest danger in this connection is that unregulated fishing by the citizens of one state or lack of uniform regulations on the part of both states will deplete the stock of fish. For many years the Great Lake fisheries were regulated only by the local authorities in the United States and Canada, but in April, 1946, a convention was signed by the two countries, setting up a commission to prescribe uniform methods of conserving the fish population.

Regulation of international intercourse. The regulation of international commerce and communication by the state has increased in extent and complexity since the end of World War I. Such regulation is part of the general situation, but it takes effect in principle at the boundary and thus becomes in one aspect a boundary function. Boundaries have become increasingly less permeable. Before 1914 travelers were not generally required to have passports to cross European borders, but in the period between the two wars this requirement became quite common.

The United States and other American countries erected barriers to another type of traveler—the immigrant. In addition, attempts to solve economic difficulties along nationalistic lines led to higher tariff barriers, import quotas, controls on foreign exchange, and other forms of "invisible tariff." Finally, the restrictions on individual liberty imposed by the totalitarian governments made many an international boundary not only a line of restriction on trade, but a line separating two sets of values regarding the books one should read, one's political opinions, one's taste in music, or the kind of blood that should flow in one's veins.

A partial offset to this trend toward autarchy was the continued vigor of efforts toward unity in the means of transportation and communication. In respect to postal service, the Universal Postal Union, founded in 1874, practically abolishes the boundaries between its members. Within recent years it included the territories of nearly every state and dependent area in the world. Railway and inland waterway unification has been most effective when handled on a regional basis.

As a result of a series of railway agreements beginning in the last century it was possible, by 1939, to move on standard gauge track, in standardized types of cars, over the railways of all Europe from the Spanish-French border to the western boundary of the U. S. S. R. Customs formalities for freight traffic were reduced to a minimum by arrangements for the transit of goods across intervening countries in sealed cars. The general principle of freedom of navigation on inland waterways accessible to more than one country was enunciated at the Congress of Vienna in 1815, and has been applied to many streams. International regimes promoting navigation on the Rhine and the Danube offered two of the best examples of international organization before the advent of Nazism. The League of Nations sponsored several agreements designed to promote international intercourse, such as the Convention and Statute on the Freedom of Transit, signed at Barcelona in 1921.

Solving Boundary Problems

Boundary disputes, as such, cause friction between nations, but they do not generally cause war unless they are linked with overlapping territorial claims of considerable extent or unless one or both parties have ulterior motives in keeping disputes alive. At the very heart of the problem of peaceful settlement of such disputes, then, is the necessity for some restraint on the will of individual states. This need calls for a world organization possessing both the machinery for peaceful settlement and sufficient backing from the world community to command respect and to speak with authority. In spite of its eventual failure, the League of Nations made a beginning at setting up machinery for investigation and settlement of territorial and boundary questions. It remains for the United Nations to complete the unfinished task.

Readjustment of boundaries may not bring satisfaction, but may only deepen the sense of injustice for one or both sides. Even if a boundary change seems to meet the requirements of justice, restrictive policies regarding trade and circulation on the part of one or both states may counteract whatever value the physical location of the line may have. The remedy for many border difficulties, then, lies not in changing the location of the boundary but in changing its functions. Abolition of numerous local restrictions and perhaps the institution of international border regimes after the pattern of Upper Silesia might be partial goals. In the broader field of international trade and intercourse the way is pointed by the United States trade agreements program linked with the name of Cordell Hull, the International Civil Aviation Agreements signed at Chicago in 1944, the Bretton Woods Monetary Agreements of the same year, and the achievements in unifying the means of intercourse, such as those discussed above. If restrictions on movement across international boundaries were no greater than across municipal and county boundaries in the United States, boundary disputes between nations would be far fewer.

No matter whether all boundary disputes are eventually settled by international machinery, or whether the restrictive functions of boundaries are at length completely abolished, the services of the proficient boundary-maker will always be in demand. The man who can combine skill in the earth sciences and social sciences with political sense and a gift for negotiation is in a position to contribute much to the settlement of boundary problems and the cause of international harmony.

CHAPTER 37 | # Population Factors in International Affairs

THE world at present holds in excess of two billion inhabitants. If each person were allowed sufficient standing room (one and one-half by two feet), the earth's total population could be crowded into an area about *one seventh the size of Rhode Island.* Actually, however, the preponderant number of people are widely scattered throughout the land hemisphere * with densities ranging from less than one person in several hundred miles in the large areas of Siberia, the Amazon basin, the Sahara, and Australia, to the more than a thousand persons per square mile in the urbanized industrial areas of the United States and Europe, in the agricultural areas of the Monsoon basins and valleys of southeast and eastern Asia, and in the Nile Valley of Egypt. These more than two billion persons are living under the sovereign authority of approximately eighty governments. As a result of the shrinking linear dimensions of an "Air Age World," which has brought increased political contacts among these national entities, more people are brought into actual "neighborly" and direct relationship in further developing the interdependence of the world's population than in any previous period of history.**

The varied characteristics of the world's

* The land hemisphere is the half of the earth's surface that includes the greatest area of land having 88 per cent of the land area and 93.8 per cent of the world's population.

** There are more than 150 separate political entities in the world, although many can be grouped into the world's empires. Of these political entities, 69 are listed in a table in Appendix B, pages 569–70, and are assumed to be potential members of the United Nations. As of May 1, 1948, 58 nations had joined the United Nations.

population create an outstanding problem, and at the same time tend to be the reason for much of the interdependence of some regions. The cultural background of two groups of people may complement one another to the benefit of all mankind and especially to each other. On the other hand, the two groups may conflict with one another and consequently create friction that may result in serious diplomatic and military activities if not settled by peaceful compromise. Thus, variations in demographic structure and trends are closely related to international political problems.

World developments may alter the population structure and characteristics within any area or region of the earth's surface. Migrations may alter the ethnic composition of the population. Also economic well-being may favor improved health and sanitation conditions that lower death rates and perhaps reduce birth rates, and thus cause a changed age and sex structure of the population. Again, variations in the way that people make a living may change the rural-urban ratio, which reflects variations in the occupational patterns of a country.

In general, the problems of population are ever changing. The dynamic nature of the world's population in itself is basic to the problems of political geography. Population in any region is rarely unchanging in numbers. Usually it is growing or declining as people move and trade throughout the world. Even though most of the world's population will be born, will grow up, will work, and will die within the same political unit, many other persons, as a result of wars, famines, or the urge of the "push-pull" drive to better themselves, will migrate and perhaps create international and national problems. Likewise, the changing composition of those more or less stationary population groups may be related to nationalistic tendencies, which stimulate international friction. Consequently, since variations exist in the characteristics of a population from place to place throughout the world, and in lesser degree from time to time, the study of the world's population is a continuing responsibility of students of international affairs.

National Greatness in Terms of Man Power

Population numbers and man power are not always synonymous. Nevertheless, the military strength of nations is usually related to the size and composition of the population. More important, however, is the effective organization of the population and the technical skills developed by them. Contrast Japan and its 73 million persons, with China and its 450 million in the long years of bitter conflict from 1931 to 1945. More people might make Australia stronger economically and politically; whereas fewer people might make India stronger, potentially, if not actually, and give that country a bigger voice in world affairs. Population numbers alone certainly have not been the basis of the world position of Great Britain as the center of one of the most powerful empires. On the other hand, approximately the same number of people in Brazil have not achieved an economic or political power even approaching that of the British Isles.

Why do numbers alone mean so little in determining political and economic power? All populations of the world must secure for themselves the essentials of living, namely, food, clothing, and shelter. In some countries all, or practically all, of the people are engaged in these activities related to mere subsistence. Consequently, these countries have little man power or economic surplus to devote to the improvement of their levels of living through scientific or educational and personal service pursuits. It has been estimated that approximately 60 per cent of the world's population is engaged in the essential activities involved in securing food, clothing, and shelter. It is impossible to determine how many are producing only for their own

countries; there is considerable variation from country to country in the proportion of the population thus engaged. In western European countries approximately a fourth of the total population is so engaged, in contrast with two thirds in eastern Europe.

Man power is a significant factor in a study of peace-time as well as wartime economies. Countries producing a surplus of either essential or nonessential commodities can soon develop trade and become a source of commodities for countries not able to produce all that they need or desire. The fewer people required to produce for domestic use, the better chance any country has of acquiring a surplus of commodities for trading purposes. A survey of occupational groups, therefore, has importance in studies of regional interdependence.

The most significant item with regard to the size of population is the way in which the people of various countries have developed and utilized the available natural resources, whether within or outside the boundaries of their own countries. It is possible for small countries to develop high levels of living through the effective use of their national human and natural resources, and by the development of favorable trade relations with other regions. In many cases, such as Switzerland, a small country may attain a significant position in the world group of nations. In other cases, such as England, the Netherlands, and Belgium, the natural and human resources of relatively small countries have been supplemented by the utilization of the resources and the man power of empire areas much larger and more populous than the home countries. The interrelations between available man power and resources within a small nation, or between home country and empire area are so highly complicated that they also become important considerations in national economic policies. Whatever the relationships, however, the trend of the man power available locally within a nation is a factor of pre-eminent importance in assessing the present and potential disposition of resources.

Distribution and Density of the World's Population

The world's population is distributed very unevenly throughout the countries of the world. A substantial proportion lives in areas with more than 500 persons per square mile; whereas 43.5 per cent of the total land area of the world (including ice caps) is occupied by people in densities of less than 1 person per 4 square miles. Of tremendous significance is the fact that more than a billion people, or half of the world's total population, live in India, China, Japan, and the islands of the southwestern Pacific on about 8.7 per cent of the total land area of the earth.

Twelve per cent of the world's population live in cities of 100,000 and over. This urban population is not uniformly distributed among the continental land masses. For example, only 4 per cent of the population of Africa is concentrated in large cities, whereas in the Americas 30 per cent of the population is found in cities over 100,000. It is striking to note the high proportion of the population in large cities occurring in Oceania and Australia, where 38 per cent of the ten million people live in cities of 100,000 and over. This condition is partly due to the emphasis on port activities in Australia and New Zealand.

The continental distribution of the world's population is far from proportionate to the continental areas. Africa with 23 per cent of the world's area has only 7 per cent of the world population, whereas Europe with only 4 per cent of the world's area has 18 per cent of the world population. And Asia with only 30 per cent of the area has 54 per cent of the population, whereas the Americas with 28 per cent of the world's area have only 13 per cent of the world's total population . More than two billion persons live outside of the continental United States; in general, the Americas as a whole, when compared with Europe and Asia, present a very sparsely populated picture.

Within the continental areas, population concentrations reflect the land use and industrial patterns, and are closely related to the land forms of mountains, plains, valleys, and plateaus. Climatic variations and soil differences are important factors in limiting population settlement. The population potential of regions, and thus of national entities, is a reflection of the present and potential carrying capacity of the areas in question. An area favorable only for agricultural utilization cannot support as many people as one adapted to urban industrial development.

Many large areas, such as those found in Western Australia, are now considered unsuitable for any intense utilization. Such environmental limitations in the frontier areas of population settlement are uppermost in importance in analyzing the potential position of a country among the nations of the world. Thus, an understanding of the densely and sparsely populated areas of the world provides a basis for the study of international problems.

Densely populated areas of the world. The largest areas of great population densities are located in Europe and Asia. Europe, China, and India each has very roughly the same proportion of the world's population and land area. It must not be assumed, however, that their respective population problems are the same. Although densities as high as 600 or more persons per square mile are to be found in the industrial areas of northwest Europe, and in the lowland plains and valleys of China and India, these great densities are not confined to industrial areas alone. In Europe over 20 per cent of the people live in cities of 100,000 and over, but, on the other hand, in India and China only about 4 per cent of the total population live in cities of this size. Europe's high density is that of an urbanized industrial region, whereas the high densities of India and China are primarily those of intense agrarian economies.

In China the distribution of population is closely related to topography and climate. Large areas of China are sparsely settled, and the areas of dense settlement are geographically localized. Rough hill land forty to fifty miles inland is very sparsely populated; one Chinese population authority has gone so far as to state that approximately 87 per cent of the area of China has less than 35 persons per square mile. The highly developed agricultural lowlands of the river valleys emphasize the strong relationship between population distribution and topography. The Red Basin in Szechwan province is one of the best defined concentrations as related to topography. Even here, however, the fifty-three million persons are not uniformly distributed and some areas of hill country and low valley bottom land tend to show up with remarkably high population densities.

There is also great diversity in the population density within the great agricultural producing areas of China. For example, in the Spring Wheat Region, where the conditions of climate, soil, and topography are not so favorable for agriculture, the density is about 850 per square mile of crop area. On the other hand, in the Southwestern Rice Region the density runs as high as 2,500 per square mile of crop area. In extreme cases, the density runs as high as 4,000 in some localities. The greater density in the rice regions is the result of a climate favorable to rice production that supplies three times as much food per unit area as do the wheat region crops.

The total population of India, with an enormous increase of 50 million in ten years, represents as many people as in all of Europe excluding the U. S. S. R. Approximately 180 million people live in the densely populated Ganges-Punjab region, a concentration where the density is over 600 per square mile in extensive rural areas. This portion of India showed an increase in population of from 20–25 per cent in the decade 1931–41. The only area of decline during the intercensual period was in the sparsely populated area of inhospitable Baluchistan. In general, rice production throughout India has failed to keep pace with population growth. Consequently, since rice imports go mainly to urban centers, the rural areas of necessity have had to lower per capita consumption of rice and turn to other foods.

For the most part the island areas of the world have relatively large populations in proportion to their areas. The British Isles with their 50 million, the Japanese Islands with their prewar 70 million, and the 185 million of the other islands of Asia and Oceania together represent about 16 per cent of the total population of the world living on only 3 per cent of the total land area. Tropical native and commercial agriculture in the islands of southeast Asia has led to concentrations along the coastal regions. This coastal alignment of agricultural development is also characteristic on the peninsulas of southeast Asia. Notable increases and concentrations of population are found in Burma, Sumatra, the southeast portion of Siam, and the south peninsula of Celebes. In large measure the population concentrations in Monsoon Asia occur at elevations below 3,000 feet in areas having more than 40 inches of rainfall annually and with an average January temperature of not less than 32° F. The people are settled in the rice areas of the valley plains along the major rivers, in the deltas, or on other coastal plains.

Sparsely populated areas of the world. More than two fifths of the land areas of the world have densities of less than one person per 4 square miles. The sparsely populated areas of Siberia; the desert areas of Africa, Australia, and Arabia; the extreme wet areas of the Amazon basin; and the forests and tundra of northern Canada stand out on a population map as regions with relatively few people. Except in pastoral and nomad areas the population concentrations seem to be localized on the best lands in the valleys or plains near available transportation routes. Even in the vast areas of northern Siberia there has been little spread of the population outward from the east-west trans-Siberian railway zone. In North America the distribution of population in the sparsely populated western and northwestern regions is largely in terms of transportational alignments. In general, the sparsely populated areas of the tropics are the extremely rainy areas and the extremely dry areas. Scattered population exists along the water or land transportational routes and in the oasis areas of the deserts.

For the most part, the sparse areas of the world are in the interiors of continental masses in contrast to the more densely populated coastal margins. This world pattern may favor the desire of man to seek routes to other lands in the setting up of contacts and trade. Migrations and the dispersal of populations inland tend to follow rivers and natural routes, which later may be followed by rail or highways. The tendency for populations to be concentrated near the coast or in the low plains areas is indicated by the fact that a high proportion of the world's large cities are located at elevations below 1,600 feet.

The 163 million people of Africa are widely distributed in densities varying from less than one in several hundred square miles in the Sahara to near 2,000 per square mile along the Nile in northern Egypt. The relatively dense areas of Nigeria and the adjoining coastal area with about 30 million, and the Lake Victoria area with 15 million stand out more significantly than that of South Africa with its better-known 10 million. The 20 million people of northwest Africa form a regional concentration apart from the rest of the continent. In contrast with South America, the distribution of population south of the Sahara is not peripheral. Contacts with the outside are thus more difficult and the transportation problems arising in either moving goods and raw materials in or out of the area are more pronounced.

Trends of the World's Population Growth

Present rates of growth. The world's population increases between 25 and 30 million persons each year. This increase is equal to approximately the population of prewar Poland or of Spain or the combined population of the states of New York, Pennsylvania, and New Jersey. Some students have estimated that the world's population increases 1.16 per cent each year; others assume a lesser rate. The present rates of growth, and their variations from country to country, have received increasing attention in recent years.

Little is known concerning the rates of population growth prior to the last 150 years. Europeans and their descendants increased from about 200 million in 1800 to almost 600 million at the beginning of World War I. This increase of Europeans and their scattering to other continents changed the political and economic situation through the increase of trade and cultural contacts throughout the world.

In northwestern Europe population increase was relatively slight during the decade 1930–40. The number of children per family decreased from more than five in the 1870's to about two in the 1930's. In many areas, therefore, the number of births was not much larger than the number of deaths. If this reduced family size continues, the total number of births will soon be less than the total number of deaths because an average family size of two cannot completely replace a generation.

REGIONS AND COUNTRIES WITH DECLINING RATES OF GROWTH. Practically all regions of the world have participated in the population increase of the last three centuries. Nevertheless, the rates vary from place to place and from time to time. Although the continent of Europe has provided immigrants for large areas in the Americas and in Oceania, much of Europe today is characterized by declining rates of population growth. Western Europe, while undergoing industrialization and urbanization, the test of modern civilization, first experienced a lowering of death rates. Later, as a small family pattern replaced the large family pattern essential to group survival in the subsistent agrarian economies of the ancient and medieval worlds, birth rates also began to decline. Before World War II much of northwestern and central Europe was not permanently replacing its existing population. This demographic transition from high mortality and high fertility rates to low mortality and low fertility rates occurred first in the so-called advanced nations of Western civilization. As this transition progresses, slow growth, relative stability, and eventual decline replace rapid rates of population increase characteristic of the early period of modernization. Already the demographic transition is well advanced in all of Europe except the extreme south and east; in the United States and Canada; and in Australia, New Zealand, and the Union of South Africa. These countries are of special interest to an Anglo-American world position, but include less than a fifth of the world's population.

Many areas of the world that will continue to have population growth for at least another generation or so already show tendencies to change from high fertility to low fertility. Such areas are the Soviet Union, Japan, eastern and southern Europe, and parts of Latin America. Another fifth of the world's population lives in these areas.

Thus, areas now having 40 per cent of the world's population show a decline in fertility that eventually may result in ending population growth. All such areas except Japan and Soviet Asia are in Europe, the Western Hemisphere, and Oceania, and for the most part already are industrialized and urbanized, or are in the process of becoming modernized.

REGIONS OF HIGH POTENTIAL GROWTH. The great agricultural areas of Asia and Africa have strong potential growth possibilities. India and Java have added vast numbers to their populations in recent decades. Although census and vital statistics data are inadequate or even lacking for many areas of Asia, it is estimated that the population of the continent increased about 30 per cent, or more than 250 million, in the 40 years from 1900–40. The absolute increase of 50 million for India from 1931–41 is a large number, but due to the huge size of the base population it is not an excessive average annual percentage rate of growth.

As the world's population has increased and people have traveled more throughout the world, new population problems have developed. National and international problems have arisen as a result of the migrations, which caused a mixing of racial, social, and economic groups. Many economic and social developments have taken place as people have moved about the world and have settled in new areas. In some instances areas have become overpopulated for high levels of living if food and raw materials from the outside were not available. Usually people have gone to new areas in order to secure a more profitable return from their activities. For the most part, however, the good lands of the world have been settled and few areas of any great importance are now open for new settlement. At the present time a great international problem exists to find politically feasible settlement areas for some of the oppressed peoples of Europe who do not wish to go back to their prewar homes. In all likelihood, if agricultural settlement is decided upon as the solution, a study of the marginal lands of the world may reveal areas suitable for settlement and development for a number of additional persons at a satisfactory level of living.

Problems of human fertility and mortality are related to the settlement capacity of regions and nations. Naturally it is the desire of most peoples to live longer and better and to enjoy life more completely. If more people live longer, however, even with no change in the birth rates, there will be more people in the world. Levels of fertility and mortality, patterns of migration, the levels of living developed within an area, and the natural physical conditions to be utilized by the people are all important factors in any study dealing with the maximum number of people an area can support under minimum and desirable living conditions.

Past rates of growth. In 1650 the world's population was only about 500 million persons. Today the population of more than two billion represents an increase of 300 per

cent in 300 years (see the chart on this page). Prior to 1650 the many famines, plagues, and public disorders tending to increase death rates led to slow and irregular population increases. Since 1800, with the development of

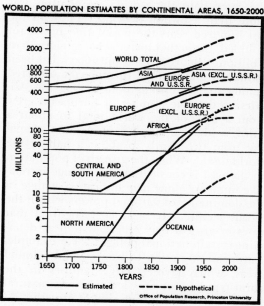

WORLD: POPULATION ESTIMATES BY CONTINENTAL AREAS, 1650-2000

NOTE: The projections in the above chart are described by Frank W. Notestein, "Population—The Long View," in *Food in International Relations*, Harris Foundation Lectures, 1944 (Chicago: University of Chicago Press). The chart, a combination of two charts that appear in Dr. Notestein's paper, is presented in *The Annals of the American Academy of Political and Social Science*, "World Population in Transition," Kingsley Davis, "The World Demographic Transition," page 2.

science and improved medical care, as well as better transportation facilities, life became more secure; children and adults lived longer; and the world's population in absolute numbers increased enormously. It must be recognized, however, that early population estimates may have been under-enumerated; and if such an error exists, the actual increases have been less than is believed.

The grouping of population into the various national units has changed greatly over the years. The Five Great Nations of today —the United States of America, Great Britain, the Soviet Union, China, and France— together hold sovereignty over about 55 per cent of the earth's land area and about 65 per cent of the population. In 1815 they possessed only about 36 per cent of the land area and in 1668 only about 18 per cent, with correspondingly smaller proportions of the world's population.

From 1650 to 1850 the population of the world more than doubled; in other words, at the later date the world's population was more than a billion persons. Thus, in the last hundred years the population has again doubled, the actual increase being more than a billion. Between 1800 and 1900 it has been estimated that more of this increase occurred among the Europeans than among the Asiatics, so that the number of Europeans grew from a fifth of the world total to about a third, with the number of Asiatics changing from two thirds to about a half of the world total. When the growth of population in the past is considered, this change in relative numbers alone may indicate a change in the dominance of national powers within the world picture. It must be recognized that rates of growth may reflect as well as determine certain national policies. For example, European migration to frontier and colonial areas, which favored large families in the rural type of economy, led to a large natural increase and thus a high rate of growth. As factors in growth limitation, famine and disease have not been so common in Western rural areas as they have in India and China. In many Asiatic areas the primary action favoring rapid growth during the last century was the development of transportation facilities that aided in famine relief and brought a resultant lowering of mortality, especially that of infants.

Many factors are involved in the development of population trends. In the areas of dense population, such as India, Java, Formosa, Korea, China, Egypt, and the Caribbean, the colonial type of economy prevails. Population is densely distributed, fertility is high, and mortality is high although variable. The presence or absence of growth depends on the state of political order, the abundance of food, and the incidence of epidemic diseases. On the other hand, in such regions as parts of Central and South America, and Central Africa, population growth has been slow and the areas have remained sparsely populated in comparison with Egypt and much of Asia.

Future populations. Students of population are often queried concerning the number of persons that could live in the world. Since the population-supporting capacity of areas of the world can be anyone's guess, many estimates have been made and much has been written on the subject. Although the writings of Malthus in the earlier 1800's discussed the problems of population growth and control, his work was not entirely original and he recognized that he had not stated the last word on the many phases of the population problem. The emphasis that Malthus placed on the relationship between population and subsistence has long been studied in its many ramifications, and his teachings are still recognized as fundamental for some areas of the world.

A number of factors are involved in the problem of population potentials. Many assumptions are necessary in order to estimate future populations. More than half of the world's population is still subject to high birth and death rates. The areas having population growth primarily limited by high death rates include many countries of Asia and Africa, but they differ in present densities of population and potential carrying capacity. It must be remembered, however, that present density does not necessarily provide a basis on which potential populations can be determined. Theoretical future populations can be determined by projecting past rates of growth and present trends into the future on the basis of some assumptions as to patterns of change. The capacity of any region to support population depends on many conditions. In determining the potential carrying capacity of a region, the type of the present economy, the agricultural pattern, the modernization and urbanization pattern (wherein the population is capable of buying items from other regions), and the interregional and international trade factors are all involved. In addition, religious and social factors, standards of living, and health conditions all must be considered in establishing population potentials. Consequently, any figure given as a future population must be considered relatively, and only for comparison with other areas, rather than as an absolute figure for any single country or region.

Hypothetical estimates of population growth, made by the Office of Population Research of Princeton University indicate a world total for the year 2000 of 3.3 billion people (see the chart on page 533). The scholars of this office believe this projected evaluation is conservative; it is based on an assumption of a slightly accelerated growth between 1940 and 1970 and a sharp curtailment after the latter date. Of this hypothetical world total, approximately 1.9 billion people would be in Asia. The North American figure of 176 million is in decided contrast to the vast increase projected for Asia, as is also the figure of 21 million for Oceania, with Australia and New Zealand making up the principal parts. Some increase is assumed beyond 1970, granting a more widespread diffusion of the European and American demographic pattern throughout Asia. Population estimates probably are as accurate as any predictions concerning the future generation because the next adult generation has already been born and will be the group to produce the oncoming generation.

Always in analyzing population growth and the capacity of an area to support more people, consideration must be given to increased agricultural productivity, improvement in the sanitation and health conditions, more and better transportation and communication facilities, and the possibility of the area being developed to produce specialized raw materials and to become a market for goods produced elsewhere. In other words, can the levels of living be raised, either through the development of the resources of the area, or through the development of specialization and interdependence with other areas?

In any case, the world as a whole does not seem to be in any immediate danger of becoming overpopulated. The problem is more one of enabling the world's population to live and work together in closer harmony, and at the same time raising standards so that the overpopulated agricultural areas can support more people through industrialization.

Political Significance of the Composition of the World's Population

Relative importance of ethnic groups. Many of the political problems of the world arise because of the variations in the composition of the world's population. Social and economic differences among the people of various regions are, in most cases, due in part to the variations in religion or nationality, or in occupation, or even to age and sex differ-

ences within the population groups. In view of all of these demographic variations there is little wonder that conflicts arise among the world's population. Through democratic education, however, we should learn to be tolerant of these differences and take them into consideration in working out the solutions to political problems.

RACES. Much has been written concerning the political significance of the racial questions of the world. The term *race* is hard to define, but here it may be used in a broad sense to mean skin color. Although the "white," or Caucasian, race as thus defined comprises roughly only half of the world's population, it directly or indirectly controls a much larger proportion through colonial affiliation and economic development. Regardless of the right or wrong of an "empire" policy, if racial hatreds are developed they greatly influence the political policies of countries and endanger world peace. All countries need to foster foreign policies that give greater emphasis to carrying out the idea of world cooperation.

RELIGIONS. Religion plays a significant role in the life of most individuals. Religious and political authority may or may not be vested in a single power, or even in parallel powers, but in any case religion exerts a great influence upon the life and policies of a nation. Although there are many different religious sects and denominations, most of the world's population is grouped into the Christian, Jewish, Moslem, Hindu, and Chinese religions. Christians may number as many as three quarters of a billion persons, whereas Moslems and Hindus number about 250 million each. Chinese and related religions comprise another 500 million. Thus, Christians, with approximately a third of the world's population, must recognize the religious differences in the other two thirds in order completely to understand international as well as national political problems.

Many religions have had a great influence upon the economic, social, and political life, and are close to the state even though not a part of it. Religious taboos on marriage and family relations have especially important demographic repercussions. The fact that widow remarriage is not allowed among the Hindus in India and that the marrying age is around 15 or 16 years means that many girls become widows in their twenties and not being allowed to remarry, do not produce as many children as they might without this taboo. Thus, without this curtailment, India's rate of natural increase would be even greater. Many actual practices and customs as favored or forbidden by religions are important factors in determining the rates of growth of population.

NATIONALITIES. Nationality as a means of differentiation is another factor to be considered in the ethnic composition of population groups. Place of birth may or may not indicate nationality or citizenship. The citizenship of the parents may indicate the nationality of the child. In many cases, nationality of population groups is one of the strongest political ties. It is a strong social, economic, and even a "yardstick" of class distinction in many communities. Of especial significance in the consideration of nationality groups is the fact that people have often migrated and settled in new areas and have colonized as specific "alien groups." Such alien groups may remain distinctly separate as minority groups or they may become assimilated through intermarriage. Many of the problem areas of the world, especially those of Europe, exist in part because ethnic lines cut across political borders. In the main, these problems are more social and cultural than economic. However, if a geographic area is utilized efficiently and persons are successfully making a living, ethnic problems may disappear or at least become insignificant.

Relative importance of occupation groups. One of the outstanding differentiations used in classifying the world's population is the grouping into "urban" and "rural" categories. Difficulties arise, however, in distinguishing urban from rural groupings because different countries use different systems of population classification, and towns of a certain size may be considered rural in one country and urban in another. Nevertheless, urban-rural comparisons are significant in relation to occupational groups, which in turn may be the significant indication of the economic position of a country. A country largely rural and agricultural in character holds a very different position or status in world affairs than a neighbor with a large industrial and urbanized population. One is a producer of raw materials, and the other a consumer and, in turn, a producer of finished products. As a country develops industrially and becomes more urban, its dependence on other regions increases. More international problems usually arise as the resulting export and import trade increases. Consequently, a study of the urban and rural relationships of the political entities of the world will reveal agricultural and industrial patterns. Countries, such as the United States and the Soviet Union, that have both types of areas possess an advantage. Other countries, such as the United Kingdom, the Netherlands, and Belgium, that are predominantly industrial, have developed empires and thus have economic and political control over both industrial and agrarian areas.

Closely related to an increasing urban proportion in the total population of countries are the trends in the rates of natural increase. It seems to be a normal development for death rates to decrease first, and then, with somewhat of a lag, for birth rates to decline. For cultural, social, and economic reasons fewer births per 1,000 persons in the reproductive ages generally occur among urban populations than among rural populations. In turn, this tendency affects the natural increase of the country as a whole and the absolute numbers of the population, present and future.

There are some countries, largely agricultural in character, that have developed a relatively large urban population. Australia, which has 59 per cent in cities of 5,000 and over, and Uruguay, which has 56 per cent, hold significant positions as exporters of agricultural raw materials; and the larger political and social urban centers have shown increases comparable with those in the cities of countries that have much larger populations. Such cities as Melbourne, Adelaide, and Montevideo have ranking status among the large city areas of the world.

Sex ratios, or the number of men per 100 women, may vary in terms of rural and urban classifications, and also in terms of the type of industry in cities. Women are commonly employed in textile and other light industries, and men in the so-called heavy iron and steel industry or in mining areas. Correlations often exist, therefore, between sex composition, rural-urban ratios, occupations, and the type of economy in an area.

Relative importance of age and sex groups. An important consideration in describing the population of any political unit is its breakdown into age and sex groups (see the chart on page 539). The national significance of such an analysis is threefold. First, the entire population cannot be called the working population. The 15–65 age group, especially of males, indicates the man power available to develop and utilize the resources of an area. Second, age groups by sex indicate the portion of the population in the reproductive age groups upon which the birth rates depend. Third, in time of either war or peace, the age groups by sex indicate the potential military man power available for defense or aggression as the case may be, depending upon the political aspirations of those in charge.

WORKING GROUPS. As has been indicated previously in this chapter, approximately three fifths of the world's population are engaged in the three types of subsistence occupations providing food, clothing, and shelter. In countries like India and China approximately three fourths of the population are so engaged. On the other hand, the United States and the countries of western Europe have more than three fourths of their total population available for "non-subsistence" occupations. Such countries have personnel available to develop the art, literature, and research needed to raise the country to a more advanced cultural stage. If properly utilized, this part of the working population can produce for peaceful activities and the betterment of mankind instead of developing a nationalistic creed of hate and a feeling of superiority.

About a third of the total population of the United States is normally in the 15–65 male age group. This group is the significant portion of the population upon which the economic status of a country depends. It is the group that is engaged in the many productive occupations supplying the essential needs of the population as well as the surplus essential to a highly developed exchange economy.

REPRODUCTIVE GROUPS. The relative proportions of a total population in the various age groups have important economic and political implications. They also affect rates of population growth. A large proportion of persons in the age group under 15 years will mean a large number in the reproductive group in the next generation. The absolute numbers of youth represent the manpower of the next generation. Education of this group in the fashion of Nazi Germany would have great political import upon the peace of the world. A "young" population, such as found in the U. S. S. R., assures a country of adequate man power probably for several generations in the future. On the other hand, the high proportion of the population in the upper age groups found in France, Sweden, and England presents a different picture involving a difficult set of problems. The economic and cultural patterns that affect the size of family also limit the biological maximum use of the younger age groups. Similarly, religious customs restricting the recognition of divorce and remarriage may restrict reproduction. Germany, Italy, and Japan attempted to raise birth rates through national policies in order to encourage a continued growth for an assured reproductive group and for the maintenance of future man power.

MILITARY MAN POWER. A very significant series of studies were made during World War II concerning the potential military man power of the Axis Powers and the United Nations. The basis of these studies was the age-sex distribution within each of the countries. Although of extreme significance during time of war for combat purposes, it is hoped that during peace the age group of 15–35 years of age as part of the 15–65 age group can be engaged in productive activities creating goods for trade and commerce, and producing commodities for the betterment of mankind. Again it must be emphasized that man power alone in absolute numbers is not the basis of world leadership. Of greater importance than numbers are the methods by which these people have adapted themselves to their environment.

Population Policies and Controls

Policies regarding international migrations. Completely free international migration has seldom existed during the history of mankind. Economic, political, and social restrictions have limited and in many cases prevented mass movements of people for purposes of permanent settlement. Immigration restrictions, put into operation by many countries, have served as factors in the development of social and nationalistic attitudes.

ECONOMIC LIMITATIONS. Economic conditions may cause a desire to leave one's home and seek better living conditions elsewhere. Often, however, these same conditions may under some circumstances prevent the desired migration. It is no small matter for families to leave places they have known as home for generations to seek new fortunes in unknown lands. In many instances economic handicaps were overcome when some of the family migrated first and sent money back for part or all of the family.

Subsidized resettlement programs may be developed in order to attract labor or occupational groups. For example, the Matanuska Valley Project was developed in Alaska during the 1930's in order to induce settlers to go there. Australia today is interested in securing new settlers, although admission favors persons of specified Caucasian extraction.

In many cases the mass transfer of peoples has been for the economic benefit of certain population groups. The importation of Negroes into the United States, although it created one of the most difficult social problems of the world, was a profit-dominated movement. The attraction of southern Europeans to northeastern United States for industrial labor contributed to the economic benefit of both employer and employee. It has been estimated that more than 60 million Europeans migrated to other continents during the century between 1820–1930. Of these, approximately 38 million came to the United States and about 30 million remained.

CULTURAL LIMITATIONS. Since the early 1920's the United States has had immigration quotas for most national groups based on national citizenship and previous immigration. Restrictions on the immigration of Asiatics reflected the early fears of a "Yellow Peril." Australia and New Zealand have held similar attitudes toward Chinese and Japanese immigration by favoring "white" immigrants, especially those of British extraction. Even with this policy of a "White Australia," about 70,000 migrants per year are now desired, a number that would tend to establish a stationary population of 7 or 8 million. Some, however, favor a more liberal immigration policy that would lead to a white population of from 20 to 25 million.

Another group of limitations on migration are those placed on the rights of alien residents. Many of the restrictions are real and may be implied by law, and others are merely the results of racial or national prejudices. There are both cultural and economic limitations relating to employment and the community in which the immigrants may work and live.

It often is recommended that an international migration authority be established in order that migration might become an international undertaking with the world problems agreed upon by the countries involved. Recommendations concerning settlement of new lands and exchange of labor as well as many other such problems could be presented country by country.

Policies regarding internal migration. Movement about one's own country is not new. Whether travel is by caravan or airliner, however, unrestricted internal migration is not possible. Such policies as the Homestead Act and the building of railroads into frontier areas, as exemplified in the prairie provinces of Canada, have stimulated internal migration and resettlement of agricultural persons. Policies of this type may be largely internal, but may nevertheless have an affect upon international migration if foreign groups are favored by the provisions of such policies.

Policies regarding natural increase. Policies regarding natural population increase can be discussed under three headings—birth rates, death rates, and health and sanitation conditions.

BIRTH RATES. The belief that countries should have population policies regarding growth is becoming increasingly prevalent. During the last generation lack of growth by a nation came to be viewed with alarm. Population policies are not always consciously planned. For example, preservation of the family has been uppermost in the organization of China for centuries. The question has been raised regarding the maintenance of this concept if and when modern industrialization and urbanization occur in China.

The traditional democratic concept of a population policy regarding growth has been that the determination of family size is the proper concern of the individual family rather than that of the nation. It is true that higher

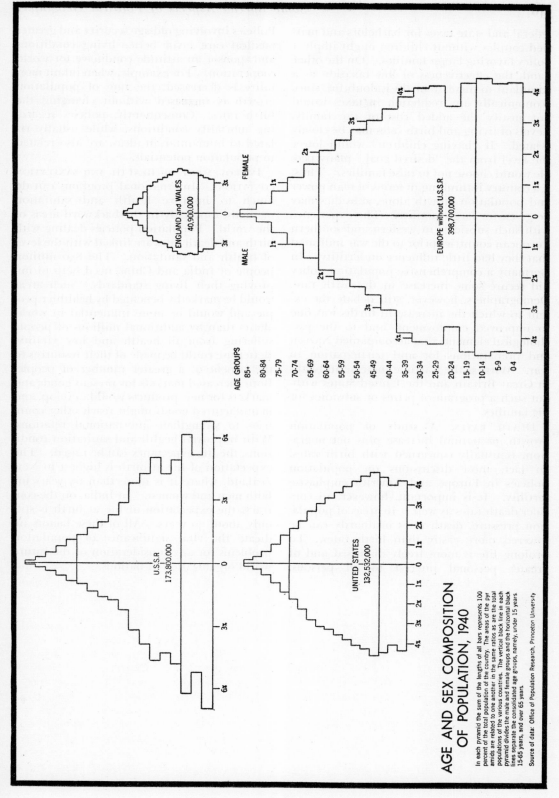

AGE AND SEX COMPOSITION
OF POPULATION, 1940

In each pyramid the sum of the lengths of all bars represents 100 percent of the total population of the country. The areas of the pyramids are related to one another in the same ratios as are the total populations of the various countries. The vertical black line in each pyramid divides the male and female groups, and the horizontal black lines separate the consolidated age groups, namely, under 15 years, 15-65 years, and over 65 years.

Source of data: Office of Population Research, Princeton University federal and state taxes for bachelors and married couples without children might imply a policy favoring larger families. On the other hand, the effectiveness of low taxation as a stimulant to increase births is doubtful, since economically any reduction in taxes would not justify the added cost of the family. Levels of living and birth rates may be closely related. If "having children" would lower the level from the "desired goal," many people would choose not to raise families. Thus, if a country is thinking in terms of man power and population growth alone, subsidies may be given for large families. The experience with such subsidies in western and southern European countries prior to the war indicated that they had little influence on fertility. In Germany a comprehensive population policy did secure some increase in the birth rate. Demographers, however, still debate the extent to which the increase in births was due to improved employment, and to the psychological elements that accompanied Nazism and preparations for and participation in war. Witness the wartime increase in births in Great Britain and the United States without such a program of prizes or subsidies for big families.

DEATH RATES. A study of population growth, or natural increase plus net migration, is usually concerned with birth rates. In fact, most discussions on population policies in Europe and America emphasize fertility. It is important, however, to consider death rates as well. In areas of population pressure, death rates ordinarily can be lowered more easily than birth rates. To prolong life is more freely discussed and of greater personal interest to all persons.

Policies involving old-age security and greater medical care favor better living conditions and sponsor an attitude conducive for world cooperation. For example, when infant mortality is decreased, the rate of population growth is increased without changing the birth rates. Consequently, policies regarding mortality conditions, while usually related to humanitarian ideas, are also related to population potentials.

IMPROVEMENT OF HEALTH AND SANITATION CONDITIONS. International programs can do much to improve health and sanitation methods, especially in the backward areas of the world. Population policies dealing with birth and death rates are linked with the level of health and sanitation. The 850 million people of India and China need help in improving their living standards. Such areas would be markedly benefited by healthier people and would be more influential in world affairs than by additional millions of people suffering from ill health and low vitality. Better use could be made of their resources to the benefit of a greater number of people. Both increased markets for present goods and markets for new products would develop, and manufactured goods might reach other countries to strengthen international relations. With improved health and sanitation conditions, the life expectancy can be raised. The expectation of life at birth is highest in New Zealand, where it is more than 65 years for both men and women. In India, on the contrary, the expectation of life at birth is still only about 30 years. All of these factors indicate the vital significance of population problems for any consideration of the future world organization of nations.

CHAPTER 38 | Grand Strategy of World War II

THE best point of vantage for the study of the strategy involved in any large-scale military encounter will be found in the command center of the force that holds the initiative. To the commander who has the initiative belong the decisions and plans that determine the course of the military operations. The defender, in turn, is compelled to shape his plans and operations to meet and hold the enemy's attack, while looking to the moment when a successful defense may enable him to launch the counter stroke that will restore strategic equilibrium, and possibly permit him to seize the initiative. Applying this principle to the global strategy of World War II, one must first look through the Axis reading glass as he examines the various campaigns that began with Japan's seizure of Mukden, September 18, 1931. The tempo of the campaigns increased by fits and starts to September 1, 1939, when Germany's invasion of Poland opened the major phase of the war, and terminated finally in the Axis defeats at El Alamein, Stalingrad, and Midway. After those turning points had been passed, the student's observation post should be moved to the command centers of the Allied Nations.

Meaning and Application of Grand Strategy

Definition. Strategy has finally come of age. Its swift evolution in the twentieth century has seen it stretch the bounds of the concept expressed in the standard definition: "the science and art of employing the armed strength of a belligerent to secure the objects of a war." The definition can be made to fit the facts if armed strength is conceived as a belligerent's total resources: human, raw material, productive plant. All rate as assets in the total sum of a nation's war potential; all become targets under the attack techniques developed in World War II. If the two great wars of the present century provide a fair basis of appraisal, the belligerents covered by the above definition may be interpreted as the mass of the world's peoples, divided into two hostile camps. Lastly, war in the fullest sense is no longer limited to armed hostilities. Germany's early bloodless victories were no less acts of war than the clashes between armed forces that followed. The objects of a war, in short, may be and often have been attained without the firing of a shot. Such a victory, won at no cost except what is paid for military preparation, shows strategy at peak effectiveness.

For such all-out aggression, and no less for the defense against it, the military historian has coined the expression "grand strategy." In Edward Mead Earle's words: "The highest type of strategy—sometimes called grand strategy—is that which so integrates the policies and armaments of the nation that the resort to war is either rendered unnecessary or is undertaken with the maximum chance of victory." * That definition is broad enough to cover the offensive and defensive policies and actions of both war and peace. It would be applicable no less to the maintenance of world security by the United Nations than to the local, regional, and global conflicts of the past.

* E. M. Earle, and others, *Makers of Modern Strategy* (Princeton University Press, 1944), p. viii.

541

Evolution. The evolution of grand strategy from the older, more limited, concept may be traced to three main causes. First, the French Revolution of 1789 brought in its train the modern world's readoption of the ancients' basic principle of the nation in arms. With that step the obligation of all citizens to make some contribution—eventually an unlimited contribution—to the war effort gained general acceptance. Second, the mounting tide of inventions in the same period was channeled by Napoleon I and later military leaders into the rapid and continuous increase in the firepower of their armies. Each such step brought a new drain on the commodity and industrial resources of the nations, and an added premium on the destruction of the enemy's resources as well as his armed forces. Third, the resultant trend toward all-out war was promptly recognized—and advocated—by General Karl von Clausewitz, who lived from 1780 to 1831.[*] The planned ruthlessness of the Axis' campaigns, including the bloodless conquests that preceded Germany's invasion of Poland, stems back directly to the thesis first expounded in modern times by that high priest of German militarism.

Military estimate of the situation; factors involved. A modern defense plan—or one of aggression—begins with an estimate of the situation. It is, in brief, a detailed analysis of all the factors bearing on the problem under consideration. For an individual combat unit in the theater of operations, such an estimate may be relatively simple. The estimates which, on the other hand, underlie the application of a nation's military potential in the formulation and execution of national policy are extremely comprehensive and highly detailed. The factors considered fall under six general heads: geographical, political, economic, demographic, psychological, and military. A glance at that list indicates that every item is duly weighed which bears, however remotely, on both the immediate and long-range war potential of one's own country, the potential enemy, and also of

[*] Karl von Clausewitz, *On War*, translated by O. J. M. Jolles (Random House, 1943). Little notice was first taken of Clausewitz's contribution to military theory. In fact, full implementation of his views occurred only when the German General Staff prepared for World War I.

other powers that might enter the picture as co-belligerents or as neutrals of various shades.

Analysis of the factors provides the basis for a conclusion that recommends a specific line of action. Due consideration is at the same time given to any alternatives that may be deemed sound. At that point the planning and strategy section of the military general staff takes over, decides on a line of strategy, and implements its decision with the draft of a detailed plan. Standard modern practice of the leading powers has made such plans subject to constant revision in order to keep pace with any changes that may occur in the factors on which the basic estimate was made.

The Strategic Situation in August, 1939

The Axis. History records no modern instances in which a nation was so well prepared as was Germany in 1939 for the swift and complete destruction of her immediate victims. The military disadvantages of her interior position had been converted into assets by such preliminary moves as Germany's bloodless conquests of Austria and Czechoslovakia, the military alliance concluded with Italy on May 22, 1939, and the non-aggression pact signed with the Soviet Union on the following August 23.[*] Moreover, the almost completed Westwall stood as a strong barrier against any possible Anglo-French attack. Internal political unity had been firmly established in both Germany and Italy through a combination of persuasion and compulsion, along with the liquidation of dissidents and unwanted minorities. Economic planning and legerdemain had given the Axis a production plant ideally suited to the support of major war and vast reserves of raw materials obtainable only from the outside world. In addition, there had been developed a substantial range of synthetic sub-

[*] Each of those steps fitted into the well-articulated strategy of conquest ordered by the Nazi hierarchy and implemented by its military instruments. Whatever doubts may have existed on that score prior to the Nuremberg trial of Germany's leading war criminals disappeared when the secret state documents offered in evidence disclosed every incriminating detail of the German plans. Germany, for example, had ready her plan for the conquest of Soviet Russia at the very hour when the two powers were signing their nonaggression pact.

stitutes for strategic items that might run short in the event of a prolonged war.

The demographic and psychological cross section of the German nation of that day discloses high levels of intelligence, physical fitness, mechanical skills, and enthusiasm for a program of conquest. Men deemed most suitable for military training had been welded into a military force incomparably superior to the armed forces of any other country at that time. Its armament was new and of the most advanced design, with extreme emphasis on the development of the air arm and the armored elements of the ground forces.

Germany's European partner in aggression suffers heavily by comparison. Italy, geographically vulnerable to sea and air attack, seriously deficient in both materials and production plant, lacking in the vital items of training, psychological stability, and zest for war, threatened to be more of a liability than an asset to Germany. A short and successful war would have lessened the hazard, while permitting Germany to capitalize Italy's potential in neutralizing a substantial part of the strength of the Axis' opponents. And the German strategists had planned a short and successful war.

In Japan, Germany counted on the accession of a powerful ally. On the warpath since 1931, Japan had roused the hostility of all the peoples listed by Germany as actual or potential enemies. Secret exchanges of views between Berlin and Tokyo had disclosed the immediate mutuality of objectives, paving the way for the complete adherence of Japan to the Axis cause on September 27, 1940. True, both Berlin and Tokyo had their misgivings about the ultimate division of the world's loot, but that was a problem for a future day.

Anti-Axis Europe. History affords few examples of national self-delusion in matters involving the life or death of a people that surpass the folly of the military estimates arrived at by the leaders of France and Britain in the years down to 1939. First, miscalculations began with the gross undervaluation of the rate at which Germany was rearming and the results already obtained in that direction. The French and British statesmen could not dismiss their obsession with the concept of a "disarmed" Germany who in 1939, they felt, had made only a partial comeback to her one-

time status as leading Continental power. Second, the same statesmen made estimates no less in error when they summed up the war potential of Britain, France, and the lesser states that might be included in an Axis scheme of aggression. Among other things, they failed to discount their own paper strength by the vast amounts of obsolete and obsolescent armament, much of it dating back to the previous war, that entered into the sum. Third, they apparently overlooked the enormous accretion to the Axis military potential that would result from its swallowing up of neighbor states, as Hitler had forecast in his *Mein Kampf*. Such an accomplishment would go far toward wiping out the disadvantages entailed by the Axis' interior position, with the result that her opponents around the periphery would be left facing an all but hopeless situation. Fourth, anti-Axis leadership had counted so heavily and so long on the deep-seated and mutual hostility between Teuton and Slav that its estimates left out the possibility of a shift in Soviet Russia's foreign policy.

Such mistakes were as much responsible for the policy of appeasing the Axis as the weight of a public opinion that favored a program of peace at almost any price. Much the same situation prevailed in the United States. True, our military experts had grave doubts as to the outcome of a war between the Axis and its logical opponents. On the other hand, the American people in the days of the "great illusion" were overwhelmingly opposed to any policy, including that of effective rearmament, that might lead to the involvement of the United States in a European war.

The one important variant from this tide of self-deception was to be found in Soviet Russia. Her experience with the successive purges of key personnel in government and the armed forces who were found guilty of disloyal contacts with Germany had left its mark. Moreover, Soviet espionage had established the facts of Germany's military strength and of the Western Powers' weakness.

The long-term possibilities. The above considerations were applicable chiefly to a short war, the war as planned by the Axis. For the longer term, Axis planning had to weigh such possibilities as a shift in Soviet Russia's policies, effective resistance by the

Anglo-French forces (in the event that Britain could not be persuaded to stand aside while the Axis entrenched itself as master of Europe), and the intervention of the United States. If all those possibilities were resolved against the Axis' interest, it would face a repetition of the multifront war that broke German resistance in 1918. Nazi plans looked to the elimination of this hazard by the use of false promises and threats to keep prospective victims quiescent until they could be knocked out in succession. Soviet Russia was to be no exception. And Japan, bitterly hostile to the United States, was expected to keep that nation too fully occupied to make her weight felt in Europe before Germany had mastered the Euro-African world. The low state of the United States' military preparations and the political strength of her isolationists figured heavily in that estimate.

War Plans in 1939

Germany. Wartime propaganda is responsible for the mistaken but widely held view that the German High Command was ready in 1939 with a fully integrated plan for: (1) conquest of the Euro-African world; (2) Japan's conquest of East Asia and the Pacific Islands; (3) joint Axis attack from several directions on the Western Hemisphere; (4) some final settlement, not yet defined, with Japan. Nothing could be further from the truth. On the other hand, good evidence exists that the Nazi dreamers in high position were fully committed to that grandiose scheme of conquest. Germany's military planners in her General Staff, by contrast, thought and acted in terms of one step at a time, expecting to digest each conquest as a prelude to the next act of aggression.

Even so, they failed to think through some of their projected moves. Little if any consideration was given, for example, to the possibility that Soviet Russia might intervene on her own behalf in the occupation of Poland, an oversight that created a sorry mess when the German and Soviet invading columns overran each other. Nor was there any prepared plan for the prompt invasion of Britain after the campaign on the Continent had destroyed most of the British land forces. Lastly, the technological development of such vital items as radar and the proximity fuse for artillery ammunition was repeatedly delayed for extended periods. Obsessed with Germany's immediate superiority in armament and the theory of a short war, the German strategists froze research and development in order to get volume production of standardized equipment.

Hitler's ideas, or "intuition," helped further to confuse the German situation. Like the Allied military leaders, the German High Command often went wrong, at least to 1943, in overestimating the strength of the Axis' opponents. Hitler frequently overruled his generals. And almost until the peak of the tide of German success Hitlerian intuition proved correct. Thereafter his amateur judgment and leadership became responsible for many of Germany's worst military mistakes.

Whatever the disagreements between Hitler and his generals, it is reasonably clear that in 1939 Germany's immediate program of conquest was five-fold: (1) to knock out Poland, exposing Soviet Russia to an invasion scheduled for a later date; (2) to seize Denmark and Norway, leaving Sweden surrounded and thus compelled to fit into the Axis system of economic exploitation; (3) to overrun France and the Low Countries; (4) to give Britain, exposed to complete and final disaster, the opportunity to make peace under an arrangement where her future existence would rest on Germany's sufferance; (5) to destroy Soviet Russia's military power, bringing the richest areas of her European lands under Germany's permanent control. The last move necessarily entailed the satellization or conquest of the Balkan area prior to the invasion of the Soviet Union.

The Allies. Defensive strategy, scaled down in some respects to the level of passive defense, guided the Allied military leaders in 1939. Soviet Russia's abstention from the hoped-for alliance against Axis aggression modified the application of the plan little, if at all. With France deemed secure behind the great concrete and steel barrier of the Maginot Line, a British Expeditionary Force to come in on France's left flank to aid in buttressing the Low Countries against a German offensive, and the sea lanes denied to German shipping, the 1918 blockade was to be reimposed until Germany succumbed. The appalling weaknesses of that outdated concept, placing its dependence on fortresses instead of trained, highly maneuverable forces, were fully disclosed in the spring of 1940.

Strategic Operations through 1942

Early results. Within less than two years after her blitzkrieg attack on Poland, Germany had made herself master of all western, central, and southeastern Europe. The neutrality of three unconquered states (Sweden, Switzerland, and Turkey) was precariously maintained by their substantial conformance with Germany's terms of economic behavior. Spain, benevolently inclined toward the Axis' cause, offered a possible route to Gibraltar, the capture of which would have resulted in the closing of the Mediterranean to Allied traffic. And the whole vast occupied area, including Italy, was swiftly being welded into one vast war machine. Italy, salvaged from military disaster in Greece and again in North Africa, had been demoted to the status of satellite. By air, submarine, and occasional surface raider Germany had struck savagely and effectively at Britain's homeland, navy, and shipping.

The situation had shaped up to the point where a full-scale offensive against the Soviet Union offered promise of destroying her as a military power, and thereby enabling Germany to exploit the vast resources of Russia. At the same time, a double pincer operation by way of North Africa and southwest Asia was expected to give Germany control of the Suez, gateway to direct contact with Japan. Both the actual successes scored and the seemingly greater opportunities for further successes that beckoned to Axis strategy added up to sums never before contemplated by a military conqueror. For an overall picture of Axis successes, see the map on page 547.

A more careful examination of the situation, however, discloses weaknesses of varying gravity in the German situation. The prolonged effort in 1940–41 to destroy British resistance by aerial bombing had cost the Luftwaffe losses that it was never able to recoup. And despite the damage suffered by Britain, her output of war goods in the spring of 1941 was heavier than before the Battle of Britain. Germany's submarine war had likewise fallen short of expectations. The partial elimination of this handicap to Allied shipping was accomplished despite Ireland's refusal to permit Britain the use of three major Irish ports.

Transatlantic routes into Britain were reduced to the two lying north and south of Eire. By the end of the war Eire's interpretation of the rules of neutrality was to cost the Allied Nations vast, though undetermined, numbers of ships, cargoes, and crews.

Within the conquered areas of Europe, the first shock of military disaster had been replaced by growing resistance and sabotage. Their collective and cumulative effect told increasingly on German power, a fact tacitly admitted by the Germans when they countered with reprisals whose ferocity and scale were till then unknown to modern warfare.

Across the Atlantic the once promising buds of Nazi activities in Latin America had been mostly shorn off by the states affected. Only the Argentine Republic remained a strong focal center of pro-Axis policy and action. More important was the swift reversal of sentiment in the United States, now become the "arsenal of democracy." Fifty of her World War I destroyers had been reconditioned and turned over to the British navy. The Lend-Lease Act of March, 1941, opened to the Axis' opponents a reservoir of American goods and services that, by the end of the war, reached a money value of more than $42,000,000,000. And the United States was at last rearming rapidly and effectively, with an objective clearly discernible from the growing hostility of her people for the Axis.

All of the above factors weighed against Germany's chances of success in the event of a long war. But all could be discounted if the planned drive against the Soviet Union brought a repetition of earlier Nazi successes. There could be no doubt as to the success of Germany's initial onset. Could she, however, destroy the main Russian armies and, with them, the Russian will to fight? While Germany was rounding out her Nazi empire, the Soviet armies had been busily extending the Union's territory by occupying part of Finland, the Baltic States, eastern Poland, and Bessarabia. Those gains gave Russia added space in which to maneuver, the space she was to trade for time in the coming test with Germany.

German failure on the Eastern Front. As on the Marne in 1914, so again on the Eastern Front German strategy failed of success on several occasions by a narrow margin. The last gasp of the final offensives in the closing months of 1942 found the three major bastions of the Russian line—Leningrad, Moscow, and Stalingrad—still in the Soviet hands. Germany's failure must be charged to a number of causes, among them her diffusion of effort, division of counsels (with Hitler superseding his generals after the unsuccessful drive for Moscow in late 1941), emphasis on the seizure of territory rather than the destruction of the Russian armies, underestimation of her opponent's strength, and material aid furnished Soviet Russia by Britain and the United States. Then, too, the savage ruthlessness of Germany's conduct of the war brought reprisals, with interest, a factor that eventually cut heavily into German strength as Russia's guerrilla fighters perfected their techniques of war behind the German lines.

As a result, when the turn of the military tide came after the Russian victory at Stalingrad, Germany's strategists found the effective strength of their Eastern armies so far reduced that no real German offensive was ever again possible in that theater. At that juncture Hitler insisted on a strategy of defense in place. His military advisors argued in vain for a large-scale withdrawal to a more defensible line. Hitler's rejection of that policy played perfectly into the Allied Nations' strategy, aimed at the destruction of the Axis' armed forces.

German failures in the Near East. The German plan to close the double jaws of a giant pincer, by way of Turkey and the Levant from the north, and North Africa from the south and west, has been mentioned. In 1941 and again in 1942 Marshal Erwin Rommel's *Afrika Korps* was stopped just short of its Egyptian objective by last-ditch British defense efforts. In each instance the German High Command failed by a small margin to give their outstanding commander the wherewithal of men and supplies to accomplish his mission. And in 1942 the diversion of American tanks, planes, guns, and trucks from training needs at home to the rearmament of the British in Egypt figured heavily in the outcome.

Nazi fifth column efforts to secure control of Syria, Iraq, and Iran had in the meanwhile (1941) been stamped out by quick countermoves of the Allied forces. As a result, the projected German drive through Turkey would have called for the diversion of a greater total of strength than Germany could spare so long as Turkey stood firm on her neutrality.

In October, 1942, the heavily reinforced British Eighth Army broke through desperate German resistance at El Alamein to open a campaign that ended with the surrender to General Eisenhower of the last remnants of the Axis forces in Africa the following May. German miscalculations, particularly as to the strength of the Allies, were largely responsible for that Axis disaster. Heavy credit must also be given to the air and submarine raids on Germany's supply lines across the Mediterranean which, in the summer and fall of 1942, cut the inflow of Rommel's supplies by more than half. Nevertheless, prior to El Alamein, Rommel's defeat was so far from being counted on as a foregone conclusion that, in the summer of 1942, the Anglo-American Combined Chiefs of Staff were giving serious consideration to a plan based on the assumption that: (1) Vichy France and Turkey would be forced into full collaboration with the Axis; (2) Rommel would secure Egypt and the Suez area; (3) the Allied forces would be forced to set up a defense south of the Sahara.

The United States entry into the war: Effects on Axis strategy. Pearl Harbor radically altered the grand strategy of all the belligerents. Axis calculations included a swift and convincing Japanese success. Occupation of Australia and of India by Japan would be a prelude to a junction with the European Axis by way of the Near East. A first step to that end was to be a carrier-borne air attack on the United States Pacific Fleet at Pearl Harbor in sufficient strength to assure the destruction or, at least, the prolonged immobilization of the fleet. Thereafter Japan could exploit her marked sea-and-air superiority in the Far Eastern theater, while her submarines were cutting the greatly lengthened Allied supply line from the United States to Australia. At the same time Japan's territorial conquests were to be developed into a fully integrated system of island fortresses and bases against which America's growing forces would presumably strike in vain.

An all-out submarine campaign against Allied shipping in the Atlantic at a time when most of the United States' naval strength was occupied in the Pacific was expected to block the flow of American supplies to Britain and

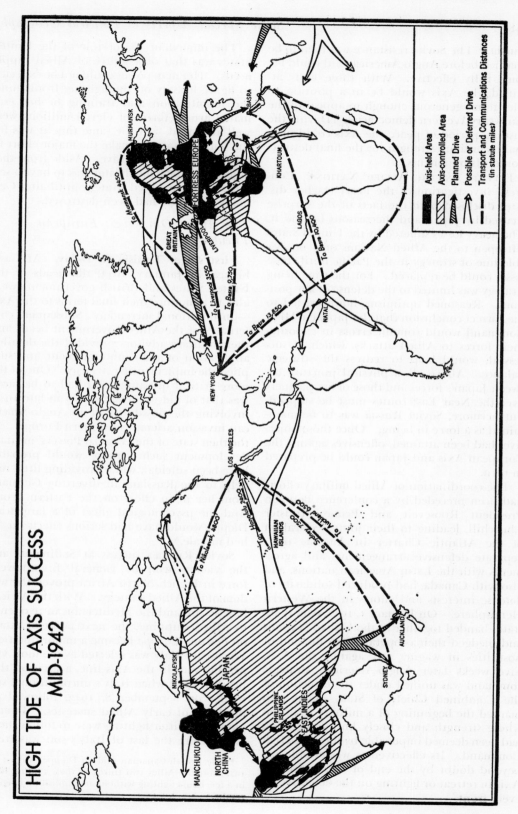

HIGH TIDE OF AXIS SUCCESS
MID-1942

Legend:
- Axis-held Area
- Axis-controlled Area
- Planned Drive
- Possible or Deferred Drive
- Transport and Communications Distances (in statute miles)

MURMANSK
BASRA
KHARTOUM
LAGOS
FORTRESS EUROPE
GREAT BRITAIN
LIVERPOOL
NEW YORK
NATAL
To Murmansk 4450
To Murmansk 4450
To Liverpool 3550
To Basra 9750
To Basra 10,400
To Basra to Lago
To Basra 13,850

LOS ANGELES
HAWAIIAN ISLANDS
To Nikolaevsk 4800
To Honolulu 2400
To Sydney 7300
To Auckland 6500
NIKOLAEVSK
JAPAN
PHILIPPINE ISLANDS
EAST INDIES
MANCHUKUO
NORTH CHINA
SYDNEY
AUCKLAND

Russia. The Soviet resistance was then to be smashed before Anglo-American aid could become fully effective. With those ends attained, the Axis would be in a position to offer terms generous enough to appeal to the war-weary Western democracies. During the ensuing period of peace the Axis could marshal its military strength for the final destruction of its opponents.

EFFECTS ON THE ALLIED NATIONS. Congress' investigation of the Pearl Harbor disaster disclosed both the facts of the surprise secured by Japan and the reasons behind it. The heavy losses suffered by the United States left open to the Allied Nations only one viable line of strategy in the Pacific until those losses could be replaced. For the time being strategy was limited to the defense of key positions. Reasoned optimism, however, led to the correct conclusion that the Japanese High Command would commit errors in exposing their forces to Allied attacks, which, if successful, would help to redress the strategic balance. Above all, a physical juncture between Japan's forces and those of her partners over the Near East routes must be stopped. Furthermore, Soviet Russia was to be maintained as a force in being. Once those objectives had been attained, offensives against the European Axis and Japan could be prepared in turn.

The coordination of Allied military efforts had been preceded by a conference between President Roosevelt and Prime Minister Churchill, leading to their joint declaration of the Atlantic Charter in August, 1941. Separate defensive arrangements and agreements with the Latin American nations, and also with Canada, had produced solidarity of defense interests and efforts in the Western Hemisphere. On January 1, 1942, twenty-six states banded together as the United Nations and pledged their cooperation to the end of hostilities in waging war against the Axis. Five weeks later Anglo-American strategic command was unified under the direction of the Combined Chiefs of Staff. That step marked the beginning of a military coalition whose strength and closely knit integration had been deemed impossible by the Axis High Command. Its effectiveness was established beyond doubt by the end of 1942, with the Axis in retreat or fighting on the defensive on every front.

The immediate major role of the United States was that of a source of Allied supply needs. Her man power could not be expected to figure heavily on the fighting fronts until the mobilization and training of her estimated armed forces of eleven millions were well advanced. At the same time it was for the United States to make the major effort in blocking Japan's offensive. Aside from that objective the Pacific theater was to have a secondary role in Allied strategy until after Germany and Italy had been destroyed.

The Allied Offensives: European Theater

First stage: Tunisia to D-day. At Casablanca, in January, 1943, the heads of the United States and British governments were able to announce their final terms to the Axis —unconditional surrender. Subsequent conferences of the Allied government heads and their military advisors provided the detailed application of that announcement and supplied the implementing strategy. One of the more critical questions that had to be faced was that of aid to Soviet Russia in late 1942, involving the possibility of an Anglo-American invasion attempt in western Europe. In the then state of the Western Powers' military development such a move would probably have been suicidal, while providing little real help to the Russians in diverting Germany from her main effort on the Eastern Front. And the psychological effect of a large-scale Dieppe would have had serious effects on Allied morale.*

Soviet Russia's success at Stalingrad and the victory won by General Eisenhower's force in French North Africa proved the wisdom of the Allied strategy. With the African base secure and the Mediterranean re-opened to Allied shipping, the next point of attack on *Festung Europa* became a major question. War-weary Italy was selected as the most vulnerable spot in the Axis line, a decision that justified itself when Italy's unconditional surrender on September 8, 1943, followed on the heels of early Allied successes. Twenty months of bitter fighting were to follow, however, before the last of Italy's soil was freed

* The British-Canadian raid on Dieppe, August 19, 1942, cost the Allies two thirds of their raiding force in a few hours fighting without accomplishing tangible results.

from Axis control, for Italy had become a secondary theater while preparations were pushed for the creation of the invasion force in Britain against the day of the major invasion of Europe, scheduled for the late spring of 1944.

The Axis submarine menace had long since been reduced to a costly nuisance by Allied countermeasures. The aerial bombing of Axis military and industrial targets by thousand-plane raids became routine in 1943. Arms and supplies were moving in quantity to resistance groups in Axis-occupied lands, and in great volume to Soviet Russia. The Soviet forces, moreover, were moving ahead in successive offensives that, by the spring of 1944 were striking into the Balkans. Rounding out the process was a well-developed psychological offensive acquainting the German people and their victims in the occupied areas with the truth of the military situation.

There remained the great question as to whether Germany could throw back the coming Allied invasion. No less important was the question of whether German science and war industry had the ability to produce enough of its projected secret weapons in time to affect the outcome. Foremost among these was the V-1, jet-propelled bomb, designed to be fired from continental launching sites and planes against the Allied military bases in Britain. Less advanced in development was the V-2 rocket, greater in range and much greater in radius of destruction than the V-1 weapon. Unlike the V-1, its velocity was too great for any defense through interception or anti-aircraft fire. Lastly, there were the questions of where Germany could find the man power to replace her dwindling armies on the Eastern Front, to maintain an adequate defense in western Europe, and to restore her bombed-out productive plant. German strategy hoped to find the answer to such questions in a defense so strong that the Allies' losses would compel them to grant an honorable peace, well buttered with permanent territorial gains for the Axis.

Second phase: D-day to Germany's surrender. Allied invasion plans made provision, at least in theory, for several landings in Europe. That secret was purposely left unguarded with the intention that German espionage would ascertain the facts, and that Axis defense forces would accordingly be dispersed. The deception was enhanced by the sudden appearance of "invasion fleets" at Britain's east-coast ports.* Well guarded, however, was the secret that a single landing in force was to be made on the Cotentin Peninsula of France, followed in due course by a second landing in southern France. To understand the pincer drives of the Allies, see the map on page 550.

Today, as always, the forced landing on a hostile shore is regarded as one of the most difficult of all military maneuvers. Nature provides as serious difficulties as does enemy opposition; then multiplies them with its storms. Allied strategy found its answer in a wide range of devices contributed by science and industry, sufficient in their sum to overcome the worst effects of the almost unprecedented storms that struck the invasion force. Air attack, as planned, isolated the immediate theater of operations by the destruction of the enemy lines of communication over a perimeter extending a hundred miles inland. Naval escort sealed off the seaway approaches from enemy interception; overhead cover was provided by fighter planes. Low-level bombing and naval bombardment overwhelmed the German's shore installations.

The strategic concept throughout was bold, though never out of line with the quality of the forces trained to execute it. The resultant speed and scope of the victories scored by the fall of 1944 exceeded the anticipations of the Allies as well as the enemy. Nevertheless, in spite of the loss of a million men in six months of fighting, the Germans were able to make a last stand at their Siegfried Line and in Holland north of the Rhine. In December a last German offensive in Belgium set back the Allied plans for a matter of weeks. By that time Germany had called to the colors her *Volkssturm*, a mass levy of all males between the ages of fifteen and sixty. Her armed forces had already been heavily diluted by the draft of prisoners of war, men who would serve only under compulsion of death. Such a ragtag of soldiery was no match for the Allied drives that in the spring of 1945 rolled forward simultaneously on the Western, Italian, and Eastern Fronts.

In the end a devastated Germany could get

* Most of the "ships" were inflated rubber models, indistinguishable at an aerial observer's height from the real thing.

no more than the unconditional surrender terms laid down by the Allies at Casablanca more than two years earlier.

The Allied Offensives: Pacific Theater

The disastrous defeat inflicted on Japan's naval and carrier-borne forces at Midway in

the Allied forces had been developed as fully as that of quality, Japan must succumb.

A few question marks remained, however, to confront the strategists in both camps. Could China, wholly cut off from outside help except for the dribble of supplies flown in from India, remain a force in being? And would not China's capitulation release

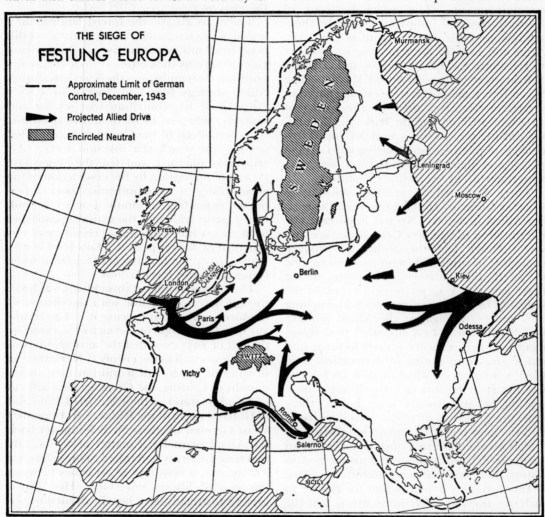

THE SIEGE OF

FESTUNG EUROPA

— — — Approximate Limit of German Control, December, 1943

▶ Projected Allied Drive

▨ Encircled Neutral

June, 1942, brought an end to her dream of victory and swollen empire. To that point she had exploited with great success her initial naval-and-air superiority. But even her victories had revealed grave weaknesses in her equipment and the training of her forces. Such revelations could not fail to convince either the Japanese or United States military leaders that, when the element of quantity of

enough Japanese forces and supplies to enable her to establish herself so securely in her newly won domain that the Allied peoples would balk at paying the price of ultimate victory?

The Allies' strategic answers to those and other queries took several directions, all combining into a shift from passive to active defense, mounting into the offensive wherever opportunity offered. China's defense was to be bolstered by increased supplies and the detail of United States' personnel for training of Chinese troops. The extreme extensions of Japanese military control, particularly those that threatened our communications with Australia and the northern defenses in the Aleutians, were to be lopped off. Submarine and air attacks on Japan's shipping routes were planned to prevent her exploitation of

and military leaders—the atomic bomb. Whether it could in fact be developed into a practical weapon was still a question.

In spite of the relatively small forces that could be spared from the task in Europe the overall strategic plan succeeded beyond all expectations. Once the bloody fighting for the seizure of the Solomons-New Guinea ladder had ended with Allied success in the spring of 1944, "island-hopping" by lengthen-

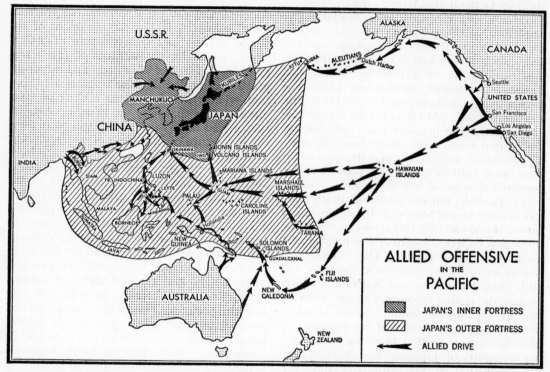

ALLIED OFFENSIVE
IN THE
PACIFIC

JAPAN'S INNER FORTRESS
JAPAN'S OUTER FORTRESS
ALLIED DRIVE

her newly won resources. Ultimately, all effective Japanese contacts of the Japanese homeland with the outside world were to be severed. And, once the initiative was surely ours, key points in the widely scattered enemy holdings were to be seized and converted into Allied bases. To follow the course of the ensuing offensive, see the map on this page.

High priority in the Allied plan was given to the seizure of bases in the Marianas, lying less than 1,500 miles from Tokyo. That distance is within the practical bombing range of the B-29 plane, scheduled to carry destruction to Japan's highly vulnerable industrial and military plant. And beyond the B-29 loomed a secret technological project, known only to a handful of scientific authorities

ing strides left many vital Japanese holdings completely isolated and useless for defense purposes. General MacArthur's swift success (1944–45) in the recapture of the Philippines signified that Japan's homeland was in vital danger. Japan's navy, merchant shipping, and war industry took terrific punishment from the swiftly rising tempo of Allied air and sea attack, which threatened the complete extinction of those arms. In the China and Burma theaters Japanese defeats became in 1945 the normal news of the day. And when both Okinawa and Iwo Jima fell, after fanatical defense efforts that inflicted heavy losses on the attackers, the continuation of Japanese resistance had become military folly.

At that juncture Japan launched a succession of peace overtures through neutral channels, none of which measured up to Allied insistence on the terms laid down at Casablanca—unconditional surrender. For the final blow two great operations were planned, the first calling for the seizure of Kyushu in the late fall of 1945, the second to be aimed at Honshu and scheduled for the spring of 1946. Combat divisions hardened in the European theater were shifted to the Pacific to build up General MacArthur's invasion force. Naval and air elements were similarly expanded. No cheap victory was expected if the do-or-die tactics of the Japanese continued. Such tactics had been responsible for the introduction of a new technique, the *Kamikaze,* or suicide flyer, whose plane became a flying bomb, directed by its pilot into an enemy vessel. At Okinawa the *Kamikazes* had inflicted the heaviest losses suffered by the United States navy throughout the war. Thousands of such planes and the men to fly them were held in reserve by Japan for the last-ditch defense of her homeland.

It is possible, but not probable, that fanatical defense would have won better terms for Japan, if one can give full credence to the information collected by American intelligence agencies in Japan after V-J Day. That possibility vanished utterly when, early in August, 1945, Hiroshima and Nagasaki in turn became the testing laboratory of the effectiveness of the atomic bomb. Soviet Russia's intervention in the war and her invasion of Manchuria were further blows to the surviving remnants of Japanese morale. Against the opposition of his militarists, Emperor Hirohito announced to the Allies his willingness to accept their terms, a statement followed by Japan's formal surrender on board the U. S. S. *Missouri* in Tokyo Harbor, September 2, 1945.

The Strategy of Peace Enforcement

The United States and Britain discovered in the flames of war the power to forge an effective fighting instrument. Without disparaging Soviet Russia's contribution to the defeat of Germany and her Balkan satellites, it becomes increasingly clear that military collaboration between the Anglo-American combine and the Soviet Union was never easy. Neither was it on a basis of that kind of understanding which welds military allies into a common force. At times, in fact, cooperation became tenuous and highly uncertain. Two other powers, China and France, threw their weight into the struggle so far as their limited means permitted.

When press commentators coined the expressions "Big Five" and "Big Three" as labels for these Allies' power combinations, it was only a step to the point where the wishful thinking of millions in many nations had sketched the design of continuing international solidarity in the establishment of enduring peace. Less than two years after Germany's surrender the outlines of the peacemakers' sketch had dimmed; and superimposed over its fading lines appears a tracery that, when studied, suggests a clash of arms more violent than any yet known. Against that mixed background we begin to discern the emergence of new lines of strategy. On the one hand, the world's peoples have indicated overwhelmingly their desire of assurance against any recurrence of armed aggression, from whatever quarter. Beginning with the draft at San Francisco of a plan for a United Nations organization designed to protect the security of all, and thence down to the discussion in the U N Assembly and Security Council on such major problems as world disarmament and the international control of atomic power, there has been no difficulty in getting thumping majorities to support any proposition that offers promise of lasting peace. Good will of that kind is to be had in abundance. More than good will, however, is needed to achieve the desired objective.

To begin with, the utter ruin that has befallen Germany and Japan has left in both Europe and Asia vast areas of power vacuum. Throughout the occupied zones, and also in unoccupied areas no less vast in extent, devastation and low-subsistence levels, often at the near-starvation level, have been the common picture for months, now beginning to sum up into years. And in China, continuing civil war calls on 450,000,000 people for the last pulse-beat of human endurance. Such conditions are by no means uncommon to human history. In the past they have led without exception to capitalization by individual powers whose leaders saw in the weakness of their neighbors the golden chance for low-cost conquest.

By V-E Day the repetition of that historical trend of progression had become an established fact. Central Europe had become an enclave securely held by the armed forces of Soviet Russia and her satellites. Not long after, the security of Turkey and Iran, and also of friendly Greece as well, was sharply threatened. And Manchuria, China's sole well-developed workshop, had been left a gutted junkheap by the Russian armies. Moscow's official declarations that the demands of her national security are sufficient explanation of her moves to establish "friendly neighbors" around her periphery have enlisted sympathy in some quarters. Just so for her actions in Manchuria, explained on the ground of her need of reparations. Such arguments became less plausible, however, when Premier Stalin told his people that a capitalist and communist system cannot live side by side in the same world, a situation that, in his opinion, can be resolved only by war.

Stalin's bold pronouncement produced no immediate repercussions. European Socialists declared that a socialized, economically restored western Europe would bridge the gap between the capitalistic Americas and the Communized areas. Their optimism was short-lived. The damage suffered by this middle world during the war, transforming it into a political and economic vacuum, and Soviet Russia's pursuit of her objectives showed what was in prospect for that vacuum. "Free elections and democratic procedures" in the liberated areas of east central Europe soon produced Communist governments, even where that party polled a small minority of the vote. At the same time, successive Communist-led strikes and sabotage in western Europe were directed at the breakdown of reconstruction.

Popular reaction in areas outside the Russian-dominated zone played an important part in the increasingly strong stand of the western states against further aggression. The sharp down trend in the Communist vote in such countries as Italy and France, followed by the dropping of Communists from the cabinets in both these countries, told volumes. A vital element in this development was the hope of economic recovery roused by the European Recovery Program (ERP) launched in 1947. Soviet Russia and her satellites reacted violently. Their newly organized Cominform declared economic and political war on ERP, calling on Communists the world over to sabotage its operations. And in Greece, where Communist-led rebels continued their civil war, neighboring satellite states gave increased support to the rebels.

The most serious crises developed in 1948, shortly after Yugoslavia's persistent refusal to become a Soviet puppet state ended in her break with the Cominform. Though her government remained as completely Communist as at any time since Tito's rise to power, this *demarche* was a definite breach in the solidarity of the Soviet bloc. Under those circumstances the presence of three western powers in Berlin became in Moscow's eyes a salient projected into the Red-controlled area. Moreover, the economic integration of the western occupied zones of Germany was being followed by steps looking to political union of that area. Russia's answer was a progressive blockade of Berlin that in June, 1948, reached the point of isolating that city from all water and land communication with the western zones. The U. S.–British countermove was the inauguration of the airlift to Berlin. Direct conferences with the Soviet representatives and the action of the UN Security Council to break the blockade proved unavailing.

Thus, before the year-end the lines between the collectivized, Russian-dominated East and the democratic West had hardened. At the same time the situation in the Far East, where Communist armies were sweeping south and threatening to take over all China, had become highly fluid. The specter visioned by Harold Mackinder, in which a "Heartland" power drives to dominance over the Old World, had become an even greater threat than in the hour of Hitler's triumphs. The "fringe lands" of Europe reacted with moves looking to the knitting together of their several economies. The first conferences to that end quickly turned to the more crucial matter of joint security. Before the end of 1948 the broad lines of a Western Union had been marked out, with Britain, France, and the Benelux nations collaborating as the key group. Direct aid from the United States in the form of arms and military equipment, and the assurance of support from that country and Canada in a crisis were sought. The next move was up to the newly elected Democratic Administration in Washington.

CHAPTER 39 | Geography in Future World Politics

POLITICS, present or future, cannot realistically be divorced from man's activity upon the earth. Political geography may well be thought of as the "earth factors" or "distribution patterns" in politics—the variants of "place" and "space." Thus geography provides a fundamental but not unchanging "frame of reference" within which national and international political organizations exist and operate. Political problems, as well as their solutions, are involved in this relationship.

The density and distribution of population in any political area; resources in farm, forest, fishery, and mineral wealth; surface configuration and climate with their many ramifications; access to the sea lanes and airways; and location as to neighboring political areas—these are some of the significant "place" and "space" factors. The importance of such earth factors in politics rests, first, on their fundamental relation to human wants and needs. Even in politics the age-old requirements of food, clothing, and shelter have by no means been displaced by liberty, fraternity, and equality. Second, a substantial part of the importance of the earth factors derives from an unequal distribution of the world's goods from area to area. Political stresses and strains are partially related to the fact that nature appears generous and benign in some areas at some times, but elsewhere seems to yield the earth's treasures in a most niggardly fashion. Finally, the importance of these factors is enhanced by the marked differential modification in the natural pattern that appears because of man's greater activities in one region than in another. Existing

resources may have been well developed in one political area but neglected in an equally rich neighboring area.

Various earth factors, operating jointly in simple, or, more often, complex interrelation with cultural, economic, technological, and political factors provide the basis of political life. To be sure, factors not primarily geographic, or not geographic at all, relating rather to the race and culture of particular people or relating to the particular period may greatly overshadow the earth factors in particular instances. Thus, these several variables, though they differ in importance from place to place and from problem to problem, are all necessarily involved in some complex fashion. The rate of exploitation of petroleum reserves in Saudi Arabia, for instance, depends not solely upon the presence of subsurface oil resources and the knowledge and technology adequate to get the oil out of the ground and move it to where it can be used. In addition, available supplies in other areas must be taken into account; as must supposed requirements of peace and war, as well as the political treaties and trade agreements that the interested political groups may have made.

If, then, the basic factors and their interrelations are so complex even as regards a particular aspect of the politics of Saudi Arabia, how can the geography of future world politics be intelligently examined or even speculated about logically? Is not the venture more foolhardy than enlightening—a case of murky crystal gazing? To this doubt the geographer replies that some of the factors, particularly the earth factors, are to some extent capable of being constructively evaluated. These factors are less rapidly and unpredictably variable and are better established as to trend, direction, and probable magnitude than are those unrelated to the physical qualities of the earth itself. That is, they are more truly a frame of reference, partly for inherent reasons, partly because they have been better explored and measured.

But in any analysis involving the factors of political geography there is a large element of uncertainty in future prediction. Though the way a people lives and works changes but slowly, the harvest from the land and the sea of food, wood, and fibers increases or declines not alone with changes in soil type from area to area but with yearly fluctuations in weather and long-term depletion or conservation of resources. Equally important are man's needs, the effort he makes, his technology, his economic organization, and his political structure as it aids or hinders his more basic efforts. Will not new technology make present resources of land and energy of little value or useless? Is it possible that through new techniques future international organization will mold anew the fundamental economic pattern of the world?

The geographer, more earth-bound perhaps and certainly dealing more in the "by and large" than the nuclear physicist or the specialist in hydroponics, visualizes only partial modification with time, not abolition of the geographic forces and factors involved. The principle of comparative areal advantage, of the geographical division of labor, is with us now and will be with us in the future. Nature did not make countries equal; man through force may modify boundaries, yet utterly fail to equalize or balance political areas. Through political agreement tariffs may be lowered and barriers to a free flow of goods and people removed; even then there will be those countries that have more and those that have less of any particular resource. Of that which they have, some will develop and use more, others less. To recognize this principle is not to be deterministic but merely to arrive at a non-static theory of geography and politics, that is, to recognize these fields as co-variants, each related to, vitally affected by, and modifying the other. Thus cautiously the future of geography in world politics may be explored.

The Population Variable

Density of population, particularly if that density is comparatively high or is increasing rapidly, generates political problems. Witness the calls, valid or invalid, that have gone out to the world for "living space" or "co-prosperity spheres." Witness the spilling over in the past of the more densely populated East of the United States into the comparatively unoccupied lands of the middle and western parts of the continent, once claimed by other countries. Witness the wars and fears of a population-static France, in competition with states on the east showing continued population expansion.

Equally, increase of population density makes for geographical problems, problems of man in his space and resource relations. Essentially, it increases competition in securing the necessities of life—at least beyond some optimum density. The man-land ratio, a geographic concept of crude support potential, is unfavorably affected by increasing density. Increased population pressure on the land in some cases stimulates the forces of external expansion and migration. The same situation may have domestic consequences. Resulting internal pressures react upon the internal social, economic, and political structure; that is, tenant versus landlord, urban versus rural, factory versus farm, tariff protection versus export subsidy, and even isolationism versus internationalism. In one way or another all of these points of friction are aspects of that man-land ratio.

As developed in Chapter 37, it seems clear enough that the present striking differences in population density between the Orient and the Occident will be still further intensified during the next decades. Though it is possible that the decline in Scandinavia, for example, can be halted or even reversed, the most acute students of the problem find little probability of that latter possibility becoming an actuality. In the same vein, there seems to be little probability that restrictive Western social philosophy, including birth control, will become widely accepted in the Orient in the near future. The probable result, then, is increased density in an area already densely populated and a decline in one that, by comparison at least, is not over-populated.

But if those areas that seem likely to remain centers of what we call Western civilization were to be filled more nearly to capacity, would a balance thereby be achieved in the world picture? Probably not. One student of the problem, Griffith Taylor, has estimated the capacity population for such areas at white standards: North America, 700,000,000; Europe, 385,000,000; South America, 115,000,-000; South Africa, 82,000,000; and Australasia, 62,000,000; giving a total of only slightly more than half of the present world population. There is, however, no present indication that such areas will so expand, nor other areas cease expansion.

The political and economic world has had considerable experience with increasing population density—that of the Western World has increased rapidly in the past three centuries. But what can be foreseen of the political results of a likely, though not inevitable decline? There would seemingly be provided a basis—economic, cultural, and psychological—for fear and tension, regardless of whether migration is or is not permitted to areas of declining population. International political organizations will be unable to escape consideration of this problem. Whether there will be authority to support "sanitary" measures in the areas of expansion seems questionable, at least in the near future. World economic organization may well be able to encourage and facilitate resource development and industrialization in the overcrowded areas. But there is a limit to the results to be obtained by those means as well as a further question of whether some aspects of such development, as irrigation, may not actually encourage additional expansion of population. What can or will be done about migration into areas of low population density, tropical or otherwise, remains to be seen. The finding and application of adequate solutions to the problems of population in areas of decline are even more uncertain.

Politically, the problem of whether representation on world committees and in international organizations shall be allocated in relation to population is due to come up from time to time. It would hardly seem to be an emerging trend to accept per capita representation, at least not so long as some of the areas facing population stability or even a decline in numbers are politically the most active and the major support of the international organization. And admittedly the concept of equal per capita representation has its limits in a world in which education, skills, technology, and wealth are highly variable from area to area. How valid, for example, is the concept when New Zealand, which has high standards of education and living and a democratic government, is contrasted with areas of equal population that have little education of the people and governments that are far from representative?

The Land Variable

Populated land implies the cultivation of food unless other factors are unfavorable. During the war we repeated not without truth: "Food will win the war and write the peace." Hungry men can hardly be expected to have peace in their hearts. Abundant food, then, is a cornerstone of any realistic attempt at world peace, more potent than fair words of diplomats or fine treaties. Without the inventory of world land resources on the basis of agricultural quality, now proposed but not yet activated by the Food and Agricultural Organization of the UN, only some general facts can be indicated and some possible political aspects pointed out.

The amount of cropped land, considering land now used with comparative intensity for food, fiber, or pasture crops, varies sharply in relation to total area from continent to continent (table, page 558). Thus, Europe has relatively intense cropping; Australia much less so. Again, the cropped land per capita is fully four times as large in amount in Anglo America as in Latin America.

That the large per cent of total area of the world not used for crops is more than a "frontier" situation that will be corrected by further settlement and increased population is suggested by an examination of the map on the facing page, based on rainfall and temperatures. Also that a large percentage of some continents is semiarid or arid, that is, less than 20 inches of rainfall per year, and not well adapted to most types of intensive cropping that do not require irrigation becomes apparent from the data in the table on page 558.

The total land that might otherwise be suited to intensive food production by cropping is still further lessened by a multitude of natural factors, such as too much rain, "climatic risk," drought, altitude, short growing season, unfavorable soil, and poor drainage. These factors have been consciously or unconsciously taken into account by the world's farmers in their age-long trial and error methods. Some can be partially overcome by modern technology, even by economic organization that makes experimentation and risk-bearing less hazardous.

But there are also economic margins to be considered along with, rather than separately needed in larger amounts? How much more? What of overproduction, local or world-wide? What solutions can be found for what appears to be emerging technological obsolescence of some products of the land, for example, cotton and natural rubber? Will they go the way of indigo, replaced by synthetics? In the drafting of international agreements on agricultural products to what extent shall the industrialists and importing

REGIONS UNSUITABLE FOR CROP GROWTH

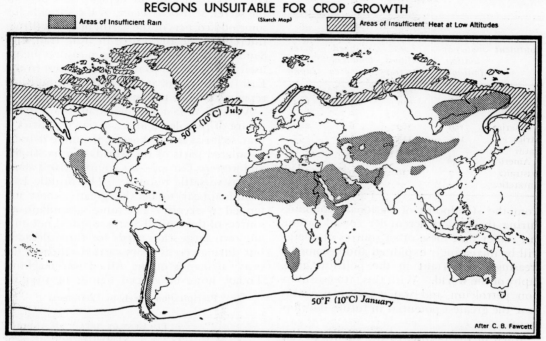

Areas of Insufficient Rain   (Sketch Map)   Areas of Insufficient Heat at Low Altitudes

50° F (10°C) July

50°F (10°C) January

After C. B. Fawcett

from, the natural margins. Emphasis on national production and world demand, technology employed, and risk capital supplied are all pertinent factors. How much food does the world need and want; what will it be willing to pay for it? In any case there is no doubt that the world can have more of most products from the land if there is sufficient demand. To effectuate increased production forests can be cleared, wet lands drained, dry lands irrigated or cropped by mechanized "dry farming" methods, plants and animals made more productive by applied genetics, better technology employed, risk capital supplied, and/or more labor used.

Therein lie many political problems, present and future, national and world. How much national self-sufficiency as to food is necessary or desirable? What foods are countries be favored with cheap raw materials; to what extent shall the consumer be represented as well as the producer? Shall agriculture in general or only particular crops be subsidized? In what size units is agriculture most efficiently carried on for specific products and areas? How does size of unit accord with political stability? To what extent shall mechanization be required or encouraged? Might it not be better to produce much of the world's food by concentrating production in the areas best adapted thereto, using the best known methods, fertilization, and other innovations? Would it be possible to encourage new agricultural development in semiarid areas, the tropics, or areas recently considered to have too short a growing season for successful cropping? These and other questions along similar lines will constitute the future political geography of the land variable.

The Energy Variable

The new and startling source of power, politically and otherwise, is, of course, atomic energy. We shall assume, however, that atomic energy will not displace other sources

Cropped Land in Relation to Population and Total Area

Continent	Approximate population (millions)	Estimated cropped land (millions of acres)	Approx. % cropped land is of total area	Cropped acres per capita
Asia	1,150	800	7.0	.69
Europe	525	570	23.0	1.04
Anglo America	150	360	6.0	2.40
Africa	165	115	1.6	.74
Latin America	138	70	1.5	.53
Australia	7	16	0.8	2.29
Antarctica	—	—	—	—

from the standpoint of national economics during the period hereunder consideration; but rather that these other sources of energy will be increasingly exploited and become increasingly important in the political geography of the world. With this latter assumption petroleum and water power probably have the greatest potential in future development.

Much of the politics of the twentieth century up to the present could be written validly, not around the direct struggle of the "isms," but around the indirect and no less acute struggle for slaves—not human slaves but the far more versatile and valuable slave, extraneous energy. The resultant of such energy is heat, light, and power, which in turn make possible the multiple goods and services of modern civilization, called by the economist "place" and "form" utility.

We may quickly write off as of inconsequential importance to the modern political world as sources of energy the tides, the wind and sun (directly), wood, and the various vegetable oil seeds and cereals sometimes used as fuel. Coal, however, is the bulwark as a source of energy in the world of fuel. It still is an important item in commodities moved in trade and is a prime prerequisite in such

politically important major industries as iron and steel. Politically, coal is the basis of the territorial struggle for the Ruhr and Upper Silesia, and to a lesser extent for the Donets Basin and North China. And the British coal mines are fundamental in the political as well as the economic reconstruction of the United Kingdom.

But the prize energy resource in the present and near future is petroleum. In the presence or absence of oil deposits lies part of the secret, if it be a secret, of the struggle for some odd corners of the earth; of the multiple interests of the Big Three in Iran, Iraq, and Saudi Arabia; of the strong measures being used by the Dutch to retain an interest in the East Indies; and of at least part of the political repercussions in regions of Latin America.

A pertinent fact to be noted in regard to the future of petroleum and associated politics is that, so far as is now known, the more densely populated parts of the world—China, India, and western Europe—are comparatively short of this versatile resource. The Middle East would appear to be the great, almost untapped reservoir. The once abundant resources of the United States supplied not only our own large-scale needs for three decades, but during recent years carried much of the heavy demands of the Allied war machine. Today, however, official figures in 1944 in-

Precipitation Levels by Continents

Continent	PER CENT OF AREA WITH ANNUAL PRECIPITATION		
	Under 20 inches	20–40 inches	Over 40 inches
Asia	67	18	15
Europe	47	49	4
Anglo America	52	30	18
Africa	54	18	28
Latin America	16	8	76
Australia	66	22	12
Antarctica	—	—	—

dicated that proven reserves of the United States constituted only an eighteen-year supply at the prewar (1935–39) annual rate of consumption. Though new discoveries will be made, they will probably occur at a declining rate. Moreover, consumption is likely to increase with the continued expansion of the automobile and aircraft industries, at least as long as petroleum products are available at reasonable cost. In addition, the large reserves of oil shale and the possibilities of using alcohol and synthetic fuel from coal do not yet provide much basis for complacency.

Politically these facts of geography will probably be resolved in some manner by international agreement. Witness the several attempts made in recent years to arrive at an International Petroleum Agreement. As for the United States, exploration for petroleum, conservation, stockpiling of existing supplies, and greater use of nondomestic sources will almost certainly take place.

The other major source of energy likely to play an increasingly important part in politics is that obtained from falling water. Unlike petroleum, it is not exhausted by use; wastage consists in not harnessing the potential power. Fundamentally, the distribution of water power, particularly unutilized water power, differs strikingly from that of petroleum. Africa with its large areas of plateau far above sea level and heavy tropical rainfall has something like forty per cent of the world's potential. India and China also have a large potential as yet unharnessed.

The location of this undeveloped power, which might mean so much to populations now without notable amounts of extraneous energy for industrialization or betterment of living standards, raises politico-economic problems. How is its development to be accomplished? The scientists and engineers to do the work along with the needed machinery presumably can be obtained in due course from countries more advanced technologically. But what of political arrangements for financing? Is it a matter for unilateral action, as by the Export-Import Bank of the United States; or is it a matter for international financing, the International Bank perhaps? And what of repayment? Will the development of water power be the means of producing goods directly for repayment, or will multilateral trade be the goal? Such new development requires capital goods and in the long run becomes the basis for expansion of the world's trade. But in the shorter term readjustment and contraction, or even loss of markets that technologically more advanced countries now hold, may result.

In the United States water power and the electricity obtained from it have become the core of regional development—the Tennessee Valley Authority and Columbia River Basin developments. These projects have also been a factor in the movement to spread industry and to raise rural living standards. Will similar projects be less of a catalytic factor internationally? One can anticipate the question arising of whether African power shall be used on that continent for industry, air conditioning, irrigation, and for other regional innovations, or whether it shall be transmitted (when engineering science permits) to areas of present higher population density and more advanced technological development, for instance, the Mediterranean Basin.

In summary, the United States, as might be expected, outranked all other countries in the utilization of power in the prewar world. Energy consumption totaled three to four times that of the United Kingdom. Germany used only approximately half as many kilowatts equivalent per capita and Japan only one sixth as many as the United States. Canada and some countries of western Europe, however, ranked moderately close to the United States in per capita utilization.

Shifting to a consideration of the potential aspects (see the chart on page 560) with the concomitant of future political strength, one finds that only the U. S. S. R. may look forward to the development of energy resources that approach the level possible for the United States. The United Kingdom, even with its coal, is a serious contender only because of the resources of the Commonwealth-Empire. Future development of resources in Africa, Brazil, Canada, China, and India will help to balance the now distinctly unbalanced world development of energy resources, but even with full development in those areas it appears that the United States and the U. S. S. R. will remain strikingly in the forefront.

Other Resource Variables

One writer on the subject of mineral reserves in the United States, former Secretary of the Interior Harold Ickes, declared:

. . . the plain fact is that we cannot afford another prolonged war in 20 or 30 years. . . .

The prodigal harvest of minerals that we have reaped to win this war has bankrupted some of our most vital mineral resources. We no longer deserve to be listed with Russia and the British Empire as one of the "Have" nations of the world.

ENERGY RESERVES AND THEIR UTILIZATION IN 1937 (MAJOR COUNTRIES ONLY)

We should be listed with the "Have Nots" such as Germany and Japan.

It should be burned into our consciousness that we do not have an inexhaustible supply of minerals—the sinew that makes this country mighty. Our minerals are not inexhaustible and (are) irreplaceable. Unlike wheat and corn, new crops of minerals do not appear from year to year. Further, the faster we grow in industrial strength and military potency, the more rapidly we dissipate our mineral resources—the very basis of our military and industrial power.

As indicated in the chart on this page, even the United States with its great array of min-

must be accumulated as contingency reserves. As regards some items, less economic sources must be maintained as standby or emergency sources. These resources may be synthetic or natural and in some cases they must necessarily come from outside the borders of the United States.

Not only does more active exploration of the world seem probable, but also the bulk of future discoveries of new resources seem sure to be in parts of the world now less well explored than the United States. However, these other areas are unlikely to prove notably

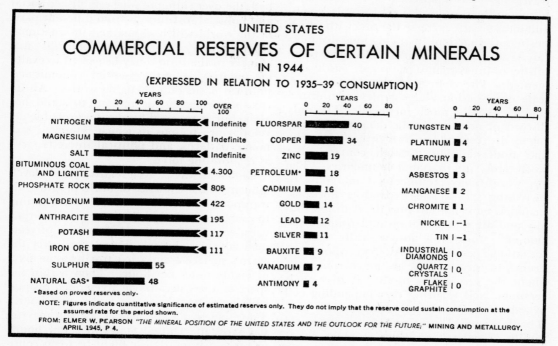

eral resources does not have within its own borders all the types needed in a complex industrial civilization. In the case of several strategic minerals its supply will last only a very few more years. Those of which less than twenty years' supply exists even at the present rate of usage are especially critical. In the case of a fair number of necessary agricultural products, for example, natural rubber, sisal, and kapok, foreign areas provide the entire supply. The future political geography of the United States will entail careful study of the sources of each of such items. If the future supply from these sources is assured through international organization, so much the better. Otherwise, stockpiles

better balanced in resources within their own borders than is the United States. This future outlook in turn puts a premium on a peaceful world, or, that failing, on political and economic arrangements with complementary areas to insure the United States access to items needed.

But in spite of the heavy drain on some vital resources in some areas during the past few decades, ways and means will probably be found to obtain or substitute for such items. To bear out this contention, there is no clear indication that any of the major political units are soon to lose a ranking world position because one or more of their domestic resources is near exhaustion. Leadership and dominance in international affairs are much too complex a matter for such a condition to have catastrophic results. Besides, since trade channels and political arrangements are still available, international agreements allocating scarce items among the world's users may be anticipated.

The Time Variable

General aspects. The political geography of the future must take at least brief notice of the degree to which communication and travel have been speeded up. New techniques in the transportation of people, goods, and ideas greatly increase the ease with which business transactions involving long distances can be successfully executed. In turn, possibilities of intercommunication are vastly augmented. The chances of success for large-scale organization and complex administration are thereby much increased. The only discordant note lies in the dangers of building up distrust and hate rather than sympathy and understanding through contacts that freely cross international boundaries. The two world wars were fomented on a globe of increasing speeds and expanding horizons; mankind must not fall into the delusion that any and all transportation and communication on a world scale automatically carry international good will. All responsible governments, for example, are much concerned about the sovereignty of the air over their territory, well realizing that impending evil as well as good may approach from the skies. The time variable thus forces upon the world family of nations an issue of great consequence to future global stability—that of utilizing speed for the mutual advantage of all concerned rather than allowing it to become a tool in the hands of power-hungry aggressors and bring destruction and chaos to the world.

The physical expressions of the time variable are many. Air transportation, with the breath-taking speed at which commercial passengers, cargo, and mail can be carried, is perhaps the most impressive and far reaching. Keeping pace with the airplane, however, are the development of the radio and radiophone, the improvement of the transoceanic cable, and the surging progress of television. These and other innovations in rapid communication facilitate the merging of cultures between basically different environments and enhance the opportunity for extending political control from a powerful center over increasingly greater distances.

The time variable presages a more closely integrated world in which the status of small political units may become uncertain. Can a small nation contain a sufficient diversity of resources and effect a sufficient industrial capacity with which to meet the growing needs of its population? Can a small nation hope to survive a war when it has no possibility for "defense in depth"? Whether for good or bad, the over-riding of long-established social and political institutions from different parts of the world will have marked international repercussions. International political machinery in the future may be geared to evaluate and provide for the essential economic and political needs of a changing world. An increasing tendency for nations to stand not alone but as regional blocks is a probable development—regions in which resources, economic patterns, and political interests serve as the binding force.

Global airways. As a relatively new development in the sequence of world progress, air transportation has exerted and is continuing to exert a tremendous impact upon the time variable. Over a span of thousands of years man advanced his maximum speed over the earth's surface from a jog trot to some sixty or eighty miles per hour. Then within the space of a few decades he accelerated his possible pace to some 300 miles per hour.* Traveling by air the average person may today cross the United States in a few hours, or make a transatlantic flight between continental United States and continental Europe from one day to the next. Just what this increased speed has meant to the people of the world becomes strikingly apparent in terms of its impact on economic and political affairs.

Within two years after the end of World War II more than 200 commercial airlines were regularly operating over the airways of the world. In 1947 each of seventy-four separate countries and possessions supported at least one air carrier officially approved by its

* The speeds used in these examples represent the maximum available to the average traveler. At a time when airliners are cruising at 300 miles per hour experimental aircraft may be able to travel at well over twice that speed, but years must pass before such speeds are representative in mass travel.

respective government. The airlines ranged in size from a globe-circling American company to a tiny Canadian concern with a route only twenty-two miles in length. More than two fifths of the world's postwar airlines function as international carriers, with their route patterns extending beyond the territory of their home country. The gigantic world network formed by the composite of all airlines testifies to the existence of the modern Air Age about which so much has been said and written (see the map on pages 564–65). In a relatively short time the Air Age has passed from a popular magazine or Sunday supplement conjecture to a reality.

Three factors were essential to the establishment of a system of air routes providing interregional transportation on a global scale. First, the airplane as an instrument of transport had to be made a technical success. Aeronautical engineers experimented to construct aircraft capable, under diverse environmental conditions, of making dependable take-offs, flights, and landings. At the outset planes were a novelty for the adventurous; next they became a luxury for those who would pay a premium to overcome gravity; recently they emerged as an established means of travel for a rapidly increasing proportion of the world's population. The heavy demands on airpower in World War II acted as a huge subsidy in accelerating the development of more and more efficient aircraft—not only fighters and bombers, but cargo planes which, in their peacetime version, carry passengers, mail, express, and freight.

Second, the airplane as an instrument of commerce had to prove an economic success. There had to be adequate payloads to warrant profitable operation of airlines over wide areas and for long distances. Business men, government officials, pleasure seekers, and individuals traveling for personal reasons have accepted the airplane as a practical mode of transportation, their numbers assuring its feasibility from the standpoint of the profit motive. Also, as operation has become more efficient, more cargo is being shipped by air; the rapid transfer of commodities has proved advantageous in many fields of endeavor.

Third, even after technical and economic success had become realities, the airplane faced still another hurdle, that of securing the *right* to fly. Thus, political jurisdiction over

flying space, or sovereignty of the air, became a vital international issue. At one end of the scale was a possible "free air" policy whereby planes would be permitted to come and go at will, irrespective of the national ownership or control of the territory over which they were flown. At the other end was a possible "closed air" policy whereby the planes of one country could lawfully be excluded from the flying space over another country. Actually, the present status of air sovereignty approaches the "closed air" rather than the "open air" policy, although mutual (bilateral) agreements between countries extend reciprocal rights that permit international operations. Most governments allow the aircraft of other countries to land on their territory provided the same privileges are granted in return. However, it is uncommon for any airline to carry traffic between points *within* a foreign country.

The political bases underlying the international air routes show wide variations from country to country. In Europe all important airlines are government monopolies, or "chosen instruments." Before World War II these carefully controlled state airlines, under the guise of commercial carriers, were largely used to promote political prestige, to link together scattered units of empires, and in the case of some nations, to facilitate political intimidation and military aggression. As a result of such practices the development of legitimate commercial traffic suffered. In the postwar world air carriers in Europe continue to be government instruments, but much more emphasis is placed on the great traffic potentials that exist.

The United States with its heritage of free enterprise has elected to certificate a number of commercial airlines to fly over international routes. A policy of "regulated competition" has resulted in the assigning of specific zones, or "traffic generating areas," to each of several air carriers. The Civil Aeronautics Board made the route awards to airline companies already established in the field of commercial flying, basing their selections on (1) the past records of the companies themselves, (2) the economic necessity of the routes to be flown, and (3) the political significance and strategical value of linking certain foreign areas with the United States. Two American flag airlines cross the Pacific, three

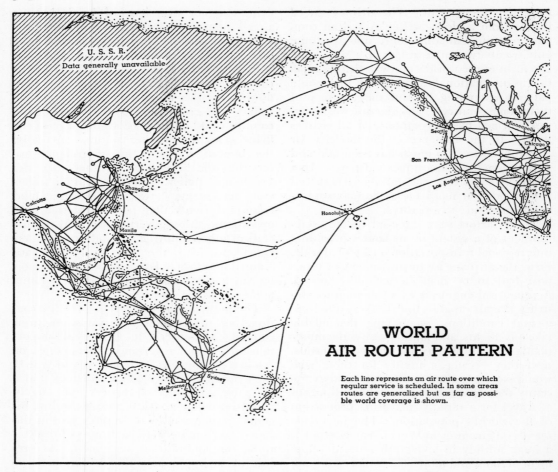

**WORLD
AIR ROUTE PATTERN**

Each line represents an air route over which
regular service is scheduled. In some areas
routes are generalized but as far as possible world coverage is shown.

cross the Atlantic, and several extend their
routes southward into Latin America.

As an exception to the general world pattern of air routes, Soviet Russia has thus far
been unwilling to open her air space to foreign aircraft. Within Russian territory a
nation-wide air transportation system is
operated by the government. In addition,
numerous air routes connect Moscow and
large cities (mainly national capitals) of eastern and central Europe. Over these routes
schedules are not generally made known to
the public and travel is largely limited to
"priority" passengers who have Soviet sanction.

The world's air route pattern is impressive,
and almost any city of importance, whether it
lies in a highly industrial region or a remote
tropical area, can be reached by regularly
scheduled airliners. By utilizing the "ocean
of the air" most peoples of the earth have

available a method of transportation free of
the many barriers that beset surface travel.
As a further advantage, air travel is normally
from three to seven times as fast as land travel
and from six to twelve times as fast as water
travel. Air travel is global in scope; ocean
travel is at best semi-global; land travel is regional.

Despite the great strides of air transportation toward effecting what is popularly called
a "shrinking world," the entire structure of
commercial operation is predicated upon
political rights and close regulation. In contrast, ships upon the sea can with but few legal
obstructions come and go at will. They
travel across the oceans of the world and
through the narrow seas; for a fee they may
enter any port where there chances to be
cargo. When imposed, shipping restrictions
spring from the competitive nature of travel
regulation rather than a nation's hesitancy

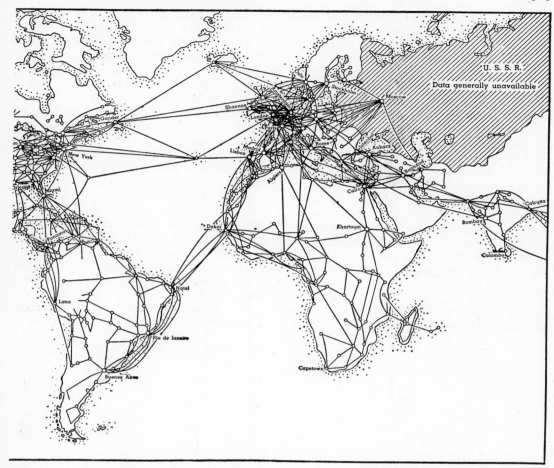

to allow foreign ships to approach its shore. Air travel can carry the "freedom of the seas" to the freedom of "open air" in a world of trust and cooperation, but it can breed hatred and force the building of impenetrable legal barriers in a world of suspicion and intense nationalism. The ability to overcome political hazards will be the crucial test in the continued development of global airways.

The Variable Economic Pattern

The geographic pattern of production, processing, transport, markets, and consumption does not remain static. The resulting oscillations have had their repercussions on the political world. Certainly much of the legislation and perhaps much of the political waxing and waning of particular parties in power appear to be related to instabilities in the economic pattern. Not merely the striking effect of deep depression or high boom

but the slower and more local development of new resources and exhaustion of old reserves are to be considered as part of the economic variable in politics.

New technology gives value to old waste products. Faster and cheaper transport permits the economic exportation to new markets formerly not accessible. To some degree previously not the case, areas have more of a chance than formerly to specialize in the products they can best produce. The competitive area tends to become world wide, except as governmental and nongovernmental agreements and restrictions limit the effective scope of new economic possibilities.

The tariff has long been a much-used political means of restricting the competition of foreign areas with domestic production. The more recent private cartel and the intergovernmental commodity agreements have as their purpose the control of supply, markets, and prices.   The results are mixed and opinions as to the value or disadvantages frequently depend on whether one is the producer or the consumer, the importer or the exporter.   In any case the pattern of trade is changed from what it would otherwise be, and in this process national and international political aspects are involved.

As to the future, the economic pattern of the world may possibly become more stabilized than has recently been true.   On the financial front the International Monetary Fund exists to assist in stabilizing currency. The International Bank will provide funds for development of resources and industries. The Food and Agriculture Organization will bring more facts to bear on the world's agriculture and perhaps implement additional development in some areas.

Finale

This is our world—the home of more than two billion individuals.   Political organiza-tion in major and minor units is an outstand-ing characteristic of the world pattern.   Man has found it useful or necessary to group him-self with his fellow men in these various units, still short of world-wide in size.   These polit-ical units not only form a part of the mosaic of world patterns but act upon and react to the multitudinous and multifarious facts of geography, whether they be physical, eco-nomic, or social.

It is these broad glimpses of our world— the question of how much of what is where and what of it?—that have provided the theme of many preceding pages.   We have looked and looked, through the eyes of the political scientist and the geographer— broadly but perchance not too hastily to gain the broad and stronger lines.   And finally we have pondered briefly the political geography of the future, the variants of "space" and "place" in the mist of time yet to be.   Geog-raphy will unquestionably be there then, along with politics.

APPENDIX A

Area and Population of the Countries of the World

(Fall, 1947)

Countries	LAND AREA *		POPULATION		Latest census or estimate date
	Thousands of sq. miles	Per cent of world total	Thousands of persons	Per cent of world total	
WORLD TOTAL	50,997	100.0	2,227,976	100.0	
AFRICA:					
Egypt	383	0.8	17,626	0.8	1944-E
Ethiopia	350	0.7	5,300	0.2	1936-E
Liberia	43	0.1	1,500	0.1	1941-E
Union of South Africa	473	0.9	10,522	0.5	1941-E
AMERICAS:					
Argentina	1,080	2.1	14,131	0.6	1945-E
Bolivia	507	1.0	3,596	0.2	1945-E
Brazil	3,286	6.4	41,565	1.9	1940-C
Canada	3,462	6.8	11,507	0.5	1941-C
Chile	286	0.6	5,024	0.2	1940-C
Colombia	440	0.9	9,390	0.4	1943-E
Costa Rica	23	0.05	747	0.03	1945-C
Cuba	44	0.1	4,779	0.2	1943-C
Dominican Republic	19	0.04	1,768	0.1	1941-E
El Salvador	13	0.03	1,997	0.1	1946-C
Ecuador (including Galápagos Is.)	100	0.2	3,086	0.1	1941-E
Guatemala	42	0.1	3,284	0.1	1940-C
Haiti	10	0.02	2,719	0.1	1941-E
Honduras	44	0.1	1,201	0.1	1945-C
Mexico	760	1.5	22,227	1.0	1945-E
Nicaragua	49	0.1	1,095	0.05	1945-E
Panama	29	0.1	632	0.03	1940-C
Paraguay	150	0.3	1,141	0.05	1945-E
Peru	501	1.0	7,023	0.3	1940-C
United States	2,977	5.8	138,955	6.2	1945-E
Uruguay	72	0.1	2,203	0.1	1942-E
Venezuela	347	0.7	3,951	0.2	1941-C
ASIA					
Afghanistan	250	0.5	12,000	0.5	1946-E
China [1]	3,877	7.6	455,900	20.4	1946-E
India and Pakistan	1,576	3.1	388,998	17.5	1941-C
Iran (Persia)	628	1.2	15,055	0.7	1940-E
Iraq	117	0.2	3,700	0.2	1939-E
Japan Proper (omitting Kuril Islands) [2]	148	0.3	73,079	3.3	1940-C
Korea	85	0.2	24,326	1.1	1940-C
Lebanon	3	0.01	1,028	0.05	1942-E
Philippine Islands	114	0.2	16,971	0.8	1941-E
Saudi Arabia	597	1.2	4,520	0.2	1941-E

* Omits ice caps of Greenland and Antarctica.

[1] China. This estimate excludes Outer Mongolia but includes Tibet, Manchuria, Sinkiang, and Formosa.

[2] Japan. An official estimate of 71,996,477 persons is given for November 1, 1945. This excludes portions of Hokkaido, the Ogasawara Islands of Tokyo-to, the islands of Oshiasgun in Kagoshima-ken, Okinawa-ken, and Karafuto (Japanese Sakhalin). Also excluded are persons in Army barracks and ships at sea and 42,099 persons in institutions, prisons, and correction houses. It is possible that this figure is under-enumerated by one and a half million persons.

Siam (Thailand)	200	0.4	15,718	0.7	1940-E
Syria	73	0.1	2,704	0.1	1941-E
Transjordan	35	0.1	300	0.01	1939-E
Turkey (including Hatay)	296	0.6	18,871	0.8	1945-C
Union of Soviet Socialist Republics (Europe and Asia) [3]	8,414	16.4	202,467	9.1	1941-E
Yemen	75	0.1	3,500	0.1	1941-E
EUROPE:					
Albania (including Saseno)	11	0.02	1,106	0.05	1941-E
Austria	32	0.1	6,650	0.3	1939-C
Belgium	12	0.02	8,247	0.4	1943-E
Bulgaria [4]	43	0.1	8,557	0.4	1942-E
Czechoslovakia (including Sudetenland) [5]	49	0.1	14,200	0.6	1945-E
Denmark and Faeroes	17	0.03	4,074	0.2	1945-C
Finland (including Aland Islands) [6]	117	0.2	3,887	0.2	1942-E
France (including small gains from Italy)	213	0.4	40,516	1.8	1946-E
Germany (1937 area west of Oder and Neisse rivers) [7]	138	0.3	59,595	2.7	1939-C
Great Britain and Northern Ireland (including Channel Islands and Isle of Man)	94	0.2	47,786	2.1	1940-E
Greece (including Dodecanese)	51	0.1	7,336	0.3	1940-C
Hungary [8]	36	0.1	9,314	0.4	1941-C
Iceland	40	0.1	130	0.01	1945-E
Ireland (Eire)	27	0.1	2,963	0.1	1942-E
Italy [9]	117	0.2	45,500	2.0	1946-E
Netherlands	13	0.03	9,076	0.4	1942-E
Norway (including Svalbard)	149	0.3	3,001	0.1	1943-E
Poland [10]	120	0.2	32,390	1.5	1939-E
Portugal	35	0.1	7,709	0.3	1940-C
Rumania [11]	92	0.2	16,409	0.7	1945-E
Spain	195	0.4	25,878	1.2	1940-C
Sweden	173	0.3	6,674	0.3	1945-E
Switzerland	16	0.03	4,266	0.2	1941-C
Yugoslavia [12]	97	0.2	17,000	0.7	1946-E
OCEANIA AND AUSTRALIA:					
Australia and Tasmania	2,975	5.8	7,197	0.3	1941-E
New Zealand	103	0.2	1,639	0.1	1942-E

[3] U.S.S.R. Included in this area are the following: U.S.S.R. within 1939 boundaries, the Baltic states, Finnish annexations, Bessarabia, Northern Bucovina, Poland east of the Curzon Line, Konigsberg area of East Prussia, Ruthenia, Karafuto (Japanese Sakhalin), and the Kuril Islands. The total population within the larger area is estimated in terms of the last census for each of the annexed areas. The addition of Tannu Tuva increases the total area by 63,000 square miles and the population by 65,000.

[4] Bulgaria. Area includes prewar territory plus Southern Dobruja.

[5] Czechoslovakia. This estimate covers Bohemia-Moravia-Silesia and Slovakia.

[6] Finland. This estimate omits from the prewar area the 1940 cession to the U.S.S.R. and the Petsamo commune.

[7] Germany. Assuming the postwar area, the 1939 census figure is applied to the area west of the Oder and Niesse rivers.

[8] Hungary. The 1946 area of Trianon Hungary is assumed to be postwar Hungary which is almost the same as prewar Hungary.

[9] Italy. The 1947 area is assumed to be that of prewar Italy, minus the area of the Free Territory of Trieste, the Yugoslav Cession, and small losses to Albania and France.

[10] Poland. An estimated area of postwar Poland includes prewar Poland west of the Curzon Line with minor adjustments, part of East Prussia, Danzig, and the Polish administered area of the Soviet Zone of Occupation in Germany.

[11] Rumania. The 1945 area is assumed to be the 1941 area which excluded Bessarabia, Northern Bucovina and Southern Dobruja; plus Northern Transylvania as included in the 1941 census of Hungary.

[12] Yugoslavia. The 1947 area is assumed to be that of prewar Yugoslavia plus a large part of Venezia Giulia, the enclave of Zara, and Cherso, Lussino, and Lagosta islands.

NOTE: There are more than 150 separate political entities in the world, although many can be grouped into the world's empires. Of these political entities, 81 are now recognized as independent countries, and 58 countries were members of the United Nations as of spring, 1948. The above table excludes microstates and certain states of uncertain status.

APPENDIX B

States of the Postwar World

(as of May 1, 1948)

Country	Capital	Type of government	Member of United Nations
AFRICA:			
Egypt	Cairo	Kingdom	Yes
Ethiopia	Addis Ababa	Empire	Yes
Liberia	Monrovia	Republic	Yes
Union of South Africa	Pretoria	Dominion	Yes
AMERICA:			
Argentina	Buenos Aires	Republic	Yes
Bolivia	La Paz	Republic	Yes
Brazil	Rio de Janeiro	Republic	Yes
Canada	Ottawa	Dominion	Yes
Chile	Santiago	Republic	Yes
Colombia	Bogotá	Republic	Yes
Costa Rica	San José	Republic	Yes
Cuba	Havana	Republic	Yes
Dominican Republic	Ciudad Trujillo	Republic	Yes
El Salvador	San Salvador	Republic	Yes
Ecuador	Quito	Republic	Yes
Guatemala	Guatemala City	Republic	Yes
Haiti	Port-au-Prince	Republic	Yes
Honduras	Tegucigalpa	Republic	Yes
Mexico	Mexico City	Republic	Yes
Nicaragua	Managua	Republic	Yes
Panama	Panama City	Republic	Yes
Paraguay	Asunción	Republic	Yes
Peru	Lima	Republic	Yes
United States	Washington	Republic	Yes
Uruguay	Montevideo	Republic	Yes
Venezuela	Caracas	Republic	Yes
ASIA:			
Afghanistan	Kabul	Kingdom	Yes
Burma	Rangoon	Republic	Yes
Ceylon	Colombo	Dominion	No
China	Nanking	Republic	Yes
Iran	Tehran	Kingdom	Yes
Iraq	Baghdad	Kingdom	Yes
Japan	Tokyo	Empire	No
Lebanon	Beirut	Republic	Yes
Mongolian People's Republic	Ulan Bator	Republic	No
Nepal	Katmandu	Kingdom	No
Pakistan	Karachi	Dominion [1]	Yes
Philippine Islands	Manila	Republic	Yes
Saudi Arabia	Mecca	Kingdom	Yes
Siam	Bangkok	Kingdom	Yes
Syria	Damascus	Republic	Yes
Transjordan	Amman	Kingdom	No
Turkey	Ankara	Republic	Yes
Union of India	New Delhi	Dominion [1]	Yes

[1] Period of transition.

U. S. S. R.	Moscow	Republic	Yes
Byelorussia	Minsk	Republic	Yes
Ukraine	Kiev	Republic	Yes
Yemen	San'a	Kingdom	Yes
EUROPE:			
Albania	Tirana	Republic	No
Austria	Vienna	Republic	No
Belgium	Brussels	Kingdom	Yes
Bulgaria	Sofia	Republic	No
Czechoslovakia	Prague	Republic	Yes
Denmark	Copenhagen	Kingdom	Yes
Finland	Helsinki	Republic	No
France	Paris	Republic	Yes
Germany	Berlin	Republic [2]	No
Great Britain	London	Kingdom	Yes
Greece	Athens	Kingdom	Yes
Hungary	Budapest	Republic	No
Iceland	Reykjavik	Republic	Yes
Ireland (Eire)	Dublin	Republic	No
Italy	Rome	Republic	No
Luxembourg	Luxembourg	Grand Duchy	Yes
Netherlands	Amsterdam	Kingdom	Yes
Norway	Oslo	Kingdom	Yes
Poland	Warsaw	Republic	Yes
Portugal	Lisbon	Republic	No
Rumania	Bucharest	Republic	No
Spain	Madrid	Kingdom	No
Sweden	Stockholm	Kingdom	Yes
Switzerland	Bern	Republic	No
Yugoslavia	Belgrade	Republic	Yes
AUSTRALIA and OCEANIA:			
Australia	Canberra	Dominion	Yes
New Zealand	Wellington	Dominion	Yes

[2] 1918–45.

NOTE: A number of other countries may be specifically noted: the European microstates of less than 200 square miles (Andorra, Liechtenstein, Monaco, San Marino, and Vatican City); the Himalayan state of Bhutan; the Arabian state of Oman and others; and certain countries that have recently attained or are attaining self-government (Indonesia, Jewish and Arab Palestine, Korea, Viet-Nam, and possibly Tibet).

APPENDIX C

Territorial Changes and New States since World War II

EUROPE

Petsamo province	Ceded to U. S. S. R. by Finland in 1944; confirmed by peace treaty, 1947.
Karelian Isthmus and Salla area	Ceded to U. S. S. R. by Finland in 1940; confirmed by peace treaty, 1947.
Eastern Poland (Western Ukraine and Western Byelorussia)	Ceded to U. S. S. R. by Poland in 1945.
Subcarpathian Ruthenia	Ceded to U. S. S. R. by Czechoslovakia in 1945.
Northern Bukovina and Bessarabia	Ceded to U. S. S. R. by Rumania in 1940; confirmed by peace treaty in 1947.
Southern Dobruja	Ceded to Bulgaria by Rumania in 1940; confirmed by peace treaties in 1947.
Bratislava bridgehead	Ceded to Czechoslovakia by Hungary in peace treaty of 1947.
Konigsberg area (Northern part of East Prussia)	Transferred to Russian administration in 1945; formal cession certain in German peace treaty.
Germany east of Oder-Neisse line (Including former Free City of Danzig and southern East Prussia, but excluding northern East Prussia)	Transferred to Polish administration in 1945; cession of whole or part of area dependent upon German peace treaty.
Little St. Bernard Pass, Mont Cenis, Mont Thabor-Chaberton, Briga-Tenda areas	Ceded to France by Italy in peace treaty of 1947.
Saseno	Recognized as Albanian territory in Italian peace treaty of 1947.
Eastern Venezia Giulia (Including Cherso, Zara, and Lagosta)	Ceded to Yugoslavia by Italy in peace treaty of 1947.
Free Territory of Trieste	Area relinquished by Italy in peace treaty of 1947 and constituted as a Free Territory under the international control of the Security Council of the United Nations.
Territorial boundary rectifications	Requested by Czechoslovakia, Luxembourg, Belgium and the Netherlands with respect to Germany but unsettled in 1947.
Saar	French economic integration and political custody realized in 1947 at the expense of Germany.
Klagenfurt Basin in Carinthia	Yugoslav claims to this Austrian territory not settled in 1947.
Czechoslovak boundary rectifications with Austria	Subject to conversations between the two countries in 1947.
Dodecanese Islands	Ceded to Greece by Italy in peace treaty of 1947.
Estonia, Latvia, Lithuania	Annexed to Soviet Union in 1940, reoccupied in 1945; annexation of these three Baltic states not recognized by the United States.
Iceland	Termination of union with Denmark under common king, 1944.

AFRICA

Libya, Eritrea, Italian Somaliland	Relinquishment of sovereignty by Italy in peace treaty of 1947; Council of Foreign Ministers to determine nature of trusteeship within one year of ratification of Italian peace treaty; failing in this, the General Assembly of the United Nations to determine the nature of the trusteeship.
Tanganyika	United Nations trusteeship under Great Britain, 1946.
Ruanda-Urundi	United Nations trusteeship under Belgium, 1946.
Togoland	United Nations trusteeship under Great Britain, 1946.
Togoland	United Nations trusteeship under France, 1946.

Cameroons .... United Nations trusteeship under Great Britain, 1946.
Cameroons .... United Nations trusteeship under France, 1946.
Southwest Africa .... Technically a mandate as Union of South Africa refuses to
                                             accept trusteeship but demands annexation.
Tangier .... Restoration of international control, 1945.

ASIA AND THE PACIFIC

Independence and partition:
India .... British withdrawal, August, 1947.
  Pakistan
  Union of India or Hindustan
Palestine .... Decision of United Nations, November, 1947.
  Jewish state
  Arab state
  Jerusalem—"corpus separatum"; international
    regime under Trusteeship Council of United
    Nations.

Independence without partition:
Mongolian People's Republic .... From China, 1945.
Republic of the Philippines .... From the United States, 1946.
Kingdom of Transjordan .... From Palestine mandate of Great Britain, 1946.
Republic of Syria .... From French mandate, 1941.
Republic of Lebanon .... From French mandate, 1941.
Republic of the Union of Burma .... From Great Britain, 1948.
Ceylon .... Dominionhood in British Commonwealth of Nations, 1948.

Promised de jure or de facto independence:
Korea
Viet-Nam in Indo-China
Republic of Indonesia in the East Indies.

Emergence from isolation:
Yemen
Nepal

Territorial changes:
Tannu Tuva .... Annexed from China by the U.S.S.R., 1945.
Kushka area .... Settlement of boundary dispute between Afghanistan and
                                             the U.S.S.R., Kushka conceded to the U.S.S.R., 1946.
Territory of the Pacific Islands .... Granted to the United States as a strategic trusteeship un-
  (Former Japanese Mandated Islands of the Caro-   der the Security Council of the United Nations by the Se-
  lines, Marshalls, and Marianas)   curity Council, 1947.
Ryukyus, Bonins, Volcanoes, and Marcus .... Disposition of these former Japanese island areas not set-
                                             tled in 1947.
Kurils and Southern Sakhalin .... Handed to Soviet Union at Yalta Agreement, 1945.
  (Former Japanese possessions)
Formosa and the Pescadores .... Returned to China by Cairo Declaration, 1943.
  (Former Japanese possessions)
Territory of New Guinea .... United Nations trusteeship under Australia, 1946.
Western Samoa .... United Nations trusteeship under New Zealand, 1946.
Nauru .... United Nations trusteeship under Australia, New Zealand,
                                             and Great Britain, 1947.

THE AMERICAS

No important territorial changes (1942–47) except for Ecuador-Peru boundary.

APPENDIX D

Area and Population of the World's "Empires"

(Prior to World War II)

"Empires"	AREA *		POPULATION	
	Thousands of sq. miles	Per cent of world total	In thousands	Per cent of world total
WORLD	50,997	100.0	2,176,785	100.0
UNITED STATES: TERRITORIES AND POSSESSIONS	3,693	7.2	150,147	6.9
Continental United States	2,977	5.8	131,669	6.0
Territories and Possessions	716	1.4	18,478	0.9
BRITISH EMPIRE	13,236	26.0	511,741	23.5
Great Britain and Northern Ireland, including Channel Islands and Isle of Man	94	0.2	46,217	2.1
Remainder of Empire	13,142	25.8	465,524	21.4
CHINA (23 PROVINCES) AND DEPENDENCIES	4,435	8.7	443,000	20.4
China (23 Provinces)	2,198	4.3	400,000	18.4
Dependencies	2,237	4.4	43,000	2.0
FRANCE AND POSSESSIONS	4,349	8.6	101,900	4.8
France	213	0.4	41,900	1.9
Possessions	4,136	8.2	60,000	2.9
NETHERLANDS AND POSSESSIONS	803	1.6	69,882	3.2
Netherlands	13	0.03	8,829	0.4
Possessions	790	1.6	61,053	2.8
BELGIUM AND POSSESSIONS	935	1.8	21,195	1.0
Belgium	12	0.02	8,092	0.4
Possessions	923	1.8	13,103	0.6
SPAIN AND POSSESSIONS	331	0.6	27,386	1.3
Spain	195	0.4	25,878	1.2
Possessions	136	0.3	1,508	0.1
PORTUGAL AND POSSESSIONS	971	1.9	18,034	0.8
Portugal	35	0.1	7,709	0.3
Possessions	936	1.8	10,325	0.5
ITALY AND POSSESSIONS	1,040	2.0	45,247	2.1
Italy	120	0.2	42,445	2.0
Possessions	920	1.8	2,802	0.1
DENMARK AND DEPENDENCIES	894	—	3,905	0.2
Denmark	16	0.03	3,844	0.2
Dependencies (including Greenland)	878	—	180	—
AUSTRALIA AND DEPENDENCIES	3,159	6.2	7,453	0.3
Australia	2,975	5.8	6,678	0.3
Dependencies	184	0.4	775	0.03
NEW ZEALAND AND DEPENDENCIES	104	0.2	1,629	0.1
New Zealand	103	0.2	1,574	0.1
Dependencies	1	—	55	—
JAPAN AND DEPENDENCIES	262	0.5	105,384	4.8
Japan	148	0.3	73,114	3.3
Dependencies	114	0.2	32,270	1.5

* Greenland and Antarctica Ice Caps are omitted except for Danish empire.

Bibliography

PART ONE

THE NATURE AND SCOPE OF POLITICAL GEOGRAPHY

Chapter 1: Political Geography and Its Point of View

W. A. BROWNE, "A New Prospectus for Geography," *Journal of Geography,* Vol. XXXIX, No. 1 (January, 1940). A geographer outlines the task ahead of American geography.

C. H. LAWRENCE, *New World Horizons* (Duell, Sloan and Pearce, 1942) pp. 9–23. An excellent popular treatment of the wartime impact of geography upon the American people.

R. PEATTIE, *Geography in Human Destiny* (Stewart, 1940). A unique and challenging statement of the importance of geographical factors in human affairs.

———, *Look to the Frontiers* (Harper, 1944), Chapters I, II, and XI. A very excellent popular presentation of the meaning of geography, the significance of regionalism, and arguments for and against the existence of small national states.

G. T. RENNER, "Air Age Geography," *Harper's* (June, 1943). A discussion of geographical relationships changed by aviation.

———, *Human Geography in the Air Age* (Macmillan, 1942), Chapters 1, 2, 3, 4, and 5. A semi-technical discussion of the meaning and point of view of modern geography with especial reference to the age of aviation.

———, AND ASSOCIATES, *Global Geography* (Crowell, 1944), Chapters 1, 2, 3, 9, 22, and 24. Brief surveys of some of the elements of geography, together with an analysis of America's need for geographic study.

N. J. SPYKMAN, *American Strategy in World Politics* (Harcourt, Brace, 1942). A straightforward evaluation of modern political relations and a discussion of the power potentials of various regions.

———, *The Geography of the Peace* (Harcourt, Brace, 1944), Chapters I, II, and III. A realistic discussion of the applications of geography in war and peace.

J. R. SMITH, *Geography and Our Need of It* (American Library Association, 1928). A definition of geography, political geography, and politico-geographic problems.

S. VAN VALKENBURG, ET AL., *America at War* (Prentice-Hall, 1942), Chapters 1, 4, 5, and 6. A comprehensive survey of the factors which make for national strength.

———, *Elements of Political Geography* (Prentice-Hall, 1939). An extensive discussion of the basic factors in political geography.

H. W. WEIGERT, V. STEFANSSON, ET AL., *Compass of the World* (Macmillan, 1944), Chapters 26, 27, and 28. Three very penetrating discussions of human resources and population problems in international affairs.

C. L. WHITE, AND G. T. RENNER, *Geography: An Introduction to Human Ecology* (D. Appleton–Century, 1936), Chapters XXVII, XXVIII, XXIX, XXX. A careful discussion of the spatial factors in geography.

———, *Human Geography: An Ecological Study of Society* (Appleton-Century-Crofts, 1948), Chapter 40. An attempt to formulate a geographical theory of human society.

Chapter 2: The Substance and Scope of Political Geography

I. BOWMAN, *The New World* (World Book, 1928), Chapter I. An excellent discussion of politico-geographic problems and their nature.

R. H. BROWN, "An Outline in Political Geography," *Journal of Geography,* Vol. XXXIV, No. 6 (September, 1935). A tentative outline for the study of political geography at an elementary level.

W. T. CHAMBERS, "Geopolitics of the United States of America," *Proceedings and Transactions, The Texas Academy of Science, 1943,* XXVII (Oct. 2, 1944). A cogent statement of the geopolitical status and motives of the United States.

G. CLARK, *A Place in the Sun* (Macmillan, 1937). Perhaps the best discussion in the English language of the question, "Do colonies pay?"

A. DORPALEN, *The World of General Haushofer*

(Farrar and Rinehart, 1942), pp. 89–104. A discussion of the index factors or indicators in geopolitics as viewed from a German standpoint.

RICHARD HARTSHORNE, "Recent Developments in Political Geography," *American Political Science Review,* XXIX (October, December, 1935). The best résumé of the nature and compass of political geography up to 1935.

T. V. KALIJARVI, ET AL., *Modern World Politics* (T. Y. Crowell, 1945). Contains an excellent chapter on geopolitics.

C. H. LAWRENCE, *New World Horizons* (Duell, Sloan, and Pearce, 1942), pp. 24–39. A brief popular discussion of geopolitics.

R. PEATTIE, *Look to the Frontiers* (Harper, 1944), Chapters V, VI, VII, VIII, IX, X. A series of discussions of boundaries aimed at statesmen and treaty makers.

G. T. RENNER, *Human Geography in the Air Age* (Macmillan, 1942), Chapter 8. A realistic discussion of geopolitics in the age of air power.

———, "Peace by the Map," *Collier's* (June 3, 1944). A revision of the Heartland theory in the light of air power.

———, "Maps for a New World," *Collier's* (June 6, 1942). A discussion of what changes in states and boundaries would be necessary to reduce international problems to the minimum, as of 1941.

———, AND ASSOCIATES, *Global Geography* (T. Y. Crowell, 1944), Part IV. Discussions of major geopolitical problems by a symposium of wartime writers.

N. J. SPYKMAN, *America's Strategy in World Politics* (Harcourt, Brace, 1942). A geopolitical classic, short on geography, long on political science.

———, *The Geography of the Peace* (Harcourt, Brace, 1944), Chapters IV and V. A brief but discerning statement of some geopolitical fundamentals.

S. VAN VALKENBURG, *Elements of Political Geography* (Prentice-Hall, 1939), Parts One, Two, Six, and Seven. Discussions of the world pattern of states, territorial changes, and colonialism.

———, ET AL., *America at War* (Prentice-Hall, 1942), Chapter 3. A very fine discussion of the application of physiography to military operations.

H. W. WEIGERT, AND V. STEFANSSON, ET. AL., *Compass of the World* (Macmillan, 1944), Chapters 12, 13, 18, and 25. A wartime symposium on geopolitics.

C. L. WHITE, AND G. T. RENNER, *Geography: An Introduction to Human Ecology* (D. Appleton–Century, 1936), pp. 20, 26–27. An outline for the study of political geography.

D. S. WHITTLESEY, *The Earth and the State* (Holt, 1939). One of the best basic textbooks in political geography.

Chapter 3: The History and Development of Political Geography

ISAIAH BOWMAN, "Geography vs. Geopolitics," *The Geographical Review,* XXXII (October, 1942), 646–658. An excellent analysis of German geopolitics in contrast to general geography.

———, *The New World, Problems in Political Geography* (Fourth Edition, World Book, 1928). A political study by a distinguished American in the field of political geography.

ANDREAS DORPALEN, *The World of General Haushofer; Geopolitics in Action* (Farrar & Rinehart, 1942). A careful selection of material in geopolitics translated largely from German sources and accompanied by comments by Dorpalen.

RUSSELL H. FIFIELD, "Geopolitics at Munich," *Department of State Bulletin,* XII (June 24, 1945), 1152–1162. Official publication.

ANDREW GYORGY, *Geopolitics, The New German Science* (Berkeley, University of California Press, 1944). An excellent analysis of German geopolitics; very scholarly and well documented.

RICHARD HARTSHORNE, "Recent Developments in Political Geography," *American Political Science Review,* XXIX (October, December, 1935), 785–804, 943–966. An excellent and scholarly study on the evolution and scope of political geography.

SIR HALFORD MACKINDER, *Democratic Ideals and Reality* (Holt, 1942). Source material on general geopolitics within the framework of conditions existing in 1919.

———, "The Round World and the Winning of the Peace," *Foreign Affairs,* XXI (July, 1943), 595–605. The reflections of the distinguished British geographer on the Heartland in 1943.

ALFRED T. MAHAN, *The Influence of Sea Power upon History, 1660–1783* (Little, Brown, 1898). An authoritative study of sea power and its influence upon history, especially from 1660–1783.

NICHOLAS JOHN SPYKMAN, *America's Strategy in World Politics* (Harcourt, Brace, 1942). A careful portrayal of the geopolitical aspects of American foreign policy in world politics.

———, *The Geography of the Peace* (Harcourt, Brace, 1944). A brief but concise study of a geopolitics for the United States, well illustrated with maps.

ROBERT STRAUSZ-HUPÉ, *Geopolitics: The Struggle for Space and Power* (Putnam, 1942). A detailed discussion of geopolitics for the general reader.

SAMUEL VAN VALKENBURG, *Elements of Political Geography* (Prentice-Hall, 1939). A study relating to the principles of political geography

and contributing to a delineation of the field.

HANS W. WEIGERT AND VILHJALMUR STEFANNSON, Editors, *Compass of the World* (Macmillan, 1944). A selection of articles relating to political geography by a distinguished group of contributors.

DERWENT WHITTLESEY, *The Earth and the State* (Holt, 1939). An outstanding contribution to political geography by an American author.

PART TWO

THE WORLD POWERS

Chapter 4: Geographic Foundations of Continental United States

WALLACE W. ATWOOD, *The Physiographic Provinces of North America* (Fourth Edition, Ginn, 1940). A well-written and illustrated regional physiography for undergraduates.

ISAIAH BOWMAN, *The New World, Problems in Political Geography* (World Book, 1928). Covers many problems in world political geography up to 1928.

R. H. FIFIELD AND G. E. PEARCY, *Geopolitics in Principle and Practice* (Ginn, 1944). Chapter 5 is up to date and helpful on the United States.

C. F. JONES AND G. G. DARKENWALD, *Economic Geography* (Macmillan, 1941). Gives a complete picture of the economic geography of the United States in relation to the rest of the world.

H. H. McCARTY, *The Geographic Basis of American Economic Life* (Harper, 1940). A regional geography of the United States from the economist's point of view.

BERNHARD OSTROLENK, *Economic Geography of the United States* (Irwin, 1941). A complete and up-to-date economic geography of our country.

A. E. PARKINS AND J. R. WHITAKER, Editors, *Our Natural Resources and Their Conservation* (Wiley, 1936). A symposium survey of our conservation problems.

GEORGE T. RENNER AND ASSOCIATES, *Global Geography* (Crowell, 1944). Has several good chapters pertaining to problems in political geography pertinent to the United States.

E. C. SEMPLE AND C. F. JONES, *American History and Its Geographic Conditions* (Houghton Mifflin, 1933). Shows the relationship between historical events and the geographic environment.

J. R. SMITH AND M. O. PHILLIPS, *North America* (Harcourt, Brace, 1940). An interestingly written regional geography at college level.

N. J. SPYKMAN, *America's Strategy in World Politics* (Harcourt, Brace, 1942). A thought-provoking and realistic approach to American international problems.

S. VAN VALKENBURG, *America at War* (Prentice-Hall, 1942). A symposium covering several aspects of American geography and its influence in World War II.

———, *Elements of Political Geography* (Prentice-Hall, 1939). Approaches political geography through a study of its elements; therefore good for reference and preliminary reading for those interested in regional political geography.

C. L. WHITE AND E. J. FOSCUE, *Regional Geography of Anglo-America* (Prentice-Hall, 1943). A factual survey of the geography of the various regions north of the Mexican border.

DERWENT WHITTLESEY, *The Earth and the State* (Holt, 1939). A thoughtful regional and topical political geography for more advanced students.

Chapter 5: The United States as a World Power

T. A. BAILEY, *Woodrow Wilson and the Lost Peace* (Macmillan, 1944). A critical analysis of Woodrow Wilson's foreign policy, written in a lively vernacular.

BAILEY, *Woodrow Wilson and the Great Betrayal* (Macmillan, 1945). The great betrayal indicated in the title of this book is that the United States by failing to support Woodrow Wilson's program of peace contributed to one of the supreme tragedies of history. By critical commentary the author tries to assess responsibility for this "betrayal" among the President, his advisers, Congress, and the people.

S. F. BEMIS, *A Diplomatic History of the United States* (Holt, 1942). A standard and comprehensive general history, to which the student is referred for greater detail on the subjects suggested in this chapter.

————, *The Latin American Policy of the United States* (Harcourt, Brace, 1943). Explains the historical background of Continental and New World defense, with much stress on the liquidation of imperialism, the doctrine of nonintervention, and the inter-American peace system.

W. T. R. FOX, *The Super-Powers* (Harcourt, Brace, 1944). Analysis of the power and position of the United States, Great Britain, and the Soviet Union, and their responsibility for peace today.

A. W. GRISWOLD, *The Far Eastern Policy of the United States* (Harcourt, Brace, 1938). A scholarly study of the advances and recoils of American Far Eastern Policy, 1899–1934.

————, "The Influence of History Upon Sea Power," *The Journal of the American Military Institute,* Vol. IV. A 1939 critique of Mahan's imperialism and defensive strategy in the light of history since 1900, particularly stressing air power.

A. T. MAHAN, *The Interest of America in Sea Power, Present and Future* (Little, Brown, 1897). A classic analysis of the naval problems of the United States at the close of the nineteenth century.

G. C. MARSHALL, *The Winning of the War in Europe and the Pacific* (Biennial Report of the Chief of Staff of the United States Army 1943 to 1945, to the Secretary of War). A wonderfully illuminating overall picture of the strategy of global victory, accompanied by excellent maps.

DEXTER PERKINS, *Hands Off—A History of the Monroe Doctrine* (Little, Brown, 1941). The best general account of the Monroe Doctrine. It is a distillation of the author's learned multi-archival researches published in three previous volumes, brought down to date of 1941.

————, *America and Two Wars* (Little, Brown, 1944). A thoughtful analysis of the continuous expansion of American influence as a world power, and particularly the interests of the United States in the two world wars of the twentieth century.

J. W. PRATT, *Expansionists of 1898* (Baltimore, Johns Hopkins Press, 1936). A scholarly study

of the ideological factors behind the Spanish-American War.

HAROLD AND MARGARET SPROUT, *The Rise of American Naval Power* (Princeton University Press, 1939). Also, *Toward a New Order of Sea Power* (Princeton University Press, 1943). These two volumes present the best general account of American naval development in the twentieth century.

N. J. SPYKMAN, *The Geography of the Peace* (Harcourt, Brace, 1944). New squints and angles on the geographical position of the United States as a world power in peace and war.

————, *America's Strategy in World Politics* (Harcourt, Brace, 1942). A cool analysis of fundamental problems of hemispheric defense. Spykman saw the defense of the New World resting on an American base in England.

Chapter 6: The Soviet Union: A Land Mass Power

AMERICAN-RUSSIAN CHAMBER OF COMMERCE, *Handbook of the Soviet Union* (Day, 1936). Excellent source of factual data.

AMERICAN-RUSSIAN INSTITUTE, *The Soviet Union Today* (Second Edition, 1945). An outline study with bibliography presenting much current data.

ISAIAH BOWMAN, *The New World, Problems in Political Geography* (Fourth Edition, World Book, 1928). An old book but still essential for geopolitical background.

GEORGE B. CRESSEY, *The Basis of Soviet Strength* (Whittlesey House, 1945). The best single volume on the geography of the U. S. S. R. now available.

H. VON ECKARDT, *Russia* (Knopf, 1932). A good history of Russia written by an outsider.

R. H. FIFIELD AND G. E. PEARCY, *Geopolitics in Principle and Practice* (Ginn, 1944). An elementary text of political geography, sound and informative.

Great Soviet World Atlas (Moscow, Scientific Editorial Institute, 1938). One of the world's best atlases; an important source of geopolitical information.

A. HRDLIČKA, *The Peoples of the Soviet Union* (Washington, Smithsonian Institution, 1942). A short but excellent study of the various Soviet nationalities.

T. V. KALIJARVI AND ASSOCIATES, *Modern World Politics* (Second Edition, Crowell, 1945). The greatly improved second edition containing excellent political material.

H. J. MACKINDER, *Democratic Ideals and Reality* (Holt, 1919 and 1942). The explanation of a basic idea underlying the Heartland controversy.

P. MALEVSKY-MALEVITCH, Editor, *Russia, U. S. S. R.* (Payson, 1933) and *The Soviet Union Today* (Paisley, 1936). A complete pro-Russian handbook and supplement.

N. MIKHAILOV, *Land of the Soviets* (Furman, 1939). The best regional geography of the Soviet Union by a Russian.

M. N. POKROVSKII, *Brief History of Russia,* two volumes (International, 1933). A study by a Russian historian.

GEORGE T. RENNER AND ASSOCIATES, *Global Geography* (Crowell, 1944). Stimulating and comprehensive consideration of U. S. S. R. in parts of the book.

H. WEIGERT AND V. STEFANSSON, Editors, *Compass of the World* (Macmillan, 1944). An excellent collection of essays on various geopolitical topics.

Chapter 7: The Soviet Union in World Politics

WILLIAM H. CHAMBERLIN, *The Russian Enigma* (Scribner, 1943). A critical analysis of the Soviet State by a newspaper correspondent with much Russian experience. Objective in the best sense.

GEORGE B. CRESSEY, *The Basis of Soviet Strength* (Whittlesey House, 1945). An extremely competent compendium of economic and geographical facts, combined with sound political, economic, and strategic interpretation concerning the Soviet Union.

DAVID J. DALLIN, *The Big Three* (New Haven, Yale University Press, 1945). An interpretation of the positions and political and strategic interrelationships of the United States, the United Kingdom, and the Soviet Union. Provocative.

———, *Russia and Postwar Europe* (New Haven, Yale University Press, 1943). A well-documented commentary on Soviet foreign policy between the wars that attempts to avoid the extremes of anti- or pro-Soviet bias.

———, *Soviet Russia's Foreign Policy, 1939–1942* (New Haven, Yale University Press, 1942). A detailed and well-organized exposition and interpretation of the foreign relations of the Soviet Union during the critical years 1939–42.

ROBERT J. KERNER, *The Urge to the Sea* (Berkeley, University of California Press, 1942). A study by a competent historian of one of the main motives of expansion of the Russian state and of the pattern of its realization.

MAX M. LASERSON, *The Development of Soviet Foreign Policy in Europe, 1917–1942, a Selection of Documents* (New York, Carnegie Endowment for International Peace, 1943). A well-chosen compendium of treaties and documentary texts bearing upon Soviet foreign policy during the period 1917–42.

HALFORD J. MACKINDER, *Democratic Ideals and Reality* (Holt, 1919). One of the early great writers in geopolitical literature. Absolutely essential.

FRANK W. NOTESTEIN, ET AL., *The Future Population of Europe and the Soviet Union* (Princeton University, Office of Population Research, Geneva, League of Nations, 1944). A statistical population study combined with sound deductive analyses of population trends.

SIR BERNARD PARES, *A History of Russia* (Knopf, 1944). The outstanding English language history of Russia, written with great objectivity and insight.

PITIRIM A. SOROKIN, *Russia and the United States* (Dutton, 1944). An interesting thesis development of sociological and geographical heritages held in common by these two great powers pointing the way to understanding.

NICHOLAS J. SPYKMAN, *The Geography of the Peace* (Harcourt, Brace, 1944). A prime motivation to international thinking. A natural companion piece of Cressey's *Basis of Soviet Strength.*

BENEDICT H. SUMMER, *A Short History of Russia* (Reynal & Hitchcock, 1943). A short, popular history by a competent English scholar using a refreshing topical approach.

TIMOTHY A. TARACOUZIO, *War and Peace in Soviet Diplomacy* (Macmillan, 1941). A carefully documented diplomatic history throwing valuable light upon the causes of the recurrent shifts of Soviet foreign policy.

GEORGE VERNADSKY, *A History of Russia* (New York, New Home Library, 1944). A standard cultural and political history of Russia.

Chapter 8: Great Britain and the Dependent Empire

JAMES T. ADAMS, *Empire on the Seven Seas* (Scribner, 1940). An interesting and valuable consideration of the rise of the British Empire, showing the periods of growth and decline.

RAOUL BLANCHARD AND RAYMOND E. CRIST, *A*

Geography of Europe (Holt, 1935). A study of the economic and human geography of Europe including the British Isles.

British Security (Royal Institute of International Affairs, Toronto, Oxford University Press, 1946). A timely consideration of the problems of security published after World War II.

ALBERT DEMANGEON, *The British Isles* (London, William Heinemann, Ltd., 1939). A valuable study of the human and physical geography of the area.

C. B. FAWCETT, *Political Geography of the British Empire* (Ginn, 1933). Standard study of the political geography of the Empire by an authority in the field.

GEORGE HUBBARD, *The Geography of Europe* (Appleton-Century, 1937). A reliable text on the subject.

ALFRED E. KAHN, *Great Britain in the World Economy* (New York, Columbia University Press, 1946). A valuable study of the economic aspects of Great Britain in the modern world.

NICHOLAS MANSERGH, *The Irish Free State* (Macmillan, 1934). An analysis of the development of the Irish Free State.

Political and Strategic Interests of the United Kingdom (New York, Oxford University Press for the Royal Institute of International Affairs, 1939). Based on the political and military conditions prevailing before World War II.

C. G. ROBERTSON AND J. BARTHOLOMEW, *An Historical Atlas of Modern Europe, 1789–1922* (Second Edition, New York, Oxford University Press, 1924). A standard atlas on the subject.

L. D. STAMP AND S. H. BEAVER, *The British Isles* (Longmans, Green, 1937). A reliable text on the geography of the British Isles.

The British Empire (New York, Oxford University Press for the Royal Institute of International Affairs, 1937). A reliable publication on the Empire under the auspices of a famous institute.

G. M. TREVELYAN, *English Social History* (Longmans, Green, 1944). A contribution to the knowledge of the social development of the area.

SAMUEL VAN VALKENBURG AND ELLSWORTH HUNTINGTON, *Europe* (Wiley, 1935). A standard text on the geography of Europe including the British Isles.

ALBERT VITON, pseud., *Great Britain: An Empire in Transition* (Day, 1940). A realistic study of the Empire before the full impact of World War II.

Chapter 9: The British Commonwealth of Nations

R. L. BUELL, *Native Problem in Africa,* two volumes (Macmillan, 1928). A lengthy discussion of the problems concerning the natives and immigrants.

Cambridge History of the British Empire, seven volumes published (Cambridge, Cambridge University Press, 1929–41; also Macmillan). Volume VI deals with Canada and Newfoundland; Volume VII with Australia and New Zealand; and Volume VIII with South Africa. These volumes are probably the best reference books available for the whole of the present chapter.

ROBERT M. DAWSON, Editor, *The Development of Dominion Status, 1900–1936* (New York, Oxford University Press, 1937). A valuable study on the political development of the Dominions.

C. B. FAWCETT, *Political Geography of the British Empire* (Ginn, 1933). The best one-volume book on the topic; Chapter 6, especially good with regard to world position and economics.

W. FITZGERALD, *Africa, Social, Political and Economic Geography* (Third Edition, Dutton, 1939). A good general geography stressing the economic factors.

R. A. MACKAY AND C. B. ROGERS, *Canada Looks Abroad* (New York, Oxford University Press, 1938). The best short book dealing with the international relations of Canada.

WALTER NASH, *New Zealand: A Working Democracy* (Duell, Sloan and Pearce, 1943). A good study of contemporary New Zealand.

GRENFELL PRICE, *Australia Comes of Age* (Melbourne, Georgian House, 1945). A recent study by an Australian geographer discussing many of the political and social problems confronting Australians.

A. SIEGFRIED, *Canada* (translated by H. H. and Doris Hemming) (Harcourt, Brace, 1937). A study of the Dominion by a well-known French publicist.

GRIFFITH TAYLOR, *Australia: An Advanced Geography* (Second Edition, Dutton, 1943). This volume deals rather fully with the settlement of a warm, arid environment by folk of British ancestry.

————, *Canada's Role in Geopolitics* (Canadian Institute of International Relations, Toronto, Ryerson Press, 1942). A small book which gives the geographical aspects of Canada's relations to the world about her.

GRIFFITH TAYLOR, *Canada: An Advanced Geography* (London, Methuen & Co., Ltd., 1946). This volume includes a detailed study of the environment and its effects on the various cultural stocks composing the Canadian nation.

ERIC A. WALKER, *The British Empire: Its Structure and Spirit* (New York, Oxford University Press for the Royal Institute of International Affairs, 1943). A reliable book on the structure of the British Empire in modern times.

PART THREE

EUROPE

Chapter 10: The German Reich: European Pivotal Area

ISAIAH BOWMAN, *The New World, Problems in Political Geography* (Fourth Edition, World Book, 1928). Somewhat out of date still one of the best basic books on the problems of political geography. The broadly drawn historical background is invaluable in understanding the present scene.

ANDREAS DORPALEN, *The World of General Haushofer, Geopolitics in Action* (Farrar & Rinehart, 1942). An excellent interpretive anthology of the thinking and writings of Haushofer and his fellow geopoliticians.

J. FAIRGRIEVE, *Geography and World Power* (Eighth Revised Edition, Dutton, 1941). An excellent, penetrating analysis of the influence of geographic conditions upon the evolution of world powers, ancient and modern.

Hearings on the Elimination of German Resources for War, Committee on Military Affairs, United States Senate, S. Res. 107 and S. Res. 146 (United States Government Printing Office, 1945), Parts I, II, and III. A thorough study of Germany's economic power and industrial and financial penetration of Europe.

ADOLF HITLER, *Mein Kampf* (Reynal & Hitchcock, 1939). Background of the philosophy of the National Socialist movement in Germany.

J. F. HORRABIN, *An Outline of Political Geography* (Knopf, 1942). A thought-provoking outline of geopolitical problems, greatly enhanced in value by a number of excellent, simplified maps.

G. D. HUBBARD, *The Geography of Europe* (Appleton-Century, 1937). An intensive study of the continent and its people with an intelligent interpretation of its life and problems.

M. H. KUSCH, "Structure of Elbe River Traffic," *Economic Geography,* XIII (January, 1937), 53–66. A thorough analysis of the economic significance of the river.

PRINCE HUBERTUS LÖWENSTEIN, *After Hitler's Fall,* *Germany's Coming Reich* (London, Faber & Faber, Ltd., 1934). A discussion of Germany's role in the world by a German idealist.

R. I. SCHNEIDER, "The Port of Hamburg," *U. S. Bureau of Foreign and Domestic Commerce,* Department of Commerce, Foreign Port Series No. 1 (Government Printing Office, 1930). An informative, thorough, technical study.

F. H. SIMONDS AND B. EMENY, *The Great Powers in World Politics* (New Edition, American Book, 1939). An interpretive handbook on national policies of the world before World War II. It includes, appended, all important international treaties since 1918.

G. TAYLOR, *Environment and Nation* (University of Chicago Press, 1936). A graphic representation of the history, culture, and politics of the various nations of Europe given from an organic point of view.

SAMUEL VAN VALKENBURG AND ELLSWORTH HUNTINGTON, *Europe* (Wiley, 1935). An excellent, informative textbook.

DERWENT WHITTLESEY, *German Strategy of World Conquest* (Farrar & Rinehart, 1942). A study of German geopolitics and its meaning to us. Contains useful bibliography.

———, *The Earth and the State* (Holt, 1939). A scholarly study of the relationship between national growth, geography, and human institutions, especially law.

Chapter 11: The Low Countries between the Great Powers

Note: The references cited below do not represent all that were consulted in the preparation of this chapter.

ERNST BAASCH, *Hollaendische Wirtschaftsgeschichte* (Jena, Germany, Gustav Fischer, 1927). A good economic history of the Netherlands, but with some typical German biases. Contains bibliography.

J. F. BOGARDUS, "The Population of the Netherlands," *Economic Geography*, VIII (January, 1932), 43–52. A brief discussion of the density and distribution of population in the Netherlands.

ARTHUR L. BURT, "The Role of Rotterdam," *Canadian Geographical Journal*, XXIV (January, 1942), 34–51. Discusses the relationships between the port of Rotterdam and its hinterland.

LAURENT DECHESNE, *Histoire Économique et Sociale de la Belgique depuis les Origines jusqu'en 1914* (Liége, Belgium, J. Wykmans, 1932). Excellent economic history of Belgium. Bibliography.

A. DEMANGEON AND L. FEBVRE, *Le Rhin, Problèmes d'Histoire et d'Économie* (Paris, Armand Colin, 1935). A discussion of the Rhine and its economic importance from the past to the present.

JAN-ALBERT GORIS, Editor, *Belgium* (Berkeley, University of California Press, 1945). Treats Belgium and the Belgian Congo from various points of view; 30 chapters by 28 authors; pertinent are chapters IX, XI, XII, XIV. The geographic treatment is rather unsatisfactory. Selected bibliography.

J. A. VAN HAMEL, *Nederland Tusschen de Mogendheden* (Amsterdam, van Holkema en Warendorf, 1918). A discussion of the position of the Netherlands between the Great Powers. Bibliography.

J. VAN HINTE, Editor, "La Néerlande, Études générales sur la Géographie des Pays-Bas," *Tijdschrift van het Koninklijk Nederlandsch Aardrijkskundig Genootschap*, LV (Livr. 4, 1938), 537–696. Eight authors; articles on the physical, social, and economic geography of the Netherlands; bibliographies.

K. JANSMA, "Drainage of the Zuider Zee," *Geographical Review*, XXI (October, 1931), 574–583. A brief discussion of the plans for the drainage of the Zuider Zee and the creation of the Ijssel Lake.

BARTHOLOMEW LANDHEER, Editor, *The Netherlands* (Berkeley, University of California Press, 1943). Treats both the Netherlands and the Dutch colonies from various points of view; 27 chapters by 21 authors; pertinent are Chapters I to V, and VIII to XI. The geographic treatment is too brief.

M. A. LEFÈVRE, *L'Habitat Rural en Belgique* (Liége, Belgium, Vaillant-Carmanne, 1926). A study of settlements in Belgium. Bibliography.

ROELOF SCHUILING, *Nederland, Handboek der Aardrijkskunde*, I, II, and Supplement (Sixth Edition, Zwolle, Nederland, N. V. Drukkerij en Uitgeverij, van de Erven, J. J. Tijl, 1934–41). This standard work on the geography of the Netherlands contains brief, but excellent bibliographical references.

SAMUEL VAN VALKENBURG AND ELLSWORTH HUNTINGTON, *Europe* (Wiley, 1935), Chapter XXVII, "The Netherlands," pp. 330–343; Chapter XXVIII, "Belgium and Luxembourg," pp. 344–350. These chapters are written by a geographer who has first-hand knowledge of the countries and of their geographic literature.

P. VIDAL DE LA BLACHE AND L. GALLOIS, *Géographie Universelle*, Volume II, A. Demangeon, *Belgique-Pays Bas, Luxembourg* (Paris, Armand Colin, 1927). A standard work on the geography of the Low Countries and Luxembourg.

BERNARD H. M. VLEKKE, *Evolution of the Dutch Nation* (New York, Roy Publishers, 1944). A history of the genesis and the growth of the Dutch nation with emphasis upon the social aspects of history.

Chapter 12: France and Its Geographical Setting

ISAIAH BOWMAN, *The New World, Problems in Political Geography* (Fourth Edition, World Book, 1928). *The New World* first appeared after World War I to assist people to interpret the problems in political geography of the countries and colonies involved in the war. Later additions have revised the interpretations in the light of later developments.

D. W. BROGAN, *France Under the Republic, 1870–1939* (Harper, 1940). Historical; political; geographic—interpretative of events through the sixty-nine years of the Third Republic. It is indeed "The Development of Modern France" as its title published in England designates it.

SHEPARD B. CLOUGH, *France* (Scribner's, 1939). A history of national economics, 1789–1939; traces policies and accomplishments through 150 years of France's performance.

ERNST R. CURTIUS, *The Civilization of France* (Macmillan, 1932). The civilization of France is discussed from its natural and its historical bases, reaching the intellectual life, religion, and education.

W. M. DAVIS, *A Handbook of Northern France* (Cambridge, Harvard University Press, 1918).

Written for the A. E. F. to use enroute and in France; the maps, diagrams, and text combine to interpret this part of France for World War I.

FLORENCE GILLIAM, *France* (Dutton, 1945). Well written, full of personal touches, historical references, valid interpretations.

R. K. GOOCH, *Regionalism in France* (Century, 1931). Regionalism in administration, both centralized and decentralized aspects. Economic regionalism is well worth reading. The book describes a method of applying administration of government to the country.

GEORGE D. HUBBARD, "France," in *The Geography of Europe* (Appleton-Century, 1937). A broad view of many aspects of the geography of each country of Europe; designed for a text.

EDWARD M. HULME, *Wandering in France* (Caldwell, Idaho, The Caxton Printers, Ltd., 1941). Delightful travelogue. Many touches of history as castle, chateau, painting, river, or city are seen. Well illustrated.

PIERRE MAILLAND, *France* (New York, Oxford University Press, 1943). An interesting interpretation of France and French people during the invasion and three years of occupation. It is history and vivid political geography.

HELEN H. MILLER, *France, Crossroads of a Continent,* Headline Series No. 49 (New York, Foreign Policy Association, 1944). Catches much of the spirit in the political relations between France and her neighbors, Britain and Germany. Interesting comments on French colonies.

ANDRÉ MORIZE AND HOWARD C. RICE, *An Introduction to France* (Macmillan, 1938). Twenty topics or chapters. Quoted texts in French open each and a bibliography follows.

HILDA ORMSBY, *France* (London, Methuen & Co., Ltd., 1931). A regional and economic geography of the country by its ten physical units with a bibliography, mostly in French, after each chapter.

MARGARET R. SHACKLETON, "France," in *Europe* (Longmans, Green, 1934). Regional geography of Europe; general survey of structure, relief, climate, vegetation, race, and language. France is discussed by physical regions.

JOSEPH J. SPENGLER, *France Faces Depopulation* (Durham, Duke University Press, 1938). Discusses the questions involved in a thorough fashion; well documented. Considers local and occupational variations, emigration, immigration, colonial theory, and practice. Bibliographies.

Chapter 13: Switzerland: A Successful Neutral

H. BOESCH, "Basle, Switzerland: A Port Terminal," *Economic Geography*, XII (July, 1936), 259–264. The importance of Basle as an inland port of entry for goods consigned to Switzerland.

ISAIAH BOWMAN, *The New World, Problems in Political Geography* (Fourth Edition, World Book, 1928). An excellent treatment of problems in political geography as they existed at the time of publication.

R. C. BROOKS, *Civic Training in Switzerland* (University of Chicago Press, 1930). Treats with the various mechanisms of civic training in the life of the Swiss.

F. C. ERICKSON, "Transhumance in the Land Economy of Schächenthal," *Economic Geography*, XIV (January, 1938), 38–46. Deals with the quasi-nomadic pastoral economy in a high mountain valley of Switzerland.

W. FRIEDERICH, *Die Schweiz* (Lippincott, 1938). Designed as a German reader, it presents various phases of Swiss life during its historical development.

J. FRÜH, *Die Schweiz* (St. Gallen, Switzerland, 1930). An excellent and exhaustive study of the geographical and historical development of Switzerland.

A. LATT, *Unsere Schweizer Heimat* (Zürich, Orell Fussli Verlag, 1935). A book designed for Swiss in foreign lands. It outlines Switzerland's historic, economic, and social development.

W. E. RAPPARD, *The Government of Switzerland* (Van Nostrand, 1936). An excellent presentation on the development of the Swiss Government.

Rapport sur le Commerce et l'Industrie de la Suisse en 1944 (A Swiss government publication). A report on the condition of commerce and industry of Switzerland during World War II.

W. RICHTER, "The War Pattern of Swiss Life," *Foreign Affairs*, XXII (July, 1944), 643–648. Political and economic problems facing Switzerland toward the close of World War II and methods employed by the Swiss to meet them.

C. W. SCHMIDT, *Die Schweiz* (Berlin, Karl Voegels, 1930). Presents physical, economic, and social background material for German tourists to Switzerland.

M. R. SHACKLETON, *Europe, A Regional Geography* (Third Edition, Longmans, Green, 1942),

Chapters 23 and 24. A regional study of the Alpine region and Switzerland.

S. Van Valkenburg, *Elements of Political Geography* (Prentice-Hall, 1939). Especially valuable for an evaluation of the elements of political geography.

———, and Ellsworth Huntington, *Europe* (Wiley, 1935), Chapter 36. A regional study of Switzerland.

Derwent Whittlesey, *The Earth and the State* (Holt, 1939). A worthy contribution to the field of political geography dealing with the areal differentiation of the world's principal states and legal codes, especially those of western Europe.

Chapter 14: Italy in the Mediterranean

W. O. Blanchard, "White Coal in Italian Industry," *Geographical Review*, XVIII (April, 1928), 261–273. A good review of the localization of the hydroelectric power development and its future potentialities.

Count Antonio Cippico, *Italy, The Central Problem of the Mediterranean* (New Haven, Yale University Press, 1926). An interesting and brief summary of the Italian point of view on Italy's international position.

Philip M. Copp, "Italy's Food in War and Peace," *Foreign Commerce Weekly* (United States Department of Commerce), XII, No. 9 (August 28, 1943), 3 ff. Very good in appraising Italy's critical diet deficiencies and food problems.

Bruno F. A. Dietrich, "The Italian Harbors on the Adriatic Sea," *Economic Geography*, VII (April, 1931), 202–209. Excellent account of the development and nature of these harbors.

Ruth Sterling Frost, "The Reclamation of the Pontine Marshes," *Geographical Review*, XXIV (October, 1934), 584–595. An excellent review of this highly advertised project of the Fascist Regime and what it really means to Italy.

Dino Grandi, "The Foreign Policy of the Duce," *Foreign Affairs*, XII (July, 1934), 553–566. Provides a good insight of how a national regime can use geographic necessity to excuse or defend its foreign policy.

Constantine E. McGuire, *Italy's International Economic Position* (Macmillan, 1927). Chapters I, II, V, VI, VII. Provides an understanding of Italy's financial position under the Fascist policy before the advent into aggressive imperialism.

Office of War Information, "Italy's Economy, The Situation Now," *Foreign Commerce Weekly* (United States Department of Commerce), XVII,

No. 8 (Nov. 18, 1944). A good overall presentation of Italy's reconstruction problems from the economic angle.

John Patric, "Imperial Rome Reborn," *The National Geographic*, LXXI, No. 3 (March, 1937), 269–325. Should be read as a vivid reminder of the processes of the totalitarian state.

Arthur S. Riggs, "Inexhaustible Italy," *The National Geographic*, XXX (October, 1916), 273–368. Provides a fine background for feeling and appreciating the cosmopolitan development and achievements of Italy.

Count Carlo Sforza, *Contemporary Italy* (Dutton, 1944). Should be read in order to evaluate the political machinations of a dictator and to show how political expediency may displace helpful policies.

Victor E. Sullam, "Fundamentals of Italian Agriculture," *Foreign Agriculture*, VII, No. 12 (December, 1943). Excellent for an evaluation of Italy's greatest occupation. Pertinent details relating to postwar problems are given.

———, "Recent Developments in Italian Agriculture," *Foreign Agriculture*, IX, No. 5 (May, 1945). Outlines effectively the rehabilitation problems confronting Italy's agriculture.

Sumner Welles, Editor, *Guide to the Peace* (Dryden, 1945), "Italy," pp. 82–88. Provides a factual basis for estimating Italy's problems with statements of attitude toward Italy's reconversion into the family of nations.

Derwent Whittlesey, *The Earth and the State* (Holt, 1939), pp. 263–303, 368–393. Pertinent analyses of geographic locations and features as permanent springboards of international affairs.

Chapter 15: Spain and Portugal: Powers of the Past

John Bartholomew, *Oxford Advanced Atlas* (Fourth Edition, New York, Oxford University Press, 1931). Standard reference atlas for college study of Europe.

W. O. Blanchard, "The Cork Oak," *Journal of Geography*, XXV (October, 1926), 241–249. Detailed discussion of the industry created by the cork oak.

———, and E. R. Blanchard, "The Grape Industry of Spain and Portugal," *Economic Geography*, V (April, 1929), 183–193. An excellent reference for information on this important industry of the peninsula.

———, and S. S. Visher, *Economic Geography of Europe* (McGraw-Hill, 1931). A text with more emphasis on economic geography.

J. F. Bogardus, *Europe* (Harper, 1934). Standard text on the geography of Europe. The chapter on the Iberian Peninsula contains some maps and cross sections that aid one in picturing the peninsula.

CHARLES E. CHAPMAN, *A History of Spain* (Macmillan, 1918). An extremely complete history of Spain in English based on the four-volume work *Historia de España y de la Civilización Española*, by Rafael Altamira y Crevea.

JAMES FAIRGRIEVE, *Geography and World Power* (Eighth Edition, Dutton, 1941). A standard work in political geography, one of the first texts discussing the relation between political power and geography.

J. P. GOODE, *School Atlas* (Revised Edition, Rand, McNally, 1943). A standard atlas for American student reference.

GEORGE D. HUBBARD, *The Geography of Europe* (Appleton-Century, 1937). Standard text on European geography with a good interpretation of human response to the environment.

L. W. LYDE, *The Continent of Europe* (Macmillan, 1920). An excellent reference for the geology and structure of Europe in general.

MARION I. NEWBIGIN, *Southern Europe* (Second Edition, London, Methuen & Co., Ltd., 1943). Introduced by a study of the Mediterranean region as a whole, the physical and regional geography of the Iberian Peninsula is discussed in detail.

M. R. SHACKLETON, *Europe, A Regional Geography* (Third Edition, Longmans, Green, 1942). A good picture of regional geography of the peninsula.

W. M. THOMPSON, "Portugal, the Country and the People," *Geographical Review*, VI (August, 1918), 147–155. Subject matter of the article suggested by the title; old but basic.

J. F. UNSTEAD, "Geographical Regions of Iberia," *Scottish Geographical Magazine*, XLII (1926), 159–170. Detailed regional studies of the peninsula.

SAMUEL VAN VALKENBURG AND ELLSWORTH HUNTINGTON, *Europe* (Wiley, 1935). Following a geographic interpretation of Europe as a whole, specific nations and groups of nations are discussed in some detail.

Chapter 16: The Five Fenno Scandic Countries

D. R. BERGSMARK, "Agricultural Land Utilization in Denmark," *Economic Geography*, XXI (April, 1925), 206–214. The geographic basis of Danish agriculture and its areal distribution are well demonstrated.

HUGO ADOLF BERNATZIK, *Lapland* (London, Constable & Co., Ltd., 1937). An interesting, beautifully illustrated story of the Lapps.

ISAIAH BOWMAN, *The New World, Problems in Political Geography* (Fourth Edition, World Book, 1928). Especially helpful in picturing relationship between economic-geographic conditions and political problems.

MARQUIS CHILDS, *Sweden, The Middle Way* (New Haven, Yale University Press, 1936). An excellent description of social and economic organization and development in this progressive land.

THE GEOGRAPHICAL SOCIETY OF FINLAND, *Atlas of Finland*, 1925. One of the best atlases from the point of view of cartography and comprehensiveness ever published by any country.

AXEL JOHAN JOSEF GUINCHARD, *Sweden; Historical and Statistical Handbook*, two volumes (Government Printing Office of Sweden, prepared for the San Francisco Exposition, 1915). Excellent articles, photographs, and maps.

GEORGE D. HUBBARD, *The Geography of Europe* (Appleton-Century, 1937). Comprehensive treatment of all phases of geography for each nation.

ELLSWORTH HUNTINGTON, "Farms and Farm Villages of Sweden," *Journal of Geography*, XXXVII (March, 1938), 85 ff. Portrays the landscape pattern of rural Sweden.

J. JOESTEN, "Scramble for Swedish Iron Ore," *Foreign Affairs*, XVI (January, 1938), 347–350. Illustrates the pressure placed on small nations possessing minerals valued by large countries.

L. W. LYDE, *The Continent of Europe* (Macmillan, 1930). Especially helpful because of its interpretive historical approach and detailed descriptions of subregions.

AGNES ROTHERY, *Denmark—Kingdom of Reason* (Viking, 1937). A popular author's significant description and interpretation of the remarkable Danes.

VILHJALMUR STEFANSSON, *Iceland, The First American Republic* (Doubleday, Doran, 1939). All phases of Icelandic life are discussed in the author's usual readable style.

EUGENE VAN CLEEF, *Finland—The Republic Farthest North* (Columbus, Ohio State University Press, 1929). An American geographer's analysis of Finnish problems.

SAMUEL VAN VALKENBURG AND ELLSWORTH HUNTINGTON, Europe (Wiley, 1935). Excellent regional descriptions of each country.

MAURICE ZIMMERMANN, "États Scandinaves, Régions Polaires Boréales," *Géographie Universelle*, Volume III (Paris, Armand Colin, 1933).

One of the best and most complete treatments of Scandinavian geography.

Chapter 17: Poland: A Perpetual Problem

RAYMOND L. BUELL, *Poland, Key to Europe* (Third Edition, Knopf, 1939). A politico-geographic history beginning with the Partition. Describes economic situation, minorities, and many other problems.

Concise Statistical Yearbook of Poland (Warsaw. Annually up to German Occupation in 1939). A publication of the Chief of Bureau of Statistics.

EDWARD H. L. CORWIN, *Political History of Poland* (New York, The Polish Book Importing Co., 1917). From early beginnings to World War I. Biographical, political, illustrated; many maps.

ROMAN DYBOSKI, *Poland* (London, Ernest Benn, Ltd., 1933). Historical and descriptive from pre-Partition times. Discusses minorities, economic life, literature, art, education, and government.

"Economic Life," *Polish Encyclopedia*, Volume III (Geneva, Atar, 1922). Many authors. Detailed elaborate study of various phases of Polish economic life.

EUROPEAN CONFERENCE ON RURAL LIFE, *Poland* (Geneva, 1940). National monograph on the country.

MONICA MARY GARDNER, *Poland* (Fourth Edition, London, A. and C. Black, Ltd., 1942). Intimate pictures of daily life and familiar scenes described with charm by a friend of the Polish people.

INSTITUTE FOR STUDY OF MINORITY PROBLEMS, *Questions of Minorities* (Warsaw, 1932). The Polish and non-Polish populations of Poland based on census of 1931.

ROBERT MACHRAY, *Poland, 1914–1931* (London, George Allen and Unwin, Ltd., 1932). Historical and biographical, rather than geographic; a valuable summary of political, military, diplomatic, and economic events, recording conferences and treaties.

WACLAW NALKOWSKI, *Poland as a Geographic Entity* (London, George Allen and Unwin, LTD., 1917). A clear-cut analysis of the geographic situation of Poland and the influence of position on Polish history and national character.

WILLIAM FIDDIAN REDDAWAY, ET AL., Editors, *The Cambridge History of Poland* (Cambridge, Cambridge University Press, 1941). Beginning with the early Saxon period (1696–1733) Poland's story is told by more than 20 authors. Although the book is a history it constantly touches upon Polish geography and the literature and spirit of the people.

SIMON SEGAL, *The New Order in Poland* (Knopf, 1942). The New Order of the Nazi occupation and government in Poland. A well-balanced description of this New Order in practice.

M. R. SHACKLETON, *Europe, A Regional Geography* (Longmans, Green, 1934), pp. 220–227, 269–285. On the geologic and geographic foundations the author describes the economic and political development of the country.

STANISLAW SLAWSKI, *Poland's Access to the Sea* (London, Eyre and Spottiswoode, Ltd., 1925). Slawski was a member of the Harbor and Waterways Board of Danzig. He examines the question from many angles and presents East Prussia's claims. Geography, legal bases, and economic use of the sea.

ANN SU CARDWELL (pseud.), MARGARET LOW (Stump) SUPER, *Poland and Russia* (Sheed and Ward, 1944). A thorough search for facts. Covers the last 25 years of Polish-Soviet relations. Three hundred years of history are reviewed in Chapter I. Bibliography of 75 titles and two appendices. Gives Molotov's report to the Supreme Soviet.

Chapter 18: The Lesser Countries of Central Europe

JOSEF CHMELAR, *National Minorities in Central Europe* (Prague, Orbis, 1937). Brief factual summaries of existing conditions in 1936.

M. W. FODOR, *Plot and Counter-Plot in Central Europe* (Houghton Mifflin, 1937). Covers the expansion of German influence along the Danube.

G. E. R. GEDYE, *Betrayal in Central Europe* (Harper, 1939). A reliable journalistic report.

Hungary, British Survey Handbooks (Macmillan, 1945). Probably the best short available summary of factual information in English.

O. I. JANOWSKY, *People at Bay: The Jewish Problem in East-Central Europe* (New York, Oxford University Press, 1938). A consideration of a serious problem of the area.

JOHN LEHMANN, *Down River: A Danubian Study* (London, Cresset Press, Ltd., 1939). An interpretation of life and landscape of the Danubian states, by a Leftist sympathizer.

EMIL LENGYEL, *The Danube* (Random House, 1939). Colorful description of all the nations along the Danube.

C. A. MACARTNEY, *Problems of the Danube Basin* (Macmillan, 1942). A brief, competent background survey by a British expert.

STOYAN PRIBICHEVICH, *World without End* (Reynal & Hitchcock, 1939). A readable survey, good on the peasant mentality.

JOSEPH S. ROUCEK, Editor, *Contemporary Europe* (Van Nostrand, 1941). Chapter IX, pp. 171–192, is entitled "Czechoslovakia and Her Minorities."

——, "Socio-Graphic Aspects of the Minorities Problem of Czechoslovakia," *Journal of Central European Affairs*, III (July, 1943), 183–197. A consideration of a significant topic.

——, "The 'Free Movements' of Horthy's Eckhardt and Austria's Otto," *Public Opinion Quarterly*, VII (Fall, 1943), 466–476. An interesting discussion about two controversial people.

——, Editor, "A Challenge to Peacemakers, Conflicting National Aspirations in Central and Eastern Europe," *The Annals of the American Academy of Political and Social Science*, CCXXXII (March, 1944). This study clearly reveals the challenge long offered to statesmen by this area.

——, "Sociological Aspects of the Minorities Problem," *New Europe*, IV (July–August, 1944), 12–13. A consideration of an important phase of the problem of minorities.

H. W. STEED, *The Antecedents of Post-War Europe* (Graduate Institute of International Studies, New York, Oxford University Press, 1932). Gives a survey primarily of the evolution of the Habsburg problem in the century before World War I.

Chapter 19: The Balkan States: Peninsular Rivals

The Balkan States, Part I, *Economic* (New York, Oxford University Press, 1936). A review of the economic, financial, and geographic developments, prepared by the Royal Institute of International Affairs.

FREDERIC W. L. KOVACS, *The Untamed Balkans* (Modern Age, 1941). A cursory survey of Balkan history emphasizing the necessity for a drastic solution of the agrarian problem.

DAVID MITRANY, *The Effect of the War in Southeastern Europe* (New Haven, Yale University Press, 1936). What World War I did to the methods of government and economic life.

STOYAN PRIBICHEVICH, *World without End* (Reynal & Hitchcock, 1939). An absorbing if discursive promenade through the history, politics, folklore, and culture of the Balkan Peninsula.

JOSEPH S. ROUCEK, *The Politics of the Balkans* (McGraw-Hill, 1939). A compact description of the social realities of the various Balkan countries.

——, "Southeastern Europe—A Study in Geographic Disunity," Chapter 31, pp. 545–561, in G. T. Renner and Associates, *Global Geography* (Crowell, 1944). A clear discussion of a complicated area.

——, "Geopolitics of the Balkans," *World Affairs Interpreter*, XV (January, 1945), 419–440. The word "geopolitics" is well applied to the Balkans.

——, "The Balkans as a World Problem," *Journal of Geography*, XXXIV (1938), 286–296. Analyzes the socio-geographic aspects of the Balkans.

——, "The Balkans: Key to World War II," *World Affairs Interpreter*, XI (July, 1940), 179–197. Shows the important role of the Balkans in world events.

——, "Hitler Over the Balkans," *World Affairs Interpreter*, XII (July, 1941), 136–152. Covers also the geographical aspects of Hitler's invasion.

——, "World War II and the Balkans," *Social Education*, V (March, 1941), 187–189. Written prior to Hitler's invasion of Yugoslavia and Greece.

F. SCHEVILL AND W. M. GEWEHR, *The History of the Balkan Peninsula* (Harcourt, Brace, 1933). The revised edition of the best general history of the Balkans in English.

BARBARA WARD AND OTHERS, *Hitler's Route to Baghdad* (Norton, 1939). Useful chapters on the political and economic problems of respective countries.

REBECCA WEST, *Black Lamb and Grey Falcon* (Viking, 1941). A beautifully written book on the peasant mentality of the Yugoslavs.

PART FOUR

ASIA

Chapter 20: Turkey and the Straits

THOMAS ANTHEM, "Russia and the Dardanelles," *The Contemporary Review,* CLXVIII (October, 1945), 222–226. A brief historical analysis, excellent as a counterpart to Graves, *Briton and Turk.*

ELIAHU BEN-HORIN, *The Middle East* (Norton, 1943). The theme of this book is its subtitle, "Crossroads of History." Chapter 1 analyzes Turkey politically under the title, "An Empire Falls to Pieces."

GEORGE B. CRESSEY, *Asia's Lands and Peoples* (McGraw-Hill, 1944). A recent regional geography by a ranking American geographer—a must for any part of Asia.

SIDNEY B. FAY, *The Origins of the World War* two volumes (Macmillan, 1928). A distinguished American historian includes a discussion of the relationships of Turkey and the Straits to the origins of World War I.

PHILIP GRAVES, *Briton and Turk* (London, Hutchinson & Co., Ltd., 1941). The position of Britain is analyzed and traced throughout history.

———, *The Question of the Straits* (London, Ernest Benn, Ltd., 1937). Most detailed discussion on this problem available. Author is a well-known authority on the problems of Turkey.

HARRY N. HOWARD, "The Montreux Convention of the Straits, 1936," *Department of State Bulletin,* XV, No. 375 (September 8, 1946).

———, "Problem of the Turkish Straits; Principal Treaties and Conventions (1774–1936)," *Department of State Bulletin,* XV, No. 383 (November 3, 1946). Nobody has done more thorough work on the problems of this region than Professor Howard, now with the Department of State. The above two articles give a summary of the Montreux Convention and list all important conventions and treaties with regard to the Straits.

ERNEST JACKH, *The Rising Crescent* (Farrar & Rinehart, 1944). A political interpretation of Turkey from 1908 to World War II by a diplomat who was long on the scene.

EMIL LENGYEL, *Turkey* (Random House, 1941). Largely historical but gives a clear picture of the Turkish mentality. Written in popular style.

L. W. LYDE, *The Continent of Asia* (Macmillan, 1938). A standard British text giving physical descriptions and economic bases of Asia's regions.

ARTHUR E. MODDIE, "The Straits and the World," *The London Quarterly of World Affairs,* XII, No. 2 (July, 1946). The eminent British geographer discussed the Straits and its setting in today's world. An important paper.

L. DUDLEY STAMP, *Asia, A Regional and Economic Geography* (Dutton, 1938). Includes a good physical treatment of Turkey and southwest Asia.

B. H. SUMNER, *A Short History of Russia* (Reynal & Hitchcock, 1943). One of the short histories of Russia. Russian historical interest in the Straits is discussed together with an analysis of her position in the whole southern area.

CHESTER M. TOBIN, *Turkey, Key to the East* (Putnam, 1944). Written by an impressed visitor, this book presents a clear insight into Turkey's present stand as a modern nation.

SUMNER WELLES, Editor, *Guide to the Peace* (Dryden, 1945). Sketches of individual countries are helpful in covering highlights of the geography, history, and political aspects.

Note: For the physical aspects of European Turkey, almost any standard text on the geography of Europe has a few pages devoted to this area.

Chapter 21: The Arab World

GEORGE ANTONIUS, *The Arab Awakening* (Lippincott, 1939). A discussion of the character of Arab aspirations and their historical development.

JOHN S. BADEAU, *East and West of Suez: The Story of the Modern Near East,* Headline Series, No. 39 (Foreign Policy Association, 1943). The former Dean of the College of Arts and Sciences of the American University of Cairo gives a brief but excellent review of Near Eastern problems.

British Admiralty Handbooks, *Syria, Arabia, Palestine and Transjordan* (British Admiralty, 1920). A reliable survey of the problems of the individual countries, of importance to anyone going into more details.

GEORGE B. CRESSEY, *Asia's Lands and Peoples* (McGraw-Hill, 1944). The chapter on southwestern Asia contains much valuable geographic material.

PHILIP K. HITTI, *History of the Arabs* (Macmillan, 1937). The most comprehensive work on recent history of the Arabs.

A. K. HOURANI, *Syria and Lebanon* (New York, Oxford University Press, 1946). A detailed discussion of the problems of the two republics of the Near East. Of special value for the student interested in details of the region.

P. W. IRELAND, *Iraq* (Macmillan, 1938). An excellent detailed survey of one of the most important countries in the Near East.

W. C. LOWDERMILK, *Palestine, Land of Promise* (Harper, 1944). A well known soil conservationist discusses the soil problems of Palestine and its future. Of special interest is the discussion of the proposed Jordan Valley Authority and its possibilities for the land and the inhabitants.

VERNON MCKAY, "The Arab League in World Politics," *Foreign Policy Reports,* November 15, 1946. In the usually dependable manner of the Foreign Policy Association, this brief article gives an excellent presentation of the background and purposes of the Arab League.

ROBERT E. NATHAN, O. GASS, AND D. CREAMER, *Palestine: Problem and Promise* (American Council on Public Affairs, 1946). A comprehensive economic study of Palestine by a group of recognized economists.

E. C. SEMPLE, *The Geography of the Mediterranean Region* (Holt, 1931). Probably one of the most important books in the geography of the region. Although written several years ago, its facts are still reliable today.

E. A. SPEISER, *The United States and the Near East* (Cambridge, Harvard University Press, 1947). An authoritative presentation of the problems of the Near East, with the necessary political, economic, geographic, and social analysis. The most up-to-date book on the region and its problems.

L. D. STAMP, *Asia, A Regional and Economic Geography* (Dutton, 1938). Although slightly outdated the chapter on Arab Asia discusses in great length the geographic structure of the Near East.

K. S. TWITCHELL, *Saudi Arabia* (Princeton University Press, 1947). One of the best books on

a given region in the Near East. It contains a wealth of geographic, social, and political material that is vital in the understanding of current problems in this peninsular country.

S. VAN VALKENBURG, *Whose Promised Lands? A Political Atlas of the Middle East and India,* Headline Series, No. 57 (Foreign Policy Association, 1946). A simple discussion of geographic and political factors of the countries of the Near East by a well-known political geographer.

Numerous articles have been published during the last years on various aspects of the Near East. For the student interested in a more detailed survey of the individual areas, the following list is given as a guide:

R. J. BARR, "Postwar Trade Prospects in Egypt, Iraq, Palestine," *Foreign Commerce Weekly,* United States Department of Commerce, June 30, 1945.

E. DEGOLYER, "Preliminary Report of the Technical Oil Mission to the Middle East," *Bulletin of the American Association of Petroleum Geologists,* July, 1944.

W. IRWIN, "The Salts of the Dead Sea and River Jordan," *Geographical Journal,* LXI (1923), 428–440.

JAMES M. LANDIS, "Middle East Challenge," *Fortune,* 32 (September, 1945), 161–188.

GRANT S. MCCLELLAN, "Palestine and America's Role in the Middle East," *Foreign Policy Reports,* July 1, 1945.

R. H. SANGER, "Ibn Saud's Program for Arabia," *The Middle East Journal,* I (April, 1947), 180–190.

AFIF I. TANNOUS, "Agricultural Collaboration in the Middle East," *Foreign Agriculture* (April–May, 1947).

The Editors of Fortune Magazine, "The Great Oil Deals," *Fortune* (May, 1947).

Chapter 22: The Middle East States of Iran and Afghanistan

ELIAHU BEN-HORIN, *The Middle East* (Norton, 1943). A satisfactory discussion of the problems of the Middle East.

GEORGE B. CRESSEY, *Asia's Lands and Peoples* (McGraw-Hill, 1944). This is valuable for geographic material on Iran and Afghanistan.

————, *The Basis of Soviet Strength* (Whittlesey, 1945). This book should be read during any study of the Middle East.

L. P. ELWELL-SUTTON, *Modern Iran* (London,

George Routledge & Sons, Ltd., 1942). A rather thorough treatment of historical, geographic, economic, and political conditions affecting Iran.

JOHN N. GREELY, "Iran in Wartime," *The National Geographic Magazine*, LXXXIV (August, 1943), 129–156. A description of Iran during World War II, including map showing transportation routes.

WILLIAM HARBERTON, "Anglo-Russian Relations Concerning Afghanistan, 1837–1907," *University of Illinois Studies in the Social Sciences*, XXI (Urbana, 1937). This should be studied to understand Anglo-Russian diplomacy.

HARRIS FOUNDATION LECTURES, *The Near East* (University of Chicago Press, 1942). A source of information concerning Arab unity, British policy in the Near East, and social changes.

HANS KOHN, *Western Civilization in the Near East* (New York, Columbia University Press, 1936). Valuable for an understanding of the what, where, and why of conditions in countries east of the Mediterranean.

JAMES M. LANDIS, "Middle East Challenge," *Fortune*, XXXII (September, 1945), 161–188. An enlightening argument urging Americans to study the Middle East.

A. K. LOBECK, *Physiographic Diagram of Asia* (New York, The Geographical Press, Columbia University, 1945). Essential for an understanding of the physiography and the geography of Asia.

BARONESS RAVENSDALE, "Old and New Persia," *The National Geographic Magazine*, LXXVI (September, 1939), 325–355. A running description of changes taking place in Iran.

MORTON B. STRATTON, "British Railways and Motor Roads in the Middle East, 1918–1930," *Economic Geography*, XX (April, 1944), 116–129. Study of conditions affecting development of communication.

———, "British Railways and Motor Roads in the Middle East, 1930–1940," *Economic Geography*, XX (July, 1944), 189–203. Sequel to above article.

SIR PERCY SYKES, *A History of Afghanistan*, two volumes (Macmillan, 1940). One should study these volumes thoroughly before discussing the Afghans. Also valuable material concerning Iran.

MAYNARD OWEN WILLIAMS, "Afghanistan Makes Haste Slowly," *The National Geographic Magazine*, LXIV (December, 1933), 731–769. Description of changes taking place in Afghanistan.

Chapter 23: The Complexity of India and Burma

VERA ANSTEY, *The Economic Development of India* (Longmans, Green, 1931). A standard work on the economy of India.

H. N. BRAILSFORD, *Subject India* (Day, 1943). A critical analysis of British rule in India.

H. G. CHAMPION, "Preliminary Survey of the Forest Types of India and Burma," *Indian Forest Records*, New Series I, No. 1 (1936). An authoritative treatment of India's forests.

J. L. CHRISTIAN, *Modern Burma* (Berkeley, University of California Press, 1942). An accurate account of Burma's economic, political, and social development.

R. COUPLAND, *The Indian Problem* (Toronto, Oxford University Press, 1944). A well-balanced, comprehensive study of the constitutional problem in India. The book is organized in three parts with a short summary of each.

G. B. CRESSEY, *Asia's Lands and Peoples* (McGraw-Hill, 1944). A good general textbook on the geography of Asia.

SIR JOHN CUMMING, *Modern India: A Cooperative Survey* (New York, Oxford University Press, 1932). An excellent series of articles. Each chapter is written by an authority on the subject.

W. E. DUFFET AND A. R. HICKS, *India Today: The Background of Indian Nationalism* (Day, 1942). Contains much valuable information in brief form.

C. B. FAWCETT, *A Political Geography of the British Empire* (Ginn, 1933). A standard textbook on political geography written by one of Britain's foremost authorities.

G. S. GHURYE, *Caste and Race in India* (Knopf, 1932). A detailed study of the Indian Caste System.

L. W. LYDE, *The Continent of Asia* (Macmillan, 1938). A good general textbook on the geography of Asia with stress on the physical aspects.

LORD MESTON, *Nationhood for India* (New Haven, Yale University Press, 1931). An analysis of India's readiness for self-government.

T. A. RAMAN, *Report on India* (Toronto, Oxford University Press, 1943). A book written in a popular style by an Indian giving a clear, objective analysis of the Indian situation.

L. D. STAMP, "Burma: An Undeveloped Monsoon Country," *Geographical Review*, XX (January, 1930), 86–109. An excellent analysis of the country's geography in brief form.

Sir Frederick Whyte, *India: A Bird's-Eye View* (Toronto, Oxford University Press, Royal Institute of International Affairs, 1943). A short account of the political situation in India.

Chapter 24: The Foundations of Modern China

J. L. Buck, *Land Utilization in China,* three volumes (University of Chicago Press, 1937). A monumental work, primarily on Chinese agriculture, based upon a study of 38,000 farm families in twenty-two provinces. Includes descriptions, charts, photographs, maps, and statistics.

Claude A. Buss, *War and Diplomacy in Eastern Asia* (Macmillan, 1941). One of the best surveys of the international politics of eastern Asia before Pearl Harbor.

China and Japan (Royal Institute of International Affairs, 1941). A careful study of modern relations between China and Japan.

George B. Cressey, *Asia's Lands and Peoples* (McGraw-Hill, 1944). This excellent textbook of Asia has several chapters devoted to Greater China, presenting both topical and regional views.

A. J. Grajdanzev, *Formosa Today* (New York, Institute of Pacific Relations, 1942). An informative handbook with geographical, economic, and political data.

Kenneth Scott Latourette, *The Development of China* (Houghton Mifflin, 1937). An excellent study of the history and culture of China.

Owen Lattimore, *Inner Asian Frontiers of China* (American Geographical Society, 1940). An authoritative consideration of the interior frontiers of China from a geographical-political viewpoint.

Harold S. Quigley, "China Today," *International Conciliation,* October, 1944, pp. 591–626. An excellent account of China in 1944 before the defeat of Japan in 1945.

Marthe Rajchman, *New Atlas of China* (Day, 1941). Useful for transportation routes in Greater China.

David Nelson Rowe, *China Among the Powers* (Harcourt, Brace, 1945). A study of the position of China among the leading nations of the world.

Jules Sion, *Asie des Moussons, Chine-Japon,* Géographie Universelle (Paris, Armand Colin, 1928). The standard French source for the Far East.

L. Dudley Stamp, *Asia: An Economic and Regional Geography* (London, Methuen & Co., Ltd., 1929). An English text stressing physical geography. Good for regions of China.

Sun Yat-sen, *The International Development of China* (Putnam, 1929). Problems of industrial development are considered in an enlightened manner.

Payson S. Treat, *The Far East* (Harper, 1935). A general text covering the history of the Far East.

Theodore H. White and Annalee Jacoby, *Thunder Out of China* (Sloane, 1946). An interesting account of recent developments in China.

Chapter 25: Korea, Indo-China, and Siam: Historic Asiatic Buffers

George B. Cressey, *Asia's Lands and People* (McGraw-Hill, 1944). The most recent geography of Asia with excellent regional material.

Herbert G. Deignan, *Siam—Land of Free Men,* War Background Studies, No. 8 (Washington, The Smithsonian Institution, 1943). A concise sketch of Siam featuring the historical evolution since prehistoric times.

Thomas E. Ennis, *French Policy and Developments in Indo-China* (University of Chicago Press, 1936). A thorough treatment of the political aspects of Indo-China, centering upon French contacts and colonial administration.

Pierre Gourou, *Land Utilization in French Indo-China* (New York, Institute of Pacific Relations, 1945). An up-to-date study from a reliable source.

A. J. Grajdanzev, *Modern Korea* (New York, International Secretariat, Institute of Pacific Relations, distributed by Day, 1944). Excellent coverage on geographical, political, and related phases of the country. A straightforward presentation that makes interesting reading. Contains valuable appendices including relatively up-to-date bibliographical references.

H. B. Hulbert, *The History of Korea,* two volumes (Seoul, Korea, 1905). An old but authentic history of Korea prior to the Japanese annexation.

Hoon K. Lee, *Land Utilization and Rural Economy in Korea* (University of Chicago Press, 1936). A complete analysis of Korean agricultural activities. Some attention is also devoted to mining, forestry, and other types of land use. Numerous tables and maps give an excellent statistical interpretation of the country's basic occupations.

SHANNON McCUNE, "Climatic Regions of Korea and Their Economy," *Geographical Review*, XXXI (January, 1941), 45–99. A rather detailed treatment of the geography of Korea from the physical standpoint.

Map of Korea (Washington, Korean Affairs Institute, Inc., 1945). Authentic for detail in place geography.

M. FREDERICK NELSON, *Korea and the Old Orders in Eastern Asia* (Baton Rouge, Louisiana State University Press, 1945). A study dealing with the international status of Korea. Diplomatic relations with the Western nations are well analyzed.

ROBERT L. PENDLETON, "Land Use in Northeastern Thailand," *Geographical Review*, XXXIII (January, 1943), 15–41. A scholarly study of recent geographic aspects of Siam.

CHARLES ROBEQUAIN, *Economic Development of French Indo-China* (translated) (New York, Oxford University Press, Auspices of the Institute of Pacific Relations, 1944). A detailed study treating the national economy of the country. The approach is strictly academic. Included is a supplement of recent developments (1939–43) that relates Indo-China's part in World War II.

L. DUDLEY STAMP, *Asia: An Economic and Regional Geography* (London, Methuen & Co., Ltd., 1929). A basic background text from the standpoint of the physical structure of the Asiatic continent.

VIRGINIA THOMPSON, *French Indo-China* (Macmillan, 1937). A general treatment of all aspects of the country, though not from a geographer's point of view.

———, *Thailand, The New Siam* (Macmillan, 1941). A reliable study of modern Siam.

H. M. VINACKE, *A History of the Far East in Modern Times* (Crofts, 1941; also Knopf, 1928). Standard text for the region; used widely in official circles. A chapter on Korea deals specifically with the position of Korea in relation to China and Japan.

CARLE C. ZIMMERMAN, "Some Phases of Land Utilization in Siam," *Geographical Review*, XXVII (July, 1937), 378–393. Although written before acute Japanese pressure this article gives an insight to the geographical pattern of the country.

Chapter 26: The Japanese Isles

GEORGE ALEXANDER BALLARD, *The Influence of the Sea on the Political History of Japan* (London, John Murray, 1921). This British vice admiral traced the evolution of the Japanese fleet.

CLAUDE A. BUSS, *War and Diplomacy in Eastern Asia* (Macmillan, 1941). An excellent survey of international relations in the Far East on the eve of the Pacific War.

BASIL HALL CHAMBERLAIN, *Things Japanese* (London, John Murray, 1902). A work in encyclopedic style by one of the greatest authorities on early Japanese lore.

Contemporary Japan (The Foreign Affairs Association of Japan, prewar periodical). A Japanese periodical in English containing valuable articles on the country.

JOHN GOETTE, *Japan Fights for Asia* (Harcourt, Brace, 1943). Excellent reportage of a correspondent who follows Japanese armies through early stages of their war with China.

R. B. HALL and A. WATANABE, "Landforms of Japan," *Papers of the Michigan Academy of Science, Arts, and Letters*, XVIII (1932), 157–207. Detailed physiographic analysis for those interested in further study on this phase of the Japanese Islands.

Industrial Japan (New York, Institute of Pacific Relations, compiled by the Research Staff of the International Secretariat of the Institute, 1941). An insight into Japanese economy by Japanese authors.

RYOICHI ISHII, *Population Pressure and Economic Life in Japan* (University of Chicago Press, 1937). A thorough demographic analysis of Japan and resulting national economy. Censuses and population trends from early times to the middle 1930's are especially well presented in this valuable book.

T. V. KALIJARVI AND ASSOCIATES, *Modern World Politics* (Second Edition, Crowell, 1945). Chapter XXVIII, "Japan, China, and Their Neighbors," gives a good survey of the political highlights of this important region.

ARTHUR J. MARDER, "From Jimmu Tennō to Perry: Sea Power in Early Japanese History," *The American Historical Review*, LI (October, 1945), 1–34. Covers the earliest Japanese naval history. Especially valuable because Japanese sources were used.

JOHN E. ORCHARD, *Japan's Economic Position* (Whittlesey, 1930). Basic material on economic and industrial conditions of prewar Japan. Data is largely the result of extensive field work.

WILLARD PRICE, *Japan's Islands of Mystery* (Day, 1944). An interesting book on the Mandated Islands that played such an important role in the Pacific phase of World War II. The book was widely used by U.S. military forces as a "guide" as they advanced through the islands.

G. B. SANSOM, *Japan: A Short Cultural History* (Revised Edition, Appleton-Century, 1943). This work is standard for the earlier period in Japanese history.

TATSUJI TAKEUCHI, *War and Diplomacy in the Japanese Empire* (Doubleday, Doran, 1935).

An excellent study of Japanese political institutions largely in the first quarter of the twentieth century.

GLENN T. TREWARTHA, *Japan, A Physical, Cultural, and Regional Geography* (Madison, University of Wisconsin Press, 1945). The only up-to-date regional treatment of the area; written by a competent American geographer familiar with Japan.

PART FIVE

AUSTRALASIA AND AFRICA

Chapter 27: Africa: A Study in Colonialism

W. O. BLANCHARD AND S. S. VISHER, *Economic Geography of Europe* (McGraw-Hill, 1931), pp. 469–479. Ten pages of excellent discussion on the economic geography of Mediterranean Africa.

A. H. BRODRICK, *North Africa* (New York, Oxford University Press, 1943). A small volume containing some worthwhile material in the Mediterranean portion of Africa.

L. BROOKS, *Africa* (University of London Press, Ltd., 1925). A good short description of the African continent.

J. DOWD, *The Negro Races,* Volume I (Macmillan, 1907), Volume II (Neale, 1914). A comprehensive description of the Negro, Bantu, Negrito, and other African peoples.

W. FITZGERALD, *Africa* (Dutton, 1944). A standard treatment of the regions, peoples, and history of Africa.

J. W. GREGORY, *Africa—A Geography Reader* (Rand, McNally, 1928). A meritorious elementary description of Africa.

W. G. KENDREW, *Climates of the Continents* (New York, Oxford University Press, 1927), Part I. This is the best published description of African climatology.

EMIL LUDWIG, *The Nile* (Viking, 1937). The biography of a river, containing good history and geography.

H. O. NEWLAND, *West Africa—A Handbook of Practical Information* (London, Daniel O'Connor, 1922). One of the best treatments of history, peoples, industries, and governments of West Africa.

GEORGE T. RENNER, "Economic Adjustments in Liberia," *Economic Geography,* VII (April, 1931), 189–201. The historical and regional geography of this little-known Negro republic.

———, "The Sudan: A Tropical Famine Zone," *Matériaux pour L'Étude des Calamités* (Société de Géographique de Genève), October–December, 1926. An analysis of climatic factors in Africa.

E. H. L. SCHWARZ, *A South-African Geography* (Blackie and Son, 1921). A standard physiographic treatment of Africa, with emphasis upon the southern portion.

H. L. SHANTS AND C. F. MARBUT, *Vegetation and Soils of Africa* (American Geographical Society, 1923). The best general account of the vegetation of Africa.

C. L. WHITE AND G. T. RENNER, *Geography—An Introduction to Human Ecology* (Appleton-Century, 1936). Various sections present a treatment of the climates, soils, vegetation, fauna, and human ecology of Africa.

R. ZON AND W. N. SPARHAWK, *Forest Resources of the World,* two volumes (McGraw-Hill, 1923). Contains a description and appraisal of the forests of Africa.

Chapter 28: A Strategical Appraisal of Africa

ARMY SPECIALIZED TRAINING PROGRAM, *Geographical Foundations of National Power,* Army Service Forces Manual M 103–1 (Government Printing Office, 1944), pp. 53–58; 87; 120–122. A brief but excellent discussion of the French and Italian colonies in Africa.

ISAIAH BOWMAN, *The New World, Problems in Political Geography* (Fourth Edition, World Book, 1928), Chapter XXXIII and portions of Chapters II to VIII. This is by far the best discussion of the geopolitical problems of the African colonies.

G. CLARK, *The Balance Sheet of Imperialism* (New York, Columbia University Press, 1936). A careful, dispassionate discussion of costs, advantages, and profits of colonialism.

J. FAIRGRIEVE, *Geography and World Power* (Eighth Revised Edition, Dutton, 1941). A good discussion of the geographical factors underlying European colonialism.

J. W. GREGORY, *Africa—A Geography Reader* (Rand McNally, 1928), Chapters XXIV and XXV. A concise discussion of the European partition of Africa.

J. F. HORRABIN, *An Outline of Political Geography* (Knopf, 1942), Chapters II to IV; VIII. A concise geographical analysis of world history.

H. J. MACKINDER, *Democratic Ideals and Reality* (Holt, 1919 and 1942). Various sections in this little book show the strategic values and world relations of Africa.

GEORGE T. RENNER, "How the United Nations Must Police the World," *American Magazine*, CXXXVI (September, 1943), 30–31. The maps and text show Africa's strategic position in the age of naval power and in the age of air power.

———, "New Lands for Europe's Uprooted Millions," *American Magazine*, CXL (November, 1945), 34–35; 134–137. A discussion of possibilities for European settlement on the continent of Africa.

———, "The Drama of Rubber," *Current History*, XXXIII (December, 1930), 405–409. An account of American rubber growing in Liberia.

F. L. SCHUMAN, *International Politics* (McGraw-Hill, 1937), Chapters IX and X. An excellent discussion of the colonial systems and foreign policies of the leading national states.

N. J. SPYKMAN, *America's Strategy in World Politics* (Harcourt, Brace, 1942), pp. 91–96; 101–103; 121–123. The geography of international relations from an American viewpoint. The author gives a brief but lucid appraisal of Africa.

S. VAN VALKENBURG, *Elements of Political Geography* (Prentice-Hall, 1939), Chapters II and VI. An excellent summary of territorial changes in Africa, and of the French colonies.

H. G. WELLS, *Outline of History* (Macmillan, 1921), pp. 141–147; 342–417; 483–488; 487–604, 801–811; 977–987. A bird's eye view of the history of Africa from ancient to modern times.

DERWENT WHITTLESEY, *The Earth and the State* (Holt, 1939). This book is basic to any understanding of politico-geography theory.

Chapter 29: The Malay Archipelago and Oceania

Atlas van Tropisch Nederland, Topografischen Dienst (Batavia, Topographical Service, 1938). An excellent atlas containing a wide variety of source materials.

J. O. M. BROEK, *The Economic Development of the Netherlands Indies* (New York, International Secretariat, Institute of Pacific Relations, 1942). Particularly valuable for its summary of current economic problems.

———, "The Economic Development of the Outer Provinces of the Netherlands Indies,' *Geographical Review*, XXX (1940), 187–200. Contrasts the recent expansion of agriculture in the Outer Provinces with the relatively stable agricultural economy on Java.

H. A. BROUWER, *The Geology of the Netherlands East Indies* (Macmillan, 1925). The standard reference book in English on the subject.

E. H. G. DOBBY, "Settlement Patterns in Malaya," *Geographical Review*, XXXII (1942), 211–232. An interesting short article on types of land settlement in Malaya.

RUPERT EMERSON, *Malaysia* (Macmillan, 1937). This volume emphasizes the political framework in Malaya, but contains valuable comparisons with the Netherlands Indies.

J. S. FURNIVALL, *Netherlands India* (Macmillan, 1944). One of the best volumes in English on the political, social, and economic history of the area. Particularly valuable for its description of the Culture System.

R. L. GERMAN, *Handbook to British Malaya* (London, Malayan Information Agency, 1935). A handy compendium of miscellaneous statistics and summaries.

Indisch Verslag (Indies Report), Vol. II, *Statistisch Jaaroverzicht van Nederlandsch-Indie over het Jaar 1937* (Statistical annual abstract of the Netherlands Indies for the year 1937) (Batavia, 1938). This official statistical summary is published each year, and contains invaluable social and economic source material.

J. E. C. MOHR, *The Soils of Equatorial Regions* (translation by R. L. Pendleton) (Ann Arbor, Edwards Brothers, 1944). This is not only the standard treatise on tropical soils in general, but contains excellent data on soil potentialities in the Netherlands Indies.

KARL PELZER, *Pioneer Settlement in the Asiatic Tropics* (American Geographical Society, Special Publication No. 29, 1945). This recent publication presents a number of interesting descriptions of settlement projects and associated problems in different parts of Malaysia.

J. B. SCRIVENOR, "The Physical Geography of the Southern Part of the Malay Peninsula," *Geographical Review*, XI (1921), 351–371. The title is self-explanatory.

AMRY VANDENBOSCH, *The Dutch East Indies* (Third Edition, Berkeley, University of California Press, 1942). A standard reference volume, particularly valuable for its description of current economic, social, and political problems.

S. VAN VALKENBURG, "Agricultural Regions of Asia, Part VIII, Malaysia," *Economic Geography*, XI (1935), 227–246, 325–337; "Part IX, Java," XII (1936), 25–44. A concise description of the principal agricultural areas of the Netherlands Indies.

C. A. VLIELAND, "The Population of the Malay Peninsula," *Geographical Review*, XXIV (1934), 61–78. Contains a description of the main culture groups and races, with an excellent discussion of the migratory laboring classes.

Chapter 30: The Philippine Islands

WILLIAM F. BROEICKE, "Future of Philippine Mining," *Far Eastern Survey*, XIV (October 24, 1945), 300–303. A mining engineer gives a realistic view of the future of Philippine mining.

COMMONWEALTH OF THE PHILIPPINES, Commission of the Census, *Census of the Philippines: 1939*, five volumes (Manila, Bureau of Printing, 1940). A complete census taken on January 1, 1939; agricultural census is for the 1938 crop year.

GEORGE B. CRESSEY, *Asia's Lands and Peoples* (McGraw-Hill, 1944), pp. 538–548. The best single, brief, geographic treatment of the islands.

ALDEN CUTSHALL, "Mineral Resources of the Philippine Islands," *Scientific Monthly*, LIV (April, 1942), 295–302. A general treatment of the islands' mineral resources.

———, "The Philippine Islands and Their People," *Journal of Geography*, XLI, No. 6 (September, 1942), 201–211. Background material on the Philippines.

———, "Trends of Philippine Sugar Production," *Economic Geography*, XIV (April, 1938), 154–158. Trends and problems of the Philippine sugar industry.

RUPERT EMERSON, LENNOX A. MILLS, and VIRGINIA THOMPSON, *Government and Nationalism in Southeast Asia* (New York, International Secretariat, Institute of Pacific Relations, 1942), Part II, Chapter II, pp. 53–69 and Part III, Chapter II, pp. 145–158 treat the Philippines. The first reference is a brief treatment of the government and its development; the second chapter considers parties and factions of national importance.

W. C. Forbes, *The Philippine Islands*, two volumes (Houghton Mifflin, 1928) (Revised and abridged into a single volume, Cambridge, Harvard University Press, 1945). A good description and analysis by a former governor-general; treatment is largely historical.

"The Future of the Philippines," *Amerasia*, IX, No. 14 (July, 1945), 211–221. The prewar economy, political-economic relations with the United States, problems of rehabilitation, and alternatives for American action.

W. H. HAAS, Editor, "The Commonwealth of the Philippines," *The American Empire* (University of Chicago Press, 1940), pp. 306–370. A general survey of Philippine geography.

JOSEPH RALSTON HAYDEN, *The Philippines: A Study in National Development* (Macmillan, 1942). The best and most complete sociopolitical work on the Philippines.

GRAYSON L. KIRK, *Philippine Independence* (Farrar & Rinehart, 1936). Includes some stimulating arguments against Philippine independence.

HERBERT W. KRIEGER, *Peoples of the Philippines*, War Background Series No. 4 (Washington, Smithsonian Institution, 1942). The origin and characteristics of the people who live in the Philippines.

KARL J. PELZER, *Pioneer Settlement in the Asiatic Tropics*, Special Publication No. 29 (American Geographical Society, 1945). Contains an excellent treatment of government-sponsored settlement areas in the islands.

CATHERINE PORTER, *Crisis in the Philippines* (Knopf, 1942). A good description of conditions in the Philippines in 1941.

ROBERT L. PENDLETON, "Land Utilization and Agriculture in Mindanao, Philippine Islands," *Geographical Review*, XXXII (April, 1942), 180–210. A detailed study of land utilization in the frontier of the Philippines.

WALTER WILGUS, "Economic Outlook for the Philippines," *Foreign Policy Reports*, XXI, No. 14 (October 1, 1945), 202–207. A realistic view of Philippine economic possibilities after July 4, 1946.

PART SIX

LATIN AMERICA

Chapter 31:   The Caribbean: An American Mediterranean

FRED CARLSON, *Geography of Latin America* (Prentice-Hall, 1944), Chapters XX to XXXII. A brief summary of the geography of Caribbean lands.

H. HERRING, *Good Neighbors* (New Haven, Yale University Press, 1941), Chapters IV to VII. A brief, interesting account of the lands and people.

PRESTON E. JAMES, *Latin America* (Odyssey, 1942), Parts III and IV. A detailed survey of the regional geography.

CHESTER L. JONES, *The Caribbean Since 1900* (Prentice-Hall, 1936). An objective survey of the major historical developments in the Caribbean region.

ROBERT PLATT, J. K. WRIGHT, J. C. WEAVER, AND J. E. FAIRCHILD, *The European Possessions in the Caribbean* (American Geographical Society, 1941). An excellent survey of the colonial possessions.

FRED J. RIPPY, *Latin America and the Industrial Age* (Putnam, 1944). An interesting collection of essays on the development of Latin America's resources through science and technology.

——, *The Caribbean Danger Zone* (Putnam, 1940). A useful interpretation of strategy and diplomacy in the Caribbean area.

J. RUSSELL SMITH AND M. OGDEN PHILLIPS, *North America* (Harcourt, Brace, 1940). Contains interesting regional material on North American lands below the Rio Grande.

N. J. SPYKMAN, *America's Strategy in World Politics* (Harcourt, Brace, 1942), Part II. A realistic analysis of the position of the United States in Caribbean affairs.

OTIS P. STARKEY, *Barbados* (New York, Columbia University Press, 1939). Written originally as a dissertation for the doctorate this study is of value for a complete economic analysis of a small West Indian island.

S. VAN VALKENBURG, *America at War* (Prentice-Hall, 1942). A chapter by Earl B. Shaw in this symposium deals with our Atlantic defenses in World War II and shows the strategic relationship between the Caribbean region and the United States.

A. P. WHITAKER, Editor, "Mexico Today," *Annals of the American Academy of Political and Social Science,* 208 (March, 1940), 1–186. A comprehensive survey of modern Mexico.

A. CURTIS WILGUS, Editor, *The Caribbean Area* (Washington, The George Washington University Press, 1934). An excellent volume of seminar conference lectures on the Caribbean area.

M. W. WILLIAMS, *The People and Politics of Latin America* (Ginn, 1930, Second Edition, 1938), Chapters XVIII to XXII. A summary of the major historical developments.

Chapter 32:   The United States of Brazil

JOÃO PANDIA CALOGERAS, *A History of Brazil,* Inter-American Historical Series (Chapel Hill, University of North Carolina Press, 1939). A clear and readable historical account, written by a Brazilian.

GILBERTO FREYRE, *Brazil: An Interpretation* (Knopf, 1945). A series of lectures on the social aspects of modern Brazilian life; a good account of the individual personality of Brazil.

EARL PARKER HANSON, *The Amazon: A New Frontier?* Headlines Series (New York, Foreign Policy Association, 1944). A compact essay on the part the Amazon may play in the future.

CARYL P. HASKINS, *The Amazon* (Doubleday, Doran, 1943). The story of the world's greatest river and its watershed that includes not only Brazil but five Spanish-speaking nations.

GERTRUDE E. HEARE, *Effects of the War on Brazil's Foreign Trade,* International Reference Service (United States Department of Commerce, May, 1945). Of importance in gauging Brazil's economic potential; includes statistical studies of Brazilian trade.

BENJAMIN H. HUNNICUTT, *Brazil Looks Forward* (Rio de Janeiro, Brazilian Institute of Geography and Statistics, 1945). An optimistic and nontechnical review of Brazil's industry, commerce, technical problems, and social outlook.

PRESTON E. JAMES, *Brazil* (Odyssey, 1946). The most recent standard geography of Brazil.

JOSÉ JOBIM, *Brazil in the Making* (Macmillan, 1943). A detailed study of the industrial and commercial factors involved in the rise of Brazil as a power.

KARL LOEWENSTEIN, *Brazil under Vargas* (Macmillan, 1942). A guide to understanding the political forces at work in Brazil.

J. F. NORMANO, *Brazil: A Study of Economic Types* (Chapel Hill, University of North Carolina Press, 1935). An economic history of Brazil.

HENRY ALBERT PHILLIPS, *Brazil: Bulwark of Inter-American Relations* (Hastings House, 1945). A journalistic treatment of Brazil's position as a leader in the affairs of the Western Hemisphere.

ROBERT S. PLATT, *Latin America* (McGraw-Hill, 1942), Chapter X. Field studies of farms, mines, plantations, fisheries, and other units of the Brazilian economy make this a valuable and interesting treatment.

ADRIAN RONDILEAU (translator), "People and Scenes of Brazil," excerpts from the *Revista Brasileira de Geografía* (Rio de Janeiro, Servicio Gráfico do Instituto de Geografía e Estatística, 1945). A series of Brazilian sketches of unusual interest in defining the relation between the landscape, the economy, and the social strata.

JOSEPH A. RUSSELL, "Fordlandia and Belterra," *Economic Geography*, XVIII (April, 1942), 125–145. An account of the Ford rubber plantation experiments in the Amazon Valley, of value in assessing the possibilities of populating inland tropical Brazil.

T. LYNN SMITH, *Brazil: People and Institutions* (Baton Rouge, Louisiana State University Press, 1946). A study of the roots of Brazilian society.

Chapter 33: The States of the Rio de la Plata

Argentina, American Nation Series No. 1 (Washington, Pan American Union). This booklet outlines briefly statistical, geographical, and historical facts about Argentina. It is well illustrated with views of cities, architectural structures, agricultural activities, etc. A similar publication is available on Uruguay and Paraguay.

Foreign Commerce Weekly, United States Department of Commerce, Supt. of Documents (Government Printing Office). In addition to current news items pertaining to economic data, this publication often carries summaries of current trade regulations as reported by the American embassies in Buenos Aires, Montevideo, and Asunción.

Foreign Commerce Yearbook, United States Department of Commerce, Supt. of Documents (Government Printing Office). These yearbooks contain current and historical statistical data for each country; area, population, cities, agricultural statistics, exports and imports of principal commodities by quantity and value, trade with principal countries, etc. A reliable source of statistical information.

SAMUEL G. INMAN, *Latin America: Its Place in World Life* (Harcourt, Brace, 1942). Written by an outstanding historian on Latin America.

PRESTON JAMES, *Latin America* (Odyssey, 1942), Chapters IX to XI, pp. 264–370. These three chapters should be required reading. This is probably the most comprehensive, well-integrated, geography text on the Latin American countries including the River Plate lands. The geographic regions of Argentina are especially well presented, but the historical and ethnological aspects are also treated in quite some detail.

C. F. JONES, *South America* (Holt, 1930). A thorough regional treatment including several chapters on River Plate lands. An excellent analysis of the factors basic to the meat industry of Argentina and Uruguay.

RAYMOND JOSEPHS, *Argentina Diary* (Random House, 1944). This is essentially a compilation of observations made by an American newspaper reporter. He was the Argentine correspondent for *PM* and *Variety*.

ROBERT S. PLATT, *Latin America—Countryside and Regions* (McGraw-Hill, 1942), Chapters VIII and IX. This source consists of a collection of field studies with particular emphasis on basic units of human occupance.

YSABEL F. RENNIE, *The Argentine Republic* (Macmillan, 1945). This book is essentially a political history of Argentina. Much of the material was obtained by the author from primary sources and through personal interviews. It is an interesting attempt to explain the birth of various political philosophies in Argentina and why modern Argentina is what it is. (A summary of this book would make an interesting and informative term paper or class report.)

R. H. WHITBECK, *The Economic Geography of South America* (McGraw-Hill, 1931), Chapters 9–13. A standard college text for South America with excellent background material on basic crops and industries.

JOHN W. WHITE, *Argentina, the Life and History of a Nation* (Viking, 1942). A political, social, and economic history from the earliest days of Spanish colonization to the present. The author gives his version of answers to questions about Argentina—such as: Why does Argentina fluctuate so violently between democracy and dictatorship? What is the secret of England's hold on the nation? The author's observations and interpretations are drawn from twenty-five years of constant association with the leaders and the people of Latin America. Chapters 20–29 should be required reading.

A. CURTIS WILGUS, *Latin America in Maps* (Barnes and Noble, 1943). Each of the countries of South America is introduced with a brief résumé of historical and ethnological background together with a general description of the geographic regions. The book contains a concise summary of the political and economic development of each country and pertinent topics are well supplemented with numerous maps presenting geographic, historic, economic, and political data. The subject of boundary disputes between countries is included.

Chapter 34: Pacific South America

ISAIAH BOWMAN, "Ecuador-Peru Boundary Dispute," *Foreign Affairs*, XX (July, 1942), 757–761. A penetrating analysis of the hundred-year dispute by America's leading political geographer.

———, *The New World, Problems in Political Geography* (Fourth Edition, World Book, 1928), pp. 673–681. Not a new book but an excellent political geography of the world. Gives the background for comprehending much of what is now taking place on the international stage. Anywhere "flare-ups" come from old problems.

C. C. COLBY, Editor, *Geographical Aspects of International Relations* (University of Chicago Press, 1938). In this volume are two studies dealing with the problems of the area: (1) Preston E. James, "The Distribution of Peoples in South America," pp. 217–240, and (2) Robert S. Platt, "Conflicting Territorial Claims in the Upper Amazon," pp. 243–276.

H. FOSTER BAIN AND THOMAS T. READ, *Ores and Industry in South America* (Harper, 1934). Probably the most authoritative presentation of South America's mineral situation available in the English language. Also contains a valuable résumé of the industrial situation.

HAROLD E. DAVIS, "Democracy in Latin America," *World Affairs*, XXII (June, 1944), 111–118. So different from the customary point of view of a North American that each student should read it.

W. J. DENNIS, *Tacna and Arica* (New Haven, Yale University Press, 1931). A critical study of this important question.

CHARLES C. GRIFFIN, Editor, *Concerning Latin American Culture* (New York, Columbia University Press, 1940). Chapter VI, "The Significance of Native Indian Culture in Hispanic America" deals with the great regional differences in the strength of aboriginal cultural influences caused by the varying degrees of culture of the Indians when the Spaniards came.

PRESTON E. JAMES, *Latin America* (Odyssey, 1942). An accurate, authoritative, and comprehensive geography of Latin America.

PHILIP A. MEANS, "The Incas: Empire Builders of the Andes," *The National Geographic Magazine*, LXXIII (February, 1938), 225–264. An interesting, penetrating, well-balanced, and accurate presentation of the Incas by one of the few unquestioned authorities on the subject. Excellent illustrations in color.

GEORGE M. McBRIDE, *Chile: Land and Society,* Research Series No. 19 (American Geographical Society, 1936). The most accurate and interesting account of the subject in the English language.

ALBERTO ARCA PARRO, "Census of Peru, 1940," *The Geographical Review*, XXX (January, 1942), 1–20. Presentation of the salient material regarding Peru's first census in 64 years by the country's technical advisor to the Central Census Committee.

A. GRENFELL PRICE, *White Settlers in the Tropics,* Special Publication No. 23 (American Geographical Society, 1939). Probably the best treatise of white settlement in the tropics. Shows that the future lies in scientific investigation and that political and economic policies will never succeed unless based upon facts thus established.

WILLIAM L. SCHURZ, *Latin America* (Dutton, 1941). A mature appraisal by one who lived and worked in Latin America for many years; who traveled widely and observed critically.

FERNANDO DE LOS RIOS, "South American Perplexities," *Foreign Affairs*, XX (July, 1942), 650–662. Reasons behind much of what happens in Pacific South America.

GEORGE SOULE, DAVID EFRON, AND NORMAN T. NESS, *Latin America in the Future World* (Farrar & Rinehart, 1945). Recent and useful in evaluating what is in store for Pacific South America as well as for the rest of Latin America.

PART SEVEN

SOME SPECIAL ASPECTS OF POLITICAL GEOGRAPHY

Chapter 35: Political Geography of the Oceans

BERNARD BRODIE, *Sea Power in the Machine Age* (Princeton University Press, 1941). Surveys the development of the steam warship from the time of Robert Fulton to the dreadnaught of our times.

PHILIP GOSSE, *The History of Piracy* (Longmans, Green, 1932). Explains the conditions, geographical and social, which preceded the rise of piracy; traces its periodical rises and declines, its forms and fortunes, and depicts acts of certain individuals.

RUSSELL GRENFELL, *Sea Power* (Doubleday, Doran, 1941). A treatise on the policies of England as a sea power.

VINCENT TODD HARLOW, Editor, *Voyages of Great Pioneers* (New York, Oxford University Press, 1929). An illuminating history of great voyages, such as the travels of Marco Polo the Venetian, Columbus, Vasco da Gama, the Search for the Northwest Passage, and others.

JAMES FRANCIS HORRABIN, *An Outline of Political Geography* (Knopf, 1942). An outline of world history from the geographers' point of view, showing how geographical factors have influenced the development and relationship of societies and states from ancient times to the present.

League of Nations, *The Network of World Trade* (Geneva, League of Nations, 1942). Presentation of magnitude and composition of world trade, systems of unilateral trade, trade groupings, exchange rates, etc.

LIONEL W. LYDE, *The Continent of Europe* (London, Macmillan, 1924, Fourth Edition, Macmillan, 1930). Emphasizes the peninsular character and influence of Europe. Included are world and regional relations; the surrounding oceans and seas; the influence of relief and climate upon environment, etc.

H. J. MACKINDER, "The Geographical Pivot of History," *The Geographical Journal*, XXIII (1904). A classic discussion of geography and its influences upon history and mankind.

E. G. MEARS, *Pacific Ocean Handbook* (Delkin, 1944). A factual presentation of data on the Pacific Basin, including maps, charts, graphs, etc.

ELIZABETH MONROE, *The Mediterranean in Politics* (New York, Oxford University Press, 1938). A discussion of the Mediterranean in the political stage before World War II with the interests of Britain, France, Italy, Spain, and Turkey involved.

JOHN MURRAY, *The Ocean* (Holt, 1913). Deals with methods and instruments of deep sea research, the properties of the water, ocean life and marine deposits.

PAUL MORGAN OGILVIE, *International Waterways* (Macmillan, 1920). Presents the evolution of the principles of international waterways; a reference to the treaties, conventions, laws, and other fundamental acts governing the international use of waterways.

GEORGE T. RENNER AND ASSOCIATES, *Global Geography* (Crowell, 1944). Approaches the problems of the world from the viewpoint of global geographical influences; considers both political area and geographical area.

JOHN HOLLAND ROSE, *Man and the Sea* (Houghton Mifflin, 1936). A presentation of the stages in maritime and human progress.

PAUL SCHUBERT, *Sea Power in Conflict* (Coward-McCann, 1942). An account of sea warfare from 1939 to 1941, including the attack on Pearl Harbor.

E. C. SEMPLE, *Influences of Geographic Environment* (Holt, 1911). Based on Ratzel's "Anthropogeography." Discusses operation of geographic factors in history, classes of geographic influences, society and state in relation to the land movements of peoples, and the geographical significance, etc.

NATHANIEL SOUTHGATE SHALER, *Sea and Land* (Scribner, 1894). Sets forth the influence exerted on life of man by the features of coasts and oceans.

ARTHUR MACCARTNEY SHEPARD, *Sea Power in Ancient History* (Little, Brown, 1924). Story of the navies of classical Greece and Rome to the fall of the western division of the Roman Empire.

HENRY C. STETSON, "Oceanography," *Smithsonian Report* (1943), 219–244. Discusses the science of oceanography and the meaning of the term, and its divisions. Summary of the historical background given.

HENRY STROMMEL, *Science and the Seven Seas* (New York, Cornell Maritime Press, 1945). An up-to-date scientific discussion of the contents and behavior of the ocean.

RAY H. WHITBECK AND OLIVE J. THOMAS, *The Geographic Factor* (Century, 1932). A forthright treatment of the influences of such geographic factors as peninsulas, seas, oceans, shorelines, relief, climate, etc., upon the peoples of the world; considers world and regional relationships.

DERWENT WHITTLESEY, *The Earth and the State* (Holt, 1939). A scholarly treatment of political geography in terms of resources, regions, relief, and political area.

JAMES ALEXANDER WILLIAMSON, *The Ocean in English History* (Oxford, The Clarendon Press, 1941). A discussion of the oceanic influence upon English history from the time of Columbus to the present.

Chapter 36: Boundaries in International Relations

Note: This list is not intended to be exhaustive, but only to give samples of works dealing with different phases of boundary problems. For more extensive reading the student should consult the bibliographies in the works listed. The bibliographies given by Boggs and Jones are especially useful.

VITTORIO ADAMI, *National Frontiers in Relation to International Law* (New York, Oxford University Press, 1927). Especially good for discussion of problems of delimiting and demarcating different types of lines, with many examples from European history.

S. WHITTEMORE BOGGS, *International Boundaries, A Study of Boundary Functions and Problems* (New York, Columbia University Press, 1940). A comprehensive survey, approaching boundary problems from both the topical and the regional standpoint. The primary reference for use with this chapter.

C. J. CHACKO, *The International Joint Commission between the United States of America and the Dominion of Canada* (New York, Columbia University Press, 1932). The work of the commission dealing with all boundary waters along the Canadian frontier.

CHARLES C. COLBY, Editor, *Geographic Aspects of International Relations, Lectures on the Har-*
ris *Foundation, 1937* (University of Chicago Press, 1938). See especially the chapters on West Africa by Whittlesey, boundary problems of Europe by Hartshorne, and territorial claims in the Upper Amazon by Robert S. Platt.

C. B. FAWCETT, *Frontiers, A Study in Political Geography* (New York, Oxford University Press, 1918). This short but surprisingly complete study discusses the factors of frontier development, functions, and types. When reading the last chapter, bear in mind the events of the last quarter century.

Frontiers of the Future, Lectures Delivered under the Auspices of the Committee on International Relations on the Los Angeles Campus of the University of California, 1940 (Berkeley and Los Angeles, University of California Press, 1941). See especially the chapters on natural frontiers by Broek, political frontiers by Steiner, and Latin-American boundary controversies by Hussey.

RICHARD HARTSHORNE, "Geographic and Political Boundaries in Upper Silesia," *Annals of the Association of American Geographers*, XXIII (December, 1933), 195–228. A study of the relationships between boundaries and the physical and cultural features of the landscape.

GORDON IRELAND, *Boundaries, Possessions and Conflicts in South America* (Cambridge, Harvard University Press, 1938). Factual summaries of the controversies. A later volume by the same author deals with North America and the Caribbean.

STEPHEN B. JONES, *Boundary-Making, A Handbook for Statesmen, Treaty Editors and Boundary Commissioners* (Washington, Carnegie Endowment for International Peace, Division of International Law, 1945). A practical guide for those entrusted with the task of laying down boundaries, introduced by a good discussion of the philosophy of boundaries and boundary-making. Numerous references to former practice.

GEORGES KAECKENBEECK, *The International Experiment of Upper Silesia, A Study in the Working of the Upper Silesian Settlement, 1922–1937* (New York, Oxford University Press, 1942). The functioning of this boundary as viewed from the legal standpoint. Complements Hartshorne's geographic approach to some extent.

SIR HARRY OSBORNE MANCE, *International River and Canal Transport* (New York, Oxford University Press, Royal Institute of International Affairs, 1944). Discusses the general principles and problems of inland waterway transportation across international boundaries and specific problems of each of the world's main international waterways.

RUTH D. MASTERS, "International Organization of European Rail Transport," *International Conciliation* (May, 1937), 487–544. An account of the promotion of freedom of transit across boundaries by European railroads.

A. E. MOODIE, *The Italo-Yugoslav Boundary, A Study in Political Geography* (London, George Philip & Son, Ltd., 1945). A case history of one of the most difficult boundary problems of Europe. Physical geography, historical claims, ethnography, and the unity of trade areas were factors entering into the problem.

NICHOLAS JOHN SPYKMAN, "Frontiers, Security, and International Organization," *Geographical Review*, XXXII (July, 1942), 436–447. Discusses the obsolescence of frontier and buffer states as defense zones, and increasing importance of the total power potential of the state. Do you agree with his estimate of the efficacy of international organization?

SARAH WAMBAUGH, *Plebiscites Since the World War, with a Collection of Official Documents* (Washington, Carnegie Endowment for International Peace, 1933). Accounts of the individual plebiscites and an estimate of the value of plebiscites in general after World War I.

Chapter 37: Population Factors in International Affairs

The American Academy of Political and Social Science, *World Population in Transition* (Philadelphia, 1945). A series of articles covering various aspects of regional and international population problems.

A. M. CARR-SAUNDERS, *World Population: Past Growth and Trends* (Oxford, The Clarendon Press, 1936). This is a basic study of population growth and related population problems.

D. V. GLASS, *Population Policies and Movements in Europe* (Oxford, The Clarendon Press, 1940). This book includes a lengthy appendix with excellent definitions and explanations of life tables, rates of growth, and other demographic measures.

International Labor Office, *World Statistics of Aliens: A Comparative Study of Census Returns 1910–1920–1930* (Geneva, 1936). Studies and reports, Series O (Migration) No. 6. A study for international problems of aliens, with data for an historical approach.

EUGENE M. KULISCHER, *The Displacement of Population in Europe* (Montreal, International Labour Office, 1943). This is a basic source of information on population movements resulting from the war up to the early months of 1943.

League of Nations, Economic Intelligence Service, *Statistical Year-Book of the League of Nations, 1941/42* (Geneva, 1943). This yearbook provides data on area, population, vital statistics, rates, and life tables, and should be used as the basic source for all demographic information including clarification and definitions of terms.

FRANK LORIMER, *The Population of the Soviet Union: History and Prospects*, Office of Population Research, Princeton University (Geneva, League of Nations, 1946). This study includes a series of 22 maps prepared by the Division of Geography and Cartography, United States Department of State, relating to the population problems of the U. S. S. R.

Milbank Memorial Fund, *Demographic Studies of Selected Areas of Rapid Growth* (New York, 1944). Studies included were a part of the proceedings of a conference on population problems sponsored by the Milbank Memorial Fund.

National Bureau of Economic Research, *International Migrations* (New York, 1929–1931). This is a basic source of data on international migrations.

FRANK W. NOTESTEIN AND OTHERS, *The Future Population of Europe and the Soviet Union* (Geneva, League of Nations, 1944). This study is representative of the many excellent studies being produced by the Office of Population Research. Detailed tables of projections to 1970 by five-year intervals for countries of Europe and the U. S. S. R. Many maps are included.

KARL J. PELZER, *Population and Land Utilization* (New York, Institute of Pacific Relations, 1941). This is a good source for statistical information in the many tables included on all countries of the Pacific area.

E. F. PENROSE, *Population Theories and their Application with Special Reference to Japan* (Stanford University, California Food Research Institute, 1934). A general discussion of population problems, and a discussion of Japan is included.

Population Index (Princeton, New Jersey, School of Public Affairs, Princeton University, and the Population Association of America, Inc., January, 1934–January, 1946). This bibliographic quarterly contains demographic materials by subject and usually includes a detailed research article on some population subject of current interest.

The Statesman's Year-Book (Macmillan, 1947). This is an all-around reference source for late population estimates including ethnic and occupation estimates with discussions of the political organization for all countries of the world. An annual publication.

WARREN S. THOMPSON AND P. K. WHELPTON, Estimates of Future Population of the United States, 1940–2000 (Government Printing Office, 1943). This study, prepared by the National Resources Planning Board, includes many possible alternate trends for the future population of the United States.

THOMPSON, Population Problems (Third Edition, McGraw-Hill, 1942). This basic text shows the methods utilized in dealing with population problems. Many of the examples, however, are for the United States rather than for foreign countries.

United States Department of Commerce, Bureau of the Census, and Library of Congress, General Censuses and Vital Statistics in the Americas (Government Printing Office, 1942). This book includes an annotated bibliography of historical census and current vital statistics of the Americas. Although no statistics are included, this publication gives complete coverage of officially published census materials.

United States, The Library of Congress, Census Library Project, Recent Censuses in European Countries (Washington, 1942). This is the most complete list of the latest (prior to 1942) European censuses and their coverage, although earlier censuses are not listed. Some enumerations taken during the war are now available and are not included in this bibliography.

Chapter 38:   Grand Strategy of World
              War II

ARMY SPECIALIZED TRAINING DIVISION, Atlas of World Maps, M–101 (Government Printing Office, 1943). Maps and charts covering the power factor in national and world politics.

————, Geographical Foundations of National Power, ASF Manual 103–1 (Government Printing Office, 1944), Section I, 1–32. Examination of the elements that sum up the nations' potential, peace or war.

————, Geographical Foundations of National Power, M–103–3 (Government Printing Office, 1944), 30–113. Survey of the potential of the Axis and the Allied Powers, as translated into action in World War II.

GENERAL H. H. ARNOLD, Official Reports (Information and Education Division, ASF, Washington, D. C.).

HANSON BALDWIN, "America at War," Foreign Affairs, all issues from April, 1942 to October, 1945. Interim reports on strategic and major tactical developments, World War II.

BUREAU OF PERSONNEL, U. S. NAVY, Foundations of National Power (Princeton University Press, 1945). Comprehensive survey, by nations and areas, of the elements of power.

Department of Social Sciences, Raw Materials in War and Peace (West Point, N. Y., United States Military Academy Press, 1947). The raw materials factor as an element of power during the period 1944–47.

E. M. EARLE AND OTHERS, Makers of Modern Strategy (Princeton University Press, 1944), vii–xi. Analysis of the contributions to strategy of the great innovators, from Machiavelli to Hitler.

LADISLAS FARAGO AND OTHERS, The Axis Grand Strategy (Farrar & Rinehart, 1942), 29–80; 495–580. Axis objectives, means, and techniques, viewed at flood tide of Axis operations.

J. H. E. Fried, The Exploitation of Foreign Labour by Germany (Montreal, International Labour Office, 1945), 1–12; 30–70; 82–89. Exhaustive survey of one of the worst elements of German strategy.

T. V. KALIJARVI AND OTHERS, Modern World Politics (Second Edition, Crowell, 1945), 3–58; 167–185; 275–338; 387–451; 466–471; 477–660. Power politics, wartime and postwar.

ADMIRAL E. J. KING, U. S. Navy at War (Official Reports published by United States News, Washington).

GENERAL G. C. MARSHALL, The United States at War, all reports to include final (The United States News, Washington, October 10, 1945).

BREHON SOMERVELL, Army Service Forces (Official Reports issued by Information and Education Division, ASF, Washington, D. C.).

HANS W. WEIGERT AND VILHJALMUR STEFANSSON, Editors, Compass of the World (Macmillan, 1944). Modern geopolitics, with emphasis on the importance of the north polar area in postwar strategy.

Chapter 39: Geography in Future World Politics

KARL BRANDT, *The Reconstruction of World Agriculture* (Norton, 1945). One volume that approaches the agricultural problem of the world from a broad point of view.

C. B. FAWCETT, "The Numbers and Distribution of Mankind," *The Scientific Monthly*, 64 (May, 1947), 389–396. A recent summary statement of what is known on this important problem of how many of us are where.

Food and Agricultural Organization of the United Nations, World Food Survey (Washington, 1946). The outstanding present survey of world diets.

G. H. KNIBBS, *The Shadow of the World's Future: Or the Earth's Population Possibilities and the Consequences of the Present Rate of Increase of the Earth's Inhabitants* (London, Ernest Benn, Ltd., 1928). An older but standard work on the resource-population problem.

OLIVER J. LISSITZYN, *International Air Transport and National Policy* (New York, Council on Foreign Relations, 1942). The most authoritative treatment on international air routes and their political aspects up to and including the beginning of World War II.

HOWARD A. MEYERHOFF, "Some Social Implications of Natural Resources," *The Annals of the American Academy of Political and Social Science*, 249 (January, 1947), 20–31. Our complex industrial civilization is examined on a broad front with a view to ascertaining implications and "laws" of resource use.

CHARLES J. V. MURPHY, "The Polar Concept—It Is Revolutionizing American Strategy," *Life*, XXII (January 20, 1947), 61–62. A stimulating account of a subject made popular through the development of the airplane.

HAROLD AND MARGARET SPROUT, Editors, *The Foundations of National Power* (Princeton University Press, 1945). Pages 604–690 consider especially the strength of the Americas.

FRANK T. STOCKTON, *Natural Resources: Their Relation to Power and Peace,* Citizens Pamphlet 4 (Lawrence, University of Kansas, Bureau of Government Research, 1947). A simple statement of the present situation of the major areas of the world with respect to space and resource factors.

ROBERT STRAUSZ-HUPÉ, *Geopolitics, the Struggle for Space and Power* (Putnam, 1942). One of the more readable books on the subject.

GRIFFITH TAYLOR, *Environment, Race and Migration* (University of Chicago Press, 1937). Part of this study deals with potential population carrying capacities of areas of the world and methods of measurement thereof.

J. P. VAN ZANDT, *Civil Aviation and Peace* (Washington, Brookings Institution, 1944). International conflicts in aviation are analyzed and a policy is proposed that would be mutually beneficial and which might assure economic stability, prosperity, and peace.

———, *The Geography of World Air Transport* (Washington, Brookings Institution, 1944). Outlines the basic setting of the air transport problem and reviews fundamental geographic and economic relations governing international air policies.

HANS W. WEIGERT AND VILHJALMUR STEFANSSON, Editors, *Compass of the World* (Macmillan, 1944). A symposium on geopolitics with several chapters relating to air age geography. Careful consideration is given to world airways and to polar flying.

ERICH W. ZIMMERMANN, *World Resources and Industries* (Harper, 1933). A good standard text on resources of the areas of the world.

Questions and Topics for Further Study

PART ONE

The Nature and Scope of Political Geography

Chapter 1: Political Geography and Its Point of View

Study Questions:

1. List eight significant services performed by geographers during World War II.

2. Under what name did the American public learn about political geography during World War II? What erroneous inferences did they make regarding political geography?

3. How old is geography? How old is that subdivision of the subject known as political geography?

4. What is geopolitics? For what three principal purposes did the German National Socialists use it?

5. What factors underlay the Germans' perversion or distortion of political geography?

6. Contrast the basic thinking of American social scientists with that of German and other European social scientists.

7. Is science moral or immoral? Give reasons for your answer.

8. What utility does political geography possess during peacetime?

9. What is the commonly accepted definition of geography? How many major subdivisions of geography are there? What is the regional aspect of each of these?

10. How many national states are there in the world? What causes the number to vary?

11. Name the five categories of geographical size into which states and other political areas may be divided? Give one specific illustration of each?

12. Name the major factors of powerhood as applied to states.

13. Into what five classes of powerhood may the world's states be divided?

14. What trends may be noted during the past half century as to the number and size of the World Powers?

15. In what three general areas do the strong states of the world tend to cluster?

Suggested Topics:

1. Government service by geographers during World War I, during the *New Deal* program, and during World War II.

2. The early history of geography.

3. Reasons for the neglect of geography in American education.

4. The field of geography and the relation of geography to its subdivisions.

5. The diminutive national states of Europe.

6. The ancient Greek city-states.

7. The evolution of Rome as a state.

8. The World Powers.

9. The Minor Powers.

10. Former European states which have disappeared from the map.

Chapter 2: The Substance and Scope of Political Geography

Study Questions:

1. What three schools of thought are there in political geography? What is the primary objective in studying political geography under each concept?

2. Why is there no single definition of the subject which will suit all political geographers?

3. In what general direction has political geography developed in France? In Germany? In the U. S.? Explain.

4. What is a political region or political area?

5. List the 5 physical properties of a political region.

6. List the 4 social characteristics of a political region.

7. List the 7 structural elements or anatomical parts of a political area or region.

8. How many classes of geopolitical problems are there?

9. What 5 desiderata enter into the study of geopolitics or political geography?

10. Why is it usually impossible to give the answers to geopolitical problems?

SUGGESTED TOPICS:

1. Geography as physiography.
2. Geography as landscape morphology.
3. Geography as human ecology.
4. The relation of political geography to political science.
5. The relation of political geography to economic geography and social geography.
6. "Schools of thought" in political geography.
7. American public reactions to geopolitics during World War II.
8. Two decades of Geopolitik in Germany.
9. Nationality as a factor in the U. S. S. R.
10. The cores of European states (or Asiatic states, or Latin American states).

Chapter 3: The History and Development of Political Geography

STUDY QUESTIONS:

1. Name some of the earliest scholars who delved into problems of political geography.
2. Cite several examples of practical geopolitics in world history.
3. What part has geopolitics played in the history of modern Germany?
4. State the essential concepts in the geopolitics of the Men of Munich.
5. What was the influence of Friedrich Ratzel on political geography?
6. Show the relationship between the ideas of the organic state and *Lebensraum*.
7. What was Kjellén's plan for studying the state?

8. Summarize the teachings of Captain Alfred Thayer Mahan.
9. What geopolitical factors contributed to the naval supremacy of Great Britain during most of the nineteenth century?
10. Compare the ideas of Mackinder and Spykman relative to the geopolitical structure of the world.
11. What was the relationship between Haushofer and Hitler and between the geopoliticians and the Nazis?
12. Cite at least three instances where Haushofer and Hitler would disagree.
13. To what extent was Haushofer an original thinker?
14. Describe the world political outlook as developed by the Men of Munich.
15. Name several major geopolitical problems of the postwar world.

SUGGESTED TOPICS:

1. Early contributions to political geography.
2. An analysis of the present foundations of power.
3. A critique of Ratzel's ideas.
4. The influence of air power upon the teachings of Mahan.
5. The validity of Mackinder's Heartland thesis.
6. The validity of Spykman's Rimland thesis.
7. Relationship between Haushofer's geopolitics and Hitler's policies.
8. The Japanese as geopoliticians without portfolio, 1900–45.
9. A practical geopolitics for the United States.
10. Political geography and "One World."

PART TWO

THE WORLD POWERS

Chapter 4: Geographic Foundations of Continental United States

STUDY QUESTIONS:

1. List in chronological order all the major acquisitions of the United States within its continental borders; beyond its continental borders.
2. Has our security from invasion become less or greater in the past fifty years? Explain.
3. Do the Great Lakes make a good international boundary for the United States? the 49th Parallel? the Rio Grande?
4. What advantages do our ocean boundaries have over our land boundaries?

5. What would be the disadvantages of having a long narrow shape instead of the compact shape as we do in the United States?
6. What natural difficulties would have beset the Japanese had they landed on our west coast in World War II and tried to move eastward to conquer us?
7. What is the advantage of having a great variety of climates within the United States?
8. Why are the Great Lakes such an important inland waterway?
9. What five minerals would you select as being the most important in the national economy of the United States? Give reasons.

10. What are the ten most important agricultural commodities in the United States and where are they produced? Which ones are exported in quantity?

11. List all the important factors favoring a great manufacturing industry in the United States.

12. Are our industrial plants located advantageously or otherwise from a strategic point of view? Why?

13. What advantages do trucks have over trains in hauling freight short distances? How can air cargo aid future industrial economy?

14. Would you suggest that the number of immigrants permitted to enter the United States be increased? Decreased? Why?

15. Do you consider that the United States has serious minority group problems? Why or why not?

SUGGESTED TOPICS:

1. Geopolitical aspects of our westward movement.

2. Boundary problems between the United States and Canada.

3. Geopolitical aspects of the American synthetic rubber industry.

4. Surpluses and deficiencies in the food supply of the United States.

5. Power resources of the United States.

6. Political friction between Argentina and the United States and its economic implications.

7. America's oil supply of the future.

8. Interstate barriers to trade.

9. The United States reviews its immigration policy.

10. Politico-geographic problems in American international air transportation.

Chapter 5: The United States as a World Power

STUDY QUESTIONS:

1. What is meant by the statement: "Behind the Cuban Question lay the Isthmian Question?"

2. How has the Panama Canal been a life-line for the whole New World as well as the United States in the two world wars of our times?

3. Which has the greater potential of world power: the "Heartland" of Asia, or the "energy-land" of North America?

4. Has recent history shown the acquisition of the Philippine Islands to have been the "Great Aberration" of American foreign policy?

5. What was the trust that the powers put in Japan in the Washington Treaties of 1922, when they left her supreme in the Far East?

6. What is meant by the British Empire as "a world archipelago"?

7. What, in 1940, were the strategical implications involved in speaking of the United States in North America as an island continent surrounded by a hostile Old World?

8. Assuming that imperialism is the exercise of dominion over alien peoples, how did the United States rank among the imperialistic powers at the apogee of its imperialism?

9. Does the liquidation of America imperialism after World War I suggest that there will be a reassertion and expansion of American imperialism after World War II?

10. How did the Hague Court decision put a premium on the use of force for the collection of contract debts and damages to foreign nationals?

11. Do you think that the Roosevelt Corollary was a logical development of the Monroe Doctrine?

12. Did Woodrow Wilson's larger concepts of world peace balance off creditably his contemporary political mistakes in the long run of history?

13. What were the reasons which impelled the United States to liquidate the protectorates which existed in the Caribbean from 1899 to 1941?

14. What is the difference between the League of Nations Covenant and the United Nations Charter?

15. What power should be in the best position to survive a war of atomic bombs?

SUGGESTED TOPICS:

1. The geopolitical position of the Continental Republic.

2. The new order of sea power.

3. The Washington Treaties of 1922.

4. Canada the hostage.

5. The Philippines as a hostage.

6. The liquidation of American imperialism.

7. The doctrine of nonintervention.

8. The Inter-American System.

9. The emancipation of the Philippines.

10. The United Nations Charter.

Chapter 6: The Soviet Union: A Land Mass Power

STUDY QUESTIONS:

1. What reasons can be advanced for the lack of statistical data on the economic progress of the U. S. S. R.?

2. Using the factors listed in the chapter, how

does the U. S. S. R. compare in quality of major powerhood with the United States? with the British Empire? with China?

3. Which natural environmental factors aided the Russian migration across Siberia? Which were a handicap?

4. Who were the more important leaders in Russia in the past and what were their contributions?

5. What similarities may be noted between the eastward expansion of Russia and the westward movement of the United States?

6. What factors were utilized to determine the major subdivisions of the U. S. S. R.?

7. In what ways is continentality important to Soviet Russian development?

8. What are the distinguishing features of the collective and state farms?

9. What are the aims of industrial development within the U. S. S. R.?

10. Why does industrial development show an eastward trend in Soviet Russia?

11. How do you account for the lack of highway development throughout the U. S. S. R.?

12. What is the "Heartland" concept? What arguments favor and disfavor its acceptance?

13. How do you account for the high rate of natural population increase in the U. S. S. R.? What is its significance?

14. In what respects are the political structures of the U. S. S. R. and the United States similar? Dissimilar?

15. What are the advantages and disadvantages of self-sufficient, economic regionalism? Illustrate from the industrial regions of the U. S. S. R.

SUGGESTED TOPICS:

1. Problems involved in the re-settlement of large numbers of displaced people.

2. Climatic regions of the U. S. S. R.

3. The advantages and disadvantages of national economic planning.

4. The importance of the Far Eastern Provinces to Russia's internal economy.

5. Economic developments in the lesser republics.

6. Cultural contributions of the lesser nationalities.

7. Economic reconstruction in the U. S. S. R.

8. Advantages and disadvantages of a single party system.

9. The significance of commercial air transportation to the internal development of the U. S. S. R.

10. The location of the U. S. S. R. with respect to future air transport development.

Chapter 7: The Soviet Union in World Politics

STUDY QUESTIONS:

1. What is the explanation for the consistency between Soviet and Czarist foreign policy?

2. What effect did western enmity have upon the foreign policy of the Soviet Union?

3. What motivates the Russian demands for a share in the administration of defeated Japan?

4. What is the historical validity of the thesis in *Russia and the United States* by Sorokin that similar geographical and sociological heritages work for Russo-American accord?

5. Describe the influence upon Russian history of the system of waterways of Central Eurasia.

6. What effect has the shifting of Russian industrialization eastward had upon Soviet foreign policy?

7. Discuss contemporary Russian foreign policy in the light of Mackinder's "Heartland" thesis.

8. What are the underlying factors behind Russia's support of certain factions in the Balkans?

9. What are the principal issues involved in contemporary Russo-Finnish conflicts?

10. What is the nature of Russian interests in Manchuria?

11. Discuss Russian naval theory.

12. What is the significance of Russia's population trends for her position in world affairs?

13. What effect does desire for additional resources have upon Russian foreign policy?

14. What are the disadvantages inherent in Russia's geographical position?

15. What significance does the Russian policy toward racial minorities have for the U. S. S. R. in world affairs?

SUGGESTED TOPICS:

1. Background of the Russo-German Non-Aggression Pact of August 23, 1939.

2. Influence of the Russo-Japanese war upon subsequent Russian foreign policy.

3. Influence of the geography of central Eurasia upon the expansion of the Russian state.

4. Pan-Slavism.

5. The U. S. S. R. and the Chinese communists.

6. The Russian drive toward "warm water" ports.

7. Soviet air power via Arctic regions.

8. Historical antecedents of the present Russo-Polish boundary.

9. Background of current Russo-Turkish territorial disputes.

10. Focal points of British-Russian imperial competition.

Chapter 8: Great Britain and the Dependent Empire

STUDY QUESTIONS:

1. Distinguish between the terms (a) United Kingdom, (b) Great Britain, (c) England, (d) British Isles, and (e) British Empire.

2. What geographical factors have influenced the distribution of population in Great Britain?

3. What is the Celtic Culture Zone? How did it come into being? Has it any importance in political geography today?

4. What were the chief results of contact between Britain and Europe before the sixteenth century?

5. What did Britain outstrip all other western European nations in the race for colonies?

6. What were the three great eras of the British Empire? Did they differ in geographical character?

7. Why did the power of Great Britain in international affairs begin to decline after 1900?

8. What are invisible exports? Explain their importance to Great Britain.

9. How did World War I affect the economy of Great Britain?

10. What is meant by "empire free trade"? Was it a satisfactory policy?

11. Define the term "space relations." How can space relations change?

12. Are the major differences between Eire and Northern Ireland environmental, cultural, or strictly political? Explain.

13. In the future are close political and economic relations between Great Britain and the United States likely to increase or decrease? Justify your answer.

14. Within the Dependent Empire of Britain give examples of (a) a trusteeship, (b) a crown colony, (c) a condominium, (d) a protectorate, and (e) a political area with "close relations" to Great Britain.

15. Explain why the British sphere of influence is either strong or weak in (a) the Indian Ocean, (b) the Middle East, (c) the North Pacific, (d) North Africa, and (e) Southeast Asia.

SUGGESTED TOPICS:

1. Changes in the distribution of population in Great Britain since 1701.

2. Analysis of factors making for strong national feeling in Great Britain.

3. Economic factors affecting the relationship between Ireland and Great Britain in the nineteenth century.

4. The effect of insularity on the development of Great Britain as compared to Japan.

5. A comparative study of the economic resources of Great Britain, the United States, and the U. S. S. R. (Population, coal and mineral reserves, industrial development, and self-sufficiency).

6. An evaluation of the contention that Great Britain retarded the political evolution of Ireland by barring it from direct contact with the continent of Europe.

7. The importance of the Mediterranean route to Britain.

8. The importance of the Dependent Empire in British trade.

9. Emigration from Britain and the distribution of British folk in other parts of the world.

10. Geographic determination and Great Britain. An attempt to estimate the relative importance of the environmental and human factors in the development of postwar Britain.

Chapter 9: The British Commonwealth of Nations

STUDY QUESTIONS:

1. Discuss the positions of Canada, Australia, and South Africa with regard to the center of the Land Hemisphere.

2. How do these three regions differ as regards the main features of structure and climate?

3. Describe briefly the four main corridors into the central lower portion of Canada.

4. Enumerate and show on a map the early British and French settlements in Canada and Newfoundland founded prior to 1800.

5. Give a brief description of the settlement pattern in the Canadian Prairies.

6. Discuss Canada's commercial interests in the Arctic and Pacific areas.

7. What are Canada's chief links with the United States in commerce and in political matters?

8. Explain the effect of rainfall distribution on present Australian population.

9. From some satisfactory atlas (such as *Goode's School Atlas*) trace the various highland areas bordering the east coast of Australia. Describe the position of Townsville, Rockhampton, Brisbane, Sydney, Canberra, and Melbourne in regard to such highlands.

10. Show how advances of the pastoralists and miners helped in the settlement of Australia.

11. Explain the reasons for the expansion of Australian control to New Guinea.

12. What are the chief differences in environment and political control between Australia and New Zealand?

13. Explain how the topography and rainfall of South Africa affect white settlement in subtropical areas.

14. Discuss the relations of British and Dutch settlers in South Africa during the nineteenth century.

15. Discuss the position of the Negroes and Indians (from India) in the South African Union.

SUGGESTED TOPICS:

Note: The references suggested for the following topics are listed in complete form in the bibliography for Chapter 9, see pages 580–81.

1. Canadian settlement in the north of the Dominion during the next century (see Taylor's *Canada*).

2. The distribution of resources in other lands which compete with those produced in Canada (see Taylor's *Canada's Role*).

3. French social and political problems in New Brunswick and Quebec (see Siegfried).

4. The relations between Canada and the United States (see Fawcett).

5. The White Australia Policy (see Price).

6. The extent of desert lands in Australia (see Taylor's *Australia*).

7. The settlement of the Australian Tropics by Europeans (see Taylor's *Australia*).

8. The claims of the Boers in regard to the control of Transvaal (see *History of the British Empire*, Vol. VIII).

9. The Negro tribes of South Africa (see Fitzgerald).

10. South Africa's position on the world's seaways (see Fawcett).

PART THREE

EUROPE

Chapter 10:   The German Reich:
            European Pivotal Area

STUDY QUESTIONS:

1. What were the major elements of Germany's physical environment which were responsible for the slow development of Germany's unification?

2. List the five major sea ports of prewar Germany and compare their respective volumes of trade and their import and export commodities. What conditions in your estimation are responsible for the differences in their economic development?

3. Which are the principal trunk railroad lines of Germany? What areas and which industries do they serve?

4. Which are the chief navigable rivers and canals of Germany? What are the important cities along them and what are the leading industries which characterize each city?

5. List ten of the most important mineral resources of the world and show in what proportion Germany can produce these from local mines.

6. List ten chief agricultural products, five of which are food stuffs and five industrial raw materials. To what extent can German production of these supply home consumption and world markets?

7. In what areas of the world are there strong German minorities which maintained their national consciousness?

8. What are the distinguishing features of agriculture in western Germany? in the Alpine regions?

9. Discuss briefly the site and situation factors of the ten largest prewar German cities and explain their economic and/or political significance.

10. What was the Hanseatic League? What were the main geographic factors fostering the development of the Hansa?

11. What types of physical environment does the Elbe River cross in its course through Germany? What are the chief types of economic regions it traverses? What role did the river play in the development of Hamburg?

12. Why is the Rhine the most important inland waterway of Europe?

13. What was the role of the Central Highlands in the evolution of Germany?

14. How does the climatic factor affect German agriculture?

15. What are the chief results of Germany's location? (Site and situation factors)

SUGGESTED TOPICS:

1. The role of the Rhine River in the economic development of Germany.

2. The geopolitical significance of the old land tenure system of eastern Prussia.

3. The chemical industry of Germany.

4. The industrial development of the Ruhr Valley.

5. The role of the Saar coal deposits in the postwar settlements of 1918–19.

6. The development of German foreign trade since 1871.

7. The geographic background of the struggle for supremacy between Austria and Prussia.

8. Germany's boundaries since the times of the French Revolution.

9. The geopolitical evolution of Prussia.

10. The ethnic problems of Silesia.

Chapter 11: The Low Countries between the Great Powers

STUDY QUESTIONS:

1. Why is it erroneous to say that the Low Countries are the delta area of the Rhine and the Meuse rivers?

2. Why have the Loess Plains of Belgium played such an important role in the military history of western Europe?

3. Why was defense of the Netherlands by flooding so much more effective in the past than it is now?

4. What are the relationships between the early development of trade and industry in Flanders and Holland and the location and physical geography of these two regions?

5. What was the cultural, political, and economic role of the high moor areas in the Netherlands and Belgium?

6. Why does the line between Walloons and Germans lie where it does?

7. Why does the line between Flemish and Walloon on one side and French on the other lie partly in France?

8. Why has there been conflict between the Netherlands and Belgium about the Scheldt River? About the water connections between Antwerp and the Rhine?

9. Why in the past has the cultural outlook of the people of the Low Countries been mostly toward France?

10. What factors contributed toward the formation of the Dutch nation?

11. How has the Netherlands changed from a great power to a political buffer state?

12. In what respects is the commercial position of the Low Countries different now from what it was before 1850?

13. Why is the agriculture of the Low Countries so dependent upon the outside world?

14. Why are most of the industries of the Low Countries so dependent upon the outside world?

15. What are some of the political consequences of the basic features of the economies of the Netherlands and Belgium?

SUGGESTED TOPICS:

1. The Flemish Movement from 1840 to 1935.

2. Advantages and disadvantages to Luxembourg of Benelux.

3. The economic relationships between the Belgian industrial districts and the industrial region of northern France.

4. The economic relationships between the Netherlands and the German hinterland.

5. The military geography of the German invasion campaign of 1940.

6. The problem of Antwerp's connections with the Rhineland and the Ruhr.

7. The political and economic factors which reduced the Spanish (Austrian) Netherlands to a passive area from about 1600 to 1800.

8. Internal and external transportation patterns of the Low Countries.

9. The campaign of Louis XIV and his allies in the Netherlands from a geographical point of view; the effectiveness of Dutch natural defenses.

10. Economic and cultural aspects of the Eupen and Malmédy districts.

Chapter 12: France and Its Geographical Setting

STUDY QUESTIONS:

1. Of what advantage to western Europe has the Rhone-Saône Valley been in (a) Roman times, (b) modern times?

2. Compare the political units within France with those of the United States.

3. Why might France need political treaties with Poland? Czechoslovakia? Russia?

4. Why do friendly relations exist between

France and England and strife between France
and Germany?

5. What geographic factors have been responsible for the superiority of Paris among French
cities?

6. From the labor point of view how practical
is the great expansion in France of the manufacture of specialized and de luxe articles?

7. Why should Marseille outstrip Bordeaux in
size and commercial importance?

8. Why should Le Havre not be as large as
Paris?

9. Why should the Saracen influence have been
so feeble in France and so strong in Spain?

10. What reasons can be given for the excellent
and efficient railroad service in France?

11. How much of the trade of Marseille is entrepôt trade? Is the same true of Paris? Why?

12. Does the balancing of trade in French
colonies or problems of administration in them
stand as the more important of France's external
enterprises? Why?

13. Explain the geographic position of Paris
with respect to the various regions of France.

14. What do you see ahead as you examine the
large Italian, Spanish, and Belgian immigration
into France?

15. Select two industrial districts in France
other than the Paris region and characterize the
factors which lend to their importance.

SUGGESTED TOPICS:

1. French self-sufficiency.
2. The Basques as a unique population group
in France.
3. France's position on the Mediterranean Sea
and its political and economic implications.
4. Comparisons and contrasts between Caesar's
Gaul and the France of today.
5. Silk production and silk manufacture.
6. Agricultural specialties in France.
7. The inland waterways of France.
8. The Auvergne Plateau.
9. Relief and military strategy in northeastern
France.
10. Population trends in France—past, present,
and future.

Chapter 13: Switzerland: A Successful Neutral

STUDY QUESTIONS:

1. How high are the more important passes of
Switzerland?

2. What large countries border Switzerland?

3. What is the distance from the Swiss border
to Rotterdam? Genoa? Bordeaux?

4. What cantons formed the nucleus of the
early Swiss Republic? In what part of Switzerland are they located?

5. How long has Switzerland enjoyed neutrality?

6. What is the average density of population
in the various physiographic regions?

7. Why is Switzerland a country of four languages? How great a handicap is this multilingual characteristic?

8. Is there any similarity in the maps of religion and language? Explain.

9. What percentage of the land is arable?

10. What degree of self-sufficiency does Switzerland enjoy in the production of food stuffs?

11. Is Switzerland rich in minerals and metals?

12. Is Switzerland dominantly an agricultural or
industrial nation?

13. How does Switzerland offset her unfavorable balance of trade?

14. What physiographic characteristic do Zu-
rich, Luzern, and Geneva have in common?

15. Account for the efficient railway pattern in
a country as mountainous as Switzerland.

SUGGESTED TOPICS:

1. Political development of Switzerland.
2. The importance of Alpine passes in Europe's historical development.
3. Waterpower development in the Alps.
4. The history of the Romansh language.
5. The Reformation in Switzerland.
6. Transhumance in the Alps.
7. Basel as a river port.
8. The development of the watch industry.
9. The tourist industry.
10. Switzerland's export trade.

Chapter 14: Italy in the Mediterranean

STUDY QUESTIONS:

1. What countries were involved before
World War II in the strategic and political control of the Mediterranean "Waist"?

2. How does the Mediterranean "Waist" compare in strategic value to either the Strait of Gibraltar or the Suez Canal?

3. Besides some native stock and the "Itali,"
what other peoples invaded the Italian Peninsula
to become part of the population of the Roman
Empire?

4. In what way does the Mediterranean type of climate limit Italian agriculture, forestry, and industry?

5. What are the problems confronting reconstruction in postwar Italy?

6. Which of Italy's reconstruction problems should be left to her own resources?

7. What problems confront a modernization program for Italian farmers?

8. Along what lines should Italy seek to increase her international income?

9. Why does the U. S. S. R. express an interest in Italian Libya and Eritrea?

10. What advantages did Italy (including Sicily) offer to the Allies as an invasion point in "Fortress Europe" in World War II?

11. Should the Italian people be treated more leniently than the German or Japanese people in a reconversion program? Why or why not?

12. In spite of Italy's maritime position, the Italian people are often spoken of as having a continental point of view. What does this mean? Is it wholly true?

13. List the attractions Italy has for travelers from abroad and tell how you think Italy can best retain its attraction for them.

14. Do you think the Italian people are ready for a place among the family of nations? What evidence do you feel they should give of their ability to join in the family of nations?

15. Can the Italian nation support 45 million people without foreign help?

SUGGESTED TOPICS:

1. Make a study of a famous Italian contributor to modern culture, such as Marconi, Stradivari, Michelangelo, Dante, or Alegheiri.

2. Winter recreation in the Italian Alps (see the *National Geographic* for September, 1936).

3. Land tenure in Italy (see reference to Victor E. Sullam, "Recent Developments" in *Foreign Agriculture* in the bibliography for Chapter 14, page 584).

4. Primitive practices in agriculture (see same reference to Sullam).

5. The northern barrier boundaries of Italy (see Ellen C. Semple, *Geography of the Mediterranean Region*).

6. The control of the Mediterranean "Waist" (see Derwent Whittlesey, *The Earth and the State*).

7. Italy's mineral deficiencies (see C. E. McGuire, *Italy's International Economic Position;* also, Office of War Information, "Italy's Economy, The Situation Now").

8. International interests in the Mediterranean.

9. The Po River valley as the breadbasket and workshop of Italy.

10. Geopolitical problems involved in the settlement of the Trieste area.

Chapter 15: Spain and Portugal: Powers of the Past

STUDY QUESTIONS:

1. What are the significant features of the location of the Iberian Peninsula?

2. Is the historical geography of Spain and Portugal more important in a study of world political geography than that of Italy? Why?

3. What are the effects of latitudinal location on the climate of Spain and Portugal?

4. What circumstances within the Iberian Peninsula led to the independence of Portugal?

5. List and consider the factors that enabled Spain and Portugal to climb to the powerful heights where they could divide the world's lands.

6. In the decline of the two nations, Spain's loss was greater than that of Portugal. Why?

7. Sketch a map of the Peninsula, locating fifteen notable features of relief.

8. How has the character of the vegetation influenced the human economy within the Peninsula?

9. What were the principal contributions of the Moors to land utilization and social progress?

10. How have the water supplies of the Peninsula affected the distribution and social life of the people?

11. How did the mineral resources of the Peninsula figure in the diplomatic maneuvering during World War II?

12. What factors today will help in the unification of the Spanish peoples?

13. In what ways has the climate influenced the agricultural activities of the Peninsula?

14. How will the Iberian Peninsula fit into the world airway transportation net?

15. What imprints have Spain and Portugal already left upon the world?

SUGGESTED TOPICS:

1. The influence of Africa in the historical development of the Iberian Peninsula.

2. The problem of Gibraltar and its relation to Spain.

3. Minerals in Spain and Portugal.

4. Relation of the church and state in Spain.

5. The Catalonians of eastern Spain.

6. The causes of the Spanish Civil War, 1936–39.

7. Communications within the Iberian Peninsula.

8. Significance of colonies to the home country (Spain or Portugal).

9. Competition between Spain and Florida for the European citrus market.

10. The role of Lisbon as an air gateway to Europe.

Chapter 16: The Five Fenno Scandic Countries

STUDY QUESTIONS:

1. What geographic similarities are characteristic of two or more of the Fenno Scandic countries?

2. What is the geopolitical significance of the North Sea? the Baltic?

3. Alaska, located in the same latitude as Scandinavia, has not developed as complex an economy. Why?

4. Explain why Denmark is in a strategic geographical position.

5. In the past the Danes owned an extensive empire. How were they able to control it?

6. The high Danish level of living is a result partly of geography, partly of cooperatives. Explain.

7. What facts can you give to explain the Viking Age of Norway?

8. Why does Norway possess a relatively large merchant marine and many fishing boats?

9. Why was it difficult for Norway and Sweden to continue as one country?

10. Describe the distribution of population and large cities in Sweden and show to what extent geographic conditions are reflected in the population pattern.

11. Of what importance is Swedish iron ore to Germany? Explain.

12. Of what significance to Finland is the nearby position of Sweden?

13. Why is Finland's future closely tied to her ability to compete in forest products?

14. How do you explain the Russo-Finnish agreements of 1940 and 1944 which together gave to the U. S. S. R.: (a) the Petsamo area, (b) Viipuri, (c) Karelia, and (d) the Porkkala Peninsula?

15. What changes in the political status of Iceland and the Faeroes have taken place in recent times?

SUGGESTED TOPICS:

1. The international significance of Swedish iron ore.

2. Geography of the Hanseatic League.

3. Geographic aspects of Swedish neutrality in two World Wars.

4. The geopolitical basis for a Baltic-North Sea bloc.

5. Britain as a market for Scandinavian products.

6. Boundary changes in Scandinavia.

7. Early Viking raids and conquests and their geographic implications.

8. The geography of Scandinavian capitals.

9. The geopolitical significance of the U. S. S. R. in Swedish and Finnish history.

10. Geographic similarities of Alaska and Scandinavia.

Chapter 17: Poland: A Perpetual Problem

STUDY QUESTIONS:

1. Discuss the relative merits of the two Polish possibilities of developing commerce through (a) Danzig and (b) the new harbor of Gdynia.

2. What advantages and disadvantages has the Curzon Line as an eastern Polish frontier?

3. What is the meaning of the statement, "Poles have long been mediators between East and West"? Is this inter-relation finished?

4. Are Poland's frontiers any more satisfactory for the future than they have been for the past? Discuss.

5. Briefly contrast the climate of eastern Poland with that of western Poland.

6. What is involved in saying Poland is continental?

7. What trade or economic affiliations should Poland seek? Why?

8. Why should Poland have adopted the Roman alphabet sooner than Russia or Bulgaria?

9. Why has the Pole such strong nationalistic feelings?

10. Why should the Poles have a carefully considered international policy?

11. What reasons can be given for the many and varied minorities in Poland?

12. What would be a wise adjustment of the Silesian problem?

13. Why is the question of a Baltic Corridor or outlet for Poland an international problem?

14. Why has Lemberg (Lwow) become more of

a minerals town than a wood products town? Who now has the city?

15. What chance has Poland to help balance her trade by the profits of a tourist business?

SUGGESTED TOPICS:

1. Postwar boundaries of Poland.
2. The Baltic Sea as an outlet to Poland.
3. The partitions of Poland.
4. The relation between density of population and topography and resources in Poland.
5. The relative value to the Poles of a westward and an eastward outlook.
6. The agricultural possibilities in the moraine-lake region of Poland.
7. The canals of Poland: history, uses, and geography of each.
8. The question of petroleum.
9. Geographic and strategic significance of Warsaw through the centuries.
10. The interests of France and England in the continued existence of Poland.

Chapter 18: The Lesser Countries of Central Europe

STUDY QUESTIONS:

1. What are the four basic routes converging on the Danube?
2. What main races have competed for the domination of the Danube?
3. Describe the extension of the Habsburg control over the Danubian nations.
4. What have been the main pressures on the Danube in modern times?
5. Describe the shape of Czechoslovakia and point out its geopolitical weakness.
6. What is the constant element of Czechoslovakia's history?
7. What are the major resources of Czechoslovakia?
8. Describe the Sudeten problem in its historical perspective.
9. What were the main causes of the problem of the Slovaks?
10. What are the main problems facing Czechoslovakia today?
11. What were the main problems of Austria between the world wars?
12. Why did the Austrians eventually turn against the Nazis?
13. By what means did Hungary temporarily recover the lost territories?

14. How was land distributed in prewar Hungary?

15. Describe the resources of Hungary during the years 1918–38 and in the period 1938–44.

SUGGESTED TOPICS:

1. Changes in the domination of the central Danube.
2. Survey of the Habsburg expansion along the Danube.
3. The economic development of Czechoslovakia.
4. The geopolitical aspects of the Czech and Slovak problem.
5. The history of the Sudeten problem in Czechoslovakia.
6. The political history of Ruthenia.
7. The geopolitical aspects of modern Austria.
8. Nazi enslavement of Austria.
9. The minorities of Hungary.
10. A customs union for the Danube basin.

Chapter 19: The Balkan States: Peninsular Rivals

STUDY QUESTIONS:

1. What are the three traditional invasion routes of the Balkans?
2. What elements have played the most important role in the disunity of the Balkans?
3. What are the Turkish heritages in the Balkans?
4. What imperialist ambitions meet in the Balkans?
5. What role has Transylvania played in Rumania's history?
6. What are the basic problems of Rumania?
7. Why does Rumania have such a great agricultural potential?
8. How has relief been partially responsible for internal strife in Yugoslavia?
9. Why is Yugoslavia pressing for Trieste?
10. Why is Macedonia such an important element in Balkan politics?
11. Evaluate the resources of Greece.
12. What are the main future needs of Greece?
13. Why is the location of Albania strategically important?
14. Explain Bulgaria's historic drive to the Aegean.
15. How have the mountains of the Balkan Peninsula affected the national economies of the various countries?

SUGGESTED TOPICS:

1. The military use of the Balkan traditional routes during World War II.

2. The invasions and racial settlements of the Balkans.

3. The Transylvania problem.

4. The role played by Rumania's oil in World War II.

5. The role of Pan-Serbianism in Yugoslavia's history.

6. Macedonia's role in world politics.

7. Bulgaria's use of Macedonia in international politics.

8. The Dodecanese and Greek politics.

9. The role of Albania in World War II.

10. Natural geographic regions within the Balkan Peninsula.

PART FOUR

ASIA

Chapter 20:   Turkey and the Straits

STUDY QUESTIONS:

1. Distinguish between *position* and *area* in the geopolitical evolution of Turkey as a state.

2. What is the political relationship to modern Turkey of the following areas: Thrace? Armenia? Alexandretta?

3. How did the Ottoman Empire get its start? How extensive did it become?

4. What was the effect of World War I on the Ottoman Empire?

5. Compare the Treaty of Lausanne with the Treaty of Sèvres as to its effects on Turkey as a nation.

6. Could Turkey's position during World War II be regarded as strictly neutral?   Explain.

7. How has the terrain of Asiatic Turkey aided human development?   Hindered it?

8. Briefly compare the climatic characteristics of the Anatolian Plateau with those of the southwestern coastal district of Asiatic Turkey.

9. What products can Turkey best expect to export?   What imports are most needed?

10. How have the following factors affected the unity of modern Turkey: Language? Religion? Race?

11. Is the question of minority groups in Turkey serious?   Discuss.

12. Discuss the position of the Straits in the light of modern strategic developments.

13. How have British and Russian interests clashed in the Straits area in the past?

14. Why was the Straits question of political interest to Austria-Hungary?

15. Is European Turkey to be considered more Asiatic than European?   Why or why not?

SUGGESTED TOPICS:

1. The capitulations and their effect on Turkish nationalism.

2. The "Berlin-to-Baghdad" railway project.

3. The rise of the Ottoman Empire.

4. The decline of the Ottoman Empire.

5. Potentialities of Turkey as an Asiatic power.

6. Modern trends in Turkey.

7. Economic importance of the Straits.

8. British interests in the Straits.

9. American interests in postwar Turkey.

10. Geographic regions of Turkey (map and discussion justifying regions).

Chapter 21:   The Arab World

STUDY QUESTIONS:

1. Why is the military factor of such great importance in the Near East?

2. Trace the beginning of Arab nationalism and discuss its ultimate goals.

3. Give the greatest expansion of Islamic power and compare it with the present situation.

4. Discuss the reason for Britain's policy toward the Palestine question.

5. Are there any solutions to the Palestine question?   Discuss any possible solutions.

6. Give a picture of the present day oil production in the Near East.   What of the future?

7. How does the geographic factor contribute to weakness or strength in the political picture of the Near East?

8. Compare the valley of the Nile with the valley of the Tigris-Euphrates.

9. Are oases capable of yielding crops needed in modern trade?

10. Discuss the importance of the Suez Canal.

11. Discuss the natural environment of any of the Near Eastern countries.

12. List the interests of Russia, Great Britain, and the United States in the Near East.

13. Discuss the development of land transportation in the Near East during the last 50 years and

its importance to: pilgrimages; trade; strategy; Great Britain; U. S. S. R.

14. What is the influence of religion on the daily life of the people of the Near East?

15. List briefly the influence of the successive occupying forces in the Near East: Hellenistic; Ottoman; Western.

SUGGESTED TOPICS:

1. The economic resources of the Near East.

2. Irrigation in the future development of Palestine and Transjordan.

3. The Near East as a crossroads of major transportation routes.

4. The importance of Egypt to the future of Great Britain.

5. Geographic factors contributing to the strength and weaknesses of the Near East.

6. Contributions of the people of the Near East to Western culture.

7. Petroleum and international relations in the Near East.

8. United States interests in the future of the Near East.

9. The development of Arab nationalism and the Arab League.

10. A survey of the social structure of the Near East.

Chapter 22: The Middle East States of Iran and Afghanistan

STUDY QUESTIONS:

1. How is the location of Iran and Afghanistan reflected in the cultural pattern of those countries?

2. Why did the people of Central Asia over-run these countries?

3. What is the relationship between the topography of Iran and Afghanistan and the routes followed by the invaders?

4. What route would you follow in motoring from Baghdad to Kabul?

5. On an outline map of Iran draw the railways and locate the principal cities.

6. Compare the size of Iran and Afghanistan with an area of similar size in the United States.

7. Describe the changes taking place in Iran.

8. Describe the changes taking place in Afghanistan.

9. Why must changes in Afghanistan be carried out at a much slower rate than they were in Turkey?

10. Why is Russia interested in the affairs of the Middle East?

11. Why is Great Britain interested in the affairs of the Middle East?

12. What is the state of internal conditions in Iran at present?

13. Give reasons for the Middle East's being vitally interested in United Nations activities.

14. How might Russia go about obtaining control of the route out of the Black Sea in a way that would disrupt Iran?

15. What major interests does the United States have in the Middle East?

SUGGESTED TOPICS:

1. The conquests of Alexander the Great, Cyrus the Great, or Ghenghis Khan.

2. The development of British and Russian diplomacy with relation to Afghanistan and Iran.

3. The development of the petroleum industry in Iran.

4. The extent and possibilities of further industrial development in Iran.

5. The importance of the Trans-Iranian Railway during World War II.

6. Historical and modern routes into Afghanistan.

7. Education in the Middle East.

8. Europeanization of the Middle East in its effect upon the political thought of the inhabitants.

9. The trends shown by press dispatches from the Middle East in the postwar period.

10. The interest of the United States in the Middle East.

Chapter 23: The Complexity of India and Burma

STUDY QUESTIONS:

1. How has the relief of India's borderlands influenced her political and economic development?

2. List the natural regions of India and evaluate each as a nuclear core for political development.

3. What are some of the important effects of the tropical monsoon climate on the lives of the Indian people?

4. Describe the coastline of India and point out its disadvantages in the development of a maritime nation.

5. What are the chief weaknesses in Indian agriculture?

6. Where are India's principal manufacturing industries and what are the geographic bases for their location?

7. Outline the possible changes in India's trade as a result of Japan's defeat.

8. Discuss the role of religion in India.

9. Analyze the potential economic strength of Moslem Pakistan, both in the northwest and in the northeast.

10. What are the possibilities of expansion in India's irrigation system?

11. Discuss the division of India into political units and point out some of the differences in government and in economic development.

12. What are the advantages and disadvantages to India of dividing the country into Moslem India and Hindu India?

13. Describe the organization of political units in Burma and the different types of administration.

14. Outline the major differences in economy between Upper Burma and Lower Burma.

15. Discuss the advantages and disadvantages to Burma of her separation from India.

SUGGESTED TOPICS:

1. The agricultural village in India.

2. Effects of the Indian climate on Europeans.

3. Possibilities of further industrialization in India.

4. The Hindu-Moslem rift.

5. Political and economic development of the Indian States.

6. Growth of nationalism in India.

7. India's political future.

8. Development of the Moslem partition scheme.

9. Commercial rice production in Burma.

10. Burma's role in World War II.

Chapter 24: The Foundations of Modern China

STUDY QUESTIONS:

1. Distinguish between "Greater China" and "China Proper."

2. How has the number of provinces in China fluctuated from time to time? What has been the political significance of these numerical changes?

3. Why have national boundaries in China been so flexible throughout Chinese history? Are they any less flexible now?

4. What is the economic significance of the Jade Gate in Chinese history?

5. Give examples to show that there is great diversity in relief and climate in Greater China.

6. In what natural resources is China potentially rich? Discuss.

7. What are the highlights of China's agricultural economy?

8. Why is transportation so important a key to the national economy of China?

9. Contrast the rail pattern with the air route pattern. Why are they so different?

10. Evaluate each of the following factors as regards its unity or diversity within China Proper: racial characteristics; language; religion.

11. Identify the following areas in relation to political status: Formosa; Hong Kong; Kwangchowan; Tannu Tuva.

12. What is the geographic difference between Inner Mongolia and Outer Mongolia? Political difference?

13. How has Manchuria reflected a position as a focal point of international politics in the Far East?

14. Is Sinkiang a point of international tension in present-day China? Why or why not?

15. Is Tibet heading toward or away from close affiliation with China? Why? Are geographic factors a strong cause?

SUGGESTED TOPICS:

1. The Great Wall of China.

2. Population density in —— (select one of the geographic regions of China Proper).

3. The three great rivers of China and their influence upon the cultural pattern (or select one for study in greater detail).

4. Trails and roads across Greater China: ancient and modern.

5. "Treaty Ports" and their effect upon the national economy of China.

6. Occupied vs. Free China: 1937-1945.

7. The changing capitals of China (from ancient times).

8. The industrial capacity of China; its potentialities and its limitations.

9. The relationship between China Proper and (1) the Northeastern Provinces, (2) Sinkiang, or (3) Outer Mongolia.

10. The Kuomintang vs. the Communists after World War II.

Chapter 25: Korea, Indo-China, and Siam: Historic Asiatic Buffers

STUDY QUESTIONS:

1. From the ethnic viewpoint, how does Korea differ from other Far Eastern nations?

2. What is the role of agriculture in Korean economy?

3. How is agricultural progress being retarded by the tenancy problem in Korea?

4. How does Korea compare with other Far Eastern nations in mineral resources and production?

5. To what extent has industrialization been developed in Korea?

6. How practical a political and economic boundary was the 38th Parallel established between the American and Russian Zones at the end of hostilities?

7. Of what nature was Korea's foreign trade in the prewar period; what is the outlook for the future?

8. What were the ties between Indo-China and China before the entry of the French?

9. How serious is the malaria problem in Indo-China?

10. What are the nature and importance of the specialized village industries in northern Indo-China?

11. Of how much importance is Indo-China in the economy of the French Empire?

12. Trace the effects of Indian and Burman cultures in Siam.

13. Describe the everyday life of a Siamese farmer.

14. Describe the functions of the city of Bangkok.

15. Identify the geographic regions of Siam. What are the principal criteria used in delineating them?

SUGGESTED TOPICS:

1. The political and economic position of Korea under the rule of the Japanese.

2. Korea as a buffer nation.

3. Korea's struggle for independence and its justification.

4. Chinese, Japanese, and Western cultural influences in Korea.

5. The origin and growth of French influence in Indo-China.

6. The foundations for Chinese interest in Indo-China.

7. Contrasting utilization of the Mekong and Tonkin deltas.

8. Effects of the Siamese bloodless revolution of 1932.

9. The influence of the Chinese in Siam.

10. Territorial claims and changes on the Siam-Indo-China frontier.

Chapter 26: The Japanese Isles

STUDY QUESTIONS:

1. With what countries did Japan have her earliest contacts and why with those countries?

2. What have been the two greatest external geographic factors affecting Japanese history? The two greatest internal factors?

3. What lesson did Japan learn from her earlier history which accounts for her rather strong navy in World War II?

4. What factors caused Japan's lack of modern civilization as of 1850, and how did she try to correct the situation?

5. What political and geographic factors favored Japan's military strategy? What hindered?

6. Compare the position of Japan off the coast of Asia with that of Britain off the coast of Europe.

7. In what ways does Hokkaido stand apart from Honshu, Kyushu, and Shikoku in the Japanese Islands?

8. Why are the Kwanto, Kinai, and Nobi plains life centers in Japan? Are they core areas?

9. How did the resources of Manchukuo fit into the economy of Japan Proper?

10. How was religion in Japan used for purposes of nationalism?

11. Trace the population increase of Japan from the early eighteenth century to the present day. Discuss population pressure.

12. Discuss the lot of the farmer and the urban worker in prewar Japan.

13. What was the meaning of the term "Greater East Asia Co-Prosperity Sphere"?

14. Trace the expansion of the Japanese Empire in the Pacific from the 1870's to Pearl Harbor.

15. What are the major postwar problems facing Japan?

SUGGESTED TOPICS:

1. Evidences of putting opportunism into practice in Japanese history.

2. Sea power vs. land power in Japanese military strength.

3. Economic advantages and shortcomings for a strong national economy in Japan.

4. The role of Japanese commercial air transportation until 1942.

5. Urban vs. rural population in Japan.

6. The fishing industry of Japan; its economic status and political implications.

7. The Japanese Mandated Islands.

8. The Westernization of Japan.

9. The great family monopolies of Japan.

10. Recuperative power of Japan.

PART FIVE

AUSTRALASIA AND AFRICA

Chapter 27: Africa: A Study in
Colonialism

STUDY QUESTIONS:

1. How does Africa rank among the continents
in size, population, and general level of civilization?

2. Physiographically speaking, of what does
Africa consist in the main? Where and what are
the principal mountain areas? Name seven great
rivers.

3. How many types of climate occur in Africa?
What is the general pattern of their distribution?

4. Why do the northern and southern ends of
Africa receive a winter rainfall? Why do the
Sudan and the interior of southern Africa receive
only a summer rain? Why does most of equatorial
Africa receive rain at all parts of the year? Ac-
count for Africa's two desert regions.

5. Describe briefly the distribution of natural
vegetation in Africa.

6. Describe the distribution of native races over
the Sahara; the Kalihari; equatorial Africa.

7. What advantages did the Nile Valley offer
to the development of ancient civilization?

8. Contrast the colonial ambitions of Portugal
and Spain in Africa. Suggest reasons for the difference.

9. Name the former German colonies in Africa.
What sort of an empire was Germany trying to
build there?

10. Name the former Italian colonies. At what
sort of general colonial pattern was Italy aiming?

11. Describe the French empire in Africa.
What are its trunk lines of communication?

12. Describe the British empire in Africa. Is
it a land or sea empire? Why?

13. What Belgian holdings are there in Africa?
Describe the process by which they were gained.

14. Name the independent countries in Africa.
Account for their independence.

15. Describe the distribution of European
colonies and independent countries in Africa since
1875.

SUGGESTED TOPICS:

1. A brief physical description of each of the
native African races.

2. North Africa's economic and political contributions to the Roman Empire.

3. The Moslem conquest of northern Africa.

4. The African slave trade.

5. Distribution of population in Africa.

6. Resources of the Belgian Congo.

7. Arab penetration in East Africa.

8. A short history of Egyptian civilization from
prehistoric times to the present day.

9. Piracy in the Barbary States.

10. European encouragement of cotton growing in Africa.

Chapter 28:   A Strategical Appraisal of
Africa

STUDY QUESTIONS:

1. What part of Africa did the ancient Greeks
colonize? What were their chief cities?

2. What part of Africa did the Phoenicians
colonize? What was their chief city?

3. What part of northern Africa was conquered by the Romans? Name the political divisions of Roman Africa.

4. What effect did the Moslem conquest have
on northern Africa?

5. What were the results on Mediterranean
Africa of the Portuguese and Spanish discoveries
of the fifteenth century?

6. How did the opening of the Suez Canal affect the west coast of Africa? the east coast? the
north coast?

7. What geopolitical changes in Africa were
wrought by World War I?

8. What was the role of Africa in World War
II?

9. Cite four cases where the Allies appeased
the forces of fascism for so-called practical reasons,
but which in the end reduced the military-geographic value of Africa for the Allied cause.

10. What will probably be the strategic value
of Africa to the United States in the future?

11. What is meant by the author's statement
that "geography is relative and cumulative"?

12. What places in Africa might be of value as
patrol bases to an International Government?

13. What are the two principal values of colonies to the owner nations? Can you think of a
third value?

14. What areas of Africa have been settled by Europeans? What additional areas might be colonized?

15. In what part of Africa might Russia logically be interested? Why?

SUGGESTED TOPICS:

1. An account of the Punic wars.
2. Alexandrine Greek culture.
3. Rise and fall of Negro and Bantu states and "empires" in Africa.
4. Construction and control of the Suez Canal.
5. The Fashoda and Agadir incidents.
6. The international regime at Tangier.
7. The African trusteeships.
8. Desert warfare during World War II.
9. Geography of Ethiopia or Liberia.
10. The story of the Boer republics.

Chapter 29: The Malay Archipelago and Oceania

STUDY QUESTIONS:

1. What is the main reason for the homogeneity of native culture in the more settled parts of the Malay Archipelago?

2. Where are the principal agricultural areas in the Archipelago?

3. What are some of the reasons for the sparse road and railway net in the Netherlands Indies outside of Java?

4. What are the basic factors responsible for Java's great population density?

5. Give some reasons why native demands for increased representative government have been much stronger in the Netherlands Indies than in Malaya.

6. Why was the Malay Archipelago of prime significance to the Japanese in their scheme for a "Greater East Asia Co-Prosperity Sphere"?

7. What are some of the productive enterprises in the Malay Archipelago that may be adversely affected by developments during the recent war?

8. What is the explanation for the seeming contradiction between the statement that the Chinese and European groups dominate the commercial field in the Netherlands Indies and the statistics in the table on page 425 which indicate that about 80 per cent of those engaged in commerce are natives?

9. What evidences in the history of economic development indicate a high degree of adjustment of commercial production to changing external influences in the Netherlands Indies? What are some of these changing influences?

10. Why does Borneo offer much less in the way of pioneer settlement than does Sumatra?

11. Contrast the positions of the Chinese in Malaya with those in the Netherlands Indies.

12. Why has there been such a marked improvement in the world-wide handling of subject peoples during the past century?

13. Contrast the "plural societies" of the Malay Archipelago with those in the United States.

14. Compare and contrast British interests in Malaya with those of the Dutch in the East Indies.

15. What geographic factors make Singapore a great entrepôt port?

SUGGESTED TOPICS:

1. An analysis of population growth and trends in standard of living in the Netherlands Indies and comparisons with Japan.

2. The foreign trade of Malaya and the Netherlands Indies.

3. The political organization of Sarawak and the State of North Borneo.

4. The "Culture System" in the Netherlands Indies.

5. A comparison of sponsored settlement projects in southeast Sumatra with those in Mindanao. (See reference to Pelzer in bibliography).

6. The political implications of international price controls in rubber production.

7. The possibilities of agricultural expansion in the Netherlands Indies.

8. Migratory workers in Malaya and the Netherlands Indies.

9. An independent state of Malaysia—arguments for and against its creation. Consult G. H. C. Hart, *The Netherlands Indies and Their Neighbors in the Southwest Pacific,* Netherlands and Netherlands Indies Council of the Institute of Pacific Relations (1942).

10. Rivalry of European states in the Malay Archipelago during the early colonial periods.

Chapter 30: The Philippine Islands

STUDY QUESTIONS:

1. Compare the total area and population of the Philippine Islands with the area and population of the United States; with your home state.

2. In the re-occupation of the Philippines General MacArthur chose the central east coast of Leyte for his first beachhead. What advantages

did this beach possess over other possible sites for an invasion?

3. What military and naval bases does the United States have in the Philippine Islands?

4. a) Philippine farmers grow very little wheat, barley, or rye. Why?

b) According to the 1939 census there were 120,081 hectares of camotes (sweet potatoes) but only 106 hectares of potatoes. What geographic factors explain this relationship?

5. a) The Philippine sugar industry probably will never regain its prewar position. Why?

b) Is the coconut industry likely to return to its prewar status? Justify your answer.

6. Why is rope made from abaca fiber (Manila hemp) superior to rope made from other vegetable fibers?

7. Name some of the principal manufacturing industries in the Philippines.

8. Compare the customs of the Moros with those of the Christian Filipinos.

9. The most common type of home in the Philippines is the *nipa* shack. Why is it more prevalent than other types of construction?

10. Why are there so few railroads in the Philippines?

11. The Philippine Islands have a large amount of potential hydroelectric power. Why?

12. The Philippine government has been called a "one-party government." What factors have prevented a second party from occupying a major role in Philippine politics?

13. How has the United States aided rehabilitation in the Philippines?

14. What Philippine products can probably be marketed in China? In Korea? In Australia? What can each of these nations sell to the Philippine Islands?

15. a) Compare the economy of the Netherlands East Indies with the economy of the Philippines.

b) What are the cultural and political similarities of the two areas?

SUGGESTED TOPICS:

1. Trends of abaca or coconut production in the Philippines.

2. Problems of reconstruction of the Philippine mineral industry.

3. Manufacturing in the Philippine Islands.

4. The Chinese problem in the Philippines.

5. The problem of minority groups in the Philippine Islands.

6. Philippine foreign relations after July 4, 1946.

7. Agrarian and other socio-economic reforms in the Philippines.

8. A national language for the Philippines.

9. Manuel Quezón's contributions to Philippine independence.

10. Transportation problems in the Philippine archipelago.

PART SIX

LATIN AMERICA

Chapter 31: The Caribbean: An American Mediterranean

STUDY QUESTIONS:

1. Why is the Caribbean region considered a tremendously important part of the world?

2. What lands are included in the Caribbean region?

3. State points of similarity and difference between the Mediterranean and Caribbean seas.

4. Why is the Caribbean area relatively free of boundary disputes?

5. Describe the location and the direction of the main mountain system of the area.

6. What are some of the principal handicaps of the area from a physical standpoint?

7. What causes climatic diversity within the region?

8. Why do many countries and colonies specialize in one crop? What are the dangers of one-crop economy?

9. What are the chief mineral assets of the Caribbean?

10. Why has air transportation developed so rapidly as compared with roads and railroads in the West Indies? In Central America?

11. Why is there relatively little trade among the countries within the region?

12. How does the population composition of the Caribbean islands differ from the mainland countries?

13. Why did civil strife and disorder mark the

political history of most of the countries after independence was achieved?

14. Outline the successive steps which the United States has taken to secure strategic control of the Caribbean.

15. Do you believe it would be wise for the United States to try to take over all of the European colonies in the region?

16. Why is Mexico the strongest state in Caribbean America?

17. How did the Good Neighbor Policy strengthen the position of the United States in the Caribbean during the past war?

18. What is the future outlook for the region?

SUGGESTED TOPICS:

1. The Panama Canal.
2. Mineral resources of the Caribbean Region.
3. European colonies in the Caribbean—assets or liabilities?
4. American bases in the Caribbean.
5. Independence for Puerto Rico.
6. The banana industry in the Caribbean.
7. Cuba's sugar industry and its political implications.
8. Geographic bases of United States–Caribbean trade.
9. Accomplishments of the Good Neighbor Policy.
10. Land reform in Mexico.

Chapter 32: The United States of Brazil

STUDY QUESTIONS:

1. What "money crops" have dominated the Brazilian economy?

2. How would you travel from São Paulo to Manaos?

3. Why is Rio de Janeiro, not São Paulo, the principal city of Brazil?

4. Where would you build a sugar refinery in Brazil? A steel mill?

5. Briefly explain the relationship of rainfall and vegetation in the regions of Brazil.

6. What racial stock has contributed most manual labor to the development of Brazil?

7. What racial stock has given Brazil its language and manners?

8. Why is Brazil larger than the original Brazilian colonies?

9. What distinguishes the Paulistas from other Brazilians?

10. Why is the northernmost part of Brazil subject to frost?

11. How does life in the interior of Brazil differ from life in the interior of the United States?

12. Who was the outstanding personality in Brazilian history? Why?

13. About what per cent of Brazil's land is cultivated? Why so little?

14. What factors retard the population of the Amazon Valley?

15. Why is the government of Brazil encouraging new industries?

SUGGESTED TOPICS:

1. The coffee industry of Brazil.
2. Racial origins of the Brazilian people.
3. The transportation systems of Brazil.
4. The growth of heavy industries in the Brazilian core.
5. Early exploration of Brazil and its relation to modern settlement.
6. The pattern of Brazilian economic cycles.
7. Prospects for settlement and development of the Amazon interior.
8. Agricultural development and potential of the Brazilian southeast.
9. The strategic position of Brazil on global sea and air routes.
10. The relation of climate to economy in Brazil.

Chapter 33: The States of the Rio de la Plata

STUDY QUESTIONS:

1. Why does Argentina fluctuate so violently between democracy and dictatorship?

2. Who were the gauchos and what became of them?

3. What is the philosophy of revolution that characterizes Argentine politics?

4. Explain the Argentines' "Beef phobia."

5. How strong are Nazis in Argentina? Communists?

6. What are the prospects for permanent harmony between Argentina and the United States?

7. How has the Roco-Runciman Treaty affected our international relations? What countries were directly or indirectly affected by this treaty and in what way?

8. Summarize Argentina's struggle for economic sovereignty. Compare the interpretation given by Ysabel Rennie in *The Argentine Republic*, pp. 230–264, with John White's version presented in chapters 21–24 of *Argentina, the Life and History of a Nation*.

9. Outline some basic causes of political con-

flict between the United States and Argentina.

10. Summarize Argentina's trade relations with the United States.

11. Justify the contention that the Pampas are the core land of the Argentine.

12. Give several reasons why Paraguay is least advanced among the River Plate lands.

13. In what way is the apex of South America significant in naval strategy?

14. Where in the River Plate lands have there been boundary disputes? In each case state the prevailing source of friction.

15. Contrast the background of the eastern cities of Argentina with that of the western colonial cities.

SUGGESTED TOPICS:

1. Economic ties between Argentina and western Europe.

2. Historic role of the Strait of Magellan.

3. The Gran Chaco and its economic potential.

4. Patagonia as a frontier land of Argentina.

5. Uruguay as a buffer state.

6. Political parties of Argentina and their effect upon international relations.

7. The oases of western Argentina.

8. Argentine foreign trade as a reflection on the geographic pattern of the country.

9. The handicaps of Paraguay as an inland nation.

10. Rivers as arteries in Argentina, Uruguay, and Paraguay.

Chapter 34: Pacific South America

STUDY QUESTIONS:

1. Where is most of the population distributed in Pacific South America? Why is this so?

2. Thinking in terms of racial composition of the population, can you show any relation between the distribution of population in Pacific South America and the type of surface features?

3. How do sociologists believe most of the Latin American countries will solve their so-called Indian problem? What has actually occurred in Chile and Colombia?

4. Bolivia, Ecuador, and Peru are far from unified. Why? Chile, on the contrary, is unified. Explain.

5. Why is Chile's population concentrated mainly in Middle Chile?

6. Discuss political instability in Chile, particularly since World War I, and account for it. Is geography a factor?

7. What was there about the highlands of Bolivia, Ecuador, and Peru that enabled the Spaniards so easily to transplant there their semi-feudal agrarian system?

8. Tell how Bolivia's interior location has influenced her politically during the past 20 years.

9. Do Chile's shape and her three markedly contrasted types of climate play any role in her internal politics? Discuss.

10. Had Chile's long coastline anything to do with her delay in breaking with the Axis during World War II?

11. Account for the fact that the arm of government in Colombia, Ecuador, Peru, and Bolivia is feeble in governing the Indian tribes of the forested eastern plains.

12. Ever since winning her independence Bolivia has been trying to correct the maladjustments of her economic and geographic structure. Name these. World War II offered Bolivia a unique opportunity to re-orient her economy. How?

13. An eminent geographer has stated that it is "geographically wrong for Chile to hold Tacna and Arica." Do you agree or disagree? Defend your position.

14. What factors are responsible for the fact that Bolivia has always had a unitary form of government?

15. Why does not South America have any *major* industrial development at present? Is it likely that she may have in the future. Make a list of the arguments *pro* and *con*.

SUGGESTED TOPICS:

1. Distribution of white, Indian, and mestizo population groups in Peru according to regions: coastal plain, *sierra*, and *montaña*.

2. Some authorities maintain that Chile has the brightest industrial future of any South American country with the exception of Brazil. Prepare arguments *pro* and *con*.

3. The geographic background of the Chaco War.

4. The geographic basis of the agrarian system of Peru.

5. Geographic problems in the boundary dispute between Ecuador and Peru.

6. The effect of the two-or-three-product economy on the political and economic geography of Pacific South America.

7. The dependence of foreign mining companies upon native Indian labor in the high Andes.

8. Reasons for Bolivia's expropriation of American oil properties.

9. Political implications of the Pan-American Highway.

10. Chile's form (shape) as a factor in her political geography.

PART SEVEN

Some Special Aspects of Political Geography

Chapter 35: Political Geography of the Oceans

STUDY QUESTIONS:

1. Do you believe that the science of oceanography should be accorded more attention in educational institutions? Why or why not?

2. Give a brief account of the contributions of ancient thinkers to the science of oceanography.

3. What are some of the economic advantages of oceanographic investigations?

4. What are the strategic ocean passageways of the world, and to what factors does each owe its main importance?

5. Briefly, what are the important benefits to man of the preponderance of the water over land masses?

6. What are the causes of ocean currents and in what manner do they affect world climates.

7. What do you understand the term "Freedom of the Seas" to include?

8. Describe the meanings of the terms "maritime power" and "continental power."

9. Give historical examples of relationships between shore lines and history.

10. Name and describe five major organizations of the world devoted to the solution and control of problems pertaining to the world ocean.

11. How has the continental shelf of the United States acquired political significance?

12. Do you agree with the viewpoint of Friedrich Ratzel concerning the ocean as the basic source of world greatness? Why or why not?

13. Should activities of the United Nations include the task of controlling the ocean fisheries?

14. What is meant by the concept of "median lines" in boundary settlements of inland seas, rivers, and lakes?

15. What are the principal sovereign rights expressed by individual nations upon the high seas under the principles of international law?

SUGGESTED TOPICS:

1. The geographical aspects of oceanography.

2. The World-Ocean of ancient history.

3. The development of sea power since 1850.

4. The industrial potential of the World-Ocean.

5. Haushofer's conception of geopolitics and the sea.

6. Political units of Oceania.

7. Ocean currents and world climate.

8. The comparative roles of the Atlantic, Pacific, and Indian oceans in world power.

9. International law and the high seas.

10. Continentalism and oceanism in world conflicts.

Chapter 36: Boundaries in International Relations

STUDY QUESTIONS:

1. Show how the idea of core area and frontier applies to the history of the United States; of Russia; of France.

2. Egyptian boundaries, throughout most of their lengths, are geometrical lines. Why are they better international boundaries than the Nile River would be?

3. Compare the world political map and the world population map at either end of this book. How does the pattern of "straight line" boundaries compare with that of population distribution?

4. France once considered the Rhine as one of her "natural boundaries." Do cultural factors lend weight to this argument?

5. Name some factors in the general situation between the United States and Canada that make the international boundary stable and fairly satisfactory.

6. Compare the United States–Canada boundary with that between Germany and Czechoslovakia in regard to physical features, language distributions, and lines of transportation, and show how the general situation is less favorable to stability along the latter.

7. Name five boundary or territorial arbitrations during the twentieth century.

8. Would you expect a successful plebiscite to be held in an area formerly under an absolute monarch? Why or why not?

9. Show how an inaccurate treaty delimitation might contribute to international discord.

10. Would you expect the task of a mixed demarcation commission to be more complicated in Central Europe or in the Amazon valley? Explain.

11. Name several international river valleys that might be developed along the lines of the Tennessee Valley in this country. What might international valley authorities for these streams be expected to accomplish?

12. What relationship does the Atlantic Charter have to international boundary functions?

13. What physical barrier acted as a partial defense for Russia against German invasion in 1941?

14. What natural resources formed the basis for the development of the Upper Silesian industrial district? What cultural factors caused it to be split by a boundary?

15. Name some differences between the functions of state boundaries within the United States and the functions of its international boundaries.

SUGGESTED TOPICS:

1. The eastern frontier of Germany before and after World War II.

2. The part played by frontier states in expansion.

3. The boundaries of some section of Africa: their history and relationships to their physical and cultural settings.

4. Changes in the course of the Rio Grande as affecting the United States–Mexico boundary.

5. A brief history of some international frontier zone, e.g., the United States–Mexico, with especial reference to the reasons for periods of discord or stability.

6. An account of some boundary or territorial arbitration.

7. Principles of territorial allocation used at the Congress of Vienna (1815) compared with those used at the Paris Peace Conference (1919–20).

8. Give an account of the way in which a particular boundary operates in respect to all of the boundary functions discussed in the text.

9. Compare the principles governing territorial waters and freedom of ocean navigation with the Chicago Civil Aviation agreements regarding air navigation above sovereign states.

10. The United States trade agreements program and its relation to international boundary functions.

Chapter 37: Population Factors in International Affairs

STUDY QUESTIONS:

1. Discuss the relationship between industrialization and population growth.

2. How are population estimates computed?

3. Discuss the factor of national greatness in terms of absolute numbers of population.

4. What factors should be considered in discussing population-supporting capacity?

5. Why cannot a specific density of population be given as desirable for all regions of the world? Use specific examples of regions.

6. Should a world-wide policy be established in regard to population growth?

7. Should lack of population growth be considered an alarming condition? Why or why not?

8. Where are the areas of declining rates of population growth? How do these areas rank among the important countries of the world?

9. Where are the areas of great potential growth? How do these areas rank in world leadership today?

10. Why is the way in which an area is being utilized of greater significance than absolute population numbers?

11. What are the limitations in regard to international migrations of population?

12. How effective were subsidies, as used in Germany and Italy, to stimulate population growth?

13. How do language variations become an international problem?

14. Why are population projections into the future generation more sound than many other predictions?

15. Why are studies of the ethnic composition of population so important in establishing a better understanding of the policies favoring permanent world peace.

SUGGESTED TOPICS:

1. Comparison of world political entities in regard to population growth.

2. Comparison of world political entities in regard to occupation groups.

3. Comparison of world political entities in regard to literacy and other cultural factors.

4. Effects of war on future population totals.

5. Significance of ethnic composition of population to international problems.

6. Areas of great population pressure.

7. The significance of European migrations throughout the world.

8. The population policies of the United Nations.

9. Future possibilities of migrations into marginal or frontier areas.

10. Evidences of the relation of modernization and industrialization to population growth.

Chapter 38: Grand Strategy of World War II

STUDY QUESTIONS:

1. Indicate the range of resources, activities, and conditions embraced by grand strategy.

2. What developments were responsible for the evolution of grand strategy from the older concept of military strategy?

3. Cite several modern instances showing how the operation of grand strategy in peacetime attained the objectives of military conquest without bloodshed.

4. What major steps were taken by Germany after 1933 to prepare for a war of aggression?

5. Indicate the major weaknesses of the strategic situation of Britain and France in September, 1939.

6. Indicate the major weaknesses of the strategic situation of the United States on the eve of Pearl Harbor.

7. Was the Axis prepared to wage a long-term war in 1939? In December, 1941? Justify your answers.

8. What strategic dividends would the Axis have received from its capture of the Suez area? What strategic liabilities would have accrued to the Allied Nations from that event?

9. What was "the arsenal of democracy"? Why?

10. Indicate the major strategic mistakes made by Germany in her fighting on the Eastern Front.

11. Outline briefly the basic strategy pursued by the United States in the Pacific theater from Pearl Harbor to the capture of Guadalcanal.

12. Justify, in terms of strategy, the Allied Nations' demand at Casablanca for the unconditional surrender of the Axis.

13. Outline briefly the Allied strategy in breaching the walls of *Festung Europa*.

14. What was the strategic effect of the United States forces' occupation of the following: Mariana Islands, Iwo Jima, Okinawa?

15. Why must the grand strategy of world security be implemented by the effective armed force of an international body like the UN?

SUGGESTED TOPICS:

1. Analyze the strategic situation of one of the following powers or combinations, as of July 31, 1939: Germany; Great Britain and France; Soviet Russia.

2. Analyze the strategic situation of Japan on December 6, 1941.

3. Analyze the strategic situation of the United States on December 6, 1941.

4. Prepare a critique of German strategy during the period from the fall of France (1940) to the drive on Stalingrad (1942).

5. Attack, defend, or modify the statement: "Airpower won the war."

6. Atttack, defend, or modify the statement: "United States seapower in the Pacific was primarily responsible for Japan's defeat."

7. Discuss the strategic decision of the Allied Nations to concentrate their major effort in the European theater until Germany was destroyed.

8. Analyze the part played by strategic and critical materials in the grand strategy of the opponents after Pearl Harbor.

9. Discuss the influence of technology on: (1) Axis defense from December, 1942, to the fall of Japan; (2) the Allied offensive in the same period.

10. Attack, defend, or modify the statement: "The atomic bomb has rendered obsolete all previous concepts and techniques of grand strategy."

Chapter 39: Geography in Future World Politics

STUDY QUESTIONS:

1. In terms of future political geography, what appears to be the significance of Greenland? Spitzbergen? Antarctica?

2. Account for the fact that so much of the earth's land space is so thinly populated.

3. In the political geography sense give a broad comparison of the bases of strength of Soviet Russia with those of the United States.

4. Indicate some of the politico-geographic factors involved in the International Whaling Convention of 1947.

5. What appears to be the major space-place factor contributing to the disunity of China?

6. Mention five major factors contributing to favorable relations between the United States and Canada.

7. Account for Cuba's dependence on the United States. Why is Mexico less dependent?

8. How does the British Commonwealth-Empire lend itself to a world-wide international air transportation network?

9. Why should hydroelectric power have effected international relations so little and petroleum have affected them so much?

10. How can you justify the use of the terms "shrinking world" and "expanding horizons" both in connection with the Air Age?

11. Account for the close juxtaposition of great population density, as in Java, and very slight population density, as in New Guinea, and Australia.

12. Explain how the political factor lags behind the technical and commercial factors in the progress of international aviation.

13. Name some major shifts which have recently taken place in the utilization of resources. To what degree was World War II responsible?

14. How has the global air route pattern changed the major trade channels of the world?

15. Explain the term "frame of reference" as used in the chapter.

SUGGESTED TOPICS:

1. The validity of the Mackinder hypothesis of the World Island and Heartland in terms of twentieth century developments.

2. The strengths and weaknesses of the Americas as a unit under: (a) A normal peacetime economy; (b) A possible wartime economy.

3. The space and place factors which proved to be weakest in the Japanese Co-prosperity Sphere.

4. The advantages and disadvantages of Brazil and Argentina in their rise toward pre-eminence in South America.

5. De-emphasis of their "life-line" through the Mediterranean if the British develop an African base south of the Sahara (as they have announced).

6. The place-space factors, present and potential, of the Soviet–eastern European area and the American–western European areas.

7. Cartels and their effect upon international commerce between world wars.

8. Political restrictions in the expansion of global air routes.

9. The effect of air transportation on political organization and on political control of territory.

10. Location of energy resources as focal points for international stresses and strains.

Biographical Notes

SAMUEL FLAGG BEMIS: Professor of Diplomatic History and Inter-American Relations, Yale University. Director of European Mission of Library of Congress, for photoduplication of documents in European Archives relating to American History, 1927–29; Carnegie Visiting Professor to Latin-American Universities, 1937–38; Visiting Professor to Cuba, State Department Program, 1945. Ph.D., Harvard University; Litt.D., Clark University. Knights of Columbus Prize for best book of the year in American History, 1923; Pulitzer Prize in Letters, 1927. Member of American Historical Association, Massachusetts Historical Society, New Haven Colony Historical Society, American Antiquarian Society, etc. Author, *Jay's Treaty, A Study in Commerce and Diplomacy*, 1923; *Pinckney's Treaty, A Study of America's Advantage from Europe's Distress*, 1926; *The Hussey-Cumberland Mission and American Independence*, 1931; *The Diplomacy of the American Revolution*, 1935 (Second Edition, 1937); *Diplomatic History of the United States*, 1936 (Revised Edition, 1942); *The Rayneval Memoranda of 1782*, 1938; *La Politica Internacional de los Estados Unidos, Interpretaciones*, 1939; *Early Diplomatic Missions from Buenos Aires to the United States, 1811–1824*, 1940. Editor and contributor, *American Secretaries of State and Their Diplomacy*, 10 Volumes, 1927–29. Coauthor, *Guide to the Diplomatic History of the United States, 1775–1921*, 1935, with Grace Gardner Griffin.

HERMAN BEUKEMA: Professor of Social Sciences, United States Military Academy. B.S., United States Military Academy; D.Sc.Ed. (honorary), Washington & Jefferson College LL.D. (honorary), Rutgers University; LL.D. (honorary), Norwich University. Member of Council on Foreign Relations, American Association for Professional Geographers, American Political Science Association, American Military Institute, etc. Author, *The United States Military Academy and Its Foreign Contemporaries*, 1943; *Military Policy of the United States, 1775–1944*, 1944; and various articles for *Encyclopedia Americana*. Coauthor, *Geographical Foundations of National Power* (ASF Manual M-103–1, 2, 3 of the War Department), 1944; *War as a Social Institution*, 1944; *Modern World Politics*, 1945; *Contemporary Europe*, 1946; *Contemporary Foreign Governments*, 1946; *Raw Materials in War and Peace*, 1947. Organized and directed Army Orientation Course, 1941–42; organized and directed Army Specialized Training Program, 1942–44. Received Distinguished Service Medal and the Purple Heart.

SAX BRADFORD: United States Department of State. A.B., University of California at Los Angeles. Author, *The Battle for Buenos Aires*, 1943. Five years of travel, writing, and study in Argentina, Brazil, and Peru for the United States Government. Special research studies on the Inca civilization of Peru, *Collier's*. Formerly editor of Scripps newspapers, including the *Seattle Star*.

ALBERT S. CARLSON: Professor of Geography, Dartmouth College. Ph.D., Clark University. Member of Association of American Geographers, American Society for Professional Geographers, New England Geographical Conference, New Hampshire Academy of Science, Industrial Development Committee of the New England Council, etc. Articles in *Economic Geography, Journal of the Franklin Institute*, and various New England publications devoted to industrial planning and development.

ALDEN CUTSHALL: Assistant Professor of Geography, in charge of Geography at the Chicago Undergraduate Division of the University of Illinois. Ph.D., Ohio State University. Member of Association of American Geographers, American Society for Professional Geographers, Southeast Asia Institute, Illinois State Academy of Science, etc. Articles in *Economic Geography, Journal of Geography, Scientific Monthly, Indiana Magazine of History*, and *Agricultural History*. Research work on the Far East, Office of Strategic Services, 1944–46.

GORDON G. DARKENWALD: Associate Professor of Geography and Chairman, Department of Geology and Geography, Hunter College of the City of New York. Ph.D., Clark University. Member of American Society for Professional Geographers, American Association for Advancement of Science, American Meteorological Society, New York Academy of Science, etc. Coauthor, *Economic Geography*, 1941, with Clarence F. Jones. Travel in every country of Europe (as of 1938) and travel and field work in Mexico, Cuba, and all parts of the United States.

SIGISMOND DER. DIETTRICH: Chairman, Division of Geography and Geology, and Head Professor of Geography, University of Florida. Ph.D., Clark University; D.Sc., Joseph University, Budapest,

Hungary. Study and research of political geography under the late Count Paul Teleki. Member of Association of American Geographers, American Society for Professional Geographers, Hungarian Geographical Society, American Academy of Political and Social Science, Florida Academy of Sciences, etc. Numerous articles on Florida in *Geographical Review, Economic Leaflets, The Annals* and *The Quarterly Journal of the Florida Academy of Sciences,* and *Education.* Travel and field trips in Europe.

SIDNEY E. EKBLAW: Professor of Geology and Geography, University of Kansas City. Ph.D., Clark University. Member of American Society for Professional Geographers, American Meteorological Society, American Society for the Advancement of Science, American Academy of Political and Social Science, Missouri Academy of Science, etc. Coauthor, *Influence of Geography on Our Economic Life,* 1938, with Douglas C. Ridgley. Author, *Problems in Economic Geography* (workbook), 1938. Chapter in 1948 *Yearbook,* National Council of the Social Studies. Articles in *Illinois State Academy of Science, Illinois Engineer, The Business Education World,* and *Journal of Geography.*

FRANKLIN C. ERICKSON: Professor of Geography, Boston University. Ph.D., Clark University. Swiss-American Exchange Student to the University of Zürich, Switzerland. Member of Association of American Geographers, American Society for Professional Geographers, etc. Articles in *Economic Geography.* Travel and field excursions in Switzerland and other European countries.

RUSSELL H. FIFIELD: Associate Professor of Political Science, University of Michigan. Formerly Officer in Division of Research and Publication of the Department of State and American Foreign Service Officer, American Consulate General, Hankow, China. Ph.D., Clark University. Member of American Historical Association, American Political Science Association, American Society of International Law, American Foreign Service Association. Coauthor, *Geopolitics in Principle and Practice,* 1944, with G. Etzel Pearcy. Articles in *American Historical Review, American Political Science Review, The World Today* (Royal Institute of International Affairs), *Journal of Geography,* and *Bulletin of the Department of State.* Extensive travel in China, 1946.

WELDON B. GIBSON: Assistant Director for Economic Research, Stanford Research Institute, and Lecturer, Graduate School of Business, Stanford University. M.B.A., Graduate School of Business, Stanford University. Member of American Academy of Political and Social Science, American Economic Association, American Sociological Society, Institute of Aeronautical Sciences, American Historical Association, American Political Science Association, Institute of Pacific Relations, etc. Associate author, *Global Geography,* 1944. Author, *Pacific Skyways,* 1947. Travel in Europe and the Pacific area as special representative of War and State departments.

ARTHUR R. HALL: Head, Territorial Studies Section, Map Intelligence Branch, Map Division, Department of State. Ph.D., Duke University. Member of Association of American Geographers, Southern Historical Association, and Agricultural History Society, etc. Articles in United States Department of Agriculture publications. Principal work with the Department of State has been along the line of territorial and boundary problems.

GEORGE W. HOFFMAN: Assistant Professor, Department of Geography, The University of Texas. Graduate work, University of Vienna, American University, and Harvard University; Ph.D., University of Michigan. Member of the Association of American Geographers, Fellow of American Geographical Society, Foreign Policy Association. Research for the Office of Strategic Services and United States Department of State. Extensive travel in western, central, and southeastern Europe and the Middle East between 1930 and 1948.

GEORGE DAVID HUBBARD: Emeritus Professor of Geology and Geography, Oberlin College; Visiting Professor of Geography, University of Missouri. Ph.D., Cornell University. Member of Association of American Geographers, American Society for Professional Geographers, Geological Society of America, American Association for the Advancement of Science, New York Academy of Science, Ohio Academy of Science, etc. Author, *Geography of Europe,* 1937. Articles in *Journal of Geography, Journal of Geology, American Journal of Science, Economic Geography, Geographical Review, Annals of the Association of American Geographers, Bulletin of the Geological Society of America, Ohio Academy of Science Journal,* etc. Travel in Europe and participation in international geologic and geographic congresses.

BEN F. LEMERT: Associate Professor of Economic Geography, Duke University. Ph.D., Columbia University. Member of Association of American Geographers, American Society for Professional Geographers, American Association for the Advancement of Science. Published industrial studies on the South, and articles in the *Journal of Geography* and *Economic Geography.* Associate author, *Global Geography,* 1944. Travel in Europe and Latin America.

GEORGE A. LIPSKY: Assistant Professor of Political Science, University of California. Formerly on faculty of the U.S. Military Academy, Department of Economics, Government, and History. Ph.D., University of California. Member of American Political Science Association. Contributed revision of "Government of the U. S. S. R.," in *Contemporary Foreign Governments,* published at West Point.

MICHAEL MANSFIELD: Representative of First Congressional District of Montana, House of Representatives. Formerly Professor of Latin-American and Far Eastern History, Montana State University. Made confidential mission to China in 1944 at request of the late President Franklin D. Roosevelt. In 1946 visited the Far East and the Japanese Mandated Islands as a Member of the Foreign Affairs Committee and submitted a report on that investigation trip to the Congress.

SHANNON McCUNE: Associate Professor, Colgate University. Formerly Assistant Professor, Ohio State University. Ph.D., Clark University. Member of Association of American Geographers, American Society for Professional Geographers, American Association for the Advancement of Science, etc. Articles in *Geographical Review, Journal of Geography, Economic Geography, Far Eastern Quarterly,* and others. Received Medal of Freedom, Presidential decoration for non-military personnel who aided the war effort by services abroad. Birth and boyhood in Korea. Travel and research in the Far East and India, including position as Head Intelligence Officer for the Foreign Economic Administration in India, Ceylon, and China.

J. WARREN NYSTROM: Associate Professor and Head of Department of Geography, University of Pittsburgh. Ph.D., Clark University. Member of American Society for Professional Geographers, Foreign Policy Association (Executive Director, Pittsburgh Branch), etc. Author, *Surinam, Geographic Study,* 1942. Field work in the Caribbean area and the Guianas, 1941.

CLARENCE BURT ODELL: Chief, Cartographic Department, Encyclopaedia Britannica, Inc. Formerly Chief, Population and Labor Section, Division of International and Functional Intelligence, United States Department of State. Formerly Assistant Professor of Geography, University of Missouri. Ph.D., University of Chicago. Member of Association of American Geographers, American Society for Professional Geographers, National Council of Geography Teachers, Sigma Xi, and American Association for the Advancement of Science. Compilation of World Distribution of Population map for Division of Geography and Cartography, Department of State.

G. ETZEL PEARCY: Geographic Attaché, U.S. Department of State. Formerly Assistant Professor of Economic Geography, School of Commerce and Business Administration, University of Alabama. Ph.D., Clark University. American Field Service Fellow for French Universities, University of Grenoble, 1933–34. Member of Association of American Geographers, American Society for Professional Geographers, American Academy of Political and Social Science, etc. Coauthor, *Geopolitics in Principle and Practice,* 1944, with Russell H. Fifield. Articles on air transportation in *Journal of Geography* and in trade magazines. Field work in the United States, the Caribbean area, France, and Italy; travel throughout the world.

GEORGE T. RENNER: Professor of Geography, Teachers College, Columbia University. Ph.D., Columbia University; LL.D., Cornell College (Iowa). Member of Association of American Geographers, American Society for Professional Geographers, American Institute of Planners, American Geophysical Union, National Council of Geography Teachers, etc. Author, *Human Geography in the Air Age,* 1942, *Conservation of National Resources: An Educational Approach to the Problem,* 1942, and *The Air We Live In,* 1942. Editor and associate author, *Global Geography,* 1944. Coauthor, *Geography: An Introduction to Human Ecology,* with C. L. White, 1936; *Conservation and Citizenship,* with W. H. Hartley, 1940; and *Home Geography,* with E. H. Reeder, 1944; *Human Geography,* with C. L. White, 1948. More than 100 articles in *Collier's, Saturday Evening Post, American Magazine, Current History, Life, Harper's, Aero Digest,* and others. Taught political geography for more than twenty years.

JOHN KERR ROSE: Geographer, Legislative Reference Service, Library of Congress. Ph.D., University of Chicago; J.D., George Washington University. Post-Doctoral Fellow of the Social Science Research Council, 1935–36. Member of Association of American Geographers, American Society for Professional Geographers (President, 1946), American Academy of Political and Social Science, American Association for the Advancement of Science, Rural Sociological Society, Indiana Academy of Science, etc. Articles in various geographical and economics magazines. Economist with the Bunce Mission to Korea (Department of State), 1946.

JOSEPH S. ROUCEK: Chairman of the Department and Professor of Political Science and Sociology, University of Bridgeport. Ph.D., New York University. Member of American Sociological Association, American Political Science Association, etc. Author, *The Working of the Minorities System under the League of Nations,* 1929; *Contemporary Roumania and Her Problems,* 1932; *Balkan Politics,* 1948. Editor and coauthor, *Contemporary Europe,* 1941; *Sociological Foundations of Education,* 1942. Co-editor of *Introduction to Politics,* 1941. Co-author or associate author, *Our Racial and National Minorities,* 1937. (Revised Edition, 1945, titled *One America*); *Contemporary World Politics,* 1939 (Second Edition, 1940); *Contemporary Social Theory,* 1940; *Czechoslovakia: Twenty Years of Independence,* 1940; *Government in Wartime Europe,* 1941; *Modern World Politics,* 1942 (Revised 1945); *Poland,* 1945; *Global Geography,* 1944. Author of several booklets on political science, and articles in the *Hungarian Quarterly, World Affairs Interpreter, Slavonic Monthly, Journal of Central European Affairs, American Journal of Economics and Sociology, Public Opinion Quarterly, Journal of Legal and Political Sociology, The Annals of the American Academy of Political and Social Science, Social Education,* and others.

JOSEPH RAYMOND SCHWENDEMAN: Professor and Head, Department of Geography, University of Kentucky. Ph.D., Clark University. Member of Association for the Advancement of Science. Author, *Geography of Minnesota,* 1933. Articles in *Economic Geography, Journal of Geography, Journal of Education* (Minnesota), etc. Travel in Italy.

RUTH S. SUTHERLAND: Senior Geographer, Department of the Army (Office of Quartermaster General, Research and Development Branch). M.A., University of Nebraska. Member of American Society for Professional Geographers. During World War II prepared classified reports pertaining to foreign resources of strategic and critical raw materials; bilateral commodity agreements with South American countries; analyses of Western Hemisphere trade agreements in relation to United States imports and stockpiles; raw materials data sheets—a handbook for foreign procurement officials.

GEORGE TATHAM: Assistant Professor, University of Toronto. M.A., Liverpool University, England; Ph.D., Clark University. Author, "Political Geography of Southeastern Europe," *Canadian Geographical Journal,* 1941.

GRIFFITH TAYLOR: Professor of Geography and Head of Department, University of Toronto. D.Sc., University of Sydney, Australia. Fellow of the Royal Geographical Society, Fellow of the American Geographical Society, Director of Canadian Geographical Society, Fellow of the Royal Society of Canada, Foundation Fellow of Australian National Research Council. Author, *Australian Physiography,* 1910; *New South Wales,* 1911; *Climate and Weather,* 1913; *Geography of Australasia,* 1915; *With Scott—The Silver Lining,* 1916; *Australian Environment,* 1918; *Australian Meteorology,* 1920; *Physiography of MacMurdo Sound,* 1922; *Geographic Laboratory for Australia,*

1925; *Environment and Race,* 1927; *Antarctic Adventure and Research,* 1930; *Australian Description Geography,* 1931; *Environment and Nation,* 1936; *Environment, Race, and Migration,* 1937; *Australia: An Advanced Text,* 1940; *Newfoundland,* 1936; *Our Evolving Civilization,* 1946; *Urban Geography,* 1947; *Canada— An Advanced Text,* 1947; associate author, *Global Geography,* 1944. Senior geologist and leader of Western Parties in Scott's Antarctic Expedition, 1910–13; received King's Polar Medal, Polar Medal of the Royal Geographical Society, Livingstone Medal of the American Geographical Society, Thomson Gold Medal of the Brisbane Geographical Society, Syme Medal for Research. Probably the only geographer to have done field work on all seven of the world's continents and the Arctic lands north of the Circle.

L. W. TRUEBLOOD: Geographer, Department of the Army; formerly Head of the Geography and Geology Department, Judson College, University of Rangoon, Burma. M.A., Clark University. Fellow of the Royal Geographical Society, member of the Association of American Geographers, member of American Society for Professional Geographers, Southeast Asia Institute, etc. Received Civilian Medal of Merit from Office, Chief of Staff, War Department, 1946. Field work in Burma, 1936–41.

RICHARD L. TUTHILL: Professor of Geography, University of Kentucky. Ed.D., Teachers College, Columbia University. Member of American Society for Professional Geographers, American Geographical Society, etc. Associate author, *Global Geography,* 1944. Classified research projects for Military Intelligence, War Department. Research, Civil Aeronautics Board International Air Route Cases, Pan American World Airways.

JOSEPH E. VAN RIPER: Associate Professor and Chairman, Department of Geography and Geology, Triple Cities College, Syracuse University. Ph.D., University of Michigan. Member of Association of American Geographers, American Society for Professional Geographers, Michigan Academy of Science, etc. Published "The Rural Zoning Plan of Marquette County, Michigan," *Michigan Academy of Science, Arts, and Letters.* For four years during the war a specialist on terrain intelligence for the Southwest Pacific area, Military Intelligence Service, United States War Department.

WILLIAM VAN ROYEN: Professor of Geography, University of Maryland. Ph.D., Clark University. Member of Association of American Geographers, American Society for Professional Geographers, American Association for the Advancement of Science, Corresponding Member,

Netherlands Society for Economic Geography, etc. Coauthor, *Fundamentals of Economic Geography*, Revised Edition, 1942, with N. A. Bengtson; "The Netherlands West Indies, Curaçao, and Surinam," with J. K. Wright, in *The European Possessions in the Caribbean Area*, published by the American Geographical Society, 1941. Articles in *Geographical Review, Economic Geography, Monthly Weather Review, Bulletin of the American Meteorological Society, Annals of the Association of American Geographers*, and many others, including Dutch scientific publications. Part of professional training at the State University of the Netherlands, Utrecht.

ROBERT J. VOSKUIL: Chief, Cartography Branch, Map Division, United States Department of State. M.A., Syracuse University. Member of American Society for Professional Geographers, American Congress on Surveying and Mapping, etc. From September, 1943, to January, 1946, was chief of the Cartographic Section, Office of Strategic Services. Received Certificate of Merit (War Department) for wartime cartographic services in the United States and abroad as a U. S. Navy Reserve officer.

CARLETON FREDERICK WAITE: Associate Professor of Social Science, New Mexico State Teachers College. Ph.D., University of Southern California. Member of American Historical Association, American Political Science Association, American Society of International Law, etc. Published "International Military Cooperation in the Suppression of the 1900 Anti-Foreign Rising in China, with Special Reference to the Forces of the United States," 1935, and other writings on international relations. Specialty, Far Eastern affairs.

C. LANGDON WHITE: Professor of Geography, School of Humanities, Stanford University. Ph.D., Clark University. Member of Association of American Geographers, American Geographical Society, etc. Coauthor, *An Introduction to Human Ecology*, 1936, with George T. Renner; *Regional Geography of Anglo-America*, 1943, with Edwin J. Foscue. Associate author, *Global Geography*, 1944. Articles in *Journal of Geography, Economic Geography, Geographical Review, Annals of the Association of American Geographers*, and other professional publications. Academic year 1947–48 spent in Lima, Peru.

Index

Index

Aden (*see also* Near East), 103, 108, 300

Afghanistan, 313-314, 321-324 (map, 321); agriculture of, 322-323; area, comparison with United States (map), 314; mineral resources of, 323; people of, 322; population of, 321; religion and languages of, 322
  physical factors: 321-322; area, 321; climate, 322; position and extent, 320-321; topography, 321-322
  political aspects: 323-324; British and Russian acquisitions, 324; ruling family, 323-324; Russia, postwar importance to, 94; Russia, treaty with, 324; world affairs, position in, 324

Africa (*see also* under name of specific country), 393-415 (map: 1875, 406); independent states of, 406; International Africa Association, 405; population of, 6, 392; position of (map), 409; races of, 395 (map, 396); Roman Empire in (map), 397; states, number in, 6; strategic value in third World War (map), 414; territorial conquests against, 410; World War II (map), 412
  colonial exploitation: 392, 397-407; Belgium, 405-406 (map, 403); Britain, 400-401 (map, 401); France, 402-404; Germany, 404 (map, 399); Italy, 405 (map, 399); Netherlands, 398-400; Portugal, 397-398 (map, 399); Spain, 404 (map, 403)
  historical backgrounds: 395-397; early civilizations, 395-397, 408; medieval contacts, 397, 408-409; world ocean age, 409-410
  physical factors: 393-395; area, 6, 392; climate, 394-395 (maps, 394, 395); geographic features, 392; topography, 393-394 (map, 393); vegetation, 394-395
  world importance, 410-415; future prospects, 414-415; reduction of value, 412-414; strategic significance, 411-412; World War II, 411, 413-414

agriculture, world, regions unsuitable for crop growth (map), 557

air power, relative status of great powers, 36

air route pattern, world (map), 564-565

air transportation, world, 562-565

Åland Islands, 229

Alaska, 56, 514; economic value of, 38; geographical features of, 56; latitude compared with Fenno Scandia (map), 223; population of, 56; United States, acquisition by, 38, 56

Albania (*see also* Balkan Peninsula), 272, 276-277; agriculture of, 276; area of, 6, 276; boundary problems of, 277; cities of, 276; historical background of, 276-277; Italy, seizure by, 198; League of Nations, 277; population of, 277; position of, 276; resources of, 276; Russia, postwar importance to, 93-94; Saseno, acquisition of, 206; Turkish control, separation from, 284; World Wars I and II, 277

Aleutian Islands, 514

Algeria, 284, 392, 396, 402, 404, 410, 415

Allied Nations, *see* World War II

Alsace-Lorraine, 20, 139, 176

American Chamber of Commerce Journal, cited, 435n

Anatolia, definition of, 281

Andorra, 5, 7, 177

Anglo-Egyptian Sudan, 402

Angola, 221, 398

Annam, *see* Indo-China

Annobon, 404

Antarctica, area of, 6; population of, 6; states, number in, 6

Antigua (*see also* Caribbean area), 443

anti-imperialism, U. S. policy of, 59-60

Antilles, Greater and Lesser (*see also* Caribbean area), 443

Antonescu, Marshal, 266

Arabian Peninsula (*see also* Near East; Saudi Arabia), 300-301; Great Britain, area controlled by, 300-301

Arab World (map), 297; oil concessions in (map), 303

Arctic Mediterranean states (map), 513

Arctic region, Russian interest in, 95

area, of continents, 6; of states, 1, 5-6; and population of the countries of the world (table), 567-568; and population of the world's "empires" (table), 573

areas, political, 15-20

Argentina, 471-482; Brazil, territorial losses to, 461; cities of, 475; Falkland Islands, dispute over, 475; Paraguay, war against, 480; power, classification by, 9; provinces and regions (map), 473; Roca-Runciman Treaty, 481; United States, relations with, 481-482; World War I, 480; World War II, 481
  economic factors: 476-478; commerce, 476-477; communications, 478; fishing, 477; industry, 477-478; surplus, problems of, 478
  historical background: 478-481; colonial period, 478-479; early republic, 479-480; modern republic, 480-481; revolution of 1810, 479; revolution of 1930, 480; revolution of 1943, 481
  physical factors: 471-472; area, 6, 471; climate, 471-472; position and extent, 471
  regions, geographic and economic features of: 472-474; Andean, or Arid West, 473-474; Chaco, 474; Mesopotamia, 474; Pampa, 473; Patagonia, 474

armament expenditures, comparative, 106n

Armenia, 286

Arnold, H. H., quoted, 514

Aruba (*see also* Caribbean area), 443

Ascension, 103, 402

Asia (*see also* under name of specific country), area of, 6; geopolitical factors of, 279-280; population, 6; states, number in, 6

Asia Minor (*see also* Turkey), Greece, ejection from, 275

Asia's Lands and Peoples, cited, 352n

Ataturk, Kemal, 286

atomic energy in world geopolitics, 44, 64

Attlee, Clement, 121; quoted, 524

Atwood, Wallace W., cited, 496n

Australasia (*see also* under name of specific country), 122-128, 391-392; area of, 6; climate of, 122; discovery and colonization of, 391-392; population of, 6; states, number in, 6

Australia (*see also* Australasia), 122-128; Canberra

Australia (*continued*)
  Agreement, 429; cities of, 126; dependencies of, 127; environment of (map), 123; foreign relations of, 126; historical background of, 125; military strength of, 126; original inhabitants of, 391; political development of, 125-126; population of, 18, 126 (map, 123); states of, 125n
    economic factors: agriculture, 124-125; commerce, 126; mineral resources, 124
    physical factors: area, 6, 122; climate, 122-124; topography, 122-124
Austria, 249-252, 256-257; area of, 256; Balkan states, concern over, 262; cities of, 256; Denmark, war with, 227; Habsburg monarchy, 249, 251-252; Italy, alliance with, 192; historical factors of, 249-252, 256; minorities in, 256; Ottoman Empire, acquisitions from, 284; physical factors of, 249-251; Poland, partitionings of, 239; population of, 256; postwar status of, 257; resources of, 256; Russia, postwar importance to, 93-94; World War II, 256-257, 542
Austria-Hungary (*see also* Austria; Hungary), Dual Alliance, 251; historical development of, 249-252, 258; power, classification by, 9; Russia, opposition to, 84; Straits, interest in, 295
Austro-Hungarian Empire (map), 251
Axis powers, *see* World War II
Azores, 207, 221, 398

Bachka, 257, 259
Bahama Islands (*see also* Caribbean area), 443
Bahrein (*see also* Near East), 300
balance of power, in Asia, World War II,, 61-62; in Europe, World War II, 61; in Far East, as supported by United States, 59; Woodrow Wilson, disapproval of, 59
Balearic Islands, 221
Balkan Peninsula (*see also* under name of specific country), 260-277; early conquest by Bulgaria, 272; economic factors of, 260-261; foreign imperialism, heritages of, 262; physical factors of, 260; races of, 261-262; routes of, 261
    international crosscurrents: 262-263; great powers, interest of, 262; statehood, rise of, 262; Truman Doctrine, 263; wars of 1912-1913, 262; World Wars I and II, 262
Balkan States (map), 260
Baltic Entente, 69
Baltic neutralization conventions, 229
Banat, 264, 265
Banse, Ewald, 22
Baranja, 257, 259
Barbados (*see also* Caribbean area), 443
Barca, 396
Basis of Soviet Strength, The, cited, 65n
Bausteine zur Geopolitik, cited, 24n
Beard, Charles A., cited, 87n
Belgian Congo, 164-165, 405
Belgium (*see also* Low Countries), 151-166; Africa, colonization of, 392, 405-406 (map, 403); as buffer zone, 20; France, wars with, 157; Netherlands, war with, 159; power, classification by, 9; Spain, conquest by, 157-158, 159
Beneš, Eduard, Dr., 254
Ben-Horin, Eliahu, quoted, 290n
Bessarabia, 84, 88, 262n, 264, 265, 266
Beukema, Herman, 30

Bhutan, geopolitical factors of, 336; power, classification by, 9
Bismarck, Otto von, 134
Bismarck Islands (*see also* Australasia), 391
Boericke, William F., cited, 436n
Bohemia (*see also* Czechoslovakia), 252; Hussite Wars, 252n
Bolívar, Simón, 453, 494
Bolivia (*see also* Pacific South American countries), Brazil, territorial losses to, 461; Chaco War, 483, 499; revolution of 1943, 481; War of the Pacific, 499
Bolton, Herbert E., cited, 494n
Bonin Islands, 384
Borneo (*see also* Australasia; Malay Archipelago), 391, 417
Bornholm, 227
Bosnia, 262, 269
Bosnia-Herzegovina, 284
Bosporus, *see* Straits
boundaries, in international relations, 517-527; of a political area, 19-20
Boundaries, Possessions, and Conflicts in Central and North America, and the Caribbean, cited, 499n
Boundaries, Possessions, and Conflicts in South America, cited, 499n
boundary fluctuations in a frontier area (map), 518
Bouvet Island, 232
Bowman, Isaiah, 23; quoted, 13-14
Brazil, 458-470 (map, 458); area of, 6; cities of, 462-463; Paraguay, war against, 480; power, classification by, 9; regions and resources (map), 465; states, territories, cities (map), 459; World War II, 461
    economic problems: 469-470; industrial outlook, 469-470; political future, 470; postwar outlook, 469-470
    historical background: 459-462; Braganza, House of, 460; colonial period, 460-461; economic cycles, 461-462; expansion, 461; modern Brazil, 461; Napoleonic wars, 460
    human factors: 462-463; language, 463; population, 462-463; races, 462; religion, 463
    regions, geographic and economic features of: 464-469; Amazon Basin, 464-466; Coreland, 467-468; Northeast, 466-467; South, 468-469
    transportation: 463-464; airlines, 464; overland routes, 463-464; water routes, 463
Britain, *see* Great Britain
Britain, industrial (map), 101
Britain and British Seas, cited, 106n
"Britain's Trade in the Post War World," cited, 109n
British Commonwealth-Empire, *see* Great Britain
British Commonwealth-Empire: 1946 (map), 97
British Commonwealth of Nations, *see* Great Britain
British East Africa, 402
British Guiana (*see also* Caribbean area), 444
British Honduras (*see also* Caribbean area), 443
British Isles, *see* Great Britain
British Malaya, 384
Brunei, 417
Brunhes, J., 22
buffer zones, definition of, 20; Russia's current desire for, 90-95
Bukovina, 88, 90, 265, 266
Bulgaria (*see also* Balkan Peninsula), 271-272; cities of, 271-272; economic factors of, 271; geographical factors of, 271; Macedonia, 270-271; population of,

272; postwar status of, 272; Russia, postwar importance to, 93-94; Saxe-Coburg-Gotha, House of, 272; Serbia, war with, 270; Treaty of San Stefano, 270; World War I, 270-271; World War II, 272

historial background: 272; Congress of Berlin, 272; First Balkan War, 272; Second Balkan War, 272

Bulgaria and Rumania, territorial changes by peace treaties: 1947 (map), 266

Burma, 325, 337; Anglo Burmese wars, 338; cities of, 339; historical background of, 338

economic factors: 338-339; agriculture and forestry, 338; commerce, 339; industry, 339; mineral resources, 338; transportation, 339

human factors: 339; minorities, 339; population, 339; races, 339; religion, 339

physical factors: area, 337-338; boundaries, 340; climate, 338; topography, 338

political status: framework under British, 340; independence, 340; separation from India, 338

"Burma, An Undeveloped Monsoon Country," cited, 338n Burma area (map), 337

Cambodia, *see* Korea

Cambridge History of the British Empire cited, 126n

Canada, 115-121; administrative pattern of, 119; American War of Independence, 118-119; British North American Act of 1867, 120; foreign relations of, 120-121; historical background of, 117-119; military strength of, 121; population of, 1, 119-120; settled zones and cultural groups (map), 118; U. S. foreign policy toward, 53; United States, relationship with, 40

physical factors: area, 6, 115; climate, 117; position and extent, 115; topography, 116-117

economic factors: agriculture, 117; industry, 117; mineral resources, 117

Canada Looks Abroad, cited, 121n

"Canada's Role in Geopolitics," cited, 4n

Canary Islands, 221, 404

Cape of Good Hope, *see* South Africa, Union of

Cape Verde Islands, 221, 398

capital goods as factor of state power, 8

capital of a political area, location of, 18-19

Caribbean area (*see also* under name of specific country), 443-456 (map, 445); cities of, 452; political divisions of (table), 456; U. S. policy toward, 454-457; World War II, 457

economic factors: 449-451; agriculture, 449; commerce, 450-451; mineral resources, 449-450; resources, 449; transportation, 450-451

historical factors: 453-454; early Spanish monopoly, 453; independence, 453; problems of government, 453-454; Spanish American War, 453

human factors: 451-452; language, 452; population, 452; races, 451; religion, 451-452

physical factors: 444-449; area, 444; boundaries, 444-445; climate, 448-449; position and extent, 444; topography, 446-448

Carinthia, 270

Caroline Islands (*see also* Australasia; Oceania), 38, 384, 391

Celebes Islands (*see also* Australasia; Malay Archipelago), 391

Central America (*see also* Caribbean area), 443

Ceuta, 108, 221

Ceylon, 328, 336-337

Champion, H. G., cited, 330n

Chapman, Charles E., cited, 215n

Chiang Kai-shek, 343n, 344-345

Chile (*see also* Pacific South American countries), Oceania, interests in, 429; Tacna-Arica controversy, 499; War of the Pacific, 499

China, 341-357 (map, 341); air routes (map), 351; Cairo Declaration, 343n; cities of, 353; Manchuria, seizure by Japan, 344; postwar problems of, 356-357; power, classification by, 8-9; provinces of (map), 342; transportation routes (map), 349; U. S. foreign policy toward, 57-59, 61-62; World War II, 550-553

economic factors: 347-352; agriculture, 347; commerce, 351-352; industry, 351-352; mineral resources, 346-347; transportation, 347-351

geopolitical aspects: 355-356; Manchuria, 355; Mongolia, 356; Sinkiang, 355-356; Russia, postwar importance to, 92-93; Sino-Russian agreement of 1945, 355; Tibet, 356

historical background: 343-345; Anglo-Chinese War, 344; Boxer Rebellion, 344; France, treaty of 1885, 368; Great Wall of China, 343-344; Han dynasty, 344; Japanese aggression, 58, 60-61; Kuomingtang, 345; Manchu dynasty, overthrow of, 344; Republic, Provisional Chinese, 344-345; Sino-Japanese War of 1895, 343, 344; Sino-Japanese War of 1937, 344

human factors: 352-354; language, 354; population, 7, 352-353, 530-531; races, 353-354; religion, 354

physical factors: 345-347; area, 6, 345; boundaries, 343; climate, 346; position and extent, 345; topography, 345-346

political framework: 341-343; territorial changes since World War I, 343; units, political, 341-343

Chinese Turkestan (*see also* Sinkiang), Russian interest in, 86, 94

Chosen, *See* Korea

Christian, J. L., cited, 340n

Christian Science Monitor, cited, 294n

Churchill, Winston, 343n, 548

Cippico, Antonio, Count, quoted, 197

Clausewitz, Karl von, 24, 542

Climates of the Continents, The, cited, 144n

"Climatic Regions of Korea and Their Economy," cited, 361n

Coastland, Mackinder's concept of, 27

collective security, as advanced by Woodrow Wilson, 59; Soviet policy of, 88

Colombia (*see also* Caribbean area; Pacific South American countries), 444; Brazil, territorial losses to, 461; Panama Canal, refusal to ratify treaty concerning, 55

Concerning Latin American Culture, cited, 500n

Congoland, *see* Belgian Congo

continents, area of, 6; population of, 6; states, distribution of, 6

Cordon Sanitaire, 20

core area of a state, 19, 517

Corfu, *see* Greece

Corisco, 404

Corsica, 172, 173

Costa Rica (*see also* Caribbean area), 443

Crane, Katherine Elizabeth, Dr., cited, 30

credit as factor of state power, 8

Cressey, George B., cited, 65*n*, 352*n*

Crete (*see also* Greece), 207*n*

Croatia, 258, 262, 267

Cuba (*see also* Caribbean area), 443; political control by United States, 38; U. S. foreign policy toward, 54-55

Curaçao (*see also* Caribbean area), 165, 443

Cutshall, Alden, cited, 431*n*, 436*n*

Cyprus, 103

Czechoslovakia, 249-255; Allied Council of Ambassadors, 252, 255; cities of, 253; Communist *coup d'etat*, 93*n*, 255; historical *factors*, 249-252, 254-255; Hungarian Plain, loss and reacquisition of, 255, 259; Minorities Treaty, 254; Munich agreement, 254; partitioning of, 257; republic, establishment of, 254; Russia, pact of mutual assistance with, 88; Russia, postwar importance to, 93; Ruthenia, loss of, 90, 255; World War I, 254; World War II, 254, 542

   economic factors: 253-254; agriculture, 253; industry, 253; transportation, 253-254

   human factors: languages, 255; population, 255; religions, 255

   physical factors: 249-253; area, 252; climate, 252-253; position and extent, 252

   political factors: minority problems, 254; Slovak problem, 254-255; territorial problems, 255

Czechoslovakia, Twenty Years of Independence, cited, 254*n*

Dai Nihon: Greater Japan's Military Power, World Role, and Future, cited, 27*n*

Dallin, David J., cited, 87*n*

Dalmatia, 262, 269

Danish West Indies, *see* Virgin Islands

Danzig, 140

Dardanelles (*see also* Straits), 262

Davis, Kingsley, cited, 533

Deak, Francis, cited, 84*n*

Democratic Ideals and Reality, 26; cited, 27

Denmark (*see also* Fenno Scandic countries), 225-227, 515; agriculture of, 226; area of, 225; Austria, war with, 227; cities of, 226; economic factors of, 225-226; Norway, control of, 232; population of, 225; power, classification by, 9; Prussia, war with, 227; topography, 225

   world relations: 226-227; boundary problems, 227; historical background, 226-227; World War II, 227

Dennett, Tyler, cited, 31*n*

De Valera, Eamon, quoted, 113

Díaz, Porfirio, 454

disarmament, U. S. policy of, 59-60

Dobruja, Southern, 272

Dodecanese Islands, 95, 205, 273, 276, 286

Dominica (*see also* Caribbean area), 443

Dominican Republic (*see also* Caribbean area), 55, 443

Dubrovnik, 269

Dutch Guiana (Surinam), 165

Earle, Edward Mead, Dr., 26; quoted, 541*n*

Earth and the State, The, cited, 145*n*

Easter Island (*see also* Australasia; Oceania), 391, 500

Eastern North American area of power, 10

East Indies (*see also* Australasia) 391-392

East Prussia, *see* Germany

Eckardt, Hans von, cited, 67*n*

Economic Basis of Politics, The, cited, 87*n*

economic development, as factor of power, 8; of states, comparative, 1

economic patterns of a political area, 18

"Economic Relations Between the Americas," cited, 459*n*

Ecuador (*see also* Pacific South American countries), Brazil, territorial losses to, 461; Peru, war with, 500

education, as factor of state power, 7-8

Efron, David, cited, 500*n*

Egypt (*see also* Near East), 103, 108, 301-302, 392; ancient civilization, 395-396; Anglo-Egyptian Treaty, 309; area of, 6, 301, 402; British occupation of, 284, 306, 400; cities of, 301-302; France, intervention by, 55; geographic features of, 301-302; Great Britain, intervention by, 55; Napoleonic invasion of, 306; Ottoman Empire, conquest by, 306; Ottoman Empire, separation from, 284; population of, 301, 402; resources of, 301; ruling house, origin of, 306, 307

Eire (*see also* Ireland), 110-113

Eisenhower, Dwight, 546

Elements of Political Geography, cited, 14*n*

Emeny, Brooks, cited, 146*n*

England, *see* Great Britain

Environment and Nation, 142*n*

"Epic of Greater America, The," 494*n*

Epirus, 272, 275, 277

equipment, institutional, of a political area, 18

Eritrea, 206, 405, 415

Estonia, 69, 84, 88, 90

Ethiopia, 206, 392, 405, 406-407, 415

Eupen, 139

Eurasia (*see also* Asia; Europe; and under name of specific country), 131; Spykman's analysis of, 33

Europe (*see also* under name of specific country), 131-132; area of, 6, 131; economic factors of, 131-132; geographical factors of, 131; languages of, 132; physical factors of, 132; population of, 6, 131; races of, 132; religions of, 132; states, number in, 6

Europe, cited, 141*n*

Europe, Central, lesser countries of (map), 249; postwar territorial changes in (map), 259

Europe, Southeastern, physical features of (map), 250; politico-geographic regions of (map), 263; railroads of (map), 261

European area of power, 10

Europes of Napoleon and Hitler, relative sizes of (map), 28

Ezekiel, Mordecai, cited, 310*n*, 495*n*

Faeroe Islands, 225, 226, 227

Fairgrieve, James, 22

Falkland Islands, 103

Far East, U. S. foreign policy toward, 55-59

Far Eastern Advisory Commission, 92

Fenno Scandia, latitude compared with Alaska (map),

Fenno Scandic countries (*see also* under name of specific country), 222-236 (map, 224); cultural accomplishments of, 222-223; international stability of, 225; languages of, 223; physical factors of, 223-225; religions of, 223

Fernando Po, 404

Fezzan, 396

Fifield, Russell H., cited, 30*n*, 80*n*, 509*n*

Fiji Islands (*see also* Australasia; Oceania), 391; climate of, 122; British annexation of, 127

Finland (*see also* Fenno Scandic countries), 227-229, 515; Åland Islands, 229; Baltic neutralization conventions, 229; cities of, 229; Hangö, lease to Russia, 229; historical factors of, 227; Petsamo, 229; population of, 227; Porkkala Peninsula, lease to Russia, 229; postwar position of, 229; Sweden, conquest by, 229

  economic factors: 228-229; agriculture, 228; forestry, 228; industry, 229; mineral resources, 228-229

  physical factors: area, 227; position, 228; topography, 228

  Russia, armistice of 1944, 90; conquest of 1809, 84, 229; peace treaty of 1940, 229; postwar importance to, 93-94; war with, 88, 229

Foreign Agriculture, cited, 203n

Foreign Commerce Yearbook, cited, 424n

"Foreign Policy of the Duce, The," cited, 197n

Formosa (*see also* China; Taiwan), 384

France, 167-180; cities of, 178-179; cities and rivers of (map), 170; colonial empire, 179; Franco-Italian border: 1947 (map), 196; Franco-Prussian War, 142, 150, 168, 402; historical factors, 167-169, 172-173; Hundred Years' War, 168; Napoleonic Wars, 103, 108; power, classification by, 8-9; regions of (map), 169; Revolution, 168; Russia, postwar importance to, 94; Sykes-Picot agreement, 307; World War II, 543-550

  economic factors: commerce, 177-178, 180; mineral resources, 174; postwar problems, 179-180

  foreign relations: Africa, colonization of, 392, 402-404 (map, 403); Africa, territorial conquests against, 410; Alexandretta, dispensation of, 281; Algeria, acquisition of, 284; Alsace-Lorraine, 139, 176; Asia Minor, acquisitions in, 286; Balkan states, interest in, 262; Canada, colonization in, 117-118; Caribbean possessions, 443-444, 453; China, territorial rights in, 343; China, treaty of 1885, 368; Egypt, intervention in, 55; Great Britain, alliance with, prior to World War I, 104; Greece, intervention in revolution, 274; Netherlands, occupation of, 158, 159; Oceania, interests in, 429; Russia, pact of mutual assistance with, 88; Spain, policy toward, 413; Switzerland, conquests of, 185; Syria, occupation of, 306; Syria-Lebanon mandated to, 284; Tunisia, acquisition of, 284; Turkey, mutual assistance pact with, 286

  human factors: language, 169-170; people, physical characteristics of, 169; population, 175-176; races, 176; religion, 169-170

  physical factors: 170-174; area, 173; boundaries, 176-177; climate, 173-174; natural regions, 171-172; position and extent, 172-173; topography, 170-172

  political factors: administrative units, 174-175; Fourth Republic, 174, 180; nineteenth century, changes of government in, 168; postwar problems, 180; social structure, 175

Franco, Francisco, 207

French Equatorial Africa, 404

French Guiana (*see also* Caribbean area), 444

French West Africa, 404

frontier of a state, 517-518

"Future of Philippine Mining," cited, 436n

Galápagos Islands, 500

Gambia, 402

Gandhi, Mohandas K., 336

geographical pivot of history (map), 26

"Geographical Pivot of History, The," 26; quoted, 27

geography, definition of, 5; early students of, 22

Geography: An Introduction to Human Ecology, cited, 13n

Geography of the Central Andes, cited, 492n

Geography of Europe, The, cited, 141n

Geography of the Peace, The, cited, 32

"Geography vs Geopolitics," cited, 14n

geopolitical problems, external, 21; internal or domestic, 20-21; international, 21

geopolitical study, considerations of, 21

geopolitics (*see also* political geography). American, 32-33; definitions of, 4, 32; founders of, 24-33; German concept of, 3-4; German origin of, 23; German usage of, 23-24, 28-32; major considerations of, 21; misconception in the United States, 2, 3-4; national economy concept of, 13; organismic concept of, 14-15; peace, application to, 5; political ecology concept of, 13-14; political landscape concept of, 12-13; warfare, application to, 3, 5

"Geopolitics and International Morals," cited, 24n

"Geopolitics at Munich," cited, 30n

Geopolitics in Principle and Practice, cited, 80n, 509n

Geopolitics of the Pacific Ocean: Studies on the Relationship between Geography and History, 28

Geopolitik der Pan-Ideen, 32

German East Africa, 400

German Reich: 1937 (map), 138

Germany, 133-150 (map: 1871-1937, 139); Bohemia, strategic significance of, 138; Brussels Convention, 148; cities of, 148-149; East Prussia, loss of, 90, 123; German Colonial Society, 404; Heartland, struggle for, 30-31; Kiel Canal, 137, 141; location, comparative (map), 136; population of, 1, 133n, 146-148; postwar occupation zones (map), 140; power, classification by, 8-9; Russian occupation of, 92; sea power, need for, 32; Southwest Africa, loss of, 130; territorial annexations during World War II, 147; territorial losses following World War I, 139-140; Treaty of Versailles, 139-140, 146; Weimar Republic, 140, 150; world power, rise as, 54

  economic factors: 148-150; agriculture, 145, 150; commerce, 108, 150; industry, 133n, 146-147, 148; mineral resources, 145-146; transportation, 149-150

  foreign relations: Africa, colonization of, 392, 404 (map, 399); Alsace-Lorraine, 139; Balkan States, interest in, 262; Dual Alliance, 251; Great Britain, conflict of interests prior to World War I, 104; Holgoland, acquisition of, 141; Italy, alliance with, 192; Poland, partition of, 136; Samoan Islands, sovereignty over, 55-56; Straits, interest in, 295; Turkish alliance, 138; Venezuela, intervention in, 55

  geopolitics: strategy of, 504; origin and development of, 3-4, 23-24, 28-32; world political outlook, 30-32

  historical factors: 133-135; Habsburg rule, 133-134; Hohenzollern rule, 133-134; Holy Roman Empire, 123; migrations, 136-137; Reich, political evolution of, 134-135; Reich, economic

Germany, historical factors (*continued*)
   evolution of, 134-135; Reich, founding of, 134; Tartar-Mongol invasion, 136
   physical factors: 135-146; area, 1, 133*n*, 139-140; boundaries, 139-140; climate, 135, 143-144; political implications, 142-143; position and extent, 135-136, 137-139; soils, 145; topography, 135-136, 140; vegetation, 144-145
   political factors: national unity, achievement of, 147-148; Reich, evolution of, 142; Reich, final unification of, 142-143; Third Reich, 133, 150
   wars: Franco-Prussian, 142, 150; Napoleonic, 123; Thirty Years' War, 150; World War I, 150; World War II, 142-143, 147, 150, 542-553

"Germany: Zones of Occupation," cited, 133*n*

Gibraltar, 103, 108 (map, 209)

Gilbert Islands (*see also* Australasia; Oceania), 391

Global Geography, cited, 66*n*, 495*n*

Gold Coast, 402

Gourou, Pierre, cited, 366*n*

Grandi, Dino, quoted, 197

"Graphic Summary of Trade between the United States and the Other Americas," cited, 496*n*

Great Britain, 96-130; geographical areas of, 96*n*; Industrial Revolution, 103; land power of, 36; Lausanne Conference, 294; lifeline of Empire, 279; Montreux Convention, 293-294, 295; Moscow Declaration, 363; Ottawa Conference, 107; political areas, 96*n*; political control, 96*n*; population of, 104-105; population of Commonwealth-Empire, 98; power, classification by, 8-9; sea power, development of, 35-36; Sykes-Picot agreement, 307; United Kingdom, 99-113; and United States, interdependence of, 54, 61; vulnerability of, 36
   British Isles: 99-113; agriculture, 100; cities, 105; climate, 99; Eire, 110-113; England and Wales, 101-102; industry, 100-101; Northern Ireland, 110-113; population (map), 105; structure (map), 99; topography, 99-100
   Commonwealth-Empire: 96-99; languages, 98; political areas (table), 112-113; position and extent, 98; position following World War II, 96-98; religions, 98; self-sufficiency, 98-99
   Dominions (*see also* under name of specific country): 114-130; Australasia, 122-128; Canada, 115-121; climate, 115; Newfoundland, 121-122; position and extent, 114; South Africa, Union of, 128-130; topography, 114-115
   economic factors: agriculture, 103-105; commerce, 102, 103-104, 105-106; Corn Laws, 105; Empire Free Trade, 107; future outlook, 109-110; industry, 102, 103-104; policy of revitalizing economy, 107-108; strength of, 106; tariffs, 105-107; weaknesses of, 106
   Egypt, intervention in, 55; defeat of Napoleon in, 306; occupation of, 284, 306, 400
   foreign policy: Atlantic Charter, 548; Balfour Declaration, 108, 307; Balkan States, interest in, 262-263; France, alliance with, prior to World War I, 104; future outlook, 110; Germany, clash of interests with, 104; Greece, assistance in, 275-276; Greece, intervention in revolution, 274; Iran, Anglo-Soviet occupation of, 310, 316; Italy, actions against, in Italo-Abyssinian War, 294; Japan, support of, in

Russo-Japanese War, 294; Near East, 309; nineteenth century, 104; Palestine, 308-309; Panama Canal, agreement concerning, 55; Spain, 413; Straits, interest in, 292, 294-295; Turkey, mutual assistance pact with, 286; twentieth century, 104-109; United States, trade agreement with, 110; Venezuela, intervention in, 55
   historical background: 101-104; ancient and medieval, 101-102; economy, colonial, 104; Empire, first, 103; Empire, second, 103-104; 1550-1914, 102-104; geographical factors, 101; industry and commerce, 102; Ireland, 102; Scotland, 102; Wales, 101-102

Russia, alliance with, prior to World War I, 104; entente with: 1907, 84, 86; support of, in World War I, 294; twenty-year mutual assistance pact, 88
   territorial interests: Africa, colonization of, 392, 400-402 (map, 401); Arabian Peninsula, control of areas in, 300-301; Arabian Peninsula, invasion of, 306; Asia, former control of, 279; Australasia, colonization in, 392; Caribbean, possessions, 443-444, 453; China, territorial rights in, 343; Iraq, mandate in, 284; Oceania, interests in, 429; Palestine, mandate in, 284; Samoan Islands, 55; territorial acquisitions of first and second Empires, 103; Transjordan, mandate in, 284
   treaties: Anglo-Egyptian treaty, 309; London treaty, 418; Roca-Runciman Treaty, 481; Siam, treaty with, 371; Treaty of Versailles, 108
   wars: Anglo-Bernese wars, 338; Anglo-Chinese War, 344; Boer War, 294, 398-399; Crimean War, 294; Hundred Years' War, 102; Napoleonic Wars, 103; Wars of the Roses, 102; World War II, 543-553

Greater Antilles (*see also* Caribbean area), 443

Great Powers in World Politics, The, cited, 146*n*

Greece (*see also* Balkan Peninsula), 273-276; Asia Minor, ejection from, 275; Balkan Wars, territorial acquisitions from, 275; British aid, 275-276; cities of, 273-274; Dodecanese Islands, acquisition of, 205; Ionian Islands, acquisition of, 274; Macedonia, 270-271; minorities in, 275; population of, 274; political situation between World Wars I and II, 275; postwar status of, 275-276; religion in, 275; Russia, postwar importance to, 92; Smyrna, acquisition of, 286; territorial acquisition of World War I, 275; territorial losses in World War II, 275; Thessaly, acquisition of, 275; Thrace, acquisition of, 286; Turkey, war with, 293; Turko-Greek repatriation agreement, 289
   economic factors: 273-274; agriculture, 273; commerce, 273; fishing, 273; industry, 274; transportation, 274
   geographical factors: area, 273; climate, 273; position and extent, 273; topography, 273
   historical background: 273, 274-275; Byzantine Empire, 274; Peace of Adrianople, 274; revolution of 1821, 274; Turkey, conquest by, 274; William of Denmark, Prince, 274

Greenland, 225, 236, 515; area of, 236; historical background of, 226-227; population of, 236; World War II, 227, 236

Grenada (*see also* Caribbean area), 443

Griffin, Charles C., cited, 500*n*

Guadeloupe (*see also* Caribbean area), 443

Guam, Spain, colonization by, 392; United States, acquisition by, 55

Guatemala (*see also* Caribbean area), 443

Guinea, 221

Guinea, Portuguese, *see* Portuguese Guinea

Hague Convention, 516

Hainan, 343n

Haiti (*see also* Caribbean area), 55, 443

Hangö, Russia, leased by, 229

Hanseatic League, 141, 227

Hartshorne, Richard, quoted, 5, 12-13

Haushofer, Albrecht, Dr., 28

Haushofer, Karl, 14, 23-24, 25, 27-32, 512

Haushofer, Max, 24

Hawaiian Islands (*see also* Australasia; Oceania), 38, 391; geographical features of, 56-57

Hay, John, foreign policy of, 58

Hayden, J. R., cited, 432n

Heartland, Germany, struggle for, 30-31; Mackinder's concept of, 15, 26-27; Russia, in relation to, 80; Russian control of, 64; Spykman's theory of, 33

Helgoland, 141

Henlein, Konrad, 254

Herzegovina (*see also* Bosnia-Herzegovina), 262, 269

Hess, Rudolf, as Nazi sponsor of Haushofer, 29

Hettener, Alfred, 22-23

Hindustan, *see* India, Union of

Hispaniola, *see* Dominican Republic; Haiti

History of Russia, A, cited, 84n

History of Spain, A, cited, 215n

Hitler, Adolph, 147; cited, 143n; as influenced by Haushofer, 29-32; as influenced by Ratzel, 25; World War II strategy, 544, 546

Hlinka, Father, 255

Hobson, J. A., cited, 106n

Hoffman, L. A., cited, 133n

Hokkaido, *see* Japan

Holland, *see* Netherlands

Honduras (*see also* Caribbean area), 443

Hong Kong, 103, 108, 110, 343, 353n (map, 353)

Honshu, *see* Japan

Hoover, Herbert, 456

Hopper, Bruce, cited, 95n

Horthy, Admiral, 258

Hoxha, Enver, 277

Hrdlicka, A., cited, 81

Hubbard, George D., cited, 141n

Human Geography, cited, 16n

Humboldt, Alexander von, 22

Hungarian Plain, 255, 259

Hungary, 249-252, 257-259; area of, 257; cities of, 258; economic factors of, 257; foreign policy of, 259; Habsburg monarchy in, 258; historical factors of, 249-252, 258-259; land reform in, 258; physical factors of, 249-251; political factors, 258-259; Russia, postwar importance to, 93-94; Treaty of Trianon, 257, Turkey, war with, 258; Turkish control, separation from, 284; World Wars I and II, 258

    human factors: languages, 259; races, 259; religions, 259

    territorial gains and losses: Bachka, 257, 259; Baranja, 257, 259; Hungarian Plain, 255; Ruthenia, 255, 257-259; Slovakia, southern, 257-259; Transylvania, partitioned, 257-259

Huntington, Ellsworth, cited, 115n, 141n

Husayn, Grand Sharif of Mecca, 306-307

Iberian Peninsula (*see also* Spain, Portugal), 207-221; cities and railroads of (map), 219; physical features of (map), 212

Ibn Saud, 307

Iceland, 515; geopolitical features of, 235-236; historical background of, 226-227; World War II, 227

Ickes, Harold, quoted, 559-561

Ifni, 221, 404

Imperialism, cited, 106n

India (*see also* Chap. 6), 325-336; before self-government (map), 326; cities of, 331; early stages in partition (map), 336

    economic factors: 329-331; agriculture, 329; commerce, 330-331; industry, 330; mineral and forest resources, 329-330; transportation, 331

    historical factors: 328-329; British East India Company, 328; early conquests of, 328; Indian Mutiny, 328-329

    human factors: 331-333; language, 333; population, 7, 331, 531; religion, 331-333

    physical factors: 325-328; area, 6, 326; climate, 327-328; coasts and islands, 328; position and extent, 325-327; topography, 327

    political framework under the British: 333-334; boundaries and defense, 333-334; British India, 333; Indian States, 333; problems, Britain's, 334; problems, India's, 334

    political status after division: 334-336; India, Union of, 336; Pakistan, 336

India, Union of, (*see also* India), 334, 336

India and Burma, political units of (map), 335

Indian Forest Records, cited, 330n

Indo-China, 358-359, 364-369 (maps, 358, 365); agriculture of, 366-367; cities of, 366, 367; commerce of, 367, 369; French East India Company, 368; population of, 365-366; religion of, 366

    physical factors: 364-365; area, 364; climate, 364-365; topography, 364

    political factors: 367-369; Annam, 367-368; Chinese economic control, 369; French Indo-China, 368-369; Japanese control, 368, 369; Viet-Nam Republic, 368

Indonesia (*see also* Australasia; Malay Archipelago), 391

Influence of Sea Power upon History, 1660-1783, The, cited, 25n

Influence of Sea Power upon the French Revolution and Empire, 1793-1812, cited, 25n

Ingria, Russian acquisition of, 84

Inonu, Ismet, 286

Institut für Geopolitik, 24, 28-32

Intelligent American's Guide to the Peace, The, cited, 206n

internal support as factor of state power, 8

Ionian Islands, 274

Iran (Persia), 313-320 (map, 315); Anglo-Iranian Oil Company, 318, 319; Anglo-Soviet occupation of, 310; area, comparison with United States (map), 314; British interests in, 313, 321; Great Britain and Russia, occupation by, 316; Russia, postwar importance to, 92-93

    economic factors: 317-319; agriculture, 317-318;

Iran (*continued*)
    industry, 318; mineral resources, 318; transportation, 318-319
    human aspects: 316-317; cities of, 316-317; historical background, 316, minorities, 316; population, 316
    physical factors: 314-316; area, 314; boundaries, 314-315; climate, 315; position and extent, 314; topography, 315-316
    political aspects: 319-321; government, 319-320; position in world affairs, 320
Iraq (*see also* Near East), 299-300; geographic features of, 299-300; Great Britain, mandate to, 284, 307; ruling family of, 307
Ireland, 110-113; agriculture of, 111; cities of, 111; historical background of, 102, 111; industry of, 111; political status of, 111-113; population of, 111; races of, 111; religion of, 111; topography of, 110-111
Ireland, Grodon, cited, 499*n*
isolation, U. S. policy of, 59-60
"Is the Twentieth Century South America's?", cited, 495*n*
Istria, 269-270 (map, 196)
Italy, 191-200; Agreement of Rome, 198; cities of, 205; cities and railroads of (map), 195; Franco-Italian border: 1947 (map), 196; historical factors of, 192-193, 194; Italy and the Mediterranean (map), 191; physical features (map), 195; population of, 193; power, classification by, 9; races of, 192; Russia, postwar importance to, 94-95; Turkey, war with, 205; Vatican City State, 196; World War I, 192; World War II, 95*n*, 192-193, 192-549
    economic factors: agriculture, 202-203; commerce, 204; forestry and fishing, 203-204; industry, 204; postwar problems, 201-202; transportation, 204-205
    foreign policy: 206; Austria, alliance with, 192; Balkan states, interest in, 262; Germany, alliance with, 192; Venezuela, intervention in, 55
    physical factors: area, 193-194; boundaries, 194-196; climate, 200-201; position and extent, 191-192; topography, 198-200
    political factors: international stability, means of maintaining, 197-198; military expansion, 197; territorial expansion, 196-197
    territorial gains and losses: Africa, colonization of, 392, 405 (map, 399); Albania, seizure of, 198; Asia Minor, acquisitions in, 286; colonies, 205-206; Dodecanese Islands, 205, 286; Eritrea, postwar disposition of, 206; Ethiopia, 206, 405; Libya, 206, 284; San Marino, 196; Saseno ceded to Albania, 206; Somaliland, postwar disposition of, 206; territorial acquisitions following World War I, 252; Trieste, 196; Yugoslavia, cessions to, 194
    Treaty, of London, 270; of Rapallo, 198, 270; of St. Germain, 198
Italy, cited, 197*n*

Jamaica (*see also* Caribbean area), 443
James, Preston E., quoted, 497*n*
Jan Mayen Island, 232, 515
Japan, 373-389 (map, 373); cities of, 379; Empire, 1941 (table), 388; Empire, expansion to (map), 385; Haushofer's estimate of, 31-32; industrial centers (map, 381; Lansing-Ishii Agreement, 58; Perry's

visit to, 377; postwar problems, 387-389; power, classification by, 9; railroads of (map), 381; Russo-Japanese War, 86; U. S. concessions to, 58; U. S. policy toward, 58-59, 60, 61, 62; world power, rise as, 54; World War II, 543-553
    aggressive expansion: 383-387; Bonin Islands, 384; British Malaya, 384; Caroline Islands, 384; China, 58, 60, 61, 542; economic motives, 383; Formosa, 384; Indo-China, 384; Korea, 384; Kurile Islands, 384; Manchuria, 384; Marcus Island, 384; Marianas Islands, 384; Marshall Islands, 384; Netherland East Indies, 384; Oceania, interests in, 429; Pescadores, 384; Philippine Islands, 384; political motives, 384; psychological motives, 383-384; Russo-Japanese War of 1904-05, 384; Ryuku Islands, 384; Sakhalin Island, 384; Siam, 371, 384; Sino-Japanese War of 1895, 343; Sino-Japanese War of 1937, 344; tools and techniques of policy, 384-387; Volcano Islands, 384
    economic factors: 380-383; agriculture, 380; fishing, 375, 380, 516; industry, 380-382; mineral resources, 375; postwar problems, 383; transportation, 382-383
    historical factors: 375-378; ancient age, 375-376; middle age, 376-377; modern age, 377
    human factors: 378-380; language, 378; population, 378-379; races, 378; religion, 378
    physical factors: 373-375; area, 373-374; boundaries, 374; climate, 374-375; position and extent, 373; topography, 374
    Russia, declaration of war by, World War II, 88; desire for control in, 92; neutrality pact with, 88
Japanese Mandated Islands, U. S. trusteeship of, 38
Java (*see also* Australasia; Malay Archipelago), 18, 165, 391-392
Jolles, O. J. M. cited, 542*n*
Juan Fernández Islands, 500

Kamerun, 404
Kant, Immanuel, 3, 22
Karelia, 84
Karelian Isthmus, 89
Kendrew, W. G., cited, 144*n*
Kerner, Robert J., cited, 86
Kjellén, Rudolf, 14, 23, 25
Korea, 358-364 (maps, 358, 360); cities of, 363; economic factors of, 361; Japanese development of, 363; language of, 362; races of, 361-362
    historical factors: 362-363; invasions, 362-363; Japan, occupation by, 363; Russo-Japanese War of 1904-05, 363; Sino-Japanese War of 1895, 363
    physical factors: 359-361; area, 360; climate, 360-361; position and extent, 359-360; topography, 360
    postwar era: 363-364; Moscow Declaration, 363-364; United Nations Commission, 364
Kreiger, Herbert, cited, 432*n*
Kuril Islands, 90, 384
Kuwait (*see also* Near East), 300
Kwangchowan, 343
Kyushu, *see* Japan

Labrador, 121-122
Laccadives, 103

Laidler, Harry W., cited, 71n

land power, in conflict with sea power, Mackinder's theory of, 26; Haushofer's theory of, 31; Mahan's theory of, 26

Landschaft concept of geopolitics, 12n

Land Settlement in the Asiatic Tropics, cited, 434n

language as factor of state power, 7

Latin America (*see also* Caribbean area; Pacific South American countries; and under name of specific country), 441-442; area of, 441; cultural factors of, 442; languages of, 441; population of, 441; position and extent of, 441; races of, 441-442; U. S. Good Neighbor policy toward, 60, 62; United State, peace pacts with, 60; United States, relationship with, 40; World War II, participation in, 62

Latin America (Preston E. James), cited, 497n

Latin America (William L. Schurz), cited, 497n

Latin America in the Future World, cited, 500n

Latin American republics, war declarations against Axis powers (map), 62

"Latin America: United States' Achilles Heel," cited, 485n

Latvia, 69, 88, 90

Lautensach, Hermann, cited, 24n

League of Nations, 108, 110, 140, 145n, 522, 527

Lebanon (*see also* Near East), area of, 6; France, mandate to, 307; geographic features, 298-299; independence of, 308

Lebensraum concept, 14-15, 24, 25, 139, 146

Leeward Islands (*see also* Caribbean area), 443

Lesser Antilles (*see also* Caribbean area), 443

Lesser Sunda Islands (*see also* Australasia; Malay Archipelago), 391

Liberia, 392, 407; power, classification by, 9

Libya, 206, 284, 392, 405, 410

Liechtenstein, 5, 190

Life, cited, 80n

Life of Nelson, The, cited, 25n

List, Friedrich, 22

Lithuania, 69, 88, 90, 140

Livonia, 84

location of a political area, mathematical, 16; natural, 16-17; relative, 17

London Times, quoted, 108

Lodge, Henry Cabot, 54-55

"Lost Mine of Tipuani, The," cited, 497n

Low Countries (*see also* under name of specific country), British protective policy toward, 104; as buffer zone, 165; cities of, 164; cities and provinces of (map), 155; colonial empire of, 164-165; cultural development of, 159; customs union of, 165-166; geographic regions (map), 153; future outlook of, 165-166; historical background of, 159-161; Treaty of Muenster, 157, 160; vulnerability of, 154

economic factors: 160-166; agriculture, 161-162; commerce, 160-161, 165; industry, 163-164; mineral resources, 162-163; self-sufficiency, 164

historical factors: 157-159; Belgian nation, 158-159; Dutch nation, 158

human factors: languages, 158, 159; population, 162, 164; religions, 158

physical factors: area, 151; boundaries, 156-157; rivers, 151; topography, 151-157

Lozada, Enrique de, quoted, 485n

Luxembourg, 5, 166

Macao, 343

MacArthur, Douglas, 387

McCune, Shannon, cited, 360n, 361n

Macedonia (*see also* Greece), 262, 269, 270-271, 272, 275

Maček, Dr., 269

Mackay, R. A., cited, 121n

Mackinder, Halford J., Sir, 15, 22, 26-27, 512; British trade, 1896-1906, estimate of, 106

McMahon, Henry, Sir, 306-307, 308

Madagascar, 402, 404

Madeira Islands, 221, 398

Mahan, Alfred Thayer, 24, 25-26; cited, 508n; foreign policy of, 54-55, 57

Makers of Modern Strategy, cited, 541n

Malacca, 103

Malaya (*see also* Malay Archipelago), 417

Malay Archipelago, 416-428 (map, 416); area of, 416; cities of, 424-425; commercial production of (map), 423; position and extent of, 416-418; resources of, 420; strategic location of, 418-419; territorial divisions, population and area of (table), 417; topography, 419-422

economic structure: 423-427; agriculture, 426-427; commerce, 423-424; natural resources, 425-426

people: 422-423; culture groups, 422; races, 422

political factors: 427-428; colonial policies of past, 427; current conflict, 427-428; future government, plan for, 427

Malaysia (*see also* Australasia; Malay Archipelago), 391

Maldives, 103

Malmédy, 139

Malta, 103, 108

Manchukuo, *see* Manchuria

Manchuria (*see also* China), 355; gateway to (map), 355; Russian invasion of, World War II, 88

Marcus Island, 384

Marianas Islands (*see also* Australasia; Oceania), 38, 384, 391

Marmara, Sea of, *see* Straits

Marmer, H. A., cited, 507n

Marshall Islands (*see also* Australasia; Oceania), 38, 384, 391

Martinique (*see also* Caribbean area), 443

Masaryk, Thomas Garrique, 254

Maull, Otto, 28, 31; cited, 24n

Mauritius, 103, 402

Mediterranean, Eastern, surface features of (map), 296

Mediterranean basin, Russia, postwar importance to, 95

Mediterranean waist (map), 198

Mehnert, Klaus, 32

Mein Kampf, quoted, 29n

Melanesia (*see also* Australasia), 391, 428

Memel, 140

Mesopotamia, *see* Iraq

Metaxas, General, 275

Mexico (*see also* Caribbean area), 443; area of, 6; International Boundary and Water Commission of the United States and Mexico, 526; political history of, 454

Micronesia (*see also* Australasia), 391, 428

Middle East, *see* Afghanistan; Iran

Middle East—Crossroads of History, The, cited, 290n

Midway Island, acquisition by the United States, 55

Mikhailovitch, General, 269

mineral resources for fuel and power, necessity of, 44

"Mineral Resources in the Philippine Islands," cited, 436n

Mitchell, Billy, quoted, 514

Modern Burma, cited, 340n

Meldavia, *see* Rumania

Moluccas Islands (*see also* Australasia; Malay Archipelago; Oceania), 391

Monaco, 5, 177

Mongolia (*see also* China; Mongolia, Outer), 356

Mongolia, Outer, 343; Russia, interest in, 86; Russia, postwar importance to, 93

Mongolian People's Republic, 356

Montenegro, 269

Moravia (*see also* Czechoslovakia), 252

Morocco, 392, 396, 404, 406, 410, 415

Mozambique, 221, 398

Munich Agreement, 88, 254

"Mystery of Haushofer, The," cited, 29n

Natal, *see* South Africa, Union of

Natalia, 398

national economy concept of geopolitics, 13

nationalism, as factor in state growth, 6; factors of, 7

Nauru, *see* Oceania

Near East (*see also* under name of specific country), 296-312; Arab revolt of 1916, 306-307; historical and social elements, 304-307; oil production: 1946 (table), 305; Russia, postwar importance to, 95; World War I, 307; World War II, 307

    economic and strategic elements: 302-304; resources, 303-304; trade routes and communications, 302-303

    environmental elements: 297-302; boundaries, 297; topography, 297

    problems of present and future: 307-312; Arab league, 307-308; Palestine, 308-309; Great Britain, 309; United States, 309-310; economic prospects, 310-312

Nehru, Jawaharlad, 336

Nepal, 336

Ness, Norman T., 500n

Netherlands (*see also* Low Countries), 151-166; Austria, acquisition by, 160; Belgium, war with, 159; Boer War, 159; France, occupation by, 158, 159; London Treaty, 418; Peace of Utrecht, 160; Portugal, war with, 398; power, classification by, 8-9; War of Independence, 157-158, 159-160

    territorial interests: Africa, colonization of, 392, 398-400; Australasia, colonization in, 392; Caribbean possessions, 443-444, 453; Dutch East India Company, 129, 398; Oceania, interests in, 429; South America, early interests in, 460

Netherlands Guiana, *see* Surinam

Netherlands Indies (*see also* Malay Archipelago), 384, 416n, 417; area of, 165; physical features of (map), 421; population of, 165

neutrality, U.S. policy of, 59-60, 61

New Britain (*see also* Australasia), area of, 122; climate of, 122; mandate to Australia, 127

New Caledonia (*see also* Australasia; Oceania), climate of, 122; French annexation of, 127

Newfoundland, 121-122

New Guinea (*see also* Australasia), 127; area of, 122; climate of, 122; mandate to Australia, 127

New Hebrides (*see also* Australasia), climate of, 122

New Ireland (*see also* Australasia), climate of, 122; mandate to Australia, 127

New World: Problems in Political Geography, The, 13, 23

New York Times, cited, 76n, 454n, 455n

New Zealand (*see also* Australasia; Australia; Oceania), 391; area of, 122; Canberra Agreement, 429; climate of, 122; economic factors, 127-128; historical background of, 127; population of, 127; position and extent of, 127; topography of, 127; Western Samoa, mandate over, 128

Nicaragua (*see also* Caribbean area), 443; United States, establishment of control by, 55

Nigeria, 402

nonintervention, inter-American system of, 60

North America (*see also* under name of specific country), area of, 6; population of, 6; states, number in, 6

Northern Ireland (*see also* Ireland), 110-113

Norway (*see also* Fenno Scandic countries), 230-232, 515; cities of, 231-232; Denmark, control by, 232; historical background of, 226-227, 232; population of, 230; power, classification by, 9; Spitzbergen, 232; World Wars I and II, 232

    economic factors: 231; agriculture, 231; fishing, 231; forestry, 231; mineral resources, 231; water power, 231

    physical factors: area, 230; climate, 230; position, 230; topography, 230

"Notes on a Physiographic Diagram of Tyosen (Korea)," cited, 360n

Notestein, Frank W., cited, 533

Obst, Erich, 28; cited, 24n

ocean currents (map), 510

Oceania (*see also* Australasia), 391, 428-429; Canberra Agreement, 429; political aspects of, 429; South Pacific Commission, 429

    geographic aspects: 429; area, 429; population, 429; position and extent, 428-429

Oceanography for Meteorologists, cited, 509n

ocean trade routes (map), 511

oceans, political geography of, 505-516

O'Donnell, John P., cited, 495n

Ogilvie, Alan G., cited, 492n

"Oil Behind the Andes," cited, 495n

Oman (*see also* Near East), 300

Orange Free State (*see also* South Africa, Union of), 398

organismic concept of geopolitics, 14-15

Oriental area of power, 10-11

origins, of geography, 22; of political geography, 22-23

Osmeña, Sergio, 435

Pacific area (*see also* under name of specific island), German concept of U. S. role in, 32; importance of, 31-32; U.S. foreign policy toward, 55-59

Pacific South American countries, 485-501 (map, 487); boundary disputes of, 499-500; cities of, 491-492; Pacific islands, 500; political relations of, 497-498; Rio de Janeiro Conference of Foreign Ministers, 500; social problems of, 500

    economic factors: 485, 494-497; agriculture, 494-495; commerce, 496; industry, 495-496; mineral resources, 495; transportation, 496-497

    historical background: 492-494; independence,

494; pre-Columbian period, 492-493; Spanish era, 493-494

human factors: 488-491; language, 485; population, 488, 491; races, 486, 490-491; religion, 485

physical factors: 486-488; area, 486-488; climate, 486, 488; topography, 486, 488

pacifism, U. S. policy of, 59-60

Pakistan (*see also* India), 334-336

Palaus (*see also* Australasia; Oceania), 391

Palestine (*see also* Near East), 308-309; American-British Cabinet Commission, 308; Balfour Declaration, 307, 308; geographic features, 298-299; Great Britain, mandate to, 284, 307; Jordan Valley Authority, proposal of, 310-311; partition of (map), 309; problem of, 308-309

Panama (*see also* Caribbean area), 443; independence of, 55

Panama Canal (*see also* Panama Canal Zone), (map, 57); necessity for, 54; negotiations for, 54-55

Panama Canal Zone (*see also* Caribbean area), 57, 443; acquisition by United States, 38; geographical features of, 57; location of, 55

Pantelleria, 108, 197

Papua (*see also* Australasia; New Guinea), 391

Paracels, 343n

Paraguay, 471, 482-483; area of, 482; Brazil, territorial losses to, 461; Chaco War, 483, 499; economic factors of, 482-483; geographic features of, 482; history and foreign relations of, 483; people of, 483; war with Argentina, Brazil, and Uruguay, 480, 483; World War II, 483

Parró, Alberta Arca, quoted, 490-491

peacetime application of geopolitics, 5

Peace Year Books, cited, 106n

Pearcy, G. E., cited, 80n, 509n

Pelage Islands, 197

Pelzer, Karl J., cited, 434n

Peoples of the Philippines, cited, 432n

Peoples of the Soviet Union, The, cited, 81

Perim, 103

Perón, Colonel, 481

Perry, Matthew, Commodore, 377

Persia, *see* Iran

Peru (*see also* Pacific South American countries), Ecuador, war with, 500; Tacna-Arica controversy, 499; War of the Pacific, 499

Pescadores, 343, 384

Peter I Island, 232

Petsamo, 229, 515

Philippine Islands (*see also* Australasia), 384, 430-439 (map, 433); cities of, 434-435; foreign relations of, 438-439; government and politics of, 435; Independence Act of, 60; internal problems of, 436-437; Rehabilitation Act (Tydings Bill), 436; Trade Act (Bell Bill), 436; Tydings-McDuffie Act, 435; vulnerability of, 58

economic factors: 435-436; agriculture, 435-436; forestry, 436; mineral resources, 436

economic rehabilitation: 437-438; agriculture, 437; industries, 437-438; mining, 437; transportation, 437

historical factors: early colonization in, 392; Spanish exploration and settlement, 430; Treaty of Paris, 430; U. S. sovereignty of, 38, 430-431

human factors: language, 434; population, 434; races, 391, 432; religion, 432-434

physical factors: 431-432; area, 431; climate, 431; position and extent, 430, 431; topography, 431; vegetation, 432

"Philippine Islands and Their People, The," cited, 431n

Philippines: A Study in National Development, The, cited, 432n

Pilsudski, Marshal, 239

Platt, Raye R., cited, 499n

Poland, 237-248 (map, 241); Austria, conquests by, 239; boundaries, 1772-1945 (map), 238; cities of, 247; Paris Peace Conference, 239; partitionings of, 66, 84, 136; Potsdam Agreement, 248; power, classification by, 9; problems of the future, 247-248; Prussia, conquests by, 239; territorial acquisitions following World War I, 252; treaty of Riga, 239; Turkey, defeat of, 239

economic factors: 243-244; 246; agriculture, 246; commerce, 246; forestry, 243-244; fuel, 246; industry, 246; mineral resources, 243; transportation, 246; water resources, 243

historical factors: 238-240; early history, 238-239; New Republic, 239-240; partitions, 239; World War I, 239; World War II, 240

human factors: 244-246; language, 245; minorities, 245-246; population, 244; races, 238; religion, 245; social progress, 245

physical factors: 240-243; area, 237; boundaries, 237, 242-243; climate, 243; topography, 240-242

political factors: General Land Office, 239; Regency Council, 239; treaty, Polish minorities, 245

Russia, border treaty with, 90; conquests by, 239; defeat of, in 1920, 87; Eastern Poland, acquisition of, 237; East Prussia, division with, 90; postwar importance to, 93; World War I, assistance of, 88

territorial acquisitions following World War II: Danzig, 237; East Prussia, partitioned, 237; Polish Corridor, 237; Pomerania, 237; Silesia, 237

political areas (*see also* states), definition of, 15 16; economic patterns of, 18; institutional equipment of, 18; nationality of, 18; population density, 18

anatomy: boundaries, 19-20; buffer zones, 20; capital, location of, 18-19; colonies and dependencies, 20; core area, 19; domain, 19; extended area, 20

physical properties: form, 16; location, 16-17; natural resources, 17; size, 16; surface features, 17

social characteristics: economic pattersn, 18; institutional equipment, 18; nationality, 18; population density, 18

political ecology concept of geopolitics, 13-14

political geography (*see also* geopolitics), different concepts of, 12-15; definitions of, 2, 5; in Germany, 3-5, 22-24, 28-32; growth of, 22-33; origins of, 3-4, 22; in the United States, 3-5, 22-23, 32-33

topical aspects: 503-566; boundaries, 517-527; oceans, 505-516; population factors, 528-540; world politics of the future, 554-566; World War II, grand strategy of, 541-553

political landscape concept of geopolitics, 12-13

political power, principles of exercise, 2

political science, definition of, 2

Politics of the Balkans, The, cited, 262n

Politische Geographie, 22, 25

Polynesia (*see also* Australasia), 391, 428

population, age and sex composition of (chart), 539; and area of the countries of the world (table), 567-568; and area of the world's "empires" (table), 573; of continents, 6; density, average, 7; density, comparative, 1; estimates by continent (chart), 533; factors in international problems, 527-540; of a political area, 18; as factor of state power, 7; of states, 7

"Population—The Long View," cited, 533

Porkkala Peninsula, Russian fifty-year lease on, 90, 229

Portugal, 207-221; Africa, colonization in, 397-398 (map, 399); Boer War, 398-399; China, territorial rights in, 343; cities of, 218; colonies of, 220-221; *Estado Novo* constitution, 207; Netherlands, war with, 398; Papal Line of Demarcation, 209, 398, 520; power, classification by, 9; South America, early interest in, 459-460; Treaty of Tordesillas, 398, 460

    economic factors: 217-220; agriculture, 217-218; industry, 218; mineral resources, 213-214; transportation, 218-220; water resources, 214

    historical factors: 208-210; decline in power, 209-210; early history, 208; early invaders, 215; exploration and colonization, 208-209; Moorish conquest, 215-216; oceans, control of, 515; political development, 216

    human factors: languages, 216; population, 214-216; races, 217, 215-216; religion, 216-217

    physical factors: 210-214; climate, 210-211; position and extent, 207-208; topography, 211-213; vegetation, 213

Population Research, Office of, Princeton Univ., 534-535

Portuguese Guinea, 221, 398

Portuguese India, 328

Posen, 140

Potsdam Conference, 90, 248

power, air, 36; Eastern North American area of, 10; European area of, 10; factors of, 7-8; land, 26, 31, 36; national, bases of, 35; Oriental area of, 10-11; political, exercise of, 2; sea, 25-26, 32, 35-36, 54; state, factors of, 7-8; state, Kjellén's theory of, 25; states, classification by, 8-10

    world, definition of, 54; factors of, 54; Germany, rise as, 54; Japan, rise as, 54; struggle for, 11; United States, rise as, 54-59; after World War II, 62-64

    world areas of, 6-7; characteristics of, 10-11; geographic features of, 7

powers, great, 1-2; comparison of, 35-36

powers, major, in comparative years, 8-9

powers, minor, in comparative years, 8-9

"Present Status of International Boundaries in South America," cited, 499n

press, as factor of state power, 7-8

Principe, 221

Prussia, Denmark, war with, 227; Poland, partitionings of, 239

Prussia, East, 140

Prussia, West, 140

Puerto Rico (*see also* Caribbean), 57, 443; area of, 57; geographical features of, 57; population of, 57; United States, acquisition by, 38

Qatar (*see also* Near East), 300

Quezon, Manuel, 435; quoted, 392

Ramirez, General, 481

Ratzel, Friedrich, 3, 14, 22, 24-25; quoted, 512

"Recent Developments in Political Geography," cited, 5n, 13n

religion as factor of state power, 7-8

Renner, G. T., 513; cited, 13n, 16n, 66n, 495n

Research Monographs on Korea, cited, 361n

Réunion Island, 404

Rhine River, International Commission of, 149

Rhodesia, 402

Rios, Fernando de los, cited, 498n

rimland, Spykman's theory of, 33

Rio de la Plata countries, *see* Argentina; Paraguay; Uruguay

Rio de Oro, 221, 404

Ritter, Karl, 22

Rivadavia, 479

Riza Khan Pahlevi, 317

Robinson, Arthur H., cited, 360n

Rogers, E. B., cited, 121n

Rommel, Erwin, 546

Roosevelt, F. D., 454n, 455n; Arabian rulers, meeting with, 310; Cairo Conference, 343n; China, hopes for, 357; Good Neighbor Policy of, 60, 456; World War II, 61-62, 548

Roosevelt, Theodore, 31; Corollary to Monroe Doctrine, 55, 60; foreign policy of, 54-55, 58

Roosevelt and the Russo-Japanese War, cited, 31n

Rosas, Juan Manuel de, 479

Ross, Colin, 32

Roucek, Joseph S., cited, 254n, 262n

"Round World and the Winning of the Peace, The," cited, 27n

Roxas, Manuel, 435

Ruanda-Urundi, 405

Rumania (*see also* Balkan Peninsula), 264-267; area of, 267; and Bulgaria, territorial changes by peace treaties, 1947 (map), 266; cities of, 264-265; economic factors of, 264; geographical factors of, 264; land, redistribution of, 264; languages of, 266; population of, 267; power, classification of, 9; Russia, armistice of 1944 with, 90; Russia, postwar importance to, 93-94; territorial acquisitions following World War I, 252; Transylvania problem, 257, 265, 267; World War II, 266

    historical background: 265-266; Convention of Paris, 265; Hohenzollern-Sigmaringen line, 265; Russo-Turkish War of 1774, 265; territorial acquisitions following World War I, 265; Treaty of Berlin, 265

    political factors: abdication of King Carol II, 265-266; abdication of King Michael, 266; fascism, rise of, 265; government following World War I, 265; minorities, prewar, 266; Russia, control by, 266; territorial gains and losses in World War II, 266; postwar status, 266-267

Russia, 65-95; air power of, 36; Alaska, sale of, to the United States, 67; Austria-Hungary, opposition of, 84; Balkan States, importance of, 262-263; Boer War, effects of, 86; Chinese Turkestan (Singkiang), interest in, 86; cities of, 76-78; Congress of Berlin, 84; Congress of Vienna, 84; Crimean War, 84, 294; Dodecanese Islands, desire for bases in, 95; fur trade, entrance into, 66-67; Greece, intervention in revolution, 274; Hague Conferences, 87; Iran, Anglo-Soviet occupation of, 310, 316; Japan, fishing agreements with, 516; Korea, economic penetration of, 86; land power of, 36; Manchuria, economic penetration of, 86; North America, expansion into, 67; Outer Mongolia, interest in, 86; Persia, drives against, 86; resources of, 2; Romanov, House of, 66; Russo-Japanese War, 384; Russo-Turkish wars, 84; Soviet sector decree, 515; Spanish Civil War, significance of, 88; Spitzbergen, desire for bases on, 95; Sweden, conflict with, 84; U. S. S. R., states comprising, 68; World War I, separate peace with Germany in, 87; World War II, 544-553

  agriculture: 72-73; arable land, 73; collectivization, 73; objectives of, 72-73

  economic structure, internal: 71-79; agriculture, 72-73; capitalistic system, elimination of, 71; five-year plans, 71-72; government control and/or ownership, establishment of, 71; industry, 73-78; New Economic Policy, 71; Revolution, significance of, 71; transportation, 78-79

  Finland, armistice of 1944, 90; conquest of 1809, 84; control of, 229; peace treaty of 1940; war with, 88, 229

  foreign policy, pre-soviet: 83-87; Anglo-Russian Entente of 1907, 84, 86; expansion, area concept of, 86-87; expansion, power concept of, 87; expansionist drives, 83-86; Great Britain, alliance with, prior to World War I, 104; Quadruple Alliance, post-Napoleonic, 87

  foreign policy, 1917-1941: 87-88; Britain, 87; collective security, 88; Czechoslovakia, pact of mutual assistance with, 88; France, pact of mutual assistance with, 88; German-Japanese Anti-Comintern Pact, 88; Germany, 87; Germany, nonaggression treaty with, 88; Japan, neutrality pact with, 88; League of Nations, 88; Munich Pact, effect of, 88

  foreign policy, World War II: 88-89; Great Britain, twenty-year mutual assistance pact, 88; Manchuria, invasion of, 88; Japan, declaration of war on, 88; Moscow Declaration, 363; Poland, sponsorship in, 88; Potsdam Conference, 90; Rumania, armistice of 1944, 90; Yugoslavia, sponsorship in, 88

  foreign policy, postwar: 89-95; cooperation, program of, 89; San Francisco Conference, 89; Sino-Russian agreement of 1945, 355; strategic frontiers, drive toward, 89-90; U. N. Security Council, 89; world position, 89; zone of security, 89, 90-95

  foreign policy, regional: Afghanistan, 94; Albania, 93-94; Arctic, 95; Austria, 93-94; Bulgaria, 93-94; China, 92-93; Chinese Turkestan (Sinkiang), 94; Czechoslovakia, 93; Finland, 93-94; France, 94; Germany, 90-92; Greece, 92; Hungary, 93-94; Iran, 92-93; Italy, 94-95; Japan, 92; Mediterranean, 95; Near East, 95; Outer Mongolia, 93; Poland, 93; Rumania, 93-94; Scandinavia, 95; Turkey, 92; Yugoslavia, 93

  geopolitical problems: 79-82; heterogeneity, 81; industrial capacity, 82; international responsibility, 82; military security, 80-81; political stability, 81-82

  historical development: 66-68; central Eurasia, conquest of, 83-86; eastward movement, 66-68; European phase, 66

  human factors: language, 71; literacy, 72; population, 68, 81; races, 70; religion, 71

  industry: 73-78; industrial regions, 75-78; mineral resources, 74-75, 515; Northern Sea Route, Administration of, 514; objectives, 73-74

  physical factors: area, 6, 36, 67, 68; boundaries, 67-68; climate, 68; position and extent, 67

  Poland, assistance to, in World War II, 88; defeat by, in 1920, 87; partitionings of, 66, 84, 239

  political structure: 68-71 (charts, 68, 70); Czarist Empire, collapse of, 68; political units, integration of, 69-71; political units, modern, 68-69; Revolution, Bolshevik, 68; Supreme Soviet of the U. S. S. R., 70

  power, classification by, 9; emergence as major, 65-66; factors of, 65-66; future, 2, 36

  Siberia, conquest of, 86; first expedition into, 67; population of, 67*n*

  Straits, interest in, 84, 292-294; Lausanne Convention, 293, 294; Montreux Conference, 293-294; Potsdam Conference, 294; Treaty of Unkiar Skelessi, 293

  territorial acquisitions: Bessarabia, 84*n*; Carpatho-Ukraine region, 90, 255; Caucasus and Transcaucasia, 86; East Prussia, partitioned, 90; Estonia, 84; Ingria, 84; Karelia, 84; Karelian Isthmus, 89; Kurile Islands, 90; Livonia, 84; Ottoman Empire, 284; Poland, partitioned, 66, 69, 84; Porkkala Peninsula, fifty-year lease on, 90; Sakhalin, 90; Siberia, 86; Turkestan, 86

  transportation: 78-79; airways, 79; railways, 78-79; waterways, 79

  Treaty, of Adrianople, 84; of Bucharest, 84*n*; of nonaggression, Soviet-German, 88; of Nystadt, 85; Polish-Russian border; 1945, 90; of Portsmouth, 86; of Rapallo, 87-88; of San Stefano, 270; of Tilsit, 84

  U. S. S. R., incorporation into: Bessarabia, 88, 90; Bukovina, 88, 90; Estonia, 88, 90; Latvia, 69, 88, 90; Lithuania, 69, 88, 90; Tannu Tuva, 90

Russia, cited, 67*n*

Russia in the Postwar Period, cited, 87*n*

Russian state, growth of (map), 85

Ruthenia (*see also* Carpatho-Ukraine; Czechslovakia), 252, 255, 257, 258, 259

Ryukyu Islands, 384

Sahara Desert, 394

St. Helena, 103, 402

St. Lucia (*see also* Caribbean area), 443

St. Thomas and Prince's Island, 398

St. Vincent (*see also* Caribbean area), 443

Sakhalen Island, 90, 384

Sala-y-Gomez, 500

Salazar, António de Oliveira, Dr., 207

Salvador, El (*see also* Caribbean area), 443; power, classification by, 9

Salonika, 275

Samoan Islands (*see also* Western Samoa), acquisition by the United States, 55-56

Sánchez, Luis-Alberto, quoted, 498

San Marino, 5, 196

San Martín, 479

Santo Domingo, *see* Dominican Republic; Haiti

São Thomé, 221

Sarawak, 417

Saseno, 206, 277

Saudi Arabia (*see also* Near East), 300; agricultural plans for, 312; geographic features of, 300; mineral resources, 312; U. S. oil interests in, 310

Scandinavia (*see also* Fenno Scandic countries; and under name of specific country), Russia, postwar importance to, 95

Schleswig-Holstein, 139, 227

Schurz, William L., quoted, 497n

Scotland (*see also* Great Britain), historical background of, 102

Sea, The, cited, 507n

sea power, in conflict with land power, Mackinder's theory of, 26; Haushofer's theory of, 31; Mahan's theory of, 25-26; nineteenth century, rearrangement in, 54; and political action, 508-509; strategic bases and passageways, 508; world's great navies, 507-508

Semple, Ellen Churchill, 22, 24

Serbia (*see also* Yugoslavia), 262, 267, 269, 272; Bulgaria, subjection of, 272; power, classification by, 9

Serbs-Croats-Slovenes, Kingdom of, 269

Seward, William H., 56

Seychelles, 103, 402

Shikoku, *see* Japan

Shotwell, James T., cited, 84n

Siam, 358-359, 369-372 (maps, 358, 365); Britain, treaty with, 371; cities of, 370; races of, 370; religions of, 369-370
    economic factors: agriculture, 371; transportation, 370-371
    physical factors: 370-371; area, 370; position and extent, 370; topography, 370
    political factors: 371-372; independence, 371; Japanese, 371; postwar status, 371-372

Siberia, *see* Russia

Sierra Leone, 402

Silesia, Upper (*see also* Czechoslovakia), 139-140, 252, 526

Simonds, Frank H., cited, 146n

Singapore, 103, 108, 418 (map, 424)

Sinkiang (*see also* China; Chinese Turkestan), 355-356

Slovakia (*see also* Czechoslovakia), 252, 257, 258, 259

Slovenia, 269

Smuts, General, 110

Smyrna, 286

Social-Economic Movements, cited, 71n

Socotra Islands, 103

Solomon Islands (*see also* Australasia; Oceania), climate of, 122; Australia, mandate to, 127

Somaliland, postwar disposition of, 206

Somaliland, British, 103, 402

Somaliland, French, 402, 404

Somaliland, Italian, 405

Soule, George, cited, 500n

South Africa, Union of, 128-130, 400; Boer war, 130, 398-399; cities of, 130; economic factors of, 129; environment of (map), 128; foreign relations of, 130; historical background of, 129; political units of (map), 128; population of, 130, 402; Southwest Africa, mandate to, 130; World War II, 130
    physical factors: area, 6, 128, 402; climate, 128-129; topography, 128

South America (*see also* Latin America; and under name of specific country), apex of (map), 475; area of, 6; Inca Empire of (map), 493; physiography of (map), 489; population of, 6; states, number in, 6

"South American Perplexities," cited, 498n

South Seas, *see* Oceania

Southwest Africa, 130, 404

Soviet Conquest of the Far North, The, cited, 95n

Soviet Union, *see* Russia

Soviet Union Today, The, cited, 68

Spain, 207-221; Allied appeasement policy toward, 413; cities of, 218; Civil War, 207; Civil War, non-intervention pact of Allied powers during, 413; Netherlands, War of Independence of, 157-158, 159-160; power, classification by, 8-9; Treaty of Tordesillas, 460; World War II, 413-414
    economic factors: 217-220; agriculture, 217-218; industry, 218; mineral resources, 213-214; transportation, 218-220; water resources, 214
    historical factors: 208-210; decline in power, 209-210; early history, 208; early invaders, 215; exploration and colonization, 208-209; Moorish conquest, 215-216; oceans, control of, 515; Papal Line of Demarcation, 209, 520; political development, 216
    human factors: languages, 216; population, 214-216; races, 207, 215-216; religion, 216-217
    physical factors: 210-214; climate, 210-211; position and extent, 207-208; topography, 211-213; vegetation, 213
    territorial interests: Africa, colonization in, 404 (map, 403); Caribbean, early monopoly in, 453; colonies, 220-221; Philippines and Guam, colonization of, 392; South America, early interests in, 459-460, 478-479, 493-494

Spanish Morocco, 211, 404

Speiser, E. A., cited, 297n

Spitzbergen, 232; Russian desire for bases on, 95

Spratly Islands, 343n

Spykman, Nicholas J., 32-33

Stambolisky, Premier, 272

Stamp, L. D., cited, 338n

Staten som lifsform, 25

states (*see also* political areas), area of, 1, 5-6; as basis of geopolitical study, 5; definition of, 5; development, comparative, 1; distribution by continent, 6; factors of growth, 6; populations, comparative, 1, 7; of the postwar world (table), 569-570; power, classification by, 8-10
    factors of power: capital goods, 8; credit, 8; economic development, 8; education, 7-8; external relationships, 8; internal support, 8; nationalism, 7; physical resources, 7; population, 7; press, 7-8; religion, 7-8; technology, 8; tradition, 7

Statistical; annual abstract of the Netherlands Indies for the year 1937, cited, 424n

"Status of Countries in Relation to the War, August 12, 1945," cited, 30

Stefánik, General, 254

Stefansson, Vilhjalmur, cited, 24n, 513, 514

Stevens, W. O., cited, 508n

Straits (Bosporus, Sea of Marmara, Dardanelles), 291-295 (map, 291); Istanbul, 292; future importance of, 295; location, importance of, 291; physical aspects of, 291-292
    political issues: 292-295; Austria-Hungary and Germany, 295; Great Britain, interest of, 294-

295; historical background of, 292-293; international commission, controlled by, 286, 295; Potsdam Conference, 294; Russia, interest of, 293-294; Truman Doctrine, 292

"Un Sud Americano en Norte América," cited, 498n

Suez Canal, 98, 103, 108, 284, 302, 400, 410 (map, 301)

Sullam, Victor B., cited, 203n

Sulzberger, C. I., cited, 76n

Sumatra (*see also* Australasia; Malay Archipelago), 165, 391

Sun Yat-sen, Dr., 344-345

Surinam (Netherlands Guiana) (*see also* Caribbean area), 444

Sverdrup, H. U., cited, 509n

Sweden (*see also* Fenno Scandic countries), 232-235, 515; cities of, 235; Finland, conquest of, 229; cooperatives, 235; core areas of, 235; foreign relations of, 235; population of, 232; power, classification by, 9; Russia, conflict with, 84

economic factors: forestry, 234; industry, 234-235; mineral resources, 234

physical factors: area, 232; position, 233; topography, 232

Switzerland, 181-190; boundaries of, 181; cities of, 186; military strength of, 189; political structure of, 185 (map, 184); power, classification by, 9; railroads and airlines (map), 183; topography of, 181-182; World War II, 189

economic factors: agriculture, 187-188; commerce, 188-189; industry, 188; transportation, 188

historical background: prior to Swiss confederacy, 182-184; development of Swiss nation, 184-185; France, defeats by, 185

human factors: languages, 186-187 (map, 186); population, 186; races, 182-184; religions, 187; religions, distribution on (map), 187

Syria (*see also* Near East), Alexandretta, 281, 286; Arab revolts in, 307

Syria, Greater, 298

Syria-Lebanon, France, mandate to, 284, 307; France, occupation by, 300; geographic features of, 298-299; independence of, 308

Tahiti, French annexation of, 127

Taiwan, 343

Tanganyika (German East Africa), 404

Tangier, 404, 410

Tanna Tuva, People's Republic of, 90, 356

Tasmania (*see also* Australasia; Australia), 391; climate of, 122

Taylor, Griffith, cited, 142n; quoted, 4, 556

territorial changes and new states since World War II (table), 571-572

Teschen, Duchy of, 252

Thailand, *see* Siam

Thessalonica, 272

Thessaly, acquisition by Greece, 275

Thrace, 262n, 272, 281, 286

Tibet (*see also* China), 356

Timor, Portuguese (*see also* Malay Archipelago; Oceania), 207, 221, 392, 417

Tiso, Father, 255

Tito, Marshal, 269

Togoland, 404

Toward World Prosperity, cited, 310n

Transjordan (*see also* Near East), 299; geographic features of, 299; Great Britain, mandate to, 284; independence, 309; ruling family, 307

Transvaal, *see* South Africa, Union of

Transvaal Republic, 398

Transylvania, 257, 258, 259, 265, 266

Treitschke, Heinrich von, 22

Trieste, 196, 269-270

Trinidad (*see also* Caribbean area), 443

Tripoli, 396

Tristan da Cunha, 103, 402

Truman, Harry S., 429, 506

Tunisia, 284, 392, 396, 404, 406, 410, 413-414, 415

Turkestan, Russian conquest of, 86

Turkey (*see also* Balkan Peninsula), 281-295; Alexandretta, acquisition of, 281; Armenia, Turkish, 281; Britain and France, mutual assistance pact with, 1939, 286; Bulgaria, conquest of, 272; cities of, 289; Egypt, defeat of Napoleon in, 306; German alliance with, 138; Macedonia, control of, 270; modern Turkey (map), 282; Ottoman Empire, disintegration of (map), 285; Ottoman Empire, fifteenth to nineteenth centuries (map), 283; power, classification by, 9; Russia, postwar importance to, 92; Straits, 286, 291-295; treaty of Unkiar Skelessi, 293; Turko-Greek repatriation agreement, 289

economic factors: 289-291; agriculture, 290; industry, 290; mineral resources, 290; transportation, 290-291

historical evolution: 282-287; Greece, war with, 274, 293; Hungary, war with, 258; Italy, war with, 205; Lausanne Convention, 286, 293, 294; Montreux Convention, 286, 294; Ottoman Empire, 282-284; republic formed, 286; revolution by Young Turks, 284; Russo-Turkish wars, 84; Treaty of San Stefano, 270; Treaty of Sèvres, 286, 293; World War I, territorial losses following, 284-286; World War II, 286-287

human factors: 288-289; languages, 288; minorities, 288-289; population, 289; races, 288; religions, 288

physical factors: 281, 287-288; area, 281; boundaries, 281; climate, 288; position and extent, 281; topography, 287-288

Turkey at the Straits, cited, 84n

Turkish Empire, disruption of, 262

Tuthill, Richard L., Dr., cited, 7

Ukraine, *see* Russia

Union of South Africa, *see* South Africa, Union of

United Kingdom, *see* Great Britain

United Nations, 9, 62, 110, 308-309, 364, 405, 528, 548, 552, 556, 569-570; United States as seat of, selection of, 40

United States of America, 37-64; air power of, 36; American Persian Gulf Command, 310; atomic power, development of, 44; cities of, 51-52; factors of strength, 37-52; geographical features of, 36; geopolitics, growth of, 32-33; and Great Britain, interdependence of, 54, 61; land forms, major (map), 41; military bases in Latin America, 62; Moscow Declaration, 363; political geography, introduction of, 3; power, classification of, 9; precipitation zones (map), 41; sea power of, 36; Spykman's theory con-

United States of America (*continued*)
cerning, 33; vulnerability of, 38-40, 54; as world power, 63; World War II, 545, 546-553

economic factors: 42-50; agriculture, 45-46; commercial reserves of certain minerals (chart), 561; industry, 46-48; mineral resources, 43-45; self-sufficiency, 46; soils, 43

foreign policy: 53; Atlantic Charter, 62, 548; Balkan states, 263; Bretton Woods Monetary Agreements, 527; Caribbean area, 54-55, 454-456; China, 57-59, 61-62; Cuba, 54-55; Far East, 55-59, 60, 61-62; Great Britain, trade agreement with, 110; International Civil Aviation Agreements, 527; Japan, 58; Lansing-Ishii Agreement, 58; Latin America, Good Neighbor Policy, 60, 62, 498; League of Nations, 59; Mahan's formula for, 57; Monroe Doctrine, Clark Memorandum on, 60; Mexico, 526; Monroe Doctrine, twentieth century interpretation of, 58-59; Monroe Doctrine, Theodore Roosevelt Corollary to, 55; Near East, 309-310; nineteenth century, 53; Pacific, 55-59; Pact of Paris, 59; Philippine Islands, 58, 60; Spain, 413; Spooner Amendment, 55; Triple Alliance, significance of, 61-62; following Washington Conference of 1922, 59-60; World War I, 59; World War II, 61-62; following World War II, 62-64; Yalta Conference, 310

historical factors: 53; nineteenth century, 53; Spanish American war, 54-58; world power, rise as, 54-59

human factors: language, 52; living standards, 48; people, attainments of, 52; population of, 18, 50-52; population density (map), 51; religion, 52

physical factors: area, 6, 40; boundaries, 38-39; climate, 41-42; forests, 1620 (map), 42; forests, 1940 (map), 43; position and extent, 39-40; topography, 40-41; vegetation, 42

territorial interests: Australasia, colonization in, 392; Caribbean, establishment of control over, 55; Caribbean possessions, 443; Near East, interests in, 297; Oceania, interests in, 429; Panama Canal, 54-55; Straits, interest in, 292, 295; territorial acquisitions of, 37-38, 55-58; territorial acquisition, 1783-1853 (map), 37; transportation: 48-50; airlines, commercial (map), 50; air routes, 49; highways, 48-49; pipelines, 50; railroads, 48; water routes, 49

Treaty, Clayton-Bulwer, 55; with Panama, 55; with Nicaragua, 454

United States and the Near East, The, cited, 297n
United States of Brazil, *see* Brazil
UNRRA, 261
Urge to the Sea, The, cited, 86n
Uriburu, General, 480
Uruguay, 471, 483-484; Brazil, territorial losses to, 461; economic factors of, 484; geographic features of, 483-484; history of, 484; Paraguay, war against, 480; population of, 484
U. S. S. R. (*see also* Russia), cities of (map), 76; industrial regions and railroads (map), 75; political divisions (map), 69; and its peripheral spheres of interest, 91
"L'Utilisation du Sol en Inochine Francaise," cited, 366n

Vallaux, C., 22
Van Valkenburg, Samuel, cited, 141n; quoted, 14
Vargas, Getulio, 461
Vatican City state, 196; area of, 5; population of, 7
Venezuela (*see also* Caribbean area), 444; Brazil, territorial losses to, 461; Germany, intervention by, 55; Great Britain, intervention by, 55; Italy, intervention by, 55; Hague Permanent Court of Arbitration, 55
Vernadsky, George, cited, 84n
Viet-Nam, *see* Indo-China
Virgin Islands (*see also* Caribbean area), 57, 443; geographical features of, 57; United States, acquisition by, 55
Voivodina, 269
Volcano Islands, 384

Wake Island, acquisition by United States, 55
Wales (*see also* Great Britain), historical background of, 101-102
Walker, E. A., cited, 130n
Wallachia (*see also* Rumania), 272
Walsh, Edmund A. cited, 29n; quoted, 24
War, On, cited, 542n
warfare, application of geopolitics in, 3, 5
Washington Nine Power Treaty of 1922, 58
Washington treaties of 1931, 1934, 1937, 61
Wasserman, Max J., quoted, 310
Weigert, Hans W., cited, 24n
Welles, Sumner, quoted, 206
Westcott, Allan, cited, 508n
Western Samoa, New Zealand, control by, 128
West Indies (*see also* Caribbean area), (map), 446
White, C. Langdon, cited, 13n, 16n, 495n
Whittlesey, Derwent, 23; cited, 145n; quoted, 12
"Why U. S. Export Trade Booms: Handicaps of War-Torn Lands," cited, 496n
Willis, Bailey, cited, 499n
Wilson, Woodrow, World War I, policy in, 59
Windward Island (*see also* Caribbean area), 443
work per capita, comparative, 44
"World Demographic Transition, The," cited, 533
World Island, concept of, 26-27; Haushofer's interest in, 32; Russia in relation to, 91
World War II (*see also* under name of specific country), 541-553; allied offensive in the Pacific (map), 551; siege of Festung Europa (map), 550; high tide of Axis success (map), 547

Yanqui in Patagonia, A, cited, 499n
Yemen (*see also* Near East), geographic features of, 300-301
Yugoslavia (*see also* Balkan Peninsula), 267-271; Bachka, acquisition and loss of, 257; Baranja, acquisition and loss of, 257; cities of, 268; economic factors of, 268; Italy, boundary problems with, 194-196; population of, 268; power, classification by, 9; races of, 268; Russia, assistance in World War II, 88; Russia, postwar importance to, 93; Sarajevo, assassination of Archduke Francis Ferdinand at, 267; territorial acquisitions following World War I, 252; territorial losses in World War II, 269

historical factors: 268-269; Balkan Wars of 1912-13, 269; Berlin, Treaty of, 269; Karageorgevitch dynasty, 269; Kosovo, Battle of, 269; political areas, 269; Turkish domination, 269

physical factors: area, 268; position and extent, 267; topography, 267-268

political factors: King Alexander, assassination of, 269; federal union, establishment of, 269; post-World War I problems, 269; Raditch, assassination of, 269; World War II, 269

territorial problems: 269-271; Carinthia, 270; London, Treaty of, 270; Macedonia, 270-271; Rapallo, 270; Trieste, 269-270

Zanzibar, 400, 402, 406

Zeitschrift für Geopolitik, 23-24, 28-32

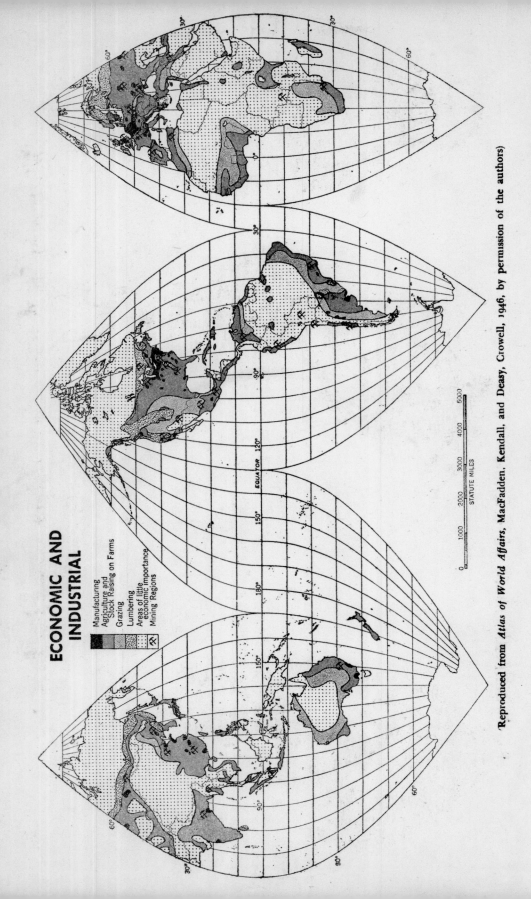

ECONOMIC AND INDUSTRIAL

Manufacturing
Agriculture and
Stock Raising on Farms
Grazing
Lumbering
Areas of little
economic importance
Mining Regions

STATUTE MILES

0   1000   2000   3000   4000   5000

Reproduced from *Atlas of World Affairs*, MacFadden, Kendall, and Deasy, Crowell, 1946, by permission of the authors)